*The Language of God –*
*Yah's Nature Revealed Through His Creation*

*Part Four -*
*The Language of God in Prophecy*
A Dynamic New Look at Bible Prophecy Using God's
Symbolic Language as the Key to Understanding
Dramatic Core Events on the Day of the Lord

Copyright © 2004-2013
By: Helena Lehman

*Pillar of Enoch Ministry Books*

Copyright © 2004-2013 by Helena Lehman
Copyrighted and Published in the United States of America by
Pillar of Enoch Ministry Books, 1708 N. 77th Avenue
Elmwood Park, IL 60707

10 Digit ISBN: 0-9759131-3-1 / 13 Digit ISBN: 978-0-9759131-3-0
First Printed Edition: July 2006 - Second Edition: October 2006
Third Edition: December 2006 - Fourth Edition: January 2007
Fifth Edition: March 2007 - Sixth Edition: May 2007
Seventh Edition: August 2007 - Eighth Edition: October 2007
Ninth Edition: November 2007 - Tenth Edition: February 2008
Eleventh Edition: April 2008 - Twelfth Edition: June 2008
Thirteenth Edition: July 2009 - Fourteenth Edition: November 2009
Fifteenth Edition: April 2010 - Sixteenth Edition: December 2010
Seventeenth Edition: March 2011 - Eighteenth Edition: August 2011
**Nineteenth Edition: November 2013**

**All Rights Reserved.**
No part of this book's text, charts, or illustrations may be used without permission from Helena Lehman. All the non-quoted text and rendered illustrations in this book are her original work and may not be copied or used without permission and possible royalty payment. For permission to use any portion of this copyrighted work, contact the author at the above address or via the e-mail address supplied below.

**Questions?** E-mail the author at: **helena@pillar-of-enoch.com**
Read excerpts from, and purchase all "Language of God" Series books online at:
**http://pillar-of-enoch.com**

---

**Publisher's Cataloging-in-Publication data**

Lehman, Helena.
 The language of God in prophecy / by Helena Lehman.
 p. cm.
 "Nineteenth Edition"
 Series: The language of God -- Yah's nature revealed through His creation, part four.
 ISBN 978-0-9759131-3-0

1. Bible--Prophecies. 2. Symbolism in the Bible. 3. Prophecy--Christianity. 4. Bible--Criticism, interpretation, etc. 5. Egypt in the Bible. 6. Great Pyramid (Egypt)--Miscellanea. 7. Cosmology, Ancient. I. Title. II. Series.

BS647.2 .L2 2008
220.1521--dc22                              2006901504

## Dedication and Acknowledgements

This book is dedicated to all those saints who will live through, and die during the Great Tribulation. May this book serve as a guiding light to them - and a beacon of hope shining through the terrible darkness of that coming time of trouble.

## Author's Notes

In the Old Testament, whenever the expression "the LORD God" or "the LORD" is used, it actually says "Yahweh Elohim" or "Yahweh" in Hebrew. I have therefore chosen to use God's Name Yahweh instead of the generic term "LORD" and the title Elohim instead of "God" in the expression "LORD God" and have restored the phrase "Yahweh Elohim" to all Bible quotations where it appears in the original Hebrew. In addition, I have chosen to use Christ's Hebrew/Aramaic Name "Yahshua" instead of the Greek name Jesus, where the "Yah" in Yahshua is the contracted form of "Yahweh," as found in the expression "Hallelu-YAH!" A detailed explanation of my reasons for this is found at my web site: http://pillar-of-enoch.com.

All Scriptural quotations in this book (unless otherwise noted) are from the PC Study Bible using either the Holy Bible: New International Version ®, Copyright © 1973, 1978, 1984 by the International Bible Society; or the New King James Version of the Bible, Thomas Nelson, Inc. © 1982. The printed edition of the New International Version referred to in the Bibliography was also used. The origins of all quoted Scriptures from these two Bibles are identified with the abbreviation (NIV) for the New International Version and   for the New King James Version. Due to copyright restrictions on these editions of the Bible, longer quotations of the Bible are abridged. To see the full content of each abbreviated passage, please utilize a full translation of the Bible. For the Ethiopian Book of Enoch, or 1 Enoch, the translation by R. H. Charles was used as listed in the bibliography, unless otherwise noted.

## Table of Contents

Dedication and Acknowledgements ............................................................. iii
Author's Notes ................................................................................................ iii
Table of Contents ........................................................................................... iv
Language of God Series Reader Endorsements: ....................................... xiii
The "Language of God" Book Series Summary ........................................ xiv
Author's Foreword ....................................................................................... xvii

### Chapter 1: God's Language - A Key to Prophecy ................. 1
Ammunition to Fight Spiritual Battles ........................................................... 2
Five New Prophetic Channels for the 21st Century .................................... 3
Amazing Prophecies in the Hebrew Aleph-Bet ............................................ 4
The Hebrew Alphabet Tied to the New Testament ..................................... 6
    The Alpha-Numeric Structure of the Bible .............................................. 8
The Bible Codes, the Language of God in Numbers .................................. 10
Menorahs: Miraculous Keys to Prophecy .................................................... 17
Old Testament Menorah Patterns ................................................................ 18
    Chanukiah Showing Jewish Feasts Prophetic Fulfillment ..................... 22
    Chanukiah Showing Christ's Reversal of History .................................. 23
New Testament Menorah Patterns ............................................................... 25
    Menorah Formed By Sayings of the Crucified Christ ............................ 26
The New Testament: A Triple Chanukiah .................................................... 27
A Menorah Within A Menorah: The Seven Prophetic Epistles ................. 30

### Chapter 2: Amazing Prophecies in the Psalms ................. 39
The Prophetic Five-Fold Structure of the Psalms ....................................... 40
The Psalms and the Five Ages of Mankind ................................................. 43
The Psalms Defy the Dual Nature of Prophecy .......................................... 46

*Amazing Fulfilled Prophecies from Selected Psalms* .................................. 47
*The Hallel Psalms and the Great Tribulation* ............................................ 60
*Psalms 110 to 118: Nine Branches of a Prophetic Chanukiah* ................ 71
*Psalms 118 and 119: The Victory Songs of the Saints* ............................ 79
*The Hallel Psalms and the Hebrew Finial Letters* .................................... 84
*The 1994 Jupiter Bombardment linked to Psalm 94!* .............................. 87

## Chapter 3: Why The Pillar of Enoch Was Built .................. 91
*The Pillar of Enoch: Designed by God, and Built by Men* ....................... 92
*How The Great Pyramid Conveys Knowledge* ......................................... 97
*Piazzi Smyth's Findings Concerning the Great Pyramid* ...................... 100
*Not All Sacred Structures in Egypt are "Egyptian"* ............................... 102
*Hidden Pyramid Prophecies in Stone* .................................................... 104
*The Pillar of Enoch's Fivefold Message* ................................................. 105
*The Great Pyramid's Connections to Astronomy* .................................. 107
*Advanced Geometry and Math in the Pillar of Enoch* .......................... 113
*Sacred Geometry: the Mathematical Code of Creation* ....................... 116
    Map - Giza: Navel of the World ............................................................ 117

## Chapter 4: The Pillar of Enoch's Amazing Prophetic Design. 123
*The Pillar of Enoch's Entrance: A Symbol For Death* ............................ 124
*The Subterranean Chamber: A Symbol for Hell* .................................... 125
    Interior Layout of the Great Pyramid .................................................. 126
    Prophetic Numbers in the Great Pyramid's Design ........................... 127
*The Lamb's Grotto and the Ascending Passages* .................................. 128
*The Queen's Chamber: Symbol of Baptism and Resurrection* .............. 130
*The Jubilee Passage, and Christ's Millennial Kingdom* ......................... 132
*The Grand Gallery & King's Chamber: A Temple to Yahweh?* ............. 133
    Equinoxes and Solstices Mark the Solar Year at Giza ........................ 137
*The King's Chamber & Djed Pillars: Connected to Christ?* ................... 142
*The Star Gospel Targeted by the Great Pyramid* .................................. 149
    From Chapter 11 of "The Language of God in Humanity:" ............... 150

Taurus and Orion Depicting Christ's Sacrifice ........................................ 153
Orion, Auriga, & Perseus Treading Satan Underfoot ......................... 155
Great Pyramid Star Shaft Alignments In 2500 BC ............................. 159
*Strange Acoustics and Anomalies within the Great Pyramid ................. 162*
*The Great Pyramid as a Scriptural Symbol for Christ .............................. 167*
*The Christ Angle Inside The Great Pyramid ............................................. 170*
Illustration of the Christ Angle in the Great Pyramid ....................... 171
*A Stone Memorial to Yahshua as Creator ................................................. 172*

## Chapter 5: Pyramid and Tabernacle: Divinely Designed ........ 177

*The Ark and the Coffer: Symbols for the Risen Christ? ......................... 179*
*A Shared Design in the Pillar of Enoch and Tabernacle ......................... 181*
Chart Showing Fivefold Tabernacle-Pyramid Connection .................. 182
Plan of Desert Tabernacle Showing Links to Great Pyramid ............ 185
*The Most Holy Place, and the King's Chamber ...................................... 188*
*The Pillar of Enoch and Tabernacle: Temples to Yahweh! ...................... 192*
Soul Being Judged in Judgment Hall of Osiris ................................. 196
The Hidden Gospel Message Inside the Great Pyramid ................... 198
Chart Comparing the Pillar of Enoch and the Tabernacle ................ 200

## Chapter 6: The Great Sphinx - Symbol For Christ .................. 205

*The Sphinx In Egyptian History and Myth ............................................... 206*
The Great Sphinx: Gazing Toward Eternity from the Past ................ 208
The Sphinx Enclosure and Associated Temples at Giza .................... 209
Khnum and Neith In Their Connection With Shem .......................... 212
*The Sphinx and the Gospel in the Stars ................................................... 214*
*Antediluvian Genius in Construction of Sphinx and Pyramid ............... 217*
Leo and Virgo Tied to the Great Sphinx .......................................... 218
*The Great Sphinx as an Astronomical Marker ........................................ 220*
Tabernacle, Great Pyramid, 12 Tribes/Zodiac Correlations ............ 222
*The Sphinx, Orion, the Aquarian Age, and the Last Day ....................... 223*

## Chapter 7: The Language of Prophecy and the Last Day ....... 233

*Is "The Day of the Lord" One Single Day? ............................................. 234*

*The Lord's Day, and The Two Battles of Armageddon* ............................ 238
*The Concept of the Great Day at the Time of Christ* ............................. 239
*Enoch's 7000 Years or "Ten Times Seven Hundred" Years* ................... 245
*The Cherubim and the Thirteen Great Days* ........................................ 254
    Depiction of Ezekiel's Four-Winged Cherub ........................................ 255
    Depiction of Revelation's Six-Winged Cherub ...................................... 257
*The Thirteenth Apostle: Paul* ............................................................... 260
*Heaven Mirrored On Earth: Christ & His Twelve Apostles* .................... 262
*The Solar System and the Zodiac: Mirrors of Israel* .............................. 265
*Are Heaven and Earth Entwined?* ........................................................ 267
*Thirteen: A Sign That Evil Will Be Replaced With Good* ........................ 270
*Can The Ten Lost Tribes of Israel Be Found?* ....................................... 272
*The Serpent Trail of the Tribe of Dan* .................................................. 282
*The Last Day: Judgment Mixed with Blessing and Mercy* ..................... 285
*The Joys of Christ's Millennial Rule* ..................................................... 288
*Everlasting Life In The New Heaven, and New Earth* ........................... 293

# Chapter 8: More Signs of the Day of the Lord's Arrival ........ 297
*Fulfilled Prophecies Signifying the Last Day's Arrival* ........................... 298
*2010 Through 2016: Prophetic Years in the Great Pyramid* ................. 302
*The Great Pyramid Antechamber - Key To The Tribulation* .................. 304
    Antechamber's Interior Measurements and Date Correlations ......... 308
    Antechamber and Tribulation Timeline Layover Graphic ................... 312
    Comet ISON at Perihelion on November 28th, 2013 ......................... 316
*End Time Herald: Blood Moon Over Orion on Dec. 21, 2010* ............... 317
    Blood Moon Over Orion's Sword - December 21st, 2010 ................... 318
    Grand Cross in Heaven on the Winter Solstice of 2010 ...................... 319
    Dec. 21st, 2010 Lunar Eclipse in Taurus With Sun in Scorpio ........... 320
    Signs in the Heavens, 3rd of Tammuz, June 19th, 2012 ..................... 324
*Daniel's Seventy Weeks And The Rebirth Of Israel* .............................. 325
*Seventy Times Seven: the Season of Forgiveness* ................................ 331
*The Reformation and Daniel's Seventy Weeks* ..................................... 332

Enoch's Prophecy of the Seventy Generations ......................................... 334
A Prophecy Hidden in the Autumn Feasts of Israel ............................... 335
The Rapture and the Coming of the Antichrist ...................................... 341
Identifying the Spirit of the Antichrist .................................................. 343
Will A New Temple Be Built On The Last Day? ..................................... 346

# Chapter 9: The United States and Israel in Prophecy............351

The Lie of British Israelism: Spiritual Israel is Global! ......................... 354
Joseph, The Fruitful Bough - The Material Blessing ............................. 356
The United States as Ephraim ................................................................ 357
America's Connection to the Number Thirteen .................................... 361
The Mazzaroth's Connection to the USA and Israel............................. 365
    America - A Symbol for the Zodiac, and Ancient Israel ..................... 366
Dire Consequences for Apostasy in the USA......................................... 368
America's Connection to Jubilees and the Great Pyramid.................... 374
    Front and Back Sides of the Great Seal of the United States ........... 375
The US Great Seal's Connection to the Ecuador Artifacts .................... 376
    Ecuador Artifact Depicting 13-Tiered Pyramid ................................ 378
    Ecuador Star Gospel Artifact - Set of 13 Cups................................... 379
    Ecuador Star-Gazer Artifact Featuring Sacred Star Triangle.............. 381
The US Constitution's Number Connection to the Bible ..................... 383
What is the Beast from the Sea in Daniel and Revelation? .................. 388
The Altar of Pergamum - The Throne of Satan ..................................... 396
The Amazing Hidden Prophecy In Psalm 108 ....................................... 402
Ezekiel 38 & 39: The USA and Israel in Great Peril Together............... 406
The Freemasonry Among America's Founding Fathers ...................... 413
Washington's Vision Tied to Daniel, Enoch, & Ezekiel......................... 415
How Zechariah Verified the Role of the USA in Prophecy! .................. 424
    Two Messianic Centaurs Confront Scorpio's Evil .............................. 426
    The Great Seal Tied to the Star Gospel .............................................. 430
The Antichrist and the Erosion of American Civil Rights ..................... 432
Enoch's Prophecy of the Seventy Shepherds of Israel .......................... 433

## Chapter 10: The Antichrist and Woman Riding the Beast ..... 439

*Are England and Judah's Throne Linked?* .................................................... *439*
*Enoch's Prophecy Of The Unicorn - A Symbol For Christ* ..................... *442*
*Daniel's Unicorn and the Antichrist* ......................................................... *450*
    Royal Coat of Arms Used By British Monarchs ................................. 451
*The Harlot and the Beasts from the Sea and the Earth* ....................... *453*
*The Woman Who Rides The Beast* ........................................................... *456*
    Heraldic Device of Prince Charles of Wales ....................................... 465
*Is There A False Bloodline of Christ?* ....................................................... *467*
*Is Mary Magdalene The Same Person As Mary of Bethany?* .............. *472*
*What Was Mary Magdalene's Role In Yahshua's Life?* ........................ *474*
    Hidden Messages In DaVinci's "Last Supper" ................................... 475
*Why Was The Apostle Thomas Called A Twin?* ..................................... *484*
*The Antichrist: Heir to the Throne of England/Judah?* ....................... *489*
*The Star Gospel Key to the Beasts of Revelation* .................................. *496*
    Star Gospel Surrounding Draco, Hercules and Cepheus .................. 500
*The Mysterious Firstfruits From The Dead* ............................................ *505*

## Chapter 11: The Rapture and Woman Clothed with the Sun 511

*Come Up Here and Come Away! - Clues For Two Raptures* ................ *522*
*How To Prepare For the Rapture* .............................................................. *526*
*The Rapture Revealed in the Parable of the Ten Virgins* ..................... *528*
*The Fate of the Foolish Virgins* ................................................................. *531*
*The Testing of the Foolish Virgins* ........................................................... *534*
*The Signs That The Great Tribulation Is Near* ....................................... *538*
*The Joel Prophecy Fulfillment By Fire* ..................................................... *540*
*Great Pyramid Targets The 2010 Summer Solstice* ............................... *544*
    Giza Solar and Stellar Alignments Targeting 2010 AD ..................... 545
*The Strong Delusion of the Antichrist* .................................................... *549*
*Why the Post-Tribulation Rapture View Doesn't Make Sense* ............ *554*
*The Rapture Connection to the Sign of the Son of Man* ...................... *558*

*The Woman Clothed With The Sun And Comet ISON ........................... 571*
    Four Comets Tell A Prophetic Story, Nov. 23rd, 2013 ...................... 578
    Comet ISON And The Woman Clothed With The Sun ..................... 581
    Woman Clothed with the Sun, September 3BC ............................... 582
    Woman Clothed with the Sun, October 2013 .................................. 583
    Meaning of November 3rd, 2013 Solar Eclipse in Libra .................... 586
    ISON Cutting Serpens And Draco In Half ......................................... 588
*The Bittersweet Meaning Behind Nova Delphinus 2013 ....................... 592*
    Star Gospel Surrounding Nova Delphinus 2013 ............................... 594
    Aquarius With Pisces, The Sign of Jonah In Heaven ........................ 595
*Who Are the 144,000 Witnesses? ............................................................ 596*
*Yahweh God's Wrath Sent From Heaven To Earth! ................................ 603*
*Why Is God Judging The Nations Today? ................................................ 607*

# Chapter 12: Sacred Astronomy as a Prophetic Tool ............... 611
*Amazing Ties Between Revelation and the Star Gospel ........................ 612*
*Sacred Astronomy and Catastrophism In The New World .................... 616*
*The Remarkable Mayans ........................................................................ 617*
*The Giza - Teotihuacán Connection ....................................................... 620*
*The Prophetic Quality of the Mayan Calendar ....................................... 623*
*The Mayan World End and the Great Tribulation ................................. 628*
*Paganism's Prophetic Counterfeits For End Time Events ..................... 630*
*What the Star Gospel Reveals on December 21st, 2012 ....................... 632*
    Meaning of Heavenly Signs on December 21st, 2012 ...................... 634
    Star Gospel for Draco, Hercules, Ophiuchus & Bootes .................... 636
*The Amazing Heavenly Anti-Peace Sign of 2012 .................................... 641*
*The White Horse: Symbol of the Gospel Being Preached ..................... 642*
    The Two Messianic Centaurs In The Heavens ................................. 643
*The Riders on the Red, Black, and Pale Horses ..................................... 645*
    Another View of the Star Gospel on December 21st, 2012 ............. 647
*The Anti-Peace Sign and the Mayan End Date ....................................... 650*
    Anti-Peace Sign In Heaven On December 21st, 2012 ...................... 651

| | |
|---|---|
| *The Chanukiah Formed by the Anti-Peace Sign in Heaven* | *652* |
| Chanukiah Formed at Noon on December 21st, 2012 | 653 |
| *The Perseus Prophecy - Three Comets With A Message* | *654* |
| Hyakutake & Hale-Bopp Crossing Al Ghoul in 1996-97 | 659 |
| *Prophetic Celestial Sign Portents From 1996 Thru 2008* | *661* |
| Comet Holmes in Perseus in 2007 and 2008 | 663 |
| *Jupiter, Saturn, and Uranus: Cosmic Spiritual Messengers* | *664* |
| The Allegorical Meaning of Jupiter and Uranus | 667 |
| Jupiter & Uranus over Pegasus & Pisces Fish: July 11, 2010 | 668 |
| *Eclipses and Conjunctions Heralding the Wrath to Come* | *671* |
| August 1st, 2008 - 1st of Av Solar Eclipse # 1 | 674 |
| July 22nd, 2009 - 1st of Av Solar Eclipse # 2 | 675 |
| Solar Eclipse Over Easter Island - July 11th, 2010 | 677 |
| Earth's Longitudinal Meridians Connected to the Zodiac | 680 |
| Jupiter-Uranus Conjunction on Feast of Tabernacles 2010 | 687 |
| Winter Solstice 2010 Blood Moon Over Orion | 688 |
| January 4th, 2011 Solar Eclipse in Sagittarius | 689 |
| June 15th, 2011 Lunar Eclipse in Scorpio and Taurus | 690 |
| December 10th, 2011 Lunar Eclipse in Taurus and Scorpio | 691 |
| Solar Eclipse of November 13th, 2012 | 695 |
| *Comet ISON as a Herald of the Rapture* | *696* |
| Comet ISON "Born" In Virgo On Nov. 17th-18th, 2013 | 699 |
| *The Blood Moon Tetrad of 2014 Through 2015* | *700* |
| *Is The 2014 Sukkot Blood Moon Post First Rapture?* | *701* |
| Blood Moon on Feast of Tabernacles, October 8th, 2014 | 703 |
| *The Sixth Seal Pole Shift or Sudden Destruction* | *705* |
| Lunar Eclipse Over Easter Island - April 4th, 2015 | 710 |
| Ominous Solar Eclipse of March 20th, 2015 | 711 |
| Solar Eclipse on August 21st, 2017 | 713 |
| Heavenly Signs at Giza on September 20th, 2017 | 714 |
| Blood Moon Triads of 2011 and 2018 | 718 |

# Appendix ..................................................................... 721

Biblical Chronological Time Chart ............................................. 722
A Summary of the Mazzaroth - Gospel in the Stars ................ 724
Jewish Civil and Sacred Years and Feast Days ......................... 726
Chart Showing 13,000 Years from Creation to Eternity .......... 728

# Bibliography By Subject ............................................................ 731

Pre and Post Flood History, Ancient and Recent ............................... 731
Ancient Judeo-Christian Manuscripts and Commentaries ................. 734
Pre-Flood Wisdom: Sacred Astronomy/Gospel in the Stars ............. 734
Judeo-Christian Religious Eschatology and Exegesis ........................ 736
Christian Apologetics – Defending the Bible ..................................... 738
Antediluvian/Ancient Technology and Civilization ........................... 739
Creation – Catastrophism – Refuting Evolution ................................ 741
Dinosaurs, Fallen Angels, Giants, and the Nephilim ........................ 742
Paganism: False Religious Mythology ................................................ 743

# Index ............................................................................................ 747

*About the Author* ............................................................................ 797
Pillar of Enoch Ministry Book Order Form ....................................... 799

## *Language of God Series Reader Endorsements:*

"As an aspiring writer myself, I realize the amount of work that goes into writing a book such as you have so masterfully done in yours. The research that you have put into these works is incredible, and the fact that you can synthesize it all into a flowing, unique work is commendable." - Walter Rogoza, M. Div, Ontario, Canada

"Lehman has the ability to take heavy, deep facts and turn them into an enjoyable page turner. Anyone interested in the stars, in scripture, in history and in mysteries will delight in this fascinating book series." - Bruce Collins, Monster Radio Book Reviewer, and Big Finale Internet Radio Talk Show Host

"Helena displays an in-depth knowledge of the Bible, and has presented some very interesting and thoughtful insights evoked from her journey with God. If you are interested in Bible allegories and prophecy, this book series is well worth the read." - James Johnson, Ohio, USA

"I have read many books on subjects like the 7 Feasts, the Tabernacle, the Sabbath, Enoch, the Pyramids, the Zodiac, and the Nephilim, etc., but no author before you has ever tied them together, and then shown how they fit in YAH's Holy plan. Your books are truly inspired by the Holy Spirit." - Joyce Tapia, Texas USA

"Your books and contacts have helped get me through tough times. The scope and content of your books is truly amazing. I am sure you will bless many others, as you have me." - Nancy Shonkwiler, Indiana, USA

## The "Language of God" Book Series Summary

**Author's Note:** This book is the last in a series of four books that sprang from one book entitled: "The Language of God - Yah's Nature Revealed Through His Creation." Since the other books are frequently referred to in this book, the content of the entire series is summarized here, and it is highly recommended that this book be read in conjunction with the other books in the series.

All the books in the Language of God series are available for purchase from author Helena Lehman at the Pillar of Enoch Ministry web site at www.pillar-of-enoch.com, and through local bookstores, BarnesandNoble.com, Amazon.com, and Amazon.co.uk. You can also e-mail the author at helena@pillar-of-enoch.com, or write to: Pillar of Enoch Ministry, 1708 N. 77th Avenue, Elmwood Park, IL 60707-4107, USA, for more information about the "Language of God" Book Series.

**Book One, "The Language of God in the Universe"** takes a profound new look at Sacred Astronomy, the Gospel in the Stars, and their connection to the Bible. By understanding the allegorical Language that God utilizes to communicate to mankind, and applying it to the Zodiac and the Bible, both are shown to be filled with similar prophetic imagery. Many allegorical ties between the Bible and the Gospel in the Stars are revealed, and once mysterious prophetic Scriptures suddenly make sense. The Universe and the forty-eight constellations of the ancient Zodiac are like biblical parables on a giant scale. They tell a compelling story that fully agrees with the Bible, and the unfolding of biblical history. The Magi who found Christ likely knew this, and the book examines their possible use of Sacred Astronomy to locate His whereabouts in Bethlehem in 3 BC.

Secondly, the parable-like allegories found in our Solar System, upon the Earth, and in various elements of nature are explored. By seeking the Language of God apparent in every created thing, each layer of Yah's creation can reveal startling truths about our Creator, His love of mankind, and His desire to save us from our worst enemies: Satan and our fallen nature.

**Book Two, "The Language of God in Humanity"** explores what it means to be created in God's image, and how this reflects God's ultimate purpose for humanity. First, it shows how the dual witness of the Gospel in the Stars, and the Bible reveal God's allegorical Language of love to humanity. Then, using the knowledge of love revealed in these witnesses, Blood Covenant ceremonies like Communion are shown to symbolically communicate the correct basis for all human and divine social relationships.

Next, by comparing the familial relationships between God and His human children, "The Language of God in Humanity" shows how all people serve as living parables, and potential members of God's family. Using the Language of God as a key, the parables of Yahshua (Jesus), and biblically based festivals such as Passover, Chanukah, and Sukkot also take on far deeper meanings. This fervent new look at Judeo-Christianity also deciphers the prophetic elements in biblically inspired religious buildings such as the Desert Tabernacle, and rituals such as Communion, baptism, and blood sacrifice - and shows how vital and relevant they still are to humanity today.

**Book Three, "The Language of God in History"** reinterprets history and archeology within a biblical framework. It does so by refuting the atheistic humanism behind modern archeological, scientific, and historical viewpoints. Then the evidence is examined through a biblical worldview, revealing how many ancient structures appear to have originally been designed not to honor Pagan deities, but the one true God. By deciphering the Language of God hidden in the sacred edifices of our ancestors, some startling conclusions are drawn concerning the spiritual teachings of the godly people before the Flood - especially the prophet Enoch.

Next, using facts found in the Bible and Ethiopian Book of Enoch, the scourge of the Nephilim on humanity, the possible causes of the Great Flood, and the swift Post-Flood devolution of mankind into sin are explored - as Noah and Shem's righteous witness were forgotten, and Yahweh's truths were perverted just as they had been prior to the Flood. Finally, the rise and fall of ancient Israel, the facts behind their migrations in the Diaspora, and the re-immergence of Israel in modern times are discussed in preparation for the study of biblical prophecy in the final book of this series.

**Book Four, "The Language of God in Prophecy"** is an explosive new exploration of the parable-like images used in biblical, and extra-biblical prophecies regarding the End Times. Prophecies in Ezekiel, Daniel, the Psalms, Revelation, Ethiopian Enoch, the Great Pyramid, the

Great Sphinx, the Mayan Calendar, and the memoirs of George Washington are explored to disclose the End Time roles of many nations, while dismantling the false doctrines behind British Israelism, and Anti-Semitism.

This book also examines the prophetic roles of the United States, the British Commonwealth, and modern Israel, and challenges many incorrect notions about God's vision for the End Times. In addition, the Great Pyramid and Great Sphinx are focused on, revealing their role as symbolic repositories of the complex scientific, spiritual, and prophetic knowledge of the godly antediluvian descendents of Seth. This study reveals that the Sethites had a keen knowledge of the coming Messiah revealed in the Gospel in the Stars, and a clear picture of End Time events - long before the Bible was written.

This startling view of End Time prophecy - with its urgent message that the Great Tribulation, and the end of Satan's reign on Earth may be imminent - will challenge many hardened Bible skeptics, and is sure to spur a renewed interest in God, His Son, the Gospel in the Stars, and biblical prophecy.

## *Author's Foreword*

When I began writing about the subject of this book series back in 1991, I was motivated by a desire to share all that Yahweh was showing me about His marvelous Plan of Salvation, and the divine Language that has communicated it to mankind since the dawn of time. However, after finding much resistance in the Christian publishing industry to these teachings, I temporarily gave up my dream of getting published. Ten years passed, during which my fascination for God's hidden language led me to continue researching the subject, though I doubted I'd ever be able to share my ideas on any grand scale.

Nonetheless, in 2002, after years of extensive Bible Study and historical research, God challenged me to apply the knowledge I had accrued to my original 350-page manuscript. I therefore began to rewrite it and - by early 2003 - my manuscript had become over 1500 pages long! When I sought a publisher, I found out that this manuscript had now become far too long for one book. In fact, though the two Christian publishing editors I contacted thought my book was fascinating, they advised me to divide my material into three or four books, and consider self-publishing. This is because, though they liked the book, they felt some of my theological ideas were too speculative for mainstream Christian publishers, and far too Christian for the New Age market.

Though I felt very discouraged, the Holy Spirit continually rekindled my desire to share what I know, and motivated me to work even harder to accomplish my goal. After spending the rest of 2003 dividing, organizing, and expanding my writings on the Language of God into four massive books, I began learning to self-publish, which took another year. Over that year, I taught myself many new skills, including how to design a cover, format a book, and insert a Table of Contents and Index. Since I drew interior illustrations for my books, I also had to learn how to create usable graphics, and correctly place them into my manuscript.

Since beginning this gargantuan task on my own, I have found it to be highly rewarding, though extremely time-consuming. Nonetheless, my excitement over the revelations God has given me to share motivates me to press forward. And so I persist in my task - with a firm eye on the ultimate goal, which is to reach many people for Christ before He returns. As I do so, I continually hope and pray that God will richly bless, and expand my endeavor to share what I know. Please help me in that task by sharing this book's message with everyone you know.

The way I see it, the information contained in this book series about God's silent, hidden language has always been "out there." It's just been misinterpreted for thousands of years. That's why, when most Christians hear the word "Zodiac," and the idea that it has godly spiritual knowledge to share with us, they automatically think or say: "Oh, that's fortune-telling, and it's evil." I get pretty tired of conversations like this:

ME: "Hi, I'm Helena Lehman, and I've written a book series that explores the allegorical Language that God uses to communicate to us in nature. My first book is called 'The Language of God in the Universe.' It discusses the many ways that God reveals Himself to mankind in the Zodiac, the Universe, and upon the Earth. A female Christian scholar named Frances Rolleston first wrote about it in the 1800's, in a book called 'Mazzaroth.' Later, another Christian scholar named Joseph Seiss verified and expanded her findings in his book: 'The Gospel in the Stars.' Have you heard of the Star Gospel?"

CHRISTIAN BEING ADDRESSED: "Oh, Yes, I have, but I've been told that the Gospel in the Stars is something evil, and though godly men have attempted to turn it to good ends, it's still evil."

Or: "The Star Gospel? I don't think that's godly, because, if it isn't in the Bible, it's probably Satanic and evil."

When I explain that the Bible has all sorts of allegorical allusions to the Zodiac running through it, Christians usually react with skepticism, or say that they don't think the Bible should be read allegorically, because there are not supposed to be any hidden meanings in Scripture. However, they are blithely overlooking the fact that many of the prophetic books in the Bible are filled with language that cannot be accurately interpreted unless it is simultaneously viewed as literal *and* allegorical! They also haven't asked (or don't want to contemplate) the big question I once asked, and sought the answer to, which is:

"If men like Enoch, Noah, and Abraham were righteous men in God's eyes, where did they get their knowledge of God in order to be deemed righteous?"

After all, there was not supposed to be a written record of God's Plan of Salvation back then. Of course, godly people could have received some truths through divine revelation, in dreams, and by being filled with the Holy Spirit. They also would have had certain oral traditions that were handed down by godly men. But could they have gotten to know God through these channels well enough to be translated for their righteousness, like Enoch was? I doubted it, so I sought more answers.

As I searched, I noted that all the patriarchs prior to the time of Moses acted as priests, and offered blood sacrifices on behalf of their people. I then discovered that the rite of Communion is actually a Blood Covenant ceremony, such as the one Yah initiated with Abraham. For years, I was satisfied that the Blood Covenant ceremony was the basis for the righteousness of men before the Bible because it teaches that God exists, that we need redemption from sin, and that God metes out justice if any blood pact we make as a promise to love our neighbors is broken.

But there were still so many burning questions that I'd asked when reading about structures such as the Great Pyramid, which seems to communicate so many Judeo-Christian spiritual truths, and shares so many connections and parallels with objects in the Bible. There is astronomical, scientific, mathematical, and spiritual knowledge locked inside the design of the Great Pyramid that no mere dream or vision could communicate, and the only possible connection I could initially see between the Great Pyramid and Blood Covenant ceremonies was that this pyramid might have served as some sort of sacred Covenant pillar.

That thought struck a deep cord in my soul, and I suddenly knew that I was onto something big. The further I explored this avenue of thought, the more I learned about the source of antediluvian spiritual knowledge, which was much more than the allegorical implications of the Blood Covenant ceremony. In fact, I discovered that the whole world and the Universe around us are silently communicating many profound spiritual truths to us - truths that are identical to ideas found in the Holy Bible. Sadly, however, because of Nimrod's defiance against God, the divine parables locked into Creation were turned to evil ends when created things like humanity, the Nephilim, the Fallen Angels, the Sun, Moon, Earth, constellations, and planets were deified and worshipped.

In this book series, I explore how and why this allegorical knowledge was perverted, and how to reinterpret the available data with the guidance of the Holy Spirit and an understanding of how the symbolic Language of God works in parabolic form. I also show that the Universe has an incredibly complex spiritual story to tell us, and that all Creation is also a treasury of prophetic knowledge. In particular, this final book in the series focuses on the power of the Language of God in prophecy, especially in connection with Sacred Astronomy and the Gospel in the Stars.

In this book, I cover many different proofs pointing to the possibility that we are now in the Last Day spoken of throughout the

Book of Revelation. Furthermore, I show biblical and extra-biblical proofs that Yahshua our Messiah is coming soon! It is my hope that many people will find this book's revealed teachings efficacious in their spiritual walk with God, and that many will be saved through it before Christ's Second Coming.

# Chapter 1: God's Language - A Key to Prophecy

*"For there is nothing hidden which will not be revealed, nor has anything been kept secret but that it should come to light."* - Mark 4:22

If you are venturing into this book series for the first time with this volume, you may not fully understand what is meant when the Language of God is referred to. Therefore, for purposes of clarity, let me offer this definition: Simply put, the Language of God is the universal pictorial and metaphorical language that God utilized to reveal deep spiritual truths to humanity within the structure of created things, and in certain religious rituals. This allegorical language permeates everything that has been made, and is a silent testimony to the existence of God, His love for humanity, and His desire for our salvation, and our returned love.

In the first book of the "Language of God" Book Series, we explored the Language of God in the Universe, the stars, our Solar System, and on our Earth. We also did an extensive study of the Gospel in the Stars locked into the ancient, 48-constellation Zodiac. In Book Two, we delved deeply into the Language of God revealed in biblical symbols, rituals, holidays, and people. In Book Three on history, we sought to discover how the ancients understood the Language of God, and how they revealed their knowledge of it in their religious rituals, in their use of symbols, and in their magnificent monolithic architecture. We also attempted to place archeological findings into a biblically based chronology, or historical timeline.

Now, in this book, we are going to explore the fascinating subject of biblical prophecy, and how it is best deciphered when the Language of God found in the rich symbolism of the Gospel in the Stars is applied. As my study into the Language of God deepened and grew, I discovered that the allegorical imagery of the Language of God revealed in the stars runs throughout all biblical prophetic literature.

Every star and constellation, and every book of the Bible, has prophetic imagery in it - even in the places that can also be taken literally. The allegorical symbolism in biblical prophecy is tied to the Star Gospel because they are both platforms for revealing God's prophetic knowledge, His Spirit, and His revealed Will throughout History. Designed to enlighten both men and angels, the Gospel in the Stars is deeply connected to the Bible in many ways. Throughout this book series, it has been shown that God's prophetic knowledge is revealed in many biblical symbols, as well as the Gospel in the Stars. Now, we are going to embark on an exciting voyage through a sea filled with wave upon wave of colorful, imaginative, yet often seemingly meaningless prophetic symbolism, and - using the Gospel in the Stars - we are going to decipher the symbol code that hides their secret meaning.

When biblical prophecies are understood through allegories hidden in our world, and throughout the Universe, these prophecies suddenly fill the muddled sea of prophecy with vibrant life, and bring every prophetic detail into deep clarity. This is because the hidden Language of God fills the Star Gospel with inspired symbolism used in the Bible, and the stars are best understood through the Bible. My goal in this book series is to give everyone the ability to read - and hopefully to understand - Yahweh's symbolic prophetic language in the Bible, and the Universe. In this way, it is my hope that everyone who reads this book will have a deeper and richer understanding of God's prophetic will for humanity. It is also my hope that they will repent if they have not already done so, will be saved, will be spared the horror of the Great Tribulation, and will make themselves ready to take part in the wonderful future that God has planned for those who love Him.

## *Ammunition to Fight Spiritual Battles*

This book is about to take you on a great spiritual journey that began in the Garden of Eden, and will culminate in the New Jerusalem. As believers make this journey, many are tempted to wander off the straight and narrow path that leads to everlasting life. Each time they wander, however, believers open themselves to attacks from the enemy, and Satan is always waiting for an opportunity to *destroy* God's children. But something few Christians realize is that Satan is not just out for righteous blood. He will be satisfied with nothing less than the total extermination of the human race, and will do anything to destroy all humanity - even those who mistakenly worship him!

Remember that Satan is an angelic being who fell because of his pride. He could not stand the idea of one day being ruled over by the

# Chapter 1: God's Language - A Key to Prophecy

human children of God that he was originally created to care for. Satan could not accept that those who love Christ are destined to rule over not just the angels, but also all of Yahweh's Creation - as co-rulers with Christ. Therefore, Satan and his demonic hosts declared war - not just on humanity, but also on all the creatures, and the Creation that humanity is destined to govern! For this reason, you can be sure that Satan or his demons have been behind every inhumane atrocity that man has committed against man, and every horrifying act of violence done to the other living creatures on this planet.

Nonetheless, Yahweh and His Son Yahshua (Jesus) are all-powerful allies, and those who love the one triune God Yahweh have not been left defenseless! They have been given divine power through the Holy Spirit, which is continually replenished in believers when they engage in prayer, worship, and praise to God. Through these things, believers have the power to conquer Satan and other demonic enemies, and to protect themselves against their desire to destroy them. In addition, they have been given God's Word in the Bible and in the Gospel in the Stars. These Two Witnesses have been provided to guide every true child of God through this dark world - until the time that it and they are clothed with God's pure light in eternity. What a glorious time that will be!

To make it harder for Satan to destroy the testimony of His two great prophetic witnesses, Yahweh placed hidden messages to His righteous servants throughout them. If the Holy Spirit does not indwell the reader, however, they will not be able to accurately see these hidden messages from God to His children. Many examples of these hidden messages in the Bible's prophetic literature are discussed in this book. There is literally layer upon layer of prophetic knowledge hidden in the Bible - often in the most unlikely places.

## *Five New Prophetic Channels for the 21st Century*

Remarkably, five once deeply hidden prophetic channels were not discovered until the 19th and 20th Centuries. These new prophetic channels to spiritual enlightenment require much careful study to master; yet the rewards for doing so are great. This is because these new channels into God's infinite mind have the most profound information to share with humanity in this Last Day, which began at the dawn of the 21st Century. These five new sources of prophecy are:

1. **The Bible Codes** found in the Old Testament
2. The hidden prophecies in **the Bible's Book of Psalms**

3. The mystical **Menorah Patterns** found in Scripture
4. The prophecies in **the Great Pyramid and Sphinx** at Giza
5. The **prophecies in 1 Enoch and the Book of Revelation** that are tied to **the Gospel in the Stars**

These five messengers were given to reveal God's plan for the End Times at the proper time. As such, they are full of secret meanings that were not to be understood until this time in history. As End Time messengers, they were intended to direct the paths of those who live on the threshold of the Tribulation period, and who may soon have to face the terror of this most perilous time in history. This book will attempt to show that people are without a doubt living in the era just before the Tribulation. It will also show what believers need to watch for as they move closer to the Wedding Supper of the Lamb, and Christ's Millennial Rule.

Through these five new prophetic channels, this book shares many prophecies that were once hidden from the world, but have now been revealed fully through the Language of God. All these prophecies were given to guide those who love Yahshua until the Rapture, and to see those who are left behind through the short but terrifying rule of the Antichrist. In addition, new prophetic interpretations that were given to me by the Holy Spirit are shared here. After years of keeping silent regarding the revelations Yahweh has shown me, they are now being revealed, and I pray that they will be of great spiritual value to all of Yah's beloved children.

Before launching into a systematic discussion of Bible prophecy, however, let me make something perfectly clear. Though I am saved, I am still a mortal, sinful human being, and though I believe that my interpretations of prophecy were God-given, I may be wrong on some points, or dates. Therefore, please prayerfully consider all that is about to be shared, and ask Yahshua, and His Spirit to give you true spiritual discernment, and prophetic foresight. May Yahshua bless you on your quest to understand biblical prophecy, and may this book help you to reach the desired destination, which is everlasting life with Yahshua. Amen!

## *Amazing Prophecies in the Hebrew Aleph-Bet*

Let's begin our study of prophecy by considering how the Hebrew alphabet in the Bible is encoded with secrets. In John 1:1, we are told that:

## Chapter 1: God's Language - A Key to Prophecy

*"In the beginning was the Word, and the Word was with God, and **the Word was God.**"*

Yahshua also told us that:

*"**I am the Alpha and Omega**, the First and the Last, and the Beginning and the End."*

Since Yahshua is called the Word, or Word of God, and the Alpha and Omega - which are the first and last letters in the Greek, alphabet - it stands to reason that He is telling us that every letter of the alphabet has a sacred meaning that pertains only to Him, and that defines who He is. It also suggests that, since the Bible is considered the essence of the Word, or Son of God in written form, then every letter and word in the Bible is the literal Word of God, and has some special meaning to share with us. It is as if every letter in the Bible were a cell in Yahshua's body!

Something else is also being suggested by Yahshua's statement that He is *"the Alpha and Omega, the First and the Last, and the Beginning and the End."* As the First and the Last, Yahshua is telling us that He knows everything that has happened, or ever will happen. Furthermore, by telling us that He is *"the Beginning and the End,"* Yahshua is alluding to the fact that He created everything, and He will also destroy and re-create everything in its due time. Finally, by saying He is the Alpha and Omega, Yahshua is telling us that every letter of His Word contains a special prophetic message to everyone who loves God, and reveals divine truths about our God and Savior.

Uncannily, though these prophetic statements about Yahshua as the Word of God, and Alpha and Omega appear *only* in the New Testament, the Jews have long taught that every letter in their alphabet has a sacred meaning, and therefore every word of the Old Testament written in Hebrew is sacred! That is why they show such a great reverence for God's Word. Interestingly, the Greek and English alphabets were both derived from the Proto-Hebrew and Phoenician alphabets, which are virtually identical. In fact, the word "alphabet" is directly derived from Hebrew. Formed by the names for the first two letters of the Hebrew alphabet, "Aleph-Bet" is the composite Hebrew word for their alphabet.

In the Old Testament, there are many instances where the Hebrew Aleph-Bet provides a hidden structure for the way God's revealed Word is recorded. For example, several of the Psalms are acrostics, meaning that each successive verse of the Psalm begins with a successive letter of the twenty-two letters in the Hebrew Aleph-Bet. These acrostic Psalms are fully discussed in the next chapter. In addition to this, before the time of Christ, the Old Testament was divided into 22 sections instead of 39. In his book "The Mystery of the Menorah and the Hebrew Alphabet," J. R. Church shows the original divisions between the Old Testament books, and how they correspond to the Hebrew Aleph-Bet. A chart showing his and my findings can be found on pages 8 and 9.

## The Hebrew Alphabet Tied to the New Testament

In addition, J. R. Church saw that the New Testament has an underlying structure based on the Hebrew Aleph-Bet, and its message to the Jews is unmistakable. This underlying alphabetic structure is found in all twenty-seven books of the New Testament, and loudly proclaims that the New Testament writings are the literal Word of God, and are just as sacred as the Old Testament! Let's examine how this connection can be made.

The Hebrew alphabet has twenty-two main letters, with five additional final forms for five of the letters, making a total of twenty-seven letter symbols, though there are still only twenty-two basic sounds attributed to these letters. Amazingly, there are also twenty-seven books in the New Testament! Since each letter of the Hebrew alphabet also serves as a number, Hebrew numerals and words are intimately connected, and are mutually sacred. In His book "The Mystery of the Menorah and the Hebrew Alphabet," J. R. Church showed the numerical meaning of each letter of the Hebrew alphabet, their allegorical associations, and how they relate thematically to the books of the Bible that they are associated with. This is shown in the alphabetic chart in this chapter.

The chart was made to show how the Hebrew Aleph-Bet provides a hidden structure to the Old Testament, New Testament, and the twenty-two chapters of the Book of Revelation. My table makes it clear that this does not appear to be a coincidence. Uncannily, each of the twenty-two chapters in the Book of Revelation have a theme that ties in with the hidden meanings behind each corresponding Hebrew alphanumeric letter symbol, and this same sequence of letters and themes correspond with the twenty-seven books of the New Testament. Even more uncannily, though, five New Testament books are left over after the twenty-two regular letters of the Hebrew alphabet are applied. These five books correspond to the special finial form of five Hebrew letters, which also serve as numeric symbols for the numbers 500, 600, 700, 800, and 900.

In ancient times, many cultures besides the Israelites used their letter symbols as numbers. The ancient Romans are one prominent example, with their use of letters to denote various Roman numerals. In

## Chapter 1: God's Language - A Key to Prophecy

Jewish circles, the system of recognizing the allegorical meanings of numbers and letters is called Gematria. This, in turn, is a part of mystical Judaism, which is recorded in the Kabbalah and Zohar. In one form of Jewish Gematria, or numerology, a person's name is analyzed by finding its Hebrew letter equivalents, then adding the numbers for these letters together to find the name's underlying numerical value. In Chapter Ten, we will explore this Jewish form of numerology in regard to the number 666, and its connection to the Antichrist's name.

Applying the principles of Gematria, J. R. Church discovered that each chapter of the Book of Revelation has an acrostic form that correlates with every basic letter of the Hebrew alphabet. Due to my understanding of Revelation as a book specifically tied to the Great Day of the Lord, the fact that Revelation acts as a complete acrostic suggests that it contains a complete record of the events that will occur on the Day of the Lord. It also suggests that the Book of Revelation was written especially to minister to, and guide believers living in that Last Day. In Chapter Seven, we will discuss what the Last Day is and how it connects to the Book of Revelation.

Before moving on to the next section on the Bible Codes, it is interesting to note here that Messianic Jewish scholars have long recognized that the New Testament is full of far less discrepancies, and makes much more sense when it is assumed that the original texts of the New Testament were written in Hebrew and Aramaic before being translated into Greek and Latin. Throughout this book series, examples have been given where the text makes more sense when a Hebrew or Aramaic source text is assumed. In Chapter Ten, my two final examples concern Simon, called "the leper," and Yahshua's stepfather Joseph, who was called a "carpenter."

The information in this chapter shows the obvious connection of the New Testament with the Hebrew Alphabet. This lends great support to the idea that the entire New Testament was once written in Hebrew or Aramaic. It is also clear that Yahweh wanted every book in the New Testament as we have it today to be recognized as sacred Scripture - with no exceptions. Therefore anyone who rejects even one book of the Bible is rejecting a portion of the true and holy Word of God.

In addition to the correlations found by J. R. Church, my studies have shown me that some Apocryphal Books may correspond with the Aleph-Bet structure of the Old and New Testament. For example, there are five sets of New Testament books that bear the same writer's name, and a complimentary message. These are 1 and 2 Corinthians, 1 and 2 Thessalonians, 1 and 2 Timothy, 1 and 2 Peter, and 1, 2, and 3 John.

## The Alpha-Numeric Structure of the Bible

| Name, Number, & Theme of Hebrew Letter | Corresponding Books of Old Testament | Corresponding Portion of New Testament & Revelation |
|---|---|---|
| Aleph (A, 1) - King, Beginning, Creation | Genesis | Matthew; Revelation Ch. 1 |
| Bet (B, 2) - House, Temple | Exodus | Mark, Revelation Ch. 2 |
| Gimel (G, 3) - Love, Mercy, Culmination | Leviticus | Luke, Revelation Ch. 3 |
| Dalet (D, 4) - door | Numbers | John, Revelation Ch. 4 |
| Hay (H, 5) - Breath of God (Holy Spirit) | Deuteronomy | Acts, Revelation Ch. 5 |
| Vav (V, 6) - Completion, Redemption | Joshua | Romans, Revelation Ch. 6 |
| Zayin (Z, 7) - struggle for survival | Judges, Ruth | 1 Corinthians, Rev. Ch. 7 |
| Chet - (Ch, 8) life, grace, transcendence | 1 & 2 Samuel | 2 Corinthians, Rev. Ch. 8 |
| Tet (T, 9) - serpent, objective good | 1 & 2 Kings | Galatians, Rev. Ch. 9 |
| Yod (Y, 10) - metaphysics, creation | 1 & 2 Chronicles Psalm 110 | Ephesians, Rev. Ch. 10 2010 AD, Delay no longer! |
| Kaf (K, 20) - crown, accomplishment | Ezra, Nehemiah Psalm 111 | Philippians, Rev. Ch. 11, 2011 AD |
| Lamed (L, 30) - Teaching, learning | Esther Psalm 112 | Colossians, Rev. Ch. 12 2012 AD |
| Mem (M, 40) - water, revealed, concealed, baptism | Job Psalm 113 | 1 Thessalonians, Rev. Ch. 13, 2013 AD |
| Nun (N, 50) - soul, | Psalms - | 2 Thessalonians, |

# Chapter 1: God's Language - A Key to Prophecy        Page 9

| | | |
|---|---|---|
| faithfulness, emergence, Heaven | Psalm 114 | Rev. Ch. 14, 2014 AD |
| Samech (S, 60) - support, divine presence, memory | Proverbs Psalm 115 | 1 Timothy, Rev. Ch. 15, 2015 AD |
| Ayin (70) eye, sight, insight | Ecclesiastes Psalm 116 | 2 Timothy, Rev. Ch. 16, 2016 AD |
| Pey (P, 80) - mouth, speech | Song of Solomon Psalm 117 | Titus, Rev. Ch. 17, 2017 AD, Christ's Return |
| Tsadek (Tz, 90) - righteousness, humility | Isaiah Psalm 118 | Philemon, Rev. Ch. 18, 2018 AD, Millennium Begins |
| Koph (K, Q, 100) - holiness, cyclic growth | Jeremiah, Lamentations Psalm 119 | Hebrews, Rev. Ch. 19 To 2118 AD |
| Reysh (R, 200) - the wicked, evil | Ezekiel - 3rd Temple | James, Rev. Ch. 20 To 2228 AD |
| Shin (Sh, 300) - Divine power and provision | Daniel | 1 Peter, Rev. Ch. 21 To 2328 AD |
| Tav (T, 400) - truth, perfection, conclusion, end | Twelve Minor Prophets | 2 Peter, Rev. Ch. 22 To 2428 AD... |
| Then there are the five finial letters: **The 5 Finial Letters:** | **Possibly correspond to:** | **NOTE:** The remaining finial letters apply to the rest of the Millennial Kingdom, leading to the New Heaven and Earth! |
| Finial Kaf (K, 500) | Book of Jubilees | 1 John - Baruch, Ch. 6 |
| Finial Mem (M, 600) | Book of Jasher | 2 John - Epistle of Barnabus |
| Finial Nun (N, 700) | 1 & 2 Esdras | 3 John - Book of Jubilees |
| Finial Pey (P, 800) | 1 & 2 Maccabees | Jude - Book of Jasher |
| Finial Tsadek (Tz, 900) | Book of 1 Enoch | Revelation - Book of 1 Enoch, 2928 - 3000AD, New Heaven and Earth |

Just as in the Old Testament, these five multi-part sections can be seen as one book. If this is done, however, the five finial Hebrew letters have no counterpart unless five Apocryphal books are added. This is also true of the Old Testament. In the last portion of the table that appears on page 9, there are some suggestions as to which Apocryphal books might be included to allow both the Old and New Testament to be divided into twenty-seven sections, instead of twenty-two. Interestingly, some of these Apocryphal books appear to be relevant to both the Old and New Testament, and therefore appear in both sections.

## *The Bible Codes, the Language of God in Numbers*

In addition to the literal and allegorical messages found in every letter of the Hebrew alphabet, and the structure they provide throughout the Bible, there is a hidden numerical code that runs throughout the Old Testament, especially within the Pentateuch, or Torah. Findings from applying these numerical codes to the Bible has revealed that the entire Old Testament is riddled with prophecies that can only be numerically discerned, and that underlie the basic written words of the Bible.

Dubbed "the Bible Codes" by the Jewish scholars who discovered them, this hidden code system in the Bible was theorized about in the past, but unproven until modern times. This is because the Bible Codes are based on highly complex numerical patterns that require a sophisticated computer program to be found. When these equidistant number sequences are applied to Hebrew and Aramaic Bible texts, and the resulting equidistant letter strings, or ELS's are read sequentially as words, they often reveal prophetic statements about Yahshua the Messiah, and other major past events in the Bible. However, many of them also appear to predict prophetic events *in the future* as well.

The Bible Codes are found when certain number sequences are used to count the Hebrew letters in the Old Testament. For example, in his book "His Name is Jesus – The Mysterious Yeshua Codes", Messianic Jewish Scholar Yacov Rambsel discovered that, counting from the first letter in Genesis 1:1, every fiftieth Hebrew letter found in sequence spells the Hebrew word "Torah." Rambsel also found similar sets in 386-letter intervals in all five books of the Torah or Pentateuch. For example, starting with the fourth letter in the twelfth word of Exodus 3:14 and counting every 386th letter in sequence spells the name of our Savior in Hebrew: "Yeshua" or "Yahshua." This is also true of the 386-letter sequence beginning with the fourth letter in the first word of Leviticus 22:14. In fact, **the name of our Savior Yahshua is found twelve times in 386-letter intervals throughout the whole Pentateuch.** Even the way to

## Chapter 1: God's Language - A Key to Prophecy

find this number sequence using the fourth letter is revealing, since Yahshua was born at the end of the Fourth Great Day, or Millennium following the creation of Adam.

Related to the Bible Code spelling the name of Yahshua in the books of the Old Testament, two sets of words relating directly to the Messiah can be found. Using equidistant letters strings or sequences, Rambsel discovered that the Hebrew words for "truth" and then "wisdom" are repeatedly spelled with the adjacent letters to those spelling the name "Yahshua" at 386-letter intervals. This reveals that Yahshua is the source of all truth and wisdom. Indeed, no other man in history more accurately told the truth, or shared more wisdom than Yahshua did. There is therefore little likelihood that these 386-letter sequences spelling Yahshua's Name and the words for two of His greatest gifts to humanity are a mere coincidence. On the contrary, they appear to be a miraculous affirmation that all of God's Word is truth!

In light of all the amazing prophecies that the Bible Codes appear to reveal, the scholars who unlocked our ability to find them have given us a powerful tool to prove that the Bible is the inspired Word of God. In this regard, many hidden prophetic words, or phrases have been found encoded directly into related biblical texts. In the book "Bible Code Bombshell" by Sherman, R. Edwin for example, two mega-clusters of words and phrases relating directly to the life and ministry of Christ are found in two highly important Bible passages about the Messiah. These are found in the 53rd chapter of Isaiah, and the 37th chapter of Ezekiel. Uncannily, Edwin is a Jew who did not believe that Yahshua was the Messiah until he discovered these two mega clusters, and became a believer based partly on his exploration of the Bible Codes.

Since the discovery of the Bible Codes, no one has been able to disprove their existence, or veracity. Various Bible Codes run throughout the Old Testament's thirty-nine separate books, suggesting that every book of the Bible is laid out in the order it was intended to be in. Furthermore, since such an elaborate and consistent encoding of the Old Testament would have been impossible for any ancient scribe, no one could have written these codes, and hidden them so perfectly without the aid of a sophisticated computer. Only Yahweh God Himself could have caused the many different authors of the Old Testament to write with this hidden code running cohesively throughout their books. Furthermore, Yahweh alone would have known what sequence the books had to be arranged in to keep the codes intact. Consequently, it appears that Yahshua, as the Word of God, formed this code as a miraculous sign. In fact, the Bible Codes appear to exist primarily to prove that the Bible is indeed the inspired Word of God to modern-day Pagans, Bible scoffers, and atheistic religious skeptics. Sadly, however, even these amazing Bible

Code proofs are being written off as coincidence by hardened skeptics who will not accept Yahshua's salvation, and will likely perish because of their hard hearts. One of them is my own brother, and I grieve for his loss.

An important point about the Bible Codes is that they are destroyed when the Bible is translated into any other language other than Hebrew or Aramaic. Hence the translations of the Old and New Testaments in Greek and English lack any trace of the Bible Codes. However, there is evidence that the New Testament was at one time written primarily in Hebrew and Aramaic. In fact, as already mentioned, a growing body of Messianic Jewish scholars has recently put forth the opinion that the New Testament did not come from original texts in Greek, but from texts originally written in Hebrew and Aramaic. It is therefore supposed that, when the original Hebrew and Aramaic texts of the New Testament were later translated into Greek, the Bible Codes in them were lost.

The primary proof for the belief that the New Testament was once written in Hebrew and Aramaic is the body of textual evidence that can be found in the Greek translations we have today. Part of this proof comes from finding words in the New Testament that only make sense when it is assumed that the words were mistranslated from Hebrew or Aramaic into Greek. For example, the possible mistranslation of the word "manger" in Yahshua's (Jesus') birth narrative in Luke's Gospel is discussed in Book Two. There, the assertions made are based on the idea that the New Testament came from Hebrew and Aramaic originals. In addition, see Chapter Ten - where the words "carpenter" and "leper" in the Gospels are analyzed as possible mistranslations from Hebrew or Aramaic.

The Bible Codes are fascinating primarily because they show that the Bible is filled with many nuances of the incredibly rich and powerful allegorical Language of God. Like the symbolic message of the starry heavens, the Bible Codes reveal that the Bible is filled with prophetic qualities that can only be discerned through an understanding of complex math and science. Just as the Mazzaroth, or Zodiac (discussed primarily in Book One), and the Great Pyramid and Great Sphinx at Giza (discussed here, and in Chapters Three, Four, Five, Six, and Eight of this book) reveal truths to us based on the astronomical and geometrical number systems surrounding them, the Bible reveals startling prophetic knowledge - especially when its hidden alphanumeric code is correctly deciphered.

There are several Bible Code prophecies that appear to have much to do with some of my prophetic interpretations in this final volume in

## Chapter 1: God's Language - A Key to Prophecy

the "Language of God" Book Series. For example, in his book "Bible Code II - The Countdown," code researcher Michael Drosnin found Bible Codes that suggest that there is a physical key to this code hidden somewhere in the land of Israel. Mr. Drosnin also found Bible Code messages suggesting that *this Bible Code Key is in the form of an obelisk that is somehow connected to a human being.* Mr. Drosnin therefore thinks a monolithic, obelisk-like structure in human form is hidden somewhere in Israel - one that may be carved with writings that are the keys for deciphering every aspect of the Bible Codes. However, this Code Key has supposedly not been found yet.

When pondering this mystery from my unique perspective, it dawned on me that the reason there is still no trace of this mysterious obelisk in Israel is because it is not located there, *but in modern day Egypt, in a section of it that once likely belonged to Shem, the son of Noah also known as Melchizedek.* This possibility was carefully explored in Book Three, "The Language of God in History". Another fact that Drosnin overlooks is that the borders of Israel are described in Genesis 15:18 as running from the Nile River in the south to the Euphrates River in the north as the territorial heritage given to Abraham by God.

Though Mr. Drosnin points to Bible Code clues that the obelisk is located in the southern end of Israel's Dead Sea area, there is a very visible candidate for the Bible Code Key that is located south, and slightly west of modern Israel in Egypt! This is the Great Pyramid at Giza, which I have dubbed the Pillar of Enoch. As will be shown in this book, this pyramidal Pillar of Enoch clearly fits the encoded descriptions of the Bible Code Key found by Michael Drosnin. For example, though obelisks are usually considered to be tall, smoothly surfaced, squared pillars that come to a pyramidion-shaped point, the square based pyramids of Egypt are pillar-like pyramidions of stone that form a more massive kind of smooth-sided obelisk.

Indeed, the Ancient Egyptians considered both obelisks and pyramids to be representations of the Sun, and their shapes to be symbolic of the Sun's life-giving rays. They therefore connected these symbols to their various Sun gods, such as Ra and Horus. Interestingly, as was shown in Book One, "The Language of God in the Universe," the Sun is also a powerful symbol for Yahweh and His Son Yahshua. This truth is also memorialized in Scripture (See Isaiah 60:1-3, Malachi 4:2). It therefore seems fitting that the Great Pyramid - as a symbol for the Sun - would be dedicated to the one and only Son of God - He who came to save us all from sin and death through His own precious blood sacrifice.

Nonetheless, despite the Great Pyramid's obelisk-like and entirely conspicuous presence, Mr. Drosnin thinks the clues in the Bible Codes hint that this obelisk is in modern-day Israel. He therefore hasn't entertained the thought that Israel's borders were once far greater than they are today. He also hasn't discovered that the top point of every obelisk ever discovered in Egypt forms a pyramidal shape, so the Great Pyramid can be seen as a greatly enlarged obelisk! Mr. Drosnin also found code words near to the occurrences of the word obelisk that suggest it contains a divine code for a human being. Uncannily, in this book, **the Great Pyramid and Great Sphinx will repeatedly be shown to be symbols for Christ, and His heavenly work on Earth.** They are therefore obelisk-like allegorical codes in stone that reveal the redemptive purpose for the greatest human being ever born, Who is the Son of God made flesh Who dwelt among us, and will one day do so again, forever!

In addition to several chapters in Book Three, Chapters Three, Four, and Five in this book carefully explore the Great Pyramid or Pillar of Enoch and disclose many of the exciting secrets hidden within it, including the fact that it is truly a secret code identifying our Messiah Yahshua, who came to us in the form of a human being that was also fully divine. These chapters also show that this same divine man is truly the author and finisher of biblical salvation, and of every word of the Bible! They will reveal that the Preincarnate Yahshua is the Bible Code-writer, and the Creator of every secret locked in the Bible and in the natural world. They will also show that Yahshua's Spirit is the ultimate Bible Code-breaker, and the ultimate Revealer of all that Yahshua has encoded into His Creation for mankind to find, ponder, and take to heart so that they can be saved.

In addition to the mysterious Obelisk Code Key, Mr. Drosnin has brought ominous future portents to light. In his first book called "The Bible Code," Michael predicts a possible comet bombardment of the Earth that could devastate this planet. Then, in his second book, one code issued a dire warning of a possible limited nuclear holocaust. Though these cataclysmic events have not happened yet, descriptions of the devastating affects of all types of wars are plainly prophesied in the Book of Revelation during the Great Tribulation.

Before we delve further into predictions of when the Tribulation could occur in this book, let me issue a note of caution about the dates given by Mr. Drosnin, myself and others mentioned throughout this book series. With great insight, Drosnin shows that the Bible Codes reveal not what will happen, but what *could* happen. In other words, Mr. Drosnin believes the codes reveal *what is likely to happen* in a given set of circumstances that take human choices, and our exercise of free will into consideration. Therefore, since the events revealed in the Bible Code are

# Chapter 1: God's Language - A Key to Prophecy

reliant on specific choices *that may or may not be made*, the prophesied event may or may not occur in the year specified - or may not occur *at all*.

Since prophetic messages are not static, but are in a state of flux based on our choices, the next section is being presented to offer my own caveat. It is an excerpt from Chapter One in "The Language of God in the Universe," the first book in "The Language of God" series. Though presented in Book One, this section has even more relevance in this book, which attempts to set times and dates for many End Time events based on Sacred Astronomy, the interpretation of Scripture, and explorations into the meanings of symbols, visions, and signs from other cultures.

**Excerpt from "The Language of God in the Universe", Chapter 2, in the section titled "Problems With Date Setting Addressed":**

As you read through this book series, please keep in mind that these are not my predictions, but *my interpretations* of signs that appear to be predictions. How do I know that my interpretations of these predictions are correct? *I don't.* I am merely reporting what appears to be a truthful and accurate interpretation of each date source. In addition, unlike some date setters, I utilize prophecies scattered throughout the Bible, as well as prophecies in the Book of 1 Enoch (i.e. the Ethiopian Book of Enoch), and a few non-biblical sources of revelatory information. One example is George Washington's vision of the destiny of the United States, which appears to be a legitimate prophetic vision, and which we discuss in Book Four *(i.e. this book)*.

Theories surrounding Sacred Astronomy that are put forth by Avi Ben Mordecai in his highly controversial and now out-of-print book: "Signs In The Heavens" were also utilized in my interpretations. Based on Sacred Astronomical and Scriptural signs, Avi Ben Mordecai pinpointed the most likely time for Christ's birthday, which was around September 11th, 3 BC. However, Avi speculated that the Rapture would occur and the Great Tribulation would begin in 2000 AD - which was incorrect.

Nonetheless, it is foolish to assume that Avi's failed prediction invalidates his entire theory. Avi never claimed to be a prophet. He simply made a miscalculation based on his belief system, which is that the Great Day of the Lord must begin with the Rapture and Tribulation period. Later in this book, when we discuss the concept of the thousand-year Great Day, I will explain why this assumption is likely incorrect, and why, though there is no way to exactly pinpoint when the Tribulation period will occur, there are many indicators that it might happen within the next fifty years of human history.

In the meantime, I have to tell the world what has been revealed to me and let them judge it according to the Spirit it is delivered in. The rest is in Yahshua's hands. In the meantime, as I step out in faith, my predictions will be made known throughout this book series. For example, in Book Four *(which is this book!)*, **it will be shown that the time of Jacob's Trouble, or the seven-year Tribulation period could begin sometime during the next decade of the 21st Century** - though there is no way to know for sure when Yahshua will return in the First Rapture.

By saying "First" Rapture, I am hinting that there may be two Raptures: one near the onset of the Great Tribulation, which is not Pre-Tribulation but Mid-Tribulation or Pre-Wrath, and one just before the Bowls of God's Wrath are poured out, when the Two Witnesses are raised up. However, keep in mind that this is a prediction, not a prophecy! For more about this, please read the section: "Come Up Here and Come Away! - Clues For Two Raptures" found in Chapter 11.

After the two Raptures and the Tribulation period, whenever they may occur, the remaining years left in the final thousand-year Great Day will be for the Millennial Rule of Yahshua on Earth. During this last Great Day, most believers expect the Rapture and Tribulation to occur at the very beginning. Using this reasoning, the Tribulation should have begun in the year 1999 or 2000 based on Avi's 6000-year timeline. However, since the Tribulation did not begin then, this supposition is incorrect. **This mistake may partly have been made because Yah's timeline could be somewhat dependant on the results of our free will.**

On the other hand, besides the fact that many Christians insist that the Day of the Lord is either 24 hours or seven years long, many also assume that the Tribulation must immediately ensue when the Lord's Day arrives. However, though God can certainly accomplish all these things in one day if He so chooses, the Book of Revelation tells us that many diverse events, such as wars, famines, and natural disasters, will come before Armageddon and Satan's imprisonment. Furthermore, all of these events are not supposed to happen in one 24-hour day. Instead, *the writer of Revelation insisted that these events unfolded before him "on the Lord's Day," and that this Day of the Lord is a thousand-year day* (Rev. 1:10, 20:2-7).

A detailed overview of the events we should expect on the Day of the Lord is given in Book Four (i.e. this book). For now, however, **it is imperative to keep in mind that the destruction of the wicked and the restoration of the Earth to Eden-like perfection have a thousand years to be fulfilled.** Those who forget this make the error of predicting a definite date rather than giving a possible time period.

# Chapter 1: God's Language - A Key to Prophecy

End of Excerpt from "The Language of God in the Universe"

## *Menorahs: Miraculous Keys to Prophecy*

The layer upon layer of allegorical and prophetic symbolism in the Bible is truly astounding. Thus far, we have explored the structure in the Bible that corresponds to the Hebrew alphabet. We also have touched upon the numerical and word repetitions found in the Bible Codes. In upcoming chapters, we will examine the amazing prophetic nature of the Psalms, and the remarkable correlations between the Great Pyramid, and the Desert Tabernacle.

**Israel's Coat of Arms**

For the moment, however, let's discuss one other repetitive, code-like symbol that runs throughout Scripture - one that is often overlooked in prophecy, but appears to have profound prophetic implications. This is the menorah, which is a national symbol for modern Israel, and appears on Israel's Coat of Arms, along with two olive branches. As shown in "The Language of God in Humanity," the menorah is a lampstand specifically related to the Ancient Israelite and Jewish culture that has many allegorical meanings. In biblical times, these lampstands had seven to nine lamps that were lighted with olive oil.

Seven-branched menorahs are specific to the Old Testament, and were used to commemorate the seventh day Sabbath, and the spring and autumn festival weeks of the Feast of Unleavened Bread, and the Feast of Tabernacles. Fascinatingly, there are seven main Old Testament Feasts, and - as shown in the illustration on page 18 - these correspond to the same seven-branched type of menorah used in commemorating them. Nine-branched menorahs, however, are specifically used in relation to the first Chanukah, and were not in common use among Jews until shortly before the time of Christ. They therefore are prophetically tied to the New Testament, and events that will find fulfillment in the Last Day.

In both types of menorahs, the center lamp has a dual role, which is to light and fuel all the other lamps. This center lamp is known as the Servant Lamp. It is also called the "Shamash" in Hebrew, meaning "brilliantly shining." The Hebrew word Shamash is also used to identify the Sun, which allegorically signifies all things that are bright, good, and right in the world. As shown in "The Language of God in the Universe," the Sun also signifies the perfect spiritual light, and goodness of our triune God Yahweh.

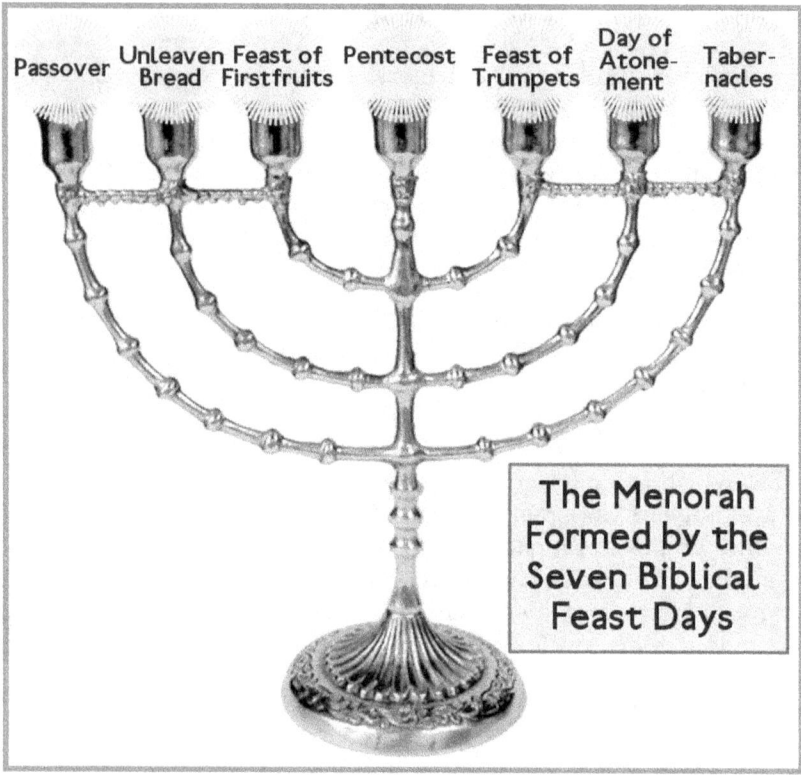

Each lamp on a seven-branched menorah pertains to one weekday, with the center, or Servant Lamp connected to Wednesday. This center lamp was designed to light and fuel all the other lamps. As was shown in Book Two, this Servant Lamp pertains to both Christ, and the role of His Holy Spirit. Now, in this book, it will be shown that each branch and lamp on a menorah has a much deeper prophetic application than was revealed in Book Two. In fact, the entire Bible is encoded with seven and nine-branched menorahs that have vital spiritual and prophetic information to share with God's people.

## Old Testament Menorah Patterns

As shown in J. R. Church's book "The Mystery of the Menorah, and the Hebrew Alphabet," the first menorah pattern encoded into Scripture is found in the structure of the first seven Hebrew words used in the Book of Genesis. These seven words not only begin the first book in the Bible, but they can tell us something very profound about our Savior.

Translated literally into English, the first seven words of the first line of the Book of Genesis read:

*"Beginning created Elohim (AT) Heaven and Earth."*

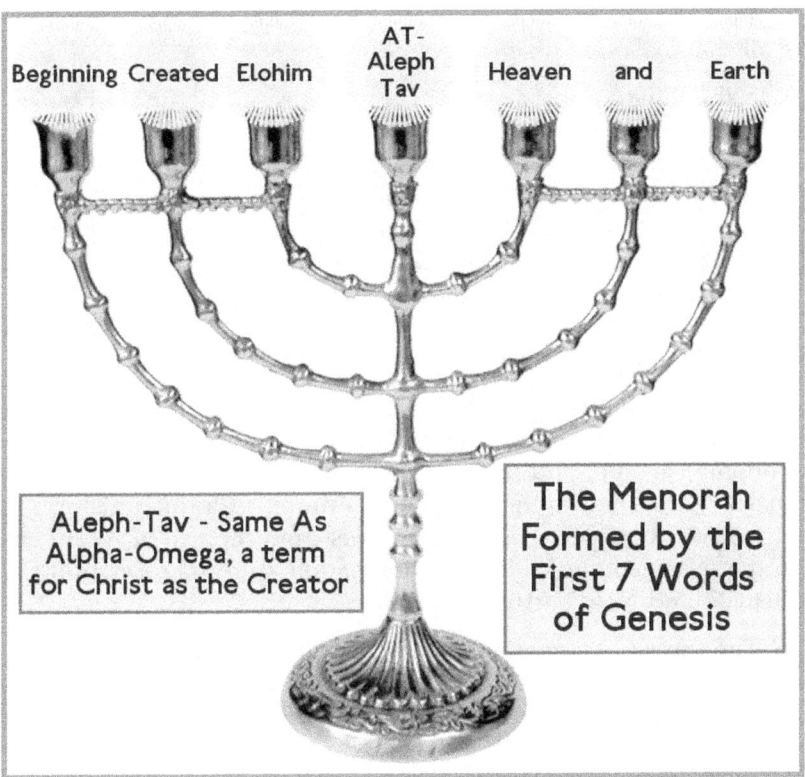

In this phrase, the fourth word has no English counterpart, because it is not a word in the usual sense. Instead, it is related to the Hebrew word "oth," meaning "sign," and it used in Genesis 1:1 to denote the preeminence of the word preceding it, which is God, or Elohim. The Hebrew letters Aleph (A) and Tav (T) form this designatory symbol. Aleph is the first letter of the Hebrew alphabet, while Tav is the last. These two Hebrew letters therefore correspond to the Greek letters Alpha and Omega, which were used to identify Christ four times in the Book of Revelation. The most complete, and self-explanatory form of this expression is found in Revelation 22:13:

*"I am the Alpha and the Omega, the Beginning and the End, the First and the Last."*

This phrase shows how the letters Alpha and Omega perfectly describe the nature, and purpose of Christ, for He is the source, or *beginning* of all life, and all Creation, and He is destined to destroy, or *end* it all, and then re-create it in an everlasting and perfect state. Yahshua was also *the first to be resurrected*, and He will be *the last to rule* over mankind at the end of time. In a very mystical sense, Christ's triune Self was all that existed at the beginning of time, and His triune Self - *united as one with His Bride the Church and the New Creation* - will be all that exists at the end of time.

In the illustration on page 19, each word in the first sentence of Genesis has been assigned to one branch in a seven-branched menorah. In this illustration, note how the Aleph-Tav symbol corresponds to the fourth, or center menorah lamp. As shown in Book Two, this is because Yahshua entered human history as a man in the fourth millennium after the Fall of Adam and Eve, and He left ordinary human history on the day He died, which was on a *Wednesday, or fourth day of the week!* As already mentioned, this fourth lamp is called the Servant Lamp, and it represents Christ as the source of light, life, and the Holy Spirit.

Another menorah pattern can be found in the first seven books of the Old Testament, which are Genesis, Exodus, Leviticus, Numbers, Deuteronomy, Joshua, and Judges. Each one of these books is thematically connected to the seven millenniums of human history. This seven thousand year period spans the ages from the Fall of Adam and Eve, to the destruction of this present creation, and the formation of the New Heaven and New Earth.

**The theme of Genesis** is birth, and the inevitability of death because of sin. As such, in Chapters 1 through 6 of Genesis, the death of Abel, and the birth and death of each patriarch in the first thousand years of human history is highlighted.

**The theme of Exodus** is being divinely chosen or elected, and finding a special dwelling place ruled by God. In the course of our lives, all of us must leave an ungodly and oppressive dwelling place (the world) to claim a divine habitation ruled by God (our hearts). Likewise, the second thousand years of human history saw Noah's election by God to survive the Flood. Noah was called by God to leave the antediluvian world filled with violence and sin behind, and to start anew in a drastically changed world full of new possibilities, and challenges.

**The theme of Leviticus**, the third book of the Bible is praising Yahweh in the House of God. In striking agreement, the third millennium saw God's choice of Abraham to be the father of His chosen people who worshipped Yahweh alone. Likewise, the third millennium saw the building of the Desert Tabernacle, and the Temple of Solomon as symbolic houses for Yahweh.

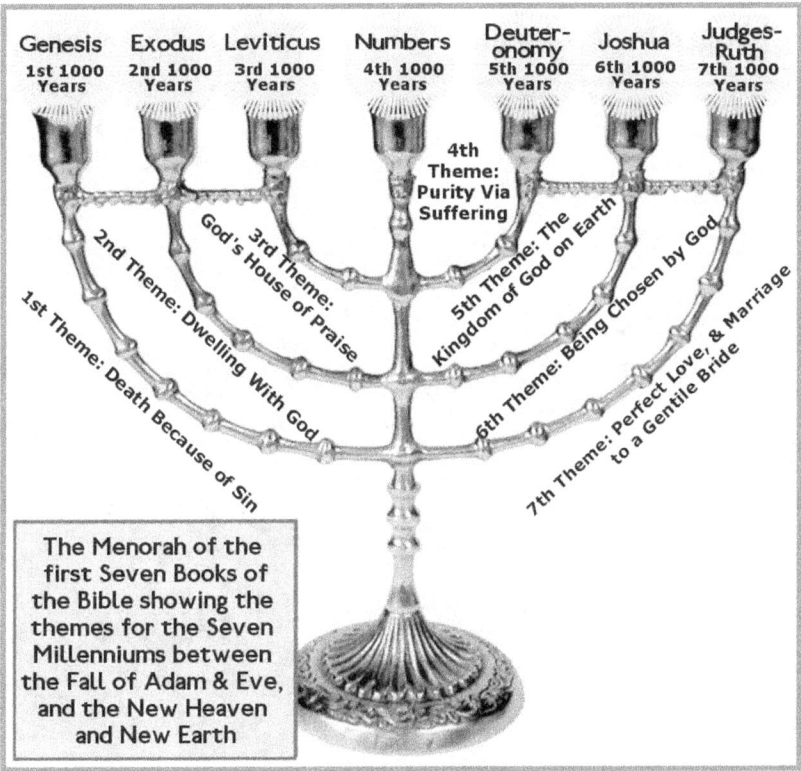

The Menorah of the first Seven Books of the Bible showing the themes for the Seven Millenniums between the Fall of Adam & Eve, and the New Heaven and New Earth

**The theme of Numbers** is purification through suffering. During the forty years that the Israelites were kept from entering the Promised Land, God shaped the Israelites into a people worthy to be called by His Name. In effect, the Israelites lost their slave identity to become a free nation ready to conquer their enemies. In juxtaposition, the Israelites experienced both the Assyrian and Babylonian captivities in the fourth millennium after the Fall. During this time, many Israelites lost their Israelite identity, were thereby freed from the yoke of the Law, and left their old heritage behind to embrace new ones in Mesopotamia and Europe.

Though these lost Israelites sadly forgot how to worship the one true God, their dissatisfaction with Paganism paved the way for them to accept the new view of the one triune God that came with Christ, who entered history at the very end of the fourth millennium! Interestingly, the Book of Numbers and the fourth millennium are connected to the center, or Servant Lamp, which represents the shepherd-like kingship of Christ, and His preeminent place as the Light of the World.

## Chanukiah Showing Jewish Feasts Prophetic Fulfillment

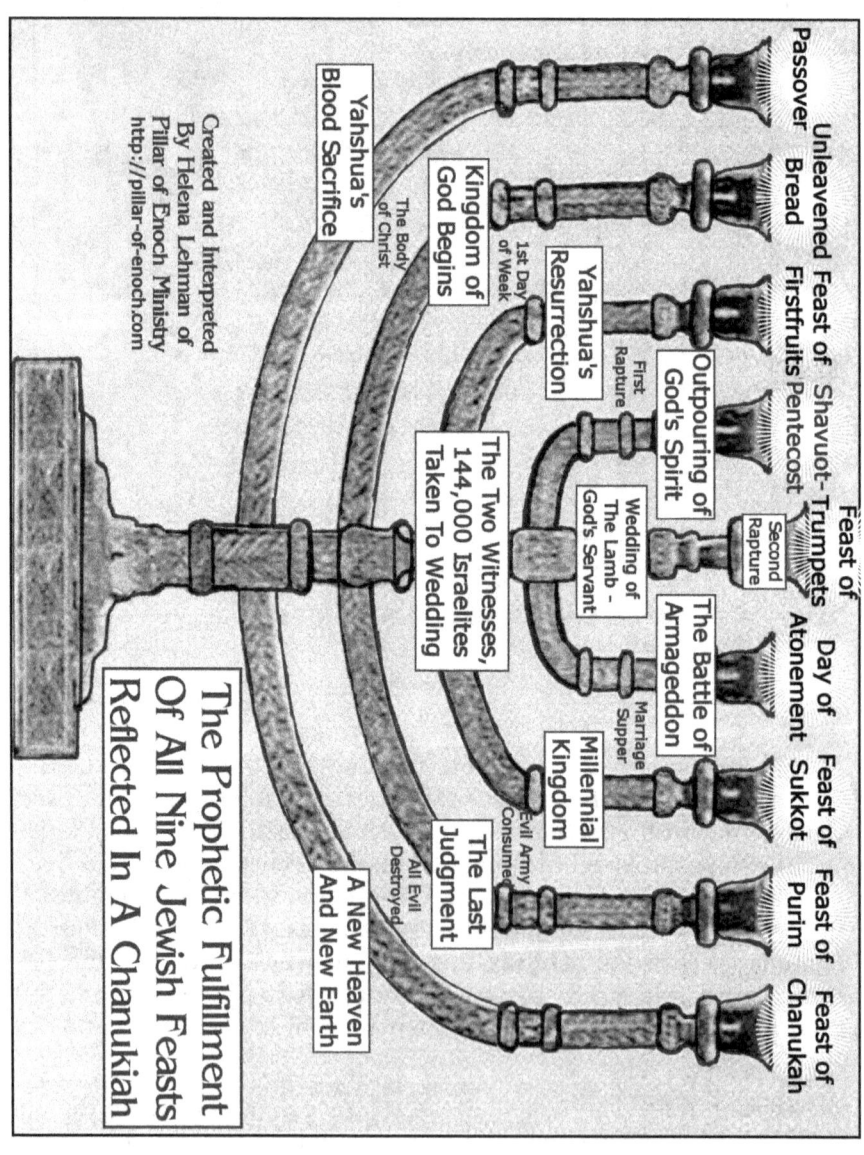

## Chanukiah Showing Christ's Reversal of History

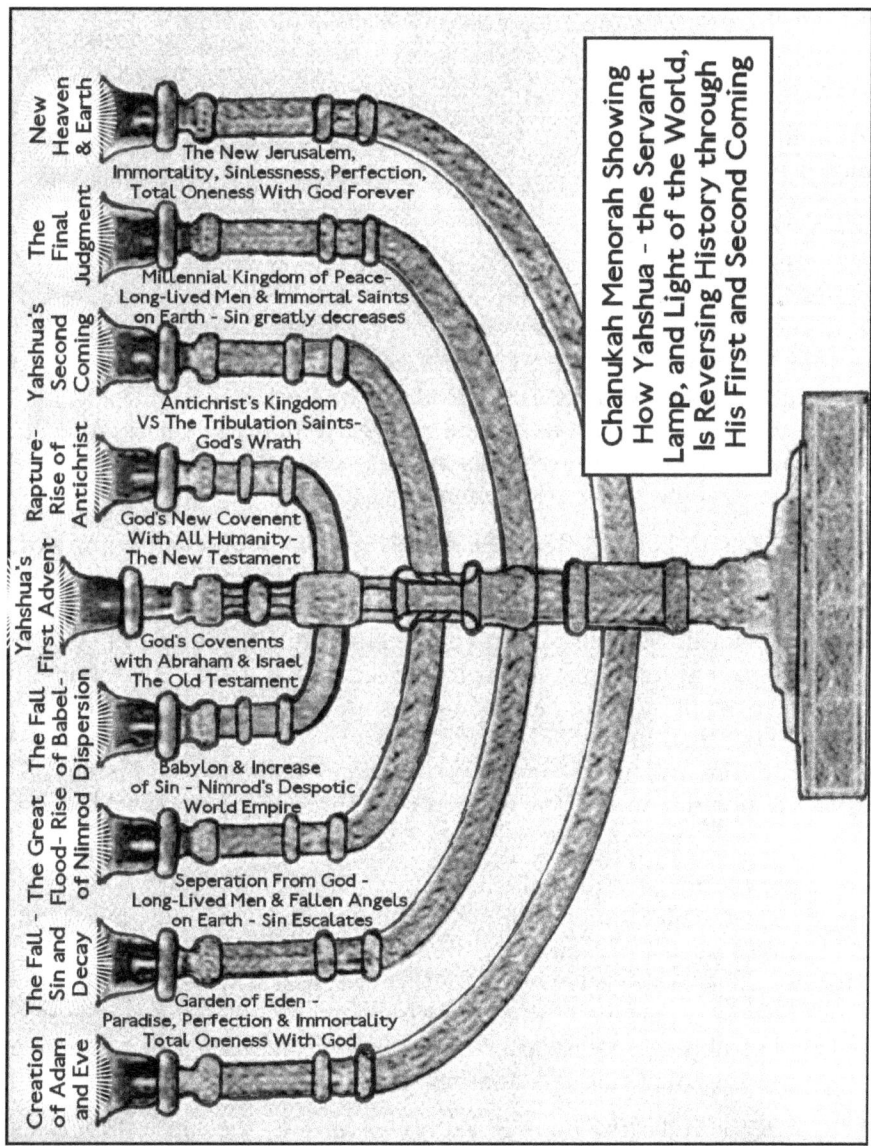

**The theme of Deuteronomy** is the establishment of God's government on Earth. This fifth book of the Bible corresponds to the fifth millennium, which began with Christ's growth, ministry, death, resurrection, and elevation to heavenly kingship. The fifth millennium also saw the tremendous outpouring of God's Holy Spirit into those who love Christ, and the establishment of the Kingdom of God inside human spirits, hearts, and minds. This building of the Kingdom of God began on Pentecost, and continues to this day. It will not be complete, however, until Yahshua returns to set up His physical kingdom on the Earth.

In Joshua, the sixth book of the Bible, being chosen by God for a special purpose is the main theme. Oftentimes, this means being rejected at first, then becoming the accepted leader. In the Book of Joshua, we find this happening to Joshua, who was rejected when he and Caleb gave a good report of the Promised Land, and urged the Israelites to take it by conquest (Numbers 14:6-10). The Israelites did not believe these two spies, threatened to stone them, and then accepted the previous testimony of the other ten - who warned that the land of Canaan was overrun with the Anakim Giants, who were the descendents of the Nephilim (Numbers 13:31-33). Forty years later, however, Joshua was chosen by Moses to lead the Israelites into the Promised Land, and to help them conquer it - just as he had wanted to do forty year before! In the process, however, the Israelites failed to wipe out the Philistines, who became the Israelite's worst opponents.

This sixth book of the Bible relates to the sixth millennium, which began with the Crusades, was punctuated by the Reformation, and the Missionary Age, and saw the establishment of Christianity throughout the known world. Most of these events helped to elevate the Messiah that the Jews rejected to the place of spiritual leadership that is His divine due in the West, while turning most Muslims into Christendom's bitterest enemies. Like their ancient Philistine counterparts, the Palestinian Arabs continue to foment hatred toward Israel and Christianity, and have played a major role in the rise of Terrorism throughout the world.

The Book of Judges is the seventh book of the Bible, and it corresponds to the seventh millennium, which represents the Millennial Rule of Christ. The theme of Judges is the people ruling one another in love, without need for a king, and their gradual victory over the Philistines. This is the way it will be during Christ's Millennial Kingdom, for all those who partake in the First Resurrection will conquer Christ's and Israel's enemies. Afterward, they will serve as priests and rulers with Christ, and they will rule one another with perfect love, rather than force!

Interestingly, the Book of Ruth was once connected to Judges as an Appendix. The subject of this eighth book in the Bible is an Israelite marrying a Gentile bride, and this is what Yahshua will do just before His reign on Earth. He will be allegorically married to a Gentile Bride - the Church, which is made up of all true believers in Christ, regardless of their cultural or national origin. This Church therefore includes former

# Chapter 1: God's Language - A Key to Prophecy

Jews who were justified by the Law, but who are now justified by Grace alone.

The menorah formed by the first seven books of the Bible shows the seven millenniums from the creation of Adam and Eve, to the New Heaven and Earth. This same span of human history can also be applied to a nine-branched Chanukiah menorah that represents a reversal of history that began with Christ's birth at the end of the fourth millennium. This can be easily seen in the Chanukiah menorah illustrations on pages 22 and 23. In the first one shown, each lamp is associated with major events in God's Plan of Salvation, with the reversal of history beginning with the fifth lamp at Yahshua's First Advent.

The second illustration compliments the first one by showing how all Nine Feasts of Israel are being fulfilled through Christ's finished work on the Cross in securing the salvation of all those who love Him. Note that the events attached to the first and ninth branches or lamps of the Chanukiahs in both illustrations literally stand outside of the seven-day week, and therefore are allegorically outside of time and eternally in God's view.

Before Yahshua came, mankind had plummeted from the perfection of Adam and Eve before they sinned into a downward spiral swirling with sin, decay, sickness, hopelessness and death. That all changed when Yahshua and His Spirit began to transform the world. Together, the Son of God and Spirit of God free people from their slavery to sin, and give them the true freedom to love God and each other as they were originally meant to before the Fall. In the end, all people will be like Adam and Eve before they sinned, yet better because they will be forever incapable of falling into the disobedience and rebellion of sin again. Hallelu-Yah for Yahshua's ability to reverse mankind's sad history!

## *New Testament Menorah Patterns*

Just as the pattern of a seven-branched menorah shines through portions of the Old Testament, the Chanukiah, or nine-branched menorah of Chanukah illuminates the spiritual landscape of the New Testament. Yet, the New Testament is also peppered with many seven-branched menorah patterns, in silent confirmation of its Old Testament foundation.

This is a sign to Jewish skeptics that the books that have shaped Christianity are as sacred as the books of the Old Testament, and should be seen as an extension and amplification of the Old Testament Word of God. Let's examine some of these menorahs.

One of the most intriguing New Testament seven-branched menorahs is found in the seven sayings that Christ uttered on the Cross before He died. Though we can't be sure of the exact order in which Christ uttered all of these phrases, their order seems to correspond to the seven Great Days of human history that began a little over six thousand years ago. For example, when Yahshua asked His Father to forgive humanity, this appears to correspond to the opening chapters of Genesis, when the Preincarnate Yahshua promised to redeem Adam and Eve after they fell.

## Menorah Formed By Sayings of the Crucified Christ

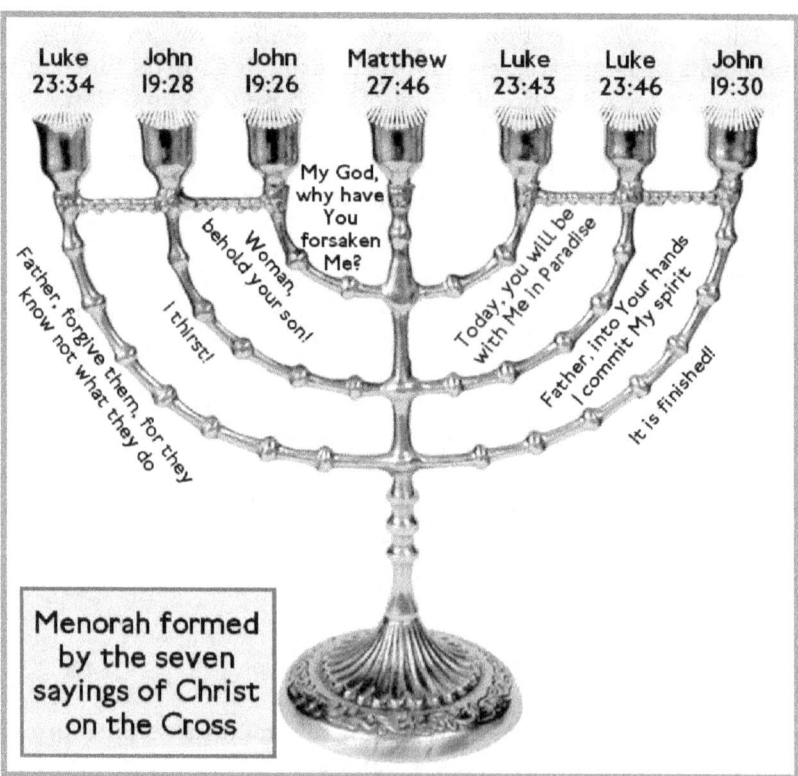

Menorah formed by the seven sayings of Christ on the Cross

At that time, Yahshua promised that the seed of the woman (Yahshua) would defeat the seed of the serpent (Satan). Next, when Yahshua said *"I thirst!"*, it suggests the great spiritual thirst people suffered in the last few hundred years before the Great Flood. At that time, the whole world was filled with evil, corruption, and violence, and no one but Noah and his kin worshipped the one true God Yahweh anymore. This is probably why God quenched the ignored spiritual thirst of those past unrepentant sinners with the Great Flood.

# Chapter 1: God's Language - A Key to Prophecy

When Yahshua uttered, *"Woman, behold your son!"*, this seems to correspond to the time of Abraham, when his promised son through Sarah was born, and God promised to offer salvation to people based on their faith in Him. Next, when Yahshua hung on the Cross and lamented *"Why have You forsaken Me?"*, He had just experienced total separation from His Father for the first time. This is because - even though Yahshua was without sin - He represented all sin, and He was dying in agony for sins He did not commit. When He did so, Yahshua became humanity's perfect sin offering. Uncannily, Yahshua's lament corresponds to the Fourth Millennium between 1000 BC and 1 BC, which saw the rise and fall of the Kingdom of Israel.

This is when God temporarily forsook His chosen people to punish them for their sins. But, one day soon, the Jews will repent of their rejection of Christ, and find salvation, and full acceptance through Him. Interestingly, Yahshua's lament corresponds with the Servant Lamp. The Servant Lamp represents Yahshua's Spirit, and God's abiding presence. But in this case, it represents the time when the Servant Lamp in the Temple was snuffed out, and the Spirit of God no longer dwelled there.

When Yahshua said *"Today, you will be with Me in Paradise,"* and *"into Your hands I commit My Spirit,"* these sayings seem connected to the moment when Yahshua rose from the dead, and the righteous saints who had died rose with Him as the Firstfruits of the First Resurrection. This began the Age of Grace, when true believers finally had full access to the Father and His Son through the Holy Spirit. Finally, Yahshua's seventh saying: *"It is finished!"* corresponds to the Seventh Millennium, when Yahshua will defeat the Antichrist, and finish His work as the ultimate leader of men during the Millennial Kingdom. Interestingly, when the end of the Millennial Rule of Christ comes, the season of repentance and forgiveness that God's mercy now offers mankind will also end.

## *The New Testament: A Triple Chanukiah*

With the exception of the Book of Revelation, which mentions the number seven many dozens of times, there are more nine branched menorahs in the New Testament than seven branched ones. Three startlingly prophetic nine-branched Chanukah-style menorahs, which are individually called a "Chanukiah", can be found by dividing the twenty-seven books of the New Testament into three distinct groups of nine. These three groups of nine New Testament books form three Chanukiah patterns that correspond to the Three Persons in the Godhead.

The fifth book in each group of nine books corresponds to the Servant Lamp of a Chanukiah. Each of these books focuses on one aspect of God's triune nature, especially the light-giving nature of each Person in the Trinity. In the first group of nine books from Matthew through Galatians, the fifth book corresponding to the Servant Lamp is the Book of Acts, where we read:

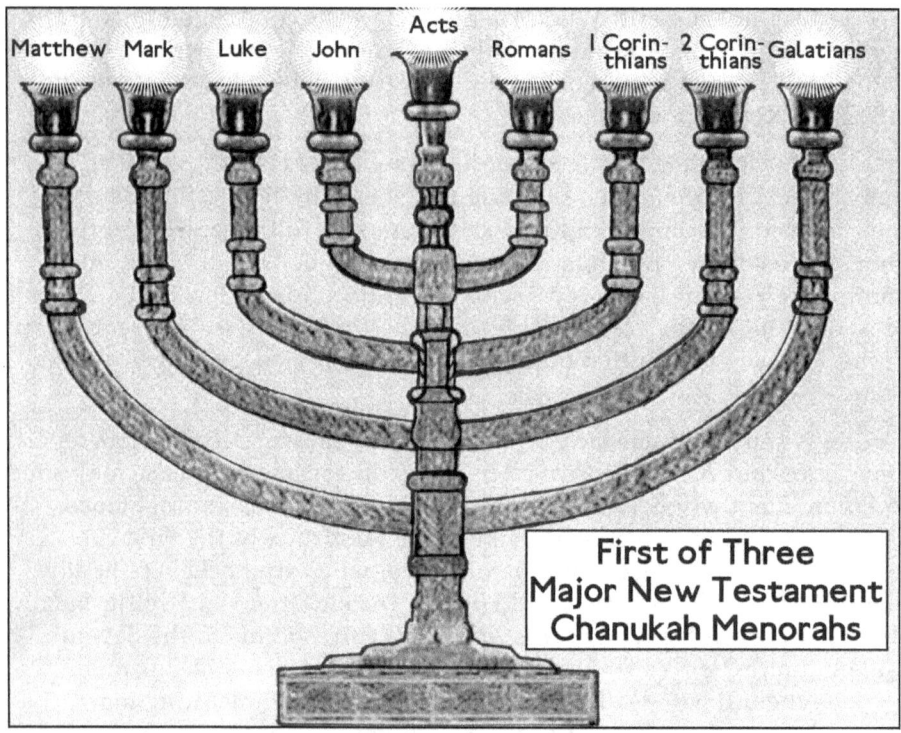

First of Three Major New Testament Chanukah Menorahs

*"Now when the Day of Pentecost had fully come, they were all... in one place. And suddenly there came a sound from heaven, as of a rushing mighty wind, and it filled the whole house...* **Then there appeared to them divided tongues, as of fire,** *and one sat upon each of them.* **And they were all filled with the Holy Spirit** *and began to speak with other tongues, as the Spirit gave them utterance."* - Acts 2:1-4

This opening passage of Acts colors the whole book, which shows the affects of that enormous outpouring of the Holy Spirit on the early spread of Christianity, and formation of the Church. Acts therefore highlights the Light of the Holy Spirit in believers.

The second group of nine books consists of Ephesians through Philemon, with the fifth book in the group being the Second Epistle to the Thessalonians. There, Yahshua is featured as the fiery Light of God's Truth, who will come to conquer the wicked on the Last Day:

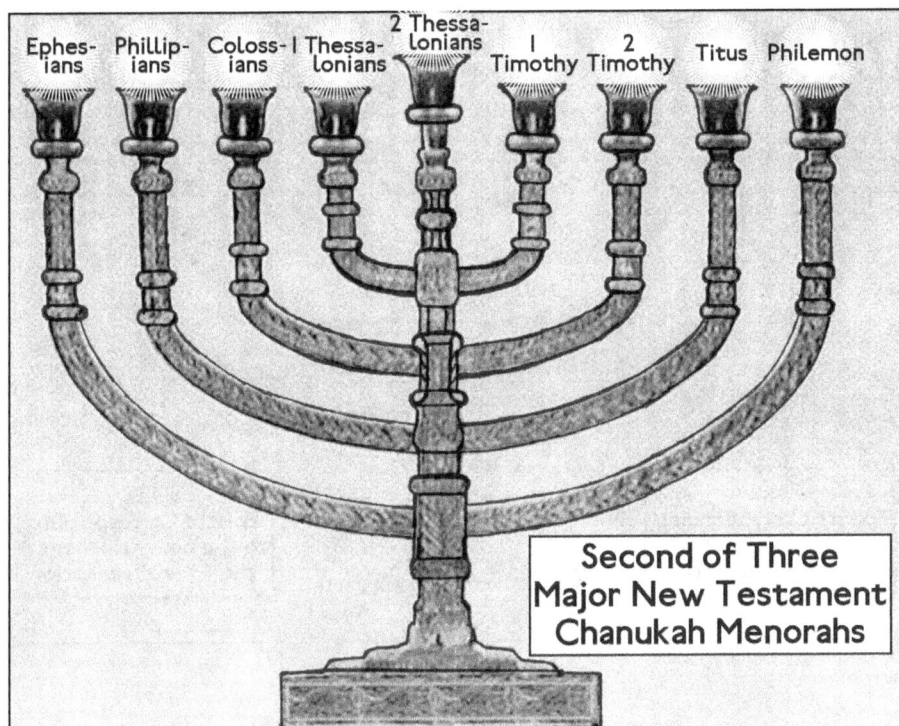

Second of Three Major New Testament Chanukah Menorahs

"God is just: He will pay back trouble to those who trouble you... This will happen when the Lord Jesus (Adonai Yahshua) is revealed from heaven in blazing fire with his powerful angels. He will punish those who do not know God and do not obey the gospel..." "And then the lawless one will be revealed, whom the Lord Jesus (Adonai Yahshua) will overthrow... and destroy by the splendor of his coming." - II Thessalonians 1:6-8, 2:8

Finally, in the third group of nine books that consists of Hebrews through Revelation, the fifth book is the First Epistle of John, where God the Father is the featured Light who gives the Light of Christ to us:

"This is the message which we have heard from Him... **that God is light and in Him is no darkness at all**. If we say that we have fellowship with Him, and walk in darkness, we lie and do not practice the truth. But **if we walk in the light as He is in the light, we have fellowship with one another, and the blood of Jesus Christ His Son cleanses us from all sin.**" - I John 1:5-7

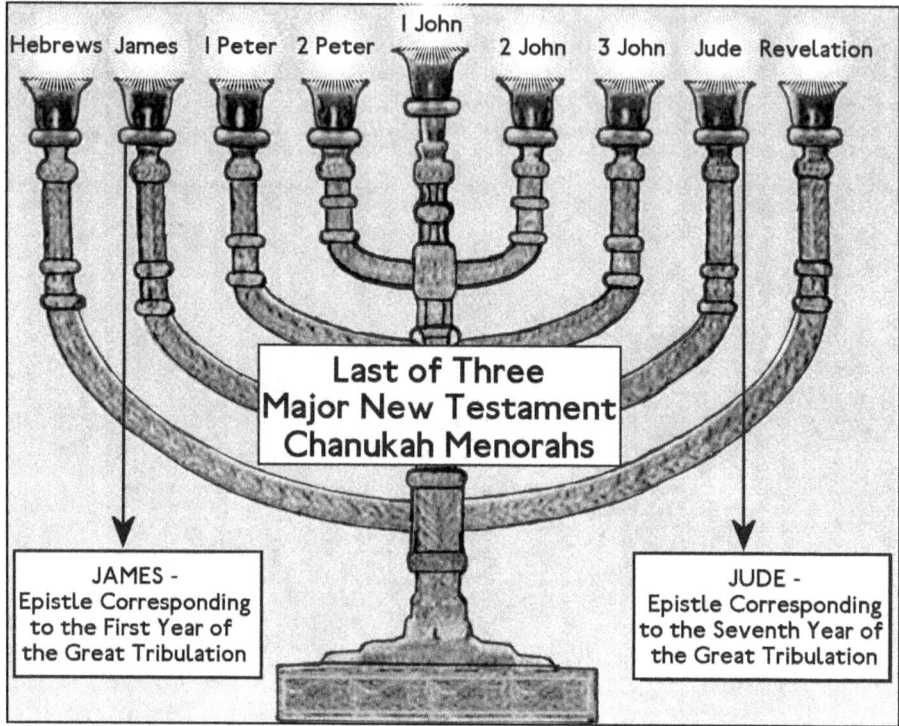

## A Menorah Within A Menorah: The Seven Prophetic Epistles

In this last group of nine books from Hebrews through Revelation, another peculiar pattern emerges that we will see again when we explore the Hallel Psalms in the next chapter. This is the fact that the first and last books of this group of nine forms a frame around the seven in between, which in turn seem clearly tied to the seven years of the Tribulation period, as shown in the illustration on this page. These seven books are James, 1 and 2 Peter, 1, 2, and 3 John, and Jude, and together they form a symbolic seven-branched menorah within a nine-branched menorah. Upon study, it can be seen that these seven books of the Bible appear to be particularly addressed to the concerns of the Tribulation Saints as they await Yahshua's Second Coming.

These seven books are epistles, or general letters of instruction to various congregations. As such, several of them are quite short. But in every case, their messages seem directed toward God's people who are suffering persecution, and who are in need of comfort. For example, in the **Epistle of James**, which appears connected to the first year of the Tribulation, James begins by addressing *"the twelve tribes which are*

## Chapter 1: God's Language - A Key to Prophecy

*scattered abroad"* (James 1:1). This seems to be referring to the 144,000 Witnesses who are sealed, or chosen from the Twelve Tribes of Israel in Revelation 7:4. Both references also suggest that all Twelve Tribes are still in existence somewhere in the world today.

James implores these tribes to be joyful even as they are tested, *"knowing that the testing of your faith brings patience"* (James 1:3). In James 2:15-17, these same people are admonished to help every brother and sister in the faith who is starving or *"naked."* Hunger and nakedness are the plight of the homeless. Therefore, in its plea to help the destitute, this passage seems tied to the war, famine, pestilence, and economic collapse suggested by the Four Horsemen of the Apocalypse in Revelation 6:2-8. But even more telling than these common points with Revelation is the fact that James refers to Elijah, who very likely may be one of the Two Witnesses mentioned in Revelation 11:3-12 that are to preach for 1,260 days. This number of days equals exactly three and one half years, or half of the Tribulation period. Uncannily, James also mentions that exact time period in reference to Elijah:

*"**Elijah** was a man with a nature like ours, and he prayed earnestly that it would not rain; and it did not rain on the land **for three years and six months.**" - James 5:17*

Since most scholars believe that the Two Witnesses will appear on the world scene either at the beginning or middle of the Tribulation period, the Book of James does indeed appear to be linked to events during the Tribulation.

This link is further strengthened when we examine the **First Epistle of Peter**, which seems connected to events in the second year of the Tribulation. In this epistle, Peter is addressing the believers in Asia Minor, which was a part of the spiritually hostile Roman Empire at the time. The hatred of Pagan Rome for Christians was a clear precursor to the hostility that the Antichrist will unleash upon anyone who seeks to know Christ during the Great Tribulation. Furthermore, in keeping with the persecution directed at Christians in the early Church, the main theme of this epistle is enduring suffering for the cause of Christ.

Over and over again, Peter admonishes his hearers to suffer through their trials without losing their faith or joy, but instead fixing their spiritual eyes *"on the salvation that is ready to be revealed in the last time"* (1 Peter 1:5), even though *"for a little while you... suffer grief in all kinds of trials"* (1 Peter 1:6). Then Peter encourages them, saying:

*"These have come so that your faith... may be proved genuine and may result in... honor **when Jesus Christ is revealed**..."* *"Therefore, prepare your minds for action; be self-

*controlled; set your hope fully on the grace to be given you **when Jesus Christ is revealed.**" - 1 Peter 1:7, 13 (NIV)*

*"But even if you should suffer for righteousness' sake, you are blessed... and always be ready to give a defense to everyone who asks you a reason for the hope that is in you... that when they defame you as evildoers, those who revile your good conduct in Christ may be ashamed. For it is better... to suffer for doing good than for doing evil. For Christ also suffered once for sins... that He might bring us to God..." - 1 Peter 3:14-18*

*"Beloved, **do not think it strange concerning the fiery trial which is to try you**, as though some strange thing happened to you; but rejoice to the extent **that you partake of Christ's sufferings**, that when His glory is revealed, you may also be glad with exceeding joy." - 1 Peter 4:12-13*

Note that, in the first two preceding passages taken from the New International Version of the Bible (or NIV), the phrase *"when Jesus Christ is revealed"* is used instead of *"the revelation of Jesus Christ,"* as found in the New King James Version (or NKJ). This is a significant difference, and it appears that the NIV is translated more faithfully in this case. Since we know that Jesus Christ is already revealed to our hearts by the power of the Holy Spirit, what does Peter mean? Could it be that this is not a reference to the action of the Holy Spirit revealing Christ to us, but an allusion to Christ's Second Coming, when He will be revealed in the flesh to all the living?

If the preceding arguments showing that the Epistle of James and the First Epistle of Peter are thematically connected to events in the first two years of the Tribulation period are true, then the **Second Epistle of Peter** should show signs that it relates to the third year of the seven-year Tribulation. This epistle admirably does so, being full of admonishments to flee evil, and behave in accordance with God's will. Furthermore, there is an emphasis in this epistle to be wary of deceptive people who can cause many to stumble:

*"But there were also false prophets among the people, even as there will be false teachers among you, who will secretly bring in destructive heresies, even denying the Lord who bought them, and bring on themselves swift destruction." - 2 Peter 2:1*

There will certainly be no shortage of false prophets during the Tribulation period! In this epistle, Peter also speaks of the end of the Day of the Lord - when this present creation will be destroyed by fire, and be replaced by a New Heaven and New Earth:

# Chapter 1: God's Language - A Key to Prophecy

> *"For this they willfully forget: that by the word of God the heavens were of old, and the earth standing out of water and in the water, by which the world that then existed perished, being flooded with water. But the heavens and the earth which are now preserved by the same word, are reserved for fire until the day of judgment and perdition of ungodly men."* - *"Nevertheless we, according to His promise, look for new heavens and a new earth in which righteousness dwells"* - 2 Peter 3:5-7, 13

The above Scripture is quite clear: In these Last Days, atheistic humanists, Pagans, and sleepy Christians have happily re-written the history of the past, omitting any reference to a world wide flood that was a just judgment for sin. Nonetheless, as shown in Books One and Three, myths and religious texts from all over the world confirm that this terrible, globally felt flood did destroy a past age of mankind as a punishment for sin. Ignoring the facts, many people living in this Last Day want nothing to do with any philosophy that includes one Supreme Creator God, or the concept of absolute good and evil. Instead, they have invented a past with no Creator, and a future with no hope.

The above Scripture also makes it clear that a future judgment - when the Earth will be destroyed by fire - has been decreed by the same "Lord" that we know as Yahshua or Jesus, the Messiah - who was our Creator God in His Preincarnate state (Colossians 1:15-17). Meanwhile, other people of our Age - though they may or may not be Christians - are more willing to accept Earth's precarious position in the Universe, and are busy trying to educate people about the real global threat of a celestial impact on the Earth.

The truth is: if the Earth were to sustain a direct impact on the level of the one that may have brought that terrible, violent Age of dinosaurs and men to an abrupt end with the Great Flood - all life on this planet could just as easily be extinguished all over again. Meanwhile, as more prudent men are busy determining ways to survive a global disaster such as a huge asteroid impact, other **people who know and believe the prophecies in the Bible know that surviving such a global disaster is ultimately dependent upon God's supernatural intervention.**

This passage also suggests that Peter was prophetically addressing the Tribulation Saints, who may wonder how much longer God will tolerate evil. Peter's answer to this question is that God is patient, and is going to give ample time for people to repent before He destroys the whole Earth by fire:

> *"The Lord is not slack concerning His promise, as some count slackness, but is longsuffering toward us, not willing that*

*any should perish but that all should come to repentance." - 2 Peter 3:9*

As will be fully explained in Chapter Seven, the Millennial Rule of Yahshua will come *after* the Great Tribulation, but *before* the destruction of this world by fire, which is an event that will happen just before the Great White Throne Judgment of Revelation Chapter 20 - an event that comes *after* the thousand year reign of Christ on Earth (See Rev. 20:4-7).

In the **First Epistle of John**, which should show some sign of being connected to the fourth year of the Tribulation, the following passage gives verification that it is speaking to the Tribulation Saints:

*"For all that is in the world... is of the world. And the world is passing away... but he who does the will of God abides forever. Little children,* **it is the last hour;** *and as* **you have heard that the Antichrist is coming, even now many antichrists have come,** *by which we know that* **it is the last hour."** *- I John 2:16-18*

Here John speaks of the Antichrist, and the many little antichrists that aid him in his sinister aims. John also repeats that *"it is the last hour,"* suggesting that the early Christians, who were under tremendous persecution, expected Yahshua to come again at any moment to save them. Could their belief in Christ's imminent return have been a prophetic call to those saints who will await Yahshua's coming in an even greater time of persecution? It seems so, especially when John states that the Antichrist will deny the deity of Christ. Though many little antichrists have done so, the Antichrist will deny the existence of both *God the Father, and the Son*:

*"Who is a liar but he who denies that Jesus (Yahshua) is the Christ (Messiah)? He is antichrist* **who denies the Father and the Son."** *- I John 2:22*

Uncannily, this passage in the First Epistle of John appears to address just what the Antichrist is supposed to do in the fourth year of the Tribulation period. Most theologians agree that the Prophet Daniel foretold that the Antichrist will make a covenant or treaty with "many" at the beginning of the Tribulation period (Daniel 9:27). After three and a half years, however, the Antichrist will break the treaty, proclaim that he is God, and set up his own image to be worshipped:

*"Let no one deceive you by any means; for that Day will not come unless the falling away comes first, and the man of sin is revealed,* **the son of perdition, who opposes and exalts himself above all that is called God** *or that is worshiped, so that* **he sits as God in the temple of God, showing himself that he is God."** *- II Thess. 2:3-4*

# Chapter 1: God's Language - A Key to Prophecy

Uncannily, this prophecy is found in the book that claims the center position in the nine branched menorah formed by the books of Ephesians through Philemon. If we see Ephesians and Philemon as framing books around the seven in between, then the Second Epistle to the Thessalonians is in the fourth position of this seven branched menorah, and may be connected to the fourth year of the Tribulation period - just as the First Epistle of John is! To strengthen the idea that John's first epistle is prophetically speaking to the Tribulation Saints, he makes the following plea:

*"And now, little children, abide in Him, that **when He appears,** we may... not be ashamed before Him **at His coming.**"* - *I John 2:28*

Here, we find two references to Christ's Second Coming in one sentence, making it clear that John expects Yahshua to return at any moment. Throughout his first epistle, John also continually speaks of Christ's character, and the future gift of everlasting life that all those who love Christ will one day receive.

Of the three epistles remaining in the group of seven beginning with the Epistle of James, the Second Epistle of John contains only 13 verses, and his third epistle only has 14, so they rank as the shortest books in the New Testament next to Jude, which follows them with only 25 verses. If these three epistles are connected in theme to the last three years of the Tribulation period, their very brevity is suggestive of the End Time prophecy in Matthew 24:22 that says: *"for the elect's sake those days will be shortened."* In this passage, could *"those days"* be a direct reference to the last three years of the Tribulation period? It is possible; since Yahshua's prophecy in Matthew speaks of the elect in the same way that the **Second Epistle of John** is addressed to *"the elect lady, and her children"* (2 John 1).

*"The elect lady"* being referring to in this epistle is likely the True Church - a "Lady" that is the Bride of Christ. Interestingly, in the Book of 1 Enoch - which is likely the oldest existing piece of apocalyptic literature ever written - *"elect ones,"* or saintly people, and "The Elect One," or the coming Messiah are referred to over a dozen times. As we will see in the upcoming discussion of the Epistle of Jude, the Book of 1 Enoch is referred to in the New Testament. This suggests that the apostles and early church fathers were familiar with Enoch's End Time teachings.

Now, just as in John's first epistle, the Second Epistle of John also speaks of the little antichrists in the world who deny that Yahshua came in the flesh:

> *"For many deceivers have gone out into the world who do not confess Jesus Christ as coming in the flesh. This is a deceiver and an antichrist."* - 2 John 1:7

During the Tribulation period, in addition to denying Yahshua's Second Coming like some smaller antichrists do, *the* Antichrist will deny that Yahshua is the Messiah, and may also proclaim that Christ was an imposter, or lesser Messiah. This is because the Antichrist, who is called *"the lawless one"* and *"the son of perdition"* in Scripture, will likely claim to be the false messiah promised in many religions, and he will perform many counterfeit miracles to prove his case:

> *"The coming of the lawless one is according to the working of Satan, with all power, signs, and lying wonders..."* - 2 Thess. 2:9

**The Third Epistle of John** is directed toward a Roman man named Gaius, and it discusses the actions of two Greeks. This suggests that the letter is aimed at a Gentile audience that is continually being confronted with Paganism, and surrounded by its followers. This is alluded to by the Pagan name Diotrephes, which means "Zeus nursed," and Demetrius, meaning "of Demeter." Zeus and Demeter were both important deities in the Classical world. In the world of the Antichrist, it is possible that these false gods will again be worshipped in the person of the Antichrist himself, who may claim to be the living personification not only of the one Creator God, but of many other Pagan deities.

In this letter, we are told that Diotrephes has rejected the wise counsel of John (3 John 9), but Gaius and Demetrius have remained faithful to the calling John entrusted them with (3 John 1, 12). This suggests that, even when it is clear by now that their world leader is the Antichrist spoken of in the Bible, a third of the Gentiles still living at this time will reject the true Christ and His teachings during the Tribulation period. This is in line with the teaching of the Book of Revelation, which suggests that a third of the people on Earth will perish for their wickedness:

> *"So the four angels... were released **to kill a third of mankind**..." "By these three plagues **a third of mankind was killed**-- by the fire and the smoke and the brimstone which came out of their mouths."* - Rev. 9:15, 18

Now we come to the seventh of the epistles tied to the Tribulation period, which is the **Epistle of Jude**. Not surprisingly, the confirmation that this epistle is connected to the last year in the Great Tribulation is apparent, for Jude refers twice in this short letter to Christ's return to judge the wicked:

## Chapter 1: God's Language - A Key to Prophecy

> *"But I want to remind you... that the Lord, having saved the people out of the land of Egypt, **afterward destroyed those who did not believe**. And the angels who... left their own abode, He has reserved in everlasting chains under darkness **for the judgment of the great day.**"* - Jude 1:5-6

> *"Now Enoch, the seventh from Adam, prophesied about these men also, saying, **'Behold, the Lord comes with ten thousands of His saints, to execute judgment on all**, to convict all who are ungodly... of all their ungodly deeds...'"* - Jude 1:14-15

In both of the preceding passages, it is clear that Jude is familiar with the apocalyptic prophecies in the Book of 1 Enoch, two of which we will focus on a bit later. In fact, the second quote from Jude is directly taken from 1 Enoch 1:9-10, while the first alludes to several Enochian scriptural passages (See 1 Enoch 54:3-5, 55:4, 56:1-4). And Jude is not alone in his knowledge of 1 Enoch. In his second epistle, Peter also alludes to the same passages as Jude:

> *"...God did not spare the angels who sinned, but cast them down to hell and delivered them into chains of darkness, to be reserved for judgment;"* - 2 Peter 2:4-5

From these references, it appears that the Book of 1 Enoch may have been required reading in the Early Church for all those who were called to teach their fellow saints. In addition, it is clear that these New Testament epistles have much to say to those of us who now live on the threshold of the Tribulation. We would therefore do well to study their messages and apply them so that we may be found worthy when Yahshua comes in the Rapture, and we can escape the terror of the Tribulation to come.

Though some of the information in the second half of this chapter is a review of J. R. Church's excellent book: "The Mystery of the Menorah and the Hebrew Alphabet," new information has been introduced here that is not in that book. Nonetheless, all of J. R. Church's books are filled with scriptural truth, and show that he has a keen understanding of the Language of God, and a great ability to decipher allegorical messages in Scripture. Though I may disagree with Mr. Church at times, especially as regards the symbol of the eagle in prophecy, I agree with him in many areas, and highly recommend all of his books.

## Chapter 2: Amazing Prophecies in the Psalms


*"I will incline mine ear to **a parable: I will open my dark saying upon the harp.**" - Psalm 49:4 (KJV)*


In his fascinating book "Hidden Prophecies in the Psalms," J. R. Church extensively documented the prophetic messages in the 150 Psalms found in the Bible. According to Mr. Church, the Psalms have a special place among the prophetic works of the Bible. This is because **the Psalms appear to prophetically represent every year in the Twentieth Century, and the first fifty years in the 21st Century.** Mr. Church refers to Psalm 49 (as quoted above) as the key to understanding the prophetic nature of the Psalms. Verse 4 of this Psalm indicates that the prophecies within the Psalms *are parables.* That is, *they are allegorical in nature, and also prophetic.* Furthermore, Psalm 49 tells us that these parables contain *"dark sayings,"* or hidden prophecies that would not be opened to our understanding until after 1949 - the year indicated by Psalm 49.

Uncannily, the number 49 indicates a period of seven times seven, or the number of days between the firstfruits offering during the Feast of Unleavened Bread, and the fiftieth Jubilee day called Pentecost. Because God chose that holy day to give the Israelites the Old Covenant Mosaic Laws, and then later gave born-again Messianic Jews, Lost Israelites, and Gentiles the New Covenant outpouring of the Holy Sprit, Pentecost is a special yearly Jubilee that signifies spiritual freedom and understanding. 1949 is also a year that is singled out in the Great Pyramid's prophetic measurements as very significant, as will be shown in Chapter Eight. It is truly remarkable how so many separate and seemingly unrelated prophetic records can concur and agree, as will be shown throughout this book.

When J. R. Church first published his book in 1986, he made a prediction that the Tribulation period might begin sometime before the year 2000. He also earmarked Psalm 94 as a very significant one. J. R. Church felt the allegorical imagery of Psalm 94 marked 1994 as the likely time when the Battle of Armageddon might occur, and Yahshua could return to Earth to set up His Millennial Kingdom. However, Mr. Church chose to revise his initial prediction in the updated 1990 edition of his book. There, Mr. Church stated that, though he felt that Yahshua intended to set up His Millennial Kingdom on Earth sometime during the period from 1991 through 2050 AD, he couldn't be certain it would occur during that time. However, the structure of, and allegorical allusions in the later Psalms highly suggest that Yahshua's Millennial Kingdom will be an earthly reality *before* 2050 AD.

Mr. Church then pointed to several places in the Psalms where strong allusions to the Tribulation, and the Millennial Kingdom were made. In every case, these sections of the Psalms were between Psalms 94 through 145. According to Mr. Church, we are now also in the Deuteronomy period of history, when the divine government of the Kingdom of God will be established forever on Earth. This means that, within the next fifty years, we should see the coming of the Antichrist during a time of widespread apostasy, then an initial period of peace, followed by an all out war amid natural disasters of epic proportions. In this book, I will show that Mr. Church may indeed be correct in his predictions - but I will do so using not just one prophetic channel, but many that all seem to be pointing to a narrow window of dates in the very near future.

## *The Prophetic Five-Fold Structure of the Psalms*

Before we explore the prophecies hidden within the Psalms, it is important to understand that their structure is based on the structure of the first five books of the Bible, which are Genesis, Exodus, Leviticus, Numbers, and Deuteronomy. Like this section of the Bible called the Pentateuch, there is a fivefold structure to the Psalms.

Each of the five sections of the Psalms reflect the basic theme of the book of the Pentateuch that it corresponds to in sequence. Hence:

1. Psalms 1 through 41 are the **Genesis Psalms**
2. Psalms 42 through 72 are the **Exodus Psalms**
3. Psalms 73 through 89 are the **Leviticus Psalms**
4. Psalms 90 through 106 are the **Numbers Psalms**, and
5. Psalms 107 through 150 are the **Deuteronomy Psalms**

It is uncanny how the theme of each book of the Pentateuch is echoed in the corresponding Psalms. For example, **the Book of Genesis'** central themes are creation, divine life or purpose, and election by Grace.

## Chapter 2: Amazing Prophecies in the Psalms

**The Genesis Psalms** are Psalms 1 through 41, and their themes correspond to those of the Book of Genesis. According to Mr. Church, these Psalms apply to the first 41 years of the 1900's, or Twentieth Century. They also seem to specifically apply to the World Zionist Movement, which began in the early 1900's.

Uncannily, the Book of Psalms is the *nineteenth book* of the Bible. Could this be an indication that the years beginning with a nineteen - 1900 through 1999 AD - are indeed numbered by Psalms 1 to 99 that correspond to every year? First, let's look at the facts of history, and the themes of the five distinct sections of the Psalms to see if this is true.

The main themes of **the Book of Exodus** are the redemption of God's chosen people, their return to, and conquest of the Promised Land, and the establishment of the Israelites in their own nation. These same desires are the force behind the World Zionist Movement, which escalated during the years connected to **the Exodus Psalms**: Psalms 42 through 72. Just as Yahweh called the Israelites out of Egypt, and Abraham out of Ur, and promised to give both Abraham and Israel's descendents the land of Canaan as a lasting inheritance, Zionist leaders Theodor Herzl and Chaim Weizmann called fellow Jews to unite an effort to reclaim the Promised Land in the early 1900's. This World Zionist Movement took root and grew - eventually leading to a mass Exodus of Jews from Europe to Palestine and the United States.

In 1942, after the slaughter of countless Jews during World War II, the Zionist Movement escalated dramatically as thousands of Jews sought freedom from oppression in Europe. The mass *exodus* of many Jews to their ancestral homeland led to the establishment of the modern nation of Israel in 1948. Amazingly, the historical events surrounding the birth and establishment of the nation of Israel during the years 1942 through 1972 are reflected allegorically in the corresponding Exodus Psalms. We will explore a few of the most compelling Exodus Psalms a bit later.

**The Book of Leviticus** is devoted to sanctification through the establishment of the priesthood, and describes the order, method, and implements of worship. Throughout the years 1973 through 1989, there was a resurgence to re-establish the Levite priesthood, and to manufacture the implements needed to re-establish Temple worship among the Jews. As a result, all the things required for the Jews to resume Temple worship are now in place except for one element: they have yet to acquire access to the Temple Mount in Jerusalem. **The Leviticus Psalms** 73 through 89 reflect this movement among the Jews in Israel, and elsewhere in the years 1973 through 1989. The historical events that affected the nation of Israel are echoed in the Psalms corresponding to the dates in which each event occurred. Due to the prophetic nature of these uncanny correlations, we will focus on them a bit later.

**The Book of Numbers** deals with the testing of our faith and the experience of our faith in action. This is also true of **the Numbers Psalms** 90 through 106. Over the period of 1973 through 2006, the nation of Israel was repeatedly under attack from her enemies in the Middle East, and elsewhere. Nonetheless, in keeping with the theme of the Book of Numbers, the violence toward Israel escalated dramatically in 1991, with the unfolding of the Gulf War. Uncannily, the year 1991 corresponds to the second Numbers Psalm, Psalm 91, and this was indeed a terrible time of testing for the nation of Israel.

The Gulf War marked a sudden resurgence in, and escalation of Arab violence toward Israel. Yet, despite the overwhelming odds against them, the Jews have prevailed over every enemy. Though there is constant unrest in Israel caused by Radical Islamic Terrorists who hate Jews and Christians, Israel is still a powerful force to be reckoned with. In addition, the people of Israel are as staunchly prepared to defend their nation's right to exist today as they were in ancient times, and as they were when Israel was reborn in 1948.

The fifth and final book of the Pentateuch is **the Book of Deuteronomy**. Its main theme is the establishment of a divine government, and the trials and tribulations associated with attempting to set up a godly kingdom in a world ruled by Satan. Likewise, Psalms 107 through 150 are **the Deuteronomy Psalms** that deal with the difficulties, and resistance that will be encountered by the righteous as they work toward the establishment of God's Kingdom here on Earth. However, these Psalms also depict the joy, elation, and happiness of God's chosen people when they see Yahshua's Millennial Kingdom firmly established on Earth. For example, the Hallel Psalms, or Psalms of Praise, which repeatedly contain the phrase "Hallelu-Yah" or *"Praise the LORD,"* are located in this section of the Psalms.

Interestingly, there are forty occurrences of the phrase: *"Praise the LORD"* running through the entire book of Psalms. This phrase therefore appears in this portion of the Bible more so than any other. Since the number 40 in the Bible often refers to a time of testing, and refining God's people through suffering, this suggests that the Deuteronomy Psalms reveal the unfolding, and completion of a severe time of testing - when God's people will be refined in the fire of affliction, and purified through suffering.

## Chapter 2: Amazing Prophecies in the Psalms

*Uncannily, this fivefold structure of the Pentateuch, and the Psalms echoes the fivefold structure of the Great Pyramid.* The five points and sides of this pyramid point to the Fifth Great Day of Creation, or the Day when the Earth was created. As shown in Chapter Three, the Great Pyramid is a stone representation of one hemisphere of the Earth. Since the number five is connected to the Earth, the corresponding fivefold structure of the Psalms and the Great Pyramid suggests that both prophetically depict events in the Fives Ages of Mankind on Earth that the prophet Daniel spoke of. They also point to the five major puncture wounds that Christ received on the Cross - the fifth wound being the spear thrust that was inflicted *after* Christ died.

### The Psalms and the Five Ages of Mankind

In another place in the Bible, the number five is also tied to the Five Ages of Mankind. This is found in Nebuchadnezzar's dream vision of the gold-headed statue of a man (Daniel 2:31-33). As discussed in Book One and Three, this statue depicts Five Ages of mankind's works. Since the Fourth and Fifth Ages both contain Iron, this suggests that the Fourth Age would directly affect the nature of the Fifth. Altogether, **the body of the gold-headed statue depicts five distinct periods in human history.** These can roughly be summarized as:

Gold head: The **Golden Age** of Egypt and Babylon

Silver torso: The **Silver Age** of Assyria

Bronze hips: The **Bronze Age** of Greece

Iron legs: The **Iron Age** of Rome, and

Iron and clay feet: The **Church Age**

The Iron Age represents the Age when Ancient Rome ruled the world in culture and politics. Though the Roman Empire eventually crumbled, its cultural values were upheld in the Church Age through the Holy Roman Empire, and in the monasteries and institutions of higher learning established by the Roman Catholic Church, Orthodox, and Protestant Churches. The cultural legacy of Rome was thereby inherited by the Western industrialized nations, which were also staunchly Christian at one time.

The fifth and final portion of the statue is its feet, which depict the Fifth Age ruled by the Catholic, Orthodox, Protestant, and Muslim nations after the fall of the Roman Empire. These iron-like and clay-like nations have created a very unstable base for the heavy metal statue above it. This represents the political and economic disparities between the Romanized West, and the Third World nations in Asia, Africa, and South America. The gaps between these nations developed slowly throughout the current Church Age, which began after Christ's Resurrection. As indicated by the stone that crushes the feet of iron and clay in Nebuchadnezzar's dream vision, this volatile and unstable mixture of weak and strong nations will eventually be overthrown, or destroyed by a supernatural stone from heaven:

> "You watched while a stone was cut out without hands, which struck the image on its feet of iron and clay, and broke them in pieces. Then the iron, the clay, the bronze, the silver, and the gold were crushed together, **and... the wind carried them away** so that no trace of them was found. **And the stone that struck the image became a great mountain** and filled the whole earth." - Daniel 2:34-35

Daniel's prophetic interpretation of this dream tells us that the stone is to become a mountain representing *"a kingdom that shall never be destroyed"* that would be set up, or established during the days of *"those kings,"* meaning the leaders of the weak and strong nations of the world after the fall of the Roman Empire. This Kingdom is the fulfillment of the Kingdom of God that was established in people's hearts after Yahshua's Resurrection from the dead:

> "And in the days of these kings **the God of heaven will set up a kingdom which shall never be destroyed**; and... it shall break in pieces and consume all these kingdoms, and it shall stand forever." - Daniel 2:44

People enter this invisible, everlasting spiritual kingdom when they accept Christ as their Savior, and receive the Holy Spirit, which is the allegorical wind in the dream vision that sweeps the fallen and crushed kingdoms of men away forever (Dan. 2:35). This dream therefore foretells Christ's Second Coming - when He will overthrow all the kingdoms of the world and set up His Millennial Kingdom. After this, He will establish an everlasting Kingdom of Peace when the New Heaven and Earth are created.

In support of Daniel's interpretation of Nebuchadnezzar's dream, we can see that today's Third World nations are weak in wealth, armaments, and/or spiritual understanding, making them the nations of clay. Two examples of these are India and China, where there is an overall lack of wealth among their beleaguered citizens, and where each nation lacks spiritual knowledge and truth. The nations of iron, on the

## Chapter 2: Amazing Prophecies in the Psalms — Page 45

other hand, are strong in arms, wealth, and/or spiritual enlightenment. Examples of these are Japan and Germany, who are strong in technological and financial wealth, and the United States, which is currently strong in all three areas, though its citizens are fast becoming as spiritually apostate as their European neighbors.

Each of the five sections of the Psalms ends with what J. R. Church dubbed the prophetic Amens. These Amens not only indicate that a given section of the Psalms has reached an end, but that it also has an overlapping prophetic application. The word "amen" means "so be it". It is an exclamation of approval over God's Word, but also an affirmation that we want God to **fulfill** His Word. Two Amens together therefore imply that the events that began to be fulfilled in that section of the Psalms will continue to be fulfilled in the next. Psalms 41, 72, and 89 all end with two Amens, while Psalm 106 ends with *only one*, coupled with a Hallelu-Yah, or *"Praise the LORD (Yahweh)!"* This is highly significant because it implies that, while the Numbers Psalms will find additional fulfillment in the Deuteronomy Section, the Deuteronomy Psalms will not need any fulfillment in the future, but will find *complete fulfillment* during the years they cover, which is from late 2006 through 2050 AD.

Uncannily, the Hallelu-Yah at the end of the Numbers Psalms also sets the theme for the Deuteronomy Psalms, which contain more mentions of the phrase *"Praise the LORD!"* than any other section of the Bible. Since the Deuteronomy Psalms deal with the establishment of God's Divine Government on Earth, the Hallelu-Yah pertaining to it suggests that God's Kingdom on Earth will be fully established during the period covered by this section. If the Kingdom of God is set up on Earth sometime between 2006 and 2050 AD, this joyful reality will cause many people on Earth to repeatedly exclaim: "Praise the LORD!"

Is it possible that Deuteronomy or the *fifth section* of the Psalms depicts the time-period leading up to, and including Christ's Millennial Kingdom - just as Nebuchadnezzar's dream depicted the setting up of the everlasting Kingdom of God on Earth in the Fifth Age? Could this mean that Psalms 106 through 150, which mark the years 2006 through 2050, will see the unfolding of the Tribulation period, and the establishment of Christ's Millennial Kingdom? This book will show many reasons to believe that this is so, and that Yahshua's Second Coming is not only near, but imminent.

## The Psalms Defy the Dual Nature of Prophecy

Many Scriptural passages like Luke 24:44 have a dualistic application, where the first half of the sentence or paragraph pertains to an earlier time, while the second half pertains to a later or future time. Acts 2:17-21, which is a reference to Joel 2:28-32, is an excellent example:

> *"(1) And it shall come to pass in the last days, says God, that I will pour out of My Spirit on all flesh; your sons and your daughters shall prophesy, your young men shall see visions, your old men shall dream dreams. And... I will pour out My Spirit in those days; and they shall prophesy. (2) I will show wonders in heaven above and signs in the earth beneath... The sun shall be turned into darkness, and the moon into blood, before the coming of the great and awesome day of the Lord. And it shall come to pass that whoever calls on the name of the Lord shall be saved." - Acts 2:17-21*

In this Scripture, the numbers 1 and 2 indicate its two thematically and prophetically different sections. Though verse 17 states that Joel's prophecy will occur *"in the last days,"* note that the first section speaks about the sudden and extensive outpouring of God's Spirit on all humanity that occurred at the first Pentecost after Christ's Resurrection. Now note the striking difference between this first section, and the second half - where the theme changes from one of jubilance in the Spirit, to ominous warnings in the heavens. Could it be that, though the first half of this prophecy pertains to the two Great Days or millenniums after Christ's Resurrection, the last half pertains to the end of that time period, which is just before Christ sets up His Millennial Rule on Earth? This indeed appears to be the case, as can be shown by comparing the preceding prophecy to the following one, which clearly pertains to Christ's Second Coming:

> *"And there will be signs in the sun, in the moon, and in the stars; and on the earth distress of nations, with perplexity, the sea and the waves roaring; men's hearts failing them from fear... for the powers of heaven will be shaken. Then they will see the Son of Man coming in a cloud with power and great glory." - Luke 21:25-27*

Now, the important thing to note through these comparisons is that Joel's prophecy has two thematically and prophetically different sections that will be fulfilled *at two different times*. Likewise, because Yahshua referred to the prophecies in the Psalms last, they likely pertain to the same last days that Joel was referring to in his prophecy.

## Chapter 2: Amazing Prophecies in the Psalms

Throughout the Bible, there are subtle indications that the prophecies contained within it will have a dual fulfillment. This is not, however, entirely true of the Psalms. This is because, with the exception of Psalms that clearly refer to Christ's First Advent like Psalm 22, the prophecies in the most of the Psalms appear to pertain primarily to *modern times*. Yahshua Himself alluded to this fact when speaking to His disciples after He rose from the dead:

> *"Then He said to them, 'These are the words which I spoke to you while I was still with you, that all things must be fulfilled which were written in the Law of Moses and the Prophets and the Psalms concerning Me.' And He opened their understanding, that they might comprehend the Scriptures." - Luke 24:44-45*

In this Scripture, Yahshua is telling His disciples that there are prophecies in the Law, the Prophets, and the Psalms concerning Him, and that these prophecies had to be fulfilled. In the way He presented them, however, Yahshua was also indicating the time period when the prophecies in these sections of the Bible would be fulfilled. Though the Psalms appear in between the Law and the Prophets, they are mentioned *last*, suggesting that the prophecies in them would be fulfilled last. In keeping with this idea, the Law and the Prophets are referred to often in the New Testament, while the Psalms are only referred to in a few places. This means that many of the prophecies in the Psalms weren't likely fulfilled during that era.

## *Amazing Fulfilled Prophecies from Selected Psalms*

If Mr. Church is correct about the prophetic nature of the Psalms that Kings David and King Solomon are attributed with writing, then Psalm 1 would prophetically correlate to the year 1901 on the Gregorian calendar, and so on. Likewise, Psalm 104 would prophetically relate to 2004. To substantiate his claims, J. R. Church has conclusively shown that many Psalms reveal a prophetic knowledge of events that occurred in the years they correlate with - especially in regard to the Jews, who are King David's descendents, and the modern nation of Israel. Some of the astounding prophecies concealed in the Psalms are highly relevant to this study of End Time events, and are focused on here to show their amazing prophetic scope.

**Psalm 13** is a Genesis Psalm, and as such, it brings the reasons for the World Zionist Movement to the forefront. This is clear from the first verses of Psalm 13, where King David prophetically anticipated the four times that Israel would suffer in exile. He did so by stating the prophetic question *"How long?"* four times, one for each kingdom that would oppress Israel, and send them into exile. These kingdoms were Babylon, Media, Greece, and Rome:

> *"**How long**, O LORD (Yahweh)? Will You forget me forever? **How long** will You hide Your face from me? **How long** shall I take counsel in my soul, having sorrow in my heart daily? **How long** will my enemy be exalted over me?"* - Psalm 13:1-2

This question *"How long?"* is found often in Scripture - both as a lament, and as a question that righteous people pose to God when they seek to know when their unjust suffering will end. In the original Hebrew version of the Psalms, the question appears eighteen times in twelve passages. Each time this phrase is uttered, it is as if David was asking God to tell him not only what trouble would befall Israel, but *when*. If we view the Psalms as a prophetic window into the fate of the Jews in the 150 years between 1901 and 2050, then a startling fact emerges. Each time David asks this question, it is in a Psalm which ties in to a year when the Jews were suffering tremendous persecution. For example, in Psalm 4, David first asked "How long?" This Psalm correlates with 1904, when the Jews were beginning to suffer from the worst pogroms ever held in Europe and Russia.

Though the first *"How long?"* appears in Psalm 4, and the last one appears in Psalm 94, this does not mean that the Jews did not suffer persecution before 1904, or that they will no longer suffer after 1994. But since this lament and question is asked four times in a row here, it indicates that the suffering the Jews had experienced over the intervening centuries was about to increase *fourfold!* Therefore, in 1904, persecution toward the Jews should have begun to escalate *dramatically* over any previous time in history, *which it did!* Likewise, when David asks this question for the last time in Psalm 94, it suggests that - sometime after 1994 - the Jews won't have to ask the question *"How Long?"* any longer, because God will permanently deliver all Jews and Christians from oppression, and exile. Like J. R. Church, I believe that we are the *last* generation - the generation that will see God's merciful answer for Israel, and the everlasting salvation of all God's people through His Son Yahshua.

In 1913, another event occurred that had many ominous implications. The Federal Reserve System in the United States was officially passed into law. This meant that the control of America's money and financial institutions had passed into private ownership, and many of those who now controlled it were Jews. This soon created chaos on the

## Chapter 2: Amazing Prophecies in the Psalms

world financial scene, and opened the way for banks to charge exorbitant interest rates on borrowed cash, while encouraging a credit-based society that would line Jewish pockets even more.

Sadly, since much of this newly realized financial power was Jewish-owned, it began to create resentment, and even outright hatred toward all the Jews in Europe, and America, and contributed greatly to the eruption of World War I in 1914. Sadly, however, only a handful of the world's Jews actually control this money to any extent. Consequently, this animosity toward all Jews was not only unfounded, it was generated by darker Satanic forces that have wanted to destroy the Jewish race since they were forged into a conquering nation in the Sinai desert 3500 years ago.

The evil events that were triggered by growing Anti-Semitism in 1913 had dire effects that would last into present times. The fact that this Anti-Semitism had initially been stirred up over the ownership of money, and control of world commerce brings a biblical warning about money to mind, which says: *"the love of money is the root of all kinds of evil"* (1 Timothy 6:10).

**Psalm 25** is also a Genesis Psalm. Interestingly, and in keeping with the theme of Genesis, its focus is on the *creation* of places of higher learning. Psalm 25 is a peculiar sort of Psalm called an *acrostic*, in which each verse in the psalm begins with a Hebrew letter. However, this acrostic does not contain all twenty-two letters in the Hebrew alphabet. Since it is incomplete, it suggests a need to gain more knowledge. In support of this, the psalm repeatedly refers to teaching. In verse 4, it says: *"Show me Your ways, O LORD (Yahweh);* **teach me Your paths.***"* Then again, in verse 5, David asks for knowledge: *"Lead me in Your truth and* **teach me***, for You are the God of my salvation."* Then, in verses 8 and 9, God's ability to teach sinners is repeated: *"Good and upright is the LORD (Yahweh); therefore* **He teaches sinners** *in the way. The humble He guides in justice, and* **the humble He teaches His way***."* Finally, in verse 12, David tells us that God teaches those who fear Him: *"Who is the man that fears the LORD (Yahweh)? Him shall He teach in the way He chooses."*

Uncannily, in April 1925, a new Jewish institution of higher learning called the Hebrew University opened on Mount Sinai. Furthermore, earlier that year in Palestine, The Haifa Institute of Technology also opened its doors. Amazingly, despite constant local Arab hostility toward the Jews in Palestine, both of these Jewish schools were able to open. Could the repeated references to teaching in Psalm 25 refer to these momentous events?

**Psalm 39** and the Genesis Psalms preceding and following it paint an extremely dismal picture for the Jews. By late 1937, the Jews in Nazi Germany had lost all human rights. They could not vote, or participate in government or the arts. They were ostracized from some stores, and were refused all humanitarian aid. In 1939, and again in 1941, Hitler decreed that, if the Jews refused to relinquish their control of world financial institutions, and it plunged the world into war again, then he vowed to see to the annihilation of the Jews in Europe. As already shown, Jewish financial power had also triggered the animosity between nations that led to World War I in 1914. When Hitler vowed to make the Jews pay for their financial power with their extermination, is it possible that many people tended to believe that the world would be better off if Christians owned the world's money, and controlled the world economy? Could this also be why they turned a blind eye to Nazi extremism and their propagandized hatred of the Jews?

**Psalm 47** is one of the Exodus Psalms, which begin with Psalm 42. The Exodus Psalms marked a new time in history when the descendents of the Jews were saved from severe oppression, and further attempts at Jewish genocide. In this regard, Psalm 47 opens with a verse that is highly prophetic of events in late November of 1947:

*"Oh, clap your hands, all you peoples! Shout to God (Elohim) with the voice of triumph! For the LORD Most High (Yahweh Elyon) is awesome; he is a great King over all the earth." - Psalm 47:1-2*

Could these joyful verses refer to the fact that the United Nations had just voted thirty-three to thirteen for the partition of Palestine into separate Jewish and Arab states? The facts of history suggest it did, because soon Jews all over the world were dancing in the streets, and praising Yahweh at the news. Verse 9 of Psalm 47 even seems to refer to the role of the dignitaries in the United Nations as *"the princes of the people,"* who planned to gather the Jews, or *"the people of the God of Abraham"* together in one place.

*"The princes of the people have gathered together, even the people of the God of Abraham. For the shields of the earth belong unto God; he is greatly exalted." - Psalm 47:9 (KJV)*

The Gentile Nations had just voted to allow the Jews a new homeland - in the very location of their former one. But the joy of the Jews over this news was a bit premature, as a confrontation with their Arab enemies was about to ensue. Nonetheless, at least for a time, the Jewish people had a right to be jubilant as they witnessed the events that

## Chapter 2: Amazing Prophecies in the Psalms

would lead to the rebirth of their nation in the Promised Land. The Holy Land is referred to as *"our inheritance"* in verse 4 of Psalm 47, which also refers to the Jews as *"the excellence of Jacob:"*

*"He will choose our inheritance for us, the excellence of Jacob whom He loves. Selah. God has gone up with a shout, the LORD (Yahweh) with the sound of a trumpet."* - Psalm 47:4-5

**Psalm 48,** like Psalm 47, begins with a jubilant voice that is reflective of the Jewish people, who would soon be rejoicing over the revival of the nation of Israel in 1948, and its recognition by the Gentile leaders who approved its formation:

*"Great is the LORD (Yahweh), and greatly to be praised in the city of our God, in His holy mountain. Beautiful in elevation, the joy of the whole earth, is Mount Zion on the sides of the north, the city of the great King"* - Psalm 48:1-2

Psalm 48, verses 4 through 8 refer to the leaders of the United Nations as kings, and speaks of the delegation that they sent to Jerusalem in 1947 to determine the state of affairs between the Jews and Arabs living there:

*"For behold, the kings assembled, they passed by together. They saw it, and so they marveled; they were troubled, they hastened away. Fear took hold of them there, and pain, as of a woman in birth pangs, as when You break the ships of Tarshish with an east wind. As we have heard, so we have seen in the city of the LORD of hosts... God will establish it forever. Selah."* - Psalm 48:4-8

In verse 7 above, the ships of Tarshish may refer to the British, who had mighty fleets that roamed the world just as the Phoenician ships of Tarshish once did in ancient times. It is interesting to note that Great Britain may have been a Phoenician colony at one time, and the source of the tin the Phoenicians sold elsewhere in the Old World. Uncannily, the British also had much to do with the formation of Israel as a Jewish state in 1948. It was the beneficence of the Gentile Nations like Britain for the plight of the Jews that gave them even more cause to dance for joy than in 1947, and gave them a major reason to shout:

*"Let Mount Zion rejoice, let the daughters of Judah be glad, because of Your judgments."* - Psalm 48:11

**Psalm 54** opens with a fervent plea for God's help against murderous *strangers*:

> *"Save me, O God (Elohim), by Your name (Ha Shem), and vindicate me by Your strength. Hear my prayer, O God (Elohim); give ear to the words of my mouth. For strangers have risen up against me, and oppressors have sought after my life; they have not set God before them. Selah."* - Psalm 54:1-3

Uncannily, just as this part of Psalm 54 suggests, the first acts of Arab Terrorism were witnessed in Israel. Masked Terrorists, who were thereby *strangers,* always carried out these extreme acts of violence against innocent Jewish civilians. This Psalm also clearly indicates that, though the Arabs view Terrorism as a religious act, the God of Israel has nothing to do with their violence inspired by Anti-Semitism, and a hatred of developed Western nations. In fact, this Psalm indicates that, despite many acts of Terrorism against Israel to come, God would protect and preserve His chosen people in Israel, and elsewhere:

> *"Behold, God is my helper; the Lord is with those who uphold my life. He will repay my enemies for their evil. Cut them off in Your truth... I will praise Your name, O LORD (Yahweh)... For He has delivered me out of all trouble; and my eye has seen its desire upon my enemies."* - Psalm 54:4-7

Though Psalm 54 is mostly in the present tense, its last verse is in the past tense, and speaks of victory against Terrorism. However, these first acts of Terrorism have not been eradicated. In fact, they have escalated dramatically in recent history, and they now affect many nations outside of Israel. Since this victory over Terrorism is a future event, this Psalm is a divine prophecy against the many Arab nations who plotted, and continue to plot these ungodly acts of violence, and a promise to Israel and her allies in the West that they will one day be able to joyfully declare that God: *"has delivered me out of all trouble; and my eye has seen its desire upon my enemies."*

These Arab Terrorist acts began in conjunction with a withdrawal of British troops from Egypt. Israelis therefore began to feel too vulnerable, and the fear of more Terrorism led some of them to act very rashly and foolishly in 1955, as we shall see.

**Psalm 55** appears to be the prophetic voice of both the Israeli people as a whole, and David Ben Gurion, a former Israeli Prime Minister who was Israel's Defense Minister at this time in history. This is because, in 1955, Israeli counter-intelligence agents plotted to, and succeeded in blowing up several British and American buildings in Egypt. Thankfully, Israeli intelligence's efforts to blame this Terrorist act on the Egyptian Muslim Brotherhood failed.

## Chapter 2: Amazing Prophecies in the Psalms — Page 53

Could the following passages be written for Ben Gurion, whose personal shame over this incident was so great that he planned to resign from office?

> "Because of... the oppression of the wicked... they bring down trouble upon me, and in wrath they hate me. My heart is severely pained within me... Fearfulness... and horror has overwhelmed me. So I said, '**Oh, that I had wings like a dove! I would fly away and be at rest.**' " - Psalm 55:3-6

When this Israeli plot was discovered, it mortified not only Ben Gurion, but also many shocked Israelis. They could not believe that their public servants had actively engaged in the same kind of Terrorist acts that they were supposed to be trying to prevent! Their cry of outrage is echoed in the following verses of Psalm 55, which speaks of the betrayal of a once trusted companion:

> "For it is not an enemy who reproaches me; then I could bear it. Nor is it one who hates me who has exalted himself against me... **But it was you, a man my equal, my companion and my acquaintance. We took sweet counsel together, and walked to the house of God in the throng.** Let... them go down alive into hell, for wickedness is... among them. As for me, I will call upon God, and the LORD (Yahweh) shall save me." - Psalm 55:12-16

Though it is highly unlikely that the deep-seated Arab hatred of Israel and the Jews in general will ever be rectified without a direct act of God, this Israeli plot, which was later dubbed the "Lavon Affair," certainly caused Arabs to hate Israel even more than they already did. This whole incident highlights an often-ignored point in God's Word. This point is that revenge is *never* justified, for it is Yahweh's place alone to judge and punish those who transgress His Laws! As it says repeatedly in Scripture:

> "Beloved, do not avenge yourselves, but rather give place to wrath; for it is written, **'Vengeance is Mine, I will repay,' says the Lord.**" - Romans 12:19

> "Rejoice, O Gentiles, with His people; for **He (Yahweh) will avenge the blood of His servants,** and render vengeance to His adversaries; He will provide atonement for His land and His people." - Deut. 32:43

> "O LORD God (Yahweh Elohim), to whom vengeance belongs-- **O God, to whom vengeance belongs,** shine forth!" - Psalm 94:1

Despite the erroneous message of countless violent Hollywood vigilante movies, these Scriptures teach that those who take justice into their own hands do so at their own peril, and inevitably will pay dearly for it as a direct breach of God's Will.

**Psalms 67 and 68** are connected to the events of the year 1967, which was the year that Israel won a great victory against her hostile Arab neighbors in what is now known as the Six-Day War. In 1967, Arab Hostilities toward Israel escalated dramatically. This is because King Hussein of Jordan, who controlled the eastern half of Jerusalem and the Temple Mount area, planned to combine his armed forces with those of Syria and Egypt to launch an all-out attack on Israel. To do so, these Arab states had already amassed their troops and weaponry in the Arab-occupied territories within Israel. In addition, King Hussein had already moved in cranes to build an Arab luxury hotel in front of the Wailing Wall, which would forever cut off Jewish prayer access to the site.

The Israelis, realizing the grave peril they were in, did not sit back and wait for the invasion. Instead, they readied their own army, and took the initiative by launching a pre-emptive strike against the Arabs on June 6th, 1967. Within hours, the Israelis destroyed the Egyptian Air Force, and captured Eastern Jerusalem and the Temple Mount area. This reunited eastern and western Jerusalem for the first time since 1948, when eastern Jerusalem had been cut off from the Jews in the western half of the city by a tall barbed-wire fence. This also put an immediate stop to King Hussein's hateful hotel plans.

In six days, the Israeli army had won the war, and captured eastern Jerusalem, the Egyptian controlled Sinai Peninsula, the Gaza Strip, the West Bank, and the Golan Heights. This finally united all of Palestine under Israeli control, and the Israeli people rejoiced in the streets at their victory. Their military victory and subsequent joy are reflected in both Psalms 67 and 68:

*"Let the peoples praise You, O God... let the nations be glad and sing for joy! For You shall judge the people righteously, and govern the nations on earth. Selah." - Psalm 67:3-4*

*"May God arise, may his enemies be scattered; may his foes flee before him. As... wax melts before the fire, may the wicked perish before God. But may the righteous be glad and rejoice... may they be happy and joyful. Sing to God... extol him who rides on the clouds-- his name is the LORD (Yahweh) -- and rejoice before him." - Psalm 68:1-4 (NIV)*

## Chapter 2: Amazing Prophecies in the Psalms        Page 55

Yes, 1967 saw a great victory for Israel, and the Israeli people had a right to be joyful. Nevertheless, the occupied land the Israelis won in the Six-Day War would continue to cause them much grief as the Arabs disputed their right to hold these lands, and Arab settlers in these regions refused to move. These unsettling developments made it impossible for Israel to claim any lasting peace, and all the efforts to get the Arabs and Israelis to come to a peaceful settlement since then have ultimately failed. Even now (as of Autumn 2010), though there are plans to create a Palestinian state within Israel that would hypothetically bring an end to the hostilities between Arabs and Jews, Scripture teaches that there will be no lasting peace in Israel until Yahshua returns to fully, and forever defeat Israel's many Gentile enemies, *including the Arabs*.

Though the Antichrist is destined to successfully establish a peace agreement between Israel and her enemies during the Tribulation period, the Antichrist himself will eventually break this agreement by defiling the newly built Jewish Temple in Jerusalem:

*"He will confirm a covenant with many for one 'seven.' In the middle of the 'seven' he will put an end to sacrifice and offering. And on a wing [of the temple] he will set up an abomination that causes desolation, until the end that is decreed is poured out on him." - Daniel 9:27 (NIV)*

This will lead to a rebellion by Israel, followed by a massive Gentile attack on Israel, and the invasion of Jerusalem - at which time Yahshua will return to defend Jerusalem, and destroy all of Israel's enemies:

*"Behold, the day of the LORD (Yahweh) is coming... For I will gather all the nations to battle against Jerusalem; the city shall be taken... Half of the city shall go into captivity, but the remnant of the people shall not be cut off from the city. Then the LORD (Yahweh) will go forth and fight against those nations, as He fights in the day of battle. And in that day His feet will stand on the Mount of Olives..." - Zechariah 14:1-4*

With the glorious return of Yahshua to Earth, the 3-1/2 year Great Tribulation will be brought to a climactic end. At that time, the Earth will be miraculously renewed, and prepared as a fitting home for Yahshua and his resurrected, immortal saints. For a thousand years from that time, these saints will serve as fellow priests and rulers with Christ. As such, they will be called to reach out in love to the still mortal inhabitants of Earth, and teach them how to lead righteous lives in keeping with Yahshua's commandments to love God, and one another. What a joyful time this will surely be for all those who love Christ, including the Jews who will finally accept and love their Messiah!

**Psalm 73** is the first of the Leviticus Psalms 73 through 89, whose themes correspond with the events of Leviticus concerning the temple and its services. Keeping with this temple theme, these Psalms were compiled by King Solomon, the builder of the first Temple to Yahweh. Uncannily, in 1973 - and in keeping with the theme of Leviticus - Jews around the world made the equivalent to a half-shekel offering toward the building of the first central house of worship for the Jews since their Temple was destroyed in 70 AD. This was the Jerusalem Great Synagogue.

The words of Psalm 73 do not pertain to the building of a temple, or synagogue, however. Instead they appear to relate to the Yom Kippur War, which erupted on October 6th, 1973. It was the Day of Atonement in Israel, and all Israel was in deep prayer and fasting on that day when the Arabs launched their surprise attack. Caught off guard, things looked dismal for Israel, and Jews the world over mourned when it appeared as if Israel might be destroyed:

*"Surely I have cleansed my heart in vain, and washed my hands in innocence. For all day long I have been plagued, and chastened every morning." - Psalm 73:13-14*

The references here in Psalm 73 to cleansing the heart and washing the hands are all in keeping with the theme of Yom Kippur, or the Day of Atonement, which is repentance. In addition, the eruption of this war on Yom Kippur certainly was a bitter *plague* on the Israeli people! But there are also echoes of hope for Israel in this psalm, and that hope came in military aid from the United States, which helped turn the tide in favor of Israel. Despite US aid, however, 3000 Israeli soldiers died in the Yom Kippur War. This may be a prophetic event, in that the number repeatedly occurs in the Bible in relation to self-sacrifice, and punishment for sin.

For example, 3000 Israelites died for worshipping the golden calf in Exodus 32:28. In Judges 16:27, Samson killed 3000 Philistines, who were Israel's worst enemies. In 2 Chronicles 4:5, we are told the Bronze Sea in Solomon's Temple held 3000 baths of water, and, in Acts 2:41, 3000 people were baptized - and allegorically died to themselves - on the day of Pentecost. Could the 3000 Israeli soldiers who died therefore have been a symbolic sacrifice made to atone for Israel's sins? Could they have served as a type of scapegoat or Azazel goat, which was killed on Yom Kippur in Temple times to pay for all of Israel's transgressions? This is suggested by the next section of Psalm 73, which speaks of the sanctuary or Temple of God and of those whom God has reserved for destruction:

> *"When I thought how to understand this, it was too painful for me--* **Until I went into the sanctuary of God; then I understood their end.** *Surely You set them in slippery places; you cast them down to destruction. Oh, how they are brought to desolation, as in a moment! They are utterly consumed with terrors. As a dream when one awakes, so, Lord, when You awake, you shall despise their image." - Psalm 73:16-20*

Though there is no Temple in Israel today, a Temple of Yahweh can now be found in the hearts of all believers who love Yahshua as their Savior. Nonetheless, though Israel has been continually blessed with aid from Christian nations like the United States, many Jews worldwide still hate Christianity and wholeheartedly reject the Messiah that their Christian allies love. Could the Israeli death toll from the Yom Kippur War therefore be God's judgment against Israel for this rejection? The number of Israeli dead in this war - 3,000 - tells us that this may indeed be the case, for those 3,000 lost Israeli lives contrast sharply with the 3,000 souls that were born-again and adopted into spiritual Israel on the day of Pentecost (Acts 2:41).

**Psalm 79 and 80** are related to two major events in Israel's history, and the history of the World. The first was the historic peace agreement reached between Egyptian President Anwar Sadat and Israeli Prime Minister Menachem Begin on the White House lawn in 1979. The second was the assassination of Anwar Sadat in 1980. In relation to these historic events, both Psalms 79 and 80 ask the question: *"How Long?"*

> *"We have become a reproach to our neighbors (the Arabs), a scorn and derision to those who are around us.* **How long, LORD? Will You be angry forever?** *Will Your jealousy burn like fire? Pour out Your wrath on the... kingdoms that do not call on Your name." - Psalm 79:4-6*

> *"O LORD God of hosts (Yahweh Elohim Tsavout),* **how long will You be angry against the prayer of Your people?** *You have... given them tears to drink in great measure. You have made us a strife to our neighbors, and our enemies laugh among themselves." - Psalm 80:4-6*

In answer to Israeli prayers for deliverance, God did finally bless Israel with an offer of friendship from Egypt. The following passages of Psalm 79 appear to reflect this merciful development, which was a major political victory for Israel:

> *"Oh, do not remember former iniquities against us!* **Let Your tender mercies come speedily to meet us***, for we have been brought very low. Help us, O God of our salvation, for the glory of Your name; and deliver us...* **Why should the nations say, 'Where is their God?'***" - Psalm 79:8-10*

This section of Psalm 79 ends with a reminder that the war against Israel is not just a blood feud between Arabs and Jews. The underlying, yet unspoken reason for all of the world's conflicts with Israel is the world's hatred of Israel's God! Satan is the ruler of this world, and he hates Israel as much as he hates every born-again believer! Perhaps that is why this psalm also contains a prophetic reference to the seven-years of the Tribulation period, when all of God's enemies will be crushed in the winepress of His wrath:

> *"And return to our neighbors sevenfold into their bosom their reproach with which they have reproached You, O Lord." - Psalm 79:12*

In confirmation of the need for the Tribulation, Psalm 80 is prophetic of the fact that the blessing of Israel that came in 1979 would not continue for long. This is because the PLO was outraged at Anwar Sadat's acceptance of Israel, and vowed to assassinate the Egyptian President in revenge. Could the following passages be speaking of Anwar Sadat as *"a vine out of Egypt,"* and as a vine that would be *"cut down"* in death by an Arab assassin's bullets?

> *"You have brought* ***a vine out of Egypt****; you have cast out the nations, and planted it." - Psalm 80:8*

> *"Return, we beseech You, O God of hosts; look down... and see, and visit* **this vine***. And the vineyard which Your right hand has planted, and the branch that You made strong for Yourself (Sadat?). It is burned with fire,* ***it is cut down;*** *they perish at the rebuke of Your countenance. Let Your hand be upon the man of Your right hand, upon the son of man whom You made strong for Yourself." - Psalm 80:14-17*

Though the above passages allude to Christ's coming sacrifice for His people as *"the vine out of Egypt"* and *"the son of man"* who was *"cut down,"* but is at God's *"right hand,"* could it be that Anwar Sadat is being prophetically commended for his offer of Peace to Israel? Furthermore, could this commendation be because Sadat had secretly come to love the God of Israel, and the Son of Man, Yahshua the Messiah? Alas, only God currently knows Anwar Sadat's true heart, but it is an intriguing possibility!

## Chapter 2: Amazing Prophecies in the Psalms

The words of **Psalm 91** appear to contain striking parallels to events that occurred in 1991, when the Gulf War that began when Iraq invaded and occupied Kuwait in August of 1990 escalated. Shortly after that war worsened, I happened to pick up a copy of Time magazine. Since I was already familiar with J. R. Church's amazing book on the Psalms, it was a real thrill to see Psalm 91 quoted from in reference to that war, and I guessed that someone on the staff of Time might be familiar with J. R. Church's revised book, which came out in 1990.

Remembering the news coverage of that war, one of the most unforgettable things about it was how the sky in, and around Kuwait was literally black with thick smoke from the burning oil wells, and how the countless oil fires were polluting the air and land. It literally looked like a vision straight from Hell. Uncannily, this is what Psalm 91 said in regard to that horrible time for Kuwait, and Israel:

*"Surely He shall deliver you from... the perilous pestilence. He shall cover you with His feathers, and under His wings you shall take refuge; his truth shall be your shield and buckler.* ***You shall not be afraid of the terror by night, nor of the arrow that flies by day, nor of the pestilence that walks in darkness, nor of the destruction that lays waste at noonday.*** *A thousand may fall at your side, and ten thousand at your right hand; but it shall not come near you. Only with your eyes shall you look, and see the reward of the wicked." - Psalm 91:3-8*

As this Psalm indicates, Iraq's invasion of Kuwait occurred under cover of night, and countless flying arrows (i.e. missiles), fiery pestilences, and severe darkness and destruction in Kuwait characterized every aspect of this war. Nonetheless, this Psalm indicates that those who love Yahweh would be spared from severe injury. Miraculously, and in keeping with the message of Psalm 91, Israel was spared from serious casualties or destruction during the war over Kuwait, despite bombardments with Iraqi Scud missiles. In addition, the US Troops and other Coalition forces that fought in this war had a remarkably low casualty rate as compared to other wars. Though Iraq lost between 20,000 and 35,000 troops, the Coalition forces only lost 240, of which 148 were Americans.

Interestingly, Psalm 91 speaks of pestilences, which is a reference to disease and sickness. After the Gulf War, thousands of US Troops complained of odd flu-like symptoms. This was dubbed the Gulf War Syndrome, and it was later determined that it may have been caused by exposure to an Iraqi manufactured nerve gas. Providentially, however, few of the troops who suffered symptoms died, or got severely ill.

## *The Hallel Psalms and the Great Tribulation*

As the last section clearly shows, J. R. Church has proven that applying certain historical events to various passages in the Psalms can be uncannily revealing. The following section, however, reveals new information about the prophetic nature of the Psalms that was shown to me while in deep study of the Hallel Psalms.

During my study, I noted that Mr. Church took a special interest in six Hallel Psalms *in the Deuteronomy (Kingdom establishment) section* of the Psalms, and pointed out that **Psalms 113 through 118 are extremely important in Jewish Liturgy.** However, Mr. Church then went on to suggest that the seven-year Tribulation period and Second Coming of Christ might occur sometime between 1996 and 2006. Avi Ben Mordecai, in his book "Signs in the Heavens" made a similar error in dating the Tribulation period - since he believed that the Tribulation period would rapidly follow the close of the six thousand years given for men's works, which likely came to a close on Nissan 1 in 2000.

Despite the fact that the real prophetic importance of the Hallel Psalms has been consistently overlooked, I believe that the Jews have been led by the Holy Spirit to focus on these psalms for a hidden prophetic reason. In my prayers, I have asked Yahweh for guidance in order to understand why J. R. Church and Avi Ben Mordecai failed in their attempts to predict the onset of the Tribulation. I have also asked to understand all of God's prophetic words concerning this terrible future time in history. In God's infinite love and mercy, those prayers appear to have been answered through my understanding of the Hallel Psalms.

After reading the remarkable prophetic correlations that Mr. Church made concerning the Psalms in his book, it occurred to me that there might be a prophetic connection between the Hallel Psalms, and the End Times. Following that hunch, I soon discovered that the Hallel Psalms may show that 2010 AD marks a significant year in history - the year before the Tribulation began. Furthermore, Psalms 111 through 118 may reveal what we have and can expect during the years 2011 through 2018 AD. In addition, as will be explained a bit later, the Hallel Psalm 110 appears to verify the date given by the measurements of the Great Pyramid for the prelude to the Tribulation period. Surprisingly, there is much correlative evidence to prove the hypothesis that the Hallel Psalms mark the time of the Tribulation. Let's explore these connections.

In previous books in the "Language of God" Book Series, I discussed the prophetic importance of several Jewish religious feasts like Passover, and Yom Kippur (a.k.a. the Day of Atonement). For at least

## Chapter 2: Amazing Prophecies in the Psalms

three millenniums, the Jewish people have read six special Psalms in connection with these feasts. These are called the Hallel Psalms or Songs of Praise, since "Hallel" is the Hebrew word meaning "praise." The six Praise Psalms are Psalms 113, 114, 115, 116, 117, and 118. In addition, **Psalm 136 was occasionally added to these six - thereby making seven Hallel Psalms - the same number as years in the Tribulation period.** Psalm 136 is called the Great Hallel, and is similar in structure to Psalm 118. Incidentally, Hallel Psalms 118 and 136 are the hymns that Yahshua and his apostles likely sang after celebrating the Passover -on the eve of Yahshua's arrest and crucifixion (Matthew 26:30; Mark 14:26).

In his book about the Psalms, J. R. Church made the observation that Psalms 111 and 112 appear to belong grouped together with the other Psalms in the Praise, or Hallel section. The Jews, however, see only Psalms 113 through 118 as true Praise Psalms. Nonetheless, like Psalm 113 and 117, Psalm 111 and 112 begin with the phrase: "Praise be to Yahweh" or "Hallelu-Yah!" Adding Psalms 111 and 112 to Psalms 113 through 117 makes a group of seven psalms - just as Psalm 113 through 118, and Psalm 136 do. Based on the prophetic visions of the prophet Daniel, *seven years* appear to be prophetically allotted for the Tribulation. It therefore is not likely to be a mere coincidence that there are also *seven Hallel Psalms*, or nine if Psalms 111 and 112 are counted. As already shown through the Chanukiah patterns running through the New Testament, and as will be shown in regard to the Great Pyramid in Chapter Five, nine is also related to the Church Age, and is a significant End Times number.

Adding fuel to my belief that the Hallel Psalms have an End Time prophetic application, it is interesting to note that **Hallel Psalm 117 is the center chapter of the Bible**. In the King James Version of the Bible, exactly 594 chapters precede Psalm 117, and 594 chapters follow it. Incidentally, **Psalm 117 is also the shortest chapter in the Bible**, containing only two verses. When I discovered this, I remembered Yahshua's prophecy in Matthew 24:22 about the terrible outpouring of Yah's Wrath during the Great Tribulation.

Since Psalm 117 relates to the year 2017, I asked myself: Is it possible that, when Yahshua said, *"unless those days were shortened, no flesh would be saved,"* His words were purposely chosen to indicate that those days to be cut short are connected to the shortest Psalm in the Bible? If so, could *"those days"* occur during or before the year 2017? If so, then could the first Hallel Psalm - Psalm 113 – herald the beginning of certain events in the Great Tribulation in the year 2013? Though this possibility intrigued me, more proof was needed before it could be entertained as correct. The biggest problem with my proposed theory was the numbers. If equated to years, Psalm 113 through 117 added up to only five years. So, though I'd discovered something important, I was missing a significant part of the puzzle. I therefore continued to study the Psalms, and read whatever explained their importance, and usage in Jewish Liturgy.

Over time, I made some remarkable discoveries about the Hallel Psalms and several of the Psalms before and after them that helped me to make the following deductions. First of all, since Psalm 117 suggests a correlation with Yahshua's prophecy that the Great Tribulation will be mercifully shortened, it likely pertains to the *end* of the Great Tribulation. If so, Psalm 113 can't be the Psalm relating to the beginning of the Tribulation. Rather, Psalm 111 is the seventh Psalm before Psalm 117. Therefore, there should be some internal evidence that Psalm 111 prophetically marks the beginning of the Tribulation period.

As the first of the traditional Hallel Psalms, Psalm 113 begins with the joyful phrase "Hallelu-Yah," as do Psalms 111 and 112. Yet this shout for joy does not appear again in the Hallel Psalms until the opening of Psalm 117, the shortest of the Psalms. Psalm 111 and 112 therefore appear to be overlooked Hallel Psalms that the Jews should have included with Psalms 113 through 117. In support of this idea, though only one verse in Psalms 111 and 112 directly identifies them with the End Times, they both contain other clues to their true importance - *but only if you know where to look!* However, even before I discovered the hidden truths in Psalms 111 and 112, I discovered another hidden truth surrounding Psalms 110 and 118. Let me explain what I found.

Though there seemed to be little to identify Psalm 111 with the Tribulation period at first, significant imagery pertaining to the Tribulation can be found in the Psalm immediately preceding it: Psalm 110! In fact, **all seven verses of Psalm 110 give a clear indication that it relates to Yahshua, the outpouring of His wrath in the Tribulation, and the establishment of His Millennial Kingdom.** In fact, its seven verses may apply to each of the seven years of the Tribulation! Since studies revealed in other parts of this book point to the year 2010 as the possible year *before* the Tribulation period begins, it seems significant that several important passages of the New Testament quote from Psalm 110, as when Yahshua indicated that He was greater than any son of David. In this regard, note that in the opening line of Psalm 110, King David identifies the Father as "Yahweh," and His Son Yahshua as "Adonai:"

## Chapter 2: Amazing Prophecies in the Psalms

*"The LORD (Yahweh) says to my Lord (Adonai): 'Sit at my right hand until I make your enemies a footstool for your feet.' " - Psalm 110:1 (NIV)*

This Old Testament passage corresponds to the following passages in the New Testament, where Christ is teaching His disciples:

*"'What do you think about the Christ? Whose son is he?' 'The son of David,' they replied. He said to them, 'How is it then that David, speaking by the Spirit, calls him 'Lord' (Adonai)? For he says, "**The Lord** (Yahweh) **said to my Lord** (Adonai): **'Sit at my right hand until I put your enemies under your feet.'**" If then David calls him 'Lord,' (Adonai) how can he be his son?" - Matthew 22:42-45 (NIV)*

In Psalm 110, it is therefore God the Father in verse 4 who calls His Son (i.e. Adonai) *"a priest forever, in the order of Melchizedek"* in verse 5. Furthermore, Yahweh proclaims that it is Yahshua as *"Adonai"* who sits at the Father's *"right hand:"*

*"The LORD (Yahweh) has sworn and will not change his mind:* **'You are a priest forever, in the order of Melchizedek.'** *The Lord* **(Adonai) is at your right hand;** *he will crush kings on the day of his wrath." - Psalm 110:4-5 (NIV)*

This Old Testament passage corresponds to the following line in the New Testament:

*"And he says in another place, "You are a priest forever, in the order of Melchizedek." - Hebrews 5:6 (NIV)*

Throughout the New Testament, Yahshua is referred to as *"the Lord,"* which is most-likely a reference to His role as *"Adonai."* King David's use of the word "Adonai" to identify Christ suggests that the apostles and disciples were not calling Yahshua "Lord," but "Adonai," which means "Master" in Hebrew. After all, as vigorous students of the Bible, these great men of faith were all likely familiar with David's use of the term to identify God's Son. The above correlations with the New Testament are therefore remarkable proof that Psalm 110 was important prophetically as it relates to Yahshua's deity and purpose. In addition, the passages quoted respectively refer to the Tribulation period and the Millennial Rule of Yahshua! In fact, all of Psalm 110 alludes to events spoken of in the Book of Revelation that will occur during the Tribulation. This is especially true of the following verses:

**"The LORD** *(Yahweh)* **will extend your** *(i.e. Yahshua's)* **mighty scepter from Zion;** *you will rule in the midst of your* enemies. **Your troops will be willing on your day of battle.** *Arrayed in holy majesty, from the womb of the dawn you will receive the dew of your youth.* **The Lord** *(Adonai - a.k.a. Yahshua)* **is at your (i.e. Yahweh's) right hand; he will crush kings on the day of his wrath. He will judge the nations,** *heaping up the dead and crushing the rulers of the whole earth." - Psalm 110: 2-3, 5-6 (NIV)*

I have added interpretations into the above Scripture (and in others throughout this book series) in parentheses. These parenthesized additions give clues to the correct reading of various Scriptures. This was done because, when translated from Hebrew into English, many Scriptures lose their power to teach accurately - as is the case with the portion of Psalm 110 just quoted, which is even harder to understand in older Bible translations. Psalm 110 has become difficult to interpret because **the translators sadly fail to distinguish between the many different words in Hebrew and Aramaic for "Lord."**

Now that the true meaning of this passage has been restored, Psalm 110 clearly appears to be telling us that Yahweh has given Yahshua the scepter with which Yahshua will rule the Earth after He conquers His enemies. When Yahshua, our *"Adonai"* comes to conquer the world, and destroy the wicked upon the Earth, His eager army of saints will be with Him. Together with Yahshua, they will help annihilate all those who oppose Yahshua's Rule. Although not a verbatim quote like in the previous cases, a section in Revelation corresponds with these verses in Psalm 110 that describe Yahshua as a conquering King. These are:

*"Now I saw heaven opened, and behold, a white horse. And He who sat on him was called Faithful and True, and in righteousness He judges and makes war..." - Rev. 19:11*

*"And the armies in heaven, clothed in fine linen... followed Him on white horses. 15 Now out of His mouth goes a sharp sword, that with it He should strike the nations. And He Himself will rule them with a rod of iron. (quoted from Psalm 2:9, and also stated in Rev. 2:27 and Rev. 12:5). He Himself treads the winepress of the fierceness and wrath of Almighty God. 16 And He has on His robe... a name written: KING OF KINGS AND LORD OF LORDS." - Rev. 19:14-16*

*"...The beast and the kings of the earth and their armies gathered together to make war against the rider on the horse and his army. But the beast was captured, and... the false prophet who had performed the miraculous signs on his behalf. With these signs he had deluded those who had received the mark of the*

beast.... The two... were thrown alive into the fiery lake of burning sulfur. **The rest... were killed with the sword that came out of the mouth of the rider** on the horse..." - Rev. 19:19-21 (NIV)

The preceding portions of the Book of Revelation correlate remarkably well with Psalm 110's references to Yahshua's Second Coming in Wrath. In these passages, Yahshua wields a sword that comes out of His mouth. This has obvious allegorical significance. First, it tells us that Yahshua is the Word of God, whose uttered words will be miraculously carried out. Yahshua therefore wields the only true magic – the magic that comes from being in love with, and joyfully doing the good and perfect Will of Yahshua's Father.

As I studied the Hallel Psalms, more clues helped me draw various conclusions concerning one of them. This key Psalm is the last of the Hallel Psalms. It is Psalm 118, which immediately follows Psalm 117 - the Psalm that may mark the End of the Great Tribulation. In Psalm 118, we find a passage that identifies Christ as *"the stone the builders* (i.e. Israel) *rejected:"*

*"**The stone the builders rejected has become the capstone;** the LORD (Yahweh) has done this, and it is marvelous in our eyes."* - Psalm 118:22-23 (NIV)

Yahshua quoted this very passage from Psalm 118 in defense of Himself against the Jewish leaders of His day. These leaders in the Jewish community were convinced that Yahshua's claims to be the Messiah were false. In retaliation, Yahshua stated that, though they rejected Him, Yahshua would one day become the "capstone" (i.e. King) of the world. Then Yahshua told them this parable:

*"He (Father Yahweh, the owner of the vineyard) had one left to send, a son (Yahshua), whom he loved. He sent him last..., saying, 'They will respect my son.' But the tenants said to one another, 'This is the heir. Come, let's kill him, and the inheritance will be ours.' So they (the Jews)... killed him, and threw him out of the vineyard (Jerusalem)."*

*"What then will the owner of the vineyard do? He will come and kill those tenants (the Jews) and give the vineyard to others (the Gentiles).* **Haven't you read...: 'The stone the builders rejected has become the capstone; the Lord** *(Yahweh)* **has done this, and it is marvelous in our eyes'?** *Then they (the Jewish leaders) looked for a way to arrest him because... he had spoken the parable against them. But they were afraid of the crowd; so they... went away."* - Mark 12:6-12 (NIV)

The quotation in Verse 10 of the preceding Scripture is taken verbatim from Psalm 118. God's Holy Name "Yahweh" occurs twenty-seven times in Psalm 118's twenty-nine verses. This Psalm therefore loudly proclaims that it is the *holy Name of Yahweh* that delivers us from evil. In effect, it implies that the people Yahweh delivers from evil know His holy Name, and *freely call upon that Name* in prayer and praise. Psalm 118 refers to Yahshua's Millennial Rule. Hence, Yahshua will become the symbolic capstone of the Great Pyramid, or Pillar of Enoch, which is a temple/altar that represents Him, and His Blood Covenant cut with mankind on Calvary. The Pillar of Enoch will therefore likely be restored to its former glory during Yahshua's Millennial Kingdom.

Incidentally, Psalm 118 falls *after* Psalm 117. Psalm 117 corresponds to 2017 AD - the year that may signal the *end* of the Great Tribulation. The King of Israel was meant to lead in the recitation of Psalm 118 with a gathering of Israelites who responded by reciting portions of the same Psalm. Psalm 118 was written and first recited by King David, whose life foreshadowed Christ's Second Coming. I therefore believe that Yahshua Himself led in reciting this Psalm with His apostles on the night of the Last Supper on the eve of Passover (Matthew 26:30). I also believe that Yahshua will be the final and everlasting King of Israel who will lead His saints in reciting this Psalm of praise, and that this event will occur immediately *after* the Great Tribulation - in 2018 AD - the first year of Christ's Millennial Rule.

As the Psalm representing the first year of the Millennial Kingdom, Psalm 118 is singled out by being specially placed in the Book of Psalms. It falls between the shortest Psalm: Psalm 117, and the longest Psalm of Praise in the Bible: Psalm 119. Psalm 119 is the longest Psalm, and hence the longest of the eight *acrostic* Psalms. Along with Psalms 9, 10, 25, 34, 37, 111, 112, and 114, Psalm 119 has verses ordered into groups beginning with consecutive letters of the Hebrew alphabet. This method of arranging some Psalms marks them as alphabetic acrostics However, **Psalm 119 holds the unique distinction of having stanzas representing all twenty-two letters of the Hebrew alphabet,** whereas the other acrostic Psalms are missing verses for one or more letters.

If you count the Psalms numbered as acrostics above, you may find that there are nine instead of eight. This is because, though our modern Bibles show Psalms 9 and 10 as separate, they are related in the Hebrew Scriptures - like two stanzas of the same acrostic poem. Prophetically, they represent the years 1909 and 1910. However, these years shared events in Jewish history that overlapped, making them *one in theme*. In fact, though all of the Psalms relate to specific years, they

## Chapter 2: Amazing Prophecies in the Psalms

may seem to be speaking of some years in hindsight. That is because the Jewish year is reckoned differently than our own. As shown in the Appendix, the Jews have two calendars, with their civil year generally beginning in September and their sacred year generally beginning in April.

According to J. R. Church in his fascinating book "Hidden Prophecies in the Psalms," the fact that seven of the eight acrostic Psalms do not represent the complete Hebrew alphabet is highly significant. As mentioned earlier, these incomplete acrostics imply that humanity needs more spiritual understanding, and more of a hunger for righteousness. This is partly because letters are what we use to record human knowledge, and missing letters imply that our knowledge is incomplete. Is it possible, however, that these incomplete acrostics also imply that Yahshua's work is not yet done, and more prophecies have yet to be fulfilled? If this is so, then **the fact that Psalm 119 is the only complete acrostic Psalm suggests that it marks the point where the prophecies in the Psalms about Yahshua - and the events leading up to the establishment of His Kingdom on Earth - will be completed by the year 2019!**

J. R. Church pointed out that Psalm 119 is not only the longest Psalm, but also the longest chapter in the Bible! It has 176 verses divided into groups of eight - making twenty-two stanzas representing each letter of the Hebrew alphabet. This dividing of the twenty-two verses into eight groups indicates that eternity and perfection, which are signified by the number eight, are being alluded to. In addition, Mr. Church noted that Psalm 119 emphasizes the Hebrew word "Debarim," or "Word," which refers to the Word of God. To the Jews, this Word is contained in the Scriptures, and in the decrees God uttered by His prophets and teachers. But, due to the opening verses of the Gospel of John, Christians call *the Messiah* the Word of God:

*"In the beginning was the Word, and **the Word was with God, and the Word was God.** He was in the beginning with God."*
*- John 1:1-2*

The word "Debarim" appears in Psalm 119 no less than forty-two times, and 42 is a number divisible by 6, which is the number of man, and 7, the number of God's Rest. Since Yahshua was fully man and fully God - as well as the Word of God - this is highly significant! It means that Psalm 119 is the signature Psalm of psalms - the Psalm that fully glorifies, and totally focuses on the spiritual importance of our Messiah. **Therefore, in Psalm 119, Yahshua's eternal nature, and perfect purpose are fully**

***revealed***. Here are just a few of the more significant verses in this Psalm that mention God's Word as found in, and through Yahshua:

> *"How can a young man cleanse his way? By taking heed according to **Your word**. With my whole heart I have sought You; Oh, let me not wander from Your commandments!* **Your word** *I have hidden in my heart, that I might not sin against You!" ... "I will delight myself in Your statutes; I will not forget **Your word**. Deal bountifully with Your servant, that I may live and keep **Your word**." ... "You have dealt well with Your servant, O LORD (Yahweh), according to **Your word**. Teach me good judgment and knowledge, for I believe Your commandments. Before I was afflicted I went astray, but now I keep **Your word**." - Psalm 119:9-11, 16-17, 65-67*

The fact that Psalm 111, the Psalm that may mark the beginning of the Tribulation period, and Psalm 112 are acrostics like Psalm 119 also has great prophetic significance. What significance they have, however, cannot really be seen until they are examined in Hebrew. In my case, an interlinear Bible made the difference! Features of these Psalms that were lost to me in English translations suddenly became obvious. So, though the meaning of the words in Psalm 111's stanzas do not tell us much about its importance in End Time events, it became apparent to me that Psalm 111 is an acrostic that is missing stanzas for certain Hebrew letters. In fact, Psalm 111 and 112 are both missing the same number of letters, and both contain exactly the same number of verses: 10. Therefore, out of the twenty-two letters in the Hebrew alphabet, they are both missing twelve letters. The ten Hebrew letters that Psalms 111 and 112 begin their verses with are Aleph (A), Gimel (G), Hey (H), Zayin (Z), Tet (T), Kaf (Ch), Mem (M), Samech (S), Pey (P), and Reysh (R).

Applying the Language of God, the ten letters represented in Psalms 111 and 112 may signify that these psalms are being addressed to the Ten Lost Tribes of Israel. Representatives of these Ten Tribes are scattered among the nations today, and many still will be when the Antichrist takes control of the world. The twelve missing letters also tell us something profound. They indicate that the people who are like the first twelve righteous patriarchs from Adam and the twelve righteous Apostles of Christ (including Paul) *will be missing* from the world scene. The fact that twelve of the twenty-two letters are missing implies that the people who represent these letters will have been taken to Heaven to enjoy the Wedding Supper of the Lamb!

Since each letter in the Hebrew alphabet has an allegorical meaning - as well as a numerical and sound value - the actual letters that are present and missing might be able to tell us something even more significant. However, my knowledge of Hebrew is too limited to explore this direction of thought at the present time. I therefore hope that someone with a greater knowledge of Hebrew will explore the possible prophetic ramifications of the missing and included letters in these acrostics, and will share their findings with others such as myself. To that end, I welcome all insights and comments from my readers, and have provided my email address at the beginning of this book - so that those interested in sharing their ideas may contact me.

Now that we've discussed a bit more about the importance of Psalm 111 as the first Psalm marking the Tribulation period, let's take a closer look at Psalm 118, the final Tribulation Psalm. As already noted, **Psalm 118 falls between the shortest and longest chapters of the Bible. It therefore appears that Psalm 118 was made to intentionally stand out from the rest of the Hallel Psalms.** Could it be because Psalm 118 is announcing a formal ceremony that will be held here on Earth after the Great Tribulation? Could it stand for the time when Yahshua will be crowned as King of kings? Yahshua is, after all, *"the stone that the builders rejected."* In Psalm 118, this rejected stone now becomes the glorified capstone, or cornerstone (Psalm 118:21-22).

Yahshua quoted from Psalm 118 in the Gospels of Matthew and Mark, referring to Himself as the Capstone. However, before He did so, Yahshua first told His Jewish audience that they would be killed, and the vineyard (Jerusalem) would be given to others (Mark 12:6-9). Approximately forty years later, this part of Yahshua's prophecy came true. In 70 AD, the Romans sacked, and utterly destroyed Jerusalem - as well as Herod's Temple. This also fulfilled Daniel's prophecy:

*"After the sixty-two 'sevens,'* **the Anointed One (Messiah or Christ) will be cut off and will have nothing.** *The people of the ruler who will come will destroy the city and the sanctuary. The end will come like a flood: War will continue until the end, and desolations have been decreed. He will confirm a Covenant with many for one 'seven.' In the middle of the 'seven' he will put an end to sacrifice and offering. And on a wing [of the temple] he will set up an abomination that causes desolation, until the end that is decreed is poured out on him."* - Daniel 9:26-27 (NIV)

In the preceding Scripture, the prophet Daniel told of the first destruction of Jerusalem. Yahshua is *"the Anointed One"* that Daniel speaks of, and He was cut off, or killed on Calvary. Later, the Roman Emperor Vespasian broke a treaty with the Jews, and set up an image of himself in the Temple built to Yahweh. This led the Jews to revolt, and consequently led the Romans to surround and destroy both Jerusalem, and the Temple in 70 AD.

As alluded to earlier, however, this prophecy is expected to find its second fulfillment in history. Many believe that this Scripture refers to events during the Great Tribulation, when the Antichrist will break a treaty with Israel, and the city of Jerusalem will again be invaded. Indeed, though Israel and Jerusalem are now in the possession of a thriving community of Jews, they are literally surrounded by their enemies on every side. Therefore, the possibility that Jerusalem will be occupied by her enemies, and will face imminent destruction is an ever-present reality.

In Matthew's Gospel, Yahshua quoted from Psalm 118 in between delivering *two* End Time parables. As in other places in the Bible, this suggests that an interval of time will pass between the End Time events that each parable prophetically refers to. After delivering the Parable of the Vineyard, Yahshua quoted from Psalm 118's passage about *"the stone the builders rejected"* (Matthew 21:33-44). Yahshua *is* that rejected stone. Nonetheless, as will be shown in Chapters Three, Four, and Five, Yahshua is the rejected stone that will one day become the symbolic capstone of the Pillar of Enoch, which represents a temple to Yah symbolically made up of all believers.

After quoting from Psalm 118, Yahshua prophesied about what it meant:

*"And **whoever falls on this stone will be broken**; but on whomever it falls, it will grind him to powder." – Matthew 21:44*

Here, Yahshua was stating that He is the Stone that makes men stumble, and the Stone that will crush the wicked on the Day of Yah's Wrath. Yahshua was therefore referring to events during the Great Tribulation, when Yahshua will destroy those who reject Him and who murder His followers.

Yahshua prophesied about these same events at the end of the Parable of the Vineyard, both in regard to the Jews in 70 AD, and in regard to the Tribulation period. After prophesying about the meaning of the rejected stone, Yahshua delivered the Parable of the Wedding Banquet. Since it comes after the Parable of the Vineyard, it speaks of events that would unfold *after* the first destruction of Jerusalem.

As was shown in Book Two, the Parable of the Wedding Banquet speaks of Yahshua's Wedding to His Bride, the True Church. It prophetically indicates that the original banquet guests were the Jewish people. But since they rejected Yahshua as the Messiah (Anointed One), the banquet became open to the non-Jewish foreigners called "Gentiles" in the Bible. So, while the Parable of the Vineyard points to the rejection of the Jews, the Parable of the Wedding Banquet foretells the acceptance of a new group of chosen people who are members of God's Kingdom by faith. Therefore, since everyone who enters the New Covenant with Christ by faith is invited to the Wedding Banquet as His symbolic Bride, Yahshua's reference to Psalm 118 - with its rejected stone becoming the capstone - seems to be well placed *between* these two parables.

## *Psalms 110 to 118: Nine Branches of a Prophetic Chanukiah*

This examination of the Hallel Psalms thus far appears to show that ***Psalm 110 and 118 are like a frame around the seven Psalms relating to the Tribulation period.*** Altogether this makes *nine Psalms* that figure in our reckoning of the timing of the Tribulation. As mentioned previously, the menorahs most favored by Jews today are "Chanukiahs" or Chanukah menorahs, which have nine branches to hold candles instead of seven. The seven branches of the original menorah signified many events in the Old Testament, including the seven days of Creation, the seventh day Sabbath, the seven biblically ordained feasts of Israel, and the seven-day Feasts of Unleavened Bread and Tabernacles. Likewise, as previously shown, the Chanukiah has prophetic connotations that pertain to the New Testament, and the Church Age. ***Psalm 110 and 118 therefore seem to serve as beacons that set the seven Psalms between them apart as holy.*** Because of this, Psalms 111 through 117 may relate directly to the seven years of the Tribulation period, which may occur from 2011 through 2017 AD.

Uncannily, more clues in all of these Psalms suggest that this assumption is correct. For example, **Psalm 111**, which is tied to 2011, is the Yom Kippur Year according to a Word of Knowledge given to me by God and described in Chapter 8 of this book. This means that it marks the final year when God's Grace will be fully available to everyone, and their names can still be written in the Book of Life. Perhaps that is why it describes the redeemed people who will eventually be taken in the Rapture as those who fear the LORD Yahweh:

*"**He provided redemption for his people**; he ordained his Covenant forever- holy and awesome is his name. **The fear of the LORD (Yahweh) is the beginning of wisdom**; all who follow his precepts have good understanding. To him belongs eternal praise." - Psalm 111:9-10 (NIV)*

This Scripture describes the faithful disciples of Yahshua, who *"provided redemption for his people."* This redemption could also refer to being set-apart to be taken in the Rapture, though the Rapture may not happen in 2011. If it is Pre-Wrath, and the years 2011 through 2017 truly do mark the Tribulation period, then the Rapture could happen as late as 2016. We simply cannot know the day or the hour. In the meantime, the Tribulation Saints that are left behind to suffer God's wrath will know that they somehow missed the mark spiritually. They will have witnessed the Rapture, and will understand what it means. As a result, those who are left behind, and who will become saints will likely know fear as they anticipate God's promised wrath. This is why this Psalm reads: *"The fear of the LORD (Yahweh) is the beginning of wisdom."* Motivated by fear, these Tribulation Saints will be ready to repentant of their sins, and to ask Yah to change them from the inside out. Likewise, **Psalm 112** suggests that Yahweh will not leave the Tribulation Saints without guidance:

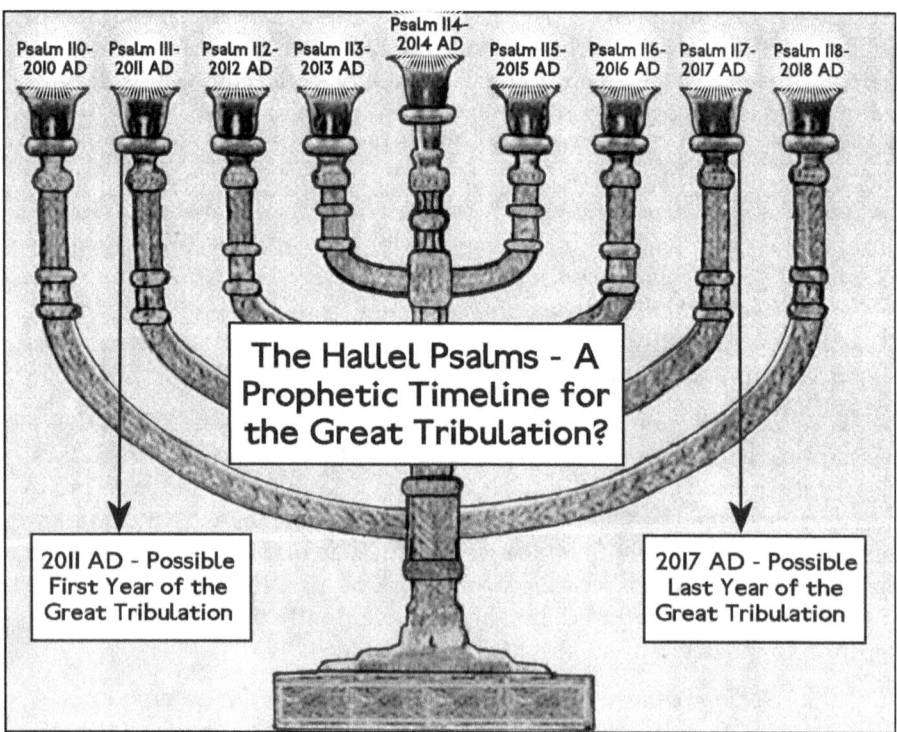

*"Unto the upright there arises light in the darkness; he is gracious, and full of compassion, and righteous."* - Psalm 112:4

Here, we see that Yahweh will send spiritual light into the darkness of the apostasy gripping the world under the Antichrist. That light will initially come from all the true believers still left on the Earth until the Rapture. After that, the Book of Revelation tells us that there will be Two Witnesses in Jerusalem and 144,000 other spiritual representatives from the Twelve Tribes of Israel evangelizing the world during the Great Tribulation, or last half of the Tribulation period. The Two Witnesses will preach to the world for the three and a half years of the Great Tribulation. Then they will be killed, but will rise again, and will then ascend to Heaven (Revelation 11:3-12). At this time, a great earthquake will strike the whole Earth, and a Second Rapture may occur then.

At the same time the Two Witnesses are preaching, the 144,000 Witnesses from the Twelve Tribes of Israel will also preach the Good News to the lost (Revelation 7:3-8). These evangelists who are marked with a seal on their foreheads (Revelation 7:4, 14:1) may be immortal, however, and therefore not subject to torture or death. This is because, *at the same time* that the Saints are taken up to heaven, the 144,000 Witnesses could be translated into imperishable physical bodies. This may be why the 144,000 are called the firstfruits (Revelation 14:4). They will be a part of *the Firstfruits of the Resurrection* into everlasting life along with Christ! This is suggested in the following Scripture:

*"For as in Adam all die, so in Christ all will be made alive. But each in his own turn: Christ, **the firstfruits**; then, when he comes, those who belong to him." - 1 Corinthians 15:22-23 (NIV)*

Here the Apostle Paul clearly teaches that Christ would rise up first, and then the firstfruits. These firstfruits rose just after Christ's resurrection, and signify the first harvest of saints that ends with the Rapture (or Raptures) of the Tribulation period:

*"Then, behold, the veil of the temple was torn in two from top to bottom; and the earth quaked, and the rocks were split,* **and the graves were opened; and many bodies of the saints who had fallen asleep were raised;** *and coming out of the graves after His resurrection, they went into the holy city and appeared to many." - Matthew 27:51-53*

This suggests that a few have already risen to everlasting life with Christ as *the firstfruits of the first stage* of the First Resurrection. We will discuss this possibility more in Chapter 8. Next, many believers will be taken in one or two Raptures, which count as the *second stage of the firstfruits* of the First Resurrection, and which may include the 144,000 Witnesses. After these immortal saints return with Christ to annihilate the wicked in the Battle of Armageddon, they will celebrate the Marriage Supper of the Lamb on Earth, which occurs *after* the Wedding of the Lamb in Heaven (Rev. 19:6-9). But before the Marriage Supper on Earth, at the end of the Great Tribulation, *the third stage of the First Resurrection will occur* and the Tribulation Saints who died as believers during the Great Tribulation will rise (Rev. 20:4-6). **There are therefore three separate stages in the First Resurrection, which collectively signify the firstfruits of God's Second Harvest.** This Second Harvest of Souls (see Book Two) will be followed by a third and final harvest at the end of Christ's Millennial Rule.

Is it possible that some who take part in the First Rapture stage of the First Resurrection will be chosen by God to stay behind as immortal witnesses for Christ during the Great Tribulation? If so, could these special saints be the 144,000 chosen out of Israel - those who will be called *the firstfruits* that will represent Yahshua during the Tribulation? **If so, these 144,000 Witnesses may be transformed into immortal life at the same time that their foreheads are marked.** This could be why Scripture states that the 144,000 Witnesses will all be alive when Yahshua returns to retrieve them and award them with a special place in Heaven (See Revelation 14:1-5).

Indestructible and unstoppable, these special representatives of Christ may serve to be the *"light in the darkness"* mentioned in Psalm 112. These 144,000 Witnesses will preach to the people left behind to suffer through the Tribulation period. Their efforts will cause millions of people from every nation to become Tribulation Saints, though some of them will subsequently be martyred (Rev. 7:9-10). These saints will, however, die knowing that they shall rise from the dead in the third stage of the First Resurrection - at the end of the Great Tribulation (Revelation 20:4-6).

In the preceding examples through Scripture, I have suggested that the First Resurrection occurs in three stages (1 Cor. 15:22-23). Though Yahshua was the first among the Firstfruits to experience the Resurrection to everlasting life, many righteous people rose from the dead shortly after Yahshua's resurrection (Matthew 27:51-52). Since Yahshua has already risen from the dead, there is no reason to assume that this resurrection of saints in the vicinity of Jerusalem was anything other than a resurrection to everlasting life. As such, these saints who had anticipated Yahshua's coming were reckoned with Christ as the Firstfruits of the Resurrection from the dead.

The second stage of the First Resurrection will occur at the time of the First Rapture (Matthew 24:37-44; Luke 17:26-37; Revelation 3:8, 4:1,

19:6-9). It is my belief that there will be two parts to this second stage, and there will be a Second Rapture just before the Bowls of God's Wrath are poured out. Those who take part in the Second Rapture will leave the Earth with the resurrected Two Witnesses, and they will accompany Christ when He comes to conquer the wicked on Earth. Finally, the third stage of the First Resurrection will occur shortly after Yahshua returns to conquer the wicked (1 Thessalonians 4:16-17; Revelation 19:11-14, 20:4-6). At that time, all the martyred Tribulation Saints will rise and be given immortal bodies. Then they will join those who have preceded them. What a glorious moment that will be!

**In Psalm 113**, we see a continuation of the message to the Tribulation Church. Here the Church is being told that great repentance and revival will sweep through their ranks. Hence, the *"barren woman"* that was the Apostate Church will become the *"happy mother of children"* or the Bride of Christ made up of millions of born-again saints:

*"He raises the poor from the dust and lifts the needy from the ash heap; he seats them... with the princes of their people.* **He settles the barren woman in her home as a happy mother of children.** *Praise the LORD (Hallelu-YAH!)."* - Psalm 113:7-9 (NIV)

In ancient times, it was considered a curse to be barren. Women who were barren were often objects of scorn, and they were sometimes shunned, or treated as outcasts in their communities. Sarah, the mother of Isaac, was barren and ashamed until she gave birth to her miraculously conceived son Isaac. This was not just any son, but the son who ended Sarah's shame, and honored her as the mother of the future father of Jacob, who was renamed Israel! This mention of a barren woman finally bearing children may therefore be a prophetic sign that the Apostate Church, which will be shunned and left behind for its inability to produce good disciples, will suddenly produce many living saints after the Rapture.

Psalm 113 also appears to reveal that Yahweh will provide shelter and protection for this new multitude of saints as they live through the Tribulation's plagues. This shelter will likely be partly provided by the wealthy among the Tribulation Saints, who may open their doors, and provide their resources to help those believers who are less fortunate. Psalm 113 suggests this when it proclaims that Yahweh *"raises the poor from the dust and lifts the needy from the ash heap; he seats them with princes."*

**In Psalm 114**, we receive the first allegorical indication of the vast destruction that will be caused by the End Time plagues that will devastate the population of the Earth during the Great Tribulation:

> *"What ails you, O sea, that you fled? O Jordan, that you turned back? O mountains, that you skipped like rams? O little hills, like lambs?* **Tremble, O earth**, *at the presence of the Lord (Adonai), at the presence of the God of Jacob..."* - Psalm 114:5-7

The preceding passages in Psalm 114 relate to the year 2014, the fourth year after the onset of the Tribulation period, which may be the first year of the Great Tribulation. Its imagery is highly suggestive of the results of a great earthquake. In fact, several terribly destructive earthquakes are mentioned in the Book of Revelation with the same poetic allegorical flare. The first earthquake is connected to an eclipse of the Sun and Moon when the Sixth Seal is opened, and it is called "great" to emphasize how terribly strong and destructive it will be:

> *"I looked when He opened the sixth seal, and behold, there was a* **great earthquake**; *and the sun became black as sackcloth of hair, and the moon became like blood."* - Rev. 6:12

In the last chapter, we will look at the prophetic meaning of several past and upcoming eclipses in relation to Daniel's Prophecy of the Seventy Weeks (Dan. 9:24-27). Incidentally, Daniel's aforementioned prophecy suggests that the Antichrist will defile the Temple of God (which could mean his body), and break his covenant with **many** (note it does NOT say Israel) half way through the fourth year of the Tribulation period. If my theory about the Hallel Psalms and their connection to the Tribulation years is correct, this may also be sometime in 2014.

**In Psalm 115**, there are prophecies about the wicked people who will follow the Antichrist, and who will be swayed to make idolatrous images of their new leader. From that time on, they will worship the Antichrist as a god:

> *"Why should the Gentiles say, 'So where is their God (Elohim)?' But our God (Elohim) is in heaven; he does whatever He pleases.* **Their idols are silver and gold, the work of men's hands.** *They have mouths, but they do not speak; eyes they have, but they do not see; They have ears, but they do not hear....* **Those who make them are like them; so is everyone who trusts in them.** *O Israel, trust in the LORD (Yahweh); he is their help and their shield."* - Psalm 115:2-9

This fall into gross idolatry is also predicted in the Book of Revelation. In fact, the poetic words used to describe this idolatry in Psalm 115 are alluded to in these correlating passages in Revelation:

## Chapter 2: Amazing Prophecies in the Psalms

*"The rest of mankind that were not killed by these plagues still did not repent...* **they did not stop worshiping demons, and idols of gold, silver, bronze, stone and wood - idols that cannot see or hear or walk.** *Nor did they repent of their murders, their magic arts, their sexual immorality or their thefts."* - Revelation 9:20-21 (NIV)

**"All inhabitants of the earth will worship the beast-** *all whose names have not been written in the book of life belonging to the Lamb..."* - Rev. 13:8 (NIV)

In **Psalm 116**, the horrible result of this worldwide surge of idolatry and wickedness is shown. It will bring great trouble to those who are faithful to Yahweh. For their refusal to worship the Antichrist, the Tribulation Saints will become persecuted, and will be hated fugitives everywhere:

*"The pains of death surrounded me, and the pangs of Sheol laid hold of me; I found trouble and sorrow. Then I called upon the name of the LORD (Yahweh): 'O LORD (Yahweh), I implore You, deliver my soul!'"* - Psalm 116:3-4

Again, the Book of Revelation agrees with the Psalms, and indicates that this slaughter of the saints will occur:

**"He was given power to make war against the saints and to conquer them.** *And he was given authority over every tribe, people, language and nation."* - Rev. 13:7 (NIV)

*"He was given power to give breath to the image of the first beast, so that it could speak* **and cause all who refused to worship the image to be killed."** - Rev. 13:15 (NIV)

These persecuted saints will have to rely on their faith in God, and their love and compassion for one another to carry them through these troubling times. Even so, Psalm 116 goes on to tell us that many of them will die as martyrs for the faith. They will be outcasts all over the world who are hunted down and then murdered as traitors and heretics. As they are killed, these saints will render their lives to Yahweh to pay their vows of fealty to Him:

*"**What shall I render to the LORD (Yahweh) for all His benefits toward me?** I will take up the cup of salvation, and call upon the name of the LORD (Yahweh). **I will pay my vows** to the LORD (Yahweh) now in the presence of all His people. **Precious in the sight of the LORD (Yahweh) is the death of His saints.**"* - Psalm 116:12-15

Yahweh mourns the loss of every martyred saint, and to atone for their suffering, He will one day give them a precious, special place in eternity. Sadly, the year 2016 will likely see millions of new saints martyred because they will refuse to deny Christ and worship the Beast.

**Psalm 117**, which correlates with the year 2017, may be the Psalm announcing the final year of the Great Tribulation. Since Psalm 117 is so short, it suggests that the Antichrist's battle to annihilate all the saints will end early in that year, or even before then - in 2016. Because 2017 may mark the time when Yahshua returns with His heavenly army to conquer the wicked and start the third stage of the First Resurrection, Psalm 117 begins with the joyful shout of Hallelu-Yah! This shout of praise will be heard from all the saints, especially the newly resurrected martyrs!

At the Last Trumpet, which may refer to Revelation's Seventh Trumpet, the Apostle Paul tells us that the dead Tribulation Saints will rise first. Then the living saints will be translated into immortal bodies as they meet Yahshua in the air:

> "According to the Lord's own word... we who are still alive, **who are left till the coming of the Lord, will certainly not precede those who have fallen asleep.** For the Lord himself will come down from heaven, with a loud command... and with the trumpet call of God, and **the dead in Christ will rise first**. After that, **we who are still alive... will be caught up together with them in the clouds to meet the Lord in the air.** And so we will be with the Lord forever." - 1 Thessalonians 4:15-17 (NIV)

The preceding Scripture tells us that the Tribulation Saints who are alive when Yahshua comes in Wrath will not precede those saints who have died as martyrs. The dead Tribulation Saints will rise first. Then the remaining saints who are alive will rise up with these risen martyrs into the air to meet Yahshua. Once transformed in the air, these now immortal saints will join Yahshua's heavenly army of saints, and they will all return to Earth to destroy the wicked together!

As mentioned earlier, this final resurrection of the martyred saints is the third part of the three-stage First Resurrection (See 1 Cor. 15:22-23; Rev. 20:4-6). The first stage occurred when Yahshua rose, and many saints in Israel rose from the dead to join Him as the Firstfruits of the Resurrection (Matthew 27:51-52). Therefore, the second phase of the First Resurrection will occur with the Rapture (or Raptures), when many saints will become immortal before God's Wrath is poured out in the Tribulation. After Armageddon, these resurrected saints will be reunited with redeemed loved ones that were martyred in the Great Tribulation. How exciting this third stage of the First Resurrection will be!

If the final stage of the First Resurrection occurs in 2017, then the two short stanzas of Psalm 117 may be the victory hymn of those resurrected Tribulation Saints. As these saints are transformed in the resurrection and then resume their fight with immortal vigor, they will announce their joy in their deliverance from certain annihilation at the hands of the Antichrist's armies:

> *"Praise the LORD (Hallelu-Yah!), all you Gentiles! Laud Him, all you peoples! For His merciful kindness is great toward us, and the truth of the LORD (Yahweh) endures forever. Praise the LORD (Hallelu-Yah)!" - Psalm 117:1-2*

## Psalms 118 and 119: The Victory Songs of the Saints

**In Psalm 118**, the victory cry of the Tribulation Saints continues. Yahshua and all the saints who will serve with Him as priests and kings will likely recite Psalm 118. As they recite this powerful Psalm of Praise, the people will recall all that Yahshua did for them when He returned in Glory:

> *"In my anguish I cried to the LORD (Yahweh), and he answered **by setting me free.**" - Psalm 118:5 (NIV)*

The preceding passage pertains to all the Tribulation Saints, especially those who are prisoners awaiting death before Yahshua's return. The next verses, however, pertain to two exclusive groups of Tribulation Saints:

> *"All the nations surrounded me, but in the name of the LORD (Yahweh) I cut them off. They surrounded me on every side, but in the name of the LORD (Yahweh) I cut them off. They swarmed around me like bees, but they died out as quickly as burning thorns... I was pushed back and about to fall, but the LORD (Yahweh) helped me. The LORD (Yahweh) is my strength and my song; **he has become my salvation**. Shouts of joy and victory resound in the tents of the righteous: '**The LORD's (Yahweh's) right hand has done mighty things**! The LORD's (Yahweh's) right hand is lifted high; the LORD's (Yahweh's) right hand has done mighty things!'" - Psalm 118:10-16 (NIV)*

The preceding verses of Psalm 118 are truly remarkable in light of information revealed in this Book. For example, this part of Psalm 118 announces that **Yahshua has become our salvation in the past tense, which suggests that His role as our Salvation will find its ultimate fulfillment in 2018!** Psalm 118 also refers to *"Yahweh's right hand."* In ancient Israel, a father would confer his deathbed blessing on his eldest, or firstborn son *with his right hand*, while the other sons were blessed with their father's *left hand*. Psalm 118 is obviously alluding to Christ as the firstborn among many brethren, and as His Father Yahweh's Right Hand. However, this appellation as God's right hand also applies to the nation of Israel as a whole. In addition, it may signify the uplifting of Ephraim, the younger son of Joseph. He too was blessed by his grandfather Jacob/Israel's *right hand*.

This portion of Psalm 118 is therefore a victory song of praise for Ephraim, the Tribe that - along with Judah and against all odds - will prevail against the Antichrist. As previously explained, Ephraim may signify the United States, as well as all Gentile believers in Christ worldwide, while Judah represents the Jews scattered among the nations, in Israel, and possibly among the British Royal Family, *whose bloodline is purported to directly descend from King David*. After Christ lifts up the Two Houses of Israel - Ephraim and Judah - among the nations, the remaining survivors of the Great Tribulation will join the people reckoned as Ephraim and Judah in singing the following section of Psalm 118. It is a hymn of joy that proclaims Christ as the symbolic gate through which we all must pass to find Salvation:

*"I will not die but live, and will proclaim what the LORD (Yahweh) has done. The LORD (Yahweh) has chastened me severely, but he has not given me over to death. Open for me the gates of righteousness; I will enter and give thanks to the LORD (Yahweh). This is the gate of the LORD (Yahweh) through which the righteous may enter." - Psalm 118:17-20 (NIV)*

Concluding this recollection of suffering and triumph that Psalm 118 suggests may occur in 2018, Yahshua's coronation as King over all the Earth is indicated. As the saints watch, they will rejoice - dancing and singing before Yahshua's throne:

**"The stone the builders rejected has become the capstone;** *the LORD (Yahweh) has done this, and it is marvelous in our eyes. This is the day the LORD (Yahweh) has made; let us rejoice and be glad in it." - Psalm 118:22-24 (NIV)*

When Yahshua assumes His rightful place upon the re-created Throne of David, He will watch the consequent celebration with great joy. At this time, Yahshua - as both King and High Priest - may re-

## Chapter 2: Amazing Prophecies in the Psalms

consecrate the Great Pyramid as a sacred stone pillar to Yahweh. This is suggested by the fact that, as mentioned previously, *the prophecy of the Capstone appears in Psalm 118*. This prophecy applies solely to Christ as the capstone, or Chief Cornerstone of the Temples built in Jerusalem, and as the apex, or pyramidion-shaped capstone of the Great Pyramid.

As outlined in the Book of Ezekiel, and suggested in the Book of Revelation, a Temple to Yahweh will likely exist in Jerusalem during the Millennial Rule of Christ. At that time, our once rejected and despised Savior Yahshua will be worshipped as God's Son, and He will truly be the Capstone of our faith, and salvation. This will be the glorious day when the saints rejoice that the Day of the Lord has come by singing: **"This is the day the LORD (Yahweh) has made;** *let us rejoice and be glad in it."* At that time, the Jews who survive the Great Tribulation will at last proclaim Yahshua as their Messiah, saying:

*"Blessed is he who comes in the name of the LORD! (Yahweh) We have blessed you from the house of the LORD (Yahweh)." - Psalm 118:26*

Following are two highly significant references to Psalm 118:26 from Matthew's Gospel, though the other Gospels also refer to this Scripture pertaining to Christ's triumphal entry into Jerusalem (See Mark 11:9; Luke 13:35; John 12:13):

*"Then the multitudes who went before and those who followed cried out, saying: 'Hosanna to the Son of David!* **Blessed is He who comes in the name of the Lord!** *Hosanna in the highest!'" - Matthew 21:9*

And:

*"...for I say to you,* **you shall see Me no more till you say,** *'Blessed is He who comes in the name of the Lord!'" - Matthew 23:39*

Can you see why these two passages present another startlingly clear proof that Psalm 118 pertains to Yahshua's Second Coming, as well as His First Advent? It lies in the fact that this Psalm was quoted when Yahshua entered Jerusalem in triumph (Matthew 21:1-10). At that time the Jews hailing Him with palm branches were saying by their words and actions that they recognized this man as *the* Messiah prophesied about in their "Tanakh," or Jewish Bible. This is because Psalm 118 is a Messianic Psalm that the Jews knew pertained *only* to the coming of their Messiah as King. In addition, they waved palm branches to show that they recognized Yahshua as the "Tzemach," or Branch of Jesse, and King

David's rightful heir. They did not know, however, that Yahshua would first have to suffer, and then die for their sins.

Later on, during the week after His triumphal entry into Jerusalem, and just before His arrest, Yahshua told the unbelieving Jews in His audience that they would not see Him again until they said *"Blessed is He who comes in the name of the Lord!"* By saying this, Yahshua was promising two things: first, that those Jews listening to Him would rise up on the Last Day, and second, that they would all accept Yahshua as their Messiah and praise Him by quoting from Psalm 118 *at His Second Coming!* Yahshua was therefore not only telling His Jewish audience that He would return to fulfill the Messiah's role as King, but likely *when* He would re-establish the throne of David - *in 2018 AD!*

We move from the song of victory in Psalm 118, to a song of praise in Psalm 119. Psalm 118 is a joyful salute to Yahshua's triumph over the wicked forces of the Antichrist, just as Psalm 119 is a song of love, delight, and praise for the newly enthroned King of kings.

**Psalm 119**, as the longest chapter in the Bible, is meant to announce the importance and greatness of this newly enthroned Messiah and King to the whole world. Mortal and immortal souls alike will lift up their eyes, and incline their ears to hear the glorious message of this long Psalm, for it is encoded with messianic themes and messages throughout. It will be a subject of much study during the Millennial Rule of Christ, when the teachings of the Torah and Tanakh, or Bible, and the teachings of the Mazzaroth, or Gospel in the Zodiac will regularly be compared, and examined. Everywhere on Earth, people will desire to know and understand Yahweh, and His Son - the Word of God. Together, the people of the world will contemplate all of God's "Words," or teachings that are found in Heaven, on Earth, and in the Bible:

> *"How can a young man cleanse his way? By taking heed according to Your word. With my whole heart I have sought You; Oh, let me not wander from Your commandments! Your word I have hidden in my heart, that I might not sin against You! Blessed are You, O LORD! (Yahweh) Teach me Your statutes!"* - Psalm 119:9-12

Throughout Psalm 119, there is an emphasis on God's Word and commandments. Yahshua, as the Word of God, is the source of both the Mazzaroth, and the Bible - the two great sources of His eternal Word, or Will. Yahshua alone is the preeminent and eternal Word of God, who was, is, and is to come – our Savior who came and left at His First Advent, and will come again in the Rapture or Raptures. Yahshua is also

## Chapter 2: Amazing Prophecies in the Psalms — Page 83

destined to return one final time to set up His Millennial Kingdom on Earth. He authored the Ten Commandments, and inspired all the Scriptures available to us. This truth is echoed in the Book of Revelation - in two passages identifying Christ as the Alpha and Omega:

> *"'I am the Alpha and the Omega, the Beginning and the End,' says the Lord, 'who is and who was and who is to come, the Almighty'... "I am the Alpha and the Omega, the Beginning and the End, the First and the Last. Blessed are those who do His commandments, that they may have the right to the tree of life..."*
> – Rev. 1:8, 22:13-14

Amazingly, the location of these statements proclaiming that Yahshua is the Alpha and the Omega, and the Beginning and the End are prophetic as well, since they are located at the very beginning and the very end of the Book of Revelation! As stated before, Psalm 119 is the only one of eight acrostic psalms in the Bible that contains verses for all twenty-two letters in the Hebrew alphabet. It therefore contains a complete picture of the Alpha and Omega, Yahshua the Anointed One.

To summarize the prophetic meaning of the Hallel Psalms, all of these psalms, and those immediately preceding and following them appear to be tied to key events in the Tribulation period. Psalm 110 acts as a sentinel heralding the imminent arrival of the Tribulation period, and serves as a summary of the events to follow. Psalm 110 refers to both the Tribulation period and the Second Coming in its entirety. It therefore appears to mark the prelude year before the full onset of the Tribulation, Uncannily, Psalm 110 represents the year 2010 on the Gregorian calendar, and the year 2010 is a significant prophetic date recorded in the design of the Great Pyramid. We will discuss the prophetic dates in the Great Pyramid further in the next chapter. As such, 2010 could be the year before the First Rapture and Tribulation, though it could begin in 2011 or 2012 as well.

Psalm 118, the last of the main Hallel Psalms, is highly important as a marker since it falls after Psalm 117 - the Psalm that may mark the year 2017 and the abrupt and triumphant *end* of the Great Tribulation. Psalm 118 appears to represent the first year of the Millennial Rule of Yahshua - the Great Day that Yahweh made so that we would all have a reason to rejoice and be glad. All the signs point to the year 2018 as the year when Yahshua may reign as High Priest and King of kings on Earth. God's Holy Name "Yahweh" occurs twenty-seven times in Psalm 118's twenty-nine verses. This Psalm therefore mightily proclaims that it is the holy Name of Yahweh that delivers us from evil. It is likely that, during the first year He rules Earth, Yahshua will lead His Covenant People in reciting Psalm 118 - along with Psalms 119 and 136 - as a song of Praise to Yahweh for their deliverance from evil.

## *The Hallel Psalms and the Hebrew Finial Letters*

In Chapter One, it was explained that there are five letters in the Hebrew Aleph-Bet that have a second, finial form. Though the five finial Hebrew letters sound the same as the letters they originate from, they have a hidden number value. As shown in my Alpha-Numeric Chart on pages 8 and 9, the five finial letters correspond to five letters that span the 11th through 18th positions in the Hebrew alphabet. Respectively, the finial Kaf corresponds to the Kaf that is the 11th letter of the Hebrew alphabet, which is associated with a crown (i.e.: the crown of the King of kings). In its original form, the letter Kaf represents Christ's crown of thorns, but in its finial form, Kaf signifies Christ's Crown of Glory in His Millennial Kingdom. In other words, the five finial letters have an opposing, and generally more positive meaning than the original meaning of the five letters they are derived from.

Keeping their duality in mind, the finial Mem meaning "concealed" (as in *forgiven, or hidden, unconfessed sin*) corresponds to the 13th letter Mem, which means "revealed;" the finial Nun meaning "rising again" corresponds to the 14th letter Nun, meaning "downfall;" the finial Pey meaning "an open mouth of praise" corresponds to the 17th letter Pey, meaning "a closed mouth of learning;" and the finial Tsadek, meaning "the righteous standing tall" is the opposite of the 18th letter Tsadek, signifying "the righteous kneeling humbly." Uncannily, the original Hebrew letters that the finial letters are derived from also correspond with the 11th through 18th chapters of the Book of Revelation!

Based on our preceding discussion of the Hallel Psalms, could it be that this is not a coincidence? Could it be that these finial letters are an encoded message to us that the years 2011 through 2018 will be significant years in human history? Furthermore, could these finial letters be telling us that the events in the eleventh, thirteenth, fourteenth, seventeenth and eighteenth chapters of the Book of Revelation correspond to the events that will take place in the years 2011, 2013, 2014, 2017, and 2018? Looking at these chapters closely, Chapter 11 of Revelation states:

"*The seventh angel sounded his trumpet, and there were loud voices in heaven, which said:* '***The kingdom of the world has***

## Chapter 2: Amazing Prophecies in the Psalms — Page 85

*become the kingdom of our Lord and of his Christ, and he will reign for ever and ever.'* And the twenty-four elders... fell on their faces and worshiped God, saying: *'We give thanks to you, Lord God Almighty, the One who is and who was, because you have taken your great power and have begun to reign.'"* - Rev. 11:15-17 (NIV)

This Bible passage suggests that the twenty-four elders are worshipping Yahshua because He has just been crowned in Heaven, and has therefore begun to reign over the kingdoms of the world on Earth. In other words, it seems that Christ will oust Satan's rule over the world of men, and take full control over every principality and power at this specified moment in time. Therefore, this Scripture melds beautifully with the Hebrew letter Kaf, which stands for the Messiah's Crown of Glory! If this passage is also meant to correspond to events in 2011, it suggests that Christ will begin His Millennial reign at the very beginning of the Tribulation period!

Interestingly, Revelation, Chapter 11 opens with an angel telling the writer of the Book of Revelation to measure the grounds for a Temple to Yahweh, though it is not actually described as being built at that time:

*"Then I was given a... measuring rod. And the angel stood, saying, 'Rise and measure the temple of God, the altar, and those who worship there. But leave out the court... for it has been given to the Gentiles. And they will tread the holy city underfoot for forty-two months.'"* - Revelation 11:1-2

Could this mean that the Tribulation period began in 2011, and that the next Temple to Yahweh in Jerusalem won't actually be completed until Yahshua begins His visible reign on the Earth a few years from now? If so, that Temple that will be built will likely fulfill Ezekiel's vision of what this future Temple will look like.

Amazingly, there are other parallels between the numeric positions and meanings of these Hebrew finial letters, and the chapters of Revelation that their original forms correspond to. For example, In Revelation, Chapter 13, Satan's evil schemes are fully *revealed* with the rise of the Beast from the Sea, the appearance of the Beast from the Earth, and the issuing of the Satanic Mark of the Beast without which no one can buy or sell anything commercially. Now, this 13th chapter describing the Antichrist's evil takeover of the world corresponds with the 13th Hebrew letter Mem, meaning "revealed," but it also conveys the idea through the finial Mem that the evil nature of this Satanic takeover will be *concealed* from the deluded people who will follow and worship the Beast!

Likewise, Revelation, Chapter 14 begins by describing the presence of the Lamb (i.e. Christ) standing on Mount Zion with the 144,000 Witnesses taken from the Twelve Tribes of Israel. This suggests that Yahshua will visit the Earth during the Great Tribulation to give encouragement to His chosen witnesses *before* He returns with His heavenly armies at the end of the Tribulation. It also suggests that all Twelve Tribes of Israel have many living representatives on the Earth today, and that 144,000 of them are very devoted to God, and will be called to serve Christ in a very special way, perhaps sometime in 2014.

These 144,000 Israelite saints have been chosen to share the Gospel of the Kingdom with the world, and to become part of the Firstfruits of the Resurrection from the dead, along with those taken in the Rapture. This suggests that the 144,000 saints will be immortal, and *incapable of being destroyed* as they witness to a lost and dying world (as discussed earlier in this chapter). This corresponds perfectly with the meaning of the 14th Hebrew letter Nun, which in its finial form symbolizes "rising up," as from the dead.

Uncannily, Nun also means "downfall," and Revelation, Chapter 14, verses 9 through 11 describes the fallen wicked who are destined to perish because they will take the identifying Mark of the Beast on their foreheads or hands. Revelation, Chapter 14, verse 8, and verses 17 through 20 also describe the downfall of the future Babylonian Empire of the Antichrist. As indicated in Revelation 14:20, the reaping of the first people to be thrown into the Winepress of God's Wrath live *"outside the city,"* meaning these damned souls live *outside* the city called Babylon the Great, which will not be destroyed until later, as indicated by Revelation, Chapters 17 and 18.

Chapter 18 of Revelation begins with a recollection of the utter destruction of Babylon the Great:

> *"And he cried mightily with a loud voice, saying, 'Babylon the great is fallen... and has become a dwelling place of demons, a prison for every foul spirit, and a cage for every unclean... bird!'"* - Rev. 18:2

Because of the way it is worded, the preceding Scripture suggests that Babylon the Great *has already fallen* by this time. Since this destruction of Babylon the Great signifies the destruction of the city seat of the Evil Empire of the Antichrist, it seems logical to assume that this destruction of evil corresponds exactly with the triumphant return of Christ as the conquering King of kings. Now, as already discussed, Psalm 117 indicates that Yahshua may conquer the Antichrist, and destroy

## Chapter 2: Amazing Prophecies in the Psalms

Babylon the Great in 2017. Uncannily, Revelation, Chapter 17 describes this evil empire:

> *"And on her forehead a name was written: MYSTERY, BABYLON THE GREAT, THE MOTHER OF HARLOTS AND OF THE ABOMINATIONS OF THE EARTH. I saw the woman, drunk with the blood of the saints and with the blood of the martyrs of Jesus (Yahshua)." - Rev. 17:5-6*

It is this city called the Whore of Babylon that Yahshua the Messiah will utterly destroy, and *the aftermath* of that destruction is described in Revelation, Chapter 18. Likewise, internal evidence in Psalm 118 suggests that Christ may formally set up His Millennial Kingdom in 2018, just as Revelation, Chapter 18 suggests. Uncannily, the finial letter Pey meaning "an open mouth of praise" is associated with Revelation, Chapter 17, and suggests that the righteous will openly rejoice over the fall of Babylon the Great, which they undoubtedly shall if it is utterly destroyed in 2017. Furthermore, if Yahshua begins to set up His Millennial Kingdom on Earth in 2018, the righteous saints who will reign with Him will have every reason to "stand tall," just as the finial form of the 18th letter Tsadek indicates in association with Revelation, Chapter 18, and the year 2018.

Now, if this Scriptural proof for my hunch about the Hallel Psalms is not enough to convince skeptics, consider the following sign in the heavens that occurred in 1994, and try to refute it!

### The 1994 Jupiter Bombardment linked to Psalm 94!

In July of 1994, a large comet that had broken into 21 pieces on July 7th, 1992 was on a collision course with the planet Jupiter. Between Saturday, July 16th and Friday, July 22nd, 1994, these 21 comet fragments crashed into Jupiter's surface one by one. It has been estimated that each one of these comet fragments hit Jupiter with the force of a 200-megaton atomic bomb blast! The original comet that had orbited Jupiter for a time before breaking apart was named Shoemaker-Levy 9 after the last names of the Jewish astronomers who discovered it.

It was the 9th of Av on the Jewish calendar when the 21 pieces of Comet Shoemaker-Levy 9 began to crash into Jupiter on July 16th, 1994. The 9th of Av is a day of fasting and great mourning among Jews because some of the most terrible past events against the Jewish people occurred on this date. For example, on the 9th of Av, all but two of the 12 spies that were sent by Moses into the Promised Land gave an unfavorable report about the ability of the Israelites to defeat the people dwelling in Canaan. As a result, the Israelites wandered in the desert for 40 years. Also on the 9th of Av, both Solomon's and Herod's Temple in Jerusalem were *burned to the ground,* and utterly destroyed. If this was not bad enough, many more tragedies befell the Jews on that sad day. On the 9th of Av in 71 AD, for example, the Roman Army plowed the rubble of what had been the city of Jerusalem with salt - leveling the ground, and removing any trace of the Jewish people, and their culture. They also did this to the destroyed temple mount to prepare the city ground and temple area to be rebuilt as a new Roman colony. In this way, this prophecy of Micah was fulfilled:

> *"Therefore because of you Zion shall be plowed like a field, Jerusalem shall become heaps of ruins, and the mountain of the temple like the bare hills of the forest."* - Micah 3:12

This terrible destruction of Jerusalem partly occurred because the Jewish people had rejected their Messiah, just as Yahshua said they would do when He warned them that the destruction of their holy city was coming (Mat. 24:2; Mark 13:2; Like 21:6). That is also why Yah meted out another great blow to the Jewish people in 135 AD. On the 9th of Av that same year, the falsely proclaimed Messiah Simon Bar Kochba, and thousands of Jewish rebels who followed him perished at the hands of Rome's legions. Then, on the 9th of Av in 1290 AD, England ordered the expulsion of its entire Jewish population. This led to much suffering and hardship for the Jews, all of whom were forced to abandon their homes, forsake most of their possessions, and move to Europe.

The same thing happened to the Jews in Spain on the 9th of Av in 1492 AD. However, since this was the same year when Christopher Columbus supposedly discovered America and claimed it for Spain, it presaged a coming time when the Jews would find deliverance from persecution by fleeing to America one day. Nonetheless, due to the terrible tragedies that occurred for the Jews on the 9th of Av, it is no wonder that this day has become one of great foreboding and mourning for Jews everywhere.

In light of Sacred Astronomy's use to foretell the prophetic fulfillment of Yahweh's Will, and coupled with the foreboding nature of the 9th of Av, the remarkable bombardment of Jupiter on that date must have some vital significance for Jews, and spiritual Israel in general. In fact, when this Jupiter bombardment is analyzed critically, it reveals many startling correlations that verify other prophetic interpretations given in this chapter. For example, this comet bombardment affected Jupiter, the planet that represents the Messiah in Jewish thought. In

## Chapter 2: Amazing Prophecies in the Psalms

addition, this bombardment happened while Jupiter was in the constellation of Virgo, the Virgin. This Zodiac sign represents not only the virgin mother of Yahshua, but also the Seed of the Virgin - Yahshua and His disciples, the saints. This comet bombardment may therefore be an omen of future dire events that will hurt the figurative Body of Christ, which is the True Church.

This comet bombardment lasted seven days, which is a biblical number signifying both completion and rest. Furthermore, there was one comet that became 21 fragments that bombarded Jupiter. Now, if we look at this event mathematically, 1 plus 21 equals 22. This is the number of letters in the Hebrew alphabet, and it is therefore connected to the totality of God's prophetic word. This is why there are many prophetic allusions in the Bible to Christ as "the Beginning and the End", "the Alpha and the Omega" and "the First and the Last," as well as allusions to Yahshua as the Beginning and the End in the Great Sphinx, and in the heavenly signs of Virgo and Leo. The number 22 also suggests a period of time marking the onset and completion of some major prophetic event. Could this period of time be 22 years from 1994? If so, 1994 + 22 = 2016. Uncannily, as shown in Chapter Eight of this book, this year is also targeted by the Antechamber in the Great Pyramid at Giza as the possible year when Yahshua may return to fight the Battle of Armageddon.

Since two Jews discovered Comet Shoemaker-Levy 9, and the comet's 21 fragments hit Jupiter on the 9th of Av, could it be that these comet fragments suggest a world breakdown in the Judeo-Christian belief in a Messiah, who is represented by Jupiter? Could it also be that this time of great apostasy will reach critical proportions 21 years from 1994, which will be in 2015? Could it also be that these future dates - 2015 and 2016 - which are 21 and 22 years past 1994, are being singled out as years of great woe for the Jewish people and the Tribulation Saints? The following verses of Psalm 94 seem to refer to the invasion of cities where the Tribulation Saints dwell, and the slaughter of those who refuse to renounce their faith:

> "O LORD God, (Yahweh Elohim) to whom vengeance belongs - ...shine forth! Rise up, O Judge of the earth; render punishment to the proud. LORD (Yahweh),... how long will the wicked triumph? They utter speech, and speak insolent things; all the workers of iniquity boast in themselves. **They break in pieces Your people, O LORD (Yahweh),... They slay the widow and the stranger, and murder the fatherless.** Yet they say, 'The LORD (Yahweh) does not see, nor does the God of Jacob understand.'"

> *"They gather together against the life of the righteous, and condemn innocent blood. But the LORD (Yahweh) has been my defense, and my God the rock of my refuge. He has brought on them their own iniquity;... the LORD our God (Yahweh our Elohim) shall cut them off."* - Psalm 94:1-7, 21-23

These verses of Psalm 94 vividly describe that horrible future time of dread on the Earth when the Antichrist will attempt to destroy all the people that love Yahshua and Yahweh. Interestingly, the shortest Psalm and chapter in the Bible - Psalm 117 - directly refers to the year 2017. Therefore, this may be the year that will be mercifully shortened or nullified with Yahshua's return to end the terrors of the Great Tribulation by annihilating the Antichrist's armies that have gathered around Jerusalem - in the valley of Megiddo, or Armageddon. In light of Psalm 94's meaning, and the prophetic nature of the Psalms as a whole, it seems highly likely that Psalm 94 is linked to 1994 - the year of the Shoemaker-Levi Comet Bombardment of Jupiter.

The Hallel Psalms and Psalm 94 all appear to have prophetic connections to the seven-year Tribulation period. Furthermore, the 21 bombardments of Jupiter witnessed in heaven may point to events in 2015 AD - a year when the persecution and slaughter of Jews and Christians may begin to far exceed the horror of Hitler's death camps.

Now that we have explored the fascinating prophecies in the Psalms, we will focus on a source of biblical wisdom that is not in the Bible, but that is allegorically tied to it in many intriguing ways. In the next two chapters on the Great Pyramid, and Great Sphinx, evidence will be given that these two edifices were designed as repositories of spiritual knowledge by the righteous descendents of Seth, and that these people were knowledgeable about the celestial signs in the Gospel in the Stars. In addition, it will be shown that these monuments were built to honor Yahweh God and his Son Yahshua, and are encoded with information that appears to show the exact time when the Tribulation will occur, and when Yahshua's Millennial Kingdom will be established.

The next two chapters will also show that our ancestors knew how to apply Biblical or Sacred Astronomy to determine when the Ages of Men would come to an end - just as the Wise Men who visited Yahshua as a toddler knew when the ultimate King of the Jews would be born. They will also reveal the meanings behind the incredibly complex designs of the Great Pyramid and Great Sphinx, and the amazing intelligence, and spiritual maturity of our remotest ancestors who loved God.

## Chapter 3: Why The Pillar of Enoch Was Built

*"You have set signs and wonders in the land of Egypt, to this day..."* - Jeremiah 32:20

The above passage of Scripture indicates that Yahweh placed *"signs and wonders"* in Egypt that existed in the prophet Jeremiah's day. The Hebrew word translated as "signs" in this Scripture is "oth," which can refer to a sign or signal, as in a flag, beacon, or monument. Interestingly, "oth" can also refer to an omen, or portent of the future. This *same word* was used in Genesis 1:15 to describe the purpose of the lights God fixed in the heavens above the Earth. These lights are the Sun, Moon, planets, comets, and stars surrounding our Earth. As exhaustively shown in "The Language of God in the Universe," all of these celestial bodies are connected to the Mazzaroth or Zodiac, and all have spiritual and prophetic meanings. These signs and wonders in Egypt were therefore also likely tied in some way to Sacred Astronomy. Likewise, they were probably meant to shed light on the nature of God, and the future of mankind using the same symbolism that is found in the Gospel in the Stars.

The prophet Jeremiah implied that these signs and wonders in Egypt were visible monuments of some kind. Furthermore, through the plural form of the word "oth," Jeremiah suggested that more than one monument in Egypt was meant to convey spiritual truths to those who found and studied them. In Book Three, "The Language of God in History," these monuments were identified as the Red and Bent Pyramids at Dahshur, the Giza Complex's associated large pyramids, the Great Sphinx and the two temples found in front of the Sphinx, Stonehenge, and Easter Island.

In this chapter, we will focus on why the inspired words about Egypt in Jeremiah 32:20 are as true today as when they were penned thousands of years ago. Furthermore, we will see that Jeremiah's words can especially be applied to two incredible monuments that were built with great ingenuity and skill. The first monument is the Great Pyramid, which I often refer to as the Pillar of Enoch because I believe that Enoch the Sethite was divinely inspired to design and build it. The second monument is the Great Sphinx, which may also have been designed by Enoch, along with the other two pyramids associated with the Great Pyramid.

As we study these two magnificent monuments filled with the Language of God, it will be conclusively shown that the Pillar of Enoch was encoded with much of the scientific and prophetic knowledge that the highly intelligent and civilized antediluvians were divinely given by God. Furthermore, this knowledge was encoded in a way that people in modern times could decipher and understand. In addition, it will be shown that these monolithic religious masterpieces of stone were likely built to survive the Great Flood, and all the future Ages of mankind to be a witness to this last generation of God's Will and Power.

## *The Pillar of Enoch: Designed by God, and Built by Men*

The Great Pyramid or Pillar of Enoch is still one of the most massive, and magnificently engineered stone buildings in the world. This marvelous megalithic monument has withstood the test of time. Touted as one of the Seven Wonders of the Ancient World, it is the only one to have survived to modern times. This is no accident, but shows the supreme ingenuity, and greatness of its divine designer: Yahweh.

Since the Great Pyramid is such a remarkably complex structure, some people doubt that men of the Stone Age could have built it, and so they have hypothesized that the Pillar of Enoch was built by Pagan gods, aliens, Fallen Angels, or their evil Nephilim offspring. We will address these strange notions in the next section. But for now, let me give you many reasons to believe that men not only built the Great Pyramid, but that they encoded it with their scientific knowledge, as well as the divine knowledge they received from God through men like the prophet Enoch, who *"walked with God; and he was not, for God took him"* (Genesis 5:24).

Most Egyptologists believe that the Pharaoh Khufu, who reigned between 2551 and 2528 BC, built the Great Pyramid, while his son Khafre may have built the second largest pyramid at Giza, and the Great Sphinx. Since Khufu's reign falls well before the Great Flood of 2347 BC, it supports the idea that the Great Pyramid was built by the antediluvian ancestors of Seth and Enoch, just as stated by the Jewish historian Josephus.

# Chapter 3: Why The Pillar of Enoch Was Built

Book Three explains that the First Century Historian Josephus identified the Great Pyramid and Great Sphinx's builders as the antediluvian ancestors of Seth - the righteous branch of humanity that descended from Adam (See Josephus, Antiquities of the Jews, 1:2:3, and refer to quotations from it in Book 3). Since Enoch the Sethite was so favored by God that he was translated without seeing death, it is my belief that Enoch designed these monuments at Giza to be lasting Covenant pillars and testimonies about Yahweh and the coming Messiah that he joyfully foresaw and hopefully awaited.

In support of this, close scrutiny of every aspect of this Pyramid's construction reveals that these amazing Pre-Flood people of God encoded the entire design of the Pillar of Enoch with advanced scientific, spiritual, and *prophetic knowledge that could only have been gained through divine inspiration*. Indeed, beyond the accurate scientific, mathematical, and astronomical information found in the Pillar of Enoch, every nuance of its interior construction tells us a remarkable story of our spiritual death, decay, salvation, restoration, and ultimate triumph through Christ.

Also in Book Three, the Biblical Chronological Time Chart (also found in the Appendix of this book) was used to identify the Fourth Dynasty Pharaoh Khufu *not* as Enoch - as some scholars and legends have incorrectly done - but as Noah. If Khufu was Noah, Shem may have been the Pharaoh Khafre. However, this does not mean that either Noah or Shem actually built the Great Pyramid and Great Sphinx. Though archeologists often ignore this because it contradicts their views, a stone carving called the Inventory Stela that was found between the paws of the Sphinx suggests that Khufu and Khafre only repaired the already ancient architecture at the Giza Complex that was falling into ruin.

Due to this, a more probable candidate for the builder or designer of the Great Pyramid is Enoch the Sethite. As shown in "The Language of God in History" through numerous quotes from the Book of 1 Enoch, Book of Jubilees, and Book of Jasher, Enoch spent much time in the presence of God's holy angels learning divine wisdom. In fact, Enoch's knowledge of Yahweh Elohim was comparable to that of many Old Testament prophets, as evidenced by the ancient book that bears his name.

This Enoch was *not* the son of Cain, and is in no way connected to the god Thoth, Hermes or the false Enoch called Hermes Trismegistus that is important to those involved in Hermeticism and other esoteric or occult spiritual paths. According to my Biblical Chronology in the Appendix, Enoch the Sethite was likely born in 3381 BC, which was hundreds of years before Noah's birth in 2900 BC. Therefore, Enoch or his son Methuselah could have organized the construction of the most remarkable stone structures at Giza during their lifetimes. After Enoch's translation and Methuselah's demise, however, Noah and Shem could have been commissioned to care for the divinely inspired monuments built by their righteous predecessors.

In Book Three, I discussed the possibility that Enoch the Sethite likely designed the Great Pyramid, the two large pyramids aligned with it, and the Great Sphinx under divine inspiration, and that his sons or grandsons likely built them. It was also shown that the Fallen Angels and Nephilim likely had nothing to do with their construction. This is why I call the Great Pyramid the Pillar of Enoch.

The theory that Enoch designed the Great Pyramid per God's instruction is supported by the pyramid's base side measurements. Since the Solar Year prior to the Flood was likely shorter than it is today by a least five days, the measurements outside and inside the Great Pyramid that reflect the 365.242 days in a Solar Year today may have originally referred to the exact length of time that Enoch walked the Earth before his translation. This is based partly on the fact that, in Genesis 5:23-24, Enoch's age at the time of his translation is given as 365 years. We also discussed the possibility that - though they did not actually build the Great Pyramid complex - Noah and Shem may have restored and possibly added to it before and after the Great Flood.

Enoch is also a prime candidate for architect of the Great Pyramid and Great Sphinx because they appear to have been designed to remain a puzzle until modern times, when our levels of technology and science, and our understanding of Yahshua our Savior was great enough to unravel all of Giza's mysterious secrets. Indeed, the Book of 1 Enoch tells us that: *"I understood as I saw, but not for this generation, but for a remote one which is for to come"* (1 Enoch 1:2-3). Just as this passage says, **1 Enoch is filled with prophecies that were not written for Enoch's era, but for people far into the future.**

In fact, it seems apparent that Enoch's books were written for the generation that will witness the re-birth of Israel and Christ's triumphant return - and this appears to be the generation that was born in 1948 - a generation that will reach its 70-year "termination" in 2018. It is therefore possible that, just as God designed Enoch's written prophecies to retain their secrets until this Last Day, God designed the Great Pyramid and Great Sphinx to do so. Because Enoch's written prophecies also speak to us today, several of them will be closely examined in this book.

## Chapter 3: Why The Pillar of Enoch Was Built

Under the same divine inspiration his book was written with, Enoch likely designed the Great Sphinx and all three major pyramids at Giza hundreds of years before Noah ruled as patriarch. Subsequently, Enoch's son Methuselah may have been put in charge of building, preserving and protecting the sacred structures built at Giza. Born over 350 years before Noah, Methuselah died in his 969th year. This was just before the Great Flood - when Noah was 600 years old. Due to the city of Mennefer's close proximity to the Giza complex, Methuselah likely ruled over that city and the entire surrounding area for a time before the Great Flood. While he was ruling, Methuselah could also have organized the successive building of the Great Sphinx and the three biggest pyramids at Giza. It is also possible that - when Methuselah was too old to do so himself - Noah and Shem continued to repair and preserve the structures at the Giza Pyramid Complex - both before and after the Great Flood.

The biggest argument against an antediluvian date for the Great Pyramid and Great Sphinx comes from a footnote in Josephus' histories. There, the translator states his opinion that no man-made structure could have survived the ferocity of the Great Flood, and Josephus was therefore incorrect in assigning a Pre-Flood origin to any monuments in Egypt. Of course, this flies in the face of the fact that one man-made structure certainly did survive the Flood, and that was Noah's Ark! In addition, he ignores the fact that the Great Pyramid is the most massive and expertly designed solid stone structure on Earth. It is estimated to contain over 2.5 million limestone blocks weighing an average of 2 tons apiece, with some far more massive granite and limestone slabs interspersed throughout.

The Great Pyramid also has giant stone footings that are part of an enormously thick, *solid bedrock* foundation that is hundreds of feet deep. In short, there is no way the Great Pyramid is going to move anywhere or be destroyed unless God wills it through some cataclysmic event such as a direct hit with an asteroid or nuclear bomb, or someone wants to dismantle it, stone by stone.

As for how the Great Pyramid was built by men, it is obvious from its amazingly complex design - and the expert engineering feats that were accomplished to construct it - that its builders were intellectual giants. Though our antediluvian ancestors were physically similar to modern human beings in appearance, the Bible tells us that they lived ten to twelve times longer than we do. There are also clues in the Book of Jasher that they were far stronger than we are today. This suggests that people were much healthier prior to the Flood than they are today. In addition, it is obvious from the Books of 1 Enoch and Jubilees that Enoch and other human beings enjoyed a close relationship with the holy

Watchers that never sinned. Furthermore, these Watchers may have helped the Sethites build the Old Kingdom Pyramids in Egypt, as well as Noah's Ark.

Due to these facts, the idea that these physically robust, intellectual giants would use steep ramps made of enormous volumes of rubble to push the stone blocks used to build the Great Pyramid into place is completely absurd, as is the idea that the ramps were built in a circular fashion around the pyramid. These rubble ramps would have taken more energy and time to build and move than cutting, polishing, and placing the blocks for the Great Pyramid itself!

Others have proposed that the stones used in the Great Pyramid are actually made of some advanced form of concrete, and were poured into molds and allowed to set like concrete. While this idea has some appeal, and explains a way that the builders of the Great Pyramid could have finished such an enormous job with such apparent ease using only Stone Age tools, it does not explain the thin layers of mortar that have been found between these huge stone blocks. It also doesn't address the unfinished appearance of the outer faces of the stones, or the evidence that incised I-shaped indentations containing *iron joins* were used to hold some of the stones together.

Another interesting theory is that the ancient builders of all monolithic structures like the Great Pyramid used some form of levitation using sound waves, or vibrations caused by the Earth's magnetic field current interacting with its geothermal core. Though these are possibilities, no one has yet discovered a way to manipulate sound waves to lift anything more massive than a golf ball. In addition, magnets can't lift up heavy stony blocks unless the stone is somehow infused with the properties of heavy metals. Until these theories of generating power are fully understood and can be proven to be viable, these methods are best reserved for science fiction novels.

Though few entertain the idea, Herodotus recorded that the Great Pyramid was built using a mechanical leverage method, where a crane-like device was positioned on each step of the pyramid before the casing stones were placed and the cranes were used to lift each stone up one level at a time. This method of hoisting the stones up would require the least amount of labor and would be the fastest way to move them into place even today. When it came time to put the dazzling white facing stones into place, the same method could have been used to hoist the stones to the top of the structure first, then to each layer downward until the pyramid was completely covered.

## Chapter 3: Why The Pillar of Enoch Was Built

So why doesn't any current book on the pyramids of Egypt show this technique? Because archeologists, in support of evolution, want us to believe that the Great Pyramid - and the four other Old Kingdom pyramids similar to it - were built by people who were little more than primitive Stone Age savages, and far inferior to us since we are supposedly further up on the evolutionary ladder. We are therefore supposed to be much smarter than they were.

The Bible, however, makes it clear that mankind was intelligent from the beginning, and that people had learned to farm and domesticate animals *within one hundred years of the Fall* of Adam and Eve. So there is no reason that, by 1500 years after the Fall and 200 years before the Flood (circa 2500 BC, when the Great Pyramid was supposedly built), people could not have figured out how to build a crane, or forge iron all on their own - without any supernatural aid. Nonetheless, 1 Enoch suggests that the holy Watchers may have helped the righteous Sethites build part of the Pillar of Enoch. See Book Three for more on this.

### *How The Great Pyramid Conveys Knowledge*

Is it possible that the Great Pyramid was specifically designed by our ancestors to instruct and challenge people to think "outside the box"? If it is, then - instead of relaying information to us with words or pictures - the Great Pyramid was likely designed to do so through its complex construction. In fact, the structure of the Great Pyramid reflects many geometric, scientific, and astronomical concepts that appear to convey a multitude of spiritual truths. But, to find these spiritual truths, we need to think like scientists and mathematicians. Therefore, we can only "read" the Great Pyramid's many spiritual messages to us when we analyze it scientifically. Since Yahweh knows how curious we are, could He have inspired men to build an enormous puzzle in His honor - in the hope that we would be curious enough to discover all of its secrets? As will be shown here, this is a very real possibility.

To decipher this gigantic puzzle effectively, however, we must experience a paradigm shift in our thinking. We have to be open to the idea that the ancient builders of the Great Pyramid may have been far more technologically advanced than archeologists currently hypothesize. Large in stature and robust in health, our antediluvian ancestors may have understood more than we can - especially since we are in a far more physically and mentally diminished state than they were. Only when we are willing to accept these ideas can the Great Pyramid convey its encoded secrets. When viewed correctly, the Great Pyramid has a profound message to share with the entire world, especially believers.

The Great Pyramid of Pillar of Enoch is primarily a product of Sacred Geometry, which involves geometry and allegory working in tandem to create a meaningful design. Within a solid geometric construct, this pyramid transmits information that also involves mathematics, science, astronomy, allegory, religion, and prophecy. In fact, there is so much geometric, mathematical, scientific, and religious information being imparted in the pyramid's design that an entire book could be filled with it! This chapter shares some of the fascinating information contained within the Great Pyramid, while Book Three contains much more about this pyramid's connection to Sacred Astronomy. Like other sections in this book on the Language of God, this chapter on the Great Pyramid has some highly complex and technical information in it. This is because simplifying or omitting much of this knowledge would detract from its value to the serious scholar. After all, this book series is about the mind of God revealed through the power of the Holy Spirit and Her Language of allegory, and there is no way to simplify the mind of God, which is infinitely more complex than our own minds or any book.

Of the Seven Wonders of the Ancient World, the Great Pyramid stands alone because it is the only one still standing, and the only one of the seven that was designed as an allegorical record of what our righteous antediluvian ancestors knew about God and His incredible Creation. In fact, in light of my own research and that of others, I've drawn the firm conclusion that only godly people who knew the one triune God Yahweh could have built the Great Pyramid. This is because **the Pillar of Enoch is undeniably the greatest human representation of the Language of God ever built!** It is a powerful monument attesting to the prophetic and scientific metaphorical code Yahweh locked into the Universe.

In comparison to us, our forefathers were not primitive savages, but intellectual and spiritual giants. We are only the degenerate ancestors of the righteous antediluvian Noah and his kin - people who were blessed with good health and a remarkable longevity that far exceeded our own. Yet now, at this present time in history, we are again approaching the level of knowledge and skill that our remotest ancestors possessed. We have arrived at a time in history when many of the secrets hidden in the Pillar of Enoch can be accurately deciphered and disclosed. It is therefore a time when these words of Scripture have come true yet again:

*"No,* ***we speak of God's secret wisdom, a wisdom that has been hidden*** *and that God destined for our glory before time*

## Chapter 3: Why The Pillar of Enoch Was Built

*began.* **None of the rulers of this age understood it,** *for if they had, they would not have crucified the Lord... As it is written: 'No eye has seen... no mind has conceived what God has prepared for those who love him'* **- but God has revealed it to us by his Spirit.** *The Spirit searches... the deep things of God. For who... knows the thoughts of a man except the man's spirit within him?* **In the same way no one knows the thoughts of God except the Spirit of God."**
*- 1 Corinthians 2:7-11 (NIV)*

Born-again believers are the inheritors of this secret or hidden wisdom that is revealed by the Spirit of God. In fact, the last verse of the preceding Scripture makes it clear that it is only through the indwelling power of the Holy Spirit that we can know *"the thoughts of God,"* which is clearly an inference to the main subject of this book series: *the Language of God!* Through the same Spirit, believers can therefore see the secrets locked into the Pillar of Enoch's design far more deeply than anyone who does not have the Holy Spirit to guide them.

From books on the subject of Pyramidology, and through the guidance of the Holy Spirit, it has become clear to me that the Pillar of Enoch has amazing scientific and prophetic import, and it was constructed *before* most of the structures of Ancient Egyptian Civilization rose up around it. Contrary to the ideas of modern archeologists, it also appears that the Great Pyramid was never built as a real tomb. Instead it was always meant to be a figurative tomb representing the coming Messiah who had to die to save us from sin, and be resurrected to give us the gift of everlasting life!

This can be deduced from the fact that, unlike the tombs in the Valley of the Kings and in smaller pyramids built after the Old Kingdom, the Great Pyramid's interior surfaces lack any painted scenes or hieroglyphic inscriptions - outside of a few quarry marks that date the chambers above the King's Chamber to the time of Khufu. Incidentally, if Khufu was Noah, and Noah knew the Great Flood was going to occur, is it possible that Noah may have built the top portion of the Great Pyramid to protect its interior structure from the coming cataclysm?

This curious lack of identifying inscriptions is also true of the Pyramids of Khafre and Menkaure that are aligned with the Great Pyramid at Giza, as well as their counterparts built during the Old Kingdom: the Red and Bent Pyramids at Dahshur and the Step Pyramid of Pharaoh Djoser at Saqqara. All these pyramids are devoid of any telltale decorations or inscriptions stating their purpose. Furthermore, there were no funerary goods of any kind found in these aforementioned pyramids that would indicate that they were meant to be a Pharaoh's dwelling for eternity. In addition, of the few that had sarcophagi, these were found completely empty and devoid of the profuse decoration always associated with the tombs of wealthy Ancient Egyptian notables, especially pharaohs.

The oldest, most expertly engineered, and most massive pyramids in Egypt therefore show no evidence of ever having served as tombs. Instead, these huge stone monuments are virtually anonymous, and devoid of decoration of any kind. As such, **these pyramids clearly seem to invite men to seek their secrets beyond the limitations of art and written language.** Seemingly oblivious to the passage of time, they stand as silent sentinels beckoning to us with their hidden secrets. It truly is as if these pyramids were built as a puzzle to dare humanity to answer their incredible challenge!

The Great Pyramid or Pillar of Enoch is a remarkable stone structure for many reasons. Constructed of millions of megalithic-sized blocks, the Pillar of Enoch has withstood the test of time. It was built to last - not as a tomb for a Pharaoh, but to celebrate the life, death, and resurrection of the King of kings: Yahshua, and to impress others with His incredible greatness. In "The Language of God in History," we explored the idea that *the Pillar of Enoch is a detailed record of the religious and scientific knowledge of a lost civilization* – a civilization that went to great lengths not to be forgotten, and to preserve their knowledge of the Messiah who was destined to come.

## *Piazzi Smyth's Findings Concerning the Great Pyramid*

Is the Great Pyramid a storehouse of secret wisdom that silently asks: "Can you decipher my purpose, and the knowledge that I conceal within my structure?" Though many scientists and archeologists have tried and failed to successfully answer this challenge, a few like Piazzi Smyth (a.k.a. Charles Piazzi Smyth), E. Raymond Capt, and N. W. Hutchings were on the right track because they were viewing the Great Pyramid from a Judeo-Christian perspective.

Due to the controversial nature of his discoveries, Piazzi Smyth's theories regarding the Great Pyramid were soon under attack. It was therefore only a matter of time before someone attempted to prove Smyth wrong. Sir William Flinders Petrie later tried to do just that. Due to his high standing in the academic community, Petrie discredited much of Piazzi Smyth's findings when he found evidence that conflicted with Smyth's observations, and disputed his measurements of the Great

## Chapter 3: Why The Pillar of Enoch Was Built        Page 101

Pyramid. Even though some of Petrie's findings are still hotly disputed, the archeological elite who wanted to promote Evolution dismissed Smyth's findings, and - without doing any further investigation - accepted Petrie's findings as correct. This may be partly why Smyth resigned as Astronomer Royal for Scotland in 1888, after serving in this eminent leadership position among scientists for 43 years (1845-1888).

Deeply dissatisfied with this turn of events, some scholars later went to Egypt and verified that Smyth's measurements were not wrong, but precise and accurate. They showed that Smyth merely used different, more sensible starting points than Petrie for his measurements, and a different base level for measuring the Great Pyramid's base length and height. Unfortunately, however, the clear attempt to discredit the findings of Piazzi Smyth made by W. Flinders Petrie and his colleagues in the academic community worked well. Petrie's findings are now touted as the truth, and Piazzi Smyth's ideas are spurned as the poor scholarship, and sloppy surveying techniques of a religious fanatic.

Since then, many well-educated Christians who are interested in history have followed in Piazzi Smyth's footsteps, and have subsequently found his ideas to be both fascinating and plausible. Unfortunately, these pioneers seeking the truth about the Great Pyramid have all been ridiculed by the religious and archeological establishments of each succeeding era. Like those who have gone before me, I will also likely be labeled a religious fanatic and similarly ridiculed for my beliefs. Indeed, I have already had the dubious honor of being labeled a "pyramidiot" by some in the academic world who believe that Pyramidology is a pseudo science that only an idiot could logically accept. There is a major difference, however, between someone who tries to force their atheistic views on others (i.e. the academic community) and one who attempts to interpret the available evidence from a Biblical perspective.

Secular academic ideas are based on the concepts of humanism and atheism, which state that the biblically defined Creator God doesn't exist, and that mankind is not the most important product of the Universe. However, my views are based on the premise that mankind was created to be like their perfect and infinite Creator God, but have become fallen and finite through their sin and rebellion against God's Law. Furthermore, this same Creator God is actively involved in our world, and left clear messages of His purpose throughout the heavens and the Earth. Using a similar Biblical Worldview as a filter to interpret information, Piazzi Smyth's views on the Great Pyramid become far more than the ranting of a lunatic. Using Smyth's sound ideas and accurate measurements, I believe that the spiritual and scientific riddles that the Great Pyramid at Giza so enigmatically poses can largely be solved.

In upcoming portions of this book, you will learn that the Great Pyramid or Pillar of Enoch shares a godly purpose, and profound message with the Great Sphinx, the Desert Tabernacle, and the Temples of Solomon and Herod. You will also be shown why it is no surprise that the prophet Jeremiah made his startling declaration about Egypt at the beginning of this chapter (Jeremiah 32:20). Furthermore, you will be shown that the spiritual knowledge encoded into the Great Pyramid is a threat to Satan's schemes. If it were not a threat, why have many in our modern academia discredited all Christian views of the Great Pyramid? Furthermore, why have proponents of the New Age Movement and those who believe in aliens or demons gone to such great lengths to appropriate the Great Pyramid to substantiate their false spiritual claims?

Under a smoke screen of lies and deceit, secular humanists, alien enthusiasts, and modern Pagans have perverted nearly every truth about the Great Pyramid and Gospel in the Stars. In many cases the Pagans have done the worst damage, glossing over every truth hidden in the stars, the Bible and the Great Pyramid with a veneer of New Age philosophies supporting such lies as reincarnation, and mankind's innate godhood. It is time for this perversion of Yah's truth to end! Therefore, in this chapter, we will reclaim the Great Pyramid for Yahweh by revealing the Judeo-Christian truths firmly locked into its structure. Piazzi Smyth detected these spiritual and scientific truths within the Great Pyramid's design in the mid 1800's. Though others later embellished upon his theories, Piazzi Smyth's book about the Great Pyramid is still one of the most detailed and accurate of its kind.

## *Not All Sacred Structures in Egypt are "Egyptian"*

Let's begin our re-appropriation of the Great Pyramid, or Pillar of Enoch by placing it in the right time frame. Though historians claim the Great Pyramid was built early in Ancient Egypt's long history, I do not believe idolatrous Pagans built it. I believe it was built by men who knew the true God Yahweh, and wanted to preserve the truth about Him, and the future of mankind that had been shown to them in the constellations of the night sky. In fact, the idolatry, and Pagan philosophy so prevalent in later Ancient Egyptian culture was likely only in its infancy when the Great Pyramid was built. Many people of that time may therefore have still worshipped the True God Yahweh, and honored their Covenant with Him.

## Chapter 3: Why The Pillar of Enoch Was Built

One clear piece of evidence that the Great Pyramid is likely *not* a construction of the idolatrous culture of Ancient Egypt is that this pyramid is completely unadorned. This is patently unlike most Pagan Ancient Egyptian temples and religious structures, which were often copiously carved and painted. There are few exceptions to this rule. Intriguingly, those that do defy the artistic and architectural conventions of Ancient Egypt are the most ancient structures ever found in Egypt. Incidentally, all of these old structures were built with megalithic stone blocks. These are the Osireion near the temple of Seti I at Abydos, the Step Pyramid of Djoser at Saqqara, the Red Pyramid and the Bent Pyramid at Dahshur, and the Valley Temple, Great Sphinx, Great Pyramid and its two smaller companions at Giza - the pyramids of Khafre and Menkaure. **Among these structures, several show a complex construction style unlike anything else so far unearthed in Egypt.** In fact, structures like the Osireion and Valley Temple appear to have much in common with the megalithic stone monuments found elsewhere, like those of Easter Island (i.e. Rapa Nui) in the South Pacific Ocean, and Cuzco and Tiahuanaco in the Andes mountain region of South America.

There is also some interesting evidence supporting an immense age for the Sphinx. It has recently come to light *that the Great Sphinx shows weathering patterns that could only have been formed by rain water* flowing over the Sphinx's back over an extended period of time. However, according to geologists, Egypt has been relatively dry for the past 6000 years. Where then did all the rainwater come from? Personally, I believe that the geological estimate of when Egypt had a rainy climate is incorrect. This rainy period probably occurred much later in time – during the time of the Great Flood in 2347 BC. The heavy precipitation that fell during the yearlong period of the Great Flood, and during the possible Ice Age that followed it are, in all likelihood, the forces that left the telltale marks of water erosion on the Great Sphinx. Though much of the precipitation that fell after the Flood likely came down as snow, it would almost always have fallen as rain in Egypt, which is in the northern sub tropics.

In the case of the Valley Temple, it is obvious that the Ancient Egyptians adopted this far older structure to their own use by placing a veneer of new stone over the older unadorned walls. This was also done on other monuments in Egypt that were falling into ruin when the Egyptians repaired, or refaced them. The Great Sphinx is just one example at Giza that shows repeated stages of repair. Afterward, Egyptian artisans often profusely decorated the new interior and exterior facades on these reclaimed buildings with images of their Pagan deities, and hieroglyphic writings. However, as stated previously, the Great

Pyramid is completely devoid of decoration of any kind. In fact, all five of the Old Kingdom Pyramids at Saqqara, Dahshur, and Giza do not contain any decorative hieroglyphic writings. They are as stark, and unadorned as the Great Pyramid itself.

## Hidden Pyramid Prophecies in Stone

It is extremely interesting that the Pillar of Enoch was never totally re-appropriated by the Egyptians as other structures of its type were. There is some evidence that the Ancient Egyptians may have tampered with this pyramid a little - but only on the exterior. One ancient historian recorded that the Great Pyramid's exterior white casing stones once contained hieroglyphic writings. What hieroglyphic scripts the pyramid was decorated with, or what these writings said can't be determined, however. This is because the casing stones of fine white limestone are now missing - except for a few at the foundation level. Over the last several centuries, Muslim rulers pillaged some of the casing stones to build their palaces and mosques in the nearby city of Cairo. Then a major earthquake in the area caused the remaining casing stones to tumble into ruin at the base of the pyramid. Later, these stones were also removed to build other important buildings in Cairo.

From an archeological point of view, the loss of these casing stones was a terrible tragedy. Nonetheless, their loss turned out to be a blessing in disguise for those scientists who sought to unlock the many secrets of the Great Pyramid. This is because the measure of the core masonry - and *not* the white limestone mantle - reveals some of the measurements that connect the Great Pyramid with Astronomy, our Solar System, and our Earth. For example, the measures for the Sidereal, Tropical and Solar Years found in the Great Pyramid's exterior measurements were not at all evident until the casing stones were removed. This is an amazing fact, for it reveals that the knowledge of the Great Pyramid was meant to remain hidden until recent times.

When Piazzi Smyth explored the Great Pyramid in the 1800's - and claimed it was a prophecy in stone - he was a true pioneer - one who unlocked many mysteries hidden within the Great Pyramid on his own. Smyth was also a dedicated Christian scholar, and the first and greatest Pyramidologist of his time. Through his meticulous research, Smyth was able to correctly decipher many of the encoded secrets in the Great Pyramid's design. But if Smyth had been unable *to look beneath the original surface* of the Great Pyramid, his research wouldn't have been as fruitful. Here again we find a clear allegorical message hidden within the

Great Pyramid. It is as if it were meant to silently tell us: *"You must look beneath the surface of things to find great truth."*

Since losing its casing stones, many truths once hidden in the Great Pyramid have now been brought to light. In this chapter, many of these startling truths that were hidden for thousands of years will be disclosed. Supposing that the Great Pyramid was built in 2500 BC (though it could have been built much earlier), this mountain of stone has withstood the test of time. Once mysterious and full of secrets, this Pillar of Enoch has endured for 4500 years. This fact alone is a powerful testimony to the skill and knowledge of its builders. It has withstood the Great Flood, major earthquakes, and the ravages of pillaging, wind, weather, and time. For these reasons, and many others, this magnificently constructed pyramid deserves our careful scrutiny to determine when, why, and by whom it was built.

## *The Pillar of Enoch's Fivefold Message*

In "The Language of God in History," it was stated that the Pillar of Enoch's design is based on solid geometric principles, and reflects the number five repeatedly in the arithmetic used to calculate its interior and exterior dimensions. Like all pyramids, this pyramid is a five-sided pyramidion shape that has five corners: four at the base, plus the apex. Though the Pillar of Enoch is missing its apex, or capstone, its measurements must be reckoned using its calculated apex point for its secrets to be disclosed.

Looking at this massive pyramid's interior, the number five is found in profusion. For example, the walls of the King's Chamber are five courses high, and its walls are composed of twenty times five stones, totaling exactly 100 stones. The floor of the King's Chamber is ten times five courses from the base, on the 50th level of stone masonry, suggesting a time of Jubilee. Similarly, the floor of the Queen's Chamber is five times five courses from the base, on the 25th level of masonry. In the language of numbers, five is the number that represents the Earth, as well as God's Grace to mankind. Six is the number of mankind, since mankind was created on the sixth "Day." In addition, there are six days of work, and one day of rest in every week, so six represents the labors, or flawed works of mankind. Seven represents spiritual completeness, perfection, and rest, and is therefore Heaven's number. Eight is the number denoting superabundance and eternity. Nine is the number of finality and judgment, and ten is the number of physical perfection and completeness.

The number five is also indicated in the Antechamber, through the raised boss on the granite leaf. This half-circular granite boss - and the granite leaf carved onto it - may be a record of the measurements used throughout the Great Pyramid. This boss is raised up 1.001 inches from the granite leaf it is carved onto. This has been dubbed the Pyramid Inch, or PI, and it appears to be the basic unit of measurement used in the Pillar of Enoch. Uncannily, it is almost identical to the American inch, formerly used also in Great Britain. In addition to showing the Pyramid Inch, the boss is five PI across, and is exactly 25 PI from the east wall of the Antechamber. This shows that the Ancient Egyptian Sacred Cubit used to design the Great Pyramid is five times five Pyramid Inches, or 25 PI, which is equal to 25.025 American inches.

A period of five years is the basic unit used in all Biblical prophetic chronology. Numbers such as 40, 50, 70, 120, 1260, etc. appear in Bible prophecies, and are all multiples of five. This same correlation is found in the Great Pyramid in numbers such as 5 X 72 = 360, or the number of degrees in a circle; in 5 X 504 = 2,520, or seven times 360 degrees; and in 5 X 432 = 2160, the number of years in one twelfth of a Precessional cycle. Interestingly, note that the sum of the digits in every number multiplied by five here equals nine - the number of judgment. As will be shown later in this chapter, the numbers 2,160 and 2,520 are both reflected in the measurements of the Grand Gallery.

Uncannily, there also seems to be five possible reasons why the Pillar of Enoch was built. The Great Pyramid's fivefold message is uncovered when it is viewed as:

6. *An astronomical calendar* revealing spiritually significant dates and many scientific facts about the Earth and the Sun

7. *A technological record* of antediluvian knowledge

8. *A temple and an altar* to Yahweh proclaiming His Glory

9. *A complete testimony* of humanity's sinfulness, and their only Path to Salvation through Christ

10. *A prophecy* regarding the future of the Church, and the End of the world

In this chapter and several others, I will show why I believe that each of these five statements is true about the Pillar of Enoch.

## Chapter 3: Why The Pillar of Enoch Was Built

### *The Great Pyramid's Connections to Astronomy*

First, let me substantiate claim number one - that the Pillar of Enoch is an astronomical calendar revealing spiritually significant dates, and many scientific facts about the Earth, the Moon, and the Sun. However, before this is done, mention needs to be made about the use of Astronomy to date ancient events prior to the Flood. Upon accepting the fact that catastrophic events shaped life on Earth in the past, some people altogether reject the idea that we can still accurately date the past using Astronomy. However, as mentioned earlier, there is clear evidence that past catastrophes did not alter Earth's year, or affect the movements of the stars and planets surrounding it appreciably. In fact, the change in our Solar Year appears to be only 1.242 days longer than the 364-day year of Enoch's time before the Flood. Therefore, with slight variations made to account for this change, Astronomical dating can still be viewed as valid.

Based on my discoveries using Sacred Astronomy, it appears that the 360-degree measure of the Mazzaroth, or Zodiac was used to tell time long before the Great Flood. However, this 360-degree, circular method of time measurement does not measure 360 days, as is commonly supposed. Rather, it measures the length of one Solar year, which measures the time it takes the Sun to transit the 360-degree circle of the Zodiac, or Mazzaroth that surrounds our Earth, which would make it equal to one Tropical Solar Year.

As discussed throughout this book series, especially in Book Three, "The Language of God in History," the Ethiopian Book of 1 Enoch records that Enoch the Sethite was the major proponent of and prophet concerning Sacred Astronomy before the Flood and that he received divine revelations from Yahweh. This is how Enoch learned to decipher the heavenly record in the Zodiac, which he called *"the heavenly tablets."* The Book of Jubilees also mentions the Heavenly Tablets, where *"all the deeds of mankind"* were divinely recorded. Enoch also devoted an entire section of his book to Sacred Astronomy. It is called "The Book of the Heavenly Luminaries," and it contains much astronomical information. Amazingly, this section contains perhaps the only written record of how to construct a simple astronomical observatory called a henge for keeping an accurate calendar (1 Enoch 72:1-37). Due to their possible Enochian origins, ancient henges around the world are discussed at length in Book Three.

In his book, Enoch showed how to mark off different sets of solar co-ordinates on the horizon to create a circular henge observatory over a period of one year (1 Enoch 72:1-37). As discussed in Book One and

Three, it is therefore highly probable that Noah and all of his descendents understood the principles of Sacred Astronomy, and knew how to build a henge, and may have done so wherever they settled. Furthermore, it is fairly certain that these henges were used to keep track of time, and to spy the Signs in the Heavens that reveal the nature of the times on Earth. Interestingly, pyramids are also found all over the world, and also appear to be related to stargazing, and time keeping.

Not surprisingly then, the Bible mentions that both Moses and Elijah constructed altars that may have resembled one of Enoch's henges, and were likely similar to Stonehenge at Salisbury in England. Both Moses and Elijah may have done so by placing twelve *undressed* standing stones either in a line, or circle around an altar. Moses built his altar with twelve stones at the base of Mount Sinai after receiving instructions from God there (Exodus 20:24-25, 24:4), while Elijah built his atop Mount Horeb (1 Kings 18:31-32). Uncannily, the biblical account of Elijah's altar of twelve stones indicates that Elijah dug a trench around it, and this is a peculiar feature of many henges that have been found in the Middle East, Europe, England, and the Americas.

Though the twelve stones used by Moses and Elijah in their altars represented the Twelve Tribes of Israel, these stones also likely represented the zodiacal wheel that Jacob associated with each of his sons, especially Joseph. It is therefore no wonder that many ancient people used a circle with a dot in the center to symbolize the Sun, because it also symbolized the design of the henges they used to track the Sun's movements!

Besides showing that Enoch knew how to keep track of time using Astronomy, 1 Enoch gives us a clue that the Great Pyramid likely had a practical purpose related to Sacred Astronomy - especially if Enoch designed it! In this regard, besides the alignments of the four shafts in the Great Pyramid with four prominent stars, several scholars have noted that the Grand Gallery has a design that would make it ideal for performing astronomical observations over long periods of time. If the Grand Gallery is part of an ancient astronomical observatory, then its uppermost end may have been open to the sky before it was later purposely buried under a veritable mountain of stone. Since the Grand Gallery presently runs north to south, its opening would have faced the southern sky. As discussed in Book Three, "The Language of God in History," this would have made the Grand Gallery ideal for observing the movements of the constellation Orion, which lies southward in the sky. We will discuss the connection of the Great Pyramid's Star Shafts, which point to Orion and other constellations, a bit later.

## Chapter 3: Why The Pillar of Enoch Was Built

Enoch the Sethite was translated around 3016 BC - when he was 365.242 years old. His translation likely left a big impression on his followers, especially if God had shown them what it signified. Since Enoch was a great prophet of Yah, even Enoch's length of years on Earth may have been meant to be a prophecy. The antediluvian ancestors of Enoch who had spiritual discernment would have known this through divine revelation, and been able to determine the Post-Flood length of the Earth's Solar Year. **They also may have seen Enoch's lifespan as a key - in which each year of his life was reduced to the span of one Pyramid Inch, and then used in the construction of the Great Pyramid.** This is why the Great Pyramid is truly the Pillar of Enoch, and why the lengths of its interior passages can prophetically reflect significant years in human history.

As discussed in Book Three, Enoch may have drawn up the plans for the building of the Great Pyramid before he was translated. Because the Book of 1 Enoch tells us that Enoch spent much time in the presence of God's holy angels, and saw many powerful and prophetic visions, Enoch could have received the plans for the Great Pyramid from God, and through the Holy Spirit. If so, after he was translated, Enoch's lifespan may have been incorporated into this Covenant pillar, or pyramid's design by Enoch's righteous ancestors as a way of showing who designed it, and why. They would also have inadvertently made sure that the mathematical, and calendrical measurements used in the Great Pyramid appeared to utilize the Post-Flood length of the Solar Year.

The facts proving that the Great Pyramid is a type of calendar are both startling, and impressive. For instance, the 365.242 days in our current Tropical Solar Year is shown in the measure of any of the Great Pyramid's four sides at the base. Each base length at socket level measures 365.242 Sacred Cubits. In addition, 365.242 x 4 = 1460.968, which is the number of Sacred Cubits in one circuit of the pyramid's base. If we multiply 1460.968 by 25, we get 36,525. This is the number of Pyramid Inches in the base circuit, and the number of days in one century! As already mentioned, the Sacred Cubit is divided into 25 equal segments that are approximately 1.001 British Inches long.

Since the standard unit of measurement once used in the United Kingdom, and still used in the United States is very close to the basic Pyramid Inch used to build the Great Pyramid, this suggests that England somehow adopted Ancient Egypt's earliest system of measurement. British Israelites like Piazzi Smyth saw this point as a partial verification for the idea that the people of the British Isles are descendents of the Israelite Tribe of Joseph, or more specifically Joseph's sons Ephraim and

Manasseh. Though it does not necessarily prove this, it does suggest that both Ancient Egyptians and Ancient Israelites once found their way to Great Britain's shores in the far past. The controversial subject of British Israelism is fully covered in Book Three, and broached again here briefly in Chapter Seven.

The Great Pyramid's shape and design is also tied to the patriarch Joseph in several ways. First of all, as was shown in Book Two, the constellation of Orion is allegorically tied to Joseph, and Orion is also tied directly to the Great Pyramid. Furthermore, though the Great Pyramid is in Egypt, it was designed and built by Joseph's spiritual and literal ancestors: the Sethites. This is suggestive of the fact that Joseph also was not Egyptian, though he resided in Egypt, and was even buried there until the Exodus. Also interesting to note is that, during Joseph's reign as Vizier in Egypt, he married Asenath, the Egyptian daughter of a priest of On. Both of Joseph's sons were therefore half Egyptian, and were probably very familiar with the city of On in Lower Egypt (Genesis 41:45). On was also known as Heliopolis (i.e. "City of the Sun"), and it was the cult center of the Ancient Egyptian Sun god Amun-Ra. Is it therefore only a coincidence that Amun-Ra was associated with the Sun, and served as one of Egypt's creator gods, just as Yahweh is the one and only Creator God, and is allegorically associated with the Sun in our local Solar System?

Uncannily, the Egyptian word "On" means "stone" or "stone pillar". The ben-ben stone of the Ancient Egyptians was a pyramid-shaped object that rested on a pillar, and was intimately associated with the Sun god Amun-Ra. In this chapter, the Great Pyramid will also be shown to be a stone pillar associated with a deity - namely the Son of God, Yahshua! Could the Pillar of Enoch's missing capstone be the mysterious ben-ben stone that was once housed in a temple in On? Furthermore, could Joseph have known that the ben-ben stone, and the Pillar of Enoch it was connected to, are both symbols for the Messiah that the God of his own people promised to send in the Gospel in the Stars? Only Yahweh knows for sure! However, the time that the Israelites spent in Egypt leaves room for some other interesting possibilities.

Some Biblical scholars believe that the Israelites adopted the Egyptian Sacred Cubit during their sojourn in Egypt. Joseph was an Israelite who, like Moses, was schooled in Ancient Egyptian wisdom. Both of them could therefore have adopted the Sacred Cubit of the Egyptians as the sacred unit of measurement used in Ancient Israel. In fact, this Egyptian standard of measurement would have been very familiar to the Israelites. This is because, during the last one hundred

## Chapter 3: Why The Pillar of Enoch Was Built

years or so of their 400-year long sojourn in Egypt, the once proud Israelites were reduced to slavery, and forced to build many monuments for the Egyptian pharaoh. As a result, the sacred Egyptian cubit of twenty-five Pyramid Inches may have been used to construct both the Desert Tabernacle, and the Ark of the Covenant. This supposition will be explored more fully in Chapter Five.

Many astronomical facts are encoded into the measurements found within the Great Pyramid. For instance, the Great Pyramid's degree of slope from base to apex indicates a factor of ten to the ninth power. This is intimated by the fact that, for every ten feet one travels up any side of the pyramid toward the apex, a height of nine feet is covered. The Great Pyramid's height from the center of the base to the apex is 5813 PI, or about 485 feet, and 485 feet is equal to .091856 of a mile. Multiplying this figure by ten to the ninth power (or 1000 million miles), we get 91,856,000 miles, which is very close to the modern estimate of the mean radius of the Earth's orbit around the Sun - also known as the mean distance of the Earth from the Sun, or Astronomical Unit (AU).

The design of the Great Pyramid also shows an approximation of the Earth's mean distance from the Moon, which is currently believed to be 238,865 miles. It is found by using the Jubilee Passage, which is fully discussed in Chapter Four. The length of the Jubilee Passage is 215.9730 Pyramid Inches, or one seventh of the length of the Horizontal Passage leading to the Queen's Chamber. Placing its length in PI into the following equation, we get: 215.9730 PI X 7 X 10**7 = 1511.811 PI X 10**7 = 1,511,811 PI, which is equivalent to 238,344 miles.

Interestingly, scientists have discovered that the Moon is slowly moving *away* from the Earth, which means that it was closer to the Earth in ancient times. Furthermore, though the Moon's rate of movement away from the Earth is quite small today, it may have been much greater right after the Great Flood. In fact, the Moon's movement away from the Earth may have been *caused* by that same cataclysm! This may explain partly why the mean distance between the Earth and the Moon calculated in the Great Pyramid is smaller than its mean distance today.

The Great Pyramid also shows the length of the full cycle for the Precession of the Equinoxes. This is found in several places. It is found on the exterior by measuring the perimeter of the 35th course of blocks in the Great Pyramid, which is the thickest course of blocks among the entire 203 courses in the pyramid. This 35th course is two Sacred Cubits, or two courses in height. In this respect, it mimics the stone block above the door of the King's Chamber, which is the only stone visible in the interior that is two courses high. When dissected diagonally, this chamber block forms a 3-4-5 Right Triangle. The perimeter of the Great Pyramid's 35th course is 25,827 PI (where PI = Pyramid Inches). This is close to the 25,920 years in a Precessional cycle.

When the white limestone casing was still intact, the 35th course's measurement in Pyramid Inches would likely have precisely equaled one Precessional cycle. The sum of the Great Pyramid's two base diagonals in Pyramid Inches also equals 25,827. Again, with the casing stones figured in, this sum would have been greater. Inside the Great Pyramid, the cycle of Precession can be found by measuring the distance between the ceiling of the King's Chamber and the apex of the pyramid. This measure of 4110.5 PI is the radius of a circle whose circumference equals the approximate length of the Precession of the Equinoxes: 4110.5 X 2 X Pi (or $\pi$, which is approximately 3.1416) = 25,827.

The length of Earth's Tropical or Solar Year is found in several places in the Great Pyramid. For example, the pyramid's base side length at socket level is 9131 PI, and 9131 PI/25 = 365.24 Sacred Cubits. It can also be found by taking the whole perimeter of the base in Pyramid Inches, and dividing it by 100: (9131 PI X 4) / 100 = 365.24. In the King's Chamber, the Solar Year can be found by first finding the solid diagonal length of the King's Chamber (51.516461), which is also equal to the degree of slope used for the pyramid's sides. Then, taking the length of the Grand Gallery and finding its ratio to the solid diagonal of the King's Chamber and multiplying it by 100, we get: (1881.598/51.516) X 100 = 365.242. The length of the Antechamber leading into the King's Chamber, when used as the diameter of a circle produces a circle with a circumference of 365.242. Finally, the length of the Antechamber to the King's Chamber times Pi (116.26471 PI X 3.14159) nearly equals the length of a sidereal year, or 365.25636.

As already suggested, this reflection of the current Solar Year in the Great Pyramid may be a fluke in that the antediluvian prophet Enoch lived 365.24 years, and the Great Pyramid was likely partly designed by him, and his ancestors. If so, their design naturally would have reflected clues identifying both the designers, and the knowledge that Enoch and his ancestors were given by God. This seems plausible because the Book of 1 Enoch tells us that the length of the antediluvian Solar Year was 364 days, or 1.242 days shorter than our current Solar Year (1 Enoch 74:11).

In addition to these facts that irrevocably tie the Great Pyramid to Astronomy, its overall exterior design is meant to represent one Hemisphere of our Earth, as was shown in Book Three, and will be partly re-examined a bit later. In addition, the inside measurements of the King's Chamber are connected to the Sun, and those in the Queen's

# Chapter 3: Why The Pillar of Enoch Was Built

Chamber are connected to the Moon. In fact, as will be shown in upcoming portions of this book, the location of the Great Pyramid just outside of Cairo, Egypt serves as the ideal geographical center for cartography. In addition, the Great Pyramid itself serves as a positional record of Earth's location in the Universe - both in relation to its closest celestial neighbor: the Moon - and the main source of its ability to sustain life: the Sun. All of these facts, when viewed together, make the idea that the Great Pyramid may have served as a sophisticated celestial observatory at one time seem highly probable. See Book Three on History to find out even more about the meaning of the Great Pyramid's geographical and astronomical situation.

## *Advanced Geometry and Math in the Pillar of Enoch*

Some of the above calculations indicate that ***the Pillar of Enoch is the only pyramid in all of Egypt to show that its builders understood the value of Pi***, which is the ratio of the circumference of a circle to its diameter. In the 1850's, it was first discovered that the Pi ratio was used in determining the size of the Pillar of Enoch. For instance, the first explorers to measure the original height of this massive pyramid (measured through its center) found that it was to its base perimeter what the radius is to the circumference of a circle! In other words, ***when the radius of a circle equals the height of the Pillar of Enoch, then the circumference of that circle equals that pyramid's square base perimeter.***

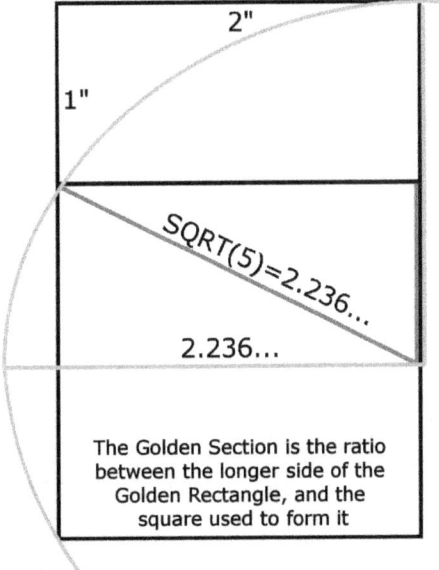

Golden Rectangle
derived from a circle
drawn with the diagonal
of a 1" X 2" Rectangle

The Golden Section is the ratio between the longer side of the Golden Rectangle, and the square used to form it

The vertical height of the Great Pyramid (taken from the base socket level to where the apex would have been if the capstone were present) is approximately 5,813 Pyramid Inches, or 232.52 Sacred Cubits. If twice the length of the base is divided by the height (2 X 365.242 / 232.52), we get 3.14159 - the approximate value of Pi ($\pi$)! Taking two times the height of the pyramid times Pi ((2 X 5,813.24) X 3.14) will give a figure close to the perimeter of its base, which is 4 X 9131 PI = 36,524 Pyramid Inches.

Besides this remarkable incidence of Pi, another advanced geometric concept is shown within the Great Pyramid's construction. Each of the four sides of the Great Pyramid forms an isosceles triangle. If a line is drawn from the apex of the Great Pyramid down one outer side to the base, this line is known as the apothem and cuts an isosceles triangle into two equal but opposite right triangles. When another line is extended from the apex to the center of the foundation of the Great Pyramid, and from the foundation center to the middle of the base perimeter, another triangle is formed. This is one half of the cross section of the Great Pyramid, and forms a right triangle with the special apothem to base side ratio of 1.618... - an irrational number known as the Golden Ratio Phi (not to be confused with Pi, which is approximately 3.1416).

Taking the sum of the length of the diagonal of a 1 X 2 rectangle (which is the square root of 5, or SQRT(5)) plus the short side of the rectangle divided by the long side of the rectangle will give us the value of Phi. This can be expressed using the equation (SQRT(5) + 1)/2. In addition, it has been mathematically proven that the use of Pi, the Golden Section, and the Golden Ratio Phi were used in the design of the King's Chamber.

The Golden Ratio or Golden Section is an irrational fraction that is derived geometrically: First, a line is drawn from the center of one side of a perfect square to one of its corners. Using this line as the radius of a circle with the midpoint of the square's side as the center of the circle, the resulting arc can be used to create a Golden Rectangle – one side of which forms the Golden Ratio. The Golden Ratio can also be found by finding the ratio of the length of one side of a Golden Rectangle with the length of one side of the square used to create the Golden Rectangle.

The Golden Spiral is another proportion used in Geometry that can be approximated with a Fibonacci Spiral. The Fibonacci Spiral shown on this page was made by drawing a quarter circle into a perfect square formed

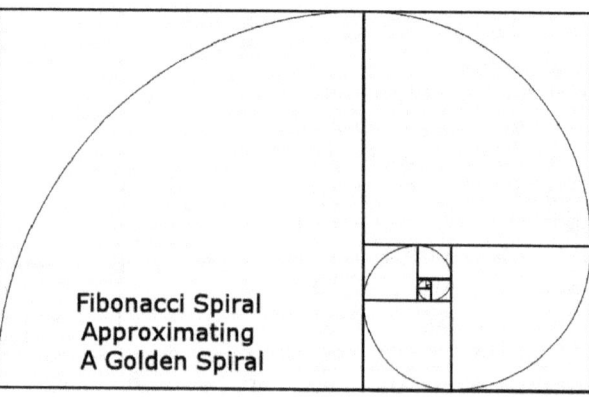

Fibonacci Spiral Approximating A Golden Spiral

## Chapter 3: Why The Pillar of Enoch Was Built

inside a Golden Rectangle, that is nested within another Golden Rectangle, square, and spiral, into still another - in logarithmic increments downward and outward, and in a potentially infinite spiral. The quarter circles are tangent to the interior of each square, and approximate the proportions of a true Golden Spiral, which is found using a logarithmic math equation. The Golden Spiral is found everywhere in nature, and gives us a glimpse of how complex, orderly, and precise everything God created is - on virtually every level.

Since these advanced geometric concepts were used by Yahshua when He created the Universe, it is no surprise that they are found used everywhere in the design of the Pillar of Enoch. As already stated, it is highly likely that Yahweh gave the plans for the Great Pyramid to Enoch, and his Sethite kin built this sacred Covenant Pillar following God's design. It is my belief that, for the Sethites to build this monument effectively, they had to understand the design concepts that God employed. This means that they knew about all of the advanced geometric elements and scientific facts encoded within the Pillar of Enoch, and they knew how to apply them thousands of years before the Greeks!

It is assumed that the Ancient Greeks discovered Pi, the Golden Rectangle, and the Golden Ratio around 1500 BC, which was at least a thousand years *after* the Great Pyramid's suspected completion date in 2500 BC. Intriguingly, all of these unique geometric ratios can only be derived when a pyramid has the Great Pyramid's height, and unique side slope angle measurement of 51 degrees, 51 minutes - approximately 52 degrees. No other pyramid among the hundreds found in Egypt contains this unique height to angle relationship, or shows this use of the Pythagorean Theorem, Pi, the Golden Ratio Phi, or the Golden Spiral.

The Pythagorean Theorem shows the relationship of the sides of a 3-4-5 right triangle. 3-4-5 right triangles are found twice in the King's Chamber. One is found in its overall dimensions, and the other is found in the enormous stone over the entrance to the King's Chamber. This chamber's length is 412 inches, the east wall diagonal is 309 inches, and the long central diagonal from either lower corner of the east wall to the opposite top corner of the King's Chamber is 515 inches. These measurements form a very large triangle with the same ratio as a 3-4-5 right triangle. Secondly, the stone over the entrance of the King's Chamber is the only stone in its walls that is two courses high, with an estimated weight of over 30 tons. The measurements of this stone's sides and central angle of 124 inches wide (124/4 = 31), by 93 inches high (93/3

= 31), by 155 inches on the diagonal (155/5 = 31) also represents a 3-4-5 Pythagorean relationship.

The remarkable stone over the entrance to the King's Chamber is visible on the Antechamber side - where it is carved with four parallel, concave grooves. Approximating one half of a tubular shape, these grooves appear to be an allegorical representation for four pillars. As will be shown in Chapter Four, these grooves may correlate with the four pillars that held up the veil separating the Holy Place from the Most Holy Place in the Desert Tabernacle, and the later Temple of Solomon.

In addition to their knowledge of the 3-4-5 right triangle, and the Golden Ratio Phi, the Great Pyramid's builders knew of Pi, which is found in the unique geometric proportions of circles and spheres. **What the use of Pi in the Great Pyramid implies is that this pyramid is meant to represent a spherical shape.** Only a pyramidion shape with the same general proportions of the Great Pyramid can serve as the geometric solution to the complex problems of squaring a circle, and cubing half of a sphere. As will be shown in upcoming portions of this book, the Great Pyramid appears to have been designed to represent not just one, but several spheres. Furthermore, these spheres are celestial in nature, and actually appear to mathematically show Earth's position in outer space!

## *Sacred Geometry: the Mathematical Code of Creation*

Having explored just a sampling of the many fascinating geometric and mathematical relationships to be found in the Great Pyramid, what does all this advanced knowledge of complex science and math tell us about the builders of the Great Pyramid? First of all, it clearly conveys the idea that its ancient builders were far more intelligent than many modern scientists would care to admit. Furthermore, *it implies that the builders knew that every divinely created thing on this planet we occupy in space has a geometric and mathematical basis for its existence!*

In other words, our remote ancestors knew that an intelligent, advanced, logical, and fully scientific design permeates every molecule and cell in the Universe. Furthermore, they knew from their own experiments that this evidence of intelligent design that permeates everything in creation could only come into existence with the aid of an intelligent, rational designer. They thereby likely concluded that an Intelligent Being far greater than themselves constructed every living thing, as well as the Universe and the Earth we inhabit!

## Map - Giza: Navel of the World

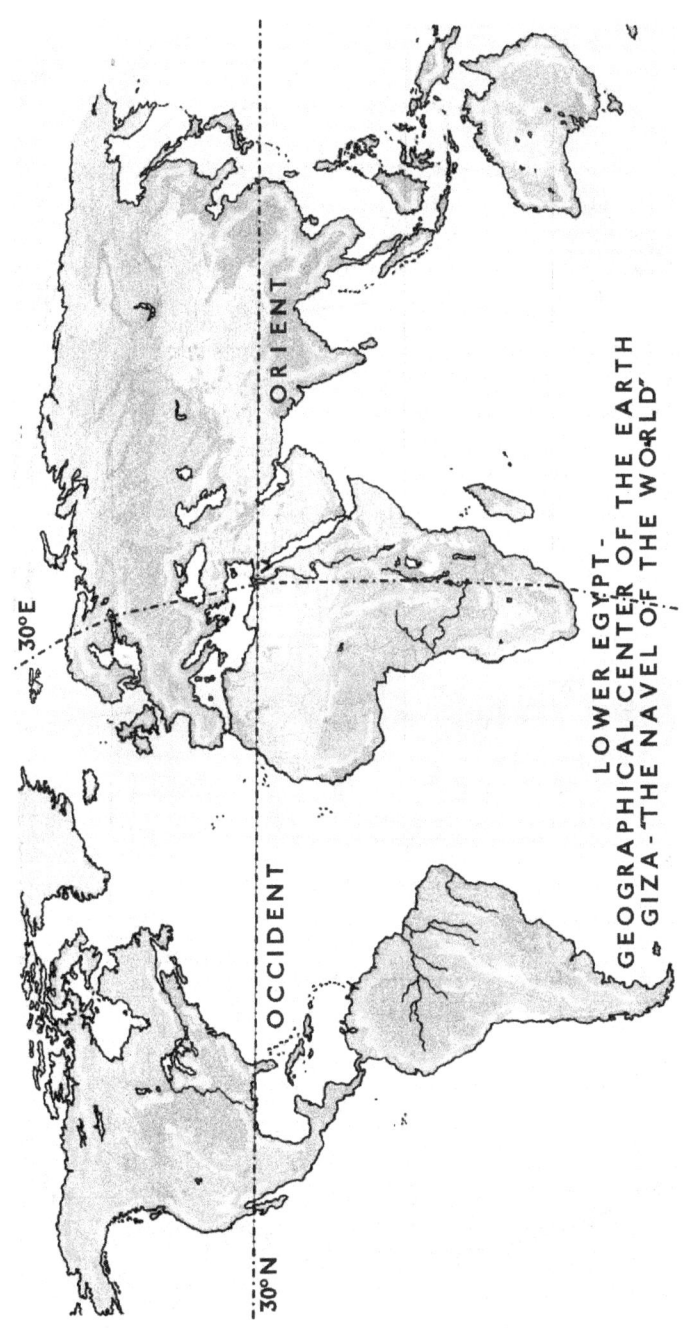

This concept is what defines both Sacred Geometry, and Sacred Astronomy, which are sciences that can work in tandem to uncover the mathematical and geometric blueprints that our Creator used to produce everything we can see, touch, hear, and feel. There is also evidence that - far in the past - these sciences were used in tandem to create a grid pattern on the Earth that correlated with a grid pattern of coordinates in the sky. This geographical grid that spanned the globe was similar to our modern longitudinal and latitudinal grid system. Likewise, we have a celestial grid system that mirrors the earthly one, and which is used to cite location and direction at sea, as well as in modern astronomy, surveying, and cartography.

In regard to map-making, Giza, and its most prominent architectural feature - the Great Pyramid - were both once known as "The Navel of the World," probably because they are located in an ideal place to center maps around. The word "Giza" is an Arabic word that means, "border." In ancient times, Egypt was divided into two sections called Upper Egypt in the south, and Lower Egypt in the northern Delta region. The dividing line between them was located at Giza. The Great Pyramid at Giza and its two smaller companions therefore may have served as a visual marker dividing the two halves of Egypt. As far as arable land area, Giza is also in the heart of Egypt.

Giza has another peculiarity in relation to the whole Earth. When viewed on an equal surface projection map, Egypt lies in the geographical middle between the Eastern Hemisphere, or Orient, and the Western Hemisphere, or Occident. In addition, the Great Pyramid's north-south longitudinal meridian is 30 degrees east of Greenwich, and it also falls on the 30th north parallel. This gives the site of the Great Pyramid another important distinction. The meridian and parallel at Giza dissect more land, and less water than any other positions on Earth. Giza is therefore the true geographical center of the world's landmasses. **This is likely one reason why Giza was once known as the "navel of the world."** In Book Three "The Language of God in History," even more compelling reasons for this designation for Giza are shown that discuss its connection to the Stonehenge monument in England.

As shown in the illustration on page 117, **Giza is the natural zero meridian of the Earth.** As such, Giza would serve as a far better zero meridian point than the one currently in use, which is Greenwich, England. This is probably why some ancient maps used the vicinity of Cairo, Egypt as the center point for their cartographic drawings of the Earth's geographical features. By truly being in the *"the heart of Egypt, at its border,"* the Great Pyramid fulfills one condition of Isaiah's prophecy.

## Chapter 3: Why The Pillar of Enoch Was Built

The prophecy of Isaiah also says that this place must serve as an altar. We therefore need to ask: "Was the Great Pyramid meant to serve as an altar?" Besides the evidence already shown in Book Three, "The Language of God in History," This book will present much compelling evidence that this specific pyramid was designed to serve a more sacred function than any other pyramid built anywhere else on Earth.

Because of the use of Pi in its construction, the Great Pyramid appears to have served as the perfect zero meridian, as well as a workable solution for the squaring of a circle. Using simple mathematics, it can be shown that *the Great Pyramid was likely designed to represent several spherical celestial bodies, including our own planet Earth*. This is one of the most remarkable facts about it. Here is how this pyramid's relationship to the Earth was mathematically proven:

First of all, each base side length of the Great Pyramid equals 9131 PI, and 9131 X 4 = 36524 PI, which is the perimeter of the pyramid's base. The perimeter of its base is 1:43200 of the Earth's equatorial circumference, which is about 24902 miles. The height of the Great Pyramid is 485 feet, which is 1:43200 of the polar radius (distance from the core to the north pole) of the Earth, which is 3949.921 miles. Incidentally, the number 43,200 is one of a series of numbers found in this pyramid that represents the Precession of the Equinoxes - a phenomenon peculiar to the Earth alone in our Solar System.

Secondly, British explorer Piazzi Smyth discovered that each side of the Great Pyramid is slightly concave - curving inward to a depth of three feet at the middle on all four sides. Later, he discovered that this curvature is a representation of the exact curvature of the Earth at the equator! This suggests that *each of the Great Pyramid's sides represents one quarter of the Earth's surface area in either the Northern or Southern Hemisphere*.

This supposition is further supported by the fact that the basic measurement used throughout the Great Pyramid - the Sacred Cubit - is very close to one ten millionth of the mean polar radius of the Earth, or one ten millionth of 3949.9 miles. Now there are 5,280 feet in a mile, and 3949.9 X 5280 = 20,855,472. If we multiply this figure by 12, we get: 250,265,664: the number of inches in the mean radius of the Earth. Since one Pyramid Inch is 1.0011 of a British Inch, we find that the radius of the Earth from its center at the equator to either pole is equivalent to 250,000,000 Pyramid Inches, or *10 Million Sacred Cubits*. This suggests that *the Great Pyramid is a ten-millionth-scale representation of the Northern Hemisphere of the Earth!* To better understand these ties between the Earth and the Great Pyramid, here is an illustration that depicts them:

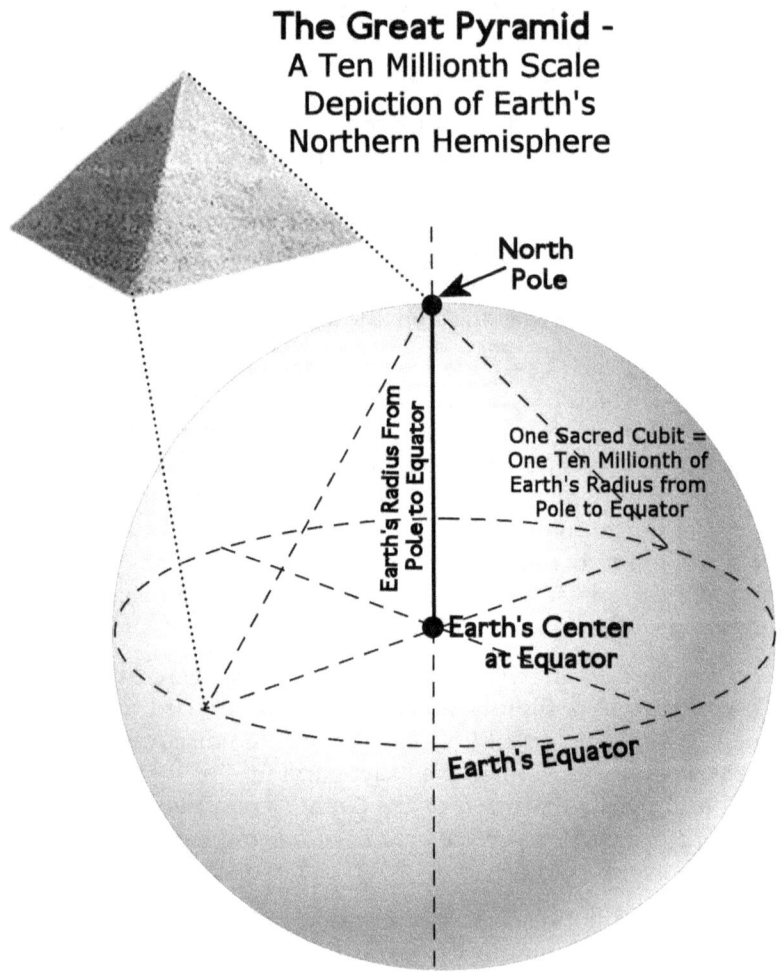

Just as startling is the fact that the Great Pyramid's dimensions represent several different spherical shapes besides our Earth. As partly shown in this book, and elaborated upon in "The Language of God in History," the Sun and Moon are also clearly alluded to in the Great Pyramid. This is partly shown in the Jubilee Passage leading into the Queen's Chamber, which represents the Moon's mean distance from the Earth, and in the height of the Great Pyramid, which shows Earth's mean distance from the Sun.

## Chapter 3: Why The Pillar of Enoch Was Built

The Queen's Chamber itself appears to represent the Moon - since the number of days in the Moon's synodic month can be found by using a complex calculation. First, the Unit Dimension or "UD" of the Queen's Chamber needs to be found. This is 92.173077 PI. Placing this figure into the following equation: 10 X UD = 10 X PI X SM − 6, where SM stands for the number of days in a synodic month, and the 6 represents "man's number" in prophecy. Thus we have: 921.73077 = 10 X 3.14159 X SM − 6. The SM or Synodic Month therefore equals 29.5305882 days, or 29 days, 12 hours, 44 minutes, and 2.76 seconds.

As will be shown a bit later, the King's Chamber, and the base of the Coffer in the King's Chamber both represent the Sun. Coupled with the knowledge that the Queen's Chamber signifies the Moon, they appear to have much allegorical religious significance. This is because the Sun symbolically represents Yahweh, and by extension, Yahshua. In addition, the Moon allegorically represents both Satan, and fallen mankind. However, the Moon also depicts the hope and joy given to the saved through spiritual baptism and rebirth in the Holy Spirit! Since a Full Moon can symbolize the affects of the Holy Spirit on a born-again believer, it seems fitting that the Moon is tied to the Queen's Chamber, with its allegorical message of resurrection and new life in Christ.

As is shown in "The Language of God in History," the Moon also symbolizes the Virgin Miriam, and is connected to the Great Pyramid through the measurements of a circle whose radius is the length of the Nile Delta from its base at Giza, to its culmination on the shore of the Mediterranean Sea. In addition, the Great Pyramid's missing capstone signifies the resurrected Christ - who was conceived as *"God With Us"* and *"the Light of the World"* in Miriam's womb. Indeed, the missing capstone also appears to signify the True Church in the Holy Spirit's allegorical womb, and that same Church's Rapture into Heaven before God's Wrath is poured out during the Great Tribulation.

## Chapter 4: The Pillar of Enoch's Amazing Prophetic Design

*"As in the days when you came out of the land of Egypt, I will show them wonders." - Micah 7:15*

In addition to the startling mathematical, geometric, and technological facts about the Pillar of Enoch, or Great Pyramid revealed in the last chapter, Arab legends say that the Pillar of Enoch recorded important events from both the past, and the future. Those who broke into the Great Pyramid in the past hoping to find these written records, however, were sorely disappointed. There isn't one spot of writing or carving inside the passages of the Pillar of Enoch. Where then were these wondrous records located? Did someone remove them in ages past, or were they recorded in an unfamiliar way? Did tomb robbers break in and steal everything of real value long before the present day? Or are there as yet undiscovered passages or chambers inside the Pillar of Enoch filled with treasure and/or writings?

Though there may be hidden chambers in the Great Pyramid that have eluded archeologists for the past century, it is my belief that, if any more passages or chambers are found, they will also prove to be as empty, and devoid of inscriptions as the existing ones are today. Along with others, I believe that **the true treasure in the Pillar of Enoch is the wisdom encoded into its design.** In effect, I believe that this prophetic knowledge was not written, but was always meant to be mathematically and metaphorically discerned.

For instance, some scholars have found that, when measuring the Great Pyramid's interior passages in Pyramid Inches (PI), a startling prophetic time line is revealed, which we will discuss in Chapter Eight. In addition to the prophetic dateline encoded in its measurements, the Great Pyramid's interior passages allegorically tell us much about our spiritual journey toward our everlasting union with Yahweh. This chapter is an overview of the spiritual metaphors locked into the interior design of the Pillar of Enoch.

The entrance to the Great Pyramid was once hidden behind a huge hinged stone, which is now missing. Instead, a huge cavern now exists around the Great Pyramid's entrance on the nineteenth course. Amazingly, the two giant stones visible over the entrance weigh at least thirty tons, yet few people stop to contemplate how these massive stones were hauled up to such a great height above the surrounding plateau. This is just one of several places inside the Great Pyramid where stones of equal or even greater mass have been utilized high above the pyramid's base. This is certainly an almost impossible engineering feat even today, yet archeologists claim that *primitive people* living over 3500 years ago supposedly managed to do this using *Stone Age tools!* As already mentioned, however, there are many reasons to believe that the accepted archeological views of who built the Pillar of Enoch, and why are based on faulty reasoning, and are therefore false.

### *The Pillar of Enoch's Entrance: A Symbol For Death*

The entrance to the Pillar of Enoch is deceptively unremarkable. Despite its seemingly modest form, however, the entrance serves to convey hidden knowledge - just as every interior and exterior feature of the Pillar of Enoch was designed to do. First of all, the entrance is narrow, conveying the idea that the path ahead is difficult to endure. Furthermore, the entrance immediately leads to a dark, seemingly endless passage that is sloped steeply downward. This conveys the idea that the path ahead is treacherous and uncertain. One false step in this passage, and a person will slide down to the bottom - possibly sustaining serious injury! Secondly, the entrance is on the nineteenth course of masonry, and nineteen is a number associated with death. This is because the Moon causes a set pattern of Solar eclipses to recur every nineteen years - and an eclipse of the Sun is an allegory for death and evil.

Though the Great Pyramid never likely served as a real tomb, it is definitely a symbolic one. First of all, since its passages are totally cut off from the light of the Sun, the Great Pyramid suggests that the people who it was built to teach were *spiritually* blind, and in spiritual darkness until they attained the enlightenment indicated by the Queen's Chamber, Grand Gallery, and King's Chamber. Secondly, Isaiah 19:19 suggests that the Great Pyramid has, and will again one day serve as a symbolic altar, which is a place where innocent animals met their deaths to pay for the sins of others - especially in a Judeo-Christian context. We will discuss both of these possibilities in Chapter Five.

## The Subterranean Chamber: A Symbol for Hell

From the natural entrance into the Great Pyramid on its north side, a cramped passageway slopes downward. When viewed allegorically, this Descending Passageway is full of symbols depicting mankind's downward journey toward Hell. This can be seen in the steep and slippery slope of the Descending Passage, as well as its narrow dimensions. Since this passage and the Ascending Passage are both barely three and a half feet high, anyone motivated to explore the inside of the Great Pyramid is forced to stoop over. This graphically depicts an unregenerated, sinful person's inability to walk upright before Yahweh. Though the Bible asks people to walk uprightly, most can't because of their sin natures. Thankfully, however, some people are able to walk upright, or be righteous because they have the Holy Spirit to help them. But they are often the exception, and not the rule.

The odd chamber at the end of the Descending Passage depicts the destination of those who fail to repent, and who therefore never learn to walk in righteousness. They are the ones bound for Hell, which is artfully depicted in the Subterranean Chamber. This chamber is deep below the surface of the Giza Plateau, and it has a rough, unfinished floor with a deep vertical pit in its center. Another seemingly pointless horizontal shaft extends beyond this pit, and it also leads to a dead end.

Some scholars have proposed that the Subterranean Chamber's floor is unfinished because its architects never completed the Great Pyramid, or decided to change the burial chamber's location after construction was well underway.

However, because the Great Pyramid shows every sign of being fully constructed, the chamber's uneven flooring was probably left that way deliberately. If so, should the Descending Passage, and the strange chamber it leads to be viewed as allegories that mean: "this downward path leads to nothingness?" This bizarre chamber's severely lopsided, treacherously slippery floor and deep vertical and horizontal shafts leading to nowhere appear to artfully represent the abyss - a bottomless pit that Satan and his followers will be cast into at the end of time!

## Interior Layout of the Great Pyramid

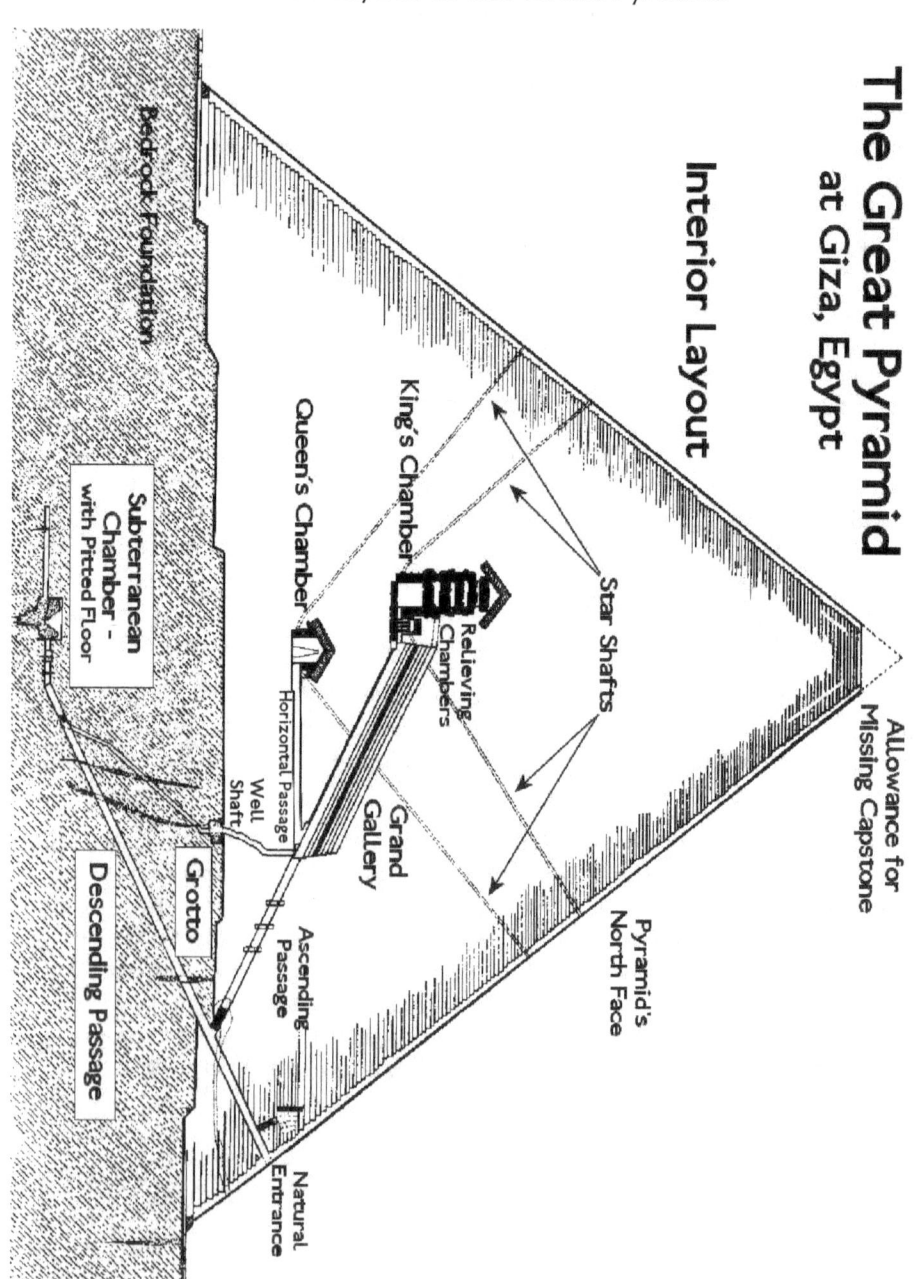

# Ch. 4: The Pillar of Enoch's Amazing Prophetic Design   Page 127

## Prophetic Numbers in the Great Pyramid's Design

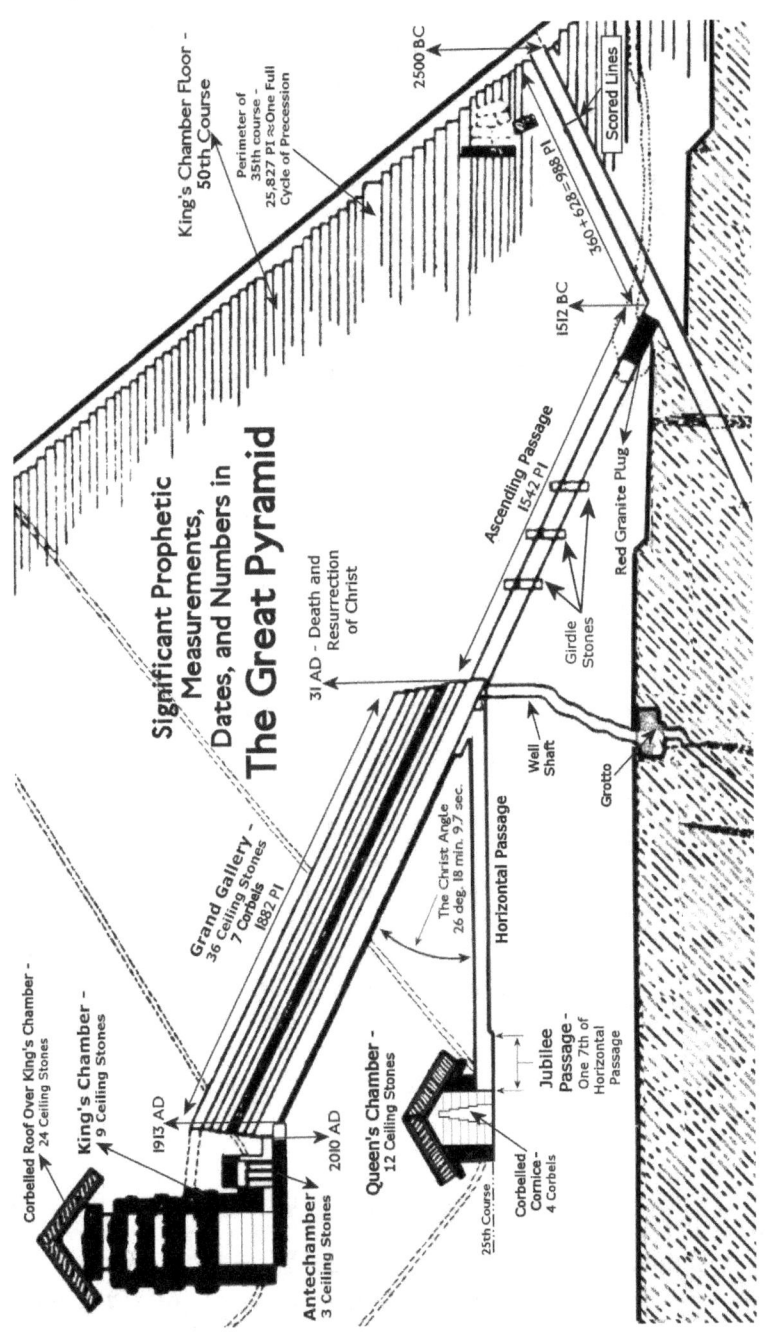

## The Lamb's Grotto and the Ascending Passages

Partway down the Descending Passage, a huge red granite plug blocks the entrance to the ascending fork. This thick, virtually impenetrable granite plug blocks the way to the Queen's Chamber at the center of the Great Pyramid, and the magnificent Grand Gallery and King's Chamber further up. Though once filled with rubble, the Ascending Passage is now clear of debris except for the granite plug. Along its ascending course, this passage has three curious design features that have been dubbed the Girdle Stones. These three sets of Girdle Stones are stones that the passage has been cut through, so they form a vertical ring around the passage. This is extremely odd, especially since the remaining blocks used in this passageway are set at the same angle as its slope. Since these are prominent design features, the Girdle Stones may represent three relatively equidistant and memorable political and spiritual events in Israelite history.

Since this blocked Ascending Passage symbolically leads away from the pit of Hell, and toward the light of God, it may represent the Old Testament Law, specifically *before* the coming of the Holy Spirit into all believers as a free gift of faith. The free giving of the Holy Spirit to all who believe occurred only after Yahshua's death and resurrection. The Ascending Passage therefore marks the time period when all people were judged by their works instead of their faith. The Israelites were burdened under the curse of the Mosaic Law at this time, and the Law proved impossible for ordinary men and women to keep.

The impassable plug at the mouth of the Ascending Passage represents our separation from God due to sin. The only way into the Ascending Passage at one time was through the Well Shaft. This uneven tunnel that leads to the beginning of the Grand Gallery contains a natural grotto that was found in the bedrock of the Great Pyramid's construction site. Inside the Grotto, a natural stone abutment can be seen that resembles the head of a *lamb*. Many have seen this naturally occurring lamb's head in stone as an image for the redemption of Christ, who is the Lamb of God. Furthermore, they see the Well Shaft as a representation of Yahshua as the *only* way of escape from the pit of Hell, and the curse of the Law.

The first half of the Well Shaft that reaches the Grotto is like the Ascending Passage leading to the Grand Gallery in that both represent the Old Testament Law, and the teachings on which Judaism was founded. ***One could never achieve righteousness by following the Law*** (Romans 9:31-33, 10:1-3; Philippians 3:6-9; 2 Timothy 1:9; Titus 3:5).

## Ch. 4: The Pillar of Enoch's Amazing Prophetic Design

Likewise, the spiritual awakening and renewal that is found through life in the Holy Spirit was virtually unattainable through the old dispensation. The Law was therefore a curse. Only the sacrifice of innocent animals kept all the Israelites from going to Hell, for none of them were able to keep the Law perfectly.

Those that sincerely repent of their sins are represented by the Grotto itself, which signifies salvation through the blood atonement ritual. Those who reached the level of the Grotto awaited the perfect sacrifice for sin represented by the lamb's head in stone: Yahshua - the Lamb of God. To allegorically go beyond the Grotto into the remaining portion of the Well Shaft leading to the Grand Gallery, a person has to be imbued with the indwelling power of the Holy Spirit. Few Israelites were baptized with the Holy Spirit prior to Christ. Those who were filled with the Spirit of God were promised future redemption because they fully believed that Yahweh intended to send a Messiah that would redeem all people from sin, and lead them to salvation. The remaining portion of the Well Shaft leading to the Grand Gallery therefore signifies those granted spiritual regeneration through their belief in, and knowledge of their need for, the full blood atonement of the Messiah to come (See John 12:41; Acts 10:43; 1 Peter 1:10-12). These people are therefore saved by their dependency on, and faith in Christ, not by doing any self-directed works.

How marvelous that Yahweh has now provided a way for us all to find salvation, and to obtain the Holy Spirit through Yahshua. Through Him alone, we can pass through the otherwise impenetrable granite plug representing our separation from God to find everlasting life. This plug was likely made of red granite to represent *righteous blood*. Yahshua's blood had to be shed to allow us a way past the impenetrable division between God and man caused by sin. The red granite used in the Great Pyramid is one of the hardest and densest types of stone in the world. It is therefore far superior in quality to the plain limestone blocks that make up the bulk of the Great Pyramid's masonry. If seen as an allegory, the red granite symbolizes heavenly things, while the plain, unfinished limestone blocks symbolize the imperfection of mankind. In support of this, Scriptures teaches that believers allegorically form the building blocks of God's Temple, and serve as citizens in God's invisible Kingdom that has been established forever within their hearts (Luke 17:21; 1 Corinth. 3:16-17).

This special reddish granite was used in only three places inside the Great Pyramid: in the King's Chamber, in the Antechamber, and in the fifteen-foot plug in the Ascending Passage. This suggests that these three granite features in the Great Pyramid have a unique, sacred purpose. Due to their red color and superior strength, they likely were meant to represent the redeeming blood of the perfect sacrifice for sin offered by our Messiah, Yahshua. As a symbol for His blood, they also represent the Blood Covenants Yahweh God made with mankind, as well as all atoning blood sacrifices that were once required for the remission of sin. The red granite artfully symbolizes the blood of animal sacrifices used in Blood Covenanting, and blood atonement rituals, but especially represents the perfect blood of Christ that was shed once and for all time on Calvary.

## *The Queen's Chamber: Symbol of Baptism and Resurrection*

Past the red granite plug, the Ascending Passage leads up to a juncture with two paths. The narrower one leads straight toward the interior of the pyramid on a level path. Called the Horizontal Passage, it was once purposely concealed beneath a stone floor at the entrance to the Grand Gallery. The Horizontal Passage opens into a small room that has been dubbed the Queen's Chamber - for lack of a better designation by Egyptologists. The Queen's Chamber is lined with the same pure white limestone used to construct the now missing casing stones for the Great Pyramid. The choice of this fine white limestone symbolizes the spiritual purity of Christ's Bride, the True Church, which will reign with Christ forever. The Queen's Chamber stands for the habitation of the righteous during Christ's Millennial Kingdom. However, due to its uneven and unfinished floor, the Queen's Chamber also signifies that righteousness is found by overcoming suffering and adversity through Christ. As will be shown a bit later, the shafts in the Queen's Chamber reveal more about the nature of this suffering, and who will suffer through it.

The pure white limestone blocks used in the walls of the Queen's Chamber, and in the Horizontal Passage leading to it are coated with an odd salty layer. This appears to have oozed out of the rock, suggesting *"the salt of the Earth"* that Yahshua once referred to (Matthew 5:13). Salt is a symbol for righteousness found through spiritual cleansing and purification. For the Christian, it represents their spiritual regeneration that begins when they are baptized and then born again with the indwelling presence of the Holy Spirit. The Queen's Chamber is therefore likely to be an allegorical representation of the rite of baptism, and the spiritual rebirth it symbolizes to true believers in Yahshua.

Interestingly, Ancient Egyptian priests scrubbed their bodies with salt before ministering in their temples. This salt rub was a way to purify

## Ch. 4: The Pillar of Enoch's Amazing Prophetic Design

the body physically so that the priests were ritually clean when they served in the temples of their gods. It is therefore likely that these highly educated men understood at least part of the symbolism behind using salt for purification. How tragic that they grasped this symbolism - but forgot the one true God, and worshipped created things instead!

For believers, the salty floor in the Queen's Chamber indicates the rocky path toward spiritual cleansing that we all must take to obtain the purity needed to obtain everlasting life. Yahshua condemned those who lose their spiritual saltiness by saying:

> "You are the salt of the earth. But if the salt loses its saltiness, how can it be made salty again? It is no longer good for anything, except to be thrown out and trampled by men." - Matthew 5:13 (NIV)

The Queen's Chamber floor - which is uneven and has no salty layer on it - aptly represents those who lose their saltiness and are only good for being trampled upon. This suggests that, though the Queen's Chamber represents the pure Bride of Christ, it also represents the Apostate Church, as well as the Jews who reject Yahshua. These are the ones who have fallen away from the truth, and that must be "made salty," or be spiritually cleansed by the dire events in the Tribulation period before they can enter Yah's Kingdom.

Just as is found in the King's Chamber, there is an empty sarcophagus in the Queens Chamber. It is sunken partly into the stone floor of the chamber, and suggests a connection to the resurrection into eternal life promised to all those who put their faith in Yahshua as the Messiah. In fact, **since the 26.3 degree Christ Angle is formed at the junction of the Horizontal Passage leading from Queen's Chamber to the Ascending Passage, this empty tomb appears to correlate perfectly with the empty tomb at Christ's resurrection** during the first stage of the three-stage First Resurrection.

Past the Horizontal Passage that leads to the entrance of the Queen's Chamber, the Ascending Passage leads directly into the impressive height of the corbel-vaulted Grand Gallery. This juncture indicates the two stages of the redemption that Yahweh founded: the first one is gained through belief in the atoning sacrifice for sin found in the crucifixion of Christ, and the second is found through obtaining the resurrection into everlasting life guaranteed by the Holy Spirit within us.

## The Jubilee Passage, and Christ's Millennial Kingdom

A level, narrow path from the Ascending Passage leads to the Queen's Chamber. Though its sides and ceiling stones are smooth, this narrow passage has a rough, unfinished floor – just as the Queen's Chamber also does. The Well Shaft, and this Horizontal Passage to the Queen's Chamber therefore appear to represent the hard road to life that few find (Matthew 7:13-14). The length of the Horizontal Passage into the Queen's Chamber can be divided into seven equal sections. The first six sections of the Horizontal Passage require a person to stoop over to pass through. This is an allegorical way of showing that it represents the narrow gate, and hard path, to everlasting life. However, this narrow part of the Horizontal Passage also represents the 6,000 years from the Fall of Adam and Eve until the Millennial Rule of Christ, as will be seen in a moment.

A large step occurs in the final seventh of the passage leading into the Queen's Chamber. This heightens the path considerably so that a man or woman of average height can stand upright in it. This higher section is known as the Jubilee Passage because it represents one-seventh of a portion, and is exactly one seventh the length of the entire Horizontal Passage. In the Bible, every fiftieth year on the Jewish calendar was a Jubilee. This Jubilee Year was the fiftieth year after seven times seven years, or forty-nine years had passed. It was a Sabbath rest for the Earth, and this is why Jewish farmers allowed their fields to remain fallow for that whole year. It was also a time when all debts were to be cancelled, prisoners were to be released, and all slaves were to be freed. In addition, every seventh year on the Jewish calendar was a Sabbath year. It was like a Jubilee year except foreign slaves and captives did not need to be set free, and debts owed by foreigners did not have to be cancelled. Only debts owed by fellow Israelites were forgiven on every Sabbath year. Yahshua referred to a Year of Jubilee when He said:

> *"The Spirit of the Lord GOD (Yahweh Elohim) is upon Me, because the LORD (Yahweh) has anointed Me to preach good tidings to the poor; he has sent Me to heal the brokenhearted, to proclaim liberty to the captives... to proclaim the acceptable year of the LORD (Yahweh), and the day of vengeance of our God; to comfort all who mourn... to give them beauty for ashes, the oil of joy for mourning, the garment of praise for the spirit of heaviness; that they may be called trees of righteousness, the planting of the LORD (Yahweh)..."* – Isaiah 61:1-3

# Ch. 4: The Pillar of Enoch's Amazing Prophetic Design

In Luke 4:17-21, Yahshua quoted from the preceding Scripture in Isaiah. The liberating, and triumphant actions toward people described in this passage of Scripture all fit the theme of the Year of Jubilee. The Jubilee portion of the Horizontal Passage in the Great Pyramid represents this same theme by being considerably higher than the first six portions of the passage. A person of average height (5 feet, 6-1/2 inches) can stand up comfortably in this Jubilee section of the Horizontal Passage, whereas a person of the same height practically has to crawl through the first six portions of the same passage. The Jubilee Passage is therefore a fitting representation of both our final salvation from sin, and the Seventh Millennium - a time when believers will be freed from their sorrows and burdens, and be able to stand tall again - without worry or care.

This Seventh Millennium is the Millennial Rule of Christ, when He will rule the whole world with justice and compassion. Later in this book, we will discuss why Yahshua's thousand-year reign can be called the Seventh Millennium, and when we might expect this time period to arrive.

## The Grand Gallery & King's Chamber: A Temple to Yahweh?

Going upward past the pathway leading to the Queen's Chamber, the corbelled Grand Gallery is reached. **This gallery is seven times higher than the Ascending Passage leading into it,** and - like the Horizontal Passage - suggests the seven millennia that may have begun with the Fall of Adam. According to the prophecies in the Bible and Book of 1 Enoch, this seven thousand year period is going to culminate with the Last Judgment - at the end of the Millennial Rule of Christ.

Like the Jubilee Passage, the level change into the Grand Gallery has allegorical significance. This is partly suggested by the feeling one gets when entering this section of the pyramid. Anyone who has traveled up the constricting Ascending Passage feels a great sense of freedom, and liberation once they reach the Grand Gallery's lofty heights. This is no accident, but alludes to freedom from the affects of sin, and a liberating rescue from damnation - two gifts that believers can find through Christ, and the baptism of the Holy Sprit.

If the level changes in the width of the Grand Gallery from floor to ceiling are counted, there are nine different sections. The top and bottom sections of the Grand Gallery forming the ceiling and the floor are both exactly three-and-one-half feet wide. The next level from the floor expands outward over the side ramps to the width of seven feet. These maximum and minimum widths of the Gallery in feet are interesting in that they suggest both the seven-year length of the Tribulation period, as well as its three-and-one-half year midpoint. This is when Daniel's prophecy of the seventy weeks suggests that the Antichrist will break his treaty with Israel. Uncannily, this connection of the Grand Gallery with the Tribulation period doesn't end there.

Between the ceiling and floor levels of its masonry, the Gallery has seven additional width changes. There is also a seven-inch wide groove running the entire length of the Grand Gallery - in the fifth corbel from the ceiling. If we view the corbel before the ceiling as representative of the Millennial Rule of Christ, and the narrow floor level as the time before the Creation of Adam and Eve, the seven level changes in between suggest the seven millennia since the Creation of mankind. However, these seven corbels also suggest a time period of seven years. **The seven-inch groove in the fourth of the seven corbel levels therefore suggests a seven-year period in the fourth of the seven millenniums, as well as seven days toward the end of the fourth year of a seven-year period.** This seven-inch groove therefore appears to graphically depict Yahshua's birth at the end of the Fourth millennium-long day since Creation, and the last week of the three and one half years of Yahshua's First Advent ministry on Earth. Passover began in the middle of this week - right after Yahshua was laid in the Garden Tomb. That week therefore ended with Yahshua's glorious resurrection from the dead into everlasting life!

This seven inch wide groove may also depict future events, such as the seven-year Tribulation period. In the middle of the seven years, the Antichrist is to be given forty-two months to rule, which is a period of three and one-half years (Revelation 13:5). This will be during the last half of the Great Tribulation, which corresponds allegorically to the three and a half days that Yahshua was officially dead. Indeed, the Antichrist will be so diabolically evil during this time period that those who witness His evil reign will likely wish they were dead, and many will die horribly from unbridled wars and Anti-Christian campaigns, virulent plagues, and catastrophic, global scale natural disasters.

Since the floor and ceiling levels in the Grand Gallery are three and a half feet wide, it suggests that the ceiling and floor levels are to act as a frame around - and a measure for - half of the seven levels in between them. Uncannily, this is exactly what Psalms 110 and 118 do around Hallel Psalms 111 through 117. As shown earlier, these seven Psalms prophetically appear to relate to the Tribulation period. The Grand Gallery therefore forms a type of Chanukiah Menorah, with Yahshua's First Advent marked in the center of the Menorah by the seven-inch groove in the fourth corbel, and the three and one half foot

## Ch. 4: The Pillar of Enoch's Amazing Prophetic Design    Page 135

span of the floor and ceiling of the Grand Gallery! This hearkens back to what was shown in Chapter 1 on the prophetic symbolism encoded into every Menorah, and to Chapter 7, where the symbolism in the Grand Gallery and its relation to Daniel's Seventieth Week are allegorically decoded.

If the seven corbels between the ceiling and floor grooves represent the seven millennia between Creation and the Last Judgment, then the ceiling and floor grooves in the Grand Gallery represent eternity itself, as well as humanity's perfect beginning in the untainted Garden of Eden, and their perfect new beginning in the New Heaven and New Earth. The seven corbel levels between the floor and ceiling grooves represent the seven divisions of heaven, the seven thousand year Creation week, the seven-day week, and the seven millennia that it will take for our final redemption to be won. The Grand Gallery also represents the path that Yahshua took before His Father Yahweh resurrected Him from the dead. In addition, the impressive corbelled Gallery represents the enlightenment, guidance, and re-birth we obtain through God's own Son Yahshua, and His indwelling Holy Spirit.

Another curious feature of the Great Pyramid are the presence of twenty-eight evenly spaced shafts cut into the two low ramps that form the base of the long east and west walls of the Grand Gallery, making a total of 56 shafts. Intriguingly, in addition to their allegorical role, these shafts may have had very practical technological applications, as will be shown later in this chapter. Furthermore, these twenty-eight pairs of shafts may have had one or more connections to Sacred Astronomy. For example, when studying Astronomy, I noted that there are twenty-eight days in a lunar month. There are also twenty-eight Celestial Mansions or Houses that the Moon is considered to pass through, or to dwell in within the course of one Solar Year.

The number fifty-six also has a fascinating celestial application, in that it can measure the times between Solar and Lunar eclipses quite accurately. As described in Book Three on History, the points where the paths of the Sun and Moon through Earth's sky intercept each other are called lunar nodes. These nodes move slowly clockwise through the year, making a complete circuit around the Earth in 18-2/3 years, or *3 circuits in 56 years*. Interestingly, the fifty-six holes in the Aubrey circle surrounding Stonehenge appear to have followed this 56-year lunar cycle, and may have been used to predict solar and lunar eclipses. Could the fifty-six shafts in the Grand Gallery have served the same purpose? If so, the Great Pyramid may indeed have served as a giant astronomical observatory at one time, with the Grand Gallery open to the sky on its southern end to view the Sun, Moon, and stars.

Fascinatingly, the number twenty-eight has another celestial application that is especially found at the latitude where Giza and the Great Pyramid are situated. In the course of a year, and only at that particular latitude, the Sun will rise over a twenty-eight degree arc on the eastern horizon. At the Spring Equinox, the Sun will rise due east. Then, over half a year, it will gradually rise further and further north of this point until it is fourteen degrees north of due east on the horizon at the Summer Solstice. At the Fall Equinox, the Sun will again be found rising at the center point due east. Then, as winter approaches, the Sun will rise further and further south until it is fourteen degrees south of due east, at the Winter Solstice. After seeing this connection of the Sun and Moon to the twenty-eight shafts in the Grand Gallery, I wondered if the twenty-eight Mansions of the Moon were designed to coincide with the position in degrees of the Sun on the eastern horizon. If so, this would partly explain why there are twenty-eight lunar mansions, rather than twenty-four or twelve, which - at first glance - seem to be numbers more in harmony with the divisions of the Zodiac.

In support of the idea that the twenty-eight paired shafts in the Grand Gallery are somehow connected to the Sun's position on the horizon during the course of one year, the causeways leading from the two biggest pyramids at Giza are angled to form a 28-degree angle. This is an architectural key indicating that the Pyramids are aligned somehow to sunrise and sunset at its farthest northern and southern positions along this 28-degree arc on the eastern and western horizons. The illustration on the next page shows the causeways on the Giza site plan. In it, note how the Great Pyramid causeway marks the Sun's position at the Summer Solstice at Giza, which is 28 degrees north of due east, while the Khafre Pyramid causeway is pointed toward the Winter Solstice, which is at 28 degrees south of due east at Giza.

Though the reason for this emphasis on the four high points of the Sun's yearly transit through the heavens at Giza is not readily apparent to the uninitiated, it makes sense to Sacred Astronomers as a reference to the purpose and ministry of Yahshua the Messiah, who was, and is *"the Sun of Righteousness"* prophetically described by Malachi (Mal. 4:2). Interestingly, the high points of Yahshua's life, ministry, death, resurrection, and Second Coming are tied to these 4 points in the Solar Year. For example, as revealed in detail in Books One and Two, Yahshua was conceived at about the time of the Winter Solstice, and was first recognized as a king by the Magi following a Winter Solstice two

# Ch. 4: The Pillar of Enoch's Amazing Prophetic Design   Page 137

years after His conception - during Chanukah. In addition, Yahshua was born at around the time of the Fall Equinox, probably during Sukkot, or the Feast of Tabernacles. Furthermore, Yahshua's death and resurrection occurred near to the time of the Spring Equinox, and His baptism by John the Baptist and the subsequent pouring out of the Holy Spirit on the Apostles at Pentecost coincided fairly closely with the Summer Solstice.

## Equinoxes and Solstices Mark the Solar Year at Giza

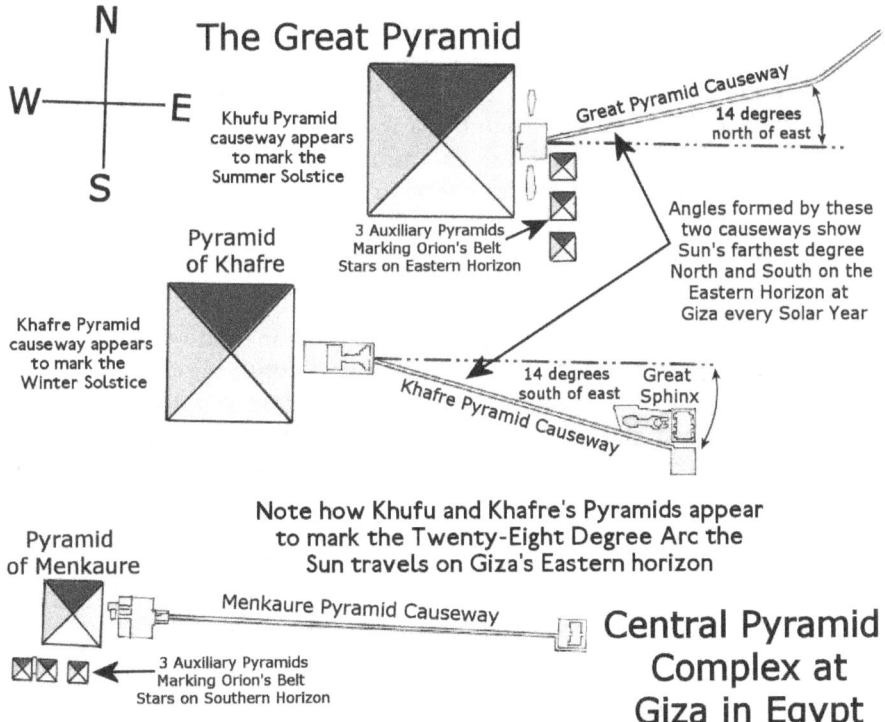

As will be shown in the final chapter about the practical application of Sacred Astronomy to events pertaining to the Tribulation and Second Coming, it also appears that the beginning of the Tribulation period was marked by a Full Lunar Eclipse over the constellation Orion's sword tip (which rests on the Ecliptic) on the Winter Solstice that fell on December 21st, 2010. Furthermore, the Signs in the Heavens tied to the Winter Solstice on December 21st, 2012 AD are directly tied to four Zodiac Signs that allude to the Four Horsemen of the Apocalypse - suggesting that the Four Horsemen were released around that time. We will discuss these alignments further in later chapters of this book.

The three small auxiliary pyramids running along the east face of the Great Pyramid - and the similar set of three along the south face of Menkaure's Pyramid - have been included in the aerial view of the Giza pyramids and their causeways on page 137. Though people writing about the Great Pyramid complex generally ignore these six pyramids, some scholars think they may mark the belt stars of Orion at certain points in history, when the belt stars were aligned on the southern and eastern horizons directly above the pyramids. We will further discuss this unusual feature of the auxiliary pyramids a bit later.

The magnificent height and symbolism of the Grand Gallery leads to the narrow Antechamber, which we will discuss more a bit later. This Antechamber opens into the largest room in the Great Pyramid: the King's Chamber. The King's Chamber's walls are made entirely of huge red granite blocks. It also contains an empty, lidless red granite Coffer. As mentioned earlier, its red granite construction suggests the color of blood, and artfully symbolizes the sacred rite of Blood Covenant and the death of Yahshua on the Cross (See Book Two for a detailed study of the sacred meaning and purpose of Blood Covenants).

The six-foot long, lidless granite Coffer to one side of the King's Chamber appears to be an empty tomb that apparently never held a body. This empty Coffer therefore appears to represent both the translation of Enoch, as well as the risen Christ. It also represents the First Resurrection to everlasting life that all believers in Christ will obtain just prior to Yahshua's Millennial Rule on Earth. The First Resurrection of the saints occurs in three stages. The first stage occurred when Yahshua rose from the dead, the second stage will occur at the Rapture, and the third stage will take place at the end of the Great Tribulation. See Chapter Seven for further explanations concerning First Resurrection.

The meaning of the granite Coffer lends some additional strength to my interpretation of the King's Chamber. As was shown in "The Language of God in the Universe," the Sun allegorically represents our triune God Yahweh. It is therefore no coincidence that the Coffer symbolizing resurrection and everlasting life through Yahshua would indicate a relationship to the Sun. This relationship is found when twice the perimeter of the Coffer's base, times 10 to the 8th power (270.45378502 PI X 10**8), is calculated. This equals 427,316 miles - close to our modern estimate of the Sun's mean radius. This fact suggests that, just as the Queen's Chamber represents the Moon, and fallen mankind reborn through spiritual baptism, the King's Chamber is meant to allegorically depict both the light of the Sun, and the Son of God that all radiant sunlight represents.

## Ch. 4: The Pillar of Enoch's Amazing Prophetic Design    Page 139

The Grand Gallery, the Antechamber, the King's Chamber, and the relieving chambers above it represent the seven thousand years leading to eternity. This is magnificently recorded in the construction of the Grand Gallery itself, which reveals some remarkable correlations between the Mazzaroth's Precessional cycle, and the prophetic reckoning of time. For example, the Grand Gallery has thirty-six ceiling slabs that correspond to both the exact number of decans in the Mazzaroth, as well as the number of ten-day weeks in an Ancient Egyptian 360-day year - to which, what were known as the five "days of chaos" were added. In addition, the Grand Gallery's corbelled walls are made up of ten courses of stone blocks. Coupled with the thirty-six ceiling stones, the number 10 X 36, or 360 is derived, and this is the number of degrees in the circumference of a circle. This confirms the idea that the Grand Gallery represents the passage of a specific amount of circular prophetic time.

That the thirty-six ceiling stones recall the exact number of decan signs in the Ancient Mazzaroth is no accident! This is suggested by the fact that these ceiling stones correspond allegorically to the heavens, as do the ceiling stones in the King's Chamber, the Antechamber, and the Queen's Chamber. For example, twelve massive stones form the gabled ceiling in the Queen's Chamber, while the nine stones in the King's Chamber ceiling and the three stones in the ceiling of the Antechamber also equal twelve when added together. These twelve ceiling stones suggest the Twelve Houses of the Zodiac and the Twelve Tribes of Israel. If the nine ceiling stones in the King's Chamber, the three ceiling stones in the Antechamber, and the thirty-six ceiling stones in the Grand Gallery are added together, there are altogether forty-eight ceiling stones – exactly the number of constellations in the Ancient Mazzaroth! The further ramifications of these facts will be explored a bit later in this chapter.

The Grand Gallery is about 28 feet high, and each of the ten courses of stone in its walls is about 24 inches high. If we divide those 28 feet by seven (as indicated by the fact that the Grand Gallery *is seven times higher* than the Ascending Passage) this allows four feet for each seventh of the Grand Gallery's height, or approximately 4 X 12 = 48 Pyramid Inches per seventh. Once again, we are confronted with two peculiar numbers. First, we can see the number 28 - the number of degrees in the solar arc on the horizon at Giza, the number of days in a lunar month, and the number of celestial houses dividing up a lunar year. Second, we see the number 48 - the number of constellations in the Ancient Mazzaroth or Zodiac. Both of these numbers suggest the full passage of a prophetic period of circular time, just as the numbers 36 and 12 do.

Thus, in addition to indicating the passage of seven millenniums, the Grand Gallery's seven 48-inch divisions in height, and seven corbels appear to indicate a shorter time span of seven full 360-degree revolutions of the forty-eight constellations of the Zodiac – or seven prophetic years. It therefore appears that the Grand Gallery is singling out the seven years of the Tribulation period! In Chapter Eight, we will closely examine the clear relationship of the Grand Gallery with the Tribulation period, and the prophetic Last Day timeline revealed in the Psalms.

The cycle of Precession is also indicated by the seven prophetic years that are allegorically depicted in the Grand Gallery's height and corbels. If these seven prophetic years of 360 days are seen as seven prophetic time periods of 360 years (7 X 360), we get the number 2,520. If we subtract 360 from this figure, we get 6 X 360 = 2,160 years, the approximate number of years it takes to change from one Zodiac sign to another due to Precession. This span of time is known as one Precessional Age, twelve of which make up a time span of 25,920 years, the length of one full Precessional cycle. Incidentally, this measure of 6 X 360 = 2,160 also alludes to the six prophetic millenniums that precede the Seventh Millennium, or the Millennial Rule of Yahshua.

As shown later in this book, and in the Chart in the Appendix taken from Book One, this six thousand year span of time began in 4003 BC and ended in 1999 AD. Earlier, it was also shown how *the measurement in Pyramid Inches of the interior passages of the Great Pyramid reveals prophetic dates.* For example, take the floor measurement from the beginning of the Grand Gallery to the doorway of the Antechamber. When each Pyramid Inch is seen as an allegory of the passage of one year, it marks a very significant span of time. This is the time between the death and resurrection of Yahshua in 31 AD (See Book Two and Chapter Eight for proof), and the year 2010 AD. Now, *the Seventh Great Day of the Lord began in 1999 AD, and the year 2010 AD corresponds to the juncture between the Great Step in the Grand Gallery and the Antechamber door, which marks the point where the Tribulation period is about to begin.* Intriguingly, eleven Jewish Sacred Calendar years will have passed between Nissan 1 or April 6th, 2000 and April 5th, 2011.

The Grand Gallery marks the seven millenniums since the Fall of mankind, while the Antechamber leading into the King's Chamber specifically represents the time of Tribulation. This factor is an important key in understanding the prophetic import of the interior passages of the Great Pyramid, which were discussed earlier. Finally, the King's Chamber itself represents the First Resurrection at the beginning of the Millennial

## Ch. 4: The Pillar of Enoch's Amazing Prophetic Design   Page 141

Rule of Christ. In a moment, we will examine why the ten layers of air and rock above the King's Chamber may signify the ten centuries that will pass during the Millennial Rule of Christ. We will also discuss why the gabled ceiling above them likely represents the Final Judgment, eternity, and the promise of everlasting life.

Amazingly, besides all the hidden knowledge in the Pillar of Enoch already revealed, there is startling proof that the King's Chamber represents the New Earth that will be created after the Millennium, while the Great Pyramid surrounding it represents the New Heavens - as well as the present Earth. This fact is proven in the King's Chamber, which, like the pyramid surrounding it, contains the values for Pi, the Golden Section, and the Golden Ratio Phi in its dimensions.

When the King's Chamber is measured across its width in Pyramid Inches, this measurement can be used as the diameter of a circle. This produces a circle with an area equal to the area of the base of the pyramid - if that area is expressed in Sacred Cubits. The King's Chamber, therefore, appears to represent Earth's celestial sphere. If we view the heavens, or atmosphere of the Earth as a larger sphere surrounding the spherical Earth, then the Great Pyramid represents that sphere, while the Earth is represented by the King's Chamber. Interestingly, in support of this hypothesis, the King's Chamber is surrounded by so much insulating stone that its internal air temperature always remains constant at 68 degrees Fahrenheit. Uncannily, this is also the average mean surface temperature of the Earth!

The King's Chamber contains an empty tomb indicating that no more death or decay will exist in the New Creation after the Millennium. Uncannily, there is a direct correlation in size and situation between the King's Coffer in the King's Chamber of the Pillar of Enoch, and the Ark of the Covenant within the Most Holy Place in the Desert Tabernacle of the Israelites. There are also amazing correlations between the Tabernacle's Most Holy Place, Holy Place, and Outer Courtyard with the King's Chamber, Antechamber, and the Grand Gallery in the Great Pyramid. *This connection implies that, like the Tabernacle after it, the Great Pyramid served as a holy temple, and an altar unto Yahweh - all in one amazingly complex edifice.*

This fact clearly suggests that the Great Pyramid, as the Pillar of Enoch, is a sacred Covenant pillar created by righteous people who loved the one true God - *and that it was not* the invention of the Paganistic Ancient Egyptians. If the Great Pyramid was finished in 2500 BC, then the Desert Tabernacle was fashioned over 1100 years later! The great span of time, and distance between the building of the Great Pyramid, and the construction of the Desert Tabernacle suggests that each edifice was built according to some hidden, universally applicable divine plan, and not by the genius of any one particular people group, or culture. We will go into much detail concerning the similarities between the Desert Tabernacle and Great Pyramid in the next chapter. There you will also find a handy chart showing the remarkable similarities between these two sacred monuments dedicated to Yahweh, and His Son.

The Pillar of Enoch's correlation with the Desert Tabernacle makes it the most amazing pillar, altar, and temple to Yahweh ever built. This is because, like the Desert Tabernacle did thousands of years later, the Great Pyramid speaks volumes without the aid of the written or spoken word. It reflects the advanced scientific and spiritual knowledge of a far distant Age, yet also reflects what can only be considered divinely given knowledge, such as the accurate prophetic dates suggested by the lengths of the interior passages, and the junctions between the passages inside the Great Pyramid. The Great Pyramid is therefore a testimony to the mental ingenuity, and spiritual depth of our remotest ancestors.

Like the Great Pyramid, the Desert Tabernacle allegorically conveys divine knowledge using the Language of God. The Desert Tabernacle's miraculous metaphorical messages are meticulously explored in Book Two, but as already mentioned, its allegorical similarity to the Great Pyramid is detailed in the next chapter. Now, let's return to our discussion of the meanings locked into the interior design of the Great Pyramid.

## *The King's Chamber & Djed Pillars: Connected to Christ?*

A very interesting design occurs above the King's Chamber - one that is allegorically overlooked in most books on Pyramidology. There, hidden from view, are five low chambers between five layers of solid stone masonry. These are currently considered to be relieving chambers that diffuse the weight of the many layers of stone above the King's Chamber. Amazingly, along with the huge gabled ceiling above them, these once hidden relieving chambers look like an arrow pointing upward when viewed in cross-section. Interestingly, a similar, but smaller scale gabled ceiling that allegorically points upward is completely visible in the Queen's Chamber. Since there is a definite correlation between the corbelled cornice in the Queen's Chamber and the corbels in the Grand Gallery, could it be possible that the gabled ceilings in the King's and Queen's Chambers also correlate somehow? Let's explore this possibility.

# Ch. 4: The Pillar of Enoch's Amazing Prophetic Design

First of all, there appears to be a correlation between this gigantic arrow-like structural device in the Great Pyramid, and the "Djed" Pillars that were so important as Ancient Egyptian amulets. Many examples of amulet-sized Djed or Tet Pillars have been unearthed throughout Egypt. Archeologists believe these Djed Pillar amulets signified stability, and may have represented the backbone of the risen Osiris. This is because Djed Pillar amulets resemble a symbolic backbone that is formed by four or five stacked "cornices" topping each pillar shaped amulet base. In comparison, there are five layers of stone between five air-filled relieving chambers above the King's Chamber, which approximate the physical characteristics of a section of a real human backbone.

Perhaps because of their similarity to the structure of a backbone, some scientists have concluded that these air-cushioned layers of stone provided architectural stability to the whole pyramid, and kept the tremendous weight of the upper courses of the Great Pyramid from crushing the internal chambers below it. However, this theory doesn't make sense because the Queen's Chamber, which has far more weight above it, does not have any relieving chambers between its gabled ceiling, and the chamber itself. If these so-called relieving chambers were built to displace the pyramid's mass in the King's Chamber, why weren't they used above the much more mass-beleaguered Queen's Chamber below?

**Are these ancient symbols allegorically connected?**

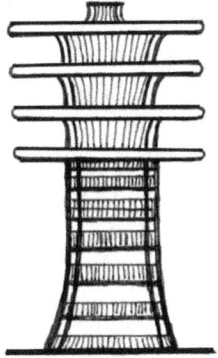

The King's Chamber in the Great Pyramid

Ancient Egyptian Djed Pillar

Regardless of what the so-called relieving chambers were actually built for, the correlation between these chambers and the King's Chamber with Djed Pillars is fascinating. Just as the King's Chamber and the relieving chambers above it symbolize everlasting life, so Djed pillar amulets symbolized the life-giving power of the god Osiris. The Egyptian word "djed" or "tet" meant "enduring" or "stable." Hence, most scholars see the Djed Pillar as a symbol of stability. However, something that endures, and is stable can also be everlasting. This is why amulets combining the Djed Pillar with the Ancient Egyptian Ankh symbol for everlasting life were made. Many examples of these Djed Pillar amulets have been found in tombs, or were placed in mummy wrappings as symbols of the Egyptian hope in a resurrection to everlasting life. Could it be that they also symbolized the backbone of Osiris, and - as such - represented Osiris' moral strength and ability to give everlasting life?

The Ancient Egyptians closely connected Djed Pillars with the god Osiris. As the resurrected god who held the keys to everlasting life, Osiris was an early, though corrupted representation of Christ. Osiris was the Egyptian god of the dead, and the ruler over eternity. He symbolized both eternity, and the resurrection into the afterlife that nearly everyone in Ancient Egypt hungered to attain at almost any cost. The Ancient Egyptians connected the god Osiris to the constellation called Orion, and this same constellation is graphically depicted in stone at Giza, in Egypt. In fact, there is a clear connection between the Great Pyramid, and the constellation of Orion/Osiris that was hinted at in Chapter Three, and will be further substantiated here. This connection appears to be an ingenious attempt by the descendents of Seth to identify the character of the anticipated Savior of the world who would one day conquer both death and sin.

The Messiah is depicted many times in the starry witness of the Mazzaroth, or Zodiac. In fact, many of the forty-eight constellations of the ancient Zodiac are tied to major events in Yahshua's ministry to mankind. As already shown, the numbers connected to the Mazzaroth are repeatedly found in the Great Pyramid, especially in the ceilings stones, such as the 36 found in the Grand Gallery, and the 12 in the King's Chamber and Antechamber. The 36 ceiling stones can be seen as 3 times 12. These three sets of 12 reflect God's Plan of Salvation, with the rite of Blood Covenant and the Gospel in the Stars governing the first dispensation connected to the twelve patriarchs from Adam to Arphaxad. Likewise, the dispensation of the Mosaic Law was connected to the Twelve Tribes of Israel, and the dispensation of Grace is connected to the Twelve Apostles.

Another example of this is found hidden above the five stone relieving chambers over the King's Chamber. There, a gabled ceiling constructed of twenty-four massive granite blocks has another hidden story to share. Symbolically, these 24 stones may represent the Twenty-four Elders seen around God's Throne in the Book of Revelation, where they worship Yahweh as the King of kings:

"Around the throne were twenty-four thrones, and on the thrones I saw **twenty-four elders sitting**, clothed in white robes; and they had crowns of gold on their heads." "And **the twenty-four elders who sat before God on their thrones fell on their faces**

## Ch. 4: The Pillar of Enoch's Amazing Prophetic Design    Page 145

*and worshiped God,* saying: *"We give You thanks, O Lord God Almighty, the One who is and who was and who is to come..."* - Rev 4:4, 11:16-17

Could the twenty-four blocks in the gabled ceiling high above the King's Chamber be a representation of the heavenly thrones of these Twenty-four Elders? Though no one is certain whom these elders are, some scholars such as me believe that they may signify the first patriarchs of the Twelve Tribes, and the Twelve Apostles. As such, they represent the connection of the Abrahamic and Mosaic Covenants with the New Covenant. Since this ceiling is over the King's Coffer connected symbolically to the Ark of the Covenant, and the Ark's lid was the symbolic Throne of God, it is likely that the King's Chamber, relieving chambers, and gabled ceiling together signify that the highest heaven - where God's Throne is now located - will be located on the Earth in eternity, as suggested by the Great Pyramid's connection to the Earth, and to Christ as our Savior and King.

The Great Pyramid's amazing connection to Christ can be seen in another intriguing analogy. This is found in the fact that the King's Chamber is connected to the Sun, which represents God the Father, the Queen's Chamber is connected to the Moon, which represents the Holy Spirit, and the Great Pyramid itself represents Christ and His Body, the Tue Church. Therefore, **the Great Pyramid's structure not only depicts the triune nature of Yahweh, but the triune nature of Christ Himself,** who is equal with the Father and the Spirit, but also fully man!

All of the ceiling stones above the relieving chambers weigh approximately 40 tons each, yet they were accurately maneuvered into place after being raised hundreds of feet above the surrounding Giza Plateau. Even with all our advanced technological knowledge, this is an engineering feat that modern humanity is virtually incapable of duplicating! Intriguingly, just as there as 24 ceiling stones above the relieving chambers, there are 24 hours in a day, and 2 times 12 equals the division between day and night on the equinoxes. Likewise, 2 times 24 equals the 48 constellations in the ancient Zodiac, which represent the 12 major Houses of the Zodiac. Therefore, 12, 24, and 48 are all numbers that deal specifically with the passage of celestial time, and are also intimately tied to God's provision for mankind throughout the Ages. To show that God's ultimate provision given thorough belief in Christ was going to be fulfilled through the Israelites, there were Twelve Tribes of Israel, and forty-eight Levite cities scattered about in Israel, just as there are forty-eight constellations scattered among the Twelve Houses of the Zodiac.

Seeing this correlation, we can look at the gabled ceiling in the Queen's Chamber to see how it compares. Uncannily, this gabled ceiling is made up of twelve massive stone blocks that correspond to the sky, the Twelve Houses of the Zodiac, the Twelve Tribes of Israel, and the 12 Apostles. Since Abraham's descendents were to be as numerous as the stars, and the patriarch Joseph saw himself and his brothers as stars in a dream vision, it seems fitting that this ceiling may represent the Twelve Tribes of Israel, as well as the Twelve Apostles who signify that all people can be adopted into Israel through faith in Christ.

Intriguingly, in a clear allegory for the sky, these twelve stones form a *gabled* ceiling that decidedly points upwards like a giant arrow toward the heavens it represents! The same is true of the gabled ceiling high above the King's Chamber, when visualized in cross-section with the relieving chambers below it. It too points upward like a giant stone imitation of an arrow. The connection of the twelve-block ceiling in the Queen's Chamber with the twenty-four blocks above the King's Chamber therefore seems patently obvious.

Now, recall my previous discussion about the date being indicated where the Ascending Passage ends, and the Grand Gallery begins. This marks the year 31 AD, the year when Yahshua likely died, and then rose from the dead. **This suggests that the Grand Gallery represents the Church Age.** It also implies that the Queen's Chamber signifies the twelve Spirit-filled Apostles who founded the Church Age, as well as the first stage of the First Resurrection. Since the Queen's Chamber once contained an empty sarcophagus like the one in the King's Chamber, its connection to the resurrection of Christ is almost certain.

At the very moment that Yahshua died on the Cross, humanity at last received the right to receive full forgiveness, and fellowship with God, Then, when Yahshua rose from the dead, and left an empty Garden Tomb as a symbol of His resurrection, all those people who repented then received the spiritual gifts of the Holy Spirit, and the right to a resurrection into everlasting life. That the gift of everlasting life in a living body was available to mankind immediately after Yahshua's resurrection is apparent from Matthew's Gospel, which indicates that righteous people who had died, and been buried were suddenly seen alive - appearing to many people around Jerusalem after Yahshua rose from the dead:

> "*...and the graves were opened; and many bodies of* **the saints who had fallen asleep were raised;** *and coming out of the graves after His resurrection, they went into the holy city and appeared to many*" (Matt. 27:52-53).

## Ch. 4: The Pillar of Enoch's Amazing Prophetic Design   Page 147

As shown in Book Two, this resurrection of the righteous among the dead at the time when Christ was risen up is the first part of the First Resurrection, which appears to occur in three stages. The first stage of this First Resurrection occurred when Yahshua rose from the dead, and the twelve stones of the ceiling in the Queen's Chamber suggest that this stage of the First Resurrection was open only to the righteous dead among the descendents of Seth, Shem, Abraham, and the Twelve Tribes of Israel. The second stage of the First Resurrection is known as the Rapture and may also have two or three stages. It will be open to God's saints alone - those who fully love Yahweh God and His Son.

After the Great Tribulation, the third stage of the First Resurrection will come. This stage is represented by the King's Chamber. At this time, all the Tribulation Saints will rise to everlasting life and will join the Saints in the Rapture. Together, those who share in the First Resurrection will serve as priests and rulers with Christ during His Millennial Kingdom:

> *"Blessed and holy is he who has part in the first resurrection. Over such the second death has no power, but they shall be priests of God and of Christ, and shall reign with Him a thousand years."* - Rev. 20:6

The Twenty-four elders in Heaven and the twenty-four gabled ceiling stones above the King's Chamber suggest this future time - when the followers of Christ will reign with Him on thrones. This is the time when all the descendents of Seth, Abraham, and Jacob who longed for the coming of the Messiah, and all of Christ's disciples who longed for His Second Coming will reign with Christ, just as the twenty-four elders in Heaven do now.

Interestingly, the pinnacle of the gabled roof in the Queen's Chamber of the Great Pyramid points to the 1913 AD date on the Great Step in the Grand Gallery. This suggests that 1913 marked the close of the Age of Grace and the *beginning* of the Age of God's Judgment of the nations - an Age culminating with the Tribulation and Second Coming of Christ. As will be shown in Chapter Eight, the number of Pyramid Inches from the pyramid entrance to the end of the Great Step leading into the Antechamber may signify the number of Solar Years that will pass from 2500 BC to 2010 AD, which may be the year just before the onset of the Tribulation period. Furthermore, the Antechamber itself may depict the Tribulation period, while the King's Chamber may be a symbol of Christ's earthly Millennial Kingdom. This is made clear in the King's Chamber by the presence of an empty Coffer, or sarcophagus, and the gabled ceiling pointing upward that is hidden above it. These are design elements that are also found in the Queen's Chamber, or - as in the case of the sarcophagus - were once found there.

If the Queen's Chamber represents the first stage of the First Resurrection, and the King's Chamber represents the third stage of the First Resurrection, then the relieving chambers above the King's Chamber most likely represent the Millennial Rule of Christ. After all, this is when immortals (suggested by the presence of the stone layers) and mortals (suggested by the empty chambers between them) will dwell together on Earth for one thousand years.

Altogether, there are ten layers of stone and open space between the King's Chamber ceiling, and the gabled ceiling atop them all. These ten layers suggest the ten centuries that make up a millennial period of time, as well as the state of the Earth during that time. Reminiscent of the iron mixed with clay symbolism found in the dream vision of Nebuchadnezzar by the Prophet Daniel, it suggests that the Earth will be filled with two very different kinds of people. On the one hand, there will be people on the Earth whose righteousness and ability to receive immortality is as strong as stone. At the same time, however, there will be mortals on Earth whose moral convictions are as insubstantial, and changeable as air.

Now, if the ten layers of rock and air leading to the gabled ceiling above the King's Chamber represent the ten centuries of the Millennial Rule of Christ, then it seems highly likely that the twenty-four stones in the gabled ceiling above these layers represents the Twenty-Four Elders who, as co-rulers with Yahshua, may help Him judge the nations at the Second Resurrection. Remember, the Second Resurrection is not to immortal life, but to *mortal* life. At this time, some who are raised will be given everlasting life, while others will be subsequently condemned to death, and destroyed in the Lake of Fire.

Though there are many analogies for Yahshua in the Mazzaroth, none are more compelling than Yahshua in His roles as Redeemer, and conquering King. This is what Orion depicts, and that may be why the Ancient Egyptians specifically identified this constellation as the heavenly representation of Osiris, their victorious god who conquered death. Uncannily, the connection of Osiris and Orion with the Great Pyramid is even more convincingly proven when the site layout of the three largest pyramids at Giza is examined in relation to the Nile River. This concept will be explained a bit later.

The preceding conclusions are partly my own, drawn through painstaking analysis of the Great Pyramid over several years. After

# Ch. 4: The Pillar of Enoch's Amazing Prophetic Design

detailed study of the facts, the correlations I subsequently reached are too perfect to be accidental. Furthermore, the symbolic spiritual meanings for each part of the interior of the Great Pyramid appear in the exact same order that they appear in the Bible. Based on their own eschatological view, other scholars have put forth similar interpretations of the symbolic meanings of the internal passages of the Great Pyramid. Now that we have explored the inside of this divinely inspired man-made mountain of stone, let's look at its prophetic and scientific significance in relation to the Giza Complex as a whole.

### *The Star Gospel Targeted by the Great Pyramid*

There are clear astronomical connections between the stars and the Great Pyramid that - due to the existence of the Gospel in the Stars - can't be a mere coincidence. First, there is the obvious connection between the three belt stars of Orion, and the three main pyramids a Giza. In addition, within both the King's and Queen's Chambers are two shafts that rise at different angles toward the sky. For lack of a better explanation by archeologists, these narrow, steeply angled shafts have been identified as airshafts. The same archeologists, however, ignore the fact that no such shafts exist in any other pyramid. **Of the hundreds of pyramids to be found in Egypt, only the Great Pyramid contains these shafts**. Given this fact, the archeological view of these shafts appears ludicrous.

Though archeologists label these narrow passages as ventilation shafts, this theory must be abandoned because **the shafts in the Queen's Chamber end before they pierce the outside of the pyramid!** Furthermore, they once ended just before they reached the walls inside the Queen's Chamber! This is why the shafts were not discovered until the late 19th Century - they were invisible from both the outside and inside of the pyramid!

Further marring their theory is the fact that a dead Pharaoh's mummy has no need of air. Why then would airshafts be needed in the tomb? Certainly not to serve the living workers who built the Great Pyramid, since there is every reason to suppose the Great Pyramid's passages and chambers were constructed as the Pyramid was erected. In fact, since there is no interior decoration of any kind in the Great Pyramid, no air-breathing workers were needed to carve decorations into the Pyramid's walls and ceilings afterward. The traditional theories behind the purpose of these supposed airshafts are therefore insensible and implausible.

The alternative theory that is still mostly rejected by many Egyptologists is that these shafts had something to do with star alignments. One theory that has been put forth with remarkable results is that ***these shafts actually point to specific stars at a specific year in history***. In practice, despite the objections of some archeologists, this theory makes much more sense. The shafts in the north walls of both the King's and Queen's Chambers point toward the northern sky, and their southern shafts point toward the southern sky. Taken as star pointers, the four shafts in the Great Pyramid tell us the following: the four shafts targeted four significant stars in their nightly transit across the north and south meridians in the sky *only* in 2500 BC. These stars were Al Nitak and Sirius in the southern sky, and Thuban and Kochab in the north. Maybe that is why the Ancient Egyptians cited each star targeted as highly important in the religious cult of Osiris.

As shown conclusively in "The Language of God in the Universe," the Great Pyramid represents Al Nitak or Zeta Orionis - the brightest star in Orion's Belt. Significantly, the southern shaft in the King's Chamber pointed to the same star in 2500 BC. This again shows the clear connection between the Great Pyramid and the constellation of Orion. Furthermore, it suggests that Orion's meaning in the Gospel in the Stars is connected to the meaning of the Great Pyramid. Since Orion is an allegory for our Savior and Redeemer Yahshua, the Great Pyramid must also have been built to represent Him in some significant way. As already shown, this is indeed the case, and even more proof of this connection can be seen when the other star shafts are analyzed. However, before examining these star shafts, here is an excerpt from Book Two that shows the true meaning of Orion - and the Giza pyramid complex which is connected to it - as a fitting symbol for Yahshua, our Savior:

## From Chapter 11 of "The Language of God in Humanity:"

Looking at Orion in relation to the other constellations around it, we can see many elements of the Gilgamesh, Osiris, and Orion stories depicted in the sky. For example, Orion's name in Ancient Egypt was "Seir" or "Prince." This was also the name of the Egyptian god-king Osiris, making Orion a royal figure like a Pharaoh, or King Gilgamesh. The strong animals that Orion boasts that he can kill are represented by the rampaging figure of Taurus, the Mighty Bull. This same bull makes his appearance in the Epic of Gilgamesh as the raging Bull of Heaven, whose breath and hooves cause earthquakes and volcanic eruptions until Gilgamesh kills it. In Osiris' case, bulls were used to plow the earth, and

## Ch. 4: The Pillar of Enoch's Amazing Prophetic Design

make it fertile with their dung - thus serving to perpetuate Osiris' blessings on Egypt as the breadbasket of the ancient world.

Originating at Orion's feet, there is a winding river that flows downward into the "outer darkness," where the darkest regions of the night sky are located. This is the constellation Eridanus, the River of Judgment. In the Gilgamesh Epic, this constellation can be identified with the Euphrates River, among other bodies of water mentioned in the story. The Milky Way also runs alongside Orion in the sky - and in Ancient Egypt, the Milky Way was the celestial counterpart of the Nile River. The Eridanus constellation can therefore also be seen as a starry depiction of the Nile River.

Nonetheless, the Eridanus constellation is not primarily a symbol for the Nile or Euphrates Rivers, but of the Jordan River! In fact, in ancient Hebrew, "Jordan" is pronounced "Yardanu", which is clearly related to "Eridanus", which is the Greco-Roman version of the Hebrew word. All of these fresh-water rivers were - and still are - conduits for trade, as well as providers of the life-giving water needed to quench thirst, and water food crops. In addition, all these rivers flow quietly through various Bible stories, providing backgrounds for major biblical events such as the divine turning of the Nile River to blood before the Exodus, the Israelite crossing of the Jordan River into Canaan, and the baptism of Christ.

Directly under Orion's feet is the sign called Lepus, known today as a dead or dying hare. But, in ancient times, this sign was seen as a serpent, whose head is biting Orion's foot. This connects well with Scorpio, the Scorpion in Greek myth that fatally wounded Orion in the heel. Scorpio is also represented by its decan called Serpens, the Serpent, both of which depict Satan at his most malevolent.

Greek myths, along with their stellar connections, are considered classic parts of our heritage today. Unfortunately, however, in a nearly successful attempt to blind all men spiritually, Satan inspired all mythological, Pagan connections made between the heavens, and various human heroes. By obliterating the true meanings behind the Zodiac symbols in the Gospel in the Stars, the first Gospel to mankind was virtually lost. Furthermore, Satan beguiled men into worshipping the constellations, stars, Sun, Moon, and planets - thereby blinding them to the knowledge and worship of the one and only triune Creator God Yahweh.

Thankfully, the Bible was written to compensate for the temporary loss of the Star Gospel, and to preserve a memory of the true allegorical and prophetic meanings behind many of the constellations. In addition, the Bible gives the actual names, and epic life stories behind the characters allegorically depicted in the vast expanses of the night sky. This is especially true for the constellation Orion, which depicts many Bible heroes. Of course, the greatest of these heroes is Yahshua, the Messiah. Just as the Egyptians called Orion "Seir," or "Prince," Christ is the Prince of Peace, and will one day literally rule as the King of kings on Earth. Orion therefore depicts Yahshua as a Conquering Prince or King.

In relation to Yahshua, the Bull of Taurus has much prophetic meaning. First of all, it signifies Christ as an atonement sacrifice - as seen in the bulls sacrificed to atone for the sins of the priests, and all Israel (Exodus 29:36; Leviticus 4:13-14), and the lambs sacrificed in atonement at Passover (Exodus 12:5-8). As explained in Book One using Gary Hazle's revelation concerning the sign of Taurus, the stars of Orion form a distinctive hourglass shape that can also be viewed as a large cup, or chalice in the sky, with the bottom of the bowl of the cup corresponding to the belts star of Orion (and the Giza Pyramid Complex, as will be shown in Books Three and Four). This can be seen as the wine cup that is used four times in a Passover meal.

In addition to this heavenly cup, there is a huge V-shape that is formed by the smaller V-shape of the Hyades star cluster in Taurus' face, and the stars marking the tips of the bull's horns. This can be seen as the tear made in a piece of unleavened bread, or the crack made in a matzo cracker on Passover. This suggests that Taurus and its decan signs Orion, Auriga, and Eridanus represent Christ's Body and Blood, and the New Covenant He made with mankind at Passover. Because Yahshua was sacrificed outside of Jerusalem like the bull used in atonement sacrifices, it shows that He died for the sins of the whole world, and to redeem both the righteous and the unrighteous when they repent and are saved.

Now, if Orion's raised sword arm is viewed as poised to slay the bull called Taurus, it shows Christ in the process of allowing His body to be sacrificed. In fact, the three belt stars of Orion may mimic the three crosses on Golgotha when Christ was crucified, and the downward sweep of the sheath of Orion's sword from the middle star may symbolize Christ's holy blood being poured out for mankind's salvation! Indeed, Christ sacrificed Himself not only for the righteous saints, but also for those who will come out of six of the Seven Churches of Revelation, which are depicted in the six brightest stars of the Pleiades. Through their repentance, these Tribulation Saints will be spiritually reborn and promised everlasting life in the Resurrection via Christ's shed body and blood! We will discuss this more in a moment.

# Ch. 4: The Pillar of Enoch's Amazing Prophetic Design   Page 153

## Taurus and Orion Depicting Christ's Sacrifice

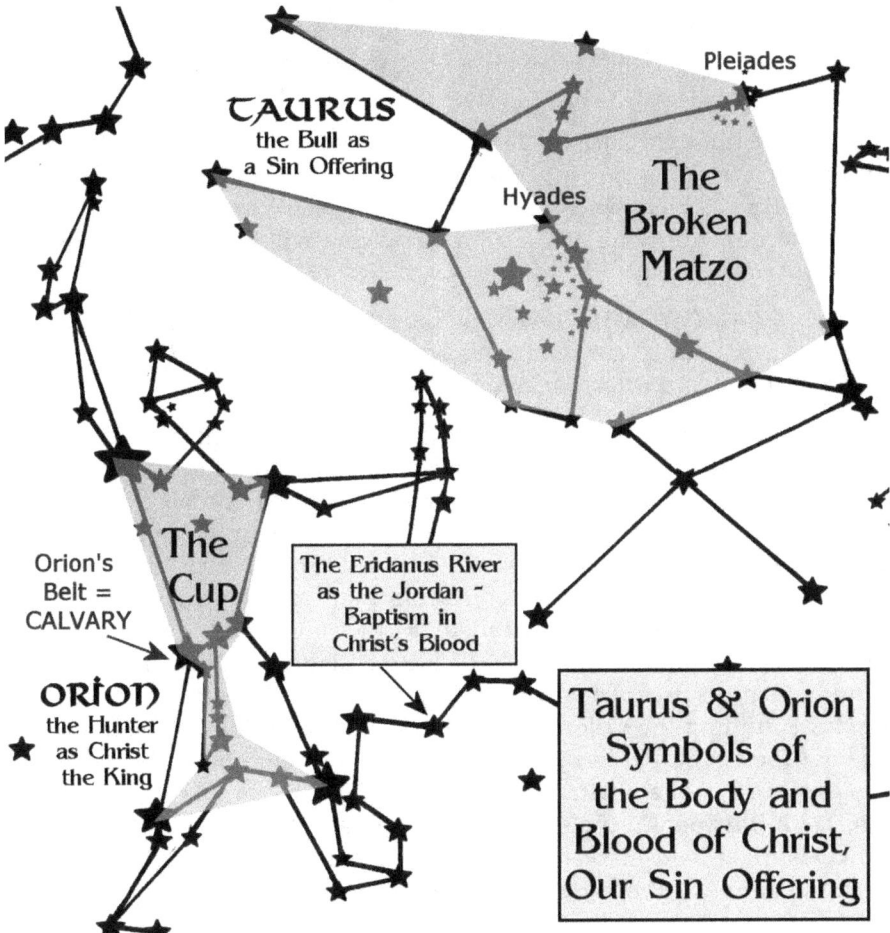

In the illustration above, Orion's hourglass shape is depicted as a Passover wine goblet (i.e. the Cup of Redemption), with the three belt stars forming the bottom of the cup. In addition, Taurus the Bull's V-shaped Hyades star cluster is depicted as the "V" formed by a torn piece of unleavened bread. Envisioned in this way, they signify the New Covenant cut with Christ's Body and Blood, which serve as the Bread of Life (John 6:35, 48), and the Living Water (John 4:10, 7:38) for all believers. As such, the Eridanus River flowing beneath Orion and Taurus can be seen as a river of water that has been tinted red with Christ's redeeming blood, and the baptism of the Spirit of God all true believers receive when they repent, and accept Christ's shed blood for the remission of their sins. This ties in perfectly with the fact that the heavenly river called Eridanus represents the Jordan River that John the Baptist baptized Yahshua in, and whose water symbolizes redemption, as well as the Blood of Christ shed from the Cross onto the barren ground of Golgotha.

Now, though Christ's death has not yet been avenged on Satan, it will be when Satan is cast into the abyss. This will initially occur after Christ returns as His own Avenger of Blood, when the Eridanus River will depict the enormous quantity of blood that will be spilled during the Battle of Armageddon:

> "And the winepress was trampled outside the city, and blood came out of the winepress, up to the horses' bridles, for one thousand six hundred furlongs." - Revelation 14:20

As the preceding Scripture conveys, **the Eridanus signifies this bloody slaughter of those who will reject the baptism of salvation found in Christ's shed blood**. As such, they will have to shed their own blood to pay for their sins. This victory over evil can be seen in the dead serpent called Lepus beneath Orion's foot, and the river of judgment and mercy called Eridanus that flows out from that same foot! This is why the star that depicts Orion's foot is called "Rigel," meaning "The Foot that Crushes," and hearkens back to the first messianic prophecy in the Bible found in Genesis 3:15! This same prophecy is revealed many times in the skies surrounding the Orion constellation, as shown in my illustration on page 518 (See page 155 in this book for a slightly modified version). In fact, as shown in the illustration on page 547 (See a similar illustration on page 218 in this book), the star called Regulus in the sign of Leo was also known as Rigel, and marks the same truth: that Christ has won the war against evil, and will one day crush Satan forever!

The preceding analogies surrounding Orion, Taurus, and the Eridanus constellation partly explains why the sign of Taurus represents the Wrath of God poured out during the Great Tribulation. However, Taurus' connection to God's Wrath can also be seen in the two horns of Taurus, which signify Joseph's two sons Ephraim and Manasseh. What people often miss about these two horns, tribes, or nations is that they dualistically serve as both proponents *and antagonists* of the Gospel of Christ at different times in history.

In fact, these horns represent the nature of the Church today, which is made up of righteous believers, as well as apostates. The right horn of the bull represents the righteous people who follow Christ in today's world, and are thus guaranteed everlasting life. Meanwhile, the

# Ch. 4: The Pillar of Enoch's Amazing Prophetic Design   Page 155

left horn of the bull signifies the Antichrist and the people who follow him, but who are still being called to repent and be saved. These tie in with the meaning of the horns or hands on the Cherubim in Ezekiel and Revelation. We will examine the roles of the two very spiritually different groups of people represented by the horns and hands of the Cherubim in Books Three and Four.

## Orion, Auriga, & Perseus Treading Satan Underfoot

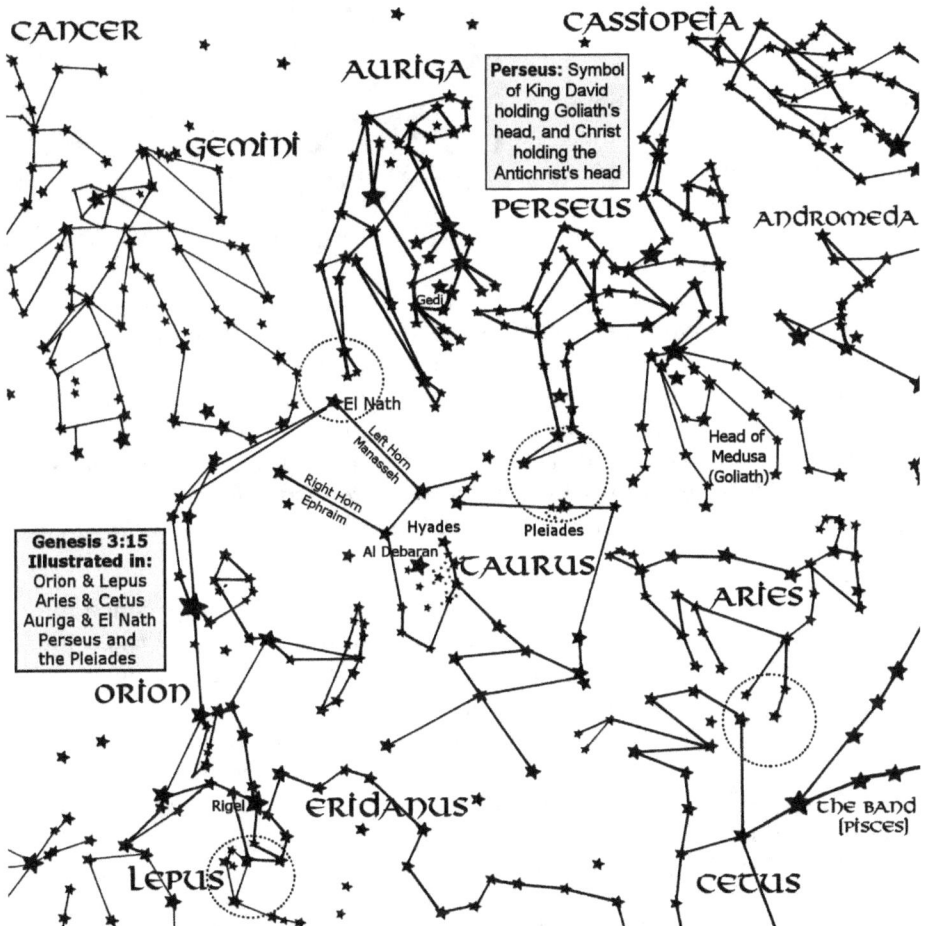

In its ultimate End Time application, Taurus depicts the evil Beast from the Sea in the Book of Revelation. Coupled with the Pleiades star cluster, which appears to be riding on Taurus' back, it also depicts six of the Seven Churches of Revelation, as mentioned earlier. This connection can be seen in the uncanny, dipper-like similarity between the pattern of the six brightest stars in the Pleiades, and the seven bright stars forming the constellations of Ursa Major and Ursa Minor, also known as the Big Dipper and Little Dipper, which are shown in the illustration on page 551 (See page 500 in this book).

Myths all over the world tell the story of how one of the original Seven Sisters, or stars that made up the Pleiades was separated somehow from the other six, but then often rejoined them at a later time. As with many Pagan myths, some truth underlies those concerning the Seven Sisters. In this case, the missing sister or star likely represents the Church of Philadelphia or Brotherly Love.

The Pleiades as 6 of the 7 Churches of Revelation

Those who allegorically belong to this one congregation - possibly signifying only one seventh of all professing believers alive today - will be taken in the First Rapture. But all apostate Christians who were never baptized with the Holy Spirit will be left behind, and - if they choose to join ranks with the Antichrist and the Woman who rides the Beast - will be severely judged. Sadly, *many professing Christians today have abandoned the true Gospel and represent the Church of Laodicea, which will be left behind in the Great Tribulation.*

Two Euro Greek Coin Featuring Europa on Bull

Uncannily, the prophetic truths concerning apostasy and divine judgment that are locked into the imagery of the sign of Taurus are being graphically depicted today in symbolism surrounding the European Union. For example, the EU Parliament Building in Strasbourg, Germany looks remarkably like either a Space Age rendition of the ruined Coliseum in Rome, or a partially constructed Tower of Babel. Significantly, the Coliseum is where many Christians were martyred, while the Tower signifies Babylon, where the Star Gospel was perverted and God was openly mocked. In addition, depictions of the woman Europa being carried on the back of a Bull representing Zeus in disguise have become a defining symbol of the EU, and are now found there everywhere - from commemorative stamps and Euro coins, to a sculpture outside the Council of Minister's Office in Brussels, Belgium.

## Ch. 4: The Pillar of Enoch's Amazing Prophetic Design

As will be shown in Book Four, people from *all* the churches on Earth today (except the allegorical, worldwide Church of Philadelphia) will be left behind to suffer God's Wrath because they are spiritually asleep. As a result, some of these apostate Tribulation churches that claim to have salvation of Christ but who aren't known by Him are to be judged, deceived, and connected to the Woman riding the Scarlet Beast in Revelation (Rev. 17:3-6). This Woman represents the false religious system of the Antichrist - a system that is allegorically sitting on the Beast representing the Antichrist's global spiritual, economic, military, and political power. Thankfully, however, there will be many who will listen to the testimony of 144,000 Witnesses and the Two Witnesses of Revelation, and they will find redemption.

**End of Excerpt from the "The Language of God in Humanity"**

This except from Book Two shows that Orion is a clear symbol of Yahshua in His roles as both a Redeemer of Sin and a Conquering King. In the horns of Taurus, we also can see the apostate and elect sides of the Church. Recognizing this duality to the Church will be extremely important in our Chapter Nine study of the place that the United States has in Bible Prophecy.

Now, as revealed in Books One, Two, and Three, the Great Pyramid, and the two other big pyramids at Giza are tied to the three belt stars of Orion. Since Orion represents Christ, the belt stars serve as the symbolic royal girdle, or belt of Christ, as well as the allegorical base of Christ's Cup of wine at the Last Supper. Indeed, these three stars may also represent the three crosses on Calvary at Christ's crucifixion! Curiously, though, the Great Pyramid doesn't represent the middle cross where the blood of Christ flowed from. As lengthily discussed in Book Three, "The Language of God in History," the middle pyramid associated with Pharaoh Khafre at Giza - with its causeway running to the Great Sphinx - actually depicts Christ's Cross and shed blood - just as the Gospels indicate. To understand this arrangement better, the illustration on page 224 shows that the star Al Nitak is clearly connected to the Great Pyramid. "Al Nitak" means "The Wounded One," or "The Slain One," while the star associated with Khafre's Pyramid was once called "Al Rai," meaning "The Bruised" - as in the Seed of the Woman who was bruised on the heel, who is Christ! In fact, all of the belt star names clearly allude to Christ's shed blood as our redemption from sin. As will be shown next, the meanings of the other constellations and stars allegorically targeted by the Great Pyramid also point to Christ, Christ's role in conquering Satan, and Christ's offering of salvation from sin.

In 2500 BC, the southern shaft in the Queen's Chamber targeted Sirius, the brightest star in the constellation Canis Major, or the Greater Dog. In the Dendera Zodiac, however, this constellation is depicted as a hawk, and is labeled "Apis," which means "the Head." The hawk, as the natural enemy of the serpent, represents Yahshua as a warrior king conquering Satan. Later in Egypt's long history, Sirius, and the constellation Canis Major became associated with Isis, the wife and sister of Osiris. However, the star name Sirius is Greek, and was derived from the original Ancient Egyptian name for that star: "Seir," which means "Prince." Incidentally, "Seir" was also the name of the god whom the Greeks called Osiris. This points to the fact that the original meaning of Canis Major was tied to the great Warrior/Redeemer that was depicted by the constellation Orion/Osiris and many other constellations in the Mazzaroth.

The northern shaft in the King's Chamber targeted Thuban (a.k.a. Alpha Draconius) in the constellation "Draco" the Dragon in 2500 BC. Thuban is in the long, coiling tail of Draco. Significantly, Thuban was the pole star for thousands of years before Precession gave that distinction to the star Polaris in Ursa Minor. All the dates cited for when the Great Pyramid may have been built fall within the time that Alpha Draconius was the pole star.

Significantly, some scholars have noted that Thuban/Alpha Draconius' circuit in the sky was once directly in line with the Descending Passage in the Great Pyramid. Furthermore, this was when Thuban served as the Pole star. This is highly symbolic, since Alpha Draconius is in the constellation Draco, which represents not only a great dragon, or serpent, but also Satan/Azazel himself! Therefore, **a star in the constellation that represented unmitigated evil ruled in the one part of the sky that never set.** This suggests that the Descending Passage was meant to allegorically represent the path to Hell and damnation.

Since the previous pole star was in such an allegorically evil constellation, it metaphorically suggests that this past age before the Great Flood was ruled over by the original serpent, or dragon called Satan. I identify Satan with the evil angel named Azazel in the Book of 1 Enoch. Maybe this is why the Bible tells us that Satan is the prince, or ruler of this world (John 12:31; 14:30; 16:11). Though the presence of the Church and the Holy Spirit are factors currently working against Satan's total control, the Spirit-filled True Church did not exist prior to Yahshua's First Advent.

# Ch. 4: The Pillar of Enoch's Amazing Prophetic Design

## Great Pyramid Star Shaft Alignments In 2500 BC

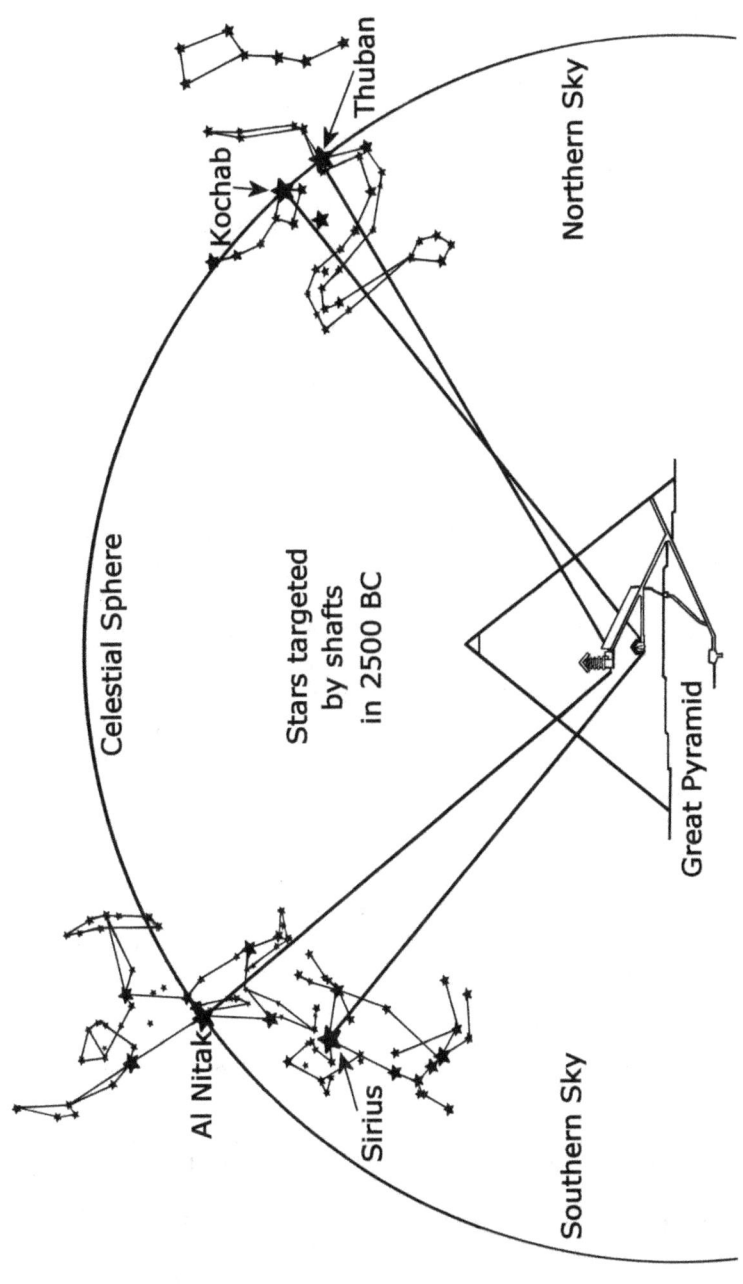

The fact that the pole star Polaris is now in the constellation of Ursa Minor is also no accident. Known today as the Lesser Bear, **Ursa Minor was not seen as a bear at all in ancient Zodiacs, but as a sheep pen, or plow.** In the Zodiac of Dendera, this constellation is shown as a plow topped by a jackal - a demonic symbol of death signifying that this sheepfold, or plot of land full of unrighteous sheep or bad seeds. It may also represent the curse of the Law and the morally lax Church of Laodicea in the End Times.

It is highly significant that the northern shaft in the Queen's Chamber pointed to the star labeled Kochab (a.k.a. Beta) in Ursa Minor in 2500 BC. The allegorical significance of this is shown through the constellations nearby. Next to Ursa Minor is Ursa Major, or the Greater Bear. This constellation is represented by a big bear in today's Zodiac, and is commonly known as the Big Dipper. However, the ancient symbol for this constellation was *a big sheepfold, or sheep pen*. This constellation therefore likely depicts the True Church, which is allegorically filled with the good sheep that Yahshua shepherds.

In contrast, Draco curves around Ursa Minor in what appears to be a deadly embrace. Since Draco allegorically depicts Satan, and the Antichrist, it suggests that the smaller sheepfold represented by Ursa Minor is currently ruled over by Satan. As shown in Book One, "The Language of God in the Universe," Ursa Minor may depict the apostate branch of the Church, which will likely suffer through the Great Tribulation. However, Ursa Minor's star names suggest that it also represents the Tribulation Saints who will be added to Yahshua's righteous sheepfold during the Tribulation period.

The location of all four star shafts in the Great Pyramid carry forward this theme of the good sheep being led by Christ, and the bad sheep led by Satan. For example, the northern shaft in the King's Chamber targets Draco, the Dragon, while its southern shaft targets the triumphant figure of Orion, the Hunter. This is a clear allusion to Christ's supremacy over Satan, and His war against evil. It is an allegory in the stars that says that Yahshua will destroy Satan by piercing through his body – the despicable body and soul of evil! The meaning of these constellations add weight to the idea that the King's Chamber may represent the Millennial Rule of Christ – a time in history when Christ's resurrected, perfected saints will reign over mortal, unsaved people.

In light of the glorious time in history targeted by the King's Chamber, it makes sense that the star shafts in it point to two allegorically complimentary constellations. Just as the god Osiris conquered death for the Egyptians, Yahshua is the triumphant figure in

## Ch. 4: The Pillar of Enoch's Amazing Prophetic Design   Page 161

Orion who will conquer the evil Dragon, sin, and death for all people, and for all time. During Christ's Millennial Rule, this will be blessedly apparent - even though the threat of evil will not be fully annihilated until the end of the thousand years is reached.

Likewise, the southern shaft in the Queen's Chamber points to Sirius in Canis Major, and represents Yahshua, the Righteous Branch. Meanwhile, the northern shaft points to Kochab in Ursa Minor. As already stated, this constellation represents the apostates and neo-pagans that will suffer through the Great Tribulation. The star Kochab, however, suggests that some will be found among this damned group that will not perish. "Kochab" means "Awaiting Him Who Comes." It therefore may signify that a righteous remnant awaiting Christ's return will come out of the Laodicean Church during the Tribulation. In sync with the meaning of the shafts, the Queen's Chamber represents Jews and Gentiles who accept Christ, both during the Age of Grace, and in the Tribulation period.

Since the Queen's Chamber allegorically corresponds to the ceremonial washing of priests and the rite of baptism, this may be one reason why the floors in the Queen's Chamber and in the Horizontal Passage were left unfinished. This may serve as a sign that a portion of Israel represented by the Queen's Chamber has spiritual business to attend to before they can enter the salvation represented by the King's Chamber.

This interpretation also makes sense of the bizarre corbelled recess that leads to nowhere in the east wall of the Queen's Chamber. This recess has five levels - four of which give the impression of being corbelled. I believe that this corbelled recess directly alludes to four of the corbels in the Grand Gallery that represent the last four thousand years of history. It therefore covers the entire time span that God's Covenant people have been in existence - from Abraham to the present. The Queen's Chamber therefore represents spiritual Israel and the True Church - those people who will become the Bride of Christ. Up until the time of the Rapture and end of this 4000 year-period, the true and apostate branches of the Church will exist together.

From the above diagrams and explanations, we can see that the Zodiac signs, and the Great Pyramid are connected astronomically, and that both have many godly spiritual meanings. We have also seen that the Great Pyramid has a sacred connection to the Bible, and an important symbolic place in dating the prophetic events that are foretold in it. All five claims made about the Great Pyramid earlier have therefore been substantiated, especially the claims that it is an astronomical record and calendar, and a storehouse of spiritual and intellectual knowledge.

Nevertheless, there are still more proofs that the five statements made about the Great Pyramid's purpose are true. In Chapter Five, for example, it will be conclusively shown that the design of the Desert Tabernacle is connected to the Great Pyramid in meaning and purpose - and this in turn shows that the Great Pyramid was designed to be a Temple to God. Also, in the next section, we will see that the Great Pyramid may also have served a utilitarian purpose, and this may account for the presence of some of the unusual structural features within it.

## *Strange Acoustics and Anomalies within the Great Pyramid*

As has already been shown through allegorical imagery, the Great Pyramid's alignment with certain stars is no accident. Many temples in Ancient Egypt were aligned with the helical rising points of stars, and may have been designed to be allegorical, earthly representations of these stars. This is because the floor plans of most Egyptian temples reflected the same threefold structure found in the Desert Tabernacle, which depicted the triune structure of a human being. Instead of the golden Ark of the Covenant, however, the inner Holy of Holies in Egyptian temples had a golden ark with hinged doors in the front that opened to reveal the idolatrous image of the god or goddess that the temple was dedicated to. The Great Pyramid, however, is devoid of any idolatrous statues, or art images. It is therefore quite unlike any other temple in Egypt.

The Great Pyramid's star shafts suggest that, among other things, it was a huge astronomical time marker. The facts already presented make it quite clear that the Great Pyramid is, and was always far more than simply the oversized tomb of a megalomaniac. Its structure is far too complex and over-designed to have merely been a tomb. Furthermore, all of the astronomical, and scientific knowledge encased within its structure marks the Great Pyramid as something far more sophisticated than any other temple, or religious monument ever devised.

The stark barrenness and great precision shown in the measurements of its interior passages suggest that the Great Pyramid was much more than a temple or astronomical observatory. In fact, the Great Pyramid may have also served another utilitarian technological purpose. This was quite compellingly demonstrated in a book entitled "The Giza Power Plant" by Christopher Dunn. In his book, Mr. Dunn noted that the Great Pyramid has many highly unusual acoustical properties that were

# Ch. 4: The Pillar of Enoch's Amazing Prophetic Design   Page 163

achieved by the pyramid's unique design, as well as the type of red granite used in its construction. In particular, the King's Chamber and Grand Gallery appear to be acoustically connected to produce a beautiful resonance through the percussive vibrations that are seismically and tidally created within the Earth. This acoustical resonance would serve no purpose if the pyramid were merely meant to be a place to inter a dead pharaoh and his grave goods, or if it was only used to study the Sun, Moon, and stars in the heavens.

Another feature of the Great Pyramid that I did not mention thus far is the damage that has been sustained by the King's Chamber. There are massive cracks along the huge granite ceiling beams on the south end of the King's Chamber that are not easily explained. Though these cracks may have been formed during a particularly strong earthquake, there is no residual damage shown anywhere else in the Great Pyramid except the King's Chamber. In addition, enough force was exerted from some unknown source within this chamber that it appears to have pushed the walls of the entire chamber out an inch past their original boundary. Yet **damage of this nature is completely lacking anywhere else in the pyramid.** On the contrary, every passage and chamber in the Great Pyramid *except* the King's Chamber shows exceptionally great mathematical and technological precision.

This raises the question that, if not an earthquake, what could have caused this isolated damage to the internal structure of the Great Pyramid? Mr. Dunn believes that an explosion of some type within the King's Chamber caused the damage there. I concur with him on that point, and speculate that the explosive force exerted on this chamber would have had to be horrendously large to cause it to expand the inch that it did. After all, there is a tremendous amount of stone weighing millions of tons surrounding the King's Chamber on all sides, including the massive forty-ton blocks of granite in the ceiling that have the cracks in them.

What could have caused this explosion inside the Great Pyramid? One possibility is that a bomb of some type was detonated within the King's Chamber. Before modern times, grave robbers, or adventurers may have set off a bomb in an effort to find a hidden doorway, or a passageway that would lead to concealed treasure. Their choice of explosive remains a puzzle, however, especially since the damage sustained in the Great Pyramid may have occurred long before the Middle Ages, when the use of gunpowder as an explosive agent became widely known.

Mr. Dunn has a far more spectacular theory of where the source of this powerful explosion came from. He believes that the Great Pyramid was a massive power plant that was meant to create usable electrical energy through sound vibrations. The energy thus generated was subsequently channeled to some sort of power relay station. There, it could be sent to various destinations, and be used to provide light, or drive machines. As an example of the uses for this power, Mr. Dunn cites the drilled holes, and cut stone blocks found throughout Egypt that show evidence that they were made using high-powered saws, and drills. Evidence of this has been found everywhere in architectural ruins and tombs. Yet, as far as archeologists ascertain, the Ancient Egyptians only had primitive stone, copper, or bronze tools at their disposal.

If the Great Pyramid were some sort of power generator, or electrical energy source, it could also have been used to propel various passenger vehicles such as the boats, planes, cars, and submarines that were described in Edgar Cayce's channeled readings. In a trance, Cayce said that these vehicles were used in the lost civilization called Atlantis. Mr. Dunn refers to Cayce's readings because the Atlantean power source described by Cayce that supposedly powered these vehicles sounds remarkably similar to the power plant that Dunn believes existed within the Great Pyramid. Though the implications of this channeled information is interesting, I do not in any way endorse the practice of channeling messages from spirits beyond our world! These messages can only be coming from demonic sources, and though they may contain glimpses of the truth, they are *always* inundated with a plethora of satanic lies.

After this Great Pyramid power plant was successfully started, Mr. Dunn believes that something went wrong with the amount of energy being produced inside it. This massive machine may then have malfunctioned in a way that caused a temporary spike in energy output. This energy output may have been so far above normal that it could not be diverted quickly enough. It therefore led to a powerful explosion inside the King's Chamber that shut down this power plant at the Giza Pyramid Complex - one that could have feasibly been in operation for thousands of years before it malfunctioned.

If the primary method for creating the energy in the Great Pyramid was the harnessing of sound vibrations, then it appears to have been a completely pollution-free source of energy! If so, **our antediluvian ancestors may have had a technologically more advanced society than our own** - with a safer form of energy, and sophisticated machines that were more environmentally friendly than anything we use today. Furthermore, it shows that these same ancient people used brilliant ingenuity to combine the practical functionality of a machine with a highly allegorical method of communicating ideas - and they did so in a way that worked almost perfectly in each case.

Mr. Dunn believes that the Great Pyramid created energy by absorbing, and channeling the vibrations of the Earth. This may have been done using Helmholtz-style resonators, which are hollow spheres of metal, or glass with one round opening. When sound vibration is introduced, these resonators amplify certain frequencies of sound vibration, creating a potential source of energy. Seven-tiered stacks of Helmholtz-style resonators (corresponding to the seven tiers in the Grand Gallery's walls) may have picked up natural vibrations from the rotation of the Earth. Evidence that there may have been 28 stacks, with seven different sized resonators in each stack, exists in the 28 precisely spaced slots that can be found along each long wall of the Grand Gallery. These may have served as anchor points for paired sets of poles that held up the stacks of resonators.

Mr. Dunn states that the unusual design of the Great Pyramid's Antechamber suggests that there were mechanisms within it meant to dampen any undesired vibrational energies created in the Grand Gallery. A significant upsurge in the vibratory resonance within the Earth would therefore be required to cause the resonators in the Great Pyramid to respond with enough sound vibration to override this energy dampening safety mechanism. Once any over-amplified sounds entered the King's Chamber, however, the vibratory energy produced would have quickly surged out of control. A terrible explosion within the King's Chamber could then have occurred, causing the odd cracks in its massive stone ceiling blocks.

Though Mr. Dunn believes a destructive power surge in sound vibration occurred in the Great Pyramid energy plant, he never suggests a known natural disaster that could have caused this destructive output. Though he notes that a powerful earthquake beneath the Great Pyramid could have done so, he doesn't name a particular instance when this may have occurred in Egypt's remote past.

If a violent earthquake caused this power surge in the Great Pyramid power plant, could the quake have been triggered by the same violent mechanism that produced the Great Flood? If the Great Flood were caused by a tremendous celestial bombardment, it would have resulted in unquestionably violent earthquakes, and massive volcanic eruptions. This, in turn, would have triggered a terrible upsurge in sound vibrations in the Great Pyramid, thereby causing the Giza Power Plant to shut down after a terrible explosion.

After this explosion, Mr. Dunn cites evidence that the Great Pyramid's internal power plant workings were repaired. Subsequently, the Great Pyramid may have been put back into use again as a power plant until another disaster possibly destroyed the civilization that utilized this tremendous source of power. If this is true, it likely happened after the Flood. Therefore, is it possible that Nimrod channeled this source of energy to power the building of his ungodly empire, and the Tower of Babel? If so, then we know from biblical references that Yahweh sent fire from heaven, and an earthquake to destroy Nimrod's world empire, and his unholy tower. Could this be the destructive force that brought the Giza Pyramid Power Plant's functionality to a crashing halt for a second and possibly final time?

The Well Shaft in the Great Pyramid appears to have been constructed to provide a way for qualified inspectors to periodically access the Grand Gallery and the Queen's and King's Chambers. This may have been done to look for damage, or to enact possible repairs when necessary. The Well Shaft may also have been created to allow the caretakers of the Great Pyramid to inspect the bedrock beneath the pyramid. This is suggested by the fact that the Well Shaft runs through two large vertical fissures in the bedrock beneath the Great Pyramid. It also appears as if the Great Pyramid's upper chambers were accessed at some point in the distant past so that plaster could be daubed into the cracks found in the ceiling stones of the King's Chamber.

The peculiarities of the Well Shaft lead to some interesting questions such as: why would such an inspection tunnel be required if the Great Pyramid were only a tomb? Furthermore, why is the Great Pyramid the *only* supposed tomb in Egypt that had a special inspection, and repair access point? Other tombs show evidence of having been entered by Egyptian priests after thieves had broken into them. However, in every other case, the priests entered by way of the *original* entrances, which were then resealed. Why then was the Great Pyramid different?

A plausible answer is that the Great Pyramid functioned as something other than a tomb. A need for inspection within the pyramid suggests that there were moving parts, or mechanisms inside that were susceptible to periodic damage, or breakdown, and would need to be repaired occasionally. If this was true, then what sort of power mechanism was contained within the Great Pyramid? Was it simply meant to produce light like a large light bulb, or was the energy that it provided used to power quarry tools, a city, a country, or even a civilization that spanned the entire planet?

# Ch. 4: The Pillar of Enoch's Amazing Prophetic Design

Regardless of the uses of its proposed energy, the possibility that the Great Pyramid may have served as a power plant in addition to its other functions is nothing short of miraculous. There is no modern technological counterpart that compares in size or scope to the Great Pyramid - especially if it once functioned as a power source. Adding this theory of the Giza Pyramid Power Plant to what has already been revealed in this book about the Great Pyramid makes one thing certain. The possibility that the Great Pyramid was a storehouse of hidden spiritual, scientific, and technological wisdom cannot be easily denied.

As witnessed in this section, there is much evidence suggesting that the Great Pyramid was purposely over designed to function on many levels of awareness, and had many interrelated purposes for its existence. For this reason, the Great Pyramid is one of the most fascinating, and enigmatic structures in the world.

## *The Great Pyramid as a Scriptural Symbol for Christ*

Thus far in this book, we have looked at some of the technological, scientific, and spiritual knowledge locked into the Great Pyramid. Now let's take a look at the allegorical spiritual meaning of the Great Pyramid and Great Sphinx. There are several messianic Bible prophecies that directly refer to the Great Pyramid. The first two appear in Isaiah. In the first, Isaiah speaks of a precious cornerstone that Yahweh has laid in Zion:

> "So this is what the Sovereign LORD (Yahweh Adonai) says: "See, **I lay a stone in Zion**, a tested stone, **a precious cornerstone** for a sure foundation; the one who trusts will never be dismayed." - Isaiah 28:16 (NIV)

According to Isaiah's prophecy, this stone is in Zion, and Zion is another name for the spiritual home of God's people in the End Times. Zion is therefore not just a physical location like Jerusalem, but the state of Grace supplied to those who are saved through repentance, and belief. Christ identified the location of this "home" when He said: "*the kingdom of God is within you*" (Luke 17:21). This home can therefore truly be found in the metaphorical temple found within all Spirit-filled believers. That is why the Prophet Isaiah also tells us that this same cornerstone in Zion is *a sanctuary,* but that this stone will nonetheless be a stumbling block for both Houses of Israel:

> "The LORD of hosts (Yahweh Tsavout), Him you shall hallow; let Him be your fear, and let Him be your dread. **He will**

*be as a sanctuary, but a stone of stumbling and a rock of offense to both the houses of Israel,* as a trap and a snare to the inhabitants of Jerusalem." - Isaiah 8:13-14

The Houses of Israel mentioned in this Scripture consist of two groups of believers: the adopted sons of Abraham that are Christians, and the natural sons of Abraham, who are Jews. In Prophecy, these Two Houses of Israel are known as Ephraim and Judah. Many Bible scholars agree that the precious cornerstone and the stumbling stone that Isaiah refers to is the Messiah Yahshua. Isaiah is therefore foretelling this current era, when many Christians have fallen away from their true faith, and Christ has become a stumbling block to them, just as He is for many Jews. Furthermore, most modern apostates view anyone who says they need Christ in their life as weak, and they insist that Biblical morality is an outdated form of intolerance - especially as regards premarital sex and homosexuality. They also claim that sin, the need for a Savior, and Salvation by Grace are outmoded ideas that need to be discarded.

These apostates want to make everyone think that everything is permissible - as long as it doesn't harm anyone else! In essence then, they have rejected morality, and turned it into a stumbling block. Instead, they favor "tolerance," which is often just another expression for turning a blind eye to sin! In effect, the new, worldwide tolerance movement is Anti-Christian, and rejects even the most basic moral principles taught by the chief cornerstone of our faith: Yahshua the Messiah.

Another Bible prophecy regarding this same Rock, stone, or chief cornerstone appears in Psalm 118, where Christ is called the capstone:

*"This is the gate of the LORD (Yahweh) through which the righteous may enter. I will give you thanks, for you answered me; you have become my salvation.* **The stone the builders rejected has become the capstone;** *the LORD (Yahweh) has done this, and it is marvelous in our eyes."* - Psalm 118:20-23 (NIV)

This reference of the capstone in Psalm 118 is highly significant, as will be shown in a moment. Long after Isaiah wrote it, Yahshua quoted this same prophecy about the capstone and applied it exclusively to Himself:

*"Jesus (Yahshua) said to them, "Have you never read in the Scriptures:* **'The stone the builders rejected has become the capstone;** *the Lord (Yahweh) has done this, and it is marvelous in our eyes'? 'Therefore I tell you that the kingdom of God will be taken away from you and given to a people who will produce its fruit.'"* - Matthew 21:42-43 (NIV)

## Ch. 4: The Pillar of Enoch's Amazing Prophetic Design   Page 169

Still later, the apostle Peter used this prophecy as he preached the Gospel to his fellow Jews. When he did, **Peter made it clear that he believed that Yahshua is the Chief Cornerstone:**

> "...let it be known to you all, and to all the people of Israel, that by the name of Jesus Christ (Yahshua the Anointed One) of Nazareth, whom you crucified, whom God raised from the dead, by Him this man stands here before you whole. **This is the 'stone which was rejected' by you builders, which has become the chief cornerstone.'** Nor is there salvation in any other, for there is no other name under heaven given among men by which we must be saved." - Acts 4:10-12

The capstone or chief cornerstone is an architectural term that often refers to the top, center stone in the lintel of an arched or corbelled doorway. In its Biblical application, it usually referred to the capstone in the main entrance doorway of the Temple of Yahweh. Interestingly, **Psalm 118 ties the symbolism of the gate of Yahweh and the capstone the builders rejected with Yahshua.** Furthermore, Yahshua calls Himself the Gate that God's faithful sheep or followers must go through to find Salvation:

> "Therefore Jesus (Yahshua) said again, 'I tell you the truth, **I am the gate** for the sheep.'" - John 10:7

The gates of Israel were often archways made of stone. As such, they would have had a capstone in the center of the archway - a capstone like the gates of Jerusalem had, and its Temple doorways may also have had. **However, this chief cornerstone or capstone could also be accurately applied to the pyramidion-shaped capstone of a pyramid.** It has already been shown that the Great Pyramid has many of the qualifications necessary to be a temple. This will be further proven in the next chapter, where the Desert Tabernacle is shown to mirror the spiritual symbolism found inside the Great Pyramid. It is therefore likely that this chief cornerstone may have pertained not only to Solomon's Temple, but also to the far older and grander Great Pyramid in Egypt.

As mentioned previously, it appears that the Great Pyramid was never finished and its missing capstone has never been found. **It was as if the Great Pyramid's builders were trying to tell us that this capstone was deliberately disregarded.** Conspicuously missing on the Giza plateau, this omitted capstone seems to be an allegory for the fact that Christ would be rejected and excluded by the Jews - those who were Yahshua's "brothers" and supposed fellow builders in establishing the Kingdom of God.

In Chapter Two, we discussed the prophecy about the stone and capstone mentioned in Psalm 118. Together with what has been revealed here, it serves to prove that the Great Pyramid may indeed be the obelisk that contains the Bible Code Key, and a key to understanding many of the spiritual revelations God gave to the ancients through His divine Language. It also shows that the Great Pyramid is truly a code in stone that identifies the God/man Yahshua the Messiah as well as the Body of Christ!

## *The Christ Angle Inside The Great Pyramid*

For those who do not wish to believe that there are other powerful testimonies about Yahweh, and His Path to Salvation that preceded the Bible, all the amazing Bible proofs I cited already will likely not be enough. For skeptics, however, there is still more proof that the Great Pyramid was divinely inspired. Let me make it clear, however, that I am *not* endorsing the use of extra-biblical works to replace Biblical Scripture. Unless these extra-biblical works agree with the teachings of the Bible in *all key respects*, they should never be regarded as true testimonies about the Living God Yah. For example, religious books such as the Koran, and the Book of Mormon do not agree with the Bible in many key respects. They either deny the deity of Christ, or introduce ideas that are not supported by the Bible at all. Unlike them, the Great Pyramid silently proclaims the truths of the Bible, and the special purpose and deity of Christ without giving any conflicting information. Let's examine further proofs of this.

Inside the Great Pyramid, the angle of the Ascending Passage is 26 degrees, 18 minutes, and 9.7 seconds. This unique angle forms an imaginary triangle at the juncture of the Horizontal Passage leading into the Queen's Chamber with the Grand Gallery above it. In fact, this angle is formed at the point where the date of Christ's birth in 3 BC is alluded to in Pyramid Inches - at the junction between the Queen's Chamber floor line and the Ascending Passage ceiling. This has been dubbed the Christ Angle. On the next page is a special diagram that I made to show how the Christ Angle is derived, and how it reveals dates surrounding Yahshua's birth, death and resurrection.

Note that the Christ Angle starts with Yahshua's birth year of 3 BC. As shown in Book One, "The Language of God in the Universe", Yahshua was born on or shortly after the Feast of Trumpets in 3 BC. The Christ Angle also shows that three and a half years passed between Yahshua's baptism by John in the Jordan River in 27 AD until His First

# Ch. 4: The Pillar of Enoch's Amazing Prophetic Design

Advent Ministry came to an end with His crucifixion death, and burial on the eve of Passover in 31 AD. This places Yahshua's baptism in the month of September in 27 AD - during the period of the Autumn Feasts of Israel. These year correlations form a Chronology of Yahshua's First Advent Life, Ministry and Death and Resurrection that I showed many proofs for in Book Two: "The Language of God in Humanity".

## Illustration of the Christ Angle in the Great Pyramid

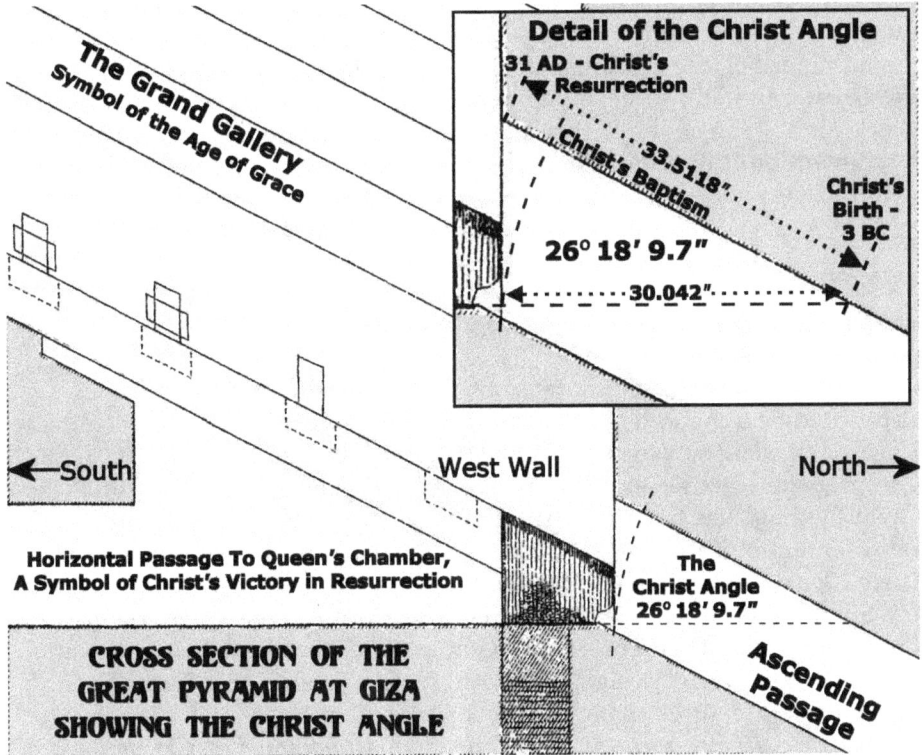

Since the discovery of this angle, its relationship to Christ and Judeo-Christianity has been proven in a rather unusual way. With the Great Pyramid as the starting point on an equal projection map, scholars have figured out that *this angle intersects three locations that are vitally important in the history of Judeo-Christianity*. This was discovered by drawing a line from the base of the pyramid due east on the map. If we then draw a second line northeastward at an angle of 26 degrees, 18 minutes, and 9.7 seconds, the Christ Angle it forms intersects the finger of the Gulf of Suez at the likely point where the Israelites entered the

Sinai wilderness during the Exodus. Next, the same angle line cuts directly through the center of the town of Bethlehem – the town in Israel where Yahshua was born! When extended still more, this same line cuts through the Jordan River - near to the ruins of the ancient city of Jericho. This is also the exact place where many Bible scholars believe the Israelites first crossed into the Promised Land after the Exodus.

As if to point to its importance, the Christ Angle is formed by the shadow of the Great Pyramid at noon on the Summer Solstice *every year*. Furthermore, as shown in Book Three and in the graphic on page 137, the causeway leading from the Great Pyramid points toward the direction of the Summer Solstice, and also points toward Israel. Therefore, it is as if the Great Pyramid has been engineered to point toward Bethlehem once a year - for as long as the Sun rises and sets on Earth! How amazing that a monument built to honor the Messiah of the World points to the location where He was born in a humble Sukkah, and where angels, shepherds, and the starry Mazzaroth bore witness to His long-awaited arrival!

## *A Stone Memorial to Yahshua as Creator*

For all the preceding reasons, the Great Pyramid as a whole appears to be a metaphor for Yahshua in His Role as Redeemer, while the King's Chamber may also be an allegory for Yahshua's role as the Creator. There are several major reasons for believing this. First of all, the Great Pyramid has been mathematically shown to be a ten-millionth-scale representation of the Earth's Northern Hemisphere. It also indicates the Earth's position in the Solar System by showing its relative distance from the Sun and Moon. Secondly, as mentioned in Chapter Three, the use of the Pythagorean Theorem, Pi, the Golden Section, and the Golden Ratio Phi were used in the design of the King's Chamber in the Great Pyramid. These design features seem to have been used in the King's Chamber to suggest that *its proportions represent the mathematical constants used in the creation of our Solar System, as well as in all material things*.

This evidence makes it almost certain that the Pillar of Enoch is also a Pillar for Christ, and the sacred ratios and proportions that were used in its design were likely put there to show allegorically *that, in essence, the Messiah is also the Creator God*. In fact, if we examine the facts, Yahshua's triune connection to the Godhead is shown in the construction of the Great Pyramid. This can clearly be seen through ideas examined closely in Book Two of this book series. There, the Sun is shown to be a clear allegory for the God the Father, and God the Son, while the Moon signifies the Holy Spirit. This is why the King's

# Ch. 4: The Pillar of Enoch's Amazing Prophetic Design    Page 173

Chamber, as a symbol for the Sun, can also signify Yahweh. In addition, it can also indicate the truth that Yahshua's mind was God's own mind. In addition, the Queen's Chamber, as a symbol for the Moon and the Holy Spirit, depicts Yahshua's own Spirit! Housed as these chambers are inside the Great Pyramid, together the three depict the triune nature of Christ, whose human body is allegorically being associated with the Earth that every human body is made up of!

Some people may balk at the suggestion that the Pillar of Enoch symbolizes Christ's triune nature, and His dual nature as fully human (via the metaphor of the Earth), and fully God (via the allegorical meanings of the Sun and the Moon), but there is no doubt that it reflects Christ's creative power. The Bible passages connected to the Great Pyramid, and all the scientific and mathematical facts embedded into its design fully support this conclusion. In fact, the Bible makes it perfectly clear that Yahshua created the Universe, and the Earth! With the Holy Spirit at His side, the Preincarnate Yahshua formed all things out of nothing using the mathematical laws that His Father set into place before Creation began:

> *"He (Yahshua) is the image of the invisible God, the firstborn over all creation. For by Him all things were created that are in heaven and that are on earth, visible and invisible, whether thrones or dominions or principalities or powers. All things were created through Him and for Him. And He is before all things, and in Him all things consist." - Col. 1:15-17*

This Scripture clearly teaches that Yahshua created the Universe. That is why there is such a remarkable connection between the Creator God Yahweh's Creation, and the geometric proportions found in the King's Chamber. Just as they are found in the King's Chamber, the use of Pi, and the Golden Ratio Phi are found constantly in the circular, spherical, and spiral constructs found in nature. They are, therefore, considered by some scholars ***to be the sacred mathematical building blocks of all matter.*** This theory is behind the mystical science of Sacred Geometry, which is related to Sacred Astronomy.

These sacred ratios are found most easily in the repeating crystal patterns that occur in the atomic structure of minerals in countless variations. Another example can be found in the ratio of the order of the leaves around certain plant stems, and in the petal number and distribution in certain flowers. These ratios can also be found in the spiral form of every DNA strand. Since they are so much a part of Creation, these geometric ratios make an excellent allegory for the act of Creation itself. They also suggest that the Creation didn't just happen by accident, but that a Being with infinite intelligence, omniscience, and omnipotence created it all.

Standing as a silent sentinel full of knowledge and truth for countless centuries, the Great Pyramid is truly a remarkable structure. This chapter has merely touched upon all of the awe-inspiring knowledge encoded into its design. Even more incredible is that this knowledge is so far reaching. Constructed 2,500 years before the Messiah was born, the Great Pyramid's encoded knowledge regarding Yahshua is nothing less than a miracle. *It is perhaps because of its bold witness for Christ that the Great Pyramid, along with the Great Sphinx, the Giza complex as a whole, and the Red and Bent Pyramids at Dahshur are the only divinely inspired edifices built by men that have withstood the test of time.* It is therefore likely no accident that many people in today's world have a fascination for all things Ancient Egyptian, especially the Great Pyramid, and Great Sphinx. Yet most of them are really unaware of the enormous amount of hidden symbolism in them announcing that Yahshua is, was, and always will be the Messiah, and King of the Universe!

Yahweh is continually calling out to all people through His Creation, the Bible, the Jews, the True Church, and the Great Pyramid. Through His divine Language in all these things, Yah is beckoning people to open their ears to hear, and their eyes to look and see all the wonders He has wrought for us to explore, and appreciate. Yet, even with all these miraculous signs of Yah's Glory still visible in today's world, many people are too blind to see it. As it says in Scripture:

> *"Even after Jesus (Yahshua) had done all these miraculous signs in their presence, they still would not believe in him. This was to fulfill the word of Isaiah the prophet: 'Lord, who has believed our message and to whom has the arm of the Lord (Yahweh) been revealed?' For this reason they could not believe, because, as Isaiah says elsewhere:* **'He has blinded their eyes and deadened their hearts, so they can neither see with their eyes, nor understand with their hearts, nor turn- and I would heal them.'** *Isaiah said this because he saw Jesus' (Yahshua's) glory and spoke about him."* - John 12:37-41 (NIV) (See also Isaiah 6:10 and 53:1)

How sad it is that so many have denied or perverted Yahweh's clear testimony about Himself found all around us. Yah made this testimony to show us that He loves us, and wants none of us to perish. Because of His great love for us, Yahshua never left us to guess on His Will, or where to find the only true Path to Salvation. He instead provided many powerful verbal and visual pictures to educate inquiring minds about the Path to Salvation from sin. The Great Pyramid is one

## Ch. 4: The Pillar of Enoch's Amazing Prophetic Design   Page 175

such visual picture meant to show us the way to salvation in Yahshua. Indeed, the Great Pyramid can be viewed as a giant parable in stone - a parable written by the Master Parable-teller Himself! It is therefore a shame that so many have chosen to ignore, or pervert the Great Pyramid's clear message to us today, especially in light of its role in prophecy.

A bit later in this book, we will explore the final and most explosively prophetic element of the Great Pyramid. This is found in the measurements of the passages within the Great Pyramid that lead up to the threshold of the Antechamber, which in turn leads into the King's Chamber. These passages may be more than spiritually and technologically symbolic elements in the Great Pyramid. They may also be giant rulers showing the prophetic passage of time leading up to the Tribulation period, and Second Coming of Christ!

## Chapter 5: Pyramid and Tabernacle: Divinely Designed

> *"We do have such a high priest... who serves in the sanctuary, the true tabernacle set up by the Lord, not by man. Every high priest is appointed to offer both gifts and sacrifices, and so it was necessary for this one also to have something to offer...* **They serve at a sanctuary that is a copy and shadow of what is in heaven...** *But the ministry Jesus (Yahshua) has received is as superior to theirs as the covenant of which he is mediator is superior to the old one, and it is founded on better promises.* **For if there had been nothing wrong with that first covenant, no place would have been sought for another."** *- Hebrews 8:1-7 (NIV)*

In Book Two, it was shown how the Desert Tabernacle and Ark of the Covenant were divinely designed to reveal important spiritual truths to us using the Language of God. Looking at the Desert Tabernacle allegorically, the symbolism in its features reflects both the three-fold construction of a man, as well as the three-fold nature, and purpose of the one True God Yahweh, and His marvelous Son. Amazingly however, this message of spiritually regenerated people, the Trinity, and the coming Messiah who would make mankind's spiritual transformation possible was being symbolically proclaimed long before the Desert Tabernacle was constructed!

As mentioned earlier, and in Book One and Three, the Great Pyramid and Great Sphinx pointed ahead to Christ 2500 years before He came! Yahshua was symbolized in every aspect of their construction, as is the Solar System, and Universe that Yahshua created to be a reflection of His purpose, and Plan of Redemption for mankind. In addition, as shown in Book Three, Enoch was the first known prophet to write about the coming of *"the Son of Man,"* who is Christ, and to teach about His pre-eminence, perfect righteousness, and kingship over all the sons of men (1 Enoch 46:1-6, 48:1-6, 62:5-16, 69:26-29, 71:14-16). This suggests that Enoch and the righteous Sethites before the Flood knew that Yahshua was coming to redeem not only mankind, but also all Creation from sin! The fact that Yahshua did so is often overlooked in attempts to interpret profound scriptural passages like this one:

> "He said, 'This is the blood of the covenant, which God has commanded you to keep.' In the same way, he sprinkled with the blood both the tabernacle and everything used in its ceremonies. In fact... without the shedding of blood there is no forgiveness. **It was necessary, then, for the copies of the heavenly things to be purified** with these sacrifices, **but the heavenly things themselves with better sacrifices than these. For Christ did not enter a man-made sanctuary that was only a copy of the true one; he entered heaven itself...** to appear for us in God's presence." - Hebrews 9:20-24 (NIV)

This Scripture is speaking about so many interrelated things. First of all, in verse 23, it clearly hints that **the Tabernacle and its furnishings are copies of heavenly things.** Furthermore, it tells us that the heavens and everything within them need redemption - just as mankind does. **This Scripture is therefore speaking of the physical heavens surrounding our Earth, NOT the Heaven where God dwells!** Coupled with the opening Scripture for this chapter, this Scripture gives a clear indication that the Desert Tabernacle was always meant to be a reflection of the heavenly Tabernacle that Yahshua created. Furthermore, we get an inkling of the truth that the Desert Tabernacle was a powerful allegorical symbol - a symbol for Yahshua's blood sacrifice for sin. It was Yahshua's sacrifice *alone* that forever redeemed the heavens, the Earth, and all living things from the clutches of sin, decay, and death.

Amazingly, as was shown in the previous two chapters, **the Great Pyramid also appears to be a reflection of heavenly things.** First of all, its external design represents our Earth. The Queen's Chamber is a symbol for the Moon, the resurrection of Christ, and the giving of the Holy Spirit, while the King's Chamber is an allegory in stone representing the Sun, as well as Christ - our Immanuel, or "God with Us." In addition, the four shafts leading from the Queen's and King's Chambers point upward toward specific stars in the heavens tied to the Star Gospel.

This suggests that the physical heavens - with its Gospel in the Stars - stood as a testimony to Christ's greatness before men were instructed to make allegorically connected copies of the heavens on Earth such as the Great Pyramid. Just as Scripture teaches that the Desert Tabernacle is a reflection of what is in the heavens - meaning the physical heavens surrounding our Earth - the Great Pyramid is a reflection of those same heavens. Likewise, just as the Desert Tabernacle is a reflection of mankind's need for redemption through Christ, the Great Pyramid

# Ch. 5: Pyramid and Tabernacle - Divinely Designed

allegorically reflects the same teachings. Before exploring my findings on the connection between the Giza Pyramid complex and the Desert Tabernacle and Temple to Yahweh, I highly recommend reviewing my teachings on this subject in Chapter Three of my book "The Language of God in History" showing this Giza - Sky correlation. In that chapter, I show the Star Gospel connection pertaining to the site layout of the Giza Pyramid Complex, as well as the fact that the Great Pyramid was meant to mark the allegorical location of God's heavenly Tabernacle - where Yahshua dwells through His Spirit.

In this book, it will be shown that ***the Great Pyramid and the Desert Tabernacle also share similarities in their physical design.*** Furthermore, it will be shown that their design represents the structure of the Universe, as well as the physical design of every born-again believer. In fact, the Earth, the stars, and all the other celestial bodies that add meaning to the Gospel in the Stars are representations of the heavenly Tabernacle spoken of in Scripture. This correlates with the idea that Yahshua came to redeem not only mankind with His precious blood, but also the entire Universe! Furthermore, though godly men built both the Great Pyramid and Desert Tabernacle, we shall see why their true author and designer is Yahweh!

In the previous two chapters, we explored the vast amounts of hidden knowledge that can be found in the Great Pyramid's design. In this chapter, we will examine all the amazing correlations between the Great Pyramid and Desert Tabernacle. We will thereby see why both of these sacred structures appear to have served as mirrors of the heavens and heralds of Yahshua's coming and purpose. To begin, let's examine some obvious correlations between the Ark of the Covenant and the Coffer in the King's Chamber.

## *The Ark and the Coffer: Symbols for the Risen Christ?*

An ark is a fancy box used for storing sacred objects. The Ark of the Covenant therefore had a practical purpose, as it was used to store the sacred relics among the Israelites. However, the Ark of the Covenant was far more than simply a storage box. It was, in fact, a powerful storehouse of spiritual knowledge in allegorical form. In fact, **every gilded portion of the Ark was an amazing allegory for Christ!** This was clearly shown in Book Two. It is therefore highly recommended that anyone reading the following section familiarize themselves with Chapter Ten in that book, which discloses many of the allegorical spiritual messages hidden within the Desert Tabernacle and Ark of the Covenant.

To see the first and most obvious correlation between the Great Pyramid and Desert Tabernacle, let's examine the peculiar dimensions of the Ark of the Covenant. The Book of Exodus tells us that the Ark of the Covenant was 2.5 cubits long, by 1.5 cubits wide, by 1.5 cubits high:

> "Then Bezalel made the ark of acacia wood; two and a half cubits was its length, a cubit and a half its width, and a cubit and a half its height." - Exodus 37:1

Curiously, this is the exact size in Sacred Cubits of the Granite Coffer in the King's Chamber. There was therefore definitely a correlation in dimensions between these two seemingly unrelated boxes. But the connection does not stop there! For example, the lidless Coffer is the only object within the King's Chamber. Likewise, the Ark was the single sacred furnishing within the Most Holy Place in the Desert Tabernacle, though it was joined by two unauthorized statues of Cherubim in Solomon's Temple.

The cubic volume of both the Ark of the Covenant and the empty Coffer in the King's Chamber are also identical. Furthermore, the cubic volume of the large bronze "sea" or basin in the courtyard of Solomon's Temple was the same as the King's Chamber - which is fifty times the volume of either the empty Coffer or the Ark of the Covenant. Interestingly, the priests used the water in the Bronze Sea to wash themselves before serving before Yahweh. The King's Chamber therefore reflects that those who are covered by the perfect nature of Christ through baptism have been washed clean by His blood. The dimensions in cubits of the Most Holy Place in the Tabernacle and the later Temple of Solomon are also precisely identical in size to the King's Chamber in the Great Pyramid, showing that all these sacred rooms were meant to be a reflection of our perfect High Priest and the blood sacrifice that He made for all Creation.

As stated earlier, it appears that the Coffer in the King's Chamber has always been meant to serve as a symbol for the risen Christ, and also as a symbol for the translation of Enoch - the man who was the probable, divinely guided designer of the Great Pyramid. As the symbol of an empty tomb, the Coffer therefore also has a direct connection to the Ark of the Covenant, which served as a symbol for Christ and of His future death and resurrection.

The lidless Coffer inside the King's Chamber corresponds exactly in symbolic meaning to the Ark of the Covenant in several ways. First of all, the Ark was an allegory for the promise of deliverance from death through resurrection. Secondly, it represented Yahshua's own Spirit

# Ch. 5: Pyramid and Tabernacle - Divinely Designed

dwelling inside each resurrected believer, which is the means by which we acquire resurrection into everlasting life. The contents of the Ark also represent Yahshua's own Spirit - through which we remember and apply the Word of God (Tablets of the Law), which are found in the Bread of Life (Manna) and in the righteous Branch of Jesse (Aaron's Staff). All these appellations can only apply to one person in history: Yahshua the Anointed One.

This is also what the empty Coffer in the King's Chamber symbolizes. It is a symbol of the risen Christ - the Son of God who conquered sin, death and decay forever on our behalf. Like the Ark, this Coffer is a silent messenger telling us all that all of us can conquer death and receive everlasting life through Christ - He who is the eternal Bread of Life - when we believe in Him.

This connection between the Ark of the Covenant and the Coffer, which were separated by huge gaps of time and distance, may seem incredible to some people - especially to skeptics who doubt the validity of the Bible. Nonetheless, these correlations between these two sacred structures are obvious and compelling - and they simply do not end with the Coffer and Ark alone. As we will see in a moment, the entire Great Pyramid was connected with the symbolism found in every aspect of the Desert Tabernacle.

## A Shared Design in the Pillar of Enoch and Tabernacle

Though many may choose to ignore it, there is an uncanny correlation between the Desert Tabernacle complex and the Great Pyramid complex that goes far beyond coincidence. First of all, as shown in the following chart, there appears to be five interior divisions in both complexes. Upon seeing these correlations, many comparisons between the Desert Tabernacle and the Pillar of Enoch can accurately be made. For instance, the Great Pyramid's exterior could have served the same purpose as the altar of burnt offering did in the Desert Tabernacle's and Temple's Courtyard.

Since the Great Pyramid may have served as a Covenant Pillar for the Sethites, offerings of oil and blood could have been poured over the Great Pyramid's dazzling white limestone casing stones - just as they were poured or sprinkled onto the bronze altar in the Tabernacle. Another spot in the Great Pyramid that seems to depict the altar of burnt offering is the red granite plug in the Ascending Passage. In addition to this, the Great Pyramid shows a five-fold construction. Though the Desert Tabernacle should be viewed as consisting of three broad sections with different purposes, there were five distinct components working within its three-fold construction. The following chart shows these five design elements and how they connect to the Great Pyramid's design:

## Chart Showing Fivefold Tabernacle-Pyramid Connection

| The Five Design Elements in the Desert Tabernacle: | The Five Interior Divisions of the Pillar of Enoch: |
|---|---|
| (1) The Entrance, and Outer Courtyard of the Desert Tabernacle | (1) Casing Stones, Entrance, Passages, and Grand Gallery of Great Pyramid |
| (2) The Altar of Burnt Offering and Bronze Sea | (2) Granite Plug, Well Shaft, and Queen's Chamber |
| (3) The Holy Place | (3) The Antechamber |
| (4) The Most Holy Place | (4) The King's Chamber |
| (5) The Ark of the Covenant | (5) The King's Coffer |

The Israelites were outside the holiest shrine of their religion, and a ten-foot high wall of white linen surrounded it on all four sides. They therefore could not see inside the Tabernacle complex at all. Similarly, the Great Pyramid's interior was sealed off from view behind four walls of casing stones made of pure white limestone. Just as the Tabernacle, and the objects in its courtyard could not be seen outside the curtain, the Grand Gallery and other internal features of the Pillar of Enoch cannot be seen from outside.

The white outer covering on both structures signifies the pure white raiment reflecting the Shekinah Glory of God that the saints will wear in Heaven (Matthew 17:2; Revelation 7:9-14, 19:14). The Tabernacle Courtyard was later referred to as the Court of the Gentiles in the Temple of Solomon. Anyone who loved Yahweh could enter into the Court of the Gentiles, as long as they were ritually clean. It therefore foreshadows the godly nations that will gather around Jerusalem in Christ's Millennial Kingdom.

Though the Ancient Israelites could not see their destiny, God had a greater plan for them than anything they could have imagined. This is seen in the Camp of Israel that surrounded the Desert Tabernacle

# Ch. 5: Pyramid and Tabernacle - Divinely Designed

Courtyard on all sides. This Israelite Camp corresponds directly with the Great Pyramid as a whole. Just as the Camp of Israel was a foreshadowing of the Millennial Kingdom of Christ, the Great Pyramid testified of the coming of the same Kingdom of God on Earth. Likewise, just as many individual stones form the Great Pyramid, God's people are the countless stones that form His holy Temple. This suggests that the entire Pillar of Enoch was meant to signify spiritual Israel, which consists of all Jewish, Israelite, and Gentile believers. Adding to this theme, the Grand Gallery of the Pillar of Enoch corresponds directly with the Tabernacle Courtyard. We will explore other startling correlations between the Grand Gallery and the Tabernacle Courtyard a bit later in this section.

Inside the Great Pyramid, the Descending Passage was completely sealed off from the Ascending Passage by a huge granite plug that represented the division between a holy God and fallen men that was caused by sin. The only way to get into the Ascending Passage from the Descending Passage at one time was through the Well Shaft. The Well Shaft connects the Descending Passage with the juncture between the Grand Gallery and the Horizontal Passage leading into the Queen's Chamber.

The Descending Passage and Subterranean Chamber in the Great Pyramid represent the effects of sin outside the Camp of Israel. It is the place outside of the Covenant of blood, and the divine Law - the place where degenerate man is completely separated from the purity, sanctity, and holiness of Yahweh. It is the place where people outside of Yah's Covenant of salvation are destined to perish, and be cast into the bottomless pit on the Last Judgment. That is why the Descending Passage ends with the Subterranean Chamber's "bottomless" pit (as described in Chapter Four).

The Well Shaft, like the Grand Gallery, alludes to the Outer Courtyard that was just inside the Tabernacle complex. In this Outer Courtyard, there was the Bronze Sea that represented the baptism of repentance, and the altar of burnt offering that symbolized God's Blood Covenant with mankind. It also foretold Yahshua's shed body and blood, and the rite of Communion.

Though only priests could enter the Tabernacle courtyard, they were sinful priests ministering before a holy God. Therefore, when they offered atonement sacrifices on the altar of burnt offering, they did it for all Israel - and for themselves also. This role of the priests foreshadowed Yahshua, who was perfect, unlike ordinary priests, and offered the perfect sacrificial lamb when He died on the Cross.

By His blood sacrifice on the Cross, Yahshua paid the full price for all our sins. In fact, the ascending Well Shaft - with its grotto that contains a stone abutment that resembles the head of a lamb - represented the altar of burnt offering, and the related sacrifice of Yahshua on the Cross. The red granite plug at the entrance to the Ascending Passage could also represent the altar of burnt sacrifice. The sacrifices offered on that altar were insufficient for salvation and therefore could never bridge the great gulf between a holy God and sinful man. However, they pointed ahead to the perfect atoning sacrifice found in Christ that is represented by the Well Shaft.

The Antechamber outside the King's Chamber corresponds to the Holy Place in the Tabernacle. The cloth curtain that hung between the Holy Place and the Most Holy Place showed the separation between the holy and invisible God Yahweh and His sin-filled, fallen Creation. This cloth curtain representing our separation from God is represented by the great stone block above the entrance to the King's Chamber. There are four parallel semi-circular grooves cut into this huge stone that resemble pillars. Uncannily, there were also four pillars of acacia wood that held up the veil separating the Holy Place from the Most Holy Place in the Desert Tabernacle (Exodus 26:31-32). This suggests that the low entryway into the King's Chamber from the Antechamber represented the veil separating sinful mankind from a holy God. Since the Antechamber depicts the final Tribulation before the Millennial Rule of Christ, its connection to the Temple veil shows that the wall of separation between Yahshua and His Church will not be completely destroyed until the Millennial Rule of Christ, when everyone that takes part in the First Resurrection will finally know and love God fully.

At one time, it is believed that there were three stone slabs in the Antechamber blocking the entrance into the King's Chamber from the Grand Gallery. A portion of one of the slabs still remains in the pyramid. This remaining granite slab is in the groove closest to the entrance to the King's Chamber, and it *is in two unbroken pieces* that appear as if they were never intended to completely fill the space they occupy. In other words, they were never meant to block the path into the King's Chamber, but merely to hamper one's entrance into it by making it difficult.

Piazzi Smyth believed that the two halves of this granite slab represented the spiritual uniting of the Houses of Israel and Judah under the leadership of Christ. This one slab in two pieces may therefore represent Israel - first in the Ten Lost Israelite Tribes recovered from all the nations on Earth, and secondly in Judah, which signifies the modern-day Jews. I partly agree with this assessment, and cover this subject at more length in Chapter Seven. However, a much more detailed overview of the meaning and purpose of the Two Houses of Israel is given in Books Two and Three of this series.

## Plan of Desert Tabernacle Showing Links to Great Pyramid

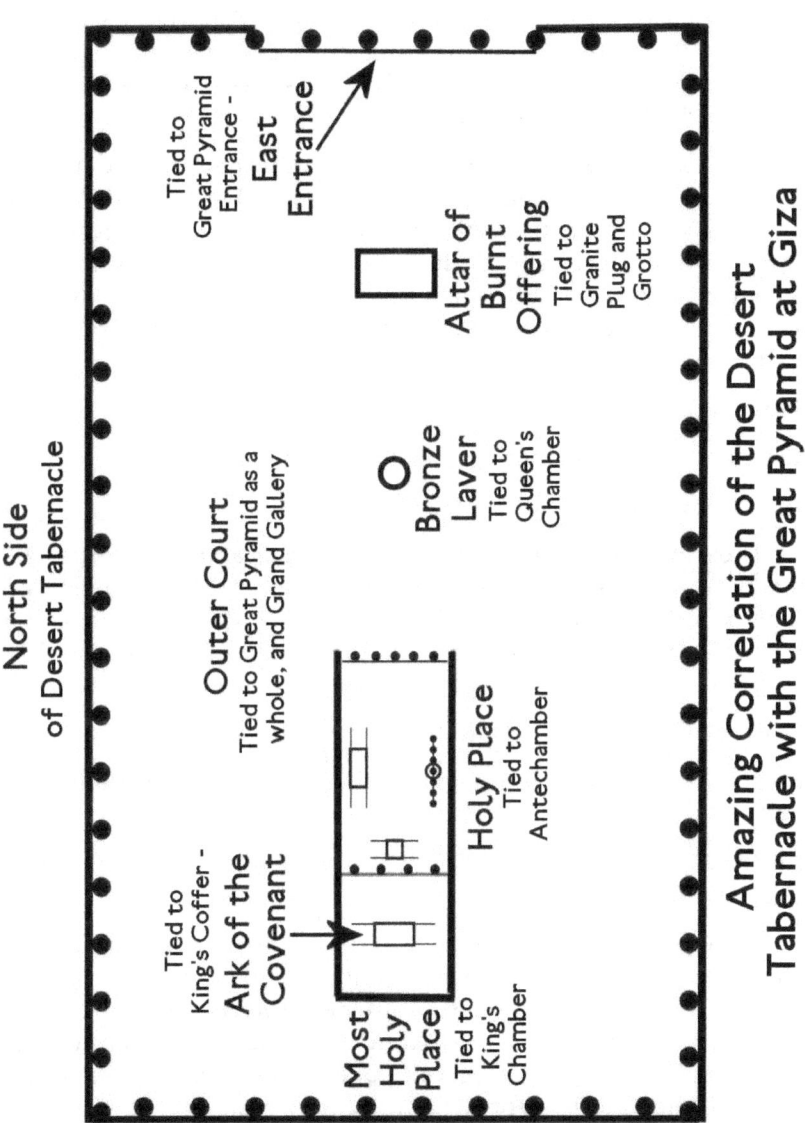

Like Piazzi Smyth, I believe that the three grooves in the Antechamber were never intended to block the way into the King's Chamber with a real sequence of three stone barriers. Rather, they appear to have an allegorical significance that is entirely in keeping with the meanings associated with other structural elements in the Great Pyramid. For example, there are three major connecting passageways in the Great Pyramid - the Descending and Ascending Passages, and the Horizontal Passage into the Queen's Chamber.

These three passageways each pertain to some aspect of our Path to Salvation. In addition, there were three ritual objects inside the Desert Tabernacle's Holy Place: the table of showbread, the golden lampstand, and the altar of incense. These allude to the threefold path we must take to find Salvation and be born-again. Like these ritual objects, the three grooves in the Antechamber's east and west walls appear to represent this path, which consists of:

1. Repentance from sin (the table of showbread),
2. Regeneration of the spirit (the golden lamp stand), and
3. Relationship with God (the altar of incense)

**These are the three R's of the Path to Salvation: Repentance, Regeneration, and Relationship.** The three ritual objects in the Holy Place that signify our path away from sin and death, and into everlasting life in Christ also represent Yahshua's role as the Messiah, This means that the three grooves in the Antechamber do also, as follows:

1. Yahshua as the Bread of Life (i.e. the showbread);
2. Yahshua as the Light of the World (i.e. the golden lampstand); and
3. Yahshua as the giver of the Holy Spirit - the key to a relationship with God in prayer (i.e. the incense)

Since the Holy Place and Antechamber are connected to the Tribulation, the ritual objects showing the Path to Salvation in Christ that were in the Holy Place are symbolic of what protects the Tribulation Saints from being deceived by the Antichrist. The Table of Showbread had two fresh loaves of bread placed upon it every day. These two loaves appear to be allegorically represented in the two granite slabs nearly touching in the groove closest to the entrance to the Antechamber.

# Ch. 5: Pyramid and Tabernacle - Divinely Designed

Just as the two loaves or piles of showbread signified the divided Kingdoms of Judah and Israel, these two stone slabs represent the Two House Church of Judah and Ephraim that form the Body of Christ. These two Houses were formed when Ancient Israel split into two kingdoms: the Kingdom of Judah, and the Kingdom of Israel. The literal and spiritual descendents of both Houses are scattered all over the world today, but are especially prevalent in modern Israel and the United States. A bit later, we will explore the ways that these two Houses can be identified in today's world.

These three symbols for Christ, like the three grooves found in the Antechamber, represent the three steps in the Path to Salvation. These are:

**The Three Steps To Salvation:**

1. Repent Of Sin, and Turn Away From It
2. Accept Christ as Messiah to Receive Forgiveness and the Holy Spirit, and:
3. Extend Christ's Love, Mercy and Forgiveness to Others -Whether Or Not They Repent!

These steps must be completed before anyone can go past the veil of sinfulness, and into the purity of the Most Holy Place represented by the King's Chamber. The three symbols for Christ found in the Holy Place represent this Path to Salvation written with the Language of God in the Bible. This path is only found in Yahshua, whose Spirit has always guided men via the Prophets of God throughout the Seven Great Days. These Seven Great Days are depicted in the seven levels of the corbelled ceiling in the Grand Gallery.

Since the Grand Gallery appears before the Antechamber, or Holy Place, and the King's Chamber, or Most Holy Place in the Great Pyramid, it is meant to correspond to the Outer Courtyard in the Desert Tabernacle, as well as to the roughly 2,000-year Age of Grace between Yahshua's death and resurrection, and the seven-year Tribulation period signified by the Antechamber. In Chapter Eight of this book, I will show what the interior measurements of the Great Pyramid Antechamber reveal about the seven-year Tribulation corresponding to the Prophet Daniel's Seventieth Week.

Now, just as there are three steps in the Path to Salvation, Yahweh God has also shown me that there are Three Steps to Evangelism, which consist of Three Gospel Messages that prepare others to be ready for the Kingdom of God, and to be ready to receive the love, forgiveness and Grace of God. **These three Gospels are the Gospel of Repentance, the Gospel of Salvation, and the Gospel of the Kingdom.** Understanding and accepting these three Gospel steps guarantee that true disciples of Christ will be ready for the First Rapture, as well as the right to rule and reign with Christ during the Millennial Kingdom of God on Earth. Simply stated, these are the three steps that Evangelists need to follow to lead others to Salvation in Christ effectively:

1. Disciples love sinners that are not yet saved by the Blood of Christ by preaching the **Gospel of Repentance** to them like John the Baptist did. This gospel convicts people of the filthiness of their sin, and their need for God's forgiveness. Just as John the Baptist did, we must get baptized by water because it is an acknowledgment of our sinfulness and need for repentance, and also of our need to die to sin and live righteously.

2. Those who have heard and accepted the Gospel of Repentance are ready to hear the **Gospel of Salvation.** This is to accept the blood sacrifice of the Son of God Yahshua, Who is the Lamb of God Who takes away the sins of the whole world. Only Yahshua or Jesus can forgive and wash away all of our sins and destroy its condemnation, freeing us to love and serve Him by filling us with His Holy Spirit. The Holy Spirit allows us to be born again so that we can be spiritually regenerated in Christ's image.

3. After that, repentant sinners that are being regenerated by the Holy Spirit are ready to hear the **Gospel of the Kingdom**, where there is no condemnation. The reason that there is no condemnation at this stage is because the repentance required, and the needed spiritual regeneration have already been done by those who are ready to enter God's Kingdom. In a nutshell, Evangelists need to remember to teach that Repentance must come before Salvation, and Salvation must come before Kingship can be bestowed upon us by the King of kings.

## *The Most Holy Place, and the King's Chamber*

Just as the Ark of the Covenant and the Coffer in the King's Chamber share a direct relationship, the King's Chamber corresponds to the Most Holy Place in the Tabernacle, as well as to the Most Holy Place in the Temples to Yahweh that once stood on the Temple Mount in Jerusalem. The Most Holy Place represents the First Resurrection, and the Millennial Rule of Christ on Earth - followed by eternity. The King's

# Ch. 5: Pyramid and Tabernacle - Divinely Designed

Chamber, as a representation of the Most Holy Place, shows the path to resurrection and everlasting life through Christ - the first-born of many.

An interesting correlation between the Great Pyramid and the Desert Tabernacle also occurs here. There are one hundred stones that make up the King's Chamber, and the size of the Desert Tabernacle was exactly one hundred square cubits. Even the measurements of the linen curtains that made up the walls of the Desert Tabernacle courtyard were one hundred cubits long on the north and south walls (Exodus 38:9-11).

As was mentioned in Chapter Four, red granite appears exclusively in three places in the Great Pyramid. These are in the 15-foot long granite plug in the Ascending Passage, in the Antechamber, and in the King's Chamber. This red granite had a special allegorical purpose. It represented blood – the blood of sacrifice and Blood Covenanting that symbolize blood redemption. Not surprisingly then, all three of these places in the Great Pyramid represent our need for Christ more strongly than any other portion of it - especially when they are viewed through their connection to the Desert Tabernacle.

Upon reading the section of Exodus that describes the construction of the Desert Tabernacle, another fascinating connection between it and the Great Pyramid revealed itself. This is found in the fact that **the Tabernacle's pure white outer linen wall was made up of ten linen sections that were each twenty-eight cubits long:**

> *"Moreover you shall make the tabernacle with **ten curtains of fine woven linen** and blue, purple, and scarlet thread; with artistic designs of cherubim you shall weave them. **The length of each curtain shall be twenty-eight cubits,** and the width of each curtain four cubits. And every one of the curtains shall have the same measurements."- Exodus 26:1-2*

Intriguingly, there are *twenty-eight vertical shafts* cut at regular intervals on the narrow ramps running up each side of the Grand Gallery. Furthermore, there are *ten courses* of finely cut and finished white limestone blocks lining each side of this beautifully constructed gallery. These facts suggest another strong correlation between the Desert Tabernacle, and the Great Pyramid. In fact, to my mind, the ten courses of white stone marked off by twenty-eight vertical shafts on either side of the 28 feet high Grand Gallery makes its connection to the Tabernacle's ten curtains that are each twenty-eight cubits long absolutely certain. The Grand Gallery's connection to the Outer Courtyard of the Tabernacle is thereby verified by these undeniable facts.

After climbing up the narrow Ascending Passage in the Great Pyramid stooped over, visitors are confronted with the magnificent corbel-vaulted Grand Gallery. Sweeping up to a height of over twenty-eight feet, the Grand Gallery has seven corbelled levels above the two stone ramps that run the entire length of the Gallery. It therefore contains nine levels made with ten courses of stone blocks. As first alluded to in Chapter One in the nine-branched Chanukiah pattern that runs through the New Testament, and in Chapter Two in nine significant Hallel Psalms, the number nine is a significant End Time number. Is it therefore possible that the nine levels of this corbelled vault may represent a Chanukah menorah, in which the two base ramps act like a frame around the seven levels in between?

Just as the Chanukiah formed by Hallel Psalms 110 through 118 are connected to the Tribulation period, the nine levels of the Grand Gallery suggest that it also represents this time period. Adding to this suggestion is the fact that the Grand Gallery is seven feet wide above the side ramps, and narrows to three and a half feet at the ceiling and the floor. Could this connection with the number seven and 3.5 - one half of seven – be suggestive of Daniel's prophecy of the Seventy Weeks (Daniel 9:24-27)? Uncannily, the fifth corbel counted from the ceiling of the Grand Gallery has *a seven-inch wide, and one-inch deep groove* carved into its entire length. *This groove therefore appears to suggest one "seven," which could simply be one seven-day week, or a seven year period.* As mentioned in Chapter Three, the week it represents may allegorically correlate with the middle of the seventieth week spoken of in Daniel's Seventy Weeks prophecy, which is the week of years when the Tribulation will occur.

The seventieth week of Daniel's prophecy refers to the week when Yahshua died, and rose from the dead, and to the future time of the Tribulation period. This seventieth week first occurred in the beginning of the fifth millennium after the Fall, just as this seven-inch wide groove occurs in the fifth level down from the ceiling of the Grand Gallery! I therefore believe it represents the beginning of Yahshua's 3-1/2 year ministry that began in 27 AD, and the tumultuous week in 31 AD when Yahshua entered Jerusalem to celebrate Passover, but then was arrested and crucified (Daniel 9:25-26). Scholars of Bible prophecy also believe that there will be a future fulfillment of this seventieth week (See Daniel 9:27). This will be at the time of the Antichrist's seven-year reign on Earth – the time when the Antichrist will break his treaty with Israel, and wage a terrible war in an effort to annihilate God's people.

# Ch. 5: Pyramid and Tabernacle - Divinely Designed

This seventieth prophetic week is also the time when the Wedding Reception/Feast of the Lamb in Heaven will likely take place. This suggests that the Grand Gallery represents more than the current Church Age. The seven-inch groove running its entire length depicts the Wedding Supper of the Lamb (as fully described in Chapter Ten), as well as the time period leading up to the concurrent seven-year Tribulation. The 3-1/2 year Great Tribulation, which culminates with the Battle of Armageddon, therefore appears to be represented by the Antechamber. Finally, the King's Chamber fittingly represents the Millennial Rule of Christ - while the relieving chambers above the King's Chamber that point upward represent the passage of the saved into Heaven, everlasting life, and eternity.

As was shown in Chapter Four, this number connection of the Grand Gallery with the seven thousand years leading to eternity doesn't appear to be a coincidence. In fact, based on the Tabernacle/King's Chamber and Grand Gallery connection disclosed here, the Grand Gallery's connection to the seven thousand years allotted for human history to unfold seems to be an inescapable fact. The Grand Gallery's height of twenty-eight times twelve Pyramid Inches (28 X 12PI) further suggests the twelve thousand years divided into the six thousand years of Creation, and followed by the six thousand years of human history. All these facts should make it abundantly clear that many obvious encoded prophetic and scientific bits of information are being conveyed to us through the structures within the Great Pyramid. Furthermore, the number correlations between the Tabernacle and the Great Pyramid cannot have been coincidence, and must have been divinely inspired.

Due to the Great Pyramid's connection with the divinely designed Tabernacle, Yahweh Himself is the only one who could have designed it. Like Moses in regard to the Tabernacle, Enoch therefore likely received direct revelations from God on how, and why to build the Great Pyramid. Being a true and dedicated prophet, Enoch then shared this divinely given knowledge with his children, and all his relations. Through two of Gods most blessed prophets - Enoch, and Moses - Yahweh likely gave mankind the blueprint for both the Great Pyramid, and the Tabernacle. This was done so that everyone in humanity would understand his or her need for Christ.

Through the symbolism of the Great Pyramid and the Desert Tabernacle, our Father Yahweh wanted to show us that we must become holy, or set-apart for divine service alongside His Son Yahshua. The Great Pyramid, like the Tabernacle after it, was a place where this process was fully laid out, and explained through the allegorical symbolism inherent in the Language of God. Due to the great importance of this information, a chart summarizing the amazing connection between the Great Pyramid, and the Desert Tabernacle appears near to the end of this chapter.

## *The Pillar of Enoch and Tabernacle: Temples to Yahweh!*

Divine revelation is the only reasonable answer for the perplexing question of why two seemingly unrelated structures in time, place, and function had nearly identical divisions, sizes and volumes. These similarities imply that both structures had a similar divine purpose. In fact, the prophet Isaiah clearly indicates that - like the Desert Tabernacle - the Pillar of Enoch will serve as an altar, and as a pillar, or temple to Yahweh during the Millennial Rule of Yahshua:

> "And the land of Judah will be a terror to Egypt... In that day five cities in the land of Egypt will speak the language of Canaan and swear by the LORD of hosts (Yahweh Tsavout)... **In that day there will be an altar to the LORD (Yahweh) in the midst of the land of Egypt, and a pillar to the LORD (Yahweh) at its border. And it will be for a sign and for a witness** to the LORD of hosts (Yahweh Tsavout) in the land of Egypt; for they will cry to the LORD (Yahweh) because of the oppressors (Judah), and He will send them a Savior and a Mighty One, and He will deliver them." - Isaiah 19:17-20

This prophecy in Isaiah stipulates that there will be an altar to Yahweh in Egypt *"in that day,"* which is a reference to the Day of the Lord, or the Last Day. Of all the ancient sacred structures in Egypt, the Pillar of Enoch stands out because it perfectly fulfills the following criteria that this altar must meet. According to Isaiah:

1. This altar must be recognized as one in the Day of the Lord
2. This Altar to Yahweh must be in the middle, or midst of Egypt
3. The Altar must be in Egypt, at its border
4. This Altar must be a pillar
5. This Altar must be a sign, or "oth," and a *witness*

As described in "The Language of God in History," the Pillar of Enoch uniquely and absolutely fulfills all the stipulations of this prophecy. It is at "Giza," which means "border." Furthermore, Giza is on the exact border between the ancient kingdoms of Upper and Lower

# Ch. 5: Pyramid and Tabernacle - Divinely Designed

Egypt, as can be seen in the drawing on this page. Since it serves as Egypt's traditional midpoint or "navel" between the two kingdoms that were united under the pharaohs, the Giza Pyramid Complex is also in the middle of Egypt. As previously shown, Giza also serves as a perfect midpoint or navel for the whole Earth.

Now, since standing stones generally served as altars all over the world in ancient times, the Great Pyramid can be viewed as a giant altar stone. As such, meat and grain offerings could have been burnt near its base, and liquid offerings to God could have been poured onto it to honor an ancient Blood Covenant. Also, as already exhaustively shown, the Great Pyramid serves as a sign and witness for Yahweh since it is fully tied to the witness of the heavens found in the Gospel in the Stars. Since the Giza Pyramid Complex can easily be seen as a collection of colossal, pyramidion-shaped Covenant pillars or Covenant altars, these pyramids are likely still relatively intact so that they can serve God as Isaiah prophesied they would in the Last Day.

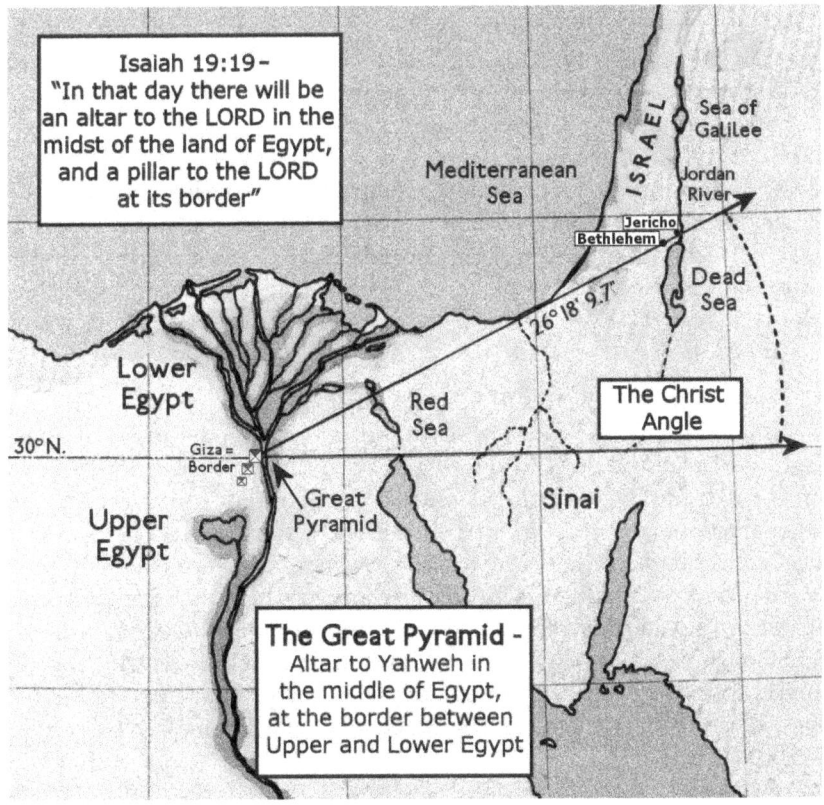

As already quoted in the last chapter, there are several other biblical prophecies that speak of the "chief cornerstone" or "capstone," which appear to refer to the capstone of the Great Pyramid, as well as to Christ. Interestingly, as noted earlier, the pyramidion-shaped capstone of the Great Pyramid can be seen as the chief cornerstone, or pinnacle stone crowning a pyramid. This stone appears to always have been missing from the Great Pyramid, suggesting that the pyramid's builders rejected it. Subsequently, it may have become the mysterious ben-ben stone that was revered by the priests of On in Ancient Egypt. How sad that these misguided priests worshipped a stone dedicated to a false god instead of the Messiah, and one triune God it represented! Nonetheless, it is fascinating to note that the patriarch Joseph was a slave in the household of Potiphar, a priest of the Ancient Egyptian god On, and subsequently married that same priests' daughter, who bore his two sons. The allegorical meaning behind this is fact is fully explored in Book Three.

Now, if the Pillar of Enoch is a symbolic altar upon which Christ, the Chief Cornerstone was allegorically offered up upon, it is possible that the Pillar of Enoch might be used as an altar unto Yahweh again during Christ's Millennial Rule. As mentioned earlier, in their ancient Judeo-Christian context, an altar was a place where innocent animals met their deaths to pay for the sins of others. Likewise, the Pillar of Enoch is a symbolic altar and prophetic stone witness that represents the ministry, death, and triumphant resurrection of Christ, our spotless Lamb. Just as the Pillar of Enoch symbolically shows in the Queen's Chamber, Grand Gallery, Antechamber, and King's Chamber, Yahshua the Messiah came to minister to a lost and dying world, to redeem all Creation from death and decay through physical resurrection, and spiritual transformation, and to judge the unrepentant.

However, though the Pillar of Enoch likely served as a Covenant pillar, altar, and temple that men could enter in the past to learn about Yahweh, and His Son, this knowledge was hidden. In addition, this pyramid's extremely steep slope, and the long length of its interior passages make exploring it extremely difficult. Furthermore, since the Great Pyramid is devoid of decoration, and is not in Jerusalem, it was never intended to replace the future Temple spoken of in Ezekiel. The Great Pyramid was only meant to be a prototype, or blueprint of the Tabernacle, or Temple of Yahweh in Heaven, as well as a reflection of the future Temple to be built in Jerusalem – a Temple whose mysteries will not be hidden, but open to the plain scrutiny of all believers in Christ as the Son of God.

# Ch. 5: Pyramid and Tabernacle - Divinely Designed

Since Yahweh instructed Moses on how to build the Desert Tabernacle, and the Tabernacle is connected to the Pillar of Enoch, this raises the question of whether or not Moses knew what Enoch's pyramidal pillar really stood for. Moses was raised as an Egyptian Prince, and - as all royal Egyptian princes were - he would have been extensively educated (Exodus 2:10). Some of the knowledge imparted to royal children was of a religious nature, and - due to allegorical references to the Great Pyramid's internal passages in the Book of the Dead - it is clear that the Great Pyramid's internal structure figured prominently in the religious ideas of the Ancient Egyptians. Therefore, Moses may have been aware of, and impressed by the scientific and spiritual knowledge that the pyramidal Pillar of Enoch silently provided.

Moses was also most definitely familiar with the system of measurements that the Ancient Egyptians used, so he would have known of the Sacred Cubit, which is 25 Pyramid Inches long. Furthermore, Moses' fellow Israelites built monuments for Pharaoh before their Exodus from Egypt. It is therefore plausible that the Israelites used the Sacred Egyptian Cubit and Pyramid Inch to build the Desert Tabernacle and the Ark of the Covenant. In fact, the identical dimensions between the King's Coffer and the Ark of the Covenant make this supposition even more likely.

But did Moses know that the Desert Tabernacle was a type, or allusion to the same spiritual ideas as the Great Pyramid? It is my belief that Moses *did indeed know* their connection, but that he did not apply what he knew of God's allegorical Language to the Tabernacle's design. In fact, it is fairly clear throughout Exodus, Leviticus, and Numbers that Yahweh gave Moses the design for every aspect of the Desert Tabernacle, as well as all the sacred implements used in priestly service to God. This therefore shows that Moses was merely a messenger of God's Will, and did not design any part of the Desert Tabernacle. It also suggests that Yahweh designed the Great Pyramid through one of His most devout servants prior to the Flood. According to the Book of Jasher, there was no greater Pre-Flood servant of God than Enoch, the seventh righteous patriarch in the line of Seth.

Though the spiritual knowledge in the Pillar of Enoch is hidden and can only be deciphered when it is diligently sought, there is evidence that the Ancient Egyptians knew some of its spiritual secrets. In fact, the unique internal design of this pyramid was repeatedly referred to allegorically in the Egyptian Book of the Dead, and in tomb paintings. Archeologists believe that the scrolls of the Book of the Dead found in Egyptian tombs were made to accompany the rich occupants of the tombs into the afterlife. Many of the extant scrolls are beautifully illustrated, and are thought to have served as a guide and tool to aid the dead soul in finding a place for itself in the spirit world.

The hieroglyphic texts on these scrolls are peppered with thematic names indicating the supposed purpose of the soul's journey through the afterlife. Interestingly, as was discussed in Book One and Three, these books all contain a section where the soul is eventually judged in the Judgment Hall of Osiris, the Egyptian god of the dead that was tied to Orion and the Great Pyramid via the Orion constellation. However, it is obvious from the occult-style magical incantations in the Book of the Dead and the myths surrounding Osiris that this false deity was a primitive and corrupted representation of the coming Messiah revealed in the Gospel in the Stars.

## Soul Being Judged in Judgment Hall of Osiris

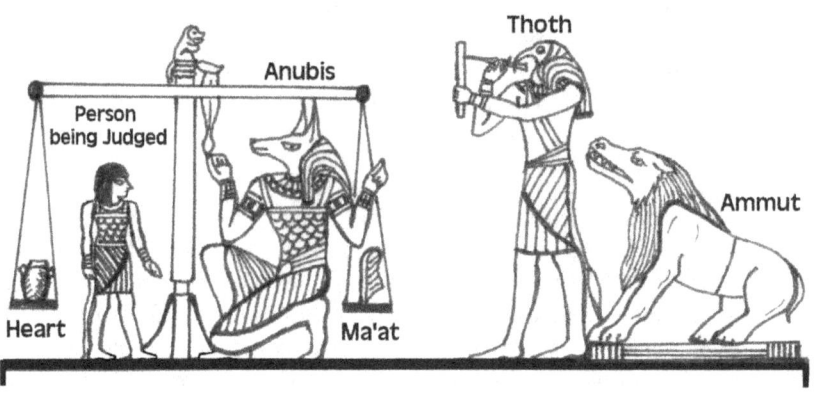

Uncannily, no one has ever suggested that people may have used these Books of the Dead as spiritual instruction manuals on how to obtain everlasting life *before* they actually died. Though these books were found in tombs, there is nothing to disprove that they were not also meant to guide the *living*. If the Book of the Dead was a guide for the living *rather than* the dead, then we can conclude that some ancient Egyptians knew that they would be judged for their actions *during* their journey through life, rather than after death. In addition, they knew that they would be judged for their sins or violations of Ma'at, and pardoned if their righteousness and justice exceeded their sin when they died. Therefore, if viewed as a guide for the living into everlasting life rather than as a guide for the dead *who we know are beyond redemption*, the correlation of the thematic place names in the Book of the Dead with the interior passages

# Ch. 5: Pyramid and Tabernacle - Divinely Designed

and chambers of the Great Pyramid are truly astounding in their implications.

For example, the Descending Passage could easily be called "the Descent," which is a term used in the Book of the Dead. Next, the Subterranean Chamber - as a symbol for the Lake of Fire and the Abyss - could easily be connected to the book's "Chamber of Ordeal," which was also called the "Chamber of Central Fire." The Well Shaft can be seen as "the Well of Life" in the Book of the Dead, and the Ascending Passage as the book's "Hall of Truth in Darkness." The Grand Gallery makes a fine symbol for the "Hall of Truth in Light" in the Book of the Dead, and the Queen's Chamber could easily be called the book's "Chamber of Regeneration."

With its clear association to the Moon, the Queen's Chamber could also be linked to the "Chamber of the Moon" in the Book of the Dead. The Antechamber with its triple grooves could well be the book's "Chamber of the Triple Veil." Finally, the King's Chamber could readily be identified as the "Chamber of the Open Tomb," or the "Chamber of the Resurrection" in the Book of the Dead, and the low passage into the King's Chamber from the Antechamber could be the book's "Passage of the Veil." The illustration on the next page shows most of these allegorical associations between the Great Pyramid and Book of the Dead, but also ties in many key Scriptures that are suggested by the pyramid's interior design.

From these associations, it is clear that the symbolic names in the Book of the Dead reflect the spiritual journey of a *living* human soul - just as is depicted in the Great Pyramid. Furthermore, these names are highly allegorical, and give clear indications of the prophetic and spiritual meanings of the passages and chambers they allude to inside the Great Pyramid. Amazingly, as shown in the illustration, there are also clear biblical connections for all these stages in spiritual growth.

Oddly, even if applied to living souls, the name of the Book of the Dead is apt. This is because all of us must die to obtain everlasting life. In fact, believers symbolically die to the world when they are baptized, so that they can be re-born in the perfect image of Christ at the point of physical death. However, though the Book of the Dead may have contained a little spiritual truth, these truths were buried under heavy layers of Pagan magic and Astrological Sorcery that were preserved in the Pyramid Texts.

# The Hidden Gospel Message Inside the Great Pyramid

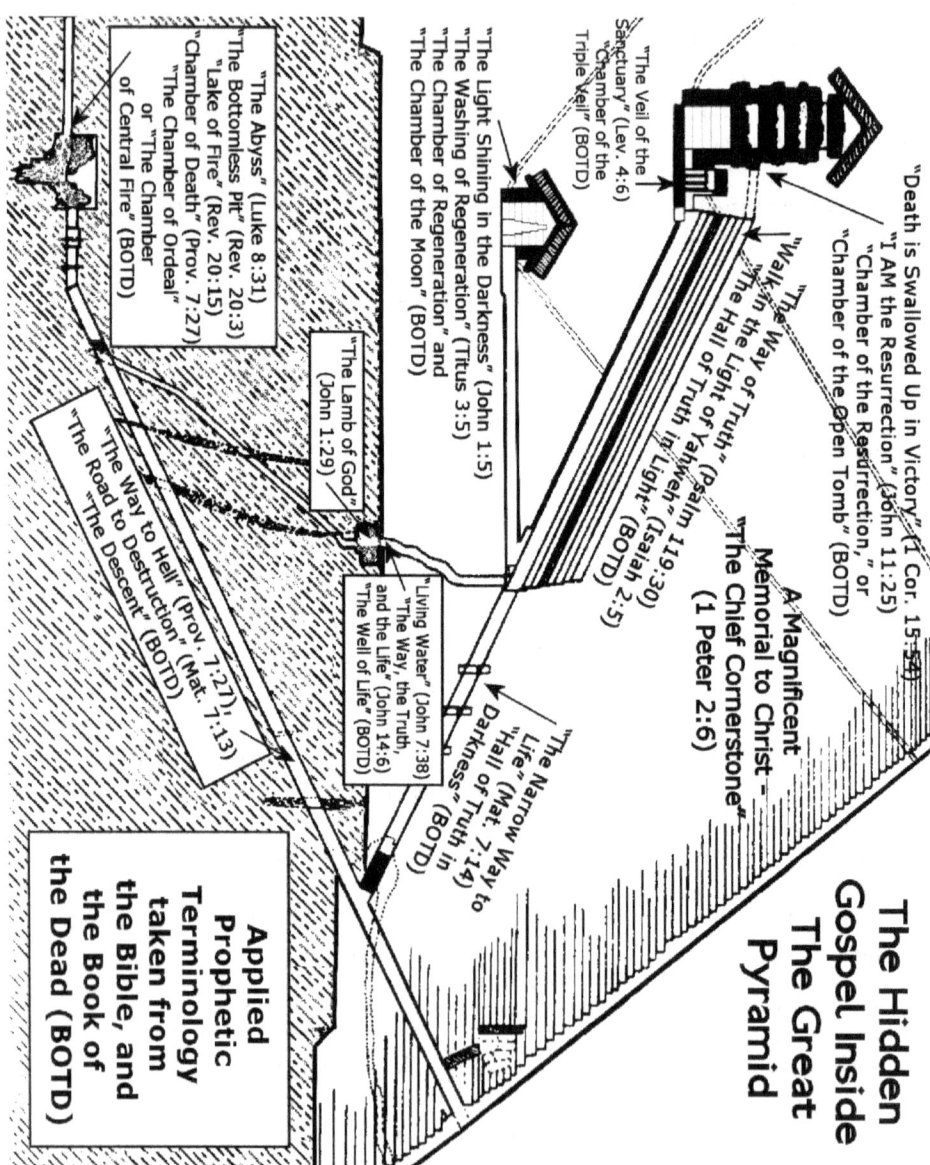

As mentioned in Book Three, "The Language of God in History," the Pyramid Texts may have originated from the false spirituality taught to the Cainites by the fallen Watchers prior to the Great Flood, and subsequently rediscovered by Arphaxad's son Cainan after the Flood. As a result of reintroducing this demonically inspired Astrological Magic after the Flood, the priests of Ancient Egypt promulgated many false spiritual teachings. Successive generations of priests were even more deluded by the demonic spirits behind their gods - whose false teachings about the Great Pyramid's symbolic features eventually obliterated the truth about their meaning.

Perhaps the biggest sin of the Ancient Egyptian priests was their belief that the Great Pyramid was physically needed to transport the dead Pharaoh into Heaven and everlasting life. As a result, they lost the true meaning of the Great Pyramid as a symbol of the only Path to Salvation open to mankind, which is through the world Redeemer who conquered death for all time: Yahshua the Anointed One. Eventually, every part of the Egyptian religion was tainted with falsehoods, and the people worshipped any god or goddess they fancied instead of the one true God Yahweh. Also, instead of worshipping the Creator, and seeking Him throughout life, the deluded Egyptians deified the Pharaoh, worshipped created things, forgot the one true God, and lost their knowledge of God's desire to reconcile us to Himself through His Son. Instead of the truth, Egyptian priests invented the magical incantations found in the Pyramid Texts and Book of the Dead that supposedly allowed people to gain power over their gods, and fool these same gods into thinking that people who had done much evil had done only good, and did not deserve to be destroyed.

This leads to questions about what falsehoods and shades of the truth Moses had been taught when he was raised as a Prince of Egypt. Was Moses taught the erroneous purpose of the Great Pyramid, or did one of his teachers (perhaps even his own Israelite family) know the allegorical spiritual truth locked into its symbolic passages? As already shown, it is highly likely that, though Moses may have initially only learned dim shades of the truth interspersed with Pagan lies, he eventually knew the Great Pyramid's connection to the Desert Tabernacle - especially since the Holy Spirit covered Moses, showed Moses the deep mysteries of God's truth, and allowed Moses to know God *face to face*.

Shortly after giving Moses the stone tablets of the Law on Mount Sinai, Yahweh gave Moses the blueprint for constructing the Desert Tabernacle (Exodus 25:9, 26:30). If Moses had any knowledge of the correct symbolic and spiritual meanings behind the Great Pyramid, the Ark of the Covenant, and the Desert Tabernacle, however, he never passed this knowledge on in the Torah. It therefore appears that the spiritual knowledge locked into the design of the Tabernacle and the Ark was meant to remain hidden until modern times, just as the knowledge hidden in the Great Pyramid was.

## Chart Comparing the Pillar of Enoch and the Tabernacle

| The Pillar of Enoch, or Great Pyramid | The Desert Tabernacle, or Tent of Meeting |
|---|---|
| **Overall Comparisons:** | **Overall Comparisons:** |
| 1. 48 Ceiling Stones corresponding to heaven:<br>9 in the King's Chamber,<br>3 in the Antechamber and<br>36 in the Grand Gallery. These suggest the 48 constellations in the ancient Mazzaroth.<br><br>2. 100 Stones in the King's Chamber walls. | 1. 48 wooden panels making up the wall of the Tabernacle Sanctuary:<br>20 each per north and south walls,<br>6 for the back west wall, and<br>2 for the back corners.<br><br>2. Volume of Tabernacle Sanctuary: 100 Square Cubits. |
| **The Grand Gallery:** | **The Outer Courtyard:** |
| 1. Ten courses of stone per wall<br><br>2. 28 feet high, 28 shafts per side<br><br>3. The Granite Plug and Well Shaft<br><br>4. The Queen's Chamber<br><br>(3 & 4 correspond to the Grand Gallery, though not part of it) | 1. Ten linen curtains<br><br>2. 28 cubits per curtain<br><br>3. The Bronze Altar<br><br>4. The Bronze Sea |
| **The Antechamber:** | **The Holy Place:** |
| 1. Three great parallel grooves<br>   a. Two granite leafs in groove farthest from the King's Chamber<br><br>2. Four parallel, concave grooves cut into the massive stone over the entrance to the King's Chamber | 1. Three objects in the Holy Place<br>   a. The table of showbread with its two piles, or loaves of bread<br><br>2. Four pillars of acacia wood holding up the veil between the Holy Place and the Most Holy Place |

## Ch. 5: Pyramid and Tabernacle - Divinely Designed     Page 201

| The King's Chamber: | The Most Holy Place: |
|---|---|
| 1. Fifty times the cubic volume of the Coffer | 1. Fifty times the cubic volume of the Ark |
| 2: Oriented east to west lengthwise with the west wall at the back | 2. Oriented east to west lengthwise with the west wall at the back |
| 3. Only Furnishing: the King's Coffer | 3. Only Furnishing: the Ark of the Covenant |
| **The King's Coffer:** | **The Ark of the Covenant:** |
| Height: 1.5 sacred cubits<br>Length: 2.5 sacred cubits<br>Width: 1.5 sacred cubits | Height: 1.5 sacred cubits<br>Length: 2.5 sacred cubits<br>Width: 1.5 sacred cubits |

    In the construction of both the Desert Tabernacle and the Great Pyramid, the key to our salvation was allegorically symbolized in the Ark of the Covenant and the empty red granite Coffer. Both of these casket sized and shaped boxes represent the risen Christ and the resurrection of the dead to everlasting life. From this association, it is obvious that both of these structures allegorically served to illustrate great spiritual truths concerning mankind's quest to find communion and oneness with Yahweh.

    The connection of the Zodiac or Mazzaroth with the Great Pyramid and Desert Tabernacle can be found in the common elements in their design. In the Desert Tabernacle, the forty-eight constellations in the Mazzaroth are alluded to in its walls, which were made of wooden panels or boards. Five horizontal bars overlaid with gold supported the walls on three sides (Exodus 26:26-29), while the front of the Tabernacle consisted of a large screen (Exodus 26:36). Each vertical wallboard was ten cubits high - making the ceiling of the Tabernacle over 20 feet up. ***48 boards were used to construct the Tabernacle's walls:*** 20 each per north and south wall, 6 for the back west wall, and 2 for the back corners (Exodus 26:15-25). Now, the Twelve Tribes of Israel surrounded the Desert Tabernacle, and each Tribe represented one sign of the Zodiac. In addition, since heaven is God's throne, there was one day to be 48 Levite cities in Israel representing God's sovereignty there. This is why all forty-eight constellations were represented in the Israelite Desert encampment via the Tabernacle's walls!

In the Great Pyramid, this same number is found by counting the sum of the ceiling stones in the King's Chamber, Antechamber, and Grand Gallery. There are nine in the King's Chamber, and three in the Antechamber, which equals twelve, the number of Zodiac signs in the Mazzaroth. In addition there are thirty-six ceiling stones in the Grand Gallery, one for each of the thirty-six decans in the Mazzaroth! Using the equation (9 + 3) + 36 = 48, we see that **there are forty-eight ceiling slabs to correspond to each of the forty-eight constellations in the heavens.**

This connection is further strengthened by the fact that the number forty-eight is found by counting the *ceiling* stones, which allegorically relate to the physical heavens. In addition, since the King's Chamber, Antechamber and Grand Gallery within the Great Pyramid correspond to the Most Holy Place, Holy Place, and Outer Courtyard in the Desert Tabernacle, they must all be allegorical representations of heavenly things.

Indeed, as shown in Chapter Four, the Great Pyramid as a whole appears to be a small-scale representation of our Earth, the Sun, the Moon, and their relative place in the Solar System, and the Universe - all expressed in angles, numbers, and allegories. In addition, as fully discussed in Book Three, the Pillar of Enoch's connection to the Giza Complex - and their mutual connection to the constellation of Orion and the Zodiac sign of Taurus - signifies that the earthly structures symbolize part of God's heavenly Temple being mirrored on Earth for the benefit of future generations. This was done by the Sethites so that we would not forget that God created the heavens and the Earth, and is sovereign over us all!

As shown through the Grand Gallery's connection with the dimensions of the Outer Courtyard of the Tabernacle, the Jews and the Church will not enter into full Salvation until they discover the true purpose and meaning of Christ. They must therefore understand the meaning and necessity of Christ's sacrificial death that allows us to be redeemed from sin and resurrected into everlasting life. **This path to everlasting life is clearly depicted by the symbols of the Antechamber and the King's Chamber - both in their connection to the Holy Place and the Most Holy Place in the Desert Tabernacle.** Yahshua's purpose is also clearly revealed in the Well Shaft and Queen's Chamber - features of the Great Pyramid that correspond to the altar of sacrifice and Bronze Sea in the Outer Courtyard of the Tabernacle.

The chart on pages 200 and 201 summarizes many of the amazing parallels in the structural design of the Pillar of Enoch and Desert Tabernacle that were revealed in this discussion into their amazing shared

## Ch. 5: Pyramid and Tabernacle - Divinely Designed

message and purpose. Doubtless there are many more connections between these two sacred structures that will become known as time goes by, for - when the time is right - God often chooses to reveal more to His earthly children. However, these revelations are only given when it might wake us up spiritually and lead us into righteousness or obedience to God instead of further rebellion and folly.

## Chapter 6: The Great Sphinx - Symbol For Christ

>  *"'And behold, I am coming quickly, and My reward is with Me, to give to every one according to his work.* **I am the Alpha and the Omega, the Beginning and the End, the First and the Last.***' Blessed are those who do His commandments, that they may have the right to the tree of life..." - Rev. 22:12-14*

The opening Scripture for this chapter makes it very clear that Yahshua has always existed, and that all matter, time, and space began - and will end - with Him. As shown in previous chapters, Yahshua is stating that He is the Alpha and Omega to tell us that He embodies every letter in the alphabet, and every word in our vocabularies. This is a direct analogy of His status as the true, and only Word of God. His appellation as the Alpha and Omega also suggests that Yahshua will ultimately have the first and last word in all disputes. Though this is first made clear in the Book of Isaiah - in connection with Christ in His role as Yahweh, the Creator (Isaiah 44:6; 48:12) - Yahshua applies it to Himself without any ambiguity in the Book of Revelation. By calling Himself *"the Beginning and the End,"* and *"the First and the Last,"* Yahshua was implying that He is the beginning and end of the Zodiac, of the Universe, and of time itself. But how, you may wonder, does this relate to the Great Sphinx, which is the subject of this chapter?

In the other books in the Language of God Book Series, it was shown that the Great Sphinx may mark both the beginning and end of the Zodiac, and the beginning and end of time. This book recaps some of the clues as to why this may be true, and reveals new ones - including the following amazing fact. The Scripture quoted at the beginning of this chapter is taken from the Book of Revelation, which is the *last* book of the Bible. Furthermore, it was taken from the *last or 22nd* chapter in that book - and its chapter number recalls the meaning of its words in numerical form! As mentioned in Chapter One, Chapter 22 of the Book of Revelation corresponds with the twenty-second, and last letter in the Hebrew Alphabet, which is the letter Tav (T). Uncannily, the Hebrew letter T recalls the Cross that Christ died upon, when He uttered the triumphant words *"It is Finished!"* (John 19:30). Note here that the numbers for this Scripture add up to 13:

$1 + 9 + 3 + 0 = 13$

Later in this book, we will explore the implications of the number 13 as the number of the Last Great Day in Prophecy, which is the final day of human history before the New Heaven and Earth are created. Since the number 13 is connected to the end of time as we know it, perhaps that is why this number is also applied to the most complete phrase referring to Yahshua as the great beginning and end of all things in the Book of Revelation, which is Revelation 22:13. In the following sections, it will be conclusively shown that the Great Sphinx allegorically recalls Christ's role as *"the Beginning and the End,"* and shows that Yahshua is the Creator of time, as well as the Creator of life and matter. For this reason, the entire Giza Pyramid Complex is truly remarkable, and worthy of our intense scrutiny. It contains the last remaining ancient wonder of the world: the Great Pyramid, and the oldest statue ever carved in stone: the Great Sphinx.

## *The Sphinx In Egyptian History and Myth*

Before moving on to our discussion of the Sphinx in prophecy, let me give a brief summary of how the Ancient Egyptians viewed the Great Sphinx, and what is currently known about the Sphinx as determined by archeological studies and temple carvings. First of all, from a cursory examination, it can easily be seen that the current appearance of the Great Sphinx is likely very different from its original design. Besides its state of ruin, its disproportionately small head has likely been carved over at least once.

This can be seen in the side view of the Great Sphinx shown in this chapter. Note how small the head appears in relation to the large size of the supine lion's body of the Sphinx. Since the Ancient Egyptians were excellent at carving objects with the correct proportions, we can assume that the Sphinx's antediluvian builders were equal to, or even more highly adept at this than their descendents. This disparity shows that the Sphinx's head has been carved over.

Intriguingly, forensic analysis has revealed that the face of the Sphinx is likely that of a Negroid woman. It is therefore not the Caucasian Pharaoh Khafre, but may be the face of a woman who ruled as Pharaoh of Egypt. However, it is not the face of Queen Hatshepsut or

# Chapter 6: The Great Sphinx - Symbol for Christ

Nefertiti, whose extant statues in museums show that they had decidedly Caucasian features like Khafre.

There is a historical candidate that could well be the culprit who defaced the Sphinx. In Book Three, we explored the idea that Semiramis, Nimrod's wife and Queen, may have carved the Sphinx to resemble herself. Folklore surrounding Semiramis indicates that she ruled as Queen after Nimrod died. Furthermore, Nimrod may have been none other than the Pharaoh Narmer. If so, both Narmer/Nimrod and Semiramis were likely Negroid in appearance, especially since Nimrod was the son of Ham's son Cush, who was considered to be the ancestor of the Negroid people groups.

Regardless of whose face is on the Great Sphinx now, however, it is likely that the face of the Sphinx was always of a woman, and was not a lion's face as some claim. This is because, as will be shown in a moment, the Sphinx serves as an astronomical marker for a specific date in history, and the priests who were in charge of caring for the Sphinx would likely have made sure its symbolism remained intact, even if it was altered. As proof of this, there is archeological evidence that the Great Sphinx was reverently repaired and restored at several points in the distant past, just as it has been recently.

The posterior of the Sphinx is actually below ground level, though its head and upper torso were carved from a naturally occurring outcropping of rock on the plateau. The antediluvians that created the

## The Great Sphinx: Gazing Toward Eternity from the Past

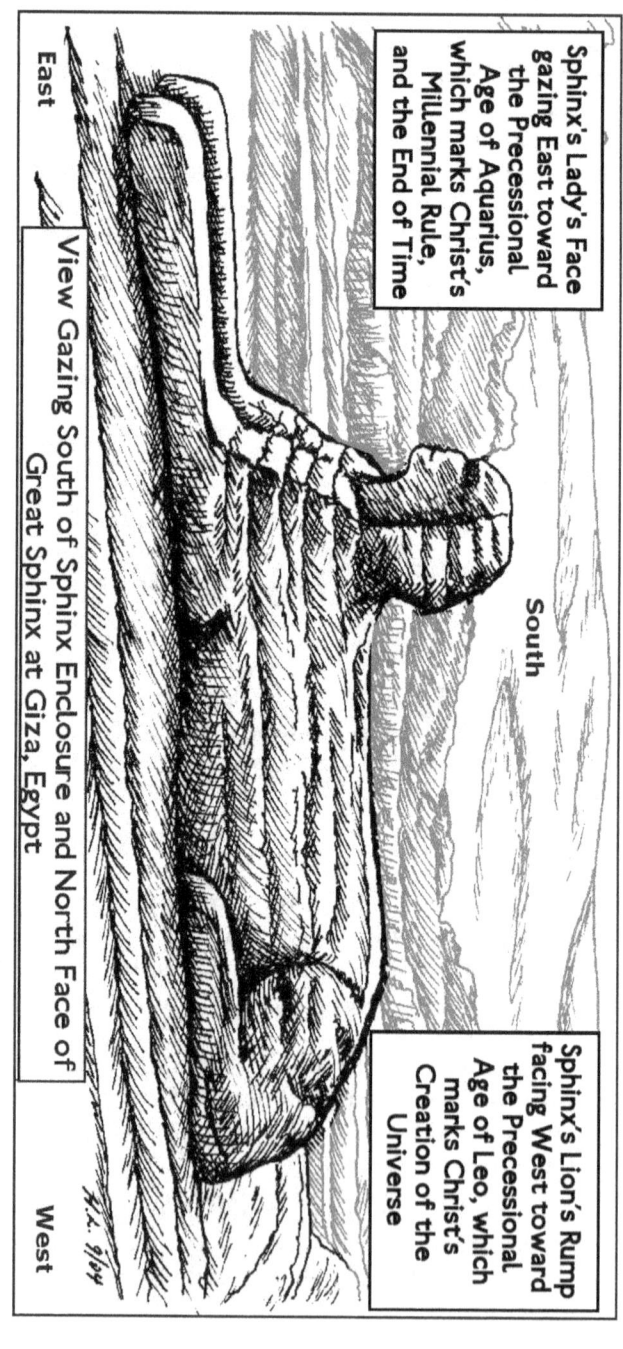

Sphinx therefore had to excavate tons of limestone from around the Sphinx to form its body, and this created the Sphinx enclosure surrounding the Sphinx. It is likely that the limestone quarried here was subsequently used to build the temples in front of the Sphinx. Also, as mentioned in Book Three, the area of the Giza Plateau around the Great Sphinx shows evidence of extreme weathering from *water* erosion in a part of the world that has been a desert for thousands of years. After this occurred, the Sphinx, the Sphinx enclosure, and the temples in front of it were re-surfaced to cover much of this weathering.

Robert Schoch, a geologist who determined that the weathering on the Sphinx was caused by water, has written extensively about this subject, and he suspects that the Sphinx and its related temples were only repaired during the reigns of the Pharaohs Khufu and Khafre. Furthermore, since geologists believe that there was little precipitation in Egypt prior to 4000 BC, Robert Schoch believes that the Sphinx is at least 6000 years old, and belongs to a much earlier epoch in human history than Khufu and Khafre's reigns.

## The Sphinx Enclosure and Associated Temples at Giza

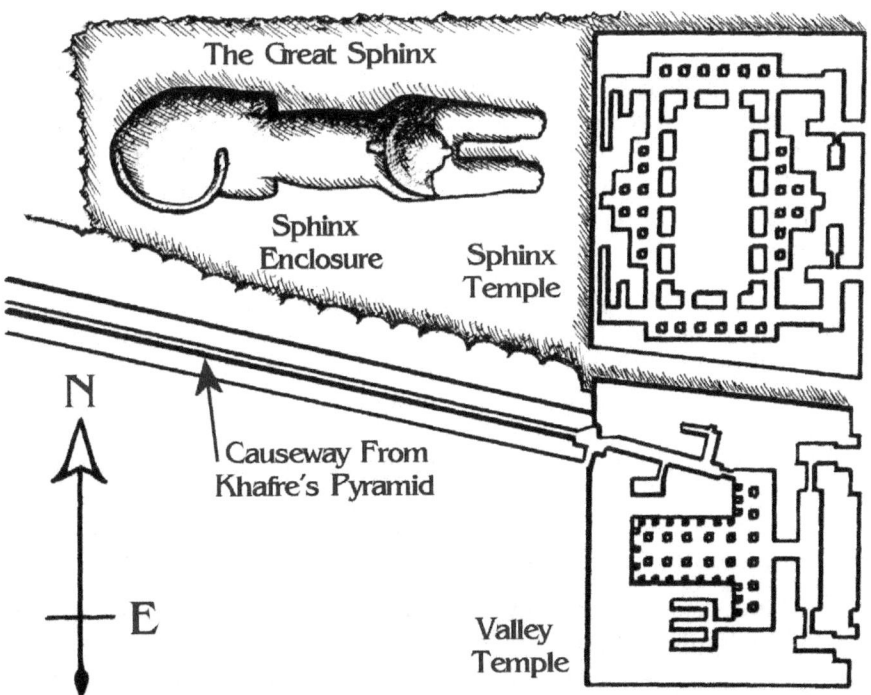

As already mentioned, the Great Pyramid and Great Sphinx may indeed belong to an earlier era; especially if Enoch's immediate children built them. However, if we follow conventional archeological suppositions, and use a strictly biblical chronology, the reign of Khufu, who is the supposed builder of the Great Pyramid, falls two hundred years *before* Noah's Flood. So, though it may have been dry in Egypt before the Flood, that climate changed dramatically when the Great Flood began. At that time, even relatively dry areas of the Earth experienced heavy precipitation, and then flooding for a year, *or more*. There is therefore every reason to believe that the advanced water weathering still visible on the Great Sphinx, and its enclosure walls occurred during the time of Noah's Flood, and perhaps for a few years afterward as the waters of the Flood slowly evaporated, and the entire world was subsequently subjected to more heavy rains, and periodic smaller-scale flooding.

Besides studying the geological features of the Sphinx, Robert Schoch and some of his colleagues conducted tests on the ground surrounding the Sphinx. These tests suggest that an open cavity exists beneath its front paws, just as the so-called "sleeping psychic" Edgar Cayce once said. Though he professed to be a Christian, Cayce was not born-again and did not consult the Holy Spirit but demons in His trance state. This is attested to by his trance teachings on reincarnation and other New Age ideas. Nonetheless, because demons are supernatural entities, some of Cayce's psychic visions proved to be accurate. In one of his psychic trances, Cayce said that a hidden chamber called the Hall of Records is beneath the paws of the Great Sphinx. Ever since Cayce made his findings public, there has been much speculation about what knowledge this hall might contain if it is ever found.

Subsequently, Egyptian archeologists have discovered that the Giza Plateau is riddled with underground passageways, and they also claim that they have discovered a chamber underneath the Great Sphinx. However, they claim that it is empty and contains no wall inscriptions. Nonetheless, many believe that these archeologists are not telling the truth. Regardless of speculations, however, the Great Sphinx already tells an amazing story that is quite visible above ground that has nothing to do with Cayce or the New Age movement he helped to perpetuate, but everything to do with Christ's Ministry and His Star Gospel.

The earliest Ancient Egyptians understood the symbolism of the Great Sphinx quite well, as is revealed within the Temple of Khnum at Esna in relation to Great Sphinx. Before exploring the depiction of the Sphinx within the Zodiac carved into the wall of this temple at Esna, however, let me tell you a bit about the god it was dedicated to. Khnum was a ram-headed deity that the earliest Egyptians identified with the Creator of Heaven and Earth, and the Maker of mankind. In this capacity, Khnum was called the "Divine Potter" and the "Father of the fathers", and he was depicted fashioning human beings with clay on a potter's wheel. This is remarkably similar to how Yahweh God is described as a Divine Potter who fashioned mankind out of clay in Scripture:

~*~ *Isaiah 64:8* ~*~

*"But now, O Lord, You are our Father;*
*We are the clay, and You are our potter;*
*And we all are the work of Your hand."*

With his Ram's Head, Khnum may have had a connection to the Zodiac sign of Aries the Ram, which is a depiction of Yahshua as the Lamb of God. This is interesting because the Pharaoh Khufu (whom I believe may have been Noah) is seen as the builder of the Great Pyramid at Giza, and his full Egyptian name was "Khnum Khufwy", which means "Khnum is my Protector", or "The Creator God is my Protector".

Another fascinating thing about Khnum is that his female consort was considered to be the goddess Neith, and I shared some very interesting information about Khnum and Neith in Book Three, "The Language of God in History". For example, the patriarch Joseph had an Egyptian wife named Asenath, which means "Follower of Neith" or "Gift of Neith". Neith was often depicted as an Archer with a bow and arrows in one hand, and she was identified with the city of Sais in the Nile Delta, which once had been the patriarch Shem's territory in his role as Melchizedek, the Priest of God Most High. That is, until Shem's feuding brother Ham wrestled this sacred territory away from Shem via his grandson Nimrod, who was also known as King Narmer - the unifier of Upper and Lower Egypt, and usurper of Shem's rightful place!

This information can shed new light on Neith's hieroglyphic symbol, which archeologists describe as two crossed arrows behind a shield alluding to Neith's role as an archer and protectress - perhaps in her connection to the Holy Spirit. Upon examining this symbol, my impression of it is that it may have also depicted two sets of horns on an oval altar, which archeologists can't see because they are not looking at these symbols with their spiritual eyes opened by the power of the Holy Spirit. With my God-given discernment, Neith's symbol looks like it may have also been meant to depict the Altar in Heaven formed by the bodies and horns of Taurus the Bull and Aries the Ram in their roles as a Sin Offering and Sacrificial Lamb.

## Khnum and Neith In Their Connection With Shem

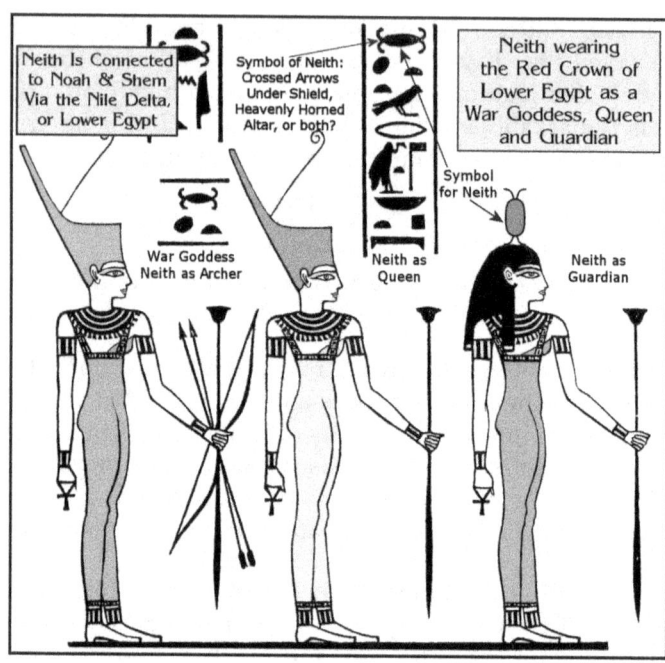

# Chapter 6: The Great Sphinx - Symbol for Christ

Perhaps, then, it is not a coincidence that the Temple of Khnum at Esna with the Mazzaroth or Zodiac on its walls has a mummified Pharaonic figure directly between the signs of Taurus and Aries depicted there, or that Esna's depictions of Virgo and Leo are pictured with a male Archer/Swordsman above them. This warrior may be a composite image of Neith the Archer tied to the Messianic constellations Bootes, which is a decan of Virgo - and Orion, which is a decan of Taurus that can be viewed as holding a sword above his head. In fact, my godly discernment tells me that the stars depicted on the stone wall panel depicting Leo and Virgo and the image of a Sphinx at Esna do not depict the stars in Virgo or Leo, but the principle stars of Orion!

If this is the case, and I believe that it is, then the people who carved this art onto the walls of the Temple of Khnum at Esna knew that Orion and Bootes depict the same Conquering Messiah or Avenger of Blood. They also knew that Leo and Virgo depicted Him as the First and the Last, and Taurus and Aries depicted Him as the Sacrificed Messiah or Kinsmen Redeemer, while Orion depicted Him as the coming Prince of princes or "Naz Seir" that they longed for. They also likely recognized the composite image of the Sphinx as a symbol of that same Messiah figure in His role as the Beginning (Virgo) and End (Leo) of all things. Though you won't find this explanation in any secular text book, it's likely because the powers that be don't want you and me to know the truth about the real origins of the greatest monuments in Egypt. Either they don't want us to see these monuments as the legacy of the righteous Sethites and Shemites, or they really have no clue about their real origins because of the satanic delusions they have been fed by wicked scholars with an evil agenda. It could also be a mixture of both. You decide.

## *The Sphinx and the Gospel in the Stars*

In the wall art of the Zodiac found in the Temple of Khnum at Esna that was shown on page 213, note the Scarab and its connection to the Winged Serpent depicting the Path of the Sun under the Sphinx that is on the panel with Virgo depicted on it. Hundreds of Scarabs have been found in Egyptian tombs, which suggest that they were important in ritual magic associated with the soul's journey in the afterlife, in mimicry of the Sun's journey through the sky. Since the Scarab or dung beetle depicted the Sun, and the Winged Serpent depicted its path

**The Actual Dung Beetle Depicting The Sun In Scarab Amulets**

through the Zodiac, the Scarab is also tied to the Solar Disk with the Serpent draped over it that crowns the Sphinx on the Esna wall depiction of Leo and Virgo. This shows that Virgo and Leo were understood to be the beginning and ending signs that the Sun passed through.

While archeologists tell us that the dung beetle was connected to the Sun and its path through the sky because of the dung beetle's habit of rolling up animal dung into a ball and laying eggs in it for the hatched larvae to feed on, the graphic on this page shows there's more to the Scarab story than they're letting on to. Though the dung beetle's behavior certainly was allegorically viewed as the Sun moving through the heavens and giving life to the world, there are 14 peculiar ray-like objects on the dung beetle - six on the beetle's crown, and four on each front leg. The six rays on the crown can be viewed as the six imaginary portals on a given horizon - as viewed through an Enochian style henge. As shown in Book Three, Enoch described these portals as the method that he used to mark the Sun's rising and setting points throughout the

## Chapter 6: The Great Sphinx - Symbol for Christ

year (1 Enoch 72:3). In addition, the four rays on each arm of the dung beetle can be seen as 8 degrees on the circle of the horizon, while the six rays on the crown can be seen as 6 more degrees for a total of 14 degrees on the horizon. Fascinatingly, at the 30 degrees North Latitude where the Great Sphinx and Pyramids at Giza are located, the Sun travels 14 degrees north of due east and 14 degrees south of due east on its journey through the seasons, which are marked by the Equinoxes and Solstices.

Now take a moment to examine the drawings of the Sphinx enclosure on page 209, and it and the Pyramids at Giza on page 157. These drawings show that the human head of the Sphinx is facing due east, while its leonine posterior is facing due west. This suggests that the Great Sphinx is a celestial marker that is pointing to the Spring and Fall Equinoxes, just as the causeway that leads from Menkaure's Pyramid to the old location of the Nile River does. I recently discovered that this supposition is perfectly true, as is shown in the graphic on page 545 of this book. This shows the Solstice and Equinox points on the western horizon behind the Sphinx - as viewed from a vantage point in the east. In this graphic, note how the Equinoxes set directly behind the head of the Sphinx. This is certainly no accident, but part of the amazing purposeful design of the entire Giza Pyramid Complex.

As a pointer, the Great Sphinx may indicate the past Age when the Zodiac sign of Virgo was on the horizon on the Spring Equinox, or the beginning of the Solar Year. Furthermore, the Sphinx's rear leonine half may be a metaphor signifying the past Age of Leo circa 10,000 BC, and its front end may be a metaphor not only for Virgo, but for Aquarius - which is the sign opposite to Leo in the Zodiac, and the sign that sunrise on the Spring Equinox will occur in throughout the Millennial Rule of Christ. As such, the Great Sphinx was designed in the far past to gaze thousands of years into the future toward the current Age of Aquarius, and the imminent arrival of Christ's Second Coming and Millennial Kingdom!

In Book Three, "The Language of God in History," and in the prior and preceding chapters of this book, it is shown that the Great Pyramid represents Yahshua our Savior in many profound and intriguing ways. It is also shown how the four major points in the Solar Year marked by the Equinoxes and Solstices as pointed to at Giza are tied to key events in Yahshua's life, and ministry. Now, it will be shown that this is also inherently true about the Great Sphinx, and that Giza is the location of two extremely ancient architectural wonders that are full of rich religious symbolism pertaining to one Person: Yahshua the Anointed

One, or Messiah. This makes the entire Giza complex a type of parable - one that was inspired by the Master Parable Teller Himself.

Like the Great Pyramid, the Great Sphinx is dated to the time of Noah, who was a young man by antediluvian standards during the Pharaoh Khufu's reign - between 2551 and 2528 BC. Now, if the Jewish historian Josephus is correct, the descendents of Seth built two structures in Egypt prior to the Flood. Khufu therefore may have been another name for Noah, and his ancestors could have built the Great Pyramid and Great Sphinx. Since the Sethites were purported to be exceptional Astronomers, it seems fitting that the two structures they likely built in Egypt work synchronously as markers pinpointing specific past and future times in astronomical history, and both appear to allegorically represent the greatest person ever born - Yahshua, the Anointed One.

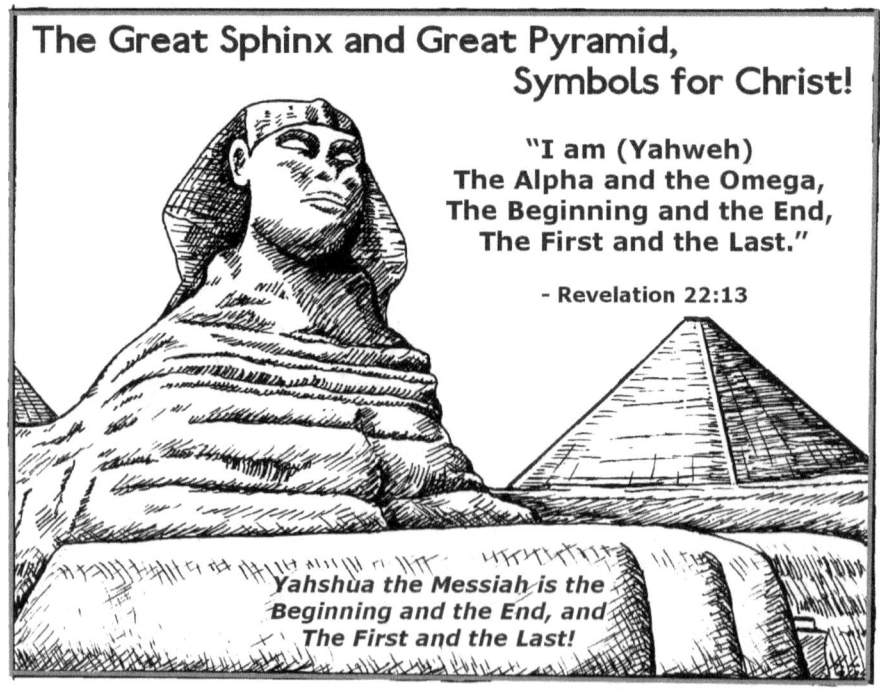

Just as Yahshua's Parables convey deep spiritual truths using nothing but everyday items and events, the builders of the Giza Pyramid Complex combined elements in our natural world to tell us a profound and complex story about a Person whose coming was vitally important not only to them, but to every future believer. Using the symbolism of the lion, and the man or woman in the Gospel in the Stars, the antediluvian descendants of Seth known as the Sethites built the Great Pyramid and Great Sphinx to tell the story they saw in the stars. Both of these monuments are architecturally and spiritually unparalleled in the entire history of humanity, and both appear to be dedicated to preserving what our antediluvian ancestors knew about the future Messiah that God promised to send.

The Great Sphinx is an apt symbol for Yahshua in His dual role as a servant and conquering king, as seen in its human head and lion's body. Through these same symbols, the Great Sphinx represents the beginning and ending signs of the Gospel in the Stars - Virgo, the Virgin Woman, and Leo, the Kingly Lion. The head of the Sphinx, with its female face, can signify both Virgo the Virgin, and Aquarius, which was depicted as a man or woman pouring water from an urn.

The third decan constellation of Virgo called Centaurus represents a centaur, which is part man and part horse. As such, it has a dual nature like Christ, who was fully God and fully man. The Centaur also has a bright star named "Toliman" in it. This star's name means "the heretofore and hereafter." This is undoubtedly a direct analogy to Christ's proclamation that He is *"the First and the Last,"* and *"the Beginning and the End."* Likewise, the Great Sphinx also signifies a beginning and an end. As mentioned previously, **the Great Sphinx marks not only the beginning and end of the Gospel in the Stars, but also the beginning and end of time.** As such, it is a clever and powerful representation of Yahshua Himself!

## *Antediluvian Genius in Construction of Sphinx and Pyramid*

In the Great Sphinx and Great Pyramid, the righteous antediluvians in the line of Seth pictured the Great Prince and Lion of Judah 2500 years before He was born! Using familiar themes in the natural world, they communicated great truths about Yahweh, and His Son Yahshua to us at Giza. They knew the Language of God, and spoke it clearly - just as Yahshua does through His Creation. The Great Sphinx contains the terrestrial imagery of a woman giving birth, and a roaring lion about to strike, and they come together to convey much about our Savior's dual role as both man and God. The Great Sphinx depicts Yahshua as He truly was - weak in His humanity, but invincible in His kingship and deity.

## Leo and Virgo Tied to the Great Sphinx

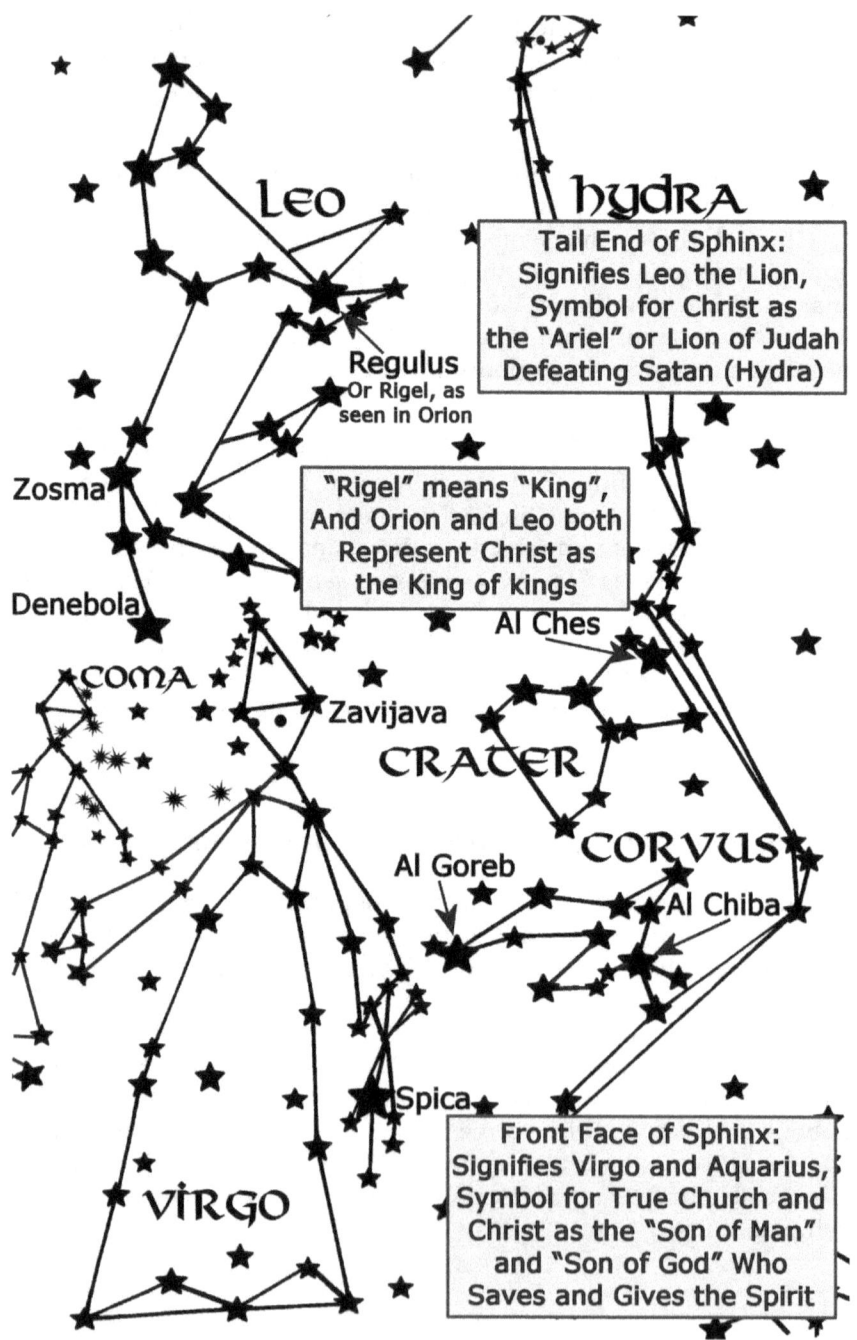

## Chapter 6: The Great Sphinx - Symbol for Christ

That the antediluvians knew enough of the coming Messiah to represent Him in such a powerful way through the symbolism of the Great Sphinx, and the Great Pyramid boggles the mind. It suggests that they knew both the Gospel in the Stars, and the prophecies of Enoch intimately. It also suggests that they were truly intellectual and spiritual giants - whose stamina and strength were as monumental as their architecture. As already mentioned, they also had a command of God's Language that goes far beyond our own in scope. The Bible supports this idea by telling us that healthy people before the Flood lived just shy of 1000 years. This is twelve times the life span that most of humanity can now achieve, which thereby gave the antediluvians a far greater potential to accrue wisdom and knowledge than we can today. It also suggests that they were physically far more robust than humanity is today.

The Bible also makes it clear that our long-lived antediluvian ancestors were far from stupid! For example, as mentioned briefly in Chapter Three, Cain was engaged in farming, and Abel was a shepherd of *domesticated* animals very early in human history (Genesis 4:2). These two activities are considered the first steps toward advanced civilizations, and they were already being done by the *second* generation from Adam and Eve, and probably within 100 years after the Fall. In addition, Cain is credited with building a city that he named after his son Enoch (Genesis 4:17). This city must therefore have been built within a few hundred years after the Fall. Cain's son Enoch was of the third generation from Adam and Eve, and this generation had grown to maturity long before the majority of the Fallen Angels arrived on Earth to mislead mankind and spawn the Nephilim.

For those who believe that all the advanced knowledge gained by humanity was introduced by aliens, the Fallen Angels, and/or the Nephilim, the Book of Jubilees indicates that the Fallen Angels did not intermarry with mankind until the time of Jared, Enoch's father (Jubilees 4:15-16). Jared was born in 3543 BC, according to the Biblical Chronology in the Appendix, and the time of Jared would coincide with his adulthood, when he was active in a leadership role over his people. This leads me to the following conclusions:

First of all, a person is not considered fully mature today until he or she has reached at least 30 years of age. Furthermore, since antediluvian men lived much longer than we do, their age at maturity was likely much older than 30 - especially since they appear to have married much later than most of humanity did in more recent ancient times. We can therefore assume that the Fallen Angel Semyaza and his fellow Fallen Angels did not arrive on Earth until Jared was at least 100 years old, which means that people developed independently of evil angelic influences for over 500 years until at least 3443 BC.

The advancements toward civilization witnessed in Cain and Abel's livelihoods between 3900 to 3600 BC therefore occurred before the Fallen Angels or Watchers, and their Nephilim offspring corrupted humanity with perverted knowledge, and encouraged militarism, extreme vanity, and a focus on demonic magic, astrology, and the occult. See "The Language of God in History" for a more thorough exploration of the extraordinary world mankind lived in prior to the Flood.

## *The Great Sphinx as an Astronomical Marker*

In the second chapter of Book One "The Language of God in the Universe", we discussed how each of the Twelve Tribes of Israel had a Zodiac sign associated with them that correlated with their placement around the Desert Tabernacle in relation to the Cardinal Signs Leo, Taurus, Aquarius and Scorpio. The first diagram on page 222 shows how the Twelve Tribes and their respective Zodiac signs were aligned around the Desert Tabernacle.

Using this correlation and connecting it with the astronomical information suggested by the Great Sphinx, I created another diagram like this. In the new diagram, imagine the Sphinx's enigmatic human face staring due east, while its leonine posterior is directed due west - on the 30th north parallel. Many scholars who have advocated that there is a Gospel in the Stars tied to the Great Pyramid and Great Sphinx contend that the face of the Sphinx represents the woman that follows the lion in the Zodiac: Virgo, the Virgin, and I agree. As explained at various points throughout this book series, Virgo is the first sign of the Mazzaroth, and neighboring Leo is the last. This assignation is evident in the earliest depictions of Virgo and Leo found in Egypt. This connection has led many Bible scholars to believe that the Great Sphinx serves as a marker proclaiming the beginning and end of the dramatic Gospel story in the Zodiac. As shown in this chapter, they are correct.

Based on the meaning of the Zodiac as a whole, it makes sense that the story of the Redeemer begins with Virgo as Eve, and later with Yahshua's mother Miriam, the virgin who gave birth to the Sun of Righteousness. It also makes sense that it ends with Yahshua, who is depicted by Leo, the Lion King of Judah coming again in triumph. Since the Sphinx is facing due east in the direction of the rising Sun, it may mean that the Zodiac sign of Virgo was on the horizon at sunrise on the

## Chapter 6: The Great Sphinx - Symbol for Christ

day when Adam was created in 4003 BC, during the Age of Virgo. If the Sun were housed in Virgo at Adam's creation, he would have begun to keep time from that starting point. It may also be pointing to the fact that Leo and Virgo are now juxtaposed on either side of the Sun on the Fall Equinox at this time in history, and we are now in the Last Day!

Though this in itself is startling, there is even more hidden symbolism in the Sphinx because *the face of the Great Sphinx can also represent Aquarius*. This sign can be depicted as a man or woman holding a water urn. If Leo is placed in the west - as the rear end of the Sphinx suggests - then Aquarius would fall due east of that point. These Zodiac signs are aligned with two of the four fixed points, which allow us to accurately place the other signs around them.

Using the Sphinx as the allegorical key, the Zodiac can be aligned consecutively - with Leo due west and Aquarius due east. With this arrangement, Taurus would then be due north, and Scorpio would be due south. Note the arrangement of the fixed points in the new diagram when compared to the diagram derived from Book One, which shows how the Twelve Tribes would have been arranged if they followed the Zodiac's current order, and how they actually camped around the Tabernacle.

In the new diagram, the Great Pyramid and Great Sphinx at Giza were used as central axis points, partly since the Great Pyramid represents the Earth and our Solar System, and the Great Sphinx signifies Christ's nature and purpose. My new diagram is based on the zodiacal alignment suggested by the Great Sphinx. In the new diagram, the Sphinx is gazing forward *toward* Aquarius. This alignment of the Zodiac therefore marks the present Age of Aquarius, when the Spring Equinox occurs in Aquarius, the Fall Equinox occurs in Leo (with Virgo opposite, in mimicry of the Sphinx!), the Summer Solstice occurs in Taurus, *and the Winter Solstice occurs in Scorpio.*

It is important to note here that the opposite alignment of the fixed signs, as shown in the diagram from Book One, marks the *beginning* of time, when the Spring Equinox occurred in the Age of Leo. Since Leo/Judah camped in the east, and Taurus/Joseph camped in the south, **the placement of the Twelve Tribes around the Desert Tabernacle suggests the Precessional position of the Zodiac at the dawn of time**.

This correlation of the Sphinx with the Zodiac - and its allegorical hint that Leo and Aquarius mark significant points in the past and future - is discussed in the book "Heaven's Mirror," by Graham Hancock and Santha Faiia. According to this well-researched book, the exact *opposite* sky to what we can see on the Spring Equinox today marked the year 10,500 BC.

# The Language of God in Prophecy

## Tabernacle, Great Pyramid, 12 Tribes/Zodiac Correlations

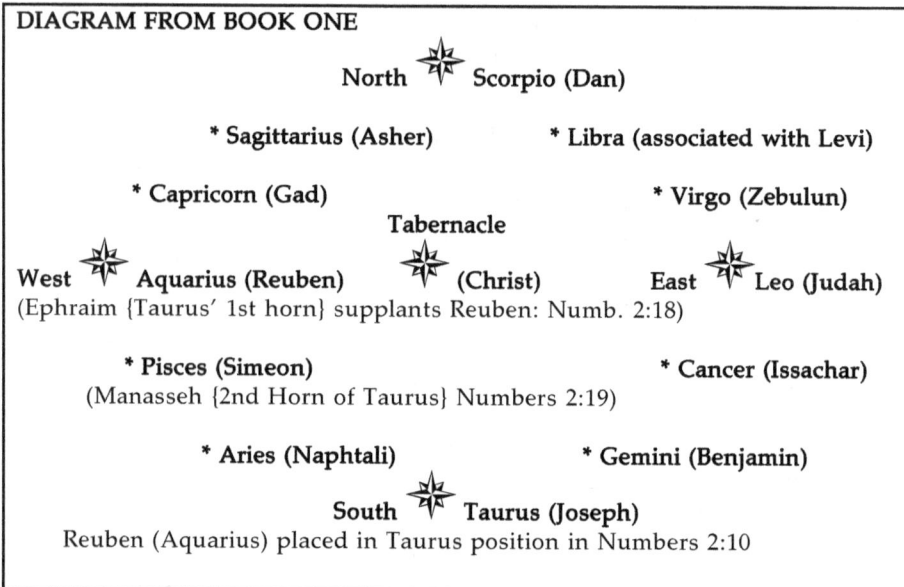

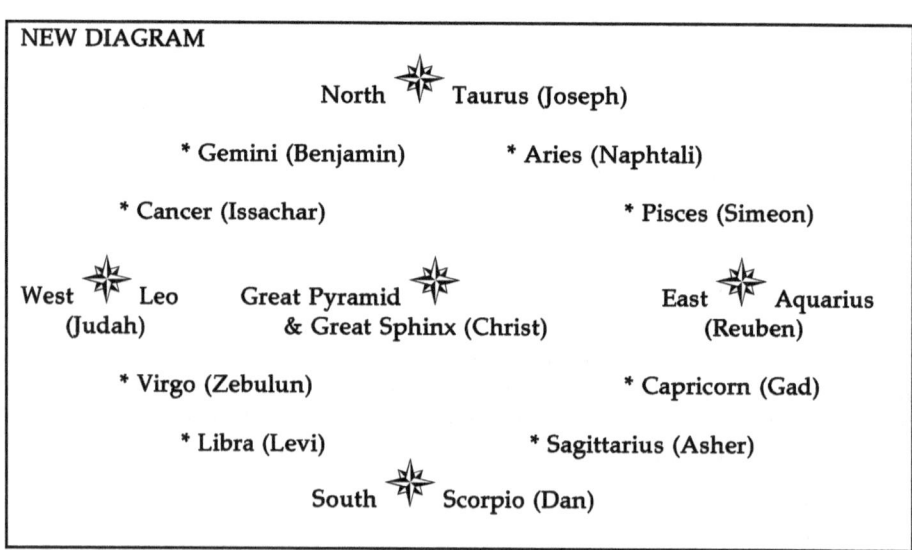

This opposite alignment of the Zodiac to our current sky therefore marked a time 12,500 years into the past. However, *the actual prophetic significance of these astronomically calculated dates were missed in Heaven's Mirror because the authors were not viewing the available evidence from a Judeo-Christian perspective.* If they had done so, they would have seen the biblical truths revealed here, and in the next section.

In the Bible, and other written Jewish sources, the Twelve Tribes of Israel have always been tied to the Zodiac - as shown in the diagrams. Note that, in these diagrams, the Tribe of Dan is associated with Scorpio. Since Scorpio is the Zodiac Sign representing unmitigated evil, it stands for Satan, and all his minions - including the Antichrist, the Nephilim, and the fallen Watchers. This may be why some have predicted that the Antichrist will be the Nephilim "Seed of the Serpent" from the Tribe of Dan.

Supporting this hypothesis, the Tribe of Dan isn't listed among the Twelve Tribes of Israel that the 144,000 Witnesses are to come out of during the Tribulation period. The Tribe of Joseph is counted twice instead, with Joseph's older son Manasseh being substituted for Dan, and Joseph being counted to represent his younger son Ephraim, who inherited Manasseh's birthright.

## The Sphinx, Orion, the Aquarian Age, and the Last Day

As already shown, the Great Sphinx is part of a complex of sacred monuments at Giza dedicated to Orion. In the Gospel in the Stars, Orion is the constellation representing Christ as a conqueror. Further showing this connection of Christ with Giza, there is the symbolism of the Great Pyramid and the Great Sphinx, which undeniably seem to reflect the nature and purpose of Christ.

Based on how the Giza pyramids mimic the arrangement of the belt stars in the constellation of Orion, and mark the placement of these three stars on the southern and eastern horizons, the entire Giza Pyramid Complex appears to be a giant astronomical clock designed to track the belt stars in Orion over an immense span of time. Interestingly, Orion is a decan of Taurus, the Zodiac sign that was in the south at the dawn of time, and is connected to the Tribe of Joseph. Not surprisingly, then, the placement of Orion on the southern horizon is also emphasized at Giza.

A comparison of the belt stars of the constellation Orion with the layout of the three biggest Pyramids at Giza can tell us much about what time period these monuments were built to convey. Note that, in the illustration, the three stars that make up the belt of Orion appear to be literally represented in the lay out, and physical volume of the three biggest pyramids at Giza. The pyramids attributed to Pharaoh Khufu (the Great Pyramid) and his successor Khafre are aligned along a central axis. However, the smallest of the three big pyramids (supposedly built by Pharaoh Menkaure) is offset slightly from the other two. From this remarkable correlation, it can be seen that these three pyramids are, in effect, an allegory for Orion.

If viewed as an allegory for Orion's belt, the Great Pyramid represents Al Nitak, the brightest star in the belt. Since the Great Pyramid represents the spherical shape of our Earth, it also suggests the spherical shape of the star it is aligned with. The pyramids of Khafre and Menkaure represent the other two stars in Orion's belt, with the pyramid of Menkaure offset from the other two pyramids exactly in the same way as the smallest star in Orion's belt is set apart from its two brighter stars. The meaning of the constellation of Orion can therefore shed much light on the study of the prophetic meaning of the names of the stars associated with it. We will cover more on this a bit later.

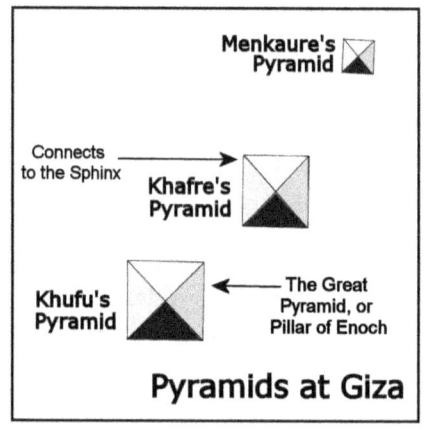

**Pyramids at Giza**

**Orion's Belt Stars**

In the diagram of the Israelite Camp from Book One, *Taurus is in the south*, and Orion is one of the three decans of Taurus. When using the Zodiac to date the time that the star shafts of the Great Pyramid point toward, several people have shown *Orion in the south*. In this position, Orion's belt stars reflect the layout of the three big pyramids at Giza *like a mirror*. In addition, the Nile River's position alongside the Giza complex mirrors the position of the Milky Way beside Orion. Uncannily, however, the sky is not mirrored at Giza as it appears today, but as it would have appeared in relation to Orion *in*

# Chapter 6: The Great Sphinx - Symbol for Christ

*10,500 BC!* This uncanny metaphor of the Universe - built on the Earth by men - is a wonderful example of how ancient people understood and applied the Language of God.

The points where the Ecliptic and Celestial Equator cross each other mark the Spring and Fall Equinoxes. The Ecliptic is the circular (east to west) path that the Sun takes through the sky as the Earth rotates on its axis. The Celestial Meridian is the great circle formed where the projection of Earth's Prime Meridian into the sky crosses the Celestial Sphere from north to south in relation to the Earth. The Celestial Equator is a projection of the Earth's equator onto the Celestial Sphere. Currently, the latitude and longitude of the Earth are found by measuring in degree increments all over the globe from the starting points of the Earth's equator running east to west and the Prime Meridian running north to south, which is currently Greenwich, England. In the sky, this same sort of square grid is derived using the Celestial Equator and the Celestial Meridian.

According to my "Starry Night" Astronomy program, the ecliptic currently crosses the Celestial Equator between Pisces and Aquarius at the Spring Equinox, and Leo and Virgo at the Fall Equinox. This will supposedly be the case until 2626 AD, when the Spring Equinox will occur just within the current arbitrary border of Aquarius. However, these borders around the constellations were imposed in relatively recent times. In actual fact, there is a fair degree of overlap between the signs of Aquarius and Pisces. As a result, the fish of Pisces that swims along the ecliptic extends into the area of Aquarius. Also, the current way we divide the sky up into sections of 30 degrees per Zodiac sign along the Celestial Equator is somewhat arbitrary. Though based on 30-degree increments of a 360-degree circle, the modern Prime Meridian at Greenwich, England appears to be fixed exactly 30 degrees out of sync with the ancient Prime Meridian, which was at Giza.

Now, if the current Prime Meridian were shifted 30 degrees east of Greenwich, as the location of the Great Pyramid near Cairo, Egypt suggests, the Celestial Meridian that is tied to it would also need to be shifted. Marked by this new sky meridian aligned with Cairo or Giza, the Spring Equinox does indeed fall squarely in the sign of Aquarius, and *it has since 2000 AD*. This means that **the Precessional Age of Pisces officially ended in 2000 AD, and the Age of Aquarius began.** If time doesn't cease to exist, the Sun will rise in Aquarius on the Spring Equinox and in Leo at the Fall Equinox for approximately the next 2,100 years.

If 10,500 BC marks the beginning of the Six Days of Creation, six Precessional Ages of 2,160 years will have past since Yahshua created the Universe, and time began - to the point when time ends, and this current Creation passes away. These six Precessional Ages represent 12,960 years of time – very close to 13,000 years. Since twelve Great Days of one thousand years each have already unfolded since the beginning, when Yahweh began His Creation of the Universe, only one thousand years are left before the real end of the world, when everything on the face of the Earth will be burned, and a New Heaven and Earth will be created.

If we stick to the 13,000-year limit of time between our finite Creation, and eternity, which is suggested by the passing of six Precessional Ages, the Creation of the Universe would have been around 10,000 BC, rather than 10,500 BC. Therefore, what could account for the 500 years difference in dates? A possible answer is found though Jewish folklore. Therein, the Jews state that Adam and Eve had been alive for seven years before they sinned. However, what if this "seven" years stands for some other full period of time? Could Adam and Eve have been perfect, and sinless, for 500 prophetic years? If so, by Jewish reckoning, 500 years would have been ten Jubilees of fifty years each, which could be considered a full period of time, or a biblical "seven."

According to Jewish reckoning, Adam and Eve were not created until toward the end of the Sixth Great Day of Creation (which fell between 5000 BC and 4000 BC). Then, sometime after their creation, Adam and Eve sinned for the first time. Biblical chronology places the time of Adam and Eve's creation at around 4003 BC. This is based on Adam's age at death, which was most likely 930 years after he presumably sinned, became mortal, and began to age. If the Fall occurred in 4003 BC, the Six Great Days of men's works began at that time, cutting God's thousand-year Great Sabbath Day of Rest short. Now, if 4003 BC dates the Fall of Adam and Eve, the year 1999 AD marked the imminent close of human history. *The Seventh Millennium is therefore already upon us!* More about what this startling fact means prophetically is covered later. For now, however, let's focus on one salient fact: *counting this final Seventh Millennium that we are now in, 13,000 years will have passed between our finite Creation, and the beginning of Eternity*.

In my book "The Language of God in History," it is noted that the Earth's Precessional movement backward through the Zodiac is a strong prophetic statement. In fact, it clearly supports my previously stated views about God's plan to reverse mankind's history! Thus far, we have explored this reversal of history as depicted in the Chanukiah Menorah. This Chanukiah pattern was shown to exist in Hallel Psalms 110 through

# Chapter 6: The Great Sphinx - Symbol for Christ

118 and in the Grand Gallery of the Pillar of Enoch. Here again, God's desire to reverse history can be seen in the heavens through the Precession of the Equinoxes.

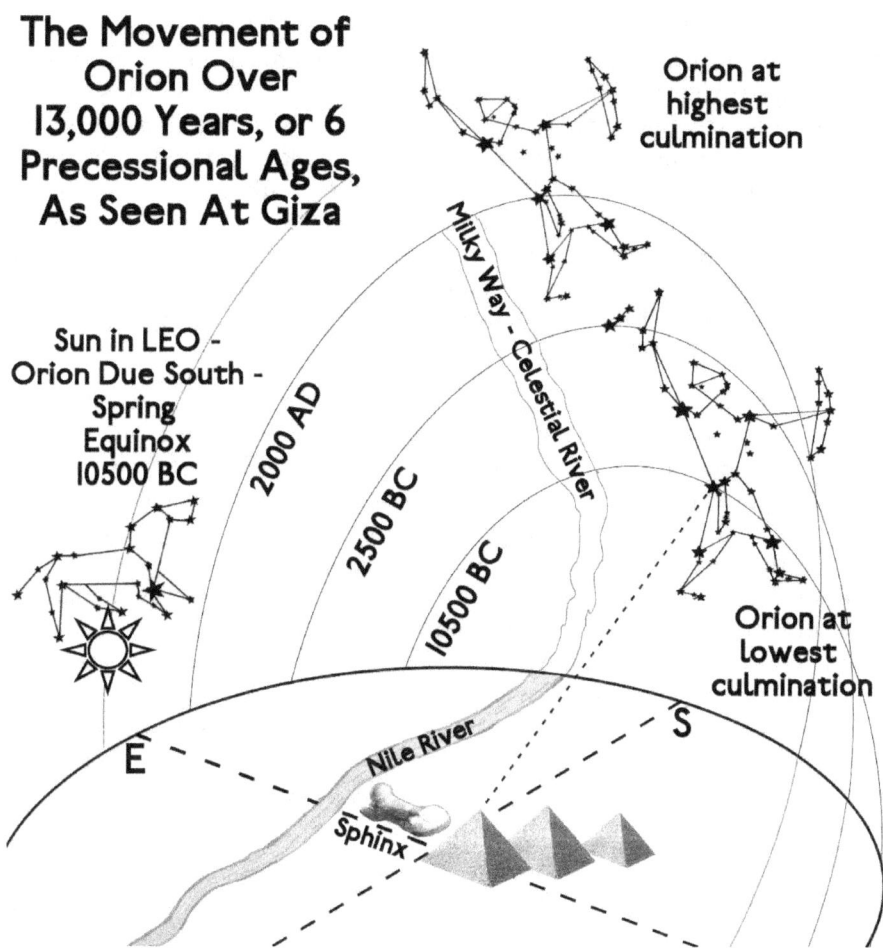

The Sun's forward motion though the twelve signs of the Zodiac marks the unfolding of six Creation Days and six thousand years of mankind's history over 12,000 years. Precession, however, marks the reversal of these same events of history over all 13,000 years of history, including the Millennial Rule of Christ, which will lead to the Creation of the New Heaven and New Earth! This truth was depicted in the Great Sphinx by the Sethites, who used a lion's body to indicate the origin of time in 10,500 BC, and a woman's face to point to the end of the Age of Aquarius, when time, as we know it, will cease to exist.

We can see this 12,000 to 13,000-year time span depicted in the celestial movements of the constellation of Orion over time, as shown on page 227. Due to the Precessional movement of the Earth, all the constellations appear to shift downward and upward in the sky over a period of approximately 25,920 years. In addition, Precession causes the Sun to shift slowly backward, passing through one Zodiac sign every 2,160 years. The constellation of Orion can be tracked to its most recent lowest and highest Precessional positions in the Southern sky over time using Astronomy programs such as Red Shift or Starry Night Pro. Using these programs we can determine when the belt stars of Orion aligned in an exact mirror image with the three biggest pyramids at Giza. We can also determine when the Great Sphinx was gazing due East at the constellation Leo on the horizon.

The only time in the past when both of these criteria were matched was during Orion's lowest culmination in 10,500 BC. At dawn on the Spring Equinox in 10,500 BC, Orion's belt would have mirrored the three biggest pyramids at Giza in position on the southern horizon, and the Sphinx would have been gazing directly toward the Zodiac sign of Leo on the eastern horizon. In addition, the three belt stars of Orion would have risen directly above the three small auxiliary pyramids along the south face of Menkaure's pyramid. This event would have occurred near the end of the Precessional Age of Leo, when the Sun still rose in Leo on the Spring Equinox. However, since the stars were not created until the Fourth Great Day of Creation, and mankind was not created until the Sixth Great Day, there were no stars or people to reckon time at the dawn of the first Creation Day (Genesis 1:13-18, 1:24-31). *It is therefore only a reference point.*

Now that we have established the time of Orion's lowest point on the horizon in relation to the Milky Way that best fits the imagery of the Nile River and Pyramids at Giza, we need to find Orion's highest Precessional position by going forward in time. **This highest position of Orion occurred in 2000 AD.** This suggests that the builders of the Great Pyramid and the Great Sphinx wanted to tell us that 10,500 BC and 2000 AD are very important. In addition, the Holy Spirit also revealed this same correlation through the Israelite Desert encampment thousands of years ago! As these correlations suggest, **the year 2000 is highly important, for it marked the beginning of a new Age on Earth - the Age of Aquarius!** This Aquarian Age also marks the beginning of the Last

## Chapter 6: The Great Sphinx - Symbol for Christ

Great Day of human history - the Age when the Millennial Rule of Christ will become a reality.

Since the antediluvian Sethites went through tremendous effort to build monuments at Giza that would last throughout the Ages, they must have really wanted to transmit a message of profound importance. Indeed, they did so, for the entire Giza complex tells mankind that the Savior promised in the Gospel in the Stars was destined to come. Furthermore, they wanted us to know the timing of Christ's First and Second Coming as a witness of God's sovereignty, and the sureness that God's Will shall be done regardless of Satan and humanity's efforts to thwart it. However, since this message was meant primarily for this present Age, humanity's understanding of these ancient monuments was closed, or hidden until this present era, when God has lifted the veil on our understanding, and allowed mankind to see the message our righteous ancestors preserved in stone as a promise, and *a warning*.

Our antediluvian ancestors also wanted to tell us the date that marked a point just before the time when God first hovered over the waters of the Great Deep, and contemplated the Creation of the Heavens and the Earth. They wanted to show us that the Precessional Age of Leo is the starting point for when God decided to create the Universe, at which time the Zodiacal wheel of Precessional time figuratively began to revolve. **10,500 BC, however, was only meant to be a reference point since the constellation of Leo, and Precession itself did not technically exist at that time.**

Beginning at the end of the Precessional Age of Leo, and for Six Millennium-long Great Days, God toiled to make the Universe. Then, sometime after Adam and Eve were first created on the Sixth Creation Day, the Seventh Millennium Day in the Precessional Age of Taurus began. This was the Day when God rested, and He likely first ordained the keeping of the seventh day Sabbath. This is also when the six thousand-year Ages of men began to unfold – but probably only when Adam and Eve first sinned. God's rest then sadly ended, and was postponed until the time of the seventh and final Great Day, which was ordained to come *after* the six Ages allotted to men had passed.

This final Great Day is none other than the Great Day of the Lord spoken of repeatedly in Bible prophecies. The Bible tells us that the coming of the Day of the Lord will herald the imminent onset of the Tribulation period. Afterward, all people who survive the Great Tribulation and are not put to death by Yahshua and His army of saints will partake in a thousand-year Sabbath rest with Yahshua as their King. It will be a time of peace, joy and prosperity on the Earth that has not been equaled since the time before the Fall, when Adam and Eve and the Garden of Eden were still untainted by sin. Still clothed with light and therefore unashamed, Adam and Eve walked with Yahweh at their side and there was no nakedness, sin, death, or sorrow to hurt them or the Universe. It has been foretold in the Bible repeatedly that a time like this will come again when Yahshua reigns as King on the Earth during His Millennial Rule. We will cover more about this blessed time of rest later in this book.

Biblical chronology traces man's history to no earlier than 4003 BC. Thus the Bible supports the idea that six thousand years have elapsed since Adam and Eve began to age, and the concept of time and aging, as we know it, began. Add to this the theory that the Six Great Days of Creation is a six thousand year period, and the Bible supports the idea that 12,000 years of time have already past. As will be shown in the next chapter, the Six Days of Creation may have been thousand-year days, and not literal 24-hour days. If so, 12,000 years have passed since the beginning of the first Creation Day, which is very close in time to the 12,500-year Precessional cycle of the constellation of Orion. According to my Biblical Chronology, the six periods of one thousand-years allotted for human history to unfold began in September of 4003 BC with the creation of Adam and technically ended in the year 1999 AD.

The end of the six thousand-year Ages of Men can be mathematically calculated with this equation: $(-4003+1+6000=1998)$. The one has been added to account for the zero point at the transition between negative to positive numbers on a linear graph. According to this calculation, the Jewish Civil Year beginning in September of 1998 that coincided with our Gregorian Year 1999 was the last year of the Sixth Millennium since the Fall of Adam and Eve. Now, since the Jewish Sacred New Year is on Nissan 1, that final year can also be seen to have ended at dusk on April 5th, 2000. This is fascinating because of the importance of Easter Island with Sethite Astronomy, and the fact that this island was discovered on Easter, April 5th, 1722. Furthermore, if my hypothesis is correct, the beginning of the Tribulation period began on the 1st of Nissan on April 5th in 2011, and we are fast approaching the mid-point of the Tribulation - when I believe that the Rapture will occur and the Great Tribulation will begin.

This book shows many reasons why I believe this. In particular, Chapters 11 and 12 in this book will explain more about Easter Island's importance as a Sethite time marker, and why I believe the Tribulation has already begun, and that most Bible Prophecy teachers are unaware of this due to their ignorance of the Signs in the Heavens and Sethite

## Chapter 6: The Great Sphinx - Symbol for Christ

Astronomy that centered around the amazing Messianic constellation Orion the Brilliant.

Since the Sixth Great Day ended on April 5th, 2000, the first year in the Seventh Millennium partly coincided with our year 2000 AD. *We have therefore reached the full circle point that marks the completion of 12,000 years of prophetic time. This also means that the Great Day of the Lord has already arrived,* and we are at the threshold of immense changes both on the Earth, and in the heavens. In Chapter Seven, the concept of thousand-year Great Days will be closely examined, and proven to be a biblical concept that makes sense of many End Time prophecies - including those found in the Book of Revelation and Book of 1 Enoch.

If the six thousand year period that God's mercy was to be extended to mankind has ended, many may be wondering why the Tribulation hasn't already begun. The answer to that is complex, and centers on the fact the Yah's mercy is so great that He has allotted a short period beyond the close of the six Ages of Men to give people a last chance to repent. This time period has been shown to the world through biblical prophecies, and the prophetic nature of the biblically ordained Jewish holidays that occur in the autumn. These amazing prophecies will be fully explored in the next few chapters of this book.

# Chapter 7: The Language of Prophecy and the Last Day

*"But **the DAY OF THE LORD will come as a thief in the night, in which the heavens will pass away with a great noise, and the elements will melt with fervent heat;** both the earth and the works that are in it will be burned up. - 2 Peter 3:10*

In the above passage, what does the phrase *"Day of the Lord"* mean to you? According to the Apostle Peter, it referred to the events leading up to the destruction of this current world by fire, and its subsequent replacement with a New Heaven and New Earth (2 Peter 3:13). Some people assume this refers to the end of the seven-year Tribulation period spoken of in the Book of Revelation, when the ungodly will be afflicted by fire and great heat (Rev. 16:8-9). Still others think that the "Day" of the Lord is the 3-1/2 year Great Tribulation, while others feel that the entire Day of the Lord refers to one literal 24-hour day. Numerous Old and New Testament prophecies refer to this Tribulation period as a time of great distress and disaster on Earth (See Jeremiah 30:7-10; Zephaniah 1:13-18; Zechariah 14:1-7, 12-16; Joel 2:1-11; Malachi 4:5-6). However, as this chapter will fully reveal, the Day of the Lord is much more than the dire event known as the Tribulation.

Due to the tremendous importance of the Tribulation and the Day of the Lord, the last half of this book focuses on these End Time prophetic events. Furthermore, they give vital information that is not found in many other current books on the subject. Therefore, please read these chapters carefully and prayerfully before casting any judgment on the startling facts about to be disclosed.

Before proceeding further, keep in mind that **the key to deciphering the allegorical symbolism in Biblical prophecy is a thorough understanding of the Language of God.** After reading all the preceding chapters, you should have a good working knowledge of the how the Language of God works - and what it can tell you when you know what to look for. Through prayer, one's mind and spirit can be keenly attuned to the power of allegories to instruct, and it becomes much easier to understand prophecies.

After my own prayers to Yahshua asking Him to help me to understand the Language of God, I found (to my surprise and delight) that the Spirit of God opened my understanding of the Bible's prophetic books. As a result, it became apparent that there is much more being divulged in these prophecies than initially meets the eye. Now, after saying your own prayer for Yahweh to open your spirit to His Language, join me as I delve into the full meaning of the phrase *"Day of the Lord."*

## *Is "The Day of the Lord" One Single Day?*

There are many different interpretations within the Messianic and Church communities of what, when, and how long the Day of the Lord will be. As already stated, some believers think the events on the Day of the Lord will occur in one single day. Though it is certainly possible that God could lay waste to the Earth and restore it to Eden-like perfection in one day, the final book of the Bible called Revelation teaches that Yahweh will do this over a one thousand year period.

One Christian theory about the Lord's Day is that it is really seven years long, and not one single day. According to this view, Yahshua will return temporarily at the beginning of the seven years - just to retrieve His saints from the Earth before the Tribulation period. This event is known as the Pre-Tribulation Rapture. Still others hold the view that the Rapture will occur before the Bowls of God's Wrath and the Battle of Armageddon. This is known as the Mid-Tribulation Rapture. Personally, I believe that there will be two Raptures - one before and one in the middle of the Tribulation.

Others believe the Day of the Lord will occur on one day. This will be at the very end of the Great Tribulation - when Yahshua will return to Earth to destroy the wicked, raise the righteous dead, and rule over the Earth as King of kings. This rapid 24-hour series of events is known as the Post-Tribulation Rapture, or simply as the Day of the Lord. However, though God unquestionably could accomplish everything prophesied in one 24-hour period, the assumption that Yahshua will do this may be incorrect - as will be shown in this chapter. Let's look at some of the many biblical prophecies about the Day of the Lord to see why. The first one introduces the Book of Revelation. Here, the Apostle John said:

# Ch. 7: The Language of Prophecy and the Last Day

*"I was in the Spirit on the Lord's Day, and I heard behind me a loud voice, as of a trumpet..." - Rev. 1:10*

This opening statement tells us that what we are about to read is a Spirit-led vision. Furthermore, since the sound of a trumpet once announced the coming of kings, the voice like a trumpet is announcing things associated with the coming of the King of kings, Yahshua our Messiah. Perhaps this is why Jews associate the trumpet with Rosh Hashanah, or the Feast of Trumpets, their New Year holiday focusing on God's Reign. Finally, this Scripture tells us that the entire book is a vision of what will occur on *"the Lord's Day."*

Since "The Lord's Day" and "The Day of the LORD," or "Day of Yahweh" are the same event, and the Book of Revelation reveals a series of events that will occur over many days, we have our first clue that "The Lord's Day" is not a mere 24-hour day, but a longer, pre-determined period of time. Incidentally, the Lord's Day is not, and never was, a reference to Sunday. Sunday is never called "the Lord's Day" in Scripture, but only *"the first day of the week"* (Mat. 28:1; Mark 16:2; Luke 26:1; John 20:1, 19). Therefore, this common misconception has no basis in fact.

The idea that the Day of the Lord is a one-day event can be dispelled through studying the entire Book of Revelation, which shows that it is a thousand year period. The Book of Revelation also clearly tells us the chain of End Time events on this thousand-year Great Day of the Lord, as this abridged section of Scripture shows:

*"He laid hold of... the Devil...* **and bound him for a thousand years;** *and he cast him into the bottomless pit, and shut him up... so that he should deceive the nations no more till* **the thousand years** *were finished.* **But after these things he must be released for a little while**... *Then I saw the souls of those who had been beheaded for their witness to Jesus (Yahshua)... And* **they lived and reigned with Christ for a thousand years.** *But the rest of the dead did not live again until the thousand years were finished. This is the first resurrection... Over such the second death has no power, but they shall be priests of God and of Christ,* **and shall reign with Him a thousand years. Now when the thousand years have expired, Satan will be released** *from his prison and will go out to deceive the nations... to gather them together to battle... They went up... and surrounded... the beloved city.* **And fire came down from God out of heaven and devoured them. The devil, who deceived them, was cast into the lake of fire***..." - Rev. 20:2-13*

# The Language of God in Prophecy

Note the repeated use of the phrase *"a thousand years"* in this section (Rev. 20:2-6). This phrase is clearly not allegorical in nature, but to be taken literally. From beginning to end, the Book of Revelation describes the unfolding of a specific sequence of events. First, there are the birth pangs of the coming Tribulation period, which occur over a long period of time, when the churches are judged according to their works (Revelation, Chapters 1-3). When this time period ends, the Tribulation period begins, and the Seals, Trumpets, and Bowls of God's Wrath are unleashed upon all the people living on the Earth at that time (Revelation, Chapters 4-18). Then Yahshua will come again to conquer the wicked, to rule the Earth, and establish an earthly Kingdom of Peace for a thousand years (Revelation, Chapters 19-20).

Now, it is interesting here to note that - according to the Jews - Adam and Eve first sinned seven years after they were created. Nonetheless, as discussed in Book One, though this seven-year period may have gone by without sin, it is still considered to be a part of the first six thousand years allotted for mankind's sinful works. Could it be that they were not supposed to be counted? Could it be that the Lord's Day did not begin in 2000 but in 2007, which is seven years later? If this is true, then Rosh Hashanah on Nisan 1 in 2007 *could have been* the official beginning of the Day of the Lord.

However, as stated earlier, Adam and Eve could have remained sinless and immortal for much longer than seven years. As this book repeatedly shows, the number 7 signifies completion, or fullness, and can mean a complete period of time other than a day or year. It therefore may be true that Adam and Eve were not created on, but fell into sin in 4003 BC. If so, their days literally began to be numbered at that time, and they needed to keep records for future generations. Hence, they needed to develop a method of keeping track of time, and Astronomy was born. Consequently, there is a good reason to believe that the Day of the Lord started in April of 2000, after the 6000 years that were divinely allotted for human history had fully passed.

The reason that the Tribulation did not begin in 1999 is likely because God granted *a delay* before the Tribulation so that more souls could be saved due to the prayers of the saints. As will be shown in the next two chapters, several divinely given prophecies besides the Psalms, and the Great Pyramid show that **the Tribulation period may be scheduled to begin after 2010** ends on Nissan 1 or April 5th, 2011. God has allotted mankind ten years of additional Grace because He doesn't want anyone to perish. As Michael Drosnin suggests in his books on the Bible Codes, this may be due to the cries of God's saints to give people

## Ch. 7: The Language of Prophecy and the Last Day

more time to repent. However, God's mercy will eventually subside so the Tribulation can begin.

Invariably, many prophecies and heavenly signs suggest that the end of 2010 or Spring or Summer of 2011 AD will be the beginning of the Tribulation period, while other prophetic signs single out 2018 as the beginning year of the thousand-year rule of Yahshua on Earth. Though these dates may have been pinpointed to warn us that the Tribulation is very near but not necessarily imminent - there are compelling reasons to believe that these dates are connected to the Tribulation itself.

Before we explore the prophecies pinpointing these dates, however, let's look at the events involving the Lord's Day, as spoken of in the Book of Revelation. First of all, Revelation insists that Christ will literally rule the world for a thousand-year period, during which Satan will be bound (Rev. 20:2-4). Furthermore, the Earth will be filled with peace, and it will be restored to pristine beauty (See Isaiah 2:4, 11:5-10, 35:4-10, 41:18-20, 51:3, 55:13). For a thousand years, mortal, and immortal people, and holy angels will work together to make Christ's Kingdom the happiest, most peaceful, and most beautiful time and place anyone can remember. Then, to weed out the last of the wicked, Satan will be released at the close of the thousand year reign of Christ, and he will tempt many unsaved people among the nations to rebel against their divine King of kings. This will precipitate a supernatural slaughter of the wicked with fire from heaven (Rev. 20:7-9). Then there will be a Great White Throne Judgment, and the remaining wicked will be destroyed in the Lake of Fire:

> *"**Then I saw a great white throne** and Him who sat on it... And I saw the dead, small and great, standing before God... And the dead were judged according to their works... Then Death and Hades were cast into the lake of fire. This is the second death.* **And anyone not found written in the Book of Life was cast into the lake of fire."** *- Rev. 20:12-15*

After the Last Judgment - when all people will be given one final chance to repent - the New Heaven, the New Earth, and the New Jerusalem will be established as the everlasting habitation of the righteous:

> *"**Now I saw a new heaven and a new earth**, for the first heaven and the first earth had passed away. Also there was no more sea.* **Then I, John, saw the holy city, New Jerusalem, coming down out of heaven** *from God, prepared as a bride adorned for her husband." - Revelation 21:1-2*

These Scriptures teach that all these chronological events do not happen in one day! They will, rather, occur on the Lord's Day that John the Revelator spoke of in his book, which is the same thing as the Day of the Lord! Furthermore, as shown in the preceding quote from the Book of Revelation, it explicitly says a thousand years are involved in Christ's Kingdom, which is also a part of the Day of the Lord. It therefore must be at least a thousand years long. I call this thousand-year time period a Great Day. This concept of a thousand-year Great Day is scriptural, as will be shown in a moment. However, first let's look at the major battles that are prophesied about as occurring on the Great Day of the Lord.

## *The Lord's Day, and The Two Battles of Armageddon*

Another way to see the reality of this thousand-year Great Day that includes the Millennial Rule of Christ is to note that there are two battles - one at the beginning, and one at the end of the Day of the Lord. Though both of these battles fit the criterion for being the Battle of Armageddon, however, they are very different events. In the first battle, for example, at Yahshua's triumphant return, swords will literally spill blood, and birds will dine on the dead people's flesh (Rev. 14:20, 19:21). However, in the second battle, fire devours the wicked, so blood is not spilled by the sword, and there will be no flesh left for the birds to dine on (Rev. 20:9).

In regard to these battles, there are other Scriptures outside of the Book of Revelation that can't be common to both battles, but exclusively refer only to one. In the Book of Jeremiah, for example, the Day of the Lord is clearly a day of vengeance against all the nations who have rejected Yahshua as their God and King. Jeremiah also describes it as a day when blood will flow from the bodies of the wicked. **For this to occur, they must be slaughtered by the sword**, but not by fire from heaven - for then there would be no blood spilled:

> *"For **this is the day of the Lord** GOD of hosts (Yahweh Tsavout), a day of vengeance, that He may avenge Himself on His adversaries. **The sword shall devour; it shall be satiated and made drunk with their blood**; for the Lord GOD of hosts (Yahweh Tsavout) has a sacrifice in the north country by the River Euphrates."* - Jeremiah 46:10

> *"For Israel is not forsaken, nor Judah, by his God, the LORD of hosts (Yahweh Tsavout), though their land was filled with sin... **Flee from the midst of Babylon**, and every one save his*

# Ch. 7: The Language of Prophecy and the Last Day

*life! Do not be cut off in her iniquity, for **this is the time of the LORD'S (Yahweh's) vengeance;** he shall recompense her. **Babylon was a golden cup in the LORD'S (Yahweh's) hand that made all the earth drunk.**" - Jeremiah 51:5-7*

With Jeremiah's talk of blood being spilled, and the golden cup of Babylon upon which all the nations become drunk, these Scriptures are clear references to the Battle of Armageddon at Christ's return, for this is when Babylon the Great is to fall (See Rev. 18:2,21).

However, the next Scripture, which is taken from the Second Epistle of Peter, seems to pertain directly to the last battle *at the end* of the Day of the Lord. This could be called the final, 24-hour Day of the Lord - when the armies surrounding Jerusalem will not be destroyed by the sword, but by a supernatural fire that is described in 2 Peter and Revelation 20:9. About this, Peter said:

*"But the day of the Lord will come as a thief in the night, in which the heavens will pass away... and the elements will melt with fervent heat; both the earth and the works that are in it will be burned up..." - 2 Peter 3:10*

The preceding Scripture cannot be referring to the battle that comes before the Millennial Rule of Christ, because all the Old Testament prophecies about this time speak of *renewal, restoration, and repair*. These sorts of actions will not be needed if the Earth is completely destroyed and then immediately made new and perfect again before Christ rules the world. Renewal and restoration can only take place on the old Earth we are familiar with, not on a world already made perfect! We will return to 2 Peter 3:10 in the next section, where - using a larger quote from Peter's second epistle - we will explore the sequence of events on the Great Day of the Lord. We will also examine other scriptural proofs supporting the idea that the Day of the Lord is a thousand years long.

## The Concept of the Great Day at the Time of Christ

The Day of the Lord is so highly important that both Yahshua and Saint Paul warn us to watch for it:

*"Be careful, or your hearts will be weighed down with dissipation, drunkenness and the anxieties of life, **and that day will close on you unexpectedly like a trap.** For it will come upon all those who live on the face of the whole earth. **Be always on the watch, and pray that you may be able to escape** all that is about to*

happen, and that you may be able to stand before the Son of Man." - Luke 21:34-36 (NIV)

> *"For **you yourselves know perfectly that the day of the Lord so comes as a thief in the night.** For when they say, 'Peace and safety!' then sudden destruction comes upon them, as labor pains upon a pregnant woman. And they shall not escape. **But you, brethren, are not in darkness, so that this Day should overtake you as a thief."** - 1 Thessalonians 5:2-4*

Yahshua and Paul's warnings imply that the Day of the Lord is an event that we should be able to recognize so that we will not be caught off guard when it comes. In fact, Paul makes it clear that his listeners *"know perfectly that the day of the Lord so comes as a thief in the night."* **Paul also says that the saints *"are not in darkness,"* meaning that they know what to watch for, and will know when the Day of the Lord is imminent.** In this chapter, we will determine what Paul's hearers knew, and what we should know, so that we are not caught unawares when the Day of the Lord arrives!

At the time of Yahshua, some Jewish Rabbis or teachers must have been familiar with the idea of Sacred Astronomy. This is evidenced in the Dead Sea Scrolls. There is an interesting text mentioned in the book "The Dead Sea Scrolls, A New Translation," by Michael Wise and colleagues. Text 58, "A Divination Text," shows that at least some of the Jews at Qumran knew about the twelve signs of the Zodiac, and noted their movements in the night sky. The following quote is from the first part of this text, which describes the positions of the Moon in relation to the signs of the Mazzaroth, or Zodiac over a one-month period:

> *"and on the seventh (day), the Archer; on the eighth and ninth, the Kid; on the tenth and eleventh, the Drawer; on the twelfth and thirteenth and fourteenth, the Fishes; on the fifteenth and sixteenth, the Ram; on the seventeenth and eighteenth, the Ox; on the nineteenth and on the twentieth and on the twenty-first, the Twins; on the twenty-second and twenty-third, the Crab; on the twenty-fourth and twenty-fifth, the Lion, on the twenty-sixth and on the twenty-seventh and on the twenty-eighth, the Virgin; on the twenty-ninth and on the thirtieth and thirty-first, the Scales. Tishri: On the first and on the second, the Scorpion..."*
> *– page 304, The Dead Sea Scrolls, A New Translation*

In the preceding quotation of the translated Qumran text, the twelve Zodiac signs are identified by their pictorial designations, and in their proper order. First, the Archer we call Sagittarius is mentioned,

# Ch. 7: The Language of Prophecy and the Last Day

followed in sequence by the Kid, known to us as Capricorn. Next, the text lists the Drawer (or Fetcher of Water) which is Aquarius, then the Fishes for Pisces, the Ram for Aries, the Ox for Taurus, the Twins for Gemini, the Crab for Cancer, the Lion for Leo, the Virgin for Virgo, and the Scorpion for Scorpio.

This text is unique among the calendar texts found at Qumran, which usually list the months by their number designations rather than their names. Nonetheless, the existence of this text at Qumran supports the Jewish use of astronomical and astrological principles around the time of Christ. The Jews at Qumran knew of all twelve symbolic names for the zodiacal signs - exactly as we know them today. Furthermore, this text contains the earliest list of the zodiacal signs ever found in Aramaic, and proves that some Jews were keeping track of stellar movements using the signs of the Zodiac near to the time of Christ.

The idea that a thousand years to God is like a day to Him was introduced in Book One, "The Language of God in the Universe", which is about the Gospel in the Stars. Scripture supports this idea:

> *"For a thousand years in Your sight are like yesterday when it is past, and like a watch in the night."* - Psalm 90:4

It is likely that Saint Paul, as a very learned man, would have been familiar with this Scripture. We also know that the Apostle Peter knew of this biblical teaching, even though he is traditionally depicted as a poor, uneducated fisherman whose knowledge of Scripture would have been rudimentary. If true, however, Peter would not remain this way. In fact, the Book of Acts and Peter's two epistles show that he often spoke eloquently and confidently in defense of the Gospel of Christ after he was baptized with the Holy Spirit. For example, just before he spoke to his fellow believers about the coming Day of the Lord, Peter explicitly mentioned the principle of reckoning days in thousand-year increments:

> *"But, beloved, do not forget this one thing, that **with the Lord one day is as a thousand years, and a thousand years as one day.** The Lord is not slack concerning His promise... but is longsuffering toward us, not willing that any should perish... But **the day of the Lord will come as a thief in the night, in which the heavens will pass away with a great noise, and the elements will melt with fervent heat; both the earth and the works that are in it will be burned up.** Therefore, since all these things will be dissolved, what manner of persons ought you to be in holy conduct and godliness, looking for and hastening the coming of **the day of God,** because of which **the heavens will be dissolved,***

*being on fire, and the elements will melt with fervent heat?"* - 2 Peter 3:8-13

In this Scripture, Peter alludes to the concept that a thousand years is as a day to God. Then Peter immediately begins to speak about the destruction of the existing heaven and Earth by fire and heat, which is accompanied by the sound of violent noise. It is as if Peter had envisioned a nuclear-type explosion encompassing the entire Universe that will completely annihilate this present Creation! This does not seem like an event that would presage Christ's Millennial Kingdom on Earth, but the end of the world. It is also obvious here that Peter possessed mystical knowledge that most of the common people of his day were unacquainted with. Could it therefore be possible that, when he was a boy, Peter had been educated nearly as well as Paul, and before either man's conversion? Using deductive reasoning, some scholars have suggested that this was indeed the case.

This supposition is supported by the fact that, before following Christ, **Simon Peter and his brother Andrew were fishing partners with James and John, the sons of Zebedee, and both families owned their own fishing boats** (Luke 5:1-11). A boat big enough to hold several fishermen and a big catch of fish would have had to be at least 18 to 20 feet long, and would require a great deal of wood to build. Since trees big enough to provide timber suitable for making boats were rare in Palestine, wood for boat making was an expensive commodity. Consequently, only men with enough capital could build, own, and operate fishing boats. The four "poor" fishermen who followed Christ therefore must have been wealthier than most Christians have been led to believe.

In the preceding Scripture (2 Peter 3:8-13), Peter suggests that this destruction of the elements by fire will occur on the Day of the Lord. However, if the Day of the Lord refers to the Great Tribulation, we know from the Book of Revelation that it doesn't end with the establishment of the New Heaven and the New Earth and the appearance of the New Jerusalem that comes down from Heaven. Rather, the Great Tribulation ends with the literal reign of Yahshua on Earth from the Old Jerusalem, and in this present Creation (Zechariah 14:3-4; Revelation 14:1, 20:6). Furthermore, the Book of Revelation foretells that the destruction of the current Creation won't occur until the end of the Millennial Rule of Christ (Revelation 20:7-15). Consequently it appears that Peter was alluding to the events *at the end* of the thousand-year "Great Day" of the Lord.

Outside of the Bible, the extra-biblical Epistle of Barnabus also alludes to the teaching that the Six Days of Creation were thousand-year Great Days, and were to be followed by six thousand years of human history. In addition, this document suggests that these millennium-long Days will culminate in another thousand-year period of rest – the Seventh Great Day when Yahshua will reign on the Earth:

> "And **God made in six days the works of his hands; and he finished them on the seventh day, and he rested the seventh day,** and sanctified it. Consider, my children, what that signifies, he finished them in six days. The meaning of it is this; that in six thousand years the Lord God will bring all things to an end. For with him one day is a thousand years; as himself testifieth, saying, Behold this day shall be as a thousand years. Therefore, children, **in six days, that is, in six thousands years, shall all things be accomplished.** And what is that he saith, And he rested the seventh day; he meaneth this; that when his Son shall come, and abolish the season of the Wicked One, and judge the ungodly; and shall change the sun and the moon, and the stars; **then he shall gloriously rest in the seventh day.**" - *Epistle of Barnabus, 13:4-6*

This epistle is attributed to the companion of Saint Paul named Barnabus, and it is dated to around the time that Paul wrote his New Testament letters. Some Bible scholars such as myself consider the Epistle of Barnabus to be canonical, though it has been somewhat corrupted. Nonetheless, it helps prove that this teaching concerning thousand-year days, or Great Days was extant in the early church.

Wise Men, or Magi like those who came to worship Christ at His birth were also still in existence in the classical world that the early church developed in. These Magi would have known how to determine the meaning of the Signs in the Heavens within the context of these Great Days.

In Book One discussing the Mazzaroth or Gospel in the Stars, the idea that the Wise Men or Magi who worshipped Christ might have been Jews or Jewish converts was entertained. If they weren't Jews, it was reasoned, why would they care about the coming Messiah and King of the Jews foretold in the Mazzaroth? In his book "The 'Lost' Ten Tribes of Israel... Found!" Steven M. Collins identifies the Magi who visited Christ as important religious dignitaries from Parthia. Collins shows that the Kingdom of Parthia, which ruled over the lands formerly held by the Assyrians and Babylonians, was likely established by displaced Israelites who had been forcibly resettled in Assyria and Babylon. Then, when Assyria and Babylon fell, these lost Israelites eventually established their own kingdom through conquest.

Regardless of who the Parthians really were, the Magi frequented the courts of the Babylonian, Persian, and Parthian kings as advisors for countless Ages, and they often shared their celestial wisdom with the rulers they counseled. These Magi were guardians of the spiritual knowledge surrounding Sacred Astronomy that had originated among the descendents of Seth and Enoch. Though this knowledge had become corrupted among the Pagans, some Magi likely still utilized the Sethite form of Sacred Astronomy to chart the heavens, and follow God's plan over the Ages.

The Wise Men who worshipped Christ likely journeyed to Jerusalem from the Kingdom of Parthia, which was a powerful kingdom that rivaled the power of Rome during the time of Christ. *As adepts in Sacred Astronomy, the Magi probably viewed the Zodiac as a prophetic depiction of a twelve thousand year period on Earth.* Of these, the Six Days of Creation were likely not seen as 24-hour days, but six 1,000-year days.

As Sacred Astronomers, the Magi would have understood that Precession plays a role in determining the timing of the final Great Day of the Lord. They would have known that six 2160-year long Precessional Ages add up to a little less than 13,000 years, and five and a half Precessional Ages totaling 12,000 years needed to pass between the dawn of the First Creation Day and the Age when the Kingdom of God would be established on Earth. The Magi also likely knew that these thirteen millennia will end after the destruction of the wicked and the triumph of good over evil on the Last Day - which is the thirteenth and final millennium.

The Biblical Chronological Time Chart in the Appendix shows that 4003 BC appears to be the starting point for when people began to age, and time began. It is now six thousand years later, and the year 1999 AD therefore likely marked the beginning of the Seventh Great Day after the Fall, and the Thirteenth Great Day since Creation began. Significantly, this Seventh Great Day arrived on March 18th, 2000, which is the REAL Rosh Hashanah or Jewish New Year, not Yom Teruah or the Feast of Trumpets. Though Yahshua may have been born around the time of the traditional Rosh Hashanah in September of 3 BC per my calculations, the Church Age truly began when He rose from the dead during Passover Week in 31 AD.

According to the prophecies that are deciphered in this book, Yahshua's Millennial Rule is to be set up during this current thirteenth millennium since Creation began. This is significant, since the number thirteen seems to play an important role in the Bible. After all, it is the number of the Apostle Paul, who was the thirteenth apostle chosen by Yahshua Himself to serve as a witness to the Gentiles.

# Ch. 7: The Language of Prophecy and the Last Day

In Book One, a handy chart showing the time span, and significant historical and spiritual events for each of these thirteen Great Days was introduced. This reference chart has been reproduced in the Appendix. In order to better follow what is being proposed in the rest of this chapter, it would be helpful to look over this chart before proceeding to read further here.

## Enoch's 7000 Years or "Ten Times Seven Hundred" Years

Before focusing our discussion on the thirteen Great Days of the Lord, let's take a look at the seven thousand years foreseen in the Book of 1 Enoch, which spanned the dawning Age of Adam and Eve, to the eternal Age of the New Heaven and New Earth. In his book, Enoch explains the spiritual events that he foresaw while reading the heavenly tablets, a written record of the deeds of men and angels that can be found in the vault of heaven.

As discussed at length in Book One and Three of the "Language of God" Book Series, these heavenly tablets are found in the relationships of the Twelve Houses of the Zodiac to each other, and in the structure and movements of the bodies in our Solar System in relation to the Zodiac. Studying the movements of, and relationships between the stars and planets, Enoch was divinely blessed with the ability to prophesy about the future in God's Name, and several of Enoch's amazing prophecies are featured in this book. The first of Enoch's prophecies that we will explore spans a period of seven thousand years. I have dubbed it Enoch's Prophecy of the 7000 Years. As you read through it, please note that the highlighted information in parentheses was added to clarify the past and future events that I believe it is describing:

> "And Enoch began to recount
>
> from the books **(in the heavens)** and said:
>
> 'I was born the seventh
>
> in the first week **(4003 to 3303 BC),**
>
> **(Enoch born in 3381 BC)**
>
> While judgement and righteousness still endured.'"
>
> "And after me there shall arise
>
> in the second week **(3304 to 2604 BC),**
>
> Great wickedness,

**(Fallen Angels and Nephilim corrupt the Earth)**

And deceit shall have sprung up;

and in it there shall be the first end..."

**(Noah's Flood is predicted)**

"And after that,

in the third week **(2603 to 1903 BC)**,

At its close,

**(NOTE: The last three hundred years of each 700-year period is reckoned as its close)**

A man (Abraham) shall be elected as

The plant of righteous judgement,

And his posterity shall become

The plant of righteousness for evermore."

"And after that

in the fourth week **(1902 to 1202 BC)**,

At its close,

Visions of the holy and righteous shall be seen,

And a law for all generations

And an enclosure shall be made for them."

**(The Mosaic Law is given, the Ark of the Covenant and Desert Tabernacle are created, and the Kingdom of Israel is established)**

"And after that

in the fifth week **(1201 to 501 BC)**,

at its close,

The house of glory and dominion

Shall be built for ever."

**(David's Throne established and Solomon's Temple built in Jerusalem as prototypes for the Rule of Christ and the True Church, but the prototypes are destroyed at the close of**

*this period. Nonetheless, Enoch vouches for their continuity elsewhere.)*

"And after that

in the sixth week *(500 BC to 200 AD)*,

All who live in it shall be blinded,

And the hearts of all of them shall godlessly

forsake wisdom.

And in it a man shall ascend;"

**(Yahshua will be born, live, die, Rise from the dead and ascend into heaven)**

"And at its close

**(the close of the birth of the Church in 70 AD)**

*The house of dominion shall be burnt with fire,*

**(The destruction of Jerusalem and the Temple by the Romans in 70 AD)**

*And the whole race of the chosen root*

*shall be dispersed."*

**(The Final Wave of the Jewish Diaspora, and the rapid spread of Christianity)**

"And after that

in the seventh week *(201 to 901 AD)*,

Shall an apostate generation arise,

**(the Papacy, the "Holy" Roman Empire, the Roman Catholic Church, the Merovingian/Magdalene Heresy, and the rise of Islam)**

And many shall be its deeds,

And all its deeds shall be apostate.

And at its close shall be elected

the elect righteous of the eternal

Plant of righteousness,

*(Abraham's plant of righteousness by faith survives in a few. These people form an oppressed but faithful Church in England and Europe.)*

*To receive sevenfold instruction*

*Concerning all His creation."*

*"And after that there shall be another,*

*The eighth week* **(902 to 1602 AD),**

*That of righteousness,"*

**(This righteousness could mean the piety of some truly saved people in the Holy Roman Empire, but the Protestant Reformation also officially began in 1517, and its roots go back to the Dark Ages)**

*"And a sword shall be given to it that*

*A righteous judgement may be executed on*

*the oppressors,"*

**(This may allude to the Crusades, which lifted a righteous sword against Islam!)**

*And sinners shall be delivered*

*Into the hands of the righteous.*

*And at its close,*

*they* **(the Protestants)** *shall acquire*

*houses (i.e. churches, or places of worship) through*

*Their righteousness, and a house*

*Shall be built for the Great King in glory for evermore*

**(This house is the True Church, made up of all born-again believers in Christ)**

*And all mankind shall look to the path of uprightness."*

*"And after that,*

*in the ninth week* **(1603 to 2303 AD),**

*The righteous judgement shall be revealed*

*To the whole world,*

*(The Day of the Lord - consisting of the Great Tribulation, and the Millennial Rule of Christ - is a time of righteous judgment)*

And all the works of the godless shall vanish

From all the earth,

And the world shall be written down for destruction."

"And after this,

In the tenth week **(2304 to 3004 AD)**,

In the seventh part (at its close), there shall be

The great eternal judgement,

**(The Great White Throne Judgment)**

In which He will execute

Vengeance amongst the angels.'

**(the Fallen Angels - including Satan - will be judged)**

"And the first heaven shall depart and pass away,

and a new heaven shall appear,

**(The New Heaven and New Earth)**

And all the powers of the heavens shall

Give sevenfold light.

And after that there will be many weeks

Without number for ever,

And all shall be in goodness and righteousness,

and sin shall no more be mentioned forever."

*- 1 Enoch 93:1-10, 91:12-17*

As can bee seen from the preceding study of the text from the Book of 1 Enoch, Enoch's Prophecy of the 7000 Years describes a series of ten ages lasting seven hundred years each, or a period of seven thousand years. Thus, Enoch was speaking of the seven thousand-year Great Days that were still well understood by Jewish Sages and the Apostles during the time of Christ.

At the beginning of this lengthy prophecy, **Enoch sees his birth in the first seven hundred years** after the Fall of Adam and Eve (4003 to 3303

BC). Since Adam and Eve fell sometime after 4003 BC and Enoch was born in 3381 BC, he was born at the end of the first seven hundred years of human existence outside of the Garden of Eden, just as he states. After that, the Fallen Angels and the Nephilim rose up and dominated the affairs of men, leading them into grievous sin.

*At the close of the second period of seven hundred years (3304 to 2604 BC), Yah approached Noah* and told him that judgment would be executed on the Earth and that Noah should build an Ark to survive the coming destruction of the wicked. After this, the Great Flood occurred, and Shem was chosen to be the ancestor of the righteous line descended from Noah. *In the third seven hundred years (2603 to 1903 BC), Noah's son Shem perpetuated a righteous remnant among the Pagans.* As the last king to hold fast to spiritual truth, Shem (a.k.a. Melchizedek, the King of Righteousness) presided over the education of Abraham in the ways of holiness. Later, it was Abraham who was specially chosen to enter into a Blood Covenant with Yahweh God.

Enoch's prophecy then tells us that, *in the fourth period of seven hundred years (1902 to 1202 BC), an enclosure would be made for the righteous.* This must have been the Desert Tabernacle, followed by the Temple of Solomon in the Kingdom of Israel *in the beginning of the fifth period of seven hundred years (1201 to 501 BC).* After this, *the sixth seven hundred years of Enoch's prophecy (500 BC to 200 AD) describes the apostasy of the Jews* who reject Yahshua as their Messiah, and the destruction of Jerusalem and the Second Temple by the Romans in 70 AD.

In the seventh period of seven hundred years, the rise of the Holy Roman Empire, the Papacy, the Merovingian heresy, and the rise of Islam are described as a time of great apostasy (201 to 901 AD). The Merovingian heresy denied that Yahshua's death and resurrection as recorded in the Gospels ever occurred, and instead claimed that Yahshua lived on to father royal children. As will be discussed in Chapter Ten, this surviving Merovingian bloodline may supply the world with the royal prince who will become the Antichrist.

Since portions of Enoch's 7000-year prophecy point to all the blatantly heretical religions that sprang up at this time, especially the one surrounding the Holy Roman Empire, is it any wonder, then, that many people in authority during this period made a sweeping effort to wipe out every last trace of the Book of 1 Enoch? Unlike the Book of Revelation, which could be written off as a description of Pagan Rome and its ultimate fall, the Book of 1 Enoch's prophecy of the Apostate Church was not so easily dismissed. This is because *it clearly gave the time period when this apostasy would arise, and this was after the fall of the Pagan*

## Ch. 7: The Language of Prophecy and the Last Day

*Roman Empire. Consequently, this apostasy would arise during the rise of the Holy Roman Empire, the Papacy, and Islam!*

Much historical information was lost during Enoch's seventh 700-year Age because the Holy Roman Empire, and the followers of Mohammed systematically destroyed any books or writings that disagreed with their vision of God, and their suppositions about God's Will for mankind. For example, during the third century AD, the Great Library at Alexandria was destroyed, and its estimated 700,000 scrolls full of arcane wisdom were used as kindling for the fire! This is just one of many reasons why this time period in history is known as the Dark Ages. This was also the period when the Book of 1 Enoch disappeared from the libraries of the West.

This destruction of all known copies of 1 Enoch was so thorough that copies only survived in Ethiopia, which at the time was well outside of the dogmatic clutches of the Holy Roman Empire, as well as Islam's oppressive reach. Interestingly, many fragments of 1 Enoch were later found in the Dead Sea Scrolls, which the Catholic Church thankfully did not destroy since they had no knowledge of their existence. One also wonders if one of the secret aims of the first Crusade was to seize and destroy any copies of 1 Enoch that might be found, and other documents that were deemed heretical by the Catholic Church.

During the eighth period of seven hundred years, Enoch foresaw the Crusades against Islam, and the rise of the Protestant Reformation (902 to 1602 AD). The Reformation officially began when the Augustinian Monk named Martin Luther nailed his Ninety-Five Theses to the door of the Castle Church of Wittenberg, Germany in 1517, though a movement against Rome and the Papacy began long before that time. This movement sought to grant all people free access to the Scriptures, as well as to challenge the unbiblical dogma taught by the Roman Catholic Church. The unscriptural ideas of Rome ranged from the deification of Yahshua's mother Mary, to the sale of Indulgences, which were "licenses to sin" that granted individuals false immunity from punishment for sin. This papal grant of immunity extended not only for life, but was supposedly recognized in that false Hell called purgatory where unrepentant people supposedly went after death to pay for their sins before going to Heaven.

At the close of Enoch's eighth week, the Protestant Church of England (a.k.a. the Anglican Church) rose to greater prominence. As discussed in Book Three, "The Language of God in History," the Protestant churches of England, Scotland, and Ireland had their roots in the latter days of the Roman Empire - *before the birth of the Holy Roman*

*Empire.* These churches were not under Papal authority in their infancy, but then later submitted to it. When Queen Elizabeth 1 came to the throne in 1558 AD, she denied and rejected Papal authority over the Church of England and placed control over it back into the hands of the English monarchy.

This separation of the Church of England from Roman/Papal authority has continued to the present, at least on the surface. Nonetheless, the Puritan religious sect in England, though Protestant in nature, was opposed to the monarchy and the Roman Catholic structure of the Church of England, or the Anglican Church. As a result, they were heavily persecuted. This is when the Puritans began to flee from England and settle on the shores of North America. Many more persecuted Protestant Christians, as well as small numbers of devotees to more mystical and arcane religious ideologies such as the Rosicrucians Freemasons followed, eventually forming the thirteen original colonies of the United States of America. Meanwhile, the tension between the Puritans, the Royalists, and the Church of England led to the English Civil War in 1648. The Puritans were on the winning side and abolished the monarchy, setting up a Republican form of government called the Commonwealth. The Puritans also tried to destroy the Church of England, which they saw as apostate. The Commonwealth soon failed, however, and the monarchy and Church of England were re-established as the ruling authorities in England.

Many of the Puritans who had supported the failed Commonwealth then left England, joining their brethren across the ocean in America. Thereafter, Puritan democratic ideas concerning government guided American colonists in setting up the original alliance between the thirteen colonies. Later, this same democratic mindset led to the Declaration of Independence, the American Revolutionary War, the formation of an American Republic, and the writing of the Constitution of the United States. For those Christian and Masonic pioneers who established and upheld Democracy in America, this victory over England's tyrannical monarchy was a great blessing that promised previously unheard of religious freedom for over 300 years. For the first time in history, a nation was formed that guaranteed and protected each person's individual right to freedom of religion, press, assembly, and the right to bear arms.

Sadly, despite the legitimate reasons for the separation of Protestant Churches from Papal authority, there is a current movement among many Protestants to reconcile themselves to the Roman Catholic Church as fellow brothers in Christ. This is an unholy alliance, however,

## Ch. 7: The Language of Prophecy and the Last Day

for the Roman Catholic Church is no friend of Christ. On the contrary, it is a brazen upholder of the false goddess worship found in their deification of Mary, Yahshua's earthly mother. Touted by some Catholics as the Queen of Heaven, Mary has become a Pagan goddess due to the many idolatrous statues of her found on Catholic Church and School grounds. How sad that, instead of simply calling Mary blessed among women, the Roman Catholic Church has deified her, and made her a curse upon those who falsely worship her!

The false goddess heretically called Mary has become a representation of the false church that upholds her. This false goddess and the Roman Catholic Church she partially represents can be identified with the Whore of Babylon spoken of the Book of Revelation (Rev. 17:1-6). This Harlot can be directly identified with the world religious movement known as the Ecumenical Movement, which began with Vatican II in the Roman Catholic Church, but later was also adopted and pushed by the Church of England. The Ecumenical Movement heretically teaches that there is no exclusive Path to Salvation, thus denying the exclusive claims of Yahshua. In addition, they teach that all faiths have a measure of the truth, and should unite under the common ground they share - even while ignoring their differences - in the favor of world peace. We will further discuss the Ecumenical Movement's wicked role in End Time prophecy a bit later.

We are now living in the ninth period of seven hundred years (1603 to 2303 AD), during which Enoch foresaw "the righteous judgment." This refers to the divine judgment of the world that the Psalms suggest began in 1900 AD. As discussed in "The Language of God in Humanity," the Parable of the Sheep and Goats and the Parable of the Weeds suggest that the goats will be separated from the sheep, and the weeds or tares will be separated from the wheat throughout the Tribulation and the Millennial Rule of Christ.

At the Judgment carried out during the Tribulation period, those who are goats and chaff will ultimately be destroyed. Until then, however, this spiritual separation of the righteous sheep from the sinful goats has resulted in the formation of two religious groups that are diametrically opposed to each other. This is why Christianity is falling out of favor in the West, and being judged as an inferior religion to erroneous Paganistic New Age philosophies. Sadly, these false religions offer the idea of flexible moral values, but there is no such thing as flexible morality, and God's moral values were carved into stone on Mount Sinai to prove it!

Nonetheless, in the last one hundred years of history, there has been a dramatic End Time rise in apostasy, and interest in Occult teachings and Paganism. As a result, true followers of Christ are being ridiculed, and persecuted as troublemakers all over the world. That is why, in this ninth period, the final remnant of the righteous will be removed from the Earth in the Rapture at the time of the Great Tribulation. During this horrible Time of Trouble, there will be a final harvest of saints before the Millennial Rule of Christ. Yahshua will then return, destroy the armies of the Antichrist, and establish the Kingdom of God on Earth. For a thousand years, Christ will reign on Earth as the perfect "Melchizedek," or King of righteousness, and everyone will live in peace. Meanwhile, the Earth will be renewed and gradually restored to resemble its original Pre-Flood splendor. What glorious times these will be - when Yahshua reigns as King of kings!

At the end of **the tenth and final seven hundred year period (2304 to 3004 AD),** Enoch envisioned the Great White Throne Judgment mentioned at the end of the Book of Revelation. At that time, Enoch foresaw the final judgment and destruction of Satan, as well as the other Fallen Angels who will lead in one final rebellion against God. These Fallen Angels and their evil human followers will fail, however, and will finally be annihilated in the Lake of Fire. Enoch's tenth and final seven hundred year period of human history also foresees the establishment of the New Heaven and the New Earth. It therefore foretells the coming of eternity, when perfection and righteousness shall be firmly established forever. This corresponds to the prophesied events of the Last Day described from beginning to end in the Book of Revelation. This Last Day (or Great Day) officially began in the year 2000 AD, and it will likely end in 3000 AD, though only God knows exactly when.

## *The Cherubim and the Thirteen Great Days*

As shown in "The Language of God in the Universe," the Living Creatures, or Cherubim are mentioned in two books of the Bible: Ezekiel and Revelation. These Cherubim or Living Creatures are highly allegorical in nature. As was shown in Book One, these Cherubim are real angelic entities that are connected to Sacred Astronomy, the Zodiac, and the Universe as a whole. This can partly be seen in the faces of the Cherubim, which represent four signs of the Zodiac. In Ezekiel, Chapter One, for example, Ezekiel mentions the lion's face of the Cherub, which signifies the sign of Leo. This lion's face is on the right side, which can be seen as the east (Ezekiel 1:10). The man's face, which Ezekiel mentions

# Ch. 7: The Language of Prophecy and the Last Day

first in this section, would therefore correlate to Aquarius, placing it in the west, or to the left - just as Ezekiel identifies it. In Chapter Ten, on the other hand, Ezekiel mentions the bull or ox's face first - without any mention of its directional orientation (Ezekiel 10:14). However, because the ox's face is mentioned first, it suggests the Precessional Age of Taurus, when the sun rose in Taurus at dawn on the Spring Equinox. This is the Age when Adam and Eve were created.

The Age of Taurus the Bull marked the beginning of the Six Great Days or Ages allotted for mankind to complete their works. Perhaps that is why the Cherubim had the overall body shape of an ox or bull, but the hands of a man:

## Depiction of Ezekiel's Four-Winged Cherub

4 Winged Cherub - Face marks Age of Taurus, Wings mark Christ's First Advent, and Age of Pisces, Right Hand and Horn Signify Christ and His Millennial Kingdom

*"Their legs were straight; their feet were like those of a calf and gleamed like burnished bronze. Under their wings on their four sides they had the hands of a man. All four of them had faces and wings..."* - Ezekiel 1:7-8 (NIV)

With their calves' feet, and man's hands, Cherubim seem to be similar to the centaurs or fauns of myth in appearance. However, the

Babylonians, Assyrians, and Israelites depicted them as bulls, often with the faces of men. Sadly, Cherubim were also worshipped in these guises, and turned into idols in Ancient Babylonia, Assyria, Greece, and Rome. Nonetheless, Cherubim are only guardians over God's Creation, and are God's servants, just as human beings are. Therefore, they should never be worshipped in any form. Though Cherubim decorated the Ark of the Covenant and the Desert Tabernacle, they were not the objects of worship there. Rather, it was God's Shekinah Glory resting over the Ark that was the focus of true Israelite worship. Sadly, however, the Israelites did resort to worshipping golden calves when they lost faith in their invisible, intangible God of truth and light, Yahweh.

In Book One, we exhaustively explored how the Cherubim show the dawn of Creation in the Precessional Age of Leo, and the onset of human history in the Age of Taurus. Now, however, God has shown me that these incredible celestial symbols have even more to tell us. This is the fact that the Cherubim in Ezekiel's visions represent the tenth of the Thirteen Great Ages, and therefore mark Christ's First Advent. However, the Living Creatures of Revelation point to the Thirteenth Great Age, and the Second Coming of Christ! Let me explain how this can be deduced.

Imagine the body of an ox, or bull. They all have four legs, a long tail, and a head with two prominent horns. A bull therefore has seven appendages of note. If the body of the cherubic bull or ox represents the Universe, each one of its appendages can be seen as allegories for each one of the Seven Great Days of Creation. The bull or ox's tail would mark the First Great Day of Creation, the four legs would mark the Second through Fifth Day of Creation, and its head with its two horns (or alternatively its hands) would mark the Sixth and Seventh Great Days of Creation, However, Yah's thousand-year divine rest day was cut short when Adam and Eve fell. Therefore, one of the Cherubim's horns, or hands are not to be counted until Yahshua comes to set up His Millennial Kingdom - when the whole world will rest from mankind's rebellion against Yah for a thousand years.

Uncannily, this may be where the symbolism of the great One-Horned Ram in one of Enoch's prophecies came from. As we will discuss in Chapter Ten, Enoch's One-Horned Ram represents Yahshua, who is God's right hand man. This links Christ to the right hand and horn of the Cherubim, which are therefore not to be counted until Christ's Second Coming! Now, if we add Ezekiel's cherubic bull's tail, four legs, and one horn to its four wings, we get a total of ten appendages. While the seven appendages common to an ordinary bull mark the Seven Days of Creation Week, the wings of the Cherubim were meant to mark four of the Six

# Ch. 7: The Language of Prophecy and the Last Day    Page 257

Great Ages, or Days of mankind's works. Looking at the chart on the next page, we can see that this period will end in 2016 AD. This could be the actual year of Christ's return, though it could be speeded up to 2014 or 2015 or delayed to 2017 or 2018 AD. Only time will tell!

## Depiction of Revelation's Six-Winged Cherub

6 Winged Cherub - Tail & Face mark Age of Leo, Wings mark Six Great Days of Mankind, Dawn of Age of Aquarius, or Day of the Lord, and Christ's Millennial Kingdom, or Cherub's Right Horn

If, as shown in Book One, Yahshua was born in 3 BC, and Adam and Eve were created in 4003 BC, then Yahshua was born in the last year of the Fourth Great Day after the Fall, or the Tenth Great Day after Creation began. Ezekiel's cherubic visions therefore showed the coming of Christ in the Fourth Great Day, which saw the end of the Precessional Age of Aries, and the dawn of the Age of Pisces, or the Church Age.

| Portion of Cherubim | 6 Days of Creation Followed By 6 Ages of Mankind's Works | 13 Great Days Since Creation Began |
|---|---|---|
| Cherubim's lion tail | First Day of Creation (Approximate) 10002 to 9003 BC | First Great Day |
| Cherubim's 1st back leg | Second Day of Creation 9002 to 8003 BC | Second Great Day |
| Cherubim's 2nd back leg | Third Day of Creation 8002 to 7003 BC | Third Great Day |
| Cherubim's 1st Foreleg | Fourth Day of Creation 7002 to 6003 BC | Fourth Great Day |
| Cherubim's 2nd Foreleg | Fifth Day of Creation 6002 to 5003 BC | Fifth Great Day |
| Cherubim's left horn | Sixth Day of Creation (Cherubim's left hand) ends 4003 | Sixth Great Day |
| Cherubim's 1st wing | First Day of Mankind's Works 4002 BC to 3003 BC | Seventh Great Day |
| Cherubim's 2nd wing | Second Day of Mankind's Works 3002 BC to 2003 BC | Eighth Great Day |
| Cherubim's 3rd wing | Third Day of Mankind's Works 2002 BC to 1003 BC | Ninth Great Day |
| Cherubim's 4th wing | Fourth Day of Mankind's Works 1002 BC to 3 BC (Yahshua born!) | 10th Great Day |
| Cherubim's 5th wing | Fifth Day of Mankind's Works 2 BC to 998 AD | 11th Great Day |
| Cherubim's 6th wing | Sixth Day of Mankind's Works 997 AD to 1998 AD + 16 (Per Autumn Feast Days) = 2015 | 12th Great Day |
| Cherubim's right horn | Yahshua's Millennial Kingdom (or, Cherubim's right hand) 2016??? | 13th Great Day |

## Ch. 7: The Language of Prophecy and the Last Day

In the Book of Revelation, the Living Creatures differ from Ezekiel's in that they each have six wings, instead of four, and have bodies like the signs they are associated with (a lion's body for Leo, etc.). Their six wings can mark the end of the Sixth Great Day of the Lord after the Fall, as well as the Twelfth Great Day after Creation. As already shown, this Sixth Day has passed, and the beginning of the Seventh Day - or Age of Aquarius - is already upon us.

Since the Living Creatures in Revelation have six wings representing the passage of the Six Ages of Mankind, they mark the coming of the thirteenth, and final Great Day of the Lord since Creation began, and the Seventh Great Day of Yah's rest that was cut short when Adam and Eve fell. Uncannily, they also mark the Sign of Scorpio governing the Winter Solstice in this Age (see the final chapter)! We are therefore at the threshold of the Millennial Rule of Christ, and the right horns and hands of the Living Creatures in the Book of Revelation are to be counted at this time in history! The chart on page 258 shows the connection of the four and six-winged Cherubim with the Thirteen Great Days or Ages. Also see the handy chart in the Appendix taken from Book One, which recaps the significant events of the Thirteen Great Days.

Earlier in this book, it was shown how the Great Sphinx is a prophecy in stone representing Yahshua as the *"the First and the Last"* (Rev. 1:11, 17, 2:8, 22:13). The Cherubim and Living Creatures also show this fact, indicating that Yahshua began His work of creating the Universe in what would have been the Precessional Age of Leo, *if* the stars and planets had existed at that time. Since Yahshua is coming a second time as the triumphant King of kings and Lion of Judah, the Zodiac sign of Leo also signifies His return. Even though the Millennial Rule of Christ will occur during the Precessional Age of Aquarius, it is the time when the last and greatest Lion King of Judah will reign on Earth - as signified by Leo, the Lion.

Finally, since Cherubim are symbols of the Universe traveling through time, and they decorated the Ark, the Tabernacle walls, and the veil within the Tabernacle in pairs, they show that the offerings given to Yahweh in the Tabernacle were meant to atone for the sins of the whole world, for all time. In addition, these Cherubim were depicted in pairs that were facing one another over the Mercy Seat, which is Christ's symbolic throne. This can be seen in the following illustration of the Ark of the Covenant, where its lid was adorned with two Cherubim facing one another:

This arrangement of the Cherubim on lid of the Ark of the Covenant that represented Christ's divinity had deep allegorical significance. Since one Cherub mirrors the other, the Cherub on Christ's symbolic left signifies the current sin-filled Creation, while the mirrored Cherub on Christ's symbolic right suggests the complete reversal of history and total eradication of sin, death, and decay that is also implied by the Chanukiah Menorah.

## The Thirteenth Apostle: Paul

The New Testament is a testimony not only to the deity of Christ - but also to the power given to one apostle in particular. How surprising that this apostle is not Peter, upon whom the Roman Catholic Church was supposedly founded! After all, there are only two short letters attributed to Peter in the New Testament. On the contrary, outside of the Gospels, the majority of the New Testament contains sermons that were written by Saint Paul! It therefore appears that Paul, who was appointed as an apostle by Christ after His Resurrection, was the legitimate replacement for Judas Iscariot. This means that the remaining eleven apostles picked a false replacement for Judas *before* Shavuot or Pentecost, when the Holy Spirit did not guide their decisions. This also means they were not acting as Christ would have - but in response to their own flesh.

Remember that Judas Iscariot lost his right to be an apostle when he betrayed Yahshua. The apostles then chose between Barsabbas and

## Ch. 7: The Language of Prophecy and the Last Day

Matthias by lots to see who would replace Judas. Consequently, the lot fell to Matthias (Acts 1:26). However, *since this is the first and last time we ever hear Matthias' name mentioned in the New Testament, one has to wonder if Yahweh or Yahshua ever ordained the choice of Matthias.* Since Matthias was chosen before the release of the Holy Spirit in power at Pentecost, it is likely that Matthias was not Yah's first choice. Yahshua Himself, on the other hand, chose Paul, and this is why Paul is often seen as the primary apostle to the Gentiles.

Yahshua called Paul (then Saul) in a vision, and asked Paul to serve Him (Acts 9:3-6). Shortly thereafter, Paul reverted from vehemently persecuting and killing Christians, to openly embracing their theology and way of life. Thus, this man who had once behaved so cruelly and mercilessly toward those who were following Christ suddenly became their protector and friend. In affect, Paul made a complete 180-degree turn in his behavior. This was due to his encounter with Christ in a vision on the road to Damascus, and for a time afterward (Acts 9:1-18). Since Paul was well educated, and highly knowledgeable about the Old Testament, he became an incredible witness for Christ to both Jews and Gentiles. Hence, *Paul - the once devoutly Jewish persecutor of Christians - became the greatest Christian Evangelist of all time.*

It can be argued that Paul - one who had never served Christ during His ministry in Judea - accomplished more for the cause of Christianity than any apostle who witnessed Yahshua's public ministry, death, and resurrection. In fact, as already noted, the New Testament consists mainly of letters that were written, dictated, or inspired by the Apostle Paul. These letters reflect Paul's earnest desire to establish Christ's kingdom on Earth in the hearts of all men regardless of sex, race, or culture. *It was therefore the thirteenth apostle's tireless efforts as a missionary that did the most to establish Christianity as the dominant world religion.*

In Paul, we see the principle of the number thirteen at work. Through this thirteenth apostle, a more righteous follower of Christ supplanted the twelfth apostle chosen by the other apostles. In addition, through Paul's missionary efforts, the apostasy and wickedness that surrounds the supposedly literal but false bloodline of Christ will ultimately be thwarted (more will be said about this later!). In addition, Paul worked tirelessly to stop the spread of the more legalistic and works-oriented form of Judeo-Christianity that was supported by Peter and James in the Jerusalem Church.

## Heaven Mirrored On Earth: Christ & His Twelve Apostles

Contemplating this act of the apostles in choosing Matthias as the twelfth among them, don't you feel compelled to ask: **Why did there have to be twelve?** One reason was so that there would be an apostolic witness to the resurrection of Yahshua to represent each of the Twelve Tribes of Israel. However, it is also possible that the twelve apostles symbolically stood for the witness of the twelve signs of the Mazzaroth or Zodiac. The twelve apostles' roles as witnesses and followers of Christ mimicked the twelve houses of the Zodiac that the Sun, which represents Yahshua as the Creator, passes through.

If we picture the Sun surrounded by the planets in our Solar System, and see it as a spiritual allegory, it is possible that *this spiritual allegory in heaven may have a symbolic correlation to what we see spiritually on Earth*. As discussed in Book One, if we view Christ as the symbolic Sun at the center, and the twelve apostles as twelve planetary bodies revolving around Christ, our Solar System is an allegory for Christ, and the twelve apostles. Furthermore, this would mean that *the changes to, and current formation of our Solar System are symbolically, and prophetically tied to human history.*

In Book One, we explored the fact that there are eleven planetary bodies in our Solar System, counting our Moon. The idea that the asteroid belt was a twelfth planet at one time was also entertained. In fact, it may have been a planet that the Babylonians worshipped as the goddess Tiamat, which was represented as a serpent-like dragon. This ties it to the sign of Scorpio, the constellation Draco, and the Tribe of Dan. But what happened to this twelfth planet?

In Book Three, we explored the idea that *a thirteenth planet* may have entered our Solar System, and destroyed the twelfth planet. The Babylonians called this "renegade" planet Marduk after their top male deity. Traveling in a retrograde path, Marduk or one or more of its moons may have crashed into and destroyed Tiamat - the planet that once orbited the Sun where the asteroid belt now is. According to Zecharia Sitchin, extraterrestrials (i.e. Fallen Angels) that once visited Earth lived on a planet in our Solar System called Marduk.

According to Sitchin, this planet's moons moved into the planet Tiamat's orbit, cleaved Tiamat in two, then smashed Tiamat's remains to bits. After witnessing Marduk's apparent power over Tiamat, Sitchin believes the star worshipping Babylonians elevated the planet Marduk to

# Ch. 7: The Language of Prophecy and the Last Day

god status. Though Sitchin, who is an avowed atheist, totally ignores biblical facts and has made many erroneous assumptions, his ideas surrounding the hypothetical existence and destructive collision of Marduk and Tiamat seem to fit the principle of Heaven being revealed on Earth and vise versa. In fact, this planetary collision may be a true cosmic allegory for the history of Israel, as will be shown in a moment.

As stated in Book Three, Jupiter's gravitational field may have captured pieces of Marduk's moons and Tiamat's largest remains. In particular, the moon Ganymede may be the other half of Tiamat that was not crushed. This large moon of icy water with a rocky core shares Tiamat's supposed composition. Meanwhile, smaller pieces of debris from the Tiamat and Marduk encounter may have formed the asteroid belt. Later, huge pieces of the planet Tiamat may have crashed into the Earth, while other fragments traveled through the rest of the Solar System. Countless impact craters on moons and planets can be found everywhere in our Solar System, and many of these may have resulted from the stellar bombardment that occurred after Marduk's moons and Tiamat smashed into one another - possibly obliterating Tiamat and damaging Marduk.

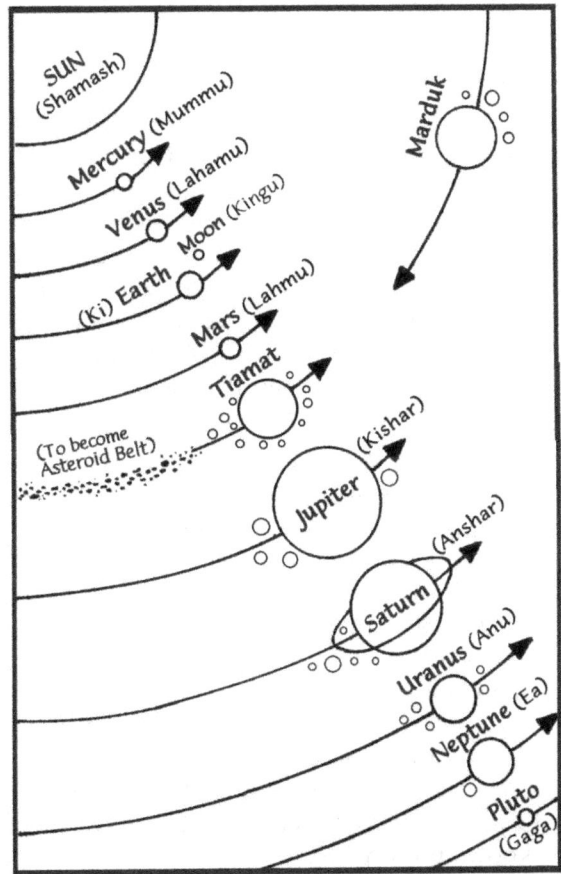

**The Solar System of the Antediluvians**
(With Corresponding Babylonian Names Added)

***The scattered pieces from both planets Marduk and Tiamat have many allegorical applications.*** For example, the fate of Tiamat and Marduk is represented in the existence on Earth of scattered groups of people who are righteous lovers of the Creator God, as well as people involved in Paganism. Both types are strewn all over the world, just as fragments of Tiamat and Marduk may have peppered the Solar System. Correspondingly, this is just what happened on the Earth after the Great Flood that may have been caused by the Marduk/Tiamat encounter.

Within a hundred years after the Great Flood in 2347 BC, Noah and Shem likely traveled all over the Earth - civilizing it while spreading the truth of Yahweh and the Gospel in the Stars. Around 2200 BC, however, it appears that Nimrod, Semiramis, their evil son Mardon (i.e.: Tammuz), and their Pagan followers began to spread their detestable Pagan beliefs and symbols wherever they conquered and ruled. In this way, over a period of several hundred years, both opposing groups likely scattered their beliefs everywhere, eventually dispersing them throughout the world. See Book Three and this book's final chapter for evidence that this occurred not only in the Old World, but in the New World as well.

This is in apparent mimicry of the heavens - in the actions and fate of Marduk, which in cleaving Tiamat apart, and scattering it about like pottery, was likely damaged. Currently, all that may remain of Tiamat and portions of Marduk are those fragments that became the asteroids in the asteroid belt, and the moons and other debris orbiting around Jupiter, Saturn, and Uranus. If this collision in outer space did occur, it serves as a powerful symbol of both the horrid effects of sin upon righteousness, and the devastating price that must be paid for rebellion against God. In this regard, the asteroid belt that came from the fragmenting of Marduk and destruction of Tiamat may represent the fragmented and destroyed Kingdoms of Babylon, Assyria, and Israel.

As if in apparent validation of the theoretical existence of the planet Marduk, a new planetoid has been discovered in the farthest reaches of our Solar System. Beyond the planet Pluto and the Kuiper belt - in a region of space known as the scattered disk - a large planetoid with at least one moon and a highly elliptical orbit has been found. Originally labeled 2003 UB 313 and known by the code name "Xena," this planetoid has now been named Eris, and is estimated to be somewhat larger than Pluto and close to our Moon in size, though it could be larger. Could this be the planet Marduk's remains, which Zecharia Sitchin claims was much larger than our Moon before its past encounter with Tiamat? If so, could some remains of Marduk be headed back toward the inner regions of our Solar System as Sitchin claims? This may indeed be the case, but only God knows the truth.

# Ch. 7: The Language of Prophecy and the Last Day

## *The Solar System and the Zodiac: Mirrors of Israel*

The story of the Israelites also mirrors the story of Marduk and Tiamat. The Kingdom of Israel fell into sin, and then was divided like Tiamat was cleaved in two by Marduk. Then, when the Kingdom of Israel fell to the Assyrians, the displaced Israelites spread out over the rest of the world like the fragments of Marduk and Tiamat may have peppered the Solar System. As the Israelites settled in other foreign lands, they brought material and spiritual blessings to whoever helped or welcomed them along the way.

It would be helpful to read Books One and Three in the Language of God Series for more background into what is being alluded to here about the planets in our Solar System. These books show that there may have been twelve celestial bodies in our Solar System that allegorically represent human individuals as well as tribes or groups of *people*. Furthermore, none of these represented a deity except the Sun, which signifies the one true God and His Preincarnate Son. Yet, it also signifies Jacob or Israel, who was a direct ancestor of the Son of God and - along with Abraham - was a spiritual father to Christ's Bride, the Church of faith.

The original planets in our Solar System, the Sun and the Moon may have been associated with the Tribes of Israel, just as the Twelve Zodiac Signs were. If so, in addition to representing the fallen Kingdom of Israel, Tiamat may also have stood for one Tribe, just as Marduk may have. Since Tiamat was destroyed, this planet likely represents an apostate Israelite Tribe that will be destroyed or *transformed*. This is the Tribe of Dan. The Babylonians symbolized Tiamat as a dragon, and since a dragon or serpent represents the Tribe of Dan, the dragon is a perfect symbol for the planet associated with the Danites. By association, **the planet Marduk may represent the half Tribe of Joseph called Ephraim, which may help to gradually reform and transform those who belong to the Tribe of Dan spiritually.**

Some scholars believe that the Tribe of Dan will continue in eternity because it is mentioned in the Book of Ezekiel as having a land allotment and place in the Millennial Temple to Yahweh, and it is fairly certain that the prophet Ezekiel foresaw the conditions in the Holy Land during the Millennial Rule of Christ. However, they are forgetting one important fact. There is a battle at the beginning and *end* of the Millennial Rule of Christ, and no one knows which spiritual side that those reckoned as the Tribe of Dan will fight on in that epic battle at the end of time.

*The Assyrians identified Marduk with their state god Asshur, whose symbol was an eagle or eagle-headed man.* Likewise, the symbol of an eagle stands for the United States. Since the United States was a rebel nation that separated from its mother country England just as Assyria separated from Babylon, their association with each other seems to fit. Indeed, the United States is still the maverick among the nations, the one nation that always seems to be marching to a different drummer than the rest of the world. The association of the United States with Assyria and Ephraim is explored further in Chapter Nine.

If the fractured half of Tiamat and pieces of Marduk or its moons formed the asteroid belt, these mixed remains may symbolize that half of Israel and the Church will be counted as repentant sinners like the Tribe of Ephraim, while the other half will be unrepentant apostates like the Tribe of Dan. As a result of their Paganism, Nimrod's Babylon and the Tribe of Dan kindled Yah's wrath. In fact, since the surviving remnants of Nimrod's kingdom and the Tribe of Dan may have done even more evil by mingling their blood with the Nephilim, Yah's wrath against them is very great and *they may never be forgiven.*

Modern-day Israelites who are apostates like the Danites of old will be reckoned as the Book of Revelation's *"Babylon the Great"*, and they will perish at the end of the Great Tribulation. Represented as the *"beast rising up out of the sea"* and the *"Red Dragon"* in the Book of Revelation, both the symbolic "Nimrod" and "Dan" of modern times will one day be utterly destroyed or overthrown. However, before modern day Babylon is destroyed, the Antichrist will attempt to destroy Israel (and possibly the USA) during the Great Tribulation. The other half of Israel that repents and is saved, however, may be spared from God's Wrath, and allowed to join in Christ's glorious return as resurrected saints.

Therefore, **we have in our Solar System a literal symbol for the prophetic Parable of the Weeds** (Matthew 13:24-30)! The related Parable of the Mustard Seed (Matthew 13:31-32) and the Parable of the Yeast (Matthew 13:33) also may prophetically apply to this cataclysmic event in our Solar System. This is because, like the good and bad seeds, two planets were fragmented into perhaps *thousands* of pieces, then were violently mixed together, and scattered across the Solar System. While the first of these three parables indicates that these good and bad seeds will be mixed together until the spiritual harvest at Armageddon, the other two parables indicate that **something very small and seemingly insignificant will eventually grow greater and more righteous than that**

# Ch. 7: The Language of Prophecy and the Last Day

*which it sprang from*. This could apply to both Israel and the United States in prophecy, as we will explore in Chapter Nine.

Viewed in light of these parables, there is tremendous spiritual and prophetic meaning locked into our Solar System, especially if Marduk's moons and all of Tiamat were smashed into pieces that hurtled through space to become asteroids, comets, and craters. As shown in Book Three, "The Language of God in History," there are many craters on the Earth and on other planets and moons in our Solar System that hint at heavy asteroid and comet bombardments in the past. Likewise, good and evil have touched every life on planet Earth, and no plant, animal, or human is immune from the effects of either. Good and evil co-exist together side by side, and it is extremely difficult for us to separate the two or remain unaffected by the evil that always seems to negate our good actions.

As stated in Book Three, some large pieces of Tiamat and Marduk's moons may have careened into the Earth, causing the Great Flood and, later, the Fall of Nimrod's Empire, and the destruction of the Tower of Babel. Also, some of the moons of Jupiter may be pieces of Tiamat and Marduk that were captured by Jupiter's immensely powerful gravity. Given Jupiter's association with our Messiah Yahshua, and the Tribe of Judah, Jupiter's many moons *may* have prophetic importance, representing certain remnants of Israel that will be especially faithful to Yahshua. Perhaps they even symbolically represent the 144,000 who will be chosen out of Israel to witness to the Tribulation Saints after the Antichrist takes control of the world.

In light of what is disclosed here, these analogies between human spiritual history and the history of our Solar System may not be mere coincidence. In fact, when the Solar System is viewed as it was intended, it seems to convey the fact that Yahweh left no ambiguity about the past, present or future of mankind and the Earth. If the hypothesis drawn here is correct, then **the actions that shaped human history on Earth exactly mimic the cataclysmic events that forever changed our Solar System.** Through these remarkable correlations, therefore, the allegorical and prophetic Language of God is shown to be miraculously evident everywhere in our Solar System.

## Are Heaven and Earth Entwined?

From the correlation in symbolism between Christ and the Twelve Apostles, the Sun and planets in our Solar System, and the Twelve Houses of the Zodiac and the Twelve Tribes, it becomes clear that

Yahweh went to great lengths to share this important truth with us: **What is witnessed in heaven must be witnessed on Earth before all things are brought to completion.** In fact, Yahshua Himself taught this truth in an example of how we should pray:

> *"your kingdom come, your will be done on earth as it is in heaven." - Matthew 6:10 (NIV)*

In the preceding Scripture, Yahshua points to the Father's Will as the determinant of what should be done on Earth *"as it is in heaven."* By analogy, **Yahshua was hinting that the heavens already display God the Father's Will.** Yahshua therefore seems to have asked us to pray that we would do on Earth *what we witness as revealed in heaven*. It is this desire that likely motivated the builders of the Great Pyramid, and Great Sphinx to mimic heaven on the Earth. With great care and brilliance, the antediluvians that believed in Yahweh made representations of Taurus' horns and Orion's Belt as they were situated at the dawn of time. Furthermore, through the symbolism of the Great Sphinx, they pointed to the beginning and end of the entire Star Gospel story as a record of the interlinked destinies of mankind and the Messiah. In doing so, they attempted to memorialize Yahweh's Will on Earth just as they had witnessed it in the heavens - written in the stars with the Language of God!

After Pentecost, the apostles, and all of Yahshua's true disciples were given a great gift. They were given all the gifts of the Holy Spirit, including the insight and ability to judge and bind evil on Earth, just *as it is already done in heaven*. Heaven and Earth are therefore entwined reflections of each other. This gift is what was behind the apostle's ability to cast out demons. Just as the Fallen Angels are to be cast out of heaven by the archangel Michael, demons can be cast into the abyss on the Earth (Mat. 12:28; Mark 3:14-15, 16:17; Rev. 12:7-9). I have personally cast demons into the abyss using this gift in fervent prayer, and I believe every Christian has the ability to do this in Yahshua's Name if they believe in the power of God, and act in faith (See Luke 8:31). This truth is revealed in the following Scriptures:

> *"I will give you the keys of the kingdom of heaven; whatever you bind on earth will be bound in heaven, and whatever you loose on earth will be loosed in heaven." - Matthew 16:19 (NIV)*

> *"I tell you the truth, whatever you bind on earth will be bound in heaven, and whatever you loose on earth will be loosed in heaven." - Matthew 18:18 (NIV)*

## Ch. 7: The Language of Prophecy and the Last Day

> *"If you forgive anyone his sins, they are forgiven; if you do not forgive them, they are not forgiven." - John 20:23 (NIV)*

In the above passages, Yahshua makes it clear that the *keys of the Kingdom of Heaven* are in understanding that we must do on Earth what we witness in Heaven. Furthermore, Yahshua was telling us that *the heavens likewise respond to what we do on Earth.* In other words, **the Solar System and Universe around us change to mimic and act as a witness to what we do spiritually on Earth, and what Yahweh already knows we will do!** This may seem unbelievable, fanciful, and far-fetched. However, there is no other way to interpret the above Scriptures logically without being guilty of limiting the power of our Creator God. It is a grievous sin to deny the real power that Yah gives us through His Holy Spirit when we believe that Yahshua is our Redeemer (Matthew 12:30-32).

It is clear from the preceding passages quoted here that all those who believe in Yahshua are being told that they have *incredible power through the Holy Spirit* at their disposal. If the choices believers make on Earth will be reflected in Heaven, then what is revealed in Heaven will be made manifest on the Earth through human actions. *This truth was disclosed repeatedly in the Bible* – in symbols like the forty-eight Levite cities, the four faces of the Cherubim, the Twelve Tribes of Israel, and Yahshua's twelve apostles. Antediluvian architecture like the Great Pyramid complex at Giza and the pyramids at Dahshur also revealed this truth *by depicting a portion of Yah's heavenly Gospel on Earth!* There is no doubt from their clear attempt to depict heaven on Earth that they were proclaiming the connection between the written Word of God in the heavens, and human actions. Could it be that they also wanted to preserve the knowledge that the heavens are transformed through time to mirror what happens on Earth? This may be exactly why they went to such great lengths to depict Heaven on Earth!

There is no doubt that the monuments built by the righteous antediluvian descendents of Seth in Egypt display this truth clearly through symbolism. As already stated throughout this book, there is also ample evidence in the Old Testament, the Language of God in the Universe, and the Gospel in the Stars that the goodness, purity and Will of Yahweh and His Son are displayed in the starry heavens. In addition, the Star Gospel displays the results of human actions in relation to God's Will (See Psalm 19:1-5; Romans 1:20).

## Thirteen: A Sign That Evil Will Be Replaced With Good

Based on the truth that whatever is disclosed on Earth through humanity will be, or already has been revealed in heaven, the choice of Matthias by the eleven apostles before Pentecost was going to have repercussions. When Paul was chosen by Christ to be the Apostle to the Gentiles, this meant there were thirteen apostles involved on the world scene. Before Christ died, He was the leader of the apostles, and could therefore be seen as the thirteenth member of an exclusive group. Since the thirteenth apostle chosen by the other apostles before Pentecost wasn't Christ, who is wholly good, could this be a God-given clue that one more of the original twelve apostles had his mind fixed on evil works instead of good? Furthermore, could it be a sign that Christians should be on the lookout for the false teachings of this evil apostle? In Chapter Ten, in the section entitled "Why Was The Apostle Thomas Called A Twin?" we will focus on one of the original twelve apostles that could well have been the second evil man in the bunch besides Judas Iscariot.

The number thirteen has long been touted as the number representing apostasy due to the Tribe of Dan's falling away into Paganism, and rebellion against Yahweh. As shown a bit later in this chapter, it appears that the Tribe of Dan is still to be viewed as a source of unrighteousness. Furthermore, some Bible scholars believe the Antichrist will hail from descendents of the Tribe of Dan. Since Dan is viewed as evil, the worthier half Tribe of Ephraim may replace the Tribe of Dan in eternity. Ephraim and Manasseh were the two sons of the patriarch Joseph that became two Half-Tribes. Manasseh, as the older brother, was originally to be reckoned as Joseph, while the younger brother Ephraim was the thirteenth Tribe destined to replace the Tribe of Dan. Their roles in history, however, were divinely switched when Jacob placed his right hand on the younger son Ephraim's head to bless him - an honor usually reserved only for the first-born (Gen. 48:13-14).

Throughout biblical history, Yah has shown that He is no respecter of human traditions. Though it was the practice among the Semites to give the major inheritance and patriarchy to their eldest sons, Yah had other ideas. Without question, Yah chose the person that He knew would make a better leader – and in many cases, ***it was the younger or lesser son that Yah chose.*** For example, it is well known that Noah had three sons named Ham, Shem, and Japheth. Less well known, however, is the fact that Japheth was the eldest son. Yet when Shem and his brothers divided the Earth between themselves after the Great Flood, Shem was allotted the best lands in the Middle of the Earth. Furthermore,

# Ch. 7: The Language of Prophecy and the Last Day

it was Shem who was chosen by Yah to be the patriarch whose bloodline would lead to the birth of the promised Messiah.

This trend continued for a long time. For example, though Abraham already had a son born to him through Sarah's handmaiden Hagar, Yah rejected Ishmael and chose Abraham's younger son Isaac as the inheritor and primary beneficiary of the Covenant promises made between Sarah, Abraham, and Yahweh. Not much later, Isaac's eldest son Esau lost his birthright to his younger brother Jacob. Jacob then became the primary recipient of the blessings associated with Yah's Blood Covenant with Abraham. Years later, Jacob's eldest son Reuben lost his birthright to his younger half brother Joseph in retaliation for Reuben's treacherous involvement in selling Joseph into slavery. Indeed, even before then, Joseph's position as the Vizier of Egypt far eclipsed Reuben's status as a wandering shepherd, thus showing that Yah honored Jacob's wisdom in loving Joseph over all his brothers.

In a similar fashion, the thirteenth apostle Paul replaced the apostle Matthias - the apostle chosen by the will of the apostles rather than the Will of God. This is because the apostles did not yet understand that choosing a twelfth apostle was not their place, for *only* Yahshua Himself could make that choice and truly know whom to pick. The fact that Paul was Yahshua's obvious choice as a replacement for Judas Iscariot must not have been lost to the eleven original apostles. Given their tremendous baptism with the Holy Spirit at Pentecost, the apostles would have understood that they had erred when they chose Matthias instead of letting the risen Yahshua choose His own representative. Saint Paul, as Yahshua's chosen representative, became the thirteenth apostle – the one meant to replace the evil one among the original twelve. In choosing a terrible persecutor of Christians such as Paul (when he was still known as Saul), Yahshua took a man who was hell-bent on evil, and transformed him into an incredible witness for Christ! **Thirteen is therefore the number signifying that evil is to be replaced with good.**

In Book Three, "The Language of God in History," this mysterious correlation of the number thirteen with apostasy was shown through the thirteenth patriarch in the bloodline of Adam through Seth. This was Cainan, the son of the godly twelfth patriarch Arphaxad. The thirteenth patriarch Cainan is identified in the Book of Jubilees as the man who rediscovered the forbidden false teachings of the Watchers that were preserved on stone tablets before the Great Flood (Jubilees 8:1-5). Instead of destroying these false teachings, Cainan preserved them, and kept his knowledge of them a secret from his more righteous family members. Later, however, Cainan inevitably led some of his own children into sin by sharing what he knew of this forbidden knowledge. Cainan therefore greatly contributed to the re-emergence of Paganism, Sorcery, Astrology, and Black Magic after the Flood.

Yet, despite Cainan's unrighteousness, he was still reckoned as one of the direct ancestors of Christ (Luke 3:36)! In this way, despite Cainan's wickedness, incredible good came out of someone who was incredibly evil. In an odd twist, even though he was ungodly, the thirteenth patriarch Cainan took part in bringing about the potential for his salvation, as well as the salvation of all Creation! As Cainan's descendent, Yahshua righted the wrongs of his forefathers, and provided a golden opportunity for all human beings who had sinned like Cainan to find salvation.

This suggests the truth that the Thirteenth Millennium – the Millennial Rule of Yahshua – will also replace evil with good. Many prophecies in the Bible refer to this Millennial Rule as a time of great renewal, restoration, and joy upon the Earth (See Isaiah 11:1-13, 49:7-13, 65:17-25; Ezekiel 34:25-31; Zechariah 14:8-11; Hosea 2:18-23). However, the events both at the beginning and end of Christ's Millennial Rule suggest that **the cup of God's Wrath will not be fully poured out until the end of the thirteenth Great Day** since Creation began. Throughout this chapter, remember that **the Thirteenth Great Day and the Seventh Great Day are referring to the same time period. This is the Millennial Kingdom** and the events leading up to it that will usher it in.

## Can The Ten Lost Tribes of Israel Be Found?

In this section, we will return to the controversial and hotly disputed subject of British Israelism, beginning with a very telling quote from Genesis:

> *"And Jacob called his sons and said, '**Gather together, that I may tell you what shall befall you in the last days**: Gather together and hear, you sons of Jacob, and listen to Israel your father.'" - Genesis 49:1-2*

Many people view British Israelism as a heresy because it is used as a way of justifying Anti-Semitism, and it has been incorrectly used to promote the faulty idea that Caucasians are superior to the other so-called races in the world today. Even though we are all descendents of Noah, and hence are the same "race," Book Three's examination of this touchy subject makes it clear that there has been both a temporal *and spiritual* fulfillment of God's promises to Judah and Israel/Ephraim. Scriptures like

## Ch. 7: The Language of Prophecy and the Last Day

the one above clearly suggest that the Twelve Tribes would all be physically represented in the last days, and this book has already made it abundantly clear that we are now living in the Last Day.

A thorough explanation of my findings concerning the prophecies surrounding Judah, Israel, and Ephraim are presented in the last chapter of Book Three. Here is a brief summary of what was revealed there. First of all, the Book of Revelation suggests that the Tribe of Manasseh, which is one of the two half-tribes of Joseph, will replace the Tribe of Dan *during the Tribulation period*. Therefore, since the Tribe of Ephraim/Joseph appears to be a permanent replacement for the Tribe of Dan in eternity (as will be shown in Chapter Nine), then the prophetic substitution of Manasseh for Dan may be tied to the fact that Great Britain is being reckoned as Manasseh, and the Antichrist may hail from Great Britain's Royalty. These suppositions will be further entertained in Chapter Ten. For now, however, we need to focus on the fact that, for this to be true, then the Tribes of Ephraim, Manasseh, and Dan should be evident somewhere on the present world scene. In fact, **since the Twelve Tribes of Israel are represented in the Book of Revelation, all twelve of these Tribes should be somewhere on the Earth today**.

From performing in-depth studies of Biblical prophecies concerning Judah and Israel, a growing number of Messianic Jews and Christians believe that there are still two Houses of Israel, just as there was when Ancient Israel split into two kingdoms. Some believe that all of Europe, the United Kingdom (Great Britain), Britain's Commonwealth Nations, the United States, and modern Israel represent the Twelve Tribes of Israel in prophecy. They believe they are partly descended from the Israelites that were scattered after being taken from the fallen Kingdom of Israel, and forced to resettle in Assyria. Though this idea has some truth to it, it is not altogether correct because it leaves out the concept of Grace, whereby Gentiles are continually being grafted into Israel.

A more balanced view of the identity of the Twelve Tribes today is especially prevalent among Messianic Jews. Some of them believe that *all* practicing Jews are to be reckoned as the Kingdom of Judah. In addition, they believe that *all* Gentile Christians allegorically and - at times - literally represent the Ten Lost Tribes of Israel. Furthermore, they consider the Ten Lost Tribes to collectively form the Tribe of Ephraim in Bible Prophecy. In this view, therefore, Two Houses or Kingdoms of Israel called Judah and Ephraim exist together, but are separated by their differing religious ideologies. Nonetheless, these Two Houses will reconcile their differences, and be reunited as one when Yahshua returns to rule over mankind.

I am deeply sympathetic to this view, and believe it lends some strength to a few of the ideas set forth in several older and far more controversial studies that arose from Scriptural searches for the whereabouts and identities of the Ten Lost Tribes of Israel. Some of these older studies are labeled British Israelism because of their emphasis on Great Britain and the nations that came from her former world empire. British Israelism insists that the prophetic Scriptures and Covenant promises of Yahweh relating to Judah and Israel are applicable in modern times. Though my research appears to indicate that this may be true to some extent, some people erroneously use this truth to "prove" that the Jews are no longer God's chosen people, and that the modern nation of Israel is not the Israel of prophecy. Furthermore, some of them foster the idea that white Anglo-Saxons are superior to all other people groups. This radical racist interpretation of Scripture, which is promulgated by some British Israelites, has caused many Christians to rightly denounce any form of British Israelism.

Denying Judah's place as part of Israel, British Israelites assume that the Western Christian nations - especially those arising from Great Britain - are to be reckoned as the true Israel of prophecy. This is known as Replacement Theology, and it attempts to prove that Britain and the nations that arose from her are physically descended from the Ten Lost Tribes of Israel. Furthermore, British Israelites believe that only Anglo-Saxon Christians are the inheritors of the New Covenant promises Yahshua made to mankind at the Last Supper. However, they are overlooking the fact that when Yahshua made His New Covenant promises to mankind at Passover, He did so in a room full of Jews, *not* Anglo-Saxons! Furthermore, blood descendents of all Twelve Tribes of Israel are still apparently represented in the current Jewish population in Israel, as well as among the Jews scattered throughout the world.

Nonetheless, much circumstantial evidence exists that supports the idea that the people of Europe, the United Kingdom, Canada and the United States are not only descended from Noah's son Japheth, but are also related to the Ten Lost Tribes of Israel *by blood*. Some of this evidence is found in Scripture. For example, as already mentioned, Yahshua's brother, the Apostle James opened his only letter in the New Testament with the phrase:

*"James, a bondservant of God and of the Lord Jesus Christ (Adonai Yahshua the Anointed One),* **to the twelve tribes which are scattered abroad***: Greetings."* - James 1:1

## Ch. 7: The Language of Prophecy and the Last Day      Page 275

What did James mean by this phrase? Was he referring only to the Jews of his time that were scattered abroad? Or was James addressing his letter to a much larger audience that included the Gentile population in *all of Europe*? An answer to these questions can be found in the writings of the First Century Jewish historian Josephus. Josephus wrote of an epistle written by Xerxes, the son of King Darius of Persia, which was sent to the Israelite prophet Ezra (i.e.: Ezdras) to be shared with the Israelites:

> *"So he read the epistle at Babylon to those Jews that went there, but he kept the epistle itself, and sent a copy of it to all those of his own nation that were in Medea. And when these Jews had understood what piety the king had toward God, and what kindness he had for Esdras, they were all greatly pleased; nay,* ***many of them took their effects with them, and came to Babylon,*** *as very desirous of going down to Jerusalem; but then* ***the entire body of the people of Israel remained in that country,*** *wherefore* ***there are but two tribes in Asia and Europe*** *subject to the Romans,* ***while the Ten Tribes are beyond the Euphrates till now, and are an immense multitude****, and not to be estimated by numbers." -* Josephus, Antiquities of the Jews, 1.5.2

In this passage, Josephus tells us that there were only two Tribes of Israel represented in the populations of Asia and Europe circa 95 AD, the estimated date for when Josephus wrote this section of his history of the Jews. By Europe, Josephus most likely meant the northern Mediterranean, Spain, and possibly Great Britain, which were under the control of the Roman Empire at one time. Those who were mentioned in Asia were the Israelites who left Babylon to return to Israel, which was considered a part of Asia by the Romans. Josephus also tells us that there was *"an immense multitude"* of Israelites *"beyond the Euphrates"*. This can only mean that they were already outside of Babylon/Parthia, and had spread out into the southeastern portion of Europe *north* of the Euphrates River. **The Ten "Lost" Tribes therefore inhabited the regions where the modern nations of Turkey, Armenia, and Azerbaijan are located today.**

From these lands north of Babylon, those many multitudes of Israelites could have crossed over the Caucasus Mountains between the Black and Caspian Seas and gone into Europe and Russia. In fact, several people groups who were located in this area at different times in history may have actually been displaced Israelite Tribes. For example, some scholars think the Scythians, a.k.a. "Sacae," who were a civilized nomadic people of the Russian steppes, were actually displaced Israelites.

Unfortunately, they base this revolutionary assertion on semantics, asserting that the word "Sacae" was derived from the Hebrew name "Isaac." Though this is possible, it isn't proof that the Scythians were Israelites.

Nonetheless, what is known of the culture of the Scythians greatly resembled Israelite culture, as did the culture of the Parthians, whose empire controlled a large section of Mesopotamia and Asia Minor during the time of Christ. In his book: "The Ten Lost Tribes of Israel - Found!", Steven Collins shows that the Parthians had a culture that shared much in common with Ancient Israel, especially in their just system of laws, and in their tolerance and kindness to foreigners.

Since the Israelites who traveled out of Parthia and went beyond the Euphrates were no longer in their homeland, they probably were considered foreigners wherever they went. They therefore likely remained a relatively migratory and war-prone people until they reached uninhabited lands farther to the north and northwest - in Europe and former Soviet Russia.

Among the Ten Lost Tribes of Israel that became the Scythians, members of the Tribe of Dan were probably included in their ranks. One clue to their presence is found in the fact that - in the 8th Century BC - the Scythians migrated to and settled in the lands just north of the Black Sea - in the most southeastern section of Europe. While there, the Scythians are thought to have named all the rivers flowing into the Black Sea, such as the Danube and Don. This could mark some of them as descendents of the Tribe of Dan. Interestingly, in their own history of their nation, the Scots claim descent from the Scythians - making it highly possible that the Scots represent one or more tribes of Israel - including the Tribe of Dan. There are also ties to several of the Tribes of Israel in the symbols used by Irish, Scottish, and British royalty - especially and ominously to the infamous Tribe of Dan. In the Bible, though there are early Danite heroes like Samson, the Danites were later known for their blatant idolatry and unrepentant rejection of the Almighty God of Israel.

The most obvious evidence of the mass migration of Israelites from Assyria and Babylon - and later from Parthia - to lands further north is attested to by the fact that many millions of Jews (who constitute all the Tribes, but especially Judah and Levi) once lived throughout Europe and Russia before the Holocaust of World War II. The return of the Jews to modern Israel from throughout Russia and Europe over the past sixty years attests to how far they actually wandered *away* from Israel. In fact, though their numbers are small, some Jews still live in every English, European, and former Russian country!

Despite a strict Jewish/Israelite tradition that forbade intermarriage with Gentile outsiders, many Jews and Israelites did marry into the Gentile populations of the countries they settled in. As they married outside of their faith and culture, the many tribal descendents of Jacob lost their identity, and were assimilated into the foreign cultures around them. These people who once had an Israelite ancestry became the Lost Israelites, also known as the Ten Lost Tribes of Israel. Therefore, *all Twelve Tribes of Israel* are likely represented in the genetic make-up of the people of modern Europe, Russia, Great Britain, and those English-speaking countries that came from Great Britain's former Empire, like the United States, Canada, and Australia.

A bit further in the same section of Josephus' histories, we are told that a band of Levites, priests, sacred singers, and servants involved in temple rites met with Ezra in order to return to Israel with him. The Old Testament Book of Ezra clearly states that only members of the Tribes of Judah and Benjamin (and a few Levites, as mentioned in Josephus) returned to Israel immediately after the Babylonian Captivity ended:

> "...and that whoever would not come within three days, according to the instructions of the leaders and elders, all his property would be confiscated, and he himself would be separated from the assembly of those from the captivity. **So all the men of Judah and Benjamin gathered at Jerusalem within three days**. It was the ninth month, on the twentieth of the month; and all the people sat in the open square of the house of God, trembling because of this matter and because of heavy rain."

> "Then Ezra the priest stood up and said to them, "You have transgressed and have taken pagan wives, adding to the guilt of Israel. Now therefore, make confession to the LORD God (Yahweh Elohim) of your fathers, and do His will; **separate yourselves from the peoples of the land, and from the pagan wives**." - Ezra 10:8-11

In the preceding passages, Ezra ordered the men of Judah and Benjamin who wished to remain faithful to Yahweh *to separate themselves from their Pagan wives*. This makes it clear that many of the Israelites had already mixed their own genes with the genetic make-up of the Gentile populations around them. In addition, many of the Israelites from the Ten Tribes that remained in Babylon later dispersed into Europe just as the Israelites from the Northern Kingdom of Israel had done before them.

After the Kingdom of Israel was divided into the Kingdom of Judah to the south and the Kingdom of Israel to the north, the Assyrians eventually conquered the northern Israelite population in 721 BC, and the Israelites living there were either slaughtered or carried away into slavery. Uncannily, this was around the same time that the Scythians began their migration into southeastern Europe, and some believe the Scythians were simply misplaced Israelites searching for a new homeland. If true, there was a migration of Israelites northward into Assyria, and beyond into Europe over a hundred years before the Kingdom of Judah fell to the Babylonians in 556 BC (as shown in my Biblical Chronology). After the Babylonian Captivity, however, **only Judah and Benjamin, and a token spattering of Levites returned to Palestine**.

Much has been learned about the two migrations of the Israelites who were scattered abroad during the two conquests of the Promised Land – first by Assyria and then by Babylon. For example, some scholars have used their knowledge of etymology to linguistically trace the path that the Ten Tribes took when they were scattered among the nations. Though it is beyond the current scope of this book to examine all of the evidence they found tracing the migrations of Israel, we will explore some of the linguistic connections that scholars have made in the next section. There we will discuss the "serpent trail" left by the Tribe of Dan in Europe.

Unfortunately, human nature being what it is, certain people have made attempts to use the possible Israelite heritage of Europe to support various types of Anti-Semitic rhetoric. For example, one misconception sometimes found among British-Israelites is that God has forsaken the Jews, and that all the once Christian nations of the West are now the true Israel of prophecy. This idea is faulty because it denies that the Jews and other Gentile nations have a rightful place in God's unconditional Covenant promises. Nonetheless, Yahweh will never reject or forsake *any* of His chosen people descended from Israel unless they ultimately reject, or break the New Covenant with Him signed with Yahshua's blood. So, though America, Britain, Britain's Commonwealth countries, and Europe are being reckoned as the Israel of prophecy, they are to be considered as *sharing* in the blessings given to Israel rather than inheriting them.

Since Yahweh is so long-suffering with the Jews, He will not condemn any among them unless they refuse to *love* and acknowledge Yahshua as the Messiah when He comes again to set up His kingdom on Earth. The erroneous doctrine that God has abandoned the Jews is often found in books written by British Israelites. Despite their doctrinally unsound Anti-Semitism, however, these scholars provide some extremely important background in interpreting End Time prophecies pertaining to the nations that descended from Israel. They do so by attempting to

## Ch. 7: The Language of Prophecy and the Last Day

identify the modern nations representing the Tribe of Joseph and Judah today. So, though the writers of older studies on the migrations of the Israelites drew some erroneous conclusions due to prejudice, they were on the right track.

Though the Bible contains prophetic messages to the Twelve Tribes of Israel in the Last Days, and this suggests that all Twelve Tribes are somewhere on the Earth today, there isn't much concrete physical proof that the theoretical connections between various nations, and the Twelve Tribes are true. However, the principles of the Language of God, and the guidance of the Holy Spirit can show us how to begin to look beyond the surface of things to find truth. Using this line of reasoning, these somewhat doctrinally unsound studies done on British Israelism still offer some compelling Scriptural, folkloric, and linguistic evidence that the Israel of prophecy is at least partially represented by the people of Europe, the United Kingdom, and its Commonwealth nations - and by extension - the United States.

Through facts found in key Scriptures, British and European history, folklore, and ancient genealogical records, British Israelites have shown that Europe may be populated with various descendents of the Ten Lost Tribes. Commensurate with this theory, they believe that the United States, the United Kingdom, and its Commonwealth Nations represent the two Tribes of Joseph. Furthermore, they assume that the Half-Tribe of Manasseh represents the United States, and the English Commonwealth represents the Half-Tribe of Ephraim.

Though this theory is based on some truth, however, it appears that the nations representing Ephraim and Manasseh may have been misidentified in most previous studies of British Israelism. In fact, the prophecies surrounding the *eldest son* called Manasseh appear to more correctly pertain to the *elder nation* called Great Britain. Likewise, the prophecies about the *younger son*, Ephraim, appear to pertain to the *younger nation* called the United States:

"*Then Israel stretched out his right hand and laid it on Ephraim's head, who was the younger*, and his left hand on Manasseh's head, guiding his hands knowingly, for Manasseh was the firstborn...."

"And Joseph said to his father, 'Not so, my father, for this one is the firstborn; put your right hand on his head.' But his father refused and said, 'I know, my son, I know. He... shall be great; **but truly his younger brother shall be greater than he, and his descendants shall become a multitude of nations.**' So he blessed them..., saying, 'By you Israel will bless, saying, "May God make you as Ephraim and as Manasseh!"' And thus **he set Ephraim before Manasseh**." - Genesis 48:14, 18-20

Many have assumed that Ephraim's "multitude of nations" mentioned in the above prophecy refers to the British Commonwealth of Nations. However, **this prophecy does not pertain to the older, but the younger brother, which figuratively could be none other than the United States**. Also, the Hebrew used in verse 18 above suggests this alternative reading: "his younger brother will become greater than he, and his descendants **shall be from a multitude of nations**." In this regard, the United States fits the prophecy perfectly, for its citizens represent people from a multitude of nations, as well as an intermingling of these nations by blood, and by culture. As Walt Whitman wrote in the preface to "Leaves of Grass,"

> *"The United States themselves are essentially the greatest poem. ....Here is not merely a nation, but a teaming **nation of nations**."*

From very early on in its history, the United States has been a nation built up of many smaller nations called states that are united by a common constitution and creed. In addition, despite this underlying unity between the different state governments, America is a melting pot of different nationalities. By 1646, settlers from England, Ireland, Scotland, Holland, Denmark, Norway, Sweden, Poland, Germany, France, Bohemia, Portugal, and many other lands were found along the Hudson River in New York *alone*. In modern times, this cultural diversity is even more obvious. In fact, nearly every nation on Earth is represented in the current population of the United States, and more immigrants from foreign nations are flocking to its shores every day in search of a better life.

Some may reject this view of the United States as the fulfillment of Israel's prophecy about Ephraim because Great Britain was once a great colonizing nation. They point out that Great Britain once controlled a vast empire covering many diverse points around the globe. The United States, on the other hand, is considered only one great nation. However, they fail to take into account that the empire that the United Kingdom ruled over has been disbanded into many separate nations like Australia, New Zealand, Zimbabwe, and South Africa. Furthermore, Great Britain's Commonwealth Nations are, for all intents and purposes, totally independent of their mother nation. In addition, the populations of all these Commonwealth nations do not equal the population of the United States! If Great Britain was Ephraim, however, it should be greater in all respects than the USA. This is indicated in Moses' deathbed prophecy concerning Ephraim and Manasseh:

## Ch. 7: The Language of Prophecy and the Last Day

*"In majesty he (i.e. Joseph) is like a firstborn bull; his horns are the horns of a wild ox. With them he will gore the nations, even those at the ends of the earth.* **Such are the ten thousands of Ephraim; such are the thousands of Manasseh.***"* - *Deuteronomy 33:17 (NIV)*

Here, some scholars like J. H. Allen, who lived at the turn of the Twentieth Century, misidentified Ephraim as Great Britain. He did so because Great Britain was a world empire at that time, and therefore had many more people under her control than the United States did. This situation, however, has now drastically changed, and Great Britain now stands predominantly separate from the nations she gave birth to. According to America's 2006 census, the United States had about 300 million people. This means that *the United States is currently the third most populated country in the world, outside of India and China, and it has about 75 million more citizens than Great Britain and all its Commonwealth Nations combined!* The population of the United States therefore far exceeds the collective populations of all the nations that Great Britain founded before her empire was dismantled.

It also cannot be denied that the United States isn't really one nation, but a group or multitude of fifty little nations that function as one through their common Constitution, and the Federal Government they have appointed to see that the U.S. Constitution is upheld. The United States is also arguably the most powerful, and wealthy "nation of nations" on Earth, and the majority of its citizens enjoy the best standard of living anywhere. Hence, just as Jacob prophesied before he died, America (Ephraim) has surpassed Britain (Manasseh) in wealth and power.

Nonetheless, Jacob's prophecy of the ox (or two unicorns) whose horns "gore" the nations pertains to both the United Kingdom, and the United States. This is because both of these nations exert tremendous control over the fashions, cultures, and lifestyle choices of people all over the world. This is also why English has become the new international language. In addition, both nations have a large army and navy with which to "gore" the nations, and both have played big roles in both major World Wars, and many smaller skirmishes throughout history. Nonetheless, even in this case, the United States has more cultural influence and military might than her mother country in today's world scene. The only way that Great Britain currently may exceed the United States is in economic strength and behind-the-scenes, sinister political and spiritual influence, as will be shown in Chapter Ten.

In Israel's deathbed prophecy regarding Ephraim and Manasseh, he tells his hearers that Manasseh will be "great." In this case, Great Britain (now known as the United Kingdom) was indeed a great nation, and even had the word "great" as part of the official country name. Israel also said that **Ephraim would eventually become greater than his older brother Manasseh.** Though Great Britain is undoubtedly one of the greatest nations on Earth, within the last one hundred years the United Stated has definitely won more esteem, attention and, at times, animosity from almost every modern nation on Earth - including the countries of Great Britain that now form the United Kingdom.

Uncannily, the major emblem of the United States gives credence to the supposition that it is to be counted as part of Ephraim, and will become a spiritual replacement for the Tribe of Dan. The national emblem of the United States is the American Bald Eagle. This is significant because, as explained in Book One and Three, the symbol of an eagle will one day replace Scorpio, the scorpion representing Dan in the heavens. Since America is still one of the most powerful nations on Earth, the connection of the United States to the triumphant, serpent-killing eagle suggests that it will fulfill a great role in End Time prophecy. Using biblical prophecies, this book will further explore the roles that the United States and some other "Israelite" nations may play in the End Times.

## The Serpent Trail of the Tribe of Dan

Since the United States uses the eagle for a symbol, it is necessary to address the fact that some people see the eagle as an evil symbol. This is because Jewish folklore indicates that the eagle was chosen as a symbol for the Tribe of Dan rather than divinely assigned to it. First, however, let me explain which symbols were originally connected to the Tribe of Dan. When Jacob gave his deathbed prophecy for his son Dan, he said the following words:

> "Dan shall judge his people as one of the tribes of Israel. Dan will be a serpent by the roadside, a viper along the path, that bites the horse's heels so that its rider tumbles backward." - Genesis 49:16-17 (NIV)

This prophecy mentions symbols closely associated with the Tribe of Dan. These are the serpent, the viper, or scorpion, a winding path, or road, a rearing horse, and a rider. Several of these symbols are tied to the Zodiac sign of Scorpio, which was assigned to Dan. In the sign of Scorpio, the symbol of a scorpion and serpent are found - with the

## Ch. 7: The Language of Prophecy and the Last Day

serpent being held at bay by the mighty man Ophiuchus, a decan of Scorpio that represents Christ in the act of treading upon Scorpio, or Satan. In addition, the constellation Hercules is a decan of Scorpio, and Hercules is treading upon the gigantic twisting form of Draco, the Dragon constellation in the northern sky. Like the scorpion, this dragon that Hercules is trampling under his feet represents the Devil. This is how the symbol of a dragon became associated with the Tribe of Dan and Satan. In addition to being a symbol for Christ as a conquering hero, the constellation Hercules represents Samson, the Danite Judge, Nazirite, and strongman of Israel (Judges 13:3-7, 15:20). Hence, the entire region of the sky in the vicinity of Scorpio has symbols connected to the Tribe of Dan.

In addition to these sinister symbols, the image of an eagle in flight can also be associated with the Tribe of Dan. Though the eagle isn't a symbol used for Dan in the Bible, Jewish folk literature indicates that the eagle was used as a symbol for the Danites. The Danite patriarch named Ahiezer, who is mentioned in the Bible (Numbers 2:25), adopted the eagle as a symbol for his tribe because he was repulsed by the serpent imagery of Dan. When Ahiezer chose the eagle, he did so to signify that he felt Dan was the enemy of the evil serpent or scorpion, not its upholder! In Book One on the Gospel in the Stars, it was noted that the eagle has long been considered the enemy of the serpent, and therefore is a symbol of good triumphing over evil. Ahiezer was therefore likely hoping that the use of an eagle symbol might change Dan's fate as *"a serpent by the roadside."* Eagle symbols also have good connotations in Scripture, and symbolize godly people throughout the ages. The use of the eagle as a benign symbol has been touched upon throughout the "Language of God" Book Series, and it will be again in Chapter Ten - in relation to Enoch's prophecy about the One-Horned Ram.

Uncannily, when studying the constellations near Scorpio, I noted that Aquila the Eagle is very near the tail of Serpens in Scorpio. The Danite leader Ahiezer may therefore have been familiar with the constellations, and chose Aquila, the Eagle sign of Capricorn over the scorpion or serpent in Scorpio. I also noted another fascinating fact. When the Bible declared that the Tribe of Dan would judge God's people, this was already memorialized in heaven - in the scales of Libra. Libra is adjacent to Scorpio on the ecliptic, and signifies divine judgment. Incidentally, the name "Dan" means "judge," and Dan was named by Jacob's beloved wife Rachel to show that God had judged her worthy of becoming a mother. Sadly, however, Dan was born not to Rachel, but to her maidservant Bilhah, who served as Jacob's concubine at Rachel's insistence, and despite Jacob's anger at Rachel for blaming him for her barrenness (Genesis 30:1-6). Dan's name was therefore likely symbolic of

God's future judgment against those representing Dan and Israel for trying to take their fate into their own hands by tampering with God's plans, and ignoring God's Will and laws just as Rachel did.

Since the United States uses the Bald Eagle as a symbol, some have suggested that the United States represents the Tribe of Dan in prophecy. However, in my own extensive studies regarding the allegorical and spiritual meanings of eagles, the only type of eagle that appears to be associated with the Tribe of Dan and the Antichrist is a fully black or red eagle, which might have two heads, a serpent's tail, and/or the clawed paws of a black leopard or bear. These symbols have been used in heraldic devices and shields to identify the people and nations that may be descended from Dan, or that can trace the "Serpent Seed" of Nephilim blood in their royal lines descended from Cain. Other heraldic symbols that may be connected to the Tribe of Dan are the serpent, dragon, rearing horse, and unicorn.

In addition to symbols, the Tribe of Dan also appears to have left etymological clues as to their whereabouts in history. Some scholars believe that the Celts consist of Israelites from the Half Tribes of Joseph, and the Tribe of Dan among others. In addition, E. Raymond Capt's book "Jacob's Pillar" shows evidence that the Celtic Royalty were already descendents of several of the Lost Tribes of Israel. He also gives clues suggesting that at least one royal Princess of Judah later married into the Celtic Royalty, which later married into the British Royal line. If so, these princesses of Judah may have been marrying into related Israelite bloodlines.

Interesting to note here is the main point that links the Tribe of Dan to this supposed royal line of Judah in Ireland. The ruling clan of Ireland was known as the "Tuatha de Danaan," which literally translates into English as the "Tribe of Dan." Though this translation is hotly disputed, it nonetheless still stands as a viable translation for this Celtic phrase. The main reason this translation is contested is because it suggests that Ireland was taken in conquest by Israelites from the Tribe of Dan, and this idea doesn't fit into traditional accounts of Celtic history.

Nonetheless, there is other evidence that the Danites wandered throughout the ancient world before settling in Scandinavia, Ireland, and Wales. In ancient times, after the Kingdom of Israel was conquered by Assyria, some scholars suggest that the people called the Danoi by the Greeks, and the Danaus by the Romans were the wandering Danites who were displaced out of Israel. These scholars also suggest that the Danites wanted to let the world know how far their wanderings and conquests would take them. Therefore, as they traveled throughout Europe, the

Danites are believed to have named many locations after their Tribal name, "Dan."

In Genesis 49:17, it says: *"Dan will be a serpent by the roadside, a viper along the path..."* This suggests that the Danites would mark their travels along the serpentine roads and rivers of the world in some way. In Ireland today, and as can be shown in locations throughout Europe, there are many Danite-inspired place names like Londonderry, Danslough, Dansower, Danmonism, Donegal City, Dunglow, Dundalke, Dundrum, Donegal Bay, Dingle, Dungarven, and Dunsmore, which means "More Dans." There is also a famous Irish ballad called "Danny Boy." Ireland is therefore filled with names that appear to derive from the Tribe of Dan. Interestingly, the Welsh people of Great Britain may also be descended from the Tuatha de Danaan, and one of the heraldic symbols of Wales is a red dragon, which is one of several symbols identifying the Antichrist, and the Serpent Seed of the Nephilim.

We will return to the subject of the Ten Lost Tribes, the Antichrist, and his association with the Tribe of Dan in Chapter Ten. There, we will examine findings showing that **an uninterrupted line of heirs descending from the royal House of Judah, and the Tribe of Dan may still exist**. For now, however, let's return to our discussion about the Great Day of the Lord.

## The Last Day: Judgment Mixed with Blessing and Mercy

The regular seventh day Sabbath was a holy day consecrated to Yah among the Israelites. It was the day that people were to rest from their own works, and do the Will of God. It was considered a good day to seek Yah's Will through reading and discussing the Scriptures, joyfully singing songs of praise and worship to God, and drawing near to Yah through prayer and meditation on His Word. Likewise the Seventh Great Day since the Fall will also be set apart as special - a holy period dedicated to pleasing Yah.

As already discussed, this Seventh Great Day corresponds to the Millennial Rule of Christ, and the Age known in Scripture as the Day of the Lord. It isn't a literal day but a thousand-year Great Day. Scripture reveals that, though most of this "Day of the Lord" is going to be a time of great blessing and renewal upon the Earth, it will nonetheless begin and end with terrible wars. The first war will begin toward the end of the 3-1/2 year Great Tribulation:

> *"And I saw the beast, the kings of the earth, and their armies, gathered together to make war against Him who sat on the horse and against His army. Then the beast was captured, and with him the false prophet who... deceived those who received the mark of the beast and... worshiped his image. These two were cast alive into the lake of fire.... And the rest were killed with the sword, which proceeded from the mouth of Him who sat on the horse. And all the birds were filled with their flesh."*
>
> *"Then I saw an angel coming down from heaven, having the key to the bottomless pit.... He laid hold of the dragon, that serpent of old, who is the Devil and Satan, and bound him for a thousand years..."* - Rev. 19:19-21; 20:1-2

After the armies gathered in the Valley of Megiddo (Armageddon) are destroyed, and Satan is imprisoned in the Abyss, Yahshua will set up His Millennial Rule, and He will reign on Earth as King of kings. At that time, Yahshua will bring true Peace to the Earth by healing the breach between Jews and Arabs, and Jews and Gentiles. In the Book of Isaiah, right after the Great Pyramid is mentioned as an altar to Yahweh in Egypt, peace between the Middle East, Israel, and the rest of the world is promised:

> *"And it (the Great Pyramid) will be for a sign and for a witness to the LORD of hosts (Yahweh Tsavout) in the land of Egypt; for they will cry to the LORD (Yahweh) because of the oppressors, and He will send them a Savior and a Mighty One (Yahshua), and He will deliver them..."* **"And the LORD (Yahweh) will strike Egypt, He will strike and heal it;** *they will return to the LORD (Yahweh), and He will be entreated by them and heal them.* **In that day there will be a highway from Egypt to Assyria,** *and the Assyrian will come into Egypt and the Egyptian into Assyria, and the Egyptians will serve with the Assyrians. In that day* **Israel will be one of three with Egypt and Assyria - a blessing in the midst of the land,** *whom the LORD of hosts (Yahweh Tsavout) shall bless, saying, 'Blessed is Egypt My people,* **and Assyria the work of My hands,** *and Israel My inheritance.'"* - Isaiah 19:20, 22-25

In this prophecy, Israel refers to the Houses of Judah and Ephraim united as one. Egypt refers specifically to the Arab Muslims of modern Egypt, Libya, and the Sudan, while Assyria means the Arabs in Iran (Ancient Assyria), Iraq, and possibly Syria and Lebanon. ***This prophecy of Isaiah therefore states that Ephraimites (Gentile believers), Israelis, and Arabs will serve Yahshua, the King of kings side by side in Jerusalem!*** Yahshua will therefore mend the rift between Abraham's two sons Isaac (Israel) and Ishmael (Arabia), and end the blood feud that the two siblings have been fighting for millennia. This is what Isaiah meant when he said that Yahweh would strike Egypt and heal it in the preceding prophetic Scripture.

In regard to this time when the Arabs will serve Yahweh, and His son Yahshua in Jerusalem, there is another pertinent Scripture:

> *"And in that day a great trumpet will sound. Those who were perishing in Assyria and those who were exiled in Egypt will come and worship the LORD (Yahweh) on the holy mountain in Jerusalem."* - Isaiah 27:13 (NIV)

This Scripture is truly awesome in light of its meaning. The phrase *"And in that day a great trumpet will sound"* is clearly speaking of the Last Day, at the Last Trumpet announcing Yahshua's victorious return. At that time, "Assyria" and "Egypt" - which may refer to all the remaining Arabs surrounding Israel at Yahshua's return - will repent and worship the true God!

Eerily, the prophecy mentions Assyria, which is modern day Iran and Iraq, and - as of the end of 2010 - the United States was still fighting a perilous war on Terrorism in Iraq and Afghanistan. Meanwhile, Iranian Terrorists are threatening to attack Israel and America with nuclear bombs and there are rumors that the United States and/or Israel may launch a preemptive strike against Iran. If so, the phrase, *"those who were perishing in Assyria"* will be fulfilled. However, the rest of this prophecy refers specifically to the end of the Great Tribulation, where *"those who were exiled in Egypt"* refers to the Jews and other people who will flee from Israel into Egypt when Israel is invaded during the battle of Armageddon. During the Great Tribulation, the armies of the Antichrist will invade Israel, and destroy part of Jerusalem (Zechariah 14:1-4). Then Christ will come again, and the dead, dying, and still living believers throughout the world that opposed the Antichrist will be raised to everlasting life.

Isn't it wonderful that Yah means to heal the many hurts of the past between three great symbolic nations: Assyria (Iran and Iraq), Israel (Messianic Jews and Gentile Christians), and Egypt (the Arabs)? In the process, Yahweh will give the Arabs an equal share in the blessed inheritance allotted to Israel, and to the repentant Christian nations of the world. At that time, there will be a symbolic "highway" built through love and friendship between the Arabs, Israel, and the West. Their hatred of one another will cease, along with the terrible threat of Terrorism. What a joyous time on Earth that will be!

## The Joys of Christ's Millennial Rule

After Christ's Second Coming, and the destruction of the Antichrist's armies, Christ will set up His earthly throne in Jerusalem, and enforce His New Covenant Laws to help humanity recover from their devastating losses during the Great Tribulation. During the millennium-long duration of Christ's benevolent leadership, the world will gradually become a happy, prosperous, and joy-filled place as the Earth is renewed, and the deserts and wastelands bloom with new life (Isaiah 35:1-2, 55:12-13). In addition, the people who choose to worship Yahweh will live in safety (Isaiah 11:6-10, 61:10-11, 66:10-14), and will know true contentment as their every spiritual, emotional, and physical need is met. In addition, once wild and ferocious animals and snakes will no longer kill and eat one another during Yahshua's reign, but will be docile like sheep, and gentle enough to be left around little children without fear of injury or death:

*"The wolf also shall dwell with the lamb, the leopard shall lie down with the young goat, the calf and the young lion and the fatling together;* **and a little child shall lead them.** *The cow and the bear shall graze... and the lion shall eat straw like the ox.* **The nursing child shall play by the cobra's hole, and the weaned child shall put his hand in the viper's den.** *They shall not hurt nor destroy in all My holy mountain,* **for the earth shall be full of the knowledge of the LORD (Yahweh)** *as the waters cover the sea. And in that day* **there shall be a Root of Jesse, who shall stand as a banner to the people;** *for the Gentiles shall seek Him"* - Isaiah 11:1-10

What a wonderful time on the Earth it will be then, when the Bible, and perhaps the Book of 1 Enoch, and the Gospel in the Stars are featured in schools around the world, and people are taught from birth to love their King Yahshua, and live by His righteous laws. During this time, every person and place on Earth will be offered the knowledge of God that was once hidden from the foolish and unsaved, and was known only to those who were wise with God's Spirit. Also at this time, the Gospel of the Kingdom *"will be preached in all the world as a witness to all the nations, and then the end will come"* (Matthew 24:14).

The preceding Scripture pertains not only to the Tribulation period, when the Word of God will be preached by the 144,000 Witnesses and the Two Witnesses, but also to the Millennial Rule of Christ. This is because there will be new generations of people born during that time who will not naturally know God, but will need to be taught about Him.

# Ch. 7: The Language of Prophecy and the Last Day

In fact, the preceding Scripture pertains even more fully to the end of Yahshua's Millennial Rule, when the true end of the world will come, and a New Earth will be created, along with a New Heaven!

The Prophet Isaiah makes it clear that this future millennium-long utopia on Earth will occur only when Yahshua, the Rod (Judge), Branch (Fruit), and Root (Life) of Jesse reigns on Earth, and judges and leads all people righteously:

> "There shall come forth a Rod from the stem of Jesse, and a Branch... out of his roots. The Spirit of the LORD (Yahweh) shall rest upon Him, the Spirit of wisdom and understanding... His delight is in the fear of the LORD (Yahweh), and He shall not judge by... His eyes, nor decide by... His ears; But with righteousness He shall judge the poor... he shall strike the earth with the rod of His mouth, and with the breath of His lips He shall slay the wicked. Righteousness shall be the belt of His loins, and faithfulness the belt of His waist." - Isaiah 11:1-5

There will be a mixture of immortal saints and mortals living upon the Earth during Yahshua's reign, and the immortal people will help the mortals to learn how to love God and each other, and how to live healthily and happily by following God's ways. As a result, most mortals will likely be so robust and healthy that they could potentially live as long as the antediluvian patriarchs did, which was just shy of 1000 years. At this time, in a complete reversal of history from the time when the Fallen Angels corrupted mankind, the immortal saints will be teaching the mortals on the Earth the ways of righteousness, and the Earth will become increasingly more filled with righteous people who love God. Also in a reversal of the past, there will be more people learning righteousness than becoming apostate at this time, and following God's Will rather than doing their own:

> "But this is the covenant that I will make with the house of Israel after those days, says the LORD (Yahweh): I will put My law in their minds, and write it on their hearts; and I will be their God, and they shall be My people. **No more shall every man teach his neighbor, and every man his brother, saying, 'Know the LORD,' for they all shall know Me,** from the least of them to the greatest... For... their sin I will remember no more." - Jeremiah 31:33-34

This Scripture makes it clear that, during the Millennial Rule of Christ, everyone will have an opportunity to know Yahshua personally. If anyone truly desires it, they will meet with Yahshua, eat with Him, and worship God through Him. No one who is seeking God's love and guidance will be denied access to Yahshua, and everyone will know who

He is, and where He resides on Earth. This Scripture is also a promise that one day all Israel will be saved, and there will be no more sin or death - forever! It is therefore a dual prophecy that pertains also to the New Heaven and New Earth, when evil will no longer exist, and every created thing will be as perfect as the Creator God who made them.

Prior to the Great Flood, some of the immortal angels called Watchers sinned by corrupting humanity with false knowledge, a warped love of sensuality, and lust for sexual perversion. During the Millennial rule of Christ, however, this trend will be completely reversed, just as the Menorah of History pictured in Chapter One shows. Instead of fallen Watchers and Nephilim deceiving humanity, the immortal saints who rule as priests and kings with Christ will teach people the ways of righteousness:

> "And they sang a new song, saying: "You are worthy to take the scroll, and to open its seals; for **You were slain, and have redeemed us to God by Your blood** out of every tribe and tongue and people and nation, **And have made us kings and priests to our God; and we shall reign on the earth.**" - Rev. 5:9-10

> "Then I saw the souls of those who had been beheaded for their witness to Jesus and for the word of God, who had not worshiped the beast or his image, and had not received his mark on their foreheads or on their hands. **And they lived and reigned with Christ for a thousand years.**" "Blessed and holy is he who has part in the first resurrection. Over such the second death has no power, but **they shall be priests of God and of Christ, and shall reign with Him a thousand years.**" - Rev. 20:4-6

These two Scriptures teach that the Saints spoken of in Revelation 5:9-10 will be joined by the Tribulation Saints spoken of in Revelation 20:4-6, and together they will co-rule with Christ. As kings and princes, these saints will enforce God's Laws and keep the peace. Meanwhile, as priests, they will gladly teach the people the meaning behind every Bible story, biblical symbol, and biblical holy day. As immortal saints, they will know the mind and Language of God fully, and will teach it perfectly.

During the Millennial Rule of Christ, the Bible makes it clear that God will still expect people to keep His commandments, and celebrate His holy feast days. Yahshua's Two Commandments, which beseech us to love God and one another, will be enforced throughout the world, as will the teachings and worship inherent in at least two of the seven Old Testament Feasts - namely Passover, and the Feast of Tabernacles.

## Ch. 7: The Language of Prophecy and the Last Day

Furthermore, those nations with mortal citizens who fail to keep God's Laws will be punished with no rain, and subsequent drought:

> *"And it shall be that whichever of the families of the earth do not come up to Jerusalem to worship the King, the LORD of Hosts (Melek Yahweh Tsavout),* **on them there will be no rain**. *If the family of Egypt will not come up and enter in,* **they shall have no rain; they shall receive the plague** *with which the LORD (Yahweh) strikes the nations who do not come up to keep the Feast of Tabernacles.* **This shall be the punishment of... all the nations that do not come up to keep the Feast of Tabernacles"* - Zechariah 14:17-19

This Scripture teaches that the whole world will be taught the meaning of, and be expected to celebrate the Feast of Tabernacles, which is a joyous autumn harvest celebration filled with symbolism that has always been tied directly to the Millennial Rule of Christ. However, it also warns that - even when Yahshua, the King of kings rules the world, there will still be unsaved nations on the Earth who will reject Yahshua, and who will refuse to keep the Feast of Tabernacles as a way of showing their objection to, and hatred of His reign!

This is why, at the end of His Millennial Rule, Yahshua will test all the mortals who yet remain on the Earth - even those who appear to be following His rules. To do this, Yahshua will release Satan for a short time in order to deceive those who are perishing:

> *"Now* **when the thousand years have expired, Satan will be released from his prison and will go out to deceive the nations**... *to gather them together to battle.... They went up... and surrounded the camp of the saints and the beloved city. And fire came down from God out of heaven and devoured them. The devil, who deceived them, was cast into the lake of fire... where the beast and the false prophet... will be tormented... forever...* **Then I saw a great white throne and Him who sat on it, from whose face the earth and the heaven fled away.** *And there was found no place for them."* - Rev. 20:7-11

The preceding passage of Scripture clearly says that evil will not be eradicated on Earth until *the end* of the Millennial Rule of Christ. At that time, those who still choose to rise up in rebellion against Christ after a thousand years of true peace will perish, and the Great White Throne Judgment will immediately follow. At that time, the preceding Scripture makes it clear that those who practice wickedness will be cast forever into the Lake of Fire. To help us avoid this horrible fate, the Bible tells us who will be cast into Hell fire, and who will be spared:

> *"Live a life of love, just as Christ loved us... But among you there must not be even a hint of sexual immorality, or of any kind of impurity, or of greed... Nor should there be obscenity, foolish talk or coarse joking, which are out of place, but rather thanksgiving.* **For of this you can be sure: No immoral, impure or greedy person-- such a man is an idolater-- has any inheritance in the kingdom of Christ and of God. Let no one deceive you... because of such things God's wrath comes on those who are disobedient.** *Therefore... live as children of light. (for the fruit of the light consists in all goodness, righteousness and truth)"* - Ephesians 5:2-9 (NIV)

In this Scripture, note that idolatrous lovers of money, promiscuous people who have sex with multiple partners outside of marriage, and people who find amusement in slanderous or obscene humor will not be allowed into the Kingdom of God. In addition to the sins listed above, the following passage indicates the traits common to unrepentant people who will perish for their sins:

> *"But know this, that in the last days perilous times will come: For men will be lovers of themselves, lovers of money, boasters, proud, blasphemers, disobedient to parents, unthankful, unholy, unloving, unforgiving, slanderers, without self-control, brutal, despisers of good, traitors, headstrong, haughty, lovers of pleasure rather than lovers of God, having a form of godliness but denying its power. And from such people turn away!"* - 2 Timothy 3:1-5

Note that the preceding Scripture uses several different words and phrase such as *"proud," "haughty,"* and *"lovers of themselves"* to describe people who have replaced the True Gospel with the erroneous cult of self-esteem that is preached in today's liberal, apostate Laodicean Church. In sharp contrast, God's people are those characterized by the fruit of the Holy Spirit, as exemplified in this Scripture:

> *"Now the works of the flesh are evident, which are: adultery, fornication, uncleanness, lewdness, idolatry, sorcery, hatred, contentions, jealousies, outbursts of wrath, selfish ambitions, dissensions, heresies, envy, murders, drunkenness, revelries, and the like; of which I tell you... that* **those who practice such things will not inherit the kingdom of God. But the fruit of the Spirit is love, joy, peace, longsuffering, kindness, goodness, faithfulness, gentleness, self-control.** *Against such there is no law. And those who are Christ's have crucified the flesh with its passions and desires."* - Galatians 5:19-25

# Ch. 7: The Language of Prophecy and the Last Day

Note here that only those who have allegorically crucified their flesh with Christ, and offered their corrupt bodies up as a living sacrifice to God can faithfully perform the fruits of the Spirit. When our current Heaven and Earth pass away, the unrepentant sinners who carelessly enjoyed satisfying the evil appetites of their flesh will be raised to life, only to be cast into Hell. This must occur to make way for the New Creation that will be as incorruptible, perfect, and as imperishable as all true believers will then be.

## *Everlasting Life In The New Heaven, and New Earth*

After all evil is eradicated, the New Heaven and New Earth will be created without the taint, or memory of sin and death. Life for the saints on the New Earth will therefore be very different than it is now in our current, fallen world:

*"Now **I saw a new heaven and a new earth, for the first heaven and the first earth had passed away. Also there was no more sea.** Then I, John, saw the holy city, New Jerusalem, coming down out of heaven from God, prepared as a bride adorned for her husband."* *"And **God will wipe away every tear from their eyes; there shall be no more death, nor sorrow, nor crying. There shall be no more pain,** for the former things have passed away." - Revelation 21:1-4*

*"**The city had no need of the sun or of the moon to shine in it, for the glory of God illuminated it.** The Lamb is its light. And the nations of those who are saved shall walk in its light... Its gates shall not be shut at all by day (there shall be no night there)."*
*"**There shall be no night there: They need no lamp nor light of the sun, for the Lord God gives them light.** And they shall reign forever and ever." -Revelation 21:23-25, 22:5*

This city will be filled with God's glorious light, making the Sun unnecessary. Also, since there will be no night there, the Moon, and stars will not be visible. This does not mean that there will not be any more night, or Gospel in the Stars in the New Creation, however. Yah's Law and Word will stand *forever!* It simply means that the saints will not have any need to sleep, or keep track of time.

In regard to the New Earth, the Scriptures quoted previously tell us that the physical laws that we are governed by now, and will still experience to some extent in the Millennial Kingdom, will not apply in eternity. We will be immortal, and will no longer know death, sorrow, weeping or pain. Hallelu-Yah! However, the first chapters of Genesis indicate that - even while Adam and Eve were immortal - they were meant to tend the Garden of Eden. They also ate of its fruit regularly before they fell into sin. Genesis also tells us that God caused Adam to fall into a deep sleep when He took Adam's rib to make Eve. All these facts suggest that our *desire* for air, water, food, and sleep will *not* cease to exist in eternity, though our absolute *need* for them will.

Since the New Earth will likely be covered by an abundant and perfect garden, there will probably be no more need to plant crops, or to harvest them. We will eat the abundant fruit of garden trees and plants like Adam and Eve, and we will never need, or want to eat animals again. All people will be vegans, just as the animals on the Earth will be. Since there will be no need for agriculture, we will no longer need to keep track of time, or seasons, and much current knowledge will likely no longer matter in the New Heaven and Earth. Also, because all people will be clothed with light, perfectly healthy, and immortal on the New Earth, the need for clothing (and sewing and weaving), doctors, and medicines will be totally unnecessary.

When the New Creations arrives, then, it will be just as taught in the First Epistle to the Corinthians:

*"Love never fails. But whether there are prophecies, they will fail; whether there are tongues, they will cease; whether there is knowledge, it will vanish away. For we know in part and we prophesy in part. But when that which is perfect has come, then that which is in part will be done away."* - *1 Corinthians 13:8-10*

Even with all our knowledge, humanity only knows *"in part,"* or partially. This means that we have probably only skimmed the surface of the lasting truths God is waiting to reveal to us. So, though much of the knowledge we have today will cease to be important, we will never be bored in the New Creation, and there will be much for us to seek, and to do in eternity. Before the arrival of this perfect New Creation, and the new knowledge it will offer, however, the Great Day of the Lord must be completed, when all people will learn that loving oneself, one's neighbor, and God is the only knowledge we currently possess that will survive, and endure throughout eternity.

As stated previously, Nissan 1 or April 6th, 2000 marked the beginning of the Seventh Great Day after the Fall of man, and the Thirteenth Great Day since the First Day of Creation. In addition, as stated in Chapter Four, **2000 AD marked the beginning of the Age of Aquarius. This means we are already in the Great Day of the Lord!** Since

# Ch. 7: The Language of Prophecy and the Last Day

we are already living in the final Day of the Lord, we are necessarily on the threshold of the beginning of the seven-year Tribulation, and the prophesied events in the Book of Revelation have already started to happen.

The terrible weather and earth changes that many believers are aware of today (but the rest of the world seems oblivious to) are just the beginning of sorrows. These are the birth pangs of the Tribulation, as Scripture warns (Matthew 24:7-9, 1 Thess. 5:2-4), and much worse is yet to come! Sadly, however, too many people are unconvinced, and are falling asleep at this crucial moment in history. As a result, many will be caught sleeping when Yahshua comes again in the Rapture (Matthew 24:42, 26:38-46; Mark 14:34-41; Luke 21:36; 1 Thess. 5:6).

In an effort to wake people up before it is too late, the remainder of this book is primarily concerned with prophecies concerning the terrible cataclysmic future moment in history called the Tribulation and the two nations that may play a major role in it - the United States and United Kingdom that are tied to the two horns of Taurus. It is also concerned with proving that **Yahweh gave us clear indications as to when the Tribulation will begin and end.** I am not speaking of the exact day or hour when it will occur, *but the years and the season* in which it will occur.

## Chapter 8: More Signs of the Day of the Lord's Arrival

*"Behold, I am coming quickly! Hold fast what you have, that no one may take your crown. He who overcomes, I will make him a pillar in the temple of My God... And I will write on him the name of My God and the name of... the New Jerusalem, which comes down out of heaven from My God. And I will write on him My new name." - Rev. 3:11-12*

In the above Scripture, Yahshua is issuing a great warning, and promise to us. First of all, Yahshua is warning us to remain faithful to Him until the end so we don't risk losing our way. Secondly, He is promising that His faithful servants will be greatly honored in the New Creation by receiving a new name that incorporates the Name of God. Therefore, just like all the angels have names that contain the title for God "El," we will have new names that incorporate the Name "Yah." In order to obtain this promise, and heed Christ's warning, however, we need to be vigilant, and to be aware of the signs of Yahshua's imminent arrival.

Unfortunately, to claim that we can't determine the season, or the year of the Day of the Lord, many point to Yahshua's statement that no one knows the exact day, or hour other than the Father Himself (see Matthew 24:36,42,44). This, however, is totally false. **Yahshua did not say that we couldn't determine the year or season, but only the day and hour. Therefore, we can determine the year that marks the season when the Tribulation is imminent.**

*"Remember... what you have received and heard; obey it, and repent. **But if you do not wake up, I will come like a thief, and you will not know at what time I will come to you.**" - Rev. 3:3 (NIV)*

This passage in the Book of Revelation makes it clear that the Tribulation period will only come as a thief in the night for those who *are asleep spiritually*. Those who do not have the baptism of the Holy Spirit will not be given the knowledge of what signs to look for. They will not know what indicators Yah left to mark the season for the end of this Age, and the coming of the Day of the Lord. However, for those who are spiritually alive and awake, there are many signs and indicators to determine when the Day of the Lord is imminent, and what to expect when it arrives.

To gain more insight into what biblical prophecies are trying to tell us using the Language of God, we have already explored the Hebrew alphanumeric structure of the Bible, the Menorah patterns in Scripture, the prophetic nature of the Psalms, and the symbolism of the Tabernacle, Great Pyramid, and Great Sphinx. We have also examined some major biblical and Enochian prophecies. In this last half of the book, we will focus on fulfilled biblical prophecies, Sacred or Biblical Astronomy, and several prophecies about the future from extra-biblical sources.

## Fulfilled Prophecies Signifying the Last Day's Arrival

There are several New Testament prophecies that indicate that we are living in the Last Day. For example, shortly before His crucifixion, Yahshua was sitting on the Mount of Olives when his many disciples came to Him privately, and asked: *"what will be the sign of Your coming, and of the end of the age?"* (Matthew 24:3). Yahshua's reply in Matthew, Chapter 24 was astounding in that it detailed the major trends in the last two thousand years of human history:

> *"For **many will come in My name, saying, 'I am the Christ,' and will deceive many.** And you will hear of wars and rumors of wars... but the end is not yet. For nation will rise against nation, and kingdom against kingdom. And there will be famines, pestilences, and earthquakes in various places. **All these are the beginning of sorrows. Then they will deliver you up to tribulation and kill you,** and you will be hated by all nations for My name's sake. And then many... will betray... and will hate one another. **Then many false prophets will rise up and deceive many.** And because lawlessness will abound, the love of many will grow cold."* - Matthew 24:5-12

First of all, Yahshua suggested that, because false messiahs would deceive many (verse 5), the Christianity of the First Century would **not** be the major world religion. Yahshua then noted that there would be many wars between nations and kingdoms, and many famines, earthquakes, and pestilences before His Second Coming at the End of the

# Ch. 8: More Signs of the Day of the Lord's Arrival

Age (verses 7 and 8). This probably gave the disciples the initial impression that Yahshua's Second Coming was yet far off. However, Yahshua then warned that believers would experience a period of tribulation when they would be greatly hated, severely persecuted, and frequently betrayed (verse 10). Since this happened to believers all over the Roman Empire during the first century because they were perceived as a threat, the apostles and disciples were led to believe that Yahshua was going to come again much sooner than He actually was. This is evident from the language in many of the New Testament epistles.

Nonetheless, though believers were severely persecuted for at least two centuries after Yahshua's death, most Bible scholars agree that this persecution was nothing compared to what has been directed toward professing Christians in the last three hundred years. Though few people today seem to be aware of it, this terrible persecution of Christians began with the Inquisition, and then increased as the Catholic Church, and rulers of the Holy Roman Empire tried to squelch every Protestant congregation that arose after the Reformation. In fact, Great Britain and the United States have been the only major bastions of Protestant Christianity anywhere in the world.

Early in the Twentieth Century, persecution of Christians rose more dramatically with the rise of Communism and other types of totalitarian dictatorships around the world. This persecution escalated again in World War II, when millions of Christians died alongside Jews in Hitler's death camps, and then soon after in Russia and China. In fact, it has been estimated that **more Christians and Jews died as martyrs in the Twentieth Century than in the previous nineteen centuries combined!**

Now, in the Twenty-First Century, this Christian tribulation does not seem to be waning, but waxing as Atheism, the New Age Movement, Wicca, Buddhism, Hinduism, and other types of false religions gain in popularity. In fact, it is clear that this is the time Yahshua warned about when He said: *"many false prophets will rise up and deceive many. And because lawlessness will abound, the love of many will grow cold"* (Matthew 24:11-12). Inevitably, with the inflexibility of the Christian stance on biblical morality, their upholding of biblical Creation, and their rejection of Darwinism, Christians are increasingly being ridiculed for their "close-mindedness" and "lack of tolerance," and are being touted as fanatical fools. Yet, despite this terrible apostate falling away and Christian persecution, Yahshua indicated that the Gospel would still manage to be preached to the whole world before He returned:

> *"But he who endures to the end shall be saved. And this gospel of the kingdom will be preached in all the world as a*

*witness to all the nations,* **and then the end will come.**" - *Matthew 24:13-14*

Taken in the current context, could Yahshua have been telling His disciples that the preaching of the Gospel to the whole world would not come until the Great Tribulation, when the persecution of Christians will be at its highest in history? After all, at this time God will appoint 144,000 Witnesses of Israel, and the Two Witnesses will also be reaching out to a world in chaos (Revelation 7:3-4, 11:3-5). Could it be that these horribly persecuted saints will finally achieve Yahshua's mandate to preach the Gospel to the whole world instead of the sleepy, largely apostate Laodicean Church, whom God will soon spit out of His mouth due to their spiritual rottenness? In light of current world events, this is highly likely! If this is true, then it is almost certain that we are indeed at the threshold of the Great Tribulation.

Other prophecies in the Bible also indicate that we are living at the close of the Age that Yahshua's first disciples had inquired about, and anticipated prematurely. For an example, take the following passages from Timothy's second epistle:

> *"But know this, that in the last days perilous times will come: For* **men will be lovers of themselves, lovers of money**, *boasters, proud, blasphemers, disobedient to parents, unthankful, unholy, unloving, unforgiving, slanderers,* **without self-control**, *brutal, despisers of good...* **haughty, lovers of pleasure rather than lovers of God,** *having a form of godliness but denying its power."* - *2 Timothy 3:1-5*

Doesn't this passage seem as though it was written for this current time in history? After all, we are living in an era when self-esteem and self-realization are considered positive forms of personal growth, despite their totally selfish and self-centered aims. Sadly, along with this marked concentration on instant self-gratification in the West, our current economy is based largely on a lust for pleasure, and desire for wealth at almost any cost. We live in a competitive, consumer-based society with a massive and totally warped emphasis on looking youthful, and being sexually attractive. This focus on staying young at almost any price has caused a massive increase in cosmetic surgery in the past thirty years. Tragically, this trend shows no signs of slowing down, but growing as more and more people attempt to hide their true age, and increase their sexual desirability in order to fit into a carnal, flesh-oriented, materialistic world where only money, power, and youth seem to have any real value.

# Ch. 8: More Signs of the Day of the Lord's Arrival

As mentioned in Chapter One, James, the brother of Yahshua also foresaw this current age of materialism and self-gratification. The following stern warning passages from his epistle seem to be directed toward people who have fallen so deeply into Satan's materialistic trap that they will be forced to live through and die in the Great Tribulation:

*"Now listen, you rich people, weep and wail because of the misery that is coming upon you. Your wealth has rotted, and moths have eaten your clothes. Your gold and silver are corroded... You have hoarded wealth in the last days. Look!* **The wages you failed to pay the workmen who mowed your fields are crying out against you. The cries of the harvesters have reached the ears of the Lord Almighty. You have lived on earth in luxury and self-indulgence. You have fattened yourselves in the day of slaughter.** *You have condemned and murdered innocent men, who were not opposing you..." - James 5:1-6 (NIV)*

Now, focus your attention on the highlighted passages in the preceding Scripture. In light of the current influx of illegal immigrants to the United States who are literally mowing our fields and harvesting our crops, could these passages be referring to them? Could this also be referring to the fact that these people know that they are being cheated of their wages, and are asking to be recognized as citizens so they will stop being paid less than the minimum wage? Sadly, in order to provide Americans with the luxurious lifestyles they crave, these illegal Mexican immigrants are being cheated of fair wages in order to do the jobs Americans would never do for so little money. In other words, it appears that America has spawned a whole new slave class to replace the loss of African American slaves after the Civil War, and especially after the success of the Civil Rights Movement.

Now, however, many Americans are blaming these illegal immigrants for America's economic woes, and are calling them criminals. Though these illegal immigrants may be criminals, many Americans have no one to blame but themselves for the millions of Latin Americans begging to be given a chance to make their permanent home here. America's desire for luxury has caused this crisis, and unless these increasingly fatter and lazier Americans want to mow their own lawns and pick their own fruit as they did twenty or thirty years ago, someone else has to do it! In the meantime, don't think God is not sympathetic to these poor immigrants who are being spitefully used to line rich businessmen's pockets, and give some Americans a level of ease and luxury that is literally killing them. Just as James 5:9 says, *"The Judge is standing at the door!"* and many lazy, greedy Americans will soon be judged for their self-indulgence at other people's expense.

Sadly, this trend toward using poorer nations and people to provide for others in wealthier nations is true everywhere in the world today, not just in America. The manufacturing sweatshops in China and other Asian countries serving the world are based on this sort of greed and desire for luxury, and the people promoting this blatant abuse of others around the world will not escape God's wrath and judgment during the Great Tribulation.

## *2010 Through 2016: Prophetic Years in the Great Pyramid*

As shown in Chapter Three, the ceiling and floor levels of the Grand Gallery in the Great Pyramid or Pillar of Enoch act as a frame around seven other levels of differing widths. Therefore, they convey the same information as the nine-branched menorah, or the nine End Time Psalms – Psalms 110 through 118. The seven widest levels in the Grand Gallery depict the seven years of the Tribulation. They also depict the Seven Ages from Adam's Creation to the New Heaven and Earth. Even more startling is the fact that the north-south length of the Grand Gallery may record the exact number of years that will pass between Christ's death and resurrection, and the beginning of the Tribulation period! Let me explain how.

The analysis of every salient feature of the Great Pyramid was revealed in this book and Book Three except for one: **when measured in Pyramid Inches (1.001 British inches), the interior passages of the Great Pyramid reveal prophetic dates.** The star shafts from the King's and Queen's Chambers give us the date of 2500 BC as the starting point. This doesn't mean the Great Pyramid was built in 2500 BC, but only that the year 2500 BC marks the beginning of the years in inches that are shown in its interior passages. In order to find the correct dates for the various divisions of the passageways, we need to subtract inches from the starting number of 2500 until we reach the zero point. From that point on, we must add inches to get the dates that correspond with the Gregorian calendar.

Some distance down from the entrance, on the wall of the Descending Passage, two straight scored lines can be found that are one Pyramid Inch apart, and run parallel to the passage. These appear to mean several things. First of all, since the scored lines are one Pyramid Inch apart, they show us the crucial measurement of one Pyramid Inch.

# Ch. 8: More Signs of the Day of the Lord's Arrival

Measuring from the original entrance to the scored lines, there are 360 Pyramid Inches. This is the number of degrees in a circle. As was shown in Chapter Four, the circle is incorporated as an integral design feature in the Great Pyramid, which among others things represents the spherical shape of the Earth, Sun, and Moon. Though the number 360 is indicated at the outset in the passage system of the Great Pyramid, I do not believe each Pyramid Inch represents a three hundred and sixty day year. Rather, it appears that **each Pyramid Inch represents one Solar Year**, or the time it takes the Sun to pass through the 360-degree circle of the Zodiac. **The Biblical Prophetic Year is therefore likely not 360 days, but the 360 degrees that the Sun takes to traverse the Zodiac** – which is currently 365.242 days.

Using this reasoning, if we subtract the first 360 Pyramid Inches from the starting date of 2500 BC indicated by the star shafts, we come up with the date of 2140 BC. Though I am uncertain of the significance of this date, it falls in the era when Nimrod ruled the world from Babylon, and built the Tower of Babel. This was also during the lifetime of Peleg. It therefore could be the date of the earthquake that caused the Earth's fractured super continent to rapidly spread apart – consequently destroying the Tower of Babel, and Nimrod's world dictatorship. However, it is more likely that the Fall of Babel occurred nearer to Peleg's death in 2037 BC, the year when Abraham was about 17 years old.

The remainder of the Descending Passage from the scored lines to its juncture with the Ascending Passage measures 628 Pyramid Inches. If we subtract 628 from 2140, we come to the year 1512 BC. Since the Exodus occurred in 1466 BC, 1512 BC may be the date when Moses finally understood that he was an Israelite, left Egypt as an outlaw, and found his way to Midian. Since Moses was 120 when he died, and this occurred forty years after he left Egypt with the Israelites (Deuteronomy 34:7), Moses would have been 80 years old at the time of the Exodus (See Exodus 7:7). If we add 80 to 1466, we arrive at the number 1546. Moses was therefore probably born in 1546 BC, making him 34 years old in 1512 BC.

The measurement of the Ascending Passage, from its juncture with the Descending Passage to the beginning of the Grand Gallery, is 1542 Pyramid Inches. When we subtract 1512 from 1542, we come to the date of 30 AD. However we need to add a one to this date to account for the lack of a zero year on the Gregorian calendar transition from BC to AD. The beginning of the Grand Gallery would therefore correspond to the year 31 AD. Amazingly, this was the year when Yahshua died on the Cross and rose from the dead, forever freeing true believers from sin and

# The Language of God in Prophecy

death (See the next section, and Book Two for proof of this). That this date signifies the beginning of the impressive Grand Gallery is no accident. As already shown, the Grand Gallery represents the spiritual ascendancy we obtain when baptized with the Holy Spirit. Gradually freed from our base sin natures, we progress upward to our goal: spending eternity with Yahshua, and reigning with Him as royal heirs in Yahshua's blessed Kingdom of Peace.

Adding the measurement of the Grand Gallery to our date of 31 AD (1882+31), we arrive at 1913 AD, the beginning of the hostilities among the nations that led to the outbreak of World War I in 1914. The Grand Gallery ends at the Great Step that leads into the Antechamber, which in turn leads into the King's Chamber. Since the King's Chamber represents the Millennial Rule of Yahshua on Earth, as well as the New Heaven to be made at its end, the date indicated by the end of the Great Step at the end of the Grand Gallery must mark the beginning of the Tribulation period. In addition, the antechamber must represent the Tribulation itself.

From measuring its height and depth, the Great Step gives us two measurements. It is 36 Pyramid Inches high and 61 Pyramid Inches deep. Adding 36 to 1913, we come to 1949, one year after the nation of Israel was formed, and *the first year* that the United Nations, and the world finally recognized Israel as an independent nation. This is also the year correlating to Psalm 49, the Psalm that indicates that the Psalms are filled with prophetic parables that would not be understood until modern times. Now **adding 61 to 1949, we come up with 2010 AD, the year that may herald the seven-year Tribulation period beginning in 2011.**

## *The Great Pyramid Antechamber - Key To The Tribulation*

In March of 2012, as I was working on an eight part article recap of my most important prophetic discoveries over the years for publication at my Pillar of Enoch Ministry Blog, God showed me how to unlock the prophetic measurements in the Antechamber of the Great Pyramid. Initially, I was baffled by these measurements because they did not fit the timeline found in the rest of the Great Pyramid's interior passages, where one Pyramid Inch equals one year.

Based on this inch to year hypothesis, the Great Step at the top end of the Grand Gallery shows three prophetic years. These are 1913, which was one year before World War I broke out; 1949, which was the year that Israel was internationally accepted as a modern nation, and

## Ch. 8: More Signs of the Day of the Lord's Arrival

2010, which the Great Pyramid may be targeting as the possible year before the final Tribulation period spoken of by the Prophet Daniel and Yahshua. Thus, if the Antechamber does truly signify the Prophet Daniel's Seventieth Week - as taught by previous scholars that have delved deeply into this subject - 2010 is being signaled out as the final year in the Age of Grace, and 2011 is being targeted as the first year of the Tribulation.

I was finally trying to make sense of this conclusion, and doing my best to salvage what I could of my ministry, which had seemingly crashed and burned when 2010 and 2011 passed without major incident. That is, if you ignored the year-round cataclysmic weather consisting of hurricanes, blizzards, massive floods, killer tornadoes, tsunamis, intense droughts, prolonged periods of scorching heat and bitter cold, and the continuing mass bird, insect, fish and animal die offs that have been occurring at unprecedented levels ever since mid-2010, and have been continuing around the world to the present. At the time, I still had no idea when the Rapture might be, or if we really were in the Tribulation or not. But that all changed on the Feast of Purim, on March 8th, 2012.

On Purim, I was suddenly shown that there is something significant about the length of the short Horizontal Passage from the Grand Gallery to the Antechamber52 PI = One Solar Year proper, which is 52.5 PI. Upon focusing on this number, God suddenly showed me that it pertains to weeks instead of years! Immediately curious and excited, I started doing the math to see what this meant on the same day, and what I found out is absolutely **astounding**! Amazingly, if we view this number as a period of weeks, it covers all of 2011.

Now, since I believe that God's Sacred Calendar is tied to the dates in the Pillar of Enoch, and not the Jewish Civil Calendar, I believe the year 2010 should be measured from it's onset on 1 Nissan or March 16th, 2010 through to it's end on the eve of 1 Nissan on April 5th, 2011. This means that, if the start of the low entrance passage into the Antechamber was targeting April 5th, 2011, the entire low passage leading into the central Antechamber was measuring the 52 weeks of the year 2011 to the beginning of 2012 on 1 Nissan, March 24th, 2012, and a bit beyond it.

Before God showed me how to read the clues in the Antechamber in 2012, what the Great Pyramid had revealed to me correlated perfectly with what I had already seen in the Hallel Psalms and the Sign in the Heavens - as revealed in this book. Unfortunately, 2010 and 2011 came and went without the Rapture that nearly every Bible Prophecy teacher insists must be a Pre-Tribulation event. So, if what God has shown me in the Hallel Psalms and the Heavenly Signs is true, it can only lead me to one conclusion: that the Rapture of the Saints is **not** a Pre-Tribulation event, but a Mid-Tribulation event consistent with the Pre-Wrath view of the Rapture. Looking into the plausibility of this conclusion after I had made it, I learned that Scripture says quite plainly that the Wrath of God begins at the Sixth Seal Judgment:

> *"'Fall on us and hide us from the face of Him who sits on the throne and from **the wrath of the lamb**! 17 **For the great day of his wrath has come**, and who is able to stand?'" - Rev. 6:16-17*

It is clear from Verse 17 that the Wrath of God begins with this Sixth Seal Judgment, and not with the first Seal as many prophecy teachers erroneously suppose! This means that the Bride of Christ and her Five Wise Virgins will experience the affects of the first four Seal Judgments tied to the Four Horsemen of the Apocalypse.

In mid 2011, I had a dream that showed me how God's Wrath will originate in Heaven so that there will be no doubt in the minds of the wicked as to Who is behind then final End Time Plagues that will devastate the entire Earth during the Great Tribulation. I will show how Revelation's Four Horsemen of the Apocalypse are tied to the Mayan End Date, and I will share a description of my dream vision that reveals the nature of the Seal and Trumpet Judgments in the final chapters of this book.

Now, counting 364 days (i.e. 52 weeks) from April 5th, 2011 per God's Sacred Calendar, we arrive at April 3rd, 2012. Adding three-and-a-half days to this, we arrive at the morning of April 7th, 2012 as the end date tied to the end of the entrance passage to the Antechamber. Amazingly, this was none other than the Feast of Passover on the 14th of Nissan in 2012! As such, this date seems to validate my Word of Knowledge from God to see the Pyramid Inches or PI in the Antechamber as **weeks** instead of years. In addition, it disproves the notion that the date thus derived is a mere coincidence. Even more remarkable is the fact that the next day - April 8th, 2012 was Easter or Resurrection Sunday. This was the day that the Firstfruits Offering was offered in the Temple to Yahweh in Jerusalem, and the day when Yahshua became the firstfruits from the dead. On this day, Yahshua ascended to Heaven briefly after rising from the dead to be presented before His Father in triumph (John 20:17). Also, note the numbers of the preceding Scripture reference. Isn't it interesting that these numbers correlate with the year 2017?

## Ch. 8: More Signs of the Day of the Lord's Arrival

If I had noted this measurement and followed God's Sacred Calendar in 2004 instead of the Jewish Civil Calendar, and I had not listened to the Prophecy Teachers, but done my own research into the timing of the Rapture, I would not have made the mistake of viewing the Feast of Trumpets on September 9th and 10th, 2010 as the possible date of the Rapture/Harpazo and start of the Tribulation. Instead, I would have seen that the Rapture is a Mid-Tribulation event, and Nissan 1 in April 2011 was more likely as the beginning date of the Tribulation period. I would also have been able to accept June 1st, 2016 as the Great Tribulation's possible end date.

The diagram on page 308 shows the prophetic dates that are hidden inside of the Great Pyramid Antechamber. These are based on counting one week per Pyramid Inch rather than one year. As shown, the dates being targeted are Nissan 1 or April 5th, 2011, Resurrection Sunday on April 8th, 2012, the 4th of Tammuz on July 1st, 2014 and the 24th of Iyar on June 1st, 2016, which is 10 days before Shavuot, the Jewish version of Pentecost. For believers familiar with the Bible, this should ring a bell, because the Bible specifically tells us that Yahshua rose up to Heaven **ten days before Pentecost**:

> "He (i.e. Yahshua) through the Holy Spirit had given commandments to the apostles whom He had chosen, 3 to whom He also presented Himself alive after His suffering by many infallible proofs, being seen by them during **forty days** and speaking of the things pertaining to the kingdom of God." - Acts 1:2-3

Now, since fifty days are counted between the day of Firstfruits during Passover Week and Pentecost or Shavuot, and we are told in Acts that Yahshua appeared to His apostles and disciples for 40 days, then it is apparent that Yahshua ascended into Heaven ten days **before** Pentecost! Furthermore, two angels appeared to the crowd that watched Yahshua rise up, and told them that He would return "in like manner":

> "Now when He had spoken these things, while they watched, He was taken up, and a cloud received Him out of their sight. 10 And while they looked steadfastly toward heaven as He went up, behold, two men stood by them in white apparel, 11 who also said, 'Men of Galilee, why do you stand gazing up into heaven? This same Jesus, who was taken up from you into heaven, will so come in like manner as you saw Him go into heaven.'" - Acts 1:9-11

# The Language of God in Prophecy

## Antechamber's Interior Measurements and Date Correlations

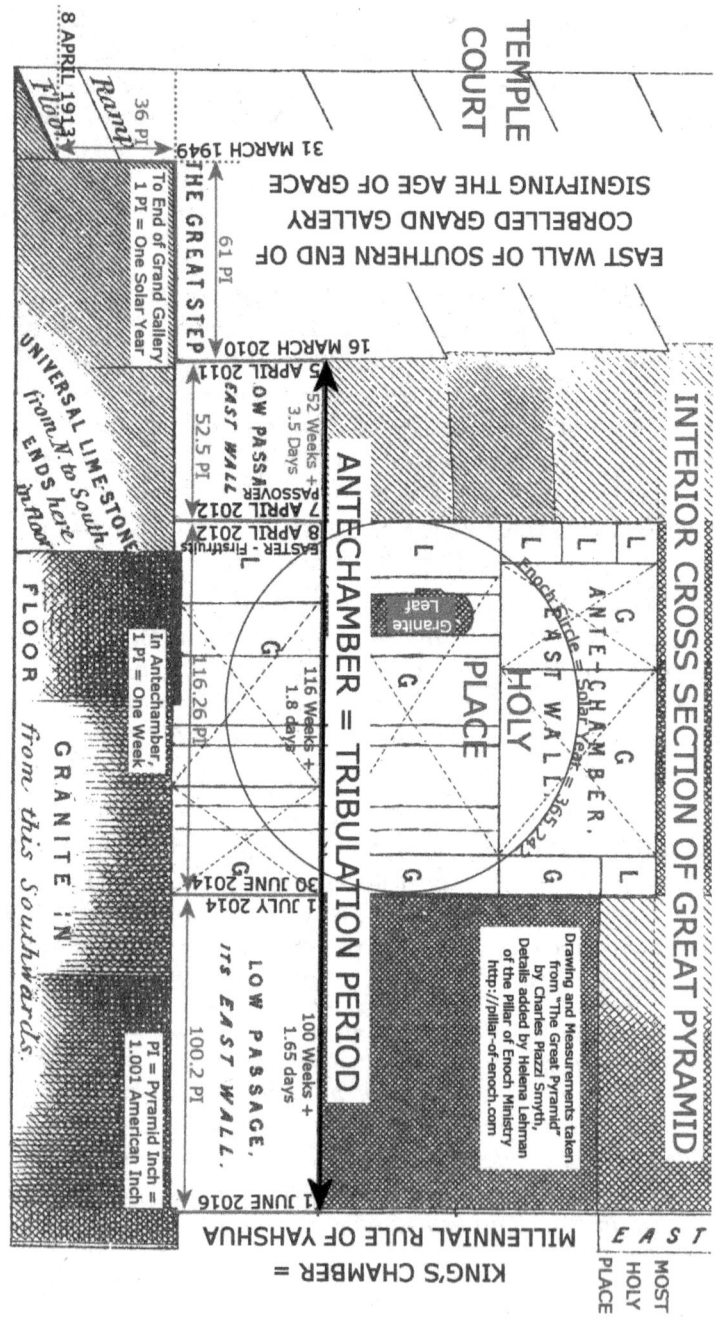

# Ch. 8: More Signs of the Day of the Lord's Arrival

This is a further corroboration that the dates I found inside the Great Pyramid Antechamber were **not** derived by mere chance, but had to have been the handiwork of the Master Designer of the Universe, God Incarnate, a.k.a. Yahshua Ha Mashiach - who worked through His prophet Enoch to create a lasting monument to His Will, purpose, and timing until the restitution of all things will be accomplished!

Perhaps this is why the Antechamber of the Great Pyramid has been called the Hall of Truth in Chaos by past Bible Scholars that have been shown the biblical significance of the Great Pyramid. These past scholars have noted that a circle whose diameter is equal to the length of the Antechamber in Pyramid Inches has a circumference that equals the fractional length of a Solar Year, which is approximately 365.242 days long. They also have called this circle the Enoch Circle because that solar number reference may also refer to the antediluvian patriarch Enoch, who was translated into Heaven without seeing death during his 365th year of mortal existence (Genesis 5:22-23).

In regard to the Enoch Circle, it is interesting to note that a circle can signify a completed period of time, as well as the Sun's path, which can be seen as the Way of Yahweh. Interestingly, the Sun is also a symbol for Yahshua, Who was called "the Sun of Righteousness" by the prophet Malachi (Malachi 4:2). Furthermore, in the Book of Revelation, Yahshua is described in this manner:

> "He (i.e. Yahshua) had in His right hand seven stars, out of His mouth went a sharp two-edged sword, and **His countenance was like the sun shining** in its strength." - Revelation 1:16

In this book, I have already revealed that the Great Pyramid Antechamber shares an allegorical connection to the Holy Place within the Desert Tabernacle and Temple to Yahweh - especially since the King's Chamber with its empty coffer shares geometric connections with the Most Holy Place and the Ark of the Covenant inside the Tabernacle. As I explained in my book "The Language of God in Humanity", the Ark of the Covenant is a symbol of Yahshua as the Word of God (the Stone Tablets), the Bread of Life (the golden jar of Manna), and the Branch of Jesse and a Priest in the order of Melchizedek (Aaron's Staff).

In addition, the contents of the Holy Place included items that all represented Yahshua and those who followed Him and His Father. These were a seven-branched golden menorah, a golden table for consecrated loaves of bread, and a golden altar of incense. Together, these objects allegorically tell us that the only way anyone can follow the Way of Yahweh is by praying continually (the incense), being a light to the world by following Yahshua, who is the Light of the World (the menorah), and by living holy and sanctified life in imitation of Yahshua, Who is the Bread of Life (the showbread). This is also the only way that anyone who is left behind will survive the coming Tribulation plagues!

Fascinatingly, though it is not shown in the above diagram, one half of the Enoch Circle can also be found on either side of the coffer in the King's Chamber. This suggests that the conditions for surviving the Tribulation and dwelling within the Millennial Kingdom of Yahshua will be the same. Tied to this fact, the coffer's connection to the Ark of the Covenant shows that only those already having resurrected bodies like Yahshua's will be perfected in the image of Christ, and will be able to keep the Law perfectly during the Millennial Rule of Christ. Everyone else will still be capable of losing their salvation until the Last Judgment that will come at its end.

Interestingly, the Antechamber has features that tie uncannily well into my Tribulation Time Chart, which I originally created in early 2011, and then completely revised in July of 2013. It is available as a free download at my Pillar of Enoch Ministry Web Site at pillar-of-enoch.com. First, note that the top outside edge of the Great Step in the Grand Gallery offers the date of 1949, which was the year that the new nation of Israel was officially recognized as a sovereign nation by the United Nations. As shown in Chapter of this book, the Prophet Daniel's Seventy Weeks Prophecy may indicate not only the 486 years from Artaxerxes' order to restore and rebuild Jerusalem to the First Advent of Yahshua, but a period of sixty-nine years, which may count the number of the Feast of Weeks or Shavuots from the Rebirth of Israel to the Second Coming of Yahshua.

Though modern Israel was officially formed in 1948, the Great Pyramid gives the year 1949 as significant, probably because a Blood Moon Tetrad on Jewish Feasts occurred beginning that year. Also, due to the Great Pyramid's connection to the star Al Nitak in Orion's Belt - and the connection of the other two large pyramids at Giza to Orion's other two Belt Stars - there is no doubt that the entire Giza Pyramid Complex is a stellar time marker.

Intriguingly, if sixty-nine years are counted from 1949, we arrive at the year 2018. This is the year that is marked by three Blood Moons by Yahweh God - just as the year 2011 was. But we arrive at May 2nd, 2017 if we count 69 years from Israel's official birthday, which was May 15th, 1948, to their Independence Day in 2017. This is shown in my "Antechamber and Tribulation Timeline Layover Graphic" on page 312, which combines my "Antechamber's Interior Measurements and Date

Correlations" graphic with my "Tribulation Timeline" graphic, which can be found at my Pillar of Enoch Ministry Web Site.

As this diagram shows, the Antechamber's end date is June 1st, 2016, which is exactly ten days before Shavuot. This is significant because Scripture tells us that Yahshua would return in the same manner as when He left, which was ten days before Pentecost or Shavuot, and the King's Chamber of the Pillar of Enoch is tied to the Millennial Reign of Yahshua. This suggests that Yahshua may return ten days before Shavuot on June 1st, 2016 to restore Jerusalem as His Kingdom Capital, and to conquer the wicked on Earth!

This will be just before the amazing 50-year Jubilee of the commemoration of the retaking of Jerusalem by the Jews during the 1967 Six Day War from their Arab enemies. The first Jerusalem Day was on June 8th, 1967, and the 50th anniversary of that date will be on June 5th, 2016, which is just four days after the Antechamber End Date. Thus, 2016 can be seen as a sacred Jubilee Year - and one that is superior to any other calculation of Jubilee years. The reason it is superior is because it was **not** determined using human reasoning, but by God in secret. Therefore, it could **only** be revealed through the unfolding of Biblical Prophecy in history.

Furthermore, since the first year of Daniel's Seventieth Week of years is 2011 - as indicated by the trio of Blood Moons marking 2011 - then the seventh year from then will be 2017, which will make 2017 a Sabbatical Year, or a year of Sabbath Rest. How fitting, then, that 2017 may mark a period of rest from all work before God restores the Earth to its Edenic beauty and the Millennial Kingdom is inaugurated.

It would be wonderful if this is indeed going to be the case, but only time will tell if these dates are referring to these events or not. For the sake of all believers, I pray that this will be so. But please realize that I am not acting prophetically here, but using logic and reasoning to apply the Words of Knowledge that God has given to me over the years. I just hope that I heard Him correctly! Therefore, I caution everyone to pray about this, and be convinced in your own mind about these things by the Holy Spirit before sharing it with others.

Concerning this time, I was given a Word of Knowledge on September 12th, 2013 that Yahshua will **not** immediately set up His Millennial Kingdom upon His return. Instead, He will go to Israel first to release His Jewish brethren from oppression in the Battle of Armageddon, thereby facilitating the conversion of the Jews to belief that Yahshua is their Messiah. Also, just before the Battle of Armageddon, Yahshua will resurrect the Two Witnesses and give everlasting life to the repentant

# The Language of God in Prophecy

Foolish Virgins. In addition, there will be a one year period of rest before Yahshua sets up His Millennial Kingdom. This could be during the Sabbatical Year of 2017, but I was not given any exact dates for these events via direct revelation. The dates given here were calculated using available facts.

## Antechamber and Tribulation Timeline Layover Graphic

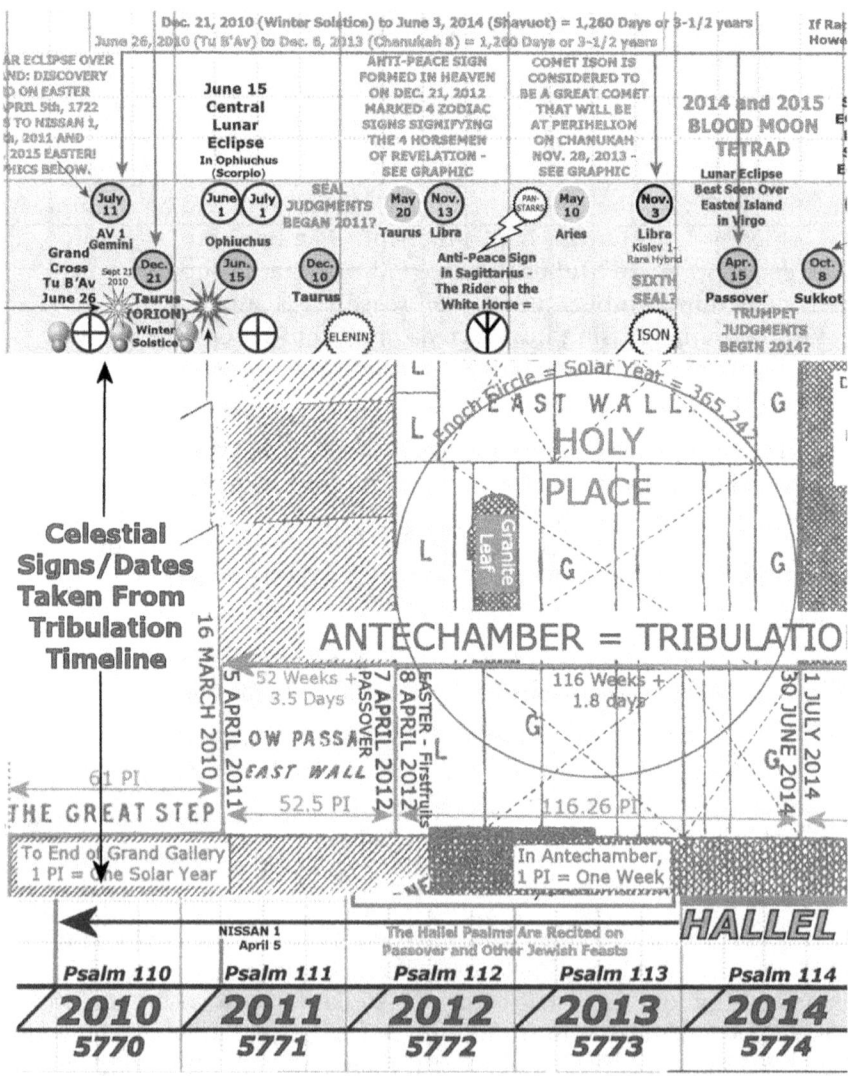

# Ch. 8: More Signs of the Day of the Lord's Arrival  Page 313

Now, Sixty-nine Solar Years will have passed between May 1948 - the month and year when Israel became a nation - and March 28th or Nissan 1 in 2017. Sixty-Nine is also the number of **weeks** that the Prophet Daniel said would pass between the order to rebuild Jerusalem, and Messiah the Prince (i.e. Yahshua):

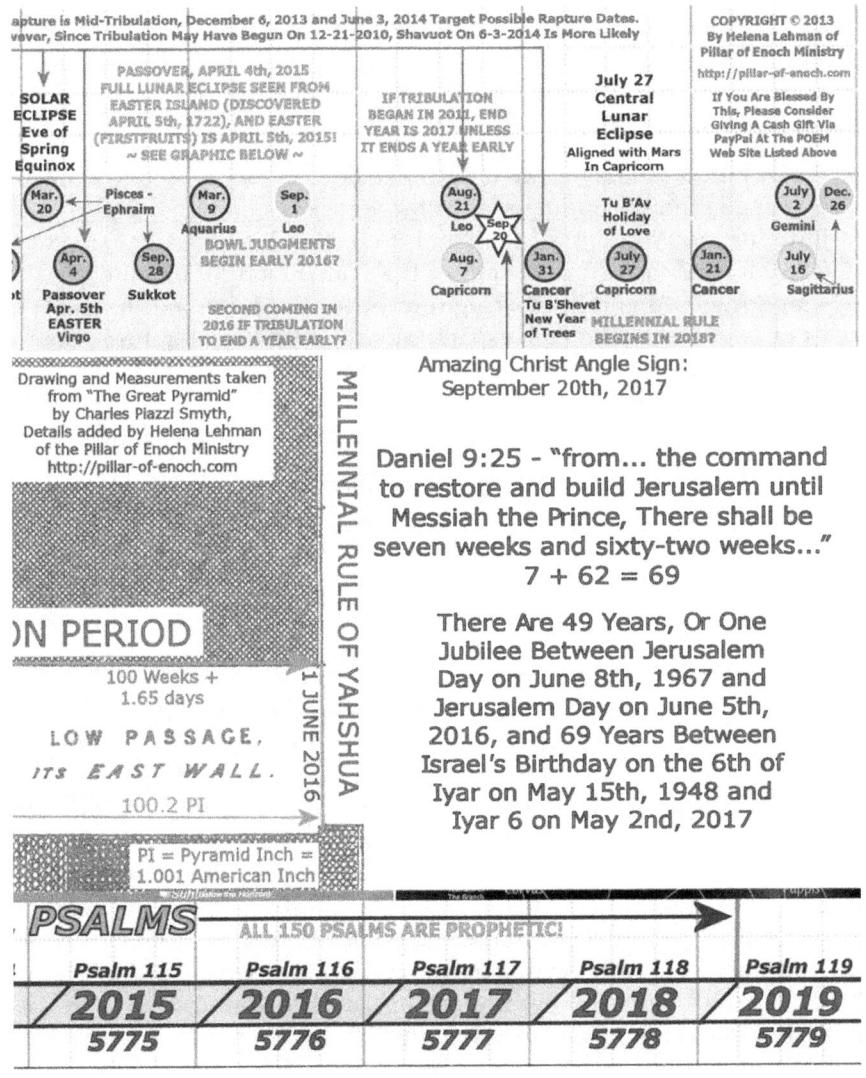

> *"Know therefore and understand: that from the going forth of the command to restore and build Jerusalem until Messiah the Prince, there shall be seven weeks and sixty-two weeks; the street shall be built again, and the wall, even in troublesome times"* - Daniel 9:25

Intriguingly, I recently read an article written by a brother in Christ on the internet that suggested that the Prophet Daniel used the word "weeks" in His Seventy Weeks Prophecy to indicate that this prophetic 70 years is to be counted from Pentecost to Pentecost, or Shavuot to Shavuot. Could this be why the two last dates in the Antechamber target June in 2014 and 2016 - the month when Pentecost or Shavuot most often occurs?

In addition to being the month of Pentecost in 2014 and Shavuot in 2016, June is the traditional month for weddings. So what better time than June for the Wedding of the Lamb to begin? Intriguingly, June of 2014 will fall not long after the first of the Four Blood Moons on Jewish Feasts marking 2014 and 2015 as significant for the Jews, and for the Two Houses of Israel as a whole. This suggests that the First Rapture may occur around June of 2014, but no one knows the day or hour. However, both the Prophet Joel and Yahshua indicated that a Full Solar Eclipse and Full Lunar Eclipse may occur just before the Rapture and Second Coming:

> *"The sun shall be turned into darkness, And the moon into blood, Before the coming of the great and awesome day of the Lord."* - Joel 2:31

> *"...and the sun became black as sackcloth of hair, and the moon became like blood."* - Rev. 6:12

Fascinatingly, as shown in my composite Antechamber - Tribulation Timeline graphic, there is a Full Solar Eclipse on November 3rd, 2013, and the first of the Blood Moons of the Lunar Tetrad on Jewish Feasts in 2014 and 2015 is on April 15th, 2014, on the evening of Passover. These could be the eclipses that will occur *before and/or during* the Sixth Seal Judgment that is described in Revelation 6:12-17. Also, if 2011 marked the first full year of the Tribulation - and three independent sources of prophetic knowledge found in the Psalms, the Heavenly Signs, and the Great Pyramid agree that it did - then the Rapture must be a Mid-Tribulation or Pre-Wrath event because it did not occur in 2010, 2011, or 2012. This agrees with another important fact. It is found from discovering that, though 1 Thessalonians 5:9 says that we are not appointed to wrath, God's Wrath is not announced as such until just before the Sixth Seal is opened, as revealed in Revelation 6:

## Ch. 8: More Signs of the Day of the Lord's Arrival

> *"I looked when He opened the sixth seal, and behold, there was a great earthquake; and the sun became black as sackcloth of hair (a full Solar Eclipse), and the moon became like blood (followed by a full Lunar Eclipse). 13 And the stars of heaven fell to the earth, as a fig tree drops its late figs when it is shaken by a mighty wind (a heavy meteor shower). 14 Then the sky receded as a scroll when it is rolled up, and every mountain and island was moved out of its place. 15 And the kings of the earth, the great men, the rich men, the commanders, the mighty men, every slave and every free man, hid themselves in the caves and in the rocks of the mountains (in their underground bunkers), 16 and said to the mountains and rocks, 'Fall on us and hide us from the face of Him who sits on the throne and from **the wrath of the Lamb! 17 For the great day of His wrath has come**, and who is able to stand?'" - Revelation 6:12-17*

This means that believers in Yahshua may not be taken in the Rapture until the first Five Seals have been opened. As shown in the last chapter of this book, the Mayan End Date on December 21st, 2012 appears to be marking the release of the Four Horsemen of the Apocalypse, or alternatively, the release of the Third or Black Horse, and the Fourth or Pale Horse. This means that 2013 and 2014 may mark the time of the Third through Sixth Seal Judgments, and the first three Trumpet Judgments.

After studying the description of the Sixth Seal Judgment given in Revelation Chapter 6, I believe that it describes a massive Pole Shift and crustal displacement of the Earth that will occur after a Full Solar Eclipse and Full Lunar Eclipse, and in conjunction with a massive worldwide earthquake. Since - as verse 17 above shows - the Great Day of God's Wrath is announced in conjunction with this cataclysmic event, it is very likely that the First Rapture will occur just before or after the Full Solar and Lunar Eclipse associated with it. Since the Sixth Seal judgment begins the outpouring of the Wrath of God, we should also expect the First Rapture to be sometime before the Pole Shift that the Sixth Seal Judgment describes.

If the Eclipses in late 2013 and early 2014 are tied to the actual unfolding of the Sixth Seal, then - if there is going to be a Pre-Wrath Rapture - it will most likely occur before the Full Lunar Eclipse on Passover in 2014. Interestingly, as shown in the illustration on page 316, a comet named Comet ISON (C/2012 S1) is scheduled to be at Perihelion, or in its closet position to the Sun, on November 28th, 2013. This is the first day of Chanukah, as well as American Thanksgiving, and there is some indication that this comet - along with four other comets that are appearing with it - may be marking a major event on God's Prophetic Calendar. Could this unprecedented 5-comet heavenly sign be a herald that the First Rapture of the Wise Virgins and the Sudden Destruction that is tied to it are very near? Could it be the Sign of the Son of Man that Yahshua told us to watch for?

## Comet ISON at Perihelion on November 28th, 2013

This illustration of Comet ISON at perihelion was created in full color for my Tribulation Timeline, which can be downloaded for free from my POEM web site at http://pillar-of-enoch.com/essays/trib-timeline.html. There is a full section in Chapter 11 of this book concerning the extraordinary 5-comet sign that is to appear in the heavens from October 2013 through January of 2014, of which Comet ISON is the most spectacular. This section includes an amazing explanation of the meaning behind Comet ISON's trajectory through the constellations in 2013 and 2014, and its possible significance as one part of the multi-layered Sign of the Son of Man that Yahshua spoke of in Matthew, Chapter 24.

# Ch. 8: More Signs of the Day of the Lord's Arrival

Since I believed at one time that the Rapture could occur in the late spring or early summer in Israel per the clues left for us in the Song of Solomon, and per a Word of Knowledge and Rapture dream that I had in 2011 that indicated late spring or early summer as the First Rapture time period, it may be sometime around June of 2014 instead of in the late Autumn of 2013. Nonetheless, as an interesting aside that could point to the Rapture being sometime in late autumn or early winter, it is later spring and early summer in the Southern Hemisphere when Chanukah occurs in the Northern Hemisphere. So, though it is unlikely, the Song of Solomon could be describing late spring and early summer in the Southern Hemisphere, when the lilies bloom there - and while it is the late autumn or early winter in the Northern Hemisphere.

Though there is no way to pinpoint the exact time of the First or Second Rapture, I believe that the First Rapture will happen at the start of the Great Tribulation, which I once believed would be three and a half years long. However, the narrow passage leading out of the Antechamber and into the King's Chamber in the Great Pyramid suggests that the Great Tribulation will only last for two years, from July 1st, 2014 though to June 1st, 2016. If the Great Tribulation starts in July of 2014, the Rapture may very well be near to the time of Pentecost or Shavuot in June of 2014.

If the Great Tribulation is to be shortened to only two years, this suggests that the references to a 3-1/2 year period in the Book of Revelation may refer to a time period stretching from the start of the seven-year Tribulation period until when the Rapture will occur and the Great Tribulation will start. Now, if Nissan 1 or April 5th, 2011 was the official beginning of the seven-year Tribulation period, 1,260 days or 3-1/2 years from that date may mark the beginning of the Great Tribulation. Using a Jewish Calendar, the Feast of Trumpets will fall 3-1/2 years later, on September 25th, 2014. However, since the Great Pyramid is tied to the star Al Nitak in Orion's Belt, it makes sense that the constellation of Orion has to figure into this equation, and this suggests that the official start of the seven-year Tribulation was on the night of the Winter Solstice in 2010.

## *End Time Herald: Blood Moon Over Orion on Dec. 21, 2010*

On December 21st, 2010, ***a spectacular Full Lunar Eclipse or Blood Moon occurred directly over the sword of Orion!*** The graphic on the next page explores the Star Gospel symbolism behind this highly important heavenly sign. In addition to this Full Lunar Eclipse over Orion, a rare celestial alignment called a Grand Cross occurred in the Heavens, as shown in the graphics on pages 318, 319 and 320.

## Blood Moon Over Orion's Sword - December 21st, 2010

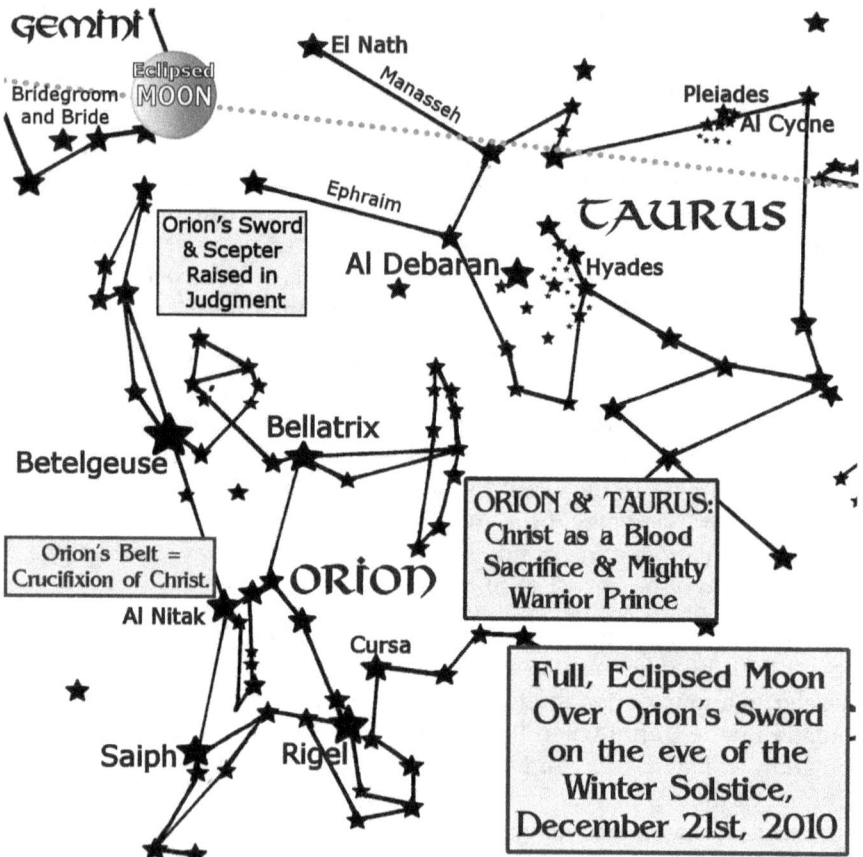

This Total Lunar Eclipse technically occurred directly on the Taurus-Gemini Meridian in the heavens where Orion's sword tip touches the ecliptic. This is a highly significant position in the heavens, as it marks the point directly between Taurus and Gemini. Since Orion is considered a decan of Taurus, this Lunar Eclipse is also targeting that Zodiac sign, as well as their earthly counterparts in the magnificent pyramids that were built by Jacob's righteous ancestors at Giza and Dahshur in Egypt.

The Taurus-Gemini Meridian has much allegorical significance. For example, while Taurus and its decan Orion signify the coming of Yahshua to destroy the nations that are aligned against God and His people in the Two Houses of Israel, Gemini signifies the resolution of all the world's conflicts with humanity's betrothal and wedding to the Lamb

# Ch. 8: More Signs of the Day of the Lord's Arrival

of God Who takes away their sins - if only they will believe in and follow Him!

Significantly, Taurus the Bull's horns represent the Tribes of Ephraim and Manasseh, as well as the apostate and faithful branches of the Church of Christ. Could it also be possible that these horns are representative of the two End Time leaders of the countries that can be most closely associated with those two tribes of Israel that descended from the patriarch Joseph, specifically Barack Hussein Obama and Prince Charles of Wales - or possibly his son William?

## Grand Cross in Heaven on the Winter Solstice of 2010

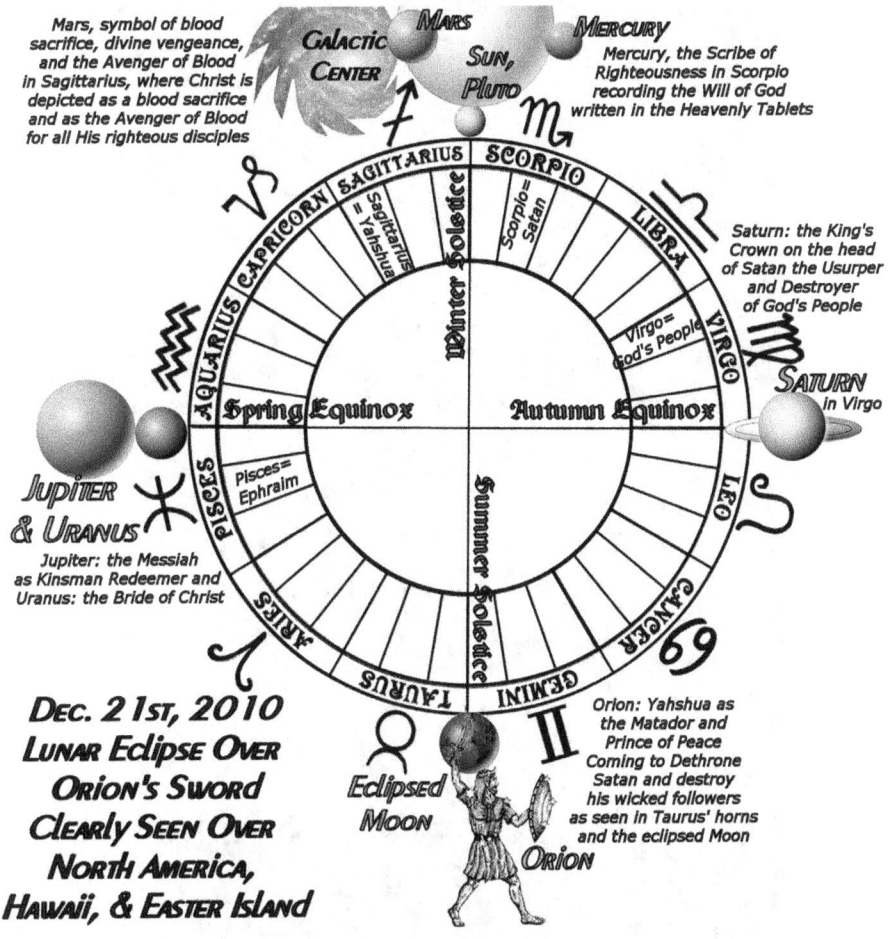

# The Language of God in Prophecy

## Dec. 21st, 2010 Lunar Eclipse in Taurus With Sun in Scorpio

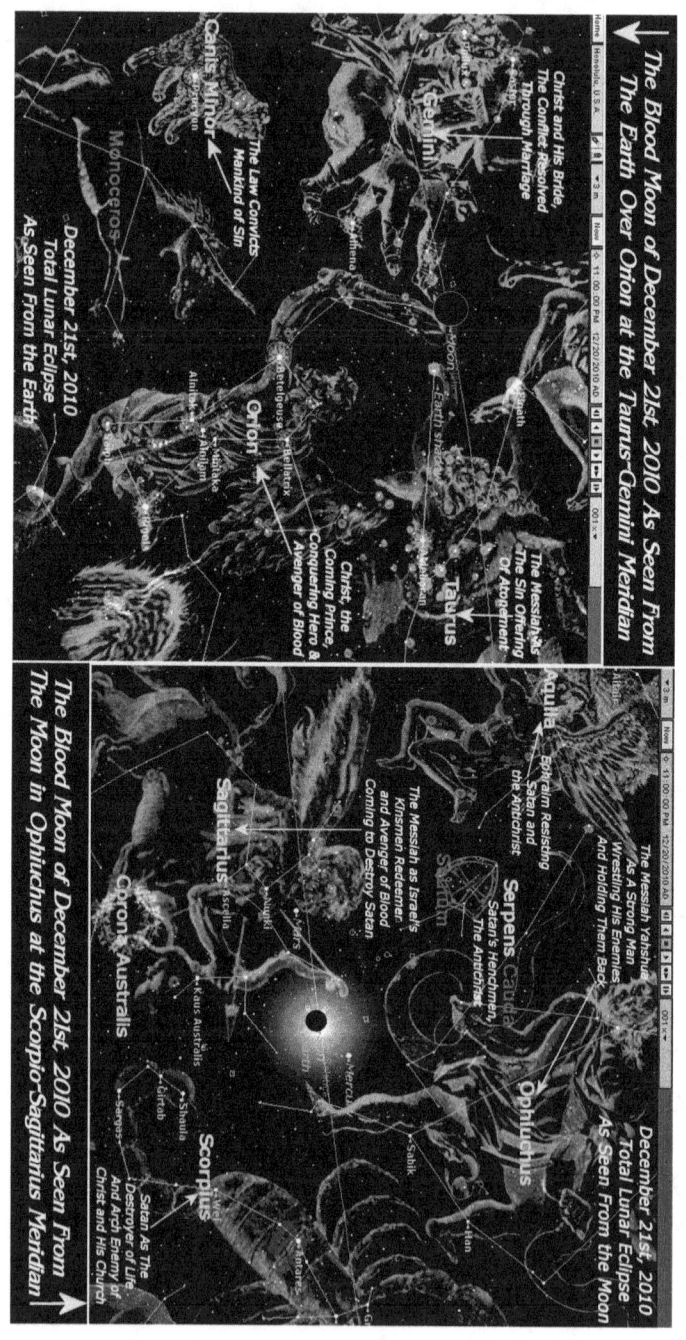

## Ch. 8: More Signs of the Day of the Lord's Arrival

Though these leaders may not turn out to be the two Antichrist figures identified by the prophet Daniel as the King of the North and the King of the South, they certainly have the credentials to fulfill those roles in Bible prophecy. Due to the fact that the two antagonists of Christ during the Tribulation may prove to be the leaders of the most powerful military machines in the world, Taurus the Bull can be seen as an enraged bull charging the allegorical Matador or Messiah signified by the constellation of Orion the Hunter. Indeed, Orion can easily be envisioned to be a proud prince or king wielding a sword and waving his regal red cape to entice the raging bull to charge and meet his death at the hands of the rightful Ruler of the World!

Incidentally, on the dawn following the Blood Moon on December 21st, 2010, the Winter Solstice Sun rose in Ophiuchus - and directly on the heavenly counterpart to the Earth's Scorpio-Sagittarius Meridian. This is shown in the illustration on page 320, which shows the Lunar Eclipse and the Solstice Sunrise on December 21st, 2010.

The earthly meridian that is tied to the Meridian running between Sagittarius and Scorpio in the heavens is tied directly to the United States or Ephraim because its earthly counterpart cuts through two of its states. These are Alaska and Hawaii, with the State of Alaska resting directly on that meridian. This meridian also runs right alongside Hawaii, with Hawaii resting on the Scorpio side of it that is also connected to Ophiuchus. Though Ophiuchus also signifies the global struggle against good and evil, it centers on the United States because of this alignment of two of its states with the Sagittarius and Scorpio Meridian. See Book Three, "The Language of God in History" for a map and detailed explanation of these Earthly meridians and their connection to the Zodiac.

In the illustration on page 320, it can be seen that the Sun is next to Ophiuchus. Many call the Decan sign of Scorpio called Ophiuchus a thirteenth sign of the Zodiac because it rests on the Ecliptic, while - with the exception of its head and pincers - the Scorpion depicted in the parent sign of Scorpio sits well below the Ecliptic. Though this seems logical, God deliberately positioned Ophiuchus as a decan to show that, while Scorpio now holds the central position in the heavens due to sin and wickedness, it and its sister sign Serpens will one day be altogether replaced by Ophiuchus riding the neighboring Eagle called Aquila to victory! Hallelu-Yah! Please study this illustration carefully and prayerfully to better understand what God is saying through the heavens on that day.

Interestingly, as I contemplated the number 13 and its connection to the thirteen original colonies of the United States one day, God gave me a Word of Knowledge that Ophiuchus partly signifies the United States and the gargantuan struggle going on within it right now between those who follow Yahshua, and those who follow Satan. He also showed me the connection of the states of Alaska and Hawaii as a symbolic Sun and Moon. See Chapter Nine in this book for more about this, as well as the connection of the USA with the Tribe of Joseph through his son Ephraim.

Due to this connection of the USA with Ophiuchus, and its connection to Taurus as the horn tied to Ephraim, Yahshua addressed this time in History with His Parable of the Wheat and the Tares in Matthew 13:24-30. I have written a detailed exploration of the meaning of this parable, which was published on my blog and linked to on my POEM Web Site at http://pilar-of-enoch.com. If you have internet access, I highly recommend reading it as a guide to understanding the mass polarization of the entire world's population into two ideological groups that are diametrically opposed to one another. You can also write to me or call me using the contact information listed on the book order form at the end of this book to request a digital copy of this study, which can be mailed or e-mailed to you.

In the illustration on page 320, Ophiuchus is depicted as a Strong Man wrestling with a giant writhing serpent that signifies Satan and his followers on the Earth. Now, in the sign of Ophiuchus, God is showing us how the Sons of Light that follow Yahshua and the Sons of Darkness that follow Satan are - and have long been - fighting a terrible war of conflicting ideologies. This war has been going on ever since the Fall of Adam and Eve, and it will not be resolved until the final conflict known as the Battle of Armageddon.

Due to this, I believe that the Blood Moon over Orion's Sword on December 21st, 2010 was a clear sign that the world government power plays that will lead to the Battle of Armageddon were about to occur, with US President Barack Obama figuring prominently in polarizing the world's warring factions for the final showdown. Sadly, this one man's efforts have secured more ground for Satan than any other President in US History. This can be seen in his rabid push for Gay Rights and the LGBT Agenda, and his ruthless denial of the rights of the unborn - with abortions even being allowed at full term now. Horribly, this amounts to nothing less than the full blown legal right for women to practice infanticide, which is the murder of an unwanted full term baby. This leads me to point to another significant feature of the Great Pyramid Antechamber.

# Ch. 8: More Signs of the Day of the Lord's Arrival

In the composite diagram of the Antechamber superimposed over my Tribulation Timeline on pages 312 and 313, the cross section of the dark Granite Leaf within the Antechamber has been labeled so that it can be easily located. Go to my diagram to identify the Granite Leaf and note the celestial event that this design feature correlates with. Amazingly, the left side of the Granite Leaf coincides with an allegorically significant Full Solar Eclipse that occurred on November 13th, 2012 near the Sethite time marker Easter Island, while the Granite Leaf itself is targeting the Anti Peace Sign that appeared in the heavens on the Winter Solstice of December 21st, 2012. This was the Mayan End Date - a date that may have been targeted by the ancient Sethites because the heavenly signs on that date are tied directly to the Four Horsemen of the Apocalypse, as will be shown in the last chapter of this book.

For now, please remember that - according to what God has shown me - the Four Horsemen of the Apocalypse began their rides already! This means that we are already in the final Tribulation period that will lead to the First Rapture and the Sixth Seal Judgment just before, or at the beginning of the Great Tribulation. Fascinatingly, the Winter Solstice in this era is targeted by the middle Pyramid at Giza that signifies the Cross of Christ. Furthermore, Yahshua's conception is tied to Chanukah, and the Chanukah before Yahshua was born began on the evening of December 14th and ended on the evening of December 21st, 4 BC. This brings us back to the Comet ISON, which reaches perihelion on the first day of Chanukah in 2013.

Fascinatingly, if we count forward 3-1/2 years from the December 21st, 2010 Blood Moon, we reach the Summer Solstice on June 21st, 2014. This is just a couple of weeks after Pentecost on June 8th, 2014, and Shavuot on June 4th, 2014. In addition, this is just one week before the date targeted by the entrance into the final low hallway between the main room of the Antechamber and the King's Chamber. The entrance to this hallway, which signifies the Great Tribulation, corresponds with the date of June 30th, 2014. This is two days after Rosh Chodesh Tammuz, or the 1st day (i.e. New Moon) of the Jewish month of Tammuz on June 28th, 2014.

Of course, the next day of July 1st, 2014 or the 3rd of Tammuz is also being targeted by the entrance to the final low passageway leading to the King's Chamber. Intriguingly, on the 3rd of Tammuz on June 19th, 2012, there was a very powerful stellar line up that had a prophetic story to tell, and a graphic I created to show what it meant appears on page 324.

# Signs in the Heavens, 3rd of Tammuz, June 19th, 2012

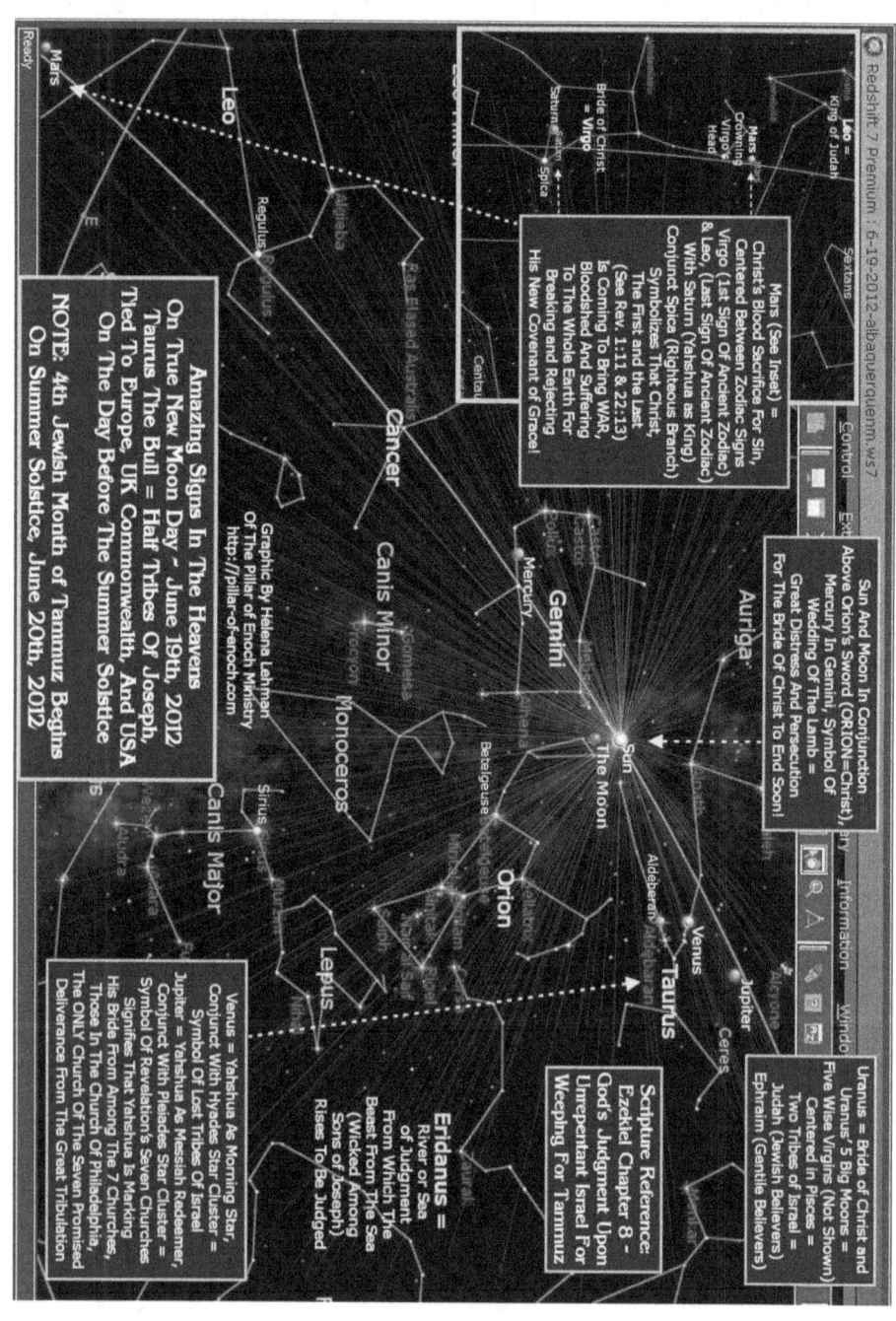

# Ch. 8: More Signs of the Day of the Lord's Arrival

Perhaps the Heavenly Signs on that day were warning of the future 3rd of Tammuz in 2014, which the Antechamber of the Great Pyramid suggests may have an even greater prophetic story to tell. Four Full Lunar Eclipses have also been marked above the Antechamber in the celestial sign portion of my composite diagram. These four consecutive Blood Moons fall on the Jewish Feasts of Passover and Sukkot - from early 2014 through late 2015 - and the last three of these Blood Moons are tied to the low passage leading from the Antechamber proper into the King's Chamber.

As shown on the diagram, this section measures the two years that fall between July 1st, 2014 and June 1st, 2016. In allegorical terms, this significantly narrowed passage in relation to the awesome height of the Grand Gallery and the King's Chamber, which is tied to the Millennial Rule of Christ respectively, suggests bowing down to oppression, hardship, discomfort, and distress. Therefore, like the low passage leading into the Antechamber, this second low passage suggests that these Blood Moons mark a terrible intensifying of sorrow and distress upon the Earth for two years between July 2014 and June 2016. We will discuss the further implications of the Signs in the Heavens marked on my Tribulation Timeline, and the Antechamber's measurements in the last two chapters of this book.

## *Daniel's Seventy Weeks And The Rebirth Of Israel*

Did you ever experience tunnel vision; when your eyes and mind contract onto one fact, and then suddenly link it together with a greater whole? This has happened to me many times as I wrote this book. However, the strongest feeling of tunnel vision that I have *ever* experienced came to me when I had the following revelation in 2006. Having read, and re-read Daniel's Prophecy of the Seventy Weeks countless times, I felt that I had a fairly good understanding of what it meant. But I didn't see one deep aspect of its meaning until prayerfully contemplating it in relation to the Tribulation period. As I sat in deep thought, I finally saw what I had failed to see before! This is the knowledge that **the command to restore and rebuild Jerusalem referred not only to the time of King Artaxerxes in 457 BC, but also to 1948 AD – the year that the modern nation of Israel was formed!** To explain why this is so, let me show you my reasoning. First, let's read the first part of the prophecy together:

> "Know therefore and understand, that from the going forth of the command to restore and build Jerusalem until Messiah the

*Prince, there shall be seven weeks and sixty-two weeks; the street shall be built again, and the wall, even in troublesome times." - Daniel 9:25*

Here Daniel tells us that there would be seven *"weeks"* and sixty-two *"weeks,"* or sixty-nine weeks from the time of the decree to rebuild Jerusalem until *"Messiah the Prince."* The *"weeks"* in Daniel's prophecy are literally called *"sevens."* This means that they not only mean literal seven-day weeks, but *groups of seven years*. In the past, this meant that - after sixty-nine weeks of years, or 483 years had passed - the expected Messiah the Jews had long awaited would appear on the scene. The first 483 years pinpointed by Daniel's prophecy fell between 486 BC, when the Babylonian Exile of the Jews officially ended, and the birth of Christ in 3 BC. The second prophetic period of 483 years partly overlaps the first one. It began in 457 BC with the Persian King Artaxerxes' decree allowing the Jews to return to Israel and rebuild Jerusalem, and ended with the baptism of Christ in 27 AD, just before Christ began His public ministry.

The seventieth week of this prophecy also has two applications – one past, and one future. In the past, it marked the period from 27 AD to 34 AD. These seven years began with Yahshua's public ministry to the Jews. After this, the prophecy says that:

**"And after the sixty-two weeks, Messiah shall be cut off, but not for Himself; And the people of the prince who is to come shall destroy the city and the sanctuary.** *The end of it shall be with a flood, and till the end of the war desolations are determined. 27 Then he shall confirm a covenant with many for one week; but in the middle of the week, he shall bring an end to sacrifice and offering. And on the wing of abominations shall be one who makes desolate, Even until the consummation, which is determined, is poured out on the desolate." - Daniel 9:26-27*

This prophecy refers to Daniel's Seventieth Week, and it is a strange prophecy in that it is purported to be spontaneously speaking about both Christ, and the Antichrist. Most Bible Prophecy teachers think that only the first verses above that are highlighted specifically pertain to Christ, and the rest of this passage is supposed to pertain to the Antichrist. But I believe that this entire passage has already been fulfilled. First, let's look at the portion that pertains to Yahshua, the Anointed One who was likely born in 3 BC, making Him 29 years old in 27 AD. Luke confirms that Yahshua was *around* 30 years old when He began His public ministry in Judea (Luke 3:23) - and if we add the 9 months that Yahshua spent in Miriam's womb - Yahshua was indeed around 30 in 27 AD! Since the need for sacrifices and offerings in the Temple in Jerusalem

## Ch. 8: More Signs of the Day of the Lord's Arrival

were no longer required after Yahshua died on the Cross, this suggests that the Messiah was cut off after one half of a week of years, or 3-1/2 years had passed, and I showed this to be true in Book Two. This pinpoints Yahshua's crucifixion to the day before Passover in 31 AD. **Yahshua's resurrection from the dead then brought the need for "sacrifice and offering" in the Temple in Jerusalem to an end.**

When Yahshua died, the curtain in the Temple was torn in two. This curtain between the Holy and Most Holy Place in the Temple served to remind men that they could have no fellowship with God without blood atonement, and no blood sacrifice could ever fully atone for sin unless it was without sin. Therefore, the torn curtain indicated that the need for animal sacrifice and blood atonement had finally come to an end through the perfect, forever-atoning sacrifice of Christ!

This leads to an interesting theory. Could it be that the *"abomination that makes desolate"* of Daniel's prophecy was placed inside the temple when the Levite priests replaced the torn curtain with a new one? Because, by doing so, they officially ignored, and repudiated God's clear message to them. This message was that mankind now had a clear way to gain a relationship with God through Christ's atoning sacrifice alone! If the Jews had been made to realize what the torn curtain truly signified, they would have recognized that God had done away with any future need for a special priesthood, or temple, and all the Levite priests would have lost their cushy positions of wealth, and authority in the Jewish Community! It is therefore likely that the Jewish Priesthood, in defiance of God, replaced the veil in the Temple, and ignored a powerful sign from God that their priesthood ceased to exist when they killed their Messiah! These Jewish priests were therefore acting in the satanic *spirit* of the Antichrist.

Now, that past seventieth "week" marking 490 years ended in 34 AD - in the proposed year of the stoning of the disciple Stephen, and the first year that Saint Paul may have served as an Apostle. Most prophecy teachers also teach that there will be a second fulfillment of Daniel's Seventieth Week after the Antichrist takes control, and it will not end until the seven-year Tribulation period ends. They infer this despite the fact that Daniel 9:25 emphatically states *"from the going forth of the command to restore and build Jerusalem until Messiah the Prince, there shall be seven weeks and sixty-two weeks."* This means that sixty-nine "weeks" will pass *before* the Messiah comes in the seventieth week.

In addition, I was one of the first people to teach that the "sevens" in Daniel's prophecy have a dual meaning. In fact, it is likely that they refer to a different *complete period* of time, specifically one year, which can be viewed as being measured from Pentecost to Pentecost - also called Shavuot or the *Feast of Weeks*. Biblically, the numbers seven, forty, fifty and seventy all allegorically imply *completion,* or a period of time that completes or fulfills an important part of Yah's Will. Therefore, if one "seven" means one year in Daniel's prophecy, then the sixty-two "weeks" or "sevens" would become sixty-two years, and the seven "weeks" would become seven years. **Daniel's prophecy could therefore be referring to a period of 70 years, as well as 490.**

Due to the previous prophetic dates already disclosed in this chapter (i.e. 2010 AD, 2017 AD and 2018 AD), this interpretation of Daniel's "sevens" has startling implications. In 1948, the modern nation of Israel was formed, and Jerusalem could again be rebuilt. 1948 is therefore the future time when *"the command to restore and build Jerusalem"* was issued! Just as in ancient times, Jerusalem has been rebuilt *"in troublesome times"* (Daniel 9:25). With the threat of Terrorism affecting the whole world, and especially Israel, it should be painfully obvious to all that Daniel's *"troublesome times"* (or time of trouble) has already arrived to some degree, but will not fully erupt until the Tribulation period begins (Daniel 12:1).

As soon as it became apparent that the "sevens" in Daniel's prophecy could also be years counted from Pentecost to Pentecost, I added 62 to 1948. The date thus derived is truly astounding! When applied as years, the 62 years in **Daniel's Seventy Weeks of years yields the date: 2010 AD - (1948 + 62 = 2010)!** This is the same exact year that the Great Pyramid gives as a possible end date before the First Rapture and beginning of the Tribulation! Hallelu-Yah for these signs! Isn't Yahweh an amazing and awesome God? **He is!** Let's further explore the ramifications of this startling revelation. Due to the nature of the Rapture, it is a time when the Messiah will be figuratively cut off *in spirit,* and *"the prince who is to come,"* or the Antichrist will appear on the scene per Daniel 9:26, as quoted above.

The application of Daniel's prophecy to the past tells us that the true Messiah Yahshua's Ministry was 3-1/2 years long, and would end when He was *"cut off,"* or removed from the world scene in 31 AD. In 31 AD, three and a half years after He began His ministry, Yahshua was crucified, died, and rose again. Likewise, the Book of Revelation says the Two Witnesses will appear three and a half years (i.e. 1260 days) after the Tribulation starts, will preach for a given period of time, and then will be miraculously raised from the dead after 3-1/2 days (Revelation 11:3-11). In the past, *"the prince who is to come"* appeared in the form of the Emperor of Imperial Rome, whose legions destroyed Jerusalem in 70 AD -

# Ch. 8: More Signs of the Day of the Lord's Arrival

nearly forty years after Yahshua rose from the dead. In the future, another removal of God's chosen representatives will occur with the First Rapture of the saints, and, later, when Revelation's Two Witnesses are resurrected at the end of the Great Tribulation. This may also be the time when Daniel 9:27 will be fulfilled.

Concurrent with this, a Second Rapture may take place when the Two Witnesses are resurrected from the dead. Others believe that this Second Rapture will happen at the end of the Tribulation. Nonetheless, most believers familiar with Bible Prophecy agree that the Antichrist will seize control of the world by the middle of the Tribulation and will attack Jerusalem sometime after that.

For the many reasons already stated in this book, it appears that the First Rapture may occur *before* or very early during the Great Tribulation, or last half of Daniel's Seventieth Week. At the First Rapture, the Holy Spirit will be temporarily removed from the Earth - along with all God's born-again children. Hence, it is a symbolic time when the Messiah can be seen as "cut off" from the Earth again. In Daniel's prophecy, this cutting off happened *after* the sixty-two weeks had passed. Counted from 1948, this 62nd week coincides with 2010 AD. This suggests that the last week of years will be the Tribulation period, beginning in the 63rd "week" or year - which was 2011. Furthermore, since Yahshua died and rose up in the middle of a week of years in the past, perhaps the First Rapture will happen in the middle of the Tribulation week as well, or around Pentecost in 2014. When the Rapture occurs, we can be certain that the Antichrist will be a prominent world leader, though he will likely not be recognizable as the Antichrist until after the Rapture.

This means that, if seven more "sevens" or years are added to 2010 AD, we arrive at 2017 AD, and ***2017 may be the last year of the Tribulation and the prelude to the Millennial Rule of Christ in 2018.*** Do you see the incredible nature of this divine disclosure? In 2011 - sixty-two years after Israel was re-born - the Tribulation period or Daniel's Seventieth Week begins. Then, sixty-nine years after 1948, the Tribulation may mercifully end with the Second Coming of Christ - if it doesn't end sooner than that. Remember, the middle of 2016 is suggested by the Antechamber in the Pillar of Enoch!

Here is a prophecy written thousands of years ago by a captive prophet named Daniel that verifies the beginning and end dates already singled out for the Tribulation period, as well as the beginning of the seventieth "week" or year - in 2018! The year 2017 may be when Yahshua is slated to return, and 2018 AD may therefore be the beginning year of

Christ's Millennial Rule. Looking back on what was discussed here, the prophetic information hidden in Daniel's Seventieth Week Prophecy can be summarized in two equations:

- 457 BC - (7 X 7) - (62 X 7) + 1 = 27 AD, when Yahshua began His Ministry as the Messiah at the beginning of a prophetic "week" of years.
- (1948 AD + 62 + 7 = 2017 AD as the 69th "week" or year, making 2018 the 70th year, when Yahshua may begin His Millennial rule as King of kings.

There it is - in plain *prophetic* English! **2018 AD falls exactly seventy years after 1948 AD, the year when modern Israel came into existence!** Adding seven "sevens" or years to sixty-two, we have sixty-nine years altogether to add to 1948, and 1948 + 69 = 2017 AD! This clearly suggests that the seven-year Tribulation period began in 2011 AD and will end sometime during (or before) 2017 AD. After this, in 2018 AD, Daniel's Seventieth "Week" will then arrive, and Yahshua may begin His reign as King on Earth for a thousand years!

Another amazing fact about these two applications of Daniel's prophecy is that the sixty-two "weeks" and seven "weeks" must be calculated in the opposite way that they were first applied for the equations to work. This suggests the reversal of history implied by the application of biblical history to the Chanukiah menorah, as shown on page 23! So, in the past, seven "weeks" came first, and then "sixty-two "weeks." In the future, however, sixty-two "weeks" will come first, and then the seven "weeks" or years of the Tribulation. If written a simpler way, the equations to calculate the First and Second Coming of the Messiah are:

- Past: 1 "seven" = 7 years, so (7 + 62) = 69 X 7 = 483 years.
- Future: 1 "seven" = 1 year, so (62 + 7) = 69 X 1 = 69 years.

Whether or not this will be the case, only time will tell. But with the Hallel Psalms, the Signs in the Heavens, and the Great Pyramid as the second, third and fourth witnesses that this is true, I am confident that we will see the Second Coming of Christ by 2017 or 2018, unless God has a more secret plan that He hasn't revealed yet. Although this contradicts the teachings of the mainstream Bible Prophecy teachers, I firmly believe that their interpretation of Tribulation events are skewed because they are ignoring the Witnesses in the Heavens, in the Hallel Psalms, and in the Pillar of Enoch.

# Ch. 8: More Signs of the Day of the Lord's Arrival

## *Seventy Times Seven: the Season of Forgiveness*

There is still another application of Daniel's Seventy Weeks Prophecy that is intimately tied to the birth of Israel as a modern nation in 1948 and the Tribulation period. It appears in one of Yahshua's teachings about forgiveness and judgment:

> *"Then Peter came to Him and said, 'Lord, **how often shall my brother sin against me, and I forgive him?** Up to seven times?' Jesus (Yahshua) said to him, 'I do not say to you, up to seven times, but **up to seventy times seven**. Therefore the kingdom of heaven is like a certain king who wanted to settle accounts with his servants.'" - Matthew 18:21-23*

Many scholars teach that Yahshua's exhortation to forgive our brethren *"seventy times seven"* times means that we must *never cease* forgiving our sinful brothers and sisters in Christ when they sin against us. However, through Daniel's *"seventy times seven,"* we are taught that this is *a specific period of time*. Furthermore, right after telling Peter to forgive his brethren up to *"seventy times seven,"* Yahshua launched right into telling the Parable of the Unmerciful Servant - *with its clear themes of future mercy and judgment* - to the Apostle Peter, and the other disciples who were present. Yahshua therefore pointedly suggests that *"seventy times seven"* does not mean "forever," but refers to a period of forgiveness leading up to a time of *judgment in the future.* Yahshua was therefore telling His disciples that the season for forgiveness would necessarily end after a period of *"seventy times seven."* After this, however, Israel and the world would be divinely judged.

If we view the modern nation of Israel as the "disciple" whom Yahshua thus instructed, it may mean that modern Israel has been given seventy "sevens," or years to repent of her hatred of outsiders, and to show mercy to the Gentile nations surrounding her, and vise versa. In addition, both the nation of Israel, and the Gentiles have been given seventy years beginning in 1948 to repent, and turn fully to Yahweh, and His Son for forgiveness of sin. However, a seven-year season of divine judgment may come in the 63rd year of this modern seventy-year period (in 2011 AD) - when no more mercy will be shown to those who refuse to repent, and be saved. Thus, 2011 to 2017 AD may be the Tribulation period - fulfilling Daniel's Seventieth Week yet again!

In the past, seventy years of mercy were literally shown the Judeans in Christ's time. Seventy-two years passed from the time that Yahshua was born to 70 AD, which was thirty-nine years after Christ's death, and resurrection. In that year, the Romans sacked, and completely destroyed Jerusalem. This suggests that Jerusalem and the Temple were spared from destruction for seventy years from the time of Yahshua's birth. After that, however, Yah's divine protection was removed, and Jerusalem and the Jewish people were judged and found wanting. Then, in 70 AD, Yah's judgment and wrath was horribly meted out against the Jews for tragically rejecting their true Messiah.

If this time period of approximately seventy years between forgiveness and judgment was applicable to the Jews of Christ's time, then it likely applies prophetically to modern Israel. If so, could seventy years be destined to pass from the time of the birth of Modern Israel in 1948, to the judgment of Israel by the Antichrist, and his unholy global army in 2017 AD? Furthermore, could this make 2017 AD the year when Christ will return in Glory to destroy the globalist enemies of the Jews, and Jerusalem? Time will tell!

This contemporary application of Daniel's Seventy Weeks is truly amazing, and serves as an excellent argument for the veracity of the information in this chapter, and previous ones. In addition, this application of Daniel's Seventy Weeks exactly verifies the encoded dates indicated by Psalms 111 through 117 in Chapter Two - suggesting that the Tribulation period will occur between 2011 and 2017 AD. It should therefore serve to give even the hard-core skeptics in this world pause to doubt their rejection of biblical prophecy! If skeptics need even more proof that Daniel's Seventy Weeks prophecy is a valid indicator of when this current world system will end, however, there is still another concrete example.

## *The Reformation and Daniel's Seventy Weeks*

When I found this next application of Daniel's Seventy Weeks, it was just too uncanny to be anything other than an act of God - as was every other application thus far explained. What Yah next showed me is incredible, yet so obvious. It lies in the date when the disgruntled Augustinian monk named Martin Luther nailed his 95 theses to the door of the Castle Church in Wittenberg, Germany. This was on October 31, 1517, and it is considered to be the beginning date of the Protestant Reformation.

A revolution in religious thinking began on that day which eventually led to the formation of many Protestant churches. These churches rejected the Pope in Rome as their spiritual leader, and instead claimed the leadership of the Bible and the Holy Spirit as the best

# Ch. 8: More Signs of the Day of the Lord's Arrival

spiritual guides available to mankind. As a result, the Roman Catholic Church in Europe persecuted Protestants heavily, and many religious reformers died in the bloody efforts of the Catholic Church to wipe out various Protestant, Esoteric or Occult religious groups. Finally, however, many of these people whose spiritual beliefs conflicted with the teachings of the Vatican found a safe haven in the United States of America, where the freedom to practice one's religion of choice is still a constitutional right, although that right is continually being challenged. Nonetheless, although many Protestant Churches still reject the Pope as their spiritual leader and claim that the Bible is sufficient as a means of knowing and following God, some are sadly returning to Rome.

The year 1517 AD, then, is the year that the Protestant Reformation began. When I read this date recently, Yah compelled me to add the number 483 to it. This is the number of years that are found in sixty-nine weeks of years. **The resulting year truly astounded me, for it is none other than 2000 AD!** Also, if we add 490 to 1517, we come to 2007 AD, which is only three years before 2010 - the probable year before the Tribulation period. Since the 1994 Comet bombardment of Jupiter linked to Psalm 94 indicated that 23 years might have to pass before the end would come, it is possible that the final seven years of Daniel's 70 "weeks" is meant to be applied to the years 2011 through 2017 AD.

The year of the Reformation was the moment that led to this present era - when all people in the West have free access to the Word of God, have a right to search the Scriptures individually, and can interpret them as the Holy Spirit leads. As there was in the past, however, a time is coming when this period of religious freedom will abruptly end. This will be when the Antichrist arises, and takes control of the World. *Daniel's Seventy Weeks prophecy seems to point to 2000 AD as the time when religious intolerance and persecution of Jews and Christians will begin to worsen throughout the world, as it surely already has.*

Here again, *we see the opposite to what happened in the past occurring in modern times*. In the past application of Daniel's Seventy Weeks Prophecy, the rebuilding of Jerusalem and its temple led to the coming of the True Christ. Seventy years after that, however, Jerusalem and the temple were again destroyed. In the modern application of this prophecy, the rebuilding of God's spiritual temple that began in 1517 AD, and the rebuilding of Jerusalem that started in 1948 AD could lead to the following events:

- The Rapture(s) of the Church between 2012 and 2018
- The Tribulation period beginning in 2011

- Jerusalem's destruction and Yahshua's return in 2016 or 2017
- The rebuilding of Jerusalem and the first year of the Millennial Reign of Christ in 2017 or 2018

## *Enoch's Prophecy of the Seventy Generations*

There is another prophecy that lends strength to my interpretation of Daniel's Seventy Weeks Prophecy. This is the Prophecy of the Seventy Generations found in the Book of 1 Enoch. There are many powerful prophecies in this book that were lost to the Church for nearly two thousand years. That finally changed at the end of the Eighteenth Century, when the Book of 1 Enoch was discovered to be part of the sacred cannon of Ethiopian Christians. It was then copied and translated into English. The following passage from this book is a prophecy about the timing of the future judgment of the Fallen Angels who sinned by taking human women as wives. After these angels were captured and bound, they were imprisoned in a dark, bottomless pit under the surface of the Earth (See Jude 1:6, Rev 20:1-3) to await judgment:

> *"And the Lord said unto Michael: 'Go, bind Semyaza and his associates who have united themselves with women so as to have defiled themselves with them in all their uncleanness. And when their sons have slain one another, and they have seen the destruction of their beloved ones,* **bind them fast for seventy generations in the valleys of the earth, till the day of their judgement** *and of their consummation, till the judgement that is for ever and ever is consummated. In those days they shall be led off to the abyss of fire: and to the torment and the prison in which they shall be confined for ever.* **And whosoever shall be condemned and destroyed will from thenceforth be bound together with them to the end of all generations.'"** *– 1 Enoch 10:11-15*

The antediluvian patriarch Enoch is attributed with recording this prophecy before his translation. Enoch was the seventh patriarch over the seventh generation of Sethites from Adam. This prophecy tells us that the Fallen Angels are to be bound *"for seventy generations."* Now, this judgment of the Fallen Angels is to occur at *"the end of all generations,"* meaning that there will be no more human generations born after these Fallen Angels are judged. Therefore, the judgment of the angels will occur **after** the Millennial Rule of Christ. This will be during the Great White Throne Judgment, which is just before the New Heaven and New Earth are created (See Rev. 20:11-15). Since 7000 years have been allotted

# Ch. 8: More Signs of the Day of the Lord's Arrival

from the Creation of Adam to the Last Judgment, if we divide it by seventy, it suggests that one human generation is approximately 100 years long. Using my Biblical Chronology on page 722, we see that Enoch was born in 3381 BC. Since the New Creation will come after the Millennial Kingdom possibly ends in 3017 AD, this leaves 6398 years between them, and 6398 divided by 70 equals 91.4. So, just as the patriarchs before the Flood died short of 1000 years, God deemed that all future generations would end shy of 100 years.

Here then, we see another prophetic "seventy times seven" in the number of generations from Enoch to the end of this fallen creation. This beautifully ties Enoch's Seventy Generations to my previous interpretations of Daniel's Seventy Weeks. Both of these periods are times of mercy and judgment, for the Millennial Rule of Christ will also be a time of mercy and judgment that occurs during Enoch's Seventy Generations. ***The prophecies reviewed in this section therefore all speak of the passage of seventy precise periods of time that will be punctuated by God's mercy and forgiveness.*** However, in the final 1000 years, or Millennial Rule of Christ, there will be wars at the beginning and end. This is when God's wrath and judgment will be heavily poured out on the wicked people of this world. Then the Great White Throne Judgment will follow, and the Fallen Angels, the demons, and all the people who followed them will be cast into the Lake of Fire forever.

## *A Prophecy Hidden in the Autumn Feasts of Israel*

In this book, it will be shown that the Antichrist is likely to be a prominent world leader by the end of the year 2010. If so, it makes sense for the First Rapture to occur before or shortly after the close of that year, which may be the final year before the Tribulation period begins. Regarding the timing of the Tribulation, God showed me the way to answer an important question raised earlier about why Yahweh did not end this world system and usher in His Son's Millennial Kingdom beginning in 1999 or 2000 AD, if that was the end of the Ages allotted to mankind.

The first great proof of the timing for the Rapture is the trio of biblically ordained religious holy days that occur in the autumn of every year, which are often called the Autumn Feasts of Israel. As stated previously in various parts of this book series, all the biblically ordained Feasts of Israel have a great deal of prophetic significance. The Spring Feasts of Israel, which include Passover, Firstfruits, the Feast of Unleavened Bread, and Pentecost or Shavuot are historically commemorative of the first Passover, the Exodus, the giving of the Law on Mount Sinai, and the conquest of the Holy Land. They also served as symbolic teaching mechanisms that pointed ahead to the ministry and purpose of Yahshua's First Advent as the Suffering Servant and Lamb of God.

When God chose and consecrated Israel for service, it led to the establishment of an earthly kingdom: the Kingdom of Israel. But even at its greatest moments during the reign of Solomon, the Kingdom of Israel was a dim reflection of the Kingdom of Heaven to come. Thankfully, however, it did lead to Yahshua's First Advent as the Suffering Servant that delivers us from sin and death through the power of the Gospel (i.e. the unleavened bread of life), and the Holy Spirit. In this way, Christians and Messianic Jews alike are all unquestionably members of the Kingdom of Heaven or Kingdom of God. When we enter the Kingdom through faith in Yahshua, His Spirit writes God's Laws in our hearts, which serve as a Tabernacle for the Holy Spirit (Luke 17:20-21; John 3:3-6). This is the Kingdom that Yahshua said was to be found within us. When the Kingdom of God was established on Pentecost, the Spring Feast days were fulfilled through Christ.

Though the Spring Feasts of Israel have been largely fulfilled, the Autumn Feasts of Israel did not find fulfillment during Yahshua's First Advent. These Autumn Feasts begin with Rosh Hashanah (a.k.a. Yom Teruah or the Feast of Trumpets), and pertain to Tabernacle or Temple worship. Rosh Hashanah or the Feast of Trumpets is the Jewish Civil New Year, and it is traditionally kept for two days. During this time, Jews and Messianics celebrate God's Sovereignty and goodness. They also make resolutions for the coming year and promises to God to keep them. After this, between the joyousness of Rosh Hashanah and the communal mourning and sadness of Yom Kippur are the nine Days of Awe or Repentance. During these nine days, people are meant to search their souls for any wrongdoing or inappropriate thoughts. Then they are to seek forgiveness for past wrongs and make amends whenever possible. They are also called to repent of these sins and make a solemn oath to refrain from future sin. This is all done in preparation for the tenth day after the Feast of Trumpets, which is the solemn Day of Atonement - a day set aside solely for fasting and the affliction of the soul in complete remorse and repentance.

As the one day in the Jewish year that God extends corporate forgiveness of sins to all those who repent, the Day of Atonement is a definite allusion to Yahshua's sacrifice on the Cross. However, the sacrifice of two goats and many other animals on the Day of Atonement

## Ch. 8: More Signs of the Day of the Lord's Arrival

only extended forgiveness for a year, while those who believe in Yahshua as the Messiah and the Son of God are *eternally* forgiven for their sins. Nonetheless, though our sins are forgiven from the moment we truly believe in and have faith in Yahshua, we cannot enter fully into fellowship with Him until we are resurrected with incorruptible bodies. This means that **Rosh Hashanah, Yom Kippur, and the week-long Feast of Sukkot are holidays with an as yet unfulfilled future application**. This is because they will not be fulfilled until Yahshua's Second Advent as King of kings and Supreme Priest and Judge.

I did not realize how significant the Autumn Feasts of Israel were, however, until after submitting the first book in this series for publication. But then something happened that changed my perspective on these Feast days forever. On September 20th, 2004, during the nine Days of Awe that were counted between the Feast of Trumpets on September 15th, and Yom Kippur, or the Day of Atonement on September 25th, 2004, I had a startling revelation. Let me explain its incredible implications. As was shown earlier in this book, the real Rosh Hashanah is likely not on the Feast of Trumpets. The true Jewish New Year is on Nissan 1, marking the beginning of the 7th Millennium on April 6th, 2000.

Now, if we count the year beginning on Nissan 1 on April 6th, 2000 as a year-long Feast of Trumpets, the nine years following it would correspond to the Nine Days of Awe. **This means that the tenth year from then beginning on March 16th, 2010 may have marked the beginning of the Yom Kippur year that ends the Church Age and precedes the first year of the Tribulation Period, which would be Nissan 1 in 2011.** It also suggests that the First Rapture may occur sometime in 2014 if it is a Mid-Tribulation event, since 2014 is three and a half years after Nissan 1 in 2011. Now, the Jews believe that all who are to be saved must have their name written in God's Book of Life by the end of Yom Kipper. This suggests that those who are to be included in the Rapture must repent of their sins and accept Yahshua as their Messiah before April 5th, 2011, which will be the end the Yom Kippur Year.

Significantly, 2010 is the year that the prophecies in the Psalms and the Great Pyramid seem to point to as the year before the Tribulation. Therefore, since Jewish Sacred Calendar begins in the Spring, the seven-year Tribulation period might have begun in the Spring of 2011 AD. Since we are not to know the exact day or hour when the Rapture will happen, however, the First Rapture could be anytime before the close of the year 2014 - if the First Rapture is to be Mid-Tribulation, and if the Tribulation did begin in 2011. Intriguingly, the Hallel Psalms, Great

Pyramid Antechamber, and Signs in the Heavens are all indicating that it did begin in 2011!

As discussed in the last chapter, the Signs in the Heavens in the Winter Solstice in 2012 show that this was the time when God's Wrath would truly begin to be poured out on the unrepentant wicked - when dreadful doses of destruction and death began to intensify dramatically all around the world. Since many believers are leaning toward a Pre-Wrath rather than a Pre-Tribulation view of the Rapture, and most only agree on one, this may be in 2014 or early in 2015.

Why this prophetic interpretation makes sense is the fact that the seven-day Feast of Tabernacles or Sukkot occurs five days after Yom Kippur or the Day of Atonement on the 15th of Tishri. This seven-day Jewish harvest festival prophetically depicts the ancient Jewish wedding feast that lasted seven days and alludes to the seven years of the Wedding of the Lamb. Sukkot alludes to the temporary nature of our mortal lives on Earth and shows that we have an eternal home and purpose that has not yet been realized - but that we are looking forward to with great joy and anticipation. This seven-day holiday therefore clearly alludes to the seven years when the saints will reside in Heaven during the Tribulation as well as to the Millennial Rule of Christ that will follow it.

Instead of spending several days feasting in Sukkot booths outdoors, the caught-up Saints will spend several years feasting in a heavenly banquet hall. Then they will return to Earth to rule with Christ during the Millennial Kingdom. This is why the Feast of Tabernacles or Sukkot will be celebrated throughout the Millennial Rule of Christ. Yahshua's thousand-year Kingdom is a temporary prelude to the final inheritance of the righteous in eternity. When eternity is ushered in, all Creation will inherit sinless perfection. At that time, death, evil, and sin will be totally annihilated, and the New Heaven and Earth will be created as our everlasting habitation.

In the Word of Knowledge that I received during the days of Awe in 2004, the five days that fall between Yom Kippur and the beginning of Sukkot can be viewed as marking five more years. These five years can be counted from April 5th, 2011 to April 9th, 2016. If this holds true, the joy that has always been associated with the first day of the week-long Feast of Tabernacles could begin anytime in early in 2016 AD. Indeed, Yahshua's Second Coming could happen a year or more before he actually sets up His Millennium-long Kingdom in order to shorten the time of the Tribulation so that all life will not be extinguished.

# Ch. 8: More Signs of the Day of the Lord's Arrival

Could this be one of the many purposes of the Autumn Feasts of Israel - to show the actual span of years when many End Time prophecies will be fulfilled? Could it be that Yahweh intends to follow the timeline of the Jewish autumn holy days, but is reckoning days as years and months as millenniums from the true beginning of the year in the spring? If so, the Seventh Millennium technically began on April 6th, 2000 with the first of the two Rosh Hashanah years. Furthermore, ten years later, the Yom Kippur year began on March 16th, 2010 and will end on April 5th, 2011. This Yom Kippur year may mark the final year that God will extend His Grace and mercy toward the unrepentant wicked.

After 2010 came to a close via the Jewish Sacred Calendar on April 5th, 2011, is it possible that God will not allow any more names to be written into the Book of Life based on their acceptance of Yahshua's sacrifice for their sins alone? Referring to my research into the heavenly End Time signs that are fully explored in the last chapter of this book, the worst years of the Tribulation period may begin in 2013 - after the December 21st, 2012 Anti-Peace Sign forms in the heavens above the Earth (See Chapter 11).

Based on the idea that there will be two Raptures, here is a summary of what I believe the Autumn Feasts of Israel allude to prophetically - in regard to the time period between the years 2000 and 2018:

- **Two Year-long Days for Rosh Hashanah beginning on Nissan 1 on April 6th, 2000 AD through to Nissan 1 on March 14th 2002** - The Day of Trumpets is traditionally celebrated for two days, so God gave mankind two years to repent of sin, thank God for His goodness, and resolve to become better people in the years ahead.

- **Nine Year-long Days of Awe or Repentance lasting from Nissan 1 on March 14th 2002 until Nissan 1 on April 5th, 2011,** which may be the first day of the first year of the Tribulation period. Fascinatingly, this day is tied to the discovery of the Sethite time marker Easter Island on April 5th, 1722. This remote island is tied to many End Time Signs in the Heavens. The Tribulation likely began between the Lunar Eclipse of December 21st, 2010 and Nissan 1 on April 5th, 2011, as will be shown in the last two chapters of this book. Since these nine years correspond to the Nine Days of Awe, they were meant to be a time of solemn reflection and repentance.

- **One Year-long Day for Yom Kippur or the Day of Atonement beginning Nissan 1 on April 5th, 2011 through to March 24th,**

2012. Note the date correlation here with the discovery of Easter Island. This was **not** an accident! If this is indeed being seen as the Yom Kippur year by God, it was the last one that unbelievers and apostates were covered under God's Grace. It is as if the Book of Life was symbolically closed, and the unrepentant wicked are now being marked for God's Wrath on that day

- **Five Year-long Days between Yom Kippur and Tabernacles beginning on March 24th, 2012 and ending on March 28th, 2017.** These five years account for the five days between Yom Kippur and the Feast of Sukkot or Tabernacles. In the middle of this period, the Second (Mid-Tribulation) Rapture may occur - along with the resurrection of the Two Witnesses. This may be in the winter of 2014, which will be three-and-a-half years after April 5th, 2011.

- **March 28th, 2017 brings us to the Jewish start of the year on Nissan 1 in 2017, which will end on Nissan 1 on March 17th, 2018.** Although this may be the year when the Tribulation will end, the Antechamber in the Great Pyramid suggests it will be around Pentecost in 2016 - about a year earlier than its seven allotted years according to the Hallel Psalms. As Yahshua indicated in Matthew 24:22, the time of the Tribulation must be shortened, or no life will survive it!

If the Tribulation is shortened, Yahshua may triumphantly return to conquer the wicked at the Battle of Armageddon sometime in 2016. Then Yahshua would also complete the last stage of the First Resurrection at that time. In any case, after all the saints return with the King of kings and the Apocalypse is over, Yahshua will likely wait to set up His Millennial Kingdom until sometime in late 2017 to mid 2018. This is based on the Heavenly Signs discussed in the last chapter, with three Full Blood Moons in January and July 2018 and January 2019 marking 2018 as a pivotal year.

This is the Word of Knowledge that Yahshua showed me during the Days of Awe in 2004. I hope many will heed its warning and repent of their sins before it is too late to be included in the Rapture. This revelation shows the timing of End Time events based on the prophetic nature of all the Jewish Feast Days found in the Bible. Since all of these Feast Days were intended to show us the nature and timing of the prophetic events on God's calendar, and I was given this revelation during the actual Days of Awe in 2004, I believe this revelation is a true word from God. Ultimately, however, all those who are reading this must judge the truth of these words for themselves. With that in mind, remember to ask the Holy Spirit to guide all of your decisions, and pray that you will not be led astray by anyone's teachings.

## *The Rapture and the Coming of the Antichrist*

Based on the witness of the Hallel Psalms, Signs in the Heavens, and Great Pyramid Antechamber, the Rapture will be a Mid-Tribulation event. There are many reasons for this that will be presented here and in the last chapter. The most significant reason why the First Rapture will likely occur before the last half of the Tribulation period is found in the strong abiding presence of the Holy Spirit in today's world. Few people are aware of how strong the presence of the Holy Spirit is on the Earth today. When Yahshua poured out His Spirit in abundance after His resurrection, amazing and miraculous things began to happen by, and for the people who lived and prayed "In His Name." This same power can be seen in the churches today that honor and invite the Holy Spirit to move in their congregations. The Holy Spirit is manifested within all true believers in Christ, and is a powerful force for good in the world. Spirit-filled believers in Yahshua are therefore the restraining forces in the world holding Satan back. This is clearly suggested by the following Scripture:

> *"Concerning the coming of our Lord Jesus Christ (Adonai Yahshua the Anointed One) and our being gathered to him, we ask you, brothers, not to become easily unsettled or alarmed by some prophecy, report or letter supposed to have come from us, saying that the day of the Lord has already come. Don't let anyone deceive you in any way,* **for that day will not come until the rebellion** *(i.e. falling away NKJ)* **occurs and the man of lawlessness is revealed, the man doomed to destruction."*

> *"And now* **you know what is holding him back***, so that he may be revealed at the proper time. For the secret power of lawlessness is already at work;* **but the one who now holds it back will continue to do so till he is taken out of the way.** *And then the lawless one will be revealed, whom the Lord Jesus (Adonai Yahshua) will overthrow with the breath of his mouth and destroy by the splendor of his coming." - 2 Thessalonians 2: 1-3, 6-8 (NIV)*

This power that holds evil back and doesn't allow it to take over completely is the Holy Spirit. In the days before the Flood, only Noah and his family were considered righteous and spiritually and genetically pure enough to be saved from destruction. In addition, Noah and his kin were the only people left on the Earth to know the powerful presence of the Holy Spirit in their lives. Though people were rarely baptized with (i.e. indwelled by) the Holy Spirit before the Advent of Christ, the Holy Spirit could fill them, and surely was guiding Noah, Shem, and possibly a few others who boarded the Ark. Furthermore, it was not until these few righteous people were removed from harm's way that the Flood came and devastated the Earth.

Though the situation today is somewhat different than before Noah's Flood, the common factor is that there are still righteous people on the Earth today who do not need to suffer through the Tribulation to get things right with God. Christ's disciples, as temples of the Living God, are a powerful restraining and binding influence against evil. Since they will not willingly allow the Antichrist to take control, they must be removed in order for Him to do so. **Since the Spirit of Yah within believers guarantees their salvation and cannot be removed from them, the believers must leave with the Holy Spirit** (2 Corinthians 1:21-22, 5:5; Ephesians 1:13-14; 2 Timothy 1:13-14). Before they are taken out of the way, however, a mass rebellion against God will come, and then they will know that their deliverance in the Rapture is near.

In the Scripture from 2 Thessalonians, Chapter 2 quoted on page 341, Paul makes it clear that the Day of the Lord won't commence until this rebellion or falling away occurs. Since I believe that the Day of the Lord is already technically underway, we should be able to identify this rebellion. This is easy, once we realize that the actual word translated as "rebellion" or "falling away" in this passage is the Greek word "apostasia," which is equivalent to our English word "apostasy." Paul is therefore telling us to watch out for a great religious falling away or time of *spiritual apostasy*. As the rapid rise of sexual immorality, the New Age Movement and Neo-Paganism in the last fifty years confirms, this great apostasy has not only begun - it is well underway!

Indeed, we are living in what has been dubbed the Post Christian Era, where the moral foundations of the Christian faith have been badly undermined by false religion and the doctrines of Humanism and Evolution. Indeed, these false religions and sciences have all but destroyed the vast majority of people's belief in the events of the Book of Genesis, such as Adam and Eve's initial perfection, their rebellion, the Fall, and the entrance of sin that leads to death. They have also severely weakened many people's belief in the need for repentance, redemption, and salvation through Christ.

Paul then goes on to tell his listeners that believers will know who the *"man of lawlessness"* or Antichrist is because he will come to power before the True Church is taken out of the way. Elsewhere, Scripture indicates that there will be many false Christs even before the Antichrist arrives, and we will see their rise also (Mat. 24:24; Mark 13:22). This has already occurred. Not only can we clearly see the cause of the apostasy such as the New Age, Paganism, Evolution and Humanism, but we can also see the many antichrists that are promulgating it, such as those found among the people who run educational and government bureaucracies throughout the world, and the leaders among the false religions.

In addition to the preceding facts, the Second Epistle to the Thessalonians has even more to say about the Antichrist. In fact, in 2 Thessalonians 2:9-12, Paul calls the Antichrist of antichrists *"the lawless one"* whose works are of Satan. Sometime after the apostasy is well underway, and the Church has been caught-up to attend the Wedding Supper of the Lamb in Heaven, the Antichrist or lawless one will emerge as a leader, and will perform *"all kinds of counterfeit miracles, signs and wonders,"* and many who are perishing will be fooled, and *"will believe the lie."*

After the Antichrist has control of the world, its armies and its resources, Scripture indicates that he will defile *"God's temple."* Since there is presently no temple to Yahweh on the Temple Mount in Jerusalem, this might mean that a third Temple will have to be built there. With the Dome of the Rock under Muslim control on the Temple Mount, however, a full scale "Jihad" or Holy War by the Arabs against Israel would erupt if the Jews ever attempted to build their Temple on the original Temple Mount right now. Nonetheless, the Antichrist will likely have the power to arrange a peace treaty between the Arabs and the Jews. Then, perhaps in exchange for their cooperation in making Jerusalem the home of some peacekeeping political body like the United Nations, the Antichrist will allow the Jews in Israel to build the Third Temple to Yahweh.

## *Identifying the Spirit of the Antichrist*

Since the Antichrist will rise to world prominence in some way before the Rapture occurs and the Tribulation period begins, it would be a blessing if believers knew how to identify the Antichrist from among the potential leaders on the world scene today. In this section, we will explore some of the prophetic and worldly signs that point to the nature and spirit of the Antichrist. Then, in Chapter Ten, we will focus on the identifying marks of the Antichrist who is to be revealed, and who will rise to world leadership. Indeed, several prominent leaders in today's world could be the Antichrist, though he hasn't yet been revealed to the world.

As discussed in the last section of Chapter One, the First and Second Epistles of John tell us that there will be many little antichrists during the Tribulation period. Indeed, many antichrists have already come and gone, such as Alexander the Great, Charlemagne, Napoleon, and Hitler, and many more will follow. Like the Antichrist who will rule over them all, an antichrist *"is the man* (or woman) *who denies that Jesus (Yahshua) is the Christ"* (1 John 2:22). In addition, John tells us that: *"every spirit that does not confess that Jesus Christ has come in the flesh is not of God. And this is the spirit of the Antichrist..."* (1 John 4:3). Finally, John teaches that: *"many deceivers have gone out into the world who do not confess Jesus Christ as coming in the flesh"* (2 John 1:7). This, John proclaims, *"is a deceiver and an antichrist."*

These Scriptures clearly teach that *anyone* who denies that Christ is fully the Son of God, or God made flesh (i.e. Emmanuel, or Elohim With Us), and fully the Son of Man (i.e. Yahshua, or Yah Saves) is an antichrist. Christ came as a mortal man with a fully divine Spirit who physically chose to die for our sins. Anyone who denies this is an antichrist. Like many of the little antichrists in the world today, the Antichrist will proclaim to be God, as well as the final Messiah of many world religions, and he will view all Christians and Jews as his enemies.

Due to the escalation of Muslim Terrorist group efforts to destroy Israel and the Christianized West, especially America, and the Muslim rejection of Yahshua as the Messiah, it should be apparent to everyone that **the extremist jihad tendencies of Muslim Terrorists make them high-profile modern antichrists.** These hate-filled people are antichrists twice over because they deny the preeminence and deity of the true Messiah Yahshua, and they blatantly break His Law to love one another by justifying the killing of innocent people in the name of their god Allah. They are children of hate, and offspring of the Devil who spawned their rejection of the only Son of God and His Father, the God of Love.

What many Christians don't realize, however, is that *all* Muslims are antichrists, not just extremist Muslims. This is because they deny Yahshua's bodily death and resurrection, and His exclusive deity, just as Atheists, Wiccans, Hindus, Buddhists, New Agers, and other Paganistic or satanic religious groups do. Indeed, **anyone in a religion that denies the God of the Bible and the coming of His Son are antichrists.** Muslims may also be unwittingly denying the God of the Bible because they do not know that their god Allah was worshipped in ancient times as a Moon

## Ch. 8: More Signs of the Day of the Lord's Arrival    Page 345

god, not the Creator God! Therefore, Allah is not the God of the Bible, even though many Muslims, Christians, and Jews mistakenly think he is!

Nonetheless, though there are many people who are antichrists, Yahshua called His disciples to *"love your enemies, bless those who curse you, do good to those who hate you, and pray for those who spitefully use you and persecute you"* (Matthew 5:44). To love their enemies, believers are called to obey the Ten Commandments and Yahshua's Commandment to *"love your neighbor as yourself"* (Matt. 22:39). Whenever they are given an opportunity, believers are also called to tell unsaved people about the Good News of Yahshua the Messiah and the Kingdom of God that He rules.

The sad truth, however, is that believers are failing miserably at reaching lost souls at this crucial hour because of their complacency and feeling of powerlessness in the face of mounting opposition to Christianity and its public expression. They are also being brainwashed into thinking that religious tolerance is the same as the social tolerance of sins like homosexuality. These, however, are not the same! Though Yahweh wants us to be tolerant of other people's beliefs, He calls us to share our own faith with them in the hope that they will see the error of their own spiritual ideologies. Furthermore, God calls all of His children to abstain from sin, and to flee from those who practice sin in all its forms. Lack of spiritual action among believers is therefore fueling the international push to establish the one world religion that the Antichrist will one day mercilessly force all people to accept.

Paganism and the spread of Islam are not just on the rise today. They are epidemics that are rapidly spreading everywhere, and no one seems immune from their invasive affects! As this Anti-Christian epidemic grows, the antichrists infected by it are joining together in an effort to unite the world under one banner and to eradicate the teachings of Judaism and Christianity, whose strong moral codes are seen as a threat to world peace. As a consequence, many modern Muslims, Pagans, New Agers are vehemently opposed to, and hateful of all things Jewish and Christian, especially Yahshua's exclusive place in the Trinity as Adonai Yahweh - the Son of God made flesh and only Way of Salvation.

Another group of antichrists in the world today have embraced the Merovingian heresy, which claims Yahshua never died on the Cross, but escaped death and fathered children in order to usher in His Kingdom at another time in history. They also deny that Yahshua is the Lamb of God who takes away the sins of the world. Among these antichrists are modern Freemasons. Having lost all connection to Christianity, many Freemasons are occultists, and some believe that

Christ's literal bloodline has been preserved in the royal bloodlines of Europe and the United Kingdom. In addition, they believe that a mortal Messiah is coming who will succeed where Christ failed, and he will arise from among existing royal lines that claim to be descended from Christ.

In addition to the Scriptures already quoted that identify the satanic spirit of the Antichrist that is already clearly at work in today's world, there are other clues in the Bible that can help us identify the Antichrist who will be a world leader before Christ's Second Coming. The nature and identity of this Antichrist of antichrists is hinted at in the Book of Daniel and other books of the Bible. The startling meanings of these prophecies are discussed in detail in Chapter Ten, where we will take a second look at the Merovingian heresy. In addition, we will examine the Bible prophecies that point to this heresy, and give clues that seem to identify the Antichrist who may arise out of it.

## *Will A New Temple Be Built On The Last Day?*

In Book Two we discussed a prophecy in the Book of Zechariah that pertained to the rebuilding of the Second Temple built by King Zerubbabel. In the Book of Revelation, symbolism tied directly to Zechariah's prophecy that the Temple to Yahweh would be rebuilt during Zerubbabel's reign was used. These are references to the two olive trees, and the two lampstands in both prophecies that are tied to the ministry of the Two Witnesses (Zechariah 4:2-14; Rev. 11:1-4). Could this be a prophetic indication that a third Temple will indeed be built during the Tribulation? The following Scripture speaks of a measuring rod used by an architect to measure and mark the layout for a proposed building:

> *"Then I was given a reed like a measuring rod. And the angel stood, saying,* **"Rise and measure the temple of God, the altar, and those who worship there... And I will give power to my two witnesses,** *and they will prophesy one thousand two hundred and sixty days, clothed in sackcloth."* **These are the two olive trees and the two lampstands standing before the God of the earth."** *- Revelation 11:1-4*

This passage strongly suggests that a new Temple to Yahweh will be built in the future. But does this passage pertain to events that will occur during the Great Tribulation as most Prophecy teachers suggest, or does it look forward to the Temple that Ezekiel described, which will stand in Jerusalem during the Millennial Rule of Christ? Many Prophecy teachers suppose that the Third Temple will be built in Jerusalem after

## Ch. 8: More Signs of the Day of the Lord's Arrival

the Palestinians have signed a false peace treaty or covenant with Israel through the mediation of the Antichrist (Dan. 9:27). Furthermore, they believe that the world at large will be living in relative peace, despite the Rapture and the pouring out of the fierce Wrath of God in the first of the Trumpet Judgments. They also believe that this treaty will allow the Jews to build a new temple on the Temple Mount in Jerusalem - perhaps even right next to the Al-Aqsa Mosque. This is all supposed because it was prophesied that - once he is inhabited by the spirit of Satan - the Antichrist will claim to be God inside "God's Temple", and subsequently demand to be worshipped as God:

*"He will oppose and will exalt himself over everything that is called God or is worshiped, so that **he sets himself up in God's temple, proclaiming himself to be God.**" - 2 Thessalonians 2:4*

Analyzing this Scripture, it says that the Antichrist *"will exalt himself over everything that is called God or is worshiped"*. From this passage, it should be clear that the Antichrist will oppose **all** of the various deities and religious feasts that are honored by humanity, and will claim that he is the only god that people may worship. Thus the One World Religion will not be the hodge-podge of different religions that the Ecumenical Movement is now forming, but a religion that demands everyone's total allegiance to the Antichrist on pain of death. This passage also says that the Antichrist will set himself up as a god in the temple of God. This passage does seem to suggest that a physical temple will be built during the Great Tribulation so that this prophecy can be fulfilled. However, Yahshua suggested, and the Apostle Paul said that the bodies of born-again believers now serve as living stones in the Temple of God (Luke 17:21; 1 Corinth. 3:16-17, 6:19-20). Therefore, this passage may mean that the Antichrist will declare that his god literally dwells within him, as he is that god, just as so many New Age spiritual paths such as the Unity School of Christianity, Rosicrucianism, Wicca and Hinduism believe.

Daniel 9:27 also says that: *"But in the middle of the week, He shall bring an end to sacrifice and offering. And on the wing of abominations shall be one who makes desolate, even until the consummation, which is determined, is poured out on the desolate."*

This Scripture speaks of a "wing of abominations" being set up that brings desolation on those who are desolate, likely due to false teaching. Before continuing, please note that the word translated as "wing" can also mean "edge" or "corner" - as in the edge or corner of **a piece of fabric**. This event is also echoed in the New Testament, where Yahshua speaks of the "abomination" in the "holy place":

> *"Therefore when you see the 'abomination of desolation,' spoken of by Daniel the prophet, standing in the holy place **(whoever reads, let him understand)**, 16 then let those who are in Judea flee to the mountains..."* - Matthew 24:15-16

Though many people believed that US President Obama fulfilled this prophecy by visiting the site of the new One World Trade Center in New York City and signing one of its top construction beams in 2012, this makes absolutely no sense because a signature or construction beam is not an abomination, and a commercial building is not a "holy place" by any stretch of the imagination. Furthermore, I firmly believe that this part of Daniel's prophecy was fulfilled in the First Century by Yahshua. The reason I believe that this fulfillment is overlooked is because the abomination was hidden from view **inside** the temple, and it had to do with the beautifully embroidered heavy curtain or veil that hung or "stood" on a set of four pillars between the Holy Place and Most Holy Place. Let me explain.

At the time of Yahshua's Crucifixion, we are told that this curtain was torn in two from top to bottom (Matthew 27:51; Luke 23:45). This event signified that the wall of separation between God and mankind due to sin had just been permanently eradicated by Yahshua's shed blood, at least for those who accept His sacrifice as our Great High Priest (Hebrews 9:11-12). But the Scriptures surrounding this event also make it abundantly clear that the Jewish priests refused to accept Yahshua as the Messiah, and they did not wish to acknowledge the miracles, including the torn veil standing in the Holy Place, or the sightings of those who had risen from the dead right after Yahshua arose three days later. This is because they did not want to lose their positions of importance, which Yahshua had just ripped away from them and the misled Jews that followed them, and given to the people who love and follow Yahshua.

Indeed, all believers are viewed as a royal priesthood in the order of Melchizedek, with Yahshua being the High Priest over them all. But since the Jewish priests refused to accept this, they would have done their best to hide any reminder of the truth. This means that the torn veil in the temple was very likely replaced. In fact, it would be highly unusual if it had not been, since it was likely seen as damaged and desecrated in the eyes of the chief priests, who refused to believe that Yahshua was the Son of God. Any new veil that these doubting priests would have placed in the Temple could therefore have been described as a "wing" of abomination to God that served to defile the Temple by hiding God's good and perfect Will that was supposed to be revealed within it.

## Ch. 8: More Signs of the Day of the Lord's Arrival    Page 349

If this veil was replaced, and I firmly believe that it was, then **Daniel's prophecy of the Abomination of Desolation may have already been fulfilled**, and may not need another fulfillment. But since prophecies can have a dual fulfillment, there is a possibility that the Antichrist may desecrate a future Temple sanctuary - one that might be built during the Great Tribulation. However, this seems highly unlikely due to the terrible judgments that God will meting out on the wicked at this time that will cause absolute chaos to ensue all over the world, such as a possible Pole Shift and Crustal Displacement and a massive, worldwide earthquake. These will come in fulfillment of the Sixth Seal Judgment, followed by the celestial bombardments of the First through Fourth Trumpets that will cause death and destruction all across the globe. I therefore find it highly unlikely that the Jews will be able to focus on building a new temple when the rest of the world is being torn apart by God!

What I feel is more likely is that the Jews may decisively win a major war against their enemies, will regain control of the Temple Mount from the Kingdom of Jordan, and will begin to prepare the foundation for the rebuilding of the temple. But this work will be interrupted because the Rapture or Catching Away will take place, along with the Sudden Destruction spoken of by the Apostle Paul:

> *"For when they say, 'Peace and safety!' then sudden destruction comes upon them, as labor pains upon a pregnant woman. And they shall not escape." - 1 Thessalonians 5:3*

This Sudden Destruction will likely be the Sixth Seal Judgment, which will effectively cause any kind of construction efforts everywhere in the world to be halted. At this time, it is also likely that the Antichrist will rise to power in the ensuing chaos. After that, it is certain that the Antichrist will attack Israel. In fact, the Antichrist may attack both Israel, and Israel's current biggest ally: the United States of America, which will be extremely weakened and vulnerable after the Rapture, when over a third of America's population will likely be taken in the Rapture.

I will show evidence for the startling claim that America will be reckoned as, and will suffer the same fate as the modern state of Israel in the next chapter, which is devoted to the United States and Israel in prophecy. This chapter is followed by a chapter focusing on the United Kingdom and Europe in prophecy, while Mexico, Central and South America will be dealt with in the last chapter.

# Chapter 9: The United States and Israel in Prophecy

> *"The LORD (Yahweh) lives who brought up the children of Israel from **the land of the north** and from all the lands where He had driven them. 'For I will bring them back into their land which I gave to their fathers.'"* - Jeremiah 16:15

The above prophecy refers to the dispersal of the Israelites from the southern Kingdom of Judah in Israel into the land of Babylon - which was northeast of Israel in Mesopotamia. This land now belongs to the countries of Iran and Iraq. The Israelites were dispersed into many other nations to the far north of them as well, most notably throughout Europe, Great Britain, and America. After the Diaspora of all the Israelites, those who returned to Israel from *"the land of the north"* came from Babylon after their captivity there. The Israelites from the Northern Kingdom of Israel that were carried away by the Assyrians, however, never returned to Israel, and became known as the Ten Lost Tribes of Israel. This prophecy was therefore only partly fulfilled in the far past. Nonetheless, as a prophecy, it will one day be fulfilled completely. In fact, it already has had a dual fulfillment with the formation of modern Israel, and also may have a triple application.

After World War II, the Jews returned to Israel from virtually every nation on Earth, especially Russia, Europe, and America – *all lands that are to the far north of Israel*. The specific identity of the land of the north in this chapter's opening prophecy was Babylon. Sometime after the Babylonians conquered Judah and carried away many Israelite captives to Babylonia, the Jews - and a handful of Levites and Benjamites - were allowed to return to their native homeland. Likewise, with the formation of modern Israel, the Jews in the countries of Iran, Iraq, and the rest of the Mid-East came flocking to their new homeland in great numbers in order to escape constant religious persecution, and the Jews in Europe followed.

The Caucasian and Mongol populations of Europe, Russia, Asia, North America, and Australia descended from Noah's son Japheth, who was likely a fair-skinned Caucasian in appearance. However, Japheth's hair was most likely black or dark brown, since seventy percent of the world's population has black or dark brunette hair shades. Shem also had Caucasian type features, though it is likely that he was middle brown in skin tone, and also had black or dark brown hair like most Semitic people do today. Incidentally, there are many people-groups on the Earth today that are Semites - not just the Jews! These include the people of modern day Turkey, Armenia, and Iran. Due to their similarities, it is likely that the descendents of Japheth and Shem intermarried and shared land regions together, just as Noah prophesied they would:

> "So Noah awoke from his wine, and knew what his younger son had done to him. Then he said: 'Cursed be Canaan; a servant of servants he shall be to his brethren.' And he said: 'Blessed be the LORD (Yahweh), the God of Shem, and may Canaan be his servant. **May God enlarge Japheth, and may he dwell in the tents of Shem; and may Canaan be his servant.**'" - Genesis 9:24-27

The above prophecy applies to Israel in general, and not the Jews (i.e. Judah) specifically; it also pertains to *hidden Israel*. That is, it applies to the Israel that arose from ancient Israelite migrations *all around the world* - even before the Diaspora of the Jews in ancient Roman times. This prophecy was uttered after an incident that involved Ham taking advantage of Noah, who was drunk on wine, and had passed out naked in his tent. As explained in my book "The Language of God in History", Ham disrespectfully stole Noah's clothes, including his special cloak of authority. Meanwhile Shem and Japheth respectfully covered their unconscious father's nakedness. They did so by walking backward to cover Noah with a cloak, thereby not viewing his nakedness at all (Genesis 9:21-23). After Noah arose, he uttered the preceding prophecy as a curse in judgment of Ham through his son Canaan.

Later, Canaan settled in the land that would one day be promised to Abraham and his descendents as an everlasting inheritance. As a result, in the process of conquering the Promised Land, the Israelites did turn the Canaanites who survived into servants - just as Noah had said. Incidentally, Ham is considered to be the ancestor of the black peoples - though he may not himself have been very dark-skinned. More specifically, Ham's son Cush is singled out as the ancestor of the Cushites - who were the direct ancestors of the Nubians and Ethiopians.

Ancient and modern demographics show that the other part of Noah's prophecy came true as well, since the descendents of Japheth spread out into the same lands assigned to Shem and they intermingled.

## Chapter 9: The United States and Israel in Prophecy

This thereby created the many varieties of Caucasians on Earth today. Asian people, due to their lighter skins, can also be classified as Caucasians, though their facial features suggest that they remained isolated from the descendents of Shem and did not intermarry with them as Japheth's descendents who wandered into Europe and the northern Mediterranean did.

According to Bill Cooper in his book "After the Flood," Ham's sons Canaan and Cush would have sired children with darker skin pigmentation due to the affects of living in a much sunnier and drier climate than Northern Mesopotamia. Nearer to the Earth's equator, dark skin is an advantageous adaptation, and allows for greater fertility in women.

Though the Jews are a distinct people group on the Earth today, the Ten Lost Tribes are mixed into many nations - including Russia and China. Evidence of this exists in China in the form of the desert-dried Takia Makan mummies. These well-preserved mummies are of people who had reddish blonde hair and typical European features. The people of southern Russia, Persia, and India can also be classified as Caucasians rather than Asians due to their decidedly Caucasian style facial features. Is it possible that, despite the great variation among Caucasian people groups, their similarities may be the result of an intermingling of the indigenous people of Europe and the Middle East with Israel's Ten Lost Tribes?

As shown in Book Three, "The Language of God in History," there is evidence that the Israelites did likely migrate all over Europe after being displaced by their Assyrian and Babylonian conquerors. Later, their Jewish counterparts followed in their footsteps after Rome destroyed Jerusalem. In addition to destroying their holy city, the Romans took many Jews as slaves, and some of them were subsequently freed to make their own fortunes around Europe and the Mediterranean.

If the Anglo-Saxon people groups in Europe, the British Commonwealth, and the Americas are the descendents of the Ten Lost Tribes of Israel, then the above prophecy concerning the ingathering of God's people from the lands to the north of Israel will be miraculously fulfilled a third time during the Millennial Rule of Christ. This will occur when Yahshua gathers all the faithful Lost Israelites from every nation at the end of the Great Tribulation. After this, Yahshua will give them a glorious new home surrounding the holy city of Jerusalem. It is in this city where Yahshua, as the rightful King of kings, will re-establish the Throne of David and the literal Kingdom of God on Earth.

## *The Lie of British Israelism: Spiritual Israel is Global!*

Though many British Israelites believe David's Throne has survived in exile in Great Britain and will be taken over by Christ when He returns, the Bible makes it clear that Christ will rule from Jerusalem and not from anywhere in the British Isles. We will examine the facts and folklore surrounding the claim that those in the British Royalty are descended from Judah in Chapter Ten. For now, however, remember that whether or not a person is descended from the Israelites will not win them a place in God's Kingdom!

The only way to inherit eternal rewards from God is to become a spiritual Israelite who worships God the Father and His Son in truth. Furthermore, it is this born-again spiritual Israel that will come out of the United States, Great Britain, Europe, the Middle East and *many other corners of the globe*, and settle in the new nation of Israel under the Millennial Rule of Christ. Many believing Jews will also come out of these nations and settle in the new Kingdom of Israel.

In order to hold all its new citizens, this future kingdom that will be ruled over by Yahshua will be much larger than the nation of Israel is today. In fact, the new Israel will likely cover as much or more land than it did during the reigns of King David and Solomon. During Christ's Millennial Rule, Israel's borders will likely stretch from the Euphrates River through Damascus in the northwest, then all along the Dead Sea and the Sinai in the south up to the borders of Egypt (1 Kings 4:21; Ezekiel 47:13-21). This means that Israel will reclaim territory from Egypt, Lebanon, Syria, and part of Jordan - in addition to counting the Arabs of those nations as adopted Israelites.

Due to Noah's curse against Ham's son Canaan, some may wonder if the Negroid peoples descended from the Hamites are excluded from Yah's Covenant promises made to Abraham and Israel. The answer is emphatically "No, they are *not* excluded!" First of all, every person on this planet is covered under the Adamic Covenant that Yahweh made with Adam and Eve when they sinned. In addition, since most black skinned people probably descended from Ham through his son Cush, they are not directly related to Canaan. Indeed, there are even several groups of black Jews in Africa that have blood ties to the Jewish people of Israel.

Besides the Ethiopian Jews who claim descent from King Solomon, an amazing tribe of Black Africans in South Africa claims to be descended from the Jews. They are called the Lemba. Though African style tribal rituals and customs heavily influence their culture, the Lemba

## Chapter 9: The United States and Israel in Prophecy

have many distinctly Jewish customs. Recently, these black people were proven to *have an exclusive Y chromosome that is unique to the Jews*. This means that the Lemba tribe is a *fellow inheritor* of Yah's Covenant promises to King David of Judah, and there may be others like them in Africa!

In Book Three of this book series, it is stressed that the concept of race is erroneous, since all people descended from the same man and woman: Adam and Eve. Furthermore, all people groups, no matter how different they appear physically, are genetically descended from Noah. This is proven by the fact that all modern people groups can successfully intermarry, bear healthy offspring, eat the same foods, use the same medicines, and die from the same causes. My focus on the migration of the Israelites is therefore not in any way meant to be an attempt to glorify the people of Europe, Great Britain, and America as physically or intellectually superior. On the contrary, the only advantage Western countries have had over other people groups have come to them through God's *material* Covenant blessings on Israel through Abraham, and later, through the *material* blessings bestowed on the descendents of the patriarch Joseph.

The Israelites were to be greatly blessed by Yah, and - as Abraham's descendents - they were meant to share their wealth and resources with the world:

*"...I will multiply your descendants as the stars of the heaven and as the sand... on the seashore....* **In your seed all the nations of the earth shall be blessed***, because you have obeyed My voice." - Gen. 22:17-18*

*"And I will make your descendants multiply as the stars of heaven; I will give to your descendants all these lands;* **and in your seed all the nations of the earth shall be blessed***; because Abraham obeyed My voice and kept... My commandments..." - Gen. 26:4-5*

In addition to the material blessings God granted to Abraham, his son Isaac and the descendents of the Israelites, Israel was to bless the whole world through Yahshua the Messiah, who is a descendent of Abraham and Jacob/Israel. However, both before and after Yahshua was born, Israelite descendents have greatly blessed the world with their spiritual knowledge and great scientific and medical discoveries. In addition, regardless of genetic descent, all people are adopted into Yah's Family as children of God when they become true believers in Christ!

*"And if you are Christ's, then you are Abraham's seed, and heirs according to the promise." - Galatians 3:29*

In addition to the Lemba, there is a small black Jewish population living in Ethiopia that calls themselves "Beta Israel," meaning "House of Israel." They are also called the "Falashas," though they consider this term meaning "outsider" to be a derogatory one. In several successive waves between 1984 and 1991, thousands of these Black African Jews migrated to Israel after suffering from persecution in their own country.

The Beta Israel may be descended from King Solomon's union with the Black African Queen of Sheba. It is said that their love affair produced a son who became the King in his mother's land. This king was Menelik 1, and he ruled in Ethiopia after the death of his mother Makeda, Queen of Sheba. When Menelik assumed the throne, he was given the title of "Emperor, and King of Kings of Ethiopia." He then founded the Solomonic Dynasty that ruled Ethiopia in an almost unbroken line for close to three thousand years. This long-lived dynasty ended with the fall of Emperor Haile Selassie in 1974. If it is true that these Jews are descended from Menelik 1, and Menelik was Solomon's son, then these Jews are of the Tribe of Judah and the lineage of David! As a result, they may have a more legitimate claim to the Throne of Judah than any other Jew or European alive today.

## *Joseph, The Fruitful Bough - The Material Blessing*

Nonetheless, as shown in Book Three, the people of Europe, Great Britain, its Commonwealth nations, and America do seem to have inherited the material, earthy blessings God promised to Israel - *especially* the Tribe of Joseph as *"a fruitful bough"* (Genesis 49:22-26). If these people groups do include descendents of the Tribes of Joseph mingled with Dan, *they have inherited an extraordinary purpose in End Times events*. Certain prophecies indicate that, though Israel will serve to bless *all* nations, the sons of Joseph would be *special blessings to the whole world*. In addition, the Tribe of Dan would serve a dual purpose, both as the tribe whose migratory routes through Europe are the most easily traced, and as the tribe that will give birth to the Antichrist. In a moment, we will examine Scriptures and history supporting these ideas.

Few people know how to identify or discern the role of the United States in Biblical prophecy. This is very odd, however, since the modern country that has the friendliest relations with Israel - and with the Jews who live in that country - is the United States. In the past fifty years since Israel became a nation, millions of Jews left many parts of the world to resettle in Israel. After thousands of years of persecution in Europe and Russia, however, far more Jews left these regions to resettle in Israel than from America. This is primarily because the Jews in America are relatively rich and well treated, whereas in Europe and Russia they were terribly persecuted for centuries. This persecution occurred most notably during World War II - when millions of Jews died horribly in Nazi concentration camps, and also afterward - in Stalin's death camps.

Now that there is a nation called Israel on the world scene, it has become apparent to many students of Biblical prophecy that the end of the world as we know it is near. Just how near was anyone's guess though until recently - when many keys to deciphering the biblical prophecies of the future came to light such as unlocking the secrets of the Gospel in the Stars, the Great Pyramid, and the Great Sphinx. In this chapter, we will focus on written prophecies and use them to show specific ways that Israel and the United States are connected. Lastly, I will show how the ancient native cultures of Mexico, Central and South America also tie into Biblical history and End Time prophecies.

## *The United States as Ephraim*

Throughout this book series, it has been suggested that the United States could be allegorically tied to Israel. If nothing else, it has certainly reaped many of the blessings that were promised to the Gentile nations through the patriarch Joseph. However, before revealing what I have discovered in reference to the United States in prophecy, let me make it clear that I do not believe any nation on Earth today has lived up to the ideals that Yahweh set forth for Israel to follow. Though the United States was once "One Nation Under God," this is no longer true. In fact, America is swiftly going the Way of Cain and Babylon, allowing people to follow after false gods of their own making, and worshipping created things instead of the Almighty God who created all things. For this reason, no nation on Earth today is truly representative of the Kingdom of God that Ancient Israel was supposed to become, but never achieved.

Nonetheless, America was founded on Christian principles, and many of the founding fathers of this nation were professing Christians who lived godly lives. In fact, despite the influence of Freemasonry in America and throughout the world, America is the only modern nation that has traditionally denied Satan's earthly rule and placed its well being in the hands of the one true God. That is why its currency still proclaims the national motto, "In God We Trust," its Pledge of Allegiance contains the line "One Nation under God," and its most popular national songs contain phrases like: "God shed His grace on thee," "And this be our motto: 'In God is our trust,'" and "God Bless America, my home, sweet home!"

To show how America fits into the biblical promises God made to Israel, we need to start at the beginning, when Yahweh made certain promises to the Tribes of Israel that Jacob delivered on his deathbed. At that time, Jacob prophetically indicated what would befall all of his son's descendents on the Last Day (Genesis 49:1-28). As shown earlier, we are already in the Last Day, and this chapter was written to tell the world that the United States is part of Israel in prophecy, and its citizens likely have an important part to play in upcoming End Time events.

Let's begin this study by clearing up a common misconception about the Tribal affiliation of the United States with Israel. Contrary to popular belief, the USA is not affiliated with Manasseh, but with Ephraim! Ephraim was the patriarch Joseph's younger son, but he inherited the birthright of the firstborn over Manasseh. As such, Ephraim became the equivalent of the Tribe of Joseph. In this chapter, we will explore many compelling facts that support the hypothesis that the United States is to be reckoned as Ephraim in prophecy. Here is the first major clue. It is found in the Gospel of John:

> *"Therefore Jesus no longer walked openly among the Jews,* **but went from there into the country near the wilderness, to a city called Ephraim,** *and there remained with His disciples."* - John 11:54

Now, though this passage does not appear at first glance to be a prophecy, remember that virtually nothing happens by accident in the Bible, and almost everything has some allegorical significance. Taking this into consideration, note what this passage is actually saying. First of all, this event chronologically happened just *before* Yahshua entered Jerusalem to celebrate the Passover, or Last Supper with His disciples. Now remember that, during the events of the Last Supper, Yahshua vowed that He would not eat the Passover again until He celebrated it with those same disciples in His Millennial Kingdom (Luke 22:15-16). This is a *very* significant detail - as will be proven in a moment.

Based on these facts, John 11:54 is telling us that - prior to His triumphal entry into Jerusalem - **Yahshua physically hid from the Jews in a "country near the wilderness,"** where He remained with His *disciples*. Now, as will be pointed out again in an upcoming prophecy, the United States is a country that was once a wilderness, and - even today with over 300 million people, it is still filled with vast stretches of unspoiled wilderness. Furthermore, unlike most other once Christian nations, the

USA is still predominantly populated with people who claim to be Yahshua's disciples - a disciple being someone who obediently follows the Way that Yahshua preached, which is the Path to Salvation detailed in the Gospels. Finally, John 11:54 states that this country near the wilderness is a city or civilized place called *Ephraim*.

As has already been shown throughout this book series, Ephraim allegorically represents one half of the True Church, which is also one of the Two Houses of Israel that will be spiritually united in marriage to Christ. Therefore, this city called Ephraim can allegorically and literally describe the True Church in America! Next, take note that this city called Ephraim is where Yahshua was said to reside until He ate the Passover, at which time He explicitly said He would not eat it again until His Millennial Rule, when the Kingdom of God is *physically* and spiritually established on Earth.

Now, the collective Church, or body of all born-again believers in America is currently the biggest and most faithful of all the churches on this planet today, and Yahshua dwells in the hearts of many Americans. Despite the rampant immorality plaguing this nation, a large segment of its Christian population is resisting the international push toward tolerance of sins like homosexuality and unhindered abortion. Is it therefore possible that America is the place near the wilderness called Ephraim that Yahshua's Spirit is residing in until Yahshua's return? Furthermore, since this book shows that we are living in the Last Day and are on the threshold of the Tribulation period, isn't it possible that the Ephraim referred to in this passage is an allegory for the True Church in the United States, which is representative of the True Church throughout the world that contains people of every nation? I believe it is!

Nonetheless, in and of itself, this passage in the Gospel of John is not conclusive proof that America is going to be reckoned in prophecy as Ephraim. More proof is required, and so this chapter is full of many convincing proofs that *America is to be reckoned as Ephraim*. In fact, the many amazing details about to be disclosed here are an excellent indication that the preceding assumptions are correct, and should be heeded by all!

Let's look at the first significant fact that points to the identity of the United States as Ephraim. The United States shares a more special bond with Israel than any other nation on Earth today - not as its conqueror, but as its *protector*. On a much less apparent level, Great Britain, which helped establish the modern nation of Israel, also currently shares this role with the United States. However, America is clearly the Gentile champion of Israel on the current world military scene.

Now, if the United States is viewed as Ephraim, and the modern nation of Israel is viewed as Judah, the following prophecy from the Book of Isaiah confirms a truth about these ancient Tribes of Israel that is true again today in that they maintain friendly relations with each other - just as they did in the far past:

> "He will set up a banner for the nations, and will assemble the outcasts of Israel, and gather together the dispersed of Judah from the four corners of the earth. Also the envy of Ephraim shall depart, and the adversaries of Judah shall be cut off; **Ephraim shall not envy Judah, and Judah shall not harass Ephraim.**" - Isaiah 11:12-13

Though this prophecy refers directly to the Millennial Rule of Christ, it has already been partially fulfilled. Today in Israel, for example, *"the outcasts of Israel"* and *"the dispersed of Judah"* are gathered together, just as this prophecy proclaimed would happen. The nation of Israel is therefore a banner to all other nations – a sign that Yahweh *is* God, and that He has guaranteed that all the prophecies He made to His chosen people will be fulfilled. This prophecy also makes it clear that Ephraim and Judah will be allied during the End Times. But where are the literal Tribes of Judah and Ephraim today? Though there are various theories about where these two Tribes are, the following views are given from my own unique perspective as a born-again disciple of Christ living in the Unites States of America.

Significantly, three nations - the United States, Great Britain and Israel - are currently staunch allies, even though some citizens of the United States and Great Britain are vehemently against their respective nation's support of modern Israel. Furthermore, there is ample evidence supporting the notion that the current monarchy of Great Britain is seated on the literal, *material* Throne of Judah, and the modern-day Israelites who are scattered throughout the world represent the nations connected to the national promises made to the people of Israel and Judah. Nonetheless, I have found in my research that the United States appears to be tied irrevocably to Israel - *not only on a material level, but also on a deeply spiritual level.* Let me explain why.

In the book, "The American Prophecies," author Michael Evans shows that the political policies of the Unites States in regard to Israel - and her mortal enemies, the Arabs - are triggering supernaturally given blessings and curses in America. Using God's Word in the Bible, Evans shows that any nation that supports Israel will share in her blessings, but anyone that supports Israel's enemies will suffer dire consequences. Mr. Evans therefore believes - as I do - that the United States has been, and

# Chapter 9: The United States and Israel in Prophecy

will be severely affected for the worse whenever it turns against Israel as a nation.

Sadly, even though the United States still appears to support Israel, it has sent weapons and financial aid to the Palestinians in Gaza, as well as to Saudi Arabia, Egypt, Syria, Iraq, and Afghanistan - all nations that are Israel's sworn enemies. In addition, the USA is supporting the division of Israel in order to give the Palestinians their own sovereign lands within modern Israel's border. However, by doing so, they have attempted to divide the birthright of Jacob, which is against God's Will.

Since America is playing the harlot in its policies toward Israel, many more curses on the land and people of the United States can only be expected - in addition to the disastrous storms, diseases, droughts, fires and foreign attacks that have already plagued this nation. If the United States does not stop interfering with Israel's ability to protect itself, and continues to pander to the Islamic nations, then even more terrible curses are surely going to be in store for Americans.

Interestingly, there is much allegorical support for the idea that the United States and Israel are prophetically linked. This can be shown through the fact that America shares many numerical connections with Israel, and also has a large Jewish population that rivals the one in Israel. In fact, America is home to over 5.4 Million Jews - close to the number of Jews in Israel, which is currently a little over 6 Million. Therefore, *the USA may share Israel's fate in prophecy.* In the following sections of this chapter, we will explore the numerical and Zodiacal connections of the United States with ancient and modern Israel.

## *America's Connection to the Number Thirteen*

Since I am a citizen of the United States, I have always wondered if this country appears in prophecy. Though most prophecy teachers ominously say it does not, my knowledge of the Gospel in the Stars has shown me that **the numbers associated with the formation of the United States have clear allegorical associations with the Star Gospel as well as Israel.** For example, the original *thirteen colonies* of the United States suggest a connection with the Twelve Tribes of Israel - one of which is considered evil. Israel was the father of twelve sons, just as Yahshua was the leader of twelve apostles. Both of these groups contained thirteen members, as do their antithesis, which is a witch's coven. Likewise, the Sun rules over the twelve houses of the Zodiac to form another group of thirteen members.

In every one of these groups of twelve centered on one leader mentioned in the Bible, however, one of the twelve is a traitor to the cause of righteousness. In the case of the patriarch Israel, it was the Tribe that sprang from Dan. In the case of Yahshua, it was Judas Iscariot. In the case of the Zodiac, it is the sign of Scorpio, and in the case of the Solar System, it was likely the destroyed planet Tiamat where the asteroid belt is now located. For more about Tiamat, see Books One and Three.

Another peculiar feature of the thirteenth member in each group is that they always suffer some sort of destruction that results in great good. In each case, the most good seems to come about through the thirteenth member elected to replace the evil member in each group. In the case of the Twelve Apostles, Paul was chosen by Yahshua to replace Judas Iscariot. In the case of the Zodiac, Aquila the Eagle may be the constellation that was divinely elected to replace the scorpion and serpent symbols in Scorpio. In the case of our Solar System, the asteroid belt is the replacement for Tiamat. In the case of the Twelve Tribes, the Book of Revelation indicates that Manasseh will be reckoned as the Tribe of Dan, while Ephraim took Joseph/Manasseh's birthright, and will be reckoned as Joseph (Rev. 7:4-8). This means that - as the nation tied to Manasseh - Great Britain is the modern representative of the Tribe of Dan, while Ephraim/America represents Joseph and is destined to replace Dan in eternity.

Examining biblical facts can substantiate the preceding claim. For example, after the Tribe of Dan sinned, God reckoned Joseph's younger son Ephraim as a thirteenth Tribe. Likewise, the United States was a nation that began with thirteen colonies. Thirteen is therefore a number that can be associated with the half-Tribe of Joseph called Ephraim that now represents the United States. Discerning this fact has led me to believe that **the United States, whose national symbol is the eagle, and who is reckoned as the Tribe of Ephraim in prophecy, will one day replace the serpent sign of Scorpio representing the Tribe of Dan.**

Following this pattern, it suggests that one of the original thirteen colonies was the symbolic "Sun" of America. At the time of the Revolutionary War, the colonies were united through the Continental Congress - whose Parliament met in Philadelphia, Pennsylvania at the time. Intriguingly, the city of Philadelphia is named after the Church of Brotherly Love in the Book of Revelation. Of the Seven Churches that are addressed in Revelation, the poor but faithful Church of Philadelphia is offered the greatest praise and rewards of any other in that Yahshua promises that they will be spared from *"the time of testing,"* which many scholars see as a reference to the Great Tribulation.

# Chapter 9: The United States and Israel in Prophecy  Page 363

Is it significant that a city named for the Church of Philadelphia figured prominently in United States history? Does it suggest that the United States is the predominant home of those who allegorically belong to that poor but loving church? Or does it simply mean that the founding fathers of the USA *hoped* that it would be? Only God knows the answers to these questions. But one thing is certain. The United States still has more professing Christian citizens than any other modern nation on Earth.

Nonetheless, as shown in the section of this book called "The Open Door and the Rapture," the Church of Philadelphia can be seen as a representation of the worldwide church of all born-again believers who actively profess their faith in Christ and continually apply His commandments to their everyday lives. In today's world of moral relativism and humanism, anyone who faithfully follows Christ's mandates in their lives will be persecuted in some way, *just as Christ promised they would be* (Matthew 5:10-12, John 15:20, 2 Cor. 4:8-10).

In the past, Philadelphia, Pennsylvania was the symbolic "Sun" of America, though it was later to be replaced by Washington, D.C. Taken from land in Maryland and Virginia, Washington D.C. isn't a State, but a city without any State affiliation. This was done so that no State would have pre-eminence over any other. Washington D.C. is the political hub around which all fifty States revolve, especially the forty-eight continental States.

If the United States is prophetically tied to Israel, this also suggests that a State that was formed from one of the original thirteen colonies was going to prove to be a source of evil and treachery. Could it be Massachusetts, where the Salem witch trials occurred? Or could it be Virginia, the State that first introduced slavery to America? Or perhaps it is Georgia, the State that once was a penal colony for criminals (much like Australia was for England). Or could it be New York - and New York City in particular? Though the other States mentioned could have been construed as villains in America's past, none of them seems particularly treacherous or rebellious now. New York City, however, is another matter!

Let's review some salient facts about New York City that make it the prime candidate to be the symbolic Judas Iscariot or Tribe of Dan in America. First of all, New York City is still the undisputed financial hub of the world - even *after* the loss of the World Trade Center. In fact, the One World Trade Center, which was built to replace the Twin Towers, is now standing with a beam signed by President Obama near its top. That beams contains words from the Bible that actually condemn America with a curse taken from Isaiah 9:10, which Rabbi Jonathan Cahn focused on in his book "The Harbinger" long before this beam was signed!

This is because, as Cahn noted in his book, that same verse of condemnation has been used by numerous Politicians in reference to America's pride in its efforts to rebuild its power and strength after the 2001 Terrorist Attack in New York City. Rather than humbling themselves and calling on all Americans to humble themselves before God to avoid more Divine Judgment, however, America's Politicians are encouraging the nation's citizens to shake their fists in defiance against God, with the prideful words of Isaiah that brought a curse to Israel highlighting their folly:

*"The Lord sent a word against Jacob, and it has fallen on Israel. 9 All the people will know - Ephraim and the inhabitant of Samaria - Who say in pride and arrogance of heart: 10 "The bricks have fallen down, but we will rebuild with hewn stones; The sycamores are cut down, But we will replace them with cedars." 11 Therefore the Lord shall set up The adversaries of Rezin against him, and spur his enemies on, 12 The Syrians before and the Philistines behind; And they shall devour Israel with an open mouth." - Isaiah 9:9-12*

Interestingly, this same Scripture not only shows why God is condemning America to Divine Judgment, but also proves my point that America is being reckoned as Ephraim. In fact, Ephraim is specifically being addressed in Isaiah 9:9!

Secondly, New York City is home to the United Nations, a political entity that may have much to do with the Antichrist's future take over of world financial and political arenas. Ominously, the United Nations appears to have a vendetta against the tiny nation of Israel, citing it more for Human Rights Violations more than any other nation on Earth. Due to these factors, New York seems to be the most likely current candidate as the evil usurper among the original thirteen colonies. If it is New York, I pray that God will show mercy on the many people of genuine faith in Christ who live there. Though only God knows if any of the original colonies will turn against his brother colonies during the Tribulation, the prophetic nature of the Star Gospel shows that **a State originating from one of the original thirteen colonies could be destined to destruction.**

Nonetheless, as Rabbi Jonathan Cahn showed in his book, not only New York, but all of America has been set up for Judgment by God by its own traitorous, treacherous leaders! But God has shown me that a remnant in America will prevail against the evil politicians and wicked corporate leaders trying to destroy them, as I will show in this chapter.

## The Mazzaroth's Connection to the USA and Israel

There is another intriguing way to determine where the United States figures in prophecy - a way that no one to my knowledge has ever noted before, but that God has shown me. It stems from the fact that the continental United States consisted of *forty-eight States* from 1912 until 1959, when Alaska and Hawaii were added. Up until that time, **the number of States was the same as the number of Levite cities in Israel and constellations in the Ancient Mazzaroth!** Could this be just a coincidence, or a highly significant clue into determining the destiny of the United States? Let's examine this clue to see what it may be trying to tell us.

Since Alaska and Hawaii are not physically part of the mainland appropriated by the United States, and do not share a common border with the other States in the Union, they are not part of the *continental* United States. There are therefore still only forty-eight States that make up the mainland United States. Could it be that these forty-eight States are meant to represent the forty-eight Levite cities, and constellations of the ancient Zodiac? One day, God gave me the answer to that question!

As I was praying to God for help in finishing this book series one day, I had an amazing vision of the United States, and its role in history. In this vision, I saw a bright blue sky where cool, cloudy Alaska suddenly appeared superimposed over a big silver crescent, and the islands of hot, sunny Hawaii were superimposed over a big yellow Sun shape. In the next instant, the forty-eight continental States were spread across the heavens beneath the Alaska Moon and Hawaii Sun. When the vision ended, it became clear to me that Alaska was being depicted as an allegorical representation of the Moon, while Hawaii was an allegorical representation of the Sun. Meanwhile, the forty-eight other States stretched out across the sky could only mean one thing: they must represent the forty-eight constellations of the ancient Zodiac!

This vision clearly showed me that **the fifty States represent the forty-eight constellations, and the Sun and the Moon that pass through the Zodiac every year!** Could this be why 50 white stars superimposed over an azure background represents every State on the US Flag? Uncannily, while researching the history of the US Flag for this book, I discovered that the thirteen stars on the original flag were intended to represent *a new constellation!*

# The Language of God in Prophecy

## America - A Symbol for the Zodiac, and Ancient Israel

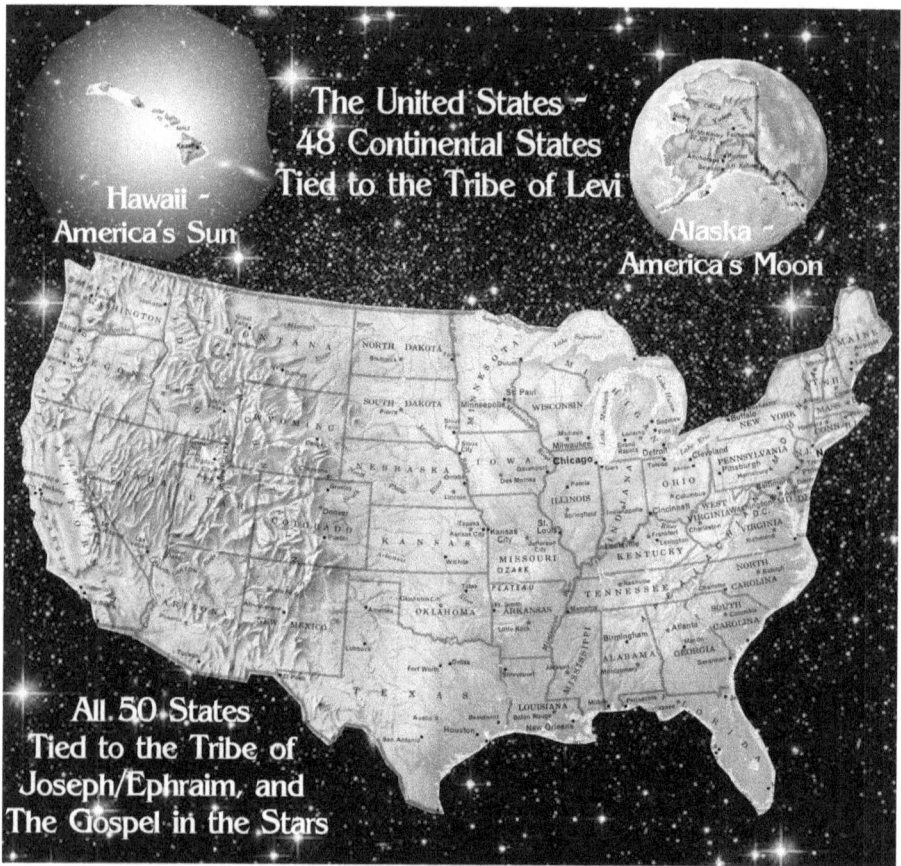

This means that what I saw in a vision was anticipated and symbolized in the US Flag *from the beginning,* as seen in very first flag of the United States pictured on the next page, which is attributed to Betsy Ross. This suggests that, coupled with the US Flag, my vision is Yahweh's way of showing all Americans how important the USA is to Him as a nation and people under God. Incidentally, the original US Flag had thirteen stars on an azure background and thirteen stripes: seven red, and six white. The stripes stand for the thirteen original colonies, which became the first thirteen States in the Union. Interestingly, the total number of the stripes in one color, 7 and 6, also indicate the year that America declared its independence from the British Empire, which was in 1776.

# Chapter 9: The United States and Israel in Prophecy

This idea that the United States is a symbolic representation of the Mazzaroth and of *literal and spiritual Israel* is also substantiated by the dream that the patriarch Joseph had when he was a boy (Genesis 37:9-11). In that dream vision,

"Betsy Ross" Style US Flag from 1777-1795

Joseph was shown that the people in his life who were signified by the Sun, Moon, and stars would one day bow down to him. Like Joseph's Israelite family, the United States represents every nation on Earth, and one day every nation will bow their heads to Christ, including the United States! But on another prophetic level, *Joseph's dream vision suggests that the United States is truly viewed as a literal part of Israel in prophecy by Yahweh, not just a spiritual part of it.*

The association of the numbers thirteen and forty-eight with the United States are prophetically significant in several other ways. First of all, the USA's connection to the number thirteen signifies that it is symbolically connected to the Sun transiting the Twelve Houses of the Zodiac, as well as to Jacob and the Twelve Tribes of Israel, and Christ and the twelve apostles. Secondly, **America's connection to the number forty-eight indicates that it shares a relationship with the Tribe of Levi and the Gospel in the Stars.**

Allegorically, the Tribe of Levi was *the spiritual center of the nation of Israel,* and - alongside the Bible and Yahshua our Messiah - the Gospel in the Stars should be a spiritual guide for the world. Since the number 48 is connected to the 48 Levite cities of refuge in Ancient Israel and the primeval Gospel in the Stars, which recognized 48 constellations, it is another indicator that America is meant to be a great source of spiritual light in this dark world. Based on the number of professing Christians in the U.S. population, and the many missionaries that U.S. congregations have sent into the world, the USA is unquestionably the statistical world leader in both numbers of missionaries and churches.

Through Moses and Aaron, the Tribe of Levi inherited the priesthood. This suggests that, besides being considered a literal part of Israel, the United States is also being reckoned as the Tribe of Levi! This means that America is being called to give more spiritual light to the world than any other nation today outside of the nation of Israel. It also means that the United States is a modern spiritual "navel of the world," just as Giza in Egypt is the physical and spiritual "navel of the world." As my friend Janice Moore pointed out to me, a navel is a scar left when a baby is severed from its mother by the cutting of the umbilical cord. It is therefore a potent symbol for the Fall of mankind, for this was when Adam and Eve were severed from their personal relationship with Yah and His Spirit. In addition, a navel is a symbol of our need for spiritual and physical redemption from sin and death. All professing Christians therefore serve to remind unredeemed sinners that they are damned without Christ. As the greatest bastion of Christianity in today's world, America is a symbolic navel of remembrance among the nations.

## *Dire Consequences for Apostasy in the USA*

If the United States is supposed to be a spiritual light to all other modern nations, it follows that the failure of this country to give that spiritual light will cause the entire nation to suffer Yah's Wrath and Judgment. Though the United States still has more Christians per capita than any other nation, the government of the United States is corrupt, and many apostate American politicians and judges frequently attack and ignore the Constitution upon which this great nation was founded. Besides the Constitutional freedoms given to American citizens including the freedom of speech and religion, the people of the USA once swore to be "One Nation Under God" - whose national and spiritual motto is "In God We Trust." But the increasing failure of the American people to honor these creeds and be a godly spiritual light in this dark world has led to great misfortune for the nation. Clear signs that the U.S. Government and many apostate or atheistic Americans are treading upon dangerous ground due to their immorality can be seen in many aspects of American society today, especially in the:

- Media promotion that homosexuality is acceptable, and should not only be tolerated, but embraced as an acceptable lifestyle

- Murder, rebellion, violence, sexual promiscuity, and pornography seen as entertainment rather than sin

- Increasing usage of mind-altering, health-damaging recreational and prescription drugs

- Legalization of abortion and euthanasia

## Chapter 9: The United States and Israel in Prophecy

- Rapid escalation of violent crimes, murders, and all kinds of theft, including electronic and identity theft
- Active promotion of Evolutionary Theory, which relegates the account of Creation in Genesis into the realm of myth
- Increasingly open hostility toward Christian morality and values in our schools and the media
- Deterioration of our legal system, which no longer supports biblical moral law, but promotes "tolerance" of sin

These immoral activities are a great affront to Yahweh, yet many Americans condone these sins by their indifference or refusal to show any outrage. Can true believers in Yah doubt that America's major national falling away from biblical morality has reaped, and will continue to reap dire spiritual consequences for American citizens? After 2001, how could anyone doubt that the material greed and moral degeneration of the USA and the rest of the world would inevitably lead to Yah's Judgment and Wrath? Indeed, though Europe and Asia had already fallen into many of the sins now becoming rampant in America (i.e. sexual immorality, promiscuity, political corruption, and apostasy) God did not begin to pour out His wrath on them immediately. Instead, Yah waited until increasing numbers of Americans followed Europe and Asia's lead by falling deeply into sin.

Currently, the world's crazy weather patterns are one of the most obvious signs that we are in the End Times. In fact, so-called "natural disasters" are increasing exponentially all over the world. In 2003 and 2004, statistics showed that there was a massive increase not only in the number, but also in the destructive power of storms, floods, earthquakes and other natural disasters *all over the world*. For example, in 2004, many regions in the United States suffered from tremendous flooding from unnaturally heavy rains in early spring that year, which continued throughout the summer. Even ordinarily dry States such as California and Nevada suffered from severe and devastating flash floods and mud slides. Later in 2004, there was unusual damage in California from drought and severe brush fires. Though common to the ecology of the Southwest, these brush fires are burning increasingly out of control. For example, brush fires burned over vast areas in Nevada, New Mexico, Arizona, and Colorado for an unnaturally long period of time in 2005. Then, in October 2007, fires ravaged Southern California, *destroying 1500 homes and burning 500,000 acres.*

In 2005 and every year since, the USA has experienced one weather extreme to another. Instead of too much rain in most regions, many States suffer from severe drought and heat. Besides drought, summer daytime temperatures continue to soar to extremely high levels. In fact, severe droughts oddly coupled with severe flooding inundated the entire globe in 2011, 2012, and 2013, and this trend shows no signs of abating. If fact, these extreme weather patterns seem to be growing worse with each passing year.

In 2005, five highly destructive hurricanes also racked the Southern coastal areas of the United States. There has never been a year in this nation's recorded history when five such storms hit the southern US coast in one season, or when two of the hurricanes were rated Category Five - the most powerful level of hurricane in destructive force. One of these was Hurricane Katrina, which flooded the city of New Orleans, caused billions of dollars in damage to property, and killed thousands of Americans.

The totally erratic weather patterns of 2005 have continued since then around the world, with record highs, lows, floods, tornadoes, hail and wind storms and droughts everywhere. This extreme weather appears to substantiate the dire scientific warnings about volatile weather due to Global Warming, and volatile weather certainly could have much to do with the plagues prophesied about in the Book of Revelation.

Environmental changes attributed to Global Warming include increased severity of storms, severe melting of polar ice caps and loss of coastal lands, massive droughts and floods, and massive species extinctions. Since these environmental plagues are connected to the birth pangs of the Tribulation, it seems likely that they are reflections of God's judgment on the wicked, and God's impatience with the Church for not continually witnessing of His soon coming to destroy the wicked people and nations that are perishing.

Now, considering that there were numerous reports that the summer of 2011 was the hottest and driest summer on record in the United States, and that many other parts of the world were hit with record heat waves that killed numerous people in 2013 and the three years prior, don't you think that many trees and shrubs - and huge swatches of grain crops and grasslands in the wilderness areas all over the world - have perished over the last few summers as a result? Furthermore, could it be that global Media outlets have underplayed it all, and we just weren't told sufficiently about the devastation it caused to become alarmed?

Records also prove that earthquakes have been increasing all over the world. For example, of the most devastating earthquakes of all time, *dozens have been in the last century alone.* One example of this was the earthquake-generated tsunami that hit the coast of Indonesia in 2005, killing over 150,000 indigenous people, and many international tourists. Then, in October 2005 a terrible earthquake hit Pakistan, killing over 80,000 people and leaving 3.3 million homeless. Another earthquake hit inland China in May 2008, killing over 80,000 and leaving 4.8 million homeless.

Then there were two massive earthquakes in early 2010 and early 2011 that should have awakened the Apostate Churches from their sinful slumber. However, they seem to have gone by almost unnoticed. The first of these severe mega quakes was the massive 8.8 Earthquake in Concepción, Chile on February 27th, 2010. This mega-earthquake not only moved the city of Concepción ten feet to the west, but also moved many other regions of South America out of their places.

In addition, this quake may have moved the Earth's axis by far more than the reported millionths of a degree, and this, coupled with increased Solar activity, may be why the world's climate patterns seem to have drastically changed since then. What made us miss it is the lack of honest reports about the amount of the Pole Shift, as well as the lack of reports about the widespread fear and terror this event likely caused in all of South America. In fact, many members of the elite may have been frightened enough by the Chile quake to seek shelter in their underground bunkers for a few days - just in case that earthquake was followed by another, even bigger one.

Then there was the 9.0 Earthquake off of Japan on March 11th, 2011 that moved that island nation about 9 feet westward out of its place, drowned tens of thousands of people, destroyed many thousands of homes, businesses, boats, ships and cars, and caused several nuclear reactors to sink into the sea. There are even reports that this earthquake also caused a slight Pole Shift, adding to the amount of shift cause by the Concepción quake a year earlier. In addition, there is the radiation poisoning of ocean water that is ongoing from the Fukushima Daiichi Nuclear Power Plant disaster that occurred because of the Japan 2011 mega quake. This destroyed nuclear reactor is still leaking high levels of radiation into the waters of the Pacific Ocean, and this could behind some of the mass fish deaths in recent years that have occurred in the bodies of water connecting to the Pacific Ocean. Due to their severity and frequency, these disasters all seem to be signs that **God is punishing the world for its apostasy, not just America.**

This trend has continued, with terrible flash floods, storms, hail, tornadoes and hurricanes severely affecting the residents in many regions of the United States. Of these disasters, Hurricane Sandy was one of the worst. In late October of 2012, Sandy hit America's East Coast with violent winds, massive flooding, some reported deaths, and the swift destruction of billions of dollars in property. In fact, some of this storm's worst affects targeted America's financial heart in Manhattan and nearby outlying areas.

The destructive force of Hurricane Sandy was so strong that the people of New York and New Jersey are still trying to recover from it today, in late 2013. For this reason, I view it as another wake up call for Americans that is somewhat similar to the 2001 destruction of the World Trade Center. Though there wasn't a huge loss of life, many thousands of Americans lost almost every material possession that they had due to the destruction Hurricane Sandy caused. How, then, can anyone miss that this event was another clear Judgment by God against the materialism and carnality of many Americans?

When the World Trade Center in New York was destroyed during the Terrorist attack on September 11, 2001, there is no doubt that Yahweh's anger was being shown over the excessive materialism of most Americans, which exceeds any other nation on Earth. *Since many Americans are greedy and selfish, they are no longer the spiritual lights of the world that they were called to be, and so they have lost Yah's divine protection!*

Eerily, the destruction of the World Trade Center echoes the destruction of the Tower of Babel. Like the ancient city of Babylon, New York City - and Manhattan in particular - is a world financial hub and the heart of America's business and economic world. As such, many multi-billion dollar international businesses and industries are headquartered there. In fact, the Twin Towers were viewed as the international heart of Capitalism by many in the financial world. Therefore, when Yahweh allowed those two gigantic pillar-like towers dedicated to "Mammon" to collapse in a terrifying avalanche of fire, smoke, bodies, and debris, Yah was sending a clear spiritual warning signal to America - and to the world!

Through this dire warning, some Americans were reminded of Christian values that too many of them had previously forgotten, or ignored. A few made some much-needed changes in the way they conducted their lives and businesses. However, the true implications of this national disaster were not really made apparent to many Americans, and too many of them refuse to believe or are woefully unaware that God is judging America and the world, and holding people accountable for their sins. That is likely why immorality is rampant, the world's economy partly collapsed in 2008, and America is being threatened by another Great Depression.

The godly values that all Americans need to uphold in order for God's blessings to be restored can partly be found in two of Yahshua's admonitions against money and wealth. The first is that *"the love of money is a root of all kinds of evil"* (1 Timothy 6:10). The second is *"store up for yourselves treasures in heaven, where moth and rust do not destroy, and where thieves do not break in and steal. For where your treasure is, there your heart will be also"* (Matthew 6:20-21).

Our focus in this life is not to be on the acquisition of wealth or material pleasures. Instead, we are to care for our needs and the needs of our families and communities in a spirit of compassion, forgiveness, brotherhood, and love. Unfortunately, however, most Americans are slaves to pleasure and leisure activities, use credit cards too much, and are very wasteful - buying far more than can be used in a given period - whether it is food, clothing, possessions or entertainment. Perhaps that is why the US economy is failing. It is most likely a form of Judgment.

Two other values that are being severely undermined in America (as in Europe) are the institutions of marriage and the family. The escalating push in the media and Hollywood for the full public acceptance of promiscuity, homosexual marriage and sexually deviant lifestyles - if allowed to go unchecked - could result in tragic moral consequences in other areas. For example, it has become a prerequisite in our schools to teach that homosexuality is perfectly acceptable! But has everyone truly considered the possible consequences of such thinking, or how offensive it is to God?

Despite the charm and good-humor that some homosexuals in the entertainment industry convey, we must not lose sight of the fact that they are blatantly unrepentant sinners. In fact, *all* abnormal sexual behaviors are considered hideous crimes in the eyes of God. Therefore, the truth is that legalizing homosexual unions and making sodomy socially acceptable could also lead to the acceptance and legalization of other sinful sexual behaviors such as polygamy, pedophilia, partner swapping, and incest! Do you doubt this possibility? Think again!

Even if we do not commit sinful acts or openly support them, our meek acceptance of them is as much a sin as actually performing these ungodly acts ourselves. Therefore, because America and the world refuses to turn away from their self-centered, immoral, and materialistic lifestyles, **the Divine Judgment and destruction of the United States and the world will continue to get worse, and will not be lifted until Christ returns to set up His Millennial Kingdom on Earth.** The dire consequences of the moral falling away occurring in the USA today will be explained in this chapter.

## America's Connection to Jubilees and the Great Pyramid

The connection of the United States of America with numbers that show its spiritual significance doesn't end with the numbers 13 and 48, for the numbers 50, 51 and 52 also figure in the "spiritual accounting" of the nation. In the Bible, the number 50 is a highly significant one. For example, there are fifty days between the Firstfruits Offering of Passover Week and the Feast of Weeks or Pentecost. Every fifty years was also to be considered a Jubilee or Great Sabbath Year, which was a very special year of rest for the land and the people of ancient Israel. On Jubilees, prisoners, slaves, and bond servants had to be set free, debts had to be forgiven, and the land had to be given rest from mining and farming.

With the selfish mindset that most Americans have today, could you imagine the chaos if the United States tried to give its citizens a Jubilee year every fifty years? Banks and creditors would be flocking to other shores rather than forgive the debts of all the indebted consumers in this country! Furthermore, instead of rejoicing and repenting, many freed prisoners would be out in force raping, murdering, and stealing without remorse, farmers and miners would be begging for government subsidies to tide them over for the year of inactivity, and virtually every servant would be demanding a year's paid vacation!

Nonetheless, 50 is a significant number in the United States in that America once gave its fifty States an unprecedented degree of freedom and responsibility for their own welfare and livelihood - more than any other nation ever did. In fact, the freedom that was once associated with a Jubilee year was upheld every year due to the faithful guidance of the Constitution of the United States. Ever since it achieved independence from Great Britain, America had become synonymous with freedom. The idea of the Jubilee Year was therefore more a part of American history than it ever was in any other nation throughout time.

The numbers 51 and 52 also have a connection to America. For example, though there are fifty States in the Union, the city of Washington D.C. is essentially separate from the fifty States - thereby changing the "count" of America's States to 51, not 50. Then there is Puerto Rico, the only major territory of the United States. Puerto Rico is not technically a territory, however. Since Guam and the Philippines became independent nations, Puerto Rico is the one remaining

## Chapter 9: The United States and Israel in Prophecy        Page 375

*commonwealth nation* of the United States. As such, Puerto Rican citizens automatically receive United States citizenship, open immigration and other privileges that people from smaller territories and foreign nations do not. **Puerto Rico is therefore the "not quite 52nd member" of the United States.**

There is a startling mathematical and prophetic connection in these facts. This can be seen in the unique angle of the Great Pyramid, or Pillar of Enoch's four sides. **Each side of the Pillar of Enoch is 51 degrees, 51 minutes, or not quite 52 degrees in slope**, and the Pillar of Enoch is the only pyramid ever built with this unique side slope angle. In addition to this, the sacred calendar henge called Stonehenge was built at 51' 51" north latitude (See Book Three) and there are a total of 48 ceiling slabs in the King's and Queen's Chambers and Grand Gallery of the Great Pyramid, which was once the number of ancient constellations and continental states in the USA.

Through these remarkable correlations, it can be clearly seen that the numbers 48 through 52 connect the United States with the Mazzaroth or Gospel in the Stars, the Pillar of Enoch, Stonehenge, and the religious and sociopolitical organization of Ancient Israel.

## Front and Back Sides of the Great Seal of the United States

Indeed - as can be seen in the preceding illustration and on the back of every US one dollar bill - a pyramid with 13 layers of masonry suggestive of the Pillar of Enoch is shown on the back side of the Great Seal of the United States.

## *The US Great Seal's Connection to the Ecuador Artifacts*

Mysteriously, the 13-tiered pyramid on the Great Seal of the United States has an identical parallel in a puzzling artifact that was discovered in Ecuador, a nation at the top of South America, and directly on the Earth's Equator. This ancient artifact was found with several other related objects that are connected not only to Sacred Astronomy, but to the messianic constellation Orion, which signifies Yahshua as a conquering King. They were found and cataloged by the German researcher Klaus Dona before being put on display in one of Berlin's many museums. This section will present these artifacts in relation to the symbols of the United States, and the possibility that the origin of the symbolism in the US Great Seal is far older, and far holier than anyone could possibly have imagined.

In Book Three: "The Language of God in History," it is explained how Noah may have started the Pre-Columbian civilizations in Mexico, Central and South America. However, I did not find out about this artifact until after that book was published! When I finally did, I immediately connected it to the research I had done in Book Three about the Sacred Astronomy of the Sethites, and the patriarch Noah's knowledge of the Star Gospel. In the photograph of the artifact on the page 378, I have superimposed a photo of the Helix Nebula in the celestial region of Aquarius the Water-Bearer, the sign that depicts Noah's deliverance in the Flood, and Yahshua's giving of the Holy Spirit.

Fascinatingly, besides alluding to Aquarius through this eye-like nebula, this artifact was found within the Aquarius Meridian of the Earth, as shown in the maps in Book Three, and the much smaller map shown on page 586 in this book. This map shows how the Zodiacal regions of the heavens were envisioned to be connected to the Earth by those who built the Great Pyramid at Giza, which was built where it is to reflect this connection. God first introduced this to me when I was working on Book Three, and it is carefully explored in that book.

The Helix Nebula almost exactly matches the oddly-shaped blue eye depicted in the apex of the Ecuador pyramid artifact, which in turn greatly resembles the pyramid on the US Great Seal. The Great Seal's eye has been traditionally referred to as the All-Seeing Eye of God, though in today's wicked world, it is being touted as a Satanically-inspired, evil Illuminati symbol. In my opinion, however, this painting of something good into something evil is clearly a case of demonic tampering and religious syncretism. The holiness of this artifact can be further seen by the inscription on its bottom, which appears next to an inlay of five gold

## Chapter 9: The United States and Israel in Prophecy

dots that depict the principle stars in Orion's Belt and sword. There, four Proto-Hebrew letters were deciphered by a master German linguist to read: "The Son of the Creator Comes"!

Since there is only one true Son of the Creator, and His Name is Yahshua, the markings on this artifact tie the 13-tiered pyramid on the US Great Seal to the Giza Pyramids that depict Orion's Belt, as well as to the Pyramid prophecy in Isaiah 19:19-20. But how this pyramid found its way onto the US Great Seal before it was discovered in Ecuador is a profound mystery. Though the temptation is there to immediately connect this symbol to the Occult leanings of the Illuminati or the Freemasons, there is a strong possibility that both the symbols on the Great Seal of the United States, and the artifacts found in Ecuador are far older and far holier than either the Illuminati or the Freemasons which both have Occult connections.

Based on the research I did in Book Three that identifies the Americas as the place where Noah may have settled after his sons divided up Eurasia and Africa among themselves after the Flood, I strongly feel that the pyramid artifact pictured above may have originated with Noah. After all, according to the available legends and evidence I uncovered, Noah may have been the founder of the early Post-Flood civilizations of the Americas that preceded the Inca, Maya, and Aztecs. This picture becomes clearer when the other artifacts found with the 13-tiered pyramid - all of which are directly connected to my most startling discoveries surrounding the Sethites and their understanding of the Mazzaroth - are brought into the discussion.

This is because Noah was one of the Magi or Wise Men of old, and a hereditary priest of God Most High in the Order of Melchizedek, as was his Son Shem. As such, Noah knew the ancient wisdom of the Star Gospel that his great grandfather Enoch had mastered. Noah therefore would have viewed the following artifacts with great reverence if they had been in his possession - given what the Messianic constellations that they target mean, and the lands they are connected to in the Middle East.

One of these artifacts consists of a set of thirteen small cups carefully fashioned out of stone that are directly tied to the Gospel in the Stars. Interestingly, one of the cups is twelve times larger than the other twelve cups. In fact, if the twelve smaller cups are filled with liquid, their combined volume will fill the largest cup in the set right to the brim. Another odd feature of these cups is that they all have inlaid dots of white and reddish-colored stone that is fluorescent under the invisible spectrum of light in the ultra violet range. On the smaller cups, the dots serve to number the twelve cups from one to twelve, while the dots on the bigger cup actually signify three constellations in the night sky associated with the constellation Orion!

## Ecuador Artifact Depicting 13-Tiered Pyramid

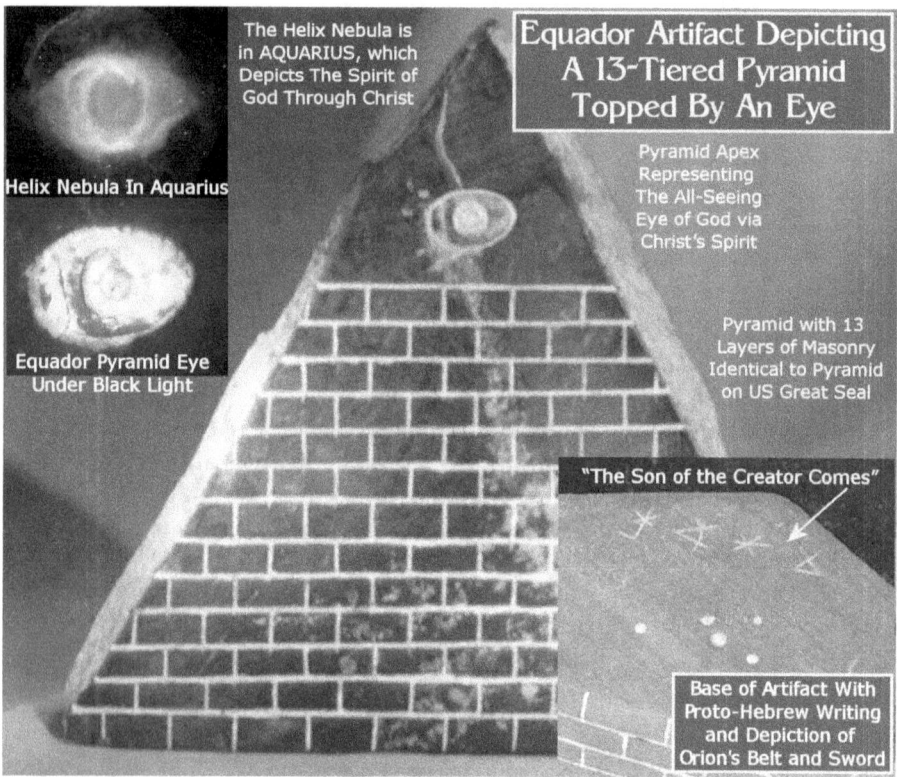

This is by far the most bizarre and compelling feature of these cups, and it is startling to me because I independently discovered the meaning behind the triangle of constellations it depicts in Book Three, "The Language of God in History"- when I did a study of the possible stellar connection of terrestrial sites other than Giza with Orion. At that time, I found a direct connection between the location of Jabal Al Lawz or Mount Sinai in Saudi Arabia and the star Procyon in Canis Minor. I also found a connection between Jerusalem and Bethlehem in the Promised Land with the stars Sirius A and B in Canis Major.

# Chapter 9: The United States and Israel in Prophecy

## Ecuador Star Gospel Artifact - Set of 13 Cups

Fascinatingly, Canis Minor and Canis Major are allegorically associated with the hunting dogs of Orion the Hunter, and Orion is one of the most Messianic, Christ-centered signs in the entire Mazzaroth. Furthermore, just as the Gospel in the Stars is hidden from ordinary view, the fluorescence of these dots under "dark" or black light appears to be a physical metaphor for the hidden or deeper aspects of the symbolic Language of God locked into the stars of the Mazzaroth, which reveal the Light of the World, Who is Yahshua. Due to the prophetic Christological meanings of these signs, there is no doubt that these three constellations are connected to Yahshua as the "Naz-Seir", "Prince of princes", or Nazarene, which is the hidden message behind Gemini, the parent sign of its decans Canis Major and Canis Minor. See Book One for a thorough explanation of the meaning of Naz and Seir in relation to Gemini, and Yahshua as the Nazarene, which may not be a word connected to His home town, but rather a reference to His prophetic role as the Son of God made flesh.

In all truth, I have never found even a hint of this particular Earth and Sky correlation in any other printed or internet-based work that I have studied. So when I saw the exact three constellations being shown on the larger of the cups, with their principle stars forming a sacred triangle just as I had envisioned in my book, I was astounded! This is because these sacred sites and constellations are directly connected to Yahweh God's dealings with the Ancient Israelites, and His Plan of Salvation through the Earthly ministry of Yahshua!

A very intriguing thing about these cups is that the center cup clearly identifies the stars of Orion, and the hour-glass shape of Orion can also be envisioned to look like a giant chalice or cup in the sky. As shown in the illustration on page 153 in this book, Orion and Taurus are both connected to the broken Matzo and cup of wine that Yahshua used at the "Last Supper" to represent the sacrifice of Himself on the eve of Passover. As such, this set of thirteen cups may have had a sacred ritual significance. In fact, I strongly feel that they did. Using my imagination, I can well picture a solemn group of 12 Sethite elders and their leader engaging in a commemorative ritual of some sort involving the wine that Noah made, which may have served to honor the future coming of the God-sent Messiah that Orion signified for them.

Though this set of cups was likely connected to a ritual involving the commemoration of the Naz-Seir in the Star Gospel, it also recalls the Patriarch Joseph, who was the "Seir" or prince among his eleven brothers, and who rose to higher prominence than them and their father Jacob. Incidentally, the male members of the House of Jacob or Israel formed a group of 13, just as Yahshua with His Twelve Apostles did.

One other object found in Ecuador that I have dubbed the "Star-Gazers" Artifact features the same star correlation as the cups that were unearthed with it. It is depicted on the next page. As can be seen, this artifact shows two odd humanoid figures that are looking up at the sky with glowing eyes, while the object of their attention is carefully laid out below them on the ground with glowing dots that are reminiscent of the stars they represent.

As in the cup set, we see the same triangle of three constellations - including Orion. But this time, we also see the six bright stars (and one dimmer star) of the Pleiades constellation that appears on the ground area near to the left foot of the figure on the right in the photos. Now, as already discussed, the Pleiades are located on the back of the Zodiac sign Taurus the Bull, and they are connected to the Seven Churches of Revelation. Furthermore, as shown and explained earlier, Taurus and Orion are connected to the Tribe of Joseph, as well as to the two Half Tribes Ephraim and Manasseh.

# Chapter 9: The United States and Israel in Prophecy — Page 381

## Ecuador Star-Gazer Artifact Featuring Sacred Star Triangle

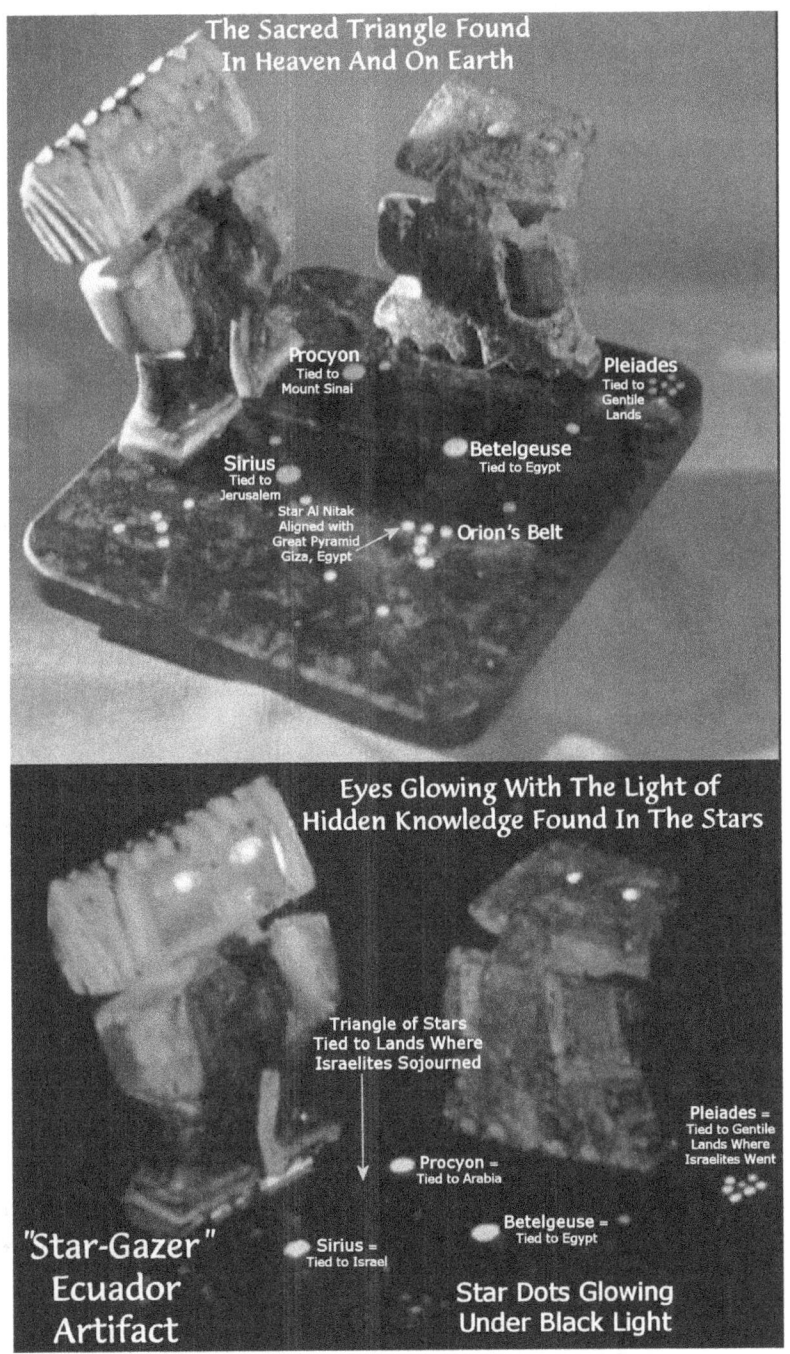

But if we stretch back even further in time, this Zodiac sign is also connected to the Antediluvian patriarchs through a prophecy in Chapter 89 the Book of 1 Enoch, where Noah and His three sons are allegorically referred to as bulls:

> *"And as I was beholding in the vision, lo, one of those four (archangels) who had come forth stoned (them) (i.e. the Nephilim) from heaven, and gathered and took all the great stars whose privy members were like those of horses (the Fallen Angels that mated with human women), and bound them all hand and foot, and cast them in an abyss of the earth." "And one of those four (angels) went to that white bull (Noah the Albino) and instructed him in secret, without his being terrified: he was born a bull and became a man, and built for himself a great vessel (the Ark) and dwelt thereon; 2 and three bulls (Noah's 3 Sons) dwelt with him in that vessel and they were covered in."* - 1 Enoch 88:3; 89:1-2

This fascinating prophecy in 1 Enoch shows that Noah and his sons were protected from the Nephilim and Fallen Angels by the Four Archangels discussed in detail in Book Three. In addition it shows that the antediluvian patriarch Noah was instructed by one of these Archangels (most likely by Uriel, the same archangel who instructed Noah's great grandfather Enoch) in the Way of Yahweh and in Sacred Astronomy. It also shows that Noah and his sons were likened to bulls. This may partly be why bulls are frequently seen in the sacred art and rituals of many ancient cultures. The bull iconography seen in ancient times was also often meant to be tied to the constellation Taurus. This is because of the hidden prophetic information that can be found when studying Taurus from an allegorical and spiritual point of view.

Based on this information, the fact that the eye-topped pyramid from Ecuador that is tied to Orion and Christ is also a symbol for the United States suggests that this nation also has a sacred purpose. Both the constellation Orion and the Great Pyramid are symbols tied to Yahshua's coming to conquer the Devil, which Christ secretly did when He died on the Cross on Golgotha - the Place of the Skull. The artifact found in Ecuador also suggests that Orion is directly tied to Christ's future return, when He will finish what He started at Golgotha by destroying the wicked at the end of the Great Tribulation.

In Chapter 12, we will explore Orion's role as a time marker for the end of the world as we know it. In the meantime, this artifact's connection to Orion, Christ and the US Great Seal suggests that many of the currently backslidden spiritual apostates living in the USA will become born-again saints doing God's Will during the Great Tribulation.

This conclusion will be further strengthened when we discuss the eagle on the front side of the Great Seal a bit later.

## *The US Constitution's Number Connection to the Bible*

There is another startling number connection between the United States and the Bible. In the Constitution of the United States, **seven articles and twenty-seven amendments** follow a short preamble. The seven articles of the Constitution help define this nation, and show that it was created to give all people certain inalienable rights regardless of race, religion or creed. Seven signifies completion and - just as the seven articles of the Constitution completely define its role in protecting the rights of U.S. citizens - the Old Testament is considered to contain the complete promises of God to Israel, as well as the full Word of God to all nations. By comparison, **though the New Testament contains prophecies and instructions for living, it does not share any revolutionary new teaching concerning God or the Messiah, but confirms that the Old Testament is fulfilled in Christ.** Therefore, just as the New Testament is complimentary to the Old Testament and was never intended to be a replacement for it, the twenty-seven constitutional amendments only clarify its seven articles.

Interestingly, seven is the number of completion and the Sabbath, and like the number thirteen, is associated with the Last Day or "Day of the Lord." In fact, the Book of Revelation would more appropriately be called "the Book of the Seventh Great Day of the Lord" since it is fully devoted to that Last Day and is filled with more prophetic references to the number seven than any other book in the Bible. The number seven is mentioned no less than fifty-five times in the Book of Revelation, and - as explained in Book One - the Star Gospel is deeply connected to its symbolism. Since the number seven signifies completion, the Book of Revelation is fittingly the last book in the Bible. Joined with the Language of God in the Old Testament, the Book of 1 Enoch, and the Gospel in the Stars, the Book of Revelation signifies Yahweh's final testimony about Himself to mankind. Together, these books are the true and defining articles of Judeo-Christianity.

Is this why, in addition to its seven articles, the Constitution of the United States has twenty-seven amendments - twenty-six in Section One and one in Section Two? After all, the twenty-seven books in the New Testament confirm and fulfill the Word of God revealed in the Old Testament. Furthermore, the Book of Revelation is the twenty-seventh and only fully prophetic book of the New Testament, so it stands alone like the twenty-seventh amendment to the US Constitution. The twenty-seven amendments to the Constitution clarify its purpose, and make it more comprehensive. Likewise, the twenty-seven books of the New Testament show Yahshua's fulfillment of the old Mosaic Law and His greater promises to God's people.

Viewing them collectively, the number correlations of the US Constitution with the books of the Bible, and those of the States with the Ancient Mazzaroth, all seem to point to an amazing connection between the United States, the Bible, Ancient Israel, and the Gospel in the Stars. This is likely not a coincidence but shows that - outside of the modern nation of Israel itself - the United States is one of several nations that have inherited the spiritual and national promises given to Israel. Perhaps that is why the North America Nebula appears in the prominent constellation called the Northern Cross, which is also known as Cygnus the Swan. Since this constellation can be seen as a beautiful, long-necked white bird or a giant cross. it is a powerful sign to Americans that their spiritual condition and ability to act as "One Nation Under God" is vital to their strength as a nation. **The number correlations coupled with these heavenly signs make it clear that the United States should be reckoned as a literal extension of the nation of Israel in the Last Days.**

Sadly, there is a current movement in America to add a new and totally immoral amendment to the United States Constitution. This is an amendment that would make same sex marriages a constitutional right by declaring that the government does not have a right to limit the definition of what constitutes a legal marriage. If it is passed, not only would it make homosexual marriage a constitutional right, it would likely lead to the legalization of polygamy and other marital and sexual abominations.

How sad that a country that has been given so much favor by the God they once honored has turned its collective back on its Divine Benefactor! How tragic that they have done so in favor of movements that promote "political correctness" and social, religious and racial "tolerance" while moving ever closer to defining devout Christians and Messianics as criminals.

In that regard, it is interesting to note that the flag favored by the Tea Party Movement that was initially fostered by the conservative Mormon media star Glenn Beck and the Dominion Theology-inspired Christian and former 2008 Vice Presidential hopeful Sarah Palin is the Gadsden Flag, with a depiction of a rattlesnake and the slogan "Don't Tread On Me" making a defiant statement as to their intentions. Due to the Pro-Gun, Anti-Big Government, Survivalist mentality of many Tea-Partiers, the US Government has labeled many of them as potential terrorists - heralding a coming time when anyone that sides with Christ and continues their rebellion against the New World Order will be cruelly treated as traitors and terrorists. Here is an excerpt from my book "The Language of God in History" that discusses the Gadsden Flag and what it may mean for Americans in the near future. It also gives a glimpse of where this chapter about the United States in prophecy is heading:

**Excerpt from Chapter 8 of "The Language of God in History:"**

The Half Tribes of Joseph are symbolized by the horns of Taurus the Bull, which symbolizes Joseph in the heavens, just as Moses prophesied on his death bed:

> "His glory is like a firstborn bull, and his horns are like the horns of the wild ox; together with them he shall push the peoples to the ends of the earth; they are the ten thousands of Ephraim, and they are the thousands of Manasseh." - Deuteronomy 33:17

Of these two horns or sons, the horn that supposedly signified Ephraim is symbolized as a white unicorn on both the Scottish and English Royal Coat of Arms. This unicorn is a symbol of the patriarch Joseph's glory or his royalty, which Manasseh - as the firstborn - was supposed to inherit. However, Joseph placed his younger son Ephraim over Manasseh as the heir to God's promises to Joseph. Therefore, despite their claims that Manasseh was numbered as the thirteenth Tribe, Ephraim was the younger son of the patriarch Joseph and the progenitor of the thirteenth Tribe of Israel by virtue of his birth, if not his inheritance. Interestingly, the ten thousands of Ephraim are symbolized as a much bigger tribe than Manasseh with her thousands in the Scripture above, and at last count, the United Kingdom - even with all her commonwealth nations added in - is still only about one third the population of the United States.

The prophecies concerning Joseph given by Jacob are different than those of Moses and do not mention a bull, but call Joseph a fruitful bough associated with archery (i.e. warfare):

> "Joseph is a fruitful bough, a fruitful bough by a well; his branches run over the wall. The archers have bitterly grieved him, shot at him and hated him. But his bow remained in strength, and the arms of his hands were made strong by the hands of the Mighty God of Jacob (From there is the Shepherd, the Stone of Israel)." - Gen. 49:22-24

Oddly enough the fruitful bough (as an olive branch with 13 leaves and fruits) and the arrows of the archer are held in the claws of an eagle on the Great Seal of the United States, but appear nowhere in the iconography of the Irish, English, or Scottish Monarchy. In addition, the United States was founded from thirteen original colonies, which allegorically alludes to Ephraim in prophecy. Furthermore, the USA has the most efficient and powerful military in the world.

The symbols of Joseph, whose son Ephraim inherited the lion's share of the blessings listed above, are connected to both the USA and the UK. But the blessings given to each nation are as different as the symbols they both hold dear. From these symbols, it can be discerned that the glory of Joseph's heritage as a Prince of Egypt belongs to the constitutional monarchy of the United Kingdom via Manasseh, the older, firstborn son, but the blessings of prosperity given to Joseph belong to the United States via Ephraim, the younger son who possesses the blessing of the firstborn.

Since these prophecies concerning Joseph were uttered, no nation on Earth has ever been as greatly blessed economically as the United States. Despite its current economic woes, American citizens still enjoy the finest standard of living compared to any other nation on Earth. Nor has any other modern country been as greatly blessed with technological and military might as the United States.

Nonetheless, the United States now stands to be eclipsed by an even greater political power: the United Kingdom. Though few people consider it, the United Kingdom is the only modern nation to have successfully controlled a world empire within the last two hundred years, and it appears to be achieving this distinction yet again through its control of the British Commonwealth, which contains 54 member states, and its power within the European Union, which contains 28 member states. As a result, the glory of the 50 United States is now fading, while the United Kingdom is set to become the revived Roman Empire prophesied about in the Book of Daniel and Revelation. Meanwhile, the Middle East is uniting under the banner of Radical Islam to set up a modern Caliphate or Babylon the Great, which may set up its headquarters in Iraq near the runs of ancient Babylon one day.

Though the UK does look like it may eclipse the USA one day soon, however, the Language of God found in symbols has a big part to play in correctly interpreting Scripture, and the tribal affiliations for Ephraim and Manasseh given by other scholars are likely wrong because they have consistently misapplied the symbols belonging exclusively to Ephraim to the British Empire. More about the Covenant promises made to the Tribe of Joseph and their fulfillment through the Ten Lost Tribes are shared in "The Language of God in Prophecy," especially in regard to Great Britain's connection to the Tribe of Judah, Dan and the half-tribe of

Manasseh, the US connection to the half-tribe of Ephraim, and the role of these half tribes of Joseph in Bible Prophecy.

For now, I wanted to point out that the USA also has a direct connection to the Tribe of Dan, but its eagle emblem suggests that it may also act as a destroyer of and godly replacement for the Tribe of Dan in prophecy. In fact, the eagle that replaced the evil serpent imagery originally associated with Dan became the symbol for the USA, which also originally had an association with serpent imagery before it was assigned the bald eagle as its symbol. This serpent imagery was first alluded to in 1751, when Benjamin Franklin wrote a satire in the Pennsylvania Gazette suggesting that the American colonists should send rattlesnakes to England as a way to thank them for their policy of sending convicted felons to America. It appeared a second time in a political cartoon drawn by Ben Franklin in 1754 that was meant to urge the eight English colonies existing at the time to unite during the French and Indian War. This cartoon wood cut showed a snake cut into eight sections that signified the colonies.

Later, serpent imagery was often adopted by the American colonies and their militias to represent their defiance against injustice. That is also why the snake appeared again in the Gadsden Flag with its warning statement: "Don't Tread on Me." This flag was created from the rattlesnake symbol and motto painted on the drum heads used by the first company of Marines formed to protect the American colonies against the British. Soon after, the first US Navy flag depicted a stretched-out version of the rattlesnake with the same motto on a background of seven red and six white stripes like that used on the original national flag of the United States. Interestingly, the rattlesnake on the Gadsden Flag has thirteen rattles at the end of its tail to reflect the number of colonies in America at that time. The rattlesnake was considered a good symbol for the American military partly

because rattlesnakes are unique to North America, have sharp, vigilant eyes, give due notice before they attack, and only strike in self-defense when they are provoked, which is seen as honorable. Over the years, this flag has been popular among US political dissidents who disagree with the government's direction. As a result, the US Government has come to view the display of this flag or its motto as extremist and a hostile act of rebellion.

Now, despite the displeasure of Ben Franklin, who preferred the wild turkey, the bald eagle was adopted as a national symbol on the Great Seal of the United States along with thirteen stars, thirteen stripes, thirteen arrows, an olive branch, and a thirteen tiered pyramid with the Eye of Providence over it signifying the blessings of God on America. Though this Great Seal is discussed in depth in Book Four, three things concerning it are important to this discussion. First of all, the constant allusions to the number 13 show that the USA is connected to Ephraim. Secondly, there is absolutely no serpent imagery of any kind on either side of the Great Seal.

This allegorically indicates that **this nation did and will again reject the evil connotations of the Tribe of Dan that it initially inherited from England** and will instead live up to its aspirations to become a force for good in the world that is symbolized by the white-headed bald eagle and its celestial counterpart called Aquila, a decan of the messianic Zodiac sign Capricorn. Though the future for America currently looks bleaker and darker than it ever has, I take heart in knowing that there still are great servants of God in America who are working behind the scenes to do God's will in eternity and who will likely have the last say in determining what part the USA will play during the Tribulation.

### End of Excerpt from "The Language of God in History"

Since the preceding book excerpt contains information that originally only appeared in Book Three, some of the Bible quotes and ideas used in it appear later in this chapter to explain America's role in history as well as its place in Yahweh God's future plans. To save time revising this book, I have left the remainder of this chapter relatively unaltered and trust that any repetition of the preceding material will only serve to further clarify and emphasize its great importance.

## What is the Beast from the Sea in Daniel and Revelation?

Perhaps the many signs of moral decay and rebellion in America such as the Tea Party Movement's use of the Gadsden Flag, the US

## Chapter 9: The United States and Israel in Prophecy   Page 389

Government's push toward marginalizing and demonizing Christians and conservatives, and the White House's new hostility toward Israel are one reason that this country may be reckoned with Israel in the Last Days. Like America, Israel is not morally right with God. They have justified immorality and engaged in unbiblical behavior toward their neighbors that has brought all sorts of trouble their way.

Though it may be done in retaliation to Muslim Terrorist attacks, fighting cruelty with cruelty has dire spiritual consequences on the people of the nation engaging in and perpetrating such behavior. Ominously, two former US Presidents (George Bush Sr. and Jr.) began the US "War on Terror." They also began using the term "New World Order" in reference to the globalization of America and its integration into the world economy and political base through the auspices of the Unite Nations, which another former US President (Franklin D. Roosevelt) helped found. This does not bode well for the many citizens of America who truly value their Constitutional freedoms and their right to bear arms.

Despite the current trend in the White House to treat Israel with contempt, several Bible prophecies offer fairly conclusive proof that the United States will be reckoned with Israel in the End Times. For example, though heavily couched in the allegorical imagery of the Language of God, the United States appears in one of Daniel's visions. In it, Daniel saw four beasts that represented four ancient kingdoms that were preparing to destroy Israel. However, like so much of God's prophetic Word in the Bible, these beasts appear to be dualistic - with an ancient and modern counterpart for each one. So that we do not miss what Yah has foreseen and foretold, let's analyze each beast in Daniel's vision of four great beasts from the sea, beginning with the lion that has an eagle's wings:

> *"Four great beasts, each different... came up out of the sea. The first was like a lion,* **and it had the wings of an eagle**. *I watched until **its wings were torn off** and it was lifted from the ground so that it stood on two feet like a man, and the heart of a man was given to it." - Daniel 7:3-4 (NIV)*

Most Biblical scholars believe that the Winged Lion in Daniel's vision is the ancient kingdom of Babylon. However, the symbol of a lion now represents the United Kingdom of Great Britain, which has a lion on its royal standard. There are also several striking comparisons that can be drawn between Ancient Babylon and the former British Empire. For instance, at one time Great Britain was a great world empire just as Babylon was. In addition, the Book of Daniel tells us that

Nebuchadnezzar went insane for seven years and there have been several past kings of England whose behavior would be classified as insane today. The best known of these insane rulers was King George the Third.

In ancient times, the kingdom of Assyria rose up out of Babylon and had the eagle as its emblem. However, Babylon eventually rose up again and attacked and vanquished Assyria. This explains why the Lion's Wings were torn off in Daniel's vision. In modern times, the eagle is the national symbol of the United States. Like Assyria, the United States rose up out of another powerful nation, fought and won a war of independence against it, and then - for a time - became one of the most formidable superpowers the world has ever known. But a time may soon come when England will again seek to have supremacy over the USA.

Interestingly, though Assyria was a Pagan kingdom in the past, modern-day Assyrians are Christians and most of them once lived in Iran, though they are now scattered all over the world. **The Assyrians left Iran because it had become a fanatical Muslim dominated land and they were being brutally persecuted for their Christian faith**. As a result, many Assyrians fled and came to live in America. Instead of Farsi or Arabic, modern Assyrians speak a form of Aramaic - the language that Yahshua spoke. Since I am one-quarter Assyrian in heritage, these facts have been known to me since I was a child. Yet I did not realize their full significance until now. All these facts suggest that the modern day country that is a counterpart to Ancient Assyria must be Christian and hated by fanatical Muslims, and the United States still fulfills that obligation - though it did much more so in the past.

Now, the Eagle was a symbol used in Ancient Rome - a Pagan empire like Assyria that was eventually transformed into the Christianized Holy Roman Empire. The Eagle's Wings being torn off the Lion could therefore symbolize the Church of England's breaking away from Papal (Roman) authority during the reign of King Henry the 8th. However, in modern times, the Eagle's Wings now represent the United States rather than Rome or the Roman Catholic Church. This also identifies the Eagle's Wings that carry the Woman Clothed with the Sun to safety as the United States, which became a safe haven for Jews and Protestant Christians to escape European and English persecution. Because of the Babylon and Assyria connection to England and the USA, Daniel's vision suggests that the United States may be attacked and possibly vanquished by its mother country in the future. Since the United Kingdom couldn't possibly win a war waged against the United States without the aid of her allies in the British Commonwealth and the

European Union, Europe's armed forces and the Commonwealth nations would have to back the UK if it ever desired to destroy the USA.

There is another prophecy pertaining to the Antichrist and the End Times that suggests that Great Britain and the United States will one day wage another war against each other. It is found in the prophecy of the Worthless Shepherd (i.e. the Antichrist) in the Book of Zechariah:

> "Then I broke my second staff called Union, breaking the brotherhood between Judah and Israel." - Zechariah 11:14 (NIV)

In a moment, we will explore a prophecy from a vision allegedly experienced by George Washington that appears to have been a genuine, godly one. In George Washington's visionary prophecy, an angelic being that appears to represent Christ coming in Glory wears a crown of light that reads "Union" - a word that aptly identifies the United States. If the United States is viewed as representative of the staff called Union in the Bible, and this staff is to be broken, it implies that it will be destroyed or weakened in some way. In Washington's vision, *this is exactly what occurs to the USA!*

This may mean that the USA, which is populated with people representing the Ten Lost Tribes, is being reckoned as modern-day Israel, while the nation of Israel is being equated with Judah or the Jews. Though representatives of the Ten Lost Tribes are also scattered throughout the United Kingdom and Europe, the severing of the current union between them and the USA may be successfully perpetrated by the Antichrist. Therefore, Zechariah's prophecy suggests that the alliance now enjoyed between the United Kingdom, the United States, Europe, and the nation of Israel will soon be violently severed.

We will explore the possibility that foreign armies might soon invade the United States a bit later. For now, however, let's return to Daniel's vision of the Beasts that rose up out of the Sea. After seeing the winged lion in his vision, Daniel envisions a second beast rising up against Israel:

> "And suddenly another beast, a second, like a bear. It was raised up on one side, and had three ribs in its mouth between its teeth. And they said thus to it: 'Arise, devour much flesh!'" - Daniel 7:5

Modern day scholars say the bear represents the Empire formed by the Ancient Medes and Persians. The modern day country with the bear as a national symbol is Russia, and there are interesting parallels between it and Medo-Persia. For example, when the Medes and Persians joined forces and seized power from Babylon, they mercilessly killed King

Belshazzar and all the members of the royal family. Likewise, when Lenin and Trotsky led the Bolshevik revolution in Russia, they wasted no time in killing the Russian Czars and their entire families. Uncannily, the names Belshazzar and Bolshevik also have a phonetic correlation. Another similarity is that the Medo-Persians had seven kings before their empire fell. Likewise, the Soviet government collapsed during the term of Mikhail Gorbechev - their seventh Premiere.

According to Daniel's prophecy, this bear would devour much flesh (i.e. kill many people). The Medo-Persian kings destroyed whole people groups in their conquests of foreign lands. King Nebuchadnezzar devastated Israel and killed all but those he brought back to Babylon as slaves - the prophet Daniel among them. Likewise, the Russian people suffered terrible persecution under the reign of dictatorial Premieres like Joseph Stalin. Similarly, in the reign of the Persian King Darius, the prophet Daniel was thrown into the lion's den because he would not agree to worship the king. Things were no different in Communist Russia. A little known fact is that **Stalin killed more Jews than Adolph Hitler, who murdered millions!** It was not just the Jews who were persecuted during the Communist era in Russia, however. Many thousands of Christians and other nonconformists were slaughtered or imprisoned because they refused to heed their Communist government's unjust demands.

After the bear, Daniel saw a third beast:

*"After that, I looked, and there before me was another beast, one that looked like a leopard. And on its back it had four wings like those of a bird. This beast had four heads, and it was given authority to rule."* - Daniel 7:6 (NIV)

Modern day scholars say the leopard represents the Greco-Macedonian Empire that was formed by Alexander the Great. The modern day country with the leopard as their national symbol is Germany. It also has a stylized black eagle on its National Coat of Arms, which harkens back to the wings on the leopard that Daniel saw in his vision. Since the eagle is black, it also suggests the color of a leopard. Alexander the Great conquered the world more swiftly than anyone else in recorded history ever did. Likewise, Adolph Hitler's army overran Europe more swiftly than any other army previously did.

Alexander the Great formed and ruled the Macedonian Empire for only twelve years before he died suddenly, still a young man. Like Alexander, Hitler also ruled as a dictator for twelve years, then died while still a relatively young man. During his rule, Hitler utilized the

## Chapter 9: The United States and Israel in Prophecy

terrible swiftness of Blitzkrieg or "Lightning War" tactics in his attempt to conquer the world. Alexander the Great was also swift and merciless in his conquest of the world. When Alexander the Great died, four generals divided his empire. Likewise, when Hitler died, four countries divided Germany into East and West Germany. These four countries were the United States, the United Kingdom, France, and Russia.

The Greco-Macedonian Empire was eventually destroyed, dividing into a western empire known as the Roman Republic and an eastern empire that was called Macedonia. Germany was also divided in two, forming West Germany and East Germany. Divided Germany represented two diverse Cold War governments formed by NATO and the Warsaw Pact - each of which had many opposing interests. Similarly, in ancient times, the Western Roman Empire had many clashes of interest with Macedonia. As a result, Rome fought against Macedonia until it eventually overcame Greek rule in the east. Rome then rose to become one of the most powerful and long-lasting world empires the world has ever known. When the Berlin Wall dividing East and West Germany fell in 1989, the West - represented by the United States, Britain and Europe - overcame the East as Communist Russia began to disintegrate and communist regimes were collapsing all over the world.

Daniel then sees the fourth and final beast rise up against the kingdom of Israel:

> *"After that, in my vision at night I looked, and there before me was **a fourth beast- terrifying and frightening and very powerful. It had large iron teeth**; it crushed and devoured its victims and trampled underfoot whatever was left. It was different from all the former beasts, and it had ten horns." - Daniel 7:7 (NIV)*

This fourth beast was the Roman Empire. The Roman legions carried iron weapons, alluding to the iron teeth of the fourth Beast. These iron weapons helped Rome's legions swiftly crush the armies around them that still used bronze weapons. It was also ancient Rome that finally destroyed the city of Jerusalem and the Second Temple in 70 AD. The modern counterpart to the Roman Empire is most likely the United Nations, which is now dominated by the European Union and the oil-rich Arab Nations of OPEC. The United Nations has plans to divide the world into ten biospheres, and this could be why the Beast in Revelation that may represent the United Nations has ten horns, which also connect it to the Beast from the Sea. In addition, the United Nations is now creating policies and laws that are binding on all its member nations, and it is extremely antagonistic to Israel, constantly issuing sanctions against it for supposed human rights violations in its fight to survive against Radical Islamic aggression.

There has been much talk in recent years of making Jerusalem the home city for the United Nations, an idea that Pope John Paul II originally suggested. This would thereby internationalize the city of Jerusalem. In past years, this idea would have been impossible to consider since Israel would not agree to surrender their control of Jerusalem. But recent reports from Israel suggest that there is now strong support for this idea there. Could Jerusalem become the capital of the United Nations? It would make sense for this to happen if the Antichrist heads the United Nations. As the Antichrist, he will seek to imitate the true Christ in every way. Since prophecy tells us that Yahshua will descend upon and reign from Jerusalem (Zechariah 14:1-11; Psalm 48-3; Isaiah 24:23; Micah 4:7), the Antichrist will also likely attempt to do so.

These nations that rise up against Israel in Daniel's vision also appear in the Book of Revelation, Chapter 13. Daniel's four beasts were said to have come up *"out of the sea"* (Daniel 7:3). They therefore correspond exactly to Revelation's *"beast rising up out of the sea:"*

> *"Then I stood on the sand of the sea. And I saw **a beast rising up out of the sea**, having seven heads and ten horns, and on his horns ten crowns, and on his heads a blasphemous name. Now the beast... was like **a leopard**, his feet were... of **a bear**, and his mouth like... **a lion**. The dragon gave him... his throne, and great authority."* - Revelation 13:1-3

Before we deal with the identity of this prophecy's dragon in Chapter Ten, we will focus on the Beast. This fearsome Beast from the Sea with seven heads and ten horns represents the nations that form the final empire of the Antichrist. This beast is likened to a leopard, a bear and a lion, suggesting that it will be formed through the uniting of Europe in the entity known as the European Union, which has many member countries, including the United Kingdom. Many scholars have identified the EU as Revelation's Beast from the Sea. Curiously, France and Germany are members of the EU that have a stylized black eagle on their National Coats of Arms – the same black eagle that Ancient Rome and Nazi Germany sported as their national symbols! It therefore appears that these nations are part of the revived Roman Empire - along with the EU as a whole - making them major players in future world events.

However, what previous scholars seem to have missed is that the United Kingdom has formed its own separate union of nations called the British Commonwealth of Nations, which as of October 2013 has 53

## Chapter 9: The United States and Israel in Prophecy

member nations in Asia, South America and Africa. To enter the Commonwealth, member nations must agree to structure their society on British legal and democratic national principles, and to support English as a first or second language. In addition, member nations must be allied to and supportive of the activities and plans of the British Royalty and the British Crown Corporation, which is run by the Bank of London. Both the corporation and the bank are based in London, England and are controlled by the British Royalty. Through its wealth and influence, the United Kingdom therefore adds considerably to the power and scope of the European Union.

The ignoble fate of the European Union can perhaps be best defined by the adopted symbols on its flag, currency, and official documents. These include a blue flag with a circle of 12 white stars, which appears to be a near copy of the azure field on the first Union Jack sewn by Betsy Ross *minus the thirteenth star that represents the USA in prophecy.* In addition, the EU has taken the myth of the goddess Europa as their defining symbol. In fact - as shown in my Book Two excerpt in Chapter Four of this book - the Euro dollar coin features a depiction of Europa riding on the back of a bull that represents Zeus in disguise. Eerily, this symbol mimics the Seven Sisters or Pleiades star cluster, which is allegorically being carried to victory by Taurus the Bull.

This symbolism in Taurus and the Pleiades was originally tied to the patriarch Joseph, and was meant to portray Christ's redeeming blood (i.e. Taurus) upon His disciples from Israel and every nation on Earth that are tied to the Seven Churches of Revelation (i.e. the Pleiades). However, **it has now been twisted into a symbol for the Beast from the Sea.** As already explained, the horns of Taurus signify two powerful modern nations tied to the Tribe of Joseph. These are the United States and the United Kingdom, and just as horns defend a bull in a fight, the US and UK are the protective powers that support the European Union.

Adding to this symbolism, the Pleiades star cluster once had seven bright stars that could be seen with the naked eye, but now only has six. This shows that six of the Seven Churches will join with the Woman who rides the Beast, and this is happening today via the Ecumenical Movement, which seeks common ground between Protestantism, Roman Catholicism, New Age Spirituality and Paganism. The Beast also represents the emergence of a global government, which has already begun via the United Nations and the setting up of the New World Order by the global elite, also known as the Illuminati. This dualistic face to Taurus, which is seen in some of the symbols in Scripture and the Star Gospel, shows that Satan and sin's ability to twist the meaning of every good symbol in the Universe is very pervasive!

The one Church that doesn't join the Whore Religion sitting on the final End Time Beast or Bull that forms the New World Order (as revealed in Chapter 17 of the Book of Revelation) is the Church of Philadelphia, and it is the only Church that is connected to the Bride of Christ, and is promised to be spared from suffering through the Great Tribulation. The Prophet Daniel had a few choice tidbits of information abut the Bride of Christ and the Five Wise Virgins who will accompany her to Heaven, as described in the Parable of the Ten Virgins. This is what he said about these saints who love and follow Christ:

> *"Those great beasts, which are four, are four kings which arise out of the earth. 18 But the saints of the Most High shall receive the kingdom, and possess the kingdom forever, even forever and ever." - Daniel 7:17-18*

> *"I was watching; and the same horn (or king, namely the Antichrist) was making war against the saints, and prevailing against them, 22 until the Ancient of Days (or Yahshua) came, and a judgment was made in favor of the saints of the Most High, and the time came for the saints to possess the kingdom." - Daniel 7:21-22*

> *"Then the kingdom and dominion, and the greatness of the kingdoms under the whole heaven, shall be given to the people, the saints of the Most High. His kingdom is an everlasting kingdom, and all dominions shall serve and obey Him." - Daniel 7:27*

These Scriptures show that the Bride of Christ and the Wise Virgins will reign and rule with Yahshua as an everlasting inheritance. See Chapter 11 for more about the Church of Philadelphia, and its connection to the Ten Virgins, the Woman Clothed with the Sun, and the New Jerusalem.

## The Altar of Pergamum - The Throne of Satan

Ominously, the May/June 2006 edition of Biblical Archeology magazine presented an article about an ancient Pagan building now called the Great Altar of Pergamum. This large colonnaded and raised altar had been excavated from the site of ancient Pergamum and rebuilt from its remains in Germany within a special section of the Berlin State Museum.

## Chapter 9: The United States and Israel in Prophecy

After its discovery, several biblical scholars were convinced that this rebuilt ruin that is now considered a priceless work of art may be the throne of Satan mentioned in connection with the ancient city of Pergamum in the Book of Revelation:

> "To the angel of the church in Pergamum write: These are the words of him who has the sharp, double-edged sword. **I know where you live - where Satan has his throne. Yet you remain true to my name.** You did not renounce your faith in me, even in the days of Antipas, my faithful witness, who was put to death in your city - where Satan lives." - Rev. 2:12-13 (NIV)

Though this throne mentioned in the Bible has long been thought of as a purely allegorical device, could it be referring to this altar that was once part of the mountaintop acropolis of ancient Pergamum? It is possible, considering that the entire structure is ringed with friezes of an epic battle between the Olympian gods and the Titans. The Titans are identified as Nephilim in Book Three, "The Language of God in History." This book shows that the Greeks, who followed the Way of Cain or the Serpent, demonized the followers of the Way of Yahweh as enemies of their false gods by depicting them as Titans. As was typical in Greek art, the Titans featured on the Altar of Pergamum were human in appearance except for the scaled serpent's tails on their bottom halves.

In Book Three, many Olympian gods are identified as the purely human, but sadly deified heroes of Judeo-Christian fame mentioned in the Bible. Due to ancestor worship and an evil process called syncretism, these great people of faith were either deified or falsely associated with the evil descendents of the Nephilim who later ruled over large segments of mankind after the Great Flood. This perversion of the truth surrounding God's heroes in the Star Gospel and the Bible with Nephilim-inspired Astrology and Pagan mythological religious beliefs was especially true in places like ancient Canaan, which became the Promised Land.

The city of Pergamum was located in Asia Minor, which was part of the Roman Empire during the days of the early Church. The Great Altar found there was dedicated to the false deities Zeus and Athena, whose images figure prominently in the friezes decorating the structure. Since the throne of Satan may now be in Germany, could Revelation's message to the Church of Pergamum be meant for the Christians living in Germany and other parts of Europe today? If so, there is no shortage of Nicolaitans in this modern allegorical Pergamum. Today, anyone who adheres to idolatrous practices such as sexual fornication, and other forms of moral laxity including idolatry in any form could be referred to as a Nicolaitan.

Ominously, President Barack Obama, who was elected to his first term in office in 2008, and who was re-elected under suspicious circumstances in 2012, has supported all forms of sexual sin, as can be seen in his promotion of the Gay Agenda in America, and the whole LBGT Movement attached to it. He also supports the despicable murder of millions upon millions of innocent lives through the process of abortion, even at late and post term. But what makes this President even more sinister than any in recent memory is the fact that he has given two speeches in Berlin, Germany, near to the museum where the Altar of Pergamum is housed.

In fact, Barack Obama visited that Berlin museum and viewed that very pagan altar dedicated to Zeus before giving a major campaign speech entitled: "A World That Stands as One" on July 24th, 2008 that outlined the proposed direction of his foreign policies if he should be elected as President of the USA. During this speech, he promised to promote good will and peace throughout the world. The fact that Obama was awarded the 2009 Nobel Peace Prize based on that speech was proof that he moved the world into believing that he could deliver on his promises. But not only has Obama failed miserably at this, but the people who awarded him the Peace Prize recently asked him to return it since he has done more to promote war rather than stop it during his entire time in office! For this reason, I have a bit more to share about Barack Obama's beliefs, behavior and foreign and domestic policies in the next chapter.

Returning to our discussion of Revelation 13:1-2 quoted earlier, the next verse in that section tells us that one of the seven "heads" of the allegorical Beast from the Sea will be mortally wounded, but will miraculously recover:

> *"And I saw one of his heads as if it was mortally wounded, and his deadly wound was healed. And all the world marveled and followed the beast." - Revelation 13:3*

Though Bible Prophecy teachers insist that this verse pertains exclusively to the Antichrist personally, I believe it represents a nation that appears to be dying, but then rises up out of its own ashes like a Phoenix to become great again. I identify this dying then resurrected nation primarily with the Roman Empire, which received a deadly wound when the Roman Empire fell. But it did not take long for it to be revived again, albeit in a weaker form. This was done under the rule of Charlemagne, or Charles the Great, who was crowned as the first Holy

# Chapter 9: The United States and Israel in Prophecy

Roman Emperor of all of western Europe in the late 8th and early 9th Centuries AD.

Like his father Pepin the Short, King of the Franks, Charlemagne became the protector of the Papacy, and fought against those who refused to submit to Papal authority. In this capacity, Charlemagne successfully removed the Lombards from power in northern Italy, and led an incursion into Muslim Spain, which was only partly successful, though it did halt the spread of Islam further into Europe. He also campaigned against the barbarous feudal civilizations to the east of his growing kingdom.

Ruthless in his approach to those who refused to submit to Rome, Charlemagne forced the Roman Catholic brand of Christianity on the barbarian civilizations he conquered on pain of death, which was accomplished by beheading. At one point, Charlemagne killed at least 4500 pagan Saxons by beheading in what is now known as the Massacre of Verden. Acts like this instilled terror into the hearts of the people Charlemagne's armies conquered, and this allowed him to form a new empire of his own, which reached its height of power by 800 AD.

On Christmas Day in that year, as a symbol of his bloody achievement, Charlemagne was crowned "Holy Roman Emperor" by Pope Leo III at Old St. Peter's Basilica that was built by Constantine at the site of the Vatican in Rome. Thus, the Roman Empire was re-born with a false "Christian" face that was anything but "Holy". This made Charlemagne the first Beast who beheaded his victims - just as it says in the Book of Revelation regarding the last Beast (Rev. 20:4). Incidentally, Charles the Great was the first Charles in a line of seven European kings with that name, and which has culminated in an eighth ruler with the name of Charles, thus fulfilling Revelation 17:11, where it says: *"The beast that was, and is not, is himself also the eighth, and is of the seven, and is going to perdition"*.

This is none other than Prince Charles of Wales, who is very likely the secret leader of the Illuminati, and a proponent of their objectives, which includes the totalitarian rule of the world, a one world religion where the elite rulers of mankind are the ultimate gods (or goddesses), and a massive reduction in the world's human population. Some of these objectives are summarized on the Georgia Guidestones, a strange and massive granite monument that was built near Atlanta, Georgia in the United States in 1980. Though this monument - which features a 10-point inscription in eight different languages - has been attributed to the Rosicrucians, it is more likely that the Illuminati have several high ranking members from the Rosicrucians in their ranks.

# The Language of God in Prophecy

In more recent times, another compelling candidate for the Beast-head with the deadly wound that was healed became Russia. After the fall of Communist Russia, the already large Muslim population in the South began to grow exponentially. Due to their rapid birth rate, the Muslims in Russia are close to outnumbering the Christian population. This has made the alliance between a Muslim-dominated Russia and its neighboring Arab states stronger, and has pitted them all against Israel or Judah, and America or Ephraim during the Great Tribulation through their alliances with Iran and Syria (Ezekiel 38:2-6). In fact, this coalition between Russian, Persian, and Arab armed forces and their subsequent war with Israel and America may form a major part of the Antichrist's international army that will be supernaturally destroyed during the Great Tribulation - when many Arab states surrounding Israel will be completely devastated (Ezekiel 39:1-6).

In fact, the conflict between Russia and the United States came to a dangerous head recently in the Civil War conflicts of 2013 in Syria and Egypt - when the USA and Russia began fighting proxy wars against each other. Ironically, US President Obama supported the Radical Muslim factions and Russia's President Putin backed the rebels fighting against them. Meanwhile, Isaiah Chapter 17's Prophecy against Damascus and Isaiah Chapter 19's Prophecy against Egypt are coming true before our very eyes! This can be seen in Syria's Civil War, which has turned sections of Damascus and many other areas in Syria into a heap of ruins. It can also be seen in Egypt, in that the Muslim Brotherhood deposed one harsh ruler for one of their own, and then the Egyptian military deposed this Radical Islamic tyrant in an effort to form a truly democratic form of government similar to the one that their neighbors in Israel utilize. As of the end of 2013, after a period of severe Christian persecution in Egypt from the Muslim Brotherhood, this has had a positive affect on the civil rights protection now being given to the millions of Coptic Christians in Egypt. This is also in a further fulfillment of Isaiah 19, which indicates that five cities in Egypt will become a beacon of God's light to the predominantly Muslim Arab nations surrounding them.

This is especially clear when the mistranslation in Isaiah 19:18 is corrected. In the King James and New King James Versions of the Bible, this passage reads: *"In that day five cities in the land of Egypt will speak the language of Canaan and swear by the Lord of hosts; one will be called the City of Destruction."* When correctly translated, the City of Destruction becomes the City of the Sun, which makes far more sense when the meaning of the rest of the passage is taken into consideration. In fact, this appears to be a veiled reference to Yahshua as the Sun of Righteousness.

This Muslim factor could also be why the United Kingdom and Europe will suddenly turn against both the USA and Israel. There is an already huge and growing Muslim population in the British Isles and Europe that is getting educated, taking over the population, and infiltrating every aspect of British and European culture and government, just as it is being done in America. In the meantime, though many of these Muslims have been indoctrinated with a fanatical desire to claim the world for Allah, most Western countries are doing nothing to stop Arab immigration into their countries or limiting the number of live births allowed per family.

This tragic situation has been heightened in the West by the concept that women have a choice on whether or not to have children or to end it with abortion. China and the Western civilization centers have also been pushing the idea that it is better to have two or less children to help protect the Earth from the destruction caused by an excessively large and environmentally irresponsible human population. Meanwhile, the Western nations' governments seem to have turned traitor against their own people by allowing virtually unrestricted immigration of Arabs, Persians and Asians into the once Caucasian West. The obvious result has been to weaken these nations from being predominantly Caucasian strongholds of Democracy and Capitalism, and gradually turning them into Socialist nations that are hostile to Judaism, and rabidly hateful of Evangelical Protestant Christianity.

Though there is some debate over the modern day identity of the Beasts in Daniel's vision, my own interpretation of their identity is based on much historical evidence. However, even if the bear represents Germany as some claim, and the leopard signifies France as some also claim, the prophetic interpretation of the Beast from the Sea as a symbol for English-led Europe, Russia, Great Britain, Asia, and the Middle East united in war as they could be through the United Nations would not change. ***The United Nations, as the unifying body between these many different countries, can clearly be seen as the potential command center for a new Roman Empire*** that now encompasses the whole world.

Incidentally, in the past, France was once part of Germany. France derives its name from the ancient people who once formed her greatest population: the Franks. The Franks were Germanic people like their neighbors to the north and south of them: the Saxons and the Lombards. They were originally inhabitants of the area of southwestern Germany know as the Rhine land, where the Rhine River flows. Eventually, however, they moved further south in conquest and invaded the territory that would one day become modern France. As mentioned earlier in this chapter, Charlemagne became the first Holy Roman Emperor and united the lands of the Franks, Lombards, and Saxons under his sole rule early in the 9th Century AD.

The next section of this chapter was derived from an article I wrote entitled "The Amazing Prophecy in Psalm 108 and the War on Terror - Are They Connected?", which was published on Internet news sites and on my blog in September of 2007. It shows that there may be a war in the Middle East between the West and the Muslim nations that sponsor Terrorism sometime soon. Though no war broke out in 2008, the alignments of the nations against Israel certainly became clear back then, and as we reach the end of 2013, it is clear that Isaiah 17's prophesied destruction of Damascus and Isaiah 19's prophecy of great unrest and change in Egypt are coming true as I write. So it is only a matter of God's timing as to when Israel will strike back at these neighboring nations that are continually threatening its security.

## *The Amazing Hidden Prophecy In Psalm 108*

In this book, I have already shown how many Psalms - especially the Hallel Psalms 110 through 118 - may be directly related to global prophetic events occurring in the years 2010 through 2018. These nine psalms appear to describe unfolding events that will usher in the most terrible time in world history outside of the Great Flood: the seven-year Tribulation period. Psalm 108 - which is directly connected to the years 2008, 2009 and beyond - gives still another potential thrilling glimpse into future world events just prior to the Tribulation. In this section, we will explore what this Psalm may foretell for the United States, the United Kingdom, the Middle East, and the rest of the world in the two years leading up to Nissan 1 in 2013 or 2014, which may near to the First Rapture, though no one knows for certain when it will be.

Throughout Psalm 108, there are many terms that apply to nations and people groups in the past, as well as to the present and future. What is doubly thrilling about this is that all the nations mentioned are directly involved with the current, globally felt war against Terrorism. To show how Psalm 108 reveals this, abridged portions of its thirteen stanzas will be quoted, and followed by interpretations of what people groups and events these verses most likely pertain to. Let's begin with the first seven stanzas:

*"O God (Elohim), my heart is steadfast; I will sing and give praise... Awake, lute and harp! I will awaken the dawn. I will*

## Chapter 9: The United States and Israel in Prophecy

*praise You, O LORD (Yahweh)... among the nations... Be exalted, O God (Elohim), above the heavens, and Your glory above all the earth; That Your beloved (i.e. Jerusalem) may be delivered, save with Your right hand, and hear me. God (Elohim) has spoken in His holiness: 'I will rejoice; I will divide (or separate) Shechem (a city of refuge in Ephraimite territory which now refers to the Palestinian allotment of land in the West Bank) and measure out (i.e. set apart) the Valley of Succoth (part of Gad's ancient territory - refers to the Palestinian occupied Gaza Strip)." - Ps. 108:1-7*

Fascinatingly, one of the two portions of land that have been portioned out to the Palestinians is the West Bank, which surrounds Jerusalem on three sides. This portion of land is called Shechem in Psalm 108, and it was rich pastureland when Jacob's sons tended their father's flocks there. It was near Shechem that Joseph made his fateful trip out into the fields to check on the welfare of his brothers, only to be beaten, imprisoned, and sold into slavery by them (Genesis 37:13-28). It was also in Shechem where Joseph was later buried.

Interestingly, the story of Joseph's slavery and later rise to power in Egypt echoes the current conflict between the West and the Muslim nations. Perhaps this is why Joseph's tomb is located in Shechem, or the West Bank, and why the Palestinians barbarically destroyed his tomb in 2003. As shown in my book "The Language of God in Humanity," Joseph's two sons Ephraim and Manasseh would come to represent two powerful Gentile nations in the Last Days: The United States (Ephraim), and the United Kingdom (Manasseh).

The Scripture *"I will divide (or separate) Shechem"* directly states that it is God's Will that there should be a separation of the West Bank from the rest of Israel through the auspices of the United States, United Kingdom, and United Nations! In double fulfillment of this, the West Bank is now separated, or divided by political strife as well since it was set up as a secular democratic state, but was quickly overrun by fundamentalist Islamic terrorist groups.

Even more fascinating is the fact that *"the Valley of Sukkoth"* in the preceding Scripture may be referring to the Gaza Strip, which is indeed measured out, or set apart from Israel and the West Bank! These two sections of land were recently given to the Palestinians in order to secure peace with them, and the rest of the Middle East. However, this grand gesture of generosity by Israel has failed miserably in winning support and friendship from the Palestinians, or other Muslim nations.

The reason this modern bid at peace is failing is bound up in the past, and directly relates to the seemingly perpetual blood feuds between

Isaac and Ishmael, and Jacob and Esau. It is also tied to the failure of the Israelites to make any lasting peace with the hated Philistines and Amalekites after their Exodus from Egypt and their conquest of Canaan.

Intriguingly, the next two stanzas of Psalm 108 tell us what nations are intimately involved with, or opposed to this dividing up of Israel in an effort to bring peace to the region. It also states which nations are under God's current control, or acting on His behalf, and also which ones are the targets of His wrath:

> *"Gilead (i.e. the grandson of Manasseh, likely referring to Canada and/or Australia today) is Mine; Manasseh (the United Kingdom) is Mine; Ephraim (the United States) also is the "helmet for My head" (or chief stronghold); Judah (the nation of ISRAEL) is My lawgiver. Moab (Syria, Iraq, and Iran) is My washpot; over Edom (Jordan, Saudi Arabia, and possibly Yemen and Oman) I will cast My shoe; over Philistia (Lebanon, Syria, Palestinian territories) I will triumph.'"* - Psalm 108:8-9

This portion of Scripture indicates that the Western nations with the most troops in Iraq and Afghanistan today, and those most closely allied with Israel today in friendship - the United States, the United Kingdom, and Canada and/or Australia - are doing God's will in the Middle East. So, no matter what people in these countries may think of their current political leaders or government decisions concerning the War on Terror, these governments are (most likely unwittingly) acting on God's behalf right now, though I must strongly emphasize here that ***this situation will change dramatically when the Antichrist becomes leader of the West*** in Europe sometime during, or after the predicted war described in Psalm 108. In addition, let me state that not every proposal regarding Israel by the United States is condoned by God. In fact, it appears that many of the tragic events that have occurred on American soil (such as 9-11, Hurricane Katrina, the California Wildfires of 2007), and the great destruction exacted on the East Coast of America by Super Storm Hurricane Sandy have partly resulted either from God's judgment against America for going too far in trying to assuage the Palestinians and in not supporting Israel, or for allowing unconstitutional attacks upon Christians, Christianity and traditional family values at home.

The remaining portion of Psalm 108 tells us that the Western nations allied to Israel are going to have a major military show down with the Islamic terrorists allied against them, which include those living in Iran, Iraq, Syria, and Saudi Arabia. Now based on my interpretation of Psalms 110 through 118 in Chapter Two, this war will likely be waged for two to three years and will break out before the First Rapture of the True

## Chapter 9: The United States and Israel in Prophecy

Church - which may occur anytime up to the end of 2014 on Nissan 1, 2015 - if the Signs in the Heavens between 2011 and 2018 are any indication. This will be near to the ominous Blood Moon on Passover of 2015. Furthermore, based on the final stanza of Psalm 108, **the armies of the West will not be able to defeat their Terrorist enemies unless the people of the West (particularly the USA) openly call upon the God of Israel to help them:**

> *"Who will bring me into the strong (or fortified) city (i.e. Babylon; a.k.a. Iraq - with its many US-built military bases surrounding it)? Who will lead me (in)to Edom (Jordan, Saudi Arabia, and possibly Yemen, and Oman)? Is it not You, O God (Elohim), who cast us off? And You, O God (Elohim), who did not go out with our armies? (OR: Elohim, will You cast us off? Elohim, will You abandon our armies?) Give us help from trouble, for the help of man is useless.* **Through God (Elohim) we will do valiantly, for it is He who shall tread down our enemies.**" - Psalm 108:10-13

In this final section of Psalm 108, the passage that reads: *"it is He who shall tread down our enemies"* suggests that God will miraculously intervene and bless Israel and the West with a temporary victory in the Middle East. It's also uncanny how this Scriptural passage is VERY reminiscent of the phrase "Don't Tread On Me" that appears on the USA's Gadsden flag. Furthermore, the lamentations and pleas to God in Psalm 109 - this psalm of prayer and lamentation is tied to events beginning in late 2009, but which might not be fulfilled until the end of 2013 or beyond. Psalm 109 indicates that this war will lead to both suffering and great spiritual revival in the land of Israel and the countries allied to it:

> *"But you, O Sovereign LORD (Yahweh), deal well with me for your name's sake; out of the goodness of your love, deliver me. For I am poor and needy, and my heart is wounded within me. I fade away like an evening shadow; I am shaken off like a locust. My knees give way from fasting; my body is thin and gaunt."* - Psalm 109:21-24 (NIV)

Psalm 109 also suggests that the resolution of this war may lead to a much greater openness among Jews and Arabs to hear the Gospel and be saved. Perhaps the miraculous events leading to this short-lived victory of Israel and the West against the Arabs will spur this revival. If so, it will lead to the sharing of the Good News of the Kingdom of God with all of Abraham's descendents through Ishmael and Isaac in preparation for the Rapture - or, if the Rapture has passed before this time - the last half of the Tribulation and the Second Coming of Christ:

> *"Help me, O LORD my God (oh Yahweh my Elohim); save me in accordance with your love. Let them know that it is your hand, that you, O LORD (Yahweh), have done it." "With my mouth I will greatly extol the LORD (Yahweh); in the great throng I will praise him. For he stands at the right hand of the needy one, to save his life from those who condemn him." - Psalm 109:26-27, 30-31 (NIV)*

Could this worldwide time of peace and revival be the result of a peace treaty between Israel and the Arab world that will be signed with the diplomatic help of a politician who either represents, or will become the Antichrist? Based on other clues in Scripture, this peace treaty will likely allow the Jews to build a new Temple adjacent to the Al-Aqsa Mosque on the Temple Mount in Jerusalem and to reinstate animal sacrifices shortly thereafter.

## Ezekiel 38 & 39: The USA and Israel in Great Peril Together

Returning to my discussion of Daniel's vision of *"the Beast from the Sea"* earlier in this chapter, I have identified what the leopard, bear, lion, and eagle represent. However, **the eagle is missing from the corresponding vision of the Beast in the Book of Revelation**. This makes sense, however, since Daniel's prophecy tells us that **the eagle will be taken out of the picture**:

> *"The first was like a lion, and it had the wings of an eagle. I watched until its wings were torn off..." - Daniel 7:4 (NIV)*

The eagle's wings were torn off - thus implying that the formidable power represented by the United States shall be excluded from the Antichrist's empire, and subsequently diminished, destroyed, or weakened (likely partly by the Rapture). Could a powerful nation like the United States be completely annihilated, however? The answer to this question is partly in the Old Testament Book of Ezekiel, Chapters 38 and 39, which describes a terrible war instigated by a prince identified as Gog, of the land of Magog, who rules over Rosh, Meshech, and Tubal:

> *"Son of man, **set your face against Gog, of the land of Magog, the prince of Rosh, Meshech, and Tubal,** and prophesy against him, and say, 'Thus says the Lord GOD (Yahweh Elohim): Behold, I am against you, **O Gog, the prince of Rosh, Meshech, and Tubal.** I will... lead you out, with all your army, horses, and horsemen, all splendidly clothed, a great company with bucklers and shields, all of them handling swords. **Persia, Ethiopia, and**

*Libya are with them, all of them with shield and helmet;* ***Gomer and all its troops; the house of Togarmah from the far north and all its troops*** *-- many people are with you.' " - Ezekiel 38:2-6*

Note here that Gog is not a nation, but a *prince* who rules Rosh, Meshech, and Tubal, in a region called Magog. Magog, Meshech, and Tubal are names of descendents of Noah's son Japheth that inhabited portions of Europe, Russia, and Asia, while Rosh might refer to a son of Benjamin (Gen. 10:2, 46:21). Many Scholars identify Rosh with Russia, and Magog has been linked to Moscow and London, implying an alliance between the two governments represented by these cities in the End Times. If so, could the prince of Gog or London rule over the European Union and modern Russia one day as the Antichrist? In Chapter Ten, we will explore the association of Gog with a prince of England. As such, the Antichrist or *"prince of Gog"* may be connected to European royalty. He may also literally be the King of the North mentioned in the Book of Daniel, who will rule over the largest empire the world has ever known outside of Ancient Babylon. Incidentally, the largest empire of all time was the British Empire, which still exists in the form of the British Commonwealth.

The huge final empire of the Antichrist will also include other nations. The historian Josephus identified Meshech with the Iberians, who ruled over portions of what is now Spain and Portugal in the first century AD. By association, Meshech is allegorically tied not only to Spain, but to all of Latin America today. Josephus also identified Tubal or Tabal as a kingdom in Asia Minor that was northeast of modern day Turkey. This links Tubal to Southern Russia, Georgia, and Azerbaijan - all of which are predominantly inhabited by Muslims.

In this End-Time army, Ezekiel identifies five other regions of the world that will join Magog in their sneak attack on Israel. These are Persia, Ethiopia, Libya, Gomer, and Togarmah. Persia refers to the lands once ruled by the Persian Empire, and may include Turkey, Armenia, Syria, Lebanon, Iraq, Iran, and northern Saudi Arabia. Gomer and Togarmah were located northeast of there - in what was once part of the southeastern Soviet Union. This area now consists of the Muslim-controlled nations of Kazakhstan, Uzbekistan, Kyrgyzstan, Tajikistan, Afghanistan, and possibly Pakistan.

The other nations listed are all found on the African continent. The biblical Ethiopia was not found where modern Ethiopia is, but was likely ancient Nubia - where modern-day Sudan is situated. Finally, ancient Libya was likely in the same locale as modern Libya, which is on the Mediterranean coast in Africa. Like Gomer and Togarmah, all of these nations are predominantly Islamic strongholds today. **At the beginning of the Tribulation period, it is highly likely that all these Islamic regions of the world will temporarily unite under an Islamic leader who will claim to be the Mahdi** or Muslim version of the Anti-Messiah, and he will become Daniel's King of the South. **These Muslim armed forces will attempt to conquer Israel and the northern (European) kingdom of the Antichrist,** which will be governed either through the European Union or United Nations:

> "At the time of the end **the king of the South shall attack him; and the king of the North shall come against him like a whirlwind,** with chariots, horsemen, and with many ships; and he shall enter the countries, overwhelm them, and pass through. **He shall also enter the Glorious Land, and many countries shall be overthrown; but these shall escape from his hand: Edom, Moab, and the prominent people of Ammon.** He shall stretch out his hand against the countries, and **the land of Egypt shall not escape.**" - Daniel 11:40-42

Since Daniel indicates that **the European Antichrist or King of the North's forces shall defeat the Islamic King of the South**, the Antichrist will eventually control all of the southern kingdom's nations including Egypt! As the newly proclaimed Mahdi, the Antichrist may temporarily put an end to Terrorism and will likely cajole the Muslim nations to sign a peace treaty with Israel. This may also be when the Israelis will be allowed to build a new temple on the Temple Mount in Jerusalem - perhaps alongside the Al-Aqsa Mosque as a symbol of the newfound (but short-lived) unity between Muslims and Jews.

Then, in the middle of the Tribulation, the Antichrist will break his treaty with Israel (and the USA), desecrate the Temple, and declare himself to be as God. This is when the Israelis will likely revolt against the Antichrist, and the Antichrist will see this as his justification for launching the war to end all wars. When he does, the European and Muslim nations controlled by the Antichrist will attack "the Glorious Land," or Israel. Since the USA can be identified with Ephraim - the largest of the Ten Lost Tribes of Israel - and likely will continue to be Israel's staunchest ally, they may be invaded at the same time. However, this prophecy also specifically says that three nations that were once to the east of ancient Israel will not be taken over by the Antichrist. These are Edom, Moab, and Ammon, which inhabited the region now known as Jordan. Though no one knows how Jordan will remain outside of the Antichrist's control, its freedom will allow Israelis fleeing Israel before the Battle of Armageddon to find a safe refuge in the uninhabited Jordanian

## Chapter 9: The United States and Israel in Prophecy

canyon city called Petra, which was once the capital city of Edom. Petra is indicated as Israel's hiding place in the "chambers" of Isaiah 26:20, and in Isaiah 63, where Christ is referred to as "the Glorious One" coming from Edom or Petra with the surviving citizens of Israel in His loving care.

There are several reasons why this prophetic section of Ezekiel may refer not only to an attack on Israel, but also to an attack on the United States. First of all, besides the many numerical and allegorical connections between the United States and Israel, there are several clear scriptural connections between them that are described in Ezekiel, Chapter 38. There, Ezekiel tells us that the lands of Magog - Rosh, Tubal and Meshech - will plan an attack on a land that was a desolate, virtually uninhabited wasteland when the prophecy was written. This land will be inhabited and prosperous, however, at the time of the prophecy's fulfillment (Ezekiel 38:8). Furthermore, the land will be populated with people gathered out of the nations (Ezekiel 38:12). There are only two countries in the world that perfectly fit this profile: the United States and Israel.

North America shows evidence that it may have been inhabited by technologically advanced, civilized people before the beautiful, rugged wilderness full of ruins that it became was resettled, farmed and civilized from coast to coast by industrious people from every nation on Earth. Likewise, Israel was a once civilized land turned desert wasteland until the Jews returned from many different lands, irrigated their ancestral homeland, and made it a beautiful place full of verdant green fields and prosperous, modern cities. Could it therefore be that the following prophecy pertains to both the United States and Israel?

> *"This is what the Sovereign LORD (Adonai Yahweh) says: On that day... you will devise an evil scheme. You will say, **'I will invade a land of unwalled villages; I will attack a peaceful and unsuspecting people** - all of them living without walls and without gates and bars. **I will plunder and loot and turn my hand against the resettled ruins and the people gathered from the nations, rich in livestock and goods, living at the center of the land.'** Sheba and Dedan and the merchants of Tarshish and all her villages will say to you, 'Have you come to plunder? Have you gathered your hordes to loot, to carry off silver and gold, to take away livestock and goods and to seize much plunder?'"* - Ezekiel 38:10-13

In the above prophecy, the Scripture says that *"Sheba and Dedan and the merchants of Tarshish and all her villages (or young lions)"* will be corresponding with the Prince of Gog who controls Magog. Tarshish is likely referring to the United Kingdom, which has always had a large and powerful navy. Thus, the young lions attached to Tarshish would be referring to her colonies and commonwealth nations. Sheba was a descendant of Ham through his son Cush, who was the father of the dark-skinned races that settled in Africa and India. In addition, it is almost certain that Sheba refers to ancient Ethiopia and the nations located in the southernmost part of the Saudi Arabian peninsula such as Yemen. Meanwhile, Dedan may refer to parts of Saudi Arabia, Pakistan and India. Furthermore, it is Yahshua as Adonai Yahweh who tells Ezekiel that the people dwelling in peace who are going to be attacked by Magog and his allies live *"at the center of the land."* This is true of both Israel and the United States. In Israel's case, they are in the center of the Fertile Crescent of the Middle East that stretches from Ethiopia in the southwest to the Persian Gulf in the northeast. In the case of the United States, its citizens inhabit the center portion of North America, with Mexico to the south and Canada to the north. In addition, there is evidence that the United States was inhabited by more sophisticated civilizations deep in the past before the time of the Native Americans (see Book Three). The ruins of these civilizations found in many abandoned mounds and pueblo-style cities attest to this fact. Therefore, the United States is like Israel in that both have prosperous and *"resettled ruins."*

The preceding examples clarify the fact that the United States is linked to, and is being reckoned as Israel in the above prophecy. Since I have already proven that the United States is a part of Israel in God's eyes, there very well could be a full-scale attack and invasion of the United States by its neighbors to the far north - mainly from Russia, China, North Korea, and Iran at the same time that they attack the nation of Israel.

Based on the fact that the Battle of Gog and Magog invasion of Israel and the USA comes at a time of peace for both nations, this attack is likely going to occur toward the middle of the Great Tribulation, which is the last 3-1/2 years of Daniel's Seventieth Week (Daniel 9:26-27). It will also likely be after the New World Order is set up, and the Antichrist has taken control of it by intrigue. This can be surmised because the Battle of Gog and Magog shares many traits in common with the Battle of Armageddon, including the fact that there will be a great earthquake and terrible hail that will kill many people, birds and fish, and destroy cities and mountain ranges (Ezekiel 38:19-22; Revelation 16:17-20), the enemies of Israel will be supernaturally defeated (Ezekiel 38:18-22, Ezekiel 39:1-6; Revelation 19:17-21), and the carrion birds will dine on the corpses of the enemy armies (Ezekiel 39:4, 17-20; Revelation 19:17-18).

# Chapter 9: The United States and Israel in Prophecy

At the time of this war, it appears that the Seven Bowls of God's Wrath will be poured out, and these will come in the form of divinely sent cataclysmic storms, earthquakes, and pestilences worldwide that will ultimately lead to the Battle of Armageddon marked by Christ's return and sound defeat of Israel's enemies. To determine more about this war, let's take a close look at the Scriptures describing this End Time attack upon Israel:

> "Therefore, son of man, prophesy and say to Gog, 'Thus says the Lord GOD (Adonai Yahweh): 'On that day when My people Israel dwell safely, will you not know it? **Then you will come from your place out of the far north, you and many peoples with you, all of them riding on horses, a great company and a mighty army. You will come up against My people Israel like a cloud, to cover the land. It will be in the latter days** that I will bring you against My land, so that the nations may know Me, when I am hallowed in you, O Gog, before their eyes.'" - Ezekiel 38:14-16

This Scripture teaches that the kingdoms of the north represented by Russia and Asia will unite with the Middle East to attack *a peaceful land without walls,* whose citizens do not have any reason to suspect such an attack (Ezekiel 38:11). However, when this mighty army does attack, it will be *"on horses."* The Hebrew word for horse is "soos," implying skipping, leaping, or flying swiftly, and with great energy. This attack is therefore prophesied to be very sudden, obvious, vigorous, and swift. One nation in particular has had no reason to suspect such an attack until recently – the United States. Sadly, this prophecy of an unsuspected attack on a peaceful land already began to be fulfilled to some degree with the Terrorist attack on America that occurred on September 11th, 2001. Since then, there have also been Terrorist bombings in Russia, England, and other countries that are relatively peaceful lands at the moment. In addition, Israel has tried unsuccessfully to be at peace with her Islamic neighbors, but is constantly being targeted by Muslim Radicals.

Nonetheless, an unwarranted air of invincibility currently seems to permeate much of America. Many Americans believe that they are relatively safe from Terrorist or enemy attacks. But while Americans were unaware, their military infrastructure has been severely compromised and eroded due to financial cutbacks. So, though Americans thinks they are essentially secure from serious Terrorist or enemy threats - its enemies in Russia, Asia and the Middle East are likely plotting to annihilate both America and Israel. Military intelligence reports tell us that the leaders of

Terrorist regimes aren't isolated to any one country, but can be found in many countries - including America. With so many places for Terrorists to hide, the threat of Terrorism as a trigger for World War III is impossible to ignore or extinguish.

Since the United States is allied to and reckoned with Israel in Ezekiel Chapter 38, the Antichrist and his armies will likely attack both nations. However, because of Yah's supernatural intervention, the United States and Israel will be able to fight back, prevail against their enemies, and will ultimately be victorious:

> *"And you, son of man, prophesy against Gog, and say, Thus says the Lord GOD (Adonai Yahweh):* **'Behold, I am against you, O Gog, prince of Rosh, Meshech, and Tubal;** *and I will turn you around and lead you on, bringing you up from the far north, and bring you against the mountains of Israel.* **Then... You shall fall upon the mountains of Israel, you and all your troops... I will give you to birds of prey... and to the beasts of the field to be devoured.** *(See Revelation 19:21) You shall fall on the open field; for I have spoken,' says the Lord GOD (Adonai Yahweh).* **'And I will send fire on Magog and on those who live in security in the coastlands.** *Then they shall know that I am the LORD (Yahweh).'"*
> - Ezekiel 39:1-6

As mentioned earlier, the above Scripture has many points in common with the Battle of Armageddon in the final chapters of the Book of Revelation, such as the supernatural nature of the defeat (Ezek. 39:2-4; Rev. 19:11-17), the fire sent to destroy Magog and Babylon the Great (Ezek. 39:6; Rev. 18:8), and the birds devouring the dead (Ezek. 39:4; Rev. 19:21). There is also an uncanny similarity between the words Magog and Armageddon suggesting a connection between the two, besides Armageddon's obvious link with the Valley of Megiddo or Jezreel Valley in northern Israel.

The similarity of Ezekiel's vision of the Battle of Gog and Magog with Revelation's prophecies concerning the Battle of Armageddon suggests that they are speaking of the same war that will end with Yahshua's return. If so, this war may rage on for one to three years before Yahshua and His heavenly army comes to rescue the beleaguered Tribulation Saints who remain alive until the end. Or it may possibly be a two-part war - with a time of uneasy peace in between.

## Chapter 9: The United States and Israel in Prophecy

### *The Freemasonry Among America's Founding Fathers*

Although many researchers now cite the fact that George Washington and several of America's other founding fathers were involved in Freemasonry to try and paint America as an Illuminati plot that was never Christian in nature, there is much historically documented evidence that George Washington was a truly God-fearing and Christ-centered leader. This is also true of several other Freemasons of high standing in America's formative years, although citing the proof of this is beyond the scope of this book. However, as a good starting point, I highly recommend the well-balanced and carefully researched book "The Secret Temple - Masons, Mysteries and the Founding of America" by Peter Levenda.

Furthermore, being a Freemason during Washington's era did not preclude being a Christian. One could be both a Christian and a Freemason without losing one's salvation back then because a Freemasonic Temple was a temple to mankind's highest ideals, not a temple to a pagan deity. Since the Bible teaches that believers are the Temples of God's Holy Spirit, Freemasons could view the highest Christian ideals that they held dear in their hearts and minds as a part of their Temple involvement. In addition, Freemasonry has a decided reverence for the Great Architect of the Universe, which is another Title for the Creator of the Universe, who is Yahweh God Almighty and Hi Son Yahshua. Since Satan is not the Creator, but desires to be the Destroyer of the Universe, the God being touted in Freemasonry can therefore be viewed as the True God Yahweh Elohim.

The American Freemasonry that was known to George Washington and several more of America's founding fathers that were powerful proponents of Democracy and Freedom was therefore not a Satanic religion, nor has it ever been touted as such. What Freemasonry is has been darkened by Satanic elements that have moved into certain branches of Freemasonry, but not all of them, and this happened after Washington - and all of America's other founding fathers - were dead and buried.

What many people who view Freemasonry with fear or suspicion do not realize is that the elements of modern Freemasonry began to form and flower during the Enlightenment period in Europe and England in the 16th through 18th centuries, and it has always been touted as a secretive men's social group that uses rituals and oaths to officiate and advance its members, but discourages the discussion of religion or politics outside of these rituals. Instead, it was a place for leaders or would-be statesmen and businessmen to discuss their livelihoods, make valuable contacts, and share their ideas on how to further the betterment of the world they lived in. Unfortunately, at various times in history, subversive and occult elements have infiltrated some Freemasonic orders. But this did not affect all of Freemasonry because each Masonic Lodge is relatively autonomous and independent of the others outside of the Masonic guidebook each Lodge utilizes to structure its behavior and activities.

Although the lie is now being promulgated that America was founded by Masons who were also occultists, scholar David Barton and others have extensively written about the fact that American Masonic teachings were decidedly Christian in tone in the far past, when most American Masons were devout Christians. However, this changed abruptly in the 19th Century, when some Masonic Lodges began to embrace the teachings of the Occult mystery schools that also flourished in England and Europe during the Enlightenment period. In response to an inquiry about the alleged influence of the Illuminati in American Freemasonry by a Christian reverend named George Washington Snyder, former US President George Washington - America's fist President and a devout Christian who was also a Freemason - wrote a letter dated October 24th, 1798, which said in part:

> *"It was not my intention to doubt that the doctrines of the illuminati and principles of Jacobinism had not spread in the United States. On the contrary, no one is more truly satisfied of this fact than I am.*
>
> *The idea that I meant to convey is was, that I did not believe that the lodges of Free Masons in this Country had, as Societies, endeavored to propagate the diabolical tenets of the first, or pernicious principles of the latter (if they are susceptible of separation). That individuals of them may have done it, or that the founder or instrument employed to found the democratic Societies in the United States, may have had these objects - and actually had a separation of the People from their Government in view, is too evident to be questioned."*

What George Washington was saying here is that the Freemasons as a Society did **not** embrace the radical doctrines of the Illuminati or Jacobins - who advocated using deceit, anarchy and excessive violence as a way to achieve their aims. But he also freely admitted that men with such ambitions did spread their venom in some Masonic Lodges, and they also certainly played a part in the American Revolution, and in the politics of his day.

# Chapter 9: The United States and Israel in Prophecy    Page 415

What George Washington could not have foreseen, however, was the success of these satanic radicals that worked to pollute American politics and Freemasonry with the Occult doctrines of the Illuminati and Jacobins. When their nefarious aims were fully achieved and unmasked in the mid-1800's, Masonic Lodges in America lost many of their professing Christian members, who were outraged by this trend. Consequently, the type of Freemasonry practiced in George Washington's America, which was decidedly Christian, mostly ceased to exist after 1850, although the Mormon Church, or the Church of Latter Day Saints has supposedly preserved a form of it as a part of their secret Temple rites that Joseph Smith - the founder of the LDS Church, and a Freemason - created his pseudo-Christian religion around.

## *Washington's Vision Tied to Daniel, Enoch, & Ezekiel*

Although it is not found in the Bible, there is another prophetic clue that verifies my preceding interpretation of Ezekiel 38 and 39, and the Book of Daniel and Revelation in light of the United States in Bible Prophecy. It comes to us in the record of a vision. This vision is not recorded in the Bible, but has so far been proven true by the unfolding of history. It is attributed to George Washington - the first President of the United States, and a devout Christian who also happened to be a high caliber Freemason of the more benign early type described in the last section of this book.

A copy of the prophecy ascribed to George Washington is preserved in the Library of Congress, where it is recorded that the vision appeared in a newspaper article first published in the National Tribune in 1859, and then was reprinted in 1880, 1931, and 1950. The account of the vision reportedly came from a well-respected officer who served under General Washington at Valley Forge named Anthony Sherman. Interviewed when he was 99 years old, Anthony related George Washington's vision to a reporter named Wesley Bradshaw. Though physically feeble, Sherman was said to still have a sharp mind that was undiminished with age. Bradshaw related that, according to Sherman, a beautiful female angel visited George Washington in the winter of 1777, at Valley Forge. **This angel then showed the future President a visionary preview of every major war that would be fought on the American mainland.** Because this vision is concerned primarily with *wars fought on American soil*, it does not mention either World War I or II, or the bombing of Pearl Harbor - since Hawaii was not an official State in the Union when this occurred. For the same reason, it also ignores the Korean War, Vietnam War, Gulf War, and both wars with Iraq.

Intriguingly, the vision was first made public in 1859, which was two years before the American Civil War - a war that was clearly predicted in the vision. For this reason, though the vision that has come down to us is not George Washington's first-hand account, it continues to hold my interest because it appears to be prophetic. In fact, certain aspects of the vision tie it in theme to the prophecies of Ezekiel and Daniel. I have included the entire vision here, with my own interpretations within it highlighted, and encased in parentheses:

"Everything about me seemed to rarify, the mysterious visitor herself becoming more airy, and yet more distinct to my sight than before. I now began to feel as one dying, or rather to experience the sensations which I have sometimes imagined accompany dissolution. I did not think, I did not reason, I did not move; all were alike impossible. I was only conscious of gazing fixedly, vacantly at my companion."

"Presently I heard a voice saying, 'Son of the Republic, look and learn,' while at the same time my visitor extended her arm eastwardly. I now beheld a heavy white vapor at some distance rising fold upon fold. This gradually dissipated, and I looked upon a strange scene. Before me lay spread out in one vast plain all the countries of the world - Europe, Asia, Africa, and America. I saw rolling and tossing between Europe and America the billows of the Atlantic, and between Asia and America lay the Pacific. 'Son of the Republic,' said the same mysterious voice as before, 'look and learn.'"

"At that moment I beheld a dark, shadowy being, like an angel floating in mid-air, between Europe and America, dipping water out of the ocean in the hollow of each hand. He sprinkled some upon America with his right hand, while with his left hand he cast some on Europe. Immediately a dark cloud rose from these countries and joined in mid-ocean. For a while it remained stationary, and then moved slowly westward, until it enveloped America in its murky folds. Sharp flashes of lightning passed through it at intervals, and I heard the smothered groans and cries of the American people." *(The American people groan under the unfair taxation of the Colonies by Great Britain, which leads to* **the Revolutionary War, and the War of 1812.** *This portion of the vision also encompasses* **the French and Indian War, and the Spanish-American War,** *all of which arose from European invaders on American soil.)*

"A second time the angel dipped water from the ocean, and sprinkled it out as before. The dark cloud was then drawn back to the ocean, in whose heaving billows it sank from view. **(This marks the end of this period of wars fought with Europeans on American soil.)** A third time I heard the mysterious voice saying, 'Son of the Republic, look and

# Chapter 9: The United States and Israel in Prophecy      Page 417

learn.' I cast my eyes upon America and beheld villages and towns and cities springing up one after another until the whole land from the Atlantic to the Pacific was dotted with them." *(The spread of America westward and the establishment of 48 of the 50 United States.)*

"Again I heard the mysterious voice say, 'Son of the Republic, the end of the century cometh, look and learn.' At this the dark, shadowy angel turned his face southward, and from Africa I saw an ill-omened spectre approach our land. *(The slavery of Africans in America is established.)* It flitted slowly over every town and city. The inhabitants presently set themselves in battle array against each other." *(The American Civil War begins.)*

"As I continued looking, I saw a bright angel, on whose brow rested a crown of light, on which was traced the word "Union," bearing the American flag, which he placed between the divided nation, and said, 'Remember ye are brethren.' Instantly the inhabitants, casting from them their weapons, became friends once more and united around the National Standard." *(This marks the end of the Civil War, the abolition of slavery, and the reuniting of all the States under one government.)*

"And again I heard the mysterious voice saying, 'Son of the Republic, look and learn.' At this the dark, shadowy angel placed a trumpet to his mouth and blew three distinct blasts; and taking water from the ocean, he sprinkled it upon Europe, Asia, and Africa. Then my eyes beheld a fearful scene: from each of these countries arose thick, black clouds that were joined into one." *(As will be verified in the next paragraph of the vision, combined forces from "Europe" (the EU nations), "Asia" (which may include Iran, Iraq, India, Pakistan, China, and North Korea), and "Africa" (most likely the Muslims in Egypt and North Africa) form a great army ruled over by the Antichrist. This army then marches on the United States (and Israel!) in what marks the beginning of World War III - possibly toward the end of the Tribulation period.)*

"And throughout this mass there gleamed a dark red light by which I saw hordes of armed men, who, moving with the cloud, marched by land and sailed by sea to America, which country was enveloped in the volume of the cloud. And I dimly saw these vast armies devastate the whole country and burn the villages, towns, and cities that I beheld were springing up." *(America's land and its people are horribly devastated by this foreign enemy invasion.)*

"As my ears listened to the thundering of the cannon, clashing of swords, and the shouts and cries of millions in mortal combat, I heard again the mysterious voice saying, 'Son of the Republic, look and learn.'

*When the voice had ceased, the dark, shadowy angel placed his trumpet once more to his mouth and blew a long and fearful blast."*

Though this is not the end of the vision, let's take a moment to ponder the word "Union" identifying the United States, and the trumpet blasts made by the shadowy angels in George Washington's vision. Could the word "Union" here be in reference to the staff called "Union" in Zechariah 11:14? Furthermore, could the trumpets in Washington's vision be connected to the trumpets, or trumpet-like voices, that will be sounded by Yah's holy angels at the beginning, during, and toward the close of the Tribulation period (Revelation 1:10; 4:1; 8:7,8,10,12-13; 9:1,13-14; 11:15)? Note especially the seventh trumpet of Revelation:

> *"Then the seventh angel sounded: And there were loud voices in heaven, saying,* **'The kingdoms of this world have become the kingdoms of our Lord and of His Christ,** *and He shall reign forever and ever!'" - Rev. 11:15*

As we will see momentarily in Washington's vision, the seventh angel of Revelation proclaims that the armies of the Earth, though powerful and destructive in their invasion of Israel and America, will be totally conquered at Yahshua's triumphant return. Besides this connection to Revelation, George Washington's vision also has an uncanny similarity with Ezekiel's vision of the great armies who go against the nation identified as Israel. As was shown in the last section, Ezekiel's "Israel" may refer to both the United States and the modern nation of Israel:

> *"You will come up against My people Israel* **like a cloud, to cover the land. It will be in the latter days** *that I will bring you against My land, so that the nations may know Me, when I am hallowed in you, O Gog, before their eyes." - Ezekiel 38:16*

The interesting parallel here with Ezekiel's vision is that George Washington sees the enemy invasion of the United States as a dark cloud forming from the water of the ocean sprinkled on the enemy nations by the angel. In this way, the watery cloud of evil allegorically seems to be tied to the *"beast rising up out of the sea"* in the Book of Revelation. In Washington's vision, however, the people who live in Africa join Europe, Russia and China in their attack on the United States. This suggests Middle Eastern and Black African Muslim involvement in the Antichrist's attack on the United States and Israel. An army formed from all these countries could easily number the 200 million soldiers that will wipe out a third of the population of the Earth (Rev. 9:16). Thankfully, this wicked

## Chapter 9: The United States and Israel in Prophecy

army will be supernaturally destroyed by Christ and His heavenly army at the Battle of Armageddon (Rev. 19:19).

In many ways, Washington's vision mimics the events seen in Ezekiel's vision of a swift and perilous invasion where all seems lost. However, just as in Ezekiel's vision, George Washington's vision ends with the supernatural intervention of Yahweh Himself, which is revealed after the formation of the "dark cloud" of attacking countries:

"Instantly a light as of a thousand suns shone down from above me, and pierced and broke into fragments the dark cloud which enveloped America. At the same moment the angel, upon whose head still shone the word "Union," and who bore our national flag in one hand and a sword in the other, descended from the heavens, attended by legions of white spirits." **(Christ returns with His heavenly army in order to save both Israel and the United States from total destruction.)**

"These immediately joined the inhabitants of America, who I perceived were well-nigh overcome, but who immediately taking courage again, closed up their broken ranks and renewed the battle. Again, amid the fearful noise of the conflict, I heard the mysterious voice saying, 'Son of the Republic, look and learn.' As the voice ceased, the shadowy angel for the last time dipped water from the ocean and sprinkled it upon America. Instantly the dark cloud rolled back, together with the armies it had brought, leaving the inhabitants of the land victorious." *(**The remaining Americans fighting against the Antichrist's army will be saved from death by Yahshua's return.** Furthermore, some of them will be transformed at Yahshua's return, becoming immortal saints who will join Yahshua's heavenly army and aid in conquering the wicked.* **Their combined victory over Satan and his armies will put an abrupt end to the Great Tribulation.)**

"Then once more I beheld the villages, towns, and cities springing up where I had seen them before, while the bright angel, planting the azure standard he had brought in the midst of them, cried with a loud voice, 'While the stars remain, and the heavens send down dew upon the earth, so long shall the Union last.' And taking from his brow the crown on which was blazoned the word "Union," he placed it upon the Standard, while the people, kneeling down, said, 'Amen.'" *(This indicates that **the United States of America will recover from the devastation of the war** and will remain "One Nation Under God" until the end of the Millennial Rule of Christ, when the heavens and the Earth will be recreated.)*

"The scene instantly began to fade and dissolve, and I at last saw nothing but the rising, curling vapor I at first beheld. This also disappearing, I found myself once more gazing upon the mysterious visitor, who, in the same voice I had heard before, said, 'Son of the Republic, what you have seen is thus interpreted: Three great perils will come upon the Republic. The most fearful is the third, passing which the whole world united shall not prevail against her. Let every child of the Republic learn to live for his God, his land, and the Union.' With these words the vision vanished, and I started from my seat, and felt that I had seen a vision wherein had been shown me the birth, progress, and destiny of the United States."

After relating his vision, **George Washington stated that this powerful encounter with an angel had shown him an outline of the history of America.** Uncannily, this vision also agrees with the prophecies in Daniel and Ezekiel regarding the fate of Israel and the United States. Just as Daniel predicted, George Washington's vision shows how the symbolic wings of the eagle in Daniel's vision that represents the United States will be torn off and left without representation in the United Nations. **Great Britain will have turned against the United States - along with Russia, Asia, Africa and Europe.** Then, under the direction of the Antichrist, they will likely unite under the banner of the United Nations. **Subsequently, the Antichrist will likely initiate an invasion of the United States at the same time that he attacks Israel, just as Ezekiel's vision indicates.** This strategically makes perfect sense since the United States is Israel's most powerful ally, and it may continue to be even after the Rapture, which may lead to a conservative-led military coup here.

Speaking of the Rapture, since the United States currently has such great military power, something drastic will have to happen to the United States to cripple it militarily before the other nations of the world attack it. This event would have to make America much more vulnerable to invasion. As such, severe economic woes coupled with the Rapture may be the likely culprit. With 25 to 45 percent of its citizens gone, the United States would be thrown into terrible chaos. The U.S. military would also be hard hit if a sizeable number of their troops mysteriously disappear. Though the United States would likely rebound somewhat from this swift and tremendous loss of citizenry, the country would suffer from outbreaks of civil unrest, wholesale looting, and general anarchy. The United States might therefore never fully recover its former strength. Given the Antichrist's evil and power-hungry nature as disclosed in the Bible, there is no doubt that the Antichrist would capitalize on any weakness in the United States when it would be advantageous for him to do so.

# Chapter 9: The United States and Israel in Prophecy

There is also the possibility that, after the Rapture (or even before), nuclear missiles originating from North Korea and other parts of Asia, Russia, or Iran and other parts of the Middle East may be launched against the United States and Israel. Such an attack would kill millions of people unless Yahweh provides supernatural intervention, as is suggested by the prophet Ezekiel (Ezekiel 38:18-23, 39:1-6). Without Yah's merciful protection, this sort of attack would severely cripple the USA and Israel, leaving them both totally vulnerable to foreign invasion. Nuclear attacks might also send the USA into a state of political and social anarchy - at least for a time.

Terrifyingly, this scenario is not at all farfetched - despite the USA's heightened security after the destruction of the World Trade Center in New York. Many believers, including myself, have had prophetic visions of nuclear bombs destroying major American cities. These visions are backed up by the fact that Russia, China, North Korea, Iran, and other Middle Eastern nations hate the United States due to its constant meddling in international affairs. Consequently, they want to destroy our country, and annihilate our culture and its dominant religion (Christianity) from the face of the Earth. Sadly, many of the leaders of these countries also hate Judaism and the Jews, and they would like nothing better than to wipe out Israel at the same time as the United States.

Despite Satan's desire to annihilate America and Israel, the Bible indicates that God will prevent their total annihilation. Ezekiel 39 indicates that God will miraculously protect the unwalled nation that undergoes the surprise attack George Washington was shown that the United States will be miraculously delivered right after *"the dark, shadowy angel placed his trumpet once more to his mouth and blew a long and fearful blast."* This is likely the seventh and Last Trumpet heralding the end of the Great Tribulation – when many things will occur simultaneously. The most important event at that time, however, will be the return of Christ with His heavenly army and their annihilation of the enemies of both Israel and America. The Apostle Matthew refers to this time with the following words:

> *"**Immediately after the tribulation** of those days the sun will be darkened, and the moon will not give its light; the stars will fall from heaven, and the powers of the heavens will be shaken. Then the sign of the Son of Man will appear in heaven, and then all the tribes of the earth will mourn, and **they will see the Son of Man coming on the clouds of heaven** with power and great glory. And He will send His angels **with a great sound of a**

*trumpet, and they will gather together His elect from the four winds, from one end of heaven to the other."* - Matthew 24:29-31

In Verse 30, which I have highlighted in the preceding Scripture, Yahshua was quoting Daniel 7:13:

*"I was watching in the night visions, and behold, One like the Son of Man, coming with the clouds of heaven! He came to the Ancient of Days, and they brought Him near before Him."* - Dan. 7:13

After utilizing this Scripture, Yahshua indicates that the final stage of the First Resurrection will begin when the Last Trumpet is sounded. At that time, God's holy angels will gather together all the surviving Tribulation Saints, and they will be *"changed - in an instant, in the twinkling of an eye"* as Paul said in 1 Corinthians 15:51-52, and they will meet Christ and the other saints in the air to become royal priests and soldiers in God's immortal kingdom (1 Thess. 4:17). The events of this glorious future moment in history are also echoed in the Book of 1 Enoch:

*"And they shall be terrified, and they shall be downcast of countenance, and pain shall seize them,* **when they see that Son of Man Sitting on the throne of his glory.** *And the kings and the mighty and all who possess the earth shall bless and glorify and extol him who rules over all, who was hidden..."* - 1 Enoch 62:5-6

*"And all the kings and the mighty and the exalted and those who rule the earth shall fall down before him on their faces, and worship and set their hope* **upon that Son of Man***, and petition him and supplicate for mercy at his hands... And* **He will deliver them to the angels for punishment, To execute vengeance on them because they have oppressed His children** *and His elect. And they shall be a spectacle for the righteous and for His elect: They shall rejoice over them, Because the wrath of the Lord of Spirits resteth upon them,* **And His sword is drunk with their blood.***"* - 1 Enoch 62:9-12

In these quotes from 1 Enoch, note that Enoch called Yahshua by the title *"Son of Man."* This is highly significant, making Enoch the first prophet of God to call the Preincarnate Yahshua the Son of Man in reference to His role as our Redeemer from sin and death. In addition, Enoch refers to the sword of wrath that Yahshua will wield on His Father's behalf. Among the many times that Yahshua spoke of the Son of Man, He was likely using this term to identify Himself with the Son of

## Chapter 9: The United States and Israel in Prophecy    Page 423

Man spoken of in 1 Enoch and Daniel. This is especially evident in the following Scriptures:

> *"For **the Son of Man** will come in the glory of His Father with His angels, and then He will reward each according to his works." - Matthew 16:27*

> *"When **the Son of Man comes in His glory**, and all the holy angels with Him, then He will sit on the throne of His glory." - Matthew 25:31*

The Book of Revelation describes harrowing scenes that mirror the passages of coming destruction in 1 Enoch, Daniel, and Matthew. In Revelation, there are numerous chilling passages about what will occur at the Last Trumpet announcing Yahshua's coming to rule as King of kings:

> *"And the kings of the earth, the great men, the rich men, the commanders, the mighty men, every slave and every free man, hid themselves in the caves and in the rocks of the mountains, and said to the mountains and rocks, '**Fall on us and hide us from the face of Him who sits on the throne and from the wrath of the Lamb! For the great day of His wrath has come**, and who is able to stand?'" - Revelation 6:15-17*

> *"Then I looked, and behold, a white cloud, and on the cloud sat One like the Son of Man, having on His head a golden crown, and in His hand a sharp sickle." - Revelation 14:14*

> *"Now out of His mouth **goes a sharp sword, that with it He should strike the nations**. And He Himself will rule them with a rod of iron. He Himself treads the winepress of the fierceness and wrath of Almighty God..." "**And the rest were killed with the sword** which proceeded from the mouth of Him who sat on the horse. And all the birds were filled with their flesh." - Revelation 19:15, 21*

All of these Scriptures appear to refer to the same time period that George Washington speaks of in his vision - the time of the Last Trumpet mentioned in Matthew 24:31. Praise Yah that His Son Yahshua will come to deliver the Tribulation Saints from certain death at the hands of their enemies! But until that time, Scripture teaches that life will literally be Hell on Earth for those who must suffer through the Great Tribulation. **Therefore, we should all make every effort to be spared from this terrible time of testing.**

If my date for the beginning of the Tribulation is correct, the invasion of the United States that George Washington foresaw and the ensuing world war will probably occur at mid-Tribulation or early 2014 and last until the end of the Tribulation between Rosh Hashanah 2016 and Rosh Hashanah 2017. Coupled with the horrible Tribulation plagues, this war will cause much death and destruction in America and the rest of the world. Therefore, time is running out for the current world we know.

After the Millennial Rule of Christ, all the fallen leaders and armies of the nations who went against Israel and the United States will be raised from the dead to attend the Great White Throne Judgment. There, the wicked will be called to account for their actions before and during the Tribulation period. How terrible it will be for them when they appear before the Supreme Judge, for those who are found wanting will meet with the terrible fate of being cast into the Lake of Fire:

> *"Then I saw a great white throne and Him who sat on it, from whose face the earth and the heaven fled away. And there was found no place for them.* **And I saw the dead, small and great, standing before God, and books were opened.** *And another book was opened, which is the Book of Life. And the dead were judged according to their works, by the things which were written in the books."*
>
> *"The sea gave up the dead who were in it, and Death and Hades delivered up the dead who were in them. And they were judged, each one according to his works. Then Death and Hades were cast into the lake of fire. This is the second death. And* **anyone not found written in the Book of Life was cast into the lake of fire.**" *– Revelation 20:11-15*

At the Great White Throne Judgment, everyone not included in the First Resurrection will be raised to life. This Second Resurrection will occur immediately after the final war at the end of the Millennial Rule of Christ. Though many people raised at this time will go on to inherit everlasting life, many more of them will perish because of their lack of repentance for their evil actions toward the saints during their lives, and their undiminished hatred of Christ.

## *How Zechariah Verified the Role of the USA in Prophecy!*

Now let's examine a startling prophecy in the book of Zechariah, which uses the imagery of several constellations in the Gospel in the Stars. This Star Gospel imagery may tell us something important about

## Chapter 9: The United States and Israel in Prophecy

the modern prophetic identities of the Tribes of Judah and Ephraim. Zechariah's messianic prophecy foretells the time when Yahshua, the King of kings returns to Jerusalem. This will likely be at His Second Coming, which is at the end of the Tribulation period. The following verses proclaim that Yahshua will *"cut off the chariot,"* or completely stop the battle raging against His saints in *"Ephraim"* and *"Jerusalem."* As I explained earlier, Ephraim represents the United States, as well as all the saints among the Gentile nations. Likewise, since Jerusalem is in the nation of Israel, it must signify the Jews living in that country, as well as the redeemed Jews around the world who have accepted Christ as their Messiah:

> *"Rejoice greatly, O daughter of Zion! Shout, O daughter of Jerusalem! Behold,* **your King is coming** *to you; he is just and having salvation, lowly and riding on a donkey, a colt, the foal of a donkey.* **I will cut off the chariot from Ephraim and the horse from Jerusalem; the battle bow shall be cut off.** *He shall speak peace to the nations; his dominion shall be 'from sea to sea, and from the River to the ends of the earth.' As for you also,* **because of the blood of your covenant***, I will set your prisoners free from the waterless pit." – Zech. 9:9-11*

Here, Yahweh is telling us that He will cut off, or stop the advance of the *"chariots,"* which equate with modern day tanks, trucks, planes, and helicopters. In addition, He will cut off the *"battle bow,"* which signifies all devices used in launching missiles against the United States, Israel, and other enclaves of persecuted Tribulation Saints. The end of the preceding quote mentions a Blood Covenant that compels Yahweh to act mercifully to Israel. This is the New Covenant that Yahshua signed in His own Blood, and that all His saints have partaken in, and upheld. Therefore, when Yahweh says, *"I will set your prisoners free from the waterless pit,"* He means that He shall deliver the Tribulation Saints from the grave in the Resurrection! The prophecy then goes on to say:

> *"'For* **I have bent Judah, My bow, fitted the bow with Ephraim***, and raised up your sons, O Zion,* **against your sons, O Greece***, and made you like the sword of a mighty man.' Then the LORD (Yahweh) will be seen over them,* **and His arrow will go forth like lightning***. The Lord GOD (Yahweh Adonai) will* **blow the trumpet***, and go with whirlwinds from the south." - Zech. 9:13-14*

## Two Messianic Centaurs Confront Scorpio's Evil

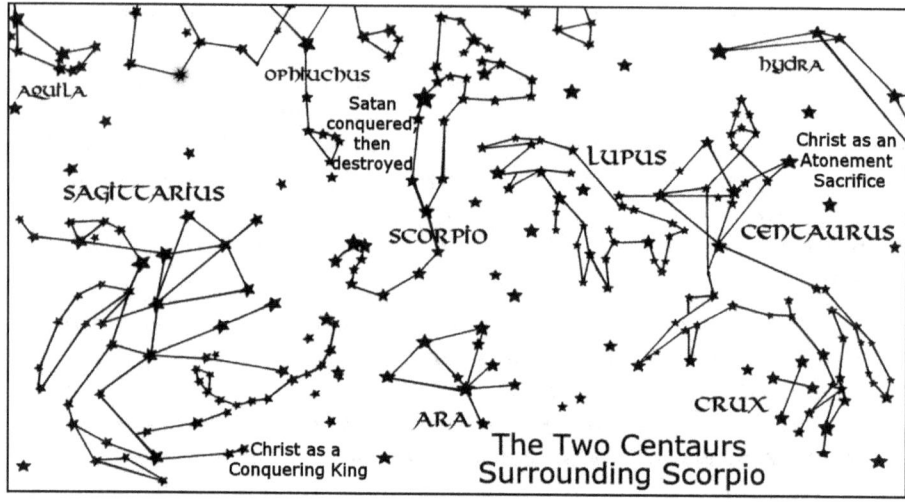

The Two Centaurs Surrounding Scorpio

Zechariah's prophecy is startling in that it exhibits clear references to the imagery in the Gospel in the Stars. Here, Yahshua - as Yahweh Adonai - blows the Shofar, or trumpet, and carries His bow, which is fitted with Ephraim, *or the saints in the United States, and elsewhere.* Ephraim serves as a symbolic arrow like Sagitta the Arrow, which is a symbol tied to Aquila the Eagle, as well as Sagittarius, the Archer of the Zodiac who is aiming his arrow at Scorpio, or Satan's heart. Yet it also refers to the prophecies that identify the USA as Ephraim, and Judah as Israel - not as they are now, but under the leadership of Christ! Meanwhile, Judah is pictured as the bow of the archer. This archer is Christ as signified by Sagittarius, the centaur in the Star Gospel that is half man, and half sacrificial animal. As such, it represents Christ's duality as both a Conquering Hero, and Redeeming Sacrifice.

In the Gospel in the Stars, the constellation Aquila the Eagle is just above Sagittarius' head. Aquila is a decan of Capricorn, and symbolizes Christ's strength, and ability to destroy the satanic Serpent. In addition, Aquila symbolizes the saints in the United States, and around the world that will one day be united with the USA in its rebellion against the Antichrist. Touching one of Aquila's wings is Sagitta the Arrow. This is the arrow (or missile) that wounds Aquila, or America, and then is utilized by Christ (as seen in Sagittarius). In fact, there is another Centaur in the Zodiac like Sagittarius called Centaurus that - in shooting Lupus with an arrow - signifies Christ wounding Himself to save us from sin. As such, it may also depict the martyred, yet now resurrected saints who will aid Christ in annihilating the armies of the Antichrist, as can be seen in the illustration on page 426.

The constellation Sagitta the Arrow wounds Aquila the Eagle, but also arms it with strength to destroy the wicked. This arrow therefore symbolizes many things. First, as the preceding Scripture indicates, the arrow is tied to Ephraim, who is shot out of the bow of Judah. But according to the following Scripture, the arrow is also Israel as a whole, not just the Tribe of Ephraim:

> "He made my mouth like a sharpened sword, in the shadow of his hand he hid me; **he made me into a polished arrow and concealed me in his quiver**. He said to me, '**You are my servant, Israel,** in whom I will display my splendor.'" - Isaiah 49:2-3 (NIV)

Here, Israel represents Yahshua and all His redeemed saints among the nations. However, when Aquila is coupled with Sagitta, the eagle and arrow also represent Israel and the United States defending themselves during a time of great peril. As shown in this chapter, this will be during the Great Tribulation, when the United States and Israel will both be engaged in a life and death struggle against the forces of the Antichrist.

Together, the two preceding Scriptures signify that, just as an arrow pierces its victim, the Jews turned Yahshua over to the Romans for crucifixion, thereby dealing Him a deathblow and piercing Him with nails, thorns, whip barbs, and a spear point instead of an arrow. Nonetheless, their evil action brought great blessing on the world, for Yahshua's death served as an atoning sacrifice for all sin. In addition, these two separate prophecies indicates that - when Christ returns as Yahweh's Avenger of Blood upon the wicked - He will be powering the bow that shoots the symbolic arrow representing His saints in the USA, and elsewhere all around the world.

These prophecies both suggest that Christ shoots the "arrow" identified as Ephraim and Israel, which represent Christ's army of saints. However, it also suggests the use of conventional or nuclear missiles against the enemies of God. Therefore, could it be that - during the final stages of the Tribulation period - Israel's peril will cause the United States to launch a portion of its nuclear or conventional missile arsenal against the Antichrist's armies, thereby bringing the wrath of the Antichrist against the United States? Despite the ferocity of the Antichrist's attack on the USA, there will likely still be saved people there fighting against the Antichrist when Christ returns. Together, they will joyfully join the saints of the world in aiding Christ as He delivers the final deathblow to

Satan's schemes. Therefore, Zechariah and Isaiah's prophecies concerning archers, bows, and arrows suggest an End Time scenario that is uncannily similar to those revealed in other prophecies discussed in this chapter that verify the role of the USA in End Time Prophecy.

In Zechariah 9:13-14, the kingdom of the Antichrist is likened to Greece, just as it was in Daniel's vision of the One-Horned Goat representing Alexander the Great and the Antichrist. Greece is symbolic of the Antichrist and his kingdom or nation because it was the forerunner to Roman rule and culture - and it is Rome, or more specifically the "Holy" Roman Empire, whom the Antichrist represents. Since this prophecy deals with the Antichrist, Zechariah also tells us that this prophecy represents the time of the Great Tribulation by its reference to blowing a trumpet. This trumpet alludes to the Last Trumpet call that will sound when Yahshua (as Yahweh Adonai in Zechariah 9:14) returns to Earth in triumph and wrath at the end of the Tribulation.

In the Gospel in the Stars, the constellation Aquila the Eagle is seen as a wounded eagle grasping the arrow that injured it in its talons. This arrow is shown in the neighboring constellation Sagitta the Arrow. In one sense, **this arrow symbolizes a terrible war, or highly devastating Terrorist attack in America - one far worse than 9-11.** Yet it also signifies the military might of the United States (the wounded eagle of Aquila) being used against the Antichrist. However, it may also symbolize the need among the believers in America and elsewhere for the supernatural sword that Yahshua will give to His saints to fight and defeat the Antichrist's armies in the Battle of Armageddon. They will be given this sword when they are translated and meet the returning Saints in the air at Yahshua's Second Coming, which could be at the time of the Second Rapture. Then these resurrected Saints will descend with the rest of Yahshua's army and fight the enemies of God with the supernatural power of the Holy Spirit. This scenario is upheld by the final passages of Zechariah's prophecy:

> "The LORD of hosts (Yahweh Tsavout) will defend them; they shall devour and subdue with slingstones. They shall drink and roar as if with wine; they shall be filled with blood like basins, like the corners of the altar. **The LORD their God** (Yahweh Elohim) **will save them in that day,** as the flock of His people. For **they shall be like the jewels of a crown, lifted like a banner over His land**..." – Zechariah 9:15-16

Here we are told that Yahweh will defend His saints, and through His power, the redeemed saints in the United States, Israel, and elsewhere will utterly defeat their enemies. After this, we are given a

## Chapter 9: The United States and Israel in Prophecy

beautiful image of the United States and Israel (and by extension, the Two-House Church of Judah and Ephraim), being exalted above the other nations of the Earth. This is why they are alluded to as jewels in Yahshua's symbolic crown of kingship. What a glorious time in history this will be!

Uncannily, the Great Seal of the United States clearly shows the allegorical connection of the United States with Aquila the Eagle, Christ, Sagitta the Arrow, the Gospel in the Stars, and the thirteenth half Tribe of Israel - Ephraim. In the illustration on page 430, note the North America Nebula in the tail of Cygnus the Swan - a giant cross-shaped constellation representing Christ and His Church. As stated in Book One, this seems to show the fact that America became a true bastion of Christian values. The swan is often used to symbolize love and peace - somewhat like a dove or olive branch. It therefore could be connected to the Olive Branch of Peace in the Bald Eagle's right talons on the Great Seal. However, the olive branch may also be symbolic of the wild and cultivated olive trees grafted together in Scripture (Rom. 11:17-25). This grafted tree symbolizes the future *union* of Jews and Gentiles under the Abrahamic and New Covenants. Meanwhile, the Bald Eagle and the arrows grasped in its left talons can clearly be tied to Aquila and Sagitta in the Star Gospel.

Above the eagle's head are the thirteen stars that represent a new constellation in the heavens. These are in the shape of a Star of David, which is unquestionably a Jewish/Israelite symbol. As shown in "The Language of God in the Universe," the Star of David is also a symbol for the Twelve Tribes of Israel, and all twelve Zodiac signs. This Star of David therefore appears to signify the symbolic crown of Christ, while the eagle signifies the USA and Christ Himself, who together are holding the branch or staff of Joseph (i.e. the Staff of Yahweh), and the arrows of Israel or Ephraim.

Joseph's dream revealed that he would be a leader among the "stars" or Tribes of Israel in the Star Gospel, and the symbolism in the Great Seal of the United States has an undeniable biblical correlation to the Tribe of Joseph and to Joseph's son Ephraim, who inherited Joseph's birthright! This symbolism in the Great Seal connecting it to the Star Gospel can also be seen in Jacob's deathbed prophecy to his son Joseph:

> *"Joseph is a fruitful bough*... *his branches run over the wall.* **The archers have bitterly grieved him,** *shot at him and hated him.* **But his bow remained in strength,** *and the arms of his hands were made strong by... the Mighty God of Jacob."* - Genesis 49:22-24

# The Language of God in Prophecy

## The Great Seal Tied to the Star Gospel

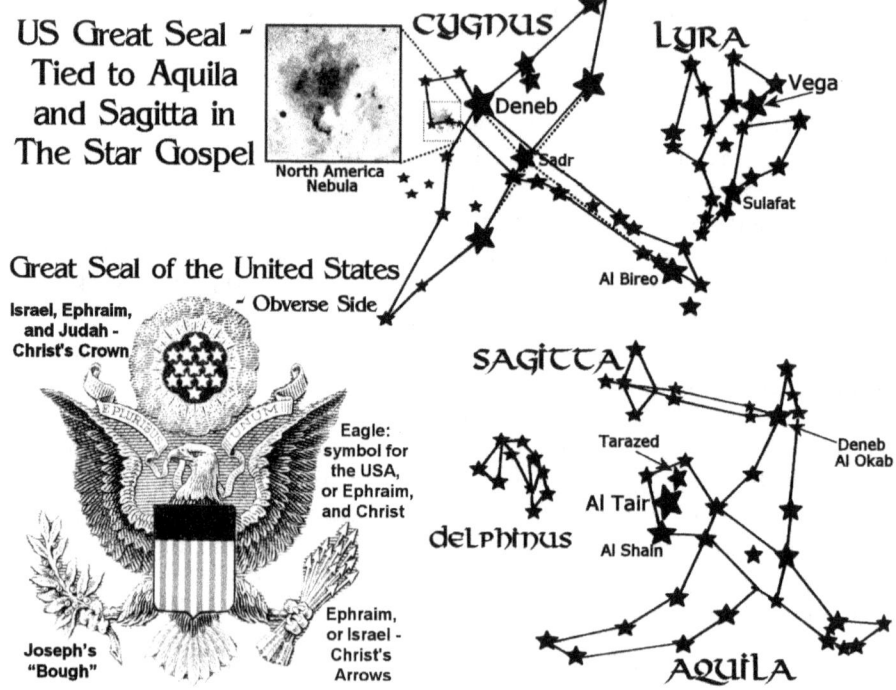

In this prophetic passage, Jacob was telling his sons what would befall them in the Last Days. This prophecy therefore applies to the Tribe of Joseph in the last two thousand years. In it, Joseph is likened to *"a fruitful bough"* or branch. This bough is considered to be an olive branch with ripe olives on it, and that is exactly what we see grasped in the Bald Eagle's right talons! In addition, the prophecy says Joseph would be hated and attacked with arrows, just as Aquila is wounded with an arrow in the Star Gospel! In 2001, the United States was attacked with figurative arrows in the form of planes piloted by Terrorists. In addition, the Islamic fundamentalists who initiated Terrorism in an effort to destroy Israel and the United States hate them both, as do many other nations like China and North Korea. In the heavens, this is shown by the Eagle Nebula, a symbol of good conquering evil that is located in Serpens - a decan of Scorpio. Serpens is a symbol of the unmitigated evil being held back by the strong man Ophiuchus - another Star Gospel symbol for Christ - and the people of the eagle, or those saints who represent the Tribe of Ephraim today.

Finally, this prophecy tells us that, despite the attacks of enemies, *"his bow remained in strength, and the arms of his hands were made strong by the hands of the Mighty God of Jacob."* This means that Ephraim would be strengthened, and protected by the God of Jacob. If the United States of America is the main representative for Ephraim in the world today, then Yahweh Elohim is its Protector, and it does not bode well that this nation is now attempting to ignore that Protector, and the divine source of its strength! However, this prophecy offers a note of hope. It says that, though Joseph/Ephraim may be sorely tested and wounded, its strength would prevail against all odds. This clearly echoes the words of George Washington's prophetic vision about the destiny of the "Union," or United States, and the uncanny way it connects it to the Staff called "Union" in Zechariah 11:14, and Joseph's "Bough" in Genesis 49:22! **All these allegorical implications conclusively tie the Great Seal and the United States to the Tribe of Joseph/Ephraim, and link their destiny together as one.**

Adding to this interpretation, the number thirteen is seen everywhere in the Great Seal - in the thirteen arrows, thirteen stripes, thirteen olives and olive leaves, thirteen stars, thirteen letters in "E Pluribus Unum", which means "Out of many, one", thirteen steps in the pyramid on the other side of the Great Seal, and thirteen letters in the motto above the pyramid: "Annuit Coeptis", meaning "He (God) has favored our undertakings". As already shown, thirteen is the number for the Tribe of Ephraim - the tribe destined to supplant or replace the Tribe of Dan. The symbolism of the Gospel in the Stars is therefore seen everywhere in the Great Seal, which is the official heraldic device for America, and uncannily shows its divinely given destiny and ultimate purpose.

Some people believe men who were involved in Freemasonry designed the Great Seal of the United States. However, the fact is that only Thomas Jefferson - who was only marginally involved in the Great Seal's design - was clearly a Mason. Furthermore, the two major players in the design of the Great Seal - Charles Thomson, the Secretary of Congress who chose the final design elements, and William Barton of Philadelphia, a lawyer and artist familiar with Heraldry - were not, and never had been Freemasons. Therefore, the symbols in the Great Seal only appear to be connected to Freemasonry because they come from common sources: Heraldry, Mythology and the Zodiac/Star Gospel - all of which are connected to the Language of God.

## *The Antichrist and the Erosion of American Civil Rights*

Because Americans have the right to bear arms, America is the only country in the world today where the civilian populace is substantially armed. This fact bears consideration in any End Time scenario, because a country filled with armed civilians poses a threat to any sort of government move to take away the civil liberties granted to Americans by the Constitution of the United States. Nonetheless, several recent Presidents of the United States and many recent Supreme Court Justices have maliciously passed laws that have undermined the civil rights of Americans - all without the American people's approval or consent.

Thankfully, as the American people become more aware of the loss of their individual freedoms under the Patriot Act and many United Nations sanctions, they are becoming rightfully alarmed, and many will not sit passively by while the government tries to take away even more of their personal freedoms. In fact, some United States citizens are forming civil rights groups or joining militia groups, and these groups could start a revolt if the erosion of their freedom is not stopped and the U.S. Constitution continues to be ignored.

Due to this, even if the Antichrist finds a way to take control of the United States Federal Government, he would likely still be hard-pressed to convince the American people to follow him without resistance. In fact, it is my firm belief that many currently apostate Americans will have already been stunned into spiritual wakefulness by the Rapture before the Antichrist tries to take full control of America. As a result, many American Tribulation Saints will likely reject any attempt at disarmament, and will instead fight against the Antichrist. When they do, this might lead to another American civil war - with people who wish to follow the Antichrist fighting against the armed citizens who do not.

Because of the great value that many Americans place in their civil rights and freedoms, it also seems inevitable that a war may ensue between America's civilians and the Antichrist's armies even before the final Battle of Armageddon begins. It is therefore possible that foreign armies will invade the continental United States and World War III will begin long before the Antichrist's armies surround and attack Israel at the end of the Tribulation period. If this does happen, America will likely be unable to come to Israel's aid at all when the Antichrist moves to destroy the Jewish people. Thankfully, however, Yahshua is destined to return to conquer the Antichrist's armies in America and in Israel during their darkest hour. Hallelu-Yah for our coming salvation!

# Chapter 9: The United States and Israel in Prophecy

## *Enoch's Prophecy of the Seventy Shepherds of Israel*

There is another prophecy that, although it does not give an exact year date, indicates that we are on the threshold of the Tribulation period. This prophecy also speaks of a fiery abyss that the wicked will be cast into. The prophecy isn't in the Bible, however. It is instead found in the Book of 1 Enoch - in Enoch's Prophecy of the Seventy Shepherds of Israel. Based on archeological evidence, even the most conservative scholars agree that the manuscript this prophecy appears in predates the New Testament by at least several hundred years. However, the Book of 1 Enoch and the Prophecy of the Seventy Shepherds may predate most of the Old Testament by a thousand years or more. In this prophecy, Enoch speaks of the shepherds or rulers who have governed Israel not just in the past, but also in the *future*.

In a vision, Enoch saw that there would be seventy shepherds of Israel:

"And **He called seventy shepherds**, and cast those sheep to them that they might pasture them, and He spoke to the shepherds and their companions: 'Let each individual of you pasture the sheep henceforward, and everything that I shall command you that do ye. And I will deliver them over unto you duly numbered, and tell you which of them are to be destroyed- and them destroy ye.' And He gave over unto them those sheep." - 1 Enoch 89:59-61

These seventy symbolic shepherds watch over the flock of sheep that figuratively are God's chosen people. The next passage tells us that Enoch saw the first group of thirty-five shepherds as unique from the other shepherds to come:

"And I saw till that in this manner **thirty-five shepherds** undertook the pasturing (of the sheep), and they severally completed their periods as did the first; and others received them into their hands, to pasture them for their period, each shepherd in his own period." - 1 Enoch 90:1-2

These first thirty-five shepherds correspond to thirty-five kings of Israel and Judah that ruled *before* the Babylonian King Nebuchadnezzar destroyed the Kingdom of Judah in 597 BC. After this, a series of foreign kings ruled over the Promised Land as shepherds. The following passage clarifies this time in history. The seventy shepherds Enoch saw were all descendents of Israel, though some of these Israelite shepherds had overlords over them who are also called shepherds:

> *"...the eyes of those sheep were blinded so that they saw not, and (the eyes of) their shepherds likewise; and they (i.e. the shepherds of the sheep) delivered them in large numbers to their shepherds (i.e. the overlords of the shepherds) for destruction, and they trampled the sheep with their feet and devoured them."* - 1 Enoch 89:74-75

Enoch sees twenty-three foreign kings ruling over Israel until the destruction of Jerusalem in 70 AD. Adding their number to the thirty-five kings who came before, a total of fifty-eight kings were foreseen as rulers over Ancient Israel:

> *"And I saw **until that twenty-three had undertaken the pasturing** and completed in their several periods fifty-eight times."* - 1 Enoch 90:5

During the reign of the twenty-three puppet shepherds, Enoch describes the destruction among the lost sheep of Israel, as well as the building and destruction of the First and Second Temple in Jerusalem (1 Enoch 89:59-76). Enoch also foresaw that, blinded by their ignorance of God's Will, many from the Twelve Tribes of Israel would be scattered abroad, and would become the victims of many enemies during the times of the two temples.

Enoch also foresaw the coming of a One-Horned Ram or Unicorn who would open the eyes of the blind sheep and lead them to salvation. Enoch's vision disclosed that there would be a period of time when the followers of this One-Horned Ram will be persecuted and killed without mercy. The enemies of the One-Horned Ram will attempt to destroy the Ram's teachings and followers, but will not succeed (1 Enoch 90:1-19). We will discuss the spiritual and temporal meanings of the unicorn, and what Enoch's unicorn means to Christians in the next chapter.

**After this, Enoch foresaw that twelve more shepherds would arise to govern over Israel.** He therefore foretold the rebirth of Israel as a nation in modern times! Sadly, Enoch tells us that this group of twelve final shepherds in Israel will do more damage to Israel spiritually than the fifty-eight bad shepherds who governed the country long before them:

> *"And I saw that man, who wrote the book according to the command of the Lord, till he opened that book concerning the destruction which those twelve last shepherds had wrought, and showed that they had destroyed much more than their predecessors, before the Lord of the sheep. And I saw till the Lord of the sheep came unto them and took in His hand the staff of His wrath, and smote the earth, and the earth clave asunder, and all*

*the beasts and all the birds of the heaven fell from among those sheep, and were swallowed up in the earth and it covered them."* - 1 Enoch 90:19

The predecessors spoken of in this prophecy were the shepherds who came *before* the emergence of someone Enoch calls "the Lord of the Sheep." This Lord of the Sheep is none other than Yahshua the Messiah: the One-Horned Ram! Since these twelve shepherds arise *after* the death and resurrection of Yahshua and the destruction of the Second Temple in 70 AD, these last twelve must belong to the modern state of Israel - a nation now ruled over by secular-minded Prime Ministers. Since these "kings" are humanistic in their outlook for Israel, they have not shepherded the people into drawing closer to Yahweh or following His Laws. As a result, many Jews in Israel no longer have faith in their heavenly Father. Yahweh will therefore judge these shepherds severely and cast them into a fiery abyss. According to the Book of 1 Enoch, they will be cast away with all the Fallen Angels who defiled themselves with women, and anyone else who is found guilty of unconfessed sins such as bitterness or lack of forgiveness and lack of repentance or impenitence at the end of the world:

*"And I saw till a throne was erected in the pleasant land (i.e. Jerusalem), and the Lord of the sheep sat Himself thereon, and the other took the sealed books and opened those books before the Lord of the sheep. And the Lord called those men the seven first white ones, and commanded that they should bring before Him, beginning with the first star which led the way, all the stars whose privy members were like those of horses, and they brought them all before Him. And He said to that man who wrote before Him, being one of those seven white ones, and said unto him:* **'Take those seventy shepherds to whom I delivered the sheep,** *and who taking them on their own authority slew more than I commanded them.' And behold they were all bound, I saw, and they all stood before Him."*

*"And the judgment was held first over the stars, and they were judged and found guilty, and went to the place of condemnation, and they were cast into an abyss, full of fire and flaming, and full of pillars of fire.* **And those seventy shepherds were judged and found guilty, and they were cast into that fiery abyss.** *And I saw at that time how a like abyss was opened in the midst of the earth, full of fire, and they brought those blinded sheep, and they were all judged and found guilty and cast into this fiery abyss, and they burned..."* - 1 Enoch 90:20-27

The twelve last shepherds of Israel will therefore be judged and found guilty along with the fifty-eight shepherd kings of Israel who came before them - with the exception perhaps of King David and King Josiah. Most from among these seventy kings, however, will perish without repenting of their sins. One easy way to test the legitimacy of Enoch's prophetic vision of the seventy shepherds of Israel is to see how closely the prophecy of the twelve last shepherds applies today. We can do this by counting how many prime ministers have ruled in the modern nation called Israel since its inception in 1948. Uncannily, *twelve* men have served in this office so far, as shown in the following list. James Johnson, a fellow scholar, friend, and enthusiast of the Book of 1 Enoch, provided me with this list when the 12th Prime Minister had not yet ruled:

1. **David Ben-Gurion** (1886-1973): Prime Minister of Israel from 1948 to 1953 and 1955 to 1963

2. **Moshe Sharett** (1894-1965): Prime Minister of Israel from 1954 to 1955

3. **Levi Eshkol** (1895-1969): Prime Minister of Israel from 1963 to 1969

4. **Golda Meir** (1898-1978): Prime Minister of Israel from 1969 to 1974

5. **Yitzak Rabin** (1922-1995): Prime Minister of Israel from 1974 to 1977, and 1992 to 1995

6. **Menachem Begin** (1913-1992): Prime Minister of Israel from 1977 to 1983

7. **Yitzhak Shamir** (1915- ): Prime Minister of Israel from 1983-1984 and 1986 to 1992

8. **Shimon Peres** (1923- ): Prime Minister of Israel from 1995 to 1996

9. **Ehud Barak** (1942- ): Prime Minister of Israel from 1999 to 2001

10. **Ariel Sharon** (1928- ): Prime Minister of Israel from 2001 to 2006

11. **Ehud Olmert** (1945- ): Prime Minister of Israel from April 2006 to present.

12. **Binyamin Netanyahu** (1949- ): Prime Minister of Israel from 1996 to 1999 and 2009 to Present.

The preceding list clearly shows that twelve men have served as Prime Ministers of modern Israel, with some of them serving more than once! Adding these twelve to the fifty-eight prior shepherds of Israel mentioned by Enoch, we find that ***Seventy men have already served as***

## Chapter 9: The United States and Israel in Prophecy

*shepherds of Israel. Since there are to be only twelve shepherds of modern Israel before all seventy of Israel's shepherds are judged, then the time before the end of this present world system must be very near.*

During the twelfth Shepherd of Israel's rule, Enoch prophesied that the persecuted sheep that follow the One-Horned Ram would be given a great sword with which to fight their enemies. As shown when this prophecy is focused on again in the next chapter, this sword is the Holy Spirit. After this, the Lord of the Sheep will smite the Earth with His Wrath, destroy the wicked, set up His own kingdom, and rule until the Last Judgment (1 Enoch 90:19-21). **Therefore, the twelfth Prime Minister of Israel is likely to be the last one to rule before the Second Coming of Christ.**

If this prophecy is true, it means that Yahshua Himself will serve as the thirteenth leader of modern Israel during His Millennial Rule! This fact again shows that the thirteenth member of any group can often turn evil into good, and replace wickedness with righteousness. In fact, the only major biblical exception to that rule was the thirteenth patriarch in the line of Adam through Seth. This was Arphaxad's apostate son Cainan, who - after the Great Flood - was instrumental in corrupting Sethite Sacred Astronomy into the Astrology first taught by the fallen Watchers prior to the Flood.

Fascinatingly, Benjamin Netanyahu's stint as Israeli Prime Minister was due to end in September of 2010 - after a period of only 18 months in office. But Netanyahu won the elections held then in late 2010 and will hold the position of Israeli Prime Minister until 2014 unless he dies in office. However, if Enoch's Prophecy of the Seventy Shepherds is to continue to hold true, either there will be no more Prime Ministers of Israel after Netanyahu leaves office or else Israel will be governed by one of its former Prime Ministers again after Netanyahu until Yahshua returns to vanquish the wicked at the Battle of Armageddon.

Since he has already been in office since 2009, Benjamin Netanyahu's position as Prime Minster is due to end someday soon. As shown in Book Two, "The Language of God in Humanity," this Feast of Israel prophetically correlates with the Rapture. However, the Rapture is even more closely tied to Pentecost and the summer harvest season in Israel, so there is a possibility that the Rapture could occur someday soon. These End Time heavenly signs are primarily explored in Chapters 8, 11 and 12 of this book.

In addition, this book has shown that there are many other prophetic indications that the First Rapture may occur sometime soon. These include the prophecies in Psalms 108, 109, and Psalms 110 through

118. Indeed, Psalms 111 through 117 appear to be tied to the seven years of the Tribulation. In addition to these prophecies, I have shown how Daniel's Prophecy of the Seventy Weeks has several different prophetic applications. Then there is the 2010 end date of the Great Step in the Grand Gallery of the Great Pyramid, and the subsequent revelation I was given of the Antechamber, which shows that the Great Tribulation may be shortened to six years rather than seven.

However, keep in mind that there is likely to be two Raptures - with one before the Great Tribulation and one occurring at its end - when the Two Witnesses are resurrected. This possibility is explored in Chapter 11 of this revised book.

## Chapter 10: The Antichrist and Woman Riding the Beast

*"Judah is a lion's whelp; from the prey, my son, you have gone up. He bows down, he lies down as a lion; and as a lion, who shall rouse him?* **The scepter shall not depart from Judah, nor a lawgiver from between his feet, until Shiloh comes;** *and to Him shall be the obedience of the people." - Genesis 49:9-10*

As mentioned in previous chapters, some nations that will make up the one world government of the Antichrist depicted by the Beast can be symbolically and literally linked to the Twelve Tribes of Israel. This fact adds much intrigue and significance to the Antichrist's take over of the world during the Tribulation period. It also makes us ask the following questions: What evidence is there that the Twelve Tribes of Israel are still in existence? If Europe, Britain, and America are part of Israel, and the Antichrist is going to lead the EU and the United Nations, is it possible that the Antichrist will be a descendent of King David of Israel, and have a legitimate claim to David's Throne, and Judah's Scepter, just as Christ does? Is the Throne of Judah still in existence somewhere on the Earth today, or did it cease to exist when Judah fell to Babylon as some scholars insist?

There are many prophecies in the Bible that refer to the rise of the Antichrist, and the signs that the Tribulation is imminent. In this chapter, we'll explore the signs that herald the coming of the Last Day, or Day of the Lord. We will also examine the signs surrounding the literal and spiritual realization of God's promises to Abraham, and their fulfillment in prophecy.

### Are England and Judah's Throne Linked?

The Scripture quoted at the beginning of this chapter suggests that King David's throne will not cease to exist until Yahshua (there identified as Shiloh) comes again to claim His rightful throne and kingdom. Remarkably, there is historical evidence that supports the validity of the claim that King David's throne was never completely overturned, and that his scepter was never fully removed, just as Yahweh promised in Scripture.

"Shiloh" is another Jewish term for the Messiah, Yahshua. Many scholars therefore say that this prophecy was fulfilled at Christ's First Advent. They reason that Yahshua is now ruling from the heavenly throne of David. However, this fails to acknowledge the fact that, even though Christ rules in Heaven, He still does not really rule on Earth. Satan is still the master of this world, and he will be until Yahshua sets up His kingdom here on Earth! King David's righteous leadership will therefore ultimately be fulfilled through Christ's future reign on Earth.

Scripture tells us that **there was a period of hundreds of years before Christ's birth when David's throne ceased to exist in Israel.** Yahshua therefore did not inherit any existing throne at that time. But the prophecy clearly states that: *"the scepter shall not depart from Judah... until Shiloh comes."* This means Yahshua should have inherited the literal throne of David, *but has not yet done so on Earth.* In addition, thousands of years have now elapsed since David's symbolic throne and scepter seemingly vanished. But since Yahweh cannot lie, the above promise that Yahweh made to Judah must somehow be upheld until Christ comes to rule as King. Only at that time can the following prophecy be fulfilled:

*"I see him, but not now; I behold him, but not near. A star will come out of Jacob; a scepter will rise out of Israel. He will crush the foreheads of Moab, the skulls of all the sons of Sheth. Edom will be conquered; Seir, his enemy, will be conquered, but Israel will grow strong."* - Numbers 24:17-18 (NIV)

In the above prophecy, each ancient country has several modern counterparts. For example, Seir signifies Egypt, Libya, and Sudan; Moab represents Lebanon, Syria, and Jordan; Sheth signifies Iran, Iraq, Kuwait, and Afghanistan; and Edom represents Saudi Arabia, Yemen, and Oman. These countries therefore represent virtually the entire modern Arab world. The preceding messianic prophecy therefore states that the Arab nations will unite to destroy Israel under the Antichrist, but will be totally defeated by a supernatural act of God. Even now, the Arabs - who are fueling the fires of Terrorism all over the world - are planting the seeds that will lead to their destruction. Praise Yah that Yahshua, our Messiah will at last subdue and convert the Muslims, Terrorism will cease, Ishmael's blood feud with his half brother Israel will finally end, and the Arabs will submit to Israel's dominion when Christ rules from Jerusalem!

# Ch. 10: The Antichrist and Woman Riding the Beast

Most Bible scholars see Numbers 24:17-18, which says: "*a star will come out of Jacob"* as a messianic prophecy concerning Christ that has not yet been fulfilled. When coupled with the prophecy concerning Shiloh in Genesis 49:10, it clearly suggests that - for them to be fulfilled - **the Messiah must have a scepter to hold, and Israel must continue to exist.** If this is true, then both Judah's Scepter (and Throne), and the nation of Israel must be present somewhere on the Earth today. In addition, David's throne must exist until Christ comes to win the Battle of Armageddon, and set up His Kingdom on Earth. If the Messiah's throne through King David is to exist until He comes to rule the Earth, David's royal bloodline must also be present somewhere on Earth. Since Yahweh never lies, it should come as no surprise that there is evidence that Yahweh kept His promises to Judah and David, and that David's lineage did continue when the Kingdom of Judah fell - *but in exile in a distant land* (Jeremiah 15:14).

Though it may seem implausible, some intriguing historical evidence, and many legends support the idea that King David's descendents arrived in Ireland, and Scotland. This happened through one or more daughters of the last King of Judah. After Judah was conquered, King Nebuchadnezzar took wicked King Zedekiah captive. Later, Zedekiah watched while his sons and heirs were killed before his eyes - after which Zedekiah's eyes were put out (2 Kings 24:7). Thereafter, Zedekiah spent the remainder of his life in prison (Jeremiah 52:10-11). It therefore appears that Nebuchadnezzar destroyed the royal line of Judah descended from David forever.

However, this was not the real end of David's royal lineage, for Scripture clearly records that some of the former King of Judah's daughters survived (Jeremiah 41:10; 43:6). After their leader Johanan killed King Nebuchadnezzar's newly appointed governor in Judea, this remnant of Judah subsequently fled to Egypt against the prophet Jeremiah's divinely given orders from Yah (Jeremiah 43:8; 44:12). Since Jeremiah prophesied that these refugees from Judah would perish in Egypt, and had warned them about it, it is assumed that all of them eventually perished. However, Jeremiah also prophesied that a few from this remnant of Judah in Egypt would escape (Jeremiah 44:14). Furthermore, Jeremiah prophesied that this tiny remnant of Judah would mingle with those they hate (i.e. the Gentiles) (Jeremiah 15:14). Isaiah also prophesied concerning the royal House of Judah, stating that this remnant of Judah's royal family will take root downward, and bear fruit upward (i.e. find a homeland, and prosper) (Isaiah 37:31-32).

Thereafter, legends suggest that at least one royal daughter of the line of Judah survived, and left Egypt accompanied by her grandfather, the prophet Jeremiah. Soon after, one or more of these princesses of Judah supposedly arrived in Ireland, married with the princes of the ruling Celtic (and therefore Lost Israelite) family, and set up a new royal dynasty. In fact, the lion symbols used in Heraldry may signify the existence of this royal bloodline, and the physical location of David's royal descendents today. In conjunction with the lion, a heraldic unicorn symbol is often used, which ties the royal line of the Tribe of Judah to the Tribes of Joseph and Dan. The following sections will explain why.

## *Enoch's Prophecy Of The Unicorn - A Symbol For Christ*

The unicorn has long been an object of fascination for many, combining the power and beauty of a white horse with a single, golden horn. Coupled with a long, flowing mane and tail, the modern and medieval European unicorn is a creature of ethereal beauty. Myths surrounding the unicorn abound, and creatures with a single horn have long been recognized as a symbol for either good or evil in cultures around the world. Few ancient unicorns, however, resemble the horse-like unicorn of today. The white, horse-like unicorn most commonly depicted today has its origins in medieval times, when it was used as a symbol for Christ. It therefore took on Christ's most notable attributes - being gentle, loving, pure, and chaste like Christ was.

Unfortunately, there are far older associations with this one-horned animal that have sinister roots, such as the unicorns of China and Babylon. In recent times, the unicorn has taken on similar occult associations, as the New Age Movement has adopted it as a symbol. To them, it represents transformation and transcendence, and as such they openly encourage their children to find their own unicorn guides. They do this in hopes that their children will ascend to the level of avatar, or ascended master faster than the rest of mortals who must supposedly live countless lives before achieving this dubious state of perfection on their own.

Regardless of the occult associations of unicorns today, unicorns undeniably represented the ultimate goodness, and holiness of Yahshua in the medieval world, as already mentioned. So there is a duality to this powerful symbol that is undisputable, and also very perplexing. How can a symbol of purity and goodness also be reckoned as a symbol for evil and unrestrained power, and how can we tell the difference if they look the same on the surface? The answer is found in the gift of spiritual discernment. This gift of the Holy Spirit allows Christians to absolutely know the difference between good and evil, and to ascertain the meanings of the symbols used for each opposing force.

As I have maintained throughout this series, Yahweh Elohim is the ultimate designer and revealer of symbols. In "The Language of God in the Universe," I showed how the cross, with its definite connection to Astronomy, is a very powerful symbol for Christ, who is the Creator of the Universe, and the Gospel in the Stars. Now, in this book, I will show that the unicorn - like the number 13, the two Enochs, and the two Cainans - has both good and bad connotations, and can represent both perfect good - and unmitigated evil. First, let's explore the benevolent side of the unicorn in folklore, the Star Gospel, and 1 Enoch.

As shown in Chapter Seven, the unicorn can be used to symbolize the right horn or hand of a Cherub, which signifies Yahshua at the right hand of His Father. This suggests that the left horn of a Cherub represents a personage that is opposite to Christ, like the Antichrist. We will examine this idea in the next section, but for now, let's focus on the unicorn as a godly symbol for Christ.

In Medieval times, the unicorn was used as a symbol for Christ. Could this be because it was found as a messianic symbol in the Book of 1 Enoch? Although 1 Enoch was supposedly lost to the West at that time, somebody in Europe or the British Isles may have had some knowledge of its prophecies. I suspect this because, in one of his prophetic visions, Enoch describes Christ and His Church as a powerful One-Horned Ram that opens the eyes of many lost sheep:

> "And I saw till **there sprouted a great horn (symbol of authority) of one of those sheep**, and their eyes were opened (they see the truth that sets them free from Satan's bondage). And it looked at them [and their eyes opened], and it cried to the sheep (the newly-saved sheep), and the rams (spiritual leaders) saw it and all ran to it. And notwithstanding all this those eagles and vultures and ravens and kites (followers of the prince of the power of the air) still kept tearing the sheep and swooping down upon them and devouring them (these devoured ones are the martyrs of God): still the sheep remained silent, but the rams lamented and cried out (the leaders begin to teach the truth). And those ravens fought and battled with it (the One-Horned Ram and His Church) **and sought to lay low its horn, but they had no power over it."**

> "All the eagles and vultures and ravens and kites were gathered together, and there came with them all the "sheep" (incorrectly translated as sheep, should say beasts - as per the next

*sentence) of the field, yea, they all came together,* ***and helped each other to break that horn of the ram.*** *And I saw till* ***a great sword*** *(i.e. the sword of the Holy Spirit)* ***was given to the sheep*** *(i.e. those who follow the One-Horned Ram), and the sheep proceeded against all the beasts of the field (the armies of the wicked in rebellion against God) to slay them (at the Battle of Armageddon), and all the beasts and the birds of the heaven fled before their face." - 1 Enoch 90:9-19*

As shown by my comments in parentheses, this section of Enoch's lengthy prophecy in chapters 89 and 90 of 1 Enoch is brimful of the allegorical Language of God. It is very rich in symbolism that must be spiritually understood before it can be correctly deciphered. First of all, as discussed in Book Two, sheep and goats represent two very different kinds of people. Goats want to lead, for example, while sheep want to follow. We can therefore deduce that the sheep in Enoch's vision are people who follow some greater cause. Likewise, Rams are horned male sheep, and their horns mark them as the leaders of the sheep who have been given the authority to lead. Since sheep were often used in Yahshua's parables to signify His followers, the sheep in Enoch's vision also represent repentant sinners, and the rams signify the spiritual leaders of the sheep. Meanwhile, the beasts of the field in Enoch's vision represent the unrepentant wicked who will perish.

Note also that all the birds mentioned in Enoch's vision are birds of prey with sharp beaks and talons. Birds of prey, as the most villainous birds, make excellent symbols for Satan's followers. Furthermore, birds are the only animals that can view the air as their natural domain. Since they rule the air, the birds in Enoch's vision likely represent the armies and servants of *"the prince of the power of the air,"* who is Satan, and his servant, the Antichrist:

*"...you once walked according to the course of this world, according to* ***the prince of the power of the air****, the spirit who now works in the sons of disobedience..." - Ephesians 2:2*

The horns and rams mentioned in Enoch's prophecy refer to leaders among the people who are working against the prince of the power of the air who is Satan. Therefore, when Enoch mentions the One-Horned Ram, or Unicorn's power to open the eyes of the sheep, he is speaking of the power of Christ and His Spirit to illumine the hearts and minds of those who love Him. The sheep whose eyes are opened may also allude directly to the 144,000 Witnesses chosen from among the descendents of the Twelve Tribes of Israel, who will act as Yah-ordained evangelists during the Tribulation period (Rev. 7:3-8). It is Yahshua's

## Ch. 10: The Antichrist and Woman Riding the Beast   Page 445

chosen sheep or disciples that the opposing nations attempt to crush. These wicked and rebellious nations that go against the One-Horned Ram and His sheep are envisioned as birds that kill and/or eat flesh, and beasts that do the same.

As discussed in the last chapter, Enoch foretold that there would be 70 Shepherds of Israel before the Messiah comes. Of these 70, only 12 Shepherds are reported for the modern nation of Israel, and according to my detailed analysis of the prophecy in Chapter 9, Benjamin Netanyahu is the 12th and last Prime Minister. That is - unless the previous Prime Minister Ariel Sharon somehow revives from his long coma, and becomes fit enough to rule before the Battle of Armageddon. Although this is remotely possible, it is extremely doubtful.

During the twelfth and last Shepherd of Israel's rule, Enoch envisioned Yahshua as the Ram with one great and powerful "horn" that opens the eyes of all the people (the sheep) that desire to know and love God. Since a horn is an instrument of protection on an animal, and an animal's horn that has been treated a special way can be used to drink from or play a tune, the horn of this Ram Who is Yahshua is allegorically referring to the Living Water and proclamations of His Word in the Bible, and in the Gospel in the Stars, which are both announcing His good and perfect Will, and that serve to awaken those who are spiritually asleep!

Enoch foresees the Battle of Armageddon, when the "rams" or male "sheep" (i.e. leaders and soldiers for Christ) of the great One-Horned Ram, or Unicorn will finally defeat their foes. Their victory is won through the *"great sword"* that signifies the Word of God, Yahshua. This is clear from the allegorical imagery used in Revelation 19:15 and 19:21 quoted earlier. Though this great sword likely signifies purely divine spiritual power, it may signify a supernatural weapon such as the Staff of Yahweh that will suddenly resurface at a crucial time for the heavily persecuted, but multitudinous body of Tribulation Saints. See Book Three for more about the wondrous Staff of Yahweh that Moses worked many miracles with.

Because the prophecy of the great One-Horned Ram in the Book of 1 Enoch mentions eagles, vultures, kites, and ravens as symbols of evil people and nations, it seems to contradict the symbol of an eagle or hawk as a godly symbol associated with heavenly things. However, as previously discussed, the Tribe of Dan was represented by an eagle to hide their identification with the serpent imagery connected with evil. In addition, the eagles used by the Danites, the Romans, European royalty, and various European nations *were always solid black, red, brown, or gold*. Not one of these nations used the image of a white bird, or white-headed bird such as the Bald Eagle as a symbol.

Though a bird of prey can be viewed as a symbol for evil, there is also Scriptural evidence that both eagles and bird's wings are symbols of God's love and protection:

> *"You have seen what I did to the Egyptians, and how I bore you on eagles' wings and brought you to Myself."* - Exodus 19:4

> *"Keep me as the apple of Your eye; hide me under the shadow of Your wings..."* - Psalm 17:8

> *"He shall cover you with His feathers, and under His wings you shall take refuge; his truth shall be your shield and buckler.'* - Psalm 91:4

> *"But those who wait on the LORD (Yahweh) shall renew their strength; they shall mount up with wings like eagles, they shall run and not be weary, they shall walk and not faint."* - Isaiah 40:31

Just as birds like eagles obviously have a dual significance in prophecy, a One-Horned White Ram may represent more than Christ and His Church. It also may represent *one nation in particular* that will rise to spiritual prominence in the End Times. As the staunchest defender of the nation of Israel in today's world, and the most "Christian" presence among the nations, the United States of America may be the nation symbolized by the one horn of the Ram representing Christ and His Church. Though there are true Christians all over the world, no other nation on Earth has as many born-again, Spirit-filled Christians per capita as the United States.

As already mentioned, the prophecy in 1 Enoch may be the source of the medieval notion that the mythical one-horned unicorn symbolized Yahshua. Since this tradition of representing Christ as a unicorn sprang up in Europe during the Dark Ages, it is likely that the Book of 1 Enoch was known to someone in that era, but was later lost. Though the written record of the connection was lost, however, the linking of the unicorn with Yahshua persisted. This is likely why the word "unicorn" was used nine times by the translator of the King James Bible for the Hebrew word "reem" that more correctly means "wild ox." As mentioned in "The Language of God in the Universe," Cherubim appear as ox-like in appearance in Ezekiel's visions, and were used to symbolize the Universe, and the Twelve Tribes of Israel. The symbol of an ox is also connected to the dual Tribe of Joseph, whose tribal standard contained a depiction of a wild bull, or ox with two horns. Here is one occurrence of the word "unicorn" in the King James Bible:

> *"Save me from the lion's mouth: for thou hast heard me from the horns of the unicorns." - Psalm 22:21 (KJV)*

The King James translation of this particular verse of Scripture has an authority that other Bible translations lack. This is because it tells us something prophetic, whereas the other translations have lost all their power to instruct due to their wording. For example, most translations tell us that the person or nation crying for help in this passage wants to be saved from both the lion's mouth, and the horns of a wild ox. However, the King James translation tells us that the supplicant is asking to be saved from the lion's mouth *by calling for help through the horn* of the unicorn!

This passage is a messianic prophecy that allegorically represents Christ's prayer as He died on the Cross. As a prophecy, it likely has a dual application. Therefore, if viewed prophetically, this passage may be telling us that the modern nation of Israel will be threatened by the jaws of the lion (i.e.: Great Britain, via the Antichrist's armies), and will call on Christ's born-again followers in America (i.e.: the horn of the unicorn) for help in her direst hour. This has already occurred in Israel's history in relation to the lion-like aggression of the Arabs toward Israel, and it will no doubt happen again.

The association made here of Great Britain with the lion was fully explained in the analysis of Daniel's and Revelation's prophecies concerning the Beast from the Sea. See Numbers 23:22, 24:8; Deut. 33:17; Job 39:9-10; Psalm 22:21, 29:6, 92:10; and Isaiah 34:7 to explore the usage of the word "unicorn" in the Kings James Version of the Bible.

There are two biblical references to a "horn" or leader that may be a symbolic allusion to Yahshua, Enoch's One-Horned Ram. These are found in Psalms 92 and 148:

> *"But my horn shalt thou exalt like the horn of an unicorn: I shall be anointed with fresh oil." -Psalm 92:10 (KJV)*

> *"And He has exalted the horn of His people, the praise of all His saints-- of the children of Israel, a people near to Him. Praise the LORD!" - Psalm 148:14*

Note that Psalm 92 is taken from the King James Version of the Bible, where the exalted horn or unicorn was taken to be an allusion to Christ. Note also that Psalm 148 is another Hallel Psalm, and begins and ends with the phrase "Hallelu-Yah!" Perhaps this is why it is not so surprising that it speaks of the exalting of the horn, or leader of the people of Israel. Since Psalm 148 is analogous to 2048 AD, it falls during the reign of Yahshua the Messiah, who will likely be the exalted leader of Israel by that time in history!

In Psalm 75, horns are also mentioned in reference to the righteous leaders who follow the Exalted Horn, Yahshua:

> *"All the horns of the wicked I will also cut off, but the horns of the righteous shall be exalted." - Psalm 75:10*

These righteous horns or leaders for Christ lead the good sheep who form the congregations of Gentile believers that are adopted into the family of Israel, and are allegorically seen as the Two Tribes of Joseph: Ephraim and Manasseh. The bull, or ox of the Zodiac sign of Taurus, which represents the Tribe of Joseph, has two horns. These two horns allegorically represent Ephraim and Manasseh - the two Tribes that descended from Joseph (Deuteronomy 33:17). Over the centuries, however, the ox metamorphosed into a horse-like unicorn. This may be why the wild ox that is connected to Joseph is called a unicorn in the King James Version of the Bible:

> *"His (Joseph's) glory is like the firstling of his bullock, and **his horns are like the horns of unicorns**... and they are the ten thousands of Ephraim, and they are the thousands of Manasseh." - Deuteronomy 33:17 (KJV)*

Since the unicorn is a prominent symbol in European and English Heraldry, could Anglo-Saxon Europeans be claiming to be connected to either one of the two horns, or Tribes of Joseph? Furthermore, could the one ram's horn in Enoch's vision that is raised to prominence over the other, is hated, and is surrounded by enemies in the End Times be one of the nations that spring from the countries connected to the Two Tribes of Joseph? If so, as already shown, two modern nations appear to fulfill the requirements for being the Two Tribes of Joseph. These are Great Britain, which is tied to Manasseh, and the United States, which is allegorically tied to Ephraim. Of these two nations, the one that seems most likely to be the One-Horned Ram of Enoch is the United States, and - by association - modern Israel. These are also the two countries that will likely be brutally attacked, miraculously saved, and specially blessed by Christ in the Last Day.

Do you see the tremendous implications of this connection? The United States and Israel may be the nations forming the one Horn of the Unicorn that represents Christ, and His Church that is now scattered among all nations. This also may be why the United States is to be reckoned as Ephraim, a great Tribe of Israel, and is to suffer the same fate as Israel. For those who wish to read a more detailed study of the history of the Ten Lost Tribes of Israel, please refer to Book Three in this book series, or to "The 'Lost' Ten Tribes of Israel... Found!" by Steven M. Collins. There, you will find detailed examinations of the prophecies, and much historical evidence supporting the modern day location of Judah's Throne, and the Ten Lost Tribes of Israel.

J. H. Allen's book "Judah's Sceptre and Joseph's Birthright" and E. Raymond Capt's book, "Jacob's Pillar" are also listed in the bibliography as resources. However, these men were British Israelites who believed in the supremacy of the Anglo-Saxon Europeans, and saw Great Britain's people as God's chosen people. As such, they believed that Great Britain is destined to rule over all the other nations, and that it was the literal location of the Throne of Judah, which will become the Throne of Christ. As will clearly be shown in this chapter, this is a dangerous heresy. Also keep in mind that all the authors listed here misidentify Ephraim as Great Britain, and also *falsely* assume that the Jews are no longer to be counted as God's Chosen People Israel. Scripture teaches, however, that anyone who believes in Yahshua as the Son of God, and Messiah are to be counted as sons, or children of God, and by extension, children of Israel (Romans 8:14; 2 Corinth. 6:18; Ephesians 1:5; Rev. 21:7), and the Jews will one day acknowledge Yahshua for who He really is:

"And I will pour out on the house of David and the inhabitants of Jerusalem a spirit of grace and supplication. **They will look on me, the one they have pierced, and they will mourn** for him as one mourns for an only child, and grieve... as one grieves for a firstborn son." - Zechariah 12:10 (NIV)

"Then the sign of the Son of Man will appear in heaven, and then **all the tribes of the earth will mourn, and they will see the Son of Man** coming on the clouds of heaven with power and great glory." - Matthew 24:30

The two preceding Scriptures pertain to the whole world, especially the Jews and Lost Tribes of Israel. Both were once ruled over by the Romans, who crucified Christ. The Gospel of Matthew calls those who mourn "tribes" to signify the Tribes of Israel. Furthermore, according to the Book of Revelation, Twelve Tribes of Israel can still be literally found somewhere on the Earth today. In addition, the "earth" being referred to in the same passage means the land where Israel dwells, and this is not just the nation of Israel, but Europe, Great Britain, and the

Americas today. Remember, I am *not* suggesting that only these nations represent spiritual Israel! On the contrary, these nations only represent the physically blessed, literal descendants of Israel - some of whom are also spiritual Israel through their faith in the true Messiah, Yahshua.

So, just as there is a good and evil Cainan, a good and evil Enoch, a good and evil unicorn, and a good and evil Messiah (or Antichrist), there is a good and evil Israel. **Beware of British Israel, which is the evil counterfeit of the real Israel made up of all believers in Christ!**

## Daniel's Unicorn and the Antichrist

As already shown, it is possible that the members of the British Royal Family are blood descendants of King David of Israel. **If so, the Antichrist could well be a member of the British Royal Family.** If this is true, The United Kingdom will lead the unholy alliance that forms Revelation's figurative Beast from the Sea. This seems apparent partly because of the symbolism behind the Coat of Arms representing the British Royal Family. This study into the Language of God should teach us all not to take any such symbols lightly. Any and every symbol can, and usually does have some prophetic significance, and virtually *nothing happens by accident!* Therefore, the fact that the Royal British Coat of Arms contains both a lion and a unicorn is no accident!

Since the One-Horned Ram that will rise to prominence over the other horn of Joseph is likely the United States/Ephraim linked to Israel, then Great Britain must represent Manasseh. Nonetheless, the appearance of the lion and unicorn on the British Coat of Arms implies that Great Britain sees itself as the modern prophesied representative of, and replacement for Ephraim *and* Manasseh, as well as Judah. Through the symbol of the unicorn, Great Britain may also be claiming to be the One-Horned Ram of Enoch's prophecy. However, there is another source of prophetic unicorn imagery in Scripture that the British Royalty could be connected to. It is found in the Book of Daniel.

Now, on the British Coat of Arms, or Shield of the British Crown shown on the next page are many symbols that supposedly show royal alliances through intermarriage. There, the golden lion - which many believe represents the Lion of Judah - stands across from a rearing white unicorn, which is a symbol supposedly tied to Christ, and the dual Tribe of Joseph. Incidentally, these same allegorical devices once appeared on the Royal Arms of the Monarch of Scotland. However, as stated previously, a rearing horse is also a symbol for the Tribe of Dan, and the unicorn on the British Coat of Arms looks like a white horse with one horn, though it has cloven feet like a goat, sheep, or bovine animal, and the tail of a bull, or ox, which shows its association with a half tribe of Joseph. Nonetheless, *since this unicorn is facing left, it is in a sinister pose, and may signify the left horn of the Cherubim, or the Antichrist, as well as the Tribe of Dan.*

## Royal Coat of Arms Used By British Monarchs

The prophecy in the eighth chapter of the Book of Daniel concerns the horn of a male goat, rather than a male sheep, or ram. After the prophecy of the One-Horned Goat is given, the angel Gabriel interprets it for Daniel:

*"The ram which you saw, having the two horns -- they are the kings of Media and Persia. And the male goat is the kingdom of Greece. The large horn that is between its eyes is the first king."*

*"And in the latter time of their kingdom, when the transgressors have reached their fullness,* **a king shall arise, having**

*fierce features, who understands sinister schemes.* His power shall be mighty, but not by his own power; he shall destroy fearfully, and shall prosper and thrive; he shall destroy the mighty, and also the holy people."

"Through his cunning he shall cause deceit to prosper under his rule; and he shall exalt himself in his heart. **He shall destroy many in their prosperity. He shall even rise against the Prince of princes; but he shall be broken** without human means." - Daniel 8:20-21, 23-25

**In the above prophecy, Gabriel discloses the identity of a two-horned ram, and a one horned goat.** The two-horned ram is reminiscent of the Bull symbolizing Taurus, as well as the Ram symbol of Aries. We are told that the two-horned ram signified ancient Media and Persia. These two kingdoms replaced other powerful kingdoms - the Medians taking over the lands of the Assyrians, and the Persians occupying the former lands of the Babylonians. In modern times, the ancient kingdom of Assyria is allegorically tied to the United States, and the kingdom of Babylonia is connected to Great Britain. This connection will be explained in a moment when we examine the prophecies in Ezekiel.

In Daniel's vision, **the Unicorn, or One-Horned Goat was Greece, and specifically represented Alexander the Great** in the past. We are also told that four kingdoms will emerge from the one *"broken horn,"* or empire forged by Alexander in his conquest of the world. At Alexander's death, his four generals divided his empire into four kingdoms. Ptolemy took Egypt and the Levant, which consisted of modern Palestine and Lebanon. Cassander took Macedonia, or what is now Greece and Albania. Lysimachus took Thrace, which consists of the Balkan Peninsula between the Adriatic and Black Seas - where parts of Hungary, Bulgaria, and Romania are located, and Seleucus eventually ruled the Seleucid Empire, consisting of what are now eastern Turkey, Syria, Iran, Iraq, Afghanistan, Pakistan, and India.

Today, these four kingdoms can be identified as four groups of nations consisting of the central Muslim, or Arab nations including Iran and Iraq, the western Greco-Roman nations of the United Kingdom, Mexico, South America, and Europe, the Slavic nations of former Soviet Russia, and the Asian countries of Pakistan, India, Southeast Asia, China, and Japan.

As mentioned earlier, and shown in "The Language of God in Humanity," Yahshua's Parable of the Sheep and the Goats allegorically shows that goats represent the damned, while sheep represent the saved.

# Ch. 10: The Antichrist and Woman Riding the Beast

The One-Horned Goat therefore represents an evil leader, and his kingdom, which is slated for destruction. The prophet Daniel tells us that this leader will *"rise against the Prince of princes."* Since the phrase *"Prince of princes"* is the same as saying *"King of kings,"* which is a title for Christ, **this one-horned goat represents a nation, or group of nations led by the Antichrist.**

The One-Horned Goat's horn that represented Alexander's empire also signifies the future Babylon the Great - the empire of the Antichrist. This latter day Babylon is not a future kingdom any longer, but already rules the world financially, and will soon rule it politically, militarily, and religiously. This is the European Union (EU), which is headed by the United Kingdom. In the rest of this chapter, we will examine Scriptures suggesting that Great Britain, Europe, and several other nations that figure prominently in End Time events will be, and already are partially ruled by the Antichrist, and his followers.

Though now nominally considered Roman Catholic, this evil empire of the One-Horned Goat is already embracing the Pagan culture of the Greeks and Romans. **Like Alexander, the Ancient Greeks and Romans rejected the idea of sin and evil, and knew nothing of the concept of Original Sin.** Likewise, in modern Europe, Christianity is considered a religion of fools by the majority, and many Europeans are now either atheistic humanists, Muslims, or professing Pagans such as Buddhists, Hindus, New Age mystics, Satanists, and Wiccans.

In the heraldic iconography employed throughout Europe and Great Britain, the one horned goat or unicorn is a symbol connected to the Half-Tribe of Joseph called Manasseh, as well as *the Tribe of Dan*. The Tribe of Dan not only represents several modern regions like Scandinavia, Ireland, Scotland, and Wales, but also allegorically represents the people throughout the world who are diametrically opposed to the good deeds and Gospel message of Yahshua, the godly One-Horned Ram, and His righteous Sheep.

## The Harlot and the Beasts from the Sea and the Earth

Using the Language of God, it should be fairly easy to further identify Babylon the Great, which is represented by a woman called a harlot. To find out more about the woman, and the Beast she rides atop of, the Old Testament gives us several clues. First of all, Babylon in the Old Testament is not only a city, but an entire region of land that worshipped the false deities of Babylon. In today's world, that same region is inhabited primarily by Muslim Arabs, who worship the old

Moon God of Babylon called Allah. Furthermore, **the Arabs are literally sitting on top of the greatest oil reserves in the world.** They therefore are figuratively riding atop an enormous black beast of economic wealth. Since the Arabs control a large chunk of the world's monetary wealth, they have used it to seize untold political power, both through the United Nations and in their dealings with every separate nation that relies on their oil reserves - which is virtually every Non-OPEC nation on Earth!

As most of the world knows, crude oil consists of the remains of dead plants and animals that were subjected to enormous heat and pressure to form the crude oil reserves on the Earth today. What people who believe in Evolution do not recognize, however, is that these oil reserves were created during the cataclysmic Great Flood of Noah. The plants and animals destroyed in this Flood died as a punishment for *evil*, for most of the world at that time was filled with unimaginable violence and bloodshed. Also, **outside of Noah and his family, all mankind had likely been completely corrupted by both sin and genetic impurity before the Flood,** as shown in Book Three on History.

In today's world, the most easily identifiable evil elements in it are the Radical Muslims, who have directed their hatred toward the God of Christianity and the people that God loves through Christ. The Radical Muslim hatred of Christianity and the democracies that Christians gave birth to that currently support Israel's Democracy have caused Terrorism in the first place. Is it any wonder then that the economy of the Beast that the Woman sits on in the Book of Revelation is fueled by and dependent upon the Arab nations that have the largest oil reserves, and therefore more economic and political power than many other nations?

The Prophet Zechariah, who spoke at length about many events that will take place on the Day of the Lord, clearly identified the Woman who rides the Beast. In it, he sees her sitting in a basket that represents iniquity, just as barrels of crude oil signify the iniquity of the Pre-Flood world:

> *"I asked, 'What is it?' He replied, 'It is a measuring basket.' And he added, 'This is the iniquity of the people throughout the land.' Then the cover of lead was raised, and there in the basket sat a woman! He said, 'This is wickedness,' and he pushed her back into the basket and pushed the lead cover down over its mouth. Then I looked up -- and there... were two women, with... wings like those of a stork, and they lifted up the basket... 'Where are they taking the basket?' I asked the angel... He replied, 'To the country of Babylonia to build a house for it. When it is*

# Ch. 10: The Antichrist and Woman Riding the Beast

*ready, the basket will be set there in its place.'"* - Zechariah 5:6-11 (NIV)

In Zechariah's vision, the woman represents not only a city or country, but also a political and religious ideology with power. This is Islam, which gives an enormous level of political and religious power to their leaders that is generally unheard of in democratic nations. The basket this woman sits in represents great wealth, since baskets were used to carry every sort of commodity in ancient times. This basket is actually a measure called an ephah, and it is placed in Babylon, so it likely represents figurative baskets, or barrels of crude oil. This all makes it quite clear that the Muslim Arab nations that control the world's oil wealth are connected to the Woman who rides the Beast in the Book of Revelation, which - like the sign of Taurus - is a symbol for the material wealth of the Gentile nations.

Uncannily, there is another Beast in the Book of Revelation that is often overlooked, which is called the Beast from the Earth:

*"Then **I saw another beast coming up out of the earth**, and he had two horns like a lamb and spoke like a dragon."* - Revelation 13:11

Note that this Beast is *"coming up out of the earth,"* just as crude oil definitely comes up out of the Earth, and all Western and developing Third World nations rely on crude oil as the primary power source for their civilizations. Likewise, the Arabs are dependant on the West for their economic wealth. The Woman who rides the Beast therefore has a clear connection to Islam and the Middle East in the Beast from the Earth. In addition, this Beast from the Earth *"exercises all the authority of the first beast in his presence, and causes the earth and those who dwell in it to worship the first beast, whose deadly wound was healed"* (Rev. 13:12). This identifies the Beast from the Earth with the False Prophet who causes people to worship the Beast from the Sea.

One factor that makes sense of this confusing picture of Babylon the Great as a Muslim and Western power is the fact that there is evidence that the Jesuit order of the Roman Catholic Church started the move toward Radical Islam in Arabia to destroy the power of the Eastern Orthodox Churches in Asia Minor that were seen as rivals to Roman Papal authority. In their efforts to protect the Papacy and the Vatican, however, the Jesuits created a monster that is now threatening to destroy all the Christian strongholds in the West as well.

Could the False Prophet mentioned in Revelation 16:13, 19:20, and 20:10 be an allusion to the Papacy in Rome? Or is it possible that it is an allusion to Mohammed, the False Prophet of Islam? It is possible that both are true. After all, the Pope - who is seen as infallible like Christ by Roman Catholics - is a sinner like all of us is therefore not infallible. In addition, no other culture on Earth today currently promotes execution by beheading except Islam, and in Revelation 20:4 it says: *"I saw the souls of **those who had been beheaded** for their witness to Jesus and for the word of God..."*

Chillingly, the Europeans and British also once practiced beheading via guillotine, axe, or sword. Therefore, this reference to beheadings could be a prophecy of a revival of that grisly practice all over the world during the Great Tribulation. In any case, whoever the False Prophet is, he or she will cause people to worship the evil, rebellious, hedonistic and humanistic god of this world who gives no Grace, offers no forgiveness, and declares blood vengeance on all who love the One True God Yahweh and/or His Son Yahshua.

## The Woman Who Rides The Beast

Thus far we have determined that the Beast from the Sea and the Beast from the Earth are symbols for great economic power and wealth - one arising from free trade and the other from the value of oil. There are, however, other layers of meaning attached to Babylon the Great and the Woman who rides the Beast. To find them, let's look at another woman spoken of in Revelation 12:1-6. This Woman is *"clothed with the Sun,"* has her head encircled by a *"garland of twelve stars,"* and gives birth to *"a male Child who was to rule all nations with a rod of iron."* This is clearly an allegorical representation of Miriam or Mary, the mother of Yahshua. As Yahshua's mother, Mary was descended from Judah, one of the twelve tribes of Israel that are signified by the twelve stars above her head. This suggests that the *"Woman clothed with the Sun"* is an allegorical depiction of Israel, and specifically of Judah, the Tribe that King David, and his royal line issued from. In addition, the Woman Clothed with the Sun signifies spiritual truth, and those who enjoy Salvation by Grace by being born-again in the Spirit.

From these connections, it appears that the Woman who rides the Beast also allegorically represents a ruler with both religious authority and political power - one who has a legitimate claim to belonging to an ancient line of priests and kings that can trace their origins all the way back to Abel and Seth - the godly sons of the first man, Adam. It can also represent the kingdom or nation that this ruler issues from or rules over. Since Yahshua or Jesus is the Son of Mary and hails from the Royal line of King David of Judah, He is the King who will one day *"rule all nations with a rod of iron."*

Now, since the Woman clothed with the Sun is both a religious and political leader, then **the Harlot riding atop the Beast from the Sea must also represent a political entity with religious power, or vise versa**. Many Protestant scholars have identified the Roman Catholic Church, and more specifically the Pope enthroned in Rome, as this Harlot. There are several reasons that suggest this identification is correct, not the least of which is that Rome is the ancient capital of the Roman Empire. In addition, Rome sits on seven hills, and could therefore represent Babylon the Great - the city that sits on seven hills in Revelation 17:9. Significantly, the Vatican - the ultimate symbol of Papal authority - is also located in Rome. Furthermore, the kings in many European countries and in Great Britain have served as either literal or figurative Holy Roman Emperors. Furthermore, the Roman Catholic Church's Popes chose or backed and crowned these Emperors. This makes the identification of the Vatican in Rome with the Harlot Woman who rides the Beast nearly certain.

This Harlot figuratively represents the entity called Babylon the Great in the Book of Revelation - both in a past and future context. Revelation tells us that this Harlot has *"committed fornication with the kings of the earth,"* and is *"drunk with the blood of the saints"* (Rev. 17:6, 18:9, and 18:24). The type of fornication spoken of in this prophecy is not sexual, but concerns ideological and economic unions. As we have seen, this aptly applies to the Muslim Arabs, who have formed political unions with the nations they hate in order to go on killing Christians and other Non-Muslims with impunity. But this Harlot can be further unmasked to show her connections to the religions and governments of the West as well as the East.

In the past - in the guise of the Holy Roman Empire - the Roman Catholic Church also worked closely with the world's governments to set up kings who were favorably disposed toward the Papacy and their desire for world spiritual domination. In effect, the kings of Europe ruled their domains politically and economically with the sanction of the Pope, and the Roman Catholic Church in turn ruled spiritually and economically through the kings they backed in an unholy alliance.

Like the Harlot of Babylon, the Roman Catholic Church can be considered to be *"drunk with the blood of the saints."* This is because it is responsible for condoning or sanctioning the deaths of millions of people. They have done so through the slaughter of the saints in the Inquisition, through pogroms and wars against the Jews and other marginalized or hated people groups, and by turning a blind eye to the Nazi and Communist Death Camps that killed millions of Jews *and Christians* in Europe, Russia, and elsewhere. The Roman Catholic Church is therefore a definite candidate for the Harlot that represents Babylon the Great.

Many scholars concur that the Book of Revelation has a past, as well as a future application. Therefore, though the Roman Catholic Church once served as the Harlot sitting on the Beast that was the Holy Roman Empire, the Harlot and the Beast upon which she rides have changed over the centuries. This is why the writer of Revelation was inspired to say that:

*"**The beast that you saw was, and is not, and will ascend** out of the bottomless pit and go to perdition. And those who dwell on the earth will marvel, whose names are not written in the Book of Life from the foundation of the world, when they see **the beast that was, and is not, and yet is**."* – Rev. 17:8

By saying the beast *"was, and is not, and will ascend,"* the writer of Revelation was saying that the Beast that was Rome existed, was destroyed, and will one day be resurrected *as a world empire*. Most believers think that this empire of the Antichrist is coming in the future as the entity called the New World Order. As already stated, however, the shocking truth is that this beastly modern Roman Empire exists *today* - albeit secretly, or *behind the scenes*. It is simply hidden and hard to identify.

Thankfully, the End Time Beast has other identifying traits by which we can discern what or who it represents. For example, we are told that: *"the seven heads* (of the Beast) *are seven mountains* (or hills) *on which the woman sits"* (Rev. 17:9). The woman mentioned in this Scripture is the Harlot who rides the Beast from the Sea. In ancient times, these seven hills, or mountains were easily identifiable with the seven hills that the city of Rome was built upon. In addition, Constantinople - the capital of the old Holy Roman Empire - *was also built on seven hills.* Since both the Beast and the Harlot seem connected to ancient Rome in some way, it may be significant that there are Roman Catholic churches and practicing Catholics in nearly every nation today, even in Muslim-dominated lands. Since the Roman Catholic Church is an international one, it could very well be the "woman" who sits on seven continental "hills."

The Book of Revelation then identifies the ten horns on this Beast from the Sea: *"the ten horns which you saw on the beast, these will hate*

## Ch. 10: The Antichrist and Woman Riding the Beast

*the harlot, make her desolate and naked, eat her flesh and burn her with fire"* (Revelation 17:16). This means that whoever this Harlot is, the End Time Beast with the ten horns that represents world political and commercial interests will succeed in destroying the Harlot utterly. If the Harlot is the Roman Catholic Church allied with apostate Protestant churches, then this suggests that the world political ruler who becomes the Antichrist will seize control of, and destroy the Vatican, and all other quasi-Christian religious centers. This will likely be when the Antichrist and the Beast will unite to wage their unholy war against Israel, the Jews, and the Tribulation Saints.

In the very next sentence, we are told: *"God has put it into their hearts to fulfill His purpose, to be of one mind, and **to give their kingdom to the beast***" (Revelation 17:17). This statement literally begs us to ask the questions: "Who is giving the kingdom to the Beast, and what kingdom is being given?" and, "Who is the leader of the End Time Beast, and what does the Beast control or represent?" If we assume that the kingdom being given has it roots in ancient Babylon and Rome, it suggests that the Beast is connected to the European nations of the European Union, as well as the OPEC nations of Arabia and South America. Since the Beast from the Sea and its ten horns also signify *international* commerce and finance, it likely refers to the United Nations, the European Union, and OPEC *combined*. In modern times, the seven mountains the Harlot sits upon could therefore figuratively represent seven major world political and economic centers such as New York, London, Brussels, Baghdad, Beijing, Tokyo, and New Delhi. They also may signify the seven continents: Africa, Eurasia, Australia, North America, South America, Greenland, and Antarctica.

The United Nations is ominously headquartered in New York City, which is also the international financial headquarters of the world, though some might argue that Brussels, Belgium and Tokyo, Japan have nearly as great a claim to that dubious honor. This is no accident, since the United Nations has long had designs on controlling world commerce. The fact that the United Nations is in the largest city in the United States does not bode well for the nation. Because, not if, but when the Antichrist takes over as the leader of the UN - and the world - the USA will be inexorably affected for the worse. In fact, if the Antichrist takes control of the United Nations, the citizens of the United States who still value their liberty and their right to bear arms will likely revolt against him. This would likely cause the Antichrist to send his armies to invade America, just as George Washington's vision and the Book of Ezekiel revealed in the last chapter.

To truly identify the End Time Beast, however, we need to figure out what the writer of Revelation meant when he told us that the Beast from the Sea had *"seven heads"* and *"ten horns."* Could this be an allegorical description of the United Nations? It is possible, since five officials from five major countries (the United Kingdom, the United States, Russia, France, and China), and *ten* other elected officials govern the United Nations. These seem to correspond closely with the seven heads and ten horns of the Beast, especially if we view the United Kingdom as three of the *"seven heads,"* which we can do if we count the United Kingdom as three countries: England, Scotland, and Ireland. This also may refer to the fact that Queen Elizabeth II has kept three Princes from ruling: her husband Prince Philip, her son Prince Charles, and her grandson Prince William. This may mean that the Antichrist will be given the power to rule over the European Union, and then gain control of the United Nations through it.

Now, let's examine the statement made in Revelation 17:18: "And the woman whom you saw is that great city which reigns over the kings of the earth." We are plainly told here that the woman or Harlot is *"a city which reigns over the kings of the earth"*. This same Harlot also rules over many nations, as shown by the horn or nations crowning the Beast's seven heads. **Therefore Babylon the Great is specifically a city that rules over a group of nations spiritually, economically and politically.**

It is fairly clear from veiled references in the Book of Revelation and Daniel that the modern-day entity called Babylon the Great is styled after the ancient city of Rome when it was the administrative center of the Roman Empire. However, *its power is or will be founded in many nations.* For many reasons, some scholars have cited New York City as the modern city that is most like the ancient cities of Babylon and Rome. Like these past cities once were, New York is a major center for international business and commerce. There: *"the kings of the earth have committed fornication with her, and the merchants of the earth have become rich through the abundance of her luxury"* (Rev. 18:3). New York is certainly a city where many globally based businesses are headquartered, and where many businessmen negotiate deals that increase their wealth on a daily basis. In fact, there is even a suburb of New York called Babylon that ominously suggests a sinister role for the biggest city in the United States.

It may therefore be no coincidence that the Twin Towers of the World Trade Center in New York City were the most representative structures in North America of the legendary Tower of Babel that Nimrod built to defy God. The fact that New York City is also the host city for the

## Ch. 10: The Antichrist and Woman Riding the Beast      Page 461

United Nations lends a great deal of credence to the assumption that New York is the modern prototype to ancient Babylon. In fact, Babylon was a world center for commerce *and religion*, and New York City is a religious world center as well. Likewise, the city of Rome is the center for commerce and religion in Europe, and has been for thousands of years. Though often overlooked, the Roman Catholic Church that is centered in Rome represents not only Catholics, but also many former Protestants who have rejoined with the Papacy via the Ecumenical Movement, as well as ordinary Protestants, which who can be defined as *protesting* Catholics, or dissatisfied members of the *Universal* Roman Church.

Another obvious, but often disregarded choice for the modern version of Babylon the Great is the city of London, a city purported to be built on seven hills like Babylon and Rome. London is the capital of the United Kingdom of Great Britain, which once controlled a world empire like Babylon, and still does if you take the British Commonwealth and British Crown Corporation into consideration. The British Royalty and the British Crown are centered in London, and the British Royal family still enjoys major political influence in the British Commonwealth countries they gave birth to, as well as in Europe. Furthermore, the Monarchs of Great Britain who rule from London are considered to be both the rulers of the Kingdom, as well as the upholders of the Anglican Church, or Church of England. Since the King or Queen of England must swear to protect and uphold the crown, the kingdom, and the Church of England, they are rulers with a priestly role, just as many ancient rulers were - including those of Israel and Babylon. In addition, as outlined in Tim Cohen's book, there are indications that the Monarchy of the United Kingdom has formed a secret alliance with the Pontiffs of Rome through the Order of the Garter.

There are other factors that tie Babylon the Great to London, and more specifically to their form of government, which is presided over by the British Monarchy. For example, since this Beast in Revelation comes out of the "sea," it suggests a power forged by ships - which could be either war or merchant ships. In this case, the seven "hills" could be "the seven seas," a term for the seven oceans of the world. This brings the British Empire to mind, since Britain's exceptionally powerful navy forged it. At the height of the British Empire in the early 1900's - the British held sway over 20 percent of the world's land, and controlled the lives of over 400 million people. This suggests that the founding nation of the British Empire - Great Britain, with London as its Capital - is tied in some way to the Beast from the Sea.

This supposition is supported by other facts. For example, in Revelation 17:15, we are told the *"waters which you saw, where the harlot sits, are peoples, multitudes, nations, and tongues."* This means that the Harlot is not represented by one country, but by many countries, and many diverse people-groups. In this case, just as was suggested a moment ago, "the waters" where the Harlot sits may refer to the oceans of the world. This would indicate that powerful navy and merchant ships initially gave the Beast from the Sea its power.

Keeping the preceding fact in mind, let's take a fresh look at the prophecies about the Harlot that represents Babylon the Great with our eyes keenly fixed on *Queen Elizabeth II*. If we picture Ireland, England, and Scotland, which are surrounded by seas on all sides, as the Beast from the Sea, then the Woman who rides the Beast as ruler is none other than Queen Elizabeth II! Lending credence to this, the Bible describes the queenly countenance of the Harlot riding the Beast, who is clothed in the regalia of her office:

> *"And I saw a woman sitting on a scarlet beast which was full of names of blasphemy, having seven heads and ten horns. The woman was arrayed in purple and scarlet, and adorned with gold and precious stones and pearls, having in her hand a golden cup full of abominations..."* - Rev. 17:4

Doesn't this bring to mind the riches that the Monarchs of England are clothed in on their coronation day? Queen Elizabeth II was just as splendidly arrayed at her coronation. Interesting to note here is the golden orb mounted with a cross that British Monarchs hold in their right hand at their coronation. Isn't this orb representing the world reminiscent of the golden cup in the Harlot's hand? Also, since the Holy Grail representing Christ's supposed bloodline is often thought to be the golden cup that Christ drank from at the Last Supper, **could the golden cup in the Harlot's hand be a symbol for the Holy Grail, and the legends surrounding it that are peculiar to the British Isles?**

In addition to these facts, there is another major detail hidden in the preceding quote from Scripture that positively identifies its connection to the Queen of the United Kingdom. This is the greatly overlooked statement that the woman *"is sitting on a scarlet beast."* Uncannily, in Tim Cohen's book: "The Antichrist and a Cup of Tea," he shows a picture of the Queen crowning her son Charles as Prince of Wales at his investiture ceremony. In a similar picture reproduced on the next page, there are three gray slate thrones. Of the three, only the center one has a short backrest - ostensibly to denote the Queen's authority over the princes who sat on either side of her. Ominously, there is a clear image of the Red Dragon of Wales carved into the gray slate on the short back of the Queen's throne. Although the dragon was not colored red, it still represented the *Red* Dragon of Wales. Therefore, Queen Elizabeth definitely *is* a woman who sits *on a scarlet beast*. This Red Dragon could be the very same one identified in the Book of Revelation 12:3. In fact, Tim Cohen mentions this Scriptural reference to the dragon, as well as the following one:

> *"Now the beast which I saw was like a leopard, his feet were like the feet of a bear, and his mouth like the mouth of a lion. The dragon gave him his power, his throne, and great authority."* - Revelation 13:2

Note that the dragon mentioned in this passage is not described as red, although most scholars concur that it is a reference to the same Red Dragon in Revelation 12:3. Uncannily, the dragon of Wales on the Queen's throne used at Prince Charles' investiture ceremony lacked any color, being a colorless gray, and it is this dragon that symbolically *"gave him (Charles) his power, his throne, and great authority."* According to the same preceding Scripture, this Red Dragon is tied to the Beast from the Sea, which *"was like a leopard, his feet were like the feet of a bear, and his mouth like the mouth of a lion."*

Uncannily, the heraldic device, or Coat of Arms for Prince Charles of Wales pictured on page 465, and the British Coat of Arms used by his mother, the Queen shown on page 451 are repeatedly decorated with a heraldic beast that most people mistake for a ferocious-looking lion. It is not, however, a lion at all, but a composite heraldic beast *with the mouth of a lion, the body of a leopard, and the heraldic feet of a bear!* A master of Heraldry will tell you that this beast represents the three countries of lineage for past Holy Roman Emperors: France (the leopard), Germany (the bear), and the United Kingdom (the lion). But this is not completely accurate, since the royal bloodlines of some past Holy Roman Emperors also supposedly originated in Spain and Italy. This heraldic beast therefore seems to be tied to the bloodlines associated with the lineage of the Merovingian kings who heretically claimed descent from a false or Anti-Christ who never died on the Cross, or rose from the dead.

Besides this lion-like beast, the heraldic device of Prince Charles of Wales features the Red Dragon of Wales, where it appears beneath the feet of the restrained unicorn. In the illustration of the flag of Wales shown on this page, note that - if the flag were printed in color, the dragon would be scarlet red, the bottom field green, and the upper field white. Peculiarly, the dragon on this flag has the head, beak, and talons of an eagle. Like an eagle, it also has wings, although they are the featherless wings of a bat instead of a bird, and a bat can be a parasitic creature that sucks the life out of other living things. In addition, this dragon has the body of a leopard and the spear-like forked-tongue and tail of a serpent. The arrow point at the end of the tail and the ridged look of its legs are also reminiscent of a scorpion's tail and stinger.

Like Revelation's Beast from the Sea, **the Welsh Red Dragon on Prince Charles' heraldic device and on the flag of Wales is a composite creature.** This suggests that Wales in the United Kingdom is somehow tied to Revelation's *"beast rising up out of the sea"*, and that it might be the source of the Antichrist who will claim dominion over Israel. Because of its composite nature, this Red Dragon of Wales also bears a striking connection to the Red Dragon in Revelation (Revelation 12:3). Like the biblical Red Dragon, the Welsh Red Dragon may be tied to the Zodiac sign of Scorpio, and what it stands for: Satan, the Nephilim Seed of the Serpent, and the Tribe of Dan.

## Heraldic Device of Prince Charles of Wales

If you still doubt that the Harlot riding on the Beast could be the rather conservative and almost saintly looking Queen Elizabeth II, it pays to consider that Revelation calls the Harlot a queen who lives luxuriously, just as Queen Elizabeth does:

*"In the measure that she glorified herself and lived luxuriously, in the same measure give her torment and sorrow; for she says in her heart, **'I sit as queen**, and am no widow, and will not see sorrow.'" - Revelation 18:7-9*

Revelation then goes on to tell us how this Harlot queen, and the world financial and spiritual empire that she reigns over and represents, will be destroyed:

> *"Therefore her plagues will come in one day-- death and mourning and famine.* ***And she will be utterly burned with fire****, for strong is the Lord God who judges her. The kings of the earth who committed fornication and lived luxuriously with her will weep and lament for her, when they see the smoke of her burning..." - Rev. 18:8-9*

Is it possible that the Book of Revelation's "beast rising up out of the sea" represents Great Britain as the initial seat of the Antichrist's world government during the Tribulation? Furthermore, if it is the Antichrist's center of operations, will Great Britain be destroyed by a nuclear bombardment or Act of God? In the Book of Revelation, we are told that *"something like a great mountain burning with fire"* will be thrown into the sea during the Tribulation period (Revelation 8:8). Furthermore, the Scripture quoted above indicates that the Harlot and her Kingdom Babylon *"will be utterly burned with fire."* Could *"the great mountain burning with fire"* be destined to hit and destroy the large island that forms Great Britain? Indeed, right after this mountain falls into the sea, we are told that *"a great star fell from heaven, burning like a torch, and it fell on a third of the rivers and on the springs of water"* (Revelation 8:10). Could the same cataclysmic event that destroys Great Britain cause this heavenly source of worldwide water pollution to occur in rapid succession?

When the Antichrist does rule, he will likely claim to be a legitimate Prince of Judah as well as the awaited Messiah that many world faiths anticipate. It is important to keep in mind that Christians and Jews are not the only religious groups expecting a Messiah to appear and set up a righteous kingdom. Buddhists, Hindus, Muslims, and many other religious groups are also expecting a Messiah of sorts. However, due to their erroneous spiritual beliefs, they will settle for a Mahdi, Messiah, Avatar, or Buddha who is much less divine, and far less righteous than Yahshua. In fact, they will settle for *the* Antichrist, a man who will be set up as an incarnation of God by the False Prophet, who will perform false miracles on the Antichrist's behalf, and will demand that everyone worship the Beast, and receive the Mark of the Beast (Rev. 13:11-18).

Though the symbolism surrounding Babylon the Great links it to several cities, one thing is absolutely certain: The Antichrist will fulfill the roles of Revelation's evil Red Dragon, and will take over the kingdom of the Harlot in the city called Babylon the Great that rides atop the Beast from the Sea. Since this Harlot represents both a political and priestly ruler over the entire world, it is likely that - after being given the leadership of the United Nations and the European Union - the Antichrist will unite with the Pope in Vatican City - the city signifying the power of the Roman Catholic Church. If so, it is likely that the Pope will serve as the False Prophet who will aid the Antichrist in his unholy schemes and proclaim this charismatic world leader to be God.

## *Is There A False Bloodline of Christ?*

The Royal family in Great Britain can trace their lineage to several European kings who led the Holy Roman Empire. There is also a currently much-publicized rumor being promulgated that these kings were literal descendents of Christ. Some popular and highly controversial books have spurred this rumor. These books include "Holy Blood, Holy Grail" and "The Messianic Legacy" by Baigent, Leigh, and Lincoln and "Bloodline of the Holy Grail" by Laurence Gardner. In fact, it is clear that books like these inspired the author Dan Brown to write his best-selling fiction thriller called "The DaVinci Code." These books all make claims that the Holy Grail is not the chalice or cup that Yahshua used at the Last Supper to initiate the New Blood Covenant ritual of Communion as is often claimed. Instead, it is alleged to be a potent allegorical symbol for something even more explosive to unsaved people: *the continuation and preservation of the literal bloodline of Christ.*

Before I proceed to discuss these books and their totally unorthodox and false views of Christ, I'd like to mention a word of extreme warning to anyone whose Biblical knowledge and faith is weak. The majority of books like the ones mentioned above persuasively deal with subjects that can weaken and undermine the religious faith of Christians who are not well versed in Scripture, or strong in their faith in Christ. These books deal with the supposed bloodline of Yahshua, linking His blood symbolically to the Holy Grail of legend. They also delve deeply into the skewed and outright heretical religious ideologies of the Knights Templar, the Masons, and the fictitious entity called the Preiur Di Sion, or Priory of Sion, which was exposed as an elaborate hoax on the television show "60 Minutes" in 2006.

The major underlying purpose of all these books is to undermine and challenge orthodox Christianity and the Bible's clear teachings about who Christ really was. They initially do so by questioning how, why, and *if* Christ died. Then they focus on the Frankish Kingdoms through the

Dark and Middle Ages, on the Merovingian heresy that arose afterward, and on their less than saintly kings who supposedly were the actual descendents of Christ. The Merovingian heresy is the false teaching that Yahshua never rose from the dead, but found His claim to immortality by fathering royal children.

Most books that promote the Merovingian heresy assert that the descendents of Christ's children eventually went on to rule Spain, Europe, and Great Britain for hundreds of years. Furthermore, these descendents of Christ and King David continue to have great influence in European politics through the current Royalty of Great Britain and their connection to the Royal Habsburg Dynasty of Europe.

Whether or not Yahshua was married or had children cannot detract from His deity or His ability to fulfill His mission of redemption and salvation for those who love Him. If Christ did have a wife and children, however, this fact appears to have been overlooked by the Gospel writers. There are, however, some purported clues in the Gospels that seem to suggest that Yahshua may have been married. There is, for example, the Wedding at Cana spoken of only in the Gospel of John. At this wedding, it is clear that Yahshua was acting as the host of the wedding, as He would have in His father's absence. This is because Yahshua was the eldest child and heir to half his father's estate. Several Bible scholars therefore have suggested that this wedding was for one of Yahshua's brothers, whose Greco-Romanized names are listed in the following Scriptures:

*"Is this not **the carpenter's son**? Is not **His mother called Mary**? And **His brothers James, Joses, Simon, and Judas**? And **His sisters**, are they not all with us? Where then did this Man get all these things?"* - Matthew 13:55-56

*"Is this not **the carpenter, the Son of Mary**, and brother of James, Joses, Judas, and Simon? And are not His sisters here with us?" And they were offended at Him."* - Mark 6:3

Before continuing this discussion about whether or not Yahshua our Messiah was married, let me digress a moment. Matthew identifies Yahshua as *"the carpenter's son,"* emphasizing that He was the son of Joseph, while Mark says Yahshua was a carpenter who was also the son of Mary. This is not a discrepancy, but shows that each Gospel writer was emphasizing a different aspect of Yahshua's identity. However, assuming that the New Testament was written in Hebrew and Aramaic, some Messianic Jews feel the word used to describe Yahshua and his stepfather

Joseph should not be translated "carpenter" at all, but "foolish carpenter."

Supporting this assessment, there is some suspicion that Yahshua and his father were called carpenters in a derogatory fashion, as in the foolish carpenter or craftsman of Isaiah 44:13-20, who fashions an idol for himself out of wood and worships it as a god. Later, however, the carpenter finds his wooden god totally useless when help is needed. If the word carpenter was used as an insult, then the people of Yahshua's hometown were calling Joseph a carpenter because they thought he was an imbecile for expecting them to worship his stepson like an idol. Likewise, the people may have called Yahshua a carpenter because He openly claimed to be the Son of God, and thus divine - making Himself greater than King David or Moses.

If there is no mistranslation, however, and Yahshua and Joseph were indeed carpenters, a common misconception is that Yahshua's family was poor, and Yahshua grew up in humble circumstances. Nonetheless, an architect or carpenter was rarely a poor man. On the contrary, architects and carpenters were skilled laborers who commanded a high price for their work. This was especially true in places like Ancient Judea and Galilee at the time of Christ, where wood was relatively scarce, and extremely costly. Due to this fact, it is probable that Yahshua and his father were not poor, but skilled laborers who had the money to purchase wood and work it. We can also assume they worked for affluent people who could pay for the labor of skilled craftsmen, and buy the raw materials they needed. Therefore, if Yahshua and Joseph were carpenters, they likely lived well on their income, and owned a nice home and other luxuries.

The plain truth is that the Roman Catholic Church promulgated the lie that Yahshua was a simple country lad who grew up in a mud-brick hut in an inconsequential small town named Nazareth. They did so to make Christ appeal to the majority of the people in the world, who were poor. The reality, however, is that our Savior's parents were not always poor, even if they had been when Yahshua was born. This is because their poverty ended the moment Yahshua was visited by the Magi! The costly gifts of gold, frankincense, and myrrh that the Parthian Wise Men presented to Yahshua and his family when they came to worship Him were worth a king's ransom, and only selling a small portion of this wealth would have kept Joseph, Miriam, Yahshua, and his siblings living in luxury for many years.

If Yahshua was wealthy, however, this should not diminish the fact the Yahshua was who He said He was: one with His heavenly Father, the Living Water, the Bread of Life, the Light of the World, and the Way, the Truth, and the Life for all mankind. In my eyes, Yahshua is far nobler if viewed as a relatively rich man who left his comfortable home and became a wandering preacher - one who relied on the generosity of others for food, clothing, and shelter, but who repaid them with a wealth of spiritual riches through His incredible, divine wisdom.

Also, as regards our Savior's official occupation, it is important to note that Yahshua was only called a carpenter or carpenter's son twice in the Gospels, whereas He was referred to as a "Rabbi," or "Rabboni," which is Hebrew for "Teacher," at least 15 times in the New King James version of the New Testament. Furthermore, Yahshua was called "Teacher" no less than 42 times! This suggests that people viewed Yahshua as one who taught others how to read, understand, and remember the Torah. The Bible is therefore quite clear that most people did *not* view Yahshua as a carpenter. Instead they clearly saw Yahshua as a learned man who was well qualified to teach others the Word of God! Yahshua was therefore a Rabbi or Preacher - *not* a carpenter.

Now, returning to the Wedding at Cana where Yahshua acted as the host, we can assume that this was no simple country wedding, but a grand affair. However, the writers of such books as "Holy Blood, Holy Grail" make it sound as if Yahshua was acting as the host of his own wedding in his father's absence! This shocking, and seemingly plausible assumption, however, ignores one prominent fact. **Yahshua was already betrothed to His true Bride, the Church!** Furthermore, it seems totally obtuse for the Gospel writers to have omitted the fact that Yahshua had a wife - much less one whom they assert was as prominent as Mary Magdalene undoubtedly was. Since they went to the trouble to tell us of the special prominence that this one woman among Yahshua's followers had, why are we never told that Yahshua was married to Mary Magdalene? In fact, even the Gnostic Gospels never say Yahshua was married, but only that Mary was His companion. Furthermore, the word companion implies friendship rather than marriage.

Those who believe that there is a surviving royal bloodline that can be traced directly to Christ think that the alleged marriage of Yahshua with Mary Magdalene was covered-up. They believe this was done in an attempt to protect the children, or carriers of the royal bloodline resulting from this union. But this leads us to ask, if Yahshua were the hoped for Messiah, why would anyone care about His bloodline? The obvious answer is that some people doubted that Yahshua was the Lamb of God who needed to be sacrificed for our sins. Nonetheless, they may have believed that Yahshua was a purely human Christ or Messiah who had a

## Ch. 10: The Antichrist and Woman Riding the Beast    Page 471

legitimate claim to David's throne, but failed to re-establish David's kingdom during His lifetime.

In support of this, it is important to point out that most of the Jews of Yahshua's era were expecting the Messiah to be a conquering leader who would liberate the Jews from oppression, re-establish the Kingdom of Israel, and force the surrounding Gentiles to keep God's laws. Thus, the idea that this leader and king had to die first to save them from sin was completely foreign to them. Though the Old Testament prophets clearly prophesied about Yahshua's suffering and death, and memorialized these events in the rituals and symbols surrounding Blood Covenant ceremonies and the Feast of Passover, many Jews still did not recognize their Suffering Servant when He died for the sins of the world.

Even Christ's apostles were initially guilty of thinking that Yahshua was going to set up a purely material Kingdom on Earth, which would elevate Israel as the unquestioned moral leader among the nations. They were therefore completely disillusioned and afraid when Yahshua was crucified like a common criminal. It was not until after Pentecost, when the apostles were baptized with all the gifts of the Holy Spirit, that they at last understood Yahshua's First Advent mission. This was to offer full redemption from sin to those who truly desired it. At that time, the apostles also realized why Yahshua promised to return. Yahshua had to finish the second half of his two-fold mission, which is to overthrow the governments of this world and set up His Millennial Kingdom - the most peaceful, prosperous, and righteous kingdom on Earth!

Unfortunately, the Bible foretells that an imposter will attempt to set up his own one-world government prior to Yahshua's Second Advent. Known in Christian circles as the Antichrist, this person will be so convincing as a Messiah-figure that he will deceive billions of people around the world. It therefore seems chillingly obvious why there has been such a plethora of books in recent years about the Holy Grail, and the possibility that the Grail is not a cup, but represents the supposed bloodline of Christ through a secret marriage. All of these books divulge many seemingly authoritative details about the mysterious history behind this bloodline, and what its purpose and future implications might be. Interestingly, people with connections to the now totally occult fraternal organization called Freemasonry have written many of these books, and **Prince Charles of Wales, through the Order of the Garter, is the official head of Freemasonry worldwide.**

## Is Mary Magdalene The Same Person As Mary of Bethany?

Many Masons or former Masons have hypothesized that a messianic bloodline may have originated from the children produced through Yahshua's secret marriage to Mary Magdalene. However, **there is not one word anywhere in the Old or New Testament that refers to a marriage between Christ and an ordinary woman.** In fact, the only marriage that is ever attributed to Christ is His future marriage to the True Church! We therefore need to compare this occult version of Mary Magdalene to the Scriptures revealing Mary Magdalene's real role in Christ's life.

In Book Two, "The Language of God in Humanity," it was shown that either Lazarus or Mary of Bethany might be *"the disciple whom Jesus loved,"* or *"the beloved disciple."* Now, in this book, it will be shown that Mary of Bethany and Mary Magdalene *are the same person*. We will start by comparing Scriptures that mention a woman who anointed Yahshua with a flask of expensive perfumed anointing oil. These Scriptures appear in all four Gospels, and all of them state that the anointing was done by a woman, and took place in the town of Bethany. However, Matthew and Mark state that this woman anointed Yahshua's head, while Luke and John indicate that she anointed Yahshua's feet and washed His feet with her hair:

> *"And **when Jesus (Yahshua) was in Bethany at the house of Simon the leper**, a woman came to Him having an alabaster flask of very costly fragrant oil, and **she poured it on His head** as He sat at the table. But when His disciples saw it, they were indignant, saying, "Why this waste? For this fragrant oil might have been sold for much and given to the poor.' But when Jesus (Yahshua) was aware of it, He said to them, 'Why do you trouble the woman? ...For in pouring this fragrant oil on My body, she did it for My burial.'"* - Matthew 26:6-12

Matthew's account of Yahshua's anointing on the head is repeated almost verbatim in Mark 14:3-9. Both indicate that the anointing was in Bethany - at the house of a man named Simon, and was done on Yahshua's head by a woman. Both also indicate that the apostles were angry with the woman for wasting money, but that Yahshua rebuked them for their ignorance of her noble cause, which was to prepare Him for burial. In addition, both seem to state that Simon was a *leper*. This is strange, because lepers are diseased and are unclean in the eyes of the Law. Therefore, no self-respecting Jew would dine with a leper!

# Ch. 10: The Antichrist and Woman Riding the Beast

In Messianic Jewish translations of this passage, the word that appears as leper in Christian translations of the New Testament has been translated as "jar merchant." This is because some Messianic Jews believe that the Gospel of Matthew was originally written in Hebrew, and the Hebrew word for leper is very similar to the word for jar-merchant. Since they also know that the apostles, who were Jews, would not have dined with a leper, they reason that Simon was not a leper at all, but a wealthy jar merchant who lived in the rich suburb of Jerusalem called Bethany. Now that we have determined that Matthew and Mark are speaking about the same woman and the same Simon, we need to determine if this woman is also the one anointing Yahshua in Luke and John's Gospels. At first glance, this does not appear to be the case. This is because Luke and John both state that this woman anointed Yahshua's feet, rather than His head. They also state that the anointing took place in the home of a Pharisee:

*"Then one of the Pharisees asked Him to eat with him. And He went to the Pharisee's house... And behold, a woman in the city who was a sinner... brought an alabaster flask of fragrant oil, and stood at His feet... and she began to wash His feet with her tears, and wiped them with the hair of her head; and she kissed His feet and anointed them with the fragrant oil. Now when the Pharisee... saw this, he spoke to himself, saying, 'This man, if He were a prophet, would know... what manner of woman this is who is touching Him, for she is a sinner.' And Jesus... said to him, 'Simon, I have something to say to you.'" - Luke 7:36-40*

Now, note here that Luke names the Pharisee as *Simon*. Is this merely a co-incidence, or is Luke's Simon the Pharisee identical to Simon the Leper or Jar Merchant, who appears in Matthew and Luke? This is possible, since there is no reason why Simon could not be both a Pharisee *and* a Jar Merchant. For that matter, there is no reason why the woman could not have anointed both Yahshua's head *and His feet* on the same occasion. Assuming that all four Gospels are eyewitness accounts of these events, the differences between them can easily be attributed to the individual personalities of the eyewitnesses, and their differing sense of what was important to emphasize.

Now, though three of the four eyewitness accounts of this anointing failed to identify the woman who anointed Yahshua, the writer of the Gospel of John plainly tells us that she was Mary of Bethany, and mentions this fact *twice:*

*"Now a certain man was sick, Lazarus of **Bethany**, the town of Mary and her sister Martha.* ***It was that Mary who***

*anointed the Lord with fragrant oil and wiped His feet with her hair, whose brother Lazarus was sick." - John 11:1-2*

*"Then... Jesus (Yahshua) came to **Bethany**, where Lazarus was... whom He had raised from the dead. There they made Him a supper; and Martha served, but Lazarus was one of those who sat at the table with Him. **Then Mary took... costly oil of spikenard**, anointed the feet of Jesus (Yahshua), and wiped His feet with her hair..." - John 12:1-3*

Due to the overlap in all four Gospel accounts of this anointing by a woman, we can be fairly certain that it was Mary of Bethany alone who anointed Yahshua with fragrant oil, and not three different women. If this is true, then what do these parallel accounts tell us about Mary's character? Though three Gospel writers are silent about Mary of Bethany's character, Luke describes this woman as a *sinner* (Luke 7:37). Nonetheless, Yahshua indicated that, by her loving actions, this sinful woman had proven herself to be repentant and deserving of much forgiveness (Luke 7:44-48). **This fact links Mary of Bethany with Mary Magdalene, who also was considered a sinner.**

Both Luke and Mark's Gospel tell us that Yahshua cast seven demons out of Mary Magdalene (Mark 16:9, Luke 8:2). Since Mary Magdalene was once demon-possessed, this implies that Mary had participated in sinful occult activities before she was exorcised, and subsequently saved - allowing her to become one of Yahshua's most devoted disciples. Since Mary Magdalene and Mary of Bethany also shared the same name, and both were among Yahshua's intimate acquaintances, their association can be proven to be far more than tenuous. Let's see what this connection suggests.

## *What Was Mary Magdalene's Role In Yahshua's Life?*

As already mentioned, two of the Gospels tell us that Yahshua cast seven demons out of Mary Magdalene (Mark 16:9; Luke 8:1-2). Since demons only plague people who have not repented of sin, and who have not sought protection from Yahweh, this implies that Mary Magdalene had sinned grievously in some way. However, the Bible *never* states that Mary Magdalene was a prostitute. On the contrary, the Gospels tell us that - though she had sinned - Mary was delivered from demon possession, and became a devoted disciple of Christ. She therefore was a reformed, repentant, and forgiven sinner.

# Ch. 10: The Antichrist and Woman Riding the Beast    Page 475

Mary Magdalene's devotion to and love for Yahshua was so great that she was there at the foot of the Cross when the other apostles and disciples had already abandoned Him (Mark 15:39-41). Mary Magdalene was also blessed with being the first person to see Yahshua in His resurrected body (Matt. 28:1, Mark 16:9-11, John 20:11-18). Furthermore, we are told that Mary Magdalene was so deeply moved by this experience that she worshipped Yahshua at His feet. But later, when Mary excitedly told the apostles that she had seen the risen Christ, they doubted her word (Mark 16:9-11).

Now let's look at the totally distorted view of Mary Magdalene that we are given through the scholars who are trying to undermine the Christian faith by touting the Merovingian heresy concerning the false bloodline of Christ. In particular, let's address some of the claims made in the fiction suspense thriller called "The DaVinci Code." According to some scholars, Leonardo DaVinci supposedly believed that Mary Magdalene was not just a disciple, but also an apostle of Christ. This supposition is hinted at in Leonardo DaVinci's famous painting depicting the Last Supper, a portion of which is shown on this page.

Among the representations of the otherwise masculine-looking apostles, there is the unmistakable image of a lovely young woman to Yahshua's right. Despite this person's feminine features, most art experts have labeled this figure as John, one of the two sons of Zebedee who were apostles. But why would anyone depict James or John so effeminately, especially when Christ Himself labeled them *"the Sons of Thunder?"* This term suggests that these two men were robust fellows with very loud, boisterous natures.

## Hidden Messages In DaVinci's "Last Supper"

In the painting, the effeminate apostle's head is tilted toward another apostle in a seeming gesture of affection. In fact, it almost appears as if she wants to lay her head on this apostle's shoulder. The object of her affection is supposedly the Apostle Peter. Here, Peter is disturbingly depicted as an old man with a scowl on his face. Furthermore, his left hand looks as if it is reaching to strangle the woman, and he is wielding a dagger in his right hand. This supposed apostle therefore looks anything but friendly. In fact, it looks as if he intends to murder the effeminate apostle to his left!

If the apostle next to this incorrectly effeminate depiction of John is indeed supposed to be Peter, and the womanly figure is Mary Magdalene - as Dan Brown asserts in "The DaVinci Code" -then Leonardo DaVinci was implying several things: that Mary Magdalene was present at the Last Supper, that she had feelings for the apostle to her right, and that this same apostle did not return her affection, but wanted to kill her. Could DaVinci also have been hinting that Mary Magdalene was unfaithful to her supposed husband, since she is tilting her head toward Peter instead of Yahshua? Or was DaVinci suggesting that Christ was not the leader at the Last Supper? It appears that DaVinci may have been hinting at both, since Scripture tells us that the disciple whom Yahshua loved laid his (or her) head on Yahshua's breast at the Last Supper:

> "Peter turned and saw that the disciple whom Jesus (Yahshua) loved was following them. (This was the one who had leaned back against Jesus (Yahshua) at the supper and had said, 'Lord, who is going to betray you?')" - John 21:20 (NIV)

There appears to be an obvious discrepancy in DaVinci's depiction of the Last Supper since - though the feminine figure is leaning her head toward a man - *it is clearly not Yahshua, who was a younger man.* Yahshua is supposed to be the central figure sitting alone at the center of the table in the painting. The Magdalene figure, however, is leaning toward the apostle identified as Peter to Yahshua's right. If these figures are Peter and Mary, could DaVinci have been suggesting that Peter, who symbolizes the Roman Catholic Church, was having an unsavory intimate relationship with Mary Magdalene that had gone sour? Others have postulated that the woman disciple in Leonardo's painting is allegorically leaning toward Christ, not Peter, and that her form fits well on Yahshua's left shoulder if moved there.

In addition to this oddity in Leonardo DaVinci's "Last Supper," there is a man seated to Yahshua's left in the painting that looks very much like Him. Some scholars suggest that this was Thomas, the Twin.

## Ch. 10: The Antichrist and Woman Riding the Beast

DaVinci therefore seemed to be hinting that Thomas looked very much like Christ. In fact, some believe DaVinci was suggesting that the central figure in the painting was not Christ at all, but the Apostle Thomas! We will discuss this heresy more in the next section. However, it is noted here because some people don't believe Yahshua died on the Cross, and this terrible heresy can weaken the faith of those who aren't baptized with the Holy Spirit, or familiar with the Gospels.

Sadly, Satan is an expert at twisting Scriptures, and misapplying them to destroy people's faith in Yahshua. For example, if we refer to the King James Version of the Bible, its translation of John 21:20 is different than the one recently quoted from the New International Version. In fact, the King James translation is truer to the original Greek, and could be viewed as saying that the beloved disciple laid his head on Peter's breast, not Yahshua's:

> "Then Peter, turning around, seeth the disciple whom Jesus (Yahshua) loved following; which also had leaned on his breast at the supper, and said, 'Lord, who is the one who betrays You?'" - John 21:20 (KJV)

Note that this Scripture says *"his breast,"* not Christ's breast, so there is confusion over whose breast is being referred to. The New International translation of the Bible tries to clear up this confusion by inserting the word "Jesus" for "his." However, in DaVinci's painting, the woman disciple's head is near Peter's breast - as could be suggested by the King James Scripture just quoted. Meanwhile, Peter is pointedly looking at this female disciple with obvious malice in his eyes. This suggests that **DaVinci believed that Mary Magdalene was the beloved disciple, and that Peter was either Christ's betrayer, or saw Mary as Christ's betrayer.**

Now, if the figures to the right and left of the central figure in DaVinci's painting are supposed to be Yahshua and Mary, then DaVinci was also suggesting that Thomas pretended to be Christ at the Last Supper, and that he may have died on the Cross instead of Christ! This also suggests that DaVinci believed the lie that the real Christ was married to Mary Magdalene, had children with her, and then posed as an apostle to escape death! Thus, DaVinci literally paints our Messiah to be a liar and a coward. Furthermore, he also implies that the Christian Scriptures are full of lies about the true nature of the Messiah.

For those who don't believe that Yahshua is the Messiah or who have doubts, such reasoning and intrigue can destroy their already weak faith, especially when presented with a plethora of supposed historical facts that seem to support these spurious deductions. But this is possible only because they are overlooking an obvious hole in the thinking of these masterminds trying to undermine and destroy people's faith in Christ. It lies in their use of the alleged fact that, though Bible Scholars believe that the Apostle John wrote the Fourth Gospel, the writer identifies himself only as *"the beloved disciple."* They use this fact to suggest that Mary Magdalene wrote the Fourth Gospel, and hence was the beloved disciple.

This deduction is difficult to refute because there is no reference anywhere in the Gospel of John that the apostle known as John ever wrote it. Though this Gospel identifies the beloved disciple with the pronoun "he," we are told nothing else about his or her identity. Some have therefore argued that Mary Magdalene could have been the author of the Fourth Gospel. However, as shown in Book Two, a more likely candidate for the role of beloved disciple was Lazarus, Mary of Bethany's brother whom Yahshua raised from the dead.

If the Gospel of John was not written by Lazarus or his sister Mary (a.k.a. Mary Magdalene), however, one thing is absolutely certain: **the Gospel of John could only have been written by a deeply spiritual person who knew Yahshua's true mission and purpose.** For example, the following Scripture clearly states that the writer of the Gospel of John knew that Yahshua was the Son of God, Son of Man, and became the Savior of the world through His death and resurrection:

> *"And as Moses lifted up the serpent... even so must the Son of Man be lifted up, that whoever believes in Him should not perish but have everlasting life. For* **God so loved the world that He gave His only begotten Son, that whoever believes in Him should not perish but have everlasting life**. *For God did not send His Son into the world to condemn... but that the world through Him might be saved. He who... does not believe is condemned already, because he has not believed in the...* **only begotten Son of God**.*" - John 3:14-18*

If the beloved disciple wrote the Fourth Gospel, he or she would never have betrayed Christ, believed that Christ was married, or that Christ was meant to save the world through one of His blood descendents. Furthermore, he or she would have vehemently denied the lies being touted by the supporters of the Holy Grail, and the false bloodline of Christ it represents!

The beloved disciple would have known that Yahshua could not be married because He was saving Himself for His mystical marriage to the True Church! In addition, he or she would have known that Yahshua

## Ch. 10: The Antichrist and Woman Riding the Beast

Himself promised to return to usher in His Kingdom on Earth, and never indicated that someone else would come in His place. There is no hint anywhere in the Bible that Yahshua intended to allow anyone else but Himself to set up the Kingdom of God on Earth. All the Old Testament prophecies and New Testament writings about Christ make it clear that this was Yahshua's privilege and purpose *alone*.

In addition to this, if we examine the facts surrounding Mary Magdalene, we come up with a far more benevolent and godly picture of her than the tarnished one she was given by the Catholic Church. For example, Mary Magdalene is reported to have been among the women who were an active part of Yahshua's ministry, and who funded it with their own possessions and wealth (Mark 15:40-41; Luke 8:1-3). These Scriptures also reveal that Mary Magdalene was a prominent disciple with access to disposable funds, and her standing and importance among the early Christians was very great - and *beyond reproach*.

Despite the position and authority Mary Magdalene had in the fledging Christian communities, many Masonic seekers of the Holy Grail assert that Mary *deliberately chose to go into hiding* after Yahshua's death, resurrection, and assumption into heaven. They also believe that people who wished to protect Yahshua's former wife Mary and her children may have carefully altered the Scriptures to keep their identity and whereabouts a secret. They even suggest that Mary had enough influence to make sure that the Scriptures were altered slightly to hide her position and relationship to Christ! However, all of these heretical suggestions can be proven to be absolutely false, as already shown. There simply is no scriptural basis whatsoever to believe that any of these conspiracy theories are true.

Nonetheless, conspiracy theories surrounding Mary Magdalene's role in Yahshua's life abound. For example, as was previously noted about John 21:20, Peter was looking at the beloved disciple when he asked about Yahshua's betrayer. **Peter's gaze therefore suggests that Peter believed that "the beloved disciple" would betray Yahshua's cause more so than any other**. This could be a veiled way of suggesting that, if Mary Magdalene believed that she had found a friend and ally in the Roman Catholic Church supposedly founded by Peter, then she may have unwittingly been unfaithful to Yahshua's cause.

If the figure of Peter in DaVinci's painting is an allegory for the Catholic Church, **could DaVinci have been suggesting that the new bishops of Rome coerced Mary Magdalene into being unfaithful to Yahshua's cause?** The dagger in Peter's hand and his threatening stance suggest this. Adding intrigue to this supposition, Scripture suggests that the beloved disciple may still be alive. Therefore, if Mary Magdalene is the beloved disciple, *she* may still be alive:

> "Peter, seeing him (the beloved disciple), said to Jesus (Yahshua), 'But Lord, what about this man?' Jesus (Yahshua) said to him, 'If I will that he remain till I come, what is that to you? You follow Me.' **Then this saying went out... that this disciple would not die.** Yet Jesus (Yahshua) did not say... that he would not die, but, 'If I will that he remain till I come, what is that to you?'" - John 21:21-23

Many scholars believe that this Scripture indicates that the beloved disciple will stay alive to serve as one of the Two Witnesses who will prophecy, preach, be killed, and be miraculously resurrected in Jerusalem during the Tribulation. Also, many people suppose that this beloved disciple is the Apostle John - a benevolent figure who will help to fulfill Yahshua's holy cause at His Second Coming. This seems to be implied by the use of masculine pronouns in the translation. However, in Book Two, it was shown that the Apostle John might not be one of the Two Witnesses, but an already resurrected member of Christ's heavenly army of saints! In addition, "The Language of God in Humanity," gives compelling reasons for believing that the beloved disciple might not be John at all - but Lazarus, Mary Magdalene's brother.

Now, let's re-examine the Scripture that says the beloved disciple will "tarry" until Christ *comes*. Could this imply that the beloved disciple will not die *at all*, but remain alive until *Yahshua's Second Coming?* If so, this may mean that the beloved disciple is not destined to experience physical death at that time, but will be translated into everlasting life when Christ returns. If the beloved disciple were Lazarus, this would circumvent his having to die again before his resurrection into everlasting life, since he already died, but was raised into a mortal existence during Christ's First Advent. Could it be that, at the time of Lazarus' resurrection, he received the gift of extreme longevity in order to wait for Christ's return? It is a possibility that seems to make sense.

Now, let's suppose the beloved disciple is Lazarus. Furthermore, let's suppose that he is still alive, and suddenly appears on the scene when the Antichrist is about to take control. Along with the Two Witnesses, and the 144,000 Witnesses out of Israel who will testify about the risen Christ, what if Lazarus plans to deny the Antichrist's claims to be the chosen Messiah and heir to the throne of David and Judah? If this were the case, you can be sure that the Antichrist would want to kill Lazarus *long before* this could happen. This means that, **to protect his or** *her life, the beloved disciple's identity must remain a secret! This is likely why no one really knows who the beloved disciple is.*

Although we can only guess about the beloved disciple's true identity, one thing is certain. If either Lazarus or Mary Magdalene wrote the Gospel of John, they both knew that Yahshua truly died, was resurrected, and was glorified with an immortal body. They also knew that Yahshua went to Heaven, and is going to come again. Therefore, if either one of these exceptional disciples is still alive, they both would be working *against* the Antichrist's carefully laid plans to take over the world. Furthermore, since the beloved disciple necessarily will oppose the Antichrist, the Antichrist would want him or her killed at any cost! If the beloved disciple's identity could be established, and his or her prolonged longevity and personal testimony became public, this is all the Antichrist would need to seek that disciple's death.

Even if the Antichrist did capture the beloved disciple, however, the Gospel of John clearly indicates that he or she would *never* betray Yahshua's cause for any reason! Instead, it is much more likely that, as a true believer in Christ, this beloved disciple would gladly face death rather than capitulate to the wishes of the enemies of God! Personally, I do not know whether Lazarus or Mary Magdalene is the beloved disciple. I also do not know for certain if either one of them may still be alive. Regardless of his or her identity, however, **I do believe that Yahshua's beloved disciple is still alive, and may serve Yahshua in some unexpected way during the Tribulation period**.

Whoever this beloved disciple is, he or she is not likely to be one of the Two Witnesses. This is because it seems that this role may already be reserved for two others: namely Enoch and Elijah. Enoch and Elijah are the only two men recorded in the Bible to have been taken up to heaven without experiencing physical death. However, they could not have been resurrected into immortal bodies at that time **since Yahshua was the First of the Firstfruits of the Resurrection** (1 Corinthians 15:20-23). Enoch and Elijah are therefore likely still mortals who are being supernaturally kept alive for their mission during the first half of the seven-year Tribulation. Because someone who is immortal cannot be killed, and the Two Witnesses must die and then be resurrected to everlasting life, they have to be mortal (Rev. 11:7-12).

Since Mary Magdalene accompanied Yahshua on His travels about Judea and Galilee, she would likely have been married, or related to someone in Yahshua's entourage. This is because male relatives such as a brother, uncle, or husband accompanied virtuous women when they traveled. It is therefore likely that Lazarus accompanied Mary as she followed Yahshua. Mary also could have been married to one of Yahshua's brothers or disciples, or related to one of His apostles. There is therefore no reason to believe Mary Magdalene was married or intimate in any way with Yahshua.

Now let's examine the one Scripture that seems to support the assumption that Mary Magdalene was *"the beloved disciple."* This happens when Yahshua, as He is dying on the Cross, asks the beloved disciple to take care of Mary, the mother of Yahshua. In the passage *just before* this event, we are told who is present at the foot of the Cross, and *none* of the male apostles are mentioned. Instead we are told **that only four of Yahshua's devoted women followers are present:**

*"Now there stood by the cross of Jesus (Yahshua) His mother, and His mother's sister, Mary the wife of Clopas, and Mary Magdalene." - John 19:25*

Note that no man is mentioned in this group. Therefore, in the next verse, it implies that the disciple whom Yahshua loved was a woman. Why then, is the beloved disciple called *"son"* there?

*"When Jesus (Yahshua) therefore saw His mother, and **the disciple whom He loved** standing by, He said to His mother, 'Woman, behold your **son**!' Then He said to the disciple, 'Behold your mother!' And from that hour that disciple took her to **his** own home." - John 19:2627*

This passage suggests that the beloved disciple was a man. Why then does the previous passage seem to contradict this? In Greek, personal pronouns are gender specific. Therefore, the highlighted pronoun "son" in the preceding Scripture implies that the beloved disciple was indeed a man. This does not mean he was literally Mary's son, however. But why is an unidentified male disciple entrusted with the care of Yahshua's mother when Yahshua had several brothers who would likely have done so without even being asked? Could it be that these brothers of Christ rejected both Yahshua and their mother for believing Yahshua's claims to be the Messiah? This is certainly implied by the following Scriptures:

*"Now the Jews' Feast of Tabernacles was at hand.*
*His brothers therefore said to Him, 'Depart from here and go into Judea, that Your disciples also may see the works that You are doing. For no one does anything in secret while he himself seeks to be known openly. If You do these things, show Yourself to the world.'* **For even His brothers did not believe in Him."** *- John 7:2-5*

## Ch. 10: The Antichrist and Woman Riding the Beast

> *"When **his family** heard about this, they went to take charge of him, for they said, 'He is out of his mind.'" - Mark 3:21 (NIV)*

The first Scripture implies that Yahshua's brothers expected the real Messiah to openly proclaim His right to the throne of Judah, as well as to perform miracles to back His claim. They also fully expected this Messiah to be unafraid and fully capable of taking His rightful place by force of arms, just as King David did. The second Scripture implies that, because Yahshua was not doing as they expected the Messiah to do, they thought that their brother was crazy! However, despite their initial disbelief in Yahshua's mission to become the perfect sacrifice for sin, we know that Yahshua's brothers James and Jude did eventually rally to Yahshua's cause. This is evident from their appearance as supporters of the Gospel message in the New Testament's book of Acts, and in the epistles attributed to them.

But how long did it take Yahshua's brothers to make this apparent about-face? At the end of the Gospel of John, the writer makes it clear that Yahshua knew His brothers had not yet accepted the New Covenant of Grace, and He therefore needed to find someone He trusted to care for his mother, who was as beloved to Him as the beloved disciple likely was, and *in the same platonic manner*.

It seems that several things are being implied in this Scripture that are not fully revealed to us. However, since nothing crucial to our salvation was being left unsaid in these passages, we must assume that Yahshua simply wanted us to know that His brothers and sisters had rejected both Him, and their mother Mary. We can also assume that Yahshua was aware that His mother's life was in danger, and she needed to be secreted away from Jerusalem. Is it therefore so impossible to believe that Yahshua entrusted His mother Mary's care with the only disciple that He could trust at the time - *a disciple that Yahshua Himself did not want identified* for obvious reasons? However, even if this beloved disciple turned out to be Mary Magdalene, her brother Lazarus, or another male disciple, this in no way suggests that Mary had a sexual love relationship with Christ! It merely suggests that *Yahshua loved and trusted Lazarus and Mary more* than any of His other disciples.

Thus far, we have ascertained that Mary Magdalene was likely not the perpetrator of this heresy that Yahshua's bloodline would lead to the eventual birth of a new Messiah. We have also determined that the beloved disciple was either Lazarus or his sister Mary of Bethany - also known as Mary Magdalene. What then, should we make of the Merovingians, who claimed to be blood descendents of Christ, and heirs to the Throne of Judah? Could one of Yahshua's brothers or apostles have posed as the risen Christ and invented this heresy to elevate himself? Since we are told in the Gospels that Yahshua may have had a twin, and definitely had several brothers who initially held Yahshua's ministry in contempt, it is a definite possibility.

## Why Was The Apostle Thomas Called A Twin?

In Chapter Seven, due to the allegorical implications of the number thirteen, it was suggested that, besides the traitorous Apostle Judas Iscariot, there may have been another evil apostle among the original twelve, and that may be why Yahshua chose the Apostle Paul as his replacement. Due to clues left for us in the Bible, the most suspect apostle is Thomas, who was also called *"the Twin"* (John 11:16, 20:24, 21:2). Among the apostles, Thomas is the only one singled out in this way, and his designation as a twin literally begs us to ask certain questions, such as: *"Why did Thomas have the nickname 'the Twin,' and if he was a twin, whose twin was he?"* Unfortunately, we are never told the reason why Thomas is called *"the Twin,"* or who he may have resembled. However, some scholars have suggested that Thomas looked like Yahshua - so much so that hardly anyone could tell them apart!

Could it be possible that Yahshua had a look-alike among His followers? If Yahshua did have a look-alike in His entourage, could this be the reason why the chief priests needed a betrayer to identify Yahshua among His disciples? Considering Yahshua's high profile ministry, it's highly *unlikely* that there was any confusion over what He actually looked like. Therefore, **unless there was someone who truly resembled Yahshua among His group of followers, there would have been no need to find someone who could positively identify him, such as Judas Iscariot.**

If Thomas did resemble Christ closely, this fact lends itself well to several decidedly heretical and patently false assumptions. For example, various apostate writers - when discussing the mysteries surrounding the Holy Grail - have suggested that Yahshua's twin may have died on the Cross so that the real Yahshua could escape and then father children – children who might one day have an opportunity to establish the Kingdom of Heaven on Earth that their father failed to do in his lifetime.

But what if the *opposite* was the case? What if this twin named Thomas looked so much like Christ that he posed as Christ *after* Christ's death and Resurrection, and subsequently taught a *different Gospel?* What if this twin's theatrics were so convincing that he amassed a loyal

## Ch. 10: The Antichrist and Woman Riding the Beast

following that did anything he asked them to, and who believed all that he said, even if it was an outright lie? Could it be a coincidence that Thomas alone is singled out in the Gospels as *doubting* that Yahshua rose from the dead - even after all the other apostles and the female disciples of Yahshua told Thomas that they had seen Yahshua appear to them, and that He was no longer dead?

Upon seeing the risen Christ, could Thomas' alleged profession of faith in John 20:28 - *"My Lord and my God!"* - have been uttered to hide the fact that he hated Yahshua and wanted to undermine His cause? Could Thomas have been the first among many antichrists who arose and tried to usurp Yahshua's place in history? If Thomas were the first Antichrist after Yahshua's resurrection, it would make sense of all the lies being touted by the many Freemasons who have recently written controversial books on the subject. It would also show that their conflicting and totally heretical Anti-Gospel has completely eroded the once Christian underpinnings of Freemasonry.

Since I unquestionably believe that the true Messiah Yahshua did die on the Cross and rise from the dead just as the Gospels teach, an imposter who posed as Christ could very well be the author of the Merovingian heresy. But if this is the case, Christians and Messianics have to ask some serious questions, such as: "What purpose could such an outright heresy serve?" Furthermore, "What could anyone possibly gain from such a bald-faced twisting and total distortion of the truth?"

The obvious answer is that there may be an underlying movement among the power mongers in our world who are seeking to control the world economy. Some people have labeled this entity, calling it the Illuminati. In addition to this organization, other more altruistic people in power want world peace, and believe that this can only be achieved through a unified one-world government with a leader at the helm that everyone will accept. Some of them also may think that - if they could present one person as a direct descendent of King David and heir to the Throne of Judah - many Jews and apostate Christians might easily fall for this deception. If this same leader could also perform miracles and rise from the dead, then many more people would likely be convinced that he was some sort of heavenly messenger such as a new Avatar, Guru, or Buddha with a divine right to rule over them.

The Bible tells us that a world leader who will convincingly pretend to be Christ is destined to rise up and control the world one day. Furthermore, we are told that the Antichrist will indeed be able to perform miracles, and that he will rise from the dead after suffering from a supposedly mortal wound:

"The coming of the lawless one is according to the working of Satan, **with all power, signs, and lying wonders...**" - II Thess. 2:9

"And I saw **one of his heads as if it had been mortally wounded, and his deadly wound was healed.** And all the world marveled and followed the beast. So they worshiped the dragon who gave authority to the beast; and they worshiped the beast, saying, 'Who is like the beast? Who is able to make war with him?'" - Rev. 13:3-4

"And he deceives those who dwell on the earth by those signs which he was granted to do in the sight of the beast, telling those who dwell on the earth to **make an image to the beast who was wounded by the sword and lived.**" - Rev. 13:14

"Then the beast was captured, and with him the false prophet **who worked signs in his presence, by which he deceived those who received the mark of the beast** and those who worshiped his image. These two were cast alive into the lake of fire burning with brimstone." - Rev. 19:20

It is clear from these Scriptures that the Antichrist will mimic the true Christ in many respects. However, whereas the true Christ will come from heaven to conquer the world, and will be accompanied by an immortal army of saints, the Antichrist will rise up as a human leader, and will likely come to power through some existing political channels. Furthermore, the Antichrist will control and lead a conventional human army wielding many horrible weapons of mass destruction. However, this conventional army will be filled with mortal soldiers. It will therefore be possible to completely annihilate this army, just as Revelation says Yahshua and his heavenly army of saints will do:

"Now I saw heaven opened, and behold, a white horse. And He who sat on him was called Faithful and True, and in righteousness He judges and makes war." - Rev. 19:11

"He was clothed with a robe dipped in blood, and His name is called The Word of God. And the armies in heaven, clothed in fine linen... followed Him on white horses. Now out of His mouth goes a sharp sword, that with it He should strike the nations. And He Himself will rule them with a rod of iron. He Himself treads the winepress of the fierceness and wrath of Almighty God. And He has... a name written: KING OF KINGS AND LORD OF LORDS. Then I saw an angel... saying to all the birds that fly... 'Come and gather together... that you may eat the *flesh of kings... the flesh of mighty men, the flesh of horses and of those who sit on them, and the flesh of all people, free and slave, both small and great.'" - Rev. 19:13-18*

Now let me digress a moment, and discuss a fact that may shed some light on this idea that there may well have been two people presenting themselves to the world as the risen Messiah immediately after Christ's resurrection. As was clearly presented in "The Language of God in History," and in Chapter Three of this book, Freemasons, esoteric spiritualists, and other occult groups are presenting a totally distorted image of the biblical patriarch Enoch in the line of Seth. Among the worst of them are the Masons who wrote the book "Uriel's Machine," which presents Enoch in the guise of a New Age-touting wise man instead of a God-fearing saint. They are trying to convince a gullible public that the Book of 1 Enoch was the product of a man who supported New Age beliefs!

These same Masons twist or falsely represent the clear history behind Enoch's origins and the formation of the Canonical Scriptures, thereby claiming that the Bible is false or corrupted! Furthermore, they use a well-known argument, which compares the similar names of the antediluvian patriarchs in the line of Cain and the line of Seth and then assumes that these patriarchal lines were not separate but identical. **They are thereby claiming that there was only one patriarch named Enoch prior to the Flood instead of two!** The falsity of their argument is clearly explained in the following excerpt from Book Three:

### Excerpt from "The Language of God in History":

"Could it be that some kingdoms traced their roots to the rebellious line of Cain instead of the righteous line of Seth? Could it also be that Cain's line survived via the part human descendents of the Nephilim who survived the Flood? Indeed, the Bible makes it clear that Cain was ostracized from his original clan, forced to leave the society he had grown up in, and was obliged to start his own. Therefore, the lines of Cain and Seth were permanently separated, and there is no reason to believe that the patriarchs in these opposing lines were the same individuals.

From the time that Cain left Adam's camp and went to live in the land of Nod, Cain's and Seth's societies developed separately. Furthermore, it is obvious from Cain's rejected attempt at appealing to the true God with offerings of fruit and grain that Cain had ignored the message behind the Blood Covenant rituals that are emphasized so strongly in the Book of Genesis. It is therefore likely that Cain had totally opposing spiritual beliefs that he passed on to his children. These two rival societies were therefore openly hostile to each other until nearer to the time of the Flood - when most of the Sethites became as violent and spiritually and genetically corrupted as their Cainite and Nephilim enemies.

Interestingly, patriarchal names in the Bible suggest the roles that each ruler played in their separate societies. For example, the name Enoch means "initiated" or "teacher." Since there is an Enoch listed in the line of Cain as well as the line of Seth, this means that both of these opposing societies had a great wise man or teacher that shaped their moral direction. However, these two separate teachers called "Enoch" touted opposing philosophies that agreed with the beliefs of the people they governed. In the case of the godly Enoch, he led his fellow Sethites to a greater understanding of and love for the one true God. In the case of Cain's son Enoch, however, he embraced the Serpent or Satan as his spiritual Father and led his descendents to do so, just as the Pharisees of Yahshua's day did. Even though these Pharisees were not related to Cain or his daughter Naamah by blood, Yahshua still identified them as children of the Devil..."

### End of Excerpt From "The Language of God in History"

Since the Freemasons and some liberal bible scholars are blatantly trying to erase the biblically clear teaching that **there were two men named Enoch prior to the Flood**, it is no small wonder that some of the same individuals are also trying to destroy the biblical depiction of Yahshua by melding Him into a false or Anti-Christ figure! Furthermore, they are doing it with the same sloppy and misleading scholarship! It therefore comes as no surprise that all of the fables that have been erected around the character of Mary Magdalene seem to be echoed in the Arthurian legends regarding Lady Guinevere. In fact, Guinevere may be an allegorical character styled after Mary Magdalene, and invented to suggest that there is a bloodline that can be traced to Yahshua the Messiah.

Let's look at the allegorical implications in the Arthurian legends. As most people familiar with the Grail romances and the legend of King Arthur are aware, Guinevere is married to King Arthur - who obviously can be viewed as a Christ figure. Furthermore, Guinevere is eventually unfaithful to Arthur by having an affair with Arthur's best friend and right-hand man - Sir Lancelot - who, as a Frenchman, would have been a Catholic. Could Lancelot therefore be an allusion to Peter and the Roman Catholic Church that he supposedly founded?

# Ch. 10: The Antichrist and Woman Riding the Beast

Since Guinevere cheated on Arthur with Lancelot, and her infidelity ultimately led to the destruction of Camelot, the Grail romances may be suggesting that the Roman Catholic Church sought to be the custodian of the bloodline of Christ by beguiling Mary Magdalene. When their attempt failed, however, the Holy Roman Empire may have decided to destroy the bloodline, which was an obvious threat to their authority. Therefore, just as the ill-fated love triangle between Arthur, Guinevere, and Lancelot supposedly helped cause the fall of the magical Kingdom of Camelot, Mary's rejection of the "protection" of the Holy Roman Empire supposedly destroyed the mysterious Kingdom of the Merovingians. In fact, Camelot may have been an allegory for that Kingdom, as well as a false version of the Kingdom of God, or Kingdom of Israel on Earth.

As stated in other portions of this book series, the Grail Romances, and the whole story of King Arthur appears to be a cleverly crafted allegory that refers to significant spiritual events in biblical history. In fact, some of the events that were poetically allegorized in the legend of King Arthur, Excalibur, and the Holy Grail are also recorded in Scripture. Still others are found in reliable ancient manuscripts that were excluded from the Bible like the Book of 1 Enoch and the Book of Jasher. These themes and ideas in the Grail Romances are therefore partially true, and they all seem to have biblical parallels. Sadly, however, not all the ideas within these legends are taken from reliable sources. In fact, all Arthurian legends and Grail Romances are fabrications that were meant to delude gullible people into falling away from the light of the Bible and the true Christ. These fables should therefore have no weight in determining the truth of the Gospel message.

## *The Antichrist: Heir to the Throne of England/Judah?*

The mysterious carriers of the bloodline that supposedly originated with Christ are said to have married into the existing royal lines throughout Europe, eventually producing the Habsburg Dynasty in Austria. Subsequently, these rulers may have married into the British royal line. This supposition can obviously lead to an intriguing question: "Are the members of the British Royalty descendents of the Royal line of David, as well as of the bloodline of Christ?"

If the members of the British Royalty can prove this to the world, one of them could also certainly claim to be the Messiah of the Jews, as well as the Christian Messiah *reincarnated*. If Prince Charles of Wales, for example, were a descendent of King David, and a descendent of Christ, his claim to be the Messiah would seem legitimate to many - especially if he could produce miracles similar to those that Yahshua performed during His First Advent. Chillingly, the Bible says that the Antichrist *will* be able to produce counterfeit miracles in order to deceive the whole world. In the following Scripture, the Antichrist is identified as *"the lawless one:"*

> *"The coming of the lawless one will be in accordance with the work of **Satan displayed in all kinds of counterfeit miracles, signs and wonders, and in every sort of evil that deceives** those who are perishing... because they refused to love the truth and so be saved. For this reason **God sends them a powerful delusion so that they will believe the lie**." - 2 Thessalonians 2:9-11 (NIV)*

Is it possible that someone in the British Royalty will one day claim to be a descendent of Christ? Could they promote the acceptance of a pretender, or Antichrist from among their ranks that will claim to be Christ? The answer to these questions may be encoded into the prophetic allegorical Language of God in the Book of Revelation. As already shown, some of Revelation's symbolic language seems tied to the British Royal Coat of Arms. In fact, its unicorn, lion and dragon-like symbols suggest that the British Royalty is tied to the Tribe of Joseph, the Welsh descendents of the Tribe of Dan, and the false kingdom of the Antichrist represented by the Beast from the Sea. This strongly suggests that the destiny of Great Britain is **not** tied to the righteous One-Horned Ram of Enoch, but to the One-Horned Goat of Daniel, and to Babylon the Great.

**There may also be good reason to believe that the person who will become the Antichrist is alive today.** In fact, he may be the prominent public figure known as *Prince Charles of Wales*. Though this suggestion may seem an outright impossibility to some, there are several good reasons to make this connection. First of all, like Revelation's Beast from the Sea, **the Red Dragon of Wales is seen repeatedly on the heraldic device for Prince Charles of Wales.** Coupled with the lion and unicorn symbolism on the heraldic devices for both the Prince of Wales, and the British Crown, this composite red dragon suggests that the United Kingdom represents a portion of Revelation's "beast rising up out of the sea", and will be the source of the Antichrist who will claim dominion over Israel. In addition to the Welsh red dragon's direct heraldic ties to Prince Charles of Wales, the name "Charles," and the number 666 are unequivocally connected to the Antichrist in the Book of Revelation:

> *"Let him who has understanding calculate the number of the beast, for **it is the number of a man: His number is 666**." - Revelation 13:18*

## Ch. 10: The Antichrist and Woman Riding the Beast

In the above Scripture, the Beast (i.e.: Antichrist) is identified as *"a man"* whose *"number"* is 666. The numerical value of the letters in the official name and title "Prince Charles of Wales" unfailingly adds up to the number 666 when Hebrew Gematria or English Numerology are applied. Furthermore, the name "Charles" means "man" or "manly." The number 666 is therefore the number of "a man" or *Charles!*

This suggests that Prince Charles is connected to the heart, feet, and eyes of "a man" spoken of in Daniel 7:3, 4, and 8 in relation to the four beasts from the sea, which are connected to the one Beast from the Sea in Revelation 17:1-5, upon whom the Harlot sits! Not only that, but Prince Charles' father is Prince Philip, *who was born Prince Philip of Greece and Denmark.* Ominously, the kingdom of the Antichrist is identified with Greece in Zechariah 9:13 and Daniel 8:21. In addition, the tribe of Dan's omission from the ranks of the Book of Revelation's 144,000 Witnesses connects the Antichrist to the Tribe of Dan, and the word "Denmark" means "Dan's Mark," or "Dan's Seed!" This is fascinating because, just as Christ is the "Seed" of the Woman in the Messianic prophecy of Genesis 3:15, the Antichrist is the "seed" of the Serpent, which is an allusion not only to Satan, but to the Nephilim, or Anakim Giants who survived the Great Flood. In that regard, has anyone ever noted how tall Prince Phillip is in comparison to Queen Elizabeth?

Other clues in the Bible that point to the princely identity of the Antichrist are the references in the Book of Daniel to *"the prince who is to come"* and *"a contemptible person who has not been given the honor of royalty:"*

> *"And after the sixty-two weeks Messiah shall be cut off, but not for Himself; and the people of* **the prince who is to come** *shall destroy the city and the sanctuary."* - *"He will be succeeded by* **a contemptible person who has not been given the honor of royalty**. *He will invade the kingdom when its people feel secure, and he will seize it through intrigue."* - Daniel 9:26; 11:21 (NIV)

Prince Charles is undeniably a Prince, just as Daniel states that the Antichrist will be. This connects the Antichrist to the *"prince of Gog"* (Ezek. 38:2-3). In addition, Prince Charles has been denied the right to rule as the King of the United Kingdom, which is most definitely a kingdom *of the north.* He therefore has not been given the honor due him as a Royal heir. This is just as Daniel intimates about the Antichrist, who in the eleventh chapter of Daniel is the **uncrowned** leader of the North who takes over the kingdom of the King of the North, and attacks and subdues the King of the South (See Daniel, Chapter 11). For that matter, Prince Charles' father Prince Phillip is also a royal heir on whom kingship has not been conferred, so there is a dual fulfillment of this prophecy in regard to the Royal Family of the United Kingdom!

This prophecy in Daniel was initially fulfilled once, where the Kings of the North were the kings of Persia and Syria, and the Kings of the South were the Ptolemaic Pharaohs of Egypt up until the time of Antiochus Epiphanes. The King of Syria, Antiochus Epiphanes ruled from 175 to 164 BC, during which time he invaded Jerusalem, and desecrated the Second Temple mount by erecting the *"abomination that causes desolation"* - a pagan altar to the false god Zeus, and Daniel speaks of Antiochus' fulfillment of this prophecy in Daniel 11:30-31:

> *"So he shall return and show regard for those who forsake the holy covenant. 31 And forces shall be mustered by him, and they shall defile the sanctuary fortress; then they shall take away the daily sacrifices, and place there the abomination of desolation."*

As a Hellenist, Antiochus, the King of the North, also tried to force the Jews in Israel to abandon their religious beliefs and festivals, and to embrace a Greco-Roman way of life under pain of death. However, the Jews soon united under the leadership of Judah the Maccabee, rebelled against Antiochus, and defeated him. Soon after this, the priests of Israel cleansed the Temple, and lit the golden menorah therein when it was re-dedicated to Yahweh. However, there was a shortage of oil in the realm due to the war, so there was only one day's worth of oil to fill the seven lamps of the menorah. Nonetheless, the Temple menorah's flames continued to burn for eight days on that one day's worth of oil, at which time new oil was found. Afterward, the Chanukah menorah, or Chanukiah was created to commemorate this miraculous event.

The reason this is being mentioned here is simple. **The events surrounding that first Chanukah are a prophetic window into the future reign of the Antichrist,** and his subsequent desecration of the Temple of God. This desecration may be referring to the corruption of the six Churches of Revelation not identified as the Bride of Christ, which only refers to the Church of Philadelphia. Therefore, the Abomination that causes Desolation may come through the Ecumenical Movement being pushed by the Vatican **and** the British Crown. The victory of the persecuted and hated Jewish and Christian people of God over this wicked movement will not occur, however, until they accept the glorious leadership of Yahshua their Messiah at His coming return to defeat the Antichrist's armies!

This brings us back to our discussion of the Chanukiah menorah in earlier chapters of this book, and how they appear to mark the prophetic unfolding of Judeo-Christianity's New Covenant with Christ. Isn't it uncanny that these nine-branched menorahs also symbolize the everlasting victory that Christ and all His risen saints will win over evil and death in eternity? This suggests that, as followers of the one true Son of God and Messiah, we ought to remember the importance of Chanukah along with the seven biblically prescribed feasts of Israel. See "The Language of God in Humanity" for more about the prophetic importance of Chanukah, as well as the Feast of Purim, which celebrates Queen Ester's heroic intervention for her people during their Babylonian captivity.

Many scholars believe that the Antichrist - in mimicry of Antiochus - will desecrate a Third Temple to be built in Jerusalem just before or at the beginning of the Tribulation period. However, Daniel's prophecy of the evil person who invades Israel, orders this desecration of holy ground, and sets himself up as a king and a god may be meant to refer to the Ecumenical Movement, which is being pushed to create a One World Religion that the Antichrist, who may be an elite descendent of the Nephilim or Seed of the Serpent, can take over when he falsely declares that he is God.

Interestingly, Prince Charles touts a lineage that links him *by blood* to Mohammed, the Prophet of Islam, and one of Prince Charles' honorary titles is: "Friend of Islam." Furthermore, it appears that the Radical Islamic kingdoms of Jordan and Saudi Arabia may be the kingdoms of Daniel's King of the South. If so, could it be that these Islamic kingdoms are being secretly controlled by Prince Charles and Princes Phillip as the *uncrowned* Kings of the North? If so, Prince Charles or his son William could be viewed as the Mahdi or Muslim Anti-Messiah that Islamic prophecies suggest will unite all Arabia, work out a false peace treaty between Islamic Fundamentalists, the Industrialized West, and Israel, and then later attack and attempt to destroy Israel.

This possible connection of the Antichrist with Islam has also found a partial fulfillment with US President Barack Obama, who grew up in the predominantly Muslim nation of Indonesia, and who shows great affection for, and support of Muslim people and beliefs. Chillingly, US President Barack Obama also has Muslim ties through his Kenyan father and Indonesian step father that go even deeper than Charles' do. Could this qualify him to play a subservient but similar role to Prince Charles during the Tribulation period?

Could Obama be the forerunner to the Antichrist, just as I supposed in an article written before Obama was elected in 2008? (See the Free Articles section at my POEM Ministry web site at http://pillar-of-enoch.com/essays/). In that sense, could Obama be like the modern antitype of John the Baptist? This certainly seems to be the case, since Obama supported the Radical Muslim rebels in Syria and Egypt. His also supports the unrest in the Middle East that was instigated by Radical, Militant Muslims that hate and seek to destroy the once Christian West. Encouraged by Obama's acquiescence, this has led Muslim Radicals in Syria and elsewhere to be bold in their heavy persecution of many Christians throughout the Middle East.

However, though President Barack Obama has proven to be a significantly malevolent leader during the Tribulation, he doesn't have nearly as many credentials linking him to the role of Antichrist as Prince Philip and Prince Charles through their connection to the European Union and British Commonwealth. This, coupled with many other factors, tie Prince Philip, Prince Charles, his sons Prince William and Prince Henry, and the British Monarchy as a whole to Daniel's *"prince who is to come,"* and Revelation's Beast from the Sea. For example, in the Book of Revelation, we are told that we will be able to identify the Beast from the Sea by *"seven kings:"*

> *"There are also seven kings. Five have fallen, one is, and the other has not yet come. And when he comes, he must continue a short time. And the beast that was, and is not, is himself also the eighth, and is of the seven, and is going to perdition. The ten horns which you saw are ten kings who have received no kingdom as yet, but they receive authority for one hour as kings with the beast." - Revelation 17:10-12*

In regard to this prophecy's *"seven kings,"* there have been seven kings named Charles who ruled over the Holy Roman Empire. These kings represent the seven heads of the Beast that the Harlot rides in the Book of Revelation (Revelation 12:3, 13:1, 17:3-9) But what of the beast who is one of the seven, but also the eighth? The answer lies with another Charles who is very prominent in the world political scene. His name is Prince Charles of Wales. Prince Charles is a direct descendent of Charles VI of Austria, the Holy Roman Emperor from 1711 to 1740, and the sixth Charles of the seven who ruled. The seventh Charles - Charles Albert of Belgium - only ruled for three years before he died.

Interestingly, the capital of Belgium - Brussels - happens to be the current capital of the European Union, and is now the European center of the world financial empire that may already be secretly ruled by the Antichrist. Now, if Prince Charles becomes the leader of a united Europe, he will be the eighth Charles to rule over the Roman Empire. If Prince Charles does, he will fulfill the prophecy: *"And the beast... is himself also the eighth, and is of the seven..."* (Rev. 17:11). Even more eerily, as if in confirmation of his possible role as the Antichrist, **Prince Charles was born in 1948 - the same year that Israel became a nation. This also ties him to "the prince who is to come" in Daniel's Prophecy of the Seventy Weeks as applied to the year 1948!**

Incidentally, Prince Charles and his mother Queen Elizabeth II are purportedly two of the richest people in the world - with combined net assets totaling billions of dollars. Furthermore, as one of the major proponents and investors in economic and financial globalization agencies, Prince Charles has been identified as one of the so-called Illuminati who now rule the world financially. If Prince Charles were to take over as the leader of the European Union, he would be the eighth Charles to rule over Europe, and also one of the seven Holy Roman Emperors by his relationship to King Charles VI. In addition, through the European Union and British Commonwealth of Nations, he could rule over a group of nations that has even greater financial and military power than the ancient Roman Empire had. This would make Prince Charles the richest man in the world by virtue of the assets he would control.

If the claim that Prince Charles may be the Antichrist sounds laughable to you, it did to me as well. That is, until I truly studied the facts disclosed in an article by Rabbi Monte Judah. Monte's entire article is available in the "Free Articles" section at http://pillar-of-enoch.com. Detailed information on this subject can also be found in the fascinating book "Antichrist, and a Cup of Tea" by Tim Cohen. Though Monte Judah and Tim Cohen have some aberrant religious beliefs that I do not share, I think they may be correct about Prince Charles being much more than he seems. These authors give many startling and believable reasons why Prince Charles (or one of his sons, particularly William) is a viable candidate for the dubious title of Antichrist. Furthermore, they explain how to calculate the numerical value of Prince Charles' name and title.

Seeing Prince Charles as a contender for the role of Antichrist is not meant to infer that there are not many saved people living in England, Scotland, Ireland, and Wales. On the contrary, many people in the United Kingdom, its Commonwealth nations, and Europe love Yahshua, are His born-again disciples, and will be highly regarded in Yahshua's Millennial Kingdom. However, the implications clearly point to the Royalty of Great Britain as the future leaders among the many nations that represent the *false* messianic kingdom of the Antichrist.

Keep in mind that it is also highly possible that a President of the United States may act as a forerunner to the Antichrist. In this regard, White House policies toward Israel under Barack Obama continue to be hostile, and this does not bode well for the people of the United States, who are already experiencing God's Judgment due to leaders like Obama, and the many liberals like him in America that are living in open rebellion against God and His Laws.

## The Star Gospel Key to the Beasts of Revelation

In this section, I will show how the Gospel in the Stars can shed a great deal of additional light on the subject of the End Time Beasts in the Book of Revelation. Though I once believed the lie that there is only one Antichrist, I now believe that, just as the Bible expressly warns, there are many antichrists in the world today. So we have to be careful about who we single out as the Antichrist. In fact, the Bible clearly warns that there is not just one, but a few Antichrist figures. The Bible says that these few are more powerful than all of the other antichrists, and they will one day collectively seize control of the world. Finally, the Bible warns that one of these few in authority will be worshiped.

This is partly revealed in the Book of Revelation, Chapter 13. The entire chapter describes two allegorical Beasts: one that is from the Sea, and one that is from the Earth. Although another Beast is described in Revelation Chapter 17, I will show that this Beast is tied to both of the Beasts in Chapter 13 a bit later. For now, let's focus on the Beasts in Revelation 13. With my strong background in Sacred Astronomy and the Gospel in the Stars, I have found several constellations that are directly tied to the Beasts in the Book of Revelation.

The first in prominence is Hydra the Serpent, whose long body runs alongside Leo and Virgo, with its head under Leo the Lion of Judah's front paws. In this case, the redeemed of Jewish Israel and the Gentile Church who are being reckoned as the Bride of Christ and the Wise Virgins are represented by Virgo the Virgin, while Leo the Lion signifies her Messiah and Crown of Salvation!

Another is Taurus the Bull, which is the first Beast in the heavens that has both a clearly good, and clearly evil connotation. The second one like Taurus with both good and evil connotations is Aries, which we will discuss in a moment. Like Hydra, Taurus is being threatened with annihilation by not one, but three heavenly Christ Figures. The first is the Messianic figure Perseus the Breaker, who is directly over Taurus' back, and signifies the Opener of the Second Seal, and the Master or Rider on the Red Horse (or Bull!) in the Book of Revelation, Chapter 6.

## Ch. 10: The Antichrist and Woman Riding the Beast

The second is Auriga the Goat Herd, who signifies Yahshua shepherding and chastising the rebellious goats in the world that refuse to be God's trusting sheep. These goats are directly connected to the goats sacrificed on the Day of Atonement. While one goat was sacrificed on the altar to God on the Day of Atonement, the other goat known as the Azazel goat was driven off of a cliff in the wilderness and left to die. The sacrificed goat represents those who are to eventually be saved, but as through the fire, while the Azazel goat signifies those who will perish forever in Hell. These goats are signified by Taurus the Bull's left horn, which is directly under the Messianic figure Auriga's foot in reference to Genesis 3:15, which is the first and most important prophecy in the entire Bible, though it tends to be overlooked due to its basic simplicity. In Genesis 3:15, it says:

*"He (i.e. Yahshua, a.k.a. Jesus) shall bruise you (i.e. Satan) on the head, and you (i.e. Satan) shall bruise Him (i.e. Yahshua) on the heel."*

This is also the same horn of Taurus that is being touched by the tip of the Messiah figure Orion's sword on the Ecliptic, showing that Orion is like Auriga as another antagonist to the Bull's ungodly power aspirations. Though Orion has been badly maligned by Occult practitioners and misinformed believers, Orion is actually one of the most powerful symbols for Christ in the heavens. This can partly be seen because the constellation Lepus directly below was depicted as a Serpent in ancient times, and its head is directly below Orion's foot. As such, it is another clear allusion to Genesis 3:15, as shown in the illustration that was excerpted from my book "The Language of God in Humanity" on page 155 in this book.

In that same book excerpt on pages 150 through 157 in this book, I explain how Taurus the Bull is directly connected to Christ in the bulls that were killed on an Altar to Yahweh outside the camp of the city as a Sin Offering. It is also connected to the Patriarch Joseph, and by extension to his Egyptian (i.e. Gentile) wife Asenath, and their two sons, Ephraim and Manasseh via the horns of Taurus, and why the mixed heritage of these two sons is important prophetically. I'll share more about this connection of the horns to Joseph's sons a bit later.

The next group of stars associated with an End Time Beast is the cluster of six bright stars on the back of Taurus the Bull known as the Pleiades. These signify the Churches that will connect themselves to the Harlot riding on the back of the Scarlet Beast, which signifies the Ecumenical Movement that will lead to the formation of the Antichrist's and False Prophet's One World Religion that is described in the Book of

Revelation, Chapter 17 as the Woman who rides the Beast. The six stars of the Pleiades signify six of the Seven Churches in the Book of Revelation. The one church NOT included in the symbolism of the Pleiades is the Church of Philadelphia, which is also the ONLY church of the seven that is identified as the Bride of Christ (See Rev. 3:12, in view of Rev. 21:2).

Incidentally, it is the Church of Philadelphia along with the Five Wise Virgins that are the only believers that Yahshua promises to protect from the Time of Trial, or the Great Tribulation (Matthew 25:6-10; Rev. 3:10). Some believe that the method of protection will involve finding cities of refuge here on Earth until Yahshua comes for us at the end of the Great Tribulation, which I think is possible for the Foolish Virgins that miss the First Rapture. Others believe we will be caught up in the air and taken to Heaven for a short time via the great Catching Away, or the Rapture. I personally believe that not one, but two Rapture events are taught in Scripture - one at the beginning of the Great Tribulation, and one near to its end. I will divulge more on this later.

The next Beast of note in the heavens is Cetus the Sea Monster. This is the Beast from the Sea that the Two Fishes of Pisces that signify the Two Houses of Israel are tied to via their enslavement to sin. However, they are being defended from this Beast's malevolent intent because its head is under the hooves of Aries the Ram. This is a good thing, because Aries is the Mazzaroth or Zodiac Sign signifying Yahshua Ha Mashiach (aka Jesus the Christ) as the Lamb of God, Whose shed blood takes away the sins of those who love Him, and frees them from the wickedness and sin that is depicted by Cetus! For this reason, Aries is often depicted with its hooves over the bands tethering the fishes of Pisces to Cetus. Unlike the Pleiades star cluster, which signifies believers who are Foolish Virgins that are either not born again or that are asleep spiritually, the fishes of Pisces signify the remnant of truly born-again believers that are doing their best to follow Yahshua, and that God has chosen for salvation and protection from His wrath and judgment due to their devotion to Christ.

Another Beast in the heavens is Scorpio the Scorpion, whose head, body and stinger are being symbolically trampled under the messianic figure Ophiuchus the Serpent Holder's feet. In this respect, Ophiuchus is also the Opener of the Fourth Seal, and the Master or Rider of the Pale Horse signified by Scorpio. Ophiuchus is also the Restrainer of the huge heavenly Serpent that is continually wrestling against this godly restraint. The one who is being restrained is Serpens the Serpent, a symbol of Satan struggling to take control of the world in the figure known as the Antichrist. This is shown in the heavens by the fact that Serpens' head is being crushed under the club in the messianic figure Hercules' hand before it can steal the Crown of Christ that is seen in the constellation Corona Borealis.

The final and most threatening of these Beast figures is Draco the Dragon, which is directly connected to the Red Dragon described as the enemy of the Woman clothed with the Sun in Revelation, Chapter 12, who signifies the True Church, or Bride of Christ and her Five Wise Virgin attendants.

> *"And another sign appeared in heaven: behold, a great, fiery red dragon having seven heads and ten horns, and seven diadems on his heads." - Revelation 12:3*

As the enemy of Yahshua's beloved saints, it's no wonder that this Red Dragon is directly connected to the Beasts in Revelation 13 and 17. Like the Beast from the Sea, the Red Dragon has seven heads and ten horns, and like the Scarlet Beast in Revelation Chapter 17, this Dragon is red. This is no coincidence, but shows us that the Red Dragon and the three other Beasts in the Book of Revelation are all connected.

In the heavens, Draco's head is being crushed under the Christ-figure Hercules' feet, while Hercules' club is raised as if to hit the head of Serpens, the writhing serpent being restrained in Ophiuchus' arms. As a Christ-figure, Hercules is keeping both satanic figures from claiming Christ's Crown, which is seen in the constellation Corona Borealis. Like Taurus and Cetus, Draco the Dragon is also diabolically interacting with the Churches of Revelation, as shown by the adjacent constellations Ursa Major, or God's Big Sheep Pen, and Ursa Minor, which is a sheep pen full of misguided and deceived people who think they are following Christ, but are not!

In this regard, please look at the illustration on the next page and note how Draco the Dragon's tail wraps around Ursa Minor in its dangerous and poisonous embrace, while Ursa Major is outside of the immediate reach of Draco's mouth and/or tail. Draco signifies two different rulers and Churches. The first of them is the Pontiff in the Vatican, who officiated at many Royal Coronations throughout European history. In this way, the Dragon or Pope gave the Beast formed by the elite its power. Meanwhile, Ursa Minor signifies the deluded sheep or congregants of the Roman Catholic Church that the Pontiff misleads. However, the Church of England, which broke away from Papal rule, also officiates at Royal Coronations within the United Kingdom, and therefore it serves as a Dragon that gives power and authority to the Beast as well.

# The Language of God in Prophecy

## Star Gospel Surrounding Draco, Hercules and Cepheus

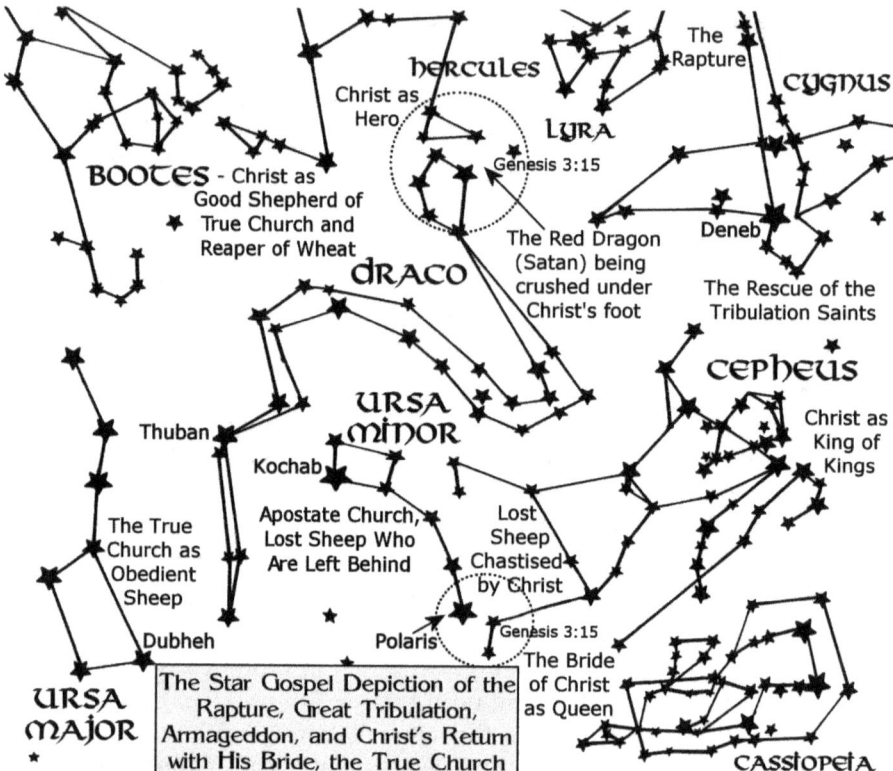

Now, note how the foot of the Messianic figure Cepheus the Crowned King is over the Pole Star Polaris located in Ursa Minor, the sheep pen full of deluded sheep or Foolish Virgins. This is an ominous sign that many of the people in the Catholic Church and apostate Protestant Churches are living under Christ's judgment and will perish without the blessing of Yahshua the King of kings. This is echoed in Psalm 91:13, where it says: *"You shall tread upon the lion and the cobra, The young lion and the serpent you shall trample underfoot."* This Scripture can also equally apply to the references to Genesis 3:15 in the Orion -Auriga -Perseus illustration on page 155.

Sadly, Yahshua's blessing is only given via our belief in, and love for Him! Therefore, those who reject Yahshua by giving His divine authority to a mere man (the Pope) and a woman (Mary) are in grave danger of either losing their salvation, or never finding it in Christ. Meanwhile, the saints who have been chosen by God to be the Bride of

Christ within the Protestant Churches are signified by Ursa Major, the big sheep pen full of Christ's righteous sheep.

The Beast from the Sea seen in Hydra and Cetus signifies the totalitarian monarchal rule of kings, as well as all forms of totalitarian government where a few rich people have absolute control over many poor, subjugated people. Though this type of government can still be seen all over the world today, the Enlightenment period in Europe and England brought a wave of change to the world, moving it away from monarchial rule to the rule of law. This had the benefit of giving some much needed control to the people over how they were governed. In the United States and Europe, this led to the development of Democratic Republics that were run by officials elected by popular vote. This government was also overseen by judges, who defined the law within the boundaries set by the various constitutions utilized in each new democratic nation.

For a long time, this form of government worked very well in the nations where it was adopted because they were populated by a largely religious populace that honored God, heeded His Laws, and also respected the rules of the land. But as the people moved further and further away from their Judeo-Christian roots, rebellion against the laws of God and men became much more commonplace. This has led to a state of near anarchy in nations that were once moral and righteous.

Because of this, the governments of these nations were eventually taken over by the elite members of society that have always hated Democracy. The reason they do is because their lives and livelihoods could be taken away at any moment by an angry mob of frustrated citizens, and as the world moves further toward anarchy, immorality and lawlessness, this fear has led some members of the elite to turn on the people they were elected to govern justly. Instead, some of them have been secretly moving behind the scenes to re-establish the totalitarian police states that protected them from harm in the past. In addition, some of the wicked leaders among the elite have been continually plotting to destroy most of the poorer people that now inhabit the Earth.

This leads us to the Bible's Beast from the Earth. As shown in the last chapter, this Beast represents crude oil. However, it also signifies nations that successfully adopted Democracy as a form of government. Their initial success, which was due to the overall godly morality of the people, led to much wealth and prosperity as the blessings of the Tribe of Joseph that is signified by Taurus the Bull. But as these nations moved away from the true faith and no longer honored God or His Laws, these Democratic forms of government became extremely corrupt.

# The Language of God in Prophecy

Like these corrupt nations, the Beast from the Earth appears benevolent (like a lamb) on the surface, but is guilty of using and manipulating the people it governs. Due to this, these Democracies are behaving more like satanic Dragons or Serpents as they move closer and closer to adopting the social structure seen in Communism and Totalitarianism. Indeed, all Serpents and Dragons, which signify corrupt governments and organized religions, tend to do this. These corrupting influences in government and religion are largely signified by Draco, Hydra, Cetus, Serpens and Scorpio in the heavens, although Taurus and the Pleiades, and several other stars and constellations do so as well, as will be shown in the next chapter.

Fascinatingly, in all of the Beast constellations, their interactions with the other constellations show that they have three major things in common. First, each depicts a Powerful Christ Figure paired up against a Satanic Beast Figure. Secondly, every Beast Figure is influencing or attacking God's Church or His people Israel in some way. This is being done through the bad Tares and Goats that Yahshua spoke of that are sown among the good Wheat and Sheep. They are a negative and evil force that is mixed into the congregations of Wheat and Sheep that signify people who love Yahweh God and do their best to follow Him and His Son Yahshua. Thirdly, every single Beast figure is being subdued and destroyed by the Christ-Figure associated with it! Therefore, these are all perfect examples of the very first prophecy in the Bible, which is found in Genesis 3:15.

Now let's focus on the horns of Taurus and Aries to see what they are trying to tell us prophetically. On that note, it pays to remember that the Priests of Israel smeared the blood of each sacrifice made in the Tabernacle and Temple on the four horns of the altar of burnt offering. The horns of Taurus and Aries represent the heavenly altar, which the altar in Israel was made to imitate. Both Taurus and Aries signify Yahshua as the Sacrifice for Sin (Taurus the Bull) burnt outside the camp of Israel, and the Atonement Sacrifice for sin (Aries the Ram) burnt inside the courtyard of the Temple/Tabernacle. Taurus the Bull is tied to Joseph, who represents the Gentile Nations that are tied to the Ten Lost Tribes of Israel.

Now, though Aries the Ram is connected to the Israelite Tribe of Naphtali, its horns signify Judah and Levi, while its body represents the Ten Lost Tribes of Israel. In Chapters 9 and 10, it was explained how the United States is tied to the Tribe of Joseph via Ephraim, as well as to Levi via the Gospel in the Stars. Meanwhile, the United Kingdom is tied to the Tribe of Judah, and to Joseph through Manasseh. The horns of Aries therefore represent the leaders among these two supposed Gentile Nations that look like a lamb in their outward benevolent rule of the people, but that speak like a dragon in destructive power and sinister authority.

At this point, we need to remember that the Bible uses horns to represent leaders. In other words, the lamb-like Beast from the Earth that speaks with great power and authority like a dragon, and will force the world to worship the Image of the Beast, and take his 666 Mark, is not one, but two leaders and authoritative bodies! In fact, as my previous exposition conveys, these two leaders are the President of the United States and the ruling Monarch of the United Kingdom. Currently these are President Barack Hussein Obama, and Queen Elizabeth II. Incidentally, Queen Elizabeth leads with the help of her husband Prince Philip, her son Prince Charles, and her grandson Prince William, who rule with her behind the scenes. As such, the Queen represents the one horn on the Beast from the Sea that subdues - or controls - three horns. Please be aware of this, and don't insist on labeling one man as the Antichrist!

Below Taurus and Aries, which signifies Democratic leadership, is Cetus the Sea Monster, which signifies the Beast from the Sea or Totalitarian Government. So, just as Aries is restraining Cetus from harming the fish of Pisces that signify the Two House Church of Judah (the Jews) and Ephraim (born-again Gentiles), the Democratic governments have restrained the power-hungry elites from seizing control again and harming the Two Fish or Houses full of the Chosen People of God signified by Pisces by adopting Freedom of Religion.

Now, all these Beasts that are found in the heavens are also revealed in the Books of Daniel and Revelation. In the Book of Revelation, Chapters 13 and 17, we are told that the Dragon, which as Draco is winding its way between two sheep pens of congregants in the Catholic and Protestant Churches - gave the Beast from the Sea (Hydra and Cetus) its power and authority. Based on the history of Europe, where the kings were crowned by the Pontiffs and Bishops of the Roman Catholic Church, this clearly identifies the Dragon as the Vatican in Rome, a city that sits on seven mountains or hills (Rev. 17:9). We are also told that the heads and horns of the Beasts represent kings. Clearly, then, the Beast is a wicked system of government that is ruled over by corrupt kings and religious leaders who assume they have a divine right to rule, just as their Fallen Angel and Nephilim forebears did.

In Chapter 13, the Mark of the Beast is revealed as being connected to the Beast from the Sea and the Beast from the Earth in relation to buying and selling, which are elements of commerce, not medicine. This means that the Mark of the Beast is likely not a medical device or therapy such as a vaccine. Instead, it will replace currency in the final Beast kingdom of the Antichrist, so that no one will be able to buy or sell anything, or draw a wage without it. It also means that the Mark is connected to Europe, which includes the United Kingdom and the Commonwealth Nations of the UK.

This suggests that the Mark of the Beast is, or will be related to the Euro. Fascinatingly, the Euro dollar is now the sole currency of the Vatican and 17 European nations, including three of the four powerful nations represented by Daniel's Four Beasts: the Lion being the United Kingdom; the Bear in its connection to Germany (and Russia); the Leopard, which is France (The Frankish Kingdoms); and the Beast with Ten Horns and Iron Teeth, which represents Rome, and the Roman Empire in its past and present forms that are found in the United Kingdom and its Commonwealth Nations. This is the Beast that was, is not and is in Revelation 17:8 and 11.

Due to the description of the Beast from the Sea as a composite creature, there is no way that this Beast is just one single person. Instead, it represents a system of powerful leaders and authorities that seize control of the whole world in a Totalitarian state. Sadly, this Beast is connected to the United States, the United Kingdom, Russia and the European Union, along with the United Nations. It has been formed from nations represented by the Leopard, Bear, and Lion, which were France (the Leopard), Germany and Russia (the Bear), and Great Britain (the Lion), respectively. In addition the USA can be connected to this Beast through the Eagle's wings that were torn off of the Lion. There is also an undeniable connection between the symbolism of Taurus the Bull and the European Union, which has romanticized and connected the Classical Greek myth of Zeus disguising himself as a bull in order to abduct the fair young maiden Europa to the European Union as a whole.

Likewise, the Beast from the Earth has two horns like a lamb, and speaks like a dragon. In this regard, it has long been known that the Bible uses horns to represent leaders. In other words, the lamb-like Beast from the Earth that will speak with great power and authority like a dragon, and will force the world to worship the Image of the Beast, and take his 666 Mark, is not one, but two leaders and authoritative bodies! Please be aware of this, and don't insist on labeling one man as the Antichrist.

There are many, and specifically not one, but two leaders and their respective governments, and one Image of the Beast that will one day control a one-world commercial empire and one-world religious

# Ch. 10: The Antichrist and Woman Riding the Beast

empire for the Dragon, who is Satan. This system has been partially identified as the Illuminati. But I believe that it is specifically tied to two powerful Western nations, and these are the United States and the United Kingdom. These nations try hard to appear harmless and good like a lamb, when in fact, they no longer are. They are being controlled by the Illuminati, who intend to use these nations to control the whole world one day soon.

I'd also like to share a word of caution regarding the Image of the Beast. Though the Beast from the Earth will cause the whole world to worship the Image of the Beast from the Sea, we are NOT told if this Image is just one person, or a group of people. So, the assumption that the Image has to be either one religious or political leader is not necessarily true. In fact, since the Image of the dragon or serpent-like, satanic Beast from the Sea represents a global political and economic entity, its image could be a logo or symbol instead of a person!

Personally, I believe the two Antichristian leaders that are connected to the two lamb's horns on the Beast from the Earth could be US President Obama and Prince Charles of Wales, and the Image of the Beast may be Prince William, who is Prince Charles' son or IMAGE. That makes three final Antichrist figures. On the other hand, the Image could be the Coat of Arms symbol of the British Monarchy, or the symbol of the United Nations or European Union, or an entirely new symbol used to represent the Antichristian One World Government that is coming.

## The Mysterious Firstfruits From The Dead

Did you know that there are strong hints in the Bible that there are secret societies today that are working to fulfill the Will of Yahweh God in this world, and so not all of them are evil? Indeed, the Bible supports the idea that some of these major players working behind the scenes aren't all working for the enemy! One of these workers, who is still likely working behind the scenes on the Earth today, was alive when Yahshua walked the Earth. This is the Beloved Disciple:

> "Then Peter, turning around, saw the disciple whom Jesus loved following, who also had leaned on His breast at the supper, and said, 'Lord, who is the one who betrays You?' 21 Peter, seeing him, said to Jesus, 'But Lord, what about this man?' 22 Jesus said to him, 'If I will that he remain till I come, what is that to you? You follow Me.' 23 Then this saying went out among the brethren that this disciple would not die. Yet Jesus did not say to him that he would not die, but, 'If I will that he remain till I come, what is

*that to you?' 24 This is the disciple who testifies of these things, and wrote these things; and we know that his testimony is true." - John 21:20-24*

In my Language of God Book Series, I explain that this Scripture hints that the Beloved Disciple might still be on the Earth today, waiting for Yahshua to return in all His Glory. My books also explain why I believe that the Beloved Disciple was not the Apostle John, but Yahshua's disciple Lazarus, the brother of Mary of Bethany, a.k.a. Mary Magdalene. In the Gospel of John, we are told that Lazarus was raised from the dead, and that Yahshua deeply loved him:

*"Therefore, when Jesus saw her weeping... He groaned in the spirit and was troubled. 34 And He said, 'Where have you laid him?' They said to Him, 'Lord, come and see.' 35 Jesus wept. 36 Then the Jews said, 'See how He loved him!' 37 And some of them said, 'Could not this Man, who opened the eyes of the blind, also have kept this man from dying?' 38 Then Jesus... came to the tomb. It was a cave, and a stone lay against it. 39 Jesus said, 'Take away the stone.' Martha... said to Him, 'Lord, by this time there is a stench, for he has been dead four days.' 40 Jesus said to her, 'Did I not say to you that if you would believe you would see the glory of God?' 41 Then... Jesus lifted up His eyes and said, 'Father, I thank You that You have heard Me... but because of the people who are standing by I said this, that they may believe that You sent Me.' 43 Now when He had said these things, He cried with a loud voice, 'Lazarus, come forth!' 44 And he who had died came out bound hand and foot with graveclothes, and his face was wrapped with a cloth. Jesus said to them, 'Loose him, and let him go.'"- John 11:33-44*

Now, since Lazarus was raised from the dead before Yahshua died and rose again, and Yahshua is the Firstfruits of the Resurrection, we can come to no other conclusion but that Lazarus rose up to a mortal life. However, this does not mean that Lazarus' longevity as a mortal wasn't affected! In other words, though Lazarus was still mortal, his life could have been supernaturally prolonged after his resurrection. If so, it could be that Lazarus is being kept alive to serve a purpose in the End Times. There are also hints in the Bible and Book of 2 Enoch that this was done for two prophets named Enoch and Elijah:

*"Enoch lived sixty-five years, and begot Methuselah. 22 After he begot Methuselah, Enoch walked with God three hundred years, and had sons and daughters. 23 So all the days of Enoch*

## Ch. 10: The Antichrist and Woman Riding the Beast

*were three hundred and sixty-five years. 24 And Enoch walked with God; and he was not, for God took him." - Genesis 5:21-24*

*"When Enoch had talked to the people, the Lord sent out darkness on to the earth, and there was darkness, and it covered those men standing with Enoch, and they took Enoch up on to the highest heaven, where the Lord is; and he received him and placed him before his face, and the darkness went off from the earth, and light came again. 2 And the people saw and understood not how Enoch had been taken..." - 2 Enoch 67:1-2*

*"Then it happened, as they continued on and talked, that suddenly a chariot of fire appeared with horses of fire, and separated the two of them; and Elijah went up by a whirlwind into heaven. 12 And Elisha saw it, and he cried out, 'My father, my father, the chariot of Israel and its horsemen!' So he saw him no more." - 2 Kings 2:11-12*

These are the only two righteous men in history that were translated into Heaven without seeing death. This fact suggests that they may be coming back to serve as the Two Witnesses of the Tribulation period, when they will finally die at the hands of the Antichrist, but will also be resurrected:

*"Now after the three-and-a-half days the breath of life from God entered them, and they stood on their feet, and great fear fell on those who saw them. 12 And they heard a loud voice from heaven saying to them, 'Come up here.' And they ascended to heaven in a cloud, and their enemies saw them." - Revelation 11:11-12*

Besides the Beloved Disciple and the Two Witnesses, there is a strong hint in the Bible that there is another group of immortal saints working behind the scenes on the Earth today that may have become very rich, and are very secretive. In fact, it is likely that they have become so shrouded in legend and mystery that no one knows the truth about them. In fact, they may have been labeled as evil or sinister out of ignorance.

The Gospel of Matthew alludes to these immortal saints in a much ignored passage of the Bible. In it, we are told that the tombs of many dead saints were opened shortly after Yahshua died on the Cross. Then, after Yahshua's Resurrection three days later, the saints whose tombs had been opened were raised from the dead and appeared to many:

*"Then, behold, the veil of the temple was torn in two from top to bottom; and the earth quaked, and the rocks were split, 52 and the graves were opened; and many bodies of the saints who*

*had fallen asleep were raised; 53 and coming out of the graves after His resurrection, they went into the holy city and appeared to many." - Matthew 27:51-53*

How is it that few pastors ever address the implications of this passage, or wonder what became of these resurrected saints? The thing that nobody seems to notice is that, since these saints rose from the dead **after** Yahshua did, they were not raised to resume a mortal life like Lazarus, but to everlasting life! This means that they could still be on the Earth today, and may have been secretly behind many events in History that have accomplished our Father God's Will in every age.

I've read articles online where people have speculated that Yahshua took these resurrected saints to Heaven with Him when He presented Himself before the Father as the Firstfruits of the Resurrection. But this doesn't make sense for several reasons. First of all, Yahshua is called the First and the Last and the Beginning and End several times in the Book of Revelation. This is partly because Yahshua was always meant to be the **first** person raised to everlasting life, and not as one of a multitude. That is why Matthew 28, verse 53 states that these first resurrected saints were raised up *after* Yahshua, not at the same time as Him. This was said to indicate that they likely did *not* take part in Yahshua's presentation as the Firstfruits of the Resurrection.

Believing that these saints accompanied Yahshua to Heaven on the day of the Firstfruits Offering in the Temple contradicts Scripture. Matthew says that these saints appeared to many in Jerusalem after they were raised up. But he never mentions their ascension to Heaven, which would have been highly significant, and should have been noted - at least in passing if it had occurred. On the contrary, the Bible says that Yahshua appeared to no one but Mary Magdalene, and that He was alone before He ascended to Heaven in secret. Furthermore, Yahshua did not return to Earth to appear to His Apostles and disciples immediately, but did so on an unspecified day. In contrast, the Gospel of Matthew suggests that the saints that were raised up after Christ appeared in Jerusalem immediately after that, and without any delay.

Since these saints were raised after Yahshua, they likely were presented to the Father after Yahshua - if they were presented at all. In fact, 40 days later, Yahshua ascended to Heaven alone while His apostles and disciples witnessed His Ascension to Heaven. This strongly suggests that the now immortal saints that were raised shortly after Yahshua could still be on the Earth today, waiting to be caught up to Heaven at a later date. This later time could be after the Two Witnesses have died and are raised up. At that time, the Two Witnesses will be caught up to Heaven

## Ch. 10: The Antichrist and Woman Riding the Beast

in what I believe will be a Second Rapture that will include those among the Foolish Virgins that have repented, and been refined in the fire of the Great Tribulation.

My point in writing this section was to raise the question of what the Beloved Disciple, as well as the group of now immortal saints that were raised after Yahshua may have gone on to do for Yahshua after their resurrections. Though it is not a crime to assume that the saints that were raised after Christ may have spent the past two millennia in Heaven with Him, it is not necessarily true. After all, the Earth is to be our everlasting habitation after the First Resurrection is complete at the end of the Great Tribulation, when the martyrs in Christ who died during the Great Tribulation will be raised to life, and will not ascend to Heaven. This is because Heaven is not our natural home, but is only meant to be a temporary place of refuge for us.

Though few in the Church want to speculate about it, there is also a very high possibility that some of the Israelite saints that were part of the Firstfruits of the Resurrection may be counted among the 144,000 Witnesses for Yahweh that will be chosen out of the Twelve Tribes of Israel during the Tribulation period. If so, those saints will be here during the Great Tribulation. So let me ask you: "Isn't it possible that these immortal saints might have chosen to stay behind on Earth to await their service during the Tribulation? Furthermore, if they did stay behind, isn't it possible that they are part of a modern top secret and wealthy organization on the Earth that is **not** evil, but is dedicated to making sure that Yahweh God's Will is faithfully carried out in these End Times?"

Please don't misunderstand me. I have no doubt that Yahweh has allowed the Devil to plant many of his wicked followers in high positions throughout the ages, including many Church and Government leaders. This has been allowed so that all people, in every age, have had the freedom to choose whose side they are on - whether for good or for evil - and what policies and actions that they will present to the world to affect change. However, Yahweh God is still ultimately in control of how much evil Satan can unleash at any given time, and God is sure of the final outcome, which includes the defeat of the Antichrist and his evil armies, and the setting up of a truly righteous kingdom on Earth afterward, which will feature Yahshua our Messiah as its everlasting King.

In reference to the coming Millennial Rule of Christ, I find it an intriguing thought the maybe some of the secret societies in the world today are *not* workers of iniquity, but followers of the Way of Yahweh that are working to achieve God's aims in these closing moments of the End Times. In fact, they could become a part of the 144,000 Witnesses, and they may even be people you know, but have no clue as to what they are really doing for a living, and Who they actually work for.

Let's hope that there truly are godly people at work today in high positions that know and love Yahweh God. In my opinion, it certainly makes sense that our Father God would have His own mighty warrior saints working with his holy angels on His behalf in this fallen world, in every age. On that note, I could not close this section without sharing that I suspect that not all of the branches of Freemasonry being practiced today and not all Freemasons are Satanic or Illuminati-controlled.

Part of my feelings in this regard comes from the godly meaning of certain symbols that can be associated with Freemasonry, like the All-Seeing Eye of God and the 13-tiered Pyramid on the US Great Seal. As shown in Chapter 9, these symbols are connected to the Ecuador Artifacts, which may be connected to Noah and Sacred Astronomy. In addition, it is a documented fact that some branches of the Freemasons keep the Christian Feasts dedicated to John the Baptist and the Apostle John, honoring these two great men of God with special ceremonies. I find this peculiarity very suggestive of the idea that Freemasonry as a whole may not have originally been an evil Occult organization, but that some of the branches within Freemasonry did **not** become perverted - just as George Washington intimated.

The Masonic commemoration of the Feast of John the Baptist on June 24th and August 29th, and the Feast of the Apostle John on December 27th suggests that there may be a link between Freemasonry and a still more secret organization headed by none other than the Beloved Disciple, who may have been Lazarus or the Apostle John, both of whom may have been resurrected during Yahshua's First Advent, with the Apostle John and John the Baptist being resurrected to immortal life just after Yahshua rose up, while Lazarus may have been resurrected to a mortal but supernaturally protected and greatly elongated life.

If this is the case, there is a possibility that these men of God may be using some of the branches of Freemasonry to do God's Will on Earth until Yahshua comes again. It is my great hope that this is so, and I pray that they will be successful in all that they do for the Kingdom of God, if that is what they aim to do.

# Chapter 11: The Rapture and Woman Clothed with the Sun

*"After these things I looked, and behold, a door standing open in heaven. And the first voice which I heard was like a trumpet speaking with me, saying, 'Come up here, and I will show you things which must take place after this.'"* - Rev. 4:1

The Rapture is a hot topic of debate in today's churches, and the above Scripture is a key passage that refers to the Rapture allegorically as an "open door" into Heaven. This chapter presents this door and many other proof texts relating to a coming Rapture before the Trumpet and Bowl Judgments are meted out on Earth during the Great Tribulation. The arguments for the Rapture presented here are given as a note of hope and comfort, which are often needed after exploring the frightening Tribulation plagues that are recorded in the Book of Revelation, as well as after focusing on the ever-growing wickedness in this world.

In the following Scripture, Yahshua speaks of His role as a thief in the night and offers proof that there will be at least one Rapture (though there may be two - one before or early in the Tribulation, and one at Mid-Tribulation, a.k.a. Pre-Wrath:

*"In My Father's house are many mansions... And if I go and prepare a place for you,* **I will come again and receive you** *to Myself; that where I am, there you may be also."* - John 14:2-3

Now, if the *"Father's house"* is in Heaven, and we are not going to go to Heaven at the Rapture, but are to be resurrected in the air and returned to Earth immediately at the end of the Tribulation, why would Yahshua need to prepare rooms for us in Heaven when He comes again? Logically, He would only need to do so if He was coming for us in surprise before the worst part of the Tribulation period begins, and needed somewhere safe to keep us for a certain period of time.

Another major reason to believe in a Rapture or Catching Away is the Apostle Paul's promises that the saints will be protected from God's Wrath, while the wicked will suffer it:

> *"Since we have now been justified by his blood, how much more shall we be saved from God's wrath through him!"* - Romans 5:9 (NIV)

> *"Let no one deceive you... because of these things the wrath of God comes upon the sons of disobedience."* - Ephes. 5:6

> *"You turned to God from idols to serve the living and true God, and to wait for... Jesus (Yahshua) who delivers us from the wrath to come."* - *"For God did not appoint us to wrath, but to obtain salvation..."* - 1 Thess. 1:9-10, 5:9

These Scriptures indicate that **Paul believed born-again Christians would always be delivered from God's Wrath.** Though they might suffer persecution, or be murdered for their faith at the hands of men, God's Wrath would only be poured out on those who have backslidden and become apostate, or those who reject Christ, hate His Gospel, and revile His saints. Since the Great Tribulation is the ultimate Wrath of God, it is wrong to suggest that God will not keep His promises to His saints during this time, or force them to suffer with the ungodly. In fact, it would be far more just for God to spare most of his faithful servants from the Tribulation.

Though at least one Pre-Wrath Rapture is nearly certain, no one knows who will be taken, who will be purposely left behind, or who will be chosen to stay behind to guide the Tribulation Saints and preach the Gospel. In this regard, only one thing is absolutely *certain*: Yahshua is knocking at the door of everyone's heart and saying: *"Behold, I stand at the door and knock"* (Revelation 3:20). When they open that symbolic door, Yahshua will come into their hearts through the Holy Spirit and they will be spiritually transformed. Blessed are they who let God's Spirit into their hearts, and listen to Her instruction. They alone will believe the signs that herald Christ's imminent return:

> *"Behold, I am coming as a thief. Blessed is he who watches, and keeps his garments, lest he walk naked and they see his shame."* - Revelation 16:15

In this Scripture, staying awake is an allegorical reference to being spiritually ready for Yahshua's arrival. Likewise, references in Scripture to those who are sleepy or asleep suggest that they are either falling into apostasy, or do not believe in Christ's imminent return and will *"go naked,"* meaning that they will suffer through the Great Tribulation without protection from calamity or assurance of salvation until they repent. On the other hand, those who stay awake will keep their *"clothes"* or righteousness.

## Ch. 11: The Rapture and Woman Clothed with the Sun    Page 513

Adding to this analogy is the fact that all living things are necessarily clothed with physical bodies. In humanity's case, bodies of flesh, bone and light served as our clothes until we became conscious of sin, and needed clothing for protection from the elements, and to repress the animalistic tendencies that sin causes. Since this is true, could this Scripture be trying to tell us that keeping our clothes means keeping our bodies in the resurrection?

The only way to avoid almost certain death during the Great Tribulation is to be physically removed from the Earth in the Rapture. Many worldwide pestilences and catastrophes will hit the Earth during the Great Tribulation, as will be discussed in detail a bit later in this chapter. Considering the ferocity of these terrifying events, absolutely no one will be physically safe on Earth unless they are already immortal like the angels or they are supernaturally protected by God. The horrifying truth is that more people and animals - both good and bad - will likely die during the Great Tribulation than at any other time in history outside of the Great Flood.

For many Christians, the idea of the Rapture offers them the hope of deliverance from what will surely be the most horrible time in human history. However, some Messianic Jews and Christians believe this is a false hope, and they use all sorts of persuasive arguments from Scripture to attempt to prove that the Rapture is not taught in the Bible. Ninety percent of their arguments against the Rapture, however, are based on a faulty interpretation of Scriptures that speak about either the First Rapture, Second Rapture, *or* the last stage of the multi-stage First Resurrection. When they erroneously lump passages pertaining to these *three different events* into one category, they create a great deal of unnecessary confusion. When all these passages about the two Raptures and the First Resurrection are studied carefully, however, these three events they speak about become apparent.

First of all, it's important to remember some distinctions between the First and Second Rapture. While the First Rapture will likely occur at the beginning of the Great Tribulation period, the Second Rapture stage of the First Resurrection will likely occur toward the end of the Great Tribulation - *at the Last or Seventh Trumpet*. Consequently, the saints who are caught up at the Seventh Trumpet will take part in Christ's triumphant return to Earth, with all of them riding white horses like their King and their already glorified peers! Furthermore, **while the First Rapture is likely to occur during a time of relative peace and safety, the Second Rapture will occur during a time of great unrest and fear.**

It's also important to know that both the First and Second Rapture will occur without warning, and though no one may actually see the beloved Thief Yahshua stealing away millions of believers all over the world, they will see his angels when they come to collect the elect from all over the world. Scripture also tells us that His coming will be marked by many signs in the Sun, Moons and stars, and in the distress of the nations on the Earth as the End Time plagues intensify. It is also my contention that Yahshua's various comings and goings to and from this Earth has been - and will surely continue to be - broadcast with the Sign of Jonah and the Sign of the Son of Man in the heavens, which we will discuss in this chapter.

In stark contrast, the last or third stage of the First Resurrection will occur when Yahshua has already physically returned to Earth in heavenly Glory and conquered the wicked armies surrounding Jerusalem. At that time, Yahshua will resurrect and add the martyred Tribulation Saints to His Kingdom. Let's examine some of the literal and allegorical proofs in the Bible that specifically teach that the Rapture will occur. First, there is the testimony of Matthew, who recorded Yahshua as saying:

> "For as in the days before the flood, they were eating and drinking, marrying and giving in marriage, until the day that Noah entered the ark, **and did not know until the flood came and took them all away, so also will the coming of the Son of Man be. Then two men will be in the field: one will be taken and the other left. Two women will be grinding at the mill: one will be taken and the other left.** Watch therefore, for you do not know what hour your Lord is coming. But know this, that if the master of the house had known what hour the thief would come, he would have... not allowed his house to be broken into. Therefore... be ready, **for the Son of Man is coming at an hour you do not expect.** - Matthew 24:38-44

In this passage, we are told that no one will know the day or hour when Yahshua, who is the Son of Man, will come for His saints. As time goes by, many will reject the teachings of latter-day prophets who will warn them of Christ's imminent return, and they will be caught spiritually unrepentant and unprepared. Next, Yahshua said: *"one will be taken, the other left."* For those who believe in the Rapture, this passage literally speaks of that event, which will be a time of judgment. Only the righteous believers in Yahshua will be swept up out of harm's way and into Heaven itself.

## Ch. 11: The Rapture and Woman Clothed with the Sun

After speaking of those who will be taken to Heaven and those who will be left behind, Yahshua shared a short parable about the master of a certain house, and a thief who will break into the master's house at an indeterminate moment. Though, in most cases the term "master" refers to God the Father or Christ, in Matthew 24:43 it appears to refer to Satan, who is the current master of this world. Therefore, the thief must be Christ, who is coming to steal His saints away in the Rapture. This is important to know, because, in the next few lines of Matthew (Mat. 24:45-51), Yahshua talks of the master again, but this time in reference to Himself! This can be determined easily because the master being spoken of *is not the master of the house*. Instead, He is the master *of the servant, and the household* - i.e. *the people* living in the house!

This Scripture shows that, **before Yahshua comes in the First Rapture, the world will be in a state of relative peace,** and people will be going about their usual business all over the world. This scenario is impossible if Christ's coming as a thief is at the middle or end of the Tribulation period. Anyone who reads of the massive plagues and total devastation that will befall the inhabitants of the entire Earth beginning in the second or third year of the Tribulation would know that envisioning the end, or even the middle of the Tribulation as a time of peace is completely nonsensical. *Hardly anyone* will be farming or getting married at that time! Instead, **even before the Seven Trumpets and Seven Bowls of God's Wrath are delivered, everyone still living will be hiding from God's wrath in terror:**

> "And the kings... the great men, the rich men, the commanders, **the mighty men, every slave and every free man, hid themselves in the caves and in the rocks of the mountains,** and said to the... rocks, 'Fall on us and hide us from... Him who sits on the throne and from the wrath of the Lamb!" - Rev. 6:15-16

Many of these terrified sinners will finally come to their knees in repentance, and will ask Yahshua into their hearts. Undoubtedly, many of the poor souls who are left behind will quickly come to realize that they missed the boat to Heaven, and are about to sink into the horror of the Tribulation, just as the unrepentant people before the Flood. However, although these Tribulation Saints will miss the First Rapture, they may be taken up to Heaven before they have to see the worst of the devastation of the plagues and wars that will ravage the Earth. If there is a Second Rapture event at the time that the Two Witnesses are resurrected, the Tribulation saints will be spared from living through what will surely be the most terrifying time in human history outside of the Great Flood!

The Rapture is alluded to in the allegorical symbolism of a door in the Book of Revelation. As already mentioned, Yahshua said: *"Behold, I stand at the door and knock"* (Revelation 3:20). This is a Scriptural clue suggesting that only those who symbolically open that door by letting Yahshua into their lives will be saved. This door is the barrier of pride that makes us deny our sinfulness, and keeps us from inviting God to work in our lives. But when that barrier is removed through belief, repentance, and rebirth, we can enter into the very presence of God! If the closed door represents unrepentant hearts that deny God's presence, and so are separate from God, then it follows that an open door symbolically shows a repentant heart, whose access to the Messiah and His Spirit *is fully guaranteed*. It is important to keep this analogy in mind as we turn our attention to the Church of Philadelphia for a moment.

Chapters 2 and 3 in the Book of Revelation consist of personal messages from Yahshua to seven churches that once actually existed in Asia Minor. Some believe these churches represent Christianity at various stages in its two thousand year history, and though this may be true, these messages also dualistically apply to seven specific *contemporary* churches that are categorized by certain traits. When the Scriptures dedicated to the Seven Churches are read, it soon becomes apparent that the best church of the seven to be in is the Church of Philadelphia, or the Congregation of Brotherly Love. Let's examine why this is so.

The Church of Philadelphia has a name that implies that it is the only church that has truly kept Yahshua's Two Commandments, which are to love God with our whole beings, and to love our neighbors as ourselves. As taught in Book Two, "The Language of God in Humanity," anyone who can faithfully keep these Two Commandments will fulfill the whole Law, because "love is the fulfillment of the Law" (Romans 13:10). Now, among the Seven Churches, the Church of Philadelphia is the only congregation that makes loving-kindness a mission field. These loving people are addressed by Yahshua, who is called: "He who is holy, He who is true, He who has the key of David, He who opens and no one shuts, and shuts and no one opens" (Rev. 3:7). Yahshua is the only One who can open our hearts to His love, and His Word, or shut our understanding of it. In the very next sentence, Christ tells the Church of Philadelphia that they are being given "an open door":

> "See, **I have set before you an open door, and no one can shut it**; for you have a little strength, have kept My word, and have not denied My name. Indeed I will make those of the synagogue of Satan, who say they are Jews and are not, but lie - indeed I will make them come and worship before your feet, and

*to know that I have loved you. **Because you have kept My command to persevere, I also will keep you from the hour of trial which shall come upon the whole world, to test those who dwell on the earth.**" - Revelation 3:8-10*

Through this door, the people of the Church of Philadelphia are being allegorically told that they will be given full and unrestricted access to the presence of God. This can only be possible, however, if they are in Heaven! Therefore, Yahshua is telling this small and persecuted Church full of loving saints that they will be spared from *"the hour of trial,"* which refers to the Great Tribulation. However, the only way anyone can truly be spared from the Tribulation's terrible time of testing is if they are removed from the Earth. This can only be through a Rapture-like event, with the saints being completely removed from harm's way in some miraculous way. Let's examine why.

First, as already mentioned, there is no natural way that anyone could remain unscathed from the terrible plagues and destruction that will be unleashed on the Earth in God's Wrath during the Great Tribulation. Second, even though the Tribulation Saints will have the supernatural protection of the Holy Spirit, many of them will still have to suffer and die during the Tribulation, just as believers today suffer and die in calamities of every kind, and just as the Two Witnesses will also have to die. Why else would the writer of Revelation have been shown the martyrs under the altar in Revelation 6:9-11, or the countless martyred saints who specifically come out of the Great Tribulation?

*"After these things I looked, and behold, a great multitude which no one could number, of all nations, tribes, peoples, and tongues, standing before the throne and before the Lamb, clothed with white robes..." "Then one of the elders answered, saying to me, 'Who are these arrayed in white robes, and where did they come from?' And I said to him, 'Sir, you know.' So he said to me, **'These are the ones who come out of the great tribulation,** and washed their robes and made them white in the blood of the Lamb.'" - Revelation 7:9, 13-14*

This great multitude represents the saints who will die at the hands of the Antichrist, for Scripture tells us that he will make war against the saints, and will overcome and annihilate them:

*"It was granted to him **to make war with the saints and to overcome them**. And authority was given him over every tribe, tongue, and nation." - Revelation 13:7*

Sadly, though the Tribulation Saints may be protected from the worst of God's End Time plagues, they will not be protected from the Antichrist's wrath. Indeed, there is no doubt that the Antichrist will lead a world war against the saints and the Jews during the Great Tribulation. This war - the dreaded World War III or Battle of Gog and Magog described in Ezekiel 38 and 39 - will likely kill more people than any war in history, and no one but those in the Church of Philadelphia today will escape it through the Open Door into Heaven itself. This supernatural Door appears again in the next chapter of Revelation:

*"After these things I looked, and behold,* **a door standing open in heaven***. And the first voice which I heard was like a trumpet speaking with me, saying,* **'Come up here, and I will show you things which must take place** *after this.' Immediately I was in the Spirit;* **and behold, a throne set in heaven,** *and One sat on the throne." - Revelation 4:1-2*

After the churches are addressed, this Scripture tells us that the writer of Revelation heard a trumpet-like voice, and then was taken up into heaven through an open door in Heaven with symbolic meaning. From this lofty vantage point, he was then shown all the things that would take place during the Day of the Lord, the Tribulation, the Millennial Rule of Christ, the Last Judgment, and the creation of the New Heaven and New Earth.

Via analogy, the writer of Revelation's lofty vantage point in Heaven (which may be where the angels reside) is clearly what Yahshua was promising the Church of Philadelphia. Like the writer of Revelation, they are to be allowed to witness all of the events of the Great Tribulation from Heaven. Furthermore, they will become immortal, and will forevermore be sheltered from harm. Since this open door appears in Scripture just before the plagues of the Tribulation period are disclosed, it suggests that the Rapture through that open door will either take place before the Tribulation begins, or before the seal, trumpet, and bowl plagues commence.

Since the spiritual meaning of the celestial events of December 21st, 2012 are directly tied to the first Four Seal Judgments of Revelation, Chapter 6, and the Rapture is to be identified with the open door in Revelation, Chapter 4, this suggests that the Rapture may occur anytime between the opening of the First through Sixth Seals.

Interestingly, the Trumpet call of God's voice is another event associated with this open door. Could this be the Last Trumpet, as mentioned in the following Scriptures?

# Ch. 11: The Rapture and Woman Clothed with the Sun

*"Behold, I tell you a mystery: We shall not all sleep, but we shall all be changed -- in a moment, in the twinkling of an eye, at the last trumpet. For the trumpet will sound, and... we shall be changed." - 1 Corinthians 15:51-52*

The preceding Scripture likely pertains to the First Rapture event. But there is another Scripture that speaks of the resurrection of the dead that may refer to events at the end of the Great Tribulation, when the Tribulation Saints who are still alive at Christ's Second Coming will be taken up to meet with Yahshua:

*"For the Lord Himself will descend from heaven with a shout, with the voice of an archangel, and with the trumpet of God. And the dead in Christ will rise first. Then we who are alive and remain shall be caught up together with them in the clouds to meet the Lord in the air. And thus we shall always be with the Lord." - 1 Thessalonians 4:16-17*

The preceding Scripture cannot refer to the Rapture when Yahshua comes like a thief in the night because, in both cases, we are told that Yahshua will appear visibly *descending out of the clouds* just as He ascended into them before Pentecost. These passages therefore describe Yahshua's Second Coming at the end of the Tribulation. At that time, Yahshua will resurrect the saints who died during the last half of the Tribulation along with those saints who survive the Tribulation. So, where are the Saints taken in the First Rapture? The Book of Revelation tells us they are coming out of Heaven with Yahshua at His Second Coming:

*"Now I saw heaven opened, and behold, a white horse. And He who sat on him was called Faithful and True, and in righteousness He judges and makes war.* **And the armies in heaven, clothed in fine linen, white and clean, followed Him** *on white horses." - Revelation 19:11, 14*

These saints who are clothed in white linen are mentioned as being in Heaven for the first time **after the open door in Revelation 3:9 and the first Six Seals are opened in Revelation, Chapter 6:**

*"After these things I looked, and behold,* **a great multitude which no one could number,** *of all nations, tribes, peoples, and tongues,* **standing before the throne and before the Lamb, clothed with white robes,** *with palm branches in their hands, and crying out with a loud voice, saying, 'Salvation belongs to our God who sits on the throne, and to the Lamb!'" - Revelation 7:9-10*

This multitude clothed in white robes represents the Saints that are Caught Up *plus* the saints who have died and gone to Heaven between Christ's First and Second Coming.

The Parable of the Ten Virgins can help explain the nature of the Rapture. In this parable, five virgins were foolish and did not have enough oil, while five did have enough oil and were allowed to go with the Bride and Groom to the Wedding:

> *"And **at midnight a cry was heard**: 'Behold, the bridegroom is coming; go out to meet him!' Then all those virgins arose and trimmed their lamps. And the foolish said to the wise, 'Give us some of your oil, for our lamps are going out.' But the wise answered, saying, 'No, lest there should not be enough for us and you; but go rather to those who sell, and buy for yourselves.' And while they went to buy, the bridegroom came, and **those who were ready went in with him to the wedding; and the door was shut.** Afterward the other virgins came also, saying, 'Lord, Lord, open to us!' But he answered and said, 'Assuredly, I say to you, I do not know you.'" - Matthew 25:6-12*

As fully explained in Book Two, the five foolish virgins allegorically depict a group of backslidden believers without oil or the Holy Spirit. Meanwhile, the five wise virgins who have enough oil represent believers who are baptized with the Holy Spirit. Those with the oil or Spirit will be taken to Heaven to attend the Wedding Supper of the Lamb, while unsaved people without the oil of the Spirit in their hearts will be left behind. The clue to when this wedding occurs is in the statement: *"those who were ready went in with him to the wedding; and the door was shut."* Note the mention of a door that is shut. Now recall that Revelation 4:1 suggests that the Saints taken in the Rapture enter heaven *through an open door*. Afterward, this door will be closed and those left behind will panic (See Luke 13:25).

Despite the clear reasoning for the Rapture already presented, some may doubt the preceding interpretations because they erroneously believe that the Church as a whole did not recognize any Scriptural basis for a Rapture-like event until modern times. However, there is documented proof that some leaders in the Early Church saw the clues for the Catching Away left in Scripture and taught that God would rescue His saints before One only has to do a search of the Internet to find numerous documented examples. Also, we should not ignore the promptings of the Holy Spirit, Who is the Revealer of Secrets, and Who is very active at this current time in history. Remember that Yahshua said:

## Ch. 11: The Rapture and Woman Clothed with the Sun

*"No one, when he has lit a lamp, covers it with a vessel or puts it under a bed, but sets it on a lampstand, that those who enter may see the light. For **nothing is secret that will not be revealed, nor anything hidden that will not be known and come to light.** Therefore **take heed how you hear**. For whoever has, to him more will be given; and whoever does not have, even what he seems to have will be taken from him."* - Luke 8:16-18

What did Yahshua mean when He said secret or hidden things would be revealed and *"come to light?"* The verse before He said this gives the answer. In the allegorical Language of God, lamps and lampstands are allusions to prophecies and prophets. Therefore, there are hidden things in prophecy that will not be revealed *until the proper time.* This is why we are warned to *"Take heed how you hear."* If we are not listening to the prophets with our spiritual eyes open, we will not hear their message!

The Rapture is one of those secret and hidden things taught in Scripture. As such, it was meant to remain hidden until the end of the world is near. Furthermore, **the Rapture was always meant to be an exclusive event - one that is only open to the select few who have foreseen it, and wish to partake in it.** Those who refute the idea of the Rapture, and lead others to reject it will reap what they have sown, and *they will be left behind!*

It is my hope that many people will heed the warnings in this book, and that they will find salvation through Christ before it is too late to be spared from the terror of the Great Tribulation. It is time to do as Yahshua tells the Church of Philadelphia to do, and that is to hold fast to your faith, be watchful, and be prepared to go to Heaven at any time by overcoming the world through Christ:

*"Behold, I am coming quickly! Hold fast to what you have, that no one may take your crown. He who overcomes, I will make him a pillar in the temple of My God... And I will write on him the name... and the city of My God, the New Jerusalem... And I will write on him My new name."* - Revelation 3:11-12

Note here that Yahshua identifies the Church of Philadelphia with the New Jerusalem, which is described as a Bride coming down from Heaven in Revelation 20:1. For this reason, only those in the Church of Philadelphia are to be considered the Bride of Christ. I can think of no greater reward than to become a perfect visual symbol of the holy character or Name of my God and Messiah, and to become a fellow citizen of the New Jerusalem, where everyone will dwell with Yahshua in peace and safety forever! What about you? Do you want to be a citizen there too? Then make sure you have given your life to Christ today, before it is too late.

In contrast to the Church of Philadelphia, the Church of Laodicea is rich materially, but dangerously lukewarm spiritually, and Yahshua has this to say about them:

> *"I know your works, that you are neither cold nor hot. I could wish you were cold or hot. 16 So then, because you are lukewarm, and neither cold nor hot, I will vomit you out of My mouth. 17 Because you say, 'I am rich, have become wealthy, and have need of nothing' - and do not know that you are wretched, miserable, poor, blind, and naked..." - Revelation 3:15-17*

Thus, the Laodicean Church is full of people who do not need or want to be close to God because they are prosperous, protected, and have no real need of Him! Instead of a need of and love for God, this Church is full of arrogance, independence, and self-importance, making it the exact opposite of the poor and persecuted Church of Philadelphia. So, instead of promising them deliverance from the coming time of trouble, Yahshua warns the people of this Church that He is ready to spit them out unless they repent of their sins, humble themselves, and turn back to God (See Rev. 3:18). Nonetheless, even though this Church is full of unrepentant people, Yahshua still lovingly offers them a chance to change their ways:

> *"As many as I love, I rebuke and chasten. Therefore be zealous and repent. 20 Behold, I stand at the door and knock. If anyone hears My voice and opens the door, I will come in to him and dine with him, and he with Me." - Revelation 3:19-20*

Thus, Yahshua offers all of the people in the Church of Laodicea an open door to God's Grace until the Rapture, when this door will be decisively shut. If they do not repent before then, they will be left behind as the Foolish Virgins, and they will have to suffer and be refined in the fire of the first part of the Great Tribulation.

## Come Up Here and Come Away! - Clues For Two Raptures

In this section, my goal is to show that those nay-saying the Rapture for whatever reason are wrong to deny the many hints in Scripture of the reality of both a First Rapture before the Trumpet Judgments of the Great Tribulation come to pass, and a Second Rapture of the saints that will occur just before the Bowls of God's Wrath are poured out. The reason I don't cite a Pre-Tribulation Rapture as I once did is because the teachings of the mainstream Bible Prophecy Teachers do not take the Hallel Psalms, the Great Pyramid, and the Signs in the Heavens into consideration, and I have discovered that it is impossible to fully understand Bible Prophecy without these three godly prophetic channels.

One of the most beautiful passages in the Bible is found in the Song of Solomon, which is a love poem written, at least in part, by King Solomon. Though it may have been written to woo a young noble woman betrothed to him, some claim it was meant to woo the Queen of Sheba, whom legends state married Solomon and produced a son by him that became a king in the line of Judah. As a poem between a king and his bride-to-be, the Song of Solomon has many allegorical implications alluding to the imminent Wedding Supper of the Lamb with His Bride: the Two-House Church of Judah (Jewish believers) and Ephraim (Gentile believers). Upon re-reading a portion of this lovely poem recently, I noted a peculiarity that really held my attention. Note the two identical passages that are repeated in the following section and my notations identifying the prophetic meanings within the passage:

> *"My beloved (Yahshua) spoke, and said to me (His Bride the Church): 'Rise up, my love, my fair one, and come away (to Heaven). For lo, the winter is past, the rain is over and gone. The flowers appear on the earth; the time of singing has come, and the voice of the turtledove is heard in our land (in the mid to late spring). The fig tree puts forth her green figs, and the vines with the tender grapes give a good smell (unripe or abloom in spring, but ready to harvest in the mid summer and early autumn). Rise up, my love, my fair one, and come away!"* - Song of Solomon 2:10-13

Oddly, this Scripture alludes to two different seasons. The time of flowers and turtledoves singing refers to the mid to late spring and therefore alludes to anytime between Passover Week through to the Feast of Pentecost or Shavuot, which are considered to be the Jewish Spring Feasts associated with the spring harvest season. In addition, though figs appear in the spring and provide an early summer crop, the main harvest time for grapes and figs is in mid summer to late autumn. This second harvest season can therefore be associated with the Jewish Autumn Feasts, as well as to the autumn harvest festival called the Feast of Tabernacles or Sukkot.

As an additional clue, the fair Lady that the King desires is told to "come away" to dwell where the King is - not just once - but two times in reference to these two different seasons, as shown by the comments in parentheses within the section of the Song of Solomon quoted above. Since the Song of Solomon can be seen as an allegorical story about Christ's love for His Bride the True Church, it is as if Yahshua were the King asking His Bride to join Him in Heaven, where He currently resides with His Father, not once, but two different times. This passage therefore contains a double allusion to the Rapture or catching up of the Church to Yahshua's Father's House in Heaven, where Yahshua said that there are many mansions built to house His saints (See John 14:2). In addition, it suggests that there may be two separate Rapture events associated with these two harvest seasons, with one toward the beginning of the three and a half year Great Tribulation, and one near to its end.

In order to further reveal why I think that there may be two Raptures instead of one, I looked past many of the more familiar passages concerning the Rapture in favor of some more obscure ones, like the passage quoted from the Song of Solomon above. Now let's take a look at another Scripture relating to the Rapture that is tied to that earlier passage. It is found in Proverbs, portions of which have also been attributed to Solomon:

*"Do not exalt yourself in the presence of the king, and do not stand in the place of the great; For it is better that he say to you, 'Come up here,' than that you should be put lower in the presence of the prince, whom your eyes have seen." - Proverbs 25:6-7*

Note that in this passage, we are instructed not to be haughty or proud in the presence of the King, which alludes to our Heavenly Father. This is followed by a warning that we will not be invited to "Come up here" into the King and Prince's presence unless we are humble and worshipful before them both! It is obvious that the Prince being referred to allegorically here is none other than Yahshua the Messiah, the great Bridegroom who asks his betrothed to "Come away!" in the Song of Solomon. It is therefore no coincidence that the phrase "Come up here" used in Proverbs is nearly identical to the "Come away!" references in the Song of Solomon. Fascinatingly, the phrase "Come up here" is also found twice in the Book of Revelation. The first occurrence is as follows:

*"After these things I looked, and behold, a door standing open in heaven. And the first voice which I heard was like a trumpet speaking with me, saying, 'Come up here, and I will show you things which must take place after this.' Immediately I was in the Spirit; and behold, a throne set in heaven, and One sat on the throne." - Revelation 4:1-2*

## Ch. 11: The Rapture and Woman Clothed with the Sun

In the preceding Scripture, the command to "Come up here" is found in reference to an open door that allows a person to visit the throne room of Yahweh in Heaven, where the Wedding of the Lamb will no doubt take place. This command to enter through that open door is made at the beginning of the Tribulation period, before the Seals, Trumpets, and Bowls of God's Wrath are unleashed. Prophetically, this open door is an allusion to Christ's Cross, whose shed blood cleanses those who are covered by it of their sins. What many overlook, however, is that this door to escape God's coming Wrath is **only** promised to the Church of Philadelphia, or the Church of Brotherly Love. Furthermore, these believers are described as having only a little strength, which implies that the other churches of their age have no strength or power of God in them at all!

In Revelation 3:10, Yahshua said: *"Because you have kept My command to persevere, I also will keep you from the hour of trial which shall come upon the whole world."* He said this to the loving, poor and marginalized saints in the Church of Philadelphia, and it is referring to a supernaturally led Exodus of God's true servants to a heavenly place of refuge from God's Wrath. This First Rapture will occur before the Sixth Seal Judgment, which is described at the end of Chapter 6 in the Book of Revelation:

*"And the kings of the earth, the great men, the rich men, the commanders, the mighty men, every slave and every free man, hid themselves in the caves and in the rocks of the mountains, 16 and said to the mountains and rocks, "Fall on us and hide us from the face of Him who sits on the throne and from the wrath of the Lamb! 17 For the great day of His wrath has come, and who is able to stand?" - Revelation 6:15-17*

In verses 16 and 17, we are explicitly told that the Great Day of the Wrath of the Lamb (i.e. Yahshua) will come at the time that the Sixth Seal is opened. So, since we are not appointed to suffer God's Wrath (See Romans 5:9; 1 Thess. 1:10; 1 Thess. 5:9), the Rapture has to occur before it unfolds. I believe the Sixth Seal is describing a catastrophic Pole Shift and Crustal Displacement of the Earth that could kill up to one third of the Earth's human population. In fact, I believe events that are tied to this Sixth Seal Judgment have already occurred as part of the first Five Seal Judgments. These were the massive earthquakes in Chile in 2010 and Japan in 2011 that reportedly began the shifting of the Earth's axis, and helped to catastrophically change the weather patterns all over the world.

If the Sixth Seal Judgment occurs as the First Rapture unfolds, the horrific affects of this judgment will prove to be the perfect cover for the world's wicked leaders to explain away the disappearance of millions upon millions of believers worldwide, and the perfect reason for them to set up the one world government and one world religion of the Antichrist. It therefore seems likely that the First Rapture will occur just before this cataclysmic event, and before the Antichrist's world takeover.

## *How To Prepare For the Rapture*

Whether someone takes part in the Rapture or not is based on how one chooses to live their lives. If the believer in question is an intellectual or cultural Christian that is living carnally and shows no fruits of the Spirit, this is clear evidence that they are not baptized with the Holy Spirit at all regardless of their claims to believe in Christ, and they will likely be left behind. Another sign of those who are only paying lip-service to God and His Son are those who show an unwillingness to pay any heed to Yahshua's two all-encompassing commandments (See Matthew 22:36-40).

Yahshua's Second Commandment is to love one another as we love ourselves, which includes learning to truly love and care for ourselves, to love our enemies, and to bless those who curse us. Yahshua's First and Greatest Commandment to His followers is related to the second one. It is to love God our Father with our whole heart, body, mind and spirit. Every act of love that comes from a true believer must be done with selfless determination, true kindness, and sacrificial generosity. This is only possible when we are in a right relationship with God, because our Father Yahweh is the ultimate source of perfect, transcendental, brotherly love.

Loving people God's way includes leading them to Yahshua with gentle but pointed instruction in the Gospel of the Kingdom and biblical morality while caring for their needs and nurturing them. To be done God's way, our care for others should be given without any emotional manipulation, and all sexual sin and substance abuse must be swiftly dealt with as an abomination to God. This is because we are the Temples of the Living God, and need to purify ourselves accordingly (1 Corinthians 3:15-17; 1 Cor. 6:18-20; 2 Cor. 6:15-18).

Those who don't trust our Father Yahweh and His Son on a daily basis, don't attempt to discern and follow God's will in every aspect of their lives, and don't care deeply about the welfare of believers and lost souls are carnally-minded. Therefore, they are consciously or unconsciously choosing to stay on Earth rather than participate in the

## Ch. 11: The Rapture and Woman Clothed with the Sun    Page 527

Rapture. As a result, they may be left behind by default unless they choose to become born again by surrendering their lives to Yahshua before it is too late.

    To become born again, Scripture supports the idea that a person must believe the following about Yahshua Ha Mashiach (i.e. Jesus the Christ) and His First Advent and Second Advent Ministries to the world:

1. That Yahshua is the one and only Son of Yahweh Elohim, was born of a virgin Jewess in Bethlehem, and - though the Jews rejected Him - died as a sin offering for the sins of the Jewish people and the entire Gentile world on a Roman cross;

2. That Yahshua sits at the right hand of His Father in Heaven, that He will literally return to Earth one day soon in the flesh to save a remnant of the Jews and Tribulation Saints from annihilation, that He will destroy the armies of the wicked gathered against Israel, and that He will end the persecution of the saints scattered abroad with their resurrection into everlasting life;

3. That Father Yahweh raised Yahshua from the dead to show His power over sin, death, and the Devil, and to give us victory of the same through our belief in, and love for Christ;

4. That without remorse and repentance that leads us to accept Yahshua's sacrifice on the Cross to pay for our sins, there is no other means of salvation;

5. That those who refuse to repent and accept Christ's sacrifice are dead in their sins and destined to perish in Hell;

6. That Yahshua expects His followers to be filled with the Holy Spirit, to commit their lives to Him, and to have faith that He will never leave them nor forsake them;

7. That believers must reject and deny the passions, lusts and desires of the world and the flesh, allegorically take up Christ's Cross, and change for the better with the help of the Holy Spirit, who will guide them to be able to do good works in keeping with God's good and perfect Will.

8. Without Christ's help via His indwelling Spirit, no one can truly believe in Yahshua and His literal Second Coming, or be following His perfect example, as described in the previous seven points. Therefore, believers must be devoted to prayer to remain strong and protected as they await the Rapture. As Scripture says: *"rejoice always, pray without ceasing, in everything give thanks"* (1 Thess. 5:16-18).

Though Salvation is based on belief in Yahshua, we cannot simply believe that Yahshua existed and was a wise man and expect to be saved. Unless we truly believe in all these points about Yahshua and our need to truly love, follow and listen to Him, we risk not being saved at all, and being ripe for God's Wrath and Judgment (See 1 John 2 and 1 John 3 - Entire Chapters).

## *The Rapture Revealed in the Parable of the Ten Virgins*

As discussed in my book "The Language of God in Humanity", several of Yahshua's Parables are related to the subject of the Rapture and the Wedding of the Lamb at Yahshua's Father's House in Heaven. In this heavenly wedding, Yahshua will be the Groom who will come to take His Bride and five of her virgin handmaidens who are wise to the Wedding Supper in His Father's House in Heaven. The one most pertinent to this discussion in relation to the Two Rapture theory is "The Parable of the Ten Virgins" in Matthew, Chapter 25. Also known as "The Parable of the Wise and Foolish Virgins", it offers an amazing allegorical picture of events that will happen during the Tribulation period. Here is a portion of this amazing Parable that explains why there may be a need for Christ to come to catch away some of His beloved saints a second time:

> *"And at midnight a cry was heard: 'Behold, the bridegroom is coming; go out to meet him!' Then all those virgins arose and trimmed their lamps. And the foolish said to the wise, 'Give us some of your oil, for our lamps are going out.' But the wise answered, saying, 'No, lest there should not be enough for us and you; but go rather to those who sell, and buy for yourselves.' And while they went to buy, the bridegroom came, and those who were ready went in with him to the wedding; and the door was shut."* - Matthew 25:6-10

This Parable is filled with allegorical references that can be interpreted as follows. The door that was shut is referring to the open door in Revelation 3:8. This door will be opened to admit the Bride of Christ and the Five Wise Virgins, and then it will be shut. The Bridegroom, of course, is Yahshua Ha Mashiach. However, the Bridegroom also signifies all literal Jewish believers, while the Bride signifies the Israelite Tribe of Ephraim that is spoken of so often along with Judah in many Bible prophecies. In ancient times, the Ephraimites mingled among the Gentiles when they sinned against God, and they were subsequently carried away from Israel as captives and refugees by

## Ch. 11: The Rapture and Woman Clothed with the Sun    Page 529

the Assyrians around the 8th Century BC, and again by the Babylonians in the 5th Century BC.

The Ten Lost Tribes of Israel allegorically refers to two groups of believers. First, they signify the Gentiles that have hidden Israelite blood in their heritage, and have lost their Israelite identity, but still cling closely to Christ and His Cross for their salvation. Secondly, they signify the Gentiles that have been grafted into Israel as adopted sons and daughters due to their love for Christ and His Kingdom. These two groups form a special class of deeply devoted Gentile and Lost Israelite believers that are allegorically described as the Bride of Christ and her five Wise Virgin attendants. Therefore, the Bride is not formed by all believers, but represents only the elect among the people of the world whose relationship with and love for God and His Son and Spirit are beyond reproach. Meanwhile, the Wise Virgins are those who love and support the Bride, and always try to help her even though they may not be as faithful in their walk with God.

The Ephraimite Bride is signified by the true believers that spiritually belong to only one of the Seven Churches spoken of in Revelation, Chapter 2 and Chapter 3. This is the Church of "Philadelphia", or "Brotherly Love", which is filled with believers who love God with their whole heart and soul, and love others as they love God and themselves. The Five Wise Virgins that have enough oil of the Holy Spirit in their lamps signify another portion of the faithful among the spiritual and literal Israelites who also love God dearly, and do their best to follow His Laws to love one another as Yahshua loves us, although they may be a bit backslidden or weak in their execution of their faith at times. Meanwhile, the Five Foolish Virgins that don't have enough oil and are left-behind signify those who are technically saved among the Gentiles and Lost Israelites, but whose spiritual walk with God is virtually non-existent, and leaves much to be desired.

In the Parable of the Ten Virgins, five of the virgin attendants of the essentially Gentile Bride of Christ are ready to leave with her when the Jewish Bridegroom arrives to take her to His Father's House in Heaven for the wedding. However, five of the virgins attending the Bride do not get to join the bridal procession because they have to go out and buy more oil for their lamps. This oil refers to the anointing of the Holy Spirit, and harkens back to the Israelite practice of anointing everything that was to be set apart for holy service in Israel. This anointing was done with a special blend of olive oil that was scented with aromatic plant extracts including spikenard, frankincense, aloe, and myrrh.

Since five of the Ten Virgins have no oil or Holy Spirit power as the seal guaranteeing their inheritance in the Kingdom of God (See Ephesians 1:13 and Ephesians 4:30), Yahshua sadly must reprimand them by telling them that *"I do not know you."* This suggests that those who are left behind will have the appearance of godliness (being described as "virgins") without knowing God's Spirit. Since the Holy Spirit helps us know the Will of God in our lives, this means that those with little oil will have a very weak relationship with Christ, if they have any at all.

To truly "know" Yahshua, we must have a connection to Him beyond merely reading His Word in the Bible. Only those who love Yahshua have the ability to hear God speaking through words of knowledge, dreams and visions, and are able to accurately apply and interpret what the Holy Spirit shows them so it is in full agreement with the Bible. With the exception of young children, those who have not cultivated this ability by drawing near to God are the Foolish Virgins, who are to be left behind! Sadly, they will temporarily be barred from Heaven for their failure to flee from sin and procure the indwelling presence of the Holy Spirit. It is this same Spirit of God that brings true believers the spiritual gifts of love, peace, kindness, gentleness, long-suffering, visions, dreams, words of knowledge, discernment, and Christ's power to help the needy, heal the sick, rescue the outcast, and cast out demons.

The singling out of five of the ten virgin bridesmaids also suggests that Yahshua will have to leave behind about half of those who claim Yahshua as their Messiah today. This will be due to the fact that - though all these believers have accepted that Christ did exist and the He was the Son of God made flesh - they do not flee from sin and seek holiness so that they will receive the gifts of the Holy Spirit, Who is the Seal of our Salvation, and Who encourages us to do good works in keeping with God's Will.

In light of this, and the fact that the Scriptures explored earlier in this chapter clearly hint that the Rapture will occur in two distinct phases, the Parable of the Ten Virgins suggests that a Second Rapture may have to occur. This Second Rapture will be to gather up the Foolish Virgins, or the wayward believers that are not ready when Yahshua initially comes for His Bride and her Five Wise Virgin attendants.

# Ch. 11: The Rapture and Woman Clothed with the Sun

## *The Fate of the Foolish Virgins*

Exactly when the First and Second Rapture may fall within the Tribulation Period is anybody's guess, for only God the Father knows the day or hour, and He has chosen not to reveal it to His servants. Indeed, these rescues of the saints to a place of refuge and safety may not even occur during the harvest seasons that they can be associated with, but just before or after them. Nobody really knows for sure but God the Father.

But there are Scriptural hints concerning the timing of these Two Rapture events. These suggest that the First Rapture will occur toward the beginning of the Great Tribulation at the Mid-Tribulation point, and just before the Antichrist begins enforcing the Mark of the Beast to control commerce. Meanwhile, the Second Rapture may occur toward the end of Great Tribulation - at the same time that the Two Witnesses will be raised up, which is just before final Tribulation plagues known as the Seven Bowls of God's Wrath are poured out, and the Battle of Armageddon ensues.

One hint that this is true is found in the Book of Revelation, Chapter 7, where we are given a vision of the saints who have *"come out of the Great Tribulation"* and are now in Heaven praising God for their deliverance:

> *"After these things I looked, and behold, a great multitude which no one could number, of all nations, tribes, peoples, and tongues, standing before the throne and before the Lamb, clothed with white robes, with palm branches in their hands, 10 and crying out with a loud voice, saying, "Salvation belongs to our God who sits on the throne, and to the Lamb!" 11 All the angels stood around the throne and the elders and the four living creatures, and fell on their faces before the throne and worshiped God, 12 saying:*
>
> *"Amen! Blessing and glory and wisdom, Thanksgiving and honor and power and might, Be to our God forever and ever. Amen."*
>
> *Then one of the elders answered, saying to me, "Who are these arrayed in white robes, and where did they come from?" 14 And I said to him, "Sir, you know."*
>
> *So he said to me,* **"These are the ones who come out of the great tribulation,** *and washed their robes and made them white in the blood of the Lamb. 15 Therefore they are before the throne of*

*God, and serve Him day and night in His temple. And He who sits on the throne will dwell among them. 16 They shall neither hunger anymore nor thirst anymore; the sun shall not strike them, nor any heat; 17 for the Lamb who is in the midst of the throne will shepherd them and lead them to living fountains of waters. And God will wipe away every tear from their eyes."*

These saints are likely tied to the Wise Virgins in the Parable of the Ten Virgins in Matthew, Chapter 25. The Wise Virgin handmaidens who attend the Bride of Christ are ready with their spiritual lamps full of the oil of the Holy Spirit when the Bridegroom arrives to retrieve His Bride. These lamps are shining brightly for all to see, and represent the faithful walk of the Wise Virgins with Yahshua as they follow the Way of Yahweh, which is the Way of the Cross. Meanwhile, Yahshua says of the Foolish Virgins who are left behind in the Rapture that "Assuredly, I say to you, I do not know you!" This means that the Foolish Virgins are those in the Churches and Messianic Synagogues that have no personal relationship with Christ, and are not following the Way of the Cross by acting as though they are dead to the world, but fully alive in Christ.

Instead, the Foolish Virgins are flirting with the world, and are thus being unfaithful to their Bridegroom. It is this illicit love affair with the world's carnal desires and pleasures that forces Christ to leave the Foolish Virgins behind when He departs with the Wise Virgins for the Wedding of the Lamb in Heaven. The Parable of the Ten Virgins therefore makes it clear that the Foolish Virgins are a part of the Church, but are to be left behind after the First Rapture because of their unfaithfulness. This suggests that they must be cleansed in the fire of the Great Tribulation a little longer than the Wise Virgins. The fact that they are a part of the Church also suggests that they are to be rescued from the Great Tribulation also, but at a later time. In that regard, the command to "Come up here!" appears for a second time in reference to the resurrection of the Two Witnesses:

*"Now after the three-and-a-half days the breath of life from God entered them (i.e. the Two Witnesses), and they stood on their feet, and great fear fell on those who saw them. And they heard a loud voice from heaven saying to them, 'Come up here.' And they ascended to heaven in a cloud, and their enemies saw them. In the same hour there was a great earthquake, and a tenth of the city fell. In the earthquake seven thousand men were killed, and the rest were afraid and gave glory to the God of heaven." - Revelation 11:11-13*

# Ch. 11: The Rapture and Woman Clothed with the Sun

This resurrection and subsequent translation of the Two Witnesses will occur just before the Bowls of God's Wrath are poured out during the seven-year Tribulation period that is identified in Scripture as Daniel's Seventieth Week. At the time that the Two Witnesses are caught up to Heaven with the command *"Come up here!"*, it is my contention that a final wave of attendees to the Wedding of the Lamb will be snatched away with them.

This miraculous translation and snatching up of many millions of new and left behind believers that have been made worthy in the cleansing fire of suffering during the Great Tribulation may actually release an enormous amount of supernatural energy when they are translated, which in turn could trigger the massive earthquake that Scripture indicates will accompany the ascension of the Two Witnesses into Heaven. In this way, the world may easily be duped into thinking that those who are missing in this second wave of disappearances were merely lost in this fierce quake rather than saved by Yahweh's Grace and mercy. Interestingly, this is also when the last of the Seven Trumpets of Judgment will be sounded:

> *"The second woe is past. Behold, the third woe is coming quickly. Then the seventh angel sounded: And there were loud voices in heaven, saying, "The kingdoms of this world have become the kingdoms of our Lord and of His Christ, and He shall reign forever and ever!" - Revelation 11:14-15*

Could this be the Last Trumpet that the Apostle Paul spoke about in his description of the Rapture in 1 Thessalonians, as shown in the following Scripture?

> *"Behold, I tell you a mystery: We shall not all sleep, but we shall all be changed - in a moment, in the twinkling of an eye, at the last trumpet. For the trumpet will sound, and the dead will be raised incorruptible, and we shall be changed" - 1 Corinthians 15:51-52*

Even though the Book of Revelation wasn't likely written until the Apostle Paul had gone to be with the Lord, there is no reason to doubt that the Last Trumpet that Paul spoke about in the above passage could be a prophetic reference to the last or Seventh Trumpet of God's Wrath that is mentioned in the Book of Revelation. It may also be tied to the Shofars or ram's horn trumpets sounded on the Feast of Trumpets or Yom Teruah, as well as on New Moon days and other Jewish Feast Days.

Could it be that Paul, who always preached to the Jews that he found in each community before preaching to the Gentiles, was preaching to the Jews when he said the above, and that he was referring specifically to the time when many Jews will at last believe that Yahshua is the Messiah, which will be toward the end of the Great Tribulation? Furthermore, could these saved Jews be meant to be taken out of the Tribulation just before the Bowls of God's Wrath are poured out during a Second Rapture event? If so, this will likely occur when the Two Witnesses and the 144,000 Witnesses chosen at the beginning of the Tribulation are caught up to Heaven, along with the newly sanctified believers found throughout the world.

From the references in the Book of Revelation pertaining to the 144,0000, it appears that Yahshua will retrieve them and the rest of His bridal party when the Two Witnesses are raised up, as described in the Book of Revelation, Chapter 11. At that time, it may be that Yahshua will take all the believing, sanctified Jews and Gentiles on the Earth to Heaven. In Heaven, they will join the already translated Bride of Christ and the Wise Virgins in celebration until it is time for them to return to Earth with Yahshua at the Battle of Armageddon, when they will be seen riding on white horses alongside Christ. In fact, it could be Yahshua's miraculous appearance and snatching away of the carnal world's hated Messianic and Christian hostages before then that will drive the wicked in their final detestable assault on the Promised Land of Israel.

In their insane efforts to annihilate the remaining unsaved Jewish people that our Messiah nonetheless still loves, the wicked armies of the Antichrist will perish by the sword. After this, their bodies will become food for the carrion birds after their blood floods the Valley of Jehoshaphat (i.e. the Valley of Judgment) in Israel that is mentioned in Joel 3:2. When their wicked blood is shed, it will be in atonement for the murder of God's people throughout history. The Valley of Jehoshaphat can be associated with two literal valleys in Israel where several important battles in Jewish history were fought. One, the Valley of Megiddo, is to the north of Jerusalem, and one, the Kidron Valley, is to the south of it.

## *The Testing of the Foolish Virgins*

Now, though many passages in Scripture hint at a Rapture or catching up of the Church, many naysayers within the Body of Christ argue that belief in a Rapture will leave many unprepared for coming disasters and hard times, as well as the Tribulation period to come when Yahweh will pour out His wrath on mankind. Many of these naysayers think it would be a great honor to be called to fight for the cause of the

## Ch. 11: The Rapture and Woman Clothed with the Sun

righteous (by their skewed definition) during the coming time of Jacob's Trouble. These war-minded people are often filled with suspicion and hate against specific groups of non-believers or apostates and believe that God expects His followers to rise up against any and all oppressors with force of arms and deadly violence if peaceful means fail to gain them their right to life, liberty and the pursuit of happiness (as they define it, not God).

However, there is not one Scripture in the entire Brit Chadashah or New Covenant Scriptures known as the New Testament that advocates using force of arms to protect our individual liberties, or to preserve our nation, culture or lives. In fact, there are several Scriptures that tell us not to use violence for any reason, even when we are being harassed and humiliated by those who hate us for our faith. Support for this teaching is found in the following words of Yahshua:

*"You have heard that it was said, 'You shall love your neighbor and hate your enemy.' But I say to you, love your enemies, bless those who curse you, do good to those who hate you, and pray for those who spitefully use you and persecute you, that you may be sons of your Father in heaven; for He makes His sun rise on the evil and on the good, and sends rain on the just and on the unjust." - Matthew 5:43-48*

*"And suddenly, one of those who were with Yahshua stretched out his hand and drew his sword, struck the servant of the high priest, and cut off his ear. 52 But Yahshua said to him, 'Put your sword in its place, for all who take the sword will perish by the sword. 53 Or do you think that I cannot now pray to My Father, and He will provide Me with more than twelve legions of angels?'" - Matthew 26:51-53*

This message is echoed in Chapter 13 of the Book of Revelation when the Beasts that are the enemies of God are described. But even in the midst of the evil of the Beasts who rise against God, the saints are told not to use violence to defend themselves, or they will die by violence:

*"He who leads into captivity shall go into captivity; he who kills with the sword must be killed with the sword. Here is the patience and the faith of the saints." - Revelation 13:10*

Nonetheless, a few Scriptures are consistently taken out of context by those with no spiritual discernment in order to support their desire to use violence to advance the Kingdom of God. Though there may be some point in the future when hardened warriors will be specifically called by

God to fight against the Antichrist and the New World Order, just as the Israelites were called to do in the far past, there is absolutely no current provision for the use of hard violence in any of Yahshua's teachings.

On the contrary! Rather than ask us to fight with force of arms, Yahshua asks His true followers to love their enemies, bless those who curse and use them, rejoice when they are reviled and persecuted, and turn the other cheek when they are slapped in the face either emotionally or physically (See Matthew 5:38-44; Luke 6:26-35). Yahshua also asks His followers to take up their Cross and follow Him. This means that God's children need to develop a close personal relationship with Christ, to follow Him, and to longingly and expectantly pray, wait and watch for His return to Earth to rescue the Church from the coming Wrath of God upon the wicked (See Matthew 24:38-47; John 10:27-30; 2 Timothy 2:19).

Nonetheless, there are many believers today who think that they will have to live through the entire Tribulation, and that they will have to fight with physical weapons of war against God's enemies. God is aware of these backslidden believers, and He also has plans for them that do not include being a part of the First Rapture. Instead, they will be connected to the Foolish Virgins in the Church who will be left behind to work on their level of sanctification.

As we discussed earlier when examining "The Parable of the Ten Virgins", the Foolish Virgins do not have a right relationship with God or a correct view of His Kingdom. In fact, some of them think that they must win a physical Kingdom of God on Earth for Yahshua before He returns. Still others believe that the Church already represents that Kingdom, and no further one will be forthcoming. Some of these Foolish Virgins even deny that there will be a literal Second Coming of Christ to the Earth, but see the presence of the Holy Spirit in believers as the manifestation of God's promised Kingdom on Earth. Many who fall in this category are within the apostate branches of the Lutheran Church and the Roman Catholic Church, which - to their detriment - do not see the Book of Revelation as a prophecy that dualistically applies to both the past and the future.

Finally, there are some among the Foolish Virgins that recognize the Book of Revelation as a past and future prophecy, but either don't believe in the Rapture, or don't want to be taken up when it happens! Instead, they think that they may have been chosen by God to stay behind to fight against demonic spiritual principalities and powers. Some of them think they will fight the Antichrist and his armies by wielding the power of the Holy Spirit against the unseen wicked spiritual realms controlling the Devil's followers. They also believe that they will win many lost souls for Christ through evangelism and spiritual warfare during the Great Tribulation.

It could very well be true if they are among the 144,000 chosen witnesses of Israel that are chosen in the Book of Revelation, Chapter 6, right after the first Five Seals of Judgment on a sacred heavenly scroll are opened by Yahshua, Who is the Lamb of God. I believe that the 144,000 will be taken up in the First Rapture, but then will be returned to the Earth shortly after they are chosen by Yahshua in Heaven. To see my ideas concerning the 144,000 Witnesses, look for the following section of this chapter entitled: "Who Are The 144,000 Witnesses Of Revelation?"

Due to these huge doctrinal schisms between various groups of believers concerning the Tribulation period, it may be that Yahweh always intended to leave the Rapture in the realm of **choice**. In other words, it may truly be up to the individual believer to decide whether they will attend the Wedding of the Lamb in Heaven, or be left behind here on Earth to save the lost and/or fight the Antichrist and his wicked armies either through force of physical arms, or spiritual power, or both.

As a case in point, one day while I was in deep prayer, I was specifically asked by God if I would be willing to stay on Earth during the Tribulation to be a witness for Him. At that time, I knew I had a right to refuse because God knew how much I wanted to attend the Wedding Supper of the Lamb in Heaven, and He had already promised that I would be a part of it. Nonetheless, after some deep contemplation of the severe suffering I might have to experience first hand and the loss I might find from not being part of the Rapture, I told God that I would stay if it would help further His kingdom.

But I also asked that He take away my fear, and He did by promising me that those who would willingly stay behind to be witnesses would be protected and unable to be harmed. I realized then that God was trying to show me two things. First, that Revelation's 144,000 chosen ones of Israel are not all Jews, but also of the Lost Tribes of Israel like me. Second, He was showing that these saints will be immortal when they are chosen to serve God during the Tribulation, having already taken part in the Rapture!

Whether or not one chooses to believe that what I just described was a bonafide supernatural encounter with the Living God of Abraham, Scripture makes it clear that our God Yahweh loves to present paradoxes and mysteries for His human children to ponder, and, with the aid of the Holy Spirit, to eventually help them to understand and embrace these paradoxes. I believe that this is one of those: that while to go to be with Yahshua is the desire of every spiritually baptized believers' heart, the desire to stay and serve God may override that desire in certain people because they want to win souls for Christ by taking part in the spiritual harvest that will take place during the first part of the Great Tribulation. I believe that the most dedicated individuals among this group of Jewish and Israelite believers are destined to become the 144,000 Witnesses, who I will focus on at the end of this chapter.

## *The Signs That The Great Tribulation Is Near*

Taking my cue from all of my Language of God Series books, I want to stress that I am not attempting to set exact dates for the Rapture or Tribulation. Instead, I am presenting heavenly and biblical evidence that strongly suggests that the Rapture and Tribulation could be imminent, coupled with the fact that there are specific days, months and years associated with these signs that I did **not** pick or predict. They were hidden in these signs, which I have done my best to interpret using the discernment of the Holy Spirit. Both the Solar Eclipse of July 2010 over Easter Island and the Lunar Eclipse of December 2010 suggest that the Tribulation already started, and the five comets and Sign of the Woman Clothed with the Sun that appeared in October 2013 suggest that the First Rapture will be very soon. But this is relative to God's timing, which is not the same as our own! Coupling these heavenly signs with the physical evidence of the birth pains of the Tribulation that can be seen in the major increase in the amount and severity of severe weather, volcanic eruptions and earthquakes in 2010 through 2013, there is no doubt in my mind that the Rapture and Great Tribulation are fast approaching.

The political climate is even more tell-tale, with Russia and China dropping the US dollar as their monetary standard for trade and tensions between China, North Korea and the United States brewing in the North Pacific. Meanwhile, Muslim-controlled Pakistan is dangerously unstable and already has nuclear weapons in its military arsenal, and Iran is developing nuclear weapons and may soon act on its mandate to destroy Israel when nuclear warheads are readily available to them. Adding to these potential war zones, the publishing of hundreds of sensitive communications between US diplomats, embassy heads, and political leaders that made world news in November of 2010 bodes very badly for the United States and Israel in the coming months.

Personally, I believe that we are already in the final seven year Tribulation Period known as Daniel's Seventieth Week. This is partly due to the Prophecies in the Hallel Psalms, which I discussed at length earlier in this book. These are Psalms 110 through 118, and they appear to

# Ch. 11: The Rapture and Woman Clothed with the Sun

directly correlate with the years 2010 through 2018 in a prophetic sense. It also has much to do with the amazing Signs in the Heavens, which correlate with 2010 through 2018 - the same years indicated by the Hallel Psalms. To see these Signs in the Heavens at a glance, please go to my blog article explaining how to read my Tribulation Time Chart, which you can view by using this URL to get to it at the POEM web site: http://pillar-of-enoch.com/essays/trib-timeline.html. Portions of this large chart are also used for clarification and instruction in the last chapter of this book.

My Tribulation Timeline clearly shows the Heavenly Signs that I have acknowledged as highly significant End Time Prophetic markers. This includes two Triple Blood Moon Sequences marking 2011 and 2018, and the Blood Moon Tetrad on the Jewish Feasts of Passover and Tabernacles in 2014 and 2015. In this book, I have theorized that the seven-year Tribulation would be between 2011 and 2017 - based primarily on the hidden prophecies in the Psalms that tie the Hallel Psalms 110 through 118 to the years 2010 through 2018, and the finial letters in the Hebrew Aleph-Bet that connect to these Psalms by their number associations. I also came to this conclusion based on the 2010 end date connected to the last inch of the Great Step in the Grand Gallery of the Great Pyramid at Giza, which signifies the belt stars of Orion, and which in turn signify the three crosses erected at the Crucifixion of Christ.

I also theorized that the Rapture might happen around the Feast of Trumpets in 2010, based on the Messianic Jewish insistence that the Rapture is thematically tied to the Feast of Trumpets. But when this failed to materialize, I had to rethink all of my previously held notions, including the idea of the Pre-Tribulation Rapture, which is so dear to all the big name Bible Prophecy teachers.

Looking at my Tribulation Time Chart, there are two heavenly signs in the year 2010 that I believe may mark the beginning of the Tribulation period. These are the Full Solar Eclipse or Sackcloth Sun that occurred directly over Easter Island on the 1st of Av on July 11th, 2010, and the Blood Moon or Full Lunar Eclipse that occurred on the Winter Solstice of December 21st, 2010, directly over the sword of Orion. Joel 2:31 suggests that a Sackcloth Sun and a Blood Moon will occur just before the great and terrible Day of the Lord, also called the Time of Jacob's Trouble or the Great Tribulation:

> "The sun shall be turned into darkness,
> And the moon into blood,
> Before the coming of the
> great and awesome day of the Lord."

This prophecy suggests that a Full Solar Eclipse and Full Lunar Eclipse would be witnessed by much of the world just prior to the Day of the Lord, which I believe alludes to the entire seven-year Tribulation period as well as the Millennial Rule of Christ. If this is the case, and the Eclipses of July and December 2010 were the signs that the Day of the Lord were about to begin, then the Tribulation began on of after December 21st, 2010. I currently believe this for numerous reasons - not the least of which is the preceding prophecy in Joel. If the Winter Solstice of 2010 is seen as the start date, then the Tribulation would have a midpoint in June of 2014, and a projected end sometime around the Winter Solstice in 2017 - although Yahshua said that this seven year time period would be cut short, or no life would survive it (Matthew 24:22).

## *The Joel Prophecy Fulfillment By Fire*

There is another way to interpret the Joel 2:31 prophecy, however. In Joel 2:30, the prophet wrote: *"And I will show wonders in the heavens and in the earth: Blood and fire and pillars of smoke..."*. This attaches the darkened Sun and blood-color Moon in his prophecy to blood, fire and smoke, suggesting their changed appearance may be caused by the smoke and ash of intense fires in the sky. This realization came to my mind in 2013, when I did a study that showed that Joel's prophecy in relation to fire appears to be coming true today. This is when I began thinking: "Could this powerful and ominous prophecy in Joel 2:30-31 be referring to the results of the terrible bush fires that have been erupting all over the world over the past few years - especially in 2013?"

Red Sun and Sky Affect Caused By 2013 California Rim Fires

Over the past few years, there have been dozens of massive wild fire outbreaks all over the world, especially in the United States and Australia. One of these devastating fires tragically killed 19 young and dedicated firefighters in Arizona in July of 2013, along with destroying much property and a large wilderness area. Then in August 2013, the Rim Fire near Yosemite National Park in California caused the Sun to turn dark red, as shown in the August 22nd, 2013 photo shown here. As a Sacred Astronomer, I can tell you that this same phenomenon would also have

# Ch. 11: The Rapture and Woman Clothed with the Sun

been happening to the Moon at night in that region, although the Moon would tend to appear an even darker and more ominous blood red.

If we are indeed seeing Joel's Prophecy come to fulfillment right now, then it is a sure sign that the Great Day of Yahweh's Wrath is imminent! To that, I say "Maranatha!" and:

~*~ *Isaiah 40:2-4* ~*~

*"Speak comfort to Jerusalem, and cry out to her,*
*That her warfare is ended,*
*That her iniquity is pardoned;*
*For she has received from the Lord's hand*
*Double for all her sins.*
*3 The voice of one crying in the wilderness:*
*"Prepare the way of the Lord;*
*Make straight in the desert*
*A highway for our God."*

In the past, I have tried to attribute Joel's Prophetic Scripture to actual eclipses of the Sun or Moon, but it recently dawned on me that the Prophet Joel may be referring to blood, fire and pillars of smoke in relation to them for a reason! Could this reason be the many bush fires that have been caused by excessive heat and drought over the past few years?

"Firenado" Caused By Tetlin Ridge Fire, 2013

In Alaska, the Tetlin Junction Ridge Fire had been burning out of control for months at the time of this writing, in late 2013. This terrible, unstoppable fire began on May 26th, 2013, when a large lightning strike ignited some of the trees in the forest there - even though a thunderstorm had been raging at the time. On page 541 is a photo of that massive firenado, which was taken from an August 16th, 2013 video.

Incidentally, the photo of the red-tinged Sun and smoky sky over California on page 540 was taken from NASA's Astronomy Pictures of the Day (APOD) web site, which had this to say about the photo:

> "This striking, otherworldly scene really is a view from planet Earth. The ochre sky and strawberry red sun were photographed on August 22nd near the small village of Strawberry, California, USA. Found along Highway 108, that location is about 30 miles north of the origin of California's large Rim Fire, still threatening areas in and around Yosemite National Park. The extensive smoke plumes from the wildfire are easily visible from space. But seen from within the plumes, the fine smoke particles suspended in the atmosphere dim the Sun, scattering blue light and strongly coloring the sky."

Could the reference to Highway 108 in the APOD commentary on the photo be a veiled reference to the "highway for our God" mentioned in Isaiah 40:4 (as quoted earlier), as well as to the Hidden Prophecy in Psalm 108, which contains a clear prophecy concerning the United States (Ephraim) and Israel (Judah) fighting in a war together for the same cause? It is certainly possible!

Even more ominously, the blood that Joel mentions in his prophecy may not only be in reference to the blood color of the Moon and Sun when the air is filled with ash and smoke from fires. There is another possibility, and that is the blood of the many animals that die in these fires, literally bursting them apart and splattering their blood from the intensity of the heat. It also may be referring to the ever-increasing numbers of Christian martyrs that are dying for their faith in Africa, Asia and the Middle East at the same time that these fires have been raging elsewhere. Peace-loving and law-abiding Christians are being murdered at an alarming rate that has increased greatly ever since the so-called Arab Spring that has swept through the Middle Easy, causing much unrest, and the ugly rise of Radical Islam. Beginning on page 592 in this chapter, I wrote about these martyrdoms in connection with a Nova that appeared in the constellation Delphinus in August of 2013.

Regarding the judgment by fire that Joel may be referring to, a terrible fire broke out and destroyed a large section of the famous Jersey Shore boardwalk in New Jersey, USA in September of 2013 - the same boardwalk that had been devastated by Hurricane Sandy in late October of 2012. In regard to this Jersey Shore fire, America's defiance in the face

# Ch. 11: The Rapture and Woman Clothed with the Sun

of God's continuing judgment on the nation - as was documented in the book "The Harbinger" by Rabbi Jonathan Cahn - is certainly behind this boardwalk fire. Unfortunately, however, many religious Americans that are in churches that do not emphasize Bible Prophecy and the Second Coming of Yahshua as they should (and this sadly is the majority of churches) are unaware of the danger they face as America moves ever further away from a strict adherence to biblical morality.

Sadly, the move away from biblical morality may also be behind the plague of over 100 bush fires that blanketed southern Australia in reddish gloom in October of 2013. Per a believing friend who lives in Australia, I was informed that the metropolitan city of Sydney is home to many wealthy Australians, has a large Muslim population, and hosts a Gay Mardi Gras Festival every summer that is very well attended by homosexuals and transgendered people from all over the world. Unfortunately, however, the Bible teaches that homosexuality and cross-dressing are despicable sins. In fact, our Holy God Yahweh despises them so much that the punishment for them in Old Testament times was certain death without hope of pardon!

Wall of Fire - 2013 Lake MacQuarie Fires

At times, the terrible bush fires that raged through the Lake Macquarie area of Southern Australia formed 30-meter (98 feet) high walls of flame that firefighters were virtually powerless against. As such, these fires also appear to be part of the fulfillment of the Joel Prophecy, as many people have tragically died in these fires - in addition to the huge loss of homes and property that these extremely hot fires have caused due to the previous drought in the region (and drought is also a sign of judgment by God!). Here is a photo made from a video clip of the Sun over the Lake Macquarie area during the fires, which had been tinted to a reddish hue from the heavy smoke and ash in the air from the fires.

Taken together, these fires are convincing evidence that Joel's Prophecy about death-causing (i.e. bloody) fires accompanying the End Times that will darken the Sun and obscure the Moon with blood-red hues may be coming to pass this year. In the future, the Sun and Moon may also be darkened due to fire when the Sixth Seal is opened (Rev. 6:12). The darkening of the heavens at this time could be caused by this coming cataclysmic pole-shift, which will surely cause many volcanic eruptions causing many fires and throwing much smoke and ash into the air, just as described by Joel.

Due to the fact that fires and volcanic eruptions can have similar affects on the Sun and Moon as eclipses do, both Joel's and John the Revelator's prophecies may indeed have a dual application. I already discussed the 2010 Solar and Lunar Eclipse that may be attached to Joel's Prophecy. As for Revelation 6, I believe that - if a Solar Eclipse is being prophesied about - it could be the November 3rd, 2013 Hybrid Eclipse over Africa. This Hybrid Eclipse is a very rare type of eclipse, and only seven such Hybrid Eclipses have occurred since the time of Christ.

In addition, I believe the Total Lunar Eclipse on Passover, April 15th, 2014, which is the first eclipse of the Blood Moon Tetrad occurring in 2014 and 2015, may by the Blood Moon being cited in relation to the Sixth Seal. If this is true, it means that we are very close to the time of the Rapture and Great Tribulation. If not, there is another Full Solar Eclipse and Full Lunar Eclipse occurring in the early spring of 2015 that could be the eclipses being cited, though this seems too late in the Tribulation period to allow for the unfolding of the remainder of the many End Time plagues that will be meted out upon the wicked.

## *Great Pyramid Targets The 2010 Summer Solstice*

In regard to the end point of the Great Tribulation, let me redirect your attention to the Great Pyramid at Giza. This splendid altar to God in the midst of Egypt was likely built by the righteous Sethites prior to the Great Flood to preserve some very significant End Time information for this generation. As shown in this book, I have deciphered many of this pyramid's secrets using the gifts of the Holy Spirit. Following is a summary of what I have found during my many years of studying this magnificent architectural wonder, which I summarized earlier in this book.

In my drawings of the architectural layout of the Giza pyramid site, I showed that the ceremonial causeway leading from the entrance face of the middle Pyramid of Khafre at Giza in Egypt points toward the spot on the horizon where the Winter Solstice Sun rises every year in that region. This suggests that there is some connection to the Winter Solstice and the time of Christ's First and Second Advent.

## Ch. 11: The Rapture and Woman Clothed with the Sun    Page 545

## Giza Solar and Stellar Alignments Targeting 2010 AD

As shown in my book "The Language of God in the Universe", Yahshua's conception and visitation by the Magi are directly connected to the Feast of Chanukah, which happens near to the time of the Winter Solstice every year. Since conception is when life begins, Yahshua's First Advent began at the moment of His conception near to the time of the Winter Solstice in Chanukah of 4 BC - not at His physical birth, which was on or near to the Feast of Trumpets in 3 BC.

If Yahshua is going to return for His Bride in the Rapture sometime around the Winter Solstice, this may be why the Mayan Calendar date for the End of the Mayan Fifth Sun and Incan Sixth Sun also targeted a Winter Solstice. As will be shown in the next chapter, the Signs in the Heavens on December 21st, 2012 are directly tied to the first Four Seal Judgments of the Tribulation, which I believe began to be opened in 2011. This is based on the fact that the Heavenly Signs on the Mayan End Date are directly tied to Four Zodiac Signs signifying the Four Horsemen of the Apocalypse, and two of them appear **after** the Winter Solstice point on the Ecliptic, indicating that the 3rd and 4th Seals may have been opened in 2013.

Judging from the contamination of sea life in the Pacific Ocean from the ongoing Fukushima Nuclear Disaster, and the terrible prolonged droughts, floods and fires that have been plaguing the world since 2010, world food supplies are being rapidly depleted and disease outbreaks have greatly increased even as the threat of world nuclear war continue to grow exponentially as tensions between the USA, North Korea, Russia, Iran, Israel and other nations escalates.

The evidence that these seals have been opened is everywhere. In fact, massive increases in every sort of trouble have occurred in 2010, 2011, 2012 and 2013. However, based on what remains of the Tribulation plagues, we haven't seen anything yet, because the situation around the world will drastically deteriorate after the Sixth Seal is opened! The traumatic End Time events of the past few years include a huge spike in political and religious demonstrations, rioting and unrest, economic failures, a terrifying increase in bizarre or grisly murders, disgusting crimes and mass shootings, more frequent deadly earthquakes, heightened Christian persecution, numerous new sinkholes, huge and deadly storms accompanied by high winds, hail, floods, and tornadoes, many new pestilences and antibiotic resistant diseases, and millions upon millions of animal, fish, bird and bee die-offs.

Also, as shown earlier in this book, God gave me the key to unravel the date correlations for the measurements in the Antechamber of the Great Pyramid in early 2011. Like past Bible Scholars, I believe that

## Ch. 11: The Rapture and Woman Clothed with the Sun

there is a clear prophetic allegorical connection between the Tribulation period and the Antechamber. Using the dating key that God revealed, the Antechamber shows that the beginning date of the Great Tribulation may be around July 1st, 2014, and the end date may be near to June 1st, 2016, making it 21 months, or 630 days long, which is half of the projected 42 month or 1260 day reign of the Antichrist. This suggests that the Great Tribulation **will be shortened by two full years.**

In addition, to being given the key to unlock the secrets hidden in the Antechamber of the Great Pyramid, I also recently discovered that there is a fascinating Solar Alignment at Giza that ties the placement and design of the entire Giza Pyramid Complex to this current era in human history, and to the very year that may target the beginning of the Tribulation period. This can be found when viewing the location of the Summer Solstice and Equinox sunsets at Giza on the Western Horizon directly in front of the Sphinx, whose face is pointing due east.

In my illustration of the Great Sphinx and Giza Pyramids on page 545, note how both the Spring and Autumn Equinox sunset points in 2010 were directly aligned with the head of the Sphinx on the Western horizon. Since sunset is at the end of the day, this suggests a connection to the End of Days when Yahshua is about to return. Furthermore, the Summer Solstice Sun of 2010 set directly adjacent to the Great Pyramid at Giza, which represents the star Al Nitak in Orion's Belt, as well as the altar to God in the midst of Egypt spoken of in Isaiah 19:19-20.

Uncannily, Isaiah Chapter 19 is also an End Time Prophecy concerning Egypt, which started being fulfilled with the rise of many violent protests in the Muslim nations of the Middle East, which began in December of 2010 - the same year targeted by the Solar Alignments of the Equinoxes with the head of the Great Sphinx! Even more fascinatingly, the middle pyramid at Giza that signifies the Cross of Yahshua has a causeway that points in the direction of the Winter Solstice, and this Solstice occurred right around the time that the so-called "Arab Spring" erupted in the Middle East.

However, though these dates found in the Great Pyramid are intriguing, and tie in perfectly with the Signs in the Heavens between 2010 and 2018, and the Hallel Psalm year correlations, no one knows exactly when Yahshua may return. Furthermore, my calculations could be wrong. All I know for certain is that Yahshua said that He would return when the Fig Tree is ready to bloom (Matthew 24:32-33), and this Parable of the Budding Fig Tree signifies that the nation of Israel is getting ready to bloom with faith in Him. Not surprisingly, there are many signs that this is occurring right now as Messianic Jewish congregations spring up all over the world, especially in the United States - where over half of the Jewish population of the world currently resides.

In addition, the Book of Revelation says that Yahshua will return to conquer the wicked just as the Battle of Armageddon is about to begin - when the armies of the world have gathered outside of Jerusalem in the Valley of Megiddo. Though this final battle surrounding the ancient city of Jerusalem's fate could happen around June of 2016, no one knows for certain when it will be. We will simply have to trust Yahweh God to protect us and keep us in His peaceful and protective embrace as we await the return of His Son.

In that regard, there is much publicized animosity between President Obama, Israeli Prime Minister Benjamin Netanyahu, and Russian President Vladimir Putin and their respective military forces, along with the governments of China, North Korea, Egypt, Iran and Syria, which is painting a very grim picture of the future. Just as before World War I and II, the saber rattling between these nations is threatening to start World War III - a war that will most likely use nuclear and chemical weapons in many locales to kill millions before it's all over.

This is becoming an even bigger threat as the United States and United Nations try and persuade the nation of Israel to divide its lands and form a new Palestinian state. Though this solution may create a temporary peace, however, the Bible makes it clear that God will not allow this false peace to endure. I therefore have no doubt that we are already in the final seven-year Tribulation period, and may in fact already be very close to the Mid-Tribulation First Rapture. Therefore, my warning to everyone is to repent of your sins NOW, ask Yahshua into your life, turn away from whatever displeases God, and pray for God to forgive you, fill you with His Helper the Holy Spirit, and help you to keep His commandments. If you sincerely do this and prayerfully keep your eyes on Yahshua, you will surely **escape** all these things, as Yahshua promised:

> *"But take heed to yourselves, lest your hearts be weighed down with carousing, drunkenness, and cares of this life, and that Day come on you unexpectedly. 35 For it will come as a snare on all those who dwell on the face of the whole earth. 36 Watch therefore, and **pray always that you may be counted worthy to escape all these things** that will come to pass, and to stand before the Son of Man." - Luke 21:34-36*

As we await our escape in the Rapture, truly born-again believers need to remember that those who follow Yahshua will always be the hated minority in this world. We have been insulated from it in the West for too long, and it has allowed the Church to become lukewarm and promiscuous. The price for that is the world turning against those who are not lukewarm. This does not mean that we should be lukewarm. On the contrary! We need to stand for our convictions in Yahshua, no matter what. But we are not called to fight with physical force of arms. We are called to love each other, to live in peace, to turn the other cheek, to rejoice when wronged, to be joyful when beaten, and glorified when we die for the sake of Yahshua with humility - when being peaceful isn't enough to appease the blood lust of the wicked.

It's time for believers to show their true mettle and the strength of their faith. Those with great faith that are tested, and who are able to stand fast in their faith until Yahshua comes for His own, will go in the Rapture. Those with little or no faith or conviction in their faith will be tested in the fire of the Great Tribulation, and some of them will sadly perish. The final weeding out of the tares from the wheat and the goats from the sheep is being carried out right now. How we love God and one another will be the deciding factor in who will be taken, and who will be left behind. It's therefore time now for all of us to decide whose side we are on, and to live the remainder of our lives with conviction and faith!

## *The Strong Delusion of the Antichrist*

Those who deny Yahshua's literal return, and/or are too enamored with the things of this world, are in danger of falling for a total imposter called the Antichrist, who some say might be a cloned counterfeit or a literal descendant of the "seed of the Serpent." The Serpent's seed were the Nephilim or Giants of old, the "men" or "beings" of great renown. These were angel-human hybrids that grew to an immense size, and terrorized humanity before the Flood. Genesis, Chapter 6 and the Book of 1 Enoch describe the violence and inhumanity of the Nephilim that inhabited the Earth before the Great Flood.

These evil hybrid beings called Nephilim became demons when they died, and - along with their Fallen Angel sires who mated with human women in the line of Cain - they are the mastermind behind all the modern UFO sightings, Alien encounters and abductions that are being reported. This can be readily discerned because the channeled messages of these alien beings are diametrically opposed to the clear teaching of Scripture. These beings insist that they are our "makers", and they are going to return soon to lead the world into a New Age of peace and prosperity, when the exact opposite is true.

My book "The Language of God in History" goes into great depth about these evil, demonic creatures, and their unceasing agenda to wipe humanity off the face of the Earth. It also looks into a once secret organization known as the Illuminati, which is made up of people who either have literal Nephilim blood in their heritage, or are completely sold out to the Devil in one form or another. For example, some worship him in the form of Baphomet. This false deity with a goat's face and human body is directly connected to Satanism, which worships the natural world and physical pleasure and power above anything else in this life, and that literally hates Yahweh God, Who calls their unrestrained, carnal worldview sinful and wicked.

New Agers and Neo-Pagans are connected to Satanism in that they greatly value wealth, power, and physical and worldly pleasure. However, to their credit, they see a spiritual dimension to life that goes far beyond that, and which reaches into eternity. Unfortunately, they do not recognize the existence of sin and evil, and therefore do not understand the necessity of Christ's sacrifice for our sins on the Cross, which is central to the Salvation message in the Bible. They also view success as a sign of salvation, and look down upon anyone who is experiencing hard circumstances, which is against the clear teaching of Scripture that those who follow Yahshua the most closely can, and often do, suffer greatly in this life.

Then there is the deity of Gnostic Christians, which is a corruption of God the Father, the giver of physical and spiritual life. In the case of the Gnostics, their god can be viewed as the Destroyer because he is meant to destroy the physical world of the flesh. Gnostics consider the flesh evil, and only see the intellect and the spirit as worthy of everlasting life through the process of Gnosis, or gaining spiritual wisdom. This puts them in league with New Agers to some extant, but puts them completely at odds with true Christians and Jews. This is because the latter groups realize that the physical world was created good, and was meant to be everlasting, but that it was corrupted and made evil with the entrance of sin, which is rebellion against God.

Though their objectives appear to be completely different, New Agers, Satanists and Gnostics seem to have a common goal, and it is very similar to the one being touted by the beings behind the "Alien Agenda", which is none other than the Antichrist's agenda to take over the world. Like these aliens, the many false religious groups of the world tend to worship nature as a goddess, and all who follow the teachings of the false prophets and Fallen Angels as little gods.

# Ch. 11: The Rapture and Woman Clothed with the Sun

On the other hand, many of the people that have bought into this false, alien-backed brand of spirituality see the rest of humanity that does not buy into their beliefs as parasitic. As a result, many of these lost souls desire to drastically reduce the human population of the world. Some of the most rich and powerful among them are in the Illuminati, an organization of the world's elite that intends to depopulate the world, and already has moved to do this through various means. These include mass genocidal wars, and technologically manufactured disasters, plagues and diseases that are meant to wipe out anyone that does not fit into their objectives.

Though I wish it were far-fetched, some of the members of the elite Illuminati groups that run our world behind the scenes are planning to replace humanity altogether with a new and improved DNA enhanced, cybernetic creature that will have superhuman strength, and a greatly increased lifespan. This movement is known as Transhumanism, and its goals are to create a new brand of Nephilim that can defy God's Will, and practically live forever without any need for submission to God or repentance of sin.

Sadly, it is now entirely possible that scientists could create this new cybernetic race of humanoids, and may already be doing so. Some even speculate that the Antichrist will be one of them in a sense - as a cross between the Jewish bloodline of Christ and the Nephilim bloodline of the Devil. Some believe this has already been done by mixing the DNA found in the bones of humanoid giants, and those of the blood stains that were found on the Shroud of Turin, which may have been the actual burial cloth of Christ.

Though many still deny it, there is reason to believe that the carbon dating of the Shroud of Turin done in the recent past was faulty due to the medieval interweaving of newer fabric into the damaged corners of the Shroud - where the samples were taken to do the tests. Though it is difficult to believe that our heavenly Father Yahweh would allow His Son Yahshua's literal blood to be used in such an evil way, some also point to the seemingly sensationalistic claims that the late adventurer Ron Wyatt found the Ark of the Covenant hidden beneath the crucifixion site of Christ at Golgotha in Jerusalem. When documenting his claims on video (which can be found at YouTube), Ron claims to have retrieved a sample of Christ's blood that had pooled on the top of the Ark. He also claims that it proved to be "alive" when tested in a laboratory. Though these are intriguing theories, however, I can't say for certain that there is any truth to them. Only time will tell!

Some people believe that Prince William of the United Kingdom may be a clone derived through DNA splicing of normal human DNA with Christ's own DNA taken from either of the above mentioned sources. They therefore believe that William may be the Antichrist. If nothing else, it is interesting to note that the name of William's father - "Prince Charles of Wales" - adds up to 666 in both the Greek and Hebrew Gematria, and William became 30 on the Summer Solstice in 2012. On that note, I find it interesting that William was born on the Summer Solstice, and I did a study of the Heavenly Signs at his birth recently that should raise some suspicions about just who he and his father represent in God's Plan. Check the "Free Articles" page of my POEM Web Site at http://pillar-of-enoch.com for links to several online articles on this topic.

In any case, the Signs in the Heavens are telling me that the Tribulation already began, so the Antichrist has to be prominent on the world scene already, even if he isn't in control of the One World Government yet. But anyone who pays attention can plainly see that this government, which is being touted as the New World Order by several past Presidents of the United States, has been steadily worked toward in Europe, the United Kingdom, and the United States for the past 50 to 100 years. The most obvious signs of this coming One World Government and Religious system can be seen in the mass move toward Socialism and Collectivism within all the governments around the world. In addition, it can be clearly seen in that Jews, Christians, Christianity and Biblical Morality have been repeatedly marginalized, sin and sinfulness and the existence of Hell have been, and are routinely denied, and Ecumenism and the move toward a One World Religion declaring all paths to be equal have been, and continue to be persistently forced on us by our governments.

Regardless of when the Great Tribulation begins or where the bloodlines of the Beast that will go down in history known as the Antichrist originate, however, his plans will not succeed! In the end, he will perish - along with all who fall for his deceptive claims to be both the Messiah of the world, and a deity worthy of the wicked world's worship. In the meantime, we are called to watch and pray as we wait for Yahshua's Return for us in the Rapture. Here are two more Scriptures that tie directly to the Parable of the Ten Virgins to show what Yahshua's return for His Bride will be like. I have filled these with short explanatory notes in parentheses to make understanding them easier for those unfamiliar with God's prophetic Language. As you read these, remember that the symbolic door to Heaven was shut on the Foolish Virgins in the Parable of the Ten Virgins:

# Ch. 11: The Rapture and Woman Clothed with the Sun

> *"But of that day and hour no one knows, not even the angels in heaven, nor the Son, but only the Father. 33 Take heed, watch and pray; for you do not know when the time is. 34 It is like a man (Yahshua) going to a far country (Heaven), who left His house (the Church) and gave authority to His servants (the saints), and to each his work, and commanded the **doorkeeper** (the Watchmen) to watch. 35 Watch therefore, for you do not know when the master of the house (this house is the Body of Christ, and the master is Yahshua the Bridegroom) is coming - in the evening, at midnight, at the crowing of the rooster, or in the morning - 36 lest, coming suddenly, He find you sleeping."* - Mark 13:32-36

The following Scripture uses similar imagery, but is very confusing because it mentions two different masters, although this is not clear in English translations. These two masters are the big Master of the Bride and the Wise Virgins who is Yahshua, and the little master of the "house", or the "world", which is currently Satan, who has usurped Christ's place. Keep this in mind as you read this Scripture:

> *"Let your waist be girded and your lamps burning; 36 and you yourselves be like men who wait (The Wise Virgins, who are watching) for their master (Yahshua), when he will return from (at or during) the wedding, that when he comes and knocks (on the symbolic door to retrieve His Bride) they may open to him immediately. 37 Blessed are those servants whom the master (this master is Yahshua), when He comes, will find watching. Assuredly... He will gird himself and have them sit down to eat, and will come and serve them (at the Wedding of the Lamb in Heaven). 38 And if He should come in the second watch (in the First Rapture), or come in the third watch (in the Second Rapture), and find them so, blessed are those servants. 39 But know this, that if the master of the house (this house is the world, and so this master is currently Satan) had known what hour the thief (this thief is Yahshua, who will come like a thief) would come, he would have watched and not allowed his house to be broken into."* - Luke 12:35-39

So, as this section proves, the Word of God does indeed teach the concept of a special "Catching-Away" or Rapture of the Saints in many different parts of the Bible. As revealed in this section, there are also many references to the Rapture hidden away where few have looked. This was done so that no one would be able to rob the diligent student of Scripture of their blessed hope!

## *Why the Post-Tribulation Rapture View Doesn't Make Sense*

As a Watchman on the Wall that is anxiously awaiting our Messiah's glorious return, I want to commend all who are attempting to discern when Yahshua will return to rescue all those who are born-again by His Spirit and living under His Grace from total destruction. Among those of you doing so, there are many that hold to varying views of when the Rapture or catching up of God's elect saints into everlasting life and resurrection will take place.

Based on my understanding of the Scriptures after detailed study and prayer, I personally believe that the Rapture of the Church is meant to protect and preserve God's people from having to experience the worst of God's Wrath that will be poured out during the Great Tribulation. Ever since openly voicing my view that the Rapture must take place by the middle of the coming seven-year Tribulation, however, I have endured near constant attacks from people with a Post-Tribulation view of the Rapture and Second Coming. These attacks have mostly been relentless and cruel, going against all the gifts of the Ruach Ha Kodesh or Holy Spirit such as love, forgiveness, kindness and compassion. Nonetheless, I did my best to display the gifts of the Ruach when debating my differing views of the Rapture with these people.

Unfortunately, my scriptural arguments for believing in a Pre to Mid-Tribulation Rapture that are outlined below were ignored for the most part by those favoring a Post-Tribulation Rapture. Furthermore, since their arguments against my views did nothing to address the teachings of the Scriptures that I shared with them, I was not convinced that my views were wrong in any way. In addition, I was encouraged by their lack of knowledge of these Scriptures to attempt to explain here why I still hold fast to a Pre-to Mid-Tribulation Rapture view.

Part of my reason is based on my Spirit-led understanding of the type and extant of the tribulation or persecution that Yahshua mentions in Matthew Chapter 24, verses 9, 21 and 29. From my study of these and many other Scriptures, it can be shown that Yahshua was in no way referring to the Great Tribulation spoken of in the Book of Revelation. In fact, when all the Scriptures pertaining to the time of Jacob's Trouble are studied carefully, two things become clear: First, that this tribulation spoken of in Matthew Chapter 24 has already begun and is ongoing, and second, that the Rapture can in no way be at the time of the Battle of Armageddon.

All one has to do to refute the Post-Tribulation view is to know the history of the last two centuries. First, one needs to be aware of the hundreds of false prophets that arose in the 19th and 20th centuries and are arising even now that tout the joys of Atheism, Deism, and the Hinduistic, Atheistic, and Humanistic New Age Religions like Theosophy, Freemasonry, Universalism, and Rosicrucianism.

Then one needs to obtain a thorough knowledge of the horrendous events of World War II when all of Western Civilization was threatened with destruction. In view of these facts, there is every indication that the distress, persecution or tribulation of believers that Yahshua was referring to in Matthew Chapter 24 began with the imprisonment, torture and eventual slaughter of at least 8 million Jews and over 30 million Christians that perished in Europe, Russia, and Asia because of their religious beliefs and resistance to the dominant secular humanistic (and communistic) culture of their home countries.

The persecution of Christians did not end there, however. It has continued virtually unabated in places such as Africa and Asia, where Muslim terrorists have moved into many once Christianized nations or Pagan and Muslim nations with significant minorities of Christians and slaughtered, raped, impoverished, and brutalized many more millions of believers in Yahshua. But the sad truth is that most of the people in the West are oblivious or unconcerned about of the plight of millions upon millions of true believers in Christ that are suffering persecution and the thousands that are being martyred every single day for living by and preaching about the Gospel of the Kingdom of God.

With this in view, the "tribulation of those days" that Yahshua spoke of in Matthew 24:29 can only be referring to the 19th and 20th Century events that led to World War I and World War II, as well as to the early 21st Century. In any case, when the Book of Revelation is compared to Matthew Chapter 24, it can be shown that a far worse tribulation is discussed in the Book of Revelation than the one defined in Matthew Chapter 24. As proof that the Great Tribulation is not meant in Matthew Ch. 24, verses 9, 21 and 29, one must carefully read what Yahshua said in these passages and compare it to the Book of Revelation's Tribulation plagues. The following passage indicates the scope of environmental destruction that will accompany the tribulation of Matthew Chapter 24:

> "For nation will rise against nation, and kingdom against kingdom. And there will be famines, pestilences, and earthquakes in various places. All these are the beginning of sorrows." - Matthew 24:7-8

In this passage, though Yahshua mentioned an increase in earthquakes, famines (ostensibly caused by droughts and floods that cause crops to fail), and pestilences as the birth pains of the Tribulation, He nowhere mentions the near total destruction of the Earth that will take place in the Tribulation period that is graphically depicted in the Book of Revelation, Chapters 6 through 16.

In fact, by using the phrase "in various places" in Matthew 24:7, Yahshua was indicating that there would only be isolated pockets of destruction during the Tribulation discussed in Matthew Chapter 24, as was completely the case in the last century. However, in Revelation Chapter 16, a nearly global destruction of the Earth is indicated. In addition, by referring to the relative peace and calm that will be part of the human condition prior to His return, Yahshua makes it clear that the Rapture stage of His Second Coming is being spoken of in Matthew Chapter 24 and not the Armageddon stage of His return that will follow the Great Tribulation or Wrath of God detailed in the Book of Revelation. He does so by explaining that the rescue of His saints will come long before most of the plagues poured out on the wicked in the Book of Revelation. This is made clear in the following Scriptures:

> *"For as in the days before the flood, they were eating and drinking, marrying and giving in marriage, until the day that Noah entered the ark, and... the flood came and took them all away, so also will the coming of the Son of Man be. Then two men will be in the field: one will be taken and the other left. Two women will be grinding at the mill: one will be taken and the other left."* - Matthew 24:38-41

> *"And as it was in the days of Noah, so it will be also in the days of the Son of Man: They ate, they drank, they married wives, they were given in marriage, until the day that Noah entered the ark, and the flood came and destroyed them all. Likewise as it was also in the days of Lot: They ate, they drank... they planted, they built; but on the day that Lot went out of Sodom it rained fire and brimstone from heaven and destroyed them all. Even so will it be... when the Son of Man is revealed."* - Luke 17:26-30

There is no way around it: one has to read Matthew Chapter 24 in light of the Book of Revelation to avoid misinterpreting what Yahshua said. These Scriptures make it clear that, when Yahshua returns for His elect saints, the world will be in a state of relative quiet and calm such as those preceding violent storms or that can be found under the eye of a hurricane. Furthermore, this state of peace and calm will be absolutely impossible after the Seventh Trumpet and Seven Bowls of God's Wrath are poured out on the Earth! No one except those who deny that the Book of Revelation speaks of yet future events can read of the cataclysmic

## Ch. 11: The Rapture and Woman Clothed with the Sun    Page 557

events in Chapter 16 in the Book of Revelation and think that there will be peace and calm immediately before or after the Battle of Armageddon.

Read it for yourself! Revelation Chapter 8, Verse 7 says that, at the time of the First Trumpet plague: *"a third of the trees were burned up, and all green grass was burned up"*. Furthermore, Revelation Chapter 16 tells us that *"every living creature in the sea died"*, and the rivers and springs of water *"became blood"* (Rev. 16:3-4). Next, *"men were scorched with great heat"* (Rev. 16:9), and this will be so great a scorching that it will cause the Euphrates river to completely dry up, and most of the remaining trees and shrubs on the Earth to die (Rev. 16:12). After this, a thick darkness will descend on the kingdom of the Beast (Rev. 16:10). In addition to this, *"a great and terrible earthquake"* that will be far worse than any in recorded history will shake the Earth so *"the cities of the nations fell"* and *"every island fled away, and the mountains were not found"* (Rev. 16:18-20).

With no clean water to drink or to irrigate crops, a severe drought that will scorch the entire world, and the cities and mountains of the world destroyed, the Earth will be laid waste by the Bowls of God's Wrath. Virtually no trees will be left standing where the ruined cities of mankind once stood, and not one blade of grass will be left alive. Furthermore, not one fish will be left alive in the lakes, streams or oceans that will have all been turned to blood by this time!

After this, hailstones will fall on mankind - each weighing about a talent (or 50 pounds!). These will injure and kill many, and cause those who survive to blaspheme against God (Rev. 16:21). Based on the total destruction of the Earth that is outlined in Revelation Chapter 16, there is simply **no way** that people will be calmly doing business, tending fields or getting married in expectation of raising a family at the end of the Chapter 16 in the Book of Revelation. Furthermore, the following Scriptures plainly state that it will be entirely possible for true believers in the Church of "Philadelphia" or "Brotherly Love" to escape all the plagues and pestilences of the Great Tribulation and to forego seeing the Wrath of God being poured out on the wicked:

*"Watch therefore, and pray always that you may be counted worthy to escape all these things that will come to pass, and to stand before the Son of Man."* - Luke 21:36

*"For they themselves declare concerning us what manner of entry we had to you, and how you turned to God from idols to serve the living and true God, and to wait for His Son from heaven, whom He raised from the dead, even Jesus who delivers us from the wrath to come."* - 1 Thessalonians 1:9-10

*"For God did not appoint us to wrath, but to obtain salvation through our Lord Jesus Christ." - 1 Thessalonians 5:9*

*"Because you have kept My command to persevere, I also will keep you from the hour of trial which shall come upon the whole world, to test those who dwell on the earth." - Rev. 3:10*

In light of the fact that Yahshua promised to spare those who love Him from the coming pouring out of God's Wrath in the Great Tribulation, the Post-Tribulation view of the Rapture is a scripturally unsound position at best, and an outright deception at its worst.

## The Rapture Connection to the Sign of the Son of Man

The previous section of this chapter shows why the "tribulation of those days" spoken of in Matthew 24:29 is likely not referring to the final seven-year Tribulation described in the Book of Revelation, Chapters 6 through 16. My argument for this partly rests on the matter of intensity. The tribulation of the Gospel writers speak of earthquakes, wars, rumors of wars, famines and pestilences "in various places", suggesting many comparatively small disasters with a limited area of coverage. Secondly, this tribulation is reported as the beginning of sorrows, not the end:

*"For nation will rise against nation, and kingdom against kingdom. And there will be famines, pestilences, and earthquakes in various places. All these are the beginning of sorrows." - Matthew 24:7-8*

Another key to understanding the 24th Chapter of Matthew are the two distinct questions that the disciples posed to Yahshua when He told them that the city of Jerusalem and the Temple would soon be destroyed:

*"And Jesus said to them, 'Do you not see all these things? Assuredly, I say to you, not one stone shall be left here upon another, that shall not be thrown down.' Now as He sat on the Mount of Olives, the disciples came to Him privately, saying, 'Tell us, when will these things be? And what will be the sign of Your coming, and of the end of the age?'" - Matthew 24:2-3*

Note here that the disciples asked Yahshua two distinct questions. In asking: *"Tell us, when will these things be?"*, the disciples were seeking to know how to recognize when the destruction of the Temple and city of Jerusalem were near so that they could flee before it happened. But the second question, which was: *"What will be the sign of*

## Ch. 11: The Rapture and Woman Clothed with the Sun    Page 559

*Your coming, and of the end of the age?"* related to Yahshua's return to set up His Kingdom. Woefully, however, though the disciples saw Yahshua as the prophesied Messiah, they fully expected Him to conquer the Roman oppressors and re-establish David's throne and kingdom immediately after the destruction of Jerusalem. The disciples had no concept of the suffering that Yahshua was soon going to undergo as the Lamb of God and atonement sacrifice for our sins, or that there was going to be a long delay before Yahshua returned to Jerusalem to lead their fellow Jews to set up God's Kingdom.

The point here is that the disciples had no idea that the two questions covered two distinctly different time periods in history that were to be separated by over 2000 years! This means that Yahshua's reply has to be seen in this light, with a portion of it pertaining to their current time in history and a portion of it pertaining to ours. Thus, though Yahshua warned his disciples to "take heed that no one deceives you" in Matthew 24:4, they had already been deceived by their former Jewish religious leaders. In an attempt to warn His disciples that they were confused, Yahshua did not answer their first question initially, but their second one. But until the Holy Spirit was sent to baptize the disciples and Apostles on the Pentecost or Shavuot after Yahshua's death and resurrection, they did not understand Yahshua's reply in context. Furthermore, those without the Spirit are still having trouble figuring out what Yahshua meant today.

Let's examine Yahshua's prophetic words in light of the two different time periods being referred to. In verses 5 through 14 of Matthew Chapter 24, Yahshua is citing the trouble that began in the early church when Pagan Rome and the Jewish leaders saw all the new believers in Yahshua and the rapidity at which this new philosophy spread among the Gentile nations as a major threat to the established order. This era saw a huge rift form between the Jewish synagogues and Gentile Christian congregations as the Jews who rejected Yahshua's free gift of Grace insisted on keeping all the ancient religious rituals that they loved alive.

In order to do this, the Jews forcibly expelled the new believers in Yahshua from their synagogues if they did not see a need to keep the same rituals or remember the Jewish Feasts in the same way. As a result of this rift, the Gentile believers that had rejected many Jewish religious restrictions and developed their own unique rituals and view of theology based on New Covenant principles suddenly found themselves without public places of worship. This caused the schism between Messianic Jews and Gentile Christians to deepen even further, and many Jews began to hate and betray their Christian brethren by turning them in to their

Roman overseers, who mercilessly raped, pillaged, imprisoned, martyred and enslaved all of the peace-loving new believers that had the misfortune of being caught.

Eventually, though Gentile coverts fellowshipped with one another in their homes and in secret meeting places, some of them also began to congregate publicly in the synagogues of the Samaritans, who neither persecuted nor rejected Christian believers, but openly accepted them. As a result, some Gentile believers were deceived because the Samaritans had erroneously mixed Pagan and Jewish religious ideas together. As a result, some believers eventually rejected sound theology, taking on Pagan customs that the Roman Emperor Constantine would tragically also embrace.

Nonetheless, though verses 5 through 14 of Matthew Chapter 24 pertained to the Early Church age, this passage equally applies to the 20th Century AD, which the first 100 of the 150 Psalms in the Bible appear to be prophetically linked to. The Twentieth Century saw the devastating affects of a severe and prolonged economic depression, and two major world wars that threatened to destroy the Christianized civilizations of the West. In addition, this period of history saw the massive imprisonment and murder of nearly 30 million Christians and 12 million Jews in Asia, Russia, Austria and Germany. Most of these victims had been relatively peaceful, law-abiding citizens that were unjustly tortured, starved, and murdered in Nazi or Communist concentration camps. This tribulation is described in the Book of Matthew here:

> *"Then they will deliver you up to tribulation and kill you, and you will be hated by all nations for My name's sake. And then many will be offended, will betray one another, and will hate one another. Then many false prophets will rise up and deceive many. And because lawlessness will abound, the love of many will grow cold. But he who endures to the end shall be saved." - Matthew 24:9-13*

The false prophets mentioned in this passage are also are easy to identify in our age. These were the warped intellectuals of the late 19th and early 20th Centuries that inspired such religious philosophies as Mormonism, Theosophy and Rosicrucianism, and political ideologies such as Nazism and Communism. Though resembling Christianity, Mormonism professes a different Messiah than the Christ of the Bible and defines salvation in a completely different way. Adding to this deception, the two non-Christian religious ideologies that I mentioned profess the false belief that Christ was not a divinely sent Messiah, but only a wise man that became a wise spirit-being or ascended master upon His death.

# Ch. 11: The Rapture and Woman Clothed with the Sun

They also erroneously teach that everyone eventually finds salvation and ascends to a higher spiritual reality like Christ did and no particular religious ideology is superior over any other. In addition, the two major political ideologies that arose in the 20th Century developed fanatical leaders that viewed Christ and those who followed Him in truth as enemies of the state.

The religious, social and political unrest of the Twentieth Century was triggered by the rise of these destructive religious and political ideologies that led to the deprivation, imprisonment and death of many Christians and Jews in World Wars I and II. Nonetheless, throughout that terrible time of trouble, some of those who were unjustly imprisoned and brutally treated were given opportunities to witness to others about their enduring faith in Yahweh God and His Son - even in the midst of terrible suffering.

The major wars that severely affected forty years of the Twentieth Century were then followed by many devastating smaller wars such as the Korean War, the Vietnam War, the Six-Day War, and the Gulf War. Out of these wars, amidst much pain and shedding of blood, the current east-west ideological division between the Christianized moderately socialistic Western nations and the communistic, Islamic and Paganistic Eastern nations has been forged. This has placed all the world's political powers on a steep precipice of antagonism and hate from which there is no escape, and that can only lead to their eventual catastrophic demise in the wake of the Antichrist's desire to place the entire world under His evil and totalitarian control.

When this happens, the next stage of Yahshua's prophetic words will be fulfilled, for as the Antichrist maneuvers himself to take control of the world, the 144,000 and Two Witnesses will join the Tribulation Saints in winning over millions into the Kingdom of God during the Tribulation:

> *"And this gospel of the kingdom will be preached in all the world as a witness to all the nations, and then the end will come."*
> - Matthew 24:14

Before the destruction of Jerusalem, the Gospel of the Kingdom was also preached throughout the Roman Empire and beyond - as witnessed in the Apostle Paul's Missionary journeys and the journeys of Yahshua's other apostles and disciples, who were reported to have traveled throughout the known world preaching the Gospel. But when the fullness of this time of Christian evangelism and Jewish apostasy had been reached in that past era, Yahweh God sent the Romans to destroy the Temple to Yahweh and to sack Jerusalem. It was Roman soldiers that surrounded Jerusalem and carried the Pagan standards and evil emblems

# The Language of God in Prophecy

of the Roman Empire before them into the sacred city, and it was the Romans that desecrated the Temple by setting up their Pagan standards there. This served as a warning to all the believers in Yahshua living in Jerusalem to flee the city. Likewise, it will be the armies of the Antichrist that will surround Jerusalem someday soon, and it will be the Antichrist or an image of himself that will appear on the Temple mount in Jerusalem and be proclaimed as a god:

> "Therefore when you see the 'abomination of desolation,' spoken of by Daniel the prophet, standing in the holy place (whoever reads, let him understand), then let those who are in Judea flee to the mountains..." "But woe to those who are pregnant and to those who are nursing babies in those days! And pray that your flight may not be in winter or on the Sabbath." - Matthew 24:15-16

The preceding Scripture is clearly teaching about the destruction of the Temple in 70 AD and the subsequent annihilation of Jerusalem. At that time, the "abomination of desolation" referred to the Pagan standards of the Roman legions that entered, sacked and burned the Temple in Jerusalem. But we have been told that it also alludes to a future time not far off, when the Antichrist is supposed to seize Jerusalem, declare his divinity in a newly rebuilt temple, and demand to be worshipped - just like any one of the many humanistic totalitarian Communist rulers of the past century.

But I question the validity of this theory. I've already explained that the abomination of desolation during Yahshua's First Advent was likely the replacement of the torn veil in the Temple to Yahweh in Jerusalem. Could it therefore be that the abomination of desolation of this Age has to do with the Al Aqsa Mosque atop the Temple Mount today? After all, Allah is **not** Yahweh, the God of Abraham, but an ancient Pagan Moon Deity that was worshipped in Arabia long before the time of Christ. The worship of Allah on the site of the Temple to Yahweh is therefore an abomination.

References to the past with allusions to the future can be seen in these passages, which show the dichotomy of Yahshua's words through to verse 18 of Matthew Chapter 24. After verse 18, however, the tone of Yahshua's sermon changes dramatically. In the next verses, He alludes to a future time that sounds quite reminiscent of the past century, when so many false-christs appeared and tried to deceive the world:

> "For then there will be great tribulation, such as has not been since the beginning of the world until this time, no, nor ever

# Ch. 11: The Rapture and Woman Clothed with the Sun

*shall be. And unless those days were shortened, no flesh would be saved; but for the elect's sake those days will be shortened. Then if anyone says to you, 'Look, here is the Christ!' or 'There!' do not believe it. For false christs and false prophets will rise and show great signs and wonders to deceive, if possible, even the elect. See, I have told you beforehand. Therefore if they say to you, 'Look, He is in the desert!' do not go out; or 'Look, He is in the inner rooms!' do not believe it. For as the lightning comes from the east and flashes to the west, so also will the coming of the Son of Man be." - Matthew 24:19-27*

This Scripture makes it clear that the Messiah we should be expecting won't be found on Earth in any ordinary situation such as living in a house like Yahshua did during His First Advent, or out in the desert like John the Baptist. Instead, He will be seen returning from out of the heavens and coming in the clouds with great glory and the swiftness of lightning. By mentioning this, Yahshua makes it clear that verses 19 through 27 of Matthew Chapter 24 aren't directly alluding to the events of the First Century AD. Instead, since the very first verse mentions a great tribulation that will be far worse than anything that has troubled humanity since the beginning of the world until that time, it appears that Yahshua is speaking about the Great Tribulation described in the Book of Revelation. In this tribulation, the entire world will be plunged into a living hell of suffering and misery that would extinguish all life if it were not brought to an abrupt end by Yahshua's return with His angels and saints to fight at the Battle of Armageddon.

Since Yahshua was referring to the Great Tribulation in verse 19, it is natural to assume that the next verses pertain to the Great Tribulation also. Therefore, when verse 29 speaks of "the tribulation of those days", it seems logical to assume that the tribulation it is referring to would be the period immediately after the Battle of Armageddon. But, if Yahshua is referring to the Great Tribulation, then why does He mention all the tribes of the Earth being present to mourn as if they will all still be alive and well at that time?

In truth, this will certainly NOT be the case at the end of the Great Tribulation, when all the cities of the Earth will already be reduced to rubble, every island and mountain will have disappeared, and every fish, tree and blade of grass will have perished! The Great Tribulation will be the most destructive and violent period in Earth's history both in natural disasters and in mankind's hatred of God and His people. Therefore, a huge majority of the remaining people on the Earth will either be dead or living in abject misery - their bodies covered with loathsome sores, their cities toppled into piles of rubble, and their poisoned and fruitless farms scorched to cinders by the Sun. With this in mind, let's read the passage in question pertaining to the Sign of the Son of Man:

> "Immediately after the tribulation of those days the sun will be darkened, and the moon will not give its light; the stars will fall from heaven, and the powers of the heavens will be shaken. Then the sign of the Son of Man will appear in heaven, and then all the tribes of the earth will mourn, and they will see the Son of Man coming on the clouds of heaven with power and great glory. And He will send His angels with a great sound of a trumpet, and they will gather together His elect from the four winds, from one end of heaven to the other." - Matthew 24:29-31

After "the tribulation of those days" in verse 29 is mentioned, we are told that "the sign of the Son of Man" will appear in "heaven," meaning the physical heavens that surround the Earth. Thus, it will be a celestial sign connected to the Gospel in the Stars that will come during a lull in the massive fighting amongst nations seen in World Wars I and II. In addition, we are told that Yahshua will gather His elect from one end of the heavens to the other shortly after at that time. But this will not be the case after the Battle of Armageddon, since Yahshua's elect will accompany Him to fight that battle riding on white horses. Who, then, are Yahshua's angels being sent to gather up?

In other words, "the tribulation of those days" is not referring to the End Time Great Tribulation, but to the century of major wars that occurred in the 20th Century. One major clue that this is indeed the case is where the saints are when the world sees the Son of Man coming in the clouds with power and great glory. Since the angels are sent out to gather all the "elect" - or those who were predestined to be saved - from one end of earth to the other, it means that the dead and living saints have not yet been given their resurrection bodies, or been taken to Heaven in the First Rapture. If this is so, the angels will be gathering up those who are to be taken to Heaven at that time, so this coming of Christ at the time of the Sign of the Son of Man in Heaven will be at the time of the First Rapture, and **not** at the time of the Battle of Armageddon, when the elect will return riding on white horses with Yahshua:

> "Now I saw heaven opened, and behold, a white horse. And He who sat on him was called Faithful and True, and in righteousness He judges and makes war. His eyes were like a flame of fire, and on His head were many crowns. He had a name written that no one knew except Himself. He was clothed with a robe dipped in blood, and His name is called The Word of God.

# Ch. 11: The Rapture and Woman Clothed with the Sun

*And the armies in heaven, clothed in fine linen, white and clean, followed Him on white horses." - Revelation 19:11-14*

In the Book of Revelation, this army of saints is identified as the wife of the Lamb of God, meaning Yahshua's Bride the True Church. There it says:

*"Let us be glad and rejoice and give Him glory, for the marriage of the Lamb has come, and His wife has made herself ready. And to her it was granted to be arrayed in fine linen, clean and bright, for the fine linen is the righteous acts of the saints." - Revelation 19:7-8*

Now, it pays to note here that there is no mention in any of the parallel passages in Matthew, Mark or Luke that describe Yahshua's visible coming in the clouds that suggests that Yahshua is going to vanquish the wicked at that time in the Battle of Armageddon. There is, for example, no mention of Yahshua touching down on the Mount of Olives, or going to the Valley of Jehoshaphat to fight the wicked.

Instead, these passages all suggest that Yahshua is going to come down to the level of the clouds of the heavens to visibly show His Glory while His angels gather His elect saints from one end of the Earth to the other. We can therefore infer that Yahshua is not coming to fight the wicked at this time, but rather to collect and transform those who are anxiously waiting for Him to take them to Heaven in the Rapture. This parallels Yahshua's Ascension into Heaven exactly ten days prior to Pentecost or Shavuot.

Before continuing, it must be stressed here that the Jews count the 49 days between the time of the firstfruits offering and Shavuot incorrectly from the day of Passover rather than the first day of the week following the regular Sabbath during the Feast of Unleavened Bread. Because of this, their Feast of Shavuot or Firstfruits is on the wrong day.

If figured correctly, the offering of the firstfruits of the barley harvest would have been made in the Temple to Yahweh in Jerusalem on Easter or Resurrection Sunday appropriately fell on that exact day in 2011. Because this is the correct date for that offering, Shavuot actually fell on the Sunday of Pentecost on June 12th, 2011 - exactly 50 days from Easter and 3 days before the Blood Moon in the constellation Ophiuchus. Interestingly, Ophiuchus depicts Yahshua and His followers as the Restrainers of the Serpent in Ophiuchus' strong arms. This serpent constellation that is connected to Ophiuchus is called Serpens the Serpent. It signifies the Serpent Seed or followers of Satan, as well as the Rider on the Pale Horse after the First Rapture.

Now, though the First Rapture or Catching Away is tied to Pentecost and the Summer wheat harvest that follows it as a marker of the end of the Age of Grace, no one knows the exact day or hour. Furthermore, Yahshua said that He would come at a time when we least expect it. This means that it will likely not be exactly on Pentecost or any other prescribed holy day such as Yahshua's Ascension day that was ten days prior to Pentecost. Nor will it likely be on the Summer Solstice, despite the fact that many monuments that are connected to the Messianic constellation called Orion point to the Summer Solstice.

What all of the Summer Solstice and Orion-oriented ancient monuments like Stonehenge, Thornborough Henge, the pyramids at Teotihuacán, and the Pyramid complex at Giza in Egypt do strongly suggest, however, is that the Rapture will occur in the summer months between mid-June and mid-September. There are also biblical clues in the Book of Ruth and the Song of Solomon that the Rapture will be in the summertime before the Autumn Jewish Feasts. In addition, the Rapture may come in two stages. I clearly explained my reasons for believing this in the section of this chapter entitled "Come Up Here and Come Away".

Now, in regard to Yahshua's Second Coming, is it possible that Bible Scholars have been mistranslating Matthew Chapter 24, verses 29 through 31 as describing the Second Coming of Christ to do battle with the wicked when it is actually speaking of the Rapture? Could this be the time when Yahshua will come to save the elect from having to suffer through the Great Tribulation, which refers only to the last three and one half years of the seven-year Tribulation? The context of Yahshua's words in Matthew Chapter 24 in relation to the Book of Revelation suggest that the elect saints being gathered up are not going to immediately fight the wicked at that time, but that they will go to Heaven to be with Christ for a time beforehand.

In Chapter 24 of Matthew, there is another clue that the Sign of the Son of Man will appear just before the First Rapture. This clue is given where it says:

> *"But as the days of Noah were, so also will the coming of the Son of Man be. For as in the days before the flood, they were eating and drinking, marrying and giving in marriage, until the day that Noah entered the ark, and did not know until the flood came and took them all away, so also will the coming of the Son of Man be. Then two men will be in the field: one will be taken and the other left. Two women will be grinding at the mill: one will be taken and the other left. Watch therefore, for you do not know what hour your Lord is coming. But know this, that if the master*

*of the house had known what hour the thief would come, he would have watched and not allowed his house to be broken into. Therefore you also be ready, for the Son of Man is coming at an hour you do not expect." - Matthew 24:37-44*

The above passage appears immediately after Yahshua mentions the Sign of the Son of Man and the gathering up of His Bride the True Church from the four winds of Heaven. In it, Yahshua says that the coming of the Son of Man will be a surprise upon an unsuspecting world, and - as clearly shown in the Tribulation article that I referred to at the beginning of this article - there is no way that the world will be unsuspecting of Yahshua's return by the end of the Tribulation! Indeed, there is no way that they will be unsuspecting even fairly early in the Tribulation since the Pole Shift and Crustal Displacement that could potentially wipe out billions of people is connected to the opening of the Sixth Seal in Chapter Six of the Book of Revelation. It is also interesting to note here that Satan is the usurper of Christ who now serves as the ruler or prince of this dark world. Satan is therefore the one being referred to in the above Scripture as "the master of the house." Meanwhile, the thief in this passage is none other than Yahshua our Messiah coming to steal His bride away at night while his enemies are sleeping.

In Matthew 24:37-44, Yahshua makes it clear that those taken to the Third Heaven in the Rapture will be living and working alongside people that they share friendships and familial relationships with but who will be left behind. This strongly implies that these people have similar values and beliefs. Since not all of them will be taken in the Rapture, however, it implies that some are not spiritually ready. Despite the fact that they will likely share conservative Christian cultural values with those who are taken to be with Yahshua, they will not be included because they are carnal, apostate or simply not born again and will need to be refined in the fire of the Great Tribulation, which was referred to by the prophet Jeremiah as Jacob's Trouble:

*"Alas! For that day is great, so that none is like it: it is even the time of Jacob's trouble; but he shall be saved out of it." - Jeremiah 30:7*

Jeremiah also prophesied that this time of trouble for Jacob's descendents would occur after Israel is re-gathered out of exile and returned to the Promised Land:

*"I will surely save you out of a distant place, your descendants from the land of their exile. Jacob will again have peace and security, and no one will make him afraid. I am with you and will save you,' declares Yahweh." - Jeremiah 30:10-11*

It is my belief that Jacob's Trouble is connected to the Tetrad of Blood Moons or Full Lunar Eclipses that will occur in 2014 and 2015 on Passover and Sukkot in both years. To see exactly when these Blood Moons will occur, and what they might mean prophetically, see my Revised 2013 Tribulation Time Chart at my POEM Web Site, and the last chapter of this book. If the time of Israel's greatest distress falls somewhere during these Blood Moons, then this will be a time of spiritual and physical terror for both believing Jews and Gentiles who will become the Tribulation Saints, and this time is rapidly approaching. Indeed, we are certainly living in the very last moments of this apostate Age, and soon Yahweh God will destroy the governments of this world and set up a righteous theocracy that will last for a thousand years.

But, as Yahshua so eloquently warns in Matthew's Gospel, not everyone that calls themselves a believer will get to reign and serve as priests with Christ during the Millennium:

> *"Who then is a faithful and wise servant, whom his master made ruler over his household, to give them food in due season? Blessed is that servant whom his master, when he comes, will find so doing. Assuredly, I say to you that he will make him ruler over all his goods. But if that evil servant says in his heart, 'My master is delaying his coming,' and begins to beat his fellow servants, and to eat and drink with the drunkards, the master of that servant will come on a day when he is not looking for him and at an hour that he is not aware of, and will cut him in two and appoint him his portion with the hypocrites. There shall be weeping and gnashing of teeth." - Matthew 24:45-51*

Though there are many Non-Christians on this planet that reject and revile the message of the Kingdom of God through Christ, there are also many people who were raised with knowledge of the Gospel message, but that are so caught up in the pleasures, cares and worries of this world that they have completely lost their heavenly focus. As such, they are no longer being godly salt and light in the world and are doomed to be left behind in the Rapture and made to suffer through the Tribulation:

~*~ *Isaiah 13:9-11* ~*~
*"Behold, the day of the LORD (Yahweh) comes,*
*Cruel, with both wrath and fierce anger,*
*To lay the land desolate;*
*And He will destroy its sinners from it.*
*For the stars of heaven and their constellations*

## Ch. 11: The Rapture and Woman Clothed with the Sun

*Will not give their light;*
*The sun will be darkened in its going forth,*
*And the moon will not cause its light to shine.*
*"I will punish the world for its evil,*
*And the wicked for their iniquity..."*

"Immediately after the tribulation of those days the sun will be darkened, and the moon will not give its light; the stars will fall from heaven, and the powers of the heavens will be shaken." - Matthew 24:29

"But in those days, after that tribulation, the sun will be darkened, and the moon will not give its light; 25 the stars of heaven will fall, and the powers in the heavens will be shaken. 26 Then they will see the Son of Man coming in the clouds with great power and glory." - Mark 13:24-26

According to the Scriptures listed above, the Sign of the Son of Man will occur shortly after the Sun is darkened, the Moon is turned to blood and the stars fall from heaven - as in a big meteor shower. Interestingly, the Sun was darkened in a full Solar Eclipse for a third consecutive time on the 1st of Av in 2010, with similar eclipses occurring on the 1st of Av in 2008 and 2009. Furthermore, the Total Eclipse of the Sun on the 1st of Av that fell on July 11th, 2010 occurred directly over Easter Island. Then, five months later, on December 21st, 2010, the Moon turned to blood over the sword of the Messianic sign Orion, which is one of several powerful Signs that mark the coming of the Son of Man in power and glory that are found in the Gospel in the Stars. The other two of great importance are Leo the Lion, and Ophiuchus the Serpent Holder.

Now all that may remain is for the world to see the stars fall from the heavens, perhaps as in a meteorite shower that will precede the Sign of the Son of Man. This massive meteor shower could be associated with Comet ISON, or one of several annual meteor showers that are visible in Earth's skies at various times in the year, which could intensify. Significantly, two of the most visible meteor showers annually are the Perseids and Leonids, which are both associated with the Comet Swift-Tuttle. The Perseids radiate outward from the Messianic sign of Perseus the Breaker, which is above the sign of Taurus. These are prominent in late July through mid August every year. Later in the year, around November when Comet ISON will be prominent in Earth's skies, the Leonid meteorite shower originates in the region of the sky governed by the constellation Leo the Lion that signifies Yahshua coming as a conquering king. Significantly, these two meteor showers both fell between the Solar Eclipse of July 11th, 2010 and the Blood Moon of December 21st, 2010 and were reported to be unusually heavy that year!

If the Rapture will be sometime in the autumn or winter of 2013 or sometime in 2014, Scripture suggests that we should expect a heavenly disturbance such as an impressive meteor shower and an accompanying celestial event that will serve as the Sign of the Son of Man in the heavens. If the Rapture is coming soon, it is possible that the sign preceding it will be more spectacular than a simple line-up of planets in the Messianic Zodiac Signs. If so, it may include one or more comets, a Supernova, and/or some strong planetary configurations such as are found in a heavenly Grand Cross like the two that have already occurred in June 2010 and June 2011.

Yet, though the Rapture will likely be marked by a Sign of the Son of Man in the heavens surrounding the Earth that the whole world will see, there is also likely going to be another powerful sign marking Yahshua's true Second Coming to conquer the wicked at the Battle of Armageddon. I believe that this Sign of the Son of Man returning as a conquering king will center on Orion's connection to the pyramids at Giza, which were built to signify not only the belts stars of Orion, but the crucifixion of Christ that paid for all sin. However, the Great Sphinx's connection to the signs Leo and Virgo and to Yahshua as the First and the Last will also come into play. On September 20th, 2017, these special criterions will be fully met via Orion, Leo and Virgo, the Sun and Moon, and the planets Jupiter, Venus and Uranus.

A color illustration depicting this sign is centrally located on my Tribulation Time Chart. It is also shown on pages 718 and 719. The Chart shows the Signs in the Heavens over the next seven years of human history and their connection to the Hallel Psalms consisting of Psalms 110 through 119. These Psalms are traditionally read in Jewish Synagogues on every High Holy Day and appear to be prophetically connected to the years 2010 through 2019. The full chart can be viewed using on the following link to my POEM web site: http://pillar-of-enoch.com/essays/trib-timeline.html. Portions of this chart have been used in the last chapter to explain the End Time Heavenly Signs.

This chart shows the possibility that the beginning and ending years of the seven-year Tribulation may be between the middle of 2011 through to the middle of 2018 based on the amazing line up of three Blood Moons or Full Lunar Eclipses marking the beginning, middle and end of both of these years. In regard to these heavenly signs, it is important to note that Yahshua told His followers to look toward these signs to know when He would come again. This is recorded in the Gospel

# Ch. 11: The Rapture and Woman Clothed with the Sun

of Luke along with the mention of a time of increasing early distress that will suddenly cause men to fear for their lives:

> *"And there will be signs in the sun, in the moon, and in the stars; and on the earth distress of nations, with perplexity, the sea and the waves roaring; men's hearts failing them from fear and the expectation of those things which are coming on the earth, for the powers of heaven will be shaken. Then they will see the Son of Man coming in a cloud with power and great glory. Now when these things begin to happen, look up and lift up your heads, because your redemption draws near." - Luke 21:25-28*

Fascinatingly, though this passage of Scripture begins by focusing on the distress of the nations over the beginning plagues of the Tribulation that will lead to World War III, it ends by encouraging the believers who will be alive to see these troublesome times come to pass that their deliverance from the Earth in the Rapture won't be far off. Instead, they will be redeemed from the suffering of the rest of the Tribulation and carried away to the mansions in Heaven that Yahshua spoke of when He was dying on the Cross and that Yahweh God the Father has prepared for the Bride of His One and Only Begotten Son.

To that I say: "Hallelu-Yah, for that coming day of our redemption from our sinful and decaying bodies of flesh is nearly at hand! Keep looking up, my brothers and sisters in Christ, for Yahshua is coming for us in the Rapture very soon!"

## The Woman Clothed With The Sun And Comet ISON

In this section of the book, my aim is to focus on the heavenly signs surrounding another Woman in Heaven who is the exact opposite of the Harlot described in Chapter 10 of this book. She is seen in the sign of Virgo the Virgin, and she is connected not only to Mary, the mother of Yahshua, but to the Church that sprang from Yahshua's beautiful and radical teachings. In sharp contrast to the Harlot riding the Scarlet Beast in Revelation Chapter 17, this section of the book will reveal the meaning of some amazing signs appearing in Virgo, the Woman Clothed with the Sun in the closing months of 2013.

Comet ISON (C/2012 S1), which was discovered in September of 2012, Comet Lovejoy (C/2013 R1), which was discovered in September 2013 and three other comets that are now coming into view may figure into the correct identification of the year when Virgo will fulfill the role as the messianic sign of the Woman Clothed with the Sun that is tied to the

Rapture, as well as being part of the Sign of the Son of Man, and one of the End Time heavenly signs that Yahshua told us to watch for in the Sun, Moon and stars (Luke 21:25).

Comet ISON is still on track to be the Comet of the Century as far as heavenly showmanship. In addition, a previously discovered periodic comet called 2P/Encke will be faintly visible in Earth's skies at the same time as Comets ISON and Lovejoy. Like the other comets, Comet Encke will be visible from October 2013 through Chanukah and the Christmas Season. Interestingly, Comet Encke was the second periodic comet discovered after Halley's Comet, and it has been linked to destructive events on the Earth. In fact, it has been postulated that the exploding object that was behind the highly destructive Tunguska Event of 1908 may have been a piece of Comet Encke.

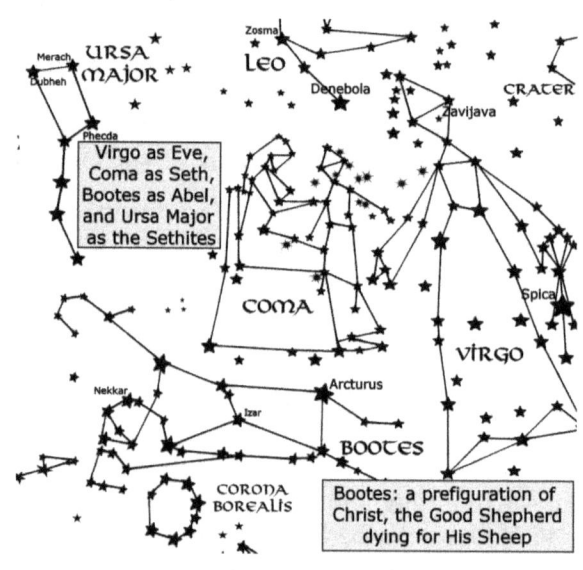

This is no surprise, since Encke was the Lord of the Earth to the Babylonians. This position belongs to Christ alone, however, so Encke symbolizes Christ's authority being usurped by Satan in the world today. But the good news is that Comet ISON's appearance suggests that Christ's coming to catch away His saints, mete out God's Wrath and regain His full authority over all the Earth is imminent!

In addition, these three comets have been joined by a fourth named Comet LINEAR C2012 X1, which was discovered in December of 2012. On October 21st, 2013, Comet LINEAR showed an outburst in brightness in the constellation Coma (or Coma Berenices), the Desired Son, which is symbolically connected to Yahshua's First Coming. In fact, Coma was anciently depicted as an enthroned woman with a little boy in her lap, as shown in the graphic above. Furthermore, the identity of that little boy is clearly tied to Christ in that Coma is a decan of Virgo, which

## Ch. 11: The Rapture and Woman Clothed with the Sun

depicts the virgin mother of Yahshua, as well as the congregation of believers who love and follow Him.

Before I continue, I want to stress here that having four comets in view simultaneously is a positively **unprecedented** event. In fact, having two prominent comets visible in the same region of the sky is a relatively rare event, and having three comets appear at once is extremely rare. But there has **never** been an incidence of four comets being visible in the sky at the same time ever in recorded history! But even more remarkable is the fact that there is a fifth comet now visible in the sky that is not in the general vicinity of the other four, but has just as important a story to tell.

This is Comet Brewington (152P), and though it's a fairly dim comet with a maximum apparent magnitude of only 8 at its brightest, it's still remarkable in that it bumps our comet count for November 2013 up to 5 visible comets, and that moves this sign from unprecedented with 4 comets visible into the realm of the **impossible**! It's also interesting to note that Comet Brewington will be moving through Aquarius the Water-Bearer - the sign of God's mercy and judgment, and the Holy Spirit - in November, and Pegasus, the White Horse for the King of kings in December! As such, it's another **clear sign** that Yahshua is coming very soon on His White Horse (Pegasus) to retrieve His Spirit-Filled Bride (Aquarius!).

In addition to being dazzled by the sight of five comets during the 2013 Holiday Season, the Earth will pass through the debris field of Comet ISON's tail around January 12th through 15th, 2014. During these three days, the Earth will likely be bombarded by many large and small size meteoroids. Ominously, because Comet ISON is so large, these meteors may not only light up the entire sky surrounding the Earth, but rain fiery havoc on the surface of our planet when some of these burning balls of debris survive their trip through our atmosphere. Since the Earth will pass through Comet ISON's debris field, it suggests a connection to the amazing Prophetic Dream I had in the summer of 2011 that is recollected at the end of this chapter. It also suggests a connection to the stars falling from heaven that are associated with the Sixth Seal Judgment - when the Wrath of God begins to be poured out from Heaven.

Interestingly, both of the new comets ISON and Lovejoy were discovered in the month of September. This is the month most often associated with the Feast of Tabernacles or Sukkot. September is also the time marking the final harvesting of crops in Israel and many other countries. As such, September and Sukkot are allusions to God's End Time Harvest of Souls that Yahshua described in the Parable of the Wheat and the Tares, which is explored in Book Two and on my POEM Blog.

Though this parable has many deeper meanings, Yahshua gave its most basic interpretation as follows:

> *"The field is the world, the good seeds are the sons of the kingdom, but the tares are the sons of the wicked one. The enemy who sowed them is the devil, the harvest is the end of the age, and the reapers are the angels."* - Matthew 13:38-40

Fascinatingly, this interpretation of the parable connects it directly to Matthew, Chapter 24's description of Yahshua gathering of His elect from one end of heaven to the other after the Sign of the Son of Man appears in heaven. As such, these comets may be heralds for the coming of the Two Witnesses, and they may also have something to do with the Sign of the Son of Man:

> *"Immediately after the tribulation of those days, the sun will be darkened, and the moon will not give its light; the stars will fall from heaven, and the powers of the heavens will be shaken. 30 Then the sign of the Son of Man will appear in heaven, and then all the tribes of the earth will mourn, and they will see the Son of Man coming on the clouds of heaven with power and great glory. 31 And He will send His angels with a great sound of a trumpet, and they will gather together His elect from the four winds, from one end of heaven to the other."* - Matthew 24:29-31

The term "sign" refers to the constellations and celestial bodies in the heavens (Genesis 1:14), and the term "Son of Man" refers to Yahshua's humanity (Matthew 11:18-19). So, we need to look at the moment in time when Yahshua became a man to find the signs of His coming. This was when He was conceived in Miriam's womb, and when He was born. Since my research has shown that Yahshua was born around Yom Kippur or Sukkot in 3 BC when the Sun was in Virgo, He would have been conceived right around the time of Chanukah in 4 BC, when the Sun was in Sagittarius. In modern times, Sukkot is still often when the Sun is in Virgo, but Chanukah most often falls when the Sun is in Scorpio, which is dominated by the constellation Ophiuchus.

Scripture clearly states that the Sign of the Son of Man will appear in the heavens. From my knowledge of Sacred Astronomy, it would make sense for God to tie this sign to the constellations that refer to Yahshua's conception and birth, and possibly also to His passion, death and resurrection. Intriguingly, the Comet ISON (C/2012 S1) is making an appearance in the constellations of Virgo and Ophiuchus, which directly relate to Yahshua's beginning or birth in Bethlehem, and His temporary end or crucifixion at Golgotha.

## Ch. 11: The Rapture and Woman Clothed with the Sun

In addition, Comet Lovejoy (C/2013 R1) was first spotted in line with the stars of Orion's Belt on September 9th, 2013, and Orion is a powerful Messianic Sign relating to the terror and triumph of Yahshua's crucifixion. Likewise, Comet LINEAR (C/2012 X1) just brightened considerably in the constellation Coma, which depicts the Virgin Miriam with her son Yahshua in her lap! Fascinatingly, Comets ISON, Encke, Lovejoy and LINEAR will be making an appearance together in the same regions of the sky from October 2013 though January 2014, and together, they tell an amazing spiritual story.

So now that we have determined that the Sign of the Son of Man is a heavenly sign that ought to be connected to Virgo and/or Ophiuchus or Orion in some way, and we have identified that three of the four comets that are appearing over the 2013 Holiday Season may be directly related to this sign (ISON, Lovejoy and LINEAR), we need to determine when this Sign will appear. As to when, I have found proof that the reference to the gathering of the elect at the time of the Sign of the Son of Man is not a reference to Christ's return to fight the Battle of Armageddon, which will come later. Instead, it is referring to Yahshua's coming for His Elect Bride and her Five Wise handmaidens before the Great Tribulation begins.

My reason for believing this has to do with a study comparing the terrible plagues and condition of the world revealed in the Book of Revelation with the end time plagues and living conditions mentioned in Matthew, Chapter 24. This study led me to understand that there is no possibility that anyone but the nation of Israel, which God will protect, and the elite hidden away in their bunkers, will be engaging in commerce, marrying, preparing food, or tending fields in a leisurely fashion after the Sixth Seal is opened during the Great Tribulation.

In contrast, Matthew 24:36-42 clearly says that people will calmly be engaging in these tasks when the Sign of the Son of Man appears in Heaven! This means that the coming of Christ for His elect spoken of Matthew, Chapter 24 is not a Post-Tribulation event, but is prior to the pouring out of God's Wrath from Heaven beginning with the Sixth Seal Judgment. To see my complete study on this topic, please read the section of this book entitled: "Why the Post Tribulation Rapture View Doesn't Make Sense".

Preliminary scientific findings show that Comet ISON is a massive comet that is likely to survive its trip around the Sun, and it will be making an impressive show in the heavens with a very long and bright coma and tail in the late autumn of 2013 and early winter of 2013 and 2014. In fact, it is already being compared to the Great Comet of 1680, with which the Comet ISON shares a similar trajectory. Though there is a great deal of uncertainty connected to the survival of any sun grazing comet, Comet ISON could be a once in a lifetime event, which is why the media is lauding it as the Comet of the Century.

The illustration of Comet ISON at Perihelion on page 316 in Chapter 8 (which is also shown on my Tribulation Timeline in the next chapter), shows Comet ISON, Comet LINEAR, and Comet Encke's possible meanings as ISON reaches Perihelion on November 28th, 2013. Intriguingly, this is the first of the eight days of Chanukah, as well as Thanksgiving Day in the United States - a holiday with plenty of allegorical associations with the Feast of Sukkot or Tabernacles.

While the Feast of Sukkot signifies the ingathering of the saints in Yahshua's Millennial Kingdom, the Feast of Chanukah marks the time of the rededication of the Temple to Yahweh in Jerusalem in ancient times. Since ancient times, Chanukah has also been lauded as "the Festival of Light" because of the miracle of the Temple Menorah that reportedly burned for eight days on one day's worth of oil. As such, Chanukah has an allegorical connection to the Foolish Virgins, who did not have enough oil (i.e. the Holy Spirit) in their lamps, and are left behind when Yahshua comes for His Bride in the Rapture.

Interestingly, on November 23rd, 2013, just before Comet ISON reaches Perihelion, the Sun will be crowning the head of Scorpio the Scorpion signifying Satan, Comet Encke will be in neighboring Libra the Scales of God's Justice, Comet ISON will be crowning Libra, Comet Linear will have passed from Coma, signifying Yahshua as the promised Seed of the Woman, into the constellation Bootes, which signifies Yahshua as a Good Shepherd and Reaper of Choice Wheat (i.e. believers).

Meanwhile, Comet Lovejoy will have just passed from Ursa Major the Big Sheep Pen full of God's Good Sheep into Canes Venatici, which is connected to Bootes the Good Shepherd as his shepherd dogs, which allegorically represents all preachers of truth who follow Yahshua. Meanwhile, Comet Brewington will be in the head region of the celestial horse Pegasus representing the proud white steed bearing Yahshua our King, and the trusty mounts of His saints. Therefore, the message hidden in the paths of these five comets on November 23rd, 2013 could read: "The Son of Man, Good Shepherd, and Master of Justice is coming on His trusty white steed to rescue His Good Sheep and the Good Preachers that guide them to do justice because they bring Him love and joy!"

The graphic depicting this moment in time, and its possible prophetic meaning appears on page 578. This graphic shows that four

## Ch. 11: The Rapture and Woman Clothed with the Sun

comets will be visible as the Sun enters Scorpio at the end of November. Though the Sun will move into the far more benevolent portion of Scorpio dominated by the constellation Ophiuchus in mid December, its time spent in Scorpio's head will be highlighted by Comet ISON and the Feast of Chanukah. This is surely no accident, but is very likely meant to be a message from Yahweh God for His People Israel that have learned to read the heavenly signs as a herald of His coming. Intriguingly, Chanukah coincides with Yahshua's conception in the Virgin Miriam's womb in December of 4 BC. It also may have coincided with the appearance of the Star of Bethlehem. Since Scripture suggests that the Wise Men found Yahshua when He was already a young toddler, it may have been near to the time of Chanukah in 2 BC, which was a little over a year after Yahshua was born in September of 3 BC.

Since Comet ISON will be making a spectacular show in Scorpio during Chanukah of 2013, it can be likened to another Star of Bethlehem. Only this time, it may be heralding another stunning blow to Satan's head when Yahshua comes for His Bride, with Comet ISON depicting the coming Wedding Procession of the Lamb to His Father's House rather than the birth of the Lamb of God in a Sukkah on Yom Kippur.

Shortly after it reaches Perihelion, ISON will pass through Ophiuchus, and Ophiuchus depicts Christ's Crucifixion. What's more, Yahshua's sacrificial death delivered a massive blow to Satan's Head by satisfying God's demand for Justice, which allowed God to extend His Grace to humanity, and to give each person a chance to find everlasting life, and to commune with God and find His protection and help until then. Since Scorpio and Ophiuchus depict this massive blow to Satan's plans to annihilate humanity, it seems fitting that it may also depict the second biggest blow to Satan's Head just before the Rapture occurs. Though there is no way of knowing exactly when the Rapture will happen, it could be this Chanukah, or sometime shortly thereafter.

In relation to the Son of God, it is interesting to note that the nickname of Comet C/2013 S1, which is "ISON", can be rendered "I Son". This is suggestive of Yahshua's Name "I AM", as well His roles as the Son of God and the Son of Man. So, if (and only if) Comet ISON survives its trip around our Sun, what this snapshot of the heavens on November 28th, 2013 may be showing is that the Son of Man (ISON) is soon going to come against Satan (Scorpio) on behalf of God's people Israel. In the near future, beginning with the Sixth Seal Judgment heralding the beginning of God's Wrath, Yahshua will punish the wicked that have repeatedly mocked and persecuted God's people.

# The Language of God in Prophecy

## Four Comets Tell A Prophetic Story, Nov. 23rd, 2013

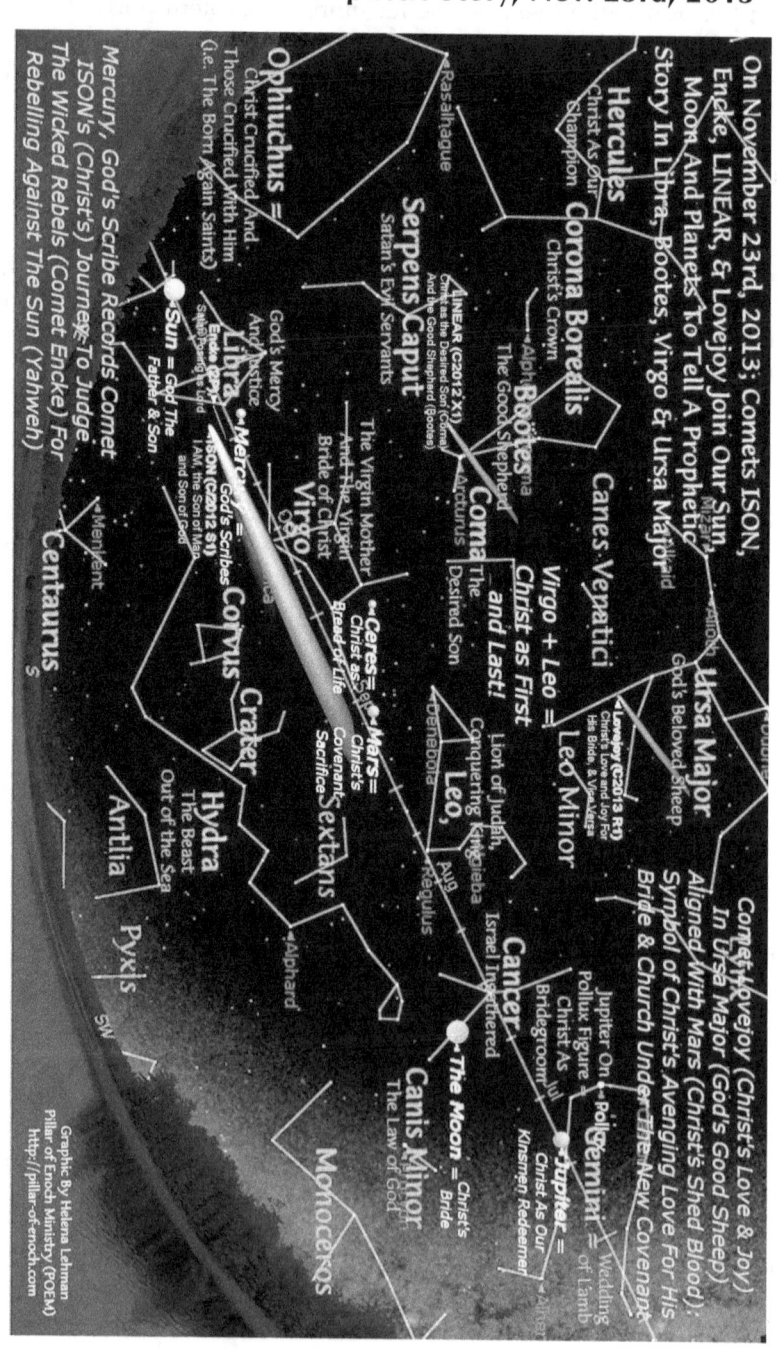

## Ch. 11: The Rapture and Woman Clothed with the Sun

Like Comet ISON, Comet Lovejoy has its own fascinating story to tell. For example, Comet Lovejoy (C/2013 R1) was officially discovered in line with Orion's Belt (the 3 Crosses on Calvary) on September 9th, 2013 (9-9). This is interesting because Orion depicts Yahshua as a Conquering King who found victory over Satan when He died for humanity's sins on the Cross, with the three bright stars in Orion's Belt signifying the three crosses on Calvary. Furthermore, the number 9 is connected to Chanukah by the nine branches of the special Menorah used during the Feast. Significantly, Chanukah always begins on Kislev 25, and Kislev is the 9th month on the Jewish Calendar - and the month when Yahshua was likely conceived. This is even more amazing if we note that Yahshua was born 9 months later in September of 3 BC. The number 9 is therefore connected to God's love and mercy - even though it is also connected to Biblical Judgment in the rejection of either God the Father or His Son Yahshua.

What's more, Comet Lovejoy will be prominent in the Constellation Ursa Major (the Good Sheep Pen) at the same time that Comet ISON is in Libra the Scales of Yahshua's Sacrificial Love and Justice around November 23rd through 26th. Together, Comet ISON and Lovejoy therefore appear to be saying: "I, the Son, am coming as a Conquering Prince, with Love and Joy to rescue my Good Sheep from the clutches of Satan!"

In addition to its powerful prophetic position at Perihelion, Comet ISON tells an amazing story with its trajectory. This became apparent to me when I saw how ISON stayed in Gemini for the first half of 2013. This is the Sign of reconciliation between warring siblings (Ishmael and Isaac; Jacob and Esau), and also of the betrothal of the Bride of Christ and the Wedding of the Lamb that ends these conflicts. Comet ISON then passed through the Beehive Cluster in Cancer in August of 2013. This is the sign of God's sheep pen of born again believers, and the Beehive Cluster is often seen as a manger (the Bread of Life) for the two bright stars on either side of the cluster that were seen as two donkeys in ancient times.

The two bright central stars in Cancer were envisioned as two donkeys by the Jews as a visual representation of the patriarch Jacob's death bed prophecy connecting the Tribe of Judah and Shiloh or the Messiah to two donkeys:

### ~ Genesis 49:10-11 ~
"The scepter shall not depart from Judah,
Nor a lawgiver from between his feet,
Until Shiloh comes;
And to Him shall be the obedience of the people.

> 11 Binding his donkey to the vine,
> And his donkey's colt to the choice vine,
> He washed his garments in wine,
> And his clothes in the blood of grapes."

Interestingly, this may be why Yahshua, as the promised Shiloh, rode into Jerusalem on two donkeys - a mother and its foal: *"They brought the donkey and the colt, laid their clothes on them, and set Him on them"* (Matthew 21:7). This may have been done in an allusion to Cancer and its connection to the Messiah. Fascinatingly, the donkeys allegorically signify Judah and Ephraim, the Two Houses of Israel, and Yahshua - as their rider - is their Master. In this way, Israel is depicted as two stubborn donkeys that eat out of the same feeding trough (the Bible and Yahshua as the Word of God), in God's Sheep Pen called Cancer or the Kingdom of God. This also shows how Israel is often working at cross-purposes to God's will, though they may be doing so unwittingly.

Next, Comet ISON passed through Leo the Lion in September 2013, and Leo is the sign alluding to Yahshua as the Lion of Judah, and the King of kings over God's Kingdom. At this point, I was very intrigued when I discovered that Comet ISON was nearly in conjunction with Mars in Leo on October 6th, 2013. This is interesting from a prophetic standpoint because of what happened in neighboring Virgo on that day. In a clear allusion to Revelation Chapter 12's Woman Clothed with the Sun - the Sun was in Virgo's body, and the New Moon was at her feet! Furthermore, the Sun and Moon were in the same relative positions that they were in over 2000 years before - on September 11th, 3 BC, when an uncannily similar sign announced the imminent birth of Christ! On pages 581 through 583 are graphics showing the similarity of the Heavenly Signs on September of 3 BC and October of 2013, followed by a composite graphic showing the Woman Clothed with the Sun combined with Comet ISON's position from early October through late November 2013.

Revelation 12's Woman Clothed with the Sun is connected to Virgo on the Feast of Trumpets on September 11th, 3 BC, which was around the time that Yahshua was born. Fascinatingly, ISON passed through Virgo in October of 2013, and Virgo is the sign of the Jewish Mother and Gentile Bride of Christ. As shown in my 440-page research book "The Language of God in the Universe", which goes into great detail about the godly meanings of the constellations, the first Sign of the Son of Man was apparent in the Sign of Virgo, which partially depicts Yahshua's Virgin mother Miriam.

## Ch. 11: The Rapture and Woman Clothed with the Sun

## Comet ISON And The Woman Clothed With The Sun

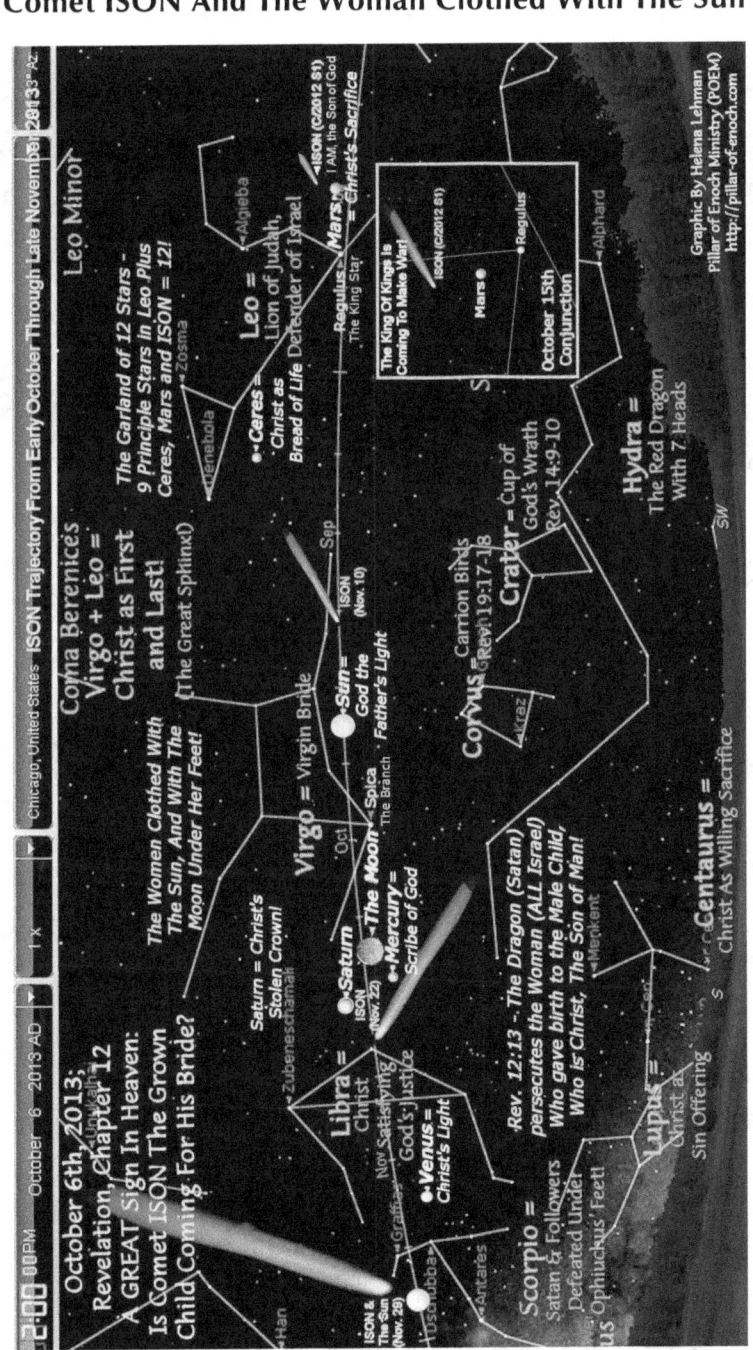

## Woman Clothed with the Sun, September 3 BC

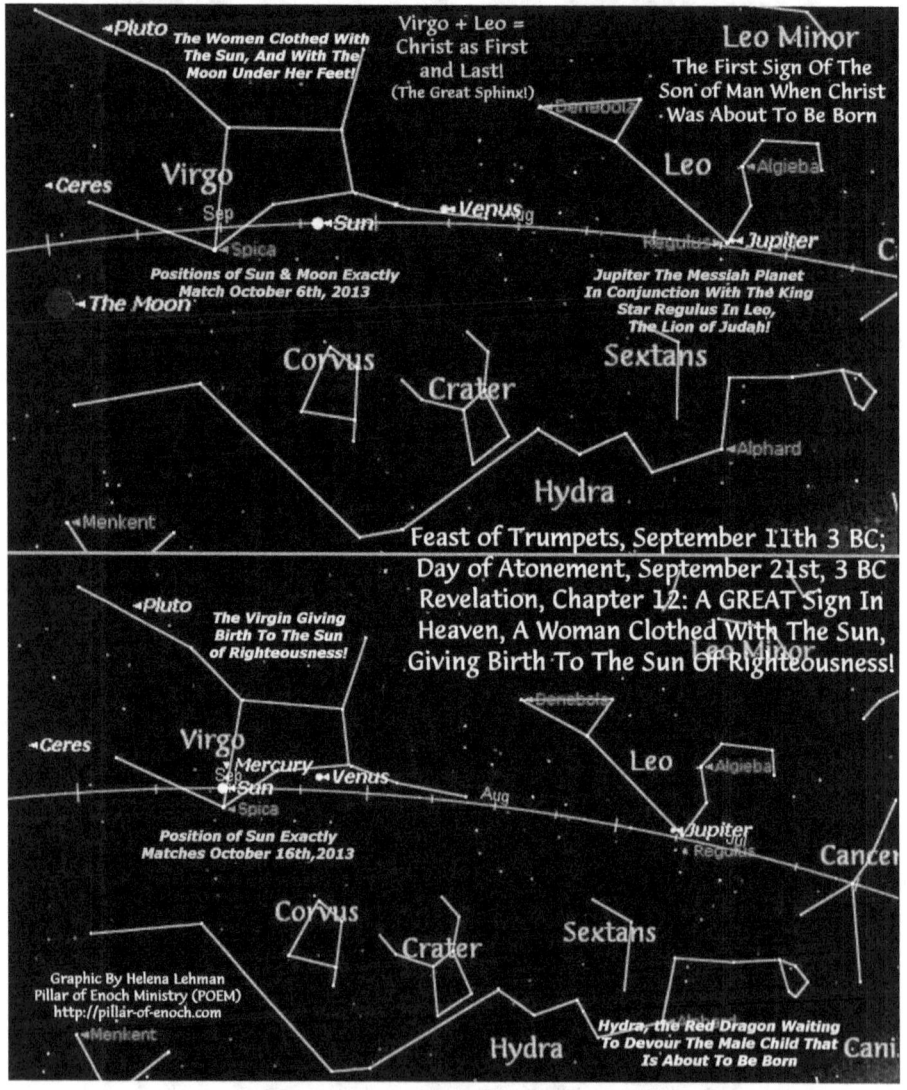

However, Virgo signifies the Bride of Christ rather than Miriam at this time in history, and Leo now signifies Yahshua coming as the King of kings in Glory rather than humbly - as He did in September of 3 BC. That is why Virgo's appearance as the Woman Clothed with the Sun and with the Moon under her feet on October 6th, 2013 is so exciting. Furthermore, the Signs of Virgo and Leo - as the first and last signs of the Ancient Zodiac - symbolize Yahshua as the First and the Last, a Title that He is given no less than four times in the Book of Revelation (Rev. 1:11, Rev. 1:17, Rev. 2:8, Rev. 22:13). Incidentally, this is what the Great Sphinx at Giza was originally meant to depict - Yahshua as the First and the Last.

## Woman Clothed with the Sun, October 2013

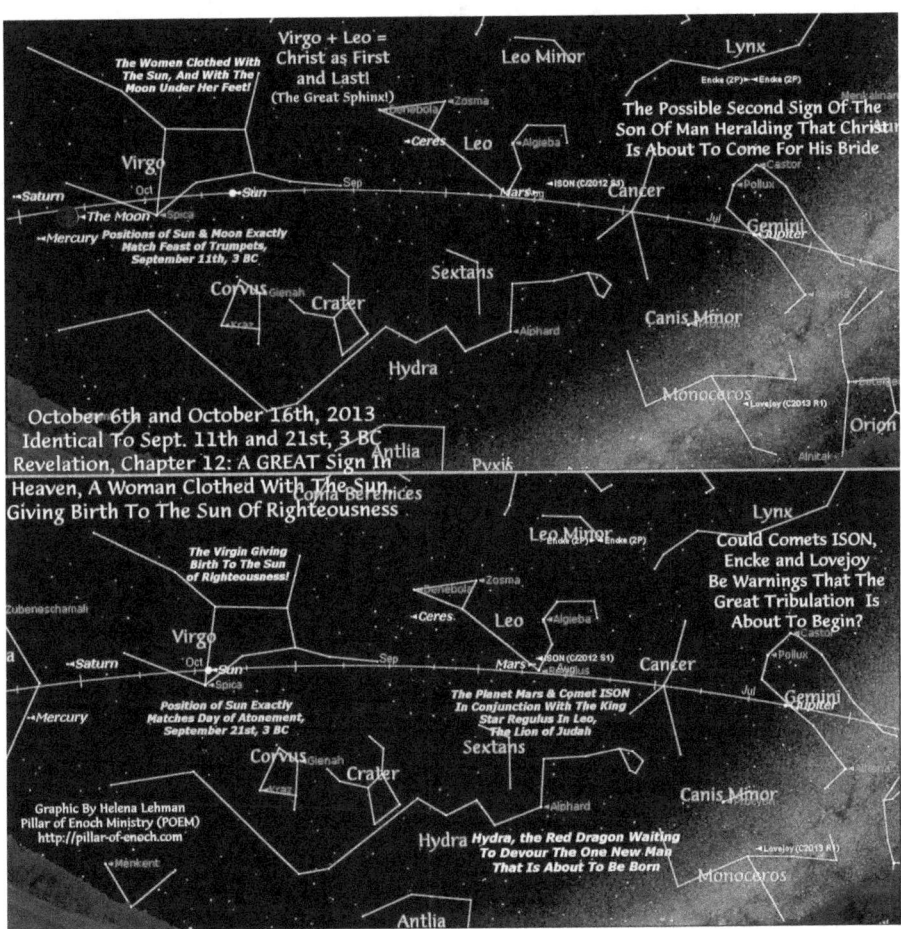

Fascinatingly, the Sign in the Heavens on Yom Kippur on September 21st, 3 BC may have signified that Yahshua was about to be born. At that time, the Red Dragon or Satan signified by Hydra the Serpent represented Satan, who sought to destroy Yahshua with Herod the Great's slaughter of the innocents (See Matthew 2:16-18). In mimicry of that moment in time, the Sign on October 16th, 2013 could be signifying that the baby about to be born is the One New Man spoken of in Ephesians 2:14-16. In other words, this could be a herald that the Rapture may be imminent.

Meanwhile, the Red Dragon or Satan is already busy inspiring the wicked to persecute, kill, and destroy born-again Christians all over the world today, thereby earning them their share in the Cup of God's coming Wrath. The new Nova discovered in the constellation Delphinus in August of 2013, which I wrote about at my POEM Blog - coupled with an increase in mysterious dolphin deaths all over the world - is a sign we have been given that highlights the plight of Christian martyrs and their families all over the world.

Though October 6th, 2013 is not on the Feast of Trumpets, the Sun is in the body of Virgo, and the Moon is at her feet - as the graphic focusing on the heavens on that day shows, and they are in the exact same positions that they were in on September 11th, 3 BC. What's more, this sign in Virgo occurred nine days before the Comet ISON, the Red Planet Mars, and the King Star Regulus were in conjunction in the sign of Leo on October 15th and 16th. So, if October 6th is seen as a type of the Feast of Trumpets, this would make October 16th, 2013 a symbolic Yom Kippur or the Day of Atonement. The illustrations on pages 582 and 583 show the strong similarities between the Sign of Yahshua's imminent birth in September of 3 BC and the Sign of the Woman Clothed with the Sun in October of 2013.

From examining the position of the Sun in September of 3 BC, I believe that Yahshua was actually born on Yom Kippur that year. This is because the Sun representing Yahshua was in conjunction with the star Spica in Virgo on September 21st, 3 BC, and this star marks the symbolic birth canal in Virgo. Fascinatingly, the Sun was also in conjunction with the star Spica on October 16th. Therefore, the Sign on October 6th through 16th, 2013 in Virgo may be a significant part of the Sign of the Son of Man that is meant to alert the Bride of Christ that her Bridegroom is coming, and the Rapture may be imminent - although it is uncertain when the Rapture will actually happen.

Now, drawing on my knowledge of Sacred Astronomy, I see this triple conjunction in Leo over the head of the constellation Hydra as an obvious allusion to our Messiah and King of kings (Leo, ISON and Regulus) coming to wage war with the Devil (Hydra, which can be seen as the Red Dragon or a large Serpent) over broken Covenants (Mars). Since Yahshua is Israel's and Judah's Kinsmen Redeemer and Avenger of Blood, Comet ISON - with its long, bright tail - can be seen as a sword of vengeance in Yahshua's mighty right hand!

## Ch. 11: The Rapture and Woman Clothed with the Sun

From Virgo, Comet ISON will pass into Libra the Scales of Justice in November 2013. Libra is the sign of God's Justice being met by Yahshua's perfect Blood Sacrifice, which is depicted in the Sign of Ophiuchus, whose right foot is above Scorpio's head.

Thus, the heavens depict the fact that Yahshua delivered a fatal blow to Satan's plans when He sacrificed Himself on the Cross to pay for our sins. At that time, Yahshua satisfied God the Father's demand for perfect justice. Because Yahshua never sinned during His mortal human walk, His blood sacrifice perfectly took away the heaviness of our sins so that we can be perfectly weighed in the balance with God's Spirit. But for those who reject Christ, there is no balance, as their sin is not blotted out by Yahshua's blood. Therefore, only judgment and damnation await them.

On November 3rd, 2013, there was a very rare Hybrid Solar Eclipse or Sackcloth Sun in the Sign of Libra the Scales of Justice that is ripe with prophetic meaning, as seen in the graphic on page 586. At the time of this eclipse, which appeared to be partial in some areas and total in others, three comets - Encke, LINEAR, and ISON - were in the same region of the sky, although these comets were not currently bright enough to be visible until dusk or before dawn.

This is an extremely rare event, especially since the fourth and fifth comets Lovejoy and Brewington were visible in the evening in neighboring regions of the sky, and five comets in the sky at once is an unprecedented, practically "impossible" event! At the time of the Eclipse, according to projections, Comet ISON will be the brightest comet of them all, and it will be visible near to the planet Mars - the symbol of Yahshua's Blood Sacrifice and New Covenant. Conversely, Mars can also be a sign of war when Christ's Blood Covenant with us is broken by the lost and the wicked.

At the time of this Hybrid Eclipse, the likes of which have only happened seven times since the birth of Christ, Mars was in the Sign of Leo, the Lion of Judah - a sign that is tied to Yahshua coming to conquer the wicked. Meanwhile, Comet Encke - a symbol of Satan usurping God's Authority - was ominously poised as if it is about to be "born" in Virgo's belly. Could this have been a sign of the full blown evil that will be born after the Rapture, just as the Sun being born in Virgo in October was a sign of the birth of the One New Man in Christ?

# The Language of God in Prophecy

## Meaning of November 3rd, 2013 Solar Eclipse in Libra

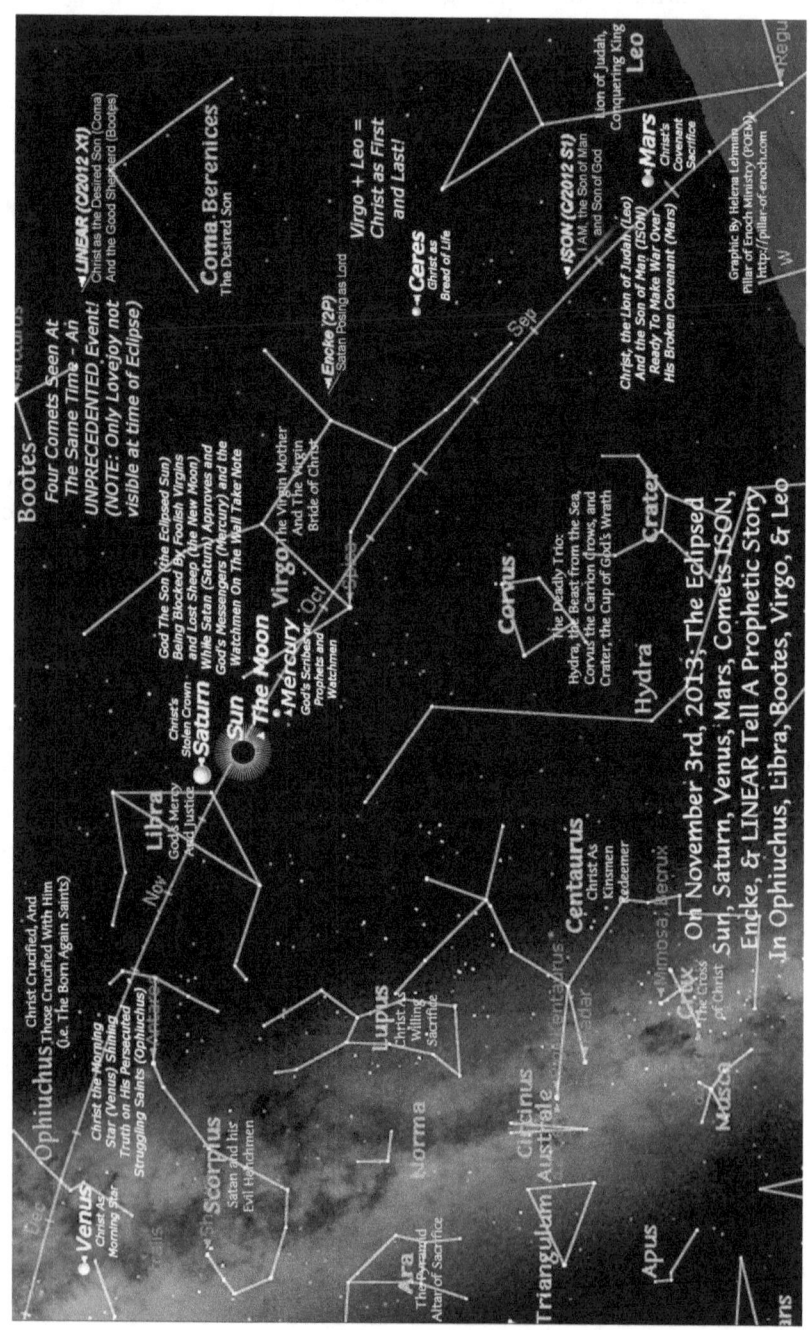

# Ch. 11: The Rapture and Woman Clothed with the Sun

Also at the time of the eclipse, the preceding graphic shows that the Sun, Moon, Mercury and Saturn were beneath Virgo's feet in Libra, the Scales of God's Mercy, Wrath and Justice. The Sun signifies God the Father as well as the Son of God, and the Moon partly signifies Yahshua's Bride. But when it covers the Sun in an eclipse, the Moon signifies those who may think that they are doing God's will, but are actually obstructing it! Meanwhile Saturn was also near to the Sun and Moon, and it is the symbol of Yahshua's Kingship and His gifts of Peace and Rest that have been usurped temporarily by Satan.

This indicates that Satan is the thief who inspires many to steel Christ's Crown and His Peace with their political and religious aspirations that oppose the reign and rule of Christ as King of kings. Meanwhile, the planet Mercury signifies the Scribes, Prophets, Watchmen and Messengers of God who are witnessing this sign and announcing its importance. Due to what Mercury represents, its close proximity to the November 3rd Solar Eclipse indicates that this is a highly important sign, especially for the people living in the islands of the Atlantic Ocean and in central Africa, where this eclipse will be best seen. Incidentally, many believers in Yahshua in central Africa are suffering under persecution and poor living conditions due to their faith in Him.

Altogether, Comet ISON will pass through Gemini, Cancer, Leo, Virgo and Libra before it reaches Perihelion on November 28th, 2013. On that day, it will be in conjunction with our Sun (God the Father) in the head of Scorpio, the sign signifying Satan and his wicked followers on the Earth. From this, I realized that - if ISON survives its close proximity to the Sun - it may be meant to show the world that God's Son (I-SON) is coming to save His Betrothed Bride and promised Wife (Gemini and Virgo) and gather His born-again Sheep (Cancer) to bring them to the Kingdom of God in Heaven (Leo) before Judging the World (Libra) and destroying the Wicked (Scorpio) with the Power of Yahweh God's Might (the Sun).

And this is NOT all! If Comet ISON survives its trajectory, it will cut through the wicked Serpent struggling against the mighty arms of the Messianic sign of Ophiuchus on December 3rd through 6th, 2013. As such ISON will allegorically cut the constellation Serpens in half! Then, on Christmas of 2013, Comet ISON will be prominently visible in the constellation called Hercules the Strongman - with Comet Lovejoy in close proximity in the same constellation. An illustration showing more about the meanings of Hercules in relation to neighboring constellations appears on page 500.

## ISON Cutting Serpens And Draco In Half

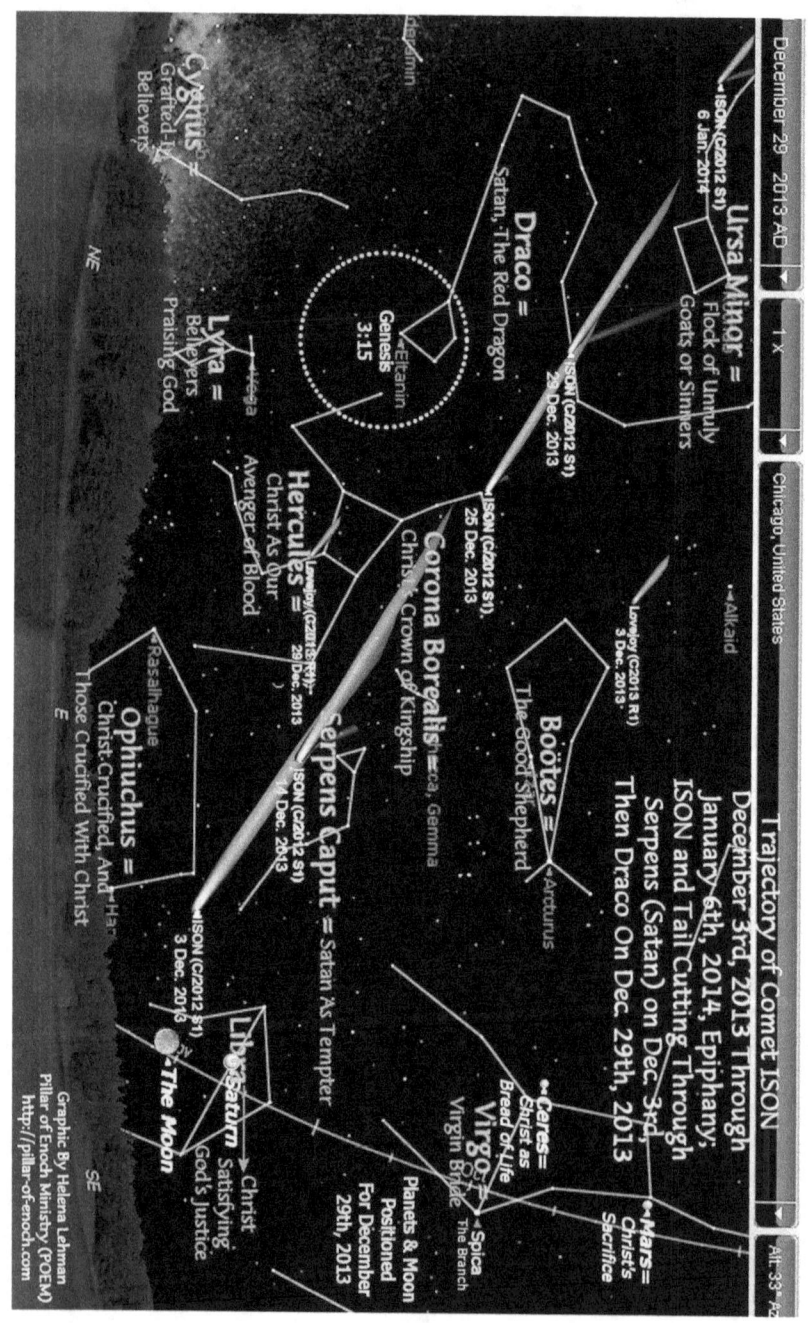

# Ch. 11: The Rapture and Woman Clothed with the Sun

Since Hercules is another allusion to Yahshua as the Mighty Man of God who conquers the wicked, these two comets in Hercules may be meant to herald the protective and defensive power of Christ's love and joy for His Bride, and the love and joy that the Bride of Christ feels toward her Bridegroom, Kinsmen Redeemer, and Avenger of Blood. Incidentally, Christmas and Chanukah are analogous to one another in God's eyes, so this is a great potential Rapture watch period. Then, just as it will do to the Satanic sign Serpens in early December, Comet ISON will cut through the body of Draco the Dragon on December 29th, 2013 - symbolically cutting this Dragon in half. Like Hydra, Draco depicts the Red Dragon of the Book of Revelation coming against God's people Israel.

However, this allegorical cutting of Serpens and Draco in half may be a symbolic indication that Satan will lose half of his followers after the Rapture, and these newly saved multitudes will work against his schemes, or die trying! This severing in half of the heavenly serpent and dragon is therefore a powerful and hopeful sign, showing that God intends to use His Tribulation Saints on Earth represented by Ophiuchus and Hercules to give a fatal blow to Satan's plans. In fact, this severing through the most evil Signs in Heaven likely is meant to relate to the further description of events in Revelation, Chapter 12 - after the Sign of the Woman Clothed with the Sun appears:

> *"And war broke out in heaven: Michael and his angels fought with the dragon; and the dragon and his angels fought, 8 but they did not prevail, nor was a place found for them in heaven any longer. 9 So the great dragon was cast out, that serpent of old, called the Devil and Satan, who deceives the whole world; he was cast to the earth, and his angels were cast out with him."* - Revelation 12:7-9

The allegorical slaying of these serpents in heaven may symbolically signify this War in Heaven, and the fact that Satan is going to step up his persecution of all who side with Yahweh God after the Rapture. It also may indicate that Yahshua's servants on Earth signified by Ophiuchus and Hercules are going to do God's Will by aligning themselves against Satan's minions represented by Scorpio, Serpens and Draco. Therefore, ISON's path appears to be heralding that the Tribulation Saints don't have much longer to wait before our Father God Yahweh exposes Satan's evil plans, fully awakens the left-behind Foolish Virgins to the truth with the Rapture, and prepares to cut the unrepentant wicked off from the face of the Earth when they reject the testimony of the 144,000 and the Two Witnesses.

A month later, on January 6th, it will be Epiphany - and the official end of the 12 days of Christmas. At this time, Comet ISON is being projected to still be visible, but much fainter. It will appear in the center of the visible arm of the Milky Way Galaxy, just above Perseus the Breaker, which represents Yahshua coming to break Satan's delusions and deceptions that are being used to fool and destroy mankind.

After this, whether Comet ISON survives its visit around our Sun or not, it is likely that Earth's orbit will pass through the debris stream left by Comet's ISON's prominent coma and tail from January 12th through 15th, 2014. This may result in a spectacular meteor shower that will be seen around the world for at least three days. If there is a great deal of particle matter in this debris stream, it could even obscure the visibility of the Sun, Moon and stars during that time.

Could this be the vehicle behind the description in Isaiah 24 and Revelation Chapter 6 of the Sixth Seal Judgment Pole Shift and Crustal Displacement? I explored the connection of these prophetic scriptures with an amazing dream I had in 2011, which is described in the section of this book entitled: "Yahweh God's Wrath Sent From Heaven To Earth!" At this time, I suspect that Comet ISON may have been the celestial object I saw in that dream, which triggered a catastrophic meteor bombardment and Pole Shift. If it is, then Comet ISON will likely survive its trajectory around the Sun to fulfill its role as an End Time Sign.

In March through May of 2014, though it will no longer be visible to the naked eye, Comet ISON will continue its journey by passing through Auriga the Goatherd, the constellation alluding to Yahshua's provision for, and love of the wayward Tribulation Saints through the worst time in human history. Significantly, the First Full Lunar Eclipse of the extremely rare 2014 - 2015 Tetrad of Blood Moons that will all fall on Jewish Feasts occurs on the night of Passover - on April 15th, 2014. At that time, Comet ISON will still be in the center of the path of the Milky Way, and in line with Orion's Sword in the center of Auriga. Then, by June of 2014, ISON will return to the heavens just above the constellation Gemini, where its trajectory began.

So what does this mean for believers watching for Yahshua's return? It means that Comet ISON coupled with Comets Encke and Lovejoy very likely could be the Sign of the Son of Man that all the world will see, and which will cause the entire world to mourn after the Rapture occurs - as described in Matthew, Chapter 24. If this is true, then the Rapture could be sometime during the eight days of Chanukah between November 28th through December 6th, 2013, or sometime shortly after that - in the days leading up to Passover Week in 2014. This would

## Ch. 11: The Rapture and Woman Clothed with the Sun

certainly be appropriate, since the Festival of Light commemorates when Yahshua was conceived, and also His discovery by the Magi.

However, as I have often noted in my other writings, in my discussion of the prophetic measurements inside the Antechamber of the Great Pyramid, and in my Revised 2013 Tribulation Timeline, the Rapture may be tied to sometime in the late spring and early summer, especially around the time of Pentecost on June 8th or Shavuot on June 4th, 2013. This time period is suggested by numerous Scriptures already discussed in this chapter, as well as the Antechamber's hidden date correlations targeting the end of June in 2014 with the opening into a greatly narrowed passage leading into the King's Chamber, which signifies Yahshua's Millennial Kingdom. Interestingly, that narrowed passage leading up to the King's Chamber entrance represents the Great Tribulation as a two year period, rather than a three and a half year period, suggesting that this terrible time of world distress will be dramatically shortened - just as Yahshua said it would be (Matthew 24:22).

In regard to Yahshua's Second Coming, the Antechamber of the Pillar of Enoch suggests that Yahshua will come to fight the Battle of Armageddon ten days before Shavuot in 2016. This is exactly the same day that Yahshua ascended to Heaven - 10 days before Pentecost or Shavuot, and 40 days after He rose from the dead. Furthermore, Scripture tells us that Yahshua will return "in like manner" as the way He left, ascending upward until His ascent was obscured by a cloud (Acts 1:9-11). This suggests that Yahshua will physically return descending bodily from a cloud on the same day that He left!

As this section shows, the Rapture described in Matthew, Chapter 24 and the Battle of Armageddon described in Revelation, Chapter 19 refer to two different events that occur at different times. Therefore, the Glorious Appearing of our Messiah and Bridegroom to retrieve His Bride will not be at the same time as Christ's return with His saints to fight the Battle of Armageddon. So the connection of the Battle of Armageddon to Pentecost does not mean that the Rapture is tied to it. In fact, it suggests that it will happen sometime before Pentecost or Shavuot!

Before closing, I want to make it clear that I do not know when the Rapture will be. I am confident that the Woman Clothed with the Sun that appeared in October of 2013 surrounded by three comets is the Sign of the Son of Man, and this is a sure sign that the Catching way of the Bride of Christ and her Five Wise Virgin Attendants will be very soon. Due to this, we need to prepare our hearts to meet Yahshua, and be ready to leave at all times. In any case, I pray that - until our beloved

Messiah Yahshua comes for us - that our Father God Yahweh will bless, guide and preserve you all.

In closing this section of the book, I want to stress here that the heavens are declaring that it is time to repent, pray and prepare the Way of Yahweh! With five comets to soon be visible in the sky this November - just after the Woman Clothed with the Sun appeared in heaven this October - the heavens are positively SCREAMING that the Day of the Lord is at hand, and the Rapture and Sudden Destruction are coming very soon! Are you ready for the greatest show of God's Mercy in the Rapture followed by the greatest show of His Wrath on Earth? If not, **now** is the time! Don't delay! Get down on your knees and beg God's forgiveness, and accept Yahshua as your Messiah before it's too late!

## The Bittersweet Meaning Behind Nova Delphinus 2013

Featured on page 594 is a graphic that I created to show the prophetic associations and meanings of the constellations surrounding a Nova that was spotted near to the tiny constellation Delphinus, the Dolphin. It was discovered on August 14th, 2013 by an amateur astronomer in Japan.

The graphic shows that the Sign of Jonah is attached to the tiny constellation Delphinus, which is primarily a symbol of baptism and resurrection. This is interesting since Yahshua said that He would only give the Sign of Jonah to the disbelieving Jews of His generation. This was in reference to the three days and nights that He was to spend in the belly of the Earth, in mimicry of Jonah's three days and nights in the belly of the big fish.

Fascinatingly, the Sign of Jonah is directly connected to Aquarius the Water-Bearer, which signifies not only the Great Flood but Yahshua giving the Holy Spirit to humanity. It is also connected to Pisces the Fishes, which is next to Aquarius, and represents the Two Houses of Israel. The allegorical meaning of the heavenly Sign of Jonah is fully explained in Book Two, "The Language of God in Humanity". An excerpt from my book regarding the Sign of Jonah is also available on my POEM Web Site in the Free Articles section. Look there for an article entitled: "Why Yahshua Gave the Sign of Jonah - A Study of Judgment & Repentance". I recommend reading it in order to understand how to identify and interpret the Sign of Jonah in the Star Gospel. On the next page is an illustration of the Sign of Jonah in Heaven that was taken from Book Two.

# Ch. 11: The Rapture and Woman Clothed with the Sun

In contrast to Aquarius, Delphinus is a decan of Capricorn, which is primarily tied to the Great Flood. So it is connected to the Days of Lot and Noah. As such, a Super Nova within it is ominous, and indicative of the Age we are in. It is clear that we are now living in the Days of Lot attached to the Gay Agenda, and the Days of Noah connected to the massive increase in genetic tampering going on under the guise of advanced medicine and science. The worldwide acceptance of homosexual love and genetic manipulation are a sure warning of the nearness of the Antichrist's kingdom, and the soon return of our Messiah Yahshua to destroy that evil kingdom forged by demons and men that worship Satan instead of God.

Delphinus is tied to the righteous people who survived the Flood. So it is indicative of the coming deliverance of true believers in the Rapture. I firmly believe that the Rapture will occur before the Nephilim (which become demonic spirits when they die) and the Fallen Angels depicted in the goat half of Capricorn reveal themselves and their demonic agenda openly here on Earth. When these evil spirits do this, they will seductively appeal to the world's leaders - just as suggested by those who falsely believe in the Alien/Demonic Agenda as a force for good.

Did you know that Capricorn is also connected to a 30-degree section of Earth's Longitudinal Meridians that runs through the Midwestern USA, Mexico, the Plains provinces in Canada, and portions of Central and South America, where many true Bible believers live? I discovered this, and revealed it in my 800-page book "The Language of God in History", which is available as a digital PDF download or as a quality paperback from my POEM web site and at Amazon.com. Since Delphinus is tied to Capricorn and its governance over part of the Americas, it could be a sign to believers in the Americas and all over the world that their deliverance from oppression in the Rapture is very near!

Since creating this graphic, I have begun to see a connection between this new Nova and the horrible news of many Christians dying as martyrs or being terribly persecuted due to the Civil Wars going on in Syria and Egypt. In addition, there has been news of many dolphins dying along the East Coast of America. I believe that there is a clear link between these dying martyrs and the dying dolphins on the East Coast and the new Nova seen in the sign of Delphinus the Dolphin.

## Star Gospel Surrounding Nova Delphinus 2013

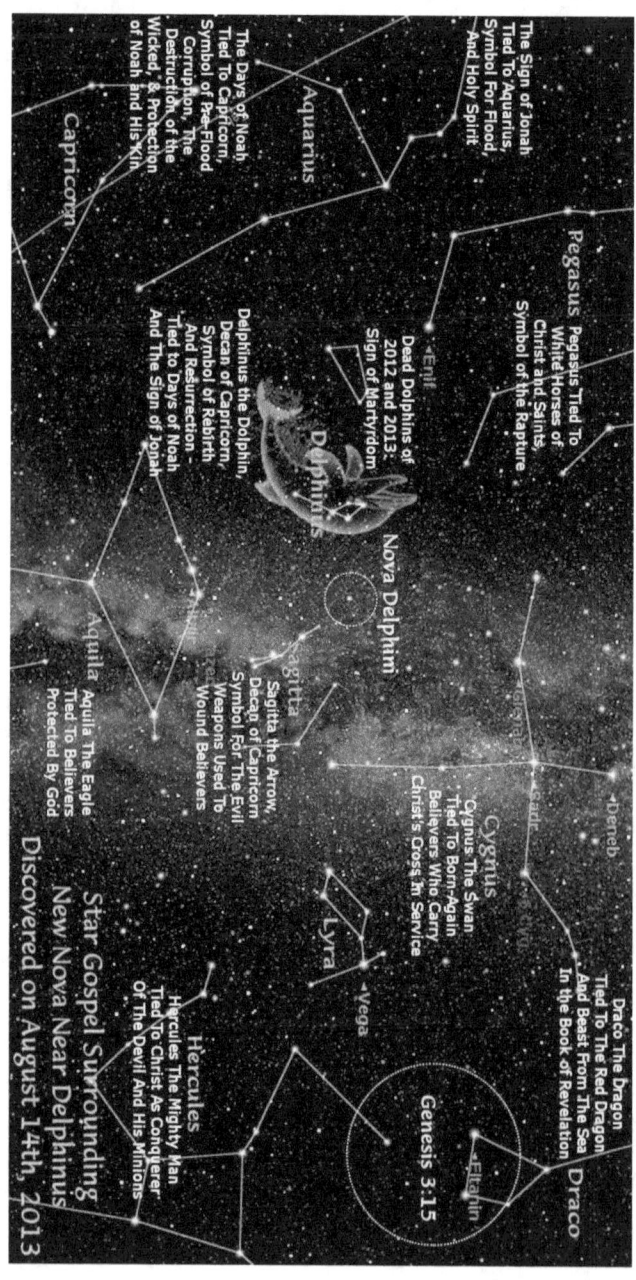

## Ch. 11: The Rapture and Woman Clothed with the Sun

### Aquarius With Pisces, The Sign of Jonah In Heaven

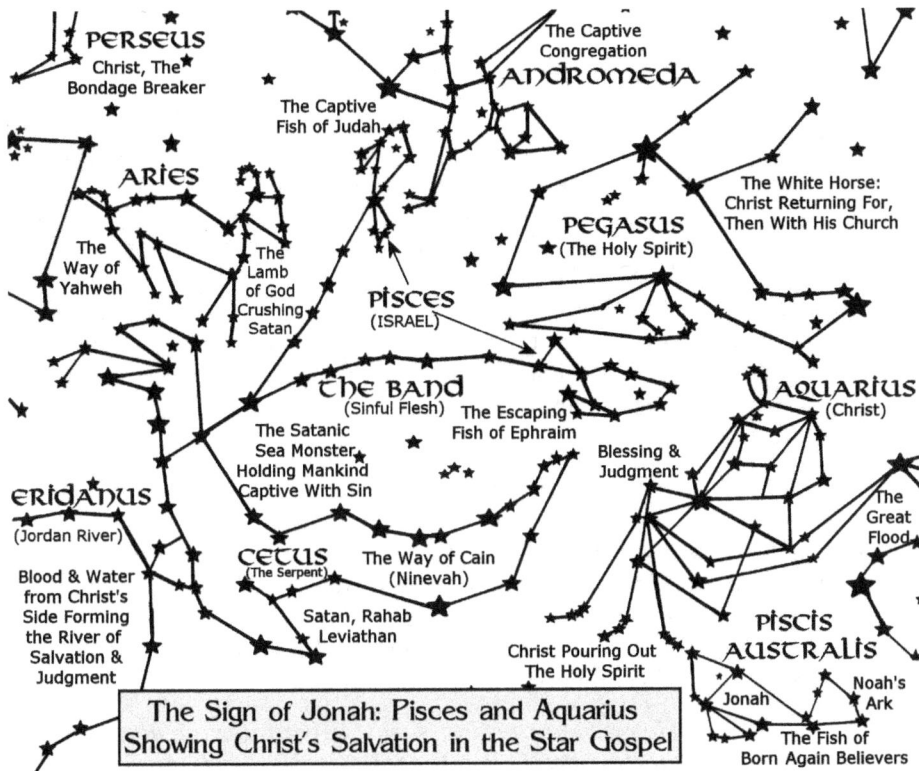

An online article about dying dolphins was published on August 20th, 2013, just 6 days after the Nova in Delphinus was discovered. This American East Coast dolphin die-off, however, is only one small part of a much greater sign that has been going on around the world. Since January of 2012, various species of bottle-nosed Dolphins have been mysteriously dying around the world in places like Cape Cod, the Gulf of Mexico, Peru and Brazil. The dead dolphins that have washed ashore in Peru alone number in the thousands since then, and this is highly unusual. Scientists are still trying to explain the bizarre deaths, and their best predictions as to the cause include virus outbreaks, parasites, toxic algae blooms, or disorientation due to loud noises from ships and oil exploration. But the truth is no one really knows why the dolphins have been beaching themselves and dying en masse in various places.

So how do I connect the persecuted and dying Christians and the dying dolphins to Delphinus? Well, first of all, the tiny constellation Delphinus represents a dolphin. So it is an obvious fit that way.

Secondly, a Nova is an exploding star that - in the process of dying - can potentially produce many more stars within the matter it interacts with. It therefore is like the action that the Christian martyrs dying right now in Egypt and other nations are having in bringing many more repentant souls to Christ.

Taking this into consideration, the sign of Delphinus allegorically signifies the baptism of the saints in the blood of Christ unto death, and a promise of the resurrection of the dead to come. It is therefore a witness to the fact that, like friendly dolphins, saints must sometimes die to produce more shining stars like them from their sacrifice! The Nova in Delphinus signifies that there will be much spiritual fruit coming from the persecution of believers that is going on in Syria, Egypt and elsewhere right now, and also that will come to those who accept Yahshua as their Messiah during the Great Tribulation.

In my opinion, it is likely that the new Nova in Delphinus was divinely sent to bring our attention to the dolphin die-offs that have been happening all over the world at the same time that the persecution of believers has stepped up. I also believe that this is a clear sign that the Fifth Seal of the Tribulation has been opened, just as the Signs in the Heavens on December 21st, 2012 indicated that the first Four Seals of Judgment were in the process of being opened. When the Fifth Seal is opened, the martyred saints cry out to Yahweh God for Justice:

> "When He opened the fifth seal, I saw under the altar the souls of those who had been slain for the word of God and for the testimony which they held. 10 And they cried with a loud voice, saying, "How long, O Lord, holy and true, until You judge and avenge our blood on those who dwell on the earth?" - Rev.6:9-10

As a result of this persecution, however, there will be new believers all over the world during the Great Tribulation - even though some of them will have to die for their faith. Though terribly tragic, their deaths will bring many others to faith in Yahshua. Therefore, these believers will **not** have been persecuted or killed in vain!

## Who Are the 144,000 Witnesses?

When it comes to deciphering who the 12 times 12,000 Israelites who become the 144,000 Witnesses are, we need to clarify their identity and ministry by actually reading and analyzing the Scriptures concerning them in the Book of Revelation, Chapter 7 and Revelation, Chapter 14, doing word studies of some of the Greek words that refer to the 144,000

## Ch. 11: The Rapture and Woman Clothed with the Sun

who are chosen out of Israel, and praying to God for guidance from His Holy Spirit to help us understand His Word.

Upon doing this, most note that Revelation 7:4 clearly indicates that the 144,000 are taken from the Twelve Tribes of Israel. However, this does not mean that the 144,000 are strictly modern Jews. In fact, as my Language of God Series Books have exhaustively shown, the modern Jews only signify a fraction of the spiritual and literal Israelites living in today's world, and throughout the ages. What is being ignored by most commentators on the 144,000 is the fact that there are the Ten Lost Tribes of Israel to consider.

The Ten Lost Tribes consist of people groups that are partly descended from the Ten Tribes dispersed throughout the known world in several successive waves. These Diaspora Israelites can allegorically and literally be associated with over a dozen Middle-Eastern, European and British nations that absorbed three waves of fleeing Israelites and Jews. These three waves occurred successively over a long period of time: once after the ancient Northern Kingdom of Israel fell to the Assyrians, at another time after the southern Kingdom of Judah fell to the Babylonians, and still later when Jerusalem and the Temple were destroyed by the Romans in 70 AD.

The remaining Two Tribes of Israel are represented by the majority of ethnic Jews today, who are descended mostly from the Tribes of Judah and Benjamin. Though there is also a remnant of Diaspora Jews living in Israel today that are descended from all Twelve Tribes, they are not part of Lost Israel, but of Judah because of their total rejection of Yahshua as their Messiah, and their hatred of the Gentiles and Gentile nations they left behind.

Though this is not true in all cases, many of the Lost Israelites of the Diaspora that live in the West have become a part of the spiritual Israelites who have been adopted into the Kingdom of God through the acceptance of Christ's sacrifice on the Cross for their sins. In Romans 11:16-24, the Apostle Paul - who was a Benjamite and therefore can be identified as a Jew - taught that the Gentile believers in Yahshua are considered to be wild olive tree branches that are grafted into the natural olive tree that signifies the Israelites naturally descended from Isaac's son Jacob/Israel.

Although they do NOT replace the Jews, the Ten Lost Tribes are reckoned with believing or Messianic Jews as equal members in the Body of Christ, and the loving congregations that form the Two-House Church of Judah and Ephraim. The Two House Church of Judah and Ephraim are referred to in several Bible prophecies as working together with Yahweh

God against Satan's schemes (See Psalm 108:7-9; Isaiah 11:12-14; Ezekiel 37:15-20; and Zechariah 9:12-14).

Revelation 14:4 also tells us that the 144,000 are Firstfruits and virgins who have not "defiled" themselves with "women". The term "Firstfruits" specifically refers to the First Resurrection, which started when Yahshua rose from the dead, bringing many righteous saints from their tombs to rise up to everlasting life shortly after Him (Mat. 27:51-53). This Firstfruits action of resurrection into immortal life will occur again in the First Rapture, which may be in the middle of the Tribulation just before the 3-1/2 year Great Tribulation begins. Furthermore, there may be a Second Rapture when the Two Witnesses are raised up and taken to Heaven just before the Battle of Armageddon ensues.

In contrast, the Second Resurrection occurs only once, and there is no guarantee that any of these poor souls will be saved after they are judged by the Law. This Last Judgment will occur at the end of the world - just before the New Heaven and Earth are created (See Revelation 20:5 and Revelation 20:11-12).

As Firstfruits, the 144,000 are part of the Firstfruits of the Resurrection, meaning that they have to be immortal saints that have been chosen at the Rapture that occurs before the last dreadful half of the Great Tribulation. Also interesting to note here is the fact that neither Revelation Chapter 7 nor 14 calls these set-apart saints "witnesses," so that term for them originated out of association. Indeed, since these saints follow and serve only the Lamb of God who is Yahshua and His Father Yahweh, they are very godly and Spirit-filled. From this, we can infer that they are also great witnesses of God's righteousness, and that they truly reflect God's character to a lost and dying world.

In addition to these things, Scripture tells us that the 144,000 are "sealed" (Rev. 7:4). Later in Revelation, we are told that this seal is on the forehead, and it is called the Seal of God (Rev. 9:4). This is reminiscent of the "tau" or cross-shaped mark that an unknown Scribe allegorically put on redeemed Jews' foreheads just before Jerusalem fell to Nebuchadnezzar (Ezekiel 9:2-4, 11). By the way, this Scribe mentioned by Ezekiel may actually be Enoch, who is called the Scribe of Righteousness in the Book of 1 Enoch (1 Enoch 12:5, 1 Enoch 15:2).

Rather than receiving a visible mark, these 144,000 saints may simply be marked by the indwelling presence of the Holy Spirit within them, which serves as an indelible and invisible seal on their foreheads. In fact, the seal of the Holy Spirit guarantees the salvation of all who are truly redeemed in Christ (Ephesians 1:13, Eph. 4:30). Before Christ, this invisible seal of the Spirit was still given to devout Israelites just as Ezekiel attested to, but they had to earn the right to receive it. In other words, they could not simply repent, believe and then be covered by the blood of Christ to sanctify themselves like humble believers may mercifully do today.

Next, we have to determine what the writer means by "virgin" and "women." Rather than meaning that the 144,000 are all men who never slept with a woman, could the writer be suggesting that these saints were never loyal to any particular church, synagogue, and/or political party? For example, the "Woman clothed with the Sun" in Revelation 12:1-6 represents the righteous Jewish/Israelite bloodline that Yahshua was descended from. As an extension of that righteous bloodline, Yahshua made us into His Church and His Body by His shed innocent blood.

Meanwhile, in Revelation 17:3-6, the "Woman sitting on a Scarlet Beast" represents the apostate churches and false religions of the Tribulation period that are "married to", or in league with corrupt bankers and dishonest politicians, and "she" worships the same Beast that they have created. This false church is described as a Harlot because of "her" association with the Roman Catholic Church, and the Ecumenical Movement being pushed by the Vatican and the British Monarchy. Sadly, Rick Warren and a host of other American preachers are now in league with Rome and London in their desire to create the New World Order, which will be the world empire of the Beast, or Antichrist. They are also working toward creating the wicked one world religion that will ride that economic Beast into perdition for eternity.

For those who don't know, the Ecumenical Movement supports the false religious doctrine that all paths lead to God, or that man is a god. In addition, ecumenical doctrines include the denial of the reality of sin, and do not teach a need for true repentance or divine forgiveness. Therefore, in Revelation 14:1 where it says: "virgins not defiled by women," it could very well mean that these saints are not political or religious activists. In fact, this description strongly suggests that the 144,000 are godly saints that live quiet and pious lives apart from worldly religious organizations and political parties, and the associated riches and excesses attached to involvement in both.

If they are truly set-apart or holy, saints who love God give themselves exclusively to Him. As a result, they no longer serve the world, or any institutions that are of the world. In other words, these saints live more like hermits who are detached from the world rather than being active in church or politics, and they are definitely not social butterflies. In fact, they serve exclusively as God's witnesses to their immediate families, friends, and acquaintances, and perhaps only reach the rest of the world through their own writings or books about their understanding of God and His desire for mankind. Incidentally, this describes my own life over the past twelve years fairly well, and someone once told me that they think I might be one of the 144,000. Though I do not claim this honor, I would be deeply humbled with gratitude if God chose me to be one of them.

There are several Scriptures that define what the nature of the 144,000 should be like. These Scriptures define the most holy or most set-apart of the saints who follow the Way of Yahweh through Yahshua. In the Epistle of John, for example, it says that those who truly love God cannot love the world, for they are mutually exclusive:

*"Do not love the world or the things in the world. If anyone loves the world, the love of the Father is not in him. 16 For all that is in the world - the lust of the flesh, the lust of the eyes, and the pride of life - is not of the Father but is of the world. 17 And the world is passing away, and the lust of it; but he who does the will of God abides forever." - 1 John 2:15-17*

The same Epistle also says:

*"He who says he is in the light, and hates his brother, is in darkness until now. 10 He who loves his brother abides in the light, and there is no cause for stumbling in him. 11 But he who hates his brother is in darkness and walks in darkness, and does not know where he is going, because the darkness has blinded his eyes." - 1 John 2:9-11*

Together, these two passages describe the nature of the 144,000. These are saints that do not love the world or the things of the world - such as wealth, fame, worldly success, and hedonism - at all, and they do not pursue mankind's approval. Instead, they seek Yahweh God's approval alone, and they love God the Father and their brethren around the world, especially those that claim to love Yahshua, but may not really "know" Him. Those who do not know Christ do not have a personal relationship with Him via the Holy Spirit, and are therefore unable to please God or live a truly set-apart or holy life.

Now, when translated correctly (as in the NIV Bible instead of the KJV or NKJ), Revelation 14:1 says that the 144,000 have Yahshua's name and His Father Yahweh's name written on their foreheads (instead of just the Father's name as in other translations). The King James Version and New King James Bibles with footnotes indicate that at least two ancient

## Ch. 11: The Rapture and Woman Clothed with the Sun    Page 601

manuscripts record that "His name and His Father's name" are written on the foreheads of the 144,000 instead of only "His Father's name". This means that these saints have Yahweh's and Yahshua's True Names always in their hearts and minds, and they have put themselves into subjection to both God the Father and God the Son, and follow their righteous Laws. It also means that the 144,000 cannot be racially pure religious Jews at all because they honor Yahshua's Name! Instead they will likely be a mixture of Spirit-filled Messianic Jews and devout Christians who may or may not keep the Jewish Feasts. Again, this is because Christians are adopted into Israel by their active relationship with God and His Son, and some are even physically descended from the Lost Israelites.

As for the purpose of the 144,000 on Earth during the Great Tribulation, it is never actually stated in Scripture, so there is an undeniable air of mystery concerning them. Nonetheless, it seems logical to assume that - due to their being chosen during the Tribulation period - these saints are meant to serve God by leading others to Christ during the Great Tribulation, which is the last 3-1/2 years of the seven-year Tribulation period. As an example of this, we need look no further than the Two Witnesses, who are called to be witnesses for God's Truth by preaching the Gospel, performing terrifying supernatural miracles to convict the evil world of God's power, and then by being resurrected from the dead and ascending into Heaven as the whole world watches (Rev. 11:3-12).

Incidentally, just as the Woman Clothed with the Sun in Revelation Chapter 12 that signifies the Two House Church is kept safe for 1,260 days, the Two Witnesses are also commissioned to preach for 1,260 days, which is 3-1/2 years or 42 months - the same length of time that the Beast from the Sea, or one world government of the Antichrist, will reign over Jerusalem - according to the following Scriptures:

> *"But leave out the court which is outside the temple, and do not measure it, for it has been given to the Gentiles. And they will tread the holy city underfoot for forty-two months." - Revelation 11:2*

> *"And he (the Beast from the Sea) was given a mouth speaking great things and blasphemies, and he was given authority to continue for forty-two months." - Revelation 13:5*

When taken together, these two Scriptures indicate that the Antichrist and his New World Order will only be in control of the world for the last half of Daniel's Seventieth Week, not the full seven years of the Tribulation. Since the Woman clothed with the Sun is protected in the "wilderness" or place of refuge for the same amount of time, doesn't it make sense that the First Rapture is tied to the middle of the Tribulation, and not the beginning?

Something few have noted about the 144,000 is that they appear with Christ on Mount Zion in Revelation, Chapter 14, and this portion of the books appears to be dealing with events after the Antichrist declares himself to be God in the middle of the Tribulation. This suggests that Christ will descend to Earth at least three and a half years before the Battle of Armageddon to Rapture the Saints and choose and commission the 144,000.

The Rapture is suggested by the fact that Revelation 14:3 says that these 144,000 saints appear to be taken up to Heaven just before the 3-1/2 year Great Tribulation so that they may sing a special worship song that only they can learn to sing. They sing this song before God's magnificent throne that is surrounded by the four Cherubim or Living Creatures and the Twenty-four Elders representing twelve godly Patriarchs and the Twelve Apostles (Rev. 4:2-7, Rev.14:2-3). If this is so, and Scripture says it is, then the 144,000 will be fully immortal, and incapable of being killed when they return to Earth to minister to their lost or apostate brethren during the Great Tribulation!

As shown in my book "The Language of God in History," Zion may not only refer to Jerusalem's Temple Mount, but to the Great Pyramid at Giza, which was built on the border between Upper and Lower Egypt by the righteous Sethites who followed Yahweh prior to Noah's Flood. This huge stone pyramid is tied to the brightest of the constellation Orion's belt stars called "Al Nitak", and this bright star may also signify an invisible location in the Third Heaven where Paradise is located, and where Yahshua now resides. In addition, both this star and the pyramid represent the Two-House Church of Israel, and specifically the Bride of Christ, who will one day forever reside in the New Jerusalem with Yahshua.

Could God's Throne be located in another dimension in the vicinity of Orion or Taurus, since Orion is a decan of Taurus? Is this the location of the heavenly Zion where the Saints will travel when the First Rapture occurs? It is possible, since scientists have long speculated that the center of the Universe may be near to the Pleiades star cluster in Taurus. In fact, that may be the reason why the brightest star in the Pleiades is named "Al Cyone", which means "The Center".

Could this imply that the Pleiades are tied to the center of the Universe, and the invisible location of God's Throne room in Heaven? It

# Ch. 11: The Rapture and Woman Clothed with the Sun

is certainly possible, a3nd it would also explain why Satan's henchmen known as demons often disguise themselves as alien beings or "Ascended Masters" and claim to be from the region of the Pleiades. Satan loves to confuse the Saints by tainting everything good that is associated with God the Father and falsely connecting these things with evil, darkness, and deception!

When taking all of these facts into consideration, one thing is clear: the 144,000 Witnesses are a very special group of believers in God's Kingdom, and they are given a unique position and a great purpose during the Great Tribulation that only Yahweh God understands fully at this time.

## *Yahweh God's Wrath Sent From Heaven To Earth!*

This section is being presented as an introduction to the last chapter of this book, which deals with the End Time heavenly signs that Yahshua told us to watch for. Though this section does not deal directly with the Rapture or any specific heavenly signs, it gives a detailed revelation about the nature of how God's Wrath will likely be meted out shortly after the First Rapture, and early in the Great Tribulation period. This entire revelation is based on a vision or waking dream I had sometime in the Summer of 2011 - in the early morning hours while I was still lying in bed and half asleep. In that dream, I believe Yahweh God showed me how His Wrath on the wicked will begin to be poured out. This is what I saw, and what I believe it means.

At the beginning of the dream, I was floating in Outer Space without any need of special gear, and I could see the entire globe of the Earth below me. Looking around me from this vantage point, I watched several terrifying events unfold.

As I looked at the Earth revolving slowly in space, I saw a massive, bright celestial body with a huge, glowing tail and several satellite objects beside and behind it whiz past the Earth. As the large, brightly shining mass leading this celestial parade passed, it disturbed the Earth's axis, and our planet began to wobble erratically to and fro in space. Then, suddenly, as the wobbling continued, the entire crust of the Earth began to shift, buckle and slide into a new position, which looked to be about 45 degrees off kilter. In this part of the dream vision, I believe I was shown the beginning of the fulfillment of the prophecy in Isaiah, Chapter 24:

# The Language of God in Prophecy

## ~*~ Isaiah 24:17-23 ~*~

"Fear and the pit and the snare
Are upon you, O inhabitant of the earth.
18 And it shall be
That he who flees from the noise of the fear
Shall fall into the pit,
And he who comes up from the midst of the pit
Shall be caught in the snare;
For the windows from on high are open,
And the foundations of the earth are shaken.
19 The earth is violently broken,
The earth is split open,
The earth is shaken exceedingly.
20 The earth shall reel to and fro like a drunkard,
And shall totter like a hut;
Its transgression shall be heavy upon it,
And it will fall, and not rise again.
21 It shall come to pass in that day
That the Lord will punish on high the host of exalted ones,
And on the earth the kings of the earth.
22 They will be gathered together,
As prisoners are gathered in the pit,
And will be shut up in the prison;
After many days they will be punished.
23 Then the moon will be disgraced
And the sun ashamed;
For the Lord of hosts will reign
On Mount Zion and in Jerusalem
And before His elders, gloriously."

After this, I watched as the Earth moved into a meteorite stream left behind by this object that triggered the Pole Shift. As the Earth moved into the debris stream, I was moved inside the Earth's atmosphere to a vantage point atop a high mountain. From there, I watched as many large and small meteorites penetrated the Earth's atmosphere and hit the Earth, causing fiery explosions, earthquakes, eruptions, tidal waves and fires all around the world, decimating both huge cities and small towns, and destroying huge swatches of vegetation and trees in the countryside.

# Ch. 11: The Rapture and Woman Clothed with the Sun

Next, I was brought up high into the atmosphere over the surface of the Earth, and - as the meteoroids continued to rain down all over the world - I saw a huge, jaggedly formed celestial object like a massive, rocky asteroid crash into the ocean, causing terrible tsunamis and flash coastal flooding near to the impact. I also saw many ships sink into the sea as the corpses of people, animals, fish, whales and other sea life began to form floating islands of death on the surface of the choppy seas surrounding the impact point.

As this occurred on the surface of the Earth, I saw another very bright comet or asteroid penetrate the upper atmosphere with a brilliant display of light and fire just like the mountain-like object had, but sometime afterward. This brilliantly glowing star-like object crashed into a large mountain range that fed many rivers, exploding before impact. I was made to understand that this was Wormwood, and I watched with fascination as its explosive impact sent massive plumes of fiery debris high into the air, which then fell over all the rivers surrounding the mountain range that it had impacted, polluting them with deadly toxins.

Finally, just before the vision ended, I watched as huge plumes of dark smoke and ash filled the sky from the impacts of countless meteoroid strikes and other celestial object impacts on the Earth. These started many fires that scorched huge sections of forests, farms and grasslands that further added to the debris already in the air from the meteoroid impacts. All this combined to blanket the Earth with clouds of thick gloom made up of smoke and smoldering, foul-smelling ashes that served to greatly diminish the amount of light from the Sun, Moon and stars that made it through to the surface.

This grim vision of the coming death and destruction accompanying God's Wrath was burned into my memory before the dream ended so that I would not ever be able to forget it. After I awoke, the Holy Spirit directed me to re-read Revelation Chapters 6 through 8, and I realized that God had just shown me what was going to take place during the first part of the Great Tribulation.

The following bulleted list shows what I saw in my dream, and what the Holy Spirit showed me in relationship to the fulfillment of the Book of Revelation's last two Seal Judgments, and first four Trumpet Judgments:

- **The Sixth Seal - Cataclysmic Earthquakes and Eruptions accompany Pole Shift, darkening the sky (Sun and Moon), destroying or flooding coastal cities, towns, and obliterating huge sections of countryside:** - *"I looked when He opened the sixth seal, and behold, there was a great earthquake; and the sun became black as sackcloth of hair, and* the moon became like blood. 13 And the stars of heaven fell to the earth, as a fig tree drops its late figs when it is shaken by a mighty wind. 14 Then the sky receded as a scroll when it is rolled up, and every mountain and island was moved out of its place." - Revelation 6:12-14

- **The Seventh Seal and First Trumpet - Heavy Meteorite Bombardments, Eruptions, Earthquakes: Seventh Seal:** *"Then the angel took the censer, filled it with fire from the altar, and threw it to the earth. And there were noises, thunderings, lightnings, and an earthquake." - Revelation 8:5 -* **The First Trumpet:** *"The first angel sounded: and hail and fire followed, mingled with blood, and they were thrown to the earth. And a third of the trees were burned up, and all green grass was burned up." - Revelation 8:7*

- **The Second Trumpet - Massive Space Object Ocean Impact, Tsunamis and Earthquakes:** *"Then the second angel sounded: and something like a great mountain burning with fire was thrown into the sea, and a third of the sea became blood. 9 And a third of the living creatures in the sea died, and a third of the ships were destroyed." - Rev. 8:8-9*

- **The Third Trumpet - Wormwood Star Impact Pollutes River-Source Mountains:** *"Then the third angel sounded: And a great star fell from heaven, burning like a torch, and it fell on a third of the rivers and on the springs of water. 11 The name of the star is Wormwood. A third of the waters became wormwood, and many men died from the water, because it was made bitter." - Revelation 8:10-11*

- **The Fourth Trumpet - Smoke And Ash From Worldwide Fires Darken The Sky:** *"Then the fourth angel sounded: And a third of the sun was struck, a third of the moon, and a third of the stars, so that a third of them were darkened. A third of the day did not shine, and likewise the night." - Revelation 8:12*

Though I can't say whether or not this dream relates to Comet ISON and the other four comets that are appearing with it in Earth's skies in October 2013 onward through early 2014, there is a good possibility that it might. Regardless of what celestial events my dream vision relates to, I feel that it will all take place soon, in order to fulfill this Scripture:

~*~ Psalm 11:5-6 ~*~
*"The Lord tests the righteous,*
*But the wicked and the one*
*who loves violence His soul hates.*
*6 Upon the wicked He will rain coals;*

# Ch. 11: The Rapture and Woman Clothed with the Sun

> *Fire and brimstone and a burning wind*
> *Shall be the portion of their cup."*

Before I finish this section of the book, I wanted to say that, because I was floating in space at the beginning of the dream, and I was unafraid of any injury from what I saw transpiring on the Earth, I believe this was a sign from God that the Rapture will take place before any of these terrible events occur on the Earth. Since the events I saw chronicle the Wrath of God from its beginning with the Sixth Seal Pole Shift Judgment, and how God's Wrath will originate from Heaven, it makes sense that the Rapture will occur before these events take place.

Please share this account with others in order to warn them that God's Wrath will be poured out on the Earth soon. What I have written here is a faithful recollection of my dream as delivered to me by God over two years ago. Incidentally, I made a series of Armageddon Internet Radio Shows that relayed what I saw in this dream, and how it relates to many End Time Prophetic Scriptures. They are archived on my ministry web site and at Vimeo.

## *Why Is God Judging The Nations Today?*

Though many deny it, there has been an exponential increase in so-called "natural disasters" and extreme weather ever since 2008 or so, and those who deny this are denying the facts. Massive and unprecedented storms, catastrophic floods and fires, deadly tornadoes (which the Bible calls whirlwinds) hail storms, persistent drought, and every pestilence imaginable have been happening with ever-increasing frequency in the past five years, and I believe these End Time plagues are "Acts of God" being sent in judgment against the nations for their ungodliness, as well as their hatred of Christianity, and their detestable treatment of the modern nation of Israel and the Jews in general.

For those who say that our Father God Yahweh doesn't send terrible storms as a sign of His displeasure with us, and that severe weather events are not a sign of God's judgment, the following Scriptures say otherwise. In fact, they explicitly say that God does indeed send storms, whirlwinds, floods and hail against mankind in judgment of their sin and rebellion against Him.

~*~ Isaiah 29:6-7 ~*~

"You will be punished by the Lord of hosts
With thunder and earthquake and great noise,
With storm and tempest, and the flame of devouring fire.

The multitude of all the nations who fight against Ariel (Israel),
Even all who fight against her and her fortress,
And distress her, shall be as a dream of a night vision."

Note here that Ariel means "Lion of God", and Yahshua is the Lion of God, as well as the "Lion of Judah". Thus, Isaiah is saying that the nations that fight against Yahshua and His saints and elect ones shall cease to exist - like a bad dream! Isaiah also said:

~*~ Isaiah 30:30 ~*~

"The Lord will cause His glorious voice to be heard,
And show the descent of His arm,
With the indignation of His anger
And the flame of a devouring fire,
With scattering, tempest, and hailstones."

Like the Prophet Isaiah, the prophet Ezekiel spoke to those of us living in this current era, when leaders around the world are speaking about *"Peace and Safety"*, although there is neither, and God will send His *"Sudden Destruction"* soon (1 Thess. 5:3). Due to this, Ezekiel warned that great hailstones, fierce storm winds (including tornadoes), and flooding rains will be sent tear down the walls of cities and homes in punishment and judgment:

*"Because they have seduced My people, saying, 'Peace!' when there is no peace - and one builds a wall, and they plaster it with untempered mortar - 11 say to those who plaster it with untempered mortar, that it will fall. There will be flooding rain, and you, O great hailstones, shall fall; and a stormy wind shall tear it down. 12 Surely, when the wall has fallen, will it not be said to you, 'Where is the mortar with which you plastered it?' 13 Therefore thus says Yahweh Elohim: 'I will cause a stormy wind to break forth in My fury; and there shall be a flooding rain in My anger, and great hailstones in fury to consume it.'"* - Ezekiel 13:10

The Prophet Ezekiel also stated that every nation that behaves like the land called Gog in coming against Israel (and "Israel" includes Jews, Christians and godly morality) will suffer from flooding rain, hail, fire and brimstone (celestial bombardments):

*"Every man's sword will be against his brother. 22 And I will bring him to judgment with pestilence and bloodshed; I will rain down on him, on his troops, and on the many peoples who are with him, flooding rain, great hailstones, fire, and brimstone.*

## Ch. 11: The Rapture and Woman Clothed with the Sun   Page 609

*23 Thus I will magnify Myself and sanctify Myself, and I will be known in the eyes of many nations. Then they shall know that I am the Lord." ~ Ezekiel 38:21-23*

Like Ezekiel, the Prophet Jeremiah also warned that God would send whirlwinds or tornadoes in Judgment in "the latter days", which means the days we are living in right now:

*~\*~ Jeremiah 23:18-20 ~\*~*
*"For who has stood in the counsel of the Lord,*
*And has perceived and heard His word?*
*Who has marked His word and heard it?*
*19 Behold, a whirlwind of the Lord has gone forth in fury—*
*A violent whirlwind!*
*It will fall violently on the head of the wicked.*
*20 The anger of the Lord will not turn back*
*Until He has executed and performed the thoughts of His heart.*
**In the latter days you will understand it** *perfectly."*

As examples, the deadly monster tornadoes that hit Oklahoma in May of 2013 and Illinois in November of 2013 can be directly connected to the advancement of the Gay Agenda in America. When the monster tornado hit near Oklahoma City on May 31st, 2013 and caused massive destruction and 5 deaths, there was a Gay Pride Parade and Festival being held in the city that day. Likewise, a Gay Marriage Bill had been passed by the Illinois legislature *twelve* days before the killer tornadoes that hit Washington, Illinois and several other towns on November 17th, 2013, which killed 8, and caused many injuries and much destruction.

In addition, God's Word says that every nation that speaks ill of either House of Israel, or that hates Jews or Christians will perish, whether their inhabitants say they love Yahshua or not. Anti-Semitism, Anti-Israel and Anti-Christian sentiments are rampant right now throughout the world, and this is why God has been judging the nations with catastrophic fires, earthquakes, storms and floods. As the prophet Jeremiah wrote:

*"Behold, I will make Jerusalem a cup of trembling unto all the people round about, when they shall be in the siege both against Judah and against Jerusalem. 3 And in that day will I make Jerusalem a burdensome stone for all people: all that burden themselves with it shall be cut in pieces, though all the people of the earth be gathered together against it."* - *"It shall be in that day*

*that I will seek to destroy all the nations that come against Jerusalem." ~ Jeremiah 12:2-3, 9*

Though these Scriptures are taken from the Old Testament, the Old Testament is also filled with God's Prophetic Word, which applies equally to everyone, whether they are Christians or Jews or some other faith. From these Scriptures, we can ascertain that Yahweh God means business when it comes to disciplining and correcting His people, and He will not be mocked! Those who go against Him in hatred of His Laws and His people Israel will pay with their lives, and no one will escape His Judgment in the end. Therefore, we who desire to please God need to take Yahshua's words to heart, loving our enemies, blessing those who curse us, and fleeing from all sin, lewdness, crass language, lust and immorality as we await the coming of our Bridegroom and King Yahshua in the Rapture.

Yet, even though the Signs in the Heavens are screaming that we are already in the Tribulation, it seems that every time there is a super storm or mega earthquake or some other form of extreme weather, there is someone claiming that it is a technologically-produced disaster. They see every killer storm or quake as either a "natural" disaster with no spiritual cause, or see it as part of some government conspiracy to depopulate the world in order to disprove God's judgment, and keep people from repenting, changing their ways, and seeking the true God Yahweh and His forgiveness and salvation. Woe to those who do this, and do not heed these expressions of God's displeasure!

# Chapter 12: Sacred Astronomy as a Prophetic Tool

> *"And there will be great earthquakes in various places, and famines and pestilences; and there will be fearful sights and great signs from heaven." - "And there will be signs in the sun, in the moon, and in the stars (this is referring to eclipses and planetary and star conjunctions, and meteor showers); and on the earth distress of nations, with perplexity, the sea and the waves roaring..." - Luke 21:11, Luke 21:25*

Thus far, several convincing proofs have been shown that indicate we are in the final Tribulation period. The testimonies locked into the Great Pyramid, the Book of Daniel, the Psalms, and the Cherubim and Beasts in the Books of Ezekiel and Revelation are powerful witnesses to us that the end of this current beastly world system is very near. We have already explored the connection between the United States and Israel, and the roles of the United Kingdom and Europe during the Tribulation period. This book has also shown how the prophecies in the Gospel in the Stars and the Book of 1 Enoch agree with the prophecies in the Bible, and clearly suggest that the Great Tribulation followed by Yahshua's Second Coming are very near.

Beyond these written proofs, there are many celestial signs connected to the Gospel in the Stars indicating that the predictions about the end of the world made in this book are correct. They are found using the Sacred Astronomy of the Sethites, which was painstakingly reconstructed in Book One, "The Language of God in the Universe," and further elaborated upon in Books Two and Three, as well as in portions of this book.

In particular, one definite date has popped up in my studies of the celestial signs that are tied to events in the Tribulation, and this is December 21st, 2012. Fascinatingly, I have discovered that this date that was touted as the Mayan date for the End of the World actually points to the end of a World Age or cycle. Via the Holy Spirit, I also was shown that this date is encoded into the Bible via allegorical Star Gospel symbolism, even though it is said to have originated with the Mayans - an indigenous New World people initially discussed in Book Three as possible descendents of the patriarch Noah and Shem. The Mayans believed that their Fifth Sun or World Age would end on December 21st, 2012 AD, and that the civilizations of this age would be destroyed by fire sometime on or after that date. This is why, after a brief recap of the prophetic symbolism in the Book of Revelation that is fully tied to the Gospel in the Stars, we will explore who the Mayans were, what they believed would happen at the end of the Fifth Sun.

## *Amazing Ties Between Revelation and the Star Gospel*

As was shown in my study of the Great Pyramid at Giza, New World cultures were not the only ones who understood or utilized Sacred Astronomy. It was also used extensively in ancient Old World cultures. It is therefore not surprising that this amazing science also has many biblical connections. The ties between the Bible and Gospel in the Stars are so extensive that all of Book One in this series was devoted to examining them. These correlations between the written and celestial Gospels prove that God's Word has always been locked into the design of the heavens surrounding our Earth.

Since celestial signs have always been visible to people, it suggests that God always intended them to instruct and guide mankind, just as His Word in the Bible and the Book of 1 Enoch are intended to. In this section, we will focus again on New Testament references to heavenly signs on the Last Day, especially those that are found in the Book of Revelation. Amazingly, this *last book* of the Bible is all about the *Last Day*, and contains more prophecies regarding this time than any other book in the Bible. In fact, as will be shown in the next section, the Four Horsemen of the Apocalypse in Chapter Four of the Book of Revelation are directly tied to four Zodiac signs that housed the major planets on December 21st, 2012.

Before we look at End Time prophecies mentioning celestial signs in the Book of Revelation, however, let's look at those found in the rest of the New Testament. One of these is in the Book of Acts. Immediately after the apostles were filled with the Holy Spirit, the Apostle Peter addressed the Jews who were witnesses to their miraculous ability to speak intelligibly in foreign languages that they did not previously know. When he did so, Peter quoted from the Prophet Joel:

## Chapter 12: Sacred Astronomy as a Prophetic Tool

> *"And it shall come to pass in the last days, says God, that I will pour out of My Spirit on all flesh; your sons and your daughters shall prophesy, your young men shall see visions, your old men shall dream dreams. And on My menservants and on My maidservants I will pour out My Spirit in those days; and they shall prophesy.* **I will show wonders in heaven above and signs in the earth beneath: blood and fire and vapor of smoke. The sun shall be turned into darkness, and the moon into blood, before the coming of the great and awesome day of the Lord.** *And it shall come to pass that whoever calls on the name of the Lord shall be saved."* - Acts 2:17-21

Here Peter quoted from Joel 2:28-32 - a passage of Scripture that recalls not only the tremendous outpouring of the Holy Spirit in the Last Days after Yahshua's First Advent, but suggests that there will be a re-awakened knowledge of the wonders that God left for mankind to discover in the heavens, and in the signs He left for them on the Earth and in all living things. This re-awakening began during the Enlightenment period in human history, which started in Europe and England in the 17th Century, and has continued to the present. Although interest in the Occult and eastern mysticism began around then also, it did pave the way for true believers to re-discover the importance of Sacred Astronomy and the Gospel in the Stars.

As was shown repeatedly in "The Language of God in the Universe," there are many amazing messages to us written in the stars surrounding our Earth, as well as on the Earth itself. These messages are written in the allegorical Language of God that runs throughout Creation, and also fills the spiritual landscape revealed in the Bible. This entire book series has shown many amazing examples of the connection between the Gospel in the Stars and the Bible. But nowhere in the Bible is this correlation between it and the stars more apparent than it is in the Book of Revelation. Uncannily, as if in silent confirmation, these correlations between the first of Yahshua's messages to mankind, and the last one in His written Word, recall the imagery of the Great Sphinx as an image for Christ, who is *"the First and the Last."* Furthermore, the phrase *"the First and the Last"* describing Christ appears *only* in Isaiah, which is the first fully prophetic book in the Bible, and in the Book of Revelation, which is the last book, and *last fully prophetic* book of the Bible (Isaiah 44:6, 48:12; Rev. 1:11,17, 2:8, 22:13).

The sacred purpose of the Astronomy surrounding the forty-eight ancient constellations of the Zodiac is constantly confirmed in the allegorical language of Scripture. This is especially true in the prophetic books, among which the Book of Revelation deals strictly with events during the thousand-year Last Day, or Day of the Lord. The remainder of this section contains information adapted from Books One and Two that shows some of the biggest connections between Revelation and the Star Gospel.

Perhaps the most remarkable correlation between the Book of Revelation and the Gospel in the Stars is that the Virgin Miriam, the mother of Christ, is represented in both at the moment when Yahshua's birth was announced in the heavens:

> "Now **a great sign appeared in heaven**: a woman clothed with the sun, with the moon under her feet, and on her head a garland of twelve stars." - Revelation 12:1

This description of the Woman Clothed with the Sun in Revelation pertains to Miriam, Christ's earthly mother, and corresponds exactly with the appearance of the sign of Virgo at sunrise on the Feast of Trumpets in September 11th, 3 BC – the date marking the time period when Yahshua may have been born in Bethlehem. As shown n Bok One, Yahshua may have been born closer to the Feast of Sukkot, and specifically on Yom Kippur or the Day of Atonement, which is five days before Sukkot or the Feast of Tabernacles.

In the Book of Revelation, a Red Dragon, which is signified by Draco the Dragon constellation, threatens to devour the child of this Woman, and she subsequently flees into the wilderness on two wings of a great eagle (Revelation 12:14). As explained earlier in this book when discussing the Prophet Daniel's vision of the four Beasts, the United States is depicted by the Eagle's Wings that are torn off of the Lion signifying the British Empire. Yahshua is the child whom the Woman Clothed with the Sun (Miriam and the Jews as a whole) gave birth to. This Sun-Clothed Woman also represents the True Church, or Bride of Christ. As such, she signifies that all who follow Yahshua as the Messiah must symbolically flee to the wilderness by learning to be in the world, but not of it, and by dying to their flesh and denying its cravings while being alive in the Spirit (John 15:19; Romans 8:9; 2 Cor. 10:3; Gal. 5:16; Col. 2:20).

The Woman Clothed with the Sun is found in heaven in the Zodiac sign of Virgo, and her divine child is seen in the symbolism of Virgo's first decan called Coma, which depicts "the Desired Son." In ancient allusions to Coma, the desired male child in the woman's arms came to represent many diverse gods, depending on the ancient origin of each succeeding myth. In Egypt, for example, he was "Shes-Nu," or "The

## Chapter 12: Sacred Astronomy as a Prophetic Tool

Desired Son" who supposedly manifested himself in the form of Horus, the hawk-headed son of the Sun god Amun-Ra. To Christians, however, this desired son is found only in Yahshua, for He was the only truly sinless Son of God outside of Adam, who was only sinless for a short time before he fell into sin.

The Red Dragon described in Revelation 12:3-4 is also a celestial symbol, which is found in the constellation Draco the Dragon, as well as in Hydra, the Sea Serpent. Hydra runs alongside the signs of Virgo and Leo in the sky today, just as it did in 3 BC. Serpens the Serpent, Draco the Dragon, and the Zodiac sign Scorpio the Scorpion are all tied in meaning with Hydra in the Star Gospel, and are synonymous with Satan, who is the deadly dragon, or serpent that threatens to devour the child of the Woman Clothed with the Sun. Of course, the Red Dragon does not act alone, but has always had his own highly wicked human henchmen and demons to carry out his pernicious plans.

The constellations Hydra the Sea Serpent, and Cetus the Sea Monster also serve as symbols for the Harlot atop the Scarlet Beast in Revelation 17:3, and the Beast from the Sea - which is synonymous with the Scarlet Beast - in Revelation 13:1-7. In Greek Myth, the constellation Andromeda represents a bound princess freed, and saved from the jaws of the Sea Monster Cetus by the Christ figure Perseus, who is found in a neighboring constellation. Perseus figures prominently in two upcoming sections of this chapter about the unusual celestial signs left by three comets that appeared in Earth's skies in 1996, 1997, 2007, and 2008

The constellation named Andromeda represents Jews and apostates without Grace who are bound to the Old Testament Law, and cursed by their failure to keep it. In addition, Andromeda signifies the many Christians in the world today who have been baptized with water, accept Yahshua as their Savior, but who do not know the Holy Spirit, or have a personal relationship with Christ.

Once born-again and freed by Grace, the trapped sinners represented by Andromeda are transformed by the renewing of their minds and hearts in Christ until they become resurrected saints, and they are re-made as perfect and immortal beings. This transformation is represented by the constellation named Cassiopeia - who signifies the saints that will partake in the Rapture, and the First Resurrection. As such, Cassiopeia the Enthroned Queen represents the True Church, and the Bride of Christ spoken of in Revelation 19:7-8. Cassiopeia appears next to the constellation Cepheus, the Crowned King in the Star Gospel. Together, they represent Yahshua, the rightful King of kings in Revelation 17:14, and His pure Bride and Queen, the True Church, who reigns with Christ in Revelation 20:6. Cassiopeia - the freed Andromeda sitting on a heavenly throne - is also the True Church that *"was given two wings of a great eagle, that she might fly into the wilderness to her place"* (i.e. find protection through the United States as the eagle's wings, and the Holy Spirit (See Revelation 12:14). This spiritual desert hiding place may also literally allude to Petra, the Edomite hiding place for Jews who flee a war-torn Israel just before Christ's return.

All four books in The Language of God Series examine the amazing connections between the Star Gospel, and prophetic Scriptures found throughout the Bible. The more one knows about God's miraculous messages to us in the stars, the easier it is to decipher Bible Prophecy, as will be shown in the following sections regarding the Mayan Fifth Sun, the Four Horsemen of the Apocalypse and the Anti-Peace Sign. These sections show even more clear ties between the Star Gospel, the Book of Revelation, and the Mayan date for the end of the Fifth Sun.

## *Sacred Astronomy and Catastrophism In The New World*

Uncannily, just as Judeo-Christian texts like Isaiah and the Book of Revelation warn of global disasters in the past and future, many Pagan religious myths agree that such world disasters have occurred - and will occur again in the not too distant future. For example, the myths of the ancient Native American Cultures that sprang up in the Americas speak of five or six Ages of mankind that ended or will end in global cataclysmic disasters. Some of these myths were discussed in Book Three. In that book, we also examined the major roles that Noah and Nimrod may have played in shaping the beliefs of the natives of the New World.

Among their religious myths, some of these New World people groups believed that a future Age was coming when the world would be destroyed by fire - a fire that is expected to physically and spiritually cleanse the Earth. This is remarkable in that, in the Scripture opening this chapter, the Apostle Peter prophesied that the world would one day be destroyed by fire for the same reason. Peter mentions the cataclysms that long ago destroyed - and will one day destroy - all human civilizations. The first cataclysm that totally changed the world was the Great Flood, just as the future cataclysm will cause the world to *"pass away with a great noise, and the elements will melt with fervent heat; both the earth and the works that are in it will be burned up"*. (2 Peter 3:5-11).

The teachings of this biblical passage are echoed in the religious myths of the Mayan Civilization in the New World - a culture that archeologists suppose developed much later than, and totally independent of any Old World Civilization. As was clearly shown in Book Three, however, the Native peoples of North and South America share too many cultural and religious elements in common with several Old World Cultures to have been totally unrelated. In fact, the New World people of Central and South America displayed much in common with the Ancient Egyptians, including the use of high-prowed, bundled reed boats, stone pyramids, mummification, a pictographic form of writing, and a mythology centered on the worship of astral deities.

Almost all the Native American people of the New World either venerated or worshipped the Sun, Moon, and certain stars and planets as gods - just like their Mesopotamian and Egyptian counterparts in the Old World. Among the ancient New World people, the predecessors of the Mayans had an especially well-developed fascination for timekeeping using Astronomy, just as the Babylonians did. This led to the development of startlingly accurate calendars that could be used to measure immense spans of time.

The complex science of timekeeping using the stars seems to have much more in common with Sacred Astronomy than Astrology, however. This is because pure Astronomy uses celestial alignments to measure times and seasons, while Astrology charts the position of celestial objects in the sky to foretell the future. As shown in Book Three, it is my contention that the beliefs of the native people of the New World stemmed not from demonic sources, but from the knowledge of Sacred Astronomy before it was corrupted.

## *The Remarkable Mayans*

Due to the fact that Noah may have influenced the culture of the Mayans considerably, the Mayan Civilization was discussed in Book Three, Chapter Nine, which covers the history of the New World in relation to the Bible. Due to the Mayan's use of Sacred Astronomy to predict the end of the Fifth Sun, which is tied to the end of the world as we know it, we will look at their civilization again in light of their spiritual beliefs, as well as their prophecy that dates the end of this current Age to December 21st, 2012 AD, or the Mayan date Baktun 13.

The Mayans were a Mesoamerican people who developed a very sophisticated civilization that supposedly flourished between 300 and 900 AD, and covered all of southern Mexico and northern Central America - in the region now known as the Yucatán Peninsula. According to archeologists, the Mayans inherited much of their culture and calendar from the Olmec Civilization that is currently dated from 1200 to 600 BC. However, some Christian scholars such as myself believe that the Olmec culture is far older, and may have been a Pre-Flood civilization. This means that the Olmecs would have been prominent in the region sometime before the Great Flood in 2347 BC. Adding strength to my hypothesis is the fact that *the starting date of the Olmec calendar is 3117 BC.*

Shortly after the Flood (around 2200 BC), I believe the Mayan Civilization began by re-appropriating some of the buildings and culture of the older Olmec Civilization. However, the Mayans were also builders and inventors in their own right. They are credited with building many beautiful and enduring stone structures in cities such as Copan, Palenque, Teotihuacán, and Tikal during their long history. Among the most stunning examples of these were tall step pyramids that were built by the Mayans, Incas and Aztecs, and served as temples and astronomical observatories.

Interesting to note here is the fact that the Babylonians used their step pyramids called ziggurats for the same things as the Mayans – to worship the heavens, count the passage of time using astronomical observations, and to read the divine omens revealed by the Sun, Moon, stars, and planets. This Paganistic star worship stemmed from a perversion of the truths once upheld by the righteous line of antediluvians that descended from Seth. These Sethites likely built some of the Old World pyramids of Egypt's Old Kingdom, especially the Bent and Red Pyramids at Dahshur, and the Great Pyramid Complex in Egypt at Giza.

Due to demonic influences, the Mayan religion turned into a barbaric blood cult that required tremendous amounts of human blood to be spilled. At some point, the Mayans had allowed their knowledge of the purity and holiness of the Sacred Astronomy discovered by the Sethites before the Flood to be perverted by demonic Nephilim bloodlust. However, despite their bloody and inhumane efforts to prolong the life of the world, the Mayans, their religion, and their civilization almost completely vanished. Beforehand, however, they and their successors the Aztecs performed countless human and animal sacrifices for the sake of a demonic lie, and also used blood taken from piercings on living people's sexual organs to smear on idols at religious festivals.

When the Mayan Civilization fell, their progeny lived on and preserved their ideas. Later, the Incas and Aztecs inherited the perverted Mayan form of Sacred Astronomy and the belief that the gods would not be satisfied with the blood of animal sacrifices alone, but sometimes required human blood to be appeased. In fact, nearly all of the indigenous cultures of Mexico, Central, and South America had this morbid obsession with human sacrifice, and a fixed interest in stellar events.

What many people do not realize when learning about the New World preoccupation with human blood sacrifices, however, is that almost all the Ancient Old World Civilizations also practiced human sacrifice - although not as often as the New World peoples did. In fact, the Israelites themselves practiced animal sacrifice in the place of human sacrifice, since Yahweh God would have required the blood of those who transgressed God's Laws to be shed unless they were redeemed with a temporary substitutionary animal sacrifice. In some cases, sins such as sexual deviations were so grievous that there was no redemption from these offenses. In these cases, the offending person's death by stoning was required to pay for his or her sins. Otherwise, their transgressions would affect the rest of the Israelites with divinely ordained curses that were afflicted on them due to their disobedience.

The records left by these Pre-Columbian Civilizations indicate that they all believed that their gods demanded the shedding of human blood for various offenses. Furthermore, they believed that if the gods received enough blood, this might delay the end of the Fifth Sun on December 21st, 2012, which they dreaded due to the fearful Civilization-destroying cataclysms that were associated with it. Driven by a lust for life, Native Americans slaughtered countless human victims to appease the demonic Nephilim gods of the New World.

In an attempt to satisfy the bloodlust of their gods, as many as 250,000 people were sacrificed a year by the Aztecs alone! Their victims were mostly warriors of neighboring enemy tribes, but women and children were also sacrificed. In addition, there is evidence that all these cultures practiced ritual cannibalism to some extant, eating the brains and dismembered bodies of children and adults. There is no doubt in my mind that these practices were vestiges of the prior influence and power of the Nephilim hybrid children of the Fallen Angels who mated with human women, and desired to rule over humanity as gods. Per the Book of 1 Enoch, the Nephilim were bloodthirsty killers that craved human and animal blood. It is also my contention that the Nephilim and the Fallen Angels eventually sought nothing less than the total genocide of the human race prior to the Flood.

The barbaric emphasis on human sacrifice seen in Mesoamerican Civilizations appears to have been accentuated by the time of the Aztecs, increasing dramatically from the amount of human bloodletting that was practiced by their Mayan and Olmec predecessors. In fact, though archeologists once thought the Mayans inherited their grisly practice of human sacrifice from the Olmecs and Toltecs that preceded them, there is much evidence that the emphasis on human sacrifice in Mayan religious practices was a later addition to their culture caused by the invasion and conquest of their cities by a rival warrior race from South America.

These violent people may have been descendants of the Nephilim Giants that also inhabited the Promised Land prior to the Israelite Conquest of Canaan. If these invaders were Nephilim or Anakim, and I believe that they were, these vile beings likely introduced human sacrifice to the Americas, and forced many Mesoamerican and North American people to fulfill the bloodlust of their new false gods with human sacrifices. In this cased, then, the evidence of cannibalism may not have been humans eating humans, but Nephilim hybrids eating humans, just as they did prior to the Great Flood.

As shown in Book Three, "The Language of God in History," it is possible that this conquest of the Mayan Civilization by hostile invaders from the south occurred within three hundred years after the Great Flood, and that the Mayans civilization flourished in Mesoamerica and South America much earlier in history than is supposed. Furthermore, certain clues suggest that the followers of Nimrod, who had already forged an empire in Mesopotamia, led this invasion - perhaps with the help of the Anakim descendents of the Nephilim who desired to destroy Noah and Shem and their descendents. Since the Bible indicates that the whole world had one set of religious beliefs and one language during Nimrod's despotic reign, it is highly likely that Nimrod conquered nearly *the entire world* in order to impose his demonically-inspired Pagan religious practices. In the process, Nimrod and his followers and the Anakim Giants who aided them almost succeeded in wiping out every last trace of the godly religious beliefs instilled in people everywhere by Noah and Shem hundreds of years earlier. This hypothesis is also explored in detail in Book Three, "The Language of God in History".

## *The Giza - Teotihuacán Connection*

Though the Mayan religion degenerated into a demonically inspired system of human sacrifice, there is evidence that the roots of their culture were inspired by the science and religion surrounding the Sacred Astronomy of the Sethites. The Mayans are accredited with building Teotihuacán, a remarkable religious temple complex about 31 miles northeast of Mexico City, in southern Mexico.

# Chapter 12: Sacred Astronomy as a Prophetic Tool

Uncannily, as was discussed in Book Three, there are remarkable similarities connecting Giza, Teotihuacán, and Sacred Astronomy that can only be seen clearly from the air. First of all, the major temples and avenues running north to south along the Street of the Dead at Teotihuacán appear to serve as a giant scale model of our own Solar System *if viewed from the air*. As shown in the drawing of Teotihuacán's site layout in this section, the Temple Complex to Quetzalcoatl serves as a representation of our Sun. What is even more remarkable is that the major avenues and associated temples running east to west along the north-south axis of the Street of the Dead appear to represent *all nine planets* in our Solar System, the Earth, our Moon, and the asteroid belt - in their correct order out from the Sun!

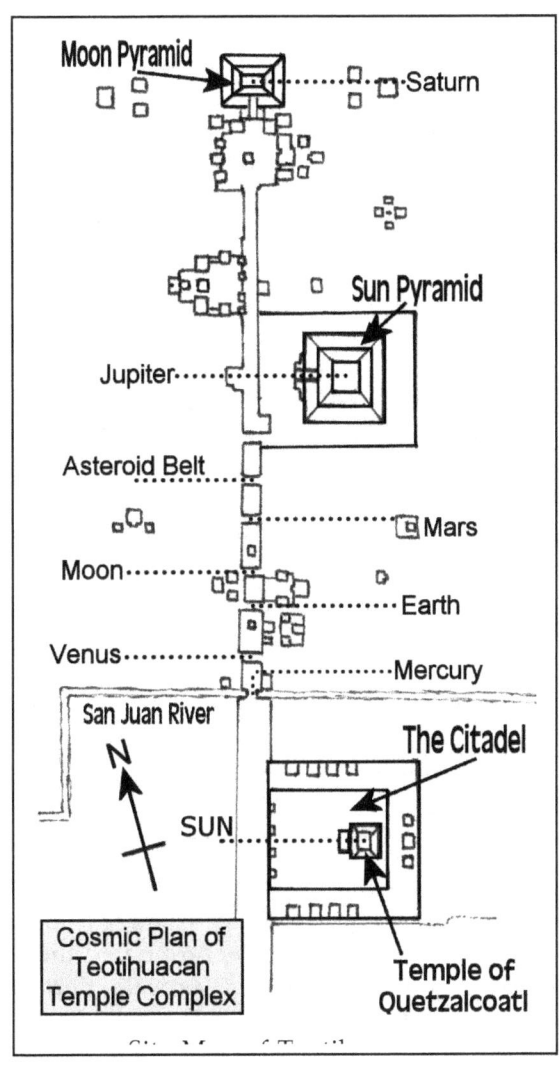

If seen as a mock up of the Solar System, we find that the so-called Pyramid of the Sun doesn't represent the Sun at all, but the Messiah planet Jupiter, and the supposed Pyramid of the Moon actually represents the planet Saturn! This raises the obvious question: "How did the Stone Age Mayans know that our Solar System has nine planets - and *an asteroid belt* - without the aid of modern high-powered telescopes?"

In addition to these startling facts, the Pyramid of the Sun at Teotihuacán and the Great Pyramid in Egypt have much in common. For example, they are both pyramidal in shape and nearly the same size at the base - though the Great Pyramid has about twice the mass of the Sun Pyramid. Another intriguing similarity between these pyramids defies explanation, in that they both have a naturally occurring hidden feature in the ground beneath them. In the Great Pyramid, it is the Well Shaft and Grotto found in the bedrock between the Descending Passageway and the Grand Gallery. In the Pyramid of the Sun, it is a cloverleaf-shaped cave that may have been formed by a now dried up subterranean spring.

Though these similarities are startling enough, there is one other connection between Giza and Teotihuacán that unquestionably shows they had a similar spiritual purpose at one time. This is the fact that ***the three pyramids at Giza, and the three biggest pyramids at Teotihuacán both appear to mirror the position of the three belt stars of Orion!*** Also, just as the Khafre Pyramid appears as tall as the Great Pyramid because it is on higher ground, the same is true of the Pyramid of the Moon at Teotihuacán, which appears as high as the Pyramid of the Sun because it is on higher ground.

Due to this connection to the belt stars of Orion - and the Messiah figure that Orion represents - it is possible that the Mayan Pyramid complex at Teotihuacán served as an altar and temple like the Great Pyramid complex at Giza. ***It is also possible that the one true God Yahweh designed Teotihuacán's site plan, just as He may have designed the Giza site.*** Though there is no direct proof of this, it can definitely be inferred by the connections to Orion, the Solar System, and the Star Gospel at Giza and Teotihuacán.

As shown in the entire Language of God Book Series, Orion is one of the most powerful Messianic symbols in the Star Gospel. Perhaps this is why men have misappropriated this powerful symbol many times in the past. One of the most prevalent erroneous connections has come from the fact that Orion is called the Hunter to connect it to the Nephilim and to Nimrod, who was called *"a mighty hunter"* in the Bible (Genesis 10:9). Though it is likely true that Nimrod saw himself as the world's Messiah that is pictured in Orion, he most certainly was **not** that Messiah, but an Anti-Messiah or Antichrist of the worst sort imaginable! See Book Three for more about Nimrod's ignoble infamy.

Despite this misappropriation, it is clear from Orion's shape as a Passover Cup or chalice, and the Orion's Belt connection to the three Crosses on Calvary that Orion was always meant to be a symbol for Christ and a few other godly heroes. Because of this, we need to ask: "Is Orion's connection with the Great Pyramid at Giza, the Sun Pyramid at Teotihuacán, and Christ a mere coincidence? Or did some Native

# Chapter 12: Sacred Astronomy as a Prophetic Tool    Page 623

Americans once worship the one true God, and the Messiah prophesied about in the Gospel in the Stars? Did they know about the Messiah's connection to Jupiter, and Teotihuacán through Orion?" In my opinion, this is the only reasonable explanation - given the obvious similarities between Teotihuacán and Giza.

Teotihuacán was supposedly built at the height of the Mayan civilization. However, some archeologists believe that the largest pyramids at Teotihuacán were built hundreds of years before the Mayan civilization arose. This would mean that the Olmecs - or some other antediluvian people before them - created the biggest pyramids at Teotihuacán. As shown in Book Three, it may have been none other than Noah himself that came to the New World. Furthermore, as the Epic of Gilgamesh suggests, it may have been Noah who started his own civilization there. After dividing up the Old World continents between his three sons awhile after the Great Flood, Noah may have decided to find peace and solitude in his own remote region of the Earth that was far from the ambitions, and schemes of his sons, and other descendents. Furthermore, as the Ecuador artifacts featured in Chapter 9 convey, there is evidence that Noah or some of his kin that understood Sacred Astronomy may have settled in Ecuador, which is right on the Earth's equator in the northernmost portion of South America.

Sadly, however, the Mayan mythology that has come down to us shows a good deal of demonic influences. As was shown so clearly in Book Three, this perversion of Sacred Astronomy likely arose because Nimrod succeeded in launching a worldwide movement to pervert the truths of the Gospel in the Stars. Therefore, though the sacred structures in Mesopotamia and the Americas may have been built using godly truths similar to those used in the Pre-Flood structures at Giza, the Post-Flood religions of the Old World Classical and New World Civilizations was largely based on a gross distortion of those truths.

## *The Prophetic Quality of the Mayan Calendar*

Despite the fact that evil men and Nephilim-inspired demons succeeded in grossly distorting Mayan religious practices with a barbaric need for human sacrifice, the Mayans had an otherwise high level of civilization marked by great refinement in pottery, textiles, and other forms of artistic expression. But by far the greatest achievement of the Mayan civilization was their extremely accurate circular calendar system. It remains one of the most accurate calendars ever devised – one that is capable of calculating immense spans of time with a high degree of precision and accuracy.

The Mayans used this calendar not only to keep records, and determine the seasons, but also to look forward and backward in time to date past events, or to pinpoint future ones. The Mayans believed that these events were calculable through the use of the same principles in astronomy that helped them to create their sophisticated calendar. Using their complex calendar, the Mayans divided the 5,125 years prior to December 21st, 2012 into five approximately 1000-year Ages or "Suns". This belief is similar to the Judeo-Christian concept of the millennium-long Great Day, and the idea that Six Great Days were destined to pass before the end of the current World Age, and the ushering in of Christ's Kingdom.

The Mayans believed that each prior Sun had ended catastrophically - with great destruction and huge losses of human and animal life. In fact, **the Mayans taught that the Fourth Sun or Age ended with a cataclysmic worldwide flood and a subsequent period of great and terrifying darkness.** This is exactly how the Bible describes Noah's Flood, which my Biblical Chronology dates to 2347 BC. There is also much evidence that the Mayans believed that their Fifth Sun would end catastrophically. The Mayans Fifth Sun corresponds to the Fifth and Sixth Great Days of the Church Age. Using their calendar, **the Mayans looked ahead and predicted that the Fifth Sun, or this current Age would end on December 21st, 2012 - accompanied by a global destruction by fire and earthquake.**

This date for the end of the Fifth Sun had great significance in the religious philosophy of the Mayans. In fact, history books on the Mayans indicate that this was the basis behind their belief in the need for human sacrifices. They were trying to delay the end of the world! Though the Mayans believed that this current Age would end by fire and earthquake, they also thought that they could prolong the coming of this terrible end by sacrificing human hearts to their gods. This grisly practice was carried on for hundreds of years by Mesoamerican peoples before the Spanish conquistadors conquered and destroyed the civilization of the Aztecs - who had succeeded the Mayans.

Amazingly, the date that the Mayans gave for the end of this current Age coincides with the year 2012 AD, which corresponds with the second year of the Tribulation period shown by the Hallel Psalms, Sacred Astronomy, and the Antechamber of the Great Pyramid. **Also, just as the Mayans predicted - and the Bible and the recent world news are telling us - this current Age is ending very violently - amid fires and earthquakes**

(**Fire:** Revelation 8:7, 9:17-18, 16:8-9; **Earthquake:** Revelation 6:12, 11:13, 16:18-20). See previous chapters for recaps of some of the worst of these fires and earthquakes.

Though New Age religious proponents teach that the end of the Mayan Fifth Sun that we are now experiencing is to be a time of great spiritual transformation and huge advancements that will promote global peace, prosperity and happiness as all living things move toward existing in harmony with one another, the transformation that true believers in Christ are seeing globally is anything but godly! In fact, the world is filled with more wickedness than ever, and seems closer to another world war with a potentially devastating nuclear component than ever before.

Many Bible scholars believe that the second year of the Tribulation will mark the beginning of *three sets of seven plagues* or judgments that are spoken of in the Book of Revelation. To begin with, one plague will accompany the opening of each of the Seven Seals (Revelation 6:1-17, 8:6-13). **One of these Tribulation plagues will be a great earthquake** that will likely be felt around the world. This will accompany the Sixth Seal, which the Bible tells us is the beginning plague of the pouring out of the Wrath of God against the ungodly:

> "I looked when He opened the sixth seal, and behold, **there was a great earthquake**; and the sun became black as sackcloth of hair, and the moon became like blood." - *Rev. 6:12*

The Book of Revelation then tells us that seven more plagues will commence with the blowing of each of Seven Trumpets (Revelation 8:7,8,10,12-13; 9:1,13-14; 11:15-19). These seven plagues will build on each other - becoming progressively worse. Significantly, three of these plagues will consist of more earthquakes (Rev. 8:5, 11:13, and 11:19). After this, a final and even more devastating set of seven plagues will come. These are the pouring out of *the Seven Bowls of God's Wrath.* **These final seven plagues will ruin whole civilizations, and destroy a large percentage of Earth's people, animals, and land by fire, great heat, and another great earthquake** (Revelation 16:1-21).

Although the fire and great heat will be terrible, however, it will *not* destroy the whole Earth. The final destruction of the Earth's surface by the fire and heat at the end of the Millennium is described in 2 Peter 3:10-12. This will occur at the end of Christ's Millennial Rule. Nonetheless, the great earthquake just before Christ's Second Coming will be more devastating than any of the other Tribulation quakes:

> *"And there were noises and thunderings and lightnings;* **and there was a... mighty and great earthquake** *as had not occurred since men were on the earth." - Rev. 16:18-20*

During the Tribulation period, much of this destruction to be caused by fires and earthquakes may result from an immense comet or asteroid collision with the Earth. The Book of Revelation speaks of two separate stellar bombardments - one of a mountain-like projectile that falls into the sea, and the other of a star that falls to Earth and pollutes the world's water supply. Based on the following Scripture, each cosmic projectile will likely come in rapid succession:

> *"Then the second angel sounded:* **And something like a great mountain burning with fire was thrown into the sea,** *and a third of the sea became blood. And a third of the living creatures in the sea died, and a third of the ships were destroyed. Then the third angel sounded:* **And a great star fell from heaven, burning like a torch, and it fell on a third of the rivers and on the springs of water. The name of the star is Wormwood.** *A third of the waters became wormwood, and many men died from the water... Then the fourth angel sounded: And* **a third of the sun was struck, a third of the moon, and a third of the stars, so that a third of them were darkened.** *A third of the day did not shine, and likewise the night." - Rev. 8:8-12*

These prophesied future cosmic bombardments of Earth in the Book of Revelation don't appear to be allegorical in nature. On the contrary, they appear to be real events that will occur during the Tribulation period. This stellar assault therefore may cause great destruction to ships and aquatic life - and widespread water pollution. In fact, this is exactly what my dream of 2011 that was recalled in the last chapter showed would happen!

In the above Scripture, the star that falls into the water is named Wormwood - a known bitter herb that has medicinal properties in small quantities, but can act as a lethal poison in high concentrations. The minerals and chemicals in this star that falls to Earth will therefore probably pollute the bodies of water it comes into contact with some sort of poisonous substance that will spread through a large swath of the world's water supply - thereby killing anyone or anything that drinks it.

If a large comet or asteroid hits the Earth, the subsequent dust and debris that would be thrown up into our atmosphere could be considerable. This initial impact debris would also likely be added to by tremendous amounts of smoke and ash from the inevitable volcanic

## Chapter 12: Sacred Astronomy as a Prophetic Tool

eruptions and earthquakes that a large-scale cosmic impact would cause. Could this be what causes the darkness that Revelation 8:12 says will obscure a third of the sun's rays during daylight, and a third of the moonlight and starlight? This is a highly probable assumption, based on the two enormous cosmic objects that this same section of Scripture describes as colliding with the Earth (Rev. 8:8-11).

The prophet Isaiah foresaw a time in the future when the Earth would be broken apart, and shaken from its place. This is something that could only occur if a large asteroid or comet moving at a high velocity cataclysmically hit the Earth:

> "Whoever flees at the sound of terror will fall into a pit; whoever climbs out of the pit will be caught in a snare. The floodgates of the heavens are opened, the foundations of the earth shake. **The earth is broken up, the earth is split asunder, the earth is thoroughly shaken. The earth reels like a drunkard, it sways like a hut in the wind;** so heavy upon it is the guilt of its rebellion that it falls - never to rise again." - Isaiah 24:18-20 (NIV)

When I first read this prophecy by Isaiah, I thought he may have been prophesying in reverse, and recalling the time of the Great Flood, or the time of the Fall of Babel since it could have been uttered equally well in reference to those past cataclysmic events. However, this prophecy appears in a section of Isaiah filled with prophecies about the Great Day of the Lord. Isaiah therefore makes it clear that **the Earth will be violently shaken and moved about during the Tribulation period, just as it likely was prior to, during, and sometime after the Flood of Noah.** Yahshua's prophecies about the coming of the Tribulation will then be fulfilled:

> "And **as it was in the days of Noah**, so it will be also in the days of the Son of Man..." - Luke 17:26

> "**For as in the days before the flood,** they were eating and drinking, marrying and giving in marriage, until the day that Noah entered the ark, and did not know until the flood came and took them all away, **so also will the coming of the Son of Man be.**" - Matthew 24:38-39

Just as Yahshua said it would, the End of this World Age has come cataclysmically, just as it did in the days of Noah. That the Mayans foresaw this future time in 2012 AD is nothing short of miraculous, especially since they foresaw the cataclysmic upheaval, death, and destruction that accompanied it, and rightly viewed its coming with great trepidation and fear. Unlike born-again believers, the Mayans could not find peace and comfort in Christ's promises of protection, resurrection, and everlasting life. Therefore, despite their advances in science and culture, the Mayans had no real hope in the future - only a demonically perverted religion that obliterated the purity of their religious beliefs based on Sacred Astronomy, and denied them the salvation and forgiveness promised to all people in the Star Gospel.

## *The Mayan World End and the Great Tribulation*

The Great Tribulation and Yahshua's Second Coming will be events like no other in history. During the Great Tribulation, for example, Yahweh will unleash the worst plagues and disasters ever to affect planet Earth outside of the Great Flood. Likewise, when Yahshua returns, He will be accompanied by a huge multitude of holy angels and shining saints riding on white horses. An event as spectacular as this has never happened in human history. Therefore, if Sacred Astronomy has any validity, **the Great Tribulation and Yahshua's Second Coming should be marked by cosmic events that have never before occurred in all of human history**. This led me to ask the question: "Could there be more significance to the date that the Mayan Calendar gives for the end of their Fifth Sun besides being a Winter Solstice?" It turns out that there is a very great significance to this date, for **it marks the date when the exact center of our Milky Way Galaxy rose helically with the morning Sun on the shortest day of the year.**

The Galactic Equator is directly between Sagittarius and Scorpio in the center of the visible arm of the Milky Way Galaxy that can clearly be seen between these two signs on a clear, dark night. On the morning of the Winter Solstice in 2012, our Sun, the Earth, and the Galactic Equator formed a conjunction that has never occurred before in recorded history. However, John Major Jenkins, who was the author of the book, "Mayan Cosmogenesis 2012," has indicated on his web site that it will take 36 years for the Sun to transit the Galactic Equator. Therefore, the conjunction of our Sun with the Galactic Equator will occur on the Winter Solstice for 35 more years in a row beginning on December 21st, 2103, and ending on December 21st, 2047. Interestingly, since the Last Great Day began in the spring of 2000, 2047 AD will mark the 48th year of the Last Great Day.

That this Galactic Alignment with the Earth and the Sun occurred on a Winter Solstice - the shortest day of the year - is certainly no accident. On this same day, people have honored the symbolic rebirth of the Sun since time immemorial, and this was a cause of much celebration in Ancient times, as it was the true start of the New Year in the eyes of

## Chapter 12: Sacred Astronomy as a Prophetic Tool     Page 629

the ancients. Perhaps this is why there is even cause for Christians and Messianics to find joy on the Winter Solstice, since Yahshua was likely conceived during Chanukah in 4 BC, and the Wise Men likely found Yahshua in Bethlehem when Chanukah was being celebrated around the time of the Winter Solstice in December of 2 BC. ***Though the worship of the Sun, or any symbol for God is a grave sin - the birth, death and resurrection of the true Son of God is a cause for great joy, and true worship!*** That is why I see such hope and joy in connection with this Galactic Alignment on the Winter Solstice of 2012. It is a sure sign that our Adonai Yahshua is coming very soon!

My cause for joy is centered on the fact that, if 2011 is the first year of the Tribulation, and the First Rapture is a mid-Tribulation event, this means the Rapture could occur anytime between the end of 2013 and the end of 2014 AD. But this will not be to escape the Tribulation altogether, but only the Wrath of God. As will be shown in this chapter, the Signs in the Heavens on December 21st, 2012 may have marked the beginning or middle of the Seal Judgments. With all the horrific plagues and disasters that have been sweeping the Earth since 2010, it seems to me that at least two of the Seals may have been opened earlier, which would mark 2012 as a possible mid point. This is a joyful thing in that I see the Seal Judgments prior to the Sixth Seal as a catalyst for repentance. Though much of the world is still not paying attention, many people who were asleep before are now putting their faith in Christ, and they will gain everlasting life through Him.

I also believe that this joyous process of people coming to Salvation in Christ will accelerate after the First Rapture. Although it is terrible that anyone should have to suffer agony in the Great Tribulation, it would be far worse to suffer in Hell for eternity. We can therefore view this terrible Time of Trouble and Testing as a joyous event for those who will be forever saved by it! We therefore should rejoice that so many saints will find Salvation in the Tribulation period rather than mourn those who - through their hatred of God - will be lost.

In his book, "Mayan Cosmogenesis 2012," John Major Jenkins also noted that this Galactic Alignment coincided with the Winter Solstice. Unfortunately, however, Jenkins doesn't see any connection between the Mayan Calendar and the patriarchs that are remembered by those with a Judeo-Christian background. Instead, he supports a Neo-Pagan, New Age spiritual worldview, and sees this Mayan End Date as marking a great spiritual step forward for mankind in general.

## Paganism's Prophetic Counterfeits For End Time Events

Sadly, like millions of other people on the Earth today, Mr. Jenkins believes that there is a coming New Age of enlightenment - when mankind as a whole will *evolve* into a higher level of existence. Although this is true in a certain sense that is truly Biblical, it won't be the way that New Agers envision it, nor will it be through their bankrupt methods of connecting with their spiritual sides. These include discovering their false godhood through meditation, crystals, and demonic encounters that free those who are so deluded from all religious and moral constraints.

According to the demons they listen to, New Age Spiritualists are waiting for the Earth to be cleansed of all the things and people that are supposedly preventing this New Age of peace and spiritual enlightenment from arriving. In actuality, however, this spiritual cleansing they are awaiting is the Rapture and Sudden Destruction, which they see as a positive and necessary development so that they and their goddess world can reach their fullest potential as gods. So, instead of the Millennial Rule of Christ, they are awaiting the coming of Satan in the form of the Antichrist, and they will worship him just as they worship themselves as gods. This total twisting of the truth was brought about by Satan, who is the instigator of all false predictions, and erroneous spiritual ideologies that either mimic, or directly oppose every Christian and Messianic teaching about the end of this current Age, and the coming of the Day of the Lord.

Satan's success in deceiving the world is very obvious at certain Internet bookstores. When doing a cursory search for books about the Mayan Calendar and their enigmatic date for the end of the world, a plethora of New Age spiritual resources will appear. Nearly all of them tout the same erroneous view of the future that Mr. Jenkins espouses. Many of them hail the Winter Solstice in December of 2012 as the date when the world was catapulted into a New Age of awareness. In New Age Spirituality, the increase in wickedness seen around the world in the acceptance of homosexuality and all other forms of sexual sin and immorality - including abortion -can be viewed as an indication that mankind has reached a new level of spiritual enlightenment that has not been seen on the Earth for millennia.

From a believer's standpoint, however, New Age Spirituality is actually a gross from of spiritual degeneration that leads to the total rejection of Biblical Morality by society. In conjunction with this counterfeit New Age Gospel, prophesied Christian events such as the Rapture, the Antichrist, and the subsequent destruction of the ungodly have similarly counterfeit explanations within New Age Spirituality. The Demonic counterfeits of Christian prophecies tout these events as methods of cleansing the Earth so this New Age of enlightenment can begin. Again - in a very perverted sense, this belief is true - but it isn't to usher in a New Pagan Age, but a New Judeo-Christian Age of righteousness – Yahshua's Millennial Rule!

Since Satan knows how to twist every truth, it should come as no surprise to believers that Neo-Pagans are being taught that the Rapture has a completely different purpose than the one given for it in the Bible. Instead of being seen as a joyful, merciful, and blessed deliverance of the righteous from needless suffering before the world is judged, New Age spiritual proponents are looking for a Rapture-like event that will remove spiritually defective humans from the Earth! These purportedly "defective" souls who disappear will be seen as the ones who are holding the world back from achieving a higher state of spiritual consciousness. Since those who disappear will be monotheistic believers in absolute right and wrong and a Savior who is the only Son of God, and these are doctrines Neo-Pagans totally reject, those who are left behind will celebrate this massive disappearance of humans as a good thing. Their celebration will be very short-lived, however, since the plagues and natural disasters of the Great Tribulation will destroy millions of these unrepentant people who are left behind.

Sadly, **there are satanic counterfeits for every Judeo-Christian belief.** Furthermore, these false spiritual views are widely held, and have rapidly spread throughout the world. Satan's counterfeit religious movement is extremely beguiling to many young people today. The United Nations has practically made it a crime for parents to discipline their children, and those who do so can be seen as criminals in the eyes of the state. For this reason, youth around the world are being taught that they do not have to listen to their parents, and that they have the right to reject their discipline.

Since so many children are being raised without proper discipline, many of them are so deeply steeped in sinful behavior and pastimes that they are almost beyond redemption. On top of this, others have developed excessive selfishness and pride. This is because spiritual arrogance is not disapproved of, but encouraged in this immoral era of "self-esteem" and "self realization." As a result, these conceited people readily reject the idea that they are fallen and sinful. Instead, they seek leaders that support their New Age ideas that all humans are little gods that have the power to create their own earthly utopias. They also naturally flock around anyone who espouses their beliefs. As such, they will readily accept the Antichrist, who will not only espouse all that they hold drear, but will be able to perform counterfeit miracles in their sight.

Many religions teach that a messiah will come to establish a New Age of peace and prosperity. As a result, the entire world is filled with people who are hungry for their messiah to appear. Sadly, the Antichrist will be able to fulfill their desire for a messiah in ways that will satisfy them. That is, until God begins to pour out His great Wrath on the world! According to the structure of Revelation, Yahweh's End Time plagues will really begin to intensify after the Sixth Seal Judgment. Thus, the Mayan date for the end of their Fifth Sun or Fifth Age actually appears to coincide with the unleashing of the Four Horsemen of the Apocalypse, who are sent when the first four of the Seven Seal Judgments are opened. Evidence for this includes the waves of limited destruction on the Earth and the great increase in wickedness that I have been documenting as a worldwide phenomenon since 2010. However, in a moment, I will show how the heavens themselves proclaimed the opening of the first four Seal Judgments on December 21st, 2012 - in more ways than one!

Tragically, however, most of the world is unaware of how perilous the times we are living in currently are. In addition, billions of unrepentant people on this planet have already fallen for Satan's lies, and are in danger of perishing forever in Hell. This is because **the stellar event that the Mayans foretold as the beginning of a cataclysmic destruction of the world has been falsely heralded as the dawn of a New Age** - an Age when there will be a One World Religion, and a Global Empire that will falsely promise world economic prosperity, and lasting world peace.

Ironically, the true and lasting versions of all these things will be achieved on Earth during Christ's Millennial Rule, but the demonically controlled Antichrist will fool the world into thinking that he can create this future utopia by purely human machinations and technology. All this will occur *before* the true Christ returns to destroy the Antichrist, and those who follow his satanic religion and government. For this reason, many who do not believe in Bible prophecies, or don't know them will be fooled by the Antichrist's convincing satanic counterfeits of godly and miraculous things, just as so many have been by the Merovingian heresy, and the many lies surrounding Christ's true nature.

## What the Star Gospel Reveals on December 21st, 2012

As previously mentioned, what marks these two very different appraisals of the future is an unprecedented astronomical event. This is when *the galactic center of the Milky Way between Sagittarius and Scorpio rose with our Sun in Scorpio/Ophiuchus on the Winter Solstice.* The center of our Galaxy has been found in the region of the sky governed by the Zodiac sign of Sagittarius, though it lies across a portion of the sky also governed by Scorpio. This has great significance since the galactic center is located between two constellations that show Christ as the victorious Archer. These are Sagittarius and Centaurus, and both of these centaurs in heaven are poised to shoot a fatal arrow into Satan/Scorpio's heart, as shown in the illustration on page 643 of this chapter. This victory over Satan happened spiritually when Christ died on the Cross, and it will happen literally when Yahshua returns from Heaven to rule the world.

The decan sign of Scorpio called Ophiuchus the Serpent Holder, which is often called the 13th Sign of the Zodiac and has a special connection to the United States both geographically and spiritually, was fully visible above the horizon just before sunrise on the Winter Solstice on December 21st, 2012. There, just before the Sun rose to obliterate their image with its light on the great stage of Earth's sky, the Strong Man signifying the redemption and protection that Yahshua's death on the Cross provided was at center stage - wrestling with Serpens the Serpent, which is a symbol of Satan and his seed. Then, as the Sun rose on the horizon, it intersected the point between Sagittarius and Ophiuchus where the center of our Milky Way Galaxy is said to be located. At the same time, the Eagle Nebula in Serpens was just above the horizon, and Aquila the Eagle was below the tail of Serpens. These Eagles symbolize the deadly enemies of the Serpent, who is Satan. As such they signify holy angels and born-again believers fighting demonic principalities and powers with God's Truth found in the Gospel in the Stars and the Bible. They also signify God's provision and protection for His people.

As mentioned in Chapters 7and 10, it is possible that the Antichrist will be a descendent of the Tribe of Dan, and Dan is connected to the sign of Scorpio in the Gospel in the Stars. This may be why the Tribe of Dan is not mentioned when the 144,000 Witnesses of God are chosen out of the Twelve Tribes of Israel in the Book of Revelation (Rev. 7:2-8). Rather, the Tribe of Manasseh is mentioned instead of the Tribe of Dan. Since 12,000 people from the Tribe of Manasseh will serve as part of the 144,000 Witnesses of Yahweh, it means that there are righteous people among this tribe, so it is not fully in rebellion against God. However, there is another sinister possibility regarding Manasseh that many people overlook because they do not know how to read the Language of God.

## Meaning of Heavenly Signs on December 21st, 2012

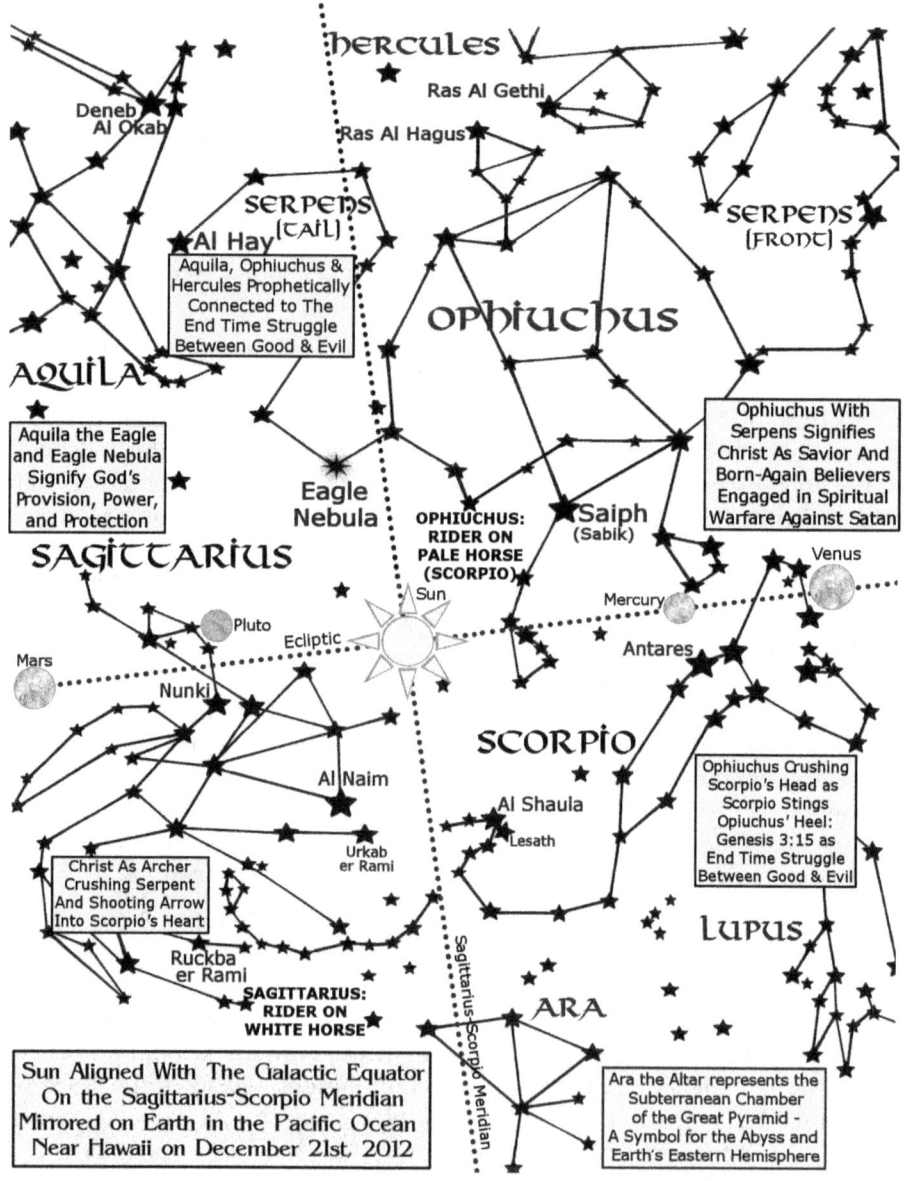

As this book has shown, the United Kingdom may represent the Tribe of Manasseh in modern times, and Prince Charles is connected to the Tribes of Dan, Judah, and Manasseh. Remember, his father Prince

## Chapter 12: Sacred Astronomy as a Prophetic Tool        Page 635

Philip is the Prince of Greece and Denmark (i.e. Dan's Mark!), and the Spartans were and the Danish are purportedly connected to the Tribe of Dan. Interestingly, if the Antichrist is Prince Charles or someone else from among the British Royalty, this designation of Manasseh with Dan in Revelation could mean that the Tribe of Manasseh will not replace the Tribe of Dan in eternity, but that *Manasseh may become like the apostate Tribe of Dan. However, the Tribe of Dan is represented in Ezekiel's Temple,* and this indicates that it will have a place in Yahshua's Kingdom as well as eternity. So though the Antichrist may come from the figurative Tribe of Manasseh, many people living in the United Kingdom and British Commonwealth will likely join Israel, the USA, and the rest of the spiritually born-again Tribe of Ephraim in fighting the Antichrist.

Though the Tribe of Dan is not recognized as part of Israel in the Tribulation period (as indicated by the replacement of Manasseh for Dan in Revelation 7:6), Dan will be honored in the Millennial Rule of Christ, as seen by the subsequent mention of Dan in Ezekiel's visions of the Millennial Kingdom (Ezekiel 48:1,2,32). This is because Ephraim will take the place of Dan, and - with Yahshua's help - will turn evil into good!

As stated earlier in this book, the Eagle Nebula located in the Serpens constellation and the sign of Aquila the Eagle are symbols for Ephraim, and this eagle symbol will replace Serpens signifying the Antichrist and Draco signifying the Red Dragon and Beast from the Sea in the heavens one day. These giant serpents in the sky are also connected to the Tribe of Dan, while the eagle's face on Ezekiel's Cherubim signifies the divinely chosen replacement for the Tribe of Dan in eternity. Meanwhile, the close proximity of these two celestial eagles to Scorpio suggests that the Tribulation Saints in the United States *and around the world* already are, and will continue to be intimately involved in this gargantuan struggle against evil that Ophiuchus represents.

Ophiuchus the Strong Man perpetually wrestles with a huge serpent, and this signifies Christ's battle with Satan, the Antichrist, and their evil followers. Meanwhile, the Eagle Nebula, and Aquila the Eagle represent Ephraim, which signifies all born-again Gentile believers in Christ that are grafted into Israel by faith, but may especially be tied to the United States in the End Times, as shown in Chapter Nine. On the following page is a graphic taken from my book: "The Language of God in History". It depicts different aspects of the spiritual struggle that the heavenly signs on December 21st, 2012 depict than the graphic that was introduced earlier in this chapter. Following the graphic is what I wrote to describe this graphic, which was taken from page 508 in Book Three:

## Star Gospel for Draco, Hercules, Ophiuchus & Bootes

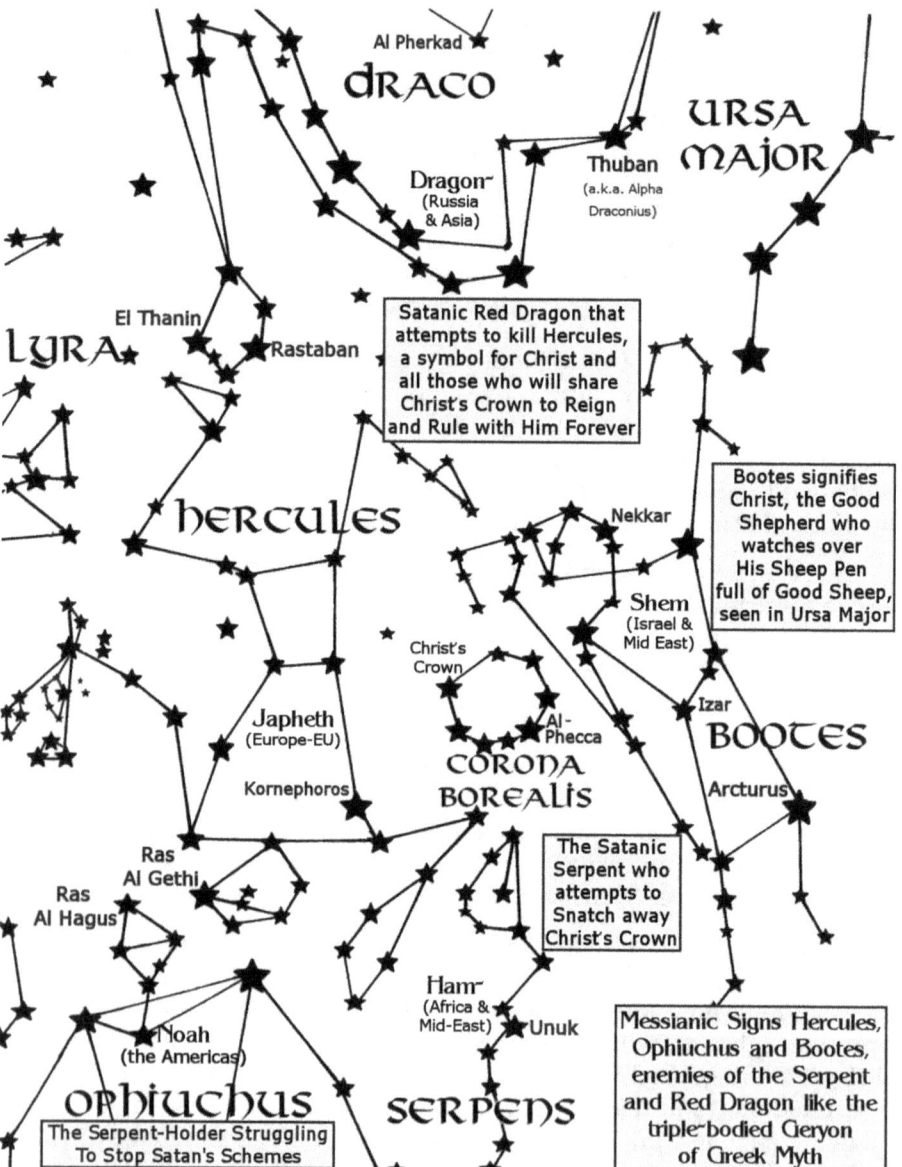

"When viewed through the Language of God rather than Greek Mythology alone, the signs of Hercules, Ophiuchus, Bootes and Draco also appear to symbolize something even more amazing. If we view Noah, who is connected to the Americas as Ophiuchus, Noah's son Shem

## Chapter 12: Sacred Astronomy as a Prophetic Tool

representing Israel and the Middle East as connected to Bootes, and Japheth as Hercules signifying the European Union, could these three signify the triple-bodied Geryon envisioned by the Greeks (see Chapter Seven! (In Book 3)), with the Geryon's single head vying for the King's Crown seen in Corona Borealis? Furthermore, could Draco symbolize Asia and Russia, and the Serpent writhing in Ophiuchus' hands that seems ready to snatch away the crown signify Africa and the Mid-East being twisted by the Jihadists and their Mahdi, who wish to steal Christ's Crown? As shown in this chapter, Scorpio signifies the Pale Horse of Revelation. Therefore, could Serpens be riding this Pale Horse of Death?" (End of Excerpt)

During the Tribulation, the wounded eagle depicted in Aquila that is connected to the Tribe of Ephraim may signify the actions of the common people of the United States and Israel - who are being called to lead the saints throughout the world in the fight against the Antichrist during the Great Tribulation. As a reward, I believe that these Tribulation Saints will earn the right to meet Christ, His Bride and His angels in the air just before the Battle of Armageddon, and they will be girded with immortality and armed with Christ's invincible might at that time. As a result, they will directly take part in the battle the Yahshua will lead to destroy the Antichrist, and they will help bring the Great Tribulation to a bloody, yet gloriously triumphant finish.

There is evidence that ***the Mayans and other cultures depicted this terrible date for the end of the world with a cross symbol drawn within a circle***. Archeological evidence shows that this cross within a circle was used as a decorative and symbolic device around the world in ancient times and was often carved into ancient temple walls. On a more mundane level, this cross within a circle allegorically represents the Sun, the equinoxes and solstices of any given year, and the four fixed signs of the Zodiac: Leo, Taurus, Aquarius, and Scorpio. However, as discussed in "The Language of God in the Universe," ***a cross within a circle can also represent the intersection of two great circles of astronomical time.***

On December 21st, 2012, the center of our Milky Way Galaxy was aligned with the rising Sun due east on the Winter Solstice. At that moment, the Precessional cross marking the beginning of the First Great Creation Day - when the Spring Equinox was in Leo and the Winter Solstice was in Taurus - was aligned in opposition with the 2012 Precessional cross with the Spring Equinox in Aquarius. This means that the diabolical sign of Scorpio was allegorically in direct opposition to the sign of Taurus. It was as if the Bull (Christ and Joseph/Ephraim) and Scorpion (Satan/Antichrist) were locked in mortal combat on the horizon.

*In my opinion, this figurative opposition marked the time when the world began to be more harshly judged for its sins.* This overlapping of the cross of the Age of Leo and the cross of the Age of Aquarius perfectly symbolizes Christ as the Alpha and Omega and makes the Cross a highly appropriate Christian symbol.

There are other interesting associations that can be made with the Mayan End Date and Christianity's teachings. For example, the Mayans had a long-count time period called a Baktun that equaled 144,000 days, or approximately 394 Solar Years. Baktun 1 of the Mayan Calendar began in our year 3114 BC, and a period of 13 times 394 years, or 5,122 years have passed from that date until Baktun 13, or December 21st, 2012. Can you see how this information ties in with Christianity? It is there; only it is difficult to see because **it is hidden in the numbers that the Mayans associated with the end of the world!** For example, the Mayans dated the end of the world as 13.0.0.0.0, or Baktun 13. Similarly, Judeo-Christian cosmology teaches that Twelve Great Ages or Days will have passed before the *Thirteenth* Great Day when Yahshua will rule on Earth. The Mayan date Baktun 13 therefore nearly coincides with the beginning of the 13th Millennium since Creation began. In addition, one Baktun is equal to 144,000 days, just as there will be 144,000 Witnesses on the Earth during the Great Tribulation.

Since these Mayan Calendar dates are so in sync with Judeo-Christian prophecies and the concept of Sacred Astronomy, it suggests that the origins of Mayan culture and their calendar had a godly beginning. Could the ancestors of the Sethites have set up this New World culture after the Flood? Could Noah and his son Shem or their godly descendants have tried valiantly to prevent this cultural center from succumbing to Nimrod's armies and his subsequent despotic rule? In Book Three, it is shown that this is a very real possibility that has been totally ignored by the archeological community, which supports Evolution and Humanism rather than Creation and Monotheism.

There is another very compelling fact that connects the origin of the accurate astronomical knowledge of the Mayans, Inca, and Aztecs with Noah and/or Shem. In the Book "Everyday Life of the Incas" by Ann Kendall, Ms. Kendall relates that **the Incas believed that the Sun had a lifecycle of one thousand years, and that five Suns had already passed**. In essence, unlike the Mayans, they did not date the Fifth Sun's end as in the future. Instead, **the Incas believed that five worlds of one thousand years each had passed, and that they were living in the Sixth Sun.** Uncannily, the Incas' Six Suns, or six 1,000-year cycles mirror the Judeo-Christian understanding that only six thousand years were allotted for

## Chapter 12: Sacred Astronomy as a Prophetic Tool

human history to unfold before this sin filled age of the world would gradually come to an end. Per Daniel's Seventieth Week and the Book of Revelation, it will end over a seven year period amid successive waves of God's Wrath being poured out on the nations who oppose and hate Jews and Christians, just as it is happening today.

The date for the close of the Inca's Sixth Sun may have been identical to the close of their Mayan predecessors' Fifth Sun: December 21st, 2012. Like the Mayans, the Incas believed that each Sun or Age began with a new world that was re-born from the ashes of the old one, and that each world "died" in some cataclysmic way when the previous Sun ended. In other words, the whole Earth was forever changed in some irreversible fashion when the new Age arrived. Yet, they also understood that each age would end gradually up to and after each End Date, and there would also be a change in the mankind's spiritual understanding. Therefore, December 21st, 2012 is only *a marker* for the time when this current evil world system of government and religious plurality will begin to disintegrate until its tumultuous and cataclysmic end at Yahshua's return several years later.

As discussed in Book One and Three, many past Jewish and Christian theologians and mystics taught that our history had a defined, glorious beginning, and ultimately will suffer a catastrophic end. Like their ancestral counterparts, some Judeo-Christian scholars who are alive today also believe that mankind, and the Earth have only been allotted six thousand years, after which Yahweh plans to judge mankind. Many also believe that the Earth and the rest of this current Creation will one day be destroyed by fire. As shown in previous chapters, however, this final and total destruction of the Earth by fire won't actually occur until the close of the Seventh Millennium, and the completion of the Millennial Rule of Yahshua, when the New Heaven and New Earth will be created.

Are the Mayan Fifth Sun, and the Incan Sixth Sun about to end with the destruction of the world we know? Is the Great Tribulation at hand? Are we in the Seventh Millennial Age of men that will usher in the destruction of this world and the establishment of a Christian New Age ruled over by Christ? Though we do not know the sure answer to all these questions, the interpretation of the combined prophecies revealed in this book unquestionably shout: "Yes!" Therefore, let each reader be forewarned. If you have not already done so, now is the time to makes things right with Yahweh.

This final chapter shows that **one must never underestimate the power of symbols!** Yahweh created these symbolic pictorial and numerical connections to show us His Will - both in Heaven, and on

Earth. All we have to do is be open to the Holy Spirit to understand these awesome symbols of Yah's all-encompassing knowledge, and wisdom. For Christians who are tuned in to Yah's Spirit, the end of the world is good news and a time that should be anticipated with joy instead of fear! The only sadness they should feel is that some backslidden or unsaved people whom they love will not be spared from the Great Tribulation. Yet, though it is the time for the destruction of the ungodly, the Great Tribulation will be a time of incredible joy and peace for those who are invited to the Wedding Supper of the Lamb. In addition, though December 21st, 2012 marks a time in the midst of the worst cataclysms to hit Earth since the Great Flood and the Fall of Babel, it is also a time of hope. This is because many apostates are now coming to a saving knowledge of Yahshua during this terrible time of testing.

All these heavenly signs that point to the end of this current evil world system, and show the sacred origins of Astronomy, should give Christians and Messianics much reason for joy and hope. We are on the threshold of the real beginning of the true New Age – the Age when Yahshua will bless the world with His perfect rule! This millennium-long Great Day of the Lord will be the true "dawning" of the Age of Aquarius, and the rise of the greatest spiritual outpouring of Grace and faith ever to be given to humanity. Though no one knows when the Great Tribulation will begin for certain, it is my firm conviction that Yahshua's golden Age of righteousness will arrive *five years after* the great destruction that will intensify on or shortly after December 21st, 2012. The means of destruction will include all of the terrible cataclysmic earthquakes and plagues mentioned in the Book of Revelation in relation to God's Wrath, which have been intensifying in strength from 2010 onward, and will not end until Christ returns sometime in 2016 or 2017 AD.

Because the end of this Age is so near, and our time is so short, I urge every reader of this book to seek to know the Creator God Yahweh and His Son Yahshua, and to love and honor God above all else as the end of this world system rapidly approaches. The time to get things right with Yahweh is **now**. Don't put off spiritual things! They are the most important aspects of every human life, and if you fail to accept Yahshua's salvation in time, you may consign yourself to spending eternity *in the oblivion of Hell*. So don't wait! If you haven't already done so, get down on your knees and ask Yahshua and the Holy Spirit into your life **today**.

## Chapter 12: Sacred Astronomy as a Prophetic Tool

### *The Amazing Heavenly Anti-Peace Sign of 2012*

Many Bible Prophecy teachers have written about the possible meanings of the cryptic symbolism found in the Book of Revelation. Among these commentaries, much has been written about the Four Horsemen of the Apocalypse found in Revelation's sixth chapter. However, none of the more popular commentaries on the Book of Revelation have noted that there is a definite Zodiac connection for many of the symbols in the prophetic language of this book.

As shown in all four books in my "Language of God" Book Series, these scriptural tie-ins to the Zodiac Star Gospel story are found throughout the many biblical prophetic scriptures, but they are especially numerous in the Book of Revelation. This suggests that we can apply Sacred Astronomy to determine the dating of key biblical prophecies, just as Enoch and his righteous Sethite descendents did prior to the Great Flood, as shown in the Pillar of Enoch, or Great Pyramid.

One aspect of this Zodiac symbolism in Revelation is found in the Four Horsemen of the Apocalypse, which are tied to four Zodiac signs, three of which appear in the illustration on this page. These horsemen begin their ride consecutively as the first four of the Seven Seal Judgments are opened. (See my book: "The Language of God in History" to see how the Four Horsemen are also tied to the Scorpio-Sagittarius Meridian and judgment). In the following sections, we will explore the Star Gospel surrounding each horseman and rider.

## The White Horse: Symbol of the Gospel Being Preached

First, let me point out that many Bible Scholars may have incorrectly seen the Rider on the White Horse as the Antichrist due to the rider's similarity to the King of kings who also will ride to conquer on a white horse:

> "Now I saw heaven opened, and behold, a white horse. And He who sat on him was called Faithful and True, and in righteousness He judges and makes war..." "Now out of His mouth goes a sharp sword, that with it He should strike the nations... He Himself treads the winepress of the fierceness and wrath of Almighty God. And He has on His robe and on His thigh a name written: KING OF KINGS..." - Rev. 19:11, 15-16

Most Bible Prophecy teachers see this Rider on the White Horse as none other than Yahshua (Jesus) the Messiah returning in Glory to set up His Kingdom on Earth. Therefore, they think that the less sensationally described rider on the white horse in Revelation, Chapter Six must be an imposter, especially since he appears at the beginning of the Tribulation period when the first of the Seven Seals is opened:

> "The Lamb opened one of the seals; and I heard one of the four living creatures saying with a voice like thunder, 'Come and see.' And I looked, and behold, a white horse. He who sat on it had a bow; and a crown was given to him, and he went out conquering and to conquer." -- Rev. 6:1-2

Note that the First Horseman of the Apocalypse or Rider on the White Horse *is given a crown* and has a bow in his hand, identifying him is an archer. However, his bow has no "arrow," which is a symbol of war and power. The lack of an arrow therefore suggests that the rider is being sent out during the false peace of the first half of the seven-year Tribulation. For the first two or three years of the Tribulation, as we have already seen, there has been relative peace. However, this time of peace has been heavily marred by ecological and geological disasters, which the deluded populace of the Earth have not been identifying as the acts of God's vengeance that they truly are. In addition, this troubled time of peace will soon end with a war against Israel, and the pouring out of the Seven Trumpets and Seven Bowls of God's Wrath.

Now, using the symbolic clarification offered by the Gospel in the Stars, the crowned archer with the bow on the white horse can be identified fairly well, because he is found perfectly represented in the starry constellation called Sagittarius, the Centaur-like Archer among the twelve major signs of the Zodiac. As depicted in the Dendera Zodiac (see the illustration on page 641), Sagittarius depicts a mounted pharaoh, or king, whose pure white horse's feet are trampling over a serpent shaped like a boat (indicating the serpent trail of Dan, and the Nephilim), while the arrow in the king's bow is aimed at the heart of Scorpio, the most Satanic symbol among the Twelve Signs of the Zodiac! This Archer King represents Yahshua, while the white horse represents His perfection, and His role as an atonement sacrifice for sin.

## The Two Messianic Centaurs In The Heavens

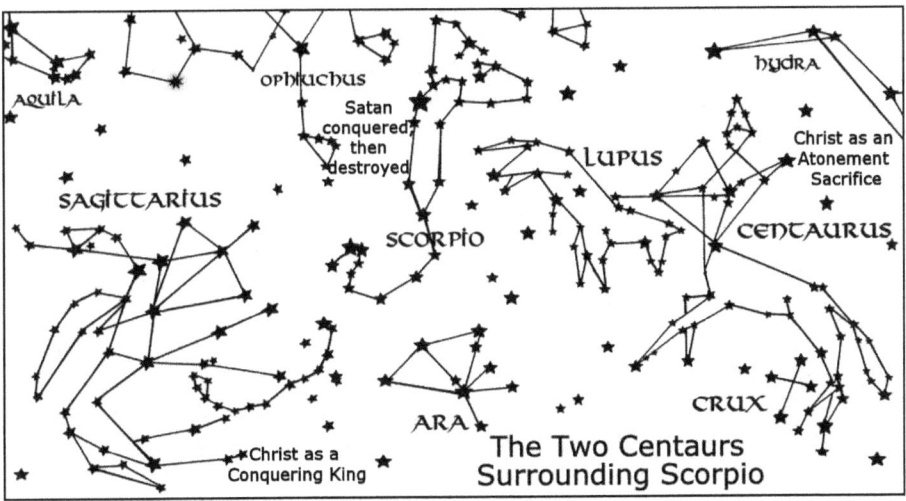

As shown in my book "The Language of God in the Universe," Sagittarius can be seen as a melding together of that first apocalyptic rider, and the white horse he is riding. In the Gospel in the Stars, this sign perfectly represents the dual-nature of Christ as both a conquering hero (the archer), and an atonement sacrifice (the hoofed, white animal) in one! There are, in fact, two centaurs in the Zodiac, as shown in the illustration on this page. Sagittarius depicts Christ coming again in triumph, while the decan of Virgo called Centaurus portrays Christ's First Advent role as an atonement sacrifice. These two centaurs are Scorpio's righteous adversaries, and their bows depict God's meting out of judgment against Satan, and his evil followers. However, these archer's bows also signify God's promises, blessings, and mercy, just as the rainbow sign given to Noah and his kin depicted God's promise to never destroy the Earth by water again. Interestingly, every rainbow symbolically aims an invisible arrow at God, showing that God would rather kill Himself than renege on any of His promises, just as He did through His Son on the Cross!

Now, as shown earlier in this book, the prophet Zechariah depicts Adonai Yahweh (i.e. Yahshua) holding a bow associated with the tribe of Judah, and an arrow tied to the Tribe of Joseph/Ephraim. These are being used to defeat God's enemies during the Battle of Armageddon:

> *"For I have bent Judah, My bow, Fitted the bow with Ephraim, and raised up your sons, O Zion, against your sons, O Greece, and made you like the sword of a mighty man. Then the LORD will be seen over them, and His arrow will go forth like lightning. The Lord GOD will blow the trumpet, and go with whirlwinds from the south. The LORD of hosts will defend them... in that day, as the flock of His people. For they shall be like the jewels of a crown, lifted like a banner over His land..." - Zechariah 9:13-16*

Note here that the bow and arrow in Zechariah's vision are being wielded by God, and those He is defending *"shall be like the jewels of a crown."* This Scripture therefore identifies the bow, and the jewels of the crown belonging to the Rider on the White Horse in the Book of Revelation! As shown in my books, Judah can prophetically refer to the Jews, especially those in the nation of Israel, while Ephraim can signify Gentile Christians living all over the world, especially those in the United States. Therefore, the Rider on the White Horse appears to be a symbol representing a messenger ensuring that the Gospel of Christ's Kingdom has been, and will continue to be preached to the whole world before the Battle of Armageddon. At that time, Yahshua and His transformed saints will conquer the Devil's kingdom, and teach about the purpose of the Kingdom of God to others.

Also, at the beginning of the Great Tribulation, God will choose 144,000 Israelites from the Twelve Tribes of Israel (which includes grafted-in Israel) to preach. Then the miracle-working Two Witnesses, and finally a mighty angel will preach the Gospel to the whole world before the fall of the Antichrist's kingdom known as Babylon the Great:

> *"Then I saw another angel ascending from the east, having the seal of the living God. And he cried... 'Do not harm the earth, the sea, or the trees till we have sealed the servants of our God on their foreheads.' And I heard the number of those who were sealed. One hundred and forty-four thousand of all the tribes of the children of Israel..." - Revelation 7:2-4*

> *"And I will give power to my two witnesses, and they will prophesy one thousand two hundred and sixty days, clothed in sackcloth."* -- Rev. 11:3

> *"Then I saw another angel flying in the midst of heaven, having the everlasting gospel to preach to those who dwell on the earth -- to every nation, tribe, tongue, and people -- saying with a loud voice, 'Hear God and give glory to Him, for the hour of His judgment has come; and worship Him who made heaven and earth, the sea and springs of water.'"* -- Rev. 14:6-7

In the preceding quote, note that this angel is preaching the Gospel of the Kingdom to the whole world, not just a few people! Thus, this angel, the 144,000, and the Two Witnesses who preach during the Great Tribulation will fulfill Christ's prophecy that:

> *"...this **gospel of the kingdom** will be preached in all the world as a witness to all the nations, and then the end will come."* - Matthew 24:14

This preaching will be faithfully carried out because Yahweh does not want even one of His human children to perish in the Lake of Fire. Therefore, Yah is, and will continue to be merciful to those who accept His Son Yahshua as Savior - even up to the end of the Battle of Armageddon! Hallelu-Yah for that!

## The Riders on the Red, Black, and Pale Horses

In the previous section, it was revealed how the Rider on the White Horse in the Book of Revelation is depicted - via Sacred Sethite Astronomy - in the Zodiac sign of Sagittarius. In addition, it was shown that this rider prophetically depicts the preaching of the Gospel of the Kingdom of God to the whole world during the pouring out of God's Wrath. This preaching will be carried out via the 144,000 Witnesses (Rev. 7:2-4), followed by the Two Witnesses (Rev. 11:3), and an angel (Rev. 14:6-7). Now, using the Language of God, let's study the meaning of the Rider on the Red Horse, who is revealed after the Second Seal Judgment is opened:

> *"When He opened the second seal, I heard the second living creature saying, 'Come and see.' Another horse, fiery red, went out. And it was granted to the one who sat on it to take peace from the earth, and that people should kill one another; and there was given to him a great sword."* - Rev. 6:3-4

Note that this rider carries a great sword, and rides a fiery red horse. As shown in my books: "The Language of God in the Universe," and "The Language of God in Humanity," the greatest sword in the Zodiac is being wielded by the messianic figure of Orion, a decan of the fiery red bull called Taurus. In addition, two of the most prominent fiery red stars in the heavens are found within Orion and Taurus. This suggests that these two constellations may depict the Rider (Orion) on the Red Horse (Taurus).

One of those two red stars is often thought of as the eye of Taurus. This bright orange-red star is called "Al Debaran", meaning "The Leader," and it signifies Christ as the spiritual leader of the congregation of righteous followers signified by the Hyades star cluster forming Taurus' face. As shown in my book: "The Language of God in History," the Red Pyramid at Dahshur in Egypt depicts the red star known as "El Debaran," and both the star and the pyramid are symbols for Christ. Likewise, just as the Sethites intended, the Great Pyramid at Giza is tied to the belt star of Orion known as "Al Nitak" or "the Wounded One." That Wounded One was Christ on the Cross, meaning that Orion and the Great Pyramid represent Christ as both atonement sacrifice and conquering Prince.

The second reddish-hued star in the Taurus region is found marking the right shoulder of Orion, a decan of Taurus and a powerful Christ figure in the Zodiac. This star is called "Betelgeuse," which means "The Branch Coming." It is one of the most massive stars in the visible Universe, with a diameter that is 600 times that of our Sun! As such, it seems fitting that Betelgeuse, and Orion as a whole actually represents Yahshua the Messiah (i.e. Jesus the Christ), the Righteous Branch that came through the righteous line of Seth, which led to the births of Shem, Abraham, Jacob and Judah.

Oddly, Orion and Taurus have two diametrically different sides that are hinted at in the two horns of Taurus, which also represent the horns of two unicorns, one turned red in rebellion, the other one turned white in perfection. On the one hand, Orion signifies Christ as an atonement sacrifice, which is also depicted by Taurus the Bull in its guise as a white unicorn stained red in sacrifice. As such, it signifies the 2,000-year Church Age sanctified by Christ's shed blood, and is a symbol of God's blessing and mercy upon the Gentiles through Christ. In its End Time application, however, Orion signifies Christ as a Great Prince conquering the red, raging unicorn side of Taurus. In this guise, Taurus becomes an uncanny metaphor for the evil Beast from the Sea in the Book of Revelation.

## Another View of the Star Gospel on December 21st, 2012

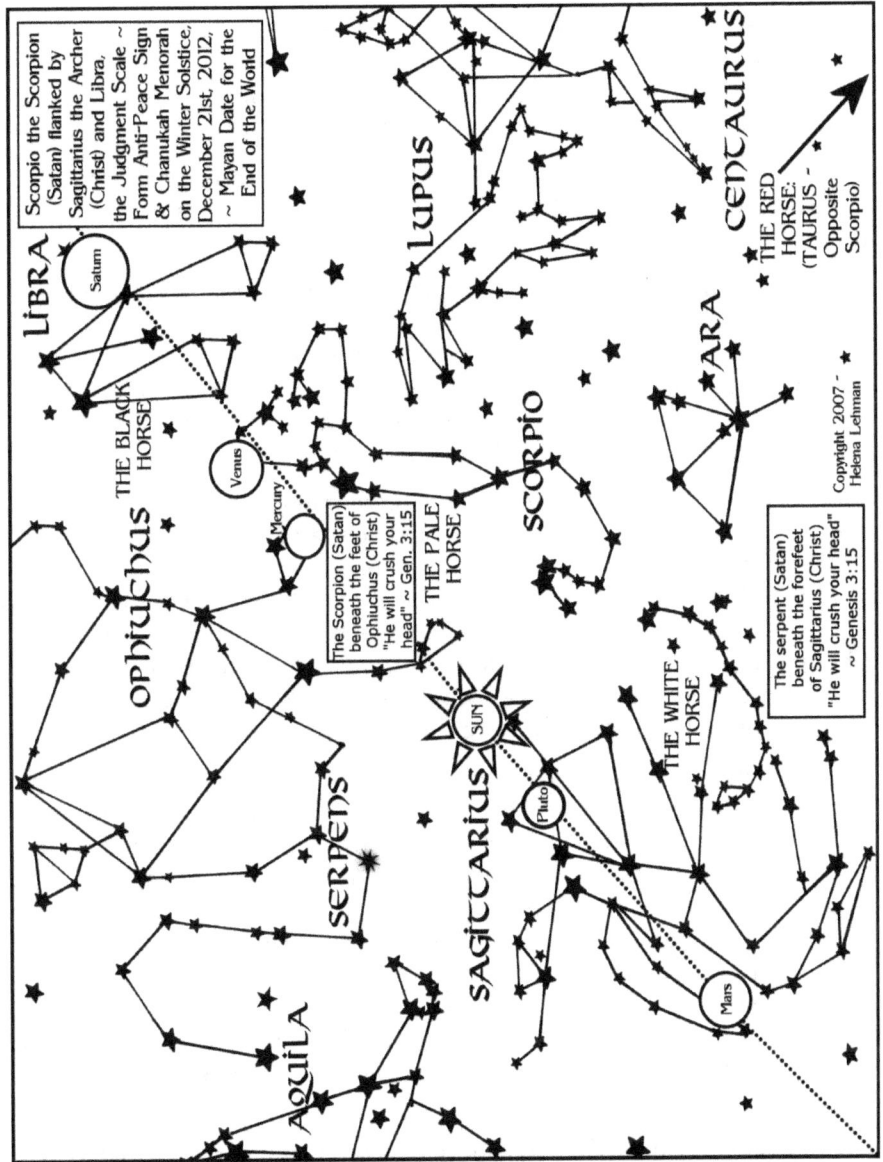

Likewise, the Pleiades star cluster on Taurus' back, which currently depicts the Seven Churches of the Church Age, will undergo a metamorphosis after the Rapture. Instead of depicting the many churches we have today, the Pleiades will represent the One World Religion of the

Whore of Babylon. Likewise, Taurus will not be a Red Bull signifying Christ's blood sacrifice for sin, but the Red Dragon or Beast from the Sea signifying the government that the fallen Woman of False Religion rides as she drinks a cup filled with the blood of many martyrs. In this way, Taurus dually represents the Antichrist's unholy economic and military might and his persecution of the Tribulation Saints.

After this fiery Rider on the Red Horse, the Third Seal is opened, and a dreadful Rider on a Black Horse with a pair of scales in his hand appears:

> "When He opened the third seal, I heard the third living creature say, 'Come and see.' So I looked, and behold, a black horse, and he who sat on it had a pair of scales in his hand. And I heard a voice in the midst of the four living creatures saying, 'A quart of wheat for a denarius, and three quarts of barley for a denarius; and do not harm the oil and the wine.'" -- Rev. 6:5-6

In the Zodiac, only one of the twelve major signs can correspond to the pair of scales in this dark rider's hands, and that is Libra, the Scales. In the Zodiac, the imbalanced scales of Libra represent the fact that all people will be judged against the perfection of Christ. Those who are not covered with His blood are seen as inferior to Him, and will be left behind in the Rapture and cast out of His Kingdom, while those who wear Christ's blood as a cloak of righteousness will pass the test, and be allowed to enter His Heavenly Kingdom, and coming Kingdom on Earth.

Interestingly, this rider's horse is black - the color most often associated with evil. Black, however, is also a color associated with grave illness, and imminent death. Furthermore, the remainder of the Scripture indicates that the Rider on the Black Horse has to do with the buying and selling of food. Since much sickness and death is caused by malnutrition, the black horse implies that much evil will come from the genetic modification of food that is occurring today, as well as the destruction of crops that extreme weather has and will cause. Soon, there will be rationing and exorbitant pricing of food supplies, and there will be great restrictions placed on buying and selling it by the One World Government of the Antichrist.

Finally, we come to the prophetic Zodiac imagery associated with the fourth Horseman of the Apocalypse - the Rider on the Pale Horse who appears at the opening of the Fourth Seal:

> "When He opened the fourth seal, I heard the voice of the fourth living creature saying, 'Come and see.' So I looked, and behold, a pale horse. And the name of him who sat on it was

*Death, and Hades followed. And power was given to them over a fourth of the earth, to kill with sword, with hunger... and by the beasts of the earth."* -- Rev. 6:1-17

Among the Twelve Signs of the Zodiac, there is one sign that has more malevolence than any of the others. This is Scorpio, which symbolizes Satan, and all the bad seeds among humanity that he fathered in his rebellion. Satan, through his sinful rebellion, brought death and destruction to Adam and Eve by beguiling them to reject Yahshua's perfect counsel. Consequently, Satan's evil has spread, and now all Creation is tainted with sin and death through the rebellion of the Fallen Angels, the Anakim, and all mankind.

If it were not for Christ, none of us would be saved, and we would only have one bleak prospect - to spend eternity in torment surrounded by evil spirits that hate us. Thank Yahweh for His Son Yahshua, who has provided a way for us to inherit eternal life with Him in perfect peace and joy - forever! This truth is shown in the illustration on page 634, where the satanic sign of Scorpio's decans called Ophiuchus and Serpens depict a strong man (Ophiuchus, or Christ) wrestling with a huge serpent (Serpens, or Satan) representing evil and rebellion. Since Ophiuchus is directly above Scorpio's mid-section, it can depict the Rider on the back of Scorpio, who - along with Serpens - depicts the dual nature of the Rider on the Pale Horse of death and sickness. On the one hand, the Rider on the Pale Horse is Ophiuchus, the god of healing as seen in Christ. However, after the First Rapture, this rider will temporarily depict the Serpent that he is holding back, who is Satan - the one who brings death and destruction instead of healing.

Interestingly, serpents and scorpions are mentioned in relation to the Fifth and Sixth Trumpet plagues in the Book of Revelation. When the Fifth Trumpet is sounded: *"locusts came upon the earth. And to them was given power, as the scorpions of the earth have power."* *"They had tails like scorpions, and there were stings in their tails. Their power was to hurt men five months"* (Rev. 9:3, 10). Then, at the Sixth Trumpet, 200 million strange, horse-like creatures cross the Euphrates out of Asia in order to kill a third of mankind with fire, smoke and brimstone, which comes out of their mouths and their serpent-like tails (Rev. 9:18-19). Here then, in the middle of the Tribulation period, we see the realization of the symbolism depicted by the Rider on the Pale Horse in Ophiuchus, Scorpio, and Serpens. Whether these 200 million creatures are analogies for soldiers in armored vehicles or some form of mutant monster like the Nephilim coming out of Asia remains to be seen. Either idea is a distinct possibility.

## The Anti-Peace Sign and the Mayan End Date

Thus far, in examining the Zodiac connection of the Four Horsemen of the Apocalypse, it has been shown how Sagittarius represents the Rider on the White Horse, Taurus signifies the Red Horse and Orion signifies the Rider, Libra signifies the Rider on the Black Horse, Scorpio represents the Pale Horse, and Ophiuchus and Serpens depict two diametrically different Riders for the Pale Horse.

Uncannily, while plotting the four Zodiac signs tied to the Four Horsemen of the Apocalypse on the Zodiacal Wheel shown on page 651, I noted that these horsemen form an astonishing Peace Symbol in the sky formed by Sagittarius, Scorpio, and Libra, which are adjacent to each other, and Taurus, which is directly opposite of Scorpio on the Zodiacal Wheel. Even more uncannily, this symbol was first used as a Peace Sign during the Anti-War Movements of the 1960's, and thereby signifies the current desire for world peace that will lead to the unholy reign and false peace of the Antichrist.

The really troubling thing about this Peace Symbol is that the four signs it is formed by do not mark the coming of eternal world peace, as so many have hoped for, but the tragic end to the temporary and partial peace that the Beast system of the Antichrist will destroy in order to bring about the Antichrist's One World Government. I therefore have dubbed this heavenly symbol as "the Anti-Peace Sign" associated with the coming of the Antichrist. As shown earlier, Scorpio was just above the horizon, and Sagittarius was just below the horizon on the Winter Solstice on December 21st, 2012, the Mayan date for the end of the Fifth Sun. At that time, the Sun and the Earth aligned with the Galactic Center of the Milky Way, unleashing a whole series of unseen End Time spiritual events. Touted as the coming of the Age of Aquarius, and the subject of intense New Age and Occult spiritual interest, this Mayan End Date signals the ending of one Age and the beginning of a new one that is to be accompanied by radical physical and spiritual changes to the world.

At sunrise, the planet Saturn hovered between Libra and Virgo, marking one downward-slanting arm of that giant heavenly Anti-Peace Sign, the planet Mars marked the opposite arm of the Anti-Peace Sign between Sagittarius and Capricorn, and the planet Mercury marked one end of the center line of the Anti-Peace Sign. Meanwhile, on the opposite side of the world - and the Zodiac - the solitary side of the center line of this Anti-Peace Sign was marked in the sky by the Messiah planet Jupiter, which was dead-center in Taurus, and hovering over the Hyades star cluster marking the True Church, as well as the Tribulation Saints who will be won for Christ by the preaching of the 144,000 Witnesses of Israel (Rev. 7:2-4), the Two Witnesses (Rev. 11:3), and a mighty angel (Rev. 14:6-7).

## Anti-Peace Sign In Heaven On December 21st, 2012

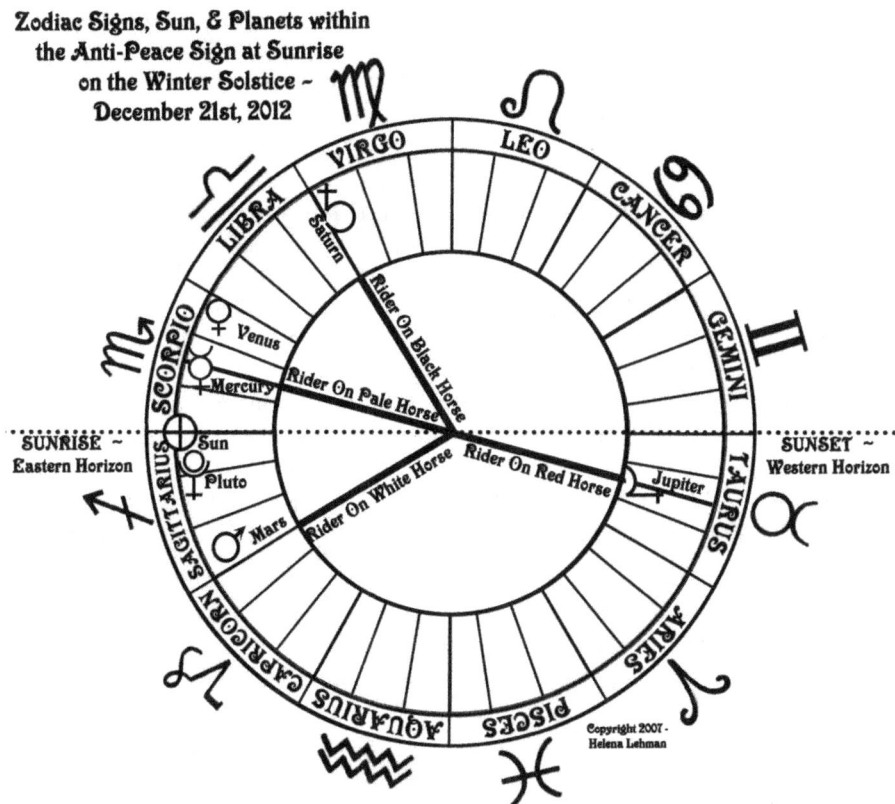

If we were to draw this Zodiac Peace Sign in its proper orientation on paper, Taurus would be at the top of the picture, while Scorpio and its neighboring signs Libra and Sagittarius would on the bottom. This shows that Christ and His saints, who are represented by the planet Jupiter and the right horn of Taurus, represent the Rider on the White Horse - except that he is a rider now armed like the Rider on the Red Horse! Meanwhile, *the Antichrist and his followers - who are marked by Scorpio on the other side of the Zodiac and Taurus' left horn - are the Rider on the Pale Horse, which is acting in direct opposition to Christ and His saints, and is pretending to be the Word of God (Mercury) and Morning Star (Venus).*

Thankfully, this is a battle that Satan and his followers cannot, and will not win! However, because this Anti-Peace sign shows Satan and Christ on opposite sides of Heaven, it appears to be marking the time when Satan is cast out of Heaven, as is described in the Book of Revelation, Chapter 12, Verses 1-17. Incidentally, Chapter 12 of Revelation may partly apply to the year 2012, as shown in the Hebrew alphabetic chart in Chapter One. This chart shows Chapters 6 through 19 in Revelation connected to the years 2006 through 2019 AD. Though all the events in those chapters don't necessarily apply to those years, there is some correlation between them.

## *The Chanukiah Formed by the Anti-Peace Sign in Heaven*

Amazingly, that is not the only sign that appeared in heaven on the morning of December 21st, 2012! What is really astounding is that the same Anti-Peace Sign allegorically formed a Chanukah Menorah tied to the number 9, which is associated with divine judgment in Scripture. The nine branches of this heavenly "Chanukiah" were marked by the three decans under each of the adjacent Zodiac signs forming the trident portion of the Anti-Peace Sign. These were Sagittarius' decans (1) Lyra, (2) Ara, and (3) Draco; Scorpio's decans (4) Ophiuchus, (5) Serpens, and (6) Hercules; and Libra's decans (7) Crux, (8) Victima, and (9) Corona Borealis.

This Chanukiah was also depicted by the line-up of planets on December 21st, 2012, with Mars in Sagittarius marking the first lamp on this Menorah in heaven, Mercury in Scorpio marking the center lamp, which is called the Servant Lamp, and Saturn in Libra marking the ninth, and final lamp - as per my illustration on page 653. The sign of Taurus depicting Christ crucified, and as a Risen King (via Orion), and the Messiah planet Jupiter depicting Christ's Crown are paired together to serve as this Chanukiah's base. It therefore represents the firm foundation of Yahshua the Messiah (i.e. Jesus the Christ), who will one day return as a conquering King - like a mighty bull in His invincible power:

> *"For no one can lay any foundation other than the one already laid, which is Jesus Christ (Yahshua the Messiah)." - 1 Corinthians 3:11*

While examining the illustrations, note that the Anti Peace Sign also forms a trident symbol, which is used as a weapon for fishing and war, suggesting both the winning of souls, and the destruction of souls.

Tridents are also associated with the false gods Poseidon, and Shiva, the Hindu god of destruction.

## Chanukiah Formed at Noon on December 21st, 2012

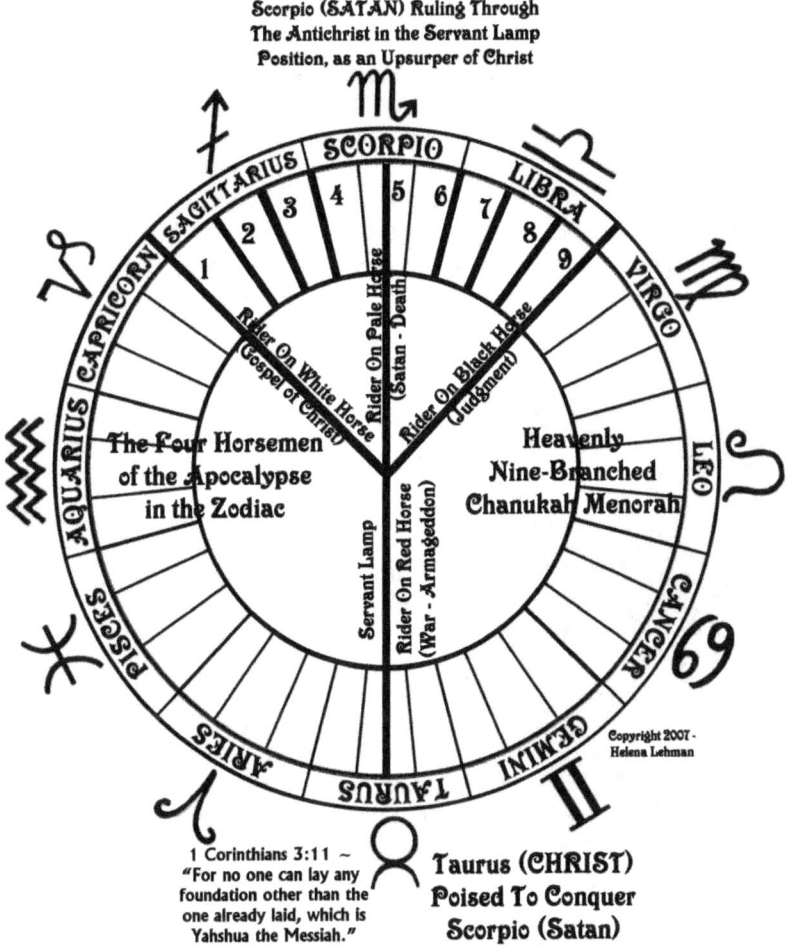

Now, based on the Hallel Psalm prophecies and the possibility that the Blood Moon over Orion's Sword on December 21st, 2010 marked the beginning of the Tribulation, December 21st, 2012 may mark the end of the second year of the Tribulation. Due to the amazing Signs in the Heavens on December 21st, 2012, and the cataclysmic events on the Earth just before and after that, it appears that Yahshua has begun to open the Seals that will lead to the Sixth Seal Judgment, and the Seven Trumpet and Bowl plagues that mark the Wrath of God in the Tribulation. This time has been marked by several Signs in the Heavens, including the darkening of the Sun in an eclipse (the Sun in sackcloth), and the reddening of the Moon in an eclipse (the Moon as if covered in blood) (Mat. 24:29; Mark 13:24-25; Rev. 6:12).

## *The Perseus Prophecy - Three Comets With A Message*

The next two sections in this chapter were derived from articles published on the Internet between January 6th and 15th, 2008 under the general headings: **"The Perseus Prophecy - A Heavenly Portent of Doom and Hope"** And **"The Amazing Heavenly Anti-Peace Sign Formed in the Zodiac by the Four Horsemen of the Apocalypse."** Together, these additional explorations of Sacred Astronomy in action add much to this study of the practical and prophetic aspects of the Gospel in the Stars.

Classical Interpretation of Perseus

Those who read my other Language of God series books should be somewhat familiar with the application of Sacred Astronomy. For those who need a refresher course concerning this ancient mystical science, or know little about it, let me offer this brief explanation.

As mentioned earlier in this book, the 1st Century historian Josephus recorded that this celestial science was perfected by the Sethites prior to the Great Flood. This science centered around interpreting the immense storybook that the One Triune God created in the heavens - a story with forty-eight star-studded constellations serving as chapters, and a host of stars, moons, planets, comets, and asteroids serving to set the stage in each.

According to the antediluvian prophet Enoch the Sethite, this celestial storybook reveals every event in human history over a period of 7,000 years - from the creation of Adam and Eve, until the Last Judgment. In the next two sections, we will examine the significant past celestial

# Chapter 12: Sacred Astronomy as a Prophetic Tool

Comet Hyakutake in 1996

events that occurred between 1996 and 2008. These past events involve both total Solar and Lunar Eclipses, and comets that were visible from various locations on Earth that appear to be issuing an ominous warning to all humanity. After that, we will focus on future celestial events up to the year 2017.

First, let's focus on the comet sightings. In 1996 and 1997, the skies over our Earth were visited with two remarkable comets. In both cases, these comets passed through the constellation called Perseus, crossing at right angles to each other over a particular star with an ominous name. That star is named "Rosh Satan" in Hebrew, which means "Head of Satan." It is also called Al Gol, or Al Ghoul, meaning "The Ghoul." In ancient times, Perseus actually foreshadowed King David's slaying of Goliath. In modern times, however, the death of Medusa signifies the much sought-after demise of another diabolical figure in history known as the Antichrist - whom Christ will one day utterly destroy.

The star Al Ghoul appears in the severed head of Medusa, which is being clutched in the heavenly Perseus' left-hand. In Greek mythology, Perseus was a warrior hero who killed the evil snake-haired gorgon called Medusa. Medusa's head, it was said, could turn anyone looking upon it into stone, which allegorically means that Medusa's Nephilim and Serpent spirit could delude anyone foolish enough to delve into her spiritually evil philosophies! The winged steed Pegasus supposedly was birthed from Medusa's blood, and Perseus rode on Pegasus when he rescued the Princess Andromeda from becoming Cetus the Sea Monster's dinner. This myth is important because it shows the evil Cainite interpretation of several constellations that are near to each other in the heavens and show a hidden knowledge of the original, divinely-written Zodiac story - the Gospel in the Stars.

Since our western version of Astrology is accredited to the ancient Greeks, it seems shocking that most scholars ignore the fact that almost all Greek religious myths are derived from the 48 ancient constellations of the Zodiac. In fact, this correlation can be seen in the mythologies of all the ancient cultures surrounding the Mediterranean Sea. If we go back to the time before the Great Flood, however, the knowledge of this Zodiac Gospel story was preserved by the Sethites - and later by Noah's son Shem, whose descendents gradually fell into sin and idolatry when they perverted the Star Gospel, and created the star-gazing astral religions of the Chaldean, Akkadian, Babylonian, and Assyrian civilizations in Mesopotamia.

Now, in the Christian view of these constellations, Perseus is an obvious allusion to Christ, while Andromeda is an allegory for Christ's Bride, the True Church. Sadly, as long as she is mortal, Christ's Bride is trapped in the clutches of sin by Satan and his demons. This can especially be seen in the figure of Cetus and the bands that tie the two Fishes of Pisces representing the Two House Church of Judah (i.e. Messianic Jews) and Ephraim (i.e. born-again Gentiles) to Cetus' neck. In addition, anyone who has read the book of Revelation knows of the white horses that the saints and Christ will ride to victory at the end of the Battle of Armageddon (Revelation 19:11-14). These white horses are depicted in the constellation Pegasus the Flying Horse, which appears above the signs of Pisces and Aquarius.

Comet Hale-Bopp in 1997

From this explanation of Perseus' meaning, it can be seen how relevant its message is to believers awaiting the Rapture and Christ's Second Coming. This is why the three comets that have passed through Perseus in the last decade are signs that the falling away that will lead to the Great Delusion signified by the head of Medusa or Satan and the star Al Ghoul are imminent and end of this evil world system is near. For example, on April 11, 1996, the Comet Hyakutake crossed over the star Al Ghoul in Perseus. Then, one year later - and on the same exact day - the amazingly brilliant Comet Hale-Bopp crossed over Al Ghoul in the opposite direction, appearing to mark a giant "X" in the sky. Could this have been one of the celestial End Time signs that the Bible forewarns us about? (See Joel 2:30-31; Luke 21:25-26.) Could this unprecedented comet crossing possibly signify that we have reached that significant time in history?

I was first introduced to this unusual comet crossing in a book connecting Stonehenge and the Great Pyramid written by the math wizard Bonnie Gaunt. Still, later I read about it in a book called "Signs of the End," by Daniel W. Matson. These authors alerted me to start paying much closer attention to unusual celestial events, and to pray for the correct interpretation of their divine meaning. This is why, when Comet Holmes entered the constellation Perseus in August of 2007, I was paying rapt attention, and I was not disappointed! Amazingly, Comet Holmes proceeded to draw a big retrograde loop through Perseus, and passed directly by its most prominent star known as Mirfak, meaning "He Who Helps." In addition, Mirfak has occasionally been incorrectly labeled "Al Genib," meaning "The One Who Carries Away."

Comet Holmes on October 30th, 2007

Before continuing, I wish to note that the term Al Genib alludes to a hero who undertakes a daring rescue of a friend from imminent danger - and which could be a reference to the coming Rapture. Now, the other bright star that the Comet Holmes will pass through - in early 2008 - is none other than Al Ghoul, a.k.a. Rosh Satan! Thus, it appears that Comet Holmes is gearing us all to look for the coming apocalyptic confrontation between our heavenly Helper and Rescuer, who is Christ, and our devilish adversary - the one infamously known as the Antichrist.

Now, let me add some fuel to the fire lighting this assumption by noting that - to the average astronomer - it seems highly unlikely that three bright comets would cross over the same constellation in less than a hundred years, much less the same exact star in a little over ten years! This leaves me to draw only one conclusion: based on the meaning of Perseus and Al Ghoul, God is telling sacred astronomers like myself that the time of Perseus confronting the Medusa is very near! In other words, the time of Jacob's Trouble that will precede Christ's return to unmask the Great Delusion of the Antichrist and bring the terrifying events in the Bible's book of Revelation to an end are about to begin!

There are other meanings to Perseus that I discovered while finishing "The Language of God in History". These are extremely eye-opening in light of the current global push towards a totalitarian, fascist One World Government and the global war on terrorism that has been downplayed in an attempt to un-demonize Islam and Muslims in general. This aspect of Perseus became clear to me when I discovered how the first recorded world dictator named Nimrod died in the Book of Jasher.

In Book Three, it was shown how Abraham was instrumental in bringing about the destruction of Nimrod's world empire. However, though Abraham brought Nimrod's evil spiritual and political ambitions to naught, it was Esau, the brother of Jacob who deliberately ambushed and murdered Nimrod, and the way Esau accomplished this feat ties this murder to Perseus. According to Jasher, Esau cut off Nimrod's head in order to kill him. So, if we see Perseus as Esau, who was one of the progenitors of the Arabs, Perseus takes on a sinister meaning.

For example, since Perseus' foot is attempting to crush the Pleiades representing the Apostate Churches, this signifies that the Muslim Arabs have been divinely allowed to attack the post-Christian Western nations and behead believers in the East because many of them are not worshipping the Almighty God who made them great, but a counterfeit god made in their own image! Indeed, the people of the West have almost completely forgotten their Christian and Democratic roots in their mad push toward Totalitarianism. In addition, believers in the East have been afraid to preach the Gospel to their radical Muslim neighbors, who have long expected their Mahdi to appear riding on a white horse, and this shows Islam's connection to Perseus.

This coming Totalitarian Government has been dubbed the New World Order by its proponents, and it is succinctly represented by the head of Medusa. In Book Three, it was also shown how the severed head of Medusa gave the Greek goddess Athena or the re-born Eve her power to delude humanity with the Serpent's evil wisdom even while setting herself up as a counterfeit goddess of light and truth. In this way, Athena in one sense signifies Eve as the giver of false wisdom. Yet in another sense, Athena is a symbol for Naamah the daughter of the Cainite Lamech who became Azazel's consort. Still later, Athena was a symbol for Nimrod's wife, who made herself into a false Angel of Light like her secret master, the Fallen Angel Azazel or Satan. Thankfully, Yahshua Himself will soon come to vanquish the Antichrist after he takes control and wars against the Tribulation Saints. At the appointed time, Christ's armies will destroy the Antichrist's armies, and Yahshua will be the one holding the severed head of the Antichrist as He shouts His victory cry!

In verification of my conclusion, there have been five Lunar Eclipses that coincided with major Jewish holidays in 1996, 1997, and 2007. In 1996, there were two total Lunar Eclipses that were ideally viewed from the Middle East, and could be clearly seen from Jerusalem, Israel. The first occurred around 12:30 a.m. on Passover, April 4th, 1996 - in the sign of Virgo, which can be seen as a symbol for Ancient Israel, as well as the virgin Bride of Christ, a.k.a. the True Church.

## Hyakutake & Hale-Bopp Crossing Al Ghoul in 1996-97

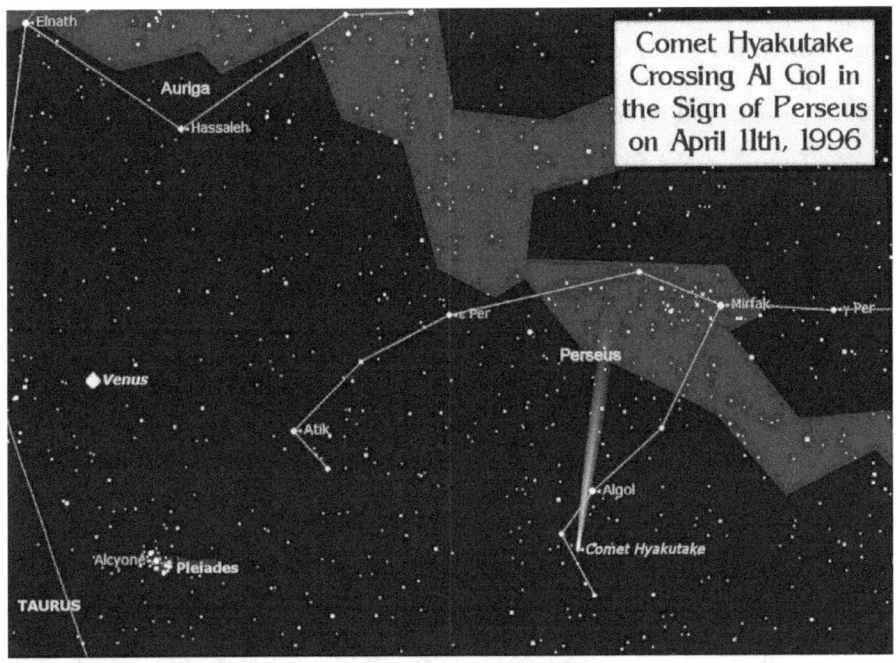

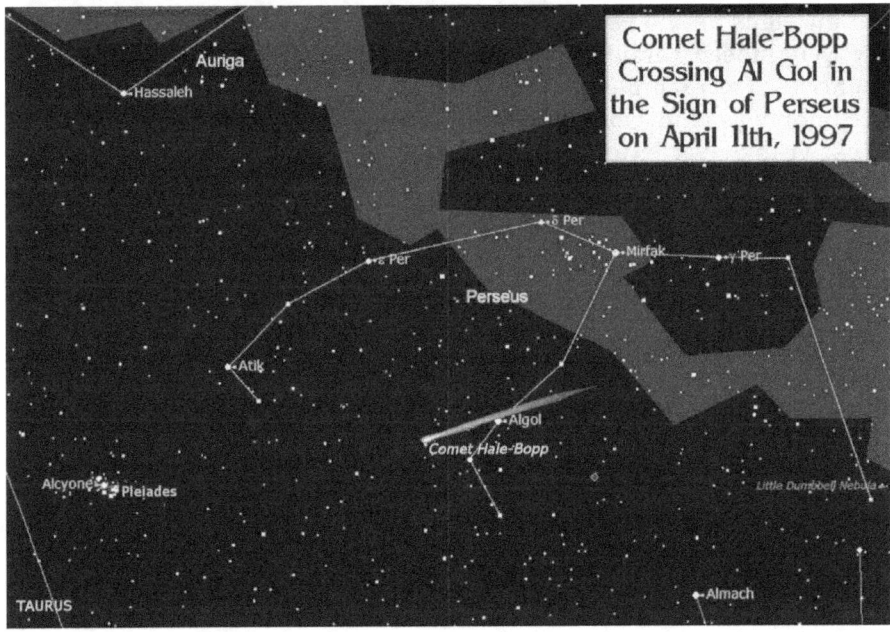

In addition - during daylight hours on that same day - the Sun, Mercury, Mars, and Saturn were in the sign of Pisces, and Jupiter was aligned with the Pleiades - and both Pisces and the Pleiades allude to Gentile and Jewish Israel! Soon after - on April 11, 1996 - Comet Hyakutake crossed over the star Al Ghoul in the constellation Perseus.

Then, on the first day of the Feast of Tabernacles - at around 4 o'clock a.m. on September 27th, 1996 - a Lunar Eclipse occurred when the Full Moon was in conjunction with the planet Saturn in the sign of Pisces. Interestingly, Pisces is allegorically connected to the fate of both Jewish and Gentile Israel, which are represented by the two fishes of Pisces. Meanwhile, the Moon signifies both the apostates in the Church, and the righteous members of Christ's Kingdom - as seen in the dark and bright faces of the Moon. In addition, Saturn represents the Sabbath, peace, and resting from work, but also can signify Satan. Since a total Lunar Eclipse fully darkens the Moon, this eclipse allegorically may have indicated that the peace that the Jews and Gentile Israel were seeking with their Muslim neighbors at that time would not come, and any attempt at peace would fail due to satanic interference.

Taken alone, the celestial signs on Jewish Feasts in 1996 appeared to be heralding that significant prophetic events were occurring or would soon occur between Gentile and Jewish Israel and the world. Coupled with the signs on the Feasts in 1997, however, there was no question that they were indeed heralding the imminent fulfillment of End Time prophecies. For example, on Purim on March 24th, 1997 - when Comet Hale-Bopp was at its closest and brightest - there was a partial Lunar Eclipse visible over Jerusalem at around 5 o'clock a.m. in the sign of Virgo. Also on that same day, the Sun, Mercury, Saturn, and Venus were in the sign of Pisces. Two weeks later, Comet Hale-Bopp followed Hyakutake's lead and crossed over the star Al Ghoul on the same calendar day - April 11th - but a year later, and in the opposite direction - completing a heavenly "X" over that sinister star.

Then, on September 16th, 1997 - at the start of the Feast of Tabernacles - another Lunar Eclipse occurred over Jerusalem. Uncannily, just as it had in 1996, the Full Moon eclipsed when it was in conjunction with the planet Saturn in Pisces! This celestial event - along with its predecessor in 1996 - was a clear sign to Israel that God was stirring up trouble for them in anticipation of the Tribulation. In fact, it seemed to be indicating that Jewish and Christian persecution would soon increase around the world - just as it surely has since then.

# Chapter 12: Sacred Astronomy as a Prophetic Tool

## *Prophetic Celestial Sign Portents From 1996 Thru 2008*

In 2007, several major celestial events occurred to strengthen my interpretation of the heavenly signs that occurred a decade earlier - in 1996 and 1997. Incidentally, 1997 was only two years before the close of the 6,000 years allotted for mankind that have elapsed between Adam's creation and the end of the Church Age. This Age ended on Rosh Hashanah, September 11th, 1999 - on the same day as the Terrorist attack that occurred two years later in 2001 at the World Trade Center in New York.

The first celestial event in 2007 was the appearance of the extremely brilliant Comet McNaught, which appeared in the sign of Sagittarius early in January. Interestingly, the centaur/archer symbol for Sagittarius signifies Christ coming to conquer Satan, sin and death via the Cross at His First Advent, and the amazingly long tail of Comet McNaught looked like the giant sword that Christ will wield in triumph when He returns in Glory.

As if in anticipation of that same event, another Lunar Eclipse occurred on Purim near to midnight on March 3rd, 2007. This one was very similar to the eclipse on Purim in 1997. Only this time, it occurred in the sign of Leo the Lion - a symbol for the Lion of Judah, who is Christ. As such, Leo represents Christ coming to assume His role as the King of Israel at the end of the Great Tribulation. At that time, Christ will conquer Israel's enemies and start His Millennial Reign on Earth. Before discussing the last celestial sign of 2007, it is interesting to note that the Feast of Purim represents the struggle of Israel against being assimilated by her Hellenized, Paganistic or humanistic and ungodly enemies such as Antiochus Epiphanes, who unsuccessfully attempted to Hellenize the Jews and force them to worship false gods.

In modern times - since there is an ever-growing awareness among Christians of their Jewish roots - Purim has taken on more significance for Christians. In addition to the victory of the Jews over the evil Vizier Haman during their forced exile in Persia, Purim now represents the desire of Christians to retain their democratic, peaceful, godly and prosperous way of life and to find protection from martyrdom. In consequence, Purim clearly symbolizes the current ideological war between the Middle East and the West - a war that is a much larger reflection of the unsettling events that led to the first Purim that was celebrated in ancient Persia (i.e. Iran and Iraq) over 2,500 years ago. A detailed overview of what Purim means for Christians can be found in my book: "The Language of God in Humanity."

The message of the Purim Eclipse compliments the meaning of the final heavenly sign that occurred near the end of 2007. Between October 23rd and November 4th that year - at the time of the Pagan Samhain festival known as Halloween - Comet Holmes grew from a very dim magnitude 17 to a very bright magnitude 2.8 that could be seen with the naked eye for over a week. This change in brightness occurred in Perseus when the comet was near to the bright star Mirfak (often erroneously labeled Al Genib). At that time, the sword-like tail of Comet Holmes was pointing directly toward the Earth. This made the comet's tail appear to disappear, and this temporarily made it look like a bright new star in Perseus.

Though Comet Holmes faded markedly in brilliance after October of 2007, it remained in the constellation Perseus - slowly doing a big retrograde loop through it. Then - just as Comets Hyakutake and Hale-Bopp did a little over a decade earlier - Comet Holmes crossed directly over the star Al Ghoul in Perseus on January 22nd, 2008. Could Comet Holmes have stayed in Perseus so long for a reason? And is there some significance to three comets visiting the sign of Perseus in the past decade? Since Medusa signifies the Great Delusion of the Serpent and the Way of Cain (See Book 3), it is likely that these comets are announcing that the Antichrist system of Secular Humanism and Satan's planned spiritual delusion of billions of wicked souls is imminent!

In order to understand what this unusual comet crossing might additionally signify, look at my illustration entitled: "Orion, Auriga & Perseus Treading Satan Underfoot" on page 155. In it, note that the very first prophecy in the Bible - Genesis 3:15 - is repeated many times in this section of the Gospel in the Stars. Also, note that Perseus is just one of many Christ-figures in the Zodiac. In fact, Orion, Auriga, and Aries all serve as dualistic representations of Christ's varied roles throughout history.

In Genesis 3:15, it says:

*"He (i.e. Yahshua, a.k.a. Jesus) shall bruise you (i.e. Satan) on the head, and you (i.e. Satan) shall bruise Him (i.e. Yahshua) on the heel."*

This prophecy signifies that at His death, Christ defeated Satan spiritually, and He will defeat the Antichrist's kingdom by crushing Satan's "head" or the seat of his power, which currently is located in Africa and the Middle East, but will later encompass all of Africa, the Middle East, Europe, Russia, and the United Kingdom.

## Comet Holmes in Perseus in 2007 and 2008

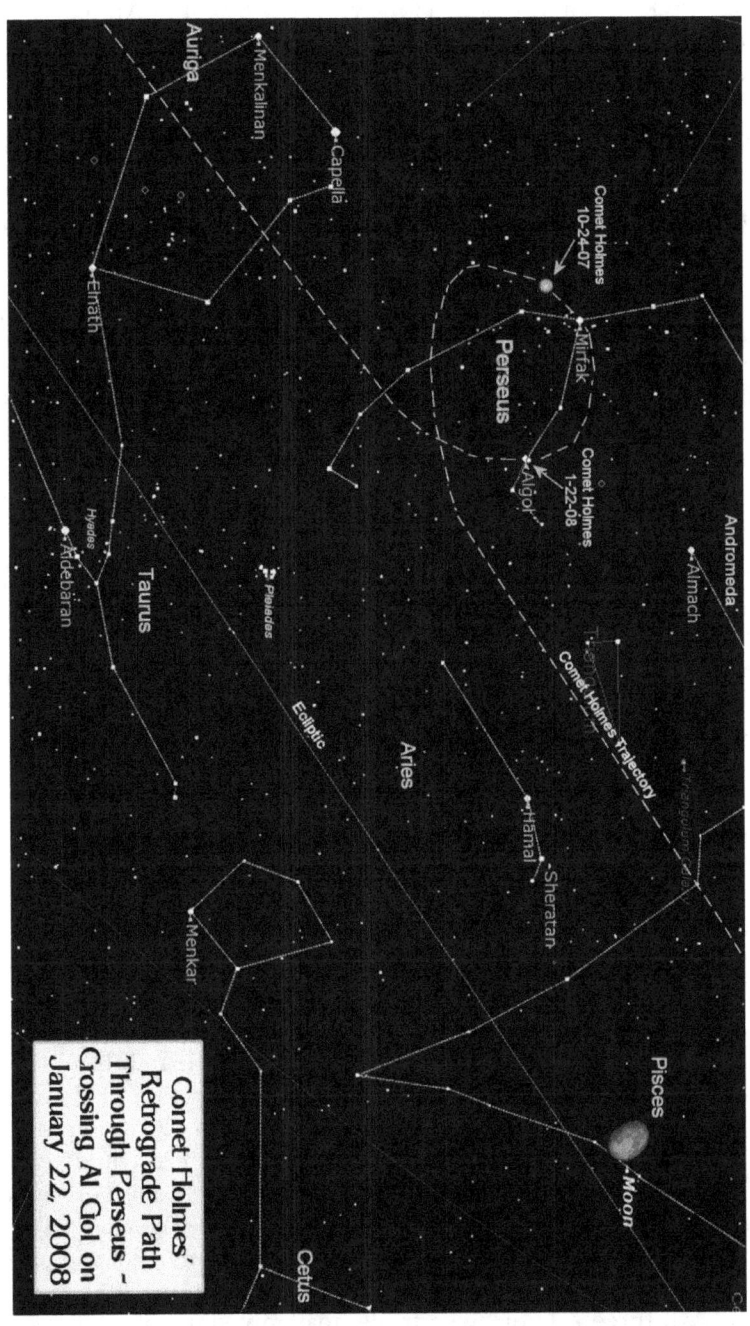

These nations will unite to form an unholy alliance that will be touted as the Kingdom of God. However, it will be the Antichrist who will rule this worldly kingdom in disguise. In support of this, Genesis 3:15 indicates that Satan will hurt Christ by biting Christ's people in the heel or severely wounding them - just as the adder or viper of the Tribe of Dan bites the horse's heels:

> "Dan shall be a serpent by the way, a viper by the path, that bites the horse's heels so that its rider (the Church) shall fall backward." - Genesis 49:17 (NIV)

The prophecies in Genesis 3:15 and Genesis 49:17 can clearly be seen in the way the Christ-figure Perseus' left foot rests over the Pleiades in Taurus the Bull: the dual unicorn. Note here that the horse in Genesis 49:17 signifies the flying horse Pegasus: a horse that is an allusion to the unicorn and bull symbols used to signify the USA, the UK, and the EU. Meanwhile, the serpent and viper of the Tribe of Dan signifies Muslim Terrorists who are allegorically biting the heels of Perseus' horse, Pegasus (i.e. the West).

Next, note that the Pleiades star cluster has a cup or dipper-like shape formed by six bright stars. These resemble the shapes of two constellations, each of which are formed by seven prominent stars. These are the Big Dipper or Ursa Major representing the True Church, and the Little Dipper or Ursa Minor, which signifies the Apostate or Antichristian Church.

## *Jupiter, Saturn, and Uranus: Cosmic Spiritual Messengers*

Regarding God's timing, there are three major sets of triple Signs in the Heavens that are earmarking 2008 through 2011 as highly significant. First, there were three Solar Eclipses on the 1st of Av, which is in the middle of a time of mourning over the loss of the Temple to Yahweh in 70 AD. These Solar Eclipses occurred on August 1st, 2008 and July 22nd, 2009 in the sign of Cancer, and on July 11th, 2010 in the sign of Gemini. The second set of signs is a triple conjunction of the planets Jupiter and Uranus in the sign of Pisces on June 6th, 2010, September 22nd, 2010, and January 4th, 2011. Then there is a third triple sign of three consecutive Total Lunar Eclipses - with the first one on the Winter Solstice of December 21st, 2010 in the sign of Taurus over Orion's upraised sword. This will be followed by a Total Lunar Eclipse on June 15th, 2011 in the sign of Scorpio and on December 10th, 2011 in the sign of Taurus. All three sets of these triple heavenly signs likely have much

## Chapter 12: Sacred Astronomy as a Prophetic Tool

to do with the imminence of the Rapture and beginning of the Tribulation.

Before we continue, however, it is important to note that the connection of heavenly signs with Bible prophecy cannot be clearly seen unless one has the baptism of the Holy Spirit and knows the spiritual meaning behind each planets' and star signs' physical and allegorical characteristics. For example, Uranus is the third largest planet in our Solar System next to Jupiter and Saturn. Now - according to the Gospel in the Stars and the Language of God that are a part of Sacred Astronomy - both Jupiter and Saturn represent Yahshua the Messiah in his differing roles. Utilizing the spiritual disciplines that righteous Sethites like Enoch and Noah understood, Jupiter, with its reddish cast suggestive of blood, can be seen to signify Yahshua as a Shepherd King, Kinsman Redeemer and Avenger of Blood. Meanwhile, Saturn with its serene blue coloration and regal rings or crowns, represents Yahshua as the Crowned King and Judge of a peaceful Universe that is finally and forever under His absolutely loving government control. However, since Satan is currently the ruler of this world, Saturn is often falsely associated with Satan in occult circles.

Because they can't be seen without the aid of powerful telescopes, the planet Uranus and its near-twin Neptune (the fourth largest planet with its own special story to tell) signify godly spiritual mysteries. The mysteries of our faith that are revealed to us by the Holy Spirit and concern the Kingdom of God are mentioned often by the Apostle Paul (Romans 11:25, 16:25; Ephesians 3:3-4, 6:19; Colossians 1:26-27). Although these planets cannot be seen with the naked eye, Uranus and Neptune have great mass and exert strong magnetic and gravitational forces on the other bodies in our Solar System. This means that they also must have a strong hidden affect on the events revealed in Enoch's Heavenly Tablets, which are the divinely written histories found in the 48 constellations of the ancient Zodiac that were authored by Yahshua when He created the Universe for His Father with the aid of the Holy Spirit.

Now, in my book "The Language of God in History," I examined Classical Mythology to show its amazing ties with the characters and events in the Old Testament historical narratives. This was done partly to prove that Nimrod's Babylon knew and bastardized the Star Gospel to invent a false religion centered around the humanistic worship of people and created things instead of the Creator God. Interestingly, the attributes and events surrounding the false gods connected to the planets Uranus and Neptune are likely deified perversions of the righteous man Noah's character and history. In keeping with the hidden aspect of

Uranus and Neptune, my book also shows that Noah was likely a hermit like his great grandfather Enoch. Like Enoch, Noah may have remained righteous by keeping himself separate from the affairs of mankind and hidden from them so that only a few knew where he dwelled or how to find him. *This suggests that those who will be counted as the Bride of Christ may need to be virtual hermits as well, with themselves and their immediate family living in the world but totally separate from and basically unconcerned with fleshly, carnal, political and organized religious pursuits.*

Amazingly, many more of the physical characteristics of Uranus have strong biblical connections. For example, Uranus has eleven faint rings and 27 known moons, but only five of its moons are truly prominent. Likewise, the Bible tells us that there were only eleven faithful apostles of Christ and there are exactly 27 books in the New Testament, with five - the four Gospels and the Book of Revelation - that are more significant than the rest. In addition, though the Hebrew alphabet has 22 letters, five of those letters having an additional finial form that were shown to be tied to the Tribulation period in Chapter Two. Oddly, Uranus is also the only planet in the Solar System whose poles point nearly directly toward the Sun. Due to this, Uranus looks as though it had been knocked over onto its side in some kind of massive cosmic collision. Allegorically, Uranus' unique tilt is also suggestive of bowing down before a great personage, and the greater celestial bodies Jupiter and the Sun signify the Preincarnate Christ and God the Father. Therefore, Uranus' tilt could signify the pure nature of true believers that are fully humble and repentant before God and His Son and not proud of their sins. Meanwhile, Uranus' eleven faint rings may signify the crowns or diadems to be worn by the eleven faithful Tribes of Israel that will form the Bride of Christ - excluding the Tribe of Dan.

Now, when pairing up the planets with the Zodiac signs and Tribes of Israel in my book "The Language of God in the Universe," I followed traditional Astrology to some extent. However, I also showed the connection of the Twelve Tribes of Israel to each of the twelve signs of the Zodiac. Interestingly, Uranus is connected to the Zodiac sign of Pisces, which signifies the Two Houses of Israel, and to the Tribe of Simeon. This is because Leah's son Reuben sinned against God and lost his birthright, so Leah's son Simeon was to became Jacob's heir. However, due to Reuben's sins, God chose Rachel's son Joseph to share in Simeon's inheritance of the spiritual and material blessings of the firstborn. In the course of studying God's choice of Joseph - whose wife Asenath was an Egyptian or Gentile - as the replacement for Reuben, the Holy Spirit also revealed to me that - as a large planet that is adjacent to

# Chapter 12: Sacred Astronomy as a Prophetic Tool

Saturn signifying Yahshua's Kingship, but which is too distant to be seen with the naked eye - Uranus may signify the Bride of Christ who is now hidden in the world, but will soon be revealed in all of her Glory as the true Queen of Heaven and Earth. Because Uranus is invisible without a telescope, this large pale blue planet also represents the mystery of the Kingdom of God (See Mark 4:11), which will become a material reality on Earth after the Wedding of the Lamb with the Bride of Christ.

## The Allegorical Meaning of Jupiter and Uranus

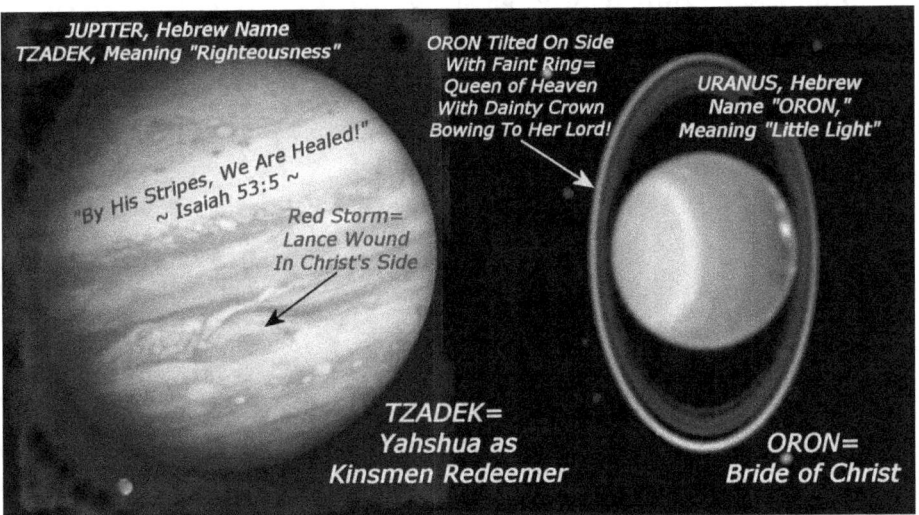

As revealed in the Parable of the Ten Virgins, only five of the Bride's virgin handmaids are taken with her to the Wedding. The five handmaids that accompany the Bride because they have enough "oil" or gifts of the Holy Spirit in their lamps signify groups of believers that are truly born-again. These believers live under Grace and actively utilize their spiritual gifts to give light to others who are in spiritual darkness. Meanwhile, the other five virgins without enough oil that are left behind signify spiritually lazy people who profess to love Yahshua, but are not born-again and do not share their faith or actively seek to draw nearer to God.

Likewise, Uranus' five prominent moons signify the Bride's five virgin handmaids that have plenty of Holy Spirit oil. Meanwhile, Uranus has twenty-two other moons, and 22 is the number of letters in the Hebrew Alphabet and in the Book of Revelation, which ends with a description of the New Jerusalem. As such, the number 22 signifies

# The Language of God in Prophecy

completion. Adding these 22 small moons to Uranus' five largest moons, this planet has 27 moons altogether - and there just happens to be 27 books in the New Testament or Brit Chadashah. Could these moons signify the 27 books of the New Testament that record the details and rules of the New Covenant? It would seem likely since Uranus signifies the Bride of Christ and the Bride should faithfully follow the New Testament, which is the only reliable earthly record of Yahshua's teachings of the concepts of Salvation and Grace.

## Jupiter & Uranus over Pegasus & Pisces Fish: July 11, 2010

Amazing Heavenly Signs, Evening of July 11th, 2010, Easter Island, South Pacific

As expounded earlier, the planet Jupiter also has much allegorical meaning. Since ancient times, Jupiter has been considered the "king" planet in association with the "king" star Regulus in Leo, as both of these celestial bodies are often found to be prominent in the sky at the births of

## Chapter 12: Sacred Astronomy as a Prophetic Tool

great personages like kings. Jupiter is therefore associated with greatness and is second only to Venus and the star Sirius in brilliance. Likewise, according to the Jewish sages, Jupiter signifies their coming Messiah and King. Not surprisingly, Jupiter was extremely prominent in the heavens at the most likely time of Christ's birth, which was between the summer of 3 BC and the winter of 2 BC. As explained in my book "The Language of God in the Universe," the retrograde movements of the planet Jupiter may have been partly behind the biblical description of the miraculous Star that the Magi followed to Bethlehem.

Due to the Judeo-Christian allegorical meanings behind the planets Uranus and Jupiter, any conjunction between them is quite significant. Not only are they a symbol for the future Wedding of the Lamb, but of Christ's great love for His Bride the True Church. Hauntingly, just as the dawning of the first day of God's Creation may have occurred on June 6th, 10,500 BC (a symbolic 666), Jupiter and Uranus will be in conjunction in Pisces for the first time in 2010 on June 6th, which is just one month before an amazing Solar Eclipse on the 1st of Av or July 11th, 2010 in the sign of Gemini.

Now, since God may have begun His act of Creation on June 6th, 10,500 BC - a date that invokes the number 666 - could it be that this number originally signified godly things? Intriguingly, there is evidence of this hidden within the Magic Sun Square, which may allegorically depict not only the Sun, which signifies Yahweh, but God's Throne room in Heaven. For further study, refer to my detailed article about the Magic Sun Square and its connection to the Great Pyramid, which can be found at my pillar-of-enoch.com web site. If so, the date of June 6th for this conjunction may be hinting that the evil perpetrated by the Antichrist whose name number is 666 will be reversed by the coming Rapture of those who love the 66 books of the Bible as well as the Second Coming of Christ. The Rapture may lead millions of unsaved people who are left behind to repent and accept Christ as their Savior before the Antichrist and his armies are destroyed at the Battle of Armageddon.

Amazingly, the Zodiac signs that these two prominent celestial events of 2010 will occur in are directly connected to both the Wedding of the Lamb and His Bride the True Church. For example, those who have read my other books will remember that the two fishes of Pisces signify the Two Houses of the Israel and the Church today. Indeed, coupled with neighboring Aquarius, the Pisces fishes form "the Sign of Jonah" that Yahshua spoke of (Matthew 12:39-40, 16:4; Luke 11:29-30). The fish swimming toward the constellation Andromeda signifies those who are bound to the Law and to salvation by works. These are the people who are under a yoke of slavery to the Law because they are not baptized with the Holy Spirit and have no lasting ability to resist sin or avoid the lusts of the flesh. They may have been baptized with water, but they have never experienced a true change of heart as a direct result of a supernatural encounter with the living God.

Meanwhile, the other fish of Pisces that is swimming along the path of the Sun called the ecliptic signifies those who are following the righteous Way of Yahweh. These redeemed souls are depicted as a fish following the literal path of the Sun as a symbol of righteousness. These are the fish caught in the harvest that are saved by Yahshua's blood and live under His Grace. Meanwhile, in its simplest sense, Gemini the Twins signifies a bond of love and a covenant union that ends the animosity between two warring family groups. In the Bible, Gemini can therefore signify the end of the antagonism between Cain and Abel, Ishmael and Isaac, Esau and Jacob, and Reuben and Joseph via acts of forgiveness and love.

In modern times, Gemini still signifies the war between Ishmael or Islam, and Isaac or Judeo-Christianity. However, though it is the resurrected Yahshua who will bring these opposing factions together one day in a truly lasting peace, the Antichrist must first appear to offer these warring parties a temporary peace that will lead to the most oppressive government and massive war in human history. This war has been dubbed the Battle of Armageddon after the word used to name the valley in the Book of Revelation where the Antichrist's multinational armies gather (Rev. 16:16). Fascinatingly, the number of the passage in Revelation that speaks of this great war is 16:16, and it is highly possible that this battle may begin in 2016 if the Tribulation begins in 2011. The valley where the battle will primarily take place can be identified with modern Israel's Jezreel Valley in the north. This valley was once in the land of the Philistines. The ancestors of the Palestinians were the Philistines, who also hated the Israelites and repeatedly tried to destroy them after the Israelites had conquered and resettled much of the Promised Land. As a result, the valley next to the ancient home of the Philistine city of Megiddo saw many terrible wars.

Now, the most amazing thing about the conjunctions of Jupiter and Uranus in Pisces in 2010 and early 2011 is that they will occur near to the center of the fish on the ecliptic, and this fish is the one that signifies the prophetic Tribe of Ephraim and the True Church, while the other fish signifies the Jewish people. Amazingly, the fish on the ecliptic has always rested directly above the back of Pegasus, the flying white horse, and this

## Chapter 12: Sacred Astronomy as a Prophetic Tool    Page 671

white horse is a symbol for the one that Yahshua will ride to victory when He returns to Earth at the End of the Tribulation (Rev. 19:11).

On Sunday, June 6th, 2010, a conjunction occurred between Jupiter signifying the Messiah and Bridegroom and the planet Uranus representing the Bride of Christ and five of her handmaids. This conjunction appeared directly over the Pisces fish that is allegorically riding the celestial horse named Pegasus, which represents the white steed that will carry our Messiah Yahshua between Heaven and Earth! Meanwhile, the Sun was centered between the horns of Taurus signifying the Tribe of Joseph, the Ten Lost Tribes of Israel and the Gentile Church, and the planet Venus representing Yahshua as the Morning Star was centered over the Pollux twin of Gemini signifying Yahshua as the Bridegroom. In allegorical cosmic terms, there truly could not be a more appropriate symbol for the return of Yahshua to claim His Bride!

At the same time as the Jupiter-Uranus conjunction, there was another conjunction between the planet Mars signifying war and blood atonement and the king star Regulus in Leo that represents Yahshua our Messiah crowned as king and coming to defeat Satan and reign victoriously over the whole Earth. Coupled with the Jupiter-Uranus conjunction in Pisces representing believing Jews and Gentiles that are God's Chosen People Israel, this Mars-Regulus conjunction suggests that the war between the righteous and the wicked will soon escalate and lead to the Second Coming of Christ represented by the sign of Leo, the Lion and King of Judah. But this is not the only witness in the stars, for this amazing double conjunction on June 6th was closely followed by other celestial signs that will be discussed in the next section.

## *Eclipses and Conjunctions Heralding the Wrath to Come*

Three triple occurrences of specific Heavenly Signs will occur between mid 2008 and the end of 2011. The first triple sign is a string of three Total Solar Eclipses in 2008, 2009 and 2010 on the 1st day of the Jewish Lunar Month of Av. The 1st of Av is nine days before a major Jewish day of lamentation and fasting called the 9th of Av, which ends a three week period of mourning over the destruction of the Temple to Yahweh in Jerusalem in 70 AD. Intriguingly, the 1st of Av falls in the middle of this time of sadness. This, coupled with the fact that there are three of these eclipses in a row, emphasizes the dire seriousness of the prophetic event that they are portending for the Jewish people.

Since the last of these eclipses falls in 2010, these eclipses seem to be heralding a terrible time of great sorrow and fasting for the Jewish people that may be coming for them in 2011. Could this be the beginning of the time of Jacob's Trouble known as the Tribulation? Could they mark the impending onset of the war between Israel and her enemies heralded by Psalm 83 and Psalm 108? The Solar Eclipse on August 1st, 2008 was best seen in the Middle East in the sign of Cancer, which represents the final spiritual harvest of the Two-House Church of Judah and Ephraim at the close of the Church Age of Pisces as well as at the end of the Millennial Rule of Christ on Earth. The Solar Eclipse on July 22nd, 2009 was also best seen in the sign of Cancer, but in Southeast Asia rather than the Middle East.

Finally, the Solar Eclipse on the 1st of Av on July 11th, 2010 occurred in the sign of Gemini the Twins and was best seen over Easter Island in the South Pacific. Fascinatingly, Gemini is a symbol for the conflict between brothers seen in Abraham's sons Isaac and Ishmael and Isaac's fraternal twin sons Jacob/Israel and Esau. However, it also signifies the resolution of the conflict via marriage - specifically the coming marriage of Yahshua to His Bride the True Church at the Wedding of the Lamb. To better explain the amazing prophetic symbolism of this triple string of Solar Eclipses on the 1st of Av between 2008 and 2010, illustrations were created using "Starry Night Backyard", which is an astronomy program, and graphics software. These illustrations can be found on several pages within this section. Of these, there are two illustrations pertaining to the Easter Island Solar Eclipse on July 11th, 2010 showing its connection with the mysterious Moai statues on Easter Island and the highly significant conjunctions between Jupiter and Uranus in the Sign of Pisces the Fishes, which signifies the Two Houses of Israel.

The Easter Island Eclipse is tied to the Scorpio-Sagittarius Longitude in the Pacific Ocean, which I gained knowledge of while finishing "The Language of God in History" in the spring of 2009. At that time, I found that the Longitudinal Meridians of the Earth that are tied to the Celestial Meridians used in astronomy programs and planispheres to chart the movement of celestial bodies in Earth's skies have a strong prophetic quality. Then, using the correlation of the Giza Pyramid Complex with Orion's Belt and the Red and Bent Pyramids at Dahshur in Egypt with the horns of Taurus, I was able to locate the alignment of the Celestial Meridians with the Earth in the orientation being indicated by the pyramids. Upon doing so, it became evident that the constellation Orion, which is symbolized as a warrior or hunter striding forward with a sword or club raised overhead, is a giant time-marker. In fact, Orion's sword-tip points to a spot on the Sun's Ecliptic that lies directly between the signs of Gemini and Taurus. This also marks a Celestial Longitude where the Summer Solstice occurs in our era.

Intriguingly, if viewed from the air, it can be seen that the processional causeway of the Great Pyramid points directly to the Summer Solstice point on the eastern horizon at that latitude, which is 14 degrees north of east. Furthermore, the Pillar of Enoch represents the brightest star in Orion's Belt, which has the name "Al Nitak." This Arabic phrase means "The Wounded One" and is allegorically referring to the wounds that our Messiah Yahshua received on the Cross. Fascinatingly, the three big pyramids at Giza also symbolize the three crosses that were erected just outside of Jerusalem when Christ was crucified. As such, the Great Pyramid signifies the cross of the repentant robber, who through his humility and remorse reflects the nature of the people within the Body of Christ and the Bride of Christ. For a more detailed written and illustrated explanation of this amazing allegorical connection of the Giza Pyramids with the crucifixion of Christ, see Book Three and Chapter Five of this book.

Since there is this undeniable correlation, could the causeway of the Great Pyramid be pointing to the Summer Solstice to indicate that this marks the season when Yahshua will return for His Bride in the Rapture? If so, could it be targeting the Summer Solstice on June 21st, 2011 as the solstice in question? It is possible. However, since no one can know the exact day or hour of the Rapture, this solstice and the summer season of 2011 could also be marking some other significant prophetic event that will involve the Body of Christ and the Jewish people residing in Israel such as the coming war between the Muslim descendents of Ishmael and the Jewish descendents of Isaac predicted by the prophetic words of Psalm 83 and Psalm 108.

No matter how else they are viewed, this triplet of 1st of Av Solar Eclipses between 2008 and 2010 is unquestionably heralding a time of unprecedented trouble for the nation of Israel and the Jews. Lending credence to the theory that these heavenly signs are heralding the coming of the Tribulation, another triple celestial sign marks not only the entire year 2011 on the Gregorian Calendar, but particularly the month of June in 2011. This triple sign is a series of Total Lunar Eclipses that will either directly or indirectly involve the sign of Taurus the Bull and its opposing sign of Scorpio. Fascinatingly, the first of these is on the night before the Winter Solstice, and the causeway of Khafre's Pyramid at Giza, which signifies the Cross of Christ, points to the Winter Solstice at that latitude. Could this be a sign that the Tribulation will begin sometime in the 2010-2011 winter season?

# The Language of God in Prophecy

## August 1st, 2008 - 1st of Av Solar Eclipse # 1

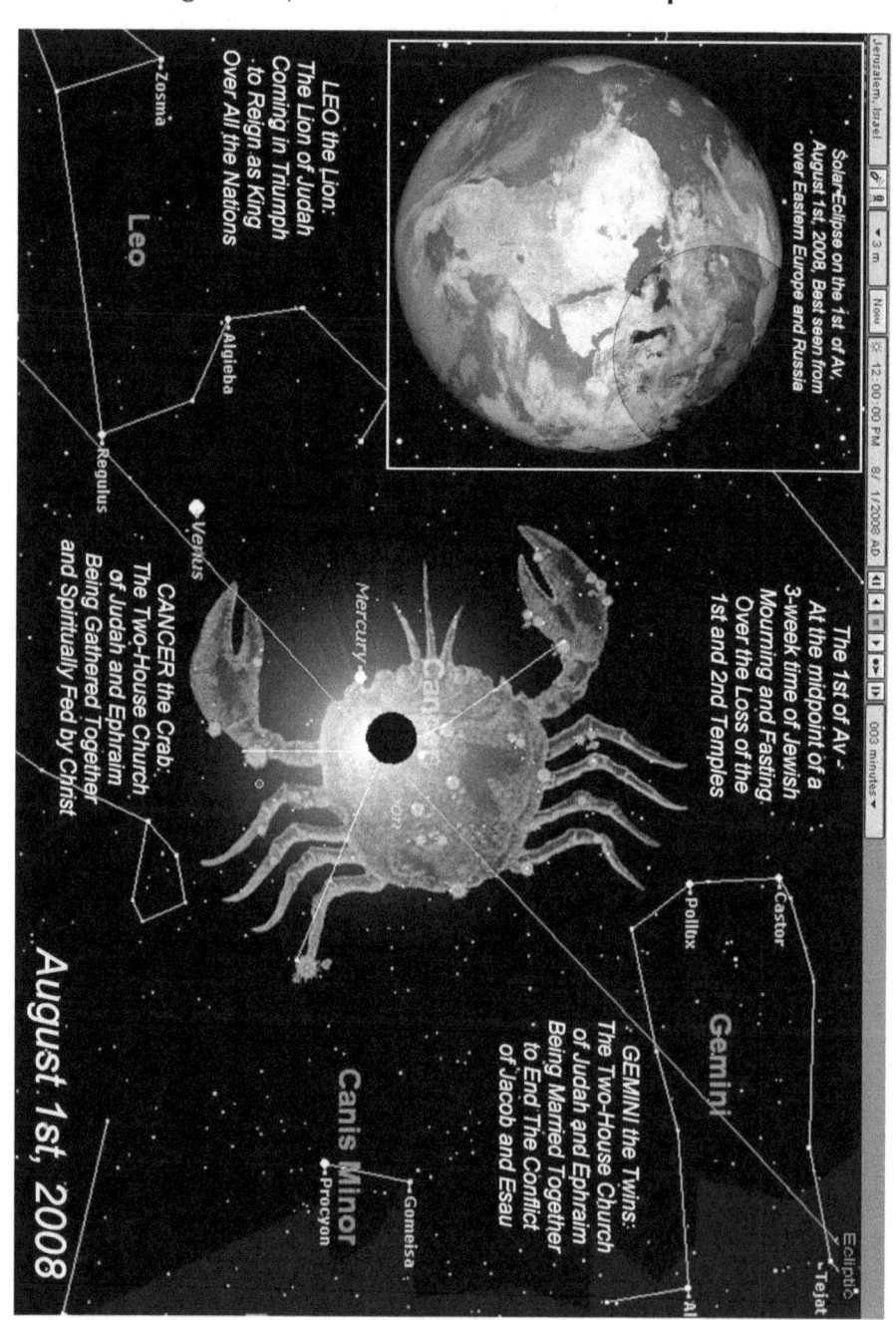

# Chapter 12: Sacred Astronomy as a Prophetic Tool  Page 675

## July 22nd, 2009 - 1st of Av Solar Eclipse # 2

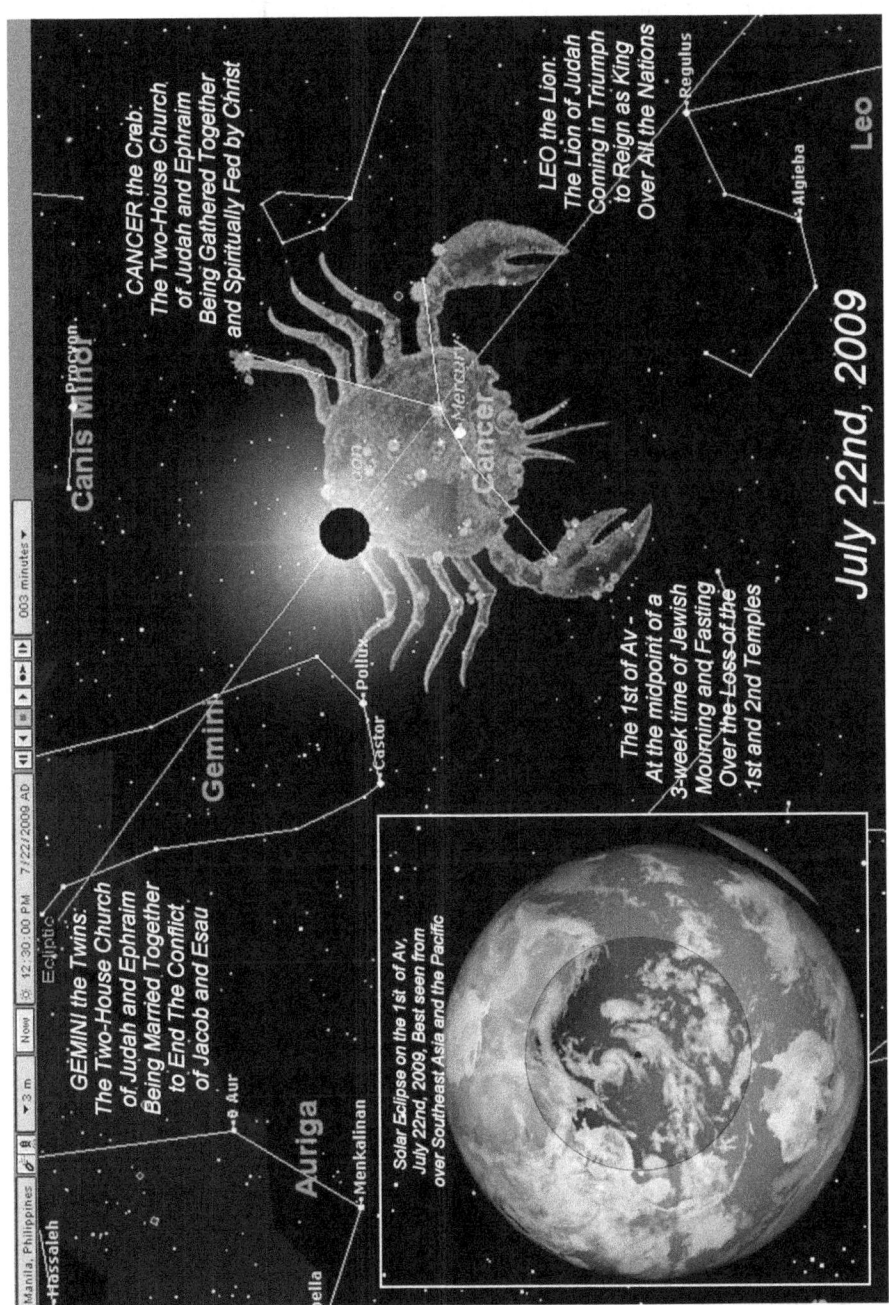

Though no one knows for certain, the fact that the Total Lunar Eclipses from December 2010 through December 2011 targeted the Celestial Meridians marking the beginning (Taurus) and the end (Scorpio) of the conflict between Jacob and Esau, Judah and Ephraim, and the ongoing conflict between the Jews and the Gentiles is certainly no accident. These conflicts that are marked by Taurus and Scorpio correspond to the 30th east longitude over Egypt and Israel, and the opposing 150th west longitude of the Earth over Alaska and Hawaii that are ominously tied not only to Scorpio, but are physically tied to the westernmost part of the USA.

Before exploring these Lunar Eclipses connected to Taurus, however, let's focus on the 1st of Av Solar Eclipses - particularly the one in 2010. On the 1st of Av on Sunday, July 11th, 2010, the Moon completely covered the Sun in a Total Solar Eclipse. Intriguingly, the 1st of Av marks the beginning of the nine days of awe leading up to the traditional 9th of Av Jewish day of mourning over the destruction of the First and Second Temples in Jerusalem. It also falls in the middle of a three-week period of mourning and lamentation that devout Jews commemorate between the 17th of Tammuz when Jerusalem was surrounded by Roman soldiers in 70 AD and the 9th of Av when the Temple to Yahweh in Jerusalem was subsequently sacked and burned.

Unlike the Solar Eclipses that occurred on the 1st of Av in 2008 and 2009, this Solar Eclipse was best be seen over Easter Island in the South Pacific, which is one of the most remote locations on the Earth. Intriguingly, Easter Island features many mysterious lava-rock cut statues called Moai. Though few seem to comment on it, these statues physically appear to be representing hundreds of starving, distressed people looking anxiously upward. Could it be that they were left there by our righteous ancestors to indicate a time when such frightening Signs in the Heavens would begin to appear over this exact spot on Earth? It would make sense, since these statues and the barren, near desolate island they have been built upon appear to accurately depict the End Times described in the Gospel of Luke and the Book of Revelation:

*"And there will be signs in the sun, in the moon, and in the stars; and on the earth distress of nations, with perplexity, the sea and the waves roaring; men's hearts failing them from fear and the expectation of those things which are coming on the earth, for the powers of heaven will be shaken." Luke 21:25-26*

*"When He opened the third seal, I heard the third living creature say, 'Come and see.' So I looked, and behold, a black horse, and he who sat on it had a pair of scales in his hand. And I*

# Chapter 12: Sacred Astronomy as a Prophetic Tool

*heard a voice... saying, 'A quart of wheat for a denarius, and three quarts of barley for a denarius; and do not harm the oil and the wine.' When He opened the fourth seal... I looked, and behold, a pale horse. And the name of him who sat on it was Death, and Hades followed with him. And power was given to them over a fourth of the earth, to kill with sword, with hunger, with death, and by the beasts of the earth."*

## Solar Eclipse Over Easter Island - July 11th, 2010

*"I looked when He opened the sixth seal, and behold, there was a great earthquake; and the sun became black as sackcloth of hair (a Solar Eclipse), and the moon became like blood (a Lunar Eclipse). And the stars of heaven fell to the earth... Then the sky receded as a scroll when it is rolled up, and every*

*mountain and island was moved out of its place (a Global Pole Shift?). And the kings of the earth... the mighty men, every slave and every free man, hid themselves in the caves and in the rocks of the mountains, and said to the(m)... 'Fall on us and hide us from the face of Him who sits on the throne and from the wrath of the Lamb! For the great day of His wrath has come, and who is able to stand?'" - Revelation 6:5-8, 12-17*

The Star Gospel surrounding the 2010 Easter Island Solar Eclipse ties in well with the symbolism of Psalm 110, and the prophecies in the Hallel Psalms indicate that Psalm 110 is tied to 2010 - the probable year before the Tribulation begins. In Psalm 110, we are told that Yahshua will sit at His Father's right hand to watch upcoming events on Earth and that He will extend His scepter from Zion, which is tied to Orion and the Great Pyramid. The day before this Solar Eclipse, the Messiah planet Jupiter and Uranus were in near conjunction over the Pisces Fish riding on the back of Pegasus, as seen in the illustration on page 668.

As shown in "The Language of God in the Universe," Jupiter signifies the Messiah Yahshua as our Savior or Kinsmen Redeemer, and Uranus with its five moons can signify Christ's Bride and her five virgin maids going to Heaven in the Rapture. Meanwhile, the fish over Pegasus signifies Ephraim or the True Church being taken to Heaven in the Rapture. Amazingly, Jupiter (Christ) and Uranus (His Bride) will remain over this Ephraimite fish through January 2011, when Jupiter and Uranus will move into conjunction one last time before moving apart again. Could this be hinting that the Rapture will come shortly after this last conjunction? If it does, it could mean that the late winter or early spring of 2011 might be a tragic time for all who are left behind! Considering that the true start of 2011 on the Jewish Sacred Calendar is Nissan 1 or April 5th, 2011, and Easter Island was discovered on April 5th in 1722 by a Dutch explorer named Jacob (i.e. Israel!) Roggeveen, the Rapture could occur before then if it is to be a Pre-Tribulation event. If so, then the Signs in the Heavens targeting June of 2011 could mark the time of the terrible war that will lead to the Antichrist's final rise to power in Daniel's 70th week - when the Antichrist will help ratify an infamous and false seven-year covenant or treaty with Israel.

Now, at the time of the 1st of Av Solar Eclipse on July 11th, 2010 over Easter Island, the Moon - which signifies the two wives of Jacob and the Two House Church of Judah and Ephraim - was positioned directly over the Sun, which was over the Pollux twin of Gemini signifying Christ as the Bridegroom. Intriguingly, the Sun also represents Yahshua as the Son of God and the Sun of Righteousness (Malachi 4:2). Incidentally, all

## Chapter 12: Sacred Astronomy as a Prophetic Tool

Solar Eclipses signify the unconstructive meddling of a woman over a male leader's good decisions such as was displayed by Sarah over Abraham and Rachel over Isaac. Sadly, a Solar Eclipse can also signify the imagined dominance that wicked humanity thinks it has over God Almighty! This is likely why Solar Eclipses have traditionally been considered negative signs of foreboding over the lands where they can be seen. Intriguingly, in every instance of these Total Solar Eclipses on the 1st of Av, the planet Mercury was also in close proximity. Since Mercury signifies Enoch the Sethite as the translated Scribe of Righteousness for Yahweh who records everything of divine prophetic significance, it is a prime indicator that the Sign in the Heavens it accompanies has a prophetic purpose.

This July 2010 Solar Eclipse occurred when the Sun was directly over the Pollux star twin of Gemini representing the Bridegroom Yahshua as well as Jacob, as shown in the illustration on page 677. Adding to this symbolism, the star Castor in Gemini the Twins can depict Yahshua's Bride the True Church as well as Esau (Arab and Persian Muslims). As such, Gemini signifies the healing of the breach between feuding brothers and warring nations. This will be brought about by a divinely sanctioned marriage that will unite the opposing parties into one loving family for all time.

Due to the heavy symbolism pertaining to the Middle-East Conflict recorded within the 1st of Av Solar Eclipses that occurred in the summers of 2008, 2009 and 2010, there is no doubt that they were intended to alert humanity that the Rapture and the time of Jacob's Trouble are imminent. Furthermore, since the Jewish religious calendar starts a new cycle on Nissan 1 or April 5th, 2011 - the same date that Easter Island was discovered - it is likely that these celestial warnings are pointing to events that could occur in the Jewish sacred year that will fall between Nissan 1 on April 5th, 2011 and Nissan 1 on March 24th, 2012.

Uncannily, there is ample evidence that the Gregorian year beginning on January 1st, 2011 is just as prophetically significant as the Jewish Sacred Year beginning on April 5th, 2011. This can be found in a series of three amazing Total Lunar Eclipses or a Blood Moon Triad that will mark the beginning, middle and end of 2011 and that will occur in Taurus and its opposing Zodiac sign Scorpio. Please go to the end of this chapter to see a graphic from my Tribulation Timeline showing this Lunar Eclipse Triad, as well as the other Triad that will mark the year 2018.

## Earth's Longitudinal Meridians Connected to the Zodiac

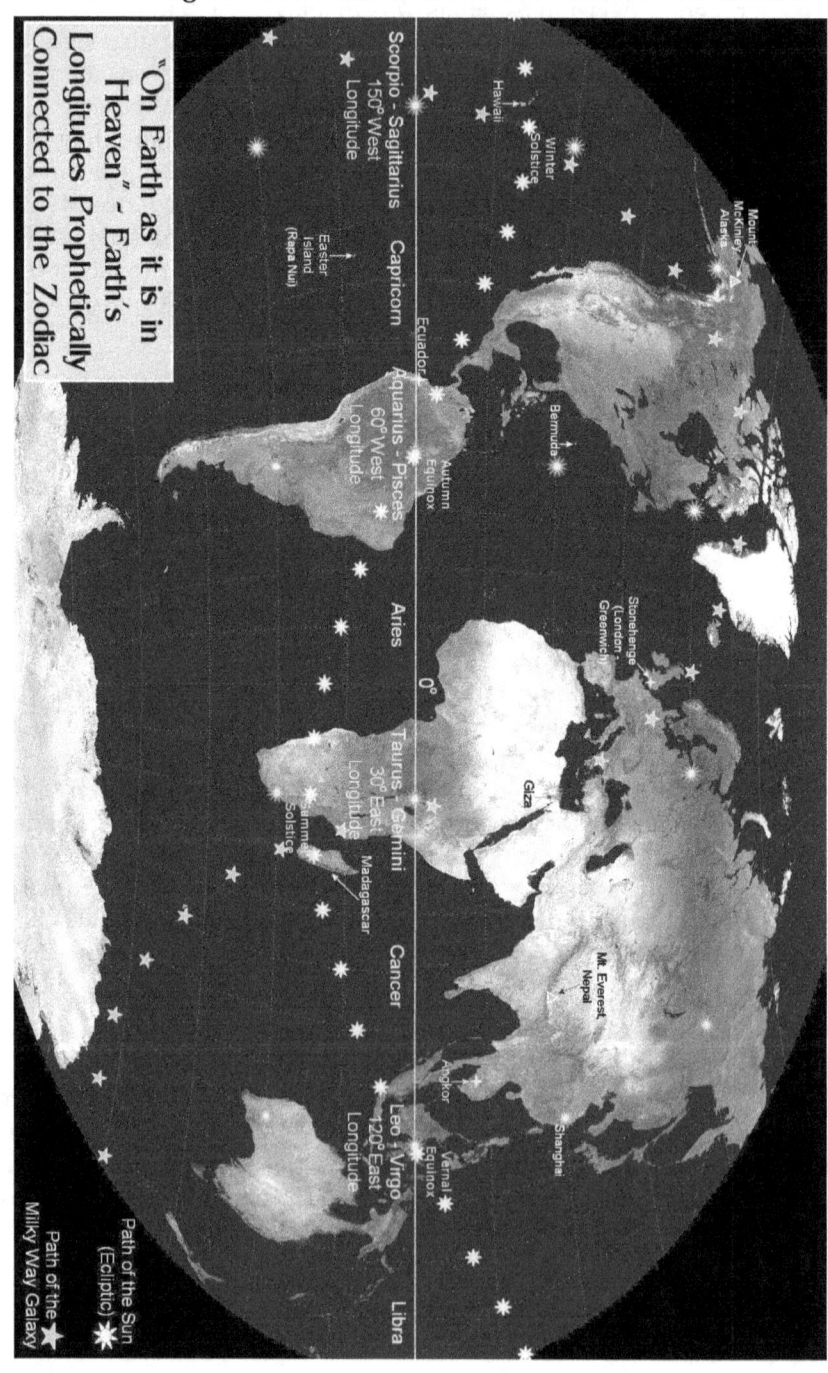

# Chapter 12: Sacred Astronomy as a Prophetic Tool

The first of these Blood Moons will occur on December 21st, 2010. On that evening just before the Winter Solstice Sun rises, this Total Lunar Eclipse will occur on the ecliptic directly between the signs of Gemini the Twins and Taurus the Bull. This is shown in the illustrations on pages 318, 320, and 688. Interestingly, Taurus signifies both God's great mercy on the Gentiles and His terrible wrath upon those who reject Him, while the sign of Gemini depicts the resolution of the Arab-Israeli conflict in the Wedding of the Lamb uniting the Two-House Church of Judah and Ephraim or the Bride of Christ.

Could this Lunar Eclipse on December 21st, 2010 be a symbol that Christ is readying for battle with His earthly enemies, the Rapture is imminent, and God's seven-year period of wrath is about to begin? As an eerie sign of the terrible wars and subsequent Wrath of God to come, this Lunar Eclipse will occur directly over the tip of the messianic constellation Orion's upraised sword. Since Orion depicts Christ, the sword that the Lunar Eclipse occurs over is the sword of Christ, and also represents His scepter! Likewise, in Psalm 110, Yahshua is seen extending His scepter from "Zion," which refers not only to Jerusalem but to the Great Pyramid and its connection to the star Al Nitak in Orion's Belt. This eclipse will be visible over much of North America, which will likely be one of the hardest hit sections of the world when the sudden disappearance of millions of believers occurs in the Rapture.

Similar to the July 11th, 2010 Solar Eclipse, this Lunar Eclipse occurring before the Winter Solstice sunrise on December 21st, 2010 was best viewed from Hawaii, Easter Island, and French Polynesia. However, this Blood Moon was also fully visible to most of the people living in North, Central and South America. On page 319, the illustration shows that this Lunar Eclipse will be accompanied by several other heavenly signs in a formation called a partial Grand Cross. On page 320, the illustration shows this same Lunar Eclipse as seen from Hawaii - a spot on the globe that was identified as an allegorical epicenter of evil lying fully within the Scorpio Meridian of the Earth in Book Three. A map that is displayed over two pages in that book is shown as a single image on page 680. It shows that these ancient Earth Meridians that are amazingly connected to the Celestial Meridians used by astronomers today. As mentioned earlier, the locations of these Meridians can be deduced from the Giza Pyramid connection to Orion's Belt and the sign of Taurus.

From the map of the Earth shown on page 680, it is easy to see that Hawaii and half of Alaska lies within the Scorpio Meridian of the Earth, and in the Star Gospel, Scorpio is a symbol of Satanic evil, pain and death. Interestingly, as revealed in Book Three, Mount McKinley in

Alaska is the second tallest mountain in the world next to Mount Everest, and at 151 degrees west of Greenwich, it lies within the Scorpio Earth Meridian. Fascinatingly, Mount McKinley also happens to be one of the coldest spots on the Earth, with recorded temperatures approaching minus 100 degrees Fahrenheit (-73°C). Furthermore, the mountain that rises up out of the Pacific Ocean to form the Big Island of Hawaii in the Hawaiian Island chain is not only the tallest peak in the world as measured from the ocean floor, but the site of two of the most active volcanoes in the world. Intriguingly, if the Zodiac were to be mapped out on the surface of the entire Earth using the orientation of Taurus and Orion that is highlighted via Egypt's biggest pyramids, Scorpio would rest dead center in the Pacific Ocean. What's more, the tail of Scorpio would rest over and mimic the curve of the Hawaiian Island chain! There is no way that this is a coincidence, but it has all the earmarks of God's hand in its design.

Two years later, on the Winter Solstice of December 21st, 2012, the heavenly Anti Peace Sign will appear in the heavens as a symbol of the destruction that will have begun whenever the Four Horsemen of the Apocalypse are released by God. After that, a highly rare Blood Moon Tetrad or series of four Total Lunar Eclipses or Blood Moons will fall on the first day of Passover and Tabernacles in 2014 and 2015. The last two times these Blood Moon Tetrads occurred was in 1949 and 1950, the year after the rebirth of Israel as a nation, and in 1967 and 1968, the year when Israel recaptured Jerusalem during the Six-Day War between Israel and her hostile Arab neighbors.

Could it be that Israel will be surrounded by the Antichrist's armies and the Battle of Armageddon will begin around Passover in 2014 and escalate even more in 2015? Could 2016 see the Second Coming of Christ a year early to end the carnage before all life on Earth is annihilated? Only time will tell, but there is no doubt that all of these heavenly signs have been left for us to ponder God's will and His ultimate purposes for Israel and the True Church at this time in history!

As shown in "The Language of God in History," volcanoes are symbolic of the intense heat needed in the forges where weapons are cast and tempered, and the Book of 1 Enoch explains that it was the Fallen Angel Azazel - also know as Lucifer or Satan - who introduced the forging of metals to mankind and taught them how to make weapons and jewelry. Sadly, this skill led all of humanity to sin far more than before due to the murderousness and lustfulness that weapons and jewelry provoked. Perhaps that is why the immense peak that rises from the depths of the world's biggest ocean's darkness to form this majestic

## Chapter 12: Sacred Astronomy as a Prophetic Tool

island within the Scorpio Meridian suggests the pride and lust of Satan, who will be thrown down to the lowest depths by Christ when He comes again in Glory to set up His Millennial Kingdom on Earth.

Though it may seem fantastic to some, my books give ample evidence to prove that our righteous ancestors were as close to Yahweh God as any Bible-educated believer is today. In fact, they understood God and knew Him on a whole different level than we modern believers are even capable of. This is because we are totally divorced from their thought processes. Too many of us live in cities of wood, metal and glass separated from nature, and can only see the stars in our dreams - if we are even motivated enough to think of them - and so few are. The majority of us are separate from nature and ignorant of what it contains for our spirits. As a result, we cannot easily grasp the beauty and spiritual power of the starry Universe and the message of failure, despair, repentance, struggle, hope, faith and everlasting promise that the Star Gospel written within it contains for all mankind.

Our righteous ancestors Enoch, Abraham, and Moses knew that future generations of mankind would be spiritually blind because of their separation from God and nature. Unlike us, they saw the Language and Mind of God in everything that He created, especially the Universe that was visible in the skies around them at night and gave them a visual divine record of everything that is, was, or ever will be. As a testimony of their ability to see, understand and love God and the future generations of mankind yet to be born that they could read about in the stars, they built incredible sacred monuments in stone to point us toward the Signs in the Heavens that warn of God's coming judgment and His promise of deliverance from that time of trouble for the faithful.

The oldest and most finely hewn of these monuments were NOT built by aliens or Fallen Angels! No way, no how, nowhere! No demon would ever leave so clear a testimony of God's love for mankind through Yahshua Ha Mashiach, the divine Savior that God memorialized forever in the ancient Zodiac! In fact, Yahshua is either directly or indirectly the subject of the entire Star Gospel! As a hint of God's message to us in the stars, Bible passages such as this one from Psalm 103 echo the separation between the Taurus Meridian in the Eastern Hemisphere and the Scorpio Meridian in the Western Hemisphere:

> *"The LORD (Yahweh) is merciful and gracious, slow to anger, and abounding in mercy. He will not always strive with us, nor will He keep His anger forever. He has not dealt with us according to our sins, nor punished us according to our iniquities.* **For as the heavens are high above the earth, so great is His mercy**

*toward those who fear Him; As far as the east is from the west, so far has He removed our transgressions from us."* - Psalm 103:8-12

Other passages in the Bible speak of the allegorical and spiritual meaning of Taurus the Bull, since bulls were once required to make sin offerings of atonement to God. These bulls were burned outside the Israelite camp as a symbol of the separation between God and man that the bull temporarily healed over by the shedding of its innocent blood and flesh. These bulls that served as the sin offerings of the Israelites were an allegorical symbol pointing to mankind's need for the shed blood of Christ to end their separation from Yahweh God once and for all time and to allow them to live as one with God forever:

*"And he said to Aaron, 'Take for yourself a young bull as a sin offering and a ram as a burnt offering, without blemish, and offer them before the LORD (Yahweh). And to the children of Israel you shall speak, saying, "Take a kid of the goats as a sin offering, and a calf and a lamb, both of the first year, without blemish, as a burnt offering, also a bull and a ram as peace offerings, to sacrifice before the LORD (Yahweh)."'"* - Leviticus 9:2-4

This sacrifice for sin was also made on the Day of Atonement. Though two goats highlighted the sacrificial offerings made that day, a bull and a ram signifying the horned altar in heaven formed by Taurus the Bull and Aries the Ram were also sacrificed just as they were in the preceding passage. Fascinatingly, the constellation known as Auriga the Goat Shepherd that twinkles above Gemini signifies the importance of the goats that were offered at these times:

*"On the tenth day of this seventh month you shall have a holy convocation. You shall afflict your souls; you shall not do any work. You shall present a burnt offering to the LORD (Yahweh) as a sweet aroma: one **young bull, one ram, and seven lambs** in their first year. Be sure they are without blemish."* - Numbers 29:7-8

Likewise the evil of the Scorpion depicted by the sign of Scorpio and the malevolence of the huge, writhing form of Serpens the Serpent that is depicted in a decan constellation belonging to Scorpio is also clearly depicted within the Bible's hallowed pages. The following passage that records God speaking to the Israelites is taken from the Book of Deuteronomy. It was delivered to Moses just before the Israelites crossed the Jordan River to enter the Promised Land. Therein, Yahweh reminded the Israelites of their deliverance from evil during their wanderings in deserts full of scorpions and serpents. Yet, though God also promised

## Chapter 12: Sacred Astronomy as a Prophetic Tool

great future blessings upon the righteous, He also issued a stern warning that contained a terrible curse upon those who disobeyed God:

> *"Be careful that you do not forget the LORD your God (Yahweh your Elohim), failing to observe his commands, his laws and his decrees that I am giving you this day. Otherwise, when you... build fine houses and settle down, and... your silver and gold increase and all you have is multiplied, then your heart will become proud and you will forget the LORD your God (Yahweh your Elohim), who brought you out of Egypt, out of the land of slavery.* **He led you through the vast and dreadful desert, that thirsty and waterless land, with its venomous snakes and scorpions. He brought you water out of hard rock. He gave you manna to eat in the desert...** *to humble and to test you so that in the end it might go well with you. You may say to yourself, 'My power and the strength of my hands have produced this wealth for me.' But remember the LORD your God (Yahweh your Elohim), for it is he who gives you the ability to produce wealth... If you ever forget... and follow other gods and worship and bow down to them, I testify against you today that you will surely be destroyed. Like the nations the LORD (Yahweh) destroyed before you, so you will be destroyed..."* - Deuteronomy 8:11-20 (NIV)

Contrary to what some apostates in the Church are claiming today, this curse upon those who forget and disobey God has not changed. Not even Yahshua, who died for our sins and rose from the dead, can change His own Word, which is the Word of His Father Yahweh. As Yahshua said: *"till heaven and earth pass away, one jot or one tittle will by no means pass from the law till all is fulfilled"* (Matthew 5:18). For this reason, Yahweh's curse upon the Israelites is an everlasting one, and it will be poured out one day upon all of the wicked, not just the foolish Israelites who have sinned without truly seeking forgiveness. Indeed, when this curse is carried out, it will not only fulfill the Book of Deuteronomy but also God's Word in the Star Gospel by using creatures carrying the poisonous and painful sting of scorpions and serpents:

> *"And he opened the bottomless pit, and smoke arose out of the pit like the smoke of a great furnace. So the sun and the air were darkened because of the smoke of the pit. Then out of the smoke locusts came upon the earth. And to them was given power, as the scorpions of the earth have power. They were commanded not to harm the grass of the earth, or any green thing, or any tree, but only those men who do not have the seal of God on their foreheads."* - Rev. 9:2-4

Due to these correlations between the Word of God in the Bible and the Gospel in the Stars, we should be seriously paying a great deal of heed to the heavenly warnings being issued by the triple Signs in the Heavens targeting 2010 and 2011 that are being talked about in this section. To that end, let me point out that the following heavenly signs are even clearer than the Solar Eclipses were in heralding the beginning of the end of this evil world system and the coming of the King of Righteousness.

To see a clear explanation of the Star Gospel message connected to the Lunar Eclipse on December 21st, 2010, see the illustrations on page 320 and page 688. This sign by itself is an ominous warning of impending judgment. However, when we look at the meaning of the partial Solar Eclipse on January 4th, 2011 that is shown in the illustration on page 689, and compare it to the illustration on page 320, it provides an even clearer forewarning that God's judgment is imminent.

On January 4th, the Sun will be eclipsed by the Moon in the sign of Sagittarius signifying Yahshua as Israel's Avenger of Blood riding upon a white horse. Meanwhile, Jupiter will move into its final conjunction with Uranus in Pisces, which is another clear sign announcing that the Rapture is also imminent. Remember that the first of these occurred on June 6th, 2010 - shortly before the July 11th, 2010 Solar Eclipse in Gemini over Easter Island. In addition, Jupiter remained close to Uranus over the Ephraimite fish of Pisces so that their second conjunction could occur on September 22nd, 2010 and their third conjunction could happen on January 4th, 2011.

Before focusing on the January 4th, 2011 Jupiter-Uranus conjunction and Solar Eclipse, let's back track for just a moment to the September 22nd conjunction. Significantly, this conjunction occurred on the same day as the Autumn Equinox in the sign of Virgo, which is a symbol of Yahshua's earthly mother Miriam as the bride of Joseph of the Tribe of Judah (suggesting the Tribe of Ephraim (Joseph) being united to Judah), and Israel as the virgin Bride of Christ. Fascinatingly, the Autumn Equinox is also an indicator that the autumn feasts of Israel are at hand, and all of these feasts have yet to be completely fulfilled in the Millennial Kingdom of Christ. In addition, the evening of September 22nd, 2010 was also the first day of the Feast of Tabernacles, a major week-long Jewish Festival celebrating the culmination of all the harvests of the summer season, the coming of the Messiah, and the ingathering of all of God's people to dwell together in the Promised Land in peace forever. See my illustration of this sign on page 687.

## Jupiter-Uranus Conjunction on Feast of Tabernacles 2010

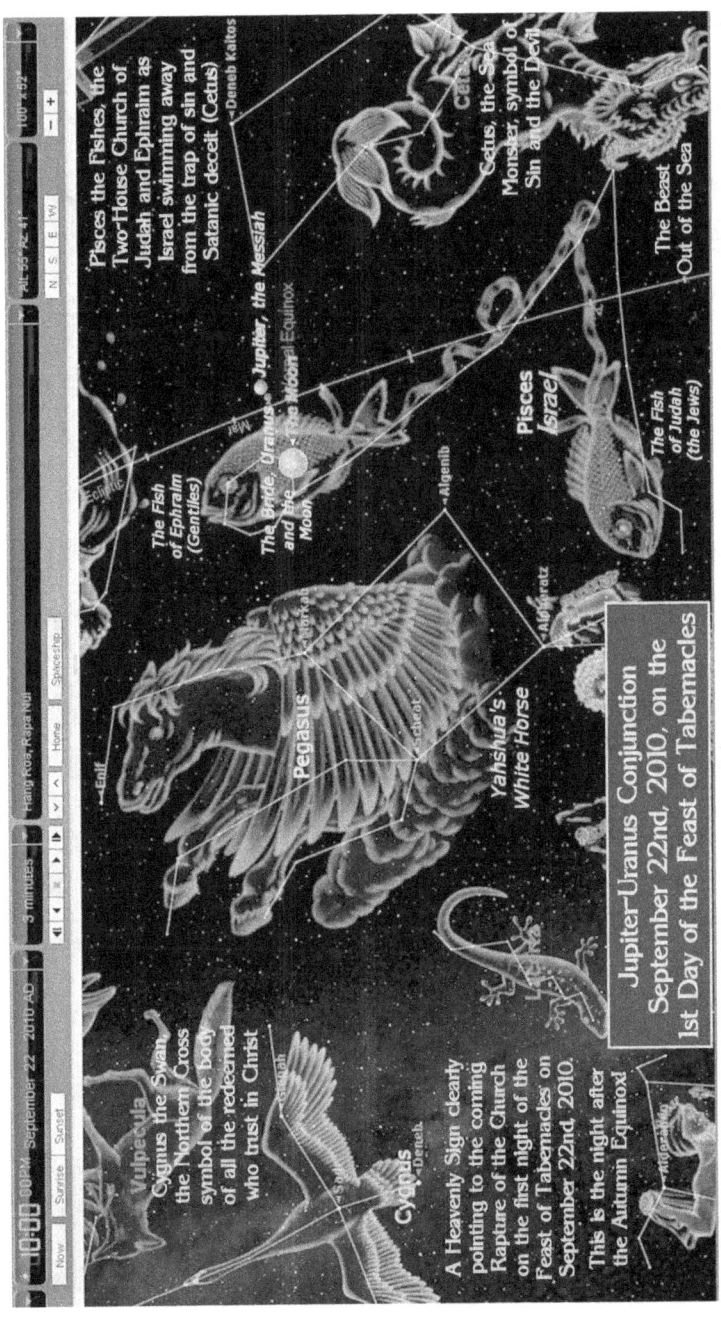

## Winter Solstice 2010 Blood Moon Over Orion

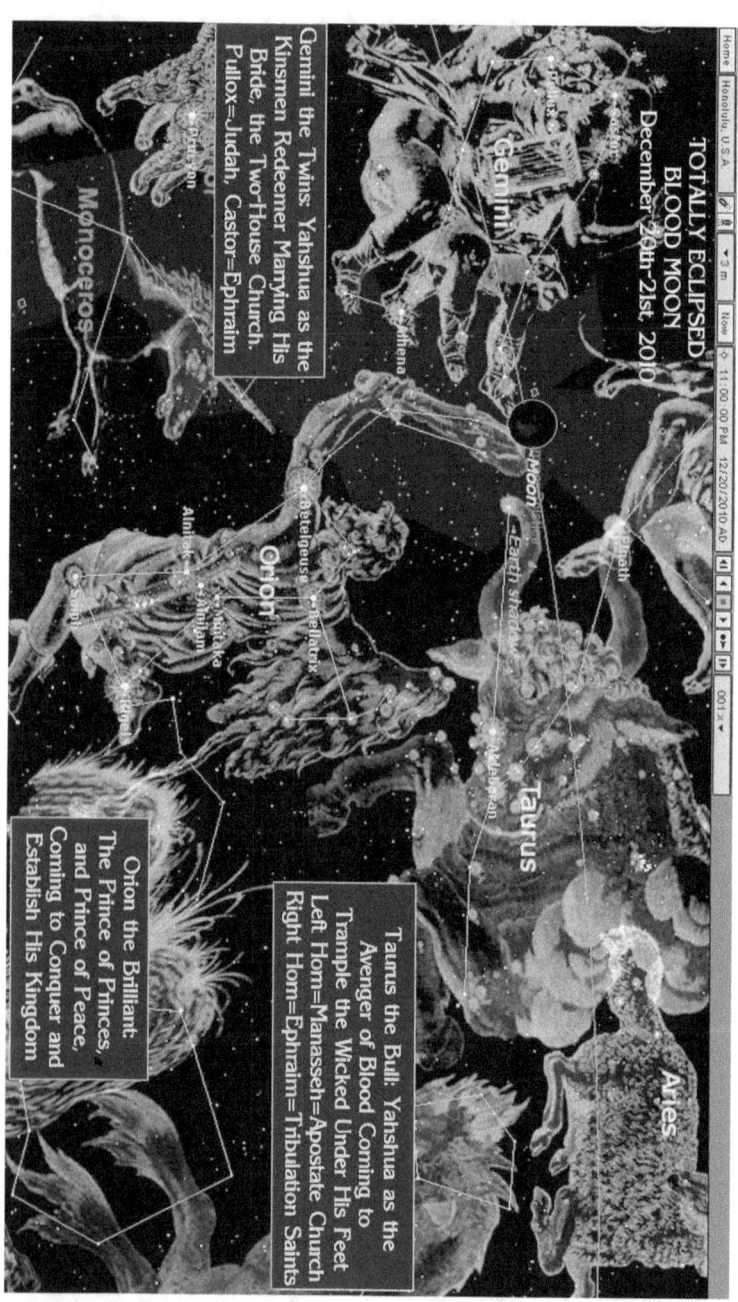

## January 4th, 2011 Solar Eclipse in Sagittarius

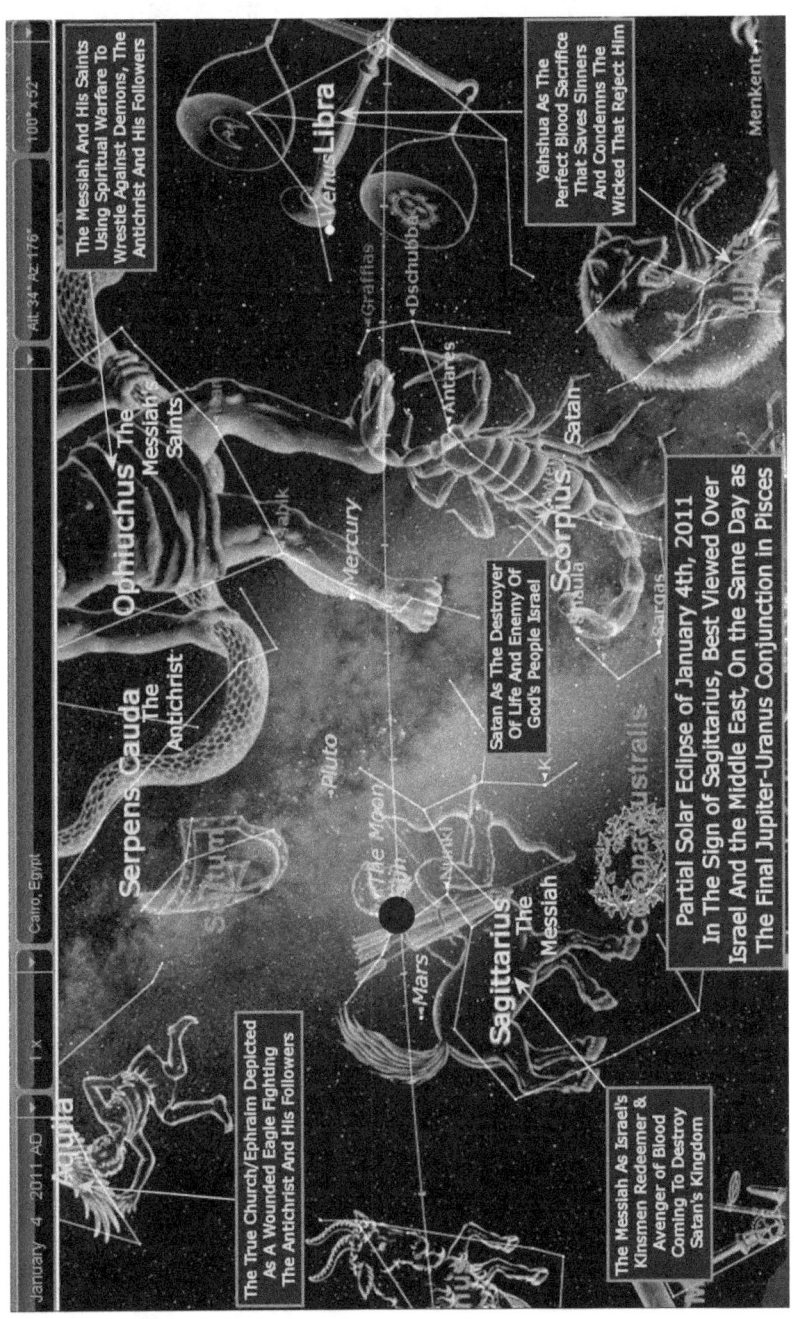

# The Language of God in Prophecy

## June 15th, 2011 Lunar Eclipse in Scorpio and Taurus

# Chapter 12: Sacred Astronomy as a Prophetic Tool  Page 691

## December 10th, 2011 Lunar Eclipse in Taurus and Scorpio

Pisces is surrounded by a very powerful section of the Gospel in the Stars. This can be seen in that the Ephraimite fish of Pisces is resting on the back of the heavenly winged horse called Pegasus, which signifies the white horses that Christ and His saints will ride at the Battle of Armageddon. To solidify this interpretation, Pegasus is suspended over the constellation called Cygnus the Swan or the Northern Cross. This heavenly white swan is a symbol of the purity and beauty of those who are saved, and who will become the spotless Bride of Christ. As revealed earlier, the North America Nebula appears in its tail, which is also the head section of the Cross of Christ that the swan actually represents. Since the United States is symbolic of the multicultural and multinational Tribe of Ephraim, and Ephraim is an allegorical reference to the Bride of Christ, this suggests that (though a political leader of the United States may play a terrible villain during the Tribulation) the United States will continue to serve as *"the helmet of God's head"* - as described in Psalm 108 - until the Rapture. Even afterward, the United States may be a refuge to many Tribulation Saints, who will resist the Antichrist and fight against his schemes through prayer, spiritual warfare, and force of arms - if God lifts His ban on it at that time.

After the Jupiter-Uranus conjunction on September 22nd, 2010, a Full Lunar Eclipse occurred over Orion's Sword on December 21st, 2010. As shown in the illustration on page 688 in this Chapter, and on pages 318 through 320 in Chapter 8 of this book, this was a very highly important sign. In fact, I strongly believe that this Blood Moon may have marked the beginning of the Tribulation period. If it did, the date correlates perfectly with the 2011 start date for the Tribulation that was revealed by the Hallel Psalms and the Great Pyramid.

Following closely after that December 2010 Blood Moon, there was a partial Solar Eclipse in the sign of Sagittarius on January 4th, 2011 representing Yahshua as Israel's Avenger of Blood. Fascinatingly, since Sagittarius borders Scorpio, this Solar Eclipse also targets the Scorpio-Sagittarius Meridian that symbolizes evil being vanquished by Yahshua as well as the western coast of the United States. This Solar Eclipse was best viewed over Israel and the Middle East, but was also visible from most of Europe and Russia, suggesting that Russia was about to stir up unrest or war in the Middle East in direct opposition to the United States, which has indeed been the case. Even more fascinatingly, the January 4th, 2011 Solar Eclipse occurred on the day after Jupiter and Uranus met for a third and last time in a perfect conjunction over the Ephraimite fish of Pisces before slowly beginning to move apart. This placed a double sign on that day indicating that Yahshua is marking those who will become His Bride for rescue in the coming Rapture, and preparing to bring about the Psalm

# Chapter 12: Sacred Astronomy as a Prophetic Tool

83/Psalm 108/Gog-Magog war. It is certainly close now, though no one knows for certain when the Rapture or the war triggering the Great Tribulation will be. But one thing is for certain. The Rapture is **not** a Pre-Tribulation event because the true start of the seven-year Tribulation period was likely on or shortly before April 5th, 2011. Therefore, since the Rapture did **not** occur beforehand, we are looking at a Pre-Wrath Rapture before or during the commencement of the Sixth Seal Judgment.

Many undeniable Signs in the Heavens are announcing that the First Rapture could happen sometime soon, such as the ones that occurred in June of 2011. On the 28th of Iyar or June 1st, 2011, for example, there was a partial Solar Eclipse that occurred in the sign of Taurus over Antarctica. Incidentally, the 17th of Iyar is the day that Noah's Flood began, and its anniversary fell on May 21st in 2011. This was the day that Noah's deliverance from death began in the Ark, which is symbolic of the re-birth signified by baptism that will lead to the First Resurrection and the First Rapture.

Though this June 1st, 2011 Solar Eclipse was rather minor visually, the location of the Sun (Yahweh) and Moon (the Church) directly at the tips of the horns of Taurus on that day signified God's redemption for sin, as well as the animosity toward God and His followers that may be manifested one day soon by two of the world's most powerful leaders in the West, specifically in the UK or EU and the USA. In addition, this Solar Eclipses' proximity to Antarctica is significant because the South Pole is located there, and Earth's poles serve as the dividers between the Taurus-Gemini Meridian and the Scorpio-Sagittarius Meridian of the Earth. If the horns of Taurus do signify the leaders of the allegorical Tribe of Ephraim or the United States as the King of the South and the allegorical Tribe of Manasseh or the United Kingdom as the King of the North, the bull fights that have been carried on in Spain for centuries in mimicry of Orion's seeming face-off with Taurus are a sign that the bullish plans of the leaders attempting to forge the New World Order in the United States, the United Kingdom and Europe definitely will lose the battle when our Messiah Yahshua returns to the Earth!

The June 1st Solar Eclipse was closely followed by a Total Lunar Eclipse or Blood Moon on June 15th, 2011 in the opposing sign of Scorpio - specifically in Ophiuchus. This ominous Blood Moon fell only three days after Pentecost, which was on June 12th, 2011. Significantly, the baptism of the Holy Spirit or Ruach Ha Kodesh was given to the Church on Pentecost, and this miraculous event has a strong allegorical connection to the purpose of the Rapture, which is re-birth, renewal and resurrection. It is therefore was a herald announcing that the Tribulation had begun, and that the time for the Mid-Tribulation First Rapture was fast approaching.

Fascinatingly, if we were to jump to the Moon to view this Lunar Eclipse, it would fall directly in the sign of Taurus. This is also true in reverse for the Blood Moons on December 21st, 2010 and December 10th, 2011. If viewed from the Moon as shown in the illustrations in this section, they would appear in the sign of Scorpio, which is Orion and Taurus' absolute opposite in spiritual meaning. These eclipses therefore may be a sign that the terrible war between the evil and darkness of Satan and the goodness and light of God that will be waged during the Tribulation will begin in earnest in 2011.

To drive this point home, God designed another Total Lunar Eclipse to appear on December 10th, 2011 in the sign of Taurus. These are connected to the December 21st, 2010 Lunar Eclipse through the Gospel in the Stars surrounding Taurus and its opposition found in Scorpio. As already shown, these two Zodiac signs represent opposing forces in the Universe and the unseen battle that is always raging between them. Could this war between good and evil that is being singled out in the heavens through these three Lunar Eclipses be reaching its climax beginning in 2011 as the first year of the Tribulation? It is possible, especially since the Great Pyramid and the Hallel Psalms also appear to be pointing to 2011 as the starting point for the time of Jacob's Trouble.

Adding even more strength to this hypothesis, another Total Solar Eclipse that was partially visible from Easter Island occurred late in the day on November 13th, 2012. As shown in the Illustration on the next page, this Solar Eclipse occurred in the Zodiac Sign of Libra the Scales. Libra is a very powerful symbol of the concept of justice and the impending judgment of the wicked. Fascinatingly, the ancient Egyptians depicted this sign as a large set of scales within the Judgment Hall of Osiris. On these scales, the Egyptians believed that a deceased human's heart would be weighed against a feather from Ma'at, their winged goddess of truth and balance. In ancient Babylon, however, Libra was seen as a round altar being grasped in the claws of Scorpio the Scorpion.

Like the scales of Libra, an altar also can convey the idea of balance and justice in that Yahshua was our Passover Lamb who died in our stead to negate the evil we have done and hide it from view with His righteousness as a covering. We are allegorically sprinkled with the blood of Yahshua when we believe in Him as the Son of God and Messiah. It is Yahshua alone who died for mankind's sins and rose from the dead so that we could be set free from the curses of sin and death through His righteous sacrifice. However, those who do not believe in Yahshua and

# Chapter 12: Sacred Astronomy as a Prophetic Tool      Page 695

hate those who do stand condemned unless they repent. Therefore, a Solar Eclipse in this sign can be an omen of coming divine Judgment on a grand scale.

## Solar Eclipse of November 13th, 2012

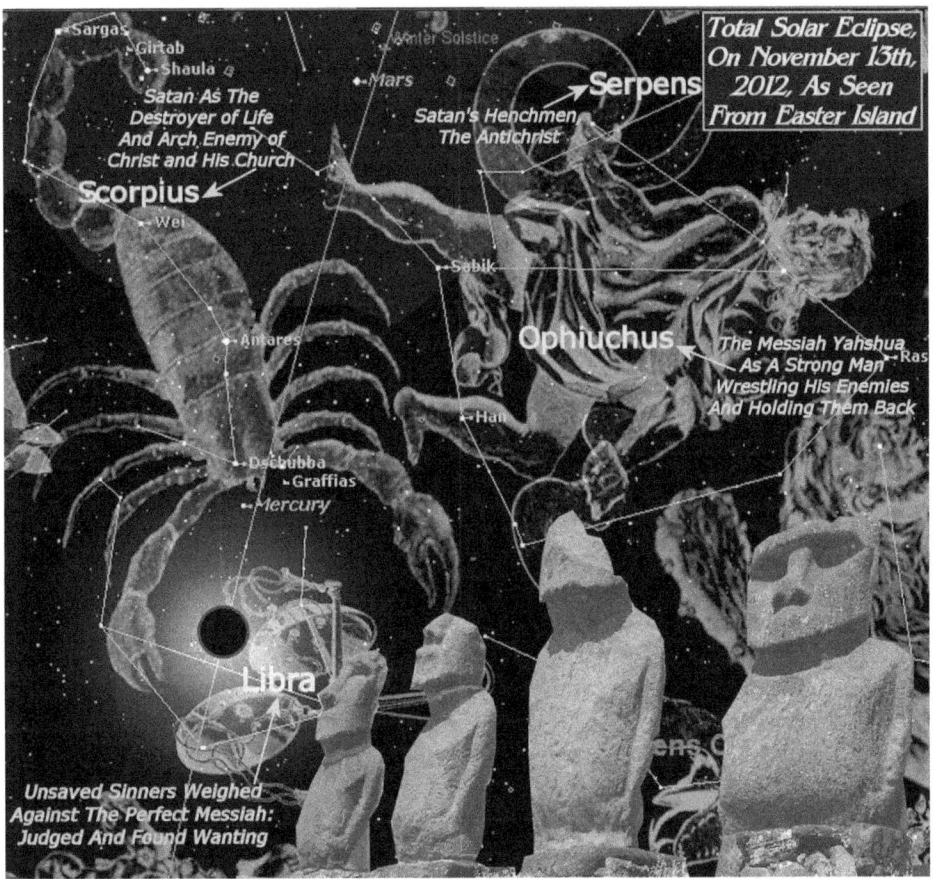

In a Solar Eclipse, the Moon can be seen as a symbol for Satan and fallen humanity that is attempting to blot out the Sun representing God the Father and His Son, and this is symbolic of Satan's pride and arrogance. If we pair this allegorical message of the Sun and Moon with the close proximity of Mercury, the Scribe of God, it suddenly takes on an extremely prophetic significance as a message from God's Heavenly Tablets to us. Now, note the presence of Mars, which portends war and bloodshed due to a broken Covenant. It is located in Sagittarius, which depicts Yahshua, the Divine Adversary coming to do battle with the wicked people in rebellion against God depicted by the Serpent and Scorpion. Viewed with these other signs, there is no doubt that the November 13th, 2012 Solar Eclipse is attempting to portray a picture of impending world judgment and strife as the battle between good and evil escalates to unprecedented levels.

Indeed, when viewed along with the amazing Signs in the Heavens that appeared on December 21st, 2012, the November 13th Solar Eclipse is nothing less than a sign that the battle between light and darkness would reach epic proportions toward the end of 2012 and on into 2013 and beyond. Coupled with the amazing stellar line-up of all the major planets, the Sun, the Earth and the Milky Way Galactic Center on the Winter Solstice on December 21st, 2012 - the Mayan Fifth Sun End Date - this November 2012 Solar Eclipse is nothing short of a trumpet blast from Heaven announcing that the beginning of the end of this evil world has come!

## *Comet ISON as a Herald of the Rapture*

In Chapters 8 and 11, I discussed the importance of Comet ISON as a prophetic sign. On November 16th, 2013, Scientists spotted a bright wing-like "U" shape forming at the front of Comet ISON as it approached the star Spica in Virgo the Virgin. This became visible upon dimming a new photograph of ISON so the comet's tail and its coma's brightness would be reduced. Now there is controversy over whether Comet ISON's recent burst in brightness and these wings forming is a sign that Comet ISON is breaking up, or if it's merely brightening due to a recent increase in Solar Flare activity on the Sun that affected the comet, actually dissipating it's coma and tail.

Comet ISON Sprouting Wings As It Approaches the Star Spica in Virgo the Virgin on November 16th, 2013

Personally, I think this is a sign from God that Comet ISON is indeed a harbinger of the coming Rapture of the

## Chapter 12: Sacred Astronomy as a Prophetic Tool

Bride of Christ and Wise Virgins depicted by Virgo the Virgin. Remember, Scripture says that the Woman Clothed with the Sun, which is seen in Virgo, *"was given two wings of a great eagle"* to go to a place of refuge before the Sudden Destruction that will overtake those who are left behind:

> *"Now when the dragon saw that he had been cast to the earth, he persecuted the woman who gave birth to the male Child. 14 But the woman was given two wings of a great eagle, that she might fly into the wilderness to her place, where she is nourished for a time and times and half a time, from the presence of the serpent." - Revelation 12:13-14*

Although this prophecy has already been fulfilled with the discovery and settling of America by Europeans and the English from the mid-17th Century onward, it may also have a future fulfillment in the Rapture. In the case of the settling of America as a safe haven from religious persecution, the time, times and half a time spoken of in Revelation in regard to the Sun-clad Woman could just as easily refer to 350 years as it does to 3.5 years.

If these times are referring to 350 years - and we count from the forming of the first settlement in America in 1607 - the 350 years ended in 1957 - right around the time when Americans began abandoning their Christian roots in favor of Eastern philosophies and Occult mysticism. Sadly this exodus from the faith in America has become so widespread that Christianity is no longer being protected, and persecution of believers is growing rapidly in America, and the world. Therefore, we are now rapidly approaching the time when there will be no safe haven for true believers left on the Earth. For this reason, God's anger has been kindled, and He has begun judging the world - as can be seen from all the extreme weather and terrible earthquakes that have been occurring globally in the last few years. This is also a sure sign that the Rapture - which is meant to protect the Bride of Christ from God's Wrath - is surely imminent.

On November 17th and 18th, 2013, as shown in the graphic on page 699, Comet ISON - which signifies Yahshua our Messiah coming in righteous judgment - was transiting over the star Spica the Branch, which is tied to Yahshua as the "Tzemach" or Righteous Branch out of Jesse and David (Isaiah 11:1-2, Jeremiah 23:4-6) at the same time that the Full Moon was transiting over the Zodiac sign of Taurus the Bull. At this time, Comet ISON passed directly over the star Spica, which marks Virgo the Virgin's birth canal, and Virgo signifies the Virgin Mary, and also the Bride of Christ. Therefore, it allegorically suggests that ISON was born from out of the Two-House Church of Judah (Messianic Jews) and Ephraim (Christians) that is signified by Virgo!

At the same time, the Full Moon moved between the Pleiades and Hyades star clusters in the body and face of Taurus the Bull. This is prophetically very important because the Full Moon is a symbol of the Church when it is full of the most spiritual light. This means it symbolizes the Church of born again believers that are spiritually mature. Since these saints fully reflect the light of God in Christ, they are members of the Church of Philadelphia.

It is also important because Taurus signifies the Tribe of Joseph, as well as the modern Gentile Nations that have been most blessed by God in the West. The two star clusters in the face of Taurus therefore represent two groups of believers that are connected to Christianity and Messianic Judaism in the West, but that have spread throughout the whole world. The Hyades cluster in Taurus' face signifies the Redeemed that will be snatched out of the remaining six of the Seven Churches or Congregations in the Book of Revelation, and taken to safety in the Rapture as a part of the Church of Philadelphia. Meanwhile, the six brightest stars of the Pleiades that are figuratively riding on Taurus the Bull's back signify the six Churches that are apostate in some way, and heavily influenced by the Ecumenical Movement's Beastly religious system, which is the Whore of Babylon. The Pleiades star cluster therefore represents the Foolish Virgins in the Churches that will be left behind after the First Rapture, and who will be tried and tested in the fire of the Great Tribulation.

It is also interesting to note here that, at the same time that Comet ISON was moving over Spica and the Moon was moving over Taurus in the heavens, Comet Lovejoy moved into Ursa Major the big Sheep Pen representing Redeemed Believers. This happened on November 18th, when ISON just passed over the Star Spica. In addition, Comet LINEAR was in Bootes, the Good Shepherd and Reaper of the Choice Wheat, and Comet Encke was near the planet Mercury at Virgo's feet, while Saturn was in Libra, the Scales of Righteous Judgment. Together with Saturn, Encke is a sign of Satan's desire to destroy the Messiah Yahshua and His born-again saints, which are figuratively represented by Comet ISON. For this reason, this sign is a very strong one that may be important from a Rapture Watch perspective.

# Chapter 12: Sacred Astronomy as a Prophetic Tool   Page 699

## Comet ISON "Born" In Virgo On Nov. 17th-18th, 2013

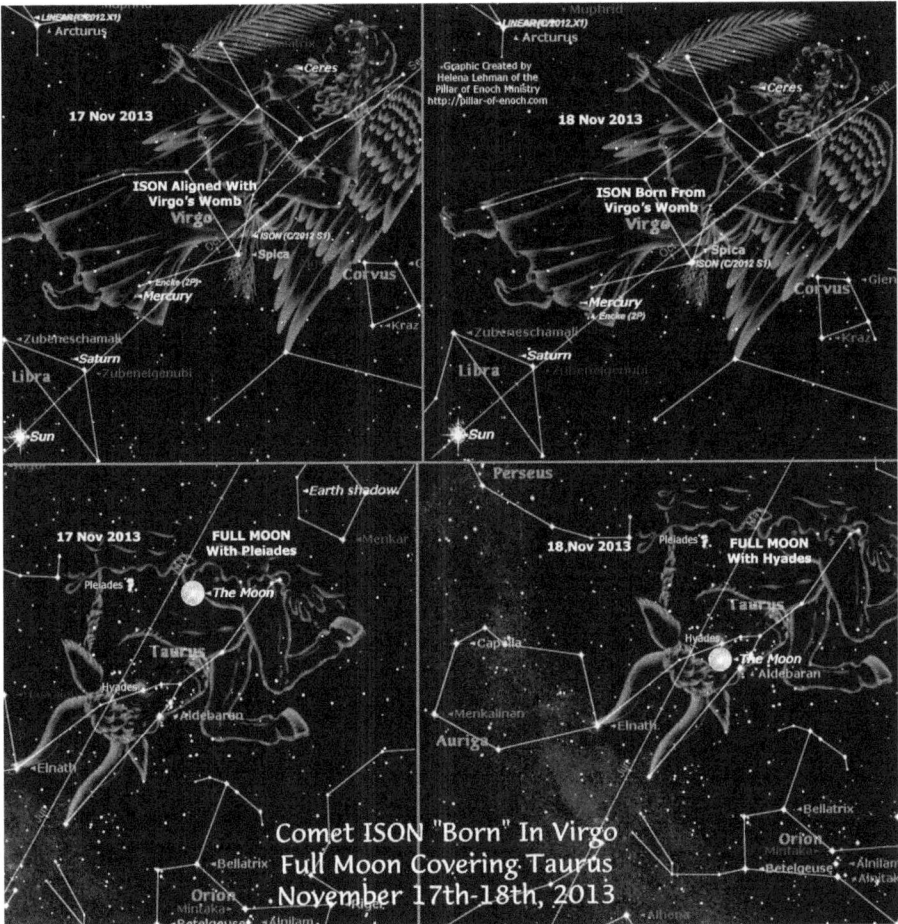

It is also highly possible that the debris field from Comet ISON's tail may cause the disturbances that I saw in my 2011 Dream, which I describe on pages 603 through 607 in Chapter 11. This dream suggests that a celestial body like Comet ISON - or some other object that hasn't been spotted yet - will lead to the massive Sixth Seal Earthquake and Pole Shift that marks the beginning of the pouring out of God's Wrath. As such, the Rapture may occur before the next set of Heavenly Signs that are tied to the Tribulation period. This is the Blood Moon Tetrad on Jewish Feasts in 2014 and 2015, which are discussed in the next section.

## The Blood Moon Tetrad of 2014 Through 2015

Above is a portion taken from my Tribulation Timeline, which shows the timing of the Four Blood Moons in the Blood Moon Tetrad that was first noticed and shared by American Pastor Mark Biltz in 2008. These highly prophetic Lunar Eclipses are framed by the prophetically powerful Hybrid Solar Eclipse of November 3rd, 2013 and the Full Solar Eclipse of March 9th, 2016. We will discuss these Eclipses - and several other Heavenly Signs during this period - in the last sections of this chapter. The Tribulation Timeline that the graphic on this page is based on is too big to properly display in this book, but it is available as a free download from my Pillar of Enoch Ministry web site at: http://pillar-of-enoch.com/essays/trib-timeline.html.

First of all, it's important to know that these Blood Moon Tetrads falling specifically on four consecutive Jewish Feasts are highly rare. In fact, only seven have occurred since the time of Christ, with this 2014 - 2015 Tetrad being the eighth, as well as the first Tetrad since the beginning of the 21st Century. Secondly, the last two Tetrads that were very similar to the 2014 - 2015 Tetrad occurred in 1940 and 1950, the year after the rebirth of Israel as a nation, and in 1967 and 1968, the year when

# Chapter 12: Sacred Astronomy as a Prophetic Tool

Israel recaptured Jerusalem during the Six-Day War between predominantly Jewish Israel and her radical Muslim enemies.

Also of high importance is the fact that the two Lunar Eclipses that fall on Passover during this Tetrad will occur in the sign of Virgo, which signified Miriam, the Jewish mother of Yahshua in the past, but which now signifies the Bride of Christ. In addition, both of these Lunar Eclipses will be visible over Easter Island, with the second one in particular of interest because it will occur on the night of Passover on April 4th, 2015, which is also the eve of Easter on April 5th, 2015, and Easter Island was also discovered on an April 5th Easter or Resurrection Sunday in 1722!

Finally, I want to draw your attention to the fact that the Eclipses that fall on the first day of Sukkot or the Feast of Tabernacles will both occur in the Sign of Pisces the Fishes. This is significant because, though the world is generally unaware of it, these two celestial fishes signify the Two Houses of Israel: Judah, which signifies the Jews, and Ephraim or the born-again Gentile believers. This Blood Moon Tetrad therefore shows that the time period that they are attached to is extremely important in the history of the Jewish people, as well as being highly significant to Gentile believers that have accepted Yahshua as their Messiah and have been grafted into Israel by their faith in, and devotion to Yahweh God.

Now let's look at some specific celestial signs during the period of 2014t through 2017 that appear to indicate that we are indeed at the close of human history as we know it, and are likely on the threshold of the Great Tribulation, followed by the Millennial Kingdom of Christ.

## *Is The 2014 Sukkot Blood Moon Post First Rapture?*

As has been repeatedly shown in previous sections of this book, the First Rapture is likely tied to the middle of the Tribulation, and will likely occur just before God's Wrath on the wicked is poured out. Marking this possibility, there is a heavenly sign alluding to the Rapture on October 8th, 2014, when there will be a Total Lunar Eclipse in the sign of Pisces representing the Two Houses of Israel. According to the Gospel in the Stars that is captured in the illustration of this Blood Moon on page 703, the Two Houses of Israel - Judah or the Jews and Ephraim or the mixed Israelite and Gentile Church - are not in sync with one another in their interpretation of who Christ is and what His sacrifice on the Cross did for humanity.

In fact, there is a big divide between them that centers on how binding the keeping of the Mosaic Law is upon believers in Yahshua as the Son of God and the perfect Passover Lamb. Some Torah-observant congregations insist that the entire Law is binding on all believers, not just the Jewish members of these congregations, and that the Law should be kept and followed in every respect that is possible without the existence of the Temple to Yahweh in Jerusalem. So, excluding the laws pertaining to animal sacrifices in the Temple, this group of believers thinks that all of the Law must be kept to the best of their ability.

Nonetheless, as shown in "The Language of God in Humanity", there is ample evidence in the New Testament that - outside of the Ten Commandments and the Book of the Covenant - the Law is only meant to be binding upon those who have not accepted Yahshua as their Messiah. Though the Law itself and the blessings and curses of the Law are still fully in effect, they have no hold on the way Christians and enlightened Messianics show their love and devotion to Yahshua. This is because Yahshua came to fulfill the Law perfectly, and to die on the Cross so that His perfection in keeping the Law could cover all those who are baptized by His blood. All of this is graphically shown in the Star Gospel surrounding this Lunar Eclipse on October 8th, 2014 that will feature the Moon in conjunction with Uranus, the planet signifying the Bride of Christ and her Five Wise Virgin handmaids.

Yahshua's desire to save His Bride and her Virgin handmaids from sin and death can be seen in the presence of Aries as the Lamb of God who takes away the sins of the world and in the Ephraimite Fish swimming along the ecliptic or path of the Sun that is the heavenly Way of Yahweh. That little fish is swimming with all its might toward the inexhaustible supply of the Holy Spirit that is depicted in the neighboring sign of Aquarius.

Thus, the Star Gospel shows that Yahshua's shed body and blood became the perfect covering for sin that allows us to appear as white as snow before God instead of as the filthy sinners that we are and will remain until we partake in the First Resurrection. With their baptism by the Holy Spirit, true believers now have God's direct guidance through their Spirit-inspired consciences, as well as through visions, dreams, and direct words of knowledge from God or his holy angels. These Spirit-filled believers living under Grace rather than the Law are the only members of the Church that will be included in the Rapture.

# Chapter 12: Sacred Astronomy as a Prophetic Tool        Page 703

## Blood Moon on Feast of Tabernacles, October 8th, 2014

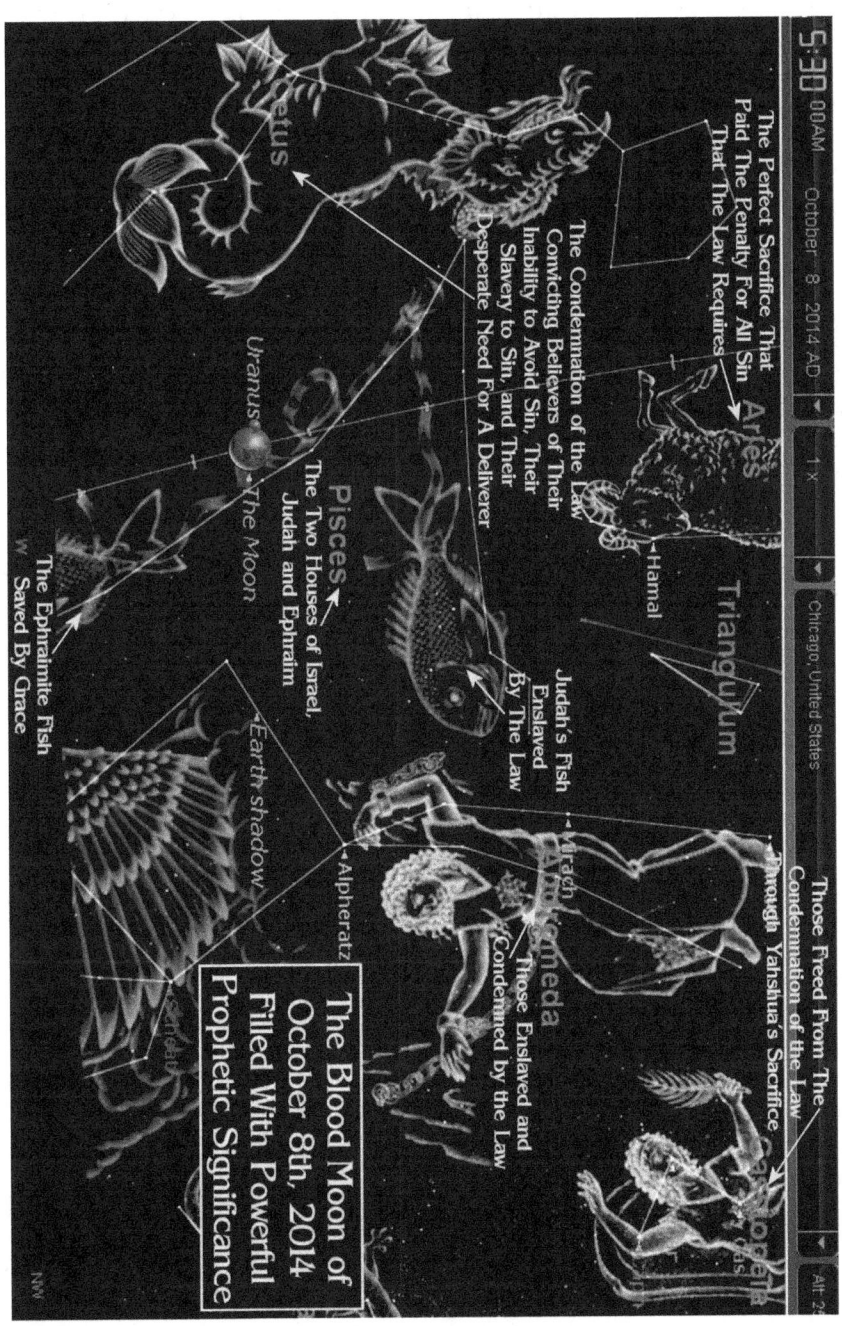

It is therefore fitting that the Lunar Eclipse on October 8th, 2014 will be on the evening of the first day of the Feast of Tabernacles, which celebrates the ingathering of all God's people during the Millennial Rule of Christ. Indeed, it can also signify the ingathering of the all the saints that will take part in the Rapture and the Wedding of the Lamb in Heaven, and it may be that this Blood Moon on the first day of Tabernacles in 2014 is meant to indicate the bad luck of those who insist on keeping the Law and rejecting the Grace, peace and freedom offered to those covered by Christ's shed blood.

In this book, I have presented much evidence that the Tribulation may be tied to Psalms 111 though 117, which are tied to the years 2011 through 2017. In addition, I discovered that Hallel Psalms 110 and 118 serve as a type of frame around the other Hallel Psalms. By examining the liturgical use and wording of Hallel Psalms 110 through 118, it appears that these psalms are truly tied to the prelude to the Tribulation, the Tribulation period itself, and the year of the restoration of Christ's Kingdom in its aftermath.

In closing this section of the book, let me point out that Yahshua was unquestionably alluding to the Rapture when He said:

> *"'In My Father's House are many mansions; if it were not so, I would have told you. I go to prepare a place for you. And... I will come again and receive you to Myself; that where I am, there you may be also. And where I go you know, and the way you know.' Thomas said to Him, 'Lord, we do not know where You are going, and how can we know the way?' Jesus (Yahshua) said to him, 'I am the Way, the Truth, and the Life. No one comes to the Father except through Me.'" - John 14:2-6*

Though some have said that these words of Yahshua do not pertain to the Rapture, and many have also denied that Yahshua is the **only** Way to Heaven, I wholeheartedly disagree with their assertions. Indeed, this passage can only pertain directly to the Rapture since our final everlasting habitation will not be in Heaven with the Father but on the Earth in the New Jerusalem with Christ. Furthermore, Yahshua said no one's prayers will be heard before the Throne of our Heavenly Father Yahweh unless they are directed through Yahshua, Who is our only true Mediator before God.

Both Yahshua and the Apostle John, who wrote the Book of Revelation, mentioned that the New Jerusalem - which will be filled with believers chosen by God to be the Bride of Christ and her Virgin attendants - would come down out of Heaven and rest on the Earth forever after the Millennial Rule of Christ:

> "He who overcomes, I will make him a pillar in the temple of My God, and he shall go out no more. And I will write on him the name of My God and the name of the city of My God, the New Jerusalem, which comes down out of heaven from My God. And I will write on him My new name." "Then I, John, saw the holy city, New Jerusalem, coming down out of heaven from God, prepared as a bride adorned for her husband. And I heard a loud voice from heaven saying, 'Behold, the tabernacle of God is with men, and He will dwell with them, and they shall be His people. God Himself will be with them and be their God.'" - Rev. 3:12 & Rev. 21:2-3

There you have it! The beautiful city called the New Jerusalem, which was built by God for mankind to dwell in forever, will one day rest on the Earth. These Scriptures serve as a potent indication that the Earth will one day be re-created to be mankind's and Yahshua's perfect and everlasting habitation for all eternity. What a glorious point beyond time that will be! Thank you Yahshua and Maranatha!

## *The Sixth Seal Pole Shift or Sudden Destruction*

After the first four Seals are opened, and the Four Horsemen are sent by God to ride over the Earth, the next event in the Book of Revelation is the opening of the Fifth Seal:

> "When He opened the fifth seal, I saw under the altar the souls of those who had been slain for the word of God and for the testimony... saying, 'How long, O Lord... until You judge and avenge our blood on those who dwell on the earth?'"... "and it was said... that they should rest a little while longer, until both the number of their fellow servants and their brethren, who would be killed as they were, was completed." - Revelation 6:9-11

This Scripture suggests that the false peace of the Tribulation period will end abruptly sometime after December 21st, 2012, and that rebellions and wars will erupt everywhere when countless Tribulation Saints begin to be imprisoned, tortured, and killed as martyrs all over the world. These persecuted contenders for the faith will then be added to the number of saints in Heaven who already await divine justice for their martyrdom at the hands of their satanic persecutors. Also, there will be four Lunar Eclipses (i.e. Blood Moons) on Passover and Tabernacles in

2014 and 2015. These suggest that the world's hatred of Jews and Christians will erupt into the War of Armageddon around that time and the Four Horsemen will continue their ominous rides.

In my book "The Language of God in History," I speculated that a shift of Earth's poles may have occurred in the past. Based on warning passages in the Book of Revelation, it is also possible that a potentially catastrophic Pole Shift may be about to occur again. Before we explore the possibility of a future Pole Shift, however, let me explain why I think a massive Pole Shift may have occurred at the time of the Great Flood. Due to the supportive evidence in ancient Judeo-Christian manuscripts like the Book of 1 Enoch, which was a canonized edition of the Ethiopian Christian Church's Bible, I believe that a massive Pole Shift and 180-degree crustal displacement happened at the time of the Flood, which, according to a strictly biblical chronology, occurred in 2347 BC. This is what the Book of 1 Enoch records about this event:

*"And all shall be smitten with fear, and the Watchers shall quake, and great fear and trembling shall seize them unto the ends of the earth.* **And the high mountains shall be shaken, and the high hills shall be made low, and shall melt like wax before the flame. And the earth shall be wholly rent in sunder,** *and all that is upon the earth shall perish, and there shall be a judgment upon all (men). But with the righteous He will make peace."* - 1 Enoch 1:5-8 (R. H. Charles Translation)

**"In those days Noah saw that the earth became inclined, and that destruction approached.** *Then he lifted up his feet, and went to the ends of the earth, to the dwelling of his great grandfather Enoch. And Noah cried with a bitter voice: 'Hear me; hear me; hear me;' three times. And he said: 'Tell me what is transacting upon the earth;* **for the earth labors and is violently shaken. Surely I shall perish with it.**" - 1 Enoch 65:1-3 (R. Laurence translation)

These passages from 1 Enoch seem to be describing the destruction that resulted from a Pole Shift and Crustal Displacement that transpired when the Great Flood occurred. The Book of Revelation also indicates that a Pole Shift and Crustal Displacement may occur again art the time of the Sixth Seal Judgment, which I believe will happen before the end of 2014. Based on the Signs in the Heavens and the Great Pyramid, the real trouble won't begin until June of 2014. Another Scripture that appears to be graphically describing a Pole Shift is in the Book of Revelation regarding the Sixth Seal Judgment:

## Chapter 12: Sacred Astronomy as a Prophetic Tool

> *"I looked when He opened the sixth seal, and behold, there was a great earthquake; and the sun became black as sackcloth of hair (a solar eclipse), and the moon became like blood (a lunar eclipse). And the stars of heaven fell to the earth (a massive meteor shower)... Then the sky receded as a scroll when it is rolled up (severe atmospheric changes), and every mountain and island was moved out of its place (massive Earth changes). And the kings of the earth... every slave and every free man, hid themselves... and said to the mountains and rocks, 'Fall on us and hide us from.... the wrath of the Lamb! For the great day of His wrath has come, and who is able to stand?'" - Rev. 6:12-17*

If you picture yourself looking up at the sky as a 180-degree magnetic Pole Shift accompanied by a similar movement of the Earth's upper crust was occurring, the sky would likely appear to be receding like a scroll being rolled up, and the sensation of vertigo would be intense. In addition, the severe crustal displacement that could be caused by this Pole Shift could be the cause of the great earthquake mentioned in Revelation 6:12. If so, this would physically move every continent and island out of its place. Then the mountains and islands of the Earth would no longer be in their original positions, but completely shifted around, making modern astronomy-based navigation impossible until new co-ordinates were established.

There are other futuristic prophecies in the Bible that support the idea that there will be a shift in the Earth's poles before the end of the Tribulation period. Note the following passage:

> *"And it shall be that he who flees from the noise of the fear shall fall into the pit, and he who comes up from the midst of the pit shall be caught in the snare; for the windows from on high are open, and the foundations of the earth are shaken. The earth is violently broken, the earth is split open, the earth is shaken exceedingly.* **The earth shall reel to and fro like a drunkard, and shall totter like a hut; its transgression shall be heavy upon it, and it will fall, and not rise again.** *It shall come to pass in that day that the LORD (Yahweh) will punish on high the host of exalted ones..." "Then the moon will be disgraced and the sun ashamed; for the LORD of hosts (Yahweh Tsavout) will reign on Mount Zion..." - Isaiah 24:18-23*

Focusing on verse 20, which says: *"The earth shall reel to and fro like a drunkard, and shall totter like a hut,"* this passage should not be viewed allegorically, but literally. Furthermore, the language is future tense, describing a future judgment of the Earth that will cause this planet to *"reel to and fro like a drunkard"* as a punishment for the iniquity of the wicked people living upon it. The idea of punishment is expressed by the passage: *"its transgression shall be heavy upon it, and it will fall, and not rise again."* Furthermore, Isaiah has this to say about this future Tribulation judgment of the Earth: *"Therefore I will shake the heavens, and the earth will move out of her place, in the wrath of the LORD of hosts and in the day of His fierce anger,"* - (Isaiah 13:13). Here, the prophet Isaiah tells us that the Earth will be moved out of its place when God's Wrath is poured out on it during the Great Tribulation. This suggests that the Earth is now fixed with a particular orbit, rotation, and axial tilt, but that its orbit, rotation, and tilt will be changed during the Great Tribulation. This Pole Shift could be further aggravated later on when the Earth is bombarded with the asteroid-like mountain of fire and a comet-like star called Wormwood that are also described in the Book of Revelation:

> *"Then the second angel sounded: And something like a great mountain burning with fire was thrown into the sea, and a third of the sea became blood. And a third of the living creatures in the sea died, and a third of the ships were destroyed. Then the third angel sounded: And a great star fell from heaven, burning like a torch, and... a third of the waters became wormwood, and many men died."* - Revelation 8:8-11

Now, it is clear from Revelation 6:12-15 that - sometime **after** the first four Seal Judgments have begun - a Total Solar Eclipse and Total Lunar Eclipse will occur around the time that the Sixth Seal is opened, but before the earthquake that will accompany the foretold Pole Shift and crustal displacement. Because the Four Horsemen of the Apocalypse are being allegorically alluded to by the Anti-Peace Sign formed in the heavens on December 21st, 2012, I originally assumed that these Seal Judgments wouldn't actually begin to be opened until that time. However, after that date in 2012, there are no more Total Solar Eclipses followed quickly by a Total Lunar Eclipse until Passover in 2015. Furthermore, if 2014 is at the mid-point of the Tribulation, this is when the Seven Trumpet judgments will end, so the eclipses in 2015 will occur far too late in time to accompany the opening of the Sixth Seal. This suggests that the Total Solar Eclipse on the 1st of Av on July 11th, 2010 and the Total Lunar Eclipse of December 21st, 2010 may be the Total Eclipses of the Sun and Moon that are being pointed to in Revelation 6:12 as signs that will occur before this Pole Shift is about to occur.

If this is true, the Anti-Peace Sign in Heaven representing the Four Horsemen of the Apocalypse that will appear in the heavens on

## Chapter 12: Sacred Astronomy as a Prophetic Tool

December 21st, 2012 may actually signify the midpoint or finish of the Seals being opened rather than the beginning of the first four Seal Judgments. In addition, it may mark a time of gradually increasing natural disasters leading up to the Pole Shift of the Sixth Seal and the Seventh Seal ushering in the Seven Trumpet Judgments.

Could the Solar and Lunar Eclipses in 2014 and 2015 be the signs that accompany the first of the Seven Trumpets of Revelation that mark the start of the last outpouring of God's Wrath on a wicked world during the Great Tribulation, as well as the beginning of the most severe persecution of the Tribulation Saints? One thing is certain: the blowing of the First Trumpet will herald the beginning of massive Earth changes that will occur via an earthquake that moves mountains and islands out of their places. In addition, many heavenly signs, including a Solar Eclipse, Lunar Eclipse, and massive meteor shower will accompany this great earthquake that will shake the foundations of the world.

Interestingly, during a Lunar Eclipse, the Moon often appears red when the eclipse is at its greatest point. Furthermore, this effect is often intensified when the Eclipse is seen from less ideal viewing areas. The Full Moons in 2014 and 2015 will all be Blood Moons, and allegorically these may mark times of much suffering and bloodshed from intense plagues and a world at war.

The Lunar Eclipses on Passover and Tabernacles in 2014 likely indicate the time when some of the Trumpet plagues will occur. After this, the outpouring of the Seven Bowls of God's Wrath can be determined by looking for a Solar Eclipse and a Lunar Eclipse in quick succession. Ominously, a total Solar Eclipse and total Lunar Eclipse or Blood Moon will occur in the spring of 2015 AD - in conjunction with major events on the Jewish calendar. Since the Hallel Psalm prophecies suggest that the Great Tribulation will end in 2017, the eclipses in 2014 and 2015 may herald the coming of the Seven Trumpet and Seven Bowl Judgments between the spring of 2014 and the end of 2017.

Fourteen days after the New Moon on the Spring Equinox in 2015 - on the evening of April 4th - it will be Passover. Intriguingly, a Lunar Eclipse will occur in the sign of Virgo on that night that will be best viewed on Easter Island. This is significant because Easter Island was discovered on Easter Sunday, April 5th, 1722, and Easter will be on Sunday, April 5th, 2015 - on the morning after the Passover Lunar Eclipse! Virgo represents the ancient kingdom and modern nation of Israel, as well as the True Church, and both serve as forerunners to the coming Millennial Kingdom of Yahshua.

## Lunar Eclipse Over Easter Island - April 4th, 2015

Could this be why Easter Island is covered with many enigmatic ancient stone statues - most of them with emaciated human torsos suggesting starvation and sickness? Could this be why their stone faces appear to be staring out in dismay at the far horizon in every direction? Could our righteous Sethite ancestors who knew Sacred Astronomy and the holy Watchers who guided them have been trying to tell us something by making Easter Island a modern archeological marvel and mystery? It is my belief that the answer to these questions is "Yes!" In fact, I am convinced that Easter Island is a giant marker pointing to terrifying earthly events that began around the time of the July Solar Eclipse over Easter Island in 2010, and will begin to reach a climax in intensity around Passover in 2015 AD.

# Chapter 12: Sacred Astronomy as a Prophetic Tool   Page 711

## Ominous Solar Eclipse of March 20th, 2015

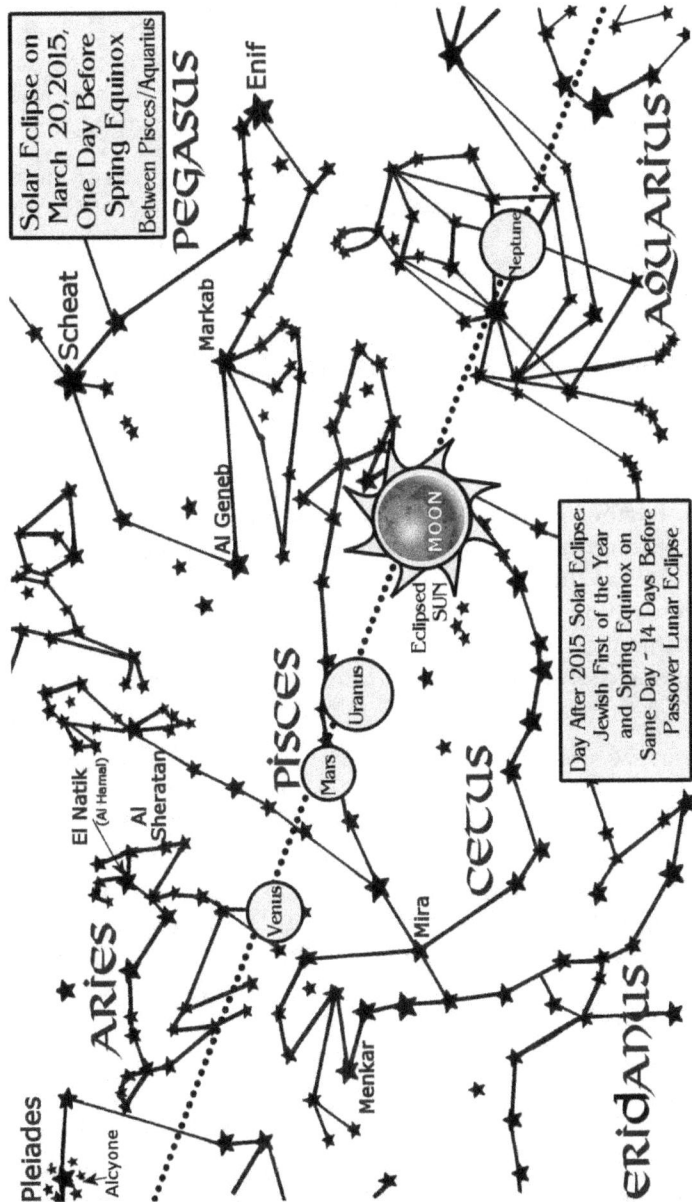

In Book Three, "The Language of God in History," it was conclusively shown that the monuments that the Sethites built on Earth to record the wisdom in the heavens are tied to the Star Gospel surrounding Orion and Taurus, which dually tell us about the purpose and nature of Christ at both His First and Second Coming. If the Sethites knew of the First and Second Advent of Christ from the Gospel in the Stars, could Easter Island's hundreds of stone statues or moai have been carved to portray the global state of mankind during the last few years before Christ's Second Coming, which may occur in 2017?

Though archeologists insist that the Easter Island stone heads were carved from solidified lava ash long after the time of Christ, some believe them to be much older. In particular, one wall carved at Ahu Vinapu on Easter Island greatly resembles ancient Pre-Flood structures made of finely fitted monolithic stone blocks that have been found around the world in places like Machu Picchu in South America, Teotihuacán in Mexico, Baalbek in Lebanon, and Giza in Egypt.

As shown in my book: "The Language of God in History," it is my belief that these disparate sites are all connected by the Sacred Astronomy of the righteous Sethite Enoch, as well as through his descendents Noah and Shem. Furthermore, it is my contention that these men wanted to leave a testimony that communicated what they believed and knew would happen in the far future. Therefore, they carved it all in stone to guide the final generation that will experience the terrifying events heralding the end of this old world system and the ushering in of a true New Age of Righteousness built on the foundation of Christ, the Bible, and the Star Gospel.

Whatever these heavenly signs portend, the pairing of these eclipses with two major Jewish calendar events in 2015 seems highly significant when viewed through the lens of biblically-based Sacred Astronomy. As shown in my book: "The Language of God in Humanity," Lunar Eclipses occurred over the Middle East on the night of the first Passover in Egypt, and on the night of the Passover when Christ was crucified! Could it be that this night of a Passover Lunar Eclipse in 2015 will also mark another significant turn of events for the Jews and Tribulation Saints?

After the Easter Island Lunar Eclipse in 2015, there will be a Total Solar Eclipse in Aquarius on March 8th, 2016 that will be best seen over Hawaii in the Earth's Scorpio Meridian. After that, the next Total Solar Eclipse won't be until August 21st, 2017, when the Sun and Moon will be in conjunction with the king star Regulus in Leo. Interestingly, the Moon will be fully centered over the Sun at exactly 12 o'clock noon that day. As shown in "The Language of God in the Universe," the star Regulus was known as the king star because ancient astrologers noted that it was often prominent in the heavens when great personages were

## Chapter 12: Sacred Astronomy as a Prophetic Tool

born. Not surprisingly, then, Regulus was in conjunction with the Messiah planet Jupiter when Christ was born. Interestingly, the sign of Leo represents Yahshua as the King of kings returning to trample the wicked under His feet! In the Star Gospel, this is indicated by Leo's placement over the long serpent form of the constellation Hydra, which - like Cetus - is another symbol for the Beast from the Sea.

From an aerial perspective, the August 21st, 2017 Solar Eclipse will cast the Moon's shadow over all of North America, possibly indicating that something prophetically significant will occur on behalf of this region of the world sometime around that date in history. Could this be close to the time when Christ, the King of kings will return with His heavenly armies to defeat the Antichrist's armies that may be invading the USA and Israel? Only time will tell, but, as shown in the following illustration, the placement of the Heavenly Signs on this day is quite compelling!

### Solar Eclipse on August 21st, 2017

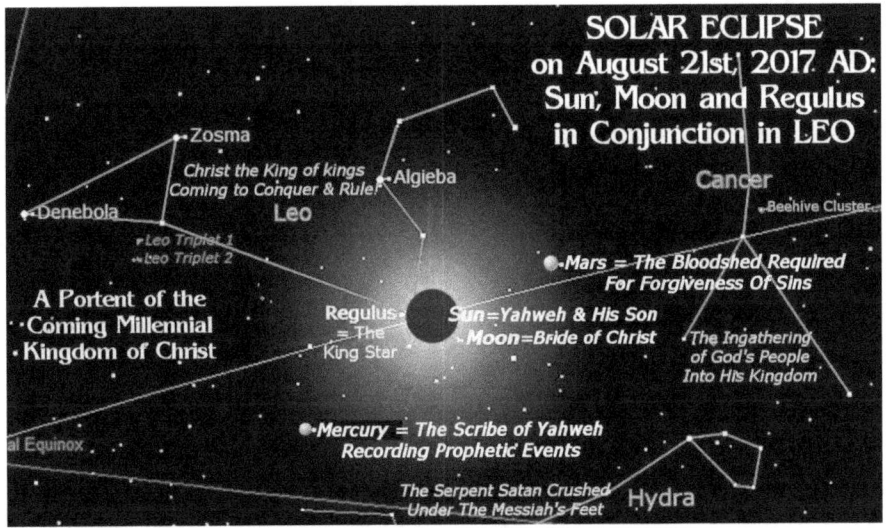

Another celestial sign indicating that Christ may return or will already be reigning on the Earth in 2017 will occur on September 20th that year, on the day before Rosh Hashanah and two days before the Autumn Equinox. On that day at dawn, the Sun and New Moon will be directly between Virgo and Leo and will form the Christ Angle with the Great Sphinx and Venus in conjunction with Regulus the king star. Uncannily, Leo and Virgo recall the imagery of the Great Sphinx with its woman's face and lion's tail that represents Yahshua as *"the First and the Last"* and *"the Beginning and the End"* (Rev. 22:13), while the planets Venus and Regulus recall Christ's role as the King of kings and bright Morning Star (Rev. 22:16). Meanwhile, the Messiah planet Jupiter will be in Virgo and the star Al Nitak, which corresponds with the Great Pyramid, will be at its zenith on the ecliptic due south in Taurus and directly above the Giza Plateau. This can be seen in the interpretive illustration on this page:

## Heavenly Signs at Giza on September 20th, 2017

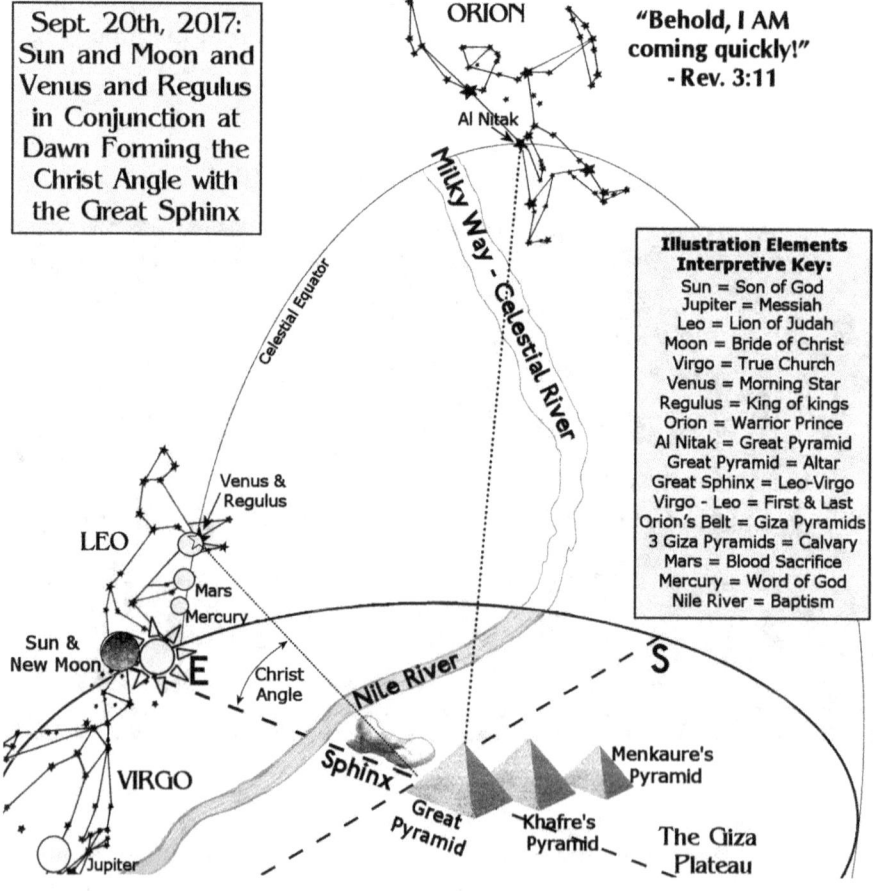

Due to these uncanny parallels in symbolism and orientation between the monuments at Giza and the heavens on September 20th, 2017, could it be that the Giza Pyramid Complex was meant to point to

## Chapter 12: Sacred Astronomy as a Prophetic Tool

that very day in history? After all, the Great Sphinx and three auxiliary pyramids on the south side of Menkaure's Pyramid appear to be heralding a time when Orion's Belt will be directly overhead in the south when the Sun rises in the east between Virgo and Leo, and in direct line with the Great Sphinx. In light of the amazing ties between Easter Island and the Lunar Eclipse on Passover in 2015, this exact correlation between the Star Gospel and the Giza Plateau seems to be far more than a coincidence. The illustration split between pages 716 and 718 was taken from my Tribulation Timeline, where you can see it in one piece and in full color. In it, I show not one but three amazing Christ Angle correlations that will occur on that day in relation to the positions of three planets with the Giza Pyramids when Orion is at the sky's zenith.

The Christ Angle of 26 degrees 18 minutes, and 9 seconds will be formed in the sky three times that day, and the first will be formed just before dawn. This angle will be formed by Uranus the "Bride of Christ" planet in Pisces the "Two Houses of Israel" and the Giza Pyramids which symbolize the three crosses on Golgotha at the Crucifixion of Christ. Next the Christ Angle will be formed by Venus the "Morning Star" in conjunction with Regulus the "King Star" and the Giza Pyramids with the horizon at dawn. Finally, just after dawn, the Christ Angle will be formed with Jupiter the Messiah planet in conjunction with Spica, the Righteous Branch or Tzemach. All of these hearken back to titles for Yahshua as the Bridegroom (Mat. 25:1), Yahshua as the Bright and Moring Star (Rev. 22:16), Yahshua as the King of kings (Rev. 19:6), and Yahshua as the Righteous Branch out of Jesse (Isa. 11:1; Jer. 23:5, 33:15:). This phenomenal correlation between the heavens and the Pyramids at Giza will occur fifteen days before the week-long Feast of Tabernacles beginning on October 6th, 2017.

Later, on the first day of Sukkot or the Feast of Tabernacles on October 6th, 2017 - at one-and-a-half hours before sunrise - Mars, the planet signifying Yahshua's Blood Atonement and Blood Sacrifice for us will rise in a brilliant conjunction with Venus, the Morning Star - which signifies Yahshua as the Star out of Jacob (Numbers 24:17), who is the Light of the World (John 8:12, 9:5). This will occur at the junction between the constellations Virgo and Leo signifying Christ as the Beginning and the End. Later that day at dawn, the Sun will rise in near conjunction with Mercury in Virgo. If Yahshua's Second Coming is sometime in 2016 or 2017, this heavenly alignment on October 6th will indeed be prophetic.

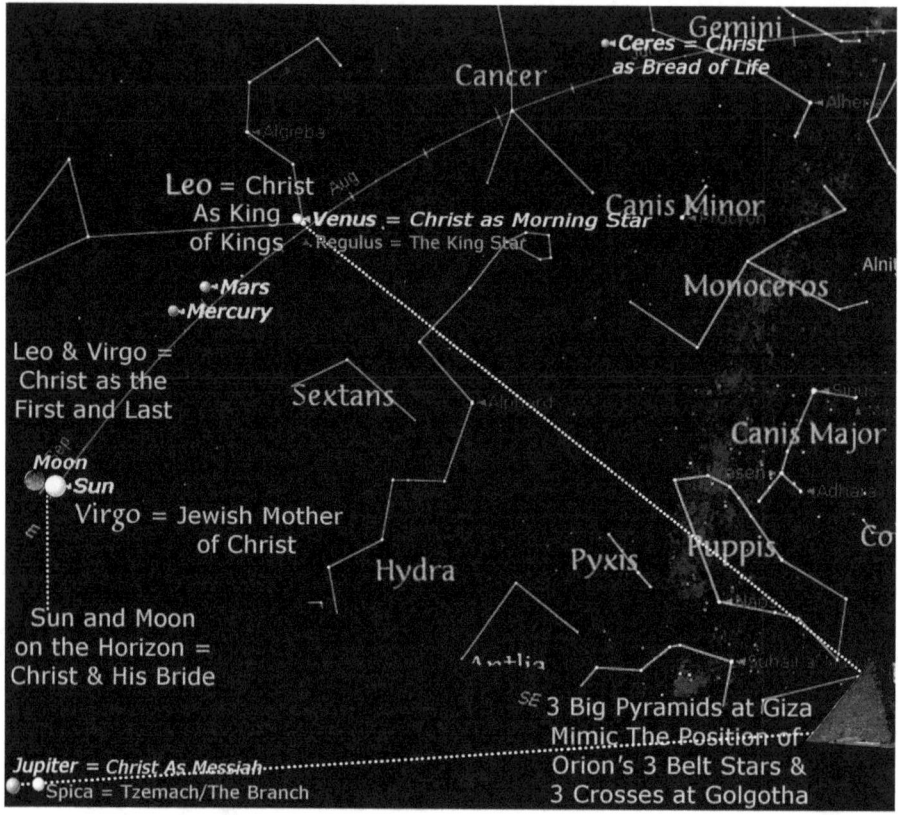

Interestingly, the symbolism behind Virgo and Leo allegorically compliment the prophetic meaning behind the Feast of Tabernacles or Sukkot, which centers on the miracle of God incarnating as a man in Christ, and dwelling or tabernacling with mankind. The week of Sukkot prefigures the miraculous First Advent (as seen in Virgo) and Second Advent of Christ (as seen in Leo), as well as His Millennial Kingdom.

Uncannily, there will be a Total Lunar Eclipse on January 31st, 2018 in the sign of Cancer, a sign representing the ingathering and uniting of all God's people Israel that is also recalled during the Feast of Tabernacles. This Lunar Eclipse will be best seen from the western coast of the United States and Mexico. Then, looking to the end of 2017 via the Jewish Sacred Calendar on Nissan 1 or March 17th, 2018, the Sun (Yahshua) and the New Moon (His Bride) will rise in conjunction over the Ephraimite Fish of Pisces/Israel representing those saved by Grace and born-again with the Holy Spirit. Therefore, the Signs in the Heavens on January 31st and March 17th, 2018 appear to support and enhance the meaning of the signs preceding it in 2017.

# Chapter 12: Sacred Astronomy as a Prophetic Tool

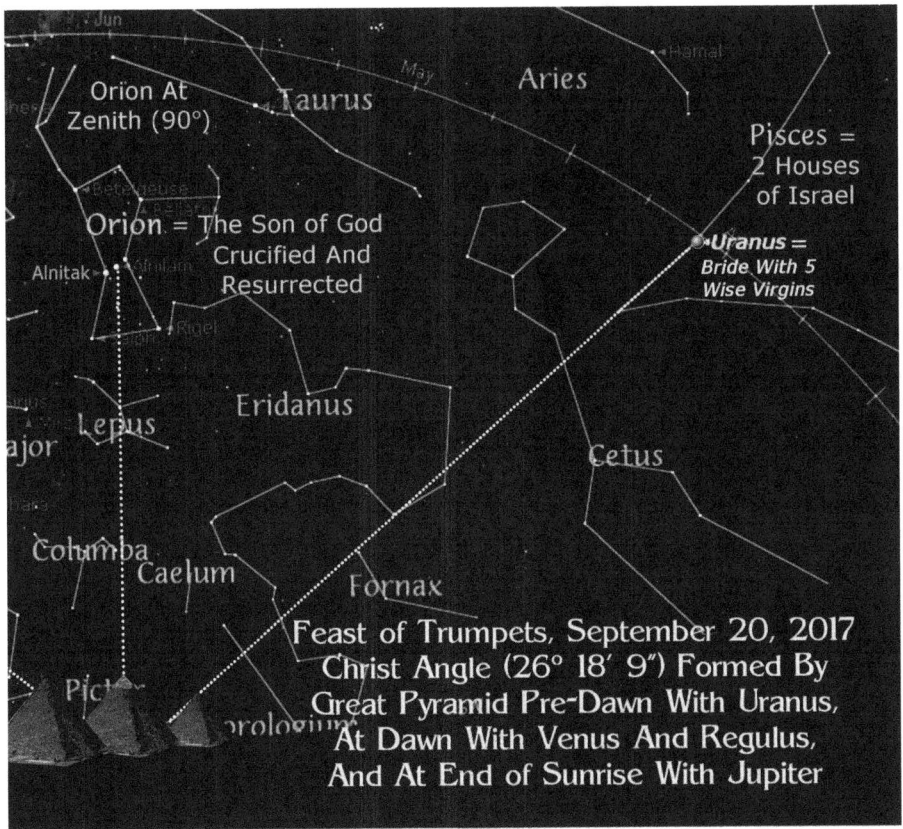

Feast of Trumpets, September 20, 2017 Christ Angle (26° 18′ 9″) Formed By Great Pyramid Pre-Dawn With Uranus, At Dawn With Venus And Regulus, And At End of Sunrise With Jupiter

Before closing this final section of the book on the Signs in the Heavens that may be announcing the timing of the Tribulation period, I wanted to seal my arguments for paying attention to these signs by focusing on two Total Lunar Eclipses in the stellar line up of amazing Heavenly Signs between 2010 and 2018 that are called Central Lunar Eclipses. **One of these Central Lunar Eclipses falls in the middle of 2011, and the next one falls in the middle of 2018, making these two eclipses exactly seven years apart.** A Central Lunar Eclipse is a Total Lunar Eclipse where all or some portion of the Moon passes directly through the center of Earth's shadow.

Central Lunar Eclipses are the longest and darkest of the different kinds of Lunar Eclipses, and they are also relatively rare, with only ten of these occurring in the next fifty years. Also of importance is the fact that, just as in 2011, the year 2018 is marked as significant by a rare line-up of three Total Lunar Eclipses or Blood Moon Triad near to the beginning, middle and end of the year on January 31st, 2018 in Cancer; on July 27th,

# The Language of God in Prophecy

2018 on the opposite side of the Zodiac in Capricorn; and on January 21st, 2019 - again in Cancer, the sign pointing to the ingathering of all God's people into His Kingdom. This marks a period of 355 days, which is a bit more than the length of one 354.37-day Lunar Year. Here are graphics derived from my full-color Tribulation Timeline showing these Lunar Triads. To see these images in color, you can download my timeline from my POEM Web Site at http://pillr-of-enoch.com.

## Blood Moon Triads of 2011 and 2018

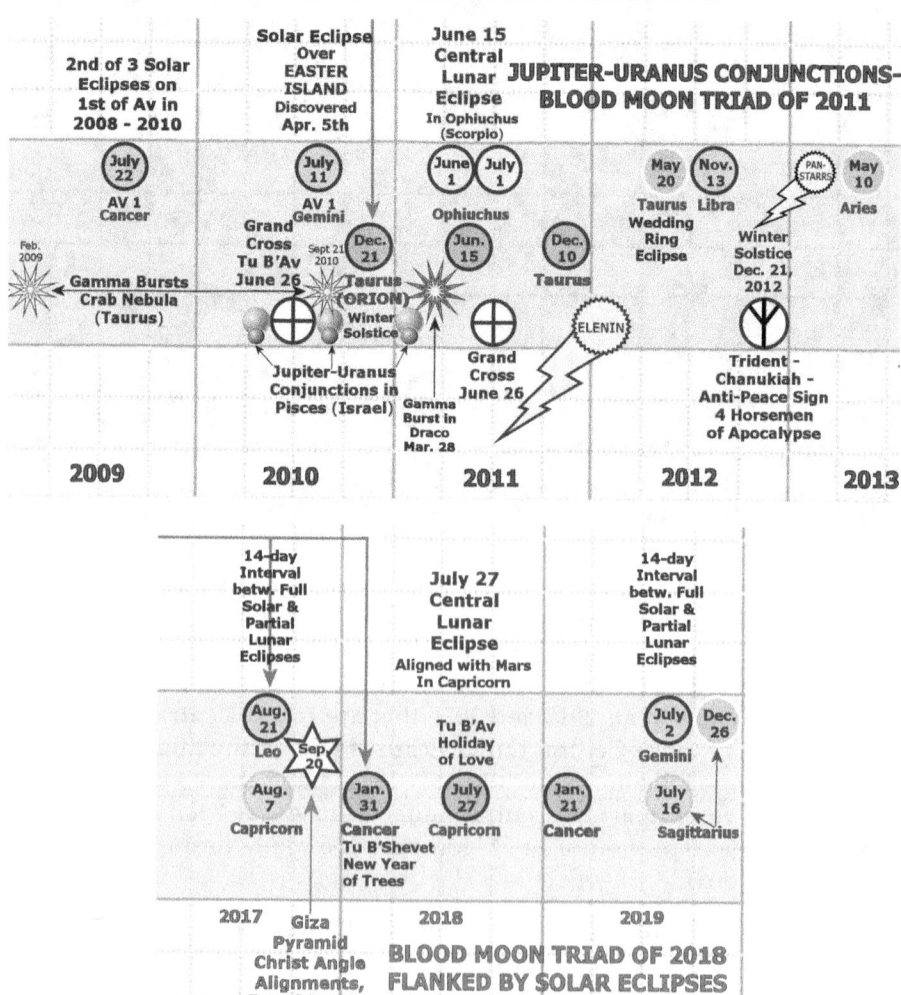

Could the Blood Moon Triads marking the beginning, middle and end of 2011 and 2018 be meant to indicate both the beginning year of the seven-year Tribulation period and the beginning year of Yahshua's Millennial Kingdom? Furthermore, could the Blood Moon of June 15th, 2011 be marking the beginning of God's full judgment and wrath on the wicked nations of the Earth? In addition, could the Central Lunar Eclipse on July 27th, 2018 be marking the time when the healing of the Earth after the Great Tribulation will be completed and Yahshua's Millennial Kingdom on Earth will be fully established? If so, it would be fitting that this would happen around the 9th of Av or Tisha B'Av, which is currently a day of Jewish mourning over the destruction of the First and Second Temples in Jerusalem.

Following the 9th of Av, the 15th of Av or Tu B'Av is already a joyous day dedicated to celebrating love, romance and marriage in Israel today, and it would become one of the most wonderful celebrations of love and marriage in history if Yahshua's Kingdom were inaugurated on that day or on Tisha B'Av in 2018! This is an intriguing possibility, especially since rabbinic traditions state that the 9th of Av will one day be turned from a day of mourning to one of rejoicing. It would certainly be a day of rejoicing if the Kingdom of God on Earth were inaugurated on that day and a worldwide Marriage Feast celebrating the everlasting unity between Jews and Gentiles in Christ was celebrated on Tu B'Av in 2018. Intriguingly, as if to frame this Blood Moon, the partial Solar Eclipses just before and after it fall on the 1st day of the 5th Jewish month of Av on July 13th, 2018 and the 1st day of the 6th month of Elul on August 11th, 2018.

In light of these amazing heavenly signs in 2017 and 2018, wouldn't it be fitting if our wonderful Savior and King Yahshua arrived in time to celebrate the Feast of Tabernacles in 2017 with His resurrected and glorified saints? To this I say, Maranatha! Come, Adonai Yahshua Ha Mashiach!

# Appendix

The charts provided in this Appendix were taken from Book One, "The Language of God in the Universe." These are the "Biblical Chronological Time Chart;" "A Summary of the Mazzaroth, or Zodiac;" "Jewish Civil and Sacred Years and Feast Days;" and the "Chart Showing 13,000 Years From Creation to Eternity." Since the information in these charts is referred to throughout this book series, they have been provided as a quick reference on the following pages:

*Biblical Chronological Time Chart* ............................................................ 722

*A Summary of the Mazzaroth - Gospel in the Stars* ................................. 724

*Jewish Civil and Sacred Years and Feast Days* ......................................... 726

*Chart Showing 13,000 Years from Creation to Eternity* .......................... 728

The biblically based chronological chart was derived using information found almost entirely in the Bible. Following this time chart are three other handy charts full of information to aid you in understanding the vast amount of knowledge presented in this book series. The first is a summary of the Gospel in the Stars that was fully explored in Book One. The second is a chart recording the Jewish sacred and civil years, and the biblical feast days associated with them. The final chart summarizes information covered in Chapter Seven in this book, which is also touched upon throughout this book series.

# The Language of God in Prophecy

## Biblical Chronological Time Chart

| Jewish Years | Chronology of Biblical Events - Partly Derived From Genesis, Ch. 5, 10, & 11 | Julian Year |
|---|---|---|
| 1 | Creation of Adam and Eve (Birthdays of Cain, Abel, and Adam & Eve's other sons and daughters not recorded, save for Seth) | 4003 BC |
| to 130 | From Creation of Adam to birth of Seth (130 years) | 3873 BC |
| to 235 | From birth of Seth to birth of Enosh (105 years) | 3768 BC |
| to 325 | From birth of Enosh to birth of Cainan (90 years) | 3678 BC |
| to 395 | Fr. birth of Cainan to birth of Mahalalel (70 years) | 3608 BC |
| to 460 | From birth of Mahalalel to birth of Jared (65 yrs) | 3543 BC |
| to 622 | From birth of Jared to birth of Enoch (162 years) | 3381 BC |
| to 687 | Fr. birth of Enoch to birth of Methuselah (65 yrs) | 3316 BC |
| to 874 | From birth of Methuselah to birth of Lamech (187 years) | 3129 BC |
| to 987 | From birth of Enoch to his Translation at age 365 | 3016 BC |
| to 1056 | From birth of Lamech to birth of Noah (182 years) | 2947 BC |
| to 1558 | From birth of Noah to birth of Shem (500 years) | 2447 BC |
| to 1656 | The Great Flood occurs - Noah is 600 years old | 2347 BC |
| to 1658 | From birth of Shem to birth of Arphaxad (102 yrs) | 2345 BC |
| to 1693 | From birth of Arphaxad to birth of Shelah (35 yrs) | 2310 BC |
| to 1723 | From birth of Shelah to birth of Eber (30 years) | 2280 BC |
| to 1757 | From birth of Eber to birth of Peleg (34 years) | 2246 BC |
| to 1787 | From birth of Peleg to birth of Reu (30 years) | 2216 BC |
| to 1819 | From birth of Reu to birth of Serug (32 years) | 2184 BC |

# Appendix

| | | |
|---|---|---|
| to 1849 | From birth of Serug to birth of Nahor (30 years) | 2154 BC |
| to 1878 | From birth of Nahor to birth of Terah (29 years) | 2125 BC |
| to 1948 | From birth of Terah to birth of Abraham (70 yrs) | 2055 BC |
| 1958 | Birth of Abraham's wife Sarah | 2045 BC |
| 1966 | Peleg dies at age 209 | 2037 BC |
| 2006 | Noah dies at age 950 | 1997 BC |
| to 2047 | From birth of Abraham to birth of Isaac (99 years) | 1956 BC |
| 2047 | Covenant of Abraham at age 99 with God | 1956 BC |
| to 2107 | From birth of Isaac to birth of Jacob (60 years) | 1896 BC |
| 2123 | Death of Abraham at age 175 | 1880 BC |
| 2158 | Noah's son Shem dies at age 600, when Isaac is 111 & Jacob is 51 years old | 1845 BC |
| to 2537 | From birth of Jacob to Israelite Exodus from Egypt 430 years later | 1466 BC |
| to 3017 | 480 years from Exodus to King Solomon's 4th Year | 986 BC |
| to 3447 | 430 years from 4th Year of Solomon's Reign to last year of King Zedekiah's Reign: Babylon conquers Israel, destroys Jerusalem and Solomon's Temple | 556 BC |
| to 3517 | 70 years from destruction of Jerusalem to prophesied end of Israel's Babylonian Exile | 486 BC |
| to 4000 | 483 years from end of Babylonian Exile to birth of Yahshua based on Daniel's 69 weeks (69 X 7=483) | 3 BC |

# A Summary of the Mazzaroth - Gospel in the Stars

| Zodiac/ Latin Mazzaroth/ Hebrew | Archetypal - Allegorical Image | Tribal and Planetary Relationship | Spiritual and Prophetic Meaning of Zodiac Signs |
|---|---|---|---|
| Virgo Bethulah | Virgin holding Branch | Zebulon, Venus | Eve & Eden before sin; Righteous Branch; Miriam, Yahshua's mother; Promised Seed of the Virgin; Eve weeping for Abel-Miriam weeping for Christ |
| Libra Mozanaim | Two Scales/ Round Altar | Levi Moses, Earth | Cain's Murder of Abel; Sin's Punishment = Death; Final Judgment; God's Law; Blood Sacrifice and Redemption through Christ |
| Scorpio Akrav | Scorpion/ Serpent Enemy: Eagle | Dan - Manasseh, Tiamat - Asteroid belt | Satan's Temptation; Knowledge of Good and Evil; War; Deceit; Rebellion and Wickedness; Greed; Pride; Destruction |
| Sagittarius Keshet | Archer With Body of Centaur | Asher, Pluto/Charon | Hope in a Messiah who will crush the Serpent in Scorpio; Yahshua, the God/Man and Desire of Ages; the Avenger of Blood |
| Capricorn Gedi | Goat Dying - Lively Fish | Gad, Saturn | Age of the Nephilim; Noah's Escape of Destruction and Death; Punishment for Earth's Corruption; Salvation from Evil |
| Aquarius Deli | Water-Bearer Pouring Water | Reuben, Neptune | Noah's Flood; Destruction leading to rebirth of Baptism; New Life; Ritual Purification; Holiness; gifts of the Spirit |

# Appendix

| Zodiac/ Latin Mazzaroth/ Hebrew | Archetypal - Allegorical Image | Tribal and Planetary Relationship | Spiritual and Prophetic Meaning of Zodiac Signs |
|---|---|---|---|
| Pisces Dagim | Two Fish Swimming Apart | Simeon/Israel as a Nation, Uranus & its Five Moons | 2 Churches from 10 Lost Tribes of Israel, & Tribe of Judah - one Apostate, one the True Church; Uranus = Bride, and 5 Moons = 5 Wise Virgins |
| Aries Taleh | Crouching Ram | Naphtali Isaac, Mars | Sacrifice; the Cross of Christ; Blood Atonement for Sin; Salvation promised through the Blood Covenant/ Communion |
| Taurus Shor; Reem | Bull charging (& bull's horns) | Joseph as Ephraim - symbolized by an Eagle, Marduk - Eris | Mercy & Judgment toward the Gentile Nations; Avengers of Blood; Deliverers of Punishment and Retribution; Agents of God's Wrath; The Great Tribulation |
| Gemini Te'omim | Twin Brothers: Bride & Groom | Benjamin - Isaac/Ishmael Jacob/Esau James/John, Mercury | Adoption by Blood Covenant; Christ's Dual Nature as God/Man and Dual Role as Priest/King; Wedding of the Lamb to the Church |
| Cancer Sartan | Crab/ Sheepfold | Issachar, Moon | Scattering of God's spiritual Sheep; Ingathering of the Redeemed; The Rapture; Spiritual Harvest; Separate Good Sheep from Evil Goats |
| Leo Aryeh | Leaping or Crouching Lion | Judah, David, Christ, Jupiter | The Lion of Judah; Yahshua as Conquering King; Pouring out of God's Wrath; Divine Judgment; Ushering in of Millennial Rule of Christ. |

## Jewish Civil and Sacred Years and Feast Days

| The Jewish Civil Calendar Year as followed from Adam's Creation | The Jewish Sacred Year in Effect After the Exodus | The Biblically Ordained Mosaic Feast Days and Their Prophetic Import |
|---|---|---|
| 7 – Tishri (Sept.-Oct.) Virgo-Libra | 1 – Abib/Nisan (Mar.-Apr.) Pisces-Aries | 1st month – 14th of Abib: Passover (Pesach) followed by six day Feast of Unleavened Bread & Firstfruits Wave Sheaf Offering on the 15th to 21st of Abib. Fulfilled at Yahshua's First Advent when He served as the Lamb of God (Passover), Bread of Life (Unleavened Bread), and Firstfruits of the Resurrection (Wave Sheaf Offering).

3rd month – 6th-7th of Sivan: Pentecost - a.k.a. Feast of Weeks, Feast of Harvest, Feast of Firstfruits (Shavuot) – 49 days/seven weeks from the wave sheaf offering at Passover, counted as the 50th (Jubilee) day. Giving of the Ten Commandments and Book of the Covenant on Mount Sinai. Fulfilled at Christ's First Advent with the Giving of the Holy Spirit after Christ's Resurrection. |
| 8 – Heshven (Oct.-Nov.) Libra-Scorpio | 2 – Iyar (Apr.-May) Aries-Taurus | |
| 9 – Chislev (Nov.-Dec.) Scorpio-Sagittarius | 3 – Sivan (May-June) Taurus-Gemini | |
| 10 – Tevet (Dec.-Jan.) Sagittarius-Capricorn | 4 – Tammuz (June-July) Gemini-Cancer | |
| 11 – Shevat (Jan.-Feb.) Capricorn-Aquarius | 5 – Av (July-Aug.) Cancer-Leo | |
| 12 – Adar (Feb.-Mar.) Aquarius-Pisces | 6 – Elul (Aug.-Sept.) Leo-Virgo | |

# Appendix

| The Jewish Civil Calendar Year as followed from Adam's Creation | The Jewish Sacred Year in Effect After the Exodus | The Biblically Ordained Mosaic Feast Days and Their Prophetic Import |
|---|---|---|
| 1 – Abib/Nisan (Mar.-Apr.) Pisces-Aries | 7 – Tishri (Sept.-Oct.) Virgo-Libra | 7th month – 1st of Tishri: New Year's Day – Feast of Trumpets (Rosh Hashanah), to be fulfilled in the Second Rapture. 10th of Tishri: Day of Atonement (Yom Kippur), to be fulfilled by the Wedding Feast/Tribulation period. 15th of Tishri: Feast of Tabernacles or Booths (Sukkot), fulfilled partly by Christ's birth, but fully fulfilled by Christ Return and the Millennial Kingdom. The 7th Jewish month heralds the arrival of the Seventh Day of the Lord and Yahshua's Second Advent roles as King of kings & Great High Priest. 

9th month – 25th of Chislev to 3rd of Tevet, Feast of Dedication - Festival of Lights (Chanukah) - Commemorates the miracle of the Temple menorah burning for eight days without needing to be refilled with oil just after the Temple was rededicated to Yahweh. Later, the Wise Men visit Christ, the Light of the World and giver of the Holy Spirit, as a toddler and present Him with costly royal gifts.

12th month - 14th – 15th of Adar, Feast of Ester, Feast of Lots (Pur; Purim) - Jews saved from slaughter in Babylon due to Queen Ester's daring intervention. |
| 2 – Iyar (Apr.-May) Aries-Taurus | 8 – Heshven (Oct.-Nov.) Libra-Scorpio | |
| 3 – Sivan (May-June) Taurus-Gemini | 9 – Chislev (Nov.-Dec.) Scorpio-Sagittarius | |
| 4 – Tammuz (June-July) Gemini-Cancer | 10 – Tevet (Dec.-Jan.) Sagittarius-Capricorn | |
| 5 – Av (July-Aug.) Cancer-Leo | 11 – Shevat (Jan.-Feb.) Capricorn-Aquarius | |
| 6 – Elul (Aug.-Sept.) Leo-Virgo | 12 – Adar (Feb.-Mar.) Aquarius-Pisces | |

# The Language of God in Prophecy

## Chart Showing 13,000 Years from Creation to Eternity

| 13,000 years - 6 Precessional Ages (approximate) | Six 1,000-Year Days of Creation, Six 1,000-Year Days of Men's Works Final Millennial Day of the Lord |
|---|---|
| Age of Leo: 10,000 BC to 8000 BC<br><br>1st and 2nd Millenniums | 1st Creation Day: Yah creates Light and separates the light from the darkness. (Gen. 1:1-5)<br><br>2nd Creation Day: Yah creates the sky to divide the waters above the Earth from the waters below. (Gen. 1:6-8) |
| Age of Cancer: 7999 BC to 6000 BC<br><br>3rd and 4th Millenniums | Third Creation Day: Yah gathers the water in one place, calling them seas, and makes dry land appear on the surface of the Earth to support all kinds of vegetation: trees, shrubs, flowers, vegetables, and fruit. (Gen. 1:9-13)<br><br>Fourth Creation Day: Yah creates the Sun, Moon, and stars to shed light (i.e. give both physical light and spiritual knowledge or enlightenment) on Earth. (Gen. 1:1-5) |
| Age of Gemini: 5999 BC to 4000 BC<br><br>5th and 6th Millenniums | Fifth Creation Day: Aquatic life of all kinds and birds of every kind are created. The Jews see this as the Day when Earth was now fully formed and ready to support life. It was therefore Earth's "birthday."<br><br>Sixth Creation Day: Yah creates all mammals and other kinds of terrestrial life, with His final creation being mankind. |
| Age of Taurus: 3999 BC to 2000 BC | God's Seventh Day Rest: Adam and Eve in the Garden of Eden, a perfect world without sin or death for seven years. Eve sins followed by Adam. **Paradise lost.** God's Seventh Day Rest Ends prematurely. Beginning of 1st Day of Men's Works: 1000-year |
| Age of Taurus - continued | Golden Age of Peace. Domestication of animals, shepherding, agriculture develops, first cities built. |

# Appendix

| | |
|---|---|
| 7th and 8th Millenniums: 1st and 2nd Days of Men's Works | 2nd Day of Men's Works: Arrival of Fallen Angels. Sin and war escalate. The Nephilim are created, further increasing wickedness and evil. The Great Flood occurs, destroying most of the Nephilim and temporarily ending mankind's moral and genetic spiral downward. Then war and conquest forge Nimrod's world dictatorship and full-blown Paganism is revived along with Earth Goddess worship, Magic, and Sorcery. Yah's destruction of Babel, and the confusion of tongues ends Nimrod's despotic rule of the world. |
| Age of Aries: 1999 BC to 0 BC<br><br>9th and 10th Millenniums: 3rd and 4th Days of Men's Works - Daniel's Kingdoms of Gold, Silver, Bronze, and Iron (Daniel 2:38-39) | 3rd Day of Men's Works: Begins with the time of Abraham and mankind's dispersion throughout the Earth after the Fall of Babel. Rise of civilization in China, the Americas. Egypt's Middle and New Kingdoms, Rise of Babylon, Assyria, then Persia. Greece rises to world power and encourages the interest and resurgence in culture, philosophy, art, and science.<br><br>4th Day of Men's Works: The Roman Republic emerges as a world power and becomes the world leader in art, science, literature, and the making of war. Christ is born in Bethlehem at the end of the 4th Day, in 3 BC. |
| Age of Pisces: 1 AD to 2000 AD<br><br>11th and 12th Millenniums: 5th and 6th Days of Men's Works - Daniel's Kingdom of Iron and those of Iron mixed with Clay (Daniel 2:33,41-43) | 5th Day of Men's Works: The Christian Age. Christ dies, is resurrected as the Firstfruits, and ascends to Heaven. The Roman Empire rises then falls. The Church has two centers: Rome in the West and Constantinople in the East while Buddhism, Hinduism, and other Pagan religions flourish in the East, with the advance of militant Islam eventually destroyed the Eastern Churches.<br><br>6th Day of Men's Works: Islam rises to prominence in the Middle East. The Crusades launched in the West during the Middle Ages against the Middle East causes Muslim Arabs to find a deep-seated hatred of the predominantly Christian West. |

# The Language of God in Prophecy

| 13,000 years - 6 Precessional Ages (approximate) | Six 1,000-Year Days of Creation, Six 1,000-Year Days of Men's Works Final Millennial Day of the Lord |
|---|---|
| Age of Pisces, continued: | 6th Day of Men's Works, continued: Islamic leaders launch a Holy War or Jihad against the West. Modern times: Terrorism begins to affect the whole world, giving rise to more government control in the West and a loss of freedom. |
| Age of Aquarius: 2001 AD to 4000 AD<br><br>13th and Final Millennium: Yah leading Men's Works, followed by the Eighth Great Day lasting all eternity<br><br>Daniel's "Stone from Heaven" that crushes the kingdoms of the Earth and becomes a far greater kingdom, Christ's 1,000-year Kingdom of Peace on Earth (Daniel 2:34-35,44). | Yah's 7th Great Day Sabbath Rest - The Day of the Lord. According to Biblical chronology, the Final Great Day of the Lord began on Nissan 1, April 6th, 2000 AD. This is the 13th Millennium since Creation began and the 7th Millennium since the Fall of mankind. This is the Age when a world government may be created, giving the Antichrist the opportunity he needs to take over the world. During this time, the Rapture will come followed by the seven-year Tribulation period.<br><br>This terrible time will end with the destruction of the Antichrist's government, the instatement of the Millennial Rule of Christ and the reinstatement of the Seventh Day Rest that Yah began at the end of the Creation Week. At the end of this final millennium of peace, evil and sin will be eradicated forever to usher in eternity, incorruptible bodies for all who are saved, no sin, a New Heaven and a New Earth.<br><br>Eighth Great Day: ***Paradise Regained!*** Life and perfection without end! Time, as we know it, ceases to exist since Eternity cannot be measured. The eternal Golden Age of Peace. |

# Bibliography By Subject

This bibliography lists research materials used for one of more of the four books in "The Language of God" Book Series. As such, it is extensive but partial. Many other magazine articles, books, pamphlets, religious reference works, and web sites were included in my research for "The Language of God" and "The Pillar of Enoch Trilogy" that are not included here.

In addition, there is much new information in this book and all the others in the Language of God Book Series that cannot be found in any book or magazine article, or on any web site (outside of the author's), but are independent conclusions and assumptions based on deductive reasoning, and God-given dreams, visions and words of knowledge that were made by the author.

Books in this bibliography are arranged by subject and author. See this book's Table of Contents for the nine subject headings and the pages that they appear on in this bibliography.

## Pre and Post Flood History, Ancient and Recent

Adkins, Lesley and Roy; Introduction to the Romans, The History, Culture and Art of the Roman Empire, 1996, Quantum Books Ltd., 6 Blundell Street, London N7 9BH, England.

Ancient Egypt, Myth and History - the religion, myths and gods explained against the background of its history, 1997, Geddes & Grosset Ltd., David Dale House, New Lanark, ML11 9DJ. Scotland.

Beechick, Ruth; Adam and His Kin - The Lost History of Their Lives and Times, 1990, Arrow Press, California, USA.

Bennett, W. H.; Symbols of Our Celto-Saxon Heritage, 1995, Herald Press Ltd, Windsor, Ontario, Canada. (The Heraldry of Israel)

Bray, Warwick; Everyday Life of the Aztecs, 1987, Dorset Press, New York, NY, USA.

Capt, E. Raymond; Abrahamic Covenant, Artisan Sales, P.O. Box 1529, Muskogee, OK 74402, USA.

Capt, E. Raymond; Jacob's Pillar, 1977, Artisan Sales, P.O. Box 1529, Muskogee, OK 74402, USA.

Capt, E. Raymond; Missing Links Discovered in Assyrian Tablets, 1985, Artisan Sales, P.O. Box 1529, Muskogee, OK 74402, USA.

Capt, Raymond E.; The Traditions of Glastonbury, 2004 Reprint, Artisan Publishers, P.O. Box 1529, Muskogee, Oklahoma 74402, USA.

Collins, Steven M; The "Lost" Ten Tribes of Israel... Found!, 1992, CPA Book Publisher, P.O. Box 596, Boring, Oregon, 97009, USA.

Cooper, Bill, B.A. Hons.; After The Flood - The Early Post Flood History of Europe, 1995, New Wine Press, Sussex, England.

Custance, Arthur C.; Noah's Three Sons - The Doorway Papers, Published online at: http://www.custance.org/old/noah/index.html

Deal, David Allen; Discovery of Ancient America, 1984, Kherem La Yah Press, Irvine, CA, USA.

Evans, Lorraine; Kingdom of the Ark, 2000, Simon & Schuster UK. Ltd., Africa House, 64-78 Kingsway, London WC2B 6AH England.

Fell, Barry; America B.C., 2004 reprint of 1976 Edition, Artisan Sales, P.O. Box 1529, Muskogee, OK 74402, USA.

Fox-Davies, Arthur Charles; The Wordsworth Complete Guide to Heraldry, 1996, Wordsworth Editions, Ltd., Cumberland House, Crib Street, Ware, Hertfordshire, SG12 9ET, England.

Gascoigne, Mike; The Forgotten History of the Western People – From the Earliest Origins, 2002, Anno Mundi Books, P. O. Box 752, Camberley, England. http://www.annomundi.co.uk

Harris, Reader, K.C.; The Lost Tribes of Israel, 2004 Reprint of the 1907 Edition, Artisan Sales, P.O. Box 1529, Muskogee, OK 74402, USA.

Hancock, Graham, & Bauval, Robert; Talisman - Sacred Cities, Secret Faith, 2004, Element Press, 77-85 Fulham Palace Road, Hammersmith, London UK.

Haywood, John, Ph.D.; Atlas of World History, 1997, published by Metro Books, an imprint of Freidman/Fairfax Publishers by arrangement with Andromeda Oxford Ltd., Abingdon, Oxfordshire, OX14 3PX, England.

Hoffmeier, James K.; Israel in Egypt – The Evidence for the Authenticity of the Exodus Tradition, 1996, Oxford University Press, 198 Madison Avenue, New York, NY 10016, USA.

Kendall, Ann; Everyday Life of the Incas, 1989, Dorset Press, New York, NY, USA.

# Bibliography

Kenyon, Douglas, Editor; Forbidden History, 2005, Bear & Company, One Park Street, Rochester, VT 05767, USA.

Kimball, Charles Scott; The Genesis Chronicles - A Proposed History of the Morning of the World., Published online at http://xenohistorian.faithweb.com/

Long, James D.; Riddle of the Exodus, 2006 Reprint, Lightcatcher Books, 842 Kissinger Ave., Springdale, Arkansas 72762, USA.

Levenda, Peter; The Secret Temple - Masons, Mysteries and the Founding of America, 2009, The Continuum International Publishing Group (now a division of Bloomsbury Publishing), The Tower Building, 11 York Road, London SE17NX

Moller, Dr. Lennart; The Exodus Case - New Discoveries Confirm the Historical Exodus, 2002, Scandinavia Publishing House, Drejervej 11-21, DK 2400 Copenhagen NV, Denmark.

Nienhuis, James I.; Ice Age Civilizations, 2006, Genesis Veracity, P.O. Box 850, 5773 Woodway Drive, Houston, TX, 77057, USA.

Reagan, David R.; America the Beautiful? - The United States in Bible Prophecy, 2003, Lamb & Lion Ministries, P.O. Box 919, McKinney, TX 75070, USA.

Roaf, Michael; Cultural Atlas of Mesopotamia and the Ancient Near East, 1999, Facts On File, Inc., 11 Penn Plaza, New York, NY 10001, USA.

Rohl, David M.; Legend, The Genesis of Civilization, 1998, Random House, London, England.

Rohl, David M.; Pharaohs and Kings, A Biblical Quest (Published in Great Britain as: A Test of Time, The Bible From Myth to History), 1995, Crown Publishers, Inc., New York, USA.

Rohl, David M.; The Lost Testament - From Eden to Exile: The Five Thousand Year History of the People of the Bible, Century, 2002, Random House UK Ltd., 20 Vauxhall Bridge Road, London, SW1V 2SA.

Rosenberg, Joel C.; Epicenter - Why the Current Rumblings in the Middle-East Will Change Your Future, Tyndale House Publishers, Inc., Carol Stream, IL 60188, USA.

Schobinger, Juan; The First Americans, 1994 English Translation, William B. Eerdmans Publishing Co., 255 Jefferson Avenue S.E., Grand Rapids, Michigan, 49503, USA.

Waddell, L.A., LL.D.; Egyptian Civilization, Its Sumerian Origin & Real Chronology and Sumerian Origin of Egyptian Hieroglyphs, CPA Book Publisher, P.O. Box 596, Boring, OR 97009-0596, USA.

Woods, Jr. PhD., Thomas E.; The Politically Incorrect Guide to American History, 2004, Regnery Publishing, Inc., One Massachusetts Ave. NW, Washington, DC 20001, USA.

## Ancient Judeo-Christian Manuscripts and Commentaries

Charles, R. H., DD.; The Book of Jubilees, 1902, Adam and Charles Black, London, England.

Charles, R. H., DD.; The Book of Enoch (from the Ethiopic), 1900? Sheldon Press, London, England. (I refer to this as the Book of 1 Enoch to distinguish it from the Book of the Secrets of Enoch, or the Book of 2 Enoch.)

Charles, R. H., DD.; The Book of the Secrets of Enoch (from Slavonic), 1896, Clarendon Press, Oxford University Press, London, England.

The NIV Study Bible, New International Version, 1985, Zondervan Bible Publishers, Grand Rapids, Michigan, USA.

The Forgotten Books of Eden, Lost Books of the Old Testament, The First and Second Books of Adam and Eve, 1980, Bell Publishing Company, USA.

The Book of Jasher - referred to in Joshua and II Samuel, 1997 reprint of the 1887 edition by J. H. Parry Publishers, Kessinger Publishing, Whitefish, MT 59937, USA.

The Epistle of Barnabus, The Lost Books of the Bible, 1979, Bell Publishing Company, New York, NY, USA.

Laurence, Richard, LL. D.; The Book of Enoch (from Ethiopic), 1980 Reprint of the 1882 Edition Published by John Thompson, Glasgow. Reprinted by Artisan Sales, Thousand Oaks, California, USA.

Mordechai, Avi Ben; Messiah, Understanding His Life and Teaching in Hebraic Context, Volumes 1, 2 & 3, 2000 edition, Millennium 7000 Communications, USA.

Morris, Henry M.; The Remarkable Record of Job, 1996, Baker Book House, Grand Rapids, Michigan, USA.

Stedman, Ray C.; Expository Studies In Genesis, Published online at: http://pbc.org/dp/stedman/genesis/index.html

Trumbull, H. Clay; The Blood Covenant, Sixth Printing, 1998

Trumbull, H. Clay; The Salt Covenant, 1999 reprint of 1899 edition, Impact Christian Books, Inc. 332 Leffingwell, Suite 101, Kirkwood, MO, 63122, USA.

Vanderkam, James C.; Enoch – A Man For All Generations, 1995, University of South Carolina Press, USA.

## Pre-Flood Wisdom: Sacred Astronomy/Gospel in the Stars

Aveni, Anthony; Skywatchers of Ancient Mexico, 1980, University of Texas Press, Box 7819, Austin, TX 78712, USA.

Banks, William D.; The Heavens Declare..., 1985, Impact Books, Inc, USA.

# Bibliography

Bauval, Robert & Gilbert, Adrian; The Orion Mystery, Unlocking the Secrets of the Pyramids, 1995, Random House, Inc., New York, NY, USA.

Bullinger, E. W.; The Witness of the Stars, (reprint of the 1893 edition) 2000, Kregel Publications, USA.

Byrd, Gary Alexander; Keys to the Kingdom - The Year 2012 - Countdown to the Apocalypse, 2007, Author House, 166 Liberty Drive, Suite 200, Bloomington, IN 47403, USA.

Davidson, D. and Aldersmith, H.; The Great Pyramid – Its Divine Message, Reprint of 1925 edition, Kessinger Publishing, Whitefish, MT 59937, USA.

DeYoung, Donald B.; Astronomy and the Bible - Questions and Answers, 1989, Baker Book House, Grand Rapids, Michigan, USA.

Gaunt, Bonnie; Stonehenge... A Closer Look, 1987 reprint, Bonnie Gaunt, 510 Golf Avenue, Jackson, MI 49203, USA.

Gaunt, Bonnie; The Coming of Jesus - The Real Message of the Bible Codes, 1999, Adventures Unlimited Press, P.O. Box 174, Kempton, IL 60946, USA.

Gaunt, Bonnie; The Magnificent Numbers of the Great Pyramid and Stonehenge, 1988, Bonnie Gaunt, 510 Golf Avenue, Jackson, MI 49203, USA.

Gaunt, Bonnie; The Stones and the Scarlet Thread, 2001, Adventures Unlimited Press, P.O. Box 174, Kempton, IL 60946, USA.

Hancock, Graham & Bauval, Robert; The Message of the Sphinx, 1996, Doubleday Canada, Toronto, Canada.

Hunkler, Tim G.; Symbolism and Coincidences of the Great Pyramid, 1998, Published online at http://www.hunkler.com/pyramids/pyramid_symbolism.html

Hutchings, Noah W.; The Great Pyramid - Prophecy In Stone, 1996, Hearthstone Publishing, P.O. Box 815, Oklahoma City, OK 73101, USA.

Kitt Chappell, Sally A.; Cahokia - Mirror of the Cosmos, 2002, The University of Chicago Press, Chicago, IL, USA.

Lockyer, J. Norman; The Dawn of Astronomy, A Study of the Temple Worship and Mythology of the Ancient Egyptians, 1997 Reprint, Kessinger Publishing, P.O. Box 1404, Whitefish, MT 59937, USA.

LaViolette, Paul, Earth Under Fire, Humanity's Survival of the Apocalypse, 1997, Starline Publications, 1176 Hedgewood Lane, Schenectady, NY 12309, USA.

Martin, Ernest L.; The Star of Bethlehem - The Star That Astonished the World, 1998, ASK Publications, P.O. Box 25000, Portland, OR 97225, USA.

Mulfinger, Jr., George; Designs and Origins in Astronomy, 1983, Creation Research Society, USA.

Mordechai, Avi Ben; Signs In The Heavens, 1999 edition, A Jewish Messianic Perspective of the Last Days and Coming Millennium, Millennium 7000 Communications, USA.

Raymo, Chet; 365 Starry Nights, an introduction to astronomy for every night of the year, 1982, Prentice-Hall, Inc., Englewood Cliffs, NJ 07632, USA.

Rolleston, Frances; The Mazzaroth; or the Constellations. Online at: http://philologos.org/__eb-mazzaroth/

Schoch, Robert M., Phd.; Voyages of the Pyramid Builders, 2003, Jeremy P. Tarcher-Penguin Group, Inc., 575 Hudson Street, New York, NY 10014, USA.

Schoch, Robert M., Phd.; Pyramid Quest - Secrets of the Great Pyramid and the Dawn of Civilization, 2005, Jeremy P. Tarcher-Penguin Group, Inc., 575 Hudson Street, New York, NY 10014, USA.

Seiss, Joseph A.; The Gospel in the Stars, 1972 Reprint of the 1882 Edition, Kregel Publications, P.O. Box 2607, Grand Rapids, MI 49501, USA.

Smyth, Piazzi; The Great Pyramid, It's Secrets and Mysteries Revealed, 1978, Gramercy Books, a division of Random House Value Publishing; Avenel, New Jersey, USA.

Tennant, Catherine; The Lost Zodiac - 22 Ancient Star Signs, What They Mean and the Legends Behind Them, 1995, Bulfinch Press - Little, Brown and Co. USA & Canada.

The Great Pyramid - Ancient Wonder, Modern Mystery, A pamphlet by Pyramid Productions, P.O. Box 1359, Westerville, Ohio, 43086 USA.

Tompkins, Peter; Secrets of the Great Pyramid, 1978, Harper & Row Publishers, Inc., 10 East 53rd Street, New York, NY 10022, USA.

## Judeo-Christian Religious Eschatology and Exegesis

Allen, J. H., Judah's Sceptre and Joseph's Birthright, 1943, A. A. Beauchamp, Publisher, Boston, Mass., USA.

Church, J. R.; Guardians of the Grail, 1989

Church, J. R.; Hidden Prophecies in the Psalms, 1990 Revised Edition

Church, J. R.; Hidden Prophecies in the Song of Moses, 1991

Prophecy Publications, P.O. Box 7000, Oklahoma City, OK, 73153, USA.

Church, J. R. & Stearman, Gary; The Mystery of the Menorah and the Hebrew Alphabet, 1989, Prophecy Publications, P.O. Box 7000, Oklahoma City, OK, 73153, USA.

Cohen, Tim; The Antichrist and a Cup of Tea, 1998, Prophecy House, Inc., P.O. Box 461104, Aurora, CO 80046-1104, USA.

Conner, Kevin L.; The Temple of Solomon - The Glory of God as Displayed Through the Temple, 1988, City Bible Publishing, 9200 NE Fremont, Portland, Oregon, 97220, USA

# Bibliography

Conner, Kevin L., & Malmin, Ken; The Covenants, 1997 Revision of original 1983 edition, City Bible Publishing, 9200 NE Fremont, Portland, Oregon, 97220, USA

DeHaan, M. R., M.D.; The Tabernacle, 1983, Lamplighter Books, a division of Zondervan Publishing House, 1415 Lake Drive, S.E., Grand Rapids, MI 49506, USA.

DeWitt, Roy Lee; Teachings From The Tabernacle, 1988, Baker Book House, Grand Rapids, MI 49516, USA.

Drosnin, Michael; The Bible Code, 1998, Touchstone Books, Rockefeller Center, 1230 Avenue of the Americas, New York, NY 10020, USA.

Drosnin, Michael; Bible Code II - The Countdown, 2002, Penguin Group (USA) Inc., 375 Hudson Street, New York, NY 10014, USA.

Evans, Michael D.; The American Prophecies - Ancient Scriptures Reveal Our Nation's Future, 2004, Warner Faith - Time Warner Book Group, 1271 Avenue of the Americas, New York, NY 10020, USA.

Gaunt, Bonnie; Jesus Christ - The Number of His Name, 1998, Adventures Unlimited Press, P.O. Box 174, Kempton, IL 60946, USA.

Hitchcock, Mark; The Complete Book of Bible Prophecy, 1999, Tyndale House Publishers, Inc. Wheaton, IL, 60189 USA.

Hunt, Dave; A Woman Rides The Beast – The Roman Catholic Church and the Last Days, 1994, Harvest House Publishers, Eugene, Oregon 97402, USA.

Hunt, Dave; Global Peace, and the Rise of the Antichrist, 1990, Harvest House Publishers, Eugene, Oregon 97402, USA.

Hutchings, Noah W.; 25 Messianic Signs in Israel Today, 1999, Hearthstone Publishing, P.O. Box 815, Oklahoma City, OK 73101, USA.

Jeffrey, Grant R.; Heaven, The Last Frontier, 1990, Frontier Research Publications, P.O. Box 129, Station "U", Toronto, Ontario, M8Z 5M4 Canada.

Jones, Dr. Stephen R.; The Seven Churches, 2004, God's Kingdom Ministries, 6201 University Ave. NE, Fridley, MN 55432, USA.

Judah, Monte; The Prince Who Is To Come, article from Yavoh Newsletter, Nov. 2001 Issue, Lion and Lamb Ministries, P.O. Box 720968, Norman, OK 73070, USA.

Kasdan, Barney; God's Appointed Times, A Practical Guide to Understanding and Celebrating the Biblical Holidays, 1993, Messianic Jewish Publishers, Lederer/Messianic Jewish Communications, 6204 Park Heights Avenue, Baltimore, MD 21215, USA.

Levy, David M.; The Tabernacle, Shadows of the Messiah: Its Sacrifices, Services, and Priesthood, 1993, The Friends of Israel Gospel Ministry, P.O. Box 908, Bellmawr, NJ 08099, USA.

LaHaye, Tim & Jenkins, Jerry B.; Are We Living In The End Times?, 1999, Tyndale House Publishers, Inc., Wheaton, IL, USA.

LaHaye, Tim & Ice, Thomas; Charting The End Times; 1999, Harvest House Publishers, Eugene, OR 97402, USA.

Lindsey, Hal; Apocalypse Code, 1997, Western Front, Ltd., Palos Verdes, California, USA.

Manty, Jeffrey A., Prophecy Code - A New Revelation For the Last Days, 2007, Wheatmark, 610 East Delano Street, Suite 104, Tucson, AZ 85705, USA.

Matson, Daniel W.; Signs of the End - A Discovery of Biblical Timelines, 2006, Inspirational Press, P.O. Box 9901, Fountain Valley, CA 92708, USA.

Martin, Dr. Walter; Essential Christianity, 1980, Regal Books, Venture, CA USA.

Rambsel, Yacov; His Name is Jesus – The Mysterious Yeshua Codes, 1997, Frontier Research Publications, Inc., P.O. Box 129, Station "U", Toronto, Ontario, M8Z 5M4, Canada.

Sherman, R. Edwin; Bible Code Bombshell, 2005, New Leaf Press, P.O. Box 726, Green Forest, AR 72638, USA.

Van Impe, Jack; 11:59 - The Countdown, 1987, Jack Van Impe Ministries, P.O. Box 7004, Troy, MI 48007, USA.

Van Impe, Jack, & Campbell, Roger F.; Israel's Final Holocaust, 1979, Jack Van Impe Ministries, P.O. Box 7004, Troy, MI 48007, USA.

Walvoord, John F.; The Rapture Question, Academic Books, Imprint of Zondervan Publishing House, 1415 Lake Drive. S. E., Grand Rapids, MI 49506, USA.

Wouk, Herman; This Is My God, The Jewish Way of Life, Little, Brown and Co., New York, NY, USA.

## Christian Apologetics – Defending the Bible

Albrecht, Mark; Reincarnation – A Christian Appraisal, 1982, Inter-Varsity Press, Downers Grove, IL 60515, USA.

Barnett, Paul, Is The New Testament History? 1986, Hodder & Stouton, Ltd., 47 Bedford Square, London WC1B 3DP, England.

Barton, David; Original Intent - The Courts, the Constitution, & Religion, 2000, WallBuilders Press, P.O. Box 397, Aledo, TX 76008, USA.

Barton, David; The Question of Freemasonry and the Founding Fathers, 2005, WallBuilders Press, P.O. Box 397, Aledo, TX 76008, USA.

Bowman, Jr., Robert M.; Why You Should Believe in the Trinity: An Answer to Jehovah's Witnesses, 1989, Baker Book House, Grand Rapids, MI 49516, USA.

Bruce, F. F.; The New Testament Documents - Are They Reliable?, 1985 Reprint, Intervarsity Press, Wm. B. Eerdmans Publishing Co., 255 Jefferson S.E., Grand Rapids, MI, USA.

# Bibliography

Caner, Emir Fethi; The Costly Call - Muslims Who Found Jesus, 2005, Kregel Publications, P.O. Box 2607, Grand Rapids, MI 49501, USA.

Caner, Ergun Mehmet, & Caner, Emir Fethi; Unveiling Islam, 2002, Kregel Publications, P.O. Box 2607, Grand Rapids, MI 49501, USA.

Gabriel, Mark A. Phd.; Islam and Terrorism, 2002, Frontline, A Strang Company, 600 Rinehart Road, Lake Mary, FL 32746, USA.

Groothuis, Douglas R.; Confronting the New Age - How to Resist a Growing Religious Movement, 1988, Inter-Varsity Press, Downers Grove, IL 60515, USA.

Groothuis, Douglas R.; Unmasking the New Age - Is There A New Religious Movement Trying to Transform Society?, 1986, Inter-Varsity Press, Downers Grove, IL 60515, USA.

Lewis, C. S.; Mere Christianity, 1952, Macmillan Publishing Company, 866 Third Avenue, New York, N. Y. 10022, USA.

Lewis, C. S.; The Screwtape Letters, 1963, Macmillan Publishing Company, 866 Third Avenue, New York, N. Y. 10022, USA.

Lewis, C. S.; The Great Divorce, 1987 Reprint, William Collins Sons and Co, Ltd., Glasgow, England.

McDowell, Josh; The New Evidence That Demands A Verdict, 1999, Thomas Nelson Publishers, Nashville, TN USA.

Sire, James W.; Scripture Twisting - 20 Ways the Cults Misread the Bible, 1980, Intervarsity Press, P.O. Box 1400, Downers Grove, IL 60515 USA.

Spencer, Robert; Religion of Peace? Why Christianity Is and Islam Isn't, 2007, Regnery Publishing, Inc., One Massachusetts Ave. NW, Washington, DC 20001, USA.

Spencer, Robert - Editor; The Myth of Islamic Tolerance, 2005, Prometheus Books, 59 John Glenn Drive, Amherst, NY 14228, USA.

Spencer, Robert; The Politically Incorrect Guide to Islam, 2005, Regnery Publishing, Inc., One Massachusetts Ave. NW, Washington, DC 20001, USA.

## Antediluvian/Ancient Technology and Civilization

Allen, J. M.; Atlantis – The Andes Solution, 1998, St. Martin's Press, Scholarly and Reference Division 175 Fifth Avenue, New York, NY 10010, USA.

Baines, John & Malek, Jaromir; Atlas of Ancient Egypt, 1994, Facts on File, Inc., 460 Park Avenue South, New York, NY 10016, USA.

Capt, Raymond E.; A Study In Pyramidology, 2002, Artisan Publishers, P.O. Box 1529, Muskogee, Oklahoma 74402, USA.

Childress, David Hatcher; Lost Cities of North and Central America, 1998 reprint, Adventures Unlimited Press, One Adventure Place, Kempton (Stelle), IL 60946, USA.

Childress, David Hatcher; Technology of the Gods - The Incredible Sciences of the Ancients, 2000, Adventures Unlimited Press, One Adventure Place, Kempton, IL 60946, USA.

Childress, David Hatcher; Vimana - Aircraft of Ancient India & Atlantis, 2004, Adventures Unlimited Press, One Adventure Place, Kempton, IL 60946, USA.

Chittick, Donald E.; The Puzzle of Ancient Man, 1997, Creation Compass, Newberg, Oregon, USA.

Collins, Andrew; Gateway to Atlantis - The Search For A Lost Civilization, 2002, Carroll & Graf Publishers, Avalon Publishing, 161 William Street, 16th Floor, New York, NY 10038, USA.

Dunn, Christopher, The Giza Power Plant – Technologies of Ancient Egypt, 1998, Bear & Company, Inc. Santa Fe, NM 87504-2860, USA.

Jacq, Christian; The Wisdom of Ptah-hotep - Spiritual Treasures from the Age of the Pyramids, 2004, Constable & Robinson Ltd., 3 The Lanchesters, 162 Fulham Palace Road, London, UK, W69ER

Joseph, Frank; The Destruction of Atlantis, Compelling Evidence of the Sudden Fall of a Legendary Civilization, 2002, Bear & Company, Rochester, Vermont 05767, USA.

Hancock, Graham and Faiia, Santha; Heaven's Mirror - Quest for the Lost Civilization, 1998, Doubleday Canada, Toronto, Canada.

Hancock, Graham; Underworld, 2002, Crown Publishers, New York, NY, USA.

Hapgood, Charles H.; Maps of the Ancient Sea Kings - Evidence of Advanced Civilization in the Ice Age, 1996 reprint, Adventures Unlimited Press, One Adventure Place, Kempton, IL 60946, USA.

Hodges, Henry; Technology in the Ancient World, 1992, Marboro Books Corp., a division of Barnes & Noble, Inc., USA.

Knight, Christopher R., and Lomas, Robert; Uriel's Machine, Uncovering the Secrets of Stonehenge, Noah's Flood, and the Dawn of Civilization, 2004, Barnes and Noble Books, Inc., USA.

Lehner, Mark; The Complete Pyramids - Solving the Ancient Mysteries, 1997, Thames and Hudson, Inc., 500 Fifth Avenue, New York, NY 10110, USA.

Noorbergen, Rene'; Secrets of the Lost Races, 1977, The Bobbs - Merrill Co, Inc., USA.

Silverman, David P., General Editor; Ancient Egypt, 1997, Duncan Baird Publishers, Sixth Floor, Castle House, 73-76 Wells Street, London, W1P 3RE, England.

# Bibliography

Wilson, Colin and Flem-Ath, Rand; The Atlantis Blueprint - Unlocking the Ancient Mysteries of a Long-Lost Civilization, 2000, Delacorte Press, USA.

Zapp, Ivar & Erikson, George; Atlantis in America – Navigators of the Ancient World, 1998, Adventures Unlimited Press, One Adventure Place, Kempton, IL 60946, USA.

## Creation – Catastrophism – Refuting Evolution

Ackerman, Paul D.; It's A Young World After All - Exciting Evidence for a Recent Creation, 1986, Baker Book House, Grand Rapids, Michigan, USA.

Allan, D. S. & Delair, J. B.; Cataclysm! - Compelling Evidence of a Cosmic Catastrophe in 9500 BC, 1997, Bear & Company, Santé Fe, New Mexico, USA.

Cuozzo, Jack; Buried Alive - The Startling Truth About Neanderthal Man, 1998, Master Books, Arkansas, USA.

Custance, Arthur C.; Evolution or Creation? - The Doorway Papers, Published online at: http://www.custance.org/old/evol/index.html

Dillow, Joseph C.; The Waters Above - Earth's Pre-Flood Water Canopy, Revised Edition, 1982, Moody Press, Chicago, Illinois, USA.

Dolphin, Lambert; On The Great Flood of Noah, Published online at: http://www.ldolphin.org/flood.shtml

Gascoigne, Mike; Impossible Theology, The Christian Evolutionist Dilemma, 2004, Anno Mundi Books. P.O. Box 752, Camberley, GU17 0XJ, England. http://www.annomundi.co.uk

Gish, Duane T., Ph.D.; The Amazing Story of Creation from Science and the Bible, 1990, Institute for Creation Research, El Cajon, California, USA.

Hancock, Graham; Fingerprints of the Gods, 1995, Doubleday Canada, Toronto, Canada.

Hapgood, Charles H.; Paths of the Poles, 1999 Reprint, Adventures Unlimited Press, One Adventure Place, Kempton, IL 60946, USA.

Lubenow, Marvin L.; Bones of Contention, A Creationist Assessment of Human Fossils, 1992, Baker Books, P.O. Box 6287, Grand Rapids, Michigan, 49516-6287, USA.

Morris, Henry M. And Parker, Gary E.; What is Creation Science?, Revised Edition, 1987, Master Books, El Cajon, California, USA.

Morris, Henry M., and Whitcomb, John C.; The Genesis Flood, The Biblical Record and It's Scientific Implications, 42nd Printing, 1998, P & R Publishing Company, Phillipsburg, New Jersey, USA.

Oard, Michael J.; An Ice Age Caused by The Genesis Flood, 1990, Institute for Creation Research, El Cajon, California, USA.

Patterson, Roger; Evolution Exposed, 2006, Answers in Genesis, P.O. Box 510, Hebron, KY 41048, USA.

Pember, G. H.; Earth's Earliest Ages, 1998 Reprint, Kregel Publications, USA.

Sarfati, Jonathan, Ph.D.; Refuting Evolution, October 1999, Seventh Printing, Master Books, Inc., P.O. Box 727, Green Forest, AR, 72638, USA.

Woodmorappe, John; Noah's Ark, A Feasibility Study, 1996, Institute for Creation Research, El Cajon, California, USA.

Velikovsky, Immanuel; Earth In Upheaval, 1955 – 11th Printing, Doubleday & Company, Inc. Garden City, New York, USA.

Velikovsky, Immanuel; Worlds In Collision, 1977, Pocket Books, New York, NY, USA.

## Dinosaurs, Fallen Angels, Giants, and the Nephilim

Alford, Alan F., Gods of the New Millennium; 1996, Hodder & Stoughton, London, England.

Collins, Andrew; Gods of Eden - Egypt's Lost Legacy and the Genesis of Civilization, 2002, Bear & Co., One Park Street, Rochester, VT, 05767, USA.

Collins, Andrew; From the Ashes of Angels, The Forbidden Legacy of a Fallen Race, 2001, Bear & Company, One Park Street, Rochester, VT, 05767, USA.

Davidson, Gustav; A Dictionary of Angels, Including the Fallen Angels, Free Press, Div. of MacMillan, Inc., 866 Third Avenue, New York, NY 10022, USA.

DeLoach, Charles; Giants – A Reference Guide from History, the Bible, and Recorded Legend, 1995, The Scarecrow Press, Inc., Metuchen, NJ, USA.

Dinosaur Dictionary, An A to Z of Dinosaurs and Prehistoric Reptiles, 2001, Tangerine Press, an imprint of Scholastic, Inc., 555 Broadway, New York, NY 10012, USA.

Gish, Duane T., Ph.D.; Dinosaurs by Design, 9th printing - 1998, Master Books, Green Forest, Arkansas, USA.

Hapgood, Charles H.; Mystery in Acambaro, 2000 reprint with forward by David Hatcher Childress, Adventures Unlimited Press, One Adventure Place, Kempton, IL 60946, USA.

Lindsay, William - Text Writer, Fornari, Giuliano - Illustrator; The Great Dinosaur Atlas, 1999, DK Publishing Inc., 95 Madison Avenue, New York, NY, 10016, USA.

Missler, Chuck; As The Days of Noah Were - Return of the Aliens?, Published online at: http://www.ldolphin.org/noahdays.html.

# Bibliography

Tanaka, Shelley; New Dinos, the Latest Finds! The Coolest Discoveries!, 2003, Madison Press Books, 1000 Yonge Street, Suite 200, Toronto, Ontario, M4W 2K2, Canada.

Taylor, Paul S.; The Great Dinosaur Mystery and the Bible, 1989, Chariot Victor Publishing, Colorado Springs, Colorado, USA.

Sitchin, Zecharia; The 12th Planet; Book One of "The Earth Chronicles," 1978, Avon Books, New York, NY, USA

Sitchin, Zecharia; The Stairway to Heaven; Book Two of "The Earth Chronicles," 1980, St. Martin's Press, New York, NY, USA.

Sitchin, Zecharia;

The Wars of Gods and Men; Book Three of "The Earth Chronicles," 1985, The Lost Realms; Book Four of "The Earth Chronicles," 1990,

When Time Began; Book Five of "The Earth Chronicles," 1993,

The Cosmic Code; Book Six of "The Earth Chronicles," 1998,

Avon Books, New York, NY, USA.

Sitchin, Zecharia; Genesis Revisited, 1991, Bear & Company, Inc., Santa Fe, New Mexico, USA.

## Paganism: False Religious Mythology

NOTE: For books about Radical Islam and Terrorism, look under "Christian Apologetics - Defending the Bible"

Baigent, Michael; From the Omens of Babylon: Astrology and Ancient Mesopotamia, 1994, Penguin - Arkana Books, 375 Hudson St., New York, NY 10014, USA.

Baigent, Michael; Leigh, Richard, & Lincoln, Henry; Holy Blood, Holy Grail, 1982, Delacorte Press, 1 Dag Hammarskjold Plaza, New York, NY 10017, USA.

Bierhorst, John; The Mythology of South America, With A New Afterword, 2002, Oxford University Press, 198 Madison Ave., New York, NY 10016-4314, USA.

Barnett, Mary; Gods and Myths of the Romans – The Archeology and Mythology of Ancient Peoples, 1996, Brockhampton Press, 20 Bloomsbury Street, London, WC1B 3QA, England.

Black, Jeremy and Green, Anthony; Gods, Demons, and Symbols of Ancient Mesopotamia – an Illustrated Dictionary, 2003, University of Texas Press, Austin, Texas, USA.

Boyce, Mary, translator and editor; Textual Sources for the Study of Zoroastrianism, 1990, University of Chicago Press, Chicago, Illinois, USA.

Bunson, Margaret; A Dictionary of Ancient Egypt, 1991, Oxford University Press, 198 Madison Ave., New York, NY 10016-4314, USA.

Classical Mythology – A dictionary of the tales, characters, and traditions of Classical Mythology, 1997, Geddes & Grosset Ltd., David Dale House, New Lanark, ML11 9DJ, Scotland,

Cotterell, Arthur; The Encyclopedia of Mythology - Norse, Classical and Celtic, Acropolis Books, imprint of Anness Publishing Ltd., Hermes House, 88-89 Blackfriars Road, London, SE1 8HA, England.

Dailey, Stephanie; Myths From Mesopotamia – Creation, The Flood, Gilgamesh, and Others, 2000, Revised Edition, Oxford University Press, Great Clarendon Street, Oxford, New York, USA.

Faulkner, R. O.; Andrews, Carol - Editor; The Ancient Egyptian Book of the Dead, 1999, University of Texas Press, Box 7819, Austin, TX 78713, USA.

Finegan, Jack; Myth & Mystery, An Introduction to the Pagan Religions of the Biblical World, 1997, Baker Book House, P.O. Box 6287, Grand Rapids, MI 49516-6287, USA.

Gardner, Laurence, Bloodline of the Holy Grail, 1996, Element Books, Ltd, Shaftesbury, Dorset SP7 8BP, England.

Gilbert, Adrian; Magi, the Quest for a Secret Tradition, 1996, Bloomsbury Publishing, 2 Soho Square, London W1B 6HB, England.

Goetz, Delia and Morley, Sylvanus G.; Popol Vuh: The Sacred Book of the Ancient Quiche Maya, 1991, University of Oklahoma Press, USA.

Heron, Patrick C.; The Nephilim and the Pyramid of the Apocalypse, 2004, Xulon Press, USA.

Hinnells, John R.; Persian Mythology; 1997, Chancellor Press, imprint of Reed International Books Ltd., Michelin House, 81 Fulham Road, London SW3 6RB, England.

Hislop, Alexander; The Two Babylons or the Papal Worship, 1959, Second American Edition of the 1916 original. The Loizeaux Brothers, Inc., USA.

Horn, Thomas R.; The Gods Who Walk Among Us, 1999, Huntington House Publishers, P.O. Box 53788, Lafayette, LA 70505, USA.

Jenkins, John Major; Maya Cosmogenesis 2012, The True Meaning of the Maya Calendar End-Date, 1998, Bear & Company, Rochester, Vermont, 05767, USA.

Johnson Jr., Robert Bowie; The Parthenon Code: Mankind's History in Marble, 2004, Solving Light Books, 727 Mount Alban Drive, Annapolis, MD 21401, USA.

Lemesurier, Peter; Decoding the Great Pyramid, 1999, Elements Books, Ltd. (Barnes and Noble Book Reprint), England.

# Bibliography

Naydler, Jeremy; Temple of the Cosmos - The Ancient Egyptian Experience of the Sacred, 1996, Inner Traditions International, One Park Street, Rochester, Vermont, 05767, USA.

New Larousse Encyclopedia of Mythology, 1989, Paul Hamlyn, London, England.

Nicholson, Paul & Shaw, Ian; The Dictionary of Ancient Egypt, in Association with the British Museum, 1995, Harry N. Abrams, Inc., New York, NY, USA.

Oakes, Lorna & Gahlin, Lucia; Ancient Egypt, An Illustrated Reference to the Myths, Religions, Pyramids, and Temples of the Land of the Pharaohs, 2002, Hermes House, a Div. of Anness Publishing Ltd., Hermes House, 88-89 Blackfriars Road, London, SE1 8HA, England.

Parker, Julia & Derek; Parkers' Astrology – The Definitive Guide to Using Astrology in Every Aspect of Your Life, 1994, Elan press – an imprint of General Publishing Co., Ltd., 30 Lesmill Rd., Toronto, M3B 2T6, Canada.

Samma, Jamie & Carson, David; Medicine Cards – The Discovery of Power Through The Ways of Animals, 1988, Bear & Company, P.O. Drawer 2860 Santa Fe, NM 87504, USA.

Sanders, Catherine Edwards; Wicca's Charm - Understanding the Spiritual Hunger Behind the Rise of Modern Witchcraft, and Pagan Spirituality, 2005, Shaw Books - WaterBrook Press, 12265 Oracle Blvd., Ste. 200, Colorado Springs, CO 80921, USA.

Waddell, L. A.; The British Edda, 1930, Christian Book Club, P.O. Box 216, Hawthorne, California, 90250, USA.

Waterson, Barbara; Gods of Ancient Egypt, 1999, Bramley Books, Ltd., Godalming Business Centre, Wooksack Way, Godalming, Surrey, GU7 1XW, England.

# Index

13-tiered Pyramid, 510
144,000 Witnesses, 73, 74, 86, 300, 480, 509, 633, 644
   as sheep with opened eyes, 444
   Dan not counted, 223
   equal number of days in one Baktun, 638
   none from Tribe of Dan in, 633
   to preach during Great Tribulation, 651
   to preach during Tribulation, 645
   will preach Word of God, 288
17th of Tammuz, 676
2009 Nobel Peace Prize
   Awarded to Obama, 398
2017 AD, 90
3rd of Tammuz, 323
9th of Av, 676
   comet hit Jupiter on, 87
   cursed day for Jews, 88
Aaron's Staff
   Branch of Jesse, 181
Abel, 220
   a shepherd, 219
abomination of desolation, 347, 492, 562
Abraham
   destroyed Nimrod's power, 658
   God's promises to him fulfilled?, 439
   was promised Isaac, 271
acrostic Psalms, 67
Acts of God, 607
Acts, Book of
   symbolic Servant Lamp, 28
Adam
   age at death, 226
   time between creation and sin, 226

Adam and Eve, 20, 25, 26, 97, 132, 134, 219, 226, 229, 230, 236, 245, 249, 255, 256, 257, 259, 294, 322, 342, 354, 355, 368, 649, 654, 722, 728, 734
Adamic Covenant, 354
Adolph Hitler
   foreshadowed in Alexander the Great, 392
   murdered millions of Jews, 392
Adonai
   meaning of, 63
Adonai Yahweh
   title for Christ, 345
   title for Yahshua, 428, 644
Afghanistan, 287, 404, 407, 440, 452
Africa, 44, 280, 354, 407, 410, 416, 417, 418, 420, 459, 662
   tied to Serpens and Draco, 637
Age of Aquarius, 221, 259, 638, 640
   tied to Mayan End Date, 650
Age of Leo, 221, 229, 256
age of materialism, 301
Age of Pisces
   tied to Church Age, 257
Age of Taurus, 255
Age of Virgo
   Adam created in, 221
Ahiezer, 283
Ahu Vinapu, 712
Al Aqsa Mosque, 562
Al Debaran
   symbol for Christ, 646
Al Ghoul, 656, 657, 662
Al Ghoul, star in Perseus, 655
Al Nitak, 150, 157, 310, 317, 547, 602, 673, 681, 714
   represents Great Pyramid, 646

tied to Great Pyramid, 224
tied to signs on Sept. 20, 2017 AD, 714
Al-Aqsa Mosque, 347, 406, 408
Alaska, 321, 322, 365, 676, 681
  America's symbolic Moon, 365
Aleph-Tav, 19
  symbol for Christ, 20
Alexander the Great
  forerunner to Adolph Hitler, 392
  symbolized by leopard, 392
Alien encounters, 549
aliens, 92
  did NOT build Great Pyramid, Teotihuacán, 683
Allah
  Babylonian Moon god, 454
  false Moon god, NOT Creator God, 344
All-Seeing Eye, 376, 510
All-Seeing Eye of God
  on US Great Seal, 376
Alpha and Omega, 83, 638
  prophetic term for Christ, 5
Alpha and the Omega, 83, 205
  describes Yahshua's purpose, 19
Alpha Draconius, 158
alphabetic acrostics, 66
altar of burnt offering, 181
altar of incense, 186
Altar of Pergamum
  Obama's visit to, 398
altars
  of twelve stones, 108
Amen, 45
America
  and Diaspora, 351
  moral decay in, 388
  synonymous with freedom, 374
  to be reckoned as Ephraim, 359
American Civil War, 416, 417
American Freemasonry, 413
  infiltrated by Illuminati in 1800's, 414
American Masonry, 414
American Revolution, 252
  Illuminati involvement in, 414
Americans
  lazy from luxury, 301
  living under false security, 411

  punished for condoning sin, 369
Amun-Ra
  god of Heliopolis, 110
Anakim, 620, 649, *Also See* Nephilim
  inhabited Promised Land prior to Israelite Conquest, 620
  Nephilim who survived Noah's Flood, 24
Ancient Egyptian priests
  deceived idolaters, 199
Ancient Egyptians
  partly understood Great Pyramid's message, 195
Ancient Egyptians, 150
Andromeda, 615
  meaning behind, 656
  signifies trapped sinners enslaved by sin, 615
  symbol for people bound to Law, 615
angel
  to preach during Tribulation, 645
  visited George Washington, 415
Anglican Church. *See* Church of England
  presided over by British Crown, 461
Anglo-Saxons, 353
  **not** superior to other people groups, 274
Ann Kendall, 638
anointing oil
  used to anoint Yahshua, 472
Antechamber
  3 ceiling stones, 139
  in Book of the Dead, 197
  in the Great Pyramid, 141, 147, 175, 182, 184, 186, 187, 189, 197, 200, 202
  interior measurements of, 187
  power dampening device?, 165
  represents Great Tribulation, 191
  represents Holy Place, 186
  represents three steps to salvation, 187
  stone slabs in, 184
  tied to Christ's judgment and forgiveness, 194
  tied to Holy Place and Tribulation, 184

# Index

Antechamber in the Great Pyramid, 89, 106, 112, 116, 129, 139, 140, 304, 309, 310, 311, 317, 322, 323, 325, 329, 338, 340, 341, 546, 547, 591
   52 PI = One Solar Year, 305
   leads to King's Chamber, 138
   targets certain dates, 306
   tied to Daniel's Seventieth Week, 305
   tied to Tribulation period, 140
Antechamber in the Great Pyramid:, 314
antediluvian architecture
   depicted the heavens on Earth, 269
antediluvian knowledge, 116
antediluvian Solar Year
   only 364 days, 112
antediluvians
   built Pillar of Enoch and Sphinx at Giza, 229
   depicted in Book of 1 Enoch, 382
   incredible architects, 217
   knew of the Star Gospel, 217
   stronger,smarter,healthier, 219
   who built the Old World pyramids, 618
Anthony Sherman, 415
Anti Peace Sign, 323
   forms trident symbol, 652
Antichrist, 4, 7, 27, 31, 34, 36, 40, 55, 68, 70, 73, 76, 77, 78, 79, 80, 82, 85, 86, 90, 134, 156, 157, 160, 186, 190, 223, 266, 267, 270, 273, 284, 285, 287, 288, 321, 326, 327, 328, 329, 332, 333, 335, 342, 343, 344, 346, 347, 349, 356, 364, 391, 394, 396, 398, 400, 404, 406, 407, 408, 410, 412, 417, 418, 419, 420, 426, 427, 428, 432, 439, 440, 443, 444, 447, 450, 451, 453, 458, 459, 460, 462, 464, 466, 480, 481, 485, 486, 490, 491, 492, 493, 494, 495, 507, 509, 517, 518, 526, 531, 534, 536, 537, 547, 549, 550, 551, 552, 561, 562, 593, 599, 601, 602, 632, 635, 637, 642, 644, 648, 650, 651, 655, 657, 658, 662, 669, 670, 678, 682, 692, 730, 736, 737
   armeis vanquished by Christ, 254
   armies to invade USA and Israel, 713
   as an abomination, 347
   as enforcer of one world religion, 345
   as viewed by New Agers, 630
   as Worthless Shepherd in prophecy, 391
   connection to number 666, 669
   could be Prince Charles, 495
   defeat of, 662
   descendent of King David?, 439
   destroyed, 637
   held back by Holy Spirit, 342
   how to identify, 343
   imposter mimicking Christ, 471
   in dark mimicry of Christ, 467
   in Perseus Prophecy, 664
   in the Star Gospel, 496, 497, 499, 503, 504, 505
   may attack USA, 420
   may be from Tribe of Dan, 633
   may be Prince Charles, 635
   of Merovingian bloodline?, 250
   rise to power heralded by heavenly signs, 650
   symbolized by left- horn of Taurus, 155
   the false god of New Age Spirituality, 630
   the false messiah expected by false religions, 632
   tied to Medusa's severed head, 658
   tied to Scorpio, 223
   to be of Nephilim or Anakim blood, 491
   to invade Jerusalem, 287
   to perform false miracles, 490
   will act like Antiochus Epiphanes, 493
   will attempt to control America, 432
   will deny deity of God and His Son, 34
   will mimic true Christ, 486
   will proclaim to be God, 344
Antichrist's armies, 90
Anti-Christian sentiments, 134, 168, 345, 609
   in Cmmunism, 299
antichrists, 343
   types of, 344
Antiochus Epiphanes, 492

Anti-Peace Sign, 339, 616, 650, 652, 654, 708
  forms Chanukiah on Dec. 21st, 2012, 652
  marked by four Zodiac signs on Zodiacal Wheel, 650
  marked by planets on 12-21-2012, 650
  on Mayan End Date, 650
Anti-Semitism, xvi, 49, 52, 272, 609
  incorrectly taught by British Israelites, 278
Anwar Sadat, 58
apostasy
  depicted by Taurus, 156
  the Last Day rebellion, 342
Apostate Christians
  will be left behind, 300
Apostate Church, 250
Apostate Churches, 658
apostle
  thirteenth, 271
Apostle John, 506
  honored by Freemasons, 510
  possibly resurrected after Yahshua was, 510
apostles, 271, *Also See* names of individual apostles
  Paul as one of the 12, 260
  were Jews, 473
April 4th, 2015
  Passover signs on, 709
April 5th
  date Easter Island discovered on, 678
April 5th, 2011, 679
  when 2011 begins per Jewish Sacred Calendar, 678
April 5th, 2015
  Easter signs on, 709
Aquarius, 215, 217, 220, 221, 222, 225, 228, 241, 255, 294, 376, 573, 592, 593, 637, 656, 669, 702, 712, 724, 726, 727, 730
  location of Helix Nebula known as Eye of God, 376
  tied to face of Sphinx, 221
Aquila, 388
  eagle star sign near Scorpio, 283
  on horizon at dawn on Maya world end date, 633

Aquila the Eagle
  as wounded eagle, 428
  symbol for Ephraim, 635
  symbol for USA, 426, 429
  tied to Sagitta the Arrow, 426
Arab hostility, 49
Arab legends, 123
Arab nations
  have largest oil reserves, 454
Arab Terrorists, 454
Arabs, 53
  control world's oil wealth, 453
  will serve Yahweh, 287
  will submit to Christ, 440
Aramaic
  spoken today by Assyrians, 390
Archer King
  symbol for Yahshua, 643
Aries
  as Atonement Sacrifice, 496, 498, 502, 503
  as Democracy with Freedom of Religion, 503
  as symbol for Israel, 502
  at Esna, 213
  connected to Khnum, 211
  in symbol for Neith, 211
  signifies Christ as Passover Lamb, 684
Ark of the Covenant, 177
  allegory for Christ, 179
  built with same cubit as Great Pyramid?, 111
  Cherubim on, 259
  decorated with Cherubim, 256
  dimensions of, 180
  measured in Sacred Cubits, 195
  symbol for Christ, 180
  symbol of resurrection and everlasting life, 201
  tied to coffer in King's Chamber, 309
Ark, of Noah, 95
Armageddon, 39, 154, 286, 287, 644, 656
  as valley of Megiddo, 90
  Battle of, 432
  Battle represented by Antechamber, 191
  Christ to win battle, 441
  two battles of, 238

# Index

where One Horned Ram is victorious, 445
Armageddon, Battle of, 644
arrow
  of Ephraim, 427
arrows
  tied to Sagitta, 429
Artaxerxes, 326
Arthurian legends
  meant to deceive, 489
  quasi-Christian allegories, 488
Meshech, 407
Ascending Passage, 170
  a narrow path to salvation, 125
  in Book of the Dead, 197
  symbol of Mosaic Law, 128
Ascension, 508, 565, 566
Asenath, 497
  means "Follower of Neith", 211
Asia, 44
  tied to Draco, 637
Asia Minor, 31, 276, 397, 407, 455
  seven churches of, 516
Assyria, 277
  in prophecy, 286, 351
  modern descendents of, 390
Assyria, Kingdom of, 390
Assyrians, 390
  god Asshur symbolized by eagle, 266
Astrology, 617, 655
astronomical observatory, 107
Athena
  as Eve, 658
Atonement, Day of, 727
Aubrey circle, 135
August 21st, 2017
  Solar Eclipse on, 712
Auriga
  as Christ, 152
  Christ as Chastiser of Lost Sheep, 497
  signifies Christ as wayward goat shepherd, 684
Australia, 404
Austria, 489
Autumn Feasts of Israel, 335, 336, 337, 339
Avi Ben Mordecai, 15, 60
Azazel, 158, 658
Azazel goat, 56, 497

Aztecs, 618, 619, 624, 638
  human sacrifice among, 618
Baalbek, 712
Babylon the Great, 86, 87, 239, 266, 453, 456, 457, 458, 462, 490
  as Muslim stronghold, 386
  centered in Rome, 460
  could be Rome, 457
  fire sent to destroy, 412
  identity of, 453
  is a city that rules over nations, 460
  linked to several cities, 466
  partly defeated by Gospel of the Kingdom, 644
  tied to London, 461
  to fall in 2017 AD?, 86
Babylon, Ancient, 266, 351, 389
  compared to United Kingdom, 389
Babylon, modern
  rich in oil, 453
Babylonian Captivity
  fate of Jews after, 277
Babylonians
  built step pyramids as sacred observatories, 618
  worshipped the heavens, 617
Baktun 13
  Mayan date for December 21st, 2012, 617, 638
bald eagle, 387, 388
Bald Eagle, 284, 429, 446
  symbol of USA, 282
Bank of London, 395
baptism, 180, 724
Barack Obama, 319, 398, 493, 494
  forerunner to Antichrist, 495
  speeches in Berlin, 398
  support of Gay Agenda, 398
Barnabus, Epistle of, 242
barren woman, 75
Battle of Armageddon, 74, 89, 234, 239, 311, 322, 340, 408, 410, 411, 412, 419, 428, 437, 444, 445, 531, 534, 548, 554, 557, 563, 564, 565, 570, 575, 591, 598, 602, *See* Armageddon
  possibly begins in 2014, 682
bear
  symbol for Russia, 391

Beast Figure, 502
Beast from the Earth, 456
   corrupt Democratic States, 501, 502, 503, 504, 505
   partly represents Islam and Western dependence on Arab oil, 455
Beast from the Sea, 155, 266, 456, 457, 458, 467
   as the United Kingdom, 462
   composite beast, 394
   confederation of nations led by Antichrist, 450
   connected to Red Dragon of Wales, 464
   connected to United Nations, 393
   depicted by Cetus, 498
   depicted by Taurus, 646
   identity of its horns, 458
   meaning of seven heads and ten horns, 460
   signifies international commerce, 459
   symbol for English-led Europe, 401
   symbol of Antichrist's kingdom, 490
   tied to Great Britain, 461, 494
   tied to Hydra and Cetus, 499, 501, 503, 504, 505
   tied to Prince Charles, 491
   tied to Scarlet Beast and Red Dragon, 615
   tied to seven kings, 494
   tied to the sign of Taurus, 395
   tied to Totalitarian governments, 501
   worshiped as god during Great Tribulation, 455
Beast with Ten Horns
   signifies Roman Empire, 504
Beast, fourth
   had iron teeth alluding to Rome, 393
Beasts
   n Revelation 13, 496
Beginning and the End, 83, 205, 717
   at Giza on Oct. 6, 2017 AD, 714
   prophetic term for Christ, 5
beheading, 399, 456
believers
   seen as spiritually defective by Neo-Pagans, 631
beloved disciple
   identity must be secret, 481
   loved Yahshua, could not betray, 481
   possible author of Fourth Gospel, 478
   still alive?, 480
Beloved Disciple
   identity of, 505, 506, 507, 509
ben-ben stone, 110
Benjamin Franklin, 387, 388
Bent Pyramid, 91, 99, 103
Berlin, 398
Beta Israel, 356
Betelgeuse
   symbol for Christ, 646
Bethany
   rich suburb of Jerusalem, 473
   Yahshua anointed there, 472
Bethlehem
   and Christ Angle, 172
   at Christ's Birth, 614
   tied to Sirius, 378
Bible
   encoded with menorah patterns, 18
   filled with hidden messages, 3
   revealed in Star Gospel, 613
   symbolized in Holy Place, 187
Bible Code, 236
Bible Code Key, 13, 14
   in the Great Pyramid, 170
Bible Code obelisk
   same as a pyramid?, 13
Bible Code prophecies, 12
Bible Codes, 3, 7, 10, 11, 12, 13, 14, 17, 735
   proof of the God who wrote them, 11, 14
biblical chronology, 230
biblical history
   alluded to in Grail Romances, 489
Big Dipper. See Ursa Major
Bilhah
   Dan's mother - a slave, 283
Bill Cooper, 353
birds of prey
   as sinister symbols, 444
birth of Israel, 94, 331
black eagle
   symbol for France, Germany, and Ancient Rome, 394
Black Magic
   re-emerged after Flood, 272
Black Sea

# Index

Israelites settled near, 276
Blitzkrieg, 393
Blood Covenant, 130, 183, 471
   Great Pyramid as Covenant pillar, 193
   promise of mercy, 425
   with Christ, 66
Blood Moon, 310, 314, 317, 321, 322, 405, 539, 544, 565, 569, 653, 681, 682, 688, 692, 693, 701, 704, 709, 719
   of June 2011, 693
   on 12-21-2010, 681
Blood Moon Tetrad, 310, 539, 544, 682, 699, 700, 701
Blood Moon Triad
   of 2011 and 2018, 719
   of 2018, 717
Blood Moon Triad of 2011, 679
Blood Moons, 694
   of 2014 - 2015, 325
   of 2014 and 2015, 682
Blood of Christ
   depicted by Eridanus, 154
bloodline
   of Christ, 346
Body of Christ, 89
   signified by Two House Church, 187
Book of 1 Enoch, 8, 15, 35, 37, 93, 94, 107, 109, 112, 133, 158, 231, 245, 249, 250, 251, 288, 334, 383, 422, 433, 435, 436, 443, 445, 446, 487, 489, 549, 598, 682, 706, 734
   Noah and sons seen as bulls, 382
Book of Jasher, 8, 93, 95, 195, 489, 734
Book of Jubilees, 8, 93, 107, 219, 271, 734
Book of Life, 71, 237, 337, 339, 340, 424, 458
Book of Revelation
   as last book of Bible, 205
   Chapter 22 tied to Hebrew letter Tav, 205
   Chapters 11 - 18 mirror events surrounding the Great Tribulation?, 84
   encoded by Hebrew alphabet, 6
   mentions number 7 more than any other Bible book, 383
   tied to Star Gospel, 641
Book of the Dead
   contained magical incantations, 196
   for living souls facing death, 197
   for the living!, 196
   tied to Great Pyramid, 195
   was mixed with spiritual truth and error, 195
Book of the Heavenly Luminaries, 107
Bootes, 636
   at Esna, 213
born-again believers, 39, 58, 75, 627, 667, 717
Born-again believers, 99
Branch of Jesse, 81
Bread of Life
   depicted by Taurus, 153
   Yahshua as, 310
Bride
   as the Bride of Christ, 20, 24, 35, 70, 75, 130, 131, 161, 265, 306, 396, 470, 492, 520, 521, 523, 524, 528, 529, 530, 532, 534, 552, 553, 565, 567, 571, 573, 575, 576, 577, 579, 580, 582, 584, 587, 589, 591, 602, 615, 637, 656, 658, 666, 667, 668, 669, 671, 672, 673, 678, 679,e681, 686, 692, 702, 704, 717, 725
Bride of Christ, 71, 161, 498, 499, 658, 697, 701, 715, See also Church of Philadelphia
   comes from Protestant Churches, 501
   given dominion over the Earth, 396
   signified by Woman Clothed with Sun, 614
   symbolized by Virgo, 496
   Uranus as symbol of, 666
Bridegroom, 524, 528, 529, 532, 553, 584, 589, 591, 610, 671, 678, 679
Brit Chadashah, 535
British Coat of Arms, 450, 464
   has sinister unicorn on it, 450
   symbols in it used in Revelation, 490
British Commonwealth, 280, 353, 386, 394, 494, 495
   British Empire in disguise, 407
   modern British Empire, 461

British Commonwealth Nations, 273, 279, 280
British Crown, 395
  part of modern British Empire, 461
British Empire, 366, 386
  connected to Ancient Babylon, 389
  still exists as British Commonwealth, 407
British Israel
  evil version of Israel, 450
British Israelism, 109, 274, 278, 354, 449
  erroneous doctrine, 274
  erroneously teaches Anti-Semitism, 279
British Israelites, 449
British Monarchy, 461, 494
British Royalty, 273, 354, 395
  Antichrist may be from, 635
  centered in London, 461
  connected to Judah?, 284
  descended from Habsburg Dynasty, 489
  in prophecy, 450
  related to Christ?, 490
  tied to Tribe of Dan and Joseph?, 490
Bronze Sea
  symbol of baptism, 180
Brussels, Belgium
  capital of EU, 494
Buddhists
  as antichrists, 344
bull
  tied to Cherubim, 256
bull fights
  symbol of End Time war, 693
bulls, 155
Cain, 93, 219, 220, 284, 487, 488, 549, 722, 724
  a farmer, 219
  built city, 219
Cainan
  13th patriarch, 271
  one good, one evil, 450
  reintroduced Astrology after Flood, 437
Cairo, 118
  built with stones from pyramids Giza, 104

Caleb, 24
calendar
  Olmec and Maya shared same, 617
California Wildfires 2007, 404
Caliphate, 386
Camelot
  allegory for Kingdom of God, 489
Camp of Israel
  corresponds to Great Pyramid, 182
Canaan, 88
  cursed by Noah, 352
  overrun with giants, 24
Canada, 404, 410
Canis Major, 158
  tied to Promised Land, 378
Canis Minor
  tied to Israelites at Mount Sinai, 378
Capricorn, 388
capstone, 70, 71, 113
  as Yahshua, 69, 81, 121, 168
  missing from Great Pyramid, 105, 110
  of Great Pyramid, 194
  signifies Christ, 66
carpenter
  as derogatory label, 469
  not poor, 469
carpenter's son, 468
Cassander, 452
Cassiopeia
  sybol of Bride of Christ, 615
Catching Away, 566
  or Rapture, 498
Caucasian genocide
  by immigration, 401
Caucasians
  descended from Japheth and Shem, 353
  **not** superior, 272
Caucasus Mountains, 275
Causeways
  at Giza, 136, 138, 215
ceiling stones
  in relation to Tabernacle, 202
  signify heaven in Great Pyramid, 139
  twelve signify Zodiac, 139
celestial marker
  in Great Sphinx, 215
Celestial Meridians, 681
celestial signs, 90, 612

# Index

celestial sphere, 141
Celtic Royalty
  married Princess of Judah?, 284
centaur. *See also:* Sagittarius, Centaurus
  depicted by Centaurus, 217
  in Zodiac, 643
  symbol for Christ, 426
  tied to Cherubim, 255
Centaurus, 217, 633, 643
Central Lunar Eclipses
  marking Tribulation period, 717
Cepheus
  signifies Yahshua coming in judgment of apostates, 500
  symbol of Yahshua as King of kings, 615
Cetus
  as Beast from Sea, 498
  signifies Totalitarian Governments, 498, 499, 501, 502, 503
  Star symbol for Beast out of Sea, 615
  symbol for Beast from the Sea, 713
Chaim Weizmann, 41
champion of Israel, 359
Chanukah, xv, 17, 25, 27, 71, 190, 317, 492, 493, 572, 574, 576, 577, 579, 589, 590, 629, 652, 727
  prophetic application of, 492
  tied to Christ's birth, 137
Chanukah, 546
Chanukiah, 25, 27, 28, 71, 134, 190, 226, 260, 330, 492, 652
  depicts reversal of history, 226
  in heaven on Dec. 21st, 2012, 652
  suggested in Grand Gallery, 190
  symbol of victory over evil though Christ, 492
Chanukiah pattern, 27, 61, 190
Charlemagne, 344, 398, 399
  aka Charles the Great, 399
  beheaded victims, 399
  first Holy Roman Emperor, 402
Charles
  name of seven Holy Roman Emperors, 494
Charles Albert of Belgium, 494
Charles the Great. *See* Charlemagne
Charles Thomson, 431

Cherubim
  as a unicorn tied to Christ, 443
  bodies like oxen, or centaurs, 255
  eagle's face replaces scorpion/serpent, 635
  faces of, 254
  horns, or hands of, 155
  mark Age of Leo, 259
  ox or bull-like, 446
  right hand and horn tied to Christ, 256
  wings mark Ages, 259
chief cornerstone, 168
Chief Cornerstone, 81, 169
  term for Christ, 194
children of God, 355, 449
China, 44, 281, 299, 302, 353, 371, 410, 417, 418, 421, 430, 442, 452, 460, 538, 728
chosen people, 20, 27, 41, 42, 52, 274, *Also See* Israel
chosen sheep, 445
Christ Angle, 131, 170, 171, 172
  formed on Sept. 20th.2017, 713
Christ Figure, 502
Christ's birth, 25
Christ's Crown
  many nations vie for it before the end, 637
Christ's Crown of Glory, 85
Christ's Resurrection, 44
Christian martyrdom, 457
Christian values
  Americans reminded of after 9-11, 372
Christianity
  opposition to, 345
  viewed as religion of fools, 453
Christians, xviii, 2, 16, 31, 33, 34, 42, 48, 50, 67, 90, 101, 156, 168, 242, 252, 261, 270, 271, 273, 274, 287, 299, 300, 333, 336, 344, 357, 367, 368, 384, 389, 390, 392, 397, 404, 414, 421, 434, 443, 446, 454, 458, 466, 467, 479, 485, 494, 512, 513, 550, 552, 555, 559, 560, 561, 568, 584, 593, 595, 601, 608, 609, 610
  called to witness to the lost, 345
Christmas, 399, 572, 587, 589, 590
Christopher Columbus, 88

Christopher Dunn, 162
Church Age, 43, 44
  depicted by Pleiades, 647
  ended in 1999, 661
  seen in Grand Gallery, 191
  tied to Age of Pisces, 257
Church Age,
  ends in 2010 AD?, 337
Church in America, 359
Church of England, 251, 252, See Anglican Church
  connected to End Time Beasts, 499
Church of Latter Day Saints, 415
Church of Pergamum, 397
Church of Philadelphia, 363, 521, 698, See also Bride of Christ
  given dominion over the Earth, 396
  keeps Yahshua's commandment to love, 516
  promised protection from Time of Trial, 498
cities of refuge
  during Great Tribulation, 498
City of the Sun, 400
civil rights
  in America, 432
civil war
  in America during Tribulation, 432
Coat of Arms
  British, 490
  featuring black eagle, 394
  for Prince Charles, 464
  of Israel, 17
  or Great Seal of USA, 429
  unicorn on Scottish and British versions, 451
Coffer
  empty as symbol of risen Christ, 180
  same dimensions as Ark, 180
  symbol of Christ's resurrection, 138
  symbol of Enoch's translation, 138
  symbol of resurrection and everlasting life, 201
  symbol of Risen Christ, 181
Coma
  symbol for Yahshua, the Desired Son, 614
Coma Berenices, 572, 575, 576, 614
comet, 89

Comet Brewington, 572, 576
Comet Encke, 572, 576, 585, 698
Comet Hale-Bopp, 656, 660, 662
Comet Holmes, 657, 662
Comet Hyakutake, 656, 662
Comet ISON, 316, 323, 571, 572, 573, 574, 575, 576, 577, 579, 580, 584, 585, 587, 589, 590, 606, 696, 697, 698, 699
Comet LINEAR, 572, 575, 576, 698
Comet Lovejoy, 571, 575, 576, 579, 587, 698
Comet McNaught, 661
Comet Shoemaker-Levy 9, 87, 89
comets, 655
  5-Comet heavenly sign of Autumn 2013, 316
  as signs, 91, 267, 538, 570, 571, 572, 573, 574, 575, 576, 577, 585, 589, 591, 592, 606, 615, 654, 655, 656, 657, 662
Commonwealth Nations, 504
  tied to Beast from the Sea, 504
Communion
  symbol of New Covenant, 467
Communism
  Anti-Christian, 299
Communist Death Camps, 458
Communist Russia
  collapse of, 393
  persecuted Jews and Christians, 392
Constantinople
  built on seven hills like Rome, 458
Constitution of the United States, 252
  civil liberties it grants are being undermined, 432
  tied to New Testament, 383
  twenty-seven amendments in, 383
contentment
  everywhere in Christ's Kingdom, 288
Continental Congress, 362
Coptic Christians, 400
corbelled cornice
  in Queen's Chamber, 142
Corona Borealis, 637
  signifies Crown of Christ, 499
Counterfeit Christianity, 631
counterfeit miracles, 632

# Index

Court of the Gentiles, 182
Covenant, 386
Covenant blessings, 355
Covenant pillar, 181
   Great Pyramid as, 109, 193, 194
Creation
   Fourth Great Day of, 228
   Seven Days of, 256
   Six Days of, 230
   Sixth Day of, 229
   Sixth Great Day of, 228
Cross
   like Hebrew letter Tav, 206
   symbol of Christ's perfect sacrifice, 184
cross within a circle, 637
   symbol for Sun, 637
Crown of Christ
   seen in Corona Borealis, 499
crude oil
   symbol of iniquity, 454
   symbol of sin, 454
Crustal Displacement, 349, 525, 567, 590, 706
cubic volume, 180
Cup of Redemption
   Orion as, 153
Cush, 207, 410
   ancestor of Negroid people, 352
Cushites, 352
Cuzco, 103
Cygnus the Swan, 429
Dahshur, 91, 99
Damascus, 261, 354, 400, 402
Daniel, 69
   foretold coming of Antichrist, 34, 346
   Prophecy of Seventy Weeks, 76
   USA in dream vision, 389
*Daniel 7*, 389, 391, 392, 393, 394, 396, 406, 422, 491
Daniel 9, 34, 55, 69, 190, 314, 326, 327, 328, 329, 347, 410, 491
Daniel W. Matson, 657
Daniel's four beasts
   re-appear in Book of Revelation, 394
Daniel's Four Beasts, 504
Daniel's sevens
   can be weeks, or *years*, 326
Daniel's Seventiy Weeks
   past and future application!, 326
Daniel's Seventy Weeks, 135, 187, 190, 310, 311, 326, 331, 332, 334, 410, 533, 538, 601, 639
   62 weeks are 62 years, from 1948 to 2010, 328
   70 Years from 1948 to 2018, 329
   applied to the Reformation, 333
   as a 77-year season of repentance and judgment, 332
   first fulfillment ended in 34 AD, 327
   gives prophetic end date, 325
   tied to Enoch's Seventy Generations, 335
   two equations of Messiah's Coming, 330
Danites, 283
dark cloud
   in Washington's vision, 418
Darwinism, 299
David Barton, 414
David Ben Gurion, 52
David's royal lineage
   continued through Zedekiah's daughters, 441
   has it survived to modern times?, 441
   linked to British Royalty?, 450
David's Throne
   coveted by Antichrist?, 439
   Yahshua sits upon the heavenly version, 440
David's Throne
   may still exist on Earth, 441
Day of Atonement, 56, 60, 336, 338, 339
   Auriga's goats tied to, 497
   in 3 BC, at Christ's Birth, 614
Day of the Lord, 7, 15, 229, 242, 285, 630
   already here!, 231
   can know year and season of, 297
   chronological events during, 237
   conclusion of, 239
   length of, 233
   Peter saw it as 1,000 years long, 241
   preceded by rebellion, 342
   revealed in Book of Revelation, 614
   same as Lord's Day, 235
   spoken of by Zechariah, 454
   the 13th Great Day since Creation, 259

Days of Awe, 336, 337, 339
  revelation shown in 2004, 340
Dead Sea Scrolls
  astronomy mentioned in, 240
  contained Book of 1 Enoch, 251
December 21st, 2010, 653, 664, 681, 686, 692, 694, 708
  Blood Moon of, 323
  Lunar Eclipse in Orion, 681
December 21st, 2012, 315, 611, 617, 640, 709
  Anti-Peace Sign in heavens on, 650
  Chanukiah in heaven, 652
  end of Mayan Fifth Sun, 619, 639
  Four Horsemen tied to, 612
  marks destruction of world by fires and earthquakes, 624
  tied to first Four Seal Judgments, 546
Declaration of Independence, 252
Dedan, 410
Demetrius, 36
Democracy, 413
Democratic Republic, 501
demons, 3
  cast out of Mary Magdalene, 474
Dendera Zodiac, 158, 160, 643
Descending Passage, 125, 183
  in Book of the Dead, 197
Desert Tabernacle, 141, 177, 180
  28 linen curtains in, 189
  48 boards in walls, 201
  built with same cubit as Great Pyramid?, 111
  conveys hidden knowledge, 142
  copy of heavenly Tabernacle, 178
  Courtyard tied to Grand Gallery, 183, 187
  decorated with Cherubim, 256
  divine design, 102
  filled with hidden knowledge, 199
  measured in Sacred Cubits, 195
  Moses knew its symbolic meaning, 195
  shows Path to Salvation, 191
  structure corresponds to Great Pyramid, 181
  threefold structure of, 162
  tied to Great Pyramid, 189
  tied to great Pyramid via Moses?, 195

Destroyer
  Satan as, 413
Deuteronomy
  theme of, 23
Deuteronomy Psalms, 40, 42, 45
  filled with Halleluyahs, 45
Diaspora, 351
Diotrephes, 36
divine judgment
  Libra as symbol of, 283
Divine Judgment
  on America, 364
Divine Potter
  Yahweh and Khnum both described as, 211
Djed Pillar, 143
Djed Pillar amulet, 143
Djed Pillars
  symbolic backbone of Osiris, 143
DNA strand, 173
Dome of the Rock, 343
Draco, 158, 160, 283, 589, 636
  depicts Red Dragon, 589
  tied to Asia and Russia, 637
  tied to Red Dragon, 499, 502, 503
  tied to Red Dragon in Revelation, 615
Dragon, 502, See Draco
  as symbol for Satan, 499, 503, 505
Dream, prophetic, 573
drought
  sent in judgment, 291, 369, 370, 557, 607
dung beetle
  as Scarab sacred to Egyptians, 214
E. Raymond Capt, 100, 284
eagle, 385, 387
  as symbol for Ephraim, 635
  as symbol for evil people, 445
  as symbol for USA, 282, 362, 406, 420
  as symbol's of God's protection, 446
  red or black for Danites, 284
  symbol for Tribe of Dan, 282
  wounded, 428
Eagle
  symbol of USA in prophecy, 390
Eagle Nebula, 633
  symbol for Ephraim, 430, 635
Eagle's wings

# Index

signify USA, 504
Eagle's Wings
  represents USA, 390
Earth
  radius of in Pyramid Inches, 119
Earth's magnetic field
  used to power ancient technology, 96
Earth's mean distance from the Moon
  reflected in Great Pyramid, 111
earthquakes
  predicted at world end., 624
Easter, 91, 103, 306, 538, 539, 565, 569, 672, 676, 678, 679, 681, 686, 694, 709
Easter Island, 103, 340, 672, 676, 678, 679, 681, 686, 694, 709, 712, 715
  discovered on April 5th, 1722, 230
  Lunar Eclipse over, on 2015 AD, 709
  Sethite time marker, 230, 323, 339
  stone statues made by Sethites?, 712
  tied to End Time Events, 710
  tied to Gospel in the Stars, 676
Eastern philosophies, 697
Ecuador artifacts, 377
  of Star Gazers, 380
  set of 13 cups depict Canis Minor and Major, and Orion, 377
  tied to US Great Seal, 376
Ecuador Artifacts, 510
Ecumenical Movement, 253, 347, 395, 461, 492, 493, 599
  helps form One World Religion, 497
  heretical teachings of, 253
  tied to Woman Riding Beast, 698
Edgar Cayce, 164, 210
Edom, Moab, and Ammon
  modern Kingdom of Jordan, 408
Egypt, 386
  as Seir, 440
Egyptian god On, 194
Egyptian Muslim Brotherhood, 52
Egyptian tombs
  Book of the Dead in, 195
Egyptian wisdom
  known to Moses and Joseph, 110
El Debaran
  red star represents Red Pyramid, 646

elect lady, 35
electrical energy
  in Great Pyramid?, 164
Elijah, 506
  constructed altar of 12 stones, 108
  mentioned in Epistle of James, 31
Emperor Haile Selassia, 356
end of the world, 226, 242, 435, 611, 617
  Mayan date for, 638
  nearness of, 357
End of the World, 611
End Time Beast, 396, 458, 459, 460
End Time Beasts, 497
  revealed in Book of Revelation, 496
End Time plagues, 632
End Time prophecies
  fulfillment of, 660
  in celestial signs, 612
End Times, 4
England, 387, 388
English
  new international language, 281
English Civil War, 252
English Commonwealth
  erroneously tied to Ephraim, 279
Enlightenment period, 413, 613
  affect on American politics, 414
Enoch, 334, 506, 712
  described Pole Shift, 706
  knew the future, 683
Enoch Circle because that solar number reference may also refer to the antediluvian patriarch Enoch, who was translated XE "translated" into Heaven without seeing death during his 365th year of mortal existence (Genesis 5 22-23). In regard to the Enoch Circle, it is interesting to note that a circle can signify a completed period of time, as well as the Sun's path, which can be seen as the Way of Yahweh. Interestingly, the Sun is also a symbol for Yahshua, Who was called, 309
Enoch the Sethite, 35, 92, 109, 654
  born in 3381 BC, 93
  designed Great Pyramid, 93, 94

taught Sacred Astronomy, 107
was translated, 93
Enoch, 7th antediluvian patriarch
   his lifespan as signature in Great Pyramid, 109
   one Cainite, the other Sethite, 488
   one good, one evil, 450
   Prophecy of 7000 Years, 245, 249
   Prophecy of the Seventy Generations, 334
   Prophecy of the Seventy Shepherds, 433
Enoch, Cain's son, 219
   evil Enoch of Freemasonry, 487
entertainment industry
   highly immoral, 373
environmental changes
   part of End Time plagues, 370
Ephraim, 80, 109, 270, 279, 281, 380, 385, 386, 387, 429, 656
   allied to Judah, 360
   as 13th Tribe of Israel, 385
   as white unicorn, 385
   linked to the USA, 450
   one of Two Houses of Israel in prophecy, 359
   symbol for Gentile believers, 635
   symbol for Gentile Church, 266
   tied to USA, 388
   to replace Tribe of Dan, 635
   united to Judah, 286
Epiphany, 590
epistles
   seven tied to Great Tribulation, 30
equidistant letter strings, 10
Eridanus constellation
   as symbol of baptism in Christ's blood, 152
   depicts Jordan River, and Blood of Christ, 154
   tied to various terrestrial rivers, 151
Eris. *See* Marduk
Esau
   lost birthright, 271
   symbol for Arabs, 658
Ethiopia, 407
   Book of 1 Enoch found there, 251
   part of Fertile Crescent, 410
Ethiopia, biblical
   likely ancient Nubia, 407

Ethiopian Book of Enoch, 15
Ethiopian Christians, 334
Ethiopian Jews, 354
etymology
   used to track Danite wanderings, 284
Euphrates River
   one border of Millennial Israel, 354
Euro dollar, 504
Europa
   goddess tied to Woman who rides the Beast, 395
Europe
   and Diaspora, 351
   Muslims in, 401
   saints in, 495
European Union, 453, 460, 504, 505
   as Beast from the Sea, 394, 459
   dominant force in United Nations, 393
   ties Taurus to Beast from the Sea, 395
   to become part of Antichrist's evil empire, 407
Evangelical Protestant Christianity
   despised under Socialist governments, 401
Eve
   as the giver of false wisdom., 658
   time between creation and sin, 226
everlasting life, 2, 4, 35, 73, 74, 99, 129, 131, 132, 134, 138, 141, 143, 144, 146, 147, 148, 152, 181, 186, 189, 191, 196, 197, 199, 201, 202, 287, 311, 424, 478, 480, 481, 508, 527, 550, 554, 577, 598
   Christ first to receive in resurrection, 508
   guaranteed to those who love Christ, 154
evil
   not eradicated until after Millennial Kingdom, 291
Evolution, 101, 343, 454, 741, 742
Evolution, Theory of
   undermines Biblical Truth, 342
Excalibur, 489
Exodus, 336
   and Christ Angle, 172
   theme of, 20
Exodus from Egypt, 404
Exodus Psalms, 41, 50

# Index

Exodus, Book of, 41
explosion
   caused damage in Great Pyramid?, 163
extreme weather
   sign of God's Judgment, 607, 610
Eye of Providence, 388
Ezra, 275, 277
Falashas, 356
Fall Equinox, 136
   current position of, 225
   Leo and Virgo highlight, 221
   signs in the heavens on, 713
   tied to Yahshua's birth, 137
Fallen Angels, 92, 94, 219, 220, 246, 254, 289, 334, 549, 649, *Also See* Watchers
   cast into abyss, 435
   did NOT build Great Pyramid, Teotihuacán, 683
   judged after seventy generations, 335
   tied to Scorpio, 223
false christs, 298
false messiah
   prophesied by false religions, 632
false messiahs, 298
False Prophet
   connected to Beast from the Earth, 455
   one world religion of, 497
fauns, 255
Feast of John the Baptist
   commemorated by Freemasons, 510
Feast of Tabernacles, 17, 290, 291, 338, 482, 523, 573, 686, 704, 717, 719, 727
   celebrated during Millennial Kingdom, 291
   celestial signs in 1996, 660
   celestial signs in 1997, 660
   in 2017 AD, 716
   in 3 BC, 614
   tied to Christ's Second Coming, 717
   tied to Yahshua's birth, 137
Feast of the Apostle John
   commemorated by Freemasons, 510
Feast of Trumpets, 235, 244, 307, 317, 336, 337, 533, 539, 546, 580, 584, 727
   Christ's birth around, 170
   in 3 BC, around Christ's birth, 614

Feast of Unleavened Bread, 565
   tied to the Exodus, 335
Feast of Weeks, 310, 328, 374, 726
Feasts of Israel
   are prophetic, 335
Federal Reserve System, 48
Fertile Crescent
   Israel at center of, 410
Fibonacci Spiral. *See* Golden Spiral
Fifth Age, 43, 45
fifth corbel, 134
Fifth Great Day, 43
Fifth Seal, 705
Fifth Sun, 639, *See* Mayan Fifth Sun
Fifth Trumpet, 649
fire
   world to be destroyed by, 616
fires
   predicted at world end., 624
First Advent, 25, 47, 81, 82, 134, 158, 171, 256, 310, 336, 440, 471, 480, 490, 510, 527, 546, 562, 563, 613, 643, 661, 726
   tied to Virgo, 717
First and the Last, 205
   and star in Centaurus, 217
   at Giza on Oct. 6, 2017 AD, 714
   prophetic term for Christ, 5
   Title for Christ in Isaiah & Revelation, 613
First Great Day of Creation, 637
First Rapture, 16, 74, 83, 156, 188, 314, 315, 316, 317, 323, 328, 329, 335, 337, 402, 437, 498, 513, 519, 522, 525, 531, 532, 536, 537, 538, 548, 553, 564, 566, 598, 602, 603, 629, 693, 701
   events before, 404
   timing of, 317
First Resurrection, 27, 74, 509, 615
   final stage at Last Trumpet, 422
   firstfruits of, 73
   in 3 stages, 138
   represented by Most Holy Place, 188
   separate from Rapture, 513
   those not included in to be judged, 424
   three stages of, 147
Firstfruit, 506
firstfruits, 39

Firstfruits, 307, 335
Firstfruits of the Resurrection, 78, 86, 506, 509
   Christ was first, 74
   Yahshua as, 508
Firstfruits Offering, 306, 374, 508
fishing boats
   luxuries in Israel, 242
five interior divisions
   in Great Pyramid & Tabernacle, 181
Five Wise Virgins, 396
   promised protection from Time of Trial, 498
Flinders Petrie, Sir William
   tried to discredit Piazzi Smyth's findings, 100
Foolish Virgins, 312, 498, 500, 509, 522, 528, 529, 530, 532, 536, 552, 576, 589
   repentant ones may form cities of refuge, 498
   tied to Woman Riding Beast, 698
forensic analysis
   of Sphinx, 206
forgiveness
   seventy-seven year season for, 331
forty-eight continental states
   symbol of starry heavens, 365
   tied to constellations, 365
Four Horsemen of the Apocalypse, 323, 616, 632, 641, 650, 654, 682, 708
   depicted by Heavenly Signs on Dec. 21st, 2012, 682
   on Zodiacal Wheel, 650
   tied to four Zodiac signs, 546
   tied to Mayan End Date, 306, 315
   tied to Mayan world-end, 612
Fourth Great Day, 11
Fourth Seal, 648
France
   connected to Germany, 401
Frankish Kingdoms, 504
Franks, 401
freedom
   hallmark of USA, 374
Freedom, 413
Freedom of Religion, 503

Freemasonry, 357, 413, 415, 431, 471, 485, 555, 738
   in America, 414
   possibly not all branches are evil today, 510
   practiced by George Washington, 415
Freemasons, 345
   not all are satanic, 510
   their Enoch is Cain's son, 487
   undermining Christianity, 485
French and Indian War, 387
Fukushima Nuclear Disaster, 371, 546
Full Moon
   symbol of the Church, 698
gabled ceiling
   above King's Chamber, 145
   above Queen's Chamber, 146
   symbol for heaven, 146
Gabriel, 452
Gadsden Flag, 384, 387, 388
galactic center, 633
Galactic Center, 696
Galactic Center of the Milky Way, 650
Garden of Eden, 230
Gay Agenda, 322, 398
   God's judgment against, 609
Gaza Strip, 54
Gemini
   connected to Yahshua as Naz-Seir or Nazarene, 379
   meaning of, 670
Genesis
   theme of, 20
Genesis 3:15, 497, 500, 502
   alluded to in Star Gospel, 497
Genesis Psalms, 41, 49, 50
genocide
   goal of Nephilim false gods, 619
Gentile Church
   symbolized by Taurus, 671
Gentile nations
   material wealth of, 455
Gentiles, 36
   believers among, 80
   given 70 year season of repentence, 331
   their Nations, 50

# Index

to be grafted into Israel, 273
geographical grid system, 118
George Washington
　391, 413, 414, 415, 416, 418, 419,
　　420, 423, 431, as Freemason, 510
　saw Americans rebelling against
　　Antichrist, 459
　saw America's deliverance from
　　annihilation, 421
　vision of America's future, 15, 391,
　　415, 418, 431
Georgia Guidestones, 399
Germany, 401
　connected to France, 401
　divided like Alexander's empire, 393
　signified by Bear, 504
　symbolized by leopard, 392
Geryon, 637
Giants, 491, 620
　in the New World, 620
　in the Promised Land, 620
　Nephilim who survived Noah's Flood,
　　24
Girdle Stones, 128
Giza, 118
　as navel of the world, 368
　center of Earth's land masses, 118
　located 30 degrees North, 215
　Sethite site before Flood, 95
　site layout similar to Teotihuacán, 622
Giza Plateau
　its underground passages, 210
Giza Pyramid Complex
　as Covenant pillars, 193
　as Orion clock, 223
　tells story of Christ, 216
Giza Pyramid Complex, 91, 95, 152,
　179, 193
　antediluvian power plant?, 164
　Navel of the World, 193
Giza Pyramid Complex, 206
Giza Pyramid Complex, 206
Giza Pyramid Complex
　in relation to Great Sphinx, 215
Giza Pyramid Complex, 223
Giza Pyramid Complex, 310
Giza Pyramid Complex, 547
Giza Pyramid Complex, 672
Giza Pyramid Complex

tied to signs on Sept. 20, 2017 AD,
　714
Giza Pyramids, 681, 715
　on September 20, 2017, 716
Glenn Beck, 384
Global Warming
　as End Time plague, 370
Glorious Land
　Israel in prophecy, 408
Glorious One
　Christ in prophecy, 409
goats
　symbol for unrepentant wicked, 444
God the Father, 29
God the Father's Will
　seen in heaven via the Star Gospel,
　　268
God's blessings
　given as reward for obedience, 373
God's Kingdom on Earth, 45
God's Sacred Calendar, 305
　used in Antechamber, 306
God's Word
　in Star Gospel, 612
God's Wrath, 16, 75, 78, 86, 121,
　154, 157, 234, 236, 266, 272, 306,
　338, 340, 512, 522, 525, 528, 531,
　533, 534, 554, 556, 557, 558, 572,
　575, 577, 590, 603, 605, 607, 632,
　639, 640, 645, 701, 708, 709, 725
　begins with Sixth Seal Pole Shift, 699
　no peace during, 517
　on the USA, 372
　only directed to the wicked, 511
Godhead, 27
Gog
　as a prince, 406, 407
Gog and Magog, Battle of
　begins Mid-Trib, leads to
　　Armageddon, 410
　connected to Daniel's battle between
　　Kings of North and South, 412
Golan Heights, 54
golden calves
　worshipped erroneously, 256
golden lampstand, 186
Golden Ratio
　used in King's Chamber, 114
Golden Ratio

in Great Pyramid, 114
Golden Ratio, 115
Golden Ratio, 116
Golden Ratio, 172
Golden Rectangle, 114, 115
Golden Section, 172, *See* Golden Ratio
  used in King's Chamber, 114
Golden Spiral, 114, 115
Golgotha, 154, 382
Gomer, 407
  Islamic southern half of former Soviet Union, 407
Good News
  Christians called to preach, 345
Gospel
  like unleavened bread, 336
  preached to world during Tribulation, 300
Gospel in the Stars, 1, 178, 241, 641
  48 constellations connected to 48 states, 367
  all about Yahshua, 683
  alluded to by Zechariah, 424
  antediluvian understanding of, 216
  concerning Tribe of Dan and Antichrist, 633
  connected to Book of Revelation, 614
  found on Ecuador artifacts, 377
  Great Pyramid tied to, 193
  heavenly witness, 3
  hidden in Book of Revelation, 612
  in Great Sphinx, 217
  in prophecy, 428
  meaning of Perseus, 655
  on Ecuador artifacts, 379
  Orion's meaning in, 622
  preserved in Zodiac, 151
  referred to in prophecy, 426
  renewed interest in Enlightenment period, 613
  reveals End Time Beasts, 496
  seen in Osiris and Orion correlation, 196
  shows God's goodness, 269
  symbols for End Time Beasts, 496, 502
  tied to Bible, 613
  tied to Book of Revelation, 383
  tied to God's written Word, 612

tied to the Great Pyramid and Great Sphinx, 220
  Wise Men knew of, 243
Gospel of John
  author not identified, 478
  identifies Mary of Bethany as anointer, 473
  written by Lazarus, or Mary?, 481
Gospel of Repentance, 188
Gospel of Salvation, 188
Gospel of the Kingdom, 188
  preached during Millennial Kingdom, 288
  preached during Tribulation, 644, 645
Grace, 25, 40, 105, 167, 236, 273, 615, 640
  Age of, 27, 147, 161
  Covenant of, 483
  Salvation by, 168
Graham Hancock, 221
Grail romances, 488
Grail Romances
  meant to deceive, 489
Grand Gallery, 106, 112, 124, 128, 129, 130, 131, 133, 134, 135, 136, 138, 139, 140, 141, 142, 144, 146, 147, 161, 163, 165, 166, 170, 182, 183, 184, 187, 189, 190, 191, 200, 202, 227, 302, 303, 304, 305, 325, 375, 438, 539, 622
  28 pairs of shafts in, 189
  28 shafts in, 135
  36 ceiling stones, 139
  a giant Chanukah menorah, 134
  an astronomical observatory?, 108
  connected to Daniel's 70 weeks, 133
  corresponds to Tabernacle Courtyard, 183
  giant Chanukah Menorah, 302
  hides prophetic dates, 310
  in Book of the Dead, 197
  marks Great Tribulation, 140
  represents freedom through Christ, 133
  represents Holy Place, 191
  tied to Chanukah menorah, 190
  tied to Christ's ministry, 194
  tied to Great Tribulation, 190
  tied to Tabernacle Courtyard, 187

# Index

granite coffer
  in Great Pyramid. *See* Coffer
granite plug, 129
  blocks Ascending passage, 128
  symbol of separation from God, 128
Great Altar of Pergamum, 396
Great Architect of the Universe
  as the Creator God, 413
Great Britain, 51, 386, 389, *See* also United Kingdom
  as One-Horned Goat, 490
  attached to Rome, 457
  colonized by Egyptians and Israelites?, 110
  established modern Israel, 359
  misidentified as Ephraim, 281
  promulgated British Israelism, 449
  seat of Antichrist's government destroyed?, 466
  sees itself as Joseph/Judah in prophecy, 450
  tied to Beast from Sea, 464
  tied to Manasseh, 279, 448
Great Day, 187, 226, 243, 254
  1000 years long, tied to Mayan Sun, 624
  of the Lord, 7
Great Flood, 26, 95, 250, 264, 267, 270, 290, 454
  cannibalism prior to, 620
  Great Pyramid built before. *See Also* Noah's Flood
  mentioned by Peter, 616
  occured in 2347 BC, 103
  Pole Shift during, 706
  work of Noah and Shem after, 264
Great Pyramid, 43, 91, 103, 337, 338, 706
  5 divisions in, 181
  a circle squared, 116, 119
  a prophetic witness, 330
  acoustical properties, 162
  advanced knowledge in, 116
  as collector of energy from sound vibrations, 165
  as heaven on Earth, 268
  as power generator, 164
  as power plant, 164
  as scientific wonder, 97
  as symbol of New Heaven, 141
  as temple to Yahweh, 162
  Bible Code Key?, 14
  built before Noah's Flood, 210
  built by Sethites, 93
  built in 2500 BC?, 302
  capstone of, 66
  Commemorates Yahshua as Redeemer, 172
  connected to Desert Tabernacle, 141
  connected to Sacred Astronomy, 108
  connected to Sun Pyramid, 622
  copy of heavenly Tabernacle, 194
  corresponds to Camp of Israel, 183
  degree of slope, 111
  described as altar in Isaiah, 192
  described by Herodotus, 96
  designed by Enoch, 94
  divinely designed as a puzzle, 94
  entrance, 123
  filled with hidden knowledge, 200
  five-fold construction corresponds to Taqbernacle, 181
  fivefold message, 106
  five-sided pyramidion, 105
  four shafts in, 150
  fulfills Isaiah's prophecy, 118
  giant altar, 193
  greater mass than Sun Pyramid, 622
  height of, 111, 113
  its hidden treasure, 123
  missing capstone, 169
  Moses knew its symbolic meaning, 195
  Navel of the World, 118
  no inscriptions in, 123, 162
  Northern Hemishpere in miniature, 172
  not a tomb, 99, 124
  not built by Pagans, 102
  on US Great Seal, 376
  over designed, 167
  parable in stone, 174
  points to year 1949, 39
  prophetic interior design of, 149
  prophetic measure of passages, 303
  prophetic measurements in, 175
  reflected length of Solar Year, 109
  reflects Solar Year, 104
  reveals prophetic dateline, 123
  Scriptures tied to design, 197

shows Earth's mean distance from Sun, 120
shows knowledge of Precession, 111
shows Path to Salvation, 191
shows possible date for Great Tribulation, 236
signifies repentant robber, 673
speaks with the Language of God, 98
stone construction of, 95
survived to testify about Christ, 174
symbol of heavenly Tabernacle, 179
symbol of Path to Salvation, 199
targeted by signs on Sept. 20, 2017 AD, 714
testimony agrees with Bible, 170
the Pillar of Enoch, 13
tied to Al Nitak, 224
tied to Al Nitak in Orion, 646
tied to Book of the Dead, 195, 197
tied to Desert Tabernacle, 191, 195
tied to Orion, 144
tied to Orion and Osiris, 196
tied to Tabernacle, 189
tied to USA, 382
tied to Zion and Orion, 678, 681
tied to Zodiac, 144
timeline within, 304
white outer covering depicts clothes of saints, 182

Great Pyramid Causeway
marks Summer Solstice, 136, 673

Great Seal of the United States, 388
displays Pyramid found in Ecuador, 375
not tied to Freemasonry, 431
tied to Aquila & Sagitta, 429
tied to Star Gospel, and Ephraim, 431

Great Sphinx, 91, 103
as heaven on Earth, 268
built before Noah's Flood, 210
built by Sethites, 93
dated to time of Noah's youth, 216
divinely designed as a puzzle, 94
face not original, 206
face of Virgo, tail of Leo, 221
face tied to Aquarius, 221
forensic analysis of face, 206
how Egyptians viewed it, 206
located at 30 degrees North, 215
marks beginning and end of time, 217
marks beginning and end of Zodiac, 205
repaired in past, 207
shows water erosion, 209
stellar meaning of, 220
symbol for Christ, 259
symbol for Virgo, Aquarius, and Leo, 217
symbol for Virgo/Aquarius and Leo, 215
symbol of Christ, 223
tied to Star Gospel on Sept. 20, 2017 AD, 713
understood by Ancient Egyptians, 210
water erosion on it caused by Great Flood?, 103

Great Step
hides prophetic dates, 310
in Great Pyramid, 304
two prophetic dates of, 304

Great Tribulation, iii, xvi, 2, 14, 15, 31, 34, 36, 40, 55, 61, 62, 65, 66, 69, 70, 73, 74, 75, 76, 78, 79, 80, 81, 83, 86, 90, 121, 134, 138, 147, 154, 156, 160, 161, 191, 229, 233, 234, 242, 249, 266, 287, 288, 300, 301, 302, 306, 307, 317, 323, 329, 346, 347, 349, 353, 362, 382, 396, 400, 410, 419, 423, 427, 428, 438, 456, 509, 511, 512, 513, 517, 518, 519, 521, 522, 524, 531, 532, 533, 534, 537, 538, 539, 544, 547, 549, 554, 555, 556, 557, 558, 563, 564, 566, 567, 575, 591, 596, 598, 601, 602, 603, 605, 628, 637, 640, 661, 708, 709, 719, 725
America during, 432
and Battle of Gog and Magog, 408
and Enoch's prophecy, 433
beginning of, 34
begins in 2011 per Daniel's 70 Weeks, 329
Bride of Christ and Five Wise Virgins protected from, 498
cities of refuge during, 498
dating of, 60
end of, 66
end too violent for Rapture event, 515
fourth year of, 35

# Index

imminent, 359
Last Trumpet to sound at end, 421
revealed in Deueronomy Psalms, 45
second year of, 31
seven epistles of, 30
seven years, 30
two Rapture events connected to, 498
very near, 4
war at end, 285
why it hasn't begun yet, 231
Great Tribulation,, 242
Great White Throne Judgment, 254, 291, 424
greed
   evil consequences of, 302
Greek mythology, 655
Greek Mythology, 636
Greeks, 637
Greenwich, England, 118
Grotto, 622
   symbol for Lamb of God, 129
   symbol of Christ's sacrifice for sin, 128
guillotine, 456
Gulf of Suez
   and Christ Angle, 171
Gulf War, 42, 59
Gulf War Syndrome, 59
Habsburg Dynasty, 468, 489
Hagar
   Ishmael's Egyptian mother, 271
hail
   sent in judgment, 270, 273, 370, 371, 410, 546, 606, 607, 608
Hall of Records, 210
Hall of Truth in Chaos
   name for Great Pyramid Antechamber, 309
Hallel Psalms, 30, 42, 60, 61, 65, 84, 90, 306, 337, 340, 341, 402
   a prophetic witness, 330
   and 2017 AD, 709
   connected to Grand Gallery?, 134
   Psalms 111-113, 62
   shows possible date for Great Tribulation, 236
   tied to Last Day, 678
Halleluyah
   at end of Numbers Psalms, 45

   *in Deuteronomy Psalms*, 45
Ham, 207
   likely darker than his brothers, 352
Hamites
   not excluded from Adamic or Abrahamic Covenants, 354
Harlot
   as Roman Catholic Church, 458
   Mary riding Beast, 253
   rides Beast from the Sea, 458
   signifies Babylon the Great, 457
harvest festival. *See* Feast of Tabernacles
Hatshepsut
   not face of Sphinx, 207
Hawaii, 321, 322, 365, 415, 676, 681, 712
   America's symbolic Sun, 365
hawk
   enemy of serpent, 158
heaven
   reveals what will happen on Earth, 270
heavenly signs
   marking Last Day, 709
heavenly tablets, 245
Heavenly Tablets, 107
heavens, 385
Hebrew Aleph-Bet, 5, 6, 7, 84, 539
Hebrew alphabet, 89
   encodes New Testament same as Old, 6
   encodes Old Testament with hidden meaning, 4
   finials connected to Great Tribulation?, 84
Hebrew Alphabet, 5, *See* Hebrew Aleph-Bet
Hebrew University, 49
Heliopolis, 110
Helix Nebula
   depicted on Ecaudor atifact as Eye of God, 376
   on Ecuador artifact and US Great Seal, 376
Helmholtz-style resonators, 165
henge
   as altar, 108
   as calendar, 107
heraldic device, 464

heraldic iconography, 453
Heraldry, 431
   English use of Unicorn, 448
Hercules, 589, 636
   symbol for Samson, a Danite, 283
Hermes, 93
Hermes Trismegistus, 93
Hermeticism, 93
Herod's Temple, 69, 88
Herodotus, 96
hidden chambers, 123
hieroglyphic texts, 196
High Priest, 80, 83, 180, 348, 727
   Yahshua as, 348
Hindus
   as antichrists, 344
history
   reversal of, 25, 260
   reversed through Christ, 289
Hitler, 50
Hollywood
   promotion of Gay lifestyle offensive to God, 373
Holy Blood, Holy Grail, 467, 470
Holy Grail, 484
   as false bloodline of Christ, 478
   supposed bloodline of Christ, 471
   symbol for Christ and Antichrist, 462
   symbol for Christ's blood, 467
Holy Place, 202
   objects inside signify Christ, 186
   symbolized Yahshua in hearts of believers, 309
   tied to Antechamber and Tribulation, 184
Holy Roman Emperor, 399, 402
Holy Roman Emperors, 457, 464
Holy Roman Empire, 43, 251, 457, 458
   Enoch's prophecy about, 250
Holy Spirit, 3, 27, 530, 573
   bird symbols for, 616
   covered Moses, 199
   depicted by Eridanus, 153
   gifts of, 146
   given by Yahshua, 726, 727
   given to apostles at Pentecost, 271
   gives believers incredible power, 269
   holding Antichrist back, 341
   outpouring of in Last Days, 613
   reveals God to us, 98
   supernatural protection of, 517
   symbolized by Queen's Chamber, 121
   ultimate Bible Code breaker, 14
Holy War, 343
homosexual marriage, 384
homosexuality
   immoral, and offensive to God, 373
Horizontal Passage, 111, 130, 131, 132, 133, 170, 183, 186, 305
   unfinished floor, 161
horns
   mark Taurus as Bread of Life, 152
   of Cherubim, 155
   of Taurus, 155
   represent Joseph's two sons, 154
House of Jacob, 380
House of Judah
   to fall, then re-emerge, 441
human blood
   demonic Mayan gods craved, 619
human sacrifice
   practiced by Maya, 624
   practiced by Mayans, 619
Humanism
   undermines Christian morality, 342
Hurricane Katrina, 370, 404
Hurricane Sandy, 404
Hutchings, N. W., 100
Hyades, 646, 650, 698
hybrid, 549
Hydra
   symbol for Beast from the Sea, 713
   symbol for Red Dragon, 615
   tied to Beast from the Sea, 496, 501, 502, 503
Illuminati, 485, 505
   in American Politics, 415
   infiltration of American Freemasonry, 414
   Prince Charles possible leader, 399
   proposed builders of Georgia Guidestones, 399
Image of the Beast, 503, 504, 505
immigrants
   being used for evil gain, 301
immorality
   consequences of, 368

# Index

immortal saints
  during Millennial Kingdom, 289
In God We Trust, 368
Inca, 638
Incan Sixth Sun, 638, 639
Incas, 618, 639
India, 44, 281, 353, 410, 417, 452, 740
Indonesia, 371
Iran, 287, 351, 352, 390, 404, 407, 417, 421, 440, 452, 538, 661
  in prophecy, 286
  tied to Assyria in prophecy, 390
Iraq, 59, 351
  enemy of Israel, 361
  in prophecy, 286
  invasion of Kuwait, 59
  US war in, 287
Ireland
  connected to Tribe of Dan, 284
  did David's descendants settle there?, 441
Iron Age, 43
iron joins
  used in Great Pyramid construction, 96
iron weapons
  used by Roman legions, 393
Isaac
  as all Israel - Gentile and Jew, 287
Isaiah
  prophesied about Great Pyramid, 192
Isaiah 9:10
  Curse Against Israel and America, 364
Ishmael
  as all Muslim Arabs, 287
Isis, 158
Islam, 250
  executes infidels by beheading, 456
  its spread into Europe, 399
  symbolized by a woman, 455
  tied to Perseus, 657
Islamic Fundamentalists, 493
Israel, 637, *See also* Spiritual Israel
  House of, 187
Israel modern nation of
  and treaty with Antichrist, 493
Israel, modern nation of, 42, 47, 51, 80, 273, 274, 304, 368, 391, 403, 404, 425, 446, 449, 538, 637
  70 year season of repentance, 331
  Antichrist's invasion of, 713
  birth of nation, 41, 325
  center of the land, with resettled ruins, like USA, 410
  Coat of Arms, 17
  connected to the United States, 357
  EndTime attack on, 411
  has unwalled villages like USA, 409
  land of resettled ruins, like USA, 410
  peaceful land attacked by Terrorists, like USA, 411
  Rebirth, 310
  refuge for persecuted Jews, 356
  tied to House of Judah, 187
  tied to United States, 448
Israelite Conquest of Canaan
  intended by God to rid the land of Nephilim Giants and their corrupted spiritual beliefs, 620
Israelites
  blessed world through Yahshua, 355
  migrated throughout Europe, 353
  practiced animal sacrifice in lieu of human sacrifice, unless stoning was required, 619
J. R. Church, 6, 37, 47, 60, 67
Jabal Al Lawz
  as Mount Sinai, 378
Jacob, 385
  deathbed prophecy of, 430
  stole Esau's birthright, 271
Jacob's Trouble, 16, 535, 539, 554, 567, 568, 657, 672, 679, 694
Jacobins
  in American politics, 414
James and John
  sons of Zebedee, 242
James, Epistle of, 30, 32
Japeth
  lost birthrihgt, 270
Japheth, 637
  likely had Caucasian features, 351
jar merchant, 473
Jared
  Enoch's father, 219
Jeremiah, 91

may have accompanied Zedekiah's daughters to Ireland, 442
Jericho
  and Christ Angle, 172
Jerusalem, 2, 41, 51, 54, 55, 56, 65, 69, 70, 73, 74, 81, 82, 85, 88, 90, 146, 152, 167, 168, 169, 182, 190, 194, 237, 239, 242, 244, 246, 247, 250, 261, 275, 277, 286, 287, 288, 291, 293, 297, 306, 310, 311, 313, 314, 325, 326, 327, 328, 329, 332, 333, 334, 343, 346, 353, 354, 358, 393, 394, 403, 406, 408, 425, 435, 440, 449, 473, 480, 483, 492, 493, 508, 514, 521, 534, 548, 551, 558, 561, 562, 565, 576, 580, 597, 598, 601, 602, 604, 609, 658, 660, 667, 671, 673, 676, 681, 682, 701, 702, 704, 705, 719, 722
  destruction in 70 AD, 434
  destruction of, 69, 332
  possible new location for United Nations, 394
  synonymous with Israel in prophecy, 425
  tied to Sirius, 378
Jerusalem Church, 261
Jerusalem Great Synagogue, 56
Jesuit order
  in league with Islam, 455
Jesus. *See* Yahshua
Jewish Civil Calendar, 305, 307
Jewish Civil New Year, 336, *See* Rosh Hashanah
Jewish Feast Days, 340, 533
Jewish Feasts
  on Blood Moon Tetrads, 699
Jewish financial power, 50
Jewish people, 50
Jewish Sacred Calendar, 140, 337, 339, 678, 717
Jews
  as slaves in ancient Rome, 353
  in prophecy, 352
  not forsaken by God, 278
Jezreel Valley, 412
  as Megiddo, 670
Jihad, 343, 730

John Major Jenkins, 628, 629
John the Baptist, 137, 154, 188, 494, 563
  honored by Freemasons, 510
  possibly resurrected after Yahshua was, 510
John, First Epistle of, 34
John, the Apostle
  beloved disciple?, 480
Jonathan Cahn, 364
Jordan River
  and Christ Angle, 172
Jordan, Kingdom of, 349, 493
  spared from Antichrist's takeover, 408
Joseph, 270, 385, 386, 395
  associated with Priest of On, 194
  earned Reuben's birthright, 271
  patriarch, 403
Joseph Smith, 415
Joseph Stalin
  killed more Jews than Hitler, 392
Joseph, patriarch, 357, 385
  learned Egyptian wisdom, 110
  married to Gentile, 497
  Naz-Seir or Prince of princes in Egypt, 380
  symbolically tied to Great Pyramid, 110
  tied to symbols of USA, 367
  Two Tribes of, 448
Joseph's birthright
  given to Ehraim, 429
Joseph's tomb, 403
Josephus, 92, 93, 95, 216, 275, 277, 407, 654
Joshua
  son of Nun, 24
Joshua, Book of
  theme of, 24
Jubilee, 39, 105, 111, 120, 132, 133, 311, 374, 726
  USA a symbol of, 374
Jubilee Passage, 111
  a 7th of Horizontal Passage, 132
  shows Earth's distance from Moon, 120
Judah, 656
  allied to Ephraim, 360
  House of, 187

# Index

united to Ephraim, 286
Judah's Scepter
  belongs to Christ, 441
Judas Iscariot
  needed because Yahshua had a twin?, 484
  Paul replaced, 260
Jude, Epistle of, 36
  quotes from Book of 1 Enoch, 37
Judeo-Christianity
  upheld in USA, 383
Judges, Book of
  theme of, 24
Judgment Hall of Osiris
  in Book of the Dead, 196
July 11th, 2010, 664, 669, 672, 676, 677, 678, 681, 686, 708
June of 2011
  significant heavenly signs of, 693
Jupiter
  in 2010, 678
  in relation to Marduk-Tiamat encounter, 263
  on Mayan End Date, 650
  represents Christ, 651
  the Messiah planet, 88, 267
Jupiter bombardment, 87, 88
Jupiter-Uranus Conjunction, 671
  of Jan. 4th, 2011, 692
  of June 6th, 2010, 669
  of Sept. 22nd, 2010, 686, 692
Jupiter-Uranus Conjunctions, 670
  of 2010 & 2011, 664
Khafre, 99, 207, 209
Khafre Pyramid causeway
  marks Winter Solstice, 136, 673
Khnum
  Ram-headed Egyptiian Creator god called Divine Potter, 211
Khufu, 99, 209
Kidron Valley, 534
King Artaxerxes
  ordered Jerusalem rebuilt in 457 BC, 325
King Arthur
  Christ figure, 488
King Darius, 275, 392

King David, 47, 354, *See* also David's Throne, David's royal lineage
  does his throne exist today?, 441
  Prince Charles a descendent?, 489
  righteous king of Israel, 436
  royal line of, 457
  symbolized by Perseus, 655
King Hussein of Jordan, 54
King Josiah
  righteous king of Israel, 436
King of kings, 286, 713
  Christ as, 254, 500
  Yahshua as, 615
King of righteousness, 254
King of the Jews, 243
King of the North, 321, 408, 491, 492, 693
  as Antichrist, 407
  will defeat Muslim King of the South in battle, 408
King of the South, 321, 408, 491, 493, 693
  Muslim alliance that attacks Antichrist, or King of the North, 408
King Zedekiah
  last King of Judah, 441
King's Chamber, 99, 105, 111, 112, 115, 121, 124, 128, 129, 131, 133, 138, 139, 140, 141, 142, 143, 144, 145, 146, 147, 148, 150, 158, 160, 161, 163, 164, 165, 166, 172, 173, 175, 179, 180, 181, 182, 184, 186, 187, 188, 189, 191, 197, 200, 202, 304, 310, 311, 317, 323, 325, 591
  9 ceiling stones, 139
  advanced Geometry inside, 172
  as symbol for New Earth, 141
  damage in, 163
  designed using Golden Ratio, 114
  entrance tied to veil in Tabernacle, 184
  gabled ceiling over, 145
  in Book of the Dead, 197
  relieving chambers represent heaven, and everlasting life, 191
  represents Most Holy Place as symbol of resurrection, 188

signifies a celestial sphere, 141
signifies the Sun, 121
symbol for Sun, 178
symbol of First Resurrection, 147
symbol of Millennial Kingdom, 147
temperature inside, 141
tied to Christ's ministry, 194
tied to Most Holy Place, 309
King's Chamber, 325
Kingdom of God, 24, 40, 44, 45, 169, 183, 187, 254, 292, 336, 345, 353, 357, 359, 405, 489, 510, 530, 535, 536, 555, 561, 568, 580, 587, 597, 644, 664, 665, 719
 established at end of 12,000 years, 244
 Uranus as symbol of, 667
 Yahshua to govern on Earth, 479
Kingdom of Heaven, 336, 484, 648
 keys to it, 269
 Kingdom of Israel fulfilled, 336
Kingdom of Israel, 27, 187, 250, 273
 dim reflection of Kingdom of Heaven, 336
 divided like Tiamat, 265
 division of, 277
 northern, 351
 tied to Tiamat, 265
 to be ruled by Christ, 354
Kingdom of Judah, 187, 351
 David's lineage survived its destruction?, 441
 destroyed by Babylon, 433
 fell to Babylonians, 278
 signified by Jews today, 273
kingdom of the Antichrist
 likened to Greece, 428
Kinsmen Redeemer
 depicted at Esna, 213
Kuwait, 59
 and Psalm 91, 59
Lady Guinevere
 as Mary Magdalene, 488
Lake of Fire, 254
 reserved for wicked, 424
Lamb of God, 498, 565
 Depicted by Aries, 211
lampstands. *See* menorah
Lancelot
 symbol for Roman Catholic Church?, 488
Language of God, 1, 4, 12, 37, 174, 386, 636
 in Holy Place symbols, 187
 in Tabernacle and Great Pyramid, 192
 part of Word of God, 383
 prayer essential to understand, 233
 understood by Sethites, 217
Last Day, 7, 94, 254
 described in Book of Revelation, 614
 has already begun!, 298
 heavenly signs tied to, 612
Last Great Day, 16, 206
Last Judgment, 133, 135, 183, 237, 310, 335, 437, 518, 598, 654
Last Supper
 depicted by Orion and Taurus, 380
 painting by DaVinci, 475
 tied to Passover, 274
Last Trumpet, 78, 287, 422, 423, 428, 518, 533
 heard in Washington's vision, 421
Last Trumpet.
 herald of First Resurrection, 513
Latin America, 407
Lavon Affair, 53
Lazarus, 473, 474, 478, 480, 481, 483, 506, 508
 as beloved disciple?, 478
 possible beloved disciple, 472
 resurrection of, 510
LBGT Movement, 398
left horn
 of Taurus as Antichrist, 155
Lemba, 354
Leo
 a Sign of the Son of Man, 569
 and Great Sphinx, 215
 and Solar Eclipse on Aug. 21, 2017 AD, 713
 as end of Zodiac, 213
 at Esna, 213
 depicts Christ on December 21st, 2012, 637
 marks dawn of time, 228
 on Sept. 20, 2017 AD, 713
 signifies Christ as conquering King, 259

# Index   Page 773

symbol for Christ as Lion of Judah, 496
symbol of Lion of Judah, 220
Leonardo DaVinci
   may have thought Christ was married, 477
   painting of Last Supper, 475
Leopard
   signifies France, 504
leper
   mistranslation of word meaning, 472
Lepus
   serpent sign beneath Orio's feet, 151
   serpent's head below Orion's foot, 497
levitation, 96
Levite priests, 327
Leviticus
   theme of, 20
Leviticus Psalms, 41, 56
Leviticus, Book of, 41
LGBT Agenda, 322
Libra
   2012 Solar Eclipse in, 694
   decans forming Chanukiah on Dec. 21, 2012, 652
   depicts Rider on Black Horse, 648, 650
   meaning of, 694
   symbl of divine judgment, 283
Library of Congress
   has Washington's vision on file, 415
Light of Christ, 29
Light of the World, 717
   Yahshua as, 309
lion
   as symbol for Christ, 637
   on British Coat of Arms, 450
Lion of Judah
   tied to lion on British Coat of Arms, 450
   tied to sign of Leo, 259
Living Creatures, 256, *See* Cherubim
lluminati, 510
Lombards, 399, 401, 402
London
   as Magog, 407
   sits on seven hills, 461
Lord of the Sheep, 435
Lord's Day. *See* Day of the Lord

Lower Egypt, 118
lunar cycle
   of 56 years, 135
Lunar Eclipse
   of Dec. 10th, 2011, 694
   of June 15th, 2011, 693
   often associated with biblical events, 712
   on Dec. 21, 2010, 681
   on Feast of Tabernacles in 1996, 660
   on Passover in 2015 AD, 715
   on Purim in 1997 and 2007, 661
   over Easter Island in 2015 AD, 709
   Passover 2014, 315
Lunar Eclipse Triad, 679
Lunar Eclipses
   three betw. Dec. 21st, 2010 & Dec. 10th., 2011, 664, 673, 679
   three that highlight 2011 as significant, 694
Lutheran Church, 536
luxury
   evil consequences of, 302
Lysimachus, 452
Ma'at, 694
   symbol of righteousness, 196
Macedonia, 393, 452
Machu Picchu, 712
Magi
   visitation of Christ tied to Chanukah, 546
Magic Sun Square, 669
Magog, 406, 407, 409, 412, 693
   connected to Armageddon?, 412
   fire sent to destroy, 412
   land prince called Gog rules, 406
Mahdi, 637, 658
   Muslim Anti-Messiah, 408
Manasseh, 110, 270, 279, 281, 380, 385, 386, 387
Manhattan
   world financial hub, 372
mankind
   intelligent from the beginning, 97
Manna
   Bread of Life, 181
Mansions of the Moon, 136
March 3rd, 2007
   Lunar Eclipse on, 661

Mardon. *See* Tammuz
Marduk
  could be Eris, 264
  fragments of, 264
  symbol for Ephraim, 266
Mark Biltz
  Pastor, 700
Mark of the Beast, 86
  connected to End Time Beasts, 503, 504
  enforced in 2013 AD?, 85
marriage
  being undermined, 373
Marriage Supper of the Lamb
  *after* Wedding of the Lamb, 74
Mars
  marks 1st Chanukiah lamp on Dec. 21, 2012, 652
Martin Luther, 332
Mary
  as deity, 500
Mary Magdalene
  a faithful disciple, 475
  accompanied by Lazarus?, 481
  conspiracy theories surround her, 479
  image tainted by false occult associations, 472
  loyal disciple, 479
  never called wife of Christ, 470
  same as Mary of Bethany, 472
  was demon-possessed, 474
  was Mary of Bethany, 470, 472, 474, 475, 476, 477, 478, 479, 480, 481, 482, 483, 488, 489, 506, 508
Mary of Bethany, 472, 473, 474, 478, 483, 506
  possible beloved disciple, 472
  same as Mary Magdelene, 472
Mary, mother of Christ
  deified as goddess, 253
Masonic Lodge, 414
Masonic Lodges
  in America, 415
  infiltrated by Illuminati, Jacobins, 414
Masonic teachings
  once Christian, not Pagan, 414
Massacre of Verden, 399
master of the house
  i.e. Satan, 515
master of the household
  i.e. Yahshua, 515
master of the servant
  i.e. Yahshua, 515
master's house
  the Earth, where Satan is master, 515
material blessings, 355, 356
materialism
  rampant today, 301
Matthew's Gospel
  originally written in Hebrew?, 473
Matthias
  chosen to replace Judas Iscariot, 270
Maya
  foresaw cataclysmic destruction in Tribulation, 632
  foresaw events of Great Tribulation, 627
Mayan Calendar, 624, 629, 630, 638
Mayan civilization
  and Teotihuacán, 623
Mayan Civilization, 616, 618, 620
  practiced human sacrifice, 618
  very advanced, tied to Noah and Shem, 617
Mayan End Date, 323, 650
  for Fifth Sun, 696
  tied to Four Horsemen, 306, 315
Mayan Fifth Sun, 612, 616, 628, 638
  corresponds to Church Age, 624
  date of its end, 650
  final Mayan Age, 619
Mayan Fourth Sun
  ended with Great Flood, 624
Mayan long-count, 638
Mayan mythology, 623
Mayan religion, 623
  called for human sacrifice, 620
Mayan Sun
  tied to Great Day, 624
Mayan World Age, 639
Mayans
  had modern knowledge of Solar System, 621
  human sacrifice among, 618
  possibly descended from Noah, 612
  used perverted form of Sacred Astronomy, 618

# Index

used step pyramids like Babylonians, 618
Mazzaroth, xviii, 82, 91, 107, 139, 144, 148, 158, 172, 200, 201, 202, 220, 240, 243, 262, 365, 375, 377, 379, 384, 721, 724, 725, 736, *See* Gospel in the Stars, *See* Zodiac
   concerning Beasts of Revelation, 498
Kochab, 161
Medeo-Persia, 391, 392, 452
Medusa, 655, 656, 657, 662
   tied to New World Order, 658
Melchizedek, 13, 63, 254, 348, 377
   as Shem, 250
   priesthood, 63
Menachem Begin, 57
Menelik 1, 356
Menkaure, 99
Menkaure's Pyramid, 715
Menkaure's Pyramid causeway
   points to equinoxes, 215
menorah
   nine-branched, 17, 25, 27, 71
   prophetic key, 17
   seven-branched, 17
      in New Testament, 25
   symbol of victory in Christ, 493
Menorah, 4, 6, 18, 37, 134, 226, 260, 290, 298, 576, 579, 652, 736
menorah pattern, 18, 20, 25
Mercury
   marks center Chanukiah lamp on Dec. 21, 2012, 652
   meaning of, 695
Merovingian heresy, 250, 345, 346, 468, 475, 632
   started by imposter of Christ?, 485
Merovingians, 483
Mesoamerican Civilizations, 619
Mesoamericans, 617
   practiced human sacrifice, 620
Mesopotamia, 351, 620
Messiah
   expected by many religious groups, 466
   Jews expected a conquering king, 471
Messiah the Prince
   Daniel's Title for Christ, 313, 314, 326, 327

messianic bloodline
   heretical belief in, 472
Messianic Jews, 39, 273, 287, 336, 468, 473, 513, 559, 597, 601, 656
Messianic Judaism, 698
meteoroids, 573, 605
meteors, 573
Methuselah, 94, 95
Mexic and northern Central America, 617
Mexicans
   America's new slave class, 301
Mexico, 357, 410, 619, 620
   Pre-Columbian civilizations of, 376
Mexico City
   Teotihuacán nearby, 620
Michael Drosnin, 13
Middle East, 386, 404, 637
   Israel at center of, 410
mighty angel
   preaches Gospel during Tribulation, 644
   to preach during Great Tribulation, 651
Mikhail Gorbechev, 392
militia groups
   in America, 432
Milky Way
   tied to Nile River, 224
Milky Way Galaxy
   aligns with Sun on December 21st, 2012, 637
Milky Way, center of. *See* galactic center
Millennial Kingdom, 8, 24, 27, 34, 39, 40, 42, 44, 45, 62, 66, 81, 83, 84, 90, 130, 140, 147, 182, 183, 188, 191, 215, 242, 244, 253, 256, 258, 272, 290, 293, 310, 311, 334, 335, 338, 340, 358, 373, 471, 495, 576, 591, 632, 635, 639, 683, 686, 709, 717, 719, 727
   as Seventh Great Day, 243
   battle before, 239
   begins in 2018 per Daniel's 70 Weeks, 330
   during Enoch's Seventy Generations, 335
   everyone will know Christ during, 289

Feast of Tabernacles celebrated during, 291
  ingathering of Israel during, 353
  judgment after final war, 424
  part of the Lord's Day, 238
  represented by Great Pyramid, and Camp of Israel, 183
  time of seen in Cherubim, 259
  time of true peace, 286
  to be set up in 2018 AD?, 87
  Tribe of Dan represented during, 635
Millennial Rule of Christ, 82, 132, 133, 134, 141, 148, 160, 184, 215, 227, 229, 238, 242, 249, 254, 259, 265, 285, 288, 291, 310, 325, 329, 334, 335, 338, 346, 360, 419, 424, 509, 518, 540, 630, 672, 704, 705, 725, 730, *See* Millennial Kingdom of Christ
  represented by Most Holy Place and King's Chamber, 188
Mirfak, 662
  star in Perseus, 657
Missionary Age, 24
Moai
  meaning of, 676
Moon
  allegorical meaning of, 660
  moving slowly away from Earth, 111
  symbol of both good and evil, 121
  symbolized in Great Pyramid, 121
  tied to Queen's Chamber, 197
  worshipped as god, 617
morality, 168
Mormon Church, 415
Morning Star
  tied to Christ, 714
Mosaic Law
  a curse, 129
Moses, 385
  as Egyptian Prince, 195
  contructed altar with 12 stones or pillars, 108
  had Holy Spirit, 199
  knew meaning of Tabernacle and Pyramid, 195
  learned Egyptian wisdom, 110

Most Holy Place, 116, 141, 180, 182, 184, 187, 188, 200, 202, 309, 327, 348
  represented by King's Chamber, 188
  tied to King's Chamber and Millennial Rule of Christ, 189
Mount Horeb, 108
Mount Sinai, 49, 108, 199, 253, 336, 726
  as Jabal Al Lawz, 378
Muslim Brotherhood, 400
Muslim nations, 43
Muslim Spain, 399
Muslims, 286
  hate Jews and Chrstians, 345
  in Russia, 400
  radical, 658
  will submit to Christ, 440
Narmer, 207
Native American Cultures
  religious myths of, 616
Native Americans, 410, 617
  knew Star Gospel?, 623
navel
  as a scar, 368
Navel of the World, 118
Nazarene
  connected to "Naz Seir", 379
Nazi Death Camps, 458
Nazi Germany, 50
  used black eagle of Ancient Rome as symbol, 394
Naz-Seir, 380
Nebuchadnezzar, 43, 44, 45, 148, 390, 392, 433, 441, 598
Nebuchadnezzar's dream, 43, 45
Negroid, 207
Neith
  female Egyptian Archer goddess and consort of Khnum, 211
  hieroglyphic symbol for, 211
Neo-Paganism. *See* Paganism
Nephilim, 24, 92, 94, 219, 220, 246, 250, 285, 290, 397, 487, 488, 618, 620, 623, 643, 649, 655, 724, 728, 744
  Antichrist to be of their kind, 491
  associated with Tribe of Dan, 284

# Index

descendents inhabited Promised Land prior to Israelite Conquest, 620
evil seed of Fallen Angels, 465
in the New World, 620
perverted Star Gospel, 397
seed of Fallen Angels, 223
Serpent Seed of Satan, and Dan, 266
tied to Scorpio, 223
Neptune, 665, 666
New Age, 253
New Age Gospel, 630
New Age Movement, 102, 342
  Anti-Christian, 299
New Age of enlightenment
  a satanic religious doctrine, 630
New Age Spirituality, 395, 630
  explanation for Rapture, 631
  their view of the Rapture and Biblical Morality, 631
  their worldview, 629
New Agers
  as antichrists, 344
New Covenant, 71, 145, 274, 278, 288, 425, 483, 493, 535, 559, 585, 668
  depicted by Taurus and decans, 153
  gives Holy Spirit, 39
  in Star Gospel, 152
  made art Passover, 274
New Heaven and Earth, 20, 206, 254, 290
  created after Millennial Kingdom, 293
  life very different when they are created, 294
New Heaven and New Earth, 32, 135, 227, 233, 245, 249, 334, 518
New Jerusalem, 242, 396
New Moon, 323
  on Sept. 20, 2017 AD, 713
New Orleans, 370
New Testament
  alphabetically encoded with hidden prophecy, 6
  filled with menorah patterns, 25
  from Hebrew-Aramaic Originals?, 12
  **its books tied to US Constitution**, 383
New World, 616, 617, 638
  date for end of age, 612
  native myths of, 616

New World cultures
  understood Sacred Astronomy, 612
New World Order, 385, 389, 395, 396, 410, 458, 536, 552, 599, 601, 693
  tied to Medusa's head, 658
New York City
  America's most villainous city?, 363
  home of United Nations/Beast from Sea, 459
  like Nimrod's Babylon, 460
  modern day Babylon?, 372
  possible candidate for Babylon the Great, 460
Nicolaitans, 397
Nile River
  tied to Milky Way, 224
Nimrod, 207, 264, 266, 658
  in league with Giants in the New World, 620
  in the Americas, 620
Noah, 26, 94, 95, 352, 636, 638, 706, 712
  as Khufu, 216
  connected to Ecuador artifacts, 377
  cursed Canaan, 352
  his deliverance from the Flood depicted by Aquarius, 376
  instructed by an angel, 382
  may be Khufu, 93
  seen as bull in Book of 1 Enoch, 382
Noah and kin
  far smarter and healthier than us, 98
Noah:, 620
Noah's Ark, 96, *See* Ark, of Noah
Noah's Flood, 246, 342, 602, 693, 724, 740
  corresponds to Maya Fourth Sun, 624
  Great Pyramid built before. *See Also* Great Flood
North America, 388, 681, 692, 713
  Prehistoric, 409
North America Nebula
  ties USA to Christianity, 429
North Korea, 417, 421, 430, 538
Northern Hemisphere
  represented by Great Pyramid, 112
northern shaft
  in King's Chamber, 160

in Queen's Chamber, 161
in Queen's Chamber, 160
Nubia
   now Sudan, 407
nuclear bombs
   visions of attacks in USA, 421
number 13
   number of Last Great Day, 206
Numbers
   theme of, 21
Numbers Psalms, 42, 45
obelisk
   Great Pyramid as, 170
   key to Bible Codes, 13
Occult doctrines
   in American Politics, 415
Occult mystery schools
   polluted American Freemasonry, 414
Occult mysticism, 697
Occult practitioners
   pervert the Star Gospel, 497
Occult teachings, 254
October 6th, 2017AD
   heavenly signs mimicked at Giza, 716
Old Covenant
   gave Mosaic Law, 39
Old Kingdom, 99, 618
Old Kingdom Pyramids, 96, 104
Old Testament
   alphabetically encoded with hidden prophecy, 5
Old World, 617
Old World Civilizations
   practiced human sacrifice, 619
Old World cultures
   understood Star Gospel, 612
Old World pyramids, 618
Olive Branch
   on Great Seal, 429
olive trees
   grafted together, 429
Olmec calendar, 618
Olmec Civilization, 618
Olmecs, 620
Olympian gods, 397
On. *See* Egyptian god On
On, or Heliopolis
   city in Ancient Egypt, 110
One Nation Under God, 368

One World Government, 505
One World Religion, 632, 647
   of False Prophet, 497
One-Horned Goat, 428, 490
   as Greece, 452
   forges an evil empire, 453
One-Horned Ram, 434, 490
   as Israel and USA in prophecy, 448
   as Unicorn, 444
   could represent one nation, 446
   Great Britain sees itself as, 450
   symbol for Christ, 443
   tied to Cherubim, 256
open door
   appears before plagues, 518
   into God's presence, 516
   leads to Heaven, 518
Ophiuchus, 283, 321, 322, 430, 498, 499, 565, 574, 575, 577, 585, 587, 589, 633, 635, 636, 649, 650, 652
   a Sign of the Son of Man, 569
   depicts Rider on Pale Horse, 649
   NOT 13th sign, but decan of Scorpio, 321
   tied to Americas, 636
Order of the Garter
   linked to Rome, 461
   tied to Freemasonry, 471
Original Sin
   concept unknown to Ancient Greeks, 453
Orion, 108, 110, 137, 144, 148, 149, 150, 151, 152, 153, 154, 157, 158, 160, 161, 196, 202, 223, 224, 228, 230, 268, 310, 317, 318, 321, 322, 379, 382, 539, 547, 566, 569, 570, 575, 579, 590, 602, 622, 646, 650, 652, 653, 662, 664, 672, 673, 678, 681, 682, 688, 膨694, 712, 715, 735
   as Christ crucified, 152
   as Cup of Redemption, 153
   as messiah figure, 497
   as Prince, 150
   as Prince of princes, 213
   as punisher of the ungodly, 497
   as Rider on Red Horse, 646
   at Esna, 213
   belt stars mimicked at Giza and Teotihuacán, 622

# Index

depicted on Ecuador artifacts, 376, 377
depicted on set of 13 cups found in Ecuador, 378
depicted on Star-Gazer Ecuador artifact, 380
depicts Last Supper with Taurus, 380
has dual meaning, 646
how it depicts 13,000 years, 228
in 10,500 BC, 225
Lunar Eclipse over on Dec. 21st, 2010, 681
symbol for Christ, 646
symbol for Yahshua, and Osiris, 148
symbol of Christ, 223
symbol of divine Matador, 693
tied to Egyptian god Osiris, 196
tied to USA, 382
weilds greatest sword in the Zodiac, 646

Orion's belt
at Giza, as in heaven, so on Earth, 268
symbolized at Giza, 138
tied to pyramid at Giza, 224

Orion's Belt, 673
depicted on Ecuador artifacts, 377
signified by Giza Pyramids, 672
targeted on Sept. 20, 2017 AD, 715

Orion's sword
tip touches ecliptic, 497

Orthodox Church, 43
Osireion, 103
Osiris, 144, 158
Egyptian god connected to Orion, 196
Egyptian god tied to Orion, 150
tied to Orion, 148

Outer Courtyard, 202
Pagan epidemic, 345
Pagan gods, 92
Paganism, 345
rapidly growing in popularity, 254

Pagans
as antichrists, 344
hate Christians, 345
pervert every Christian truth, 102

Pakistan, 371, 407, 410, 417, 452, 538
Palenque, 618
Palestinian Arabs
descendents of Philistines, 24
Palestinians, 403, 404

Papacy, 247, 250, 251, 399, 457, 461
Jesuits sworn to protect, 455
Papal authority, 252, 399, 455, 457
Parable of the Sheep and Goats, 253
Parable of the Sheep and the Goats, 452
Parable of the Ten Virgins, 396, 529, 530, 532, 536, 552, 667
explains Rapture, 520
Parable of the Unmerciful Servant
pertains to coming of Great Tribulation, 331
Parable of the Vineyard, 70
Parable of the Wedding Banquet, 70
Parable of the Weeds, 253, 266
Parable of the Wheat and the Tares, 322, 573
Parable of the Wise and Foolish Virgins. *See* Parable of the Ten Virgins
Parable of the Yeast, 266
Parthia, 243
culture like Ancient Israel's, 276
kings of, 243
Passover, 60, 335, 471, 565
Christ to celebrate in Millennial Kingdom, 359
Lunar Eclipses on, 709, 712
targeted in Antechamber, 306
tied to Christ's death and resurrection, 336
tied to Last Supper, 274
wine cup depicted in Orion, 153
Passover Lamb
Yahshua as, 694
Passover Week, 244, 307, 374, 523, 590
Path of the Sun
depicted by Winged Serpent, 214
Path to Salvation, 106, 170, 174, 186, 187, 253, 359
depicted in Holy Place, 187
shown in Great Pyramid, 186
shown in Holy Place and Pyramid Antechamber, 186
symbolized in Great Pyramid, 199
Patriot Act
violates U.S. Constitution, 432
Paul

as an apostle, 261, 270
as the murderous Saul, 261
better apostle than Matthias, 271
chosen by Christ, 261
wrote much of New Testament, 260
Peace Symbol
on Zodiacal Wheel, 650
peace treaty
false one of Antichrist, 493
Pearl Harbor, 415
Pegasus, 573, 576, 655, 656, 664, 670, 671, 678, 692
meaning of, 664
Pentateuch, 10, 40
Pentecost, 24, 46, 56, 261, 271
a Jubliee day, 39
First Rapture tied to, 566
gift of Holy Spirit, 268
targeted in Antechamber, 307, 314
tied to giving of Mosaic law and Holy Spirit, 335
Yahshua to return 10 days prior?, 307
Pergamum, 397
persecution of Christians, 299
Perseus, 615
as Esau or the Arabs, 658
as sybol of David, 655
Christ-figure smiting Satan, 664
Christian interpretation of, 656
symbol for Christ as Opener of the Second Seal, 496
Perseus Prophecy, 654
Persia
as Turkey, Armenia, Syria, Lebanon, Iran, & Iraq in prophecy, 407
kings of, 243, 275, 326, 392, 492
Persian Empire
in future prophecy, 407
Persian Gulf
End of Fertile Crescent, 410
Peter
referred to Prophet Joel, 613
Peter Levenda, 413
Peter, First Epistle of, 31, 32
Peter, Second Epistle of, 32
Peter, the Apostle, 31
as symbol for Roman Catholic Church, 479
may have been well-educated, 242

preached that fire will destroy world, 616
Petra, 616
Israel's End Time hiding place, 409
Pharaoh Djoser, 99
Pharaoh Khafre
could be Shem, 93
face not on Sphinx, 206
Pharaoh Khufu, 92, 224
as Noah, 216
not Enoch, but Noah, 93
Pharaoh Menkaure, 224
Philadelphia
in US history, 362
Philemon, 35
Phoenicians, 51
Phoenix
in mythology, 398
Pi ratio
used in Great Pyramid, 113
Piazzi Smyth, 104, 109, 119, 184
did godly survey of the Great Pyramid, 100
measurements of Great Pyramid accurate, 101
Pillar of Enoch. *See* Great Pyramid, *See* Great Pyramid
Pisces
fish over Pegasus signifies Rapture, 678
signifies Two House Church, 498, 503
symbol for Two Houses of Israel, 666
symbolof Israel, 660
tied to Two Houses of Israel, 715
Pisces fishes
meaning of, 669
Plan of Redemption, 177
Pleiades, 156, 380, 647, 660, 664, 698
depict Seven Churches of Revelation, 152
dually depicts Seven Churches and Whore of Babylon, 647
false church attacked by Arabs, 658
meaning of, 664
tied to Woman who rides the Beast, 395
PLO, 58
Polaris, 160, 500

# Index

Pole Shift, 349, 371, 525, 567, 590, 604, 605, 678, 699, 706, 707, 708, 709
   tied to Sixth Seal Judgment, 315, 607
Pole Star
   as Polaris, 500
political correctness
   offensive to God, 384
Pope
   as Antichrist, 499, 500
   seen as infallible, 456
Poseidon, 653
Post Christian Era, 342
Potiphar, 194
Precession, 140, 228
   creates Orion's 13,000 year cycle, 227
   Six Ages of, 226
Precession of the Equinoxes, 119, 227
   shown in Great Pyramid's design, 112
Precessional Ages, 244
Precessional cycle, 140
Pre-Columbian Civilizations, 619
Preiur Di Sion
   never existed, 467
Presidents of the United States, 432
Priest in the order of Melchizedek, 309
Priests of Israel
   smeared blood on altar horns, 502
priests of On, 194
Prime Meridian, 225
   should align with Giza, 225
Prime Ministers of Israel, 435
   twelve until judgment, 436
Prince Charles. *See* Prince Charles of Wales
   may be Antichrist from Tribe of Dan, 635
   tied to Tribes of Dan, Manasseh, and Judah, 634
Prince Charles of Wales, 319, 462, 464, 493, 494, 505
   as prince of Gog, 491
   born in 1948, 494
   connected to Beast from the Sea, 491
   could be Antichrist, 490
   denied kingship, 460
   descended from King David?, 489
   descended from Mohammed, 493
   eighth Charles, of Illuminati, 399
   extremely wealthy, 495
   head of Freemasonry, 471
   heraldic device's symbols, 464
   King of the North & Muslim Mahdi?, 493
   name adds up to 666, 491
   not taken seriously as Antichrist, 495
Prince Henry, 494
prince of Gog
   as a prince of London, 407
   as Prince Charles, 491
Prince of Gog, 409
Prince of princes
   depicted at Esna, 213
   Orion signifies, 379
Prince Philip, 494
   denied kingship, 460
Prince Phillip
   from Greece, tied to Antichrist, 491
prince who is to come
   both Rome and Antichrist, 328
   is Antichrist, 491
Prince William, 494, 503, 505
   denied kingship, 460
Princess of Judah
   married Celtic Royalty?, 284
Priory of Sion, 467
Procyon
   tied to Mount Sinai, 378
Promised Land, 24, 41, 397
   inhabited by Giants prior to Israelite Conquest, 620
   overrun by Giants, 24
prophecy
   five new channels, 3
Prophecy of the Seventy Generations, 335
Prophecy of the Seventy Shepherds of Israel, 433
prophetic Amens, 45
Protestant Church
   some returning to Rome, 333
Protestant Churches, 43, 252
Protestant Reformation, 248, 251, 332
   483 years before 2000 AD, 333
Protestantism, 395

Protestants
  apostate, 459
  persecuted by Catholic Church, 333
Psalm 103, 683
Psalm 108, 672
  prophecy hidden in, 402
  war described in, 404
Psalm 109, 405
Psalm 110, 60, 62, 64, 83, 678
Psalm 110 and 118, 71
Psalm 111, 62
Psalm 111 and 112, 61, 68
Psalm 111 through 118, 60
Psalm 113, 61, 75
Psalm 113 through 118, 60
Psalm 114, 76
Psalm 115, 76
Psalm 116, 77
Psalm 117, 61, 78
Psalm 118, 65, 69, 70, 79
Psalm 119, 66, 82, 83
Psalm 13, 47
Psalm 136, 61
Psalm 25, 49
Psalm 39, 50
Psalm 4, 48
Psalm 47, 50
Psalm 48, 51
Psalm 54, 52
Psalm 55, 52
Psalm 67 and 68, 54
Psalm 73, 56
Psalm 79 and 80, 57
Psalm 83, 672
Psalm 91, 42, 59
Psalm 94, 48, 90
Psalms. *Also See* Genesis Psalms, Exodus Psalms, Numbers Psalms, Leviticus Psalms, Deuteronomy Psalms.
  hidden prophetic parables in, 39
Ptolemy, 452
Puerto Rico
  in prophecy with USA, 374
Purim, 493
  celestial signs in 1997, 660
  celestial signs on, 661
  meaning of, 661
Puritans, 252
Pyramid Complex at Giza, 618
Pyramid Inch, 106, 109, 119, 195, 302, 304, 307, 309
  as a prophetic key, 123
  gives prophetic dates in Great Pyramid, 302
  measures's one prophetic year, 140
Pyramid Inches, 106, 109, 111, 112, 113, 119, 139, 140, 141, 147, 170, 191, 195, 302, 303, 304, 306
Pyramid of the Sun, 621
  cave under, 622
  tied to Jupiter, 621
Pyramid Texts, 198
pyramidion, 105
pyramidiot, 101
Pyramidology, 99, 101
Pythagorean Theorem, 115, 172
quarry marks
  in Great Pyramid, 99
Queen Elizabeth II, 462, 465
  extremely wealthy, 495
  kept 3 princes from ruling, 460
  possible Whore of Babylon, 462
Queen of Heaven
  Mary XE "Mary, mother of Christ:deified as goddess" has become a Pagan goddess due to the many idolatrous statues of her found on Catholic Church and School grounds. How sad that, instead of simply calling Mary blessed among women, the Roman Catholic Church XE "Roman Catholic Church:deified Mary" has deified her, and made her a curse upon those who falsely worship her! The false goddess heretically called Mary has become a representation of the false church that upholds her. This false goddess and the Roman Catholic Church XE "Roman Catholic Church" she partially represents can be identified with the Whore of Babylon XE "Whore of Babylon:connected to Mary as false goddess" spoken of the Book of Revelation (Rev. 17, 253

# Index

Queen of Sheba, 356
Queen's Chamber, 105, 111, 130, 170
  12 ceiling stones, 139
  gabled ceiling in, 146
  in Book of the Dead, 197
  salt in, 130
  symbol for Moon, 121, 178
  symbol of baptism, 130
  symbol of Christ's Millennial Kingdom, 130
  symbol of First Resurrection, 147
  tied to Bronze Sea, 202
  tied to Christ's ministry, 194
  unfinished floor, 161
Quetzalcoatl
  temple to, 621
Qumran, 240
Rabbi
  Yahshua as, 470
Rachel
  Jacob's beloved wife, 283
Radical Islam, 42, 386, 394, 400, 493
  created by Jesuits, 455
Radical Muslims
  see Christians is infidels to be killed, 457
Rapture, 4, 15, 16, 37, 71, 72, 73, 75, 78, 82, 86, 121, 138, 147, 161, 234, 254, 295, 305, 306, 307, 314, 315, 317, 328, 329, 333, 335, 338, 340, 341, 342, 343, 347, 349, 363, 405, 406, 420, 421, 432, 437, 498, 511, 512, 513, 514, 515, 516, 517, 518, 519, 520, 521, 522, 524, 525, 526, 527, 528, 530, 531, 532, 533, 534, 536, 537, 538, 539, 544, 548, 549, 552, 553, 554, 556, 558, 564, 565, 566, 567, 568, 570, 571, 572, 575, 576, 577, 584, 585, 589, 590, 591, 592, 593, 598, 602, 603, 607, 610, 615, 647, 649, 656, 657, 665, 669, 673, 678, 679, 681, 686, 692, 693, 701, 702, 704, 725, 727, 730, 738
  and those left behind, 515
  as viewed by New Agers, 630
  at Mid-Tribulation, 307
  before Great Tribulation, 341
  could lead to America's invasion, 420
  explained in Parable of Ten Virgins, 520
  Occult explanation for, 631
  occurs secretly, and in time of peace, 515
  Pre-Wrath, 314
  purpose of, 693
  second stage of First Resurrection, 73
  seen in fish of Pisces riding Pegasus, 678
  separate from First Resurrection, 514
  signs of in 2010 and 2011, 679
  taken to heaven in, 513
  tied to December 21, 2010 Eclipse?, 681
  timing of, 305, 511
Rapture, Pre-Wrath, 315
Raptured Saints, 73, 147, 290, 338, 428, 513, 519
rattlesnake, 384, 387
rebellion
  of apostasy in Last Day, 342
Red and Bent Pyramids
  signify horns of Taurus, 672
Red Dragon, 266, 499
  depicted by Draco and Hydra, 589
  in prophecy, 463
  of Revelation, 466
  of Wales on British Coat of Arms, 464
  serpent symbol of Nephilim Seed, 285, 464
  symbol of Wales and Prince Charles, 463, 490
  symbolized by Draco, 615
  tied to Draco and Beast from the Sea, 499
red granite, 163
  symbolic of blood atonement, 189
red granite plug, 181
Red Pyramid, 91, 99, 103
Red Pyramid at Dahshur
  depicts red star, or eye of Taurus, 646
reem, 446
Reformation, 24
Regulus
  as the King Star, 716
  at Christ's birth, 712
  king star in Leo, 668
Pope, 332
relieving chambers

above King's Chamber, 142
  gabled ceiling above, 144
  like an arrow, 146
religious tolerance, 345
resonators, 165
resurrection
  a reality, 146
Resurrection into everlasting life, 425
Resurrection Sunday, 307, 565
  targeted in Antechamber, 306
Reuben
  lost birthright, 271
Revelation Chapter 17, 496, 499, 571
Revelation Judgments
  Fifth and Sixth Trumpets, 649
  Fourth Seal, 648
  Second Seal, 645
  Seven Seals, 642
  Seven Trumpets, 625, 642
  Third Seal, 648
Revelation, Book of
  tied to Star Gospel, 614
Revelation, Chapter 13, 496
Revelation, Chapter 6, 496
reversal of history, 289
  accomplished by Christ, 25, 330
  seen in Precession, 226
Revolutionary War, 252, 362
Rider on Black Horse
  depicted by Libra, 648, 650
Rider on Pale Horse, 649
  dually depicted by Ophiuchus and Serpens, 649
Rider on Red Horse, 648
Rider on the Pale Horse
  depicted by Scorpio, 648
  is Ophiuchus, but after the Rapture, it is Serpens, 565
Rider on the Red Horse
  as Orion and Taurus, 645
  depicted by Taurus, 650
Rider on the White Horse
  depicts Sagittarius, 642, 645
  not Antichrist, but Gospel being preached, 642
Rider on White Horse
  depicted by Sagittarius, 650
right horn

  of Taurus, 154
right to bear arms, 432
Righteous Branch, 646, 697, 716
Robert Schoch
  theory about Great Sphinx, 209
Roman Catholic Church, 43, 247, 251, 252, 253, 333, 390, 457, 458, 459, 461, 467, 476, 489, 536, 599, 737
  and Mary Magdalene, 479
  as Babylon the Great, 457
  as Revelation's Harlot, 457
  built upon Peter, 260
  connected to End Time Beasts, 499, 503
  deified Mary, 253
  in league with Islam, 455
  lied concerning Christ's life, 469
  persecuted Protestants, 333
  symbolized by Lancelot?, 488
Roman Catholicism, 395
  spread of, 399
Roman Empire, 31, 43, 44, 247, 248, 250, 251, 275, 299, 386, 390, 393, 394, 397, 398, 399, 401, 428, 457, 458, 460, 467, 489, 494, 495, 561, 728, 731
  revived by Antichrist, 494
  tied to Daniel's 4th beast, 393
Roman legions
  used iron weapons, 393
Romans
  crucified Christ, 449
Rome
  built on seven hills, 457
Rosh, 407
Rosh Chodesh Tammuz
  in 2014, 323
Rosh Hashanah, 235, 236, 244, 336, 337, 339, 424, 661, 727, 730, See Also Feast of Trumpets
  may mark Second Coming in 2017 AD, 713
Rosh, Tubal and Meshech
  lands of Magog, 409
Rosicrucians
  proposed builders of Georgia Guidestones, 399
Royal Coronations

# Index

mark Churches as Babylon the Great, 499
Royalists, 252
rule of law
  in a democracy, 501
Russia, 48, 275, 276, 277, 299, 351, 353, 356, 392, 393, 401, 407, 410, 411, 418, 420, 421, 452, 458, 460, 538, 662, 692
  and Diaspora, 351
  as Rosh, 407
  head wound healed, 400
  signified by Bear, 504
  tied to bear symbol, 391
  tied to Draco, 637
  to become part of Antichrist's evil empire, 407
Ruth, Book of
  theme of, 24
Sabbath
  tied to number seven, 383
Sabbatical Year, 311, 312
Sacred Astronomers, 244
Sacred Astronomy, 15, 88, 90, 91, 107, 108, 118, 240, 510, 613, 640
  basis of time-keeping, 617
  marking End Time events, 641, 710
  Mayan use of, 617
  of the Mayans, 618
  renewed interest in Enlightenment period, 613
  taught by Enoch, 107
  used to design Great Pyramid, 98
  utilized by many ancient cultures, 612
Sacred Cubit, 106, 110, 111, 119
  known by Moses and Israelites, 195
  used in design of Tabernacle and Ark, 195
Sacred Geometry, 118
  used in Great Pyramid's design, 98
Sacrificial Lamb
  as Aries the Ram, 211
Sagitta the Arrow, 428, 429
  tied to Aquila the Eagle, 426
Sagittarius
  as Rider on White Horse, 642
  Comet McNaught in, 661
  decans forming Chanukiah on Dec. 21, 2012, 652
  depicts Rider on White Horse, 650

galactic center in, 633
in prophecy, 426
on Mayan End Date, 650
saints
  in America, 428
salt rub
  used to purify body, 130
salvation
  three steps to, 187
Salvation by Grace, 456
Salvation in Christ, 186, 188, 629
Samson
  killed 3000 Philistines, 56
  symbolized in Hercules constellation, 283
Saqqara, 99
Sarah, 271
Sarah Palin, 384
Satan
  allegorical guises of, 615
  as Azazel, 158
  his, 465
  our enemy, 2
Satanists
  as antichrists, 344
Saturn
  at Mayan End Date, 650
  marks 9th Chanukiah lamp on Dec. 21, 2012, 652
Saudi Arabia, 410
  kingdom of Daniel's King of the South?, 493
  location of Mount Sinai, 378
Saxons, 399, 401, 402
Scandinavia
  connected to Tribe of Dan, 284
Scarab
  dung beetle sacred to Egyptians, 214
  Symbol for Sun's Path at Esna, 214
Scarlet Beast
  tied to Beast from the Sea and Red Dragon, 615
Scorpio, 498, 502, 615
  as Satan, 643
  Blood Moon in, 693
  connected to Tribe of Dan, 633
  decans forming Chanukiah on Dec. 21, 2012, 652
  depicts Rider on Pale Horse, 650

depicts Satan on December 21st,, 2012, 637
marks Pacific Ocean, 682
signifes the Pale Horse, 637
tied to Tribe of Dan, 282
Scorpio Meridian, 683
scorpion
as symbol for Satan, 637
Scorpio-Sagittarius Meridian, 321, 641, 692, 693
in Pasific, 672
Scotland
Royal Arms of, 450
Scud missiles, 59
Scythians, 278
may have been Lost Israelites, 276
Sea Serpent. *See* Hydra, Cetus
Seal, 629
Seal Judgments, 708
Second Advent, 337, 471
tied to Leo, 717
Second Coming, xx, 30, 32, 35, 36, 44, 45, 46, 60, 65, 66, 81, 82, 83, 136, 137, 147, 175, 215, 229, 256, 288, 299, 338, 346, 405, 425, 428, 437, 480, 519, 520, 611, 625, 628, 656, 669, 671, 682, 712
during or after 2016, 329
indicated by heavenly signs on Oct. 6, 2017 AD?, 717
many wars, pestilences before, 298
possible in 2016, 682
Second Rapture, 73, 75, 317, 329, 428, 509, 513, 515, 522, 530, 531, 534, 553, 598
in 2014?, 329
Second Resurrection, 424
Second Seal Judgement, 645
Second Temple, 346
Seed of the Serpent, 266, 284, 285, 465
Seir, 379
Seleucid Empire, 452
Seleucus, 452
Semiramis, 207, 264
Semyaza, 219
September 11th, 3 BC, 614
September 1999
beginning of 7th/13th Great Day, 294

Serpens, 587, 589, 633
as Rider on Pale Horse, 565
depicts Rider on Pale Horse, 649
true rider of Pale Horse, 637
serpent
biting the horse's heels, 664
symbol for Tribe of Dan, 282
symbol tied to Tribe of Dan, 283
Serpent, 502
Serpent Seed
depicted by Serpens, 565
serpent trail of Dan, 643
Servant Lamp, 17, 20, 27, 28
symbol for Christ, 18
Seth, 217
Sethite Astronomy, 618
Sethites, 110, 181, 269, 334, 638, 654
as Astronomers, 216
built Giza Complex, 217
built Old Kingdom Pyramids, 618
designed Giza, 229
knew Yahweh well, 683
made Giza to depict Christ, 217
used advanced Geometry long before the Greeks, 115
Seven Ages, 302
seven articles
of US Constitution, 383
Seven Bowl Judgments, 709
Seven Bowls of God's Wrath, 411, 515, 625, 642
Seven Churches, 698
depicted by Pleiades, 647
of Revelation, 516
Seven Churches of Revelation
depicted by Pleiades, 152
Seven Days of Creation Week, 256
Seven Great Days, 26, 187
seven hills
site for wicked city in Revelation, 457
seven kings
tied to seven Holy Roman Emperors, 494
Seven Seals, 642
Seven Trumpet Judgments, 709
Seven Trumpets, 515, 625, 642
Seven Wonders of the Ancient World, 92
Seven Wonders of the World

# Index

Great Pyramid only surviving example, 98
seventh angel of Revelation, 418
Seventh Great Day, 140, 244, 285
Seventh Millennium, 231, *See* Millennial Rule of Christ
seventieth week
   time of Great Tribulation, 190
seventy times seven
   season of forgiveness lasting 77 years, 331
Seventy Weeks Prophecy, 314
shafts
   in Great Pyramid, 150
Shamash. *See* Servant Lamp
Shavuot, 335
   targeted in Antechamber, 314
Sheba, 410
Shechem, 403
sheep
   symbol for repentant sinners, 444
Sheep, 499, 502
Shekinah Glory, 256
Shem, 94, 95, 638, 712
   as Melchizedek, 250
   given Japeth's birthright, 271
   likely had Caucasian features, 352
   may be Khafre, 93
   tied to Israel, 636
shepherds
   as leaders of Israel, 433
shepherds of Israel, 436
Shiloh
   a term for Christ, 439
Shiva, 653
Shofar, 533
Sign of the Son of Man, 316, 514, 564, 566, 567, 569, 570, 572, 574, 575, 580, 584, 590, 591
Signs in the Heavens, 60, 108, 243, 338, 341, 653, 664, 676, 683, 686, 693, 696, 706, 713, 717
   a prophetic witness, 330
   clearly show that the Tribulation has begun, 610
   Easter Island as a Sethite time marker, 339
   mark June of 2011 as significant, 678
   on December 21st, 2012, 546, 629

Simon Bar Kochba, 88
Simon the Pharisee
   same as Simon the Leper, 473
Sin Offering
   as Taurus the Bull, 211
Six Ages of Mankind, 259
Six Day War, 311
Six Days of Creation
   not 24-hour days?, 244
Six Great Days, 255, 624
Six-Day War, 54, 682
Sixth Seal, 314, 708, 709
Sixth Seal Judgment, 306, 314, 323, 349, 525, 573, 575, 577, 590, 632, 699
   accompanied by Pole Shift, 349
   describes Pole Shift, 315, 706
   tied to Pole Shift, 315
   Wrath of God begins with, 306
Sixth Sun, 639
Sixth Trumpet, 649
Socialist takeover of Democratic states, 401
Solar Disk
   Scarab tied to, 214
Solar Eclipse
   meaning of, 695
   of Aug. 21st, 2017, 712
   of Jan. 4th, 2011, 692
   of July 11th, 2010, best seen over Easter Island, 676
   of June 1st, 2011, 693
   of Nov. 13th, 2012, 694, 696
   on July 11, 2010, 672
   on July 11th, 2010, 669
   on July 11th, 2010 - meaning of, 678
   on July 11th, 2010 best seen from Easter Island, 672
Solar Eclipse of November 3rd, 2013, 314
Solar Eclipses
   three on 1st of Av in 2008 thru 2010, 664, 671, 673, 676
Solar Flares, 696
Solar System, 177
   bombarded by asteroids, 263
   filled with spiritual allegories, 267
   shown at Teotihuacán, 621
   Teotihuacán model of, 621

tied to Tribes of Israel, 265
understood by Mayans, 621
Solar Year
   and length of Enoch's life, 109
   same as Enoch's lifespan, 112
   tied to Yahshua's purpose, 136
Solomon, 354
   and Queen of Sheba, 356
Son of God, 5, 13, 14, 25, 110, 138, 181, 188, 194, 265, 337, 344, 345, 348, 379, 449, 469, 478, 493, 530, 577, 587, 615, 629, 679, 694, 702
Son of Man, 422
Song of Solomon
   gives clues to Rapture timing, 317
sons of Zebedee. See James and John
sound vibrations
   power source in Great Pyramid?, 164
sound waves
   used in levitation, 96
South America, 44, 357, 619
southern shaft
   in King's Chamber, 150, 160
   in Queen's Chamber, 158, 161
Soviet Union, 407
Sphinx enclosure, 209, 215
Spica, 696, 697, 698, 716
Spirit of God, 25
spiritual clothes
   our resurrected bodies, 513
spiritual Israel, 161, 183, 367
Spiritual Israel, 88, 161, 183, 354, 367, 450
   Gentile and Jew united in Christ, 287
spiritual sleepiness
   sign of apostasy, 512
Spring Equinox
   current position of, 225
   in 10,500 BC, 228
   Menkaure's Pyramid causeway points to, 215
Spring Feasts of Israel, 335, 336
staff called Union
   and USA, 391
Staff of Yahweh, 445
Star of David
   on Great Seal, 429
   on the Great Seal of the USA, 429

Star out of Jacob, 717
star shafts
   astronomical markers, 162
   in Great Pyramid, 160
star worship, 618
Star-Gazers
   artifact found in Ecuador, 380
Step Pyramid of Djoser, 103
step pyramids of the Americas
   serve d as sacred astronomical observatories, 618
Steven Collins, 276
Steven M. Collins, 449
Stone Age, 97
Stone Age tools
   supposedly used at Giza, 96
stone over entrance to King's Chamber, 116
Stone Tablets of the Law, 199
   Word of God, 181
Stonehenge, 91, 108, 135, 375, 566, 656, 735, 740
   connection to Giza Complex, 118
stoning
   Israelite form of ritual human sacrifice, 619
Street of the Dead, 621
Subterranean Chamber
   in Book of the Dead, 197
   symbol for Hell, 125
Sudan
   once Nubia, 407
Sudden Destruction, 316, 349, 592, 608, 697
   New Age Explanation for, 630
Suffering Servant, 336
Sukkah
   where Yahshua was born, 172
Sukkot, xv, 137, 325, 337, 338, 340, 523, 568, 573, 574, 576, 717, 727, *See Also* Feast of Tabernacles
   in 3 BC, 614
Sukkoth, Valley of, 403
Summer Solstice, 136, 172, 221, 547, 552, 566, 673
   Great Pyramid causeway points to, 136
   tied to baptism of Holy Spirit, 137
Sun

# Index

signified by King's Chamber, 121
worshipped as god, 617
Sun of Righteousness, 136, 309, 400, 679
Sun Pyramid, 622
Supreme Court
    secretly eroding civil rights of Americans, 432
sweatshops, 302
synodic month, 121
Syria's Civil War, 400
Tabernacle, xiii, xv, 17, 21, 116, 141, 142, 162, 169, 177, 178, 179, 180, 181, 182, 183, 184, 186, 187, 188, 189, 191, 192, 194, 195, 199, 200, 201, 202, 220, 221, 222, 246, 250, 259, 298, 309, 336, 737, 797
Tabernacle Courtyard, 182
table of showbread, 186
Table of Showbread
    symbol of Christ as Bread of Life, 186
Takia Makan mummies, 353
Tammuz, 264
Tanakh, 81, *See* Bible
Tarshish
    as the United Kingdom, 409
Taurus, 385, 652, 697
    as Red Horse, 646
    as Sin Offering, 496, 497, 499, 501, 502, 503, 504
    at Esna, 213
    depicted by unicorn, 646
    depicts Rider on Red Horse, 650
    has dual meaning, 646
    in Perseus prophecy, 664
    in symbol for Neith, 211
    on Mayan End Date, 650
    signifies Tribe of Joseph, 448, 698
    symbol for material wealth, 455
    symbol of atonement sacrifice, 684
    symbol of End Time war as bull fight with Orion, 693
    symbolizes Christ as sin offering, 684
    targeted by Lunar Eclipses of 2010 and 2011, 673
    tied to Beast from the Sea, 395, 496
    tied to Noah and his sons, 382
Taurus as Bread of Life, 152
Taurus Meridian, 683
Taurus, horns of
    signify Ephraim & Manasseh, Apostate & True Church, 319, 671
    symbolized by Red and Bent Pyramids, 672
Taurus-Gemini Meridian, 318, 693
Tea Party Movement, 384, 388
Temple, 180
    in Jerusalem, 434
    people as, 342
    threefold structure of, 162
Temple Mount, 41, 54, 188, 343, 347, 349, 406, 408, 562, 602
Temple of Khnum at Esna
    built by followers of Yahweh, 213
    in relation to Great Sphinx, 210
    Zodiac wall art featured Scarab, 214
Temple of Solomon, 102, 180, 182
Temple to Yahweh, 56, 81, 85, 179, 265, 306, 309, 343, 346, 561, 565, 576, 664, 671, 702
    built during Tribulation, 347
    destruction in 70 AD, 676
Ten Commandments, 83, 345
Ten Lost Tribes, 275, 278
    descendents of, 279
Ten Lost Tribes of Israel, 449
    found in Gentile Christianity, 273
    from northern Kingdom of Israel, 351
    may have been Scythians, 276
    reached Russia and China, 353
    represented in world today, 274
    symbolized by Taurus, 671
Teotihuacán, 618, 620, 621, 622, 623, 712
    possibly built before Maya, 623
    similar to Giza site plan, 622
    tied to Solar System, 621
Terrorism, 24, 52, 287, 328, 440, 454, 664, 730
Terrorists
    as antichrists, 344
    possible nuclear attacks by, 287
Thanksgiving 2013
    Comet ISON to reach perihelion on, 315
The DaVinci Code, 467
    filled with lies, 475
The Harbinger

by Jonathan Cahn, 364
The Parable of the Ten Virgins, 528
Theodor Herzl, 41
Thessalonians
   Second Epistle to, 343
Third Seal, 648
Third Temple, 346, 493
   to be built in 2011 AD?, 85
Third World, 44
Third World nations, 455
thirteen colonies
   in prophecy, 361
Thirteen Great Ages, 256
thirteen members
   suggests one is evil, 361
thirteen stars
   signify a new constellation, 429
Thirteenth Great Day. *See*
   Thirteenth Millennium, *See*
   Seventh Great Day, or Day of the
   Lord
thirteenth member
   replaces evil member in groups of twelve, 362
Thirteenth Millennium
   same a Seventh Millennium, 272
thirteenth patriarch, 271
Thomas Jefferson, 431
Thomas, the Apostle
   a traitor to Christ's cause?, 484
Thoth, 93
thousand-year day. *See* Great Day
Three Gospel Messages
   steps to Evangelism, 187
Three Steps to Evangelism
   the 3 Gospel messages, 187
Throne of David, 80
Throne of Judah
   a living heir to it?, 485
   located in England?, 449
Thuban, 158
Tiahuanaco, 103
Tiamat
   as planet and false deity, 262
   fragments of, 264
   symbol for Tribe of Dan, 265
Tikal, 618
Tim Cohen, 462
time of testing, 362

Time of Trouble, 254, 629
Titans, 397
Togarmah, 407
   Islamic southern half of former Soviet Union, 407
tolerance
   condones sin, 384
Toliman
   star n Centaurus, 217
Toltecs, 620
tomb robbers, 123
Torah. *See* Pentateuch
tornadoes
   sent in judgment, 305, 370, 371, 546, 607, 608, 609
Total Lunar Eclipse, 708
Total Solar Eclipse, 708
translated, xix, 7, 12, 32, 64, 73, 78, 91, 93, 109, 240, 309, 334, 342, 347, 400, 443, 469, 473, 480, 507, 533, 534, 600
Tribe of Dan, 265, 266, 388
   Antichrist may be of, 633
   as apostates, 270
   as Seed of the Serpent, 223
   as Tuatha de Danaan, 284
   biting the horse's heels, 664
   connected to Scorpio, 282
   dual purpose of, 356
   European place names connected to, 276
   in British Royalty, 490
   not judges, but the judged!, 283
   not mentioned in Revelation, 633
   rearing horse, or unicorn as symbol of, 450
   serpent trail of, 278
   supplanted by Ephraim, 431
   symbolized by sinister unicorn, 453
   symbols tied to, 282
   tied to Scorpio, 284
   tied to Scorpio, Antichrist, and Nephilim Seed, 223, 285
   tied to terrorists, 664
Tribe of Ephraim, 270
   as spiritually born again, 635
   represents all Ten Lost Tribes in prophecy, 273

# Index

tied to United States, and number 13, 429
Tribe of Joseph, 109, 223, 279, 322, 356, 386, 429, 430, 431, 448, 450, 490
  as Ephraim, 644
  as half tribe of Ephraim, 265
  as half tribe of Manasseh, 453
  connected to Taurus and Orion, 380
  material blessings to, 356
  ox or bull as symbol of, 447
  signified by Taurus, 698
  symbolized by Taurus, 671
  tied to Ephraim, 358
  tied to sign of Taurus, 223
  tied to USA, 362
Tribe of Judah, 279, 356, 386, 442, 579, 686, 725
  tied to Jupiter, 267
Tribe of Levi
  connected to USA, 367
Tribe of Manasseh
  replaces Tribe of Dan, 633
  replaces Tribe of Dan in Revelation, 635
  tied to the UK, 634
  to replace Dan during Tribulation, 273
Tribe of Naphtali
  signified by Aries, 502
Tribulation, 388
  Christian persecution inevitable during, 300
  may begin in 2011, 629
  possibly began on April 5th, 2011, 230
  prelude has already begun!, 295
Tribulation Church, 75
Tribulation period, 15, 16, 30, 31, 32, 34, 35, 36, 39, 58, 60, 61, 62, 63, 68, 69, 70, 71, 72, 73, 74, 76, 83, 85, 90, 131, 134, 137, 140, 147, 160, 161, 175, 187, 190, 223, 233, 234, 236, 237, 253, 273, 288, 297, 302, 304, 305, 307, 317, 323, 325, 327, 328, 329, 330, 331, 膨332, 333, 335, 337, 339, 341, 343, 344, 402, 417, 418, 424, 425, 427, 439, 444, 466, 481, 493, 507, 509, 511, 515, 518, 525, 528, 533, 534, 537, 539, 540, 544, 547, 548, 556, 599, 601, 624, 626, 627, 629, 635, 638, 642, 644, 649, 666, 692, 693, 704, 705, 707, 717, 719, 727, 730
Tribulation Period, 337, 531, 538
Tribulation Saints, 30, 33, 152, 160, 267, 290, 422, 423, 425, 459, 512, 514, 515, 517, 519, 650, 658
  in 2012, 705
  in America, 432
  persecution of, 648
Tribulation Timeline, 310, 312, 314, 316, 323, 325, 539, 576, 591
trident
  in heaven on Dec. 21, 2012, 652
Trinity, 28
  Yahshua as Adonai Yahweh, 345
Tropical Solar Year
  in design of Great Pyrmaid, 109
True Church, 161, 342, 658
  as fish of Pisces, 678
  Judah and Ephraim united, 359
  signified by Woman Clothed with Sun, 614
  signified in stars by Cassiopeia, 615
  symbolized by Queen's Chamber, 121
  Yahshua's marriage to, 478
trumpet, 235, 287
Tuatha de Danaan, 284
Tubal
  as Georgia, Armenia, and Azerbaijan in prophecy, 407
tunnel vision, 325
Twelve Apostles, 380
Twelve Houses of the Zodiac
  as Enoch's heavenly tablets, 245
twelve last shepherds of Israel, 436
Twelve Tribes of Israel, 73
  and US Great Seal, 429
  can all be found among modern Jews, 274
  concerning Tribe of Dan, 633
  in the last days, 279
  present on Earth today, 449
  reflected in altars of 12 stones, 108
  represented on Earth today, 273
  should be represented on Earth today, 273
  spiritually linked to modern day nations, 439

symbolized in Great Pyramid's
    ceilings, 146
symbolized in Zodiac, 220
tied to Zodiac, 223
will supply 144,000 Witnesses, 444
Twelve Zodiac Signs
    and US Great Seal, 429
Twentieth Century
    Christian persecution rose early in,
    299
twenty-eight degree arc, 136
Twenty-First Century
    Christian persecution escalating again,
    299
twenty-seven amendments
    tied to 27 books in New Testament,
    383
twenty-seventh amendment
    stands alone like Book of Revelation,
    384
Twin Towers. See World Trade
    Center
Two Fishes of Pisces
    signify Two Houses of Israel, 498
two horns
    of Taurus, 448
Two House Church, 656
    represented in Antechamber, 187
Two House Church of Judah
    signified by Pisces, 503
Two Houses of Israel, 80, 168, 314
    sifgnified by Pisces, 498
Two Rapture Theory, 498
Two Witnesses, 3, 31, 73, 75, 157,
    300, 311, 329, 340, 346, 438, 480,
    481, 507, 508, 515, 517, 531, 532,
    533, 534, 561, 574, 589, 598, 601,
    644, 645
    appear after 3-1/2 years, 328
    not beloved disciple, nor John, 480
    to preach during Great Tribulation,
    651
    to preach during Tribulation, 645
    will preach Word of God, 288
Two-House Church, 429, 698
Tzemach, 81
U.S. Constitution, 281
UFO sightings, 549
unicorn, 281, 385

as One-Horned Goat, 428
as One-Horned Ram, 434
as symbol for goodness, 442
depicts Taurus, 646
mentioned in King James Bible, 447
more than a fantasy, 442
occult associations of, 442
on Scottish and British Coat of Arms,
    450
one good, one evil, 450
symbol for Christ, 446
symbol in Heraldry, 448
tied to Pegasus, 664
tied to Taurus, 664
Union
    staff called, and USA, 391
    term for USA in Washington's vision,
    419
United Kingdom, 109, 385, 386, 389,
    409, 499, 502, 503, 504, 505, See
    also Great Britain
    as King of the North, 693
    as Manasseh, 403
    heads EU, 453
    Muslims in, 401
    part of Beast system, 460
    royalty of, 346
    saints in, 495
    tied to Tribe of Dan, 634
United Nations, 343
    Antichrist may rule from, 459
    as Beast from the Sea, 459
    located in New York, 364
    modern counterpart to Roman Empire
    through EU, 393
    part of Beast system, 460
    possible center of modern Roman
    Empire, 401
    tied to Daniel's 4th Beast, 393
United Nations sanctions
    violate U.S. Constitution, 432
United States, 109, 273, 385, 386,
    387, 460, 538, 637
    a teaming nation of nations, 280
    and numbers 50, 51, & 52, 374
    Antichrist's invasion of, 713
    as Ephraim, 403, 425
    as injured eagle in Star Gospel, 427
    as King of the South, 693
    as spiritual navel of the world, 368

# Index

as the eagle's wings, 616
as the wounded eagle Aquila, 428
attaacked by Antichrist?, 406
bound to Israel, 359
center of the land, with resettled ruins, 410
center of the land, with resettled ruins, like Israel, 410
citizens value freedom, 432
connected to Israel, 357
connected to Tribe of Levi, 367
connection to number 13, 367
erroneously tied to Manasseh, 279
has more Christians than any other nation, 368
has unwalled villages like Israel, 409
how to identify in prophecy, 356, 361
in Bible Prophecy, 415
invasion of foreseen, 423
may be invaded during Great Tribulation, 391
most powerful nation on Earth, 281
peaceful land attacked by Terrorists, like Israel, 411
reckoned as Ephraim in Isaiah 9 9, 364
Solar Eclipse over, 713
suffering for immorality, 374
symbol depicted on Ecaudor arifacts, 382
tied to Ephraim, 431, 448
tied to House of Israel or Ephraim, 187
tied to Israel, 448
tied to Israel in End Times, 389
tied to Joseph, Ephraim, Levi, 502
tied to numbers in Bible, 383
tied to Star Gospel, 365, 367, 384
war in Iraq, 287
will be crippled after the Rapture, 420
will be punished for abandoning Israel, 360
younger nation tied to younger son of Joseph, 280
United States citizens
will rebel against Antichrist, 459
United States Federal Government, 432
unleavened bread
Taurus as, 152
Upper Egypt, 118
Uranus
as Bride of Christ, 715
Five Moons signify Five Wise Virgins, 667
meaning of, 665, 666
Uriel
angel that taught Enoch, 382
Uriel's Machine, 487
Ursa Major, 160, 499, 698
compared to Pleiades, 664
Sheep Pen full of believers from Protestant Churches, 501
tied to Pleiades, 156
Ursa Minor, 160, 161
compared to Pleiades, 664
symbol of Apostate Churches, 499, 500
tied to Pleiades, 156
US Flag
13 stars a new constellation, 365
13 stripes, 366
first version attributed to Betsy Ross, 366
US Government, 388
US Great Seal, 510
US political dissidents, 388
US Troops, 59
Valley Forge, 415
Valley of Jehoshaphat, 534, 565
Valley of Megiddo, 286, 412, 534, 548
Valley Temple, 103
Vatican, 399, 499, 503, 504
as Harlot, 457
behind Radical Islam, 455
to be destroyed, 459
Vatican II, 253
veil, 562
Venus
as Morning Star, 671, 714
Vespasian, 69
Virgin Mary, 697
Virgin Miriam
symbolized by Queen's Chamber, 121
Virgo, 89, 614, 615, 643, 650, 658, 660, 686, 696, 697, 698, 701, 709, 713, 715, 717
as beginning of Zodiac, 213

at Christ's birth, 614
at Esna, 213
on Sept. 20, 2017 AD, 713
symbol for Eve, and Mary, 220
symbol for Miriam, 614
symbol for Woman clothed with Sun, 614
Woman Clothed with the Sun, 697
Virgo, the Virgin
tied to Great Sphinx, 220
Wales
connected to Tribe of Dan, 284
War on Terror, 389, 404
Washington, D.C, 363
Watchers, 198, 220, 290, 706
Cainan preserved their false teachings, 271
fallen ones taught Astrology, 437
holy ones, 97, 710
tied to Scorpio, 223
Way of Cain, 357, 397, 662
Way of Yahweh, 397, 509
hidden in Pyramid, Temple and Tabernacle, 309
weather
changes recently due to Tribulation prelude onset, 295
weather patterns
sign of Last Day's arrival, 369
Wedding at Cana, 470
not Christ's wedding, 468
Wedding of the Lamb, 191, 314, 338, 525, 528, 532, 533, 537, 553, 579, 667, 669, 672, 681, 704, 725
*before* Marriage Supper, 74
Wedding Supper of the Lamb
depicted by groove in Grand Gallery, 191
Well Shaft, 183, 622
in Book of the Dead, 197
part of internal inspection system?, 166
symbol for Mosaic Law, 128
tied to altar of sacrifice, 202
tied to Tabernacle courtyard, 183
Wesley Bradshaw, 415
West Bank, 54, 403
Wheat, 502
whirlwinds
sent in judgment, 425, 607, 609, 644
Whore of Babylon
a city destined for destruction, 87
connected to Mary as false goddess, 253
depicted by Pleiades, 648
tied to Ecumenical Movement, 698
Wiccans
as antichrists, 344
William Barton, 431
Winged Serpent
depicts path of the Sun, 214
Winter Solstice, 136, 137, 221, 259, 317, 321, 323, 539, 540, 544, 546, 547, 628, 629, 633, 637, 650, 664, 673, 681, 682, 688, 696
and galactic alignment, 628
in 2012, 338
Khafre Pyramid points to, 136
of Dec. 21st, 2010, 681
of December 21st, 2012, 630
on December 21st, 2012, 633
tied to Christ's conception and kingship, 136
Wise Men, 90
may have come from Parthia, 244
might have been Jews, 243
Parthian Magi who gave gifts to Christ, 469
Wise Virgins, 306, 316, 528, 529, 532, 534, 553
given dominion over the Earth, 396
symbolized by Virgo, 496
Woman clothed with the Sun, 457
Woman Clothed with the Sun, 390, 396, 538, 571, 572, 580, 582, 584, 589, 591, 592, 601, 697
symbol for Mary, and Israel, 456
tied to Virgo and Miriam, 614
Woman who rides the Beast, 456
as a harlot queen, 462
as Queen Elizabeth II, 462
connected to Islam, 455
identified by Zechariah, 454
Six of the Seven Churches connected to, 395
symbolized by the Pleiades, 395
tied to Muslims and Western wealth, 455

# Index

tied to Vatican, 457
Word of God, 5, 82
    as great sword, 445
    preached by 144,000, and 2 Witnesses, 288
Word of Knowledge, 71, 306, 311, 317, 322, 338, 340
world
    to be destroyed by fire, 616
World Age
    end of, 611
    end of on 12-21-2012, 612
World Trade Center, 363
    its destruction a warning from God, 372
    like modern Tower of Babel, 460
World War I, 49, 50
World War II, 41
    catalyst for Jewish return to Israel, 351
    saw worst persecution of Jews in history, 357
World War III, 432, 518
worship
    of stars, 617
Worthless Shepherd
    prophecy of, 391
Wrath of God, 154, 306, 314, 347, 512, 536, 556, 573, 607, 654, 681
Wrath of God, 315
Xerxes, 275
Yahshua, 3, 69
    alluded to at Giza, 216
    anointed by Mary, 472
    as Adonai Yahweh, 345, 428, 644
    as Alpha and Omega, 5
    as Archer King depicted in Sagittarius, 643
    as Beginning and End, 5
    as capstone of Great Pyramid, 169
    as carpenter's son, 468
    as First and Last, 5
    as giver of Holy Spirit, 726, 727
    as Prince of Peace, 152
    as Rod of Jesse, 289
    as Son of God and Son of Man, 344
    as Son of Man, 422
    as Sun of Righteousness, 136
    as the capstone, 65, 66, 69, 169
    as the First and Last, 205
    as the Light of the World, 22
    atoning sacrifice, 427
    birth of, 614
    brothers did not believe, 483
    called teacher, rabbi 57 times in Bible, 470
    child of Woman Clothed with Sun, 614
    Creator of time and matter, 206
    depicted by Great Sphinx, 217
    depicted in Coffer and Ark, 181
    depicted in the heavens, 683
    did He have a twin?, 484
    erroneously seen as human king, not God, 470
    heresy of twin, 484
    His commandments, 345
    if married, should not affect faith, 468
    in the Bible Codes, 10
    Lamb of God, 183
    loved Lazarus and Mary, 483
    made rich by Wise Men, 469
    not married, except to Church, 478
    occult version of, 488
    possible date of His return, 311
    righted the wrongs of his forefathers, 272
    sacrifice for sin, 146
    Second Coming tied to Oct. 6, 2017 AD, 714
    symbolized in Great Pyramid, 100
    symbolized in Great Sphinx, 215
    symbolized in Tabernacle, 178
    the Word of God, 5
    thirteenth leader of modern Israel?, 437
    tied to right hand and horn of Cherubim, 256
    tied to right horn of Cherubim, 443
Yahshua Ha Mashiach, 309, 527, 528, 719
Yahshua's baptism, 170
Yahshua's heavenly army, 78
Yahshua's Ministry
    3-1/2 years long, 328
Yahshua's Parables, 216
Yahweh, 502
    as Archer, 644
    designed Great Pyramid, 115

designed Great Pyramid and Desert
   Tabernacle, 179
witness in Great Pyramid, 193
Yahweh's Right Hand, 80
Year of Jubilee, 133
Yemen, 410
Yom Kippur, 337, 338, 339, *See Also*
   Day of Atonement, *See* Day of
   Atonement
   in 3 BC, 614
Yom Kippur War, 56
Yom Kippur year, 337, 339, 340
Yom Teruah, 244, 336, 533
Yucatán Peninsula, 617
Zecharia Sitchin, 262
Zechariah's messianic prophecy, 425
Zerubbabel
   built second Temple, 346
Zeta Orionis, 150
Zeus, 36, 156, 397, 492
   Altar of Pergamum dedicated to, 398
   Greek god who raped Europa, 395
ziggurats, 618
Zion
   not a place, 167
   tied to Orion and Great Pyramid, 678, 681
Zionist Movement, 41, 47
Zodiac, 12, 89, 91, 641
   and faces of Cherubim, 254
   as heavenly tablets, 245
   Christ-figures in, 662
   concerning Beasts from Sea, 498
   connected to Tabernacle and Pyramid, 201
   depicts ministry of Christ, 144
   marks 12,000 year time period, 227
   mentioned in Dead Sea Scrolls, 240
   mirror of earthly events, 262
   Moon's connection with, 136
   Scorpio most evil sign in, 649
   Scorpio the most satanic sign, 643
   signified by ceiling stones in Great Pyramid, 139
   symbolized in Great Pyramid's ceilings, 146
Zodiacal Wheel
   Four Horsemen within, 650

## *About the Author*

Bible scholar, historian, and astronomer Helena Lehman is the author of, and artist for the non-fiction "Language of God" Book Series, and the upcoming fictional Pillar of Enoch Trilogy. She is an avid student of the Bible and ancient history, and an expert on the Gospel in the Stars, the Tabernacle, and the Great Pyramid. Her writings explore the ancient and divine roots of the Star Gospel, and their place as the cornerstone of the Language of God - a divine allegorical language of parables and symbols that permeates every book of the Bible, and all Creation.

Helena's premiere work is the four-volume "Language of God" Book Series, which reflects the accumulated knowledge of a lifetime, and challenges many traditional views of the past. It offers compelling evidence about what our righteous ancestors actually knew and believed, and how they perceived God - in light of their advanced knowledge of their world, and the Universe that God created for them. The allegorical Language of God, and the messages that God locked into the Ancient Zodiac ties the separate topics covered in each book together, and offers a feast of new ideas for every inquiring mind.

Helena has spent many years in intense research, becoming a self-made scholar in diverse areas such as ancient history, astronomy, comparative religion, and theology - where she writes on apologetics, eschatology, exegesis, and hermeneutics. She has many writing projects underway, and is available to speak at special events. For further information about Helena, her writing and speaking endeavors, or to purchase her books, visit her web site at http://pillar-of-enoch.com, or write her at helena@pillar-of-enoch.com.

Helena currently lives with her husband Steve, and daughter Miranda in the Chicago area. Steve and Helena were once childhood sweethearts, and despite thirty years of separation, they never forgot each other. When Steve found her again in 2002, Helena found an unbounded faith in miracles - a faith she holds fast to with joy as she awaits Yahshua's return.

# Pillar of Enoch Ministry Book Order Form

Name:_____

Address:_____

City:_____ State/Prov._____ Postal Code_____

E-Mail Address:_____(required)

Note: All Prices include shipping in the USA. International Customers, call Customer Service at 708-977-0115 to get rates.

| Paperback Titles at 33% OFF Autographed by Author | Price: | Qty: |
|---|---|---|
| "The Language of God in the Universe" | $24.00 | _____ |
| "The Language of God in Humanity" | $28.00 | _____ |
| "The Language of God in History" | $30.00 | _____ |
| "The Language of God in Prophecy" | $28.00 | _____ |
| "The Language of God" Series 4 Book Set | $94.00 | _____ |

| Specially Priced PDF Books on CD | Price: | Qty: |
|---|---|---|
| "The Language of God in the Universe" | $14.00 | _____ |
| "The Language of God in Humanity" | $16.00 | _____ |
| "The Language of God in History" | $18.00 | _____ |
| "The Language of God in Prophecy" | $16.00 | _____ |
| "The Language of God" Series 4 CD Set | $50.00 | _____ |

Order on the Internet at pillar-of-enoch.com for special web-only discounts and extras on all book orders, or mail orders to:

Pillar of Enoch Ministry Books, 1708 N. 77th Avenue
Elmwood Park, Illinois 60707-4107 USA

Questions? E-mail: helena@pillar-of-enoch.com
Phone: 708-977-0115

www.ingramcontent.com/pod-product-compliance
Lightning Source LLC
Chambersburg PA
CBHW071428300426
44114CB00013B/1346